CASES IN INTERNATIONAL RELATIONS

PRINCIPLES AND APPLICATIONS

EIGHTH EDITION

DONALD M. SNOW

THE UNIVERSITY OF ALABAMA

ROWMAN & LITTLEFIELD

Lanham · Boulder · New York · London

Executive Editor: Traci Crowell
Assistant Editor: Deni Remsberg
Higher Education Channel Manager: Jonathan Raeder

Credits and acknowledgments for material borrowed from other sources, and reproduced with permission, appear on the appropriate page within the text.

Published by Rowman & Littlefield
An imprint of The Rowman & Littlefield Publishing Group, Inc.
4501 Forbes Boulevard, Suite 200, Lanham, Maryland 20706
www.rowman.com

6 Tinworth Street, London SE11 5AL, United Kingdom

Seventh edition 2018

British Library Cataloguing in Publication Information Available

Library of Congress Control Number: 2019951070

ISBN 978-1-5381-3436-8 (cloth : alk. paper)
ISBN 978-1-5381-3437-5 (pbk. : alk. paper)
ISBN 978-1-5381-3438-2 (electronic)

™ The paper used in this publication meets the minimum requirements of American National Standard for Information Sciences—Permanence of Paper for Printed Library Materials, ANSI/NISO Z39.48-1992.

Contents

Preface

This book is, and through its various editions always has been, about explaining basic concepts, forces, and dynamics in international relations and how these principles help shape and guide applications to contemporary situations. As such, it has two basic missions: providing basic instruction in important dynamics of how international relations work (hopefully in a lively and engaging manner) and providing updated and relevant information and interpretation of major events helping to shape the world. These have been the goals since the first edition appeared in 2002; they remain for this, the eighth edition. After some experimentation with formats, I have adopted a "formula" of sorts, where each case study begins with a principle of operation of the international system followed by an example of events that illustrate the principle and controversies surrounding it. This division is reflected in the overall table of contents: the first nine chapters deal with underlying international relations principles, whereas the last nine chapters focus on substantive problems. The purpose is to create a coherence often missing in supplemental texts. I would like to think that, in addition to being a "reader" to accompany a comprehensive text, it could be used as a text on its own supplemented by other materials.

Like all books going through multiple editions, this one has evolved over time. This edition is distinguished by two major structural changes from previous editions. Both affect the cases in this volume. First, there are more cases than before. Most of the previous editions had fourteen cases, and this edition has eighteen. The length of each case has been reduced from about 9,000 words to a little over 6,000 words, leaving the final product about the same length as earlier editions. This restructuring replicates the organization of my *Cases in U.S. National Security*, published in 2018. The shorter chapters are more reader friendly, in the sense that each chapter can be read in one easy sitting. Second, the expansion in number of cases allows an expansion of the topics covered, thereby enhancing the book's comprehensiveness. I hope the reader will find the additions interesting, informative, and readable, and that what has been lost in the depth of past cases will be compensated for by greater topic coverage.

New to This Edition

The new configuration of the table of contents has provided both the opportunity and necessity of adding additional topics, reconfiguring some others, and eliminating yet others—particularly applications that have become less relevant since the last edition was published. There is, for instance, much less coverage of the Islamic State than in the seventh edition, for the simple reason that its star rose and then fell (largely for reasons laid out in the last edition). Topics like national overdependence on petroleum revenues (petrolism) and its impact on the current Venezuelan crisis have been added. As a quick glance at the table of contents shows, eight of the eighteen chapters are totally new to this edition. That is almost half the book, and there is not a single chapter that has not been revised and updated based on events through mid-2019.

The nine new chapters cover a wide range of topics and concerns. Four deal with principles of operation of the international system, and are thus in part I. These are chapter 2 on diplomacy, chapter 4 on the instruments of power, chapter 5 on multilateral versus unilateral approaches to conducting international relations, and chapter 6 on the universality of human rights. The other new chapters look at systemic problem areas: chapter 7 on rising and declining powers (China and Russia), chapter 9 on petrolism, chapter 13 on regional power changes in the Middle East, chapter 14 on the dilemma of stateless nations, and chapter 18 on cybersecurity and cyberwar. Other chapters with major revisions from the previous edition include chapter 10 on nuclear proliferation, chapter 12 on international population movement, chapter 15 on global climate change, chapter 16 on global resource scarcity, and chapter 17 on terrorism. In addition, more limited changes were made to chapter 8 on asymmetrical warfare and chapter 11 on global economic dynamics (including the controversy over tariffs and economic associations).

The text also introduces some new ideas and forces in the international mix. An illustrative list includes the evolving situation in Saudi Arabia, the idea of a "responsibility to protect" beleaguered peoples, the instability in Nigeria and Venezuela created by an excess dependence on petroleum revenue, the Trump administration's proposed U.S.-Mexico-Canada agreement as a successor to North American Free Trade Agreement, the evolving role of the Kurds (and the Palestinians) in their quest for their own sovereign state, differing dynamics of North Korean and Iranian proliferation, and how terrorism may change post Islamic State and Al Qaeda. There is more, but it is a broad and I hope rich menu. Dig in!

Features

What distinguishes this effort from other supplementary texts in the field? One answer is that all the chapters included in the volume are original papers written by the author specifically for this volume. The reason for doing so was to allow for more timely coverage of ongoing situations than is possible with the publication lag time of scholarly journals and their availability to readers and other compendia. It also allows casting the cases in a common format that makes it easier to compare the contents of the various cases without wading through disparate styles and formats of various authors and publications. In addition, journal articles are written for academic peers rather than more-or-less lay students, meaning they are generally rendered in language and theoretical trappings that are less than accessible to student readers. Finally, writing original chapters facilitates updating and modifying materials as events and dynamics change, which hopefully adds to the freshness, accuracy, and timeliness of the materials contained in these pages. Presenting the most contemporary set of portraits possible has certainly been a major purpose of this and earlier editions.

A word about what this book is—and is not—is appropriate at this point. It is a case book, presenting a series of individual instances of dynamics and trends within the international arena. The effort is neither inclusive nor encyclopedic; it covers selected concepts and events, not the universe of international concerns. A series of eighteen important, underlying concepts and principles of the international system have been chosen and discussed, and the discussion of these principles has been applied to contemporary, important, and interesting real-life examples. The result is not a systematic overview of the international system or its history, which is the province of core textbooks in the field. Likewise, it does not offer a unifying theoretical explanatory framework of international politics, a task that more specialized books purporting grand "theories" of international relations propound. Rather, the intent is to introduce and apply some basic concepts about international relations and how they apply in real situations.

Acknowledgments

This edition of the book is once again dedicated to my good friend and colleague, the late D. Eugene Brown. Gene and I met in 1989 at the U.S. Army War College, where we both served as visiting professors and shared an office for two years before he returned to his permanent home at Lebanon Valley College in Annville, Pennsylvania, and I returned to the University of Alabama in Tuscaloosa. In the ensuing decade, we were collaborators on several book projects; *Cases in International Relations*, which was mostly Gene's idea, was to be a continuation, even culmination, of those efforts. Unfortunately, Gene left us before the original project was complete. His shadow remains, I hope with a smile on his face.

I have also received generous and very helpful assistance from the team at Rowman & Littlefield. In particular, I would like to thank three members of the Rowman & Littlefield team. My editor, Traci Crowell (a fellow University of Colorado alum—Go Buffs), obtained the reversion of rights to me for the previous edition, and encouraged me throughout the writing process. Alden Perkins did her usual professional job turning the manuscript into a book, our third project together. Special thanks go to Deni Remsberg, who cheerfully and efficiently came to my aid when my lack of knowledge and empathy with the dynamics of electronic infernal machines left me in a bewildered panic (a recurrent burden on her). Thanks for everything, guys!

Lastly, I would like to thank the reviewers of the eighth edition: John Allen Williams (Loyola University of Chicago), John W. Dietrich (Bryant University), Lynda K. Barrow (Coe College), Rita Peters (University of Massachusetts at Boston), George Poluse (Kent State University), Marius Ratolojanahary (Northern Virginia Community College), and Matthew Wahlert (Miami University).

Donald M. Snow
Professor Emeritus
University of Alabama

PART I

Principles and Dynamics

1

Sovereignty

Dealing with Changing Norms and the International Criminal Court

Sovereignty—supreme authority—has been the most central concept and operational principle of the international order since the Peace of Westphalia ended the Thirty Years' War in 1648. Since then, sovereignty has been defined territorially as possessed by states. This has meant that state sovereignty is the principle on which world political order is grounded. Within sovereign states, there can be no authority greater than that of the state. In principle, it is absolute in scope. In practice there are infringements on the total control of the state. Sovereignty is a controversial concept, in that it is used to justify armed violence and can be a shield behind which atrocity is sometimes committed. Established sovereignty does, however, endow its possessor with international legitimacy, making it a valued commodity among political actors.

Sovereignty is pervasive, is jealously guarded by its state possessors, and is a fundamental pillar of world politics. Some states are more obsessed with protecting their sovereignty than others, but it is important to all states. The ongoing controversy over sovereignty and the sovereignty threatening implications of state practices and the International Criminal Court (ICC) vividly demonstrate the power and role of sovereignty.

The basic premise of the ICC is that individuals and groups (including states) who commit war crimes and crimes against humanity should be subject to the same kinds of penalties as individuals and groups within states—a situation that is not universally the case. Conflict arises between states and the international community because accused offenders are sometimes protected by states on sovereignty grounds. When this occurs, the sanctity of state sovereignty and the dictates of international justice come into direct conflict. In those cases, something must give.

Principle: The Concept of Sovereignty

Any discussion of the underlying philosophy, structure, or operation of international relations begins with the concept of sovereignty. Defined as "supreme authority," it is the operational base of both international and domestic political life, although with quite opposite effects on the two realms. Ever since it emerged as the bedrock organizational principle of world politics in 1648, it is, and has always been, a somewhat controversial foundation for world affairs. Controversy has surrounded matters such as the location of sovereignty (who has it?) and the extent of power that it conveys to its possessors (what can the sovereign do—and not do?), and concepts have changed over time. Disagreements about sovereignty are prominent parts of some debates about the evolving international order and the assault on its basic function is part of international dialogue.

Sovereignty has evolved over time. It emerged at a time when modern political states did not exist except in limited places such as France and England. During this period, questions of political authority still revolved around whether people owed their ultimate loyalty and even existence to sectarian authority represented most prominently by the Catholic Church or to secular monarchs in the locales where they resided. One of the most important elements of the Peace of Westphalia (the collective name given to the series of treaties that ended the Thirty Years' War) was to wrest political control from the church and to transfer that power to secular authorities. This transfer was accompanied by the effective installation of sovereignty as the basis of relations among secular political communities. A primary outcome of this "marriage" was to associate sovereignty with territorial political jurisdictions. Because those territories were essentially all ruled by absolute monarchs, the conjunction effectively created the precedent that the power of the sovereign was absolute. This association is symbolized by the fact that the monarchs of the time were also known as sovereigns.

This association has changed over time. Reflecting the political period in which it became the bellwether concept of an evolving secular state-based system, sovereignty began as a principle that legitimized and promoted authoritarian rule. That principle was challenged with the rise of democratic thought, suggesting that sovereignty was a characteristic not only of the ruler but the ruled as well. From this challenge arose the modern notion of popular sovereignty.

Origins and Evolution

Understanding how and why sovereignty came to be the major organizing principle of international relations begins with an enigma of sorts. The heart of sovereignty is territorial supremacy—whoever has sovereignty has ultimate authority in the physical territory where it is claimed and enforced. This means that in the domestic affairs of sovereign entities, sovereignty provides the basis for political *order* by endowing its possessors with the ability to develop and enforce rules and laws that provide some form of political system. It does not predetermine *who* within the jurisdiction has sovereignty or the *extent* to which it can be exercised. In domestic affairs, it is the basis for order.

The impact of sovereignty on the relations *between* sovereign territories (in modern terms, the world's states or countries) is quite the opposite. The supreme authority that sovereignty creates means that there can be no other entity that can claim or exercise any form of authority over another state, and this principle implies states cannot interfere in one another's affairs. Although this principle was never taken quite literally, the result was that international relations (the interactions between states) was effectively a state of *anarchy* (the absence of government) where no state could legally be impelled to do things it did not want or that might offend others within their sovereign domains. The only recourse that a political authority aggrieved by the actions of another sovereign state was through *self-help*, which often effectively meant the recourse to arms.

The fact that sovereignty created the justification both for order and disorder was not a concern of its early chroniclers and enthusiasts. The concept was first introduced by the French philosopher Jean Bodin in his 1576 book *De Republica*. Bodin's major concern was to promote the consolidation of the authority of the king of France over his realm. The problem that he sought to alleviate was the practice by lower feudal lords within France of effectively claiming sovereignty over their realms by charging tolls to cross their territories.

To deal with this situation, Bodin countered with the concept of sovereignty, which he defined as "supreme authority over citizens and subjects, *unrestrained by law*" (emphasis added). Bodin, who was a staunch monarchist, felt the italicized element was necessary to keep the monarch from being hamstrung by parochial laws in his quest to establish the power of the monarchy and to spread its sway over the entire country. The notion of exemption from law has fallen from common conceptions of sovereignty, but its implications remain and are part of ongoing disagreements on the meaning and controversies surrounding the concept. If the sovereign is indeed above the law, then nothing he or she does can possibly be illegal, at least when committed within the sovereign jurisdiction over which the sovereign reigns. The claim by Richard Nixon during the Watergate scandal that "if the President does it, it cannot be illegal" is an example; so is Robert Mueller's 2019 determination that President Trump could not be tried for a crime while he is in office.

Bodin was not concerned about its extension to forming the basis of international relations. The extension of the implications of sovereignty to international affairs occurred as the state system evolved and the structure of the modern state emerged in an increasing number of European states. The major publicist of this extension was the Dutch scholar Hugo Grotius, who is generally acknowledged as the father of the idea of international law. He first proclaimed state sovereignty as a fundamental principle of international relations in his 1625 book *On the Law of War and Peace*, and by the eighteenth century it was accepted as both a principle of domestic and international relations.

By the nineteenth century, the modern state system was taking form, and this entailed implications for both the questions raised earlier: with whom does sovereignty exist within sovereign jurisdictions? And how extensive are the legitimate powers that reside in the holder of sovereignty? Both remain basic questions.

The question of the locus of sovereignty was a product of greater citizen participation in the political process within evolving countries, and especially with democratization. When monarchism was universal and was accompanied by the belief that the monarch was supreme over his or her realm, it was natural to assume monarchical control over the state. When political philosophers like the Englishman John Locke and his French counterpart Jean-Jacques Rousseau made the counterclaim that the sovereign's powers were limited and could be abridged by the people, the question of the locus of sovereignty was joined. The premise of both the American and French Revolutions was that the people were the source of fundamental political legitimacy, which translated into the idea of popular sovereignty. The heart of this notion, which gradually took hold as the state system matured in Europe, was that the people were sovereign and that they voluntarily bestowed parts of that sovereignty to the state to legitimize state power and to ensure domestic order.

The idea of popular restraint suggested that there were limits on the extent of the freedom of states to act as they might want to. Within democratizing states, the major limit (or restraint) on sovereign authority was what the people would tolerate. This expression was asserted gradually: after a republican form of government was established in the United States, other states during the nineteenth century, notably France (which alternated between democratic and authoritarian rule before 1870) and Great Britain, which gradually expanded political rights, began to democratize more broadly, and this trend spread. The symbolic acts of embracing this notion in domestic politics were the UN Charter and various declarations after World War II, although full implementation of the concept has not yet occurred.

Changing Conceptions of Sovereignty

Applying changing conceptions of sovereignty to the relations *among* sovereigns has been difficult. Sovereignty as the basic principle of international relations remains largely conceptually intact, although its pervasive dominance has been selectively diluted through voluntary forfeitures by organs like the European Union. Some countries are more jealous and protective of the protections from outside interference that their sovereignty bestows upon them: the United States and China, for instance, are among the most jealous guardians of their sovereign status. Most of the attempts at change come from international efforts to limit the degree of control and even persecution to which states can subject their citizens (extensions of the idea of popular sovereignty) like the UN Declaration on Human Rights and the Convention on Genocide, both of which the United States did not ratify until the 1990s (they were first drafted in the 1940s). The nature and implications of sovereignty remain controversial in contemporary international politics for different reasons. Three of them are worth noting as examples.

The first is the connection between sovereignty and war. The most commonly stated objection to sovereignty in this regard is that the concept justifies and even glorifies war to settle difference between states—the result of international anarchy. Domestic conflict–resolving methods like justice systems with mandatory jurisdiction are unavailable for most purposes. In a system of sovereign states, after all, there is no authority to enforce international norms on states or to enforce judgments resolving disputes that arise between them. Such mechanisms are conspicuously (and purposely) missing in the relations among states. Because there can be no superior authority to that of the sovereign, no one can enforce anything against a sovereign (at least in principle). The reason is simple: states have what are generally referred to as *vital interests*, conditions on which they will not voluntarily compromise, and are thus unwilling to empower any authority that could dilute that power (the concept of national interest is the basis of chapter 3).

The second objection to sovereignty is the degree of control it gives states over their citizens, including the right to suppress and even murder individuals and groups. The assertion of this objection is largely contemporary, a postwar phenomenon reflecting global outrage in the aftermath of the genocide during the Holocaust. The notion of absolute sovereignty implies that the sovereign state has total control over those who reside within its legal boundaries. Taken literally, this means the sovereign can do anything he or she wants or can do to those citizens—including killing all or parts of the population—with no outside legal sanction or basis for interference in any atrocities arising from that treatment.

That scenario, of course, describes the Holocaust carried out by Nazi Germany against the Jewish and Roma (sometimes referred to as Gypsy) population of Germany and other countries it occupied. Rejection of this practice represents, at least implicitly, an affirmation and an advocacy of popular sovereignty. It has also been the subject of attacks that argue the assertion that government control over its citizenry is fundamental to the conceptual underpinning of the state system, and that, despite the merits of protecting people from atrocity, it should be opposed on the basis that it erodes and undermines the basic conceptual underpinning of the state system. This debate forms the core of objections to the ICC.

The third, and somewhat mitigating, factor is that sovereignty in practice has never been as sacrosanct as it is in theory. The degrees of control in the nineteenth century were not actually total, and they are less so today. Countries can and do regularly penetrate and interfere with the affairs of other countries. The attempts by Russia to influence the 2016 American presidential election were presented as something unusual and extreme, but they were not. During the Cold War, the Soviet Union regularly attempted to influence American elections by manipulating relations to make different candidates they favored or opposed look good or bad, and the United States also has a long history of interfering with elections through the use of clandestine intelligence operations to do things like financing campaigns either to elect or defeat candidates and, in the most extreme cases, to carry out "wet operations" to eliminate disfavored politicians from some countries, notably in the Western Hemisphere.

The United States is by no means the only country that engages in these kinds of violations of the state sovereignty of other countries. It is a kind of general rule of thumb that large states—those with considerable and extensive interests and the means to realize them—are more likely to cross the sovereign rights line in other countries than weaker and smaller states that lack both those levels of interests and those means. To paraphrase an old saw, with regards to the maintenance of sovereignty, the powerful states do what they can and the weak states suffer what they must.

The U.S. Position

The United States has been one of the chief proponents of the retention of maximum sovereign rights for the government. Most of the assault has focused on human rights abuses—from genocide to torture—in the form of international conventions and treaties, mostly sponsored and sanctioned under the United Nations. In general, these treaties specify things governments cannot do and prescribe penalties, up to and including criminal penalties for the leaders of countries breaking the international agreements. They also specify that acceptance includes incorporation of prohibitions within domestic laws, a clear infringement on the "right" of countries to do anything they please within their sovereign jurisdictions. As an example, the Convention against Terrorism makes the suborning or commission of torture a war crime, and its acceptance by the United States has meant that torture is a crime under American law as well. American resistance to assaults on sovereignty based in jurisdictional infringement often puts the United States at odds with its closest allies and in incongruous positions, as the ICC case illustrates.

Applications: Changing Norms and the International Criminal Court

Sovereignty as an absolute concept has been diluted in content in the contemporary world, but its basic characteristics remain powerful aspects of international political organization, making a reiteration of those qualities necessary to understanding that changing role. These include that a sovereign state possesses (and must possess) four characteristics: a recognized territory and population, recognized jurisdiction and legitimate authority over the territory and its inhabitants, autonomy from external control, and recognition by other states. The requirements are cumulative and related. A state can only be considered sovereign if it possesses all these characteristics. If any of these characteristics is lost or falls under question, the sovereignty of the entity is compromised and can be questioned. Each characteristic is sufficiently important to warrant some examination.

Territory and Population

States are inherently physical places, the delineation of which is based on political boundaries on a map. For sovereignty to be established, there must be a recognized place over which that sovereignty can be claimed, and a population that resides in that area. For this reason, for instance, it has always been controversial whether claims of sovereignty can be made for Antarctica, which has no permanent human population. One way to solve this problem is to colonize that area with people who become permanent residents. There is no accepted process or criteria for legitimizing this method.

Accepted Jurisdiction and Legitimate Authority

Claiming sovereignty also requires that the claimant has a legitimate basis for that possession that supersedes the claims of any other body and that the claimant can politically exercise control: legitimacy and authority. These characteristics are most often called into question when a group seizes another territory and attempts to rule as a sovereign. Seizures, normally the result of invasion, are illegal under international law and undermine legitimacy. Countries that are experiencing civil conflicts between internal factions for physical control of government create controversy when they claim sovereignty, as the Islamic State did in 2014.

Autonomy from Outside Control

This characteristic refers specifically to the independence of whoever claims sovereignty from outside forces. This situation occurs when a country is invaded and conquered, and the invader puts a puppet regime in nominal charge of governance. The puppet regime may claim that it is sovereign, but its claims are unlikely to be accepted by other sovereign states. The German-installed Vichy Regime in France during World War II, which consisted of French Nazi collaborators, is an example.

Recognition by Other States

The acceptance that a physical territory and its rulers possess the other characteristics leads to the bestowal by other states of the claimant's status as a sovereign state. The symbols of that acceptance include such things as formal states of recognition, the exchange of diplomatic personnel and establishment of embassies, and regular interaction between the sovereign state and its counterparts.

Although the content and meaning of sovereignty is in a state of flux or adjustment, the concept retains considerable force as conditioning parameter about how countries deal with one another and even *if* they interact. Almost all the situations derive from questions about whether different states possess all the elements of sovereignty or whether they can successfully protect their sovereignty from outside intrusion. A few examples will illustrate this continuing relevance of the concept in contemporary international affairs.

Issues and Limits

Virtually no one overtly opposes the primacy of sovereignty as the basic means by which the international system operates. Legitimacy and authority must exist at some level to avoid total anarchy, and the alternatives to a system of sovereign states would have to transfer sovereignty either to a larger, more inclusive authority or to a smaller, more atomized series of authorities. The first possibility is to transfer power to larger bodies such as international organizations or associations of states. The UN system represents a very limited example of the international organization alternative; the European Union is an example where members confer sovereignty to elements of a voluntary association. Secession and the formation of new sovereign states represents the atomization direction.

Until recently, those who would transfer elements of sovereignty to larger bodies have had the upper hand, and the ICC case illustrates the dynamics of these efforts. There has, however, been a political backlash in both Europe and the United States that these "internationalists" (to borrow a designation developed in chapter 5) have dangerously encroached on national sovereignty in ways these "unilateralists" find dangerous. In a December 4, 2018, speech in Brussels, American Secretary of State Michael Pompeo warned of the invidious impact of organizations like the United Nations, the European Union, the Organization of American States, the African Union, and even the World Bank and the International Monetary Fund as posing potential sovereignty and national security dangers to their members on these grounds.

The issue of sovereignty thus has become entangled in the widening debate about the future direction of international relations (see chapter 5). The discussions tend to focus on the most adamant defenders of national sovereignty against those who believe that some relaxation of that principle can lead to a more prosperous, safe, and even just international system than one where absolute sovereignty holds sway.

The debate can, of course, be overstated. The assertion that states do not violate one another's sovereignty has always been somewhat fictitious, and modern electronics has made the "impenetrability" of state sovereignty even more suspect (see chapter 18). The issues are also complex, contentious, and controversial, as the case of the ICC illustrates.

The International Criminal Court Conundrum

The ICC has become part of the debate about sovereignty and infringements upon it. In some ways tension is natural and inevitable. The mission of the ICC is to identify and prosecute individuals and organizations, including states, who violate international norms, mostly those associated with war crimes, and the accused perpetrators are often states or groups and organizations within them. In order to carry out its duty, the ICC must receive the cooperation of the states where war crimes occur, and sometimes this cooperation materializes. Slobodan Milosevic, the leader of Serbia whose government committed numerous crimes against humanity in Bosnia, was turned over to the ICC by his successors; he was tried and was sentenced to life imprisonment for his deeds. Bashar al-Assad, the president of Syria, has similarly been accused of war crimes but is protected from legal jeopardy by his government, which will not relinquish sovereign control. The tension arises from the dilution of sovereignty that allowing ICC jurisdiction requires.

In historical terms, this issue is relatively recent. Under traditional concepts of sovereignty, the absolute authority it confers meant that within sovereign states, sovereignty means that states could treat people any way they wanted. No state could commit illegal acts against their own citizens. Such acts are practiced in a few places like Saudi Arabia, but they have not been internationally acceptable since World War II.

The concern underlying the criminality of war crimes and other acts of inhumanity by governments is thus largely a byproduct of the twentieth and twenty-first centuries. The role of German atrocities against Jews, Roma, and others during the 1930s and 1940s—the Holocaust—was the unavoidable stimulus to international action. It must be remembered, however, that the term genocide was not invented until 1944, and that even as the Nuremberg and Tokyo trials were being organized there was some resistance and question. One American judge at Nuremberg, for example, questioned whether the Germans could be tried for murdering German Jews and Roma who were German nationals because they were under the sovereign control of the German state. War crimes before World War II had largely been confined to traditional matters of violating the conventions for fighting, and the idea of "crimes against humanity"—now a standard basis of war crimes—had not even been articulated. The sheer atrocity and horror of Axis actions during the war made an avoidance of the international problem untenable.

The Nuremberg and Tokyo trial experiences provided the initial impetus for what became the ICC. The experience revealed two basic problems a permanent body might address and solve, both the result of the ad hoc manner for adjudicating the post–World War II cases. The first was the need to constitute a procedure and structure each time a violation occurred, which was both cumbersome and uncertain. The second was the need for a set of standards and regulations about what constituted violations and the punishments available for crimes, necessary to avoid the charge that tribunals were little more than "kangaroo courts" enforcing "victor's law" rather than objective standards.

The initial effort occurred in 1948, when the UN General Assembly commissioned the International Law Commission (a private body) to study the possibility of establishing an ICC. The Commission produced a draft statute in 1954, but it appeared during the darkest days of the Cold War. Both sides objected to a permanent body that each feared (not without reason) would be used politically against it. As a result, the United Nations dropped the proposal, which lay dormant until 1989, when it was revived by Trinidad and Tobago to help combat drug traffickers exploiting the island country's sovereign space and committing atrocities against its citizens. The proposal was energized by clear human rights tragedies in the late 1980s and early 1990s in places like Rwanda and Bosnia.

The idea of a permanent tribunal illustrated vividly the clash between international order and disorder attached to sovereignty. No country officially endorses the right to commit war crimes, but occasionally such violations do occur, and the question is what to do about these instances. The old system allowed states to invoke sovereignty to avoid actions against its citizens, but the dilution of sovereign control creates the possibility of invocation for political rather than legal reasons and thus constitutes an interference with national sovereignty. Where is the proper balance between order and disorder, justice and atrocity?

Champions of the ICC contend the Court must have mandatory jurisdiction over all accusations of war crimes and that its jurisdiction must supersede sovereignty to be effective. Sovereignty, in other words, must not be a shield behind which war criminals can hide. Opponents object to the precedent for violating national sovereignty more generally and thus undermining national control of its own territory. This latter position is largely advocated by the United States.

Advantages of an ICC

A permanent ICC had several advantages over impaneling ad hoc tribunals. First, it would not have to start from scratch each time suspected war crimes were uncovered. It would have a permanent staff who could investigate and identify war crimes situations and determine appropriate courses of action in a timely manner better than could occur in its absence.

It was also hoped that a permanent body might deter future war criminals. Would, for instance, the Bosnian Serb leaders have been dissuaded from their systematic ethnic cleansing in Bosnia if they knew what fate might befall them at the hands of international justice? Would a permanent ICC have mitigated or prevented the awful slaughter in Rwanda? At the same time, the jurisdiction of the ICC only extends to those states that accept it. Would war criminal–allowing states simply not join the ICC? The end of the Cold War had encouraged a spirit of considerable but not universal international cooperation.

The pressure to do something effective about war crimes grew during the 1990s. As early as 1995, the Clinton administration actively endorsed the concept. And the movement culminated with the Rome Conference of 1998 (technically the UN Diplomatic Conference on the Establishment of a Permanent International Criminal Court). The conference produced a proposal to establish the ICC as a permanent body with authority for trying individuals accused of genocide, war crimes, and crimes against humanity. When the vote on the draft was taken, 120 states voted in favor, seven voted against, and twenty-one abstained. To come into full effect, the treaty required ratification by sixty states, a level reached in 2002, and the ICC came into formal existence on July 1, 2002. In a harbinger of future difficulties, the United States was one of the seven states to oppose the treaty and has neither signed nor ratified it. In December 2000, President Clinton signed the statute; in February 2001, President Bush announced that his government had "unsigned" it. The United States thus both advocated and opposed the treaty. As of 2019, 122 states were members.

Objections to the International Criminal Court

The United States advocating and then opposing the ICC may seem anomalous, but it represents America's conflicting views and attitudes toward its place in the world, and especially the question of sovereignty. The Clinton administration saw the ICC as a way both to demonstrate responsible American leadership and to improve the international environment (Clinton viewed not intervening in Rwanda in 1994 as his greatest failure). Others feared the loss of sovereignty joining would entail and thus opposed American membership. Objections came to focus on the potential loss of control over American forces, especially service members who might be accused of atrocities during wartime. Acceding to the treaty would force Americans to forfeit the rights of such American authorities to foreigners, a problem illustrated by periodic Afghan insistence to exercise control of an American service member accused of atrocities in that country.

There were additional elements to the American objection. For one thing, the ICC would only have jurisdiction in countries party to the treaty and noted that countries accused of atrocities could avoid prosecution simply by not signing the treaty. Saudi Arabia is a current example. The emotional heart of the objection was forcing states to relinquish their ability to protect American citizens accused of crimes outside American jurisdiction. Jennifer Elsea summarized U.S. objections in a Congressional Research Service study in 2006: "The ICC will not offer adequate due process guaranteed them under the U.S. constitution."

The U.S. position, formulated by the Bush administration but neither modified or renounced since, contains two other objections also cited by Elsea. The first is the possibility of an "unacceptable prosecutor" who would have "unchecked discretion to initiate cases." The second is the possible "usurpation of the role of the Security Council" to intervene when questionable prosecutions are proposed. Both are sovereignty questions: who controls the ICC bureaucracy and what limits are available to check sovereignty usurpation.

These distinctions are not academic. Refusal to accept mandatory jurisdiction places the United States in a rogue's gallery of other states who have not joined the ICC statute. This list contains many of the world's most populous states but also some of the world's worst human rights and war crimes offenders, including many accused of violations of offenses covered by the ICC (Russia and Syria, for instance). One motivation of many of these states, which are concentrated in Africa and the Middle East, is to avoid the ICC's reach in situations where their own leaders might be defendants. The United States would not admit such an imputation, but is there an implicated guilt by association?

Conclusion

War crimes and their elimination are not likely to go away as an international issue with strong sovereignty ties and implications. Even in a world where authoritarianism is on the apparent decline, states still violate the norms underlying the principles on which the ICC is premised, and the resort to sovereignty often provides the cover to ignore or resist enforcement. The challenge is indirect and arises from the dogged persistence of an insistence of the inviolability of state sovereignty.

The major remaining barrier to the ICC is institutionalization of enforcement. The development of antiwar crimes norms far outdistances efforts to enforce that consensus. States agree that war crimes are bad, but they are reluctant to relinquish part of their sovereignty in the name of enforcement. Sovereignty and ICC enforcement are the matters at odds.

As noted, sovereignty is the most basic conceptual foundation element in the international system. In its early evolution, absolute sovereignty meant rulers could do whatever they wanted to those in their realms, including the commission of acts that are now clearly illegal and punishable under the rules of the ICC promulgated by those states party to the statute.

The two forces, the discretionary power of the possessor of sovereignty and the defense of human rights against abuse, thus find themselves at odds in a strange way that causes both to distort their own intent. Very few staunch defenders of sovereignty embrace the extension of their adherence to the sovereignty principle to atrocity against other peoples, but the extrapolation is imbedded in their principle. Similarly, although many who champion limits on human rights abuse blame the principle of sovereignty for creating the untamed "state of nature" and the framework for abuse it creates, very few advocate the denunciation of sovereignty as a practical solution to the dilemmas that underlie the international system of injustice it has historically allowed. In the end, the sentiments that led to the formation of the ICC are like those held by advocates of absolute versus popular sovereignty. That debate effectively ended with the triumph of those who believe sovereignty ultimately resides with individuals and that the application of state sovereignty is limited by that possession. That evolution has clearly not yet taken place in the areas advocated by the ICC. But will they be?

Study/Discussion Questions

1. Define sovereignty. When did the concept emerge as a central tenet of international relations? Who were Bodin, Grotius, Locke, and Rousseau, and how did each contribute to the development of sovereignty?
2. Sovereignty has opposite effects on domestic and international relations. What are the differences? Explain the implications for international politics.
3. How has the concept of sovereignty evolved as both a dictate in domestic and international affairs? What is the U.S. position on sovereignty? Why?
4. What are the characteristics of a sovereign state? Why is sovereignty so important to states that they sometimes go to great lengths to protect that sovereignty?

1. What is the ICC? Trace the twentieth-century emergence of the perception of a need for something like the ICC, including the American role in that evolution.
2. Discuss the legislative history of the ICC. What crimes is it supposed to have jurisdiction over? Why do its supporters say it must have a permanent role in matters of war crimes? Why does the supposed need for a permanent body create controversy among both supporters and skeptics?
3. What are the major American objections to the role and mission of the ICC that have caused it not to become a member or to accept its jurisdiction? Do you find these objections compelling?
4. Why are sovereignty and the premise of the ICC conceptually at odds with one another? Is there any practical way to resolve the competing premises and implications of supporting one at the expense of the other?

Bibliography

Bodin, Jean. *Six Books on the Commonwealth.* Oxford, UK: Basil Blackwell, 1955.
Bosco, David. *Rough Justice: The International Criminal Court in a World of Power Politics.* New York: Cambridge University Press, 2014.
Brierly, J. L. *The Law of Nations* (sixth edition). New York: Oxford University Press, 1963.

Cusimano, Mary Ann, ed. *Beyond Sovereignty*. Bedford, MA: Bedford St. Martin's Press, 1999.

Dempsey, Gary. *Reasonable Doubt: The Case Against the Proposed International Criminal Court*. CATO Policy Analysis No. 311. Washington, DC: CATO Institute, 1998.

Elsea, Jennifer K. *U.S. Policy Regarding the International Criminal Court*. Washington, DC: Congressional Research Service, August 29, 2006.

Elshtain, Jean Bethke. *Sovereignty: God, State, and Self* (reprint edition). New York: Basic Books, 2012.

Grimm, Dieter (translated by Belinda Cooper). *Sovereignty: The Origin and Future of a Political and Legal Concept* (Columbia Studies in Political Thought/Political History). New York: Columbia University Press, 2015.

Grotius, Hugo. *On the Law of War and Peace*. New York: Cambridge University Press, 2012 (originally published 1625).

———. *The Rights of War and Peace: Including the Law of Nature and Nations*. New York: M. W. Dunne, 1981.

Gutman, Roy, and David Rieff, eds. *Crimes of War*. New York: Norton, 1999.

Harris, Gardiner. "Pompeo Takes Aim at Global Institutions." *New York Times* (online), December 5, 2018.

Hashami, Sohail, ed. *State Sovereignty and Persistence in International Relations*. University Park, PA: Penn State University Press, 1997.

Hobbs, Thomas. *Leviathan*. Oxford, UK: Clarendon, 1989.

Jackson, Robert. *Sovereignty: The Evolution of an Idea*. New York: Polity Press. 2007.

Kahn, Leo. *Nuremberg Trials*. New York: Ballantine, 1972.

Kersten, Mark. *Justice in Conflict: The Effect of the International Criminal Court's Interventions on Ending Wars and Building Peace*. Oxford, UK: Oxford University Press, 2016.

Krasner, Stephen D. *Sovereignty: Organized Hypocrisy*. Princeton, NJ: Princeton University Press, 1999.

Locke, John. *Two Treatises on Government*. New York: Cambridge University Press, 1988.

Lyons, Gene M., and Michael Mastanduno, eds. *Beyond Westphalia: State Sovereignty and International Relations*. Baltimore, MD: Johns Hopkins University Press, 1995.

Morgan, Edmund S. *Inventing the People: The Rise of Popular Sovereignty in England and America* (revised edition). New York: W. W. Norton, 1989.

Novak, Andrew. *The International Criminal Court: An Introduction* (Springerbooks in Law). New York: Springer, 2015.

Randolph, Christopher. *Power and Principle: The Politics of International Criminal Courts*. Ithaca, NY: Cornell University Press, 2017.

Rousseau, Jean-Jacques. *The Collected Works of Jean-Jacques Rousseau*. Hanover, NH: University Press of New England, 1990.

Schabas, William A. *An Introduction to the International Criminal Court* (fifth edition). New York: Cambridge University Press, 2017.

Sewell, Sarah, and Carl Kaysen, eds. *The United States and the International Criminal Court: National Security and International Law*. Lanham, MD: Rowman & Littlefield, 2000.

Snow, Donald M. *National Security* (seventh edition). London and New York: Routledge, 2020.

Wegner, Patrick. *The International Criminal Court in Ongoing Intrastate Conflicts: Navigating the Peace-Justice Divide*. New York: Cambridge University Press, 2015.

2

Diplomacy

Changing Methods and U.S.-Mexico Border Security

States have a variety of ways in which they deal with one another. These range from the use of armed force to the more cooperative methods. The use of envoys from the leaders of countries (or their representatives, known as plenipotentiaries) to interact with one another (what is called diplomacy) began with the first interactions between human groups as they encountered one another. In most cases, their initial interactions were probably hostile, fearful, or both, with both (or all) sides seeing people whose appearance and means of communication were alien and incomprehensible. The problem for both was what to do about this new and probably unwanted set of other humans, and the first reactions probably included the instinct to attack and vanquish the intruders or somehow to communicate with them, try to find out if their intents were hostile or fearful like their own, and to try to reach some form of accord with them. The first reaction was the prototype for war; the second was the spark of human interaction which, in the relations between groups, became diplomacy. Both processes have developed and been greatly sophisticated since. The threat of nuclear war has acted as a governor on violent resolution to many, but not all, encounters. Recent international interactions have also raised questions about both the utility and methods of diplomacy.

Understanding what is happening in the realm of diplomacy begins by examining what the term means. Most definitions emphasize two distinct aspects of what constitutes diplomacy. The first is what diplomacy does, and it emphasizes the goal of diplomacy, which is, in the words of the *Cambridge English Dictionary*, "the management of the relations between countries." Other definitions add that doing so is a "profession" or "an art or practice." The second definition emphasizes the salient characteristics and methods of those who practice diplomacy. They emphasize what is often thought of as acting "diplomatically." Thus diplomacy is depicted as "skill in dealing with people without offending them" or "skill in handling affairs without arousing hostility." The two meanings are related: the first describes the purposes of diplomacy and the second how diplomats ought to go about that task.

It is the second meaning that is in some dispute in contemporary terms. Traditional diplomacy was largely conducted in private settings involving diplomatic professionals for whom discretion and social correctness were paramount. This meant that the public was generally unaware of the content of intergovernmental discussions and thus was unable to determine if their side had "won" or "lost" the outcome, only that an accord had been reached in which both sides argued their interests had been served by the outcome. This method, private diplomacy, stands in stark contrast to methods associated with so-called public diplomacy. The current epitome of this new practice is the bombastic style of the Trump administration, which has unsettled the diplomatic community and changed the way countries deal with one another. These changes and their impact are the subject of this chapter, illustrated by international efforts somehow to negotiate and finance the controversial border wall between the United States and Mexico.

Principle: The Art of Diplomacy

Diplomatic practices and traditions are the accumulated product of a long evolution of human experience in intergroup interaction. The Greeks, Romans, Chinese, and Egyptians are all known to have developed ad hoc ways to regularize encounters between them. Thucydides' *A History of the Peloponnesian Wars*, a fifth-century BC account of wars between Athens and Sparta, is one of the first systematic explorations of how the political city-states of Greece dealt with one another; Machiavelli's *The Prince*, an account of sixteenth-century power politics, is another famous account of the accumulating practice of what became diplomatic standards. Probably the first principles that underlay the practice were connected to reciprocity and diplomatic immunity. Before these were accepted rules of interchange, negotiators could never be sure of their fate if they ventured into hostile territory to negotiate, making the profession of diplomacy decidedly perilous. The principle of reciprocity, which roughly means that the treatment of other diplomats is governed by the treatment one might expect to be accorded one's own emissaries, and diplomatic immunity, which granted safe passage and treatment to foreign emissaries, were the necessary preconditions to developing some sort of diplomatic process.

Evolution of the Diplomatic Art

The differing experience of groups from contrasting cultures, locales, and backgrounds congealed to produce what became the modern practice of diplomacy in Europe during the fourteenth and fifteenth centuries. What is now looked upon as *classic diplomacy* is most often associated with the long process that created the Peace of Westphalia that ended the Thirty Years' War in 1648. That process was elaborated in subsequent centuries to form much of the basis of modern diplomacy. A cardinal principle of that process was governmental secrecy in dealing with one another, a practice that was tolerable when most countries were not democratic and thus popular support for and information about diplomatic practice was not necessary. World War I, which was arguably the result of practices associated with secret diplomacy, created outrage at the veil of secrecy and ushered in change to something that has been labeled *modern diplomacy*. The assault of the modernizers was led by American President Woodrow Wilson, a former political science professor, and its implementation under the banner of "open covenants openly arrived at" helped shape diplomacy for the rest of the twentieth century. The wave of populism of the early twenty-first century helped spawn another "revolution" in how ***postmodern*** diplomacy is conducted. Assessing the import and likely permanence and impact of this latter phenomenon requires looking at least briefly at the other stages of diplomatic evolution.

Diplomats serve a range of roles in addition to the more glamorous and well-publicized negotiation of resolutions to differences dividing and creating conflict between them. Diplomatic missions and their personnel carry out tasks such as representing their governments at political events, issuing or validating passports and visas, assisting businesses seeking to understand or do business in foreign countries, and aiding private citizens who may need help in the country to which the diplomatic mission is accredited, to name a few of the less dramatic roles.

The heart of diplomacy, however, is face-to-face interactions between governments on matters of mutual concern and disagreement. Historically, the role of accredited diplomats—ambassadors and their staffs being the most prominent example—was crucial. Diplomats exercised considerable discretion in how they worked and what they concluded because the physical distance between national capitals and the primitive nature of communications technology meant it was impractical, even impossible, for diplomats in the field to communicate events and ask for instructions given the lag times involved. Thus plenipotentiaries were given considerable latitude in their actions. Depending on the distance between the capitals of two states engaged in a diplomatic negotiation, the time necessary to communicate with the national capital and get a response could be weeks, even months, often with considerable possible impact. The United States, for instance, declared war on Great Britain in 1812 two weeks after all the issues dividing them had been successfully resolved: the word had simply not made its way back to Washington in time. Similarly, the most famous military clash of that war, the Battle of New Orleans, took place several weeks after the truce formally ended the war.

Modern electronic technology has changed that situation and had a major impact on the structure of diplomacy along the way. Diplomats and their central governments can now communicate with one another instantaneously, so that the discretion of diplomats is greatly reduced. In addition, diplomatic missions used to be a prime source of information, but much of that function has been eclipsed by global electronic media that collect and disseminate news much faster than before (intelligence operations within diplomatic missions still collect and provide clandestine information).

There are two major impacts of these changes on modern diplomacy. First, the ambassador has effectively ceased being the country's chief negotiator with foreign governments, since his/her activities can now be closely monitored and instructions provided to the embassy in real time. The ambassador is thus not a policy maker in the classic sense. Second, electronic speed has allowed, even facilitated, the direct intervention of the chief executive and presidential staff in diplomatic efforts. The president can keep apprised of many world events (admittedly at a nonclassified level) by watching television and can communicate directly with other world leaders by picking up the telephone.

Classic Diplomacy

Classic diplomacy, of course, was developed and evolved in a very different environment than today, and thus evolution and change are to be expected. The basic purpose of diplomacy—resolving differences hopefully in a mutually satisfactory manner short of the employment of violence—remains the same. What is important to note is the principles that evolved and form the basis of modern practice and how changes in the international environment have had an impact on those methods of doing business.

Classic diplomacy, as noted, evolved in Europe—especially the Italian states and France—during a time when absolute sovereignty was the norm including, importantly, the equation of the sovereign condition with the monarch who ruled a realm. The relations between sovereign states were considered the king's business. Generally, the interactions between monarchs had little effect on the citizenry, which did not believe it had a right to question those interactions until the rise of popular sovereignty began to broaden conceptions about the national interest—where it resided and who had a voice in it. In this circumstance, international diplomacy could be conducted outside the spotlight that illuminates modern interstate relations, including the popular politicization of those actions.

The absence of public scrutiny created a veil behind which the negotiations between states could be conducted. It was a profoundly political process in that its purpose was to resolve differences between states on matters of disagreement where the two (or more) sides desired mutually exclusive outcomes that required either or both to accept outcomes they would rather not accept. How difficult this might be varied, of course, depending on how important the outcomes might be to either or both. The more important the interests involved were (see chapter 3), the more difficult the resulting bargaining might be. Unlike the more contemporary world, such interests and bargaining were almost exclusively unknown to the public. This dynamic is important because of the impact it had on reaching solutions where the sides did not get everything they initially wanted.

Secrecy provided the context for bargaining and, most importantly, the compromise that was the central purpose and outcome of the process. In most situations, the two sides would enter with contradictory demands, both of which could not simultaneously be accommodated (they both demanded some of the same things). In this situation, there were only two ways to resolve the situation: one side could physically coerce or convince the other side to accept its position through the threat or use of violence, or they could compromise and reach a solution where both got part of but not all they wanted. Because the reason for pursuing diplomacy was normally to avoid military clash, negotiating and reaching a compromise where each got part of but not all they wanted was the main goal.

Secrecy made compromise feasible. At the end of successful negotiations, both sides would announce a settlement including the claim that they had "won"—they had accomplished what they set out to attain. The nature of compromise is that both sides relent on their most desired outcome to allow the other to get something it can claim as success. Both sides get less than they wanted, meaning the claim of "victory" is normally exaggerated, but it works because secrecy means outsiders do not know initial positions and thus cannot judge if they were achieved. This allows both sides to claim a victory their populations may demand, thus settling the dispute.

Modern Diplomacy

Citizen participation in the political system changed that environment. It was the result both of political democratization that reflected the changing nature of the locus of sovereignty and growing public perceptions of the corruption of the classic situation culminating in the series of secret treaties and protocols that helped lead to World War I. The war was a massive bloodletting from which hardly any European was exempt. The old system was blamed, and democratization seemed an inevitable consequence.

U.S. President Woodrow Wilson was the primary symbol of the assault on the old system. Wilson was a former Princeton political scientist whose classic text *Constitutional Government* was an early advocacy of political democracy and a founding building block of the study of comparative politics. The chief thesis of Wilson's text was the inherent superiority of democracy to other forms of government, and Wilson firmly believed that the application of democratic principles to diplomatic practices would produce a superior, and especially more peaceful, international order.

Because American entrance into the "Great War" had proven crucial to breaking the deadlock in Western Europe, Wilson was a leading figure at the Versailles Conference, where he worked tirelessly for moving the diplomatic process to a more open and popular level. Both the diplomatic process and its outcomes in terms of various kinds of international agreements should, in his view, be open to public scrutiny that would eliminate the pattern of secret agreements secretly negotiated and implemented. His basic belief and hope were that the result would be a more peaceful world, because he maintained that the people at large would be much more reluctant to enter into arrangements that led them to war than was possible when only a few people could reach those decisions. The crown jewel of this revolution in diplomacy was the first universal political international organization, the League of Nations (see chapter 5).

The Wilsonian experiment ultimately failed, the chief symbol of which was its inability to prevent the slide into World War II. The idea of democratic participation and parameter setting on the diplomatic enterprise was not universally embraced by states that did not join the democratizing world system (Imperial Japan was a prime example) and thus clung to both the traditional values and methods. In a few cases like those of Germany and Italy, democratic processes were even used to bring antidemocratic elements to power who perpetuated the classic model. After World War II, the Cold War confrontation further impeded the universal development of a more democratic diplomatic set of practices, at least in the relations between the superpowers.

Enough of the democratic model did seep into diplomatic practice to sow the seeds of the current transition away from classic diplomacy and the erosion of its more beneficial values on both diplomatic and domestic political processes. The opening of the diplomatic process politicized diplomacy in ways to which the international system is still adjusting. Democratizing diplomacy has had the unintended consequence of politicizing the methods, particularly the expectations that surround international relations and the resolution of the kinds of disputes that formerly would be dealt with quietly by employing compromise that allowed for both sides to claim accomplishment from the same outcome. This dynamic has been largely missing in both domestic and international relations in the early twenty-first century.

Postmodern (Contemporary) Diplomacy

In 1996, Eugene Brown and I published an international relations textbook, one of the features of which was an examination of the evolution of diplomatic practices. We identified four trends we associated with "modern diplomacy," but the categories serve to frame the more contemporary period, especially the apparent merger of diplomatic methods with more domestic ways of conducting political business. With some modifications and updates, the four observations still serve as useful ways to discuss contemporary diplomatic practice. They are summarized in Table 2.1.

The first characteristic is the proliferation of different kinds of diplomatic players. This is largely a reflection of changes in the basic structure of the international system. In the classic system, diplomacy was the exclusive province of a small group of monarchical court members who were internationally recruited (it was normal for nationals from several countries to be included in any country's diplomatic corps), and they shared common outlooks, methods, and goals. After World War II, democratization entailed national diplomatic corps and thus the injection of national viewpoints that made the system less universal and, in terms of values, more parochial because diplomacy was conducted by citizens of the countries negotiating. These diplomats did not share as fully the orientation to the process and its values that earlier practitioners held.

Contemporary practice has further expanded this trend in two ways with a major effect on the structure and conduct of diplomacy. One is the addition of new countries from regions that had not historically been part of diplomatic practices and which either had different values or were inexperienced in diplomatic practices. The Democratic People's Republic of Korea (or North Korea) is an example. The second is the addition of nonstate actors, groups within or among states whose goals are sufficiently unlike those of traditional actors that their goals do not conform to traditional norms. Revolutionary groups seeking to overthrow or change national boundaries by force are examples.

Table 2.1. Characteristics of Contemporary Diplomacy

1. Expansion and diversification of the range of diplomatic players.
2. Declining autonomy of ambassadors and embassies due to centralization of decision making in national capitals.
3. Public opinion pressure for greater openness and political accountability in diplomacy.
4. Growing importance of summit diplomacy.

The second characteristic, raised earlier, is the declining role of ambassadors in actual decision making. Part of this decline is the result of improved communication that makes it easier for national governments to communicate and even negotiate with counterpart leaders, thereby allowing a leader so inclined virtually to ignore the advice of a professional diplomatic corps and its accumulated knowledge about the countries and issues with which they must deal.

The third characteristic is public demands for greater openness and accountability in diplomatic practice. This trend, of course, is part of the Wilsonian influence after World War I, the purpose of which was to create a brake on secret alliances and other elite-dominated activities. A basically unintended result, however, has been to politicize the conduct of diplomacy and, in the most deleterious sense, to inject a highly partisan element into the system that interferes with the ability to negotiate, both because the influence can be fickle and because other states with which one is negotiating may be inhibited or confused by the vagaries of the domestic politics of those with whom they are interacting.

Possibly the most dramatic, transformational change has been the degree to which heads of state now personally conduct diplomacy among themselves—summit diplomacy. This trend, which has been growing and has reached a kind of zenith in the United States with the presidency of Donald J. Trump, has several aspects. First, it can effectively cut the professional diplomats out of the negotiating process. The diplomatic corps may remain a vital link due to its procedural and substantive expertise, but it also may be possible for national leaders to ignore their advisors and conduct negotiations on subjects they do not fully understand. A classic case involved the 1986 summit between Ronald Reagan and Mikhail Gorbachev, where the two leaders agreed privately on total nuclear disarmament before aides managed to intervene and terminate the discussions (see Oberdorfer). Second, negotiations conducted in this manner tend to be more media-driven "photo ops" than serious, detailed discussions that produce detailed, concrete resolutions of problems. Summit diplomacy, in other words, tends to simplify inherently complicated, contentious problems, and along with the greater politicization inherent in executive-level involvement, often to produce inadequate outcomes. Trump's 2017 summit with the Democratic People's Republic of Korea's Kim Jong-Un in Singapore is one of many examples. These influences—simplification and politicization—are also demonstrated by the current political and diplomatic conflict between the United States and Mexico over their shared border.

Application: Negotiations and the U.S.-Mexico Border

The 1,933-mile land border between the United States and Mexico is one of the most enduring sources of international, and thus diplomatic, interaction and disagreement between the two North American powers, and it has become a highly politicized issue since Donald J. Trump became the forty-fifth American president in 2017. His obsession with building a physical barrier of some kind as a signature political issue has transformed what has been a diplomatic problem into a highly charged political problem, thereby moving the nature of any resolution process away from diplomatic practice and distorting its nature. The 2019 presidential threat to impose tariffs on Mexico for not halting illegal border crossings is an example.

The border problem is venerable. Disagreement about where the line should be and who should control what parts of it goes back at least to the nineteenth century, when large parts of what is now the American Southwest was ceded to the United States as part of the Louisiana Purchase or 1803, and it has resurfaced periodically since: as part of the conflict over the Texas Republic and its annexation to the United States in the 1840s, to the Mexican War and its settlement in 1848, forward into the early twentieth century when the United States admitted Mexican-touching New Mexico and Arizona into the Union and Pancho Villa and his bandits raided across the border.

The problem is unique and extensive. The frontier is the longest land border between a member of the "developed" and the "developing" worlds, meaning there are very different standards of living on either side of the frontier that serve to draw people across it in search of economic benefit, which remains an active part of the problem. This dynamic in turn makes the function of the border more problematical than it might otherwise be: is it, in Nevins' terms, more a gateway to facilitate movement or a line of control (barrier) to restrict that movement? The broad answer is that it is both. Its length and the broadly differing terrain and barriers along it make it difficult to fashion and enforce a policy emphasizing both the gateway and barrier functions. The border between the United States and Canada is primarily a gateway; the U.S.-Mexico border is both gateway and barrier. It is thus more complicated.

Aspects of the Border Dispute

The current political debate on erecting a physical barrier oversimplifies the issue, ignoring major (and arguably subtler and more important) aspects of the border's function than the atavism of essentially closing the border suggests. The current policy debate focuses on the problem of immigration by illegal undesirables and the problems they pose. The real dynamics of the problem are more complex and probably best served by international negotiation—diplomacy—that the current political effort virtually precludes. Traditional analyses (including my own) have focused on three essentially international problems: the question of immigration (see chapter 12), the narcotics trade that crosses the border, and terror. Evidence of the terrorist penetration is so minimal that it does not merit consideration beyond saying it is possible but has not been convincingly observed. Immigration and drugs are domestic American problems; they are also international problems, some of the solutions to which require diplomatic attention and resolution.

The Immigration Problem

That there is a constant influx of foreigners into the United States from south of the U.S.-Mexico border is a consequence of being where the less-developed world rubs against its more prosperous neighbors. It is a situation that has existed since the two countries were formed, and it probably reached its zenith in the 1990s, when implementation of the North American Free Trade Agreement stimulated the economy, producing jobs in the United States for which there were inadequate workers and thus stimulating an influx of workers to fill the void, many of whom were undocumented or "illegal." This migration was magnified by the fact that U.S. prosperity came at the expense of Mexican and Central American populations, further increasing the incentive to come north. The U.S.-Mexico-Canada Agreement is supposed to mitigate this problem.

These immigrants can be classified into three groups. The vast majority are *economic immigrants*, people who travel to the United States to make a better living than they can in their native countries; many send remittances back to their relatives and help to boost local economies. Their virtue is that they are, by and large, hard-working and honest. They can further be divided into those seeking permanent residence in the country and seasonal workers who come into the United States for seasonal jobs like food harvesting and return home after their jobs are completed. They perform tasks Americans do not want: the so-called 3-D jobs (dirty, dangerous, and difficult). Moreover, their crime rates are well below those of the general American population. Second are the *political immigrants*, asylum seekers fleeing oppression and even death in their home countries, a problem largely associated with the Central American states (Nicaragua, Guatemala, and El Salvador).

The third group, *criminal immigrants*, are the real problem. This group consists mainly of people associated with criminal cartels and organizations engaged in the narcotics business, and they migrate to organize the sale of and profit from the sale of narcotics to Americans. These "narco-gangs," many of whose members are Mexican, pose the real threat to which border security advocates refer when they advocate great line of control measures. The irony is that these measures—like the "wall"—are primarily effective against the immigrants who will not commit crimes if admitted and quite ineffective against the criminal elements, who possess monetary and other resources to surmount any barriers.

Is a stronger line of control the answer to the immigration part of the issue? It is part of the solution to slow the rate of infiltration, but it is not clear that it is effective against the real problem, which is the crime and violence associated with criminal insurgents. As officials like Utah Senator Mitt Romney point out, if one wants to cut the flow of economic immigrants, the answer is to attack their incentive, which is the availability of jobs. It violates American law to employ undocumented workers, and Romney argues that enforcing existing laws (arresting and trying employers who hire illegal workers) would reduce the jobs and the flow. The Trump administration has never implemented effective procedures for doing so. Similarly, the reason the drug lords are active is because Americans represent a ready market for their wares. A quarter century ago, one part of the solution was "demand side," reducing the market for drugs through efforts to reduce drug usage through education and the like, especially in urban areas where the problem (and thus the profits) are concentrated. When was the last time the Trump administration suggested dealing with demand for drugs as an augmentation to building a bigger barrier, which many argue will not work anyway: Former New Mexico Governor Bill Richardson once dismissed a predecessor barrier proposal, saying, "If we build a 10-foot wall, they will build an 11-foot ladder."

Drugs

If there is a core security issue of which the southern border is a central part, it is the flow of illegal narcotic drugs (especially heroin and cocaine) going northward into the United States. It is by no means a new problem: it dates to the post–American Civil War period, when wounded veterans suffering long-term effects from war wounds turned to narcotics from South America to ease their pain, and this stimulus was repeated by World War I veterans. Today, between 70 and 90 percent of the illegal drugs entering the United States come across the Mexican border. Almost all make the transit through regular points of entry, normally as physically small parts of loads of cargo in eighteen-wheeler tractor trailer trucks that the border patrol cannot adequately inspect.

The drug traffic is at the heart of whatever crisis exists surrounding the border in two ways. First, it fuels a sizable part of the drug epidemic in the United States, a public health and crime problem of significant proportions and a problem that has existed for at least three decades. Second, almost all the crime and violence associated with illegal immigration is a direct consequence of drug trafficking, because narcotics traffickers, not economic immigrants, commit virtually all the crime that forms what President Trump has labeled the "national emergency" resulting from illegal migration. A border security system designed to reduce the criminal aspect must cull out and stop the criminals.

How does one deal with narcotics-related border penetration? A barrier may be part of the answer, but it is not the solution. The trucks carrying drugs pass through regular checkpoints that would be unaffected by the wall, and the most a wall could do is provide a filter to capture some cartel members from sneaking across the border or intermingling with economic immigrants. A strategy for dealing with the narcotics problem and the associated violence it brings must have two central elements. The first is strengthening cooperation between Mexican and American officials aimed at interrupting and suppressing the movement of drugs into the United States from Mexico. This is especially the case in terms of assistance to Mexican police efforts that have been overwhelmed by the narco-cartels, and that entails suppressing the flow of arms from the United States into Mexico that have added to the firepower advantage of the traffickers. The second is a more aggressive American effort to convince Americans to eschew drug use (a revival of Nancy Reagan's 1980s "Just say no to drugs" campaign, perhaps?), thereby reducing cartel profits and aiding internal policing. A third and related initiative might be developmental assistance programs between the United States, Mexico, and Central American countries further to develop those countries so that less of their citizens will seek to leave.

Diplomacy and Border Security

If the problem posed by the Mexican-American border was simple to resolve, it would not have been around for nearly 200 years, but it has been. Most of the problem, of course, centers on movement northward by people (immigrants of one kind or another) and illicit commodities (currently narcotics), and a sensible border security system—which includes some more efficient regulation of immigration—is clearly a national priority on both sides of the border. The United States wants a less porous, more orderly system by which it can regulate movement of people and things across its frontier; Mexico and Central America want to reduce the corrosive effects of American weapons flooding across the border from the United States that end up in the hands of the narco traffickers and leave the Mexican authorities outgunned and increasingly vulnerable to the drug cartels. The result can be political destabilization in Mexico that could leak across the border and affect Americans. Central Americans need more resources for development, both to provide a better life for their citizens and to foster political reform, both of which could slow the flow of people (mostly economic immigrants) northward.

These problems are all international and interactive, and as such, they are logical candidates for diplomatic efforts between the United States and its southern neighbors. There is little evidence such efforts are occurring, or that the approach of the participants—and especially the Trump administration—tends toward the partisan political public advocacy of policies that may address some American concerns (e.g., the "Wall") but do not address the broader questions of international cooperation and have at least the implicit effect of antagonizing those with whom diplomatic efforts must be undertaken. As noted earlier, the heart of a good diplomatic process is that the maximum goals of each party are not made public at the beginning of negotiation. Those goals generally must be compromised to accommodate the maximum goals of the other, so that after an agreement is reached, both participants can publicly argue that it has accomplished the purpose it set out to achieve.

Think of the contemporary border debate in these terms. It began with the highly public announcement by the American president that there would be a border barrier the length of the frontier and that Mexico would pay for it. Mexico immediately fired back they certainly would not pay for the wall and implied they would not cooperate with its construction. Regardless of the merits of either position, they were the kind of goals one pursues in private, because announcing them publicly removes any ability to compromise without "losing" in the estimation of its own countrymen. Can Trump back away from an augmented line of control without appearing to "lose," regardless of the merits of any other parts of an agreement? Can Mexico participate in financing the wall without a similar loss of face? The answer in both cases is negative, and the large reason is that diplomatic principles were ignored and violated from the start. Other aspects of potential diplomatic negotiation like drugs entering the United States and cartel destabilization of Mexican politics, which were points on which negotiation might have proven fruitful have not, as far as is publicly known, been rigorously pursued, despite cooperation in pursuing, capturing, and incarcerating Mexican drug lord Juaquin Guzman (El Chapo).

Politics and diplomacy have clearly merged in the border security debate. Is security a real concern? Absolutely, but it has been a problem for a long time and is probably no worse than it has been in the past. What is different is that the international diplomatic problem of negotiating all or part of the problem has disappeared in the fog of postmodern political approaches to diplomacy like tariff threats to force compliance. It is hard to argue the result has been beneficial to solving the border problem.

Conclusion

Diplomacy has been the backbone method by which states have sought to solve their problems with one another in a nonviolent manner. The set of protocols and methods that have evolved over time are detailed and go beyond present concerns. The underlying rationale, however, does not. Diplomacy is, at heart, a quiet enterprise wherein the participants negotiate to reach mutually acceptable—if not always optimal—resolutions to their differences. The key element is compromise, the willingness to accept less than one might want in order to facilitate an outcome where both sides can claim success and be satisfied with the outcome. The intrusion of public political posturing upsets, even destroys, that process. Compromise becomes a dirty word, because partisans do not get everything they want and deride the diplomats who failed to achieve resolutions in which they attain all their desires—outcomes that would almost certainly be unacceptable to the other side and thus guarantee that no resolution occurs at all.

The border security debate centering on a border wall between the United States and Mexico illustrates the distortion that failing to engage in quiet diplomacy can create. At one level, there is the question of whether a physical barrier solves the problem of border security between the two countries, a legitimate national interest for which an arguably faulty implementing strategy is being advocated. In the process of a highly politicized debate in the United States, the possibility of quiet diplomatic interaction between the two states to their potential mutual benefit has been forfeited. That may be the real shame of the situation.

Study/Discussion Questions

1. What is diplomacy? What are the three stages through which it has evolved since 1648? Why is this evolution important?
2. What are the four characteristics of modern diplomacy identified in the text? Describe each and why it is important.
3. How have diplomacy and politics comingled in the contemporary world? How has that phenomenon affected the contemporary conduct of international relations?
4. Would a return to older and more prominent roles for diplomacy improve American interaction with the world? Use the wall as an example.
5. What are the basic issues that divide the United States and Mex-

ico surrounding their mutual border? Place the current imbroglio in historic context.

6. Discuss the immigration problem along the border. Discuss the various kinds of immigrants that cross the border. Do current policy efforts reflect the problem?
7. What is the nature of the drug crisis as a border security problem? Is drug (and drug dealer) penetration the real border issue? Discuss.
8. Will the wall (or some other form of barrier) solve the border security problem, or are there other approaches that should be explored?

Bibliography

Andreas, Peter. *Border Games: Policing the U.S.-Mexico Divide.* Ithaca, NY: Cornell University Press, 2009.

Berridge, G. R. *Diplomacy: Theory and Practice* (fifth edition). London: Palgrave, 2015.

Black, Jeremy. *A History of Diplomacy.* Chicago, IL: University of Chicago Press, 2010.

Bonner, Robert C. "The New Cocaine Cowboys: How to Defeat Mexico's Drug Cartels." *Foreign Affairs* 89, no. 4 (July/August 2010), 35–47.

Camp, Roderic. *Politics in Mexico: Consolidation or Decline?* New York: Oxford University Press, 2013.

Carpenter, Ted Galen. *The Fire Next Door: Mexico's Drug Violence and the Danger to America.* Washington, DC: Cato Institute Press, 2012.

Cooper, Andrew F., and Jorge Heine. *The Oxford Handbook of Modern Diplomacy* (Oxford Handbooks). Oxford, UK: Oxford University Press, 2015.

Dorman, Shawn. *Inside a U.S. Embassy: The Essential Guide to the Foreign Service* (third edition). Washington, DC: Potomac Books, 2011.

Edmunds-Poli, Emily, and David A. Shirk. *Contemporary Mexican Politics* (third edition). Lanham, MD: Rowman & Littlefield, 2015.

Farrow, Ronan. *War on Peace: The End of Diplomacy and the Decline of American Influence.* New York: W. W. Norton, 2018.

Ganster, Paul, and David E. Lorey. *The Mexican Border Today: Conflict and Cooperation in Historical Perspective.* Lanham, MD: Rowman & Littlefield, 2015.

Kennan, George F., and John Mearsheimer. *American Diplomacy: Sixtieth Anniversary Expanded Edition.* New York: Simon and Schuster, 2012.

Kerr, Pauline, and Geoffrey Wiseman. *Diplomacy in a Globalizing World.* Oxford, UK: Oxford University Press, 2017.

Kissinger, Henry A. *Diplomacy.* New York: Touchstone Books, 2011.

———. *A World Restored: Metternich, Castlereagh, and the Problem of Peace.* New York: Touchstone Books, 1999.

Kopp, Harry W., and John K. Naland. *Career Diplomacy: Life and Work in the U.S. Foreign Service* (third edition). Washington, DC: Georgetown University Press, 2017.

Kralev, Nicholas. *America's Other Army: The U.S. Foreign Service and Twenty-First Century Diplomacy* (second edition). New York: CreateSpace Independent Publishing Platform, 2015.

Lasswell, Mark, ed. *Fight for Liberty: Defending Democracy in a World of Trump.* New York: PublicAffairs, 2018.

Longo, Matthew. *The Politics of Borders: Sovereignty, Security, and the Citizen after 9/11.* New York: Cambridge University Press, 2017.

Machiavelli, Niccolo. *The Prince*. New York: Millennium Press, 2018 (originally published 1532).
Nevins, Joseph. *Gatekeepers and Beyond: The War on "Illegals" and the Remaking of the U.S.-Mexico Border* (second edition). New York: Routledge, 2010.
Oberdorfer, Don. *The Turn: From the Cold War to a New Era: The United States and the Soviet Union, 1983-1990*. New York: Poseidon Press, 1991.
O'Neil, Shannon. "The Real War in Mexico: How Democracy Can Defeat the Drug Cartels." *Foreign Affairs* 88, 4 (July/August 2009), 63–77.
Payan, Terry. *The Three U.S.-Mexico Border Wars: Drugs, Immigration, and Homeland Security* (second edition). Westport, CT: Praeger Security International, 2016.
Phelps, James R., and Jeffrey Dailey. *Border Security* (second edition). Durham, NC: Carolina Academic Press, 2018.
Rana, Kishan S., and Giles Scott-Smith. *Twenty-First Century Diplomacy: A Practitioner's Guide*. New York: Continuum, 2011.
Shifter, Michael. "Latin America's Drug Problem." *Current History* 106, no. 697 (February 2007), 58–63.
Snow, Donald M. *Regional Cases in U.S. Foreign Policy* (second edition). Lanham, MD: Rowman & Littlefield, 2018.
——— and Eugene Brown. *The Contours of Power: An Introduction to Contemporary International Relations*. New York: St. Martin's Press, 1996.
Thucydides. *A History of the Peloponnesian Wars*. New York: Penguin Books, 1954.
U.S. Government and U.S. Military. *Decision Model for U.S.-Mexican Border Security, Measures—President Trump's Proposed Border Wall, History of Security Infrastructure by ICE, CBP, DHS, Intelligence Community, Law Enforcement*. Washington, DC: U.S. Government, 2017.
Walt, Stephen. *The Hell of Good Intentions: America's Foreign Policy Elite and the Decline of American Primacy*. New York: Farrar, Straus, and Giroux, 2018.
Wilson, Woodrow. *Constitutional Government: A Study in American Politics*. New York: Amazon Digital Services, 2017 (originally published 1885).

3

National Interests and Power

Dealing with Saudi Arabia

Interests represent another primary concept in international relations. Sovereignty means those interests are defined in national terms, making the determination and protection of national interests the key operational dictate and definition of sovereignty. The basic term "interests" has multiple meanings in different contexts, but the base of the concept comes from the French term *raison d'etat* (reason of state), which establishes national interests (the values of the sovereign states) above those of other claimants. In practice, determining interests is not so easy because people within and between states disagree fundamentally on the content and relative importance of interests as they affect themselves and other states. Moreover, interests come into conflict with those of other individuals and states, and they often are different, contradictory, and not amenable to easy resolution. The competitive pursuit of national interests by the world's sovereign states is thus highly controversial, ambiguous, and conflict-producing.

The interplay of conflicting interests is at the heart of much diplomacy, whether amicably conducted or more conflictual. Ultimately, resolving conflicts of national interests requires some or all the parties do things they would rather not do, which is the definition of power.

The resolution of conflicts of interest is often idiosyncratic, influenced by a complex of factors that is unique to the relations of affected states at different times. The application in this chapter between Saudi Arabia and the United States reflects both change and uniqueness. For most of the post–World War II period, they have been close collaborators, even "friends," with oil as their great commonality. Given the nature of the Saudi monarchy, they have also been strange political bedfellows. The reduced American dependency on Persian Gulf oil and Saudi actions, such as its aggression in Yemen and royal family complicity in the murder of journalist Jamal Khashoggi, have contributed to changing perceptions of their relationship.

Principle: National Interest and Power

The term "national interest" occupies a virtually sacrosanct position in international political language. These interests represent the hierarchical values that states have. National interests and sovereignty are inextricably intertwined. Sovereignty dictates that the interests a state has are its most important concern and are called "vital interests." Preserving the state is the highest national priority and thus the supreme national interest. This attachment endows the concept of national interest with a virtually absolute importance and need for obeisance in even the most heated and contentious discussions. The primacy and necessity of preserving and promoting national interests is at the heart of international conflicts and their resolution. The use of force is one of the ways these conflicts may be resolved.

National interests are controversial. It is easy to state the definition of what constitutes an interest, but applying that definition to the substance of actual situations is difficult. The idea that there *are* conditions that serve national values is virtually unassailable; *what* those conditions may be in general or in the context of often ambiguous situations is quite another matter, and it is the basis for lively domestic and international debates about national interest that are subjective in nature and often difficult to resolve.

The Non-Intersubjective Nature of National Interest

Phrasing any issue as being in the national interest gives it an aura of great importance and gravitas, because many people equate national interest and national security. The advocacy of something as being in the national interest suggests that it is contributing to that most vital of national interests—the country's security from harm. Sometimes that equation is valid and sustainable, but at other times it is not so clearly the case, for one or both of two reasons. One is that the issue may not really be important enough for this elevation, and the other is the position the advocate has on the issue may or may not be the best way to attain the goal. The abstract idea of national interest may be rock solid, but the proposed actions made in its name may not be.

There is a formalistic way to state this problem: *intersubjectivity*. The term comes from the philosophy of science, and it refers to whether all observers can view the same phenomenon in the same way. A useful synonym for the term is objectivity, and it means that for something to be intersubjective, it must be viewable in the same way by all observers. The statement President Donald Trump is a Republican is intersubjective, because it is a fact with no embellishment or interpretation. The statement that Trump is a good (or bad) president is not intersubjective, because it requires a subjective interpretation that goes beyond objective fact to opinion, and people hold different opinions on things.

Questions of national interest are very much of this nature. Their core begins from some generally objective observation (a statement of truth), to which two additional characteristics, neither of them objective, are added. One is whether the issue is in fact a matter of interest and what degree of importance should be attached to doing something about it. The second characteristic consists of a prescription for appropriate action to alleviate whatever problem the situation creates. The first observation is generally objective: its truth or falsity can be demonstrated objectively. The other questions are subjective, because it is a matter of opinion what the nature and extent of the problem is and what needs to be done about it.

One can make questions of what is and is not in the national interest look more chaotic and contentious than they in fact are. Determining interests is an ongoing exercise within governments and analysts where there is broad agreement on the general categories of those interests and at least in general about how to handle them. The content of what is in the national interest does not change as much as do challenges to that interest and what those changes may portend. The key concept is the idea of vital interests, the sole property of sovereign states.

Operationalizing the National Interest: The Key Role of Vital Interests

Scholars and policy makers alike seek to make national interests more concrete and objective. No one doubts that national interests exist and are supreme in a system of sovereign states. Likewise, everyone agrees that not all interests are equally important, that the consequences of their non-realization differ depending on their relative importance, and that different levels and kinds of national exertion are appropriate to attain or maintain them.

The most basic distinction is made between those interests that are *vital* (VIs) for the country to realize and those that are *less-than-vital* (LTVs). VIs are generally defined as conditions that are so important to the state that it will not willingly compromise on their attainment. Achieving those interests may not always be within the power of the state, but they are the baseline of a country's sense of security. This definition helps explain why states will not allow an authority superior to themselves to adjudicate their differences, because a verdict against them could affect their vital interests and would be unacceptable and likely would be resisted or disobeyed. LTV interests, on the other hand, are matters of descending but lesser importance to the state that would cause varying but not basic discomfort or inconvenience to the state and whose non-realization may not be entirely intolerable.

The VI-LTV distinction is critical because it is generally considered the effective boundary between those situations where the state will and will not consider the recourse to violence to attain them. In simplest terms, VIs are potentially worth going to war over to ensure; LTVs do not normally justify the recourse to force. Even this distinction is less sharp than the simple statement may suggest, because there will always be disagreement about the worthiness and appropriateness of force in a specific situation. For this reason, it may be better to think of the boundary between VIs and LTVs as a "confidence interval" within which disagreement exists rather than as a sharp line.

These distinctions are important enough that they bear further elaboration both analytically and as a guide for political action. The late Donald Nuechterlein, in a 1991 text, laid out a more elaborate way of distinguishing interests based in a four-by-four matrix reproduced as Table 3.1.

The two dimensions are hierarchical in descending order of importance to the state. On the intensity dimension, the survival of the state is clearly its most intense interest, the inability of which to secure leaves other interests moot. Not all vital interests entail challenges to national survival, but they are important enough that states will engage in serious, including military, efforts

Table 3.1. Nuechterlein National Interest Matrix

	Intensity of Interest			
Basic Interest at Stake	**Survival**	**Vital**	**Major**	**Peripheral**
Homeland Defense				
Economic Well-Being				
Favorable World Order				
Values Promotion				

to attain them. Border disputes often fall into this category, such as the current conflict between the United States and Mexico over the sanctity of their common boundary. The differentiations are not precise or clearly intersubjective, but major interests are matters that would inconvenience and trouble a state (the terms of an international trade agreement might be an example) but whose non-realization would be tolerable. Peripheral interests attach to conditions the state might disfavor but to which it can adapt. The ongoing border dispute with Mexico probably belongs between vital and major intensity.

The other dimension refers to the content of interests. It is also hierarchically arranged. Clearly, matters of homeland security are of the most basic nature and can be either survival or vital in intensity, depending on how extensive the threat is. Conquests of states clearly qualify as survival in intensity; the annexation of a small part of national territory may be vital but not survival-threatening. Because the commodiousness of life within a state is related to its economic standing, economic well-being is also very important, and probably can take on the characteristic of vital or major importance depending on the situation. A favorable world order and the promotion of American values are presumably at a lower order of vitality.

The Nuechterlein matrix may help clarify some thinking about the relative priority of securing certain national interests, but it does not resolve all matters nor provide iron-clad guidance over what the country should do all of the time. All situations are to some degree unique, meaning some judgments must be made in all cases, and people will disagree about the nature and importance of given challenges to interests: into what pair of categories from the matrix does an individual situation fall? How important is it? Based on this assessment, what quality of actions are justifiable to realize the affected interest and which are not? Clearly, the most important consequential differentiation involves the boundary between VIs and LTV interests. As noted, this line is really a confidence interval (or band), because not everyone accepts the same frontier at which an interest passes from LTV to vital, and vice versa.

National and Other Levels of Interest

The concepts of sovereignty and national interest are intertwined in another way that leads some to question the idea that national interest, like sovereignty, should be as supreme and overriding as it is. The objection that is raised suggests that state sovereignty has pernicious effects and has its parallel in the definition of the supremacy of national interest as opposed to the interests of individuals and the interests that go beyond those of states (international interests).

The obvious implication of elevating national interest to conceptual supremacy is that as a result, interests at other levels occupy a lesser priority and importance, a consequence with which not everyone agrees. They are asserting other levels of interest that some argue are of equally or even arguably greater importance than those of national interest.

Objections come from both ends of a spectrum from interests that affect individual humans to those that affect the human condition. At one extreme are *individual* interests, the most important of which center on individual human rights and the conditions that maximize (or minimize) the survival and prosperity of individuals. At the other end of the spectrum are *international* interests, those conditions and actions that contribute to or detract from maximum survivability and prosperity for everyone. The levels problem exists because the pursuit of one level may come at the expense of the others. More specifically, the pursuit of national interest as the supreme value may endanger or preclude the pursuit of individual or international interests.

Individual interests represent an extension of the arguments for popular sovereignty that can be endangered by an unfettered pursuit of national interests in several ways. Probably the most obvious is when national interests collide with those of another state, are sufficiently important to both that they cannot compromise on them, and thus result in the resort to armed violence. In that circumstance, individuals may well be involuntarily required to fight in the ensuing hostilities, a participation to which those placed in harm's way may object and which certainly infringes on the pursuit of the individual right to survive.

The other competing level is international interests, conditions that transcend national boundaries and which can only be addressed by international efforts. This level becomes a concern and source of international tension and disagreement particularly when efforts to pursue national interests result in international effects that both make the disagreement over national interests greater and endanger the interests of humankind as a whole.

Possibly the most notable political science example of the clash of national and international interest levels is a construct called the ***security dilemma***. This idea was first articulated by John H. Herz in a 1951 book and referred to the situation where one state, feeling insecure in its security relationship with another state, takes actions to increase its sense of security. In the classic depiction, the threatened state builds up its military power to cancel a perceived inferiority, and this action creates a similar reaction by the other state (the dynamic is often referred as the action-reaction phenomenon) which, in the classic example, did not previously harbor animosity to the threatened state. It interprets the other's buildup as a hostile act and increases its own armament which, in turn, causes the other state to arm even more, and the situation spirals into an arms race in which both states end up being less secure than they were in the first place. This dynamic, as pointed out by scholars like Jervis and Waltz, is most destabilizing when nuclear weapons are the currency of the arms race. Waltz's *Theory of International Politics*, reprinted in 2010 before his 2013 death, remains a classic statement.

National interests are more controversial than many who emphasize them lead people to believe. The concept flows from the notion of a world of sovereign states each concerned almost exclusively with its own narrowly defined well-being. Raising national interest to supremacy, however, accentuates conflict and competition between its members and adds to the use of power—including military force—that may be invoked to get other states to do what they would prefer not to do. The concept in application is also much more fluid than its apparent immutability suggests. Interests and conflicts between them do change, as the contemporary relations between the United States and Saudi Arabia demonstrate.

Application: Dealing with Saudi Arabia

It is sometimes said by both diplomats and analysts that national interests do not change very much or very often, but that circumstances altering the level of threat to achieving those interests are subject to change and vacillation over time. Effectively, the promotion and protection of national interests thus compete with changes in the environment in which interests exist. In a system of sovereign states, these challenges often arise in the bilateral relations between countries. Recent changes in the relationship between Saudi Arabia and the United States illustrate this process in action.

The United States has historically defined its interest in the Middle East (see more detailed discussion in chapter 13) as the promotion of peace and stability in an historically unstable, contentious region. This preference reflects three traditional American preferences in the area: the safety and sanctity of Israel in a religiously hostile region, the minimization of Soviet (and presumably more recently Russian) influence, and guaranteeing access to adequate petroleum resources at a reasonable and stable price. More recently, suppressing regional sources of terrorism potentially directed at the United States has been added to the list. The Saudis, the prosperity and status of whom derive almost exclusively from oil revenues, have viewed the United States as their primary oil customer, valuable source of military acquisition, and a prime provider of protection for the Kingdom from its enemies. In addition, the Saudis, because of their evangelical state religion (Sunni Wahhabism), see the promotion of very conservative Islam as a primary goal, and this evangelism entails expanding its sway as a regional power. This goal is mainly associated with its competition with Shiite, non-Arab Iran, which is by far the most populous regional power and a formidable obstacle to a heightened Saudi role.

The interests of the two countries are asymmetrical as they impinge on one another. Especially since the breach in American relations with Iran following the fall of the Shah of Iran and the subsequent hostage crisis beginning in 1979, the United States increased its consumption of Persian Gulf oil from the Kingdom and smaller Persian Gulf states aligned with it (largely through Wahhabism) along the Gulf littoral, but the United States had other countries from which it could and did buy oil (e.g., Nigeria, Mexico, Venezuela), making the Saudis more dependent on the United States and its European allies than they were on the Saudis' oil. The dependency of Saudi Arabia on the Americans was starkly demonstrated in 1990 and 1991 during the Persian Gulf War (Operation Desert Storm) when American forces were arguably the only thing that protected the Saudis from the capture of their oil fields and refining facilities by Saddam Hussein's Iraqi invaders.

Saudi assertiveness has been at the base of some cooling in U.S.-Saudi relations. Because the Iranians have become more assertive in a number of regional conflicts such as the civil war in Syria and the support of Israel's continued denial of a Palestinian state, the monarchy in Riyadh has become more militantly anti-Iranian and has involved itself in related power struggles in the region that have some Sunni-Shia but especially Wahhabist implications in places like Qatar and Yemen. Although much of Saudi domestic and much of its foreign policy are unfamiliar and even repugnant to the United States, the two countries have remained closely aligned, with commonalities in the area of petroleum production, opposition to Iran, and more recently, warmer relations between the Saudis and the Israelis (some of this is analyzed in chapter 13).

An Odd and Asymmetrical "Friendship"

It is sometimes said that the United States and Saudi Arabia are "friends." As in the case of most international relationships, it is a misnomer, and one that the Saudis never employ. Rather, it is more appropriate to discuss the relationship between the two countries as one where they have some mutual interests, and in those situations they interact positively when it is to their mutual interest. On the other hand, when the interests of the two sides differ, and especially when the result is disagreement and lack of cooperation, the depiction of international "friendship" does not apply. There can be friendly relations between Saudi and American officials (Prince Bandar bin-Sultan, who was Saudi ambassador to Washington during the 1980s, made an ostentatious effort to befriend as many in Washington as he could), but those efforts were not emblems of general U.S.-Saudi relations.

The major commonality between the two countries is economic: both are among the wealthiest states in the world, if for very different reasons that have very different consequences for their places in the world. According to statistics published in the 2019 edition of *The World Almanac and Book of Facts*, per capita gross domestic product (GDP) for Saudi Arabia is $54,800, whereas the equivalent figure for the United States is $59,500. The American economy is diverse and has an overall strength that ranks it as a superpower (its GDP is $19.4 trillion, second largest in the world after China), whereas the Saudi GDP is about one-tenth that at $1.8 trillion. Saudi Arabia's economy and wealth is almost entirely derived from natural resources—mainly petroleum—exploitation, although the Kingdom is trying to diversify somewhat, whereas the American economy is much more diverse. The geopolitical upshot is that Saudi importance in the world is tied almost entirely to world demand for petroleum, and their strength arises from their ability essentially to "buy" influence with oil wealth: the December 2018 Saudi offer to finance the rebuilding of Syria demonstrates this use of Saudi power.

The two countries could also hardly be more different geographically and demographically. Saudi Arabia has a much smaller and less diverse population. The country's population is a little over 33 million, but 37 percent of that total was immigrants in 2017, who are imported from neighboring regions to perform physical labor and are ineligible for citizenship. The official count of citizenry is 90 percent Arab, of whom 85 to 90 percent are Sunnis, predominated by the Wahhabis (see subsequent discussion). By constitutional provision, non-Muslims are ineligible for citizenship. The country is relatively large at 830,000 square miles, but only 1.6 percent of it is arable. This contrasts with the United States, which has both the world's third largest population and geographic area.

Politically and otherwise, the countries could scarcely be more unalike. According to the *CIA World Factbook*, the Kingdom of Saudi Arabia is one of a handful of countries (basically all in the Persian Gulf region) designated as an "absolutist monarchy," meaning that the king exercises total political power in a way not seen in the West since the Middle Ages, and certainly not in the past several centuries. In terms introduced in chapter 1, the king is the sovereign with powers that have disappeared from Western practice since the rise of notions of popular sovereignty. This status sanctions extreme and summary justice against its citizens by its rulers, including accusations the regime has "dealt brutally with its critics," according to Gause. Their behavior and values caused T. E. Lawrence (quoted in Anderson) to describe the Saudi Wahhabists in the 1920s as "marginal medievalists" during his campaign in Arabia. This description stands in stark contrast with the values of the American system as a secular democracy funded on the precepts of popular sovereignty.

The other point of contrast is the role of religion in the society. The United States, of course, was founded on the principle of religious freedom and the absolute separation of church and state. The situation in Saudi Arabia could hardly be more different. When the movement to create Saudi Arabia was being contested in the 1920s, the House of Saud, which became and remains the political power in the country, aligned itself with the extremely fundamentalist Wahhabist sect of Sunni Islam. Wahhabism became the state religion of Saudi Arabia, and it is both an extremely conservative and evangelical form of Islam and is the basic faith of many of the wealthiest people in the country. The House of Saud and the Wahhabis formed an enduring alliance where the Wahhabis support the regime if it neither interferes with Wahhabi pursuits or activities. Many Wahhabist views are radically anti-Western (including anti-American), creating the seed for dissension. Their support is also crucial to Saud retention of political power. The combination of Wahhabi extremism and the level of influence wealthy Wahhabis have on the government in Riyadh creates conditions which have created schisms in U.S.-Saudi relations that have become evident recently.

Most Americans, including many political figures, know little about Wahhabism and the power its adherents have over Saudi behavior that increasingly affects adversely relations between the two countries. The relationship between the House of Saud, from whose clan the political leadership arises, and the Wahhabis is particularly intimate and powerful. The sovereign state of Saudi Arabia came into existence in 1932, declared by Abdal-Aziz bin Abdul Rahman Al Saud

(Ibn Saud), who had led the movement to expel the Ottomans and other foreigners from the land of Mecca and Medina, the birthplace and residence of Mohammed and thus the holiest land within Islam. The rise to power was the direct result of an alliance between the House of Saud and Wahhabist religious leaders, the salient (if officially unrecorded) bargain underlying which was that the Wahhabi leadership, which controlled the most wealth in the Kingdom and which is supported by many Saudis, would control the country's religious life in the form of making Wahhabism the state religion of the country, in return for which religious leaders (and their wealth) would support rule by the House of Saud. In 1992, the Saudi Basic Law requires that the king of Saudi Arabia be a direct descendent of Ibn Saud, a practice that is still in effect. The ruler knows, however, that his rule rests on Wahhabi support, meaning the religious leadership has an effective veto on Saudi policy and that violating Wahhabi practice could result in the termination of the Saud monarchy.

The problem is that Wahhabism is a particularly fundamentalist sect of Sunni Islam the precepts and preferences of which run counter to American (and most other) modern thought. It is based in a fundamentalist and literalist interpretation of Islam that seeks a return to the religious purity of the seventh century when the Prophet taught and thus employs many of the precepts of that time. Many of these are encompassed in the harshness of *sharia* law in areas of crime and harsh, summary forms of justice that are offensive to Westerners and *Salafism*, which translates as "pious forefathers" and is used to justify violence. The Wahhabi faith is also practiced in several of the other absolute monarchies in the Gulf states. Although it represents a distinctly minority position within Sunnism, its influence is magnified by where it is practiced and the consequent wealth and power of its adherents. Many of its beliefs are also shared by Abu Bakr Baghdadi and his followers in the Islamic State.

Sources of Change and Conflict

The relationship between the United States and the Kingdom of Saudi Arabia is in the process of change. The changes occurring are not yet fundamental: America still retains an interest in secure access to Saudi (and other Gulf) oil at reasonable prices and still favors regional stability, prominently including the suppression of terrorist activities emanating from Middle East sites and sources. What has changed, however, is the immediacy and vitality of America's need for Saudi oil and its toleration of some of the Saudi regional actions that impinge on the United States. Predictably, some of the latter concerns are related to the Wahhabi yoke that tethers and interacts with the geopolitical goals of the House of Saud.

The changing oil situation is a major driver in this process. As I (in *The Middle East, Oil, and the U.S. National Security Policy*) and others have pointed out, three factors have lessened American dependence on Saudi oil, which is the major lever the Saudis have had over Washington. These are the shale oil boom that has simultaneously increased American domestic energy production and stimulated the conversion of some of that concentration to natural gas, conservation efforts that have reduced American demand, and alternate, if not always stable, alternative petroleum sources such as Nigeria and Venezuela (see chapter 10). All of these decrease the dependency of the United States on Saudi Arabia and make tolerance of other forms of Saudi behavior that offends American sensitivities and runs counter to American interests less tolerable.

There are several sources of objection that were not publicized when doing so could have imperiled the American energy situation. A major irritant is Saudi involvement in 9/11. Seventeen of the twenty-one attackers were, of course, Saudi, and it was widely suspected that much of the funding for the attack came from private Saudi Wahhabi donors. Anderson states the relationship bluntly: the emergence of Osama bin Laden and Al Qaeda, he asserts, is "the most famous product of this (Saudi/Wahhabi) arrangement." The Islamic State and other fundamentalist movements have also been recipients of Wahhabi largesse that the regime feels it cannot suppress without endangering its own stability. Wahhabi influence also contributes to the authoritarian, arguably barbaric rule by the Saudi regime. Designated heir-apparent Muhammad bin Sultan (MbS) has sought to moderate this impression, but his obvious complicity in the murder of Jamal Khashoggi has undermined that effort. In addition, clumsy Saudi military efforts in Yemen have contributed visibly to the levels of starvation and other privations stemming from the civil war there between the government and Houthi rebels. Saudi excesses in using military power in the region caused the U.S. Congress to suspend authority for the president to sell arms to the Kingdom in 2019.

Conclusion

National interests are simultaneously one of the most fundamental pillars of international relations and one of its most confusing, complicated characteristics. In a system of sovereign states, the protection and promotion of national interests will always be a basic concern of the members in their relations with one another, even if they disagree on exactly what actions and policies best serve those interests in general and in specific situations.

The basic interests of countries do not change often or greatly, but circumstances and problems do, meaning much of the secret of how any country deals with its place in the world involves calculating and recalculating what serves the most important interests in different circumstances. It is that process of adaptation that undergirds much of the energy of states in their relations with one another.

The Saudi-American relationship illustrates this situation. The basic American interests for which Saudi Arabia is a part have not changed. The United States still wants and requires secure access to petroleum energy, but due to changes described earlier, it no longer must rely on oil from the Persian Gulf littoral—mostly Saudi Arabia—to guarantee meeting its needs. Recent Saudi geopolitical activism, generously infused with Wahhabi values and preferences, also make it less clear that the Saudis desire the same form of regional stability as do the Americans (see chapter 13).

At this point in time, the process of accommodation would seem clearly to lie with the Kingdom. The relationship between the two countries has not only been an odd one—it has also become very asymmetrical. When the United States bought more oil from Saudi Arabia than from any other source and was dependent on the flow of that oil to American shores, the Saudis had considerable leverage over the United States. Now that the United States does not necessarily require that source, the dependency and leverage has largely evaporated. Despite the cosmetic show of modernization being engineered by MbS, the more distasteful aspects of life in the Kingdom are becoming more obvious. Would the assassination of Khashoggi have been authorized if the royal family recognized this? Apparently the reaction was not anticipated, and relations will not return to past levels of mutual interest fulfillment until or unless they do recognize change.

It is thus not entirely clear how Saudi Arabia will react to a potentially less supportive position from the United States. The Khashoggi murder apparently ordered by MbS has had a shocked and chilling effect that goes well beyond what the Saudis must have expected. It has been emphatic. Karl Vick, writing in *Time* magazine in December 2018, dramatically described the impact as laying bare "the utter absence of morality in the Saudi-U.S. alliance." That intensity of reaction to the relationship may soften, but will it disappear altogether?

Study/Discussion Questions

1. Define the terms "interest" and "national" and how they are combined as a basic principle of international relations. Why are they so important?
2. What does it mean to say national interests are non-intersubjective? How does this make them controversial in political discussions?
3. What is the Nuechterlein matrix? Describe it and how difficult it can be to apply in individual situations. Emphasize the VI-LTV interest distinction in your discussion.
4. What is a conflict of interest? Apply the concept to individuals and states. Also, what is the problem of levels of interest? What are the competing levels? How may they conflict with national interests?
5. Discuss the role of national interests in the operational international system, using U.S.-Saudi relations as an example.
6. What is the heart of the Saudi situation in the current system? How does it affect Saudi pursuit of its national interests in the Middle East?
7. What national interests divide the United States and Saudi Arabia, specifically in terms of conflicts over Saudi influence expansion in its region (e.g., Yemen) and the influence of Wahhabism on the government? Discuss.
8. Why is the role of oil so critical to the evolution of U.S.-Saudi relations? Can and should the United States use America's decreasing need for Saudi oil to promote change in Middle East politics? Why or why not?

Bibliography

Allison, Graham T., and Dimitri K. Simes. "The National Interest." *The National Interest*, 2017.

Al-Rasheed, Madawi. *A History of Saudi Arabia* (second edition). Oxford, UK: Cambridge University Press, 2010.

———. *Muted Modernists: The Struggle over Divine Politics in Saudi Arabia*. Oxford, UK: Oxford University Press, 2016.

———. *Salman's Legacy: The Dilemmas of a New Era in Saudi Arabia*. Oxford, UK: Oxford University Press, 2018.

Anderson, Scott. *Lawrence in Arabia: War, Deceit, Imperial Folly, and the Making of the Modern Middle East*. New York: Anchor Books, 2013.

Art, Robert, and Kenneth A. Waltz, eds. *The Use of Force: Military Power and International Politics* (seventh edition). Lanham, MD: Rowman & Littlefield, 2009.

Blumi, Isa. *Destroying Yemen: What Chaos in Arabia Tells Us About the World*. Berkeley, CA: University of California Press, 2018.

Brandt, Marieke. *Tribe and Politics in Yemen: A History of the Houthi Conflict*. Oxford, UK: Oxford University Press, 2017.

Bronson, Rachel. *Thicker Than Oil: America's Uneasy Partnership with Saudi Arabia*. Oxford, UK: Oxford University Press, 2018.

Commins, David. *The Mission and the Kingdom: Wahhabi Power Behind the Saudi Throne*. London: I. B. Tauris, 2016.

Feltman, Jeffrey. "The Only Way to End the War in Yemen: Saudi Arabia Must Move First." *Foreign Affairs Snapshot*, November 26, 2018.

Firro, Tarik. *Wahhabism and the Rise of the House of Saud*. Eastbourne, UK: Sussex Academic Press, 2018.

Friedman, Thomas L. "The First Law of Petropolitics." *Foreign Policy* (May/June 2006), 28–36.

Fromkin, David. *The Independence of Nations*. New York: Praeger Special Studies, 1981.

Gause, Gregory III. "Why the United States Should Stay Out of Saudi Politics: Let the Royal Family Do Its Job." *Foreign Affairs Snapshot*, November 18, 2018.

Herz, John H. *Political Realism and Political Idealism*. Chicago, IL: University of Chicago Press, 1951.

Hill, Ginny. *Yemen Endures: Civil War, Saudi Adventurism, and the Future of Saudi Arabia*. Oxford, UK: Oxford University Press, 2017.

House, Karen Elliott. *On Saudi Arabia: Its People, Past, Religion, Fault Lines—and Future*. New York: Vintage, 2013.

Jervis, Robert. *Perception and Misperception in International Politics*. Princeton, NJ: University of Princeton Press, 1978.

Jordan, Robert W., and Steve Fiffer. *Desert Diplomat: Inside Saudi Arabia after 9/11*. Washington, DC: Potomac Books, 2015.

Kaplan, Robert D. *The Coming Anarchy: Shattering Dreams of the Post-Cold War*. New York: Random House, 2000.

Krasner, Stephen D. *Defending the National Interest: Raw Materials Investments and U.S. Foreign Policy*. Princeton, NJ: Princeton University Press, 1978.

Lackner, Helen. *Yemen in Crisis: Autocracy, Neo-Liberalism, and the Disintegration of the State*. London: Saqi Books, 2017.

McDougal, Walter A. *The Tragedy of U.S. Foreign Policy: How America's Civil Religion Betrayed the National Interest*. New Haven, CT: Yale University Press, 2016.

Nuechterlein, Donald. *America Recommitted: United States National Interests in a Reconstructed World*. Lexington, KY: University of Kentucky Press, 1991.

Riedel, Bruce. *Kings and Presidents: Saudi Arabia and the United States Since FDR. (Geopolitics in the Twenty-First Century)*. Washington, DC: Brookings, 2017.
Scott, Peter Dale. *The American Deep State: Wall Street, Big Oil, and the Attack on U.S. Democracy*. Lanham, MD: Rowman & Littlefield, 2014.
Snow, Donald M. *The Middle East, Oil, and the U.S. National Security Policy: Intractable Conflicts, Impossible Solutions*. Lanham, MD: Rowman & Littlefield, 2016.
———. *Regional Cases in U.S. Foreign Policy* (second edition). Lanham, MD: Rowman & Littlefield, 2018.
———. *National Security* (seventh edition). New York and London: Routledge, forthcoming.
Vick, Karl. "Man of the Year Edition." *Time* 192, 27–28 (December 24–31, 2018), 50.
Waltz, Kenneth. *Theory of International Politics* (revised edition). Long Grove, IL: Wavelend Press, 2010.
Ward, Terence. *The Wahhabi Code: How the Saudis Spread Extremism Globally*. Baltimore, MD: Arcade Press, 2018.

4

The Instruments of Power

Ending the Syrian Civil War

The previous chapters have laid out much of the basis for organizing and understanding the basic dynamics of international relations. The bedrock principle, of course, is sovereignty, which makes the international order anarchic if not necessarily chaotic. The normal means to regulate chaos has been diplomacy, the major purpose of which is to facilitate sovereign state actors to resolve their difference through negotiation rather than the recourse to more conflictual methods. The definition of state interests as supreme and the nonnegotiability of some matters of interests—vital interests—means the ultimate method states possess to retain or expand that which they deem to be most important to them is through self-help. Some challenge this construction, as discussed in the next chapter, but the construct remains intact.

The major method through which states realize their interests is the exercise of power, and this had led many analysts to refer to international politics as *power politics*. In an anarchical system, the member-states have conditions of existence on which they will not willingly compromise if they can avoid doing so, because those conditions are deemed vital to the state's acceptable situation in the world. It means they succeed to the extent they can muster the relevant ability to get other states to do what the state deems vital, even if those conditions are antithetical to the equally strongly held interests of others.

The generic term for how states organize their resources to impose or convince others to do what they want are known as the *instruments of power*. Broadly, this term refers to the accumulation of capabilities that the state has at its avail to convince or coerce others to accept their will. There are various categories of instruments, and one of them, diplomacy, has already been introduced. There is some disagreement about the kinds of capability that should be considered in classifying the instruments of power, and the list expands as new forces associated with technology expand the list of potential instruments.

Controversy surrounds the instruments of power concept in some quarters, because one instrument, arguably the most important or ultimate category, is the recourse to military force. Those who seek a world in which differences between countries are increasingly settled by nonviolent means decry the implicit emphasis the concept places on military force. The realist paradigm, which has been a leading construct for understanding the conflictual nature of international relations and which is still the dominant paradigm in most policy circles, illustrates this dominance with considerable clarity. At the same time, there are enough countervailing limits on the application of the instruments to suggest that their influence is not universal or straightforward in all situations, making that application difficult.

The Syrian Civil War, which has raged in that country since 2011 when it erupted as one theater of the largely abortive Arab Spring, illustrates the complexity and difficulty of applying the instruments of power construct. The carnage in that conflict has been horrendous, including over a half-million killed and over half the population made into internal or external refugees. Reaching a peace settlement to begin the process or returning normalcy to the country and its citizenry would seem an obvious goal to which applications of power would seem an approach, but this has not been the case. Prominent reasons include the conflict of basic interests and thus the inability for potentially helpful states to agree either on desired outcomes or the instrumental means to accomplish them.

Principle: The Instruments of Power

Power, the ability to get someone to do something they otherwise would not do, is a vital building block in understanding how international politics works. In one sense, all politics—domestic and international—are power based, because the heart of politics is the allocation of scarce resources among individuals and groups with different claims on that resource. The difference between domestic and international politics is contextual. Domestic politics normally proceeds within a framework of rules and practices (e.g., laws and institutions) that specify how allocations will occur and includes mechanisms for enforcing whatever choices are made. The purposeful anarchy of international politics creates a contrasting context within which there are no authoritative structures to allocate how resource conflicts are to be resolved, and in most cases, no authoritative means to enforce divisions of resources.

The result is that international politics has an inherent basis in power: states achieve their goals to the extent they can do so themselves—the principle of self-help. Lacking institutions that can resolve differences and enforce the outcomes, the result is the need to have power to be sure that outcomes are honored.

The basic concept of power is both ubiquitous and ambiguous. Power is used so generally to describe relationships in international relations that it is difficult to imagine situations that do not have a power element. At the same time, there is disagreement about what power *is*. The most common academic debate is between power as a physical commodity or attribute, and power as a relationship. The first emphasis tends to look at the attributes that a state possesses—the amount of military power is an obvious example. This approach produces concrete measures of the attributes a state has at its avail and thus allows countries to be ranked according to how much power so measured it has. It also facilitates guessing how a conflict between states will come out based on a comparison of measures of power. It also allows quantification of power attributes, an important emphasis in much modern international political analysis. Viewing power in relational terms is more subjective and less observable. It emphasizes the *percep-*

tion of relevant comparisons of power in determining the outcome of conflicts. It operates more at the psychological level of participants acting based on their perceptions of relevant factors.

The Vietnam War between 1965 and 1973 (the period of American active combat in that country) illustrates the distinction. The American purpose in intervening in that country's civil war was to assist the government of the Republic of Vietnam (RVN, or South Vietnam) to prevail in the southern half of the country, whereas the opposition members of the National Liberation Front (the military component of which was the Viet Cong) and the armed forces of the Democratic Republic of Vietnam (DRV, or North Vietnam) sought to avoid that outcome and to unify the country under their control. Because these outcomes were mutually exclusive and neither side would accept the other's victory, power would have to be imposed on one side by the other; the United States sought to augment the power of the RVN by intervening with a military force that numbered over 500,000 at its zenith.

By any objective power comparison, the United States and the RVN should have prevailed, but they did not. The application of the military instrument of power, after all, matched the world's most powerful country in military terms with an opponent that American President Lyndon B. Johnson depicted as a "piddling, piss-ant little country" (quoted in Chua). How could the United States have lost? The answer is that it applied the instruments of power incorrectly.

The mistake shows why comparisons of power are ambiguous. The comparison that showed the United States and the RVN could not lose was based in viewing power as a property rather than a relationship and was incorrect, for at least three reasons that point to power as a relational concept. First, it failed to reflect an analysis of the situation correctly. The Vietnam war was more than a territorial struggle—it was a clash over the future shape of the Southeast Asian peninsula. The Americans saw it as a territorial contest, whereas many Vietnamese saw it as an opportunity to rid themselves of a Chinese minority that controlled 70 to 80 percent of the country's wealth and was despised for it. As Chua puts it, "In effect, the U.S.-backed regime was asking the South Vietnamese to fight and die—and kill their northern brethren—in order to keep the Chinese rich." This led to the second reason, which flowed from the first: the war was simply more important to North Vietnamese than it was to the United States and the RVN. Third, the United States was backing the wrong side and in fact had little stake in the outcome. It had a lesser resolve and tired of the contest and left. The United States and its ally won the power comparison of material power, but it lost the relational battle for "the hearts and minds of men," which ultimately proved more important.

The point is that comparisons of power must take various factors into account, some of which will prove more prescient than others in concrete applications. If there is a concrete, irrefutable formula for applying the instruments of power that would allow predictions of outcomes with great accuracy, we do not have it at this time. As a result, the application of the instruments of power remains subjective, as much an art as a science.

Delineating the Instruments of Power

There is general agreement about what the concept of instruments of power is, and there is also agreement that the list is increasing. From the early days of the modern state system depicted in chapters 2 and 3, for instance, there were generally three universally acknowledged instruments: the military, economic, and political/diplomatic. These reflected the kinds of capabilities states possessed and could harness to achieve national ends. That list expanded during the twentieth century to include categories like information, intellectual prowess, financial strength, and even the sophistication of law enforcement power in different sources. Citing categories from the *U.S. Army War College Guide to National Security Issues*, *Wikipedia* adds other categories including geography, resources, population, and psychological strength to the mix. The list is expandable—for instance cybercapability (see chapter 18) could easily be added, and there will undoubtedly be more.

No list is thus comprehensive, but one can list and briefly describe the accepted candidates and how they can potentially be applied in different situations. The three traditional instruments have formed the basis for most calculations until recently. They can be thought of as ascending in potential severity, and each has a series of suboptions that can be applied in different circumstances. Diplomacy, as discussed in chapter 2, is the most "civilized" form. Its core is the use of persuasion by national diplomats and other political figures to convince an opponent to accept an outcome that one favors. To be effective, diplomacy requires a level of civility and willingness to compromise that has declined in an environment where partisan political practice, and notably political actors with little or no diplomatic training or understanding, have intruded.

Recourse to the economic instrument has increased as the use of traditional diplomacy has waned. The most common form of economic action is the threat or imposition of some form of economic sanctions against an opponent that will not conform to some demand. Tariffs are examples. The idea is to create enough economic discomfort so that the recipient will relent to the demands of the sanctioning party. The effectiveness of sanctions is mixed at best. For one thing, targets are often more resistant to being coerced by these actions than anticipated. For another, quite often sanctions have an adverse effect on the party imposing them, and relenting is hard to disguise as anything other than capitulation, an admission states are reluctant to make.

The third traditional instrument is military power. It is generally based in the threat to cause physical injury or harm if the other party fails to comply to whatever demand the threatening party issues. It is, in most cases, the most volatile form of threat, because if the threat is not honored, it may require carrying out military action, in which case both sides are likely to suffer to some degree. Military threats by nuclear weapons–possessing states have the further danger that, no matter how unlikely the prospect may be in any given situation, escalation is always possible. Less extreme uses of the military instrument include restrictions on arms sales or pulling back from military commitments.

In addition to this traditional trinity, information has become an accepted part of the arsenal of instruments. The collection of information about rivals is, of course, a venerable practice generally thought of as the product of espionage of one sort or another, but modern technology has expanded this concept. Electronic technology and the whole area of cyberspace (see chapter 18) has expanded the ability of states to interfere with the activities of opponents, as with the Russian electronic interference in the 2016 American presidential election; this is a precedent likely to spread to other countries like China and will be an ongoing source of influence on the interactions between affected countries.

The Army War College listing elaborates some of these distinctions by adding attributes that allow the implementation of various instruments. It lists factors that can enhance the effectiveness of traditional instruments by allowing augmentation of, say, economic or military power. These include physical geography (size and location, for instance), the possession of strategic natural resources, and population factors like size and support for the government. They also list psychological factors as a social indicator augmenting the ability to accomplish goals. The miscalculation of the outcome of the Vietnam War, a matter of considerable embarrassment to the Army, probably reflects its inclusion.

Limits of Power: Turkey, the United States, and the Kurds

Determining the utility of the instruments of power in specific situations is not a simple matter of counting how much of a given capability those engaged in a relationship possess and assuming whoever has the most capability will prevail. The comparison is not irrelevant, but its importance can be negative: if one party threatens actions that it clearly does not possess the capability or willingness to implement, that can affect whether its interests will prevail.

The application of the instruments is both psychological and situation-specific. The decision to accede to a demand (have power exercised against it) or not is a psychological decision that entails calculations on both sides. At least three factors are relevant to that specificity. All are leavened by the tendency, especially by the world's most powerful countries and least experienced leaders, to overestimate the utility and effectiveness of the instruments.

Situation-specificity refers to relevance of a given element of power to a specific application. The United States, for instance, is by most measures the most powerful country in the world, and the ultimate expression of that strength is nuclear weapons. But for what applications of power are those weapons effective instruments for convincing other states to accede to American interests? The answer is that the utility is circumscribed and specific to situations where those weapons are relevant—which are limited. By any measure, for instance, the United States has overwhelmingly more military power than almost any small African state. So what? Can the United States threaten to initiate a nuclear war against Upper Volta or a conventional invasion of Burkino Faso? It could issue such a threat, but nobody (and especially those at whom the threat was directed) would believe the threat or be influenced by it. The situation would simply not warrant carrying out the threat.

The use of threats to employ the instruments of power, if they are to be effective, must be believable and acceptable. Is it believable that many states would be willing to carry out major threats against very weak states knowing that such an action would be almost universally condemned by the international community? If outcomes are viewed as important enough, some states (Russia, for instance, in its annexation of Crimea) might take actions that are broadly condemned by others, but that willingness is circumscribed. The willingness to carry out some actions because of possessing certain amounts of power is certainly circumscribed by the costs in terms of prestige and humanity that might be entailed. Possessing and using the instruments of power is not a simple matter of standing bare-chested on a parapet and loudly extolling one's power. It is also a matter of determining when and how that power may or may not be relevant to the situation at hand.

As it winds down toward an uncertain ending that is the subject of the applications section of the chapter, a slice of the problem of applying relevant power to achieve the peace in the Syrian Civil War illustrates the difficulty of a straightforward application of the instruments to resolve international difficulties. That aspect of the problem is the fate of the Kurds, whose quest for statehood is the subject of chapter 14. The Kurds have been among the most valiant and effective fighters in the conflict which is, in their estimation, one theater of their goal of establishing a Kurdish state from several Middle Eastern states, none of which wants them to succeed. Among the states most opposed to the Kurds is Turkey, and one of the possible outcomes of the peace that will at some point come into being in Syria is a concerted Turkish military drive to break, even to destroy, the Kurdish independence movement by decimating the Kurds. The United States, which has had a modest but crucial presence in eastern Syria where the Kurds have primarily been the effective opponents of ISIS, announced their intention to withdraw all forces from Syria. An absolute guarantee of the safety and security of the Kurds from Turkish oppression has been a requirement the Americans have demanded from Turkey as a condition of that withdrawal.

The positions taken by Turkey and the United States and the very public way in which they have been presented virtually precludes a diplomatic solution (which is characteristic of the entire Syrian problem). The two sides have taken extreme opposite positions on the Kurds. The United States insists on an ironclad guarantee of Kurdish security, an insistence clearly aimed at the Turks. The Turks adamantly refuse, given their strongly stated position that the Kurds are terrorists whose target is the Turkish government. The Americans can only back away if the Turks capitulate (which is how the Turks see the prospect) and cannot implement their goal of withdrawal without losing face unless the Turks accede. The Turks cannot comply to the demand without publicly acceding to the demands of terrorists in their midst, an unacceptable political and national security position for the Turks who are, after all, an American ally in the North Atlantic Treaty Organization. Because the positions are public, any concession by either side will be viewed domestically in their countries as a defeat by some. Where is the possibility of resolution? The Kurds, of course, are stuck in the middle of the confrontation, largely powerless to influence the outcome of what is an existential problem for them.

The Americans and the Kurds have been cooperative forces in the eastern region of Syria that the Kurds call Rojava and claim as part of Kurdistan. This territory abuts Southern Turkey, where Kurdish separatists have operated to subvert the Turkish government as part of their national aspirations. The Turkish government has rejected the American demand as collusion with Kurdish "terrorists." The result is loggerheads, where some form of power must be effectively exerted by either the United States or Turkey. The Kurds, not unusually in their history, are caught in the middle.

The question is how to resolve this problem. It is only one part of the overall complicated set of factors and forces seeking to end a terribly bloody civil uprising that has been going on for eight years and which has decimated Syria to the point that it is not clear how that country can ever be made whole again. The effort shows how deeply conflicted interests among interested partners create an enormous tangle of instruments of power trying to settle the conflict.

Application: Ending the Syrian Civil War

The Syrian Civil War has been one of the bloodiest, most tragic events of recent political history. It began, as summarized in *Cases in U.S. National Security*, as part of the so-called Arab Spring, which broke out in Tunisia in 2010 to protest corrupt, autocratic rule in the Middle East. The movement did not achieve most of its lofty goals, but it did spin off movements in various other regional countries. It occurred most tragically in Syria.

The offshoot that became the civil war began in March 2011 in Syria as protests of the autocratic rule of Bashar al-Assad, the Shiite Alawite who had succeeded his father Hafiz but had not instituted reforms he had promised when he took office. The immediate spark occurred when teenagers were arrested for spray-painting antigovernment slogans on buildings. Police reacted harshly, arresting fifteen of the protesters, and one died under suspicious circumstances, igniting protests and violence among the Sunni Syrians who constitute about 70 percent of the country's population. The situation quickly devolved into violent clashes, as hastily assembled Sunni militias took up arms to protest the government's action. What I have described elsewhere as "the perfect maelstrom" was set spinning in the process. It continues to swirl as the government has moved to quash the resistance, but suffering remains the norm for the beleaguered Syrian people.

The tragedy for the Syrians is well chronicled but in summary provides context for the disaster in need of resolution. On the eve of the violence, the Syrian population was about 21 million. Of that number, an estimated 510,000 had been killed by March 2018 according to Syrian Observatory for Human Rights quoted in *The World Almanac and Book of Facts*, 2019 edition. In addition, at least 5 million Syrians have been driven from their homes into internal exile and at least that number has fled into external exile from which they fear return to the war zone. Estimates of what it will take to rebuild the country vary from a quarter trillion to more than a trillion dollars. All estimates are no more than refined speculation given the fluidity of the situation and the extent of physical devastation. Stated roughly, however, over half the prewar Syrian Civil War population has died or been displaced by the war, and most of the country lies in ruins. In human terms, it is a tragedy that cried out for alleviation. It is, however, caught up in a power struggle between various conflicting sides with differing objectives, none of which has adequate relevant power to impose a solution, and especially one that meets the needs of the Syrians and outsiders with some interest in the outcome.

Issues and Interested Parties

There are two sets of parties who have an interest in the outcome of the Syrian conflict and who have, with varying success, tried to force an outcome to their favor. The first set are internal, and the primary groupings are the government of Bashar al-Assad and the various opposition groups seeking to overthrow him. The second set are outside countries and movements, all of which seek a different Syrian outcome featuring a Syrian government that will be sympathetic to their positions. There are multiple groups in this category, and the positions and support they advocate contradict one another. None of these internal or external groups has demonstrated that they have adequate power to overcome the power of those that oppose them, leaving a settlement elusive.

There are factors that inhibit either internal or international efforts to bring the Syrian nightmare to an end. It is certainly in the interests of the Syrian population to end their horror, whether they have remained in their homes or been forced into a form of dislocation. Unfortunately, there are strong, countervailing interests and forces at both levels that insist on their preferred outcome and have enough power to prevent the other side from successfully applying its own instruments of power.

The internal situation is conceptually the most straightforward. The al-Assad government represents a minority of the population; the Shiites, of whom the ruling Alawites are a part, represent about 15 percent of the population, compared to the 70 percent of the population that is Sunni and from which most of the opposition groups are drawn. This comparison appears to favor the rebels, but it is misleading. Historically, the Alawites have dominated the professional Syrian military, and they are much better organized and equipped than their opposition. The government, for instance, controls the Syrian Air Force, whereas what airpower the opposition can call upon must be supplied by outsiders. Moreover, the opposition groups are weakened by their internal divisions—many of the opposition groups hate other opposition groups nearly as much as they hate the government. Cooperation has been virtually nonexistent, and outsiders seeking to find some group or leader that can unite the opposition and provide the basis for a new government have proven futile. The United States, for instance, tried in the early stages of the war to identify a rebel group or coalition to which it could direct aid to oppose the government, but could never identify a group it considered reliable and which would not end up losing those weapons to ISIS. Because of this lack of coordination among groups, they have not succeeded despite what would seem formidable numerical odds. By the end of 2018, there were widespread reports that the government was on the verge of prevailing and crushing the last organized resistance to its rule. The major impediments to achieving this end, however, have come from outside forces which, for one reason or another, oppose an outcome in which their "side" does not prevail.

Support for the government illustrates the point. In broad terms, outside help and support has come from three sources. One is Iran (including its ally Hezbollah). Their connection is partly the result of shared adherence to Shiite Islam but also contains an important element of Iranian geopolitics. The Alawite government of al-Assad provides a Shiite entry point for Iran into the Mediterranean Middle East. This provides a platform for aspiring regional power Iran to expand its influence in the region generally, but more specifically to give it a stronger physical link to Hezbollah, whose terrorist campaign against Israel is part of its attempt to cause the Israelis to abandon the West Bank to the Palestinians, a cause that Iran also supports. This linkage has benefited Syria, because Iran has allegedly provided "volunteers" from Iran and other Shiite areas to augment Syrian forces and help maintain a favorable balance of power for the government.

The second major supporter for al-Assad has been Russia. Syria provides Russia with an entry point into the region that it would not otherwise have. The arrangement is reminiscent of then-Soviet policy during the Cold War. The key physical gem in the relationship for the Russians is their naval base in Northern Syria at Tartus, which is located within the Alawite region of the country, thereby reinforcing the bond between Damascus and Moscow.

The third supporter has been Turkey, a country whose support has been the most blatantly geopolitical and least sincerely pro-Syrian. Virtually the sole interest the Turks have in the outcome is whether it will strengthen the Kurds. That concern, of course, centers along the Turkish-Syrian border area claimed by the Kurds as Rojava and parts of the Kurdish Autonomous Region of Iraq that also borders on Turkey. The Turks view the Kurds as their prime enemy in the region, and although they are at best ambivalent about the close relationship between the Syrians and Iran, they view Kurdish benefit from the outcome of the civil war as the greater of two evils. Most particularly, they fear that if al-Assad is overthrown, the ensuing chaos in Syria would allow the Kurds to consolidate their hold on Rojava, which they would then use as a launching pad for attacks (which they deem terrorist) against Turkey in support of Turkish Kurdish separatists.

The motives and methods of those supporting the Damascus regime are disparate. The Iranians and the Turks, who are themselves rivals and historic enemies, are almost entirely geopolitical. Each has a personal agenda that is motivated by personal gain (the extension of Iranian influence, Turkish frustration of the Kurds) and has little to do with the well-being of the Syrians. The Iranians have religious ties as an added incentive and have been the most active, in terms of personnel and financial/military assistance, whereas the Turks have been more restrained physically because of their North Atlantic Treaty Organization ties and the fear that any active intervention might cause the region to erupt. The Russians are the true opportunists in the equation, and they have also provided the most active assistance to the al-Assad regime. They have provided airpower to assist in suppression of the rebels and military equipment to regime forces, in addition to issuing warnings against American air actions that might cause a confrontation between them. They have also provided valuable diplomatic cover against international condemnation of Syrian chemical attacks against civilians in 2012, 2013, and 2018 in forums like the UN Security Council.

Outside support for the rebels has been spottier and less effective. The large reason for this is that there is not *a* resistance but a whole series of fragmented, feuding groups, none of which receive much general support. The fact that ISIS arose as one of those groups further taints the effort and makes outsiders, including the United States, reluctant to do much beyond counseling a negotiated settlement and keeping a token training force in the east. Because 70 percent of the Syrian citizenry is Sunni, one might expect more assistance from major Sunni states, but except for some private assistance from Saudi Arabia and the Gulf states, very little has been forthcoming. The Trump administration, with its basically isolationist view of U.S. activism in the world (see chapter 5), has shown notable reluctance to take any leadership role in an intractable conflict they maintain is really none of the United States' business. The possession of usable military power within Syria continues to favor the government augmented by its outside allies and against the Syrian rebels.

Conclusion

The instruments of power concept is simultaneously beguiling and deceptive. The dynamic it measures—how much power one state has compared to another by various measures—is appealing because it apparently allows one to predict likely outcomes of conflicts between two (or more) states when they come into conflict over some mutually desired outcome in situations of scarcity where they cannot both (or all) have all the resource they want. Knowing which side has the most power helps to predict who will prevail.

The calculation can and often proves to be deceptive. The problem is, in important ways, a matter of measurement. The concept of instruments leads one to measure those attributes that are physical, concrete, and easily measurable, and that can be misleading. It does not, for instance, account well for intangible but often critical factors like will and determination, among other psychological elements. To return to the Vietnam example, the Vietnamese had no objective physical chance against the mighty United States, but they prevailed. The reason, simply put, was that the outcome was more important to them than it was to the Americans—they wanted to win much more than did the Americans, and they succeeded. A whole genre of military strategy, what is called asymmetrical warfare, is dedicated to the development and application of ways that an inferior military force (one with less of the military instrument) can prevail over an objectively superior force (see chapter 8). It does not work all the time, but it does enough of the time that it is adopted by those in an objectively inferior position. The same kind of analysis applies to the other instruments as well.

As the application section shows, measuring outcomes is even more problematical when there are multiple participants with differing motivations and preferred outcomes. Nobody favors the suffering that has been going on in Syria since 2011, but the various state and nonstate actors have clearly differing preferences they would like to see as the outcome, and they are applying their power to bring their vision into reality. On the ground, the government forces seem close to imposing their preferred outcome, but achieving it is problematic in a situation where there are so many actors with differing commitments and capabilities that contradict and cancel out one another. Determining which instruments of power possessed by which participants will prevail is not a simple matter of putting the measurable power of two opponents in the two sides of a scale and seeing which is heavier. The instruments offer one kind of measure that is important but not always decisive. Before reaching judgments, it is necessary to incorporate both the physical and measurable elements of power and the less tangible but, in certain circumstances, equally or more important intangibles.

There is an old saying that, in paraphrase, suggests that for every concrete, complicated problem, there is an answer that is simple, straightforward—and wrong. That may not be the case for all applications of the instruments of power concept, but neat projections of outcomes based on who has the most measurable power are not foolproof either.

Study/Discussion Questions

1. Why is international politics an exercise in power? What controversies surround the concept and its application?
2. Why is it difficult but tempting to devise instruments of power to measure national power and the ability of states to exercise power in their favor?
3. What categories appear on various lists of instruments of power? List and briefly describe each.
4. Why is it difficult to apply the instruments of power to concrete situations? Use the Vietnam War and the U.S. policy of protecting the Kurds from Turkey as examples.
5. Describe the Syrian Civil War. How did it start, how has it progressed, and why have efforts to end it failed?
6. What countries and groups have supported the Syrian government in the civil war? What are the objectives of each? Do they lead to a uniform application of the instruments of power?
7. What are the possible outcomes of the Syrian conflict? Can recourse to the instruments of power help predict the eventual outcome?
8. Why did the text describe the use of the instruments of power concept as both beguiling and deceptive? Do you agree with that assessment?

Bibliography

Abboud, Samer N. *Syria: Hot Spots in Global Politics.* Cambridge, MA: Polity Press, 2015.

Abouzeid, Rania. *No Turning Back: Life, Loss, and Hope in Wartime Syria.* New York: W. W. Norton, 2018.

Ajami, Fouad. *The Syrian Rebellion.* Palo Alto, CA: Hoover Institution Press, 2012.

Art, Robert J., and Kelly M. Greenhill, eds. *The Use of Force: Military Power and International Politics* (eighth edition). Lanham, MD: Rowman & Littlefield, 2015.

Chua, Amy. *Political Tribes: Group Instinct and the Fate of Nations.* New York: Penguin Press, 2018.
D'Anieri, Paul. *International Political Power and Purpose in Global Affairs* (fourth edition). Boston, MA: Cengage, 2016.
Drew, Dennis M., and Donald M. Snow. *Making Twenty-First Century Strategy: An Introduction to Modern National Security Processes and Problems.* Montgomery, AL: Air University Press, 2006.
Ford, Robert S. "Keeping Out of Syria: The Least Bad Option." *Foreign Affairs* 96, 6 (November/December 2017), 16–22.
Fromkin, David. *The Independence of Nations.* New York: Praeger Special Studies, 1981.
Ghosn, Faten. "The Hard Road Ahead for Syrian Reconstruction." *Current History* 117, 803 (December 2018), 331–37.
Goldsmith, Leon. *Cycle of Fear: Syria's Alawites in War and Peace.* London: Hurst Publications, 2015.
Hisham, Marwan. *Brothers of the Gun: A Memoir of the Syrian Civil War.* New York: One World, 2018.
Jablonsky, David. "National Power," in J. Boone Bartholomees, ed. *The U.S. Army War College Guide to National Security Issues*, Volume 1: Theory of War and Strategy. Carlisle Barracks, PA: U.S. Army War College, 2010.
Liddell Hart, B. H. *Strategy.* New York: Meridian Press, 1991.
McHugo, John. *Syria: A Recent History.* London: Saqi Books, 2015.
Morgenthau, Hans J. *Power Among Nations* (seventh edition). Revised by Kenneth W. Thompson and W. David Clinton. New York: McGraw-Hill Educational, 2005.
Nuechterlein, Donald E. *America Recommitted: United States National Interests in a Restructured World.* Lexington, KY: University of Kentucky Press, 1991.
Phillips, Christopher. *The Battle for Syria: International Rivalry in the Middle East.* New Haven, CT: Yale University Press, 2016.
Reilly, James N. *A Shattered Land: The Modern History of Syria.* Boulder, CO: Lynne Rienner, 2018.
Schelling, Thomas G. *Arms and Influence.* New Haven, CT: Yale University Press, 1966.
Schmidinger, Jordi. *Rojava: Revolution, War, and the Future of Syria's Kurds.* London: Pluto Press, 2018.
Snow, Donald M. *Cases in U.S. National Security: Concepts and Processes.* Lanham, MD: Rowman & Littlefield, 2019 (see especially chapter 10, "Syria: The Perfect Maelstrom").
———. *The Middle East, Oil, and the U.S. National Security Policy.* Lanham, MD: Rowman & Littlefield, 2016.
———. *Thinking About National Security: Strategy, Policy, and Issues.* New York and London: Routledge, 2016.
Sorenson, David S. *Syria Is Rising: The Dynamics of the Syrian Civil War.* Westport, CT: Praeger Security International, 2016.
Stares, Paul B. *Preventive Engagement: How American Can Avoid War, Stay Strong, and Keep the Peace.* New York: Columbia University Press, 2018.
Tejel, Jordi. *Syria's Kurds: Politics and Society.* New York and London: Routledge, 2008.
Thucydides. *The History of the Peloponnesian Wars.* New York: Penguin Books, 1954.
Van Dam, Nikolas. *Destroying a Nation: The Civil War in Syria.* London: I. B. Tauris, 2017.
Waltz, Kenneth. *Realism and International Politics.* New York: Routledge, 2006.
The World Almanac and Book of Facts 2019. New York: World Almanac Books, 2019.
Worley, D. Robert. *Orchestrating the Instruments of Power: A Critical Examination of the U.S. National Security System.* Washington, DC: Potomac Books, 2015.

5

Internationalism and Unilateralism

Going It Together or Alone—The Fate of NATO

Among the most notable changes in the international order in the decade of the 2010s has been the erosion of the liberal political order that emerged from World War I as a principle for diplomatic interaction (see chapter 2). This change extended to a more cooperative world order where the diplomatic instrument of power eclipsed other forms of influence and multilateral approaches to problem solving became the norm. The rise of multilateral international organizations has been one of the most public aspects of this change.

It is an order that has never been universally embraced, and the challengers have become increasingly bold, vocal, and powerful. The most common banner under which this opposition is expressed is that of nationalism, and one way the challenge is often phrased is as an intellectual contest between internationalism and unilateralism. This construction played a major role in the Brexit decision by the United Kingdom to leave the quintessential expression of a more cooperative order, the European Union, and it has also been a major theme of the Trump administration in the United States.

Both the internationalist and nationalistic approaches have common and contrasting bases. Both, for instance, have the promotion of the interests of the state as their goal, but they fundamentally disagree about whether this goal is more effectively pursued through collective action that seeks to enlist the international system in joint actions that promote mutual security and prosperity (going it together) or whether such goals are more effectively pursued through unilateral actions wherein the benefit of others is far less important than benefits for the individual country trying to maximize its utilities (going it alone). Both approaches have been strategies pursued in the past and present; preference for one or another has always been a matter of time and circumstance.

What is known as the liberal internationalist order has been the dominant paradigm for most of the world for just over a century. Its genesis was in the nineteenth century in Europe and paralleled the democratization of the continent. It is generally associated with British Prime Minister Lord Palmerston. The liberal order was not well established enough to prevent the dynamics leading to World War I, and in its wake, it was revived by President Woodrow Wilson at the Versailles peace negotiations in 2018 (see chapter 2).

The central highlight of the new order was to be the League of Nations. The League was to be the first universal membership international organization in which countries bound themselves together to promote their common interests. In the wake of the global bloodletting between 1914 and 1918, the scourge they proposed to arrest was war, especially on the scale of the "Great War." Their proposed method was international cooperative action in the form of collective security. The conceptual dynamic was the prior agreement that should any country or coalition threaten the common peace, the membership would come together and dissuade or defeat the potential wrongdoers. The League membership was to be universal, which meant enough power should be available to deter a potential aggressor. Failing that, the goal was to defeat the transgressor of international norms militarily. The League experience provides an allegory of sorts for understanding the ongoing, and especially the current, debate between the universalists and the unilateralists.

Principle: Internationalism or Isolationism

The debate was joined after World War I. The first American-led effort to institute internationalism failed, and the second global conflagration broke out just over two decades later. Scholars and others have long debated why the League failed, and there are a variety of reasons put forward and available. They all reflect philosophical differences between supporters of the two basic positions that are both symbolically and physically present in the current debate.

Since World War I, the United States has been a featured actor in the debate between internationalism and nationalist-based isolationism. The heart of the debate is, and always has been, over whether American interaction and entanglement with international affairs should be limited or extensive, which reflects a judgment about whether American interests are best served by different levels of involvement in international affairs. For most of early American history, there was a consensus on isolation—going it alone—as the appropriate approach both to development of the United States across the continent and to isolate Americans from what many viewed as the taint of European politics—from which many European immigrants had fled across the Atlantic to the new world.

World War I broke that consensus and introduced the internationalist element into the equation. It thus began a debate over the best approach for the country that has continued to the present. Following World War I, the debate ended with a return to isolationism in the United States. World War II was widely blamed, justly or not, on American retreat from international affairs. The argument is that if the United States had been an active, committed member of the League collective security system during the 1930s, those who started the war would have been deterred by the sure prospect of a crushing defeat. Isolationism was blamed both internationally and in the United States for the second global conflagration; its advocacy after the war became a very tough "sell" that drove its advocates underground, where they remained until the early twenty-first century.

It may seem—and be—chauvinistic to center this discussion on the United States, but the post-1945 situation justifies it. The United States emerged from the war as the overwhelmingly most powerful, physically capable state, rivaled only by a Soviet Union whose power was a pale image of American capabilities. America was supreme, and most of the participants needed American economic assistance to rebuild and military power to protect them from communist predators. The Americans in the U.S. State Department and their counterparts in the British Foreign Office and elsewhere were committed internationalists who believed, in Gideon Rose's words, in a liberal order conceptualized as a "positive sum game" based on "the potential for mutual gain from voluntary, rules-based international cooperation." They created an international order based on that premise that is now under siege.

The basic premise of collective, international efforts to achieve goals is that aggregating the voice and resources of multiple countries increases the breadth and thus the effectiveness of actions. It presumes that the multiple states that agree to cooperate have sufficiently similar interests and will support collective actions enough to convince those whom they oppose that their noncompliance is futile and that conformance with the collective demands is thus necessary. For a united front to arise and be effective, those banding together must agree on the values to be enforced (including the virtue of collective action) and on the greater effectiveness and personal and systemic virtue of collective action. Most importantly, they must be willing to accept and enforce collective judgments.

The latter criterion is the most problematic, because it is likely to run afoul of strictly nationalist objections. The commitment to carry out collective judgments removes some sovereign prerogative by requiring its adherents to accept and carry out actions even if they may personally oppose or not benefit from them. This requirement places internationalists and nationalists at odds. For a collective agreement to be effective, the members must forfeit their sovereign authority over situations covered by the agreement. Sovereignty implies retention of maximum state control over all its actions, a situation that collective commitments dilute. The irony is that collective agreements are effective to the extent that someone contemplating violating them must believe in an overwhelming negative response that will not tolerate its heresy. If the international commitment is strong and unambiguous enough, the potential transgressor cannot miscalculate the consequences of disobedience. At the same time, the more automatic the commitment, the more sovereign autonomy is diluted. Sovereignty-based autonomy, in turn, may assuage nationalist desires, but it also dilutes the effectiveness of the collective arrangement, because it potentially provides an out for members and thus potentially can weaken the response to ineffectiveness.

The failure of League of Nations collective security gains meaning in those terms. The League's provisions included a commitment on the part of members to oppose war, but it stopped short of creating any automatic requirement to participate in collective actions or mechanisms to coordinate efforts. Not uncharacteristically, the failure to create an unambiguous collective response in the area of collective security was most strongly voiced by the U.S. Congressional delegation to Versailles, which insisted that only the U.S. Congress could commit American forces to military actions. President Wilson opposed the congressional declaration, but sentiment to guarantee inclusion of the Americans did not carry the day, and the League Covenant contained no automatic commitment in the event of breaches of the peace. Collective security decisions would have to be made unanimously, retaining the sovereign prerogatives of the states over any actions that might commit them. Individual member-states would determine whether they would respond to League calls for collective action—an approach sometimes known as the "hue and cry"—by which states would determine if or how they would participate in League actions. Wilson was so enraged by this action that he withdrew his support from the treaty. In the end, the United States neither signed the final Versailles agreement nor joined the League. The irony is that the League needed committed American power to enforce the peace, and it was unavailable. The League essentially collapsed as a collective security arrangement in the mid-1930s, and it was actions by isolationist opponents that, by undermining the commitment to act collectively, helped convince the Axis powers they could start the expansion that led to war with minimal fear of an effective international reaction. The debate between the internationalists and the isolationists was not concluded. It was, if anything, intensified.

The Rise of Internationalism

The isolationists "won" the interwar debate over whether collective responses to international threats were preferable to individual responses. This "triumph" was most pronounced in the United States, which was the pivotal state in any internationalist response because of its preeminent economic and potential military might. After the bruising debate at the end of World War I, the Americans retreated to "splendid isolationism," cutting off as much political interaction with the rest of the world as they could. During the 1930s, the battle cry for this movement, especially associated with Charles Lindbergh, the first person to fly an airplane solo across the Atlantic Ocean, was "America First." The answer to going it together or alone was that the United States would go it alone.

World War II, of course, discredited that position—at awful costs (an estimated 80 million people died because of the war, roughly equally divided among civilian and combatant deaths). The internationalists had lost the 1930s, but once war broke out and the allied countries united to defeat the Axis, they reemerged within the leadership of the major powers opposing fascism and went about fashioning and institutionalizing the liberal internationalist vision they brought to the postwar world.

The new order emphasized the underlying values and observations of the liberal internationalist argument and created an institutionalized system reflecting those beliefs. Those who advocated the liberal order argued that the postwar geopolitical order was in such disarray that only the United States could take the effective lead in repairing it, and that the principles of liberal internationalism were the only basis on which this reconstruction could occur. Remaining advocates of exclusionary nationalism disagreed with this assessment and the implications of its implementation (principally in the area of incursions on sovereign prerogatives). The outcomes of the war, including the looming Soviet threat, rendered them mute, although it did not convert them.

The heart of the liberal internationalist position is the need for and benefit of cooperation across state lines to strengthen and redefine international relations. This cooperation has embedded in it a belief that collective action between member states is more effective than unilateral action, and that universality of membership and participation are necessary conditions for effective action (a legacy of the League). The movement was, as Haass points out, dominated by the democratic states, which sought to use Wilsonian principles of diplomacy to "strengthen ties and foster respect for the rule of law within and between countries."

The liberal order was implemented through a series of elements that included, according to Rose, "international public goods such as global and regional security, freedom of the commons, and a liberal trading system." In other words, the order was to produce safety and access to economic opportunity through access to public goods (the "commons") and a trading system that was a positive sum enterprise.

The postwar 1940s provided a fertile geopolitical setting in which to create a series of institutional efforts to implement the liberal order. It began with the negotiation of the UN Charter in 1945 to create a successor to the failed League of Nations. Notably, it entreated all the world's countries to join and notably succeeded in getting the American commitment (the Charter was negotiated in San Francisco and the headquarters were located in New York to help ensure that outcome). Stronger collective security provisions than those of the League were also included but put in abeyance given the building Cold War confrontation. Economic well-being was fostered at the Bretton Woods meetings in New Hampshire, which produced two seminal international economic organizations, the International Bank for Reconstruction and Development (or World Bank) and the International Monetary Fund. The purposes of the International Bank for Reconstruction and Development included providing loans for rebuilding war-torn Europe and funds for the development of less prosperous areas, and the International Monetary Fund was created to stabilize international financial matters. Both remain vital institutions with headquarters in downtown Washington, DC. Bretton Woods also contained a proposal to promote global trade, but politics prevented the implementation of the World Trade Organization until 1994. This same dynamic helped, with American assistance, to create the movement that has eventuated in the European Union.

The United States took the leadership in forming three major initiatives to foster the sense of goodwill and safety the new order required, focused on the rising Cold War threat. This process was accomplished in three steps. On March 12, 1947, President Truman gave a speech where he argued the world was effectively divided into free and subjugated countries and that only the United States was physically capable of protecting the weak. The address became known as the Truman Doctrine and was initially used to provide aid to Greece and Turkey to resist Soviet intrusion. The principle was expanded through the Marshall Plan in 1948. In 1949, the United States led the establishment of its first military alliance during peacetime, the North Atlantic Treaty Organization (NATO), which is the subject of the Applications section of the chapter.

The Return of Isolationism

The consensus has eroded in the twenty-first century. The explanations are at least partially speculative. They reflect changes in the nature of international politics and relations caused by phenomena like the rise of terrorism, the slowing of the global economy and the subsequent diminution of the popularity of globalization (see chapter 11), and global activism in the form of wars—especially in the Middle East—that have drawn in the major powers and created new and unwelcome conditions such as migrant flows from those fleeing the vagaries of war or seeking economic betterment.

Rightly or wrongly, the liberal internationalist order has been blamed by some for changing events and circumstances for people. In the United States, for instance, questionable military involvements in places like Iraq, Afghanistan, and even Syria have led some to the conclusion that pursuing the liberal internationalist dream of growing global cooperation has overextended the United States in ways that diminish the situations in which it can act (see chapter 6). In Europe, the flood of refugees into the countries of the European Union, among which they can move freely, was a large part of the motivation for British withdrawal from that organization (Brexit).

The result has been to allow the reemergence of isolationism and unilateralism both in the United States and Europe. As Rose puts it, "liberalism's project ended up getting hijacked by nationalism. Large segments of many Western populations came to think the order wasn't working for them." This resurgence has been gradual in the new century. Its initial manifestation was a reaction to American failure to prevail in either Iraq or Afghanistan, which had the effect of questioning the wisdom of military activism, a prime pillar of the internationalist order. President Obama was a spokesman for dialing back American military activism, completing the withdrawal from Iraq, championing (but failing to accomplish) a withdrawal from Afghanistan, and placing strong constraints on involvement in Syria. He did not extend this drawback from overt activism to other areas like economic cooperation, but it represented a crack in the solidarity surrounding the liberal consensus and thus an opening for a broader assault. As Cohen argues, Trump "has merely accelerated a trend—that of Washington's retreat from its global responsibilities."

The attack by Trump on liberal internationalism has represented a broad philosophical and operational attack, and it has unleashed a backlash from supporters of the liberal order. Some of the condemnation has been strong and direct. In a January 2019 online *Foreign Affairs* article, Wright summarizes the Trump effect in stark terms. Trump, he says, "is the only President ever elected on a platform that explicitly rejected all of the pillars of U.S. grand strategy." Eliot Cohen, normally a reliably conservative voice, concurs, arguing, "The President has outlined a deeply misguided foreign policy vision that is distrustful of U.S. allies, scornful of international institutions, and indifferent, if not downright scornful, of the liberal international order."

These are strong words of condemnation that reflect the continuing adherence many in the foreign policy elite have for the liberal order. They reflect a reaction to the Trump view of international relations, which, as the quotes in the last paragraph indicate, is at odds with accepted practice. Trump's disdain for permanent interests and lack of support for international institutions reflects his opinion that the relations among states is a fluid, transactional enterprise wherein constancy and loyalty to others is less valued than the outcomes of individual interactions. Rose summarizes: "Trumpism is about winning, which is something you do to others. The order requires leading, which is something you do with others." This attitude reflects a more transitory, varying attitude than the liberal order promotes. According to Wright, this basic orientation is reflected in policy toward the world: "a transactional relationship with other nations, a preference for authoritarian governments over democracies, a mercantilist approach to international economic policy, a general disregard for human rights and the rule of law, and the promotion of nationalism and unilateralism at the expense of multilateralism." This list is harsh and clearly constructed by an opponent of President Trump, and it should be viewed as such. The list of preferences that it states, however, could scarcely be a more comprehensive rejection of the liberal order of the last century.

Trump views his emphasis in terms reflecting the long-running debate between liberalism and isolationism. In a speech before the United Nations in September 2018, he emphasized his conviction that the United States should act independently of others—essentially on its own—when he envisioned "a future of patriotism, prosperity, and pride" for the United States, sentiments that would clearly resonate more positively before an American than an international audience. Implicit in his assessment is a rejection of the internationalist position.

For the time being, the unilateralist position associated with Trump represents the policy of the United States. It represents a very different image of international politics than has been the norm for the past three-quarters of a century. Of practical significance in this reformulation is a contrasting image of American ongoing relations with other countries that is much more fluid than has been the case in the past. Wright summarizes that contemporary foreign policy "is one in which the Trump administration has no permanent friends and no permanent enemies." Since the late 1940s, the prime internationalist edifice by which friends and enemies have been categorized and nurtured or confronted has been NATO. The question is how NATO will adapt to a Trumpian vision that may or may not persist in the future.

Application: The Fate of NATO

The North Atlantic Treaty of 1949 is, in many ways, the crowning achievement of the liberal internationalists, and especially those in the United States who adhere to multilateral as opposed to unilateral approaches to and solutions of international problems. It succeeded because the circumstances in which it was negotiated were fortuitous. Isolationism and unilateralism were universally blamed for allowing World War II to occur, and even in the United States, most people agreed that the splendid isolationism of the 1930s had provided the encouragement the Axis powers needed and that if the United States had been a committed member of the League, the war might have been avoided. By 1949, it was also clear that the hopeful UN view of a world of cooperative powers enforcing the peace was collapsing into the Cold War. In these circumstances, the calls of those who counseled a multilateral approach to international conflict had the decided upper hand, and those who desired a traditional American withdrawal from the world had little chance of succeeding.

The dynamics that led to NATO were centered in the United States, which was by far the most powerful country in the world at the time. Its military might, symbolized by the atomic bomb, confronted a huge Soviet Red army, but its superiority was unchallenged. The Americans were also the only people whose economy escaped the ravages of the war (the war stimulated the economy and helped end the Great Depression in the United States) and possessed the world's only fully functioning, solvent economic system. Whether they wanted to or not, the world had to listen to the United States.

The structure of the postwar world of which NATO was a centerpiece was fashioned through allied cooperation during the war itself. The UN Charter was the first piece, designed to be an improved universal international organization that avoided some of the pitfalls of the League of Nations—notably in its collective security provisions and the universality of its membership. This was followed by the Bretton Woods process and the extension of American assistance to war-torn countries menaced by communism. NATO was the crown jewel in the liberal internationalist crown, and its adoption vividly demonstrated, especially in its collective security provisions, the dynamic tension between the internationalists and the unilateralists.

The North Atlantic Treaty was important from both an American and international vantage point for several reasons. Most famously, it was the first peacetime military alliance in American history. The United States had allied itself formally with other states during wartime to prosecute mutual efforts against common foes (the world wars being examples), but it was the first time it had done so during peacetime, and NATO created a military command to coordinate military preparation and war plans against its enemies. Additionally, NATO was endowed with a political arm, the Council, the job of which was to reach common political judgments. Both arms of NATO remain vital parts of transatlantic cooperation, which was part of the intent of the formation of the alliance.

The looming Soviet threat was, of course, the major operative challenge that allowed for broad support for the treaty and its commitment. Particularly after the national failure to recognize and blunt the fascist threat of the 1930s, the stage was set for international cooperation and even bipartisan cooperation within the United States. Democratic President Harry S. Truman was the leading American proponent of NATO, and he was joined in the effort by the powerful Republican chairman of the Senate foreign relations committee, Arthur Vandenburg, in leading ratification of the Treaty through the U.S. Senate. The catchphrase of that cooperation was the idea that "politics ends at the water's edge"—the idea that domestic affairs was a political battle but that when facing the rest of the world, the United States should maintain a united front.

The result was the ultimate victory for the liberal internationalists, because it tied the United States both politically and militarily to Europe and set the precedent for broader cooperation both substantively and geographically in the future. Of the greatest symbolic importance, the United States forfeited some sovereign control over its affairs—the protection of which is at the core of unilateralism—in the process. It was a wrenching experience, and one that illustrates the dynamic tension between the two preferences to this day.

The operative and most controversial provision of the NATO Treaty was Article 5, known as the collective security article and the basis on which the American commitment in advance to come to the aid of its allies is based. In one sense, it augmented the collective security provisions found in chapter VII of the UN Charter. The Charter provides for a collective security response to breaches of the peace, but also grants permanent members of the Security Council (France, Great Britain, China, the United States, and Russia/Soviet Union) a veto over any actions. Because the Soviet Union was both a permanent member and the most likely violator, the provision disabled the Council from action, which was the framers' intent in such a situation. To deal with this problem, chapter VII also contains Article 51, which provides for the formation of collective security alliances. NATO and Article 5 exemplified implementation of that provision.

The chief political objection to Article 5, expressed most strongly by American unilateralists in the Congress, was that a provision containing an automatic requirement to come to the military aid of an attacked ally violated Article 1, Section 8 of the U.S. Constitution, which reserves the exclusive right to Congress to make war, effectively transferring that power to whoever attacked a NATO country. American participation was so crucial to a successful NATO guarantee that the treaty's framers were forced to accommodate the Americans by removing automaticity of military action from the article. The result was a pledge with a hedge.

To paraphrase the formal language of the Washington Treaty, Article 5 states that an attack against any member-state is to be considered an attack against all members. In that event, the article entreats that "each and every member will consider this as an attack against all members and will take *such actions as it deems necessary, including the use of armed force, to restore and maintain the security of the North Atlantic area*" (emphasis added). The pledge is to respond to such a provocation; the hedge is what the members pledge to do if such an attack occurs. As a literal, technical matter, they are not required to do anything but to talk the matter over. There is no obligation to use force. A pledge of automatic commitment would have torpedoed ratification of the Treaty in the U.S. Senate. Instead, Article 5 creates the ability to prepare for the possibility of aggression and how to go about responding to it.

The commitment was less than the liberal internationalists wanted, because it left the likelihood of a military response ambiguous. In the event the Soviets were contemplating an invasion of Western Europe (the contingency for which NATO was designed to avoid or defeat), they would have to ask themselves what the NATO, and especially the American, response would be. Would the United States commit armed forces and stop them, possibly starting World War III, if they acted? Or would they just debate the situation and decide not to act militarily? Once nuclear weapons were introduced into the equation, the calculation became even more complicated.

The liberal internationalist/unilateralist divide thus resulted in a compromise where the price of acceptance of the treaty was a diminished physical commitment. During the Cold War, the United States sought to make the prospects more certain by stationing U.S. troops along the Iron Curtain frontier. This "tripwire," as it was known, meant American troops would be among the first killed in a Soviet thrust westward, making it more difficult to conclude a Congressional postinvasion debate with inaction. It was the best they could do.

In the seventy years since NATO came into existence in 1949, the provisions of Article 5 have only been invoked once. The occasion was the terrorist attack against New York and Washington on September 11, 2001, and it was the European allies who invoked it as a symbolic act of solidarity with their North American allies. The act further suggested a united effort and front against terrorist activity and called for cooperation among NATO members in pursuing the perpetrators and in subsequent activities against the common foe. The action stands in some contrast to remarks by President Trump questioning whether continued American participation in the alliance was worth the effort and cost in 2018.

Conclusion

Montenegro is a small country in the Balkans that was part of Yugoslavia until it dissolved in 1992. It formed a union with Serbia that lasted until 2006, when the country ended that merger and formed a union of not quite 650,000 people and borders on Serbia, Bosnia, and Herzegovina, and Albania and the Adriatic Sea. Montenegro is hardly a geopolitical powerhouse.

Montengero became the twenty-ninth member of NATO on June 5, 2017, as part of its policy of integrating itself more fully with the rest of Europe. A year later, this created the basis for a conversation between President Trump and Fox News host Tucker Carlson on the latter's talk show. Carlson asked if Montenegro's membership meant his son might be forced into military service to defend Montenegro in the event it became involved in a war. Trump replied, "They have very aggressive people. They may get aggressive and congratulations, you're in World War III. . . . That the way it (NATO) is set up." In addition to the implausibility of such an act by tiny Montenegro (with an area slightly smaller than Connecticut), the president misrepresented Article 5, which is activated only when a member is menaced, not when it attacks someone else. The point, however, is what the exchange says about the liberal interventionist/unilateralist debate.

As noted, NATO is the crown jewel of the liberal interventionists' attempt to fashion international relations on a cooperative, multilateral base rather than on a unilateralist base. Without the alliance and the NATO Council, transatlantic cooperation would be greatly reduced in an institutional sense, and the Trump administration has sought to loosen those bonds, reflecting its American nationalist philosophy that puts primary emphasis on the preservation of maximum sovereign control.

This is the current articulation of the answer to the question of the desirability of going it together or alone. The consensus surrounding the liberal preference for collective cooperation and action has been challenged in this century by a retreat to a more exclusionary, nationalist view in various parts of the world. The question is what has caused this, and part of the answer is explored in chapter 6 under the banner of human rights obligations. The more important questions are how permanent or transient this debate will be, and what will be its short- and long-term effects on international relations. In terms of NATO, is international peace better served by a strong commitment to its provisions centered around Article 5? Or would a world in which those bonds were weakened or eliminated be a better, preferable place? Because NATO is about keeping the peace in an era when general war could be catastrophic, it occupies a special place in the debate, but it ripples much more broadly through the operation of international relations.

Study/Discussion Questions

1. What are the liberal internationalist and unilateralist approaches to international relations? Compare and contrast them and their historic role in the United States.
2. The liberal internationalist philosophy has been dominant for a century. Discuss its genesis and evolution in both the United States and more widely from the League of Nations forward.
3. What are the premises of the two approaches? How did the interwar (1919–1939) experience affect the debate and shape of the post–World War II world?
4. Why is the American debate over internationalism and unilateralism so important? How has that debate evolved in the United States? What has the "Trump effect" been on contemporary discussions?
5. What is NATO? How and why has it been the centerpiece of the liberal internationalist approach to international relations since 1945?
6. The most controversial aspect of NATO is Article 5. What is the substance of that provision? What does it commit the United States and other members to do? How many times has it been invoked? When, by whom, and for what reason?
7. Discuss the role of the Soviet threat on the postwar debate over approaches to international relations. Has the situation changed enough to reopen the internationalist-unilateralist debate? Why or why not?
8. Recognizing any opinion will be a hybrid of pure positions, does internationalism or unilateralism make more sense to you? Defend your position.

Bibliography

Alcaro, Riccardo, ed. *The Liberal Order and Its Contestations: Great Powers and Regions Transiting in a Multipolar Era*. London: Routledge, 2018.

Beate, Jahn. *Liberal Internationalism: Theory, History, Practice*. London: Palgrave, 2013.

Blake, Aaron. "Trump's Montenegro Remarks Make It Abundantly Clear He Doesn't Understand NATO." *Washington Post* (online), July 18, 2018.

Carr, E. H. *The Twenty-Year Crisis, 1919-1939.* New York: Macmillan, 1939.

Chua, Amy. "Tribal World: Identity Is All." *Foreign Affairs* 97, 4 (July/August 2018), 25–33.

Cohen, Eliot A. "America's Long Goodbye: The Real Crisis of the Trump Era." *Foreign Affairs* 89, 1 (January/February 2019), 138–46.

Colgan, Jeff D., and Robert O. Keohane. "The Liberal Order Is Rigged: Fix It Now or Watch It Wither." *Foreign Affairs* 96, 3 (May/June 2017), 36–44.

Committee on Armed Services, U.S. Senate. *The North Atlantic Treaty Organization, Russia, and European Security.* Washington, DC: U.S. Senate, 2015.

Deudney, Daniel, and G. John Ikenberry. "The Liberal World: The Resilient Order." *Foreign Affairs* 97, 4 (July/August 2018), 16–25.

Gaddis, John Lewis. *Strategies of Containment: A Critical Appraisal of American National Security Policy During the Cold War* (revised and expanded edition). New York: Oxford University Press, 2005.

Haass, Richard. "How a World Order Ends and What Comes in Its Wake." *Foreign Affairs* 98, 1 (January/February 2019), 22–30.

Hazony, Yoram. *The Virtue of Nationalism.* New York: Basic Books, 2018.

Ikenberry, G. John. "The Plot Against American Foreign Policy. Can the Liberal Order Survive?" *Foreign Affairs* 96, 3 (May/June 2017), 2–9.

Jervis, Robert, et al., eds. *Chaos in the Liberal Order: The Trump Presidency and International Politics in the Twenty-First Century.* New York: Columbia University Press, 2018.

Johnston, Seth A. *How NATO Adapts: Strategy and Organization in the Atlantic Alliance Since 1950.* Baltimore, MD: Johns Hopkins University Press, 2017.

Kagan, Robert. *The Jungle Grows Back: America and Our Imperiled World.* New York: Knopf, 2018.

Kaplan, Lawrence. *N.A.T.O. 1948: The Birth of the Transatlantic Alliance.* Lanham, MD: Rowman & Littlefield, 2007.

———. *NATO Divided, NATO United: The Evolution of the Alliance.* Westport, CT: Praeger, 2004.

Kotkin, Stephen. "The Realist World: The Players Changed but the Game Remains." *Foreign Affairs* 97, 4 (July/August 2018), 10–15.

Lindley-French, Julian. *The North Atlantic Treaty Organization.* New York and London: Routledge, 2015.

Mearsheimer, John. *The Great Delusion: Liberal Dreams and International Realities.* New Haven, CT: Yale University Press, 2018.

Miller, Paul D. *American Power and the Liberal Order: A Conservative Internationalist Grand Strategy.* Washington, DC: Georgetown University Press, 2016.

Nye, Joseph S. Jr. *The Paradox of American Power: Why the World's Superpower Can't Go It Alone.* New York: Oxford University Press, 2003.

Rose, Gideon. "The Fourth Founding: The United States and the Liberal Order." *Foreign Affairs* 98, 1 (January/February 2019), 10–21.

Sexton, Jay. *A Nation Forged by Crisis: A New American History.* New York: Basic Books, 2018.

Sloan, Stanley. *Defense of the West: NATO, the European Union, and the Transatlantic Bargain.* Manchester, UK: Manchester University Press, 2016.

Smith, Tony. *Why Wilson Matters: The Origin of American Liberal Internationalism and the Crisis Today.* Princeton, NJ: Princeton University Press, 2017.

U.S. Army War College. *The Relevance of the European Union and the North Atlantic Treaty Organization for the United States in the Twenty-First Century.* Carlisle Barracks, PA: Strategic Studies Institute, 2017.
Walt, Stephen. *The Hell of Good Intentions: America's Foreign Policy Elite and the Demise of U.S. Primacy.* New York: Farrar, Straus, and Giroux, 2018.
Wright, Thomas. "Trump's Foreign Policy Is No Longer Unpredictable: Gone Are the Days of a Divided Administration." *Foreign Affairs Snapshot* (online), January 18, 2019.

6

Promoting Universal Human Rights

Responsibility to Protect?

The promotion and protection of human rights among all people of the world was another of the major priorities that emerged from World War II and formed one of the bases for the liberal internationalist agenda introduced in the last chapter. The reason for this intrusion onto the world agenda arose naturally from the horror of the prewar and wartime atrocities committed principally (but not exclusively) by the Axis powers: the Nazi Holocaust aimed at the genocide of Jews, Roma, and other minorities, and atrocities committed by the Japanese in China (the so-called Rape of Nanking) and against American service members (e.g., the Bataan death march in the Philippines). The suppression and denial of human rights was a long-standing worldwide phenomenon that did not end when the last shot was fired in the war, and violations would reemerge to form what many considered a compelling rationale for an international response to protect members of the human species from the not-so-tender ministrations of their fellow humans. The creation of international norms and institutions was the international system's response and set in motions dynamics that remain a work in progress three-quarters of a century later.

The idea of ensuring the rights of other humans does not sound like it should be a controversial proposition, but in practice it has been and continues to be. Questions tend to arise in three distinct ways. The first is the determination about what constitutes the basic entitlement people have regarding the quality of their lives. It is a profoundly political and cultural question, and one that is influenced by the often tumultuous, even hate-filled relations people within political jurisdictions and across national boundaries have toward one another. The simple fact of the matter is that the idea all humans should be treated with the same dignity as all others is not universally held.

The second question is who has responsibility for ensuring and protecting the rights of people, and this ultimately comes down to the question of who should suppress or bring to justice violators of whatever norms are violated. Because violations occur within sovereign political communities, the core centrality of sovereignty introduced in chapter 1 becomes a major factor in any discussions about human rights and their enforcement. Who determines what rights people have, and who should enforce those? The traditional answer is the state, but what if the state is itself the offender or chooses to shield offenders within its jurisdiction. Both questions, who sets standards and who enforces them, have been central matters of contention in the debate. The internationalists and unilateralists disagree vehemently on these questions, which remain central to ongoing efforts to define and enforce standards of human entitlement.

The third question is infrequently raised publicly but is crucial to efforts to fashion standards and to their enforcement: How important is the human rights question to states? It is a matter of where human rights resides in the hierarchy of national interests that states have (see chapter 3). Like the question of whether such rights exist, whether their enforcement is important enough to warrant the dedication of priority efforts would seem noncontroversial on the face of it, but it is in fact a matter of controversy. The most passive form of resistance arises from the belief that states have more interests than they can attend to properly, that it is the responsibility of government to deal with their own citizens' welfare, and that protecting others is simply beyond their capabilities. Moreover, the violation of human rights tends to occur most often and flagrantly in developing countries and thus evade the notice of many in the more developed countries. When violations reach atrocious proportions, then the world takes notice. Otherwise it may not.

Efforts have been ongoing since the 1940s to deal with the questions that drive this examination: what are human rights? Who should enforce them? And what can be done to make the guarantee of life with dignity and comfort possible? The principles section of the chapter is devoted to the record as it has evolved, including the controversies it has created. The record is certainly incomplete—basic standards of human existence are neither universally formulated nor enforced worldwide. The applications section will look at two related initiatives that emerged in the last twenty years to energize that process, humanitarian intervention and the so-called Responsibility to Protect (R2P).

Principle: Human Rights

Questions about the rights to which humans are entitled by virtue of being humans are of remarkably recent vintage in human history. The modern emergence of an assertion that humans have individual and group rights is largely a twentieth-century phenomenon that is conceptually attributable to two related intellectual forces already raised in earlier pages: sovereignty and democratization. When sovereignty was a sacrosanct property of states wielded by whoever ruled a sovereign jurisdiction, human rights were whatever the ruler (the "sovereign") said they were within his or her realm, and there was neither internal or international recourse available to dissenters. The rise of popular sovereignty and its assertion that sovereignty resides in individuals naturally extrapolates to an assertion that those individuals should have some control over the quality of their existence. Democratization in turn suggests that individuals have some rights over the selection of who sets the conditions of existence for people and the right to challenge judgments about those rules and to change both the rules and the rule makers. These propositions seem unexceptional in many parts (but not all) of the twenty-first-century world. They have not always been so.

Human rights and entitlements to certain conditions of existence have historically been heretical, and in some places apostolic, until the recent human past. Their modern emergence is, in many ways, an outgrowth of the early twentieth century and especially the trauma of World War II. The assertion and advocacy of basic human rights has been a staple part of liberal internationalism and its attempt to democratize both international and domestic politics. The impact of the Great War was traumatic and began the process of challenging the old order of absolute sovereignty. Woodrow Wilson was its leading advocate, and the added humanitarian assaults of World War II made inexorable the rise of an active movement to reform the world order. The assertion and spreading advocacy of human rights has been part of that pattern.

Two examples from the period immediately after World War II illustrate this transformation. The first is the question of genocide. Although massive extinction of peoples was not a new phenomenon and had even blighted the twentieth century (the Ottoman Turks campaign against Armenia early in the century was a case in point), the practice reached its most extreme form in the Nazi Holocaust against European Jews and Roma. The problem was that there was no word to describe such atrocity until 1944, when Ralph Lemkin, a Polish Jew, invented the term in a study of Nazi practices in occupied Europe published by the Carnegie Endowment for International Peace. This gave those organizing proceedings against excesses in the war a name for the crime for which they would try the offenders. The physical formation of tribunals represents the second example. When those who would organize the Nuremberg trials against accused Nazi mass murderers were impaneled, one jurist, a member of the U.S. Supreme Court, opined that while the Nazis could be tried for massively killing foreigners, they could not be tried for genocide against Jews and Roma who happened to be German citizens. His reason reflected conventional conceptions of sovereignty, which maintained that sovereign governments had total control over their own territories, including slaughtering population groups. The conferees rejected this interpretation, and genocide is recognized as a war crime against anyone regardless of nationality. It was not the only controversy surrounding the universality of human rights at the end of World War II and still is not.

The Content of Human Rights

When the conferees gathered in San Francisco in 1945 to fashion postwar institutions, most notably the United Nations, they hoped to create a more enduring global peace than had been the outcome in 1919, and one of their central concerns was human rights. A major obstacle they faced was how to create mechanisms that could enforce violations against people by other people, and especially governments. Before they could attack this problem, however, they had to reach agreement about exactly what conditions (or rights) that people possess and which could then be enforced. In a Western context, the general content of what conditions are encapsulated in human rights are generally agreed to, and controversies surround how and by whom to enforce them. Outside the traditional Euro-American world, disagreement exists about the content of human rights as well.

Discussions about human rights were an important part of the deliberations leading to the UN Charter. The least controversial human rights issue that the conferees faced was over the horror over the Holocaust and how to prevent the possibility of the repetition of a similar event. The condemnation of the newly minted crimes of genocide was an easy conceptual action for the new world organization, especially in the atmosphere of trials of leading German and Japanese officials who had ordered or engaged in genocidal acts during the war in Tokyo and Nuremberg. As a result, the Convention of Genocide passed without controversy in 1946.

The agreement on genocide opened the floodgates for negotiating international accords in the human rights area more generally. The first hurdle that had to be surmounted was the nature, quality, and extent that such standards would encompass. In rough terms, there were two categories of possible inclusions. The first, and least controversial, were the so-called negative or political rights, actions that governments and others were prohibited from taking toward their citizens. Denial of the right to vote is an example. The deliberations were dominated by the Western democracies, notably the United States. Many of the negative rights that were introduced and included in the discussions were taken from or modeled on rights included in the first ten amendments to the U.S. Constitution—the Bill of Rights—making it difficult for unilateralists in the United States to oppose them.

The other category of rights was the so-called social and economic, or positive, rights. The question was a matter of the quality of existence to which members of the human species are entitled by virtue of being human, and they include a long list of entitlements that were neither universally available or, in some cases, culturally acceptable in parts of the world. Universal access to education for both males and females and freedom to the unfettered right to marry are classic examples of differences in belief; equal access to medical care represents a difference in societal abilities or priorities.

There were also political problems to be overcome. Even in countries where there could be few objections in principle to most of the items that made their eventual way into the results of deliberations, there were also bases for objection, some of which were voiced most strongly and adamantly by Americans. The United States in the 1940s was not exactly an egalitarian paradise where all people enjoyed equal access to the protections and entitlements that were under discussion, and some American critics worried—with justification—that the United States might be accused of hypocrisy because some of the provisions of any agreement were not available to some Americans (e.g., African Americans and Native Americans), who might even have the temerity to demand that they be extended to them. At the same time, negotiations were occurring in an atmosphere of growing antagonism that would eventuate in the Cold War. Because the Soviet "worker's paradise" was not precisely a haven of human rights protection and promotion, international charges of hypocrisy would almost certainly occur.

The crown jewel of the early postwar human rights movement was the UN Universal Declaration on Human Rights (UDHR). It was proclaimed by the UN General Assembly (it was not introduced in the more geopolitically powerful Security Council for fear of a veto) in Paris on December 10, 1948, as General Assembly resolution 217. The obligations that signatories bind themselves are extensive and are contained in thirty articles of the agreement that individually and collectively lay out the framers' conception of human rights and entitlements.

The first nineteen articles lay out the negative rights, political and personal entitlements that governments are prohibited from denying to or withholding from its citizens. The rights asserted are comprehensive. They include "the right to life, liberty, and security" (Art. 3), prohibition on slavery (Art. 4), outlawing "torture or cruel, inhuman or degrading treatment or punishment" (Art. 5), recognition as a "person before the law" (Art. 6), equality before the law (Art. 7), "effective remedy by competent national tribunals" (Art. 8), prohibition on "arbitrary arrest" (Art. 9), "fair and full public hearings"(Art. 10), the "presumption of innocence" and a ban on unjustified imprisonment (Art. 11), no "arbitrary interference" in people's private lives (Art. 12), "freedom of movement and residence" (Art. 13), the right to seek asylum (Art. 14), the right to nationality (Art. 15), the "right to marry and to found a family" (Art. 16), the right to own property (Art. 17), freedom of "thought, conscience, and religion" (Art. 18), and "freedom of opinion and expression" (Art. 19).

Articles 20 to 28 summarize the positive rights. Like the negative rights, it is an impressive list. It includes the right to peaceful assembly and association (Art. 20); the right to "take part in the government," including its services and selection of who governs (Art. 21); "social security" and the "rights indispensable for his dignity" (Art. 22); free choice of employment, "equal pay for equal work," "just" renumeration and the right to join unions" (Art. 23); the "right of rest and leisure, including reasonable limitation of working hours and periodic holidays with pay" (Art. 24); "a standard of living adequate for the health and well-being of himself and his family" (Art. 25); the right to education (Art. 26); the right "freely to participate in the cultural life of the community" (Art. 27); and entitlement to "a social and international order in which the rights and freedoms set forth in this declaration can be fully realized" (Art. 28).

The entire UDHR has been controversial, notably because all the signatories do not honor or enforce all its provisions. The negative rights, which consciously reflect the Bill of Rights in the U.S. Constitution, are criticized less frequently, but the positive rights are by no means either universally honored or even asserted. A number of those rights, for instance, are matters of public policy debate throughout the world, including in the United States.

The UDHR opened the floodgate for the advocacy and formulation of a broad range of international human rights declarations, but they have not all been universally embraced or even been formalized in international obligations. The statute that would eventually create the International Criminal Court (ICC), as will be remembered from chapter 1, was part of the 1940s movement, but it did not reach even partial implementation until the 1990s. The clear barrier to enacting international human rights standards has been the reluctance of many states (including the United States) to submit itself to possible enforcement of those standards against itself. It has several bases.

Resistance to Human Rights Standards

The expansion or contraction of internationally enforceable human rights is, in some ways, a mirror of the broader debate over conceptualizations of the international system, a disagreement introduced in the last chapter. Those who feel that international cooperation is the best way to stabilize and expand the quality of international life (the liberal internationalists) through collective action see greater international assertion in important matters like the terms of human existence to be a logical arm of the attempt to improve the human condition generally, and they therefore support greater internationalization of the human rights process as a step in the right direction. Those who are skeptical of the desirability and effects of international jurisdiction and influence on the state (the unilateralists) emphasize the potential deleterious effects such regulations can have on the state and thus the status—including human rights—of the citizens of their states. It is thus an extension of a larger debate about international relations.

Given this construction, it is not surprising that much of the resistance to human rights expansion is expressed in terms of its deleterious effects on national sovereignty. In cases where allegations of abuses are leveled at states, the enforcement of those standards must be directed at states and usually at high-ranking officials in those states. The leaders who are alleged perpetrators are often in a political position to deny access to their countries in ways that could lead to their own prosecution, and they will virtually always base their arguments on grounds of sovereignty. There is no question that the Syrian government of Bashar al-Assad has suppressed the rights of large parts of the Syrian population in fundamental ways, but no international human rights monitors (in this case officials of the ICC) have been permitted into the country to investigate these allegations or to take punitive actions against members of the government. The reason is that such intrusion would be a violation of Syria's sovereignty, a position supported by Russia, whose veto in the UN Security Council precludes the possibility that the world body can become proactively involved in the case.

Some objections to international standards are cultural and reflect fundamental belief systems of people from different backgrounds and belief systems about the nature of human existence and the rights of authorities toward people within their sovereign jurisdictions. The assertion of universal human rights is, after all, an historically recent phenomenon, one that is often dated formally back to Woodrow Wilson's 14 Points as a reason for prosecuting World War I, and it took the vicious backlash of atrocities in World War II fully to energize the process. Because the post-1945 period has also witnessed the independence of many Afro-Asian peoples whose belief systems are different than those shared by Westerners whose values dominate the human rights movement, many of these new members of the international order also have beliefs and practices at odds with those of documents like the UDHR, and they are reluctant to accept standards in direct contraposition to beliefs and practices that are centuries old. Religious beliefs often play prominently into resistance to the values and general secularization that is imbedded in human rights.

Many of the cultural objections are based in gender. The idea of gender equality expressed as a human right that applies to both sexes was certainly part of the liberal internationalist movement in world affairs, and it is still a work in progress in large parts of the world where cultural beliefs and practices relegate women and girls to an inferior status. In some cases (such as certain fundamentalist sects of Islam such as the Wahhabism that is the state religion of Saudi Arabia) conventions place very strong restrictions on a woman's "place" in the world. These restrictions tend to be strongest and most resistant in the least developed societies, where more traditional values, often governmentally and/or religiously reinforced, tend to hold sway. The absolute monarchies of the Persian Gulf offer the purest (or most egregious, depending on one's vantage point) examples of sexual inequality, and these practices were the major target of the 1995 Beijing summit on women, at which then First Lady Hillary Clinton was a leading advocate of equalizing actions.

The failure to protect the basic human rights can be embarrassing to countries, and one way to deal with this problem is to argue that human rights are indeed protected and enforced but to restrict the ability of outsiders either to inspect evidence of this enforcement or to chronicle evidence of compliance or noncompliance. The denial of the kinds of human rights contained in the UDHR and other post-1945 documents through the United Nations (Chapter IX of the Charter—Articles 55 to 60 and the preamble, which "reaffirms faith in human rights") are evidence either of authoritarian rule or the absence of modern political and human values and are ignored by many countries. Some states may hold antihuman rights values, but it is embarrassing to admit these positions, and great efforts are usually made to obscure or downplay them. The "charm offensive" by Saudi Arabia to enhance the elevation of Muhammad bin Salman to the throne is a primary example of this attempt.

To almost everyone reading this volume, the existence of basic human rights and entitlements probably seems so obvious that one can wonder why they are the subject of controversy and uneven enforcement. One reason is that those rights, and particularly the rights of people in places where violations are the strongest and often most hideous, are not at the top of the agenda for most outsiders who might be in a physical position to do something about them. In the hierarchy of interests identified in chapter 2, human rights abuses elsewhere in the world do not rise to vital or even very important level for most outsiders, and this indifference is especially pronounced in an inward-turning international environment such as today's.

Enforcement has been the sticking point for human rights enforcement since the first efforts were mounted with initiatives like the UDHR and other 1940s proposals. The problem is both a matter of jurisdiction and appropriate, mandatory enforcement efforts and mechanisms. There has been a disconnect between the pronouncement of principles and means of enforcement since the immediate post-1945 period. That period was pregnant with institutional change beginning with the UN Charter and extending to human rights concerns. The UDHR was a seminal accomplishment in delineating standards for human existence, but it contained no provisions for enforcing those, particularly against states that might be in violation.

The ICC has been used to adjudicate some of the grossest forms of human rights abuse (e.g., charges of genocide in Rwanda and Kosovo during the 1990s), but it has proven of limited reach when governments exercise their sovereignty-based protections of human rights violators. Omar al-Bashir, the former president of Sudan, is under ICC indictment for alleged human rights/war crime violations in Darfur, but the government will not surrender him for prosecution, and there is nothing the ICC can do to force their compliance. The same is true of Syrian president Bashar al-Assad, who has been charged with gross violation connected to chemical attacks in the Syrian Civil War (see chapter 13). By contrast, former Serbian president Slobodan Milosevic, who was charged with war crimes in Kosovo, was remanded to the ICC because his successor government turned him over, and he remains incarcerated at the Hague.

Enforcement remains the chief stumbling block to realizing human rights on an international basis, and it is a situation that, at the level of international relations, is unlikely to change in the near term. State governments do not place as high a priority on assuring the rights of people at other places in the world as they do on their own sovereign priorities, including the possibility that relaxing sovereign control could result in effective international enforcement of human rights norms *against them*. The objection is, of course, never placed in quite such stark terms, but it is a dynamic that efforts to see the universal enforcement of international human rights must overcome.

Application: Humanitarian Intervention and the Responsibility to Protect

The question about the enforcement of human rights lay fallow through the Cold War. Advocacy and calls for action tended to be concentrated on situations that did not have direct Cold War implications and on situations where the UN peacekeeping model of interposing designated forces between formerly warring parties could reduce the recourse to violence and even, in the best of cases, lead to negotiated peace settlements. These situations were reasonably infrequent and peripheral, as Soviet and American interests tended to be engaged in most conflicts and where allegations of human rights abuse probably had communist-anticommunist overlays that both sides sought to avoid. The slaughter in Cambodia in the 1970s, which evoked little active international reaction, may be the best case in point.

When the Cold War ended, the world was different. In terms of violence and instability, often featuring human rights abuses, some of the most prominent were internal conflicts in multinational developing countries, where internal factions sometimes "celebrated" their freedom from colonial rule by reverting to precolonial savagery against other groups inside new political boundaries. These developing world internal conflicts are often orgies of hideous violence where human rights and even existence are brutally tested. I have discussed these extensively in places like *National Security*, seventh edition. With no Cold War overlay to provide a buffering of these events, they erupted with a vengeance in the 1990s in the Balkans and parts of the Afro-Asian world like Rwanda and the

Darfur region of Sudan. They have continued into the contemporary world in hideous campaigns in the new state of Sudan and savagery against the Houthis of Yemen and the Rohingya of Myanmar.

The international system has no adequate mechanisms to deal with the suffering these kinds of situations create. The geopolitics of assuaging human disasters has been inadequate to engender intergovernmental efforts to intervene in and relieve the human suffering that has been the result. Over half the population of Syria, after all, live in internal or external exile, where they clearly do not enjoy the conditions of life guaranteed in the documents like the UDHR.

Because state governments cannot or will not engage in effective measures to end human suffering, the impetus has moved to privately inspired efforts. The most prominent of these, both conceptual products of the 1990s, have been humanitarian intervention and the R2P. Both should be viewed as aspirational attempts to raise international awareness and spirited advocacy and action to increase the quality of human life on the planet.

The two concepts are conceptually linked. Both start from the premise that it is a moral imperative of humankind to alleviate violent denial and suppression of human rights and suffering caused by other people. As Walzer put it over a decade ago, "How much human suffering are we prepared to watch before we intervene?" The traditional answer is swathed in the concept of state sovereignty and is "quite a lot." The champions of R2P counter that the necessity to protect people from gross abuses has both a moral base (it is the morally right or correct thing to do) and that it is important enough to justify the expenditure of military force to guarantee it. It asserts, in other words, a moral vital interest in the protection of human rights that cannot be allowed to be ignored.

The arguments over this responsibility are both moral and political. The moral arguments are summarized by Nardin in a 2002 article and are familiar in content and sentiment. On one hand, "the use of force is justified not solely by self-defense but by the moral imperative to punish wrongs and to protect the innocent." At the same time, the sovereignty-based principle of non-interference asserts that "states are forbidden to exercise their authority, and certainly to use force, within the jurisdiction of other states." The former position is primarily moral in content and suggests the universality of rights regardless of political location and jurisdiction. The latter suggests that the primarily politico-legal concept of sovereignty is supreme, making humanitarian or any other kind of interference illegal. This latter contention activates the advocacy of R2P supporters. Former Australian Foreign Minister Gareth Evans, one of the most vocal supporters of the R2P position and opponents of the moral and philosophical sovereignty arguments, summarized the R2P contention in a 2008 book: "the Westphalian principles effectively institutionalized the longstanding indifference of political leaders institutionalized toward atrocities occurring elsewhere."

There are two other noteworthy factors that contribute to the reluctance of the members of the international community to embrace R2P principles operationally. One of these is the fact that rhetorical acceptance of the principle that humans have some humanitarian obligation toward the condition of others, does not always—even often—translate into a vital interest that justifies or impels armed intervention when violations occur. Proponents of internationalization of enforcement of human rights have tried to gain acceptance of adding the adjective "vital" to their entreaty—something like vital humanitarian intervention—but the idea has never gained significant international operational traction. The other problem is whether international responses can be effective in alleviating many of the worst humanitarian abuses. Many of these occur in the most intractable developing world internal conflicts, and the success of outside intervention in these kinds of situations within the resource bounds available to address them are problematic in terms of likely success (see my *The Case Against Military Intervention* for a detailed discussion). As a particularly extreme example, the massive slaughter currently going on in the Republic of South Sudan includes the gross violation of virtually all the human entitlements included in the UDHR. Whatever "responsibility to protect" may exist for the international community, it is not clear what would be effective in relieving the situation and restoring the human entitlements of South Sudanese victims of multiple abuses.

Conclusion

As a matter of public policy and advocacy, the question of human rights and how to deal with violations of those rights is anomalous and culturally charged. Most of the rights heralded in documents like the UDHR are decidedly Western in content and, in principle, are embraced or at least not openly opposed by most Westerners. How can an American, for instance, not support most of the assertions in the negative rights included in Articles 1 to 19 of the declaration? There are objections, but they are basically peripheral and generally focused on the most expansive of the rights asserted. Asylum (Art. 14) has been a recent point of contention in the United States about border security, for instance. The objections that are voiced center on the positive rights, because they assert human entitlements that are extremely egalitarian and strike some conservatives as overreaches in the political process: they are objections not to the rights in principle, but to who and how they can be achieved.

The anomaly is much more striking in parts of the developing world, where large and influential groups, often representing governments, reject some of the rights in principle. It is not unusual in traditionally based societies to deny that women have the same basic rights as men. Sometimes these objections are historically "baked" into culture, and sometimes they are religious. Some Islamic groups, for instance, not only oppose freedom of religion within their societies, but they label nonbelievers as apostate and encourage the suppression—even killing—of people of other faiths. The result can be uniform opposition to many of the negative rights. As an example, compare the list of political rights in the UDHR with Saudi law, custom, and practice. Additionally, many in both the developing and developed world simply lack the resources to implement many of the positive rights in the declaration.

The enforcement of norms intended to implement basic rights layers onto these problems. The ICC creates a legal framework for prosecuting violators of the most serious standards, but these can be evaded by not joining the court and thus accepting its jurisdiction or by excluding court officials from their sovereign jurisdictions. The UN Charter makes provision for forming forces that could impose some human rights, but those provisions have never been implemented in any meaningful way.

Advocacies of principles like humanitarian intervention and R2P are morally based responses to the inability to enforce human rights standards, especially in highly conflictual situations where governments and nongovernmental entities engage in gross, often massive atrocities against other people. It is morally difficult to ignore these situations except on sovereignty grounds that were undermined at Nuremberg and in Tokyo after World War II. Major atrocities continue, and some of these are raised in later parts of this book. All have questions about human rights and what should be done to realize them universally as text or subtext. Yet there is no concerted global effort to erase the problems. That is the true anomaly of the situation.

Study/Discussion Questions

1. What is the human rights movement? What brought it about? Include a discussion of World War II and postwar dynamics in your discussion.
2. What are the major issues surrounding human rights in international relations? Discuss each.
3. Sovereignty and human rights are competing international priorities and dynamics. How and why?
4. Discuss the process leading to the Universal Declaration on Human Rights (UDHR). What are the major categories of rights in the document? Cite examples.
5. What are the major sources of opposition to human rights and its enforcement?
6. What are humanitarian intervention and the Responsibility to Protect (R2P)? How are they related to one another? What is their status?
7. Analyze the premises of R2P human rights and international political grounds. Which arguments do you find compelling?
8. Why have human rights and applications like R2P been described in the text as anomalous? How do you feel about the human rights issue, and especially its enforcement?

Bibliography

Bellamy, Alex. *Responsibility to Protect.* Cambridge, UK: Polity Press, 2009.

———. *The Responsibility to Protect: A Defense.* Oxford UK: Oxford University Press, 2014.

——— and Tim Dunne. *The Oxford University Handbook of Responsibility to Protect.* Oxford, UK: Oxford University Press, 2016.

Bellamy, Alex, and Edward C. Luck. *The Responsibility to Protect: From Promise to Practice.* Cambridge, UK: Polity Press, 2018.

Brysk, Alison. *The Future of Human Rights.* Cambridge, UK: Polity, 2018.

——— ed. *Globalization and Human Rights.* Berkeley, CA: University of California Press, 2002.

Clapham, Andrew. *Human Rights: A Very Short Introduction.* Oxford, UK: Oxford University Press, 2015.

Donnelly, Jack. *Universal Human Rights in Theory and Practice* (third edition). Ithaca, NY: Cornell University Press, 2018.

——— and David J. Whelan. *International Human Rights: Dilemma in World Politics.* New York and London: Routledge, 2018.

Evans, Gareth. *The Responsibility to Protect: End Mass Atrocities Once and For All.* Washington, DC: Brookings Institution Press, 2008.

Ganguly, Meenakshi, and Brad Damas. "For Rohingya Refugees, There's No Return in Sight: Why They Remain Stuck in Bangladesh." *Foreign Affairs Snapshot*, June 5, 2019.

Glanville, Luke. *Sovereignty and the Responsibility to Protect: A New History.* Chicago, IL: University of Chicago Press, 2013.

Goodhart, Michael. *Human Rights: Politics and Practice.* Oxford, UK: Oxford University Press, 2016.

Grover, Sonja. *The Responsibility to Protect: Perspective on the Concept's Meaning, Proper Application, and Value.* New York and London: Routledge, 2018.

Hehir, Aidan. *Humanitarian Intervention: An Introduction.* London: Red Globe Press, 2013.

Hunt, Lynn. *Inventing Human Rights: A History.* New York: W. W. Norton, 2008.

Korey, William. *The Promises We Keep: Human Rights, the Helsinki Process, and American Foreign Policy.* New York: St. Martin's Press, 1993.

Lemkin, Ralph. *Axis Rule in Occupied Europe: Analysis and Proposals for Refugees.* Washington, DC: Carnegie Endowment for International Peace, 1944.

Menon, Rajan. *The Conceit of Humanitarian Intervention.* Oxford, UK: Oxford University Press, 2016.

Mertus, Julie. *Human Rights and Conflict: Exploring the Links between Rights, Law, and Peacebuilding.* Washington, DC: U.S. Institute for Peace Press, 2013.

Moyn, Samuel. *Not Enough: Human Rights in an Unequal World.* Cambridge, MA: Harvard University Press, 2018.

Nardin, Terry. "The Moral Basis of Humanitarian Intervention." *Ethics and International Affairs* 16, no. 1 (March 2002), 57–70.

Pinos, Jaume Castan. *Kosovo and the Collateral Effects of Humanitarian Intervention.* New York and London: Routledge, 2018.

Roosevelt, Eleanor, et al. *Universal Declaration of Human Rights* (Little Books of Wisdom). Boston, MA: Applewood Books, 2001.

Sikkink, Kathryn, Stephen C. Ropp, and Thomas Risse. *The Power of Human Rights: International Norms and Domestic Change.* Cambridge, UK: Cambridge University Press, 2010.

Snow, Donald M. *National Security* (seventh edition). New York and London: Routledge, 2020.

———. *The Case Against Military Intervention: Why We Do It and Why It Fails.* New York and London: Routledge, 2016.

———. *Thinking About National Security: Strategy, Policy, and Issues.* New York and London: Routledge, 2016.

Thakur, Ramesh, and William Melvey, eds. *Theorizing the Responsibility to Protect.* Cambridge, UK: Cambridge University Press, 2015.

UN General Assembly Resolution 217. *Universal Declaration of Human Rights.* New York: United Nations, December 10, 1948.

Walzer, Michael. *Just and Unjust Wars: A Moral Argument with Historical Illustrations.* New York: Basic Books, 2006 (originally published in 1976).
Weiss, Thomas G. *Humanitarian Intervention* (War and Conflict in the Modern World) (third edition). Cambridge, UK: Polity Press, 2016.
——— and Cindy Collins. *Humanitarian Challenges and Interventions* (second edition). New York and London: Routledge, 2016.

7

Rising and Declining Powers

China and Russia

The role of power in international relations is pervasive and forms much of the context in which states conduct their relations with one another. The problem they share is scarcity—the inability of all claimants to a resource to possess all the resource they desire or feel they need—but its core is how to deal with other states to see who receives more or less of the resource than they desire, in other words, to exercise power. When the process involves the most important interests of the state—vital interests—the interactions can be furtive and make the possession of appropriate power crucially important.

As argued in chapters 3 and 4, power is an elusive and multifunctional attribute. Definitions of what constitutes power and how its different forms apply in different situations are inherently subjective and controversial. To order this ambiguity, the most important, powerful states are those with the largest amounts of the widest variety of "instruments of power" (chapter 4). Understanding the role and function of power is further complicated because power is both an attribute that states possess and an object of some international power situations: states, in other words, use power to get more power that they can use in other situations, including with those that seek to increase their power. Much of this process is based on states' reputations: what states are *considered* most powerful.

The relative power that different states possess absolutely and compared to other states changes. Over time, some states become more powerful whereas others become comparatively less so. Those whose power is increasing compared to others are referred to as *rising powers*, whereas states whose power is comparatively shrinking are called *declining powers*. The process of rise and decline is historic and perpetual. States (or equivalent entities) emerge, rise, expand, and ultimately decline. The pattern and causes differ from epoch to epoch, but the general phenomenon seems immutable.

Since the 1990s collapse of the Cold War, it has been widely asserted that another cycle of change is occurring. The most obvious manifestation came in 1991, when the Soviet Union collapsed and its successor the Russian Federation emerged as a much weaker successor, a state in obvious and arguably irreversible decline. This left the United States the "sole superpower" for the balance of the twentieth century and arguably beyond. Russia has not accepted this reduction in status with magnanimity. As declining states usually do, the Russians have sought to reassemble and reassert the power of the former Soviet Union, and much of ongoing Russian policy under Putin can best be thought of in terms of the effort to get Russia to rise again to premier status.

The other state that is prominent in this process is the People's Republic of China. Since China began to transform its economy after the death of Mao Ze Dung in 1976, China has clearly been transformed into a rising power that is the closest power rival to the United States. It has become commonplace to refer to the twenty-first century as the "Asian Century" and to hypothesize that global power will gravitate toward the world's physically largest and most populated continent.

The rise and decline of twentieth-century relative power has both benefited and raised questions about America's continuing position in the world. The demise of the Cold War clearly benefited the relative position of the United States by effectively removing the Soviet Union from rivalry status. The rise of China, on the other hand, has left the United States with a formidable rival, although Chinese and Russian power are and have been very different. In trying to assess the relative power of the United States in the emerging order, one point of debate is over whether the United States has become, in effect, a declining power.

Principle: Rising and Declining Power

Although it is an elusive, difficult entity both to identify and physically to use, power is a basic element of international relations. The basis of much of the attempt to grasp, measure, and assess the role of power in the international system has already been introduced, principally in chapters 3 and 4, but one element that has not been explored is the competition among states for being considered more or less powerful and how states can enhance their power or avoid the perception that it is eroding. The concepts of rising and declining power contribute to that understanding.

For most Americans, this is a relatively new consideration. Since the end of the Second World War, the United States has been a, if not the, preeminent state in the world, its relative power basically unchallenged across the spectrum of measures of national power. That status has been under some question in the twenty-first century, as new competitors like China have arisen to challenge American preeminence. This has been unsettling for some Americans and has become a part of the foreign policy dialog. The result is to raise the issue of American status in the world.

The idea of rising and declining powers can help clarify and condition these concerns. The simple fact is that preeminent position in the international realm is not immutable, but is instead in a state of flux. Most of the countries that were the most important and powerful countries in the world in 1900, for instance, no longer have that status, although many of them are prosperous and in comfortable, even enviable, international positions. The international system by whatever designation has always been that way. Countries rise to positions of enhanced importance in the world, in a few cases become the preeminent territorial entities in the system, and they remain so for a time. In the long run, however, new states or other entities arise and challenge that supremacy.

The comparison of the most important or powerful countries in the world is an important consideration in a political system where self-help—or power—

remains an important determinant of national success and the ability to realize national security and interests. Power is a difficult, often even gauzy concept that is hard to pin down and the applications of which can be hard to predict. Nonetheless, power is important, and the reputation of states in power terms is important both to their status and their ability to succeed. This makes the determination of who is and is not powerful important, as well as whether the power of individual states is waxing or waning. The relative power of states and whether that power is increasing (rising) or decreasing (declining) has international currency. Thus the rankings people assign to different levels of power are important in the relations among countries. Countries will always disagree with their rankings and those of others, and the inexorable process of change will also create frictions and difficulties, some of which create danger for all involved. Understanding these dynamics both helps understand the current apparent process of change and the impact it can have on views of system dynamics.

Ranking Powers

The comparison of national power among states is a controversial, imperfect, and subjective enterprise. Wanting to know where a country ranks in the international ability to influence is a natural phenomenon in a power-driven system, and states will always seek to maximize their relative status. There are few consensual bases on which to base comparisons to which there are not exceptions, making the process of estimations both subjective and prone to disagreement and change. That said, one can make distinctions along two bases, recognizing the imprecision of the designations. These dimensions can be thought of as reputation and direction.

The first concern is national reputation. It is an estimate of how other states regard the power of a country to influence events in its region or globally. At the top of this list are the possession of nuclear weapons, and especially large nuclear arsenals. During the Cold War, the United States and the Soviet Union were the acknowledged superpowers. When the Soviet Union imploded, the United States was considered the sole superpower for the balance of the last century, and the early twenty-first century has featured the attempt of others to achieve that status. As defined before 1991 (the year the Cold War ended), the status has undergone change as Russian power has declined and Chinese power has risen, largely because of economic growth. Additionally, superpowers are generally thought of as countries whose interests and influence are global in nature.

The second category consists of *major* or *great* powers. This category is composed of countries that either were the greatest powers before superpower status eclipsed them or whose decline was otherwise caused, as in the loss of empire. The countries of the pre–World War II European balance are the obvious examples. The great powers are still consequential globally and especially within their regions, but their power is more limited than that of the most powerful states. Beneath this category are the most important *regional* states, also sometimes referred to as *pivotal*. The influence of these states is mostly limited to the physical regions of which they are part, but when superpowers or major powers deal with them in their regions, the pivotal state's influence must be accounted for. Iran and Vietnam in their regions are examples. At the bottom of the ranking are the *smaller* or *regional* states, generally smaller and less powerful states lacking the personal ability to influence matters outside the narrow physical area of which they are a part.

The other designation, which forms the basis for this chapter, is the direction in which the power of states is headed relative to the power of others. Rising powers are those states whose power and reputation is ascendant, with implications for their ability to influence global affairs in their direction. China is the most obvious rising state, with clear ambitions for superpower status. Iran is a similar example, with ambitions to become a premier pivotal state or even a great power. Declining powers are those states whose ability to influence events has decreased relative to the ability of other states. Russia after the collapse of the Soviet Union is the most obvious example, and the efforts of Vladimir Putin in the second decade of the current century can best be viewed as an attempt to arrest decline and reassert Moscow's former status.

The Impact of Rising Powers

Changes in the international status of different countries is an important element in the operation, and especially the stability, of the international system at any point in time. Following the settlement of the Napoleonic Wars in 1815, for instance, the important European states engineered a set of relations that became known as the balance of power or Concert of Europe. In that arrangement, the important European states accepted the general idea of equality of power among them and the collective settlement of differences among them. The system worked until the latter part of the century when Franco-German territorial rivalry and the German Empire's determination to rise above that equality to the status of something like a superpower broke the system's dynamic and created a power competition that took two world wars in the twentieth century to resolve.

The conclusion of the second global conflict witnessed the emergence of two rising powers, the United States and the Union of Soviet Socialist Republics (USSR), into the most prominent roles and saw the relationship elevated to mutual superpower status with the addition of nuclear weapons and the division of effective power in the world between them. When the Cold War ended, the United States was left as the sole ascendant power.

The rise of new powers always seems to follow major dislocations in previous arrangements, and the contemporary period has been no exception. The United States never aspired to be the unilateral world power in the sense of possessing a hegemonic level of power, and so it is natural that new states would aspire to rise to challenge it. The net effect of the twentieth century in affecting the new pattern has been to open the competition to countries in parts of the world previously not part of that competition. The rising power of the current century is China, which clearly alters the geopolitical map of global politics, and other countries will follow. Whether this alteration of the power map will be achieved peacefully and productively will depend to some degree on the ability of the major participants to avoid the dangers that sometimes accompany the rise and decline of states.

The Dangers of Rising Powers: Thucydides' Trap

Because they represent changes in the relative power of states and thus have some effect on the relations between states, the decline and especially the rise of new states is an unsettling phenomenon. Part of the problem is uncertainty. How much will a rising power upset the existing order, especially to the detriment of powers whose relative places they will challenge and possibly replace? What will be the nature of the change the rising power will try to implement, and how will that affect others in the system? If a rising state eclipses the position of other powers, what will be the effect on those disturbed by change? Possibly of the greatest importance, how will those being challenged react to these changes? More to the point, what will they do in the face of perceived threat both before and while it is occurring?

It is not a new question. The first major exposition of this phenomenon was recorded by the Greek historian Thucydides in the fifth century BCE. His *History of the Peloponnesian War* chronicled the long war between Athens and Sparta for supremacy, and the trigger for that conflict was the rising power relationship between the two city-states. As he described it, "It was the rise of Athens and the fear that this instilled in Sparta that made war inevitable."

The Harvard political scientist Graham Allison labeled this dynamic the "Thucydides' trap" in a 2017 *Foreign Affairs* article as a warning about the direction and growing drift in U.S.-Chinese relations. The "trap" arises from the degree of threat that a country experiences when a challenge arises from another, and especially a rival, state. It can trigger something like what is sometimes called an "action-reaction phenomenon." That situation is where one party (A) to a competition perceives a threat from the growth in power of a rival (B) and responds by building its power to a greater level than the rising competitor. The rising power (A) sees this change, views it as threatening and aggressive, and responds with another increase in power, which in turn induces the other party (B) further to increase its power. The resulting spiral may create a classic arms race that can lead to war—the trap.

Not all rising power situations result in war. The Cold War competition between the United States and the Soviet Union was clearly the result of a rising power challenging an established premier power, a prime feature of which was a classic arms race. Thucydides' trap was not sprung in this case, because each side came to realize that war between them would threaten both their existences. The dynamic was, however, intense and very deadly, and its control or elimination would clearly stabilize international politics.

The major purpose of Allison's argument is to try to manage the ongoing shift in relative power among the major powers. Change is perpetual in the international system, but its intensity varies considerably. The end of World War II created a power vacuum that caused the decline of the pre-1939 powers and the rise of the United States, the Soviet Union, and eventually China to major significance in the international system. The implosion of the Soviet Union created another major change by vastly depreciating the power of one superpower and initiating a process to see what replaced the Soviet vacuum at the top. The result has been the current period of major rise represented by China and the adaptation to decline of Russia, a process that the Russians seek desperately to reverse. The United States stands as the remaining superpower trying to cope with a rising China and a restive Russia.

Application: China and Russia

It is generally agreed that effective power in the world has been moving eastward in the twenty-first century. The centerpiece of that shift has, of course, centered on the economic and military growth of China and especially the challenge that China poses under its current leader, Xi Jinping. It is a continuing dynamic, and its effect is to challenge American power both in Asia and worldwide. Henry Kissinger, in a 2016 *Atlantic* interview, summarized the prevailing wisdom: "Our relations with China will shape the international order in the long term. The United States and China will be the world's most consequential countries." Campbell and Ratner concur: "Washington now faces its most dynamic and formidable competitor in modern history." Meanwhile, the principal challenger to American power in the twentieth century, Russia, struggles to regain its status amid almost impossible odds.

China, the Rising State

If any country in the world is an expert in the phenomenon of rising and descending in power, it is China. The country has the world's oldest continuous civilization, dating back at least seven thousand years. For most of its existence, it was the most advanced country in the world, which infused the Chinese with both a sense of their own superiority and caused them to isolate themselves from the "barbarians" (essentially anyone who is not Han Chinese). The Great Wall is the most visible physical symbol of this view of the world. This isolation insulated them from progress in the rest of the world, and China gradually fell behind competing civilizations from the West, culminating in the Century of Humiliation in the nineteenth and early twentieth centuries, when China was overrun by foreigners whom they were incapable of containing or expelling.

The period since World War II has seen the rebirth and rising of China. In 1949, mainland China fell to the Communists, who gradually (if brutally) consolidated the state. When communist founder Mao Ze Dong died in 1976, he was replaced by the diminutive Deng Xiaoping, who reformed the Chinese economy and started China on an economic trajectory that has transformed it into a formidable rival. Known as the "Four Modernizations" (agriculture, science, technology, and the military), this program also included partial capitalization of the economy by creating the Special Economic Zones (SEZs), which attracted Western businesses to China and formed working alliances with them that allowed the Chinese economy to explode. Euphemistically called "socialism with Chinese characteristics," the program transformed China from a backward developing country to a rising world power that now challenges the United States for superpower status and has caused some Americans dourly to raise questions of American relative decline. Xi Jinping appears intent on continuing the competition.

China and the United States in the World

The Chinese-American relationship has always been unique. During China's Century of Humiliation, Americans felt a strong, if not reciprocal bond with China, from the dispatch of American missionaries to the construction of a fleet of Clipper ships to foster trade with China. In the early twentieth century, the United States supported the Nationalist Chinese revolution that overthrew the old order, and they continued that support when the Mao Ze Dong's communists overthrew the Nationalists and sent them fleeing to Taiwan, where they still rule. During the Korean War, Chinese "volunteers" were a formidable opponent for the U.S. and UN effort on the peninsula. Until Henry Kissinger and Richard Nixon established links with China in the 1970s and Jimmy Carter formally recognized the People's Republic of China in 1979, the United States did not even recognize the existence of the People's Republic, preferring the fiction that the Republic of China government on Taiwan was the legitimate ruling group on both Taiwan and the mainland.

That situation has, of course, changed dramatically. When Deng announced the Four Modernizations and opened parts of China to the outside world by inviting foreign investors into the SEZs, the relations between the two countries exploded as American manufacturers moved production to lower wage China and the Chinese flooded the U.S. market with cheaper retail goods. The result has become a clear economic imbalance where the United States owes huge debts to China but where that indebtedness has created a bond whereby neither side can contemplate enormous deterioration in relations for fear of the economic consequences to itself that might accompany such a change.

China's transformation has made the country a rising power that has arguably moved it to superpower status, and that possibility has raised considerable concern in the United States. China is the second largest country in the world in land area, and its GDP has surpassed that of the United States in recent years. Chinese wealth has been partially dedicated to spreading Chinese influence in the developing world, and it has engaged in a military buildup that certainly makes it the preeminent power in East Asia and could pose a threat to American control of the Pacific Rim of Asia. At the same time, China's growth has slowed (its gross domestic product growth rate had dropped from double digits to less than 7 percent in 2017, for instance). The dragon's fire may be losing some of its heat, and this could affect its relations with the United States.

Brakes on the Chinese Miracle

Like most political change, the upward trajectory of Chinese power is not linear. China's growth is not unqualified, and the future of the Chinese miracle is neither inexorable nor entirely predictable. The Chinese continue to rise, but there are at least three qualifications to its continued meteoric ascent in the world. None suggest China will stagnate or decline; they do suggest that its growth will slow.

The clearest indicators of the slowing of Chinese growth—and presumably its expanding power in the world—are economic. The 2017 *CIA World Factbook*, for instance, showed that the economic growth rate in China had slowed to 6.9 percent in 2015, down sharply since its explosion as the Deng reforms took hold and more in line with growth in other major developing countries. There are three major contributory factors to this situation, all of which Xi Jinping must confront and solve in the upcoming years.

The first is structural. There are essentially two economic foci of the Chinese economy. The first surrounds the SEZs. These joint ventures with the West are the heart of China's economic miracle, employing about one-third of the workforce and responsible for over two-thirds of productivity, including technological innovation. The anchor that slows growth, however, are the so-called state-owned enterprises. Owned and controlled by the government (and especially the military), the state-owned enterprises are considered necessary for political control by the Chinese Communist Party, but they are an economic drag on Chinese overall growth, employing nearly 70 percent of the workforce but only responsible for about 30 percent of economic output. Xi Jinping is committed to continued communist rule (his political base) but economic expansion. The two priorities may be practically irreconcilable, and if Chinese Communist Party power remains the supreme value, the tension between them provides an anchor on continued expansion and dynamism.

The second problem is demographic. The Chinese population is aging, with larger numbers of people retiring and leaving the workforce than are joining it. The importance of this factor is two-fold. First, it means a larger burden of providing retirement benefits for elders than there is a working-age population to support it in a system where the retirement safety net is minimal. Who pays? Second, more people leaving than entering the workforce means that body of workers is shrinking, with inevitable negative effects that are difficult to solve. Many are the result of the one-child policy of the late twentieth century (when it was illegal for Chinese couples to have more than one baby). The classic mechanism for dealing with this problem is immigration, which is anathema to the notoriously racist Han Chinese. There are minorities in China (e.g., the Uighurs), but most of these people live in the western part of the country (growth is in the east) and want to secede from China anyway. One manifestation of this problem at the macro level is that the Chinese population, 1.384 billion in 2018 and projected at 1.407 billion in 2025, is expected to shrink to 1.3 billion in 2050.

The third problem is resource-based. China is energy deficient. It has huge reserves of shale oil and gas, but it is remotely located, and China has neither the technology nor the transportation network to access it. This is a potential problem the United States can exploit, because it and Canada lead the world in shale technology. In the absence of this technology, the Chinese must rely on imports, creating a vital interest in access to Middle East oil fields and control of shipping lanes like the South China Sea, both points of U.S.-China contention. At the same time, China is water-deficient. Nearly one-fifth of Chinese arable land has gone out of service since 1949 because of dropping water tables. The energy and water problems collide over shale exploitation, because shale extraction uses and fouls enormous amounts of scarce water supplies. China may remain ascendant, but as Hale and Hale pointed out in 2003, it also suffers from some of the "dragon's ailments."

Where the Sides Collide

When the rise of a power collides with the traditional interests of another, there are inevitable points of conflict. This is clearly the case in the abrasion between China and the United States. Rising states generally want to expand or reassert traditional places in the world, and the rough edges of the Sino-American relationship clearly demonstrates two of these kinds of collision: over the Democratic Republic of Korea (DPRK) and the South China Sea. At their worst, such collisions could activate the dynamics of Thucydides' trap.

Sino-American relations are a mixed bag. Their economic relations are intimate, and their economies are interrelated, but they also have points of disagreement accentuated in their 2019 "trade war" that include terms of trade and intellectual property theft. Geopolitically, they are clear rivals in their area of mutual interest, which is East Asia and the Pacific Rim. China's most important interest is in hegemony over the mainland in a modern-day version of their historical dominance of the region. Operationally, this means that China will not tolerate a hostile power on its border. The primary point of contact is North Korea. A change in the status of the DPRK could result in a unified Korea where an American-backed Republic of Korea government could threaten that imperative, and Chinese participation in talks between the United States and the DPRK must be taken in this light (see my *Cases in U.S. National Security* for a discussion).

The two sides also come into conflict over the South China Sea. That body of water stretches along the Asian coast roughly from Indonesia to Taiwan, and it is important to both countries. China covets the oil under its ocean bed, has declared the sea a territorial water (a claim denied by others), and is a transit route from the Middle East to the Pacific Rim, where oil-poor American allies get their energy. Both are contentious, but they are not candidates for Thucydides' trap unless one or both sides chooses to escalate its claims, a course unlikely if they remain closely linked economically. Their relationship is somewhat abrasive, but it is not currently highly combustible.

Russia, a Declining State with Ambitions

The Russian profile in the contemporary world has been the mirror opposite of that of China. During the Cold War, the Soviet Union/Russia was clearly the "senior partner" of the communist world and led the communist movement as the Chinese system consolidated and took off. Russia stagnated and began the process of economic decline two decades before it physically dissolved, while China was preparing for a preeminent Asian role and beginning its economic domain. As China has steadily ascended, Russia struggled with postcommunist chaos until the rise of Vladimir Putin to leadership in 2000. Russia has tried to piggyback a resurgence on oil revenues, but these efforts have been partially subverted by downward fluctuations in petroleum prices, leaving Russia a classically unstable petrolist state. Mirroring centuries of Russian history, Putin has attempted to use expansionist policies to reassert Russia's claims to superpower status. It has been only a partial success and continues in the shadow of negative trends, especially demographic, in the Russian future.

The Russian Saga

Russia has always been an enigmatic place. It sits astride the eastern part of Europe and has spread across Asia to the Pacific, making it the world's largest country in land mass, even since half the Soviet Union disappeared when the USSR dissolved. Its sheer size makes it a consequential place, but it has remained culturally and politically, as well as physically, at the fringes of a world order it seeks to join as a fully accepted member. It is culturally distinct and has been viewed as marginal by the world's powers, a status it badly wants to reverse. Much of Russia's political history has been the quest for acceptance as a great power. It achieved that status after World War II; it lost it after the Soviet Union dissolved.

Although much about Russia is mysterious from the outside (Winston Churchill's depiction of the USSR as "a riddle wrapped in a mystery inside an enigma"), its broad contours are not. By most material standards, Russia has always lagged behind the major powers, and it continues to do so today. Its claim to status is its size, and it has sought to augment its claim to world power status through relentless expansion. The sheer size and resultant power of the Soviet Union represented its high-water mark in international political terms. Along with the United States, it was the only major participant in World War II to emerge as a significant power, and its development of a large nuclear arsenal allowed it to rise to the status it had fought so long to achieve.

Unfortunately for the Russians, part of the image was an illusion, a false front that obscured flawed foundations. The Soviet Union's claim to leadership in the world was almost entirely military. Its political system was harsh and authoritarian and eventually lost the support of the people both within its borders and in places like Eastern Europe that were vassal states. The economy was essentially a developing world construct in structure and performance, leading some to refer to it as a "frozen banana republic with nuclear weapons." That economy contributed significantly to the Soviet demise in 1991.

Despite efforts to obscure the fact, the fatal weakness of the Soviet economy was evident to some by the early 1970s. Soviet academic economists called it the Era of Stagnation: by 1973, the only economic sector not in decline was vodka production. The economists adopted Mikhail Gorbachev and his wife Raisa (a colleague at Moscow State University) to publicize this fate, which helped lead to Gorbachev's ascension to power. This crisis was most strikingly obvious in science and technology (a traditional Russian strength), and especially computer development, where the Soviets lagged progressively further behind. These trends led Gorbachev in two fateful policy directives. Both because of inherent economic weakness and the progressively debilitating technological situation, he determined that he must end the Cold War and try to rejoin the world order to gain access to funds and technology. Second, in 1989, he ended a debilitating military adventure in Afghanistan that demonstrated the weakness of the iron fist and encouraged defections from both the Soviet Union and among its satellites. I discussed this progression in a three-edition series of books in the 1990s collectively titled *The Shape of the Future*.

The end of the Cold War was the beginning of Russia's decline from superpower to a lesser status. Russia was plunged into essentially a state of economic and political chaos in the 1990s with which Boris Yeltsin, the new leader, could not cope. The economy collapsed, leaving many Russians in abject poverty and misery, into which the Russian mafia jumped to exploit. Former Soviet authority and power declined to the point that the United States was enlisted to help get part of the former Soviet nuclear arsenal out of the Soviet Socialist Republics, where the loyalty and responsibility of newly independent regimes was suspect, and to engage in some inspection of those weapons to guard against nuclear accidents. This was the situation Vladimir Putin inherited when he became president in 2000.

The Limits of Russian Power and Prospects

A declining Russia was beset by two major problems that continue to bedevil Putin's dream of reasserting Russian status as a superpower. One of these is demographic: the Russian population was halved by the breakup of the USSR and has declined more since. The other is economic: Putin has addicted Russia to an economy dominated by oil sales, and the result is a petrolist state with all its inherent problems.

The demographic problem is straightforward and dire. Using U.S. Census Bureau figures, the 2019 *World Almanac and Book of Facts* documents the Russian population decline. In 1990, the last year of the Soviet Union, its population stood at about 300 million (290 million for the United States). In 2018, the estimate was 142 million, and by 2050, it is projected at 129 million. By contrast, the U.S. totals are 330 million today and projected at 398 million in 2050, three times that of Russia. Russia's population was third largest in the world; it is now ninth and falling. Factors in this dismal prospect include declining fertility rates and shortened life expectancies. Because only 7 percent of Russian land is arable, it also has trouble feeding itself. Proposed solutions include greater immigration and expansion into new territories. Neither is likely to work well.

The other problem is economic. Putin tied Russia's economy to oil revenues, making the country an effective petrolist state, with all the vagaries attached, including boom and bust cycles based on the global price of oil, corruption, and a government based on oil revenues. When oil prices are high, the system appears to work, because there is a surplus of money to spend on citizen welfare and government expansion. When oil prices fall, discontentment and associated problems return. People get less benefits, the corruption associated with petrolism increases, and the system becomes what is sometimes called a kleptocracy (the dynamics of petrolism are discussed in chapter 9). The price of oil collapsed in the early 2010s, and in a two-year period, Russian gross domestic product fell from 2 to 1.2 trillion (U.S. gross domestic product at the time was over 16 trillion). There are few projections that suggest a rebound of high oil prices in the near term.

Putin's dream is clearly a return to great-/superpower status, and both these dynamics are heavy anchors weighing it down. Clearly, Putin wants to rekindle the prestige of the Soviet days, and his long-term success and popularity are largely dependent on a return to glory for the highly nationalistic Russians. Putin, very simply, witnessed the precipitous decline of his country in the 1990s, and he is struggling to make it rise to its former status. He has, in typical Russian fashion, chosen expansion as his preferred method—into the Crimea and Eastern Ukraine for now. Expansion can bring overseas Russians into the federation, a form of immigration, but the immigration solution will not work. Only a return to high oil prices will.

Putin's Russia may be a modern Potemkin Village, but it is still an important state whose continued decline can only further destabilize world politics. Nuclear weapons mean it remains a dangerous state. It has under its permafrost and Arctic waters some of the world's largest stores of energy, which the world needs. It is still a potentially aggressive, expansionist, and politically destabilizing place—it is Russia, after all. The question is what can be done to make it a power with a status it can embrace that does not trigger Thucydides' trap.

Conclusion

The international system is clearly in a period of transition, the triggering events of which have been the demise of the Soviet Union and the progressive increase of Chinese power since the death of Mao Ze Dong and the partial capitalization of the world's most populous country. The concept of rising and declining states is an intuitively appealing way to depict the changes that are under way and how those most affected have responded to them.

Periods of transition are always unsettling to those involved, and the trajectory of change is seldom linear or entirely predictable. China has been "on a roll" for over 40 years and is still feeling its way about the extent of its place in the new order. Its contemplation has, of course, been more pleasant than that of Russia, because its place in the world has expanded whereas Russia's has shrunk. Russia is not what it used to be, and it wants to return to its former status. It is not clear what its path to redemption is or whether a rise to its former status is even possible. Uncertainty exists for both countries because of structural, and especially demographic, factors. The result is some level of uncertainty about the future. Who, for instance, predicted China's rise and Russia's decline fifty years ago?

The United States stands in the middle of this turbulence. The competition with a Soviet superpower dominated the post–World War II period, and a weaker Russia clearly resents and works to subvert its contemporary invidious comparison with U.S. status. At the same time, China's rise has created a challenge for the United States in Asia and the Pacific, and even if that change does not appear volatile today, what about the future?

Thucydides remains relevant. Athens and Sparta came in conflict because one was rising and the other feared the consequences of that rise and reacted to blunt it, activating a process that ended in war. The contemporary situation is distinguished by rising and declining forces in both directions. Avoiding Thucydides' trap is arguably more imperative now, because all three parties who could become entrapped in its dynamics have nuclear arsenals the resort to which could be catastrophic. That makes avoiding the trap even more imperative.

Study/Discussion Questions

1. What are rising and declining states? Why is the distinction important in the conduct of international relations?
2. What are the categories of powers through which states ascend (rise) or descend (decline)? Briefly describe each, including examples.
3. What is Thucydides' trap? How does it work? Why is it important, especially in the context of rising and declining states?
4. Describe China as a rising state. What caused it to rise, what problems does it pose, and what are the barriers to its continuing ascent?
5. Describe Russia as a declining state. What caused it to decline? What are its prospects of reversing that decline over the short and long haul? What problems does it pose?
6. Which state, China or Russia, poses the greatest threat to international peace and stability due to its process of rise/decline? Defend your choice.
7. Compare and contrast the process of rise/decline of the two former communist superpowers and how they affect the United States.
8. Why is the phenomenon of Chinese/Russian ascent/decline important to the United States? What is the American status in these terms? How do each pose a different problem in terms of avoiding Thucydides' trap?

Bibliography

Allison, Graham T. "China versus America: Managing the Next Clash of Civilizations." *Foreign Affairs* 96, no. 5 (September/October 2017), 80–89.

———. *Destined for War: Can America and China Escape Thucydides' Trap?* Boston, MA: Houghton-Mifflin, 2017.

Art, Robert A., and Kenneth N. Waltz, eds. *The Uses of Force: Military Power and International Politics* (seventh edition). Lanham, MD: Rowman & Littlefield, 2009.

Biden, Joseph S. Jr., and Michael Carpenter. "How to Stand Up to the Kremlin: Defending Democracy Against Its Enemies." *Foreign Affairs* 97, no. 1 (January/February 2018), 44–57.

Brown, Kerry. *CEO China: The Rise of Xi Jinping*. London: I.B. Tauris, 2016.

Campbell, Charles. "China Steps Closer to Despotism as Xi Becomes Leader for Life." *Time* 191, no. 10 (Mach 12, 2018), 5–6.

Campbell, Kurt M., and Ely Ratner. "The China Reckoning: How Beijing Defied American Expectations." *Foreign Affairs* 97, no. 2 (March/April 2018), 60–70.
Christensen, Thomas J. *The China Challenge: Shaping the Choices of a Rising Power*. New York: Norton, 2016.
Committee on Foreign Relations, U.S. Senate. *Strategic Assessment of U.S.-Russian Relations*. New York: CreateSpace, 2018.
Cumings, Bruce. "Chinese Bullying No Match for US Pacific Power." *Current History* 113, no. 764 (September 2014), 245–51.
Dawisha, Karen. *Putin's Kleptocracy: Who Owns Russia?* New York: Simon and Schuster, 2014.
Economy, Elizabeth. *The Third Revolution: Xi Jinping and the New Chinese State*. New York: Oxford University Press, 2018.
——— and Michael Levi. *By All Means Necessary: How China's Resources Quest Is Changing the World*. Oxford, UK: Oxford University Press, 2014.
Friedman, Thomas J. "The First Law of Petropolitics." *Foreign Policy* (May/June 2006), 28–36.
French, Howard W. *Everything Under the Heavens: How the Past Helps Shape China's Push for Global Power* (reprint edition). New York: Vintage, 2018.
Garver, John. *The History of the Foreign Relations of the People's Republic of China*. Oxford, UK: Oxford University Press, 2016.
Goldberg, Jeffrey. "The Lessons of Henry Kissinger." *Atlantic* 218, no. 5 (December 2016), 50–56.
Goldstein, Lyle G. *Meeting China Halfway: How to Defuse US-China Rivalry*. Washington, DC: Georgetown University Press, 2015.
Gorbachev, Mikhail. *The New Russia*. Cambridge, UK: Polity Press, 2016.
Hale, David, and Lyric Hughes Hale. "China Takes Off." *Foreign Affairs* 82, no. 6 (November/December 2003), 36–53.
Heilmann, Sebastian. *China's Political System*. Lanham, MD: Rowman & Littlefield, 2016.
Isikoff, Michael, and David Corn. *Russian Roulette: The Inside Story of Putin's War on America and the Election of Donald J. Trump*. New York: Twelve Books, 2018.
Joffe, Julia. "Putin's Game." *Atlantic* 321, no. 1 (January/February 2018), 68–85.
Kroeber, Arthur P. *China's Economy: What Everyone Needs to Know*. Oxford, UK: Oxford University Press, 2016.
Lanteigne, Marc. *Chinese Foreign Policy: An Introduction* (third edition). New York and London: Routledge, 2015.
Legvold, Robert. *Return to Cold War*. Cambridge, UK: Polity Press, 2016.
Li, Cheng. *Chinese Politics in the Xi Jinping Era: Reassessing Leadership*. Washington, DC: Brookings Institution Press, 2016.
Mandelbaum, Michael. "The New Containment: Handling Russia, China, and Iran." *Foreign Affairs* 98, no. 2 (March/April 2019), 123–31.
Nalbandov, Robert. *Not By Bread Alone: Russian Foreign Policy Under Putin*. Washington, DC: Potomac Books, 2016.
Paulson, Henry M. Jr. *Dealing with China: An Insider Unmasks the New Economic Superpower*. New York: Twelve Books, 2015.
Pei, Minxin. *China's Gang Capitalism: The Dynamics of Regime Decay*. Cambridge, MA: Harvard University Press, 2016.
Rudd, Kevin. "How Xi Jinping Views the World: The Core Interests That Shape China's Behavior." *Foreign Affairs Snapshot* (online), May 10, 2018.
Shambaugh, David. *China's Future*. Cambridge, UK: Polity Books, 2016.

Snow, Donald M. *Cases in U.S. National Security: Concepts and Processes.* Lanham, MD: Rowman & Littlefield, 2019.
———. *Regional Cases in U.S. Foreign Policy* (second edition). Lanham, MD: Rowman & Littlefield, 2018.
———. *The Shape of the Future: The Post-Cold War World* (three editions). Armonk, NY: M. E. Sharpe, 1991, 1995, 1999.
Stent, Angela. *The Limits of Partnership: U.S.-Russian Relations in the Twenty-First Century.* Princeton, NJ: Princeton University Press, 2015.
Sutter, Robert. *Chinese Foreign Relations: Power and Policy Since the Cold War.* Lanham, MD: Rowman & Littlefield, 2016.
Thucydides. *The History of the Peloponnesian War.* New York: Penguin, 1954 (originally published in the fourth century BCE).
Toal, Bernard. *Near Abroad: Putin, the West, and the Contest over Ukraine and the Caucasus.* Oxford, UK: Oxford University Press, 2017.
Trenin, Dmitri. *Should We Fear Russia?* Cambridge, UK: Polity Press, 2016.
Tsygankov, Andrei. *Russia's Foreign Policy: Change and Continuity in National Identity* (fourth edition). Lanham, MD: Rowman & Littlefield, 2016.
The World Almanac and Book of Facts, 2019. New York: World Almanac Books, 2019.

8

Asymmetrical Warfare

The Never-Ending Case of Afghanistan

How wars are fought is one of the most obvious ways in which international relations has changed since the middle of the twentieth century. The first half of the century was characterized by the ultimate applications of Western-style warfare in the form of the two world wars. Conventional warfare has been replaced by another dominant form, asymmetrical warfare, a methodology more fitting and applicable to the places where fighting now occurs—in the internal affairs of the developing states. The purposes of asymmetrical warfare—enforcing or imposing the "national" interests of various groups within or between states—has not changed so much as the ways in which it is conducted.

What is now called asymmetrical warfare is certainly not new, with roots in antiquity and tactics and strategies traceable at least back as far as Sun Tzu, the ancient Chinese military philosopher. In important ways, it is Eastern-style warfare that represents the application of principles to allow a militarily inferior force to compete with a larger and more conventionally superior force. As such, it shares commonalities with the other major form of contemporary violence, terrorism. Asymmetrical warfare is so pervasive that outside powers seeking to influence events in developing world situations find themselves drawn into developing world internal conflicts (DWICs) that they do not understand, are unprepared to fight, and lack enough interest to sustain the effort. The results are usually poor outcomes for those who intervene.

The long internal war in Afghanistan illustrates this phenomenon. Asymmetrical warfare is a long-standing part of the pattern of endemic Afghan instability, and at the time of the September 11, 2001, terrorist attacks against the United States, one of the periodic Afghan civil wars was raging. The Taliban government, under attack by a coalition of rival tribal groups, was providing sanctuary to the Al Qaeda terrorists who committed these attacks, creating an American interest where virtually no other interest had previously existed. When the Taliban refused to remand the Al Qaeda terrorists to American custody, the United States intervened to try to capture them. The attempt failed, and the United States had become involved in an asymmetrical war against the Taliban that has now lasted for almost two decades.

A basic dynamic of warfare has always been the balance or imbalance of forces possessed by the warring parties. Whenever a force inferior in numbers or quality and quantity of armaments has faced a superior force, their problem has been how to nullify the advantages of the superior force to the point that the inferior force has a chance of defeating or at least avoiding defeat at the hands of the superior force. That is the same question the contemporary asymmetrical warrior contemplates. The style of war being waged in most contemporary DWICs is the current variant of the answer to the problem.

The remaining pages of this chapter examine the challenge of asymmetrical warfare to thinking about war—its purposes, its conduct, and its outcomes. It will proceed in two sequential parts. It will examine the evolving nature of asymmetrical warfare. The discussion will move from a definition and examination of the dynamics to a brief comparison with terrorism and the difficulties that an outside conventionally armed state has intervening in these wars. Second, it will apply those observations to one of the international system's most prominent current instance of asymmetrical warfare, the war in Afghanistan.

Principle: Asymmetrical Warfare

If asymmetrical warfare is ancient, its modern prevalence combines perennial and contemporary influences and causes. Warfare has changed enormously since the end of the Cold War. The remaining conflicts in the world are mostly DWICs, internal conflicts within countries in which the major powers may have a limited interest. These wars have become the major source of military conflict in the contemporary world, a condition unlikely to change anytime soon.

The result is the rising dominance of asymmetrical warfare. Two rejoinders need to be raised. On one hand, the "new" way of war is not new or, in general principle, all that innovative. Asymmetrical warfare features the adaptations an inferior force makes when it is faced with a more powerful force with which it cannot compete successfully on the terms preferred by the superior force. The tactics and means may change, but the core rationale does not. Asymmetrical warfare is an approach to warfare, not a form of war or combat. It is a methodology, a way to organize the problem, not a method or set of battlefield or theater instructions. No two asymmetrical wars are the same, although their purposes may be. Thinking about and planning either to conduct or to counter asymmetrical situations requires considerable adaptability and openness to change.

The result is a very different contemporary global conflict environment. First, the imbalance in conventional capability between the United States and the rest of the world means no one is likely to confront the United States in large-scale conventional warfare, making necessary the adoption of different or asymmetrical approaches to negate that advantage. As Bruce Berkowitz puts it, "Our adversaries know they cannot match the United States in tanks, planes, and warships. They know they will most likely lose any war with us if they play according to the traditional rules." This innovation is the second new characteristic of the environment: the widespread adoption of asymmetrical ways to negate the advantages of overwhelming military capability and thus to reduce the military leverage greater power seems to convey. Asymmetrical approaches are intended, in Berkowitz's terms, "to change the rules to strategies and tactics that avoid our strength head-on and instead hit us where we are weak." This problem is progressive, because the core of asymmetrical warfare is constant adaptation, whereas conventional war is incremental, seeking better doctrinal solutions to problems.

The Context and Meaning of Asymmetrical War

Asymmetrical warfare is physically and conceptually different from Western-style warfare. It differs in terms of the reasons for which it is conducted, how those who carry it out think and act, and in terms of the motives of the asymmetrical warrior. Asymmetrical warfare is not only militarily unconventional but it is also intellectually unconventional, both for those who practice and oppose its application. It is a methodology, not an ideology.

The heart of asymmetrical warfare is a mindset. The potential asymmetrical warrior always begins from a position of military inferiority, and the problem is how to negate that disadvantage. Adaptability is at the heart of asymmetrical approaches to warfare. The asymmetrical warrior learns from what works and discards what does not.

As an example, Iraq attempted to confront the United States conventionally in Kuwait in 1990/1991 and was crushed. It learned from this experience that a future conflict with the United States could not be conducted in the same manner as before without equally devastating results. What to do? The answer in 2003 was to offer only enough resistance to American symmetrical force application to make the Americans think they were prevailing, while regrouping to resist an occupation that they were powerless to prevent except asymmetrically. Thus, the limited form of irregular warfare (ambushes, car bombings, and suicide terror attacks) became the primary method of resisting the occupation—convincing the Americans that the costs of occupation were not worth the costs in lives lost and treasure. It ultimately succeeded.

The Iraq experience introduced an important aspect about how the asymmetrical warrior can achieve his or her goals against an opponent it has no chance of defeating by force of conventional arms. The contrast between asymmetrical objectives in entirely internal wars (DWICs) and those in which outsiders interject themselves illustrates the point. Asymmetrical warfare works in some situations, but not in all. The secret lies in understanding what the problem is and how to approach it.

Most asymmetrical wars occur in DWIC situations. One group or another is displeased with its status and believes it can only be rectified by recourse to force. Normally, the insurgents begin their campaign at a disadvantage, less well armed and facing a government with much larger, usually conventionally armed forces. It cannot confront its opponents on their terms, and so it resorts to strategy and tactics that will allow it to shift the balance of power in its direction.

The problem is fundamentally different when an outsider intervenes to influence the outcome. The intervening party (often the United States) is likely to be so militarily superior that defeating it is unthinkable. At the same time, its Achilles heel is likely to be that it has lesser interests in the outcome and will, if engaged in protracted conflict including intervener casualties, tire of the contest and leave. This problem is known as cost-tolerance.

The Lure of Asymmetrical Warfare

Asymmetrical warfare is attractive to participants in DWICs because it works a good deal of the time when the recourse to more conventional approaches almost always fails. The Iraqi experience with the United States provides one instructive allegory, and Vietnam another. The Vietnamese who opposed the United States could not match American firepower, a lesson they learned at their first encounter with the Americans at a place called the Ia Drang Valley. Instead, they retreated to a strategy of attrition, inflicting more casualties on the Americans than the United States would eventually tolerate while absorbing enormous losses of their own. Their cause, however, was more important to them than the American mission was to the United States. American cost-tolerance was eventually exceeded, and the Americans left.

The comparative Vietnamese and Iraqi examples suggest asymmetrical situations are all different, making generalization perilous. One can begin by looking at predictable problems that asymmetrical warriors will present in the future. With no pretense of being exhaustive, at least two stand out.

First, political and military aspects of these conflicts will continue to merge, and distinctions between military and civilian targets and assets will continue to dissolve. The asymmetrical warrior will continue to muddy the distinction for two reasons. One is that he or she is likely to see conflicts as pitting societies against societies, so there is no meaningful distinction between combatants and noncombatants, whereas traditional symmetrical warfare draws sharp distinctions between the two. The other reason is that imbedding conflict within the fabric of society removes some of the advantage of the symmetrical warrior. Urban warfare, for instance, can only be waged symmetrically by concentrating firepower intensity on areas where civilians and opponents are intermingled, where traditional rules of war prohibit actions aimed at civilians, thereby inhibiting some actions, and where the problem of collateral damage (killing noncombatants) is a concern under conventional laws of war. The asymmetrical warrior usually rejects these distinctions, leaving him or her free either to attack or fight among civilians.

Second, the opposition in these kinds of conflicts often consists of nonstate actors acting out of nonstate motivations and without state bases of operation. International terrorist organizations, for instance, often carry out operations that cannot be tied to any state, and they are not clearly based in any state. This creates a problem of response for the symmetrical warrior. Whom does he or she go after? Whom does he or she attack and punish? This is a major problem the United States has faced in dealing with Al Qaeda and the Taliban in Afghanistan and Pakistan: one cannot attack the enemy without attacking the sovereign territory of an ally.

The Asymmetrical Warfare-Terrorism Nexus

There is a dynamic, reciprocal relationship between asymmetrical warfare and terrorism. Recourse to terrorism is, in some ways, a form of asymmetrical warfare, and asymmetrical warriors (as well as their symmetrical counterparts) often use terror as part of their operational tactics and strategy. As a tactical tool, terrorizing an enemy or a hostile target population may weaken the resolve or strength of that opponent, either military or civilian. A terrorist attack in a major city may soften the resolve of the target to continue resistance, as an example. Air attacks against enemy leadership have the dual purposes of eliminating important enemies and of frightening others in the vicinity.

The strategic relationship is somewhat more complicated and reflects the strength of individual asymmetrical warriors. Terrorism is generally a method of the very weak, who can mount no serious campaign to overcome an opponent but hope to gain limited objectives by frightening that opponent to the point that its cost-tolerance is overcome and it acquiesces to some terrorist demand. Purely terrorist attacks are generally not intended to achieve larger political goals, and their commission may be no more than a reminder to those attacked that the organization is capable of mayhem. Asymmetrical warfare, on the other hand, is the tool of the more robust insurgent who may not have the military strength to stand toe-to-toe with a conventional force, but whose strength is adequate to engage in military campaigns of attrition to wear down or discourage the opposition. The choice between the two techniques reflects levels of weakness.

One can draw too fine a distinction between the two kinds of organization. A terrorist organization can grow into an asymmetrical warfare force, as former Al Qaeda in Iraq did when it became the Islamic State in 2014. At the same time, if an asymmetrical force suffers enough setbacks and is visibly weakened to the point it can no longer compete in an unconventional warfare role, it may revert to the relatively less demanding role of terrorist. The retreat of the Islamic State Caliphate suggests that may have happened to it. This ability to change shape and mission is nothing new. The writings of strategists like China's Mao Zedung and North Vietnam's Vo Nguyen Giap suggest that guerrilla and conventional forces could alternate roles and methods depending on their relative situations.

Terrorism and asymmetrical warfare are part of a continuum of forms of warfare with the common purpose of trying to prevail against a materially superior opponent. Terrorists operate at the lower end of the scale both in terms of ambition and capability, and asymmetrical warriors aim to transform a position of inferiority into a situation where they can prevail. Ironically, terrorism is often "showier" in that its results are often more spectacular and visually horrific, even if they have less effect on the final outcomes of conflicts. Asymmetrical warfare approaches, on the other hand, have more serious and long-term consequences that include the overthrow and replacement of governments and territories where outsiders may have perceived interests. This latter dynamic, common to DWICs, is why outsiders—including the United States—sometimes feel the need to intervene in these situations.

The Perils of Outside Involvement

Involvement in asymmetrical DWICs is the most likely form that major power involvement in military conflict will take for the foreseeable future. Such involvements are almost always problematic, and as I have argued most extensively in *The Case against Military Intervention*, likely to be unsuccessful, very frustrating, and expensive, as the Afghanistan case application volubly demonstrates. Committing forces to these wars is often like following Alice down the rabbit's hole.

The problem of involvement is that it tends to be open-ended, as these internally based conflicts drag on in a protracted manner that is extended when outsiders become involved. The rise of asymmetrical warfare and most of the longest wars in American history have coincided: the eight-year involvement in Vietnam between 1965 and 1973, followed by the eight-years-plus invasion and occupation of Iraq (2003 to 2011) and currently culminated by the ongoing American involvement in Afghanistan (2001 to present).

The peril of involvement arises from the attempt to insert outside military might into a situation for which it is unsuited. The whole point of asymmetrical warfare is to blunt and foil the intrusion of superior conventional forces. The situations where involvement may be contemplated tend to be difficult, convoluted, and opaque in terms or the motives of the contestants, and outsiders have not shown great talent in identifying the "side of the angels" in these encounters.

The Military Dimension

Any military force contemplating insertion into a DWIC must face certain uncomfortable and unfamiliar realities. The first is the nature of the opponent, its methods, and its goals. DWICs occur in locales very unlike North America and Europe, for which most major power armed forces were designed. The "natives" in DWICs recognize they cannot fight major power militaries head-on, and so they can only compete by changing the rules and methods of the engagement. Asymmetrical forces avoid the kinds of confrontation at which they know they will lose, preferring instead more indirect forms of warfare. They consciously change the rules of engagement to make them uncomfortable for conventional forces. Declaring there are no noncombatants allows themselves to imbed themselves in civilian populations, forcing the enemy to avoid attacking them or cause collateral damage that violates the intervener's rules of engagement. The asymmetrical warrior's goal is to frustrate the enemy and overcome its cost-tolerance. The goal is achieved by frustrating the opponent to the point that it tires of the contest and leaves. The yardstick of success for symmetrical warriors is the military defeat of its enemy as preface to imposing a settlement on it. It wins by winning. By contrast, the asymmetrical warrior's strategy of attrition seeks to get the opponent to leave on its own. The opponent is not vanquished; it leaves voluntarily. The asymmetrical warrior's goal is to keep on the pressure until the enemy leaves: it wins by not losing.

The Political Dimension

Two major political dilemmas face the potential intruder into DWICs. The first is understanding them and thus what and who to support. In most DWIC situations, outsiders do not fully understand the nuances of the situations and who—if anyone—is worth supporting. DWICs tend to be about loyalty to the sides fighting, and it is often difficult trying to determine which side represents the aspirations of the population. Failing to choose the virtuous side and the side likely to prevail is a crucial problem.

The other problem surrounds the lack of intense and compelling outsider interest in the conflict. Was there, for instance, anything about any outcome that justified an eight-year commitment and the loss of over 58,000 American lives in Vietnam? Or eight years of combat and commitment in Iraq? Or the long and continuing military commitment to Afghanistan? Cases can be made on either side on all these involvements, but none are so overwhelmingly compelling as to gather universal agreement. The lack of vital interests is the culprit.

Application: The Never-Ending Afghanistan War

Unless one counts long occupations such as the U.S. Marines' two decades in Haiti between 1915 and 1934, the American military effort in Afghanistan now represents America's longest war. A satisfactory outcome seems no more imminent than it did at the beginning. Those who committed the first American forces to Afghanistan did not envision a war without end when they dispatched the first Americans there in October 2001. Their overt purpose was to attack, capture, and destroy Al Qaeda and its leader Osama bin Laden. That action, however, enmeshed the United States in a conventional civil war between the Taliban and insurgents under the banner of the Northern Alliance.

The campaign against bin Laden and Al Qaeda, of course, failed, as the terrorist leader and his followers eluded their pursuers and slipped across the border into Pakistan. Despite this inability to accomplish this primary—and universally supported—goal, the United States stayed. When the Taliban returned to reassert their domain in 2003, the United States became part of the Afghan civil war, which was not part of the original purpose.

Afghanistan is a classic asymmetrical war. On one side is the Afghan government, aided by a North Atlantic Treaty Organization (NATO)–based coalition and the United States. Thanks to outside assistance, the Afghan government possesses superior conventional force. On the other side is the insurgent Taliban, whose forces are inferior to those of the United States and its allies in physical terms. In these circumstances, the Taliban had no choice but to adopt the methodology of asymmetrical force.

The Afghan Maelstrom

Afghanistan is one of the most forbidding, unforgiving, and difficult countries in the world. It is an ancient land with a discernible history dating back three to four millennia. It has always been a harsh and contentious place whose history is punctuated by occasions in which it has united to repel foreign invaders and then fallen back into fractious disunity and violent rivalry. Afghans always seem to be fighting, either against hated outsiders or among themselves. Since 2001, it has been both.

Historic interest in Afghanistan has largely geographic bases. The country has few natural resources to exploit or physical bases for development, and it is one of the poorest countries in the world. In 2016, for instance the *CIA World Factbook* listed its three largest exports (in order) as opium, fruits, and nuts. It does have a strategic location in the heart of Asia that has made it a junction point, what the U.S. government has called a "land bridge," for travelers and traders throughout history.

Its strategic location has placed Afghanistan on the transit route or made it the object of some of history's greatest conquerors. Alexander the Great passed through in both directions as he sought to subdue India, and Genghis Khan's Golden Hordes swept through and for a time occupied this rugged land. More recently, independent Afghanistan (it originally achieved its independence in 1747) was occupied and partially subdued by Great Britain, which fought three wars there. The Soviet Union invaded Afghanistan in December 1979 in a feckless attempt to shore up a communist regime in Kabul. Like virtually all the conquerors that had come before them, the Soviets retreated ignominiously.

For most of its history, Afghanistan has been a deeply divided society, with loyalty to tribal affiliations rather than the state. Afghanistan has never evolved a strong, stable central government, and its attempts to create one have been fleeting and ultimately unsuccessful. This misery has been compounded by epidemic corruption over the sparse wealth, which continues to this day. As a March 10, 2017, *New York Times* editorial summarized the situation: "Afghanistan remains in the grip of a resolute insurgency and a kleptocratic, dysfunctional governing elite."

What passes for unity and peacefulness normally has occurred when geographically based ethnic tribal groups have had substantial autonomy and where such central regulation as existed was the result of tribal *loya jirgas* meetings, the most recent of which convened in mid-2019. Whenever a central government in Kabul has attempted to assert its authority outside the tribal council system, it has been actively resisted, often violently.

The result is an Afghan society dominated by its tribal parts with a xenophobic dislike for and suspicion of outsiders. Within the tribal structure, however, one group has traditionally been most prominent. The Pashtuns are the largest ethnic group in the country. They are further divided into competing subunits, the most prominent of which are the Durrani and the Gilzai Pashtuns. Throughout most of Afghan history, Pashtuns were in the majority in the country, and for a time the terms "Afghan" and "Pashtun" were used synonymously. Forced migration—largely to Pakistan—has cost the Pashtuns their majority status, but they retain a plurality (currently estimated as about 42 percent). Traditional Pashtun lands are concentrated in the Southern and Eastern parts of the country adjacent to and overlapping the Durand Line (the legal boundary between Afghanistan and Pakistan that is rejected as invalid by many Pashtuns). A sovereign state of Pashtunistan remains the goal of some tribal members. By some measures, the Pashtuns are a stateless nation like the Kurds.

The Pashtuns are important for two reasons. First, virtually all Afghan governments have been headed by a Pashtun and have had the active support of the Pashtuns. Hamid Karzai, the president of Afghanistan until 2014, is an urban Durrani Pashtun, but his support among the rural Gilzais who form the core supporters of the Taliban was always suspect. He was succeeded by Dr. Ashraf Ghani, a former chancellor of Kabul University and an urban Pashtun. Second, the Gilzai support base of the Taliban comes almost exclusively from rural-based Pashtuns, and most of the hotbeds of Taliban activity and control are in traditional Pashtun lands. All Pashtuns are by no means Taliban, but virtually all the Taliban are Pashtuns.

The War and U.S. Involvement

The dynamics of the current war in Afghanistan are the direct legacy of the Afghan resistance to the Soviet occupation and its aftermath. The Soviet invasion produced a fierce resistance by the various Afghan tribes, aided by, among others, the Americans. The mujahidin, as the Afghan resisters were collectively known, had two distinct elements: native Afghan tribesmen who, in typical Afghan fashion, formed a loose coalition to repel the Soviets that dissolved when the Soviets departed; and foreign fighters, mostly from other Islamic countries. Native Afghans formed the basis for both sides in the later civil war between the Taliban and the Northern Alliance. Many foreign fighters, some of whom had been recruited by a then-obscure Saudi activist named Osama bin Laden, became members of Al Qaeda.

The expulsion of the Soviets began the end of communist rule in Afghanistan. After they left, governments came and went in Kabul, but all were equally inept, corrupt, and unpopular. In reaction, a new movement primarily comprising students (talibs) from religious schools (madrassas) largely in Pakistan formed and swept across Afghanistan. In 1996, the Taliban became the government of the country. That same year, Al Qaeda was expelled from Sudan. The new Afghan government welcomed them and provided them with protection.

The Taliban government's rule—or misrule—is well documented and inevitably spawned its own opposition. Gradually, a coalition of primarily non-Pashtun tribes formed under the banner of the Northern Alliance. By 9/11, the Northern Alliance and the Taliban were locked in a full-scale civil war, the outcome of which was very much in doubt. Meanwhile, Al Qaeda continued to operate training facilities in Afghanistan, planning, among other things, the 9/11 attacks.

The United States stayed on the sidelines of this conflict before 9/11, and the United States intervened as part of the "war on terror," with Al Qaeda as its centerpiece. The U.S. entry in effect created a second conflict with its own objectives and conduct separate from and independent of the ongoing civil war. Although bin Laden's flight from the country effectively ended the military effort against Al Qaeda (because the terrorists were now in Pakistan), that did not end NATO and American involvement. Rather, the result was the formation of the new Karzai government as the representative of the victorious Northern Alliance, with American blessing. When the Taliban left, the United States and NATO remained to help mop up residual Al Qaeda and Taliban resistance and to ensure they did not return. The effect was to bifurcate the fighting into a limited and failed effort to capture Al Qaeda, a goal in the highest American interest, and a continuing civil war in which the only American interest was to maintain in power a regime that would oppose Al Qaeda's return. That interest has remained the basic rationale for the U.S. role ever since.

The Taliban began to infiltrate back into the country in 2003 to launch a new phase of the civil war with the pre-9/11 roles reversed: The Karzai-led Northern Alliance formed the core of the government and the Taliban were the insurgents. Now reconfigured as the Afghan National Army, the Northern Alliance was no more capable of defeating the Taliban than they had been before.

It has become a classic asymmetrical war. The Taliban are a formidable match for the Afghan National Army without foreign help, but they are less powerful than and incapable of defeating the NATO/American forces in symmetrical warfare. The Taliban thus adopted an unconventional, asymmetrical approach to the war, aiming most clearly at overcoming American cost-tolerance by prolonging the conflict sufficiently to turn American public opinion against the effort and force a withdrawal.

Never-Ending Conflict

The civil war in Afghanistan between the central government of Ghani aided by the International Security Assistance Force continues, and no one is publicly predicting its physical conclusion. In one sense, the protraction and lack of visible success of either side is not unusual for an asymmetrical war where neither side can vanquish the opponent and impose the kind of peace that marks conventional wars. It is even more a war of attrition than most asymmetrical wars, as its inconclusive length is a testament.

This war would hardly be of interest to the West, and specifically the United States, were it not for 9/11. American interests in Afghanistan before the terrorist attacks were decidedly marginal, and without the Al Qaeda connection, it is almost impossible to imagine that the United States would have cared enough about the outcome of the war to insert itself to affect the outcome. The clear American interest was in capturing bin Laden and his cohorts, and it failed. What was left was the internal war, in which the only discernible American interest is in victory for the side that would most oppose Al Qaeda's return.

Opposing the Taliban insurgency is a different, but in many ways more familiar, problem. The Taliban are conducting an asymmetrical campaign using largely guerrilla tactics and insurgent goals, and the Americans have responded with counterinsurgency strategy. The effort, however, is plagued by at least three difficulties. One is that the Taliban have proven to be tough, adept, and adaptive fighters defending harsh territory with which they are more familiar and comfortable than their opponents: The going is very difficult. The second problem is that the outsiders find themselves aligned with what many Afghans view as an anti-Pashtun coalition: The leadership from Karzai to Ghani are Durrani Pashtuns who have aligned themselves with other ethnic minorities like the Tajiks, who are the historic enemies of the rural Afghans who support the Taliban. Afghan history has been remarkably consistent in the sense that no government that is opposed by the Pashtuns has much chance of succeeding, and when a government is perceived to be an adjunct of urbanites in Kabul, it is doubly suspicious to Afghans from remote parts of the country. Third, the outsiders are exactly that—outsiders—and their presence is resented because they are unwelcome guests. Resistance to foreign military occupation is a universal human instinct, and it is especially strong among the Afghans.

The war in Afghanistan became asymmetrical and continues to be because of the outside intervention of the United States and its NATO allies. Prior to their involvement, the conventional civil war would likely have continued toward some internal resolution at some point. Interfering in that internal affair was not a prominent part of the rationale for intervention in the first place, but it has become the de facto reason for staying. Destroying Al Qaeda was the real goal, and the Taliban were in the way. Operationally, the anti–Al Qaeda mission in Afghanistan ended when Al Qaeda fled.

How the Afghanistan war will end depends largely on two factors that speak more to the interests of outsiders than the Afghans themselves. The first, of course, is the Al Qaeda factor. If Al Qaeda is otherwise destroyed or its return to Afghanistan successfully precluded, there is little reason for the outside world to worry about the civil war. The other is the outside, and especially the American role, which is an enigma. The longest American war in history has not been cheap. The monetary costs have been enormous. Officially, $686 billion was appropriated for the conflict between 2001 and 2014, and no one thinks that was the total bill. Most unofficial estimates fall in the $2 to 4 trillion range for outcomes that are hardly discernible. President Obama announced early in his presidency the intention to get the United States out of Afghanistan by 2014, and he failed. The Trump administration has done no better.

Where does the effort stand? Analysts disagree, but none are wildly optimistic. The *New York Times* March 10, 2017, editorial argues, "The challenges that have stymied American generals in Afghanistan for years—including havens for insurgents in Pakistan, endemic corruption and poor leadership in the Afghan military—remain unsolved." Alleged but largely unpublicized Pakistani aid to the Taliban is, according to Fair, resulting in a dismal outlook: "the situation in Afghanistan is spiraling downward as the Taliban continues to make new gains while consolidating older ones. Hopes that Pakistan would bring the Taliban to the negotiating table continue to fizzle. The reason for this is simple: Pakistan and its proxy, the Taliban, are winning." The 2017 policy response in Washington, summarized by Jones, is pessimistic: "aggressively pursue terrorists that threaten the United States, prevent Taliban forces from overthrowing the Afghan government, and encourage a more sustainable and effective Afghan government." Is this not the policy in place since 2001—which has not worked?

Conclusion

Warfare is both an ever-changing and never-changing human endeavor. The opponents change, the purposes for which wars are fought change, and the methods and tools of war change. At the same time, the fact that groups of humans find reasons to fight and kill other groups of humans remains one of history's true constants.

What is now called asymmetrical warfare is part of this march of history. The basic ideas and methods underlying this kind of war are as old as warfare itself and have been a recurring part of the historic pattern. What is arguably different is that differential fighting capabilities between countries and groups have widened to the point that asymmetrical warfare has become much more necessary for weaker participants than it was in the past. The ongoing war in Afghanistan is only the latest and most currently obvious example of this form of warfare.

Study/Discussion Questions

1. What is asymmetrical warfare? Contrast it with symmetrical warfare. Why has it arisen as the major military problem of the twenty-first century? Why is it likely to continue to be the dominant problem?
2. Where do asymmetrical wars tend to occur? What is a DWIC, why are those conflicts likely to be asymmetrical, and why is this important to the United States?
3. Discuss the problem posed by asymmetrical warfare. In what kinds of conflicts and by what kind of groups is it practiced?
4. Why has participation in asymmetrical warfare become such a large enterprise for the United States? What has the experience been? What political and military problems does it create?
5. Discuss the background and evolution of the Afghanistan war, beginning with its roots in the Afghan resistance to the Soviet occupation and leading to the 9/11 attacks. Why does the war have two distinct facets? What are they? Explain.
6. Building on the dual nature of the conflict, describe Afghanistan as an asymmetrical war. Put your discussion in the context of the Afghan historical experience.
7. How did the United States get involved in Afghanistan? What changes have occurred since the initial involvement that could or should have changed the nature of that involvement?
8. What do you think the lessons of Afghanistan should be for the United States? Discuss.

Bibliography

Ansary, Tamim. *Game without Rules: The Often-Interrupted History of Afghanistan*. New York: PublicAffairs, 2012.

Barfield, Thomas. *Afghanistan: A Cultural and Political History*. Princeton, NJ: Princeton University Press, 2010.

Barnett, Roger W. *Asymmetrical Warfare: Today's Challenge to U.S. Military Power*. Issues in Twenty-First Century Warfare. Washington, DC: Potomac Books, 2013.

Belasco, Amy. *The Cost of Iraq, Afghanistan and Other Global Terrorist Operations since 9/11*. Washington, DC: Congressional Research Service, December 8, 2014.

Berkowitz, Bruce. *The New Face of War: How War Will Be Fought in the 21st Century*. New York: Free Press, 2003.

Central Intelligence Agency. *CIA World Factbook, 2016*. Washington, DC: Central Intelligence Agency, 2016.

Coll, Steve. *Ghost Wars: The Secret History of the CIA, Afghanistan, and bin Laden from the Soviet Invasion to September 10, 2001*. New York: Penguin Books, 2004.

Editorial Board. "Afghanistan Is Now Trump's War." *New York Times*, March 10, 2017.
Ewans, Martin. *Afghanistan: A Short History of Its People and Politics*. New York: HarperCollins Perennial, 2002.
Fair, C. Christine. "Pakistan's Deadly Grip on Afghanistan." *Current History* 116, no. 789 (April 2017), 136–41.
Galula, David. *Counterinsurgency Warfare: Theory and Practice*. Westport, CT: Praeger Publishers (Praeger Classics of the Counterinsurgency Era), 2006.
Giap, Vo Nhuyen. *People's War, People's Army*. New York: Praeger, 1962.
Haass, Richard N. *War of Necessity, War of Choice: A Memoir of Two Iraq Wars*. New York: Simon and Schuster, 2009.
Jones, Seth G. "How Trump Should Manage Afghanistan: A Realistic Set of Goals for the New Administration." *Foreign Affairs Snapshot*, March 21, 2017.
———. *In the Graveyard of Empires: America's War in Afghanistan*. New York: W.W. Norton, 2009.
Kaplan, Robert D. "Man versus Afghanistan." *The Atlantic* 305, no. 3 (April 2010), 60–71.
Kaurin, Pauline M. *The Warrior, Military Ethics and Contemporary Warfare: Achilles Goes Asymmetrical*. New York and London: Routledge, 2016.
Lowther, Adam B. *Americans and Asymmetrical Warfare: Lebanon, Somalia, and Afghanistan*. Westport, CT: Praeger Security International, 2007.
Mao Ze Dung. *The Collected Works of Mao Ze Dung*. Volumes 1–4. Beijing, China: Foreign Languages Press, 1967.
Rashid, Ahmed. *Taliban: Militant Islam, Oil, and Fundamentalism in Central Asia* (second edition). New Haven, CT: Yale University Press, 2010.
Snow, Donald M. *The Case against Military Intervention: Why We Do It and Why It Fails*. New York and London: Routledge, 2016.
——— and Dennis M. Drew. *From Lexington to Baghdad and Beyond: War and Politics in the American Experience* (third edition). Armonk, NY: M. E. Sharpe, 2010.
Tomsen, Peter. *The Wars of Afghanistan: Messianic Terrorism, Tribal Conflicts, and the Failure of Great Powers*. New York: PublicAffairs, 2013.
U.S. Army and U.S. Marine Corps. *Counterinsurgency Field Manual* (U.S. Army Field Manual No. 3-24, Marine Corps Warfighting Publication No. 3-33.5). Chicago, IL: University of Chicago Press, 2007.
U.S. Marine Corps. *Afghanistan: Operational Culture for Deploying Personnel*. Quantico, VA: Center for Operational Cultural Learning, 2009.
Weston, J. Kael. *The Mirror Test: America at War in Iraq and Afghanistan*. New York: Vintage Books, 2016.

9

The Corrosive Politics of Petroleum

Nigeria and Venezuela

Petroleum energy has been a dominant influence in global life since it emerged as a replacement for wood as the major source of energy around the beginning of the twentieth century. The discovery of new and abundant supplies of petroleum around the world, a process that continues to this day, created a seemingly boundless supply of energy that allowed the massive development of much of the world to an extent that would probably have been impossible without it. That transformation reached its zenith when the United States convinced Europeans to build their World War II economies on oil-based energy. Petroleum has been the energy king ever since.

World climate change has squelched the honeymoon between petroleum and international virtue. As described in chapter 15, the use (or overuse) of petroleum as an energy source has resulted in the emission of enormous amounts of carbon dioxide into the atmosphere where it serves as an atmospheric blanket with multiple, deadly effects on the sustainability of human life as it has evolved. There is some minor disagreement on the exact nature and extent of the change that is occurring, but only the most obdurate skeptics (many of whom have some vested interest in petroleum exploitation and use) deny that the world needs to reduce drastically its burning of petroleum as the world's energy source. The conversion to petroleum energy that made life in the twentieth century more commodious and prosperous now threatens the very basis of civilization in the twenty-first century.

Because it is valuable and has produced enormous wealth for those who possess it, oil has played a role in international politics as well. Petroleum reserves are present in most parts of the world, but they are particularly abundant in certain locales, many of which are in the developing world. The most prominent and obvious example is the Persian Gulf littoral, which has been a major provider of world supplies since the 1940s, a process that has made the countries on top of which its oil domes sit fabulously wealthy and made their political regimes, many of which are otherwise anachronistic, important members of the international system. Imagine, for instance, how much time and attention the world would pay to Saudi Arabia if did not have oil. The quest to find, claim, and exploit petroleum reserves is a major enterprise with very real international consequences. The conflict over the South China Sea (chapter 7) would hardly matter if there were not oil underneath it and if Middle East–based oil tankers did not traverse it to provide oil to American Pacific allies.

There is another pernicious impact of petroleum, what is known as *petropolitics*. This phenomenon is defined by the Merriam-Webster dictionary as "the strategy of controlling petroleum sales as a way of achieving international political goals." This phenomenon was first given widespread publicity in a 2006 *Foreign Policy* article by *New York Times* columnist Thomas L. Friedman, "The First Law of Petropolitics." Friedman noted that states with dominating oil reserves that tend to gear their economic status and political life around oil and the revenues it produces tend to be transformed into unstable, often authoritarian places where the enormous amounts of wealth that petroleum generates serve to destabilize the country's politics. More fundamentally, the First Law posits that petrodollars and political liberalization, including democratization, are inversely related: the more petroleum wealth dominates a country's economic structure, the less democratic it becomes. This problem is particularly evident in developing countries lacking sound and accepted ways to deal with political rewards, which is true in many developing countries that also have large petroleum reserves but few (if any) reliable institutions to regulate their effects.

The petrolist problem has been particularly poignant since the price of oil dropped in international markets between 2012 and 2014 from around one hundred dollars per barrel to thirty dollars or less, figures from which it has not rebounded. The result has been stark and destabilizing. Countries whose economies were based on petroleum largesse no longer have those monetary resources available, and because their overall economies are otherwise poor and undeveloped, they lack the ability to replace the lost petrodollars. The result has been widespread discontent in several countries for which regimes have no answer but borrowing or a reversion to authoritarian rule that can become chaotic. In places where there is intergroup or international tension on top of this difficulty (the border area between the Sudan and South Sudan is an example), the result can be explosive. Part of this phenomenon has occurred in Russia, as introduced in chapter 7. The corrosive effects of huge amounts of oil wealth have been a problem for years in Africa's most populous country, Nigeria, and it underlies much of the tragic dynamics of Venezuela, the chaos in which became publicly notorious internationally in 2019.

Principle: Politically Corrosive Petroleum

The idea that petroleum-generated wealth could become the source of instability, violence, and unhappiness rather than the key to greater prosperity and satisfaction is initially counterintuitive. Much of the world's disparity in conditions of life, after all, derives from wildly varying conditions of living, and economic and developmental resources have virtually universally been identified as the palliative for removing disparities and providing the wherewithal for a more salutary existence for all.

The situation, and especially the contemporary environment, has not supported this optimistic view of how developmentally useful resources would be generated or used. Shortly after the turn of the millennium, the price of oil increased dramatically, and high prices were championed, encouraged, and manipulated by energy-rich countries through mechanisms such as the Organization of Petroleum Exporting Countries (OPEC). The expectation arose that price inflation was uncontrollable and likely perpetual. It was during this period that Vladimir Putin came to power in Russia, recognized the apparent oil dynamic, and began successfully to exploit it. Oil revenues became the platform both for the gaudy enrichment of some Russians (apparently including Putin himself) and the treasure he could employ to energize Russian resurgence geopolitically. For countries with significant proven or even expected oil deposits, these were heady times.

The linear projections of perpetual petrodollars were flawed on at least two counts. First, it presumed that the conditions on which the seemingly endless demands for more petroleum energy were perpetual, and they were not. The reasons included the discovery that oil deposits were more widely distributed and larger than earlier projections had suggested: oil was not as scarce as once thought. At the same time, demand began to slow, partly because of the continually rising expense of oil, and partly because of conservation efforts to reduce the burning of oil on ecological grounds: demand leveled off. Second, the more the dynamics of a global petrolist economy developed, the more its inherent contradictions became evident. Two examples, so-called Dutch disease and the resource curse illustrate this realization.

So-called Dutch disease is a product of the 1960s and was a harbinger of things to come in the petrolist phenomenon. At that time, the cause of Dutch disease was the discovery of huge deposits of natural gas under its territory, which in turn destabilized the Dutch economy. Friedman described the dynamic in his 2006 article: "What happens in countries with Dutch Disease is that the value of their currency rises, thanks to the influx of cash from the resource discovered and exploited. The result is to distort the economy by making the country's 'manufactured exports uncompetitive and its imports very cheap,' and you end up with economic distortion in the form of 'deindustrialization.'"

A broader, more contemporary version of Dutch disease is what is called the "resource curse." In general, it refers to the distortion and development of dependency on a natural resource on the economic structure and vitality of a country that allows itself to become dependent on the beneficial effects of a surge of revenue from the natural resource, in this case petroleum. Its manifestations and symptoms are numerous and ultimately pernicious. Colgan lists some of the dilatory effects, including symptoms like pervasive corruption in both government and the private sector, wasted public spending, volatile economic growth and contraction as prices of the triggering resource rise and fall, and societal instability and violence in the forms of civil war and domestic unrest. Not all states are equally vulnerable to the impacts of petropolitics nor does it always manifest itself in precisely the same way. At the same time, it is pervasive enough to merit examining its dynamics and potentials where it does or may arise as a form of corrosion in the future.

Vulnerable Settings

Not all countries that have petroleum reserves of one kind or another have proven equally vulnerable to the problems associated with petrolism, although almost all have experienced change that is associated with it. The Netherlands is, of course, the prototype, but has recovered from Dutch disease, and one can even argue that the United States has not escaped entirely, thanks to the shale oil boom that began in the mid-2010s. As profitable shale formations were discovered in the northern plain states, the result was a boom and rush to states like North Dakota, which experienced economic expansion that is associated with petroleum wealth, for instance. The most pernicious impacts, however, have occurred in relatively poor, underdeveloped countries that lack the infrastructure and government mechanisms and maturity to deal with the explosive impact of massive amounts of petrodollars into their environments without the basic physical wherewithal to absorb and create order from this intrusion.

The impact of this influx is, in some ways, idiosyncratic, making broad generalizations at least partially misleading. Moreover, instances of what can be classified as petrolist-based corrosion have been separated in time, location, and severity enough that they are difficult to compare meaningfully. The competition over the Caspian Sea oil fields involving Azerbaijan and Kazakhstan over oil discoveries in Nagorno-Karabakh during the 1990s are so different from the twenty-first-century contest between Sudan and South Sudan or the collapse of Venezuela in the mid-2010s as to make any generalizations arising from a comparison essentially meaningless.

There are, however, some general trends that appear whenever oil seeps into and corrodes a national economy. The most obvious is the psychological and institutional unpreparedness to deal with the sudden influx of vast amounts of petroleum dollars into a country. The discovery and exploitation of new oil reserves attracts international oil companies, entrepreneurs, and even national governments into the target country, and their motives are invariably to gain access—and hopefully control—over a resource that meets their needs and results in maximum profits for them. Typically, there is not a developed governmental apparatus in the country with which outsiders can institutionally deal, and in many countries, there is a "tradition" of bribery and corruption that can create incestuous relationships between multiple oil suitors and internal individuals and factions, each seeking to maximize its personal profits or the wealth of whatever group they may represent. There probably is no governmental entity to deal with the unique impacts of a resource explosion, making the enterprise more attractive to individuals and groups whose agenda may be much more personal than some notion of the public welfare. Rules of proportionality come into play: the vast oil reserves of the Niger Delta and the enormous size of Nigeria and its population make it a much richer target for attracting corrupt interactions than, for instance, the comparatively modest oil reserves of Sudan. The size of the "pie" may prove to be especially problematic in Venezuela, under whose jurisdiction lies what are currently estimated to be the world's largest reserves.

These conditions tend to recur in the developing world, where the exploitation of a variety of natural resources is occurring and where institutions and traditions are least well developed to manage the influx of petrodollars in the most productive ways. Not all the problems occur in those parts of the world generally considered classically underdeveloped (e.g., Africa and Asia), although many do. At the same time, a country like Russia, part of the classic European balance of power, has proven to be vulnerable, and Vladimir Putin's rise to and retention of power has largely been financed by petroleum revenues, many of which have been based in less than above-the-board transactions. At any rate, wherever institutional insufficiencies, corrupt and dishonest officials and power brokers, and outsider greed are simultaneously present, the corrosive impact of petroleum is a very real possibility.

Ironically, the one petroleum-rich part of the world that seems to have escaped the worst of the resource curse is the Persian Gulf region that has been the source of so much of the world's energy and whose countries and leaders have most profited from their role in world energy. The irony here is at least partially explainable by the fact that this region has some of the most anachronistic, absolutist governments in the world—including conservative monarchies that disappeared hundreds of years ago in the developing world. Often aligned with religious movements (e.g., the House of Saud-Wahhabist alliance in Saudi Arabia), these countries are so authoritarian and effectively regressive that they have managed to suppress the outbreak of the resource curse until now. One can only speculate about how long they will remain exempt.

The Consequences of the Resource Curse

Two almost entirely opposing trends make understanding the quite different effects of the resource curse important. Both center on the question of petroleum's continuing role in world politics. The first is changing demand patterns. Largely influenced by the global climate change movement, there has been a decreasing demand for fossil fuel to produce energy. The decrease has been particularly strong regarding the most polluting sources like coal, but it has extended to petroleum-based energy. Conservation of energy has been part of this change, as have efforts to find and exploit other energy technologies that do not leave a carbon residue. The result is less demand for oil, which has contributed to falling oil prices since the early 2010s and pessimism about when or whether prices will rebound. These reductions have, of course, been the major cause of the politico-economic crisis that has destabilized petrolist states accustomed to a steady stream of petrodollars.

The other change has been the discovery of more oil sources than were previously thought to exist. Around the turn of the millennium, many predictions assumed the world was reaching a tipping point in oil availability, so-called peak oil, where half the world's supply was used and availability would subsequently decline, solving the problem of carbon emissions but also creating energy crises. Since then, major new oil sources globally have been discovered, as have alternate sources such as shale oil. The world, as it turns out, is not running out of petroleum, and one major effect is that the oil deposits that many petrolist states possess are less relatively valuable than they were in the past. The world may also be running out of the capacity to absorb the carbon deposits burning petroleum creates.

The petroleum dynamic is thus changing in not entirely predictable or necessarily positive ways. Whether the existing petrolist states will return to their former economic status is open to question, as is concern with what a prolonged lessening of petroleum wealth will do to the countries that have become petrostates. At the same time, the apparent ubiquity of petroleum deposits could conceivably have a similar effect on other states in the future. Even if the burning of oil declines and even disappears, oil will remain a valuable commodity. It is, after all, the basis of much of the chemical industry worldwide and is the major "ingredient" of most plastics. Thus understanding the dynamics of petrolism is more than an historical oddity.

For countries unprepared for the flood of money it creates, petrodollars can indeed have corrosive effects on the countries that experience it—the resource curse in action. Each case is idiosyncratic to some degree, but, as suggested earlier, they do have some similarities that can be noted and exemplified in the applications section of the chapter.

The perverse impacts of petroleum have been most pronounced in countries suffering from prior political and economic underdevelopment. The political effects tend to be associated with two basic but critical phenomena. The first of these is a deficit of uniting nationalism. This problem is less severe in a highly nationalistic country like Russia, but in most of the developing world, there is not the kind of unifying sense of national identity and loyalty that leads to a desire to put the interests of the country over more parochial, group-based loyalties. Partially as a result, there is little civic sense and institutional development that puts a brake on the misuse of the outpouring of money that accompanies the oil boom forming the basis for petrolism.

There are several manifestations of this problem. The most frequent is pervasive corruption. Officials lack overarching, encompassing respect for the country as an entity and are likely to view the flood of money as a personal windfall rather than as a national opportunity. Manifestations include a strong culture of bribery, wasted public spending that benefits some but not all, and ethnically or otherwise crony-based corruption. Nepotism and kleptocracy are frequent terms associated with the phenomenon. Multinationalism becomes a frequent factor, because petroleum deposits are likely to be concentrated in the tribal lands of a subnational group that is uninterested in sharing this windfall with other groups with which it has differences. At its most extreme, the result can be that oil wealth exacerbates differences to the point of making conflict and violence worse than it might otherwise be. The Biafran War in Nigeria from 1967 to 1970 is the most extreme example.

The heart of petrolism, and thus the resource curse, is money. As oil prices steadily increased in the early 2000s and otherwise modestly successful national economies were infused with enormous amounts of money, their statuses changed both internationally and in the eyes of their own people. Countries that were geopolitically marginal suddenly became important. Some, like the oil-rich kingdoms of the Middle East, had been awash in petrodollars for decades and were only slightly affected, but countries that had been on the outside of the heart of the OPEC-controlled system suddenly found themselves at center stage in world politics, their coffers overflowing with petroleum assets that they were institutionally and psychologically unprepared to manage honestly and efficiently. Their underlying assumption about their new-found wealth was that the situation would remain: a kind of perpetual boom cycle that meant huge amounts of petrodollars would be available indefinitely. This situation fostered greed and dishonesty that was already present but unfulfilled, adding to the kleptocracy that was the dream of many.

Its prospects for politicians helped lead to the curse. In most of the new oil-rich countries, political elites were not held in high regard, and suddenly the government had large amounts of money it could dispense to the people to gain their support. In effect, governments were able to buy support from their people and to remain highly popular as long as the largesse continued. Governments like those in Russia and Venezuela received enormously high approval ratings from their populations. In Russia, for instance, the infusion of these monies erased the torpor of the 1990s with support for a leader like Putin, and in Venezuela, it did much the same for Hugo Chavez. Continuing high oil prices artificially created support for governments that had not previously had such support.

And then the bubble burst in the early 2010s. Suddenly there were not government monies to distribute, economies cratered, and enormous prosperity was replaced by dwindling resources. Klare described the resulting situation in 2017: "with oil below $50 and likely to persist at that level, they find themselves curbing public spending and fending off rising domestic discontent. The fates of their governing institutions are deeply woven onto the boom-and-bust cycles of the international petroleum economy." Because both oil and its pernicious curse are ongoing problems, examining the dynamics in concrete cases is appropriate.

Application: Nigeria and Venezuela

Nigeria and Venezuela are exemplary cases for more detailed consideration for several reasons. One is that they are large and potentially consequential developing world countries. Nigeria, for instance, has the world's seventh largest population at over 200 million living in a country about twice the size of California. That population will explode in the next three decades, making Nigeria the clearly dominant state on an African continent that itself will be the world's second most populous land mass by 2050. The land area of Venezuela is comparable but not so locally notable, given the presence of large states like Brazil and Argentina on the South American continent, but it has long been an important link in the land bridge between the Americas.

Two related factors make these two developing world countries consequential for this chapter: unstable politics and large petroleum deposits. These factors are, of course, closely related. Nigeria has been unstable since it achieved its independence in 1960, and the competition over oil revenues has been a central factor in that situation. Venezuela has a longer and more diverse history. It became an independent country in 1830 when Gran Colombia split into Colombia, Ecuador, and Venezuela. Politically, it has periods both of stability and instability: for most of the nineteenth century, for instance, it was under generally tranquil military rule, and it has been politically democratic since 1959. Political instability has been a way of life in Nigeria since birth; turmoil in Venezuela is more recent.

The common basis of concern has been petroleum. As OPEC successfully wrestled control of oil production and prices from Western oil companies in the latter parts of the twentieth century, developed countries that had built their energy systems on the premise of secure, affordable petroleum energy found themselves in an uncomfortable situation of supply and cost uncertainty. One of their strategies was to explore and try to exploit oil production in areas other than the Middle East to provide themselves some leverage with Persian Gulf–dominated OPEC. The oil deposits of the Niger Delta made Nigeria a bellwether for this strategy in Africa; the enormous oil reserves of Orinoco Belt tar sands under Northern Venezuela and Caribbean waters controlled by Venezuela made that a target as well. Petrolist-based problems have been common to both: the competition for oil wealth exacerbated preexisting instability in Nigeria; the vicissitudes of the boom-and-bust cycle fractured a more civil society in Venezuela.

Nigeria

Nigeria is, by African standards, a very large and consequential place the importance of which can only increase in the future for demographic reasons. Its 200 million citizens are the most of any African country, and the gap will explode in the coming years for sheerly demographic reasons. Projections between now and 2050 predict that population will more than double to 417 million, making it the third most populous country on the globe (the United States will drop from third to fourth at 398 million). It is also one of the most diverse places on the Earth. It has over 500 discernible tribes who speak over 1,000 languages and dialects. That diversity is dominated by three major tribes that also exemplify the problems of the country. The largest tribal grouping is the Hausa-Fulani, who are concentrated in northern Nigeria, constitute about 29 percent of the population, and are almost all Muslims. Most of the Boko Haram terrorist members are also Northerners and Muslims, and many Muslim Northerners are also strongly evangelical, seeking to spread or—depending on one's viewpoint—impose their faith on the rest. Since 1970, only one president of the country has been other than a Northerner. Their chief antagonists have been the Igbo (or Ibo) of Eastern Nigeria, including the Niger Delta under which the major petroleum deposits are located. The Igbo are Christian and compose about 18 percent of the population. The Hausa-Fulani and Igbo were the major contestants in the so-called Biafran Civil War between 1967 and 1970, when the Igbo attempted to secede from Nigeria and to create a state of Biafra that included control of the oil. The third large tribe is the Yoruba of western Nigeria, who constitute roughly 21 percent of the population and are mostly Christian or animist. Overall, the country is half Muslim, 40 percent Christian, and 10 percent animist.

Nigeria will become more important because of its demographics and notably whether it can develop the ability to achieve stability among its multiple, numerous ethno-religious groups. Its economy, however, has been highly dependent on oil reserves, production, and exports. In 2015, its proven reserves were the tenth largest in the world, and its pre-2012 exports were the fifth largest in the world. The result was a surplus of funds flooding the country, which contributed visibly to thriving corruption for which Nigeria is famous.

Since 1970, the Nigerian petroleum-based economy and its endemic corruption have been the focal points of most attention on the country. The country has always placed at or near the top of world rankings among corrupt states, but when prosperity was ensured by high oil prices, that condition was acceptable both to Nigerians and the international community, among whom the venality of the kleptocracy was accepted as part of the Nigerian culture. Dowden describes the Nigerian system as characterized by "hilariously brazen corruption" that "puts it in another league" among states. The fact that Nigerian oil was not critical to world powers but rather a backup source in the event of problems in supply from the Middle East adds to the nonchalance with which this oil-driven corruption was viewed internationally.

Nigeria has also been reasonably politically stable since the end of the Biafran Civil War in 1970. Following the conclusion of that bloodletting, the military intervened and ruled until 1999, when power was transferred to civilian rule (there were brief interludes of civilian rule during the thirty-year period of military rule, but none lasted). The Fourth Republic came to power in 2000, and despite some largely regional/sectarian conflict and pressures like what to do about the Boko Haram terrorists, it has remained intact. The fall of oil prices and the decision of the United States to suspend oil imports from Nigeria has added to an ongoing insurgent movement in the Niger Delta to create unrest and further cut oil profits, but as Dowden concluded in 2009, "The coming of democracy did not change the Nigerian system: the king is dead, long-live-who-ever-has-got-the-oil-money."

Venezuela

The situation is different in Venezuela. In Nigeria, oil wealth is a virtually interwoven component of a culture much of whose economics are imbedded in corruption and kleptocracy that oil revenues help to enable and continue. Problems of exploding demographics and latent religious/ethnic divisions may eventually cause major stress, as they did in 1967, but the resource curse is comparatively benign.

The same is not true in Venezuela, where the existence and misuse of wealth from the world's largest petroleum reserves have contributed greatly to the disintegration of the South American country to the point of internal chaos and suffering. Oil is only part of the cause of utter state failure in Venezuela, but until its politics are somehow brought under control, that oil cannot contribute to the reintegration of Venezuela back into the world system.

Division in Venezuela with economic, and thus petroleum, implications is largely based in the country's deep internal divisions centering on physical and ideological gaps in the population. The current chasm has its roots in the globalization of the 1990s. Economic globalization greatly increased productivity and wealth worldwide, but it also had differential effects internally within countries, increasing the economic gap between the wealthy and the less affluent, and this has been an ongoing problem in Venezuela. As Castenada explained in 2008, "The left stresses social improvement over macroeconomc orthodoxy, egalitarian distribution of wealth over its creation, sovereignty over international cooperation, democracy over economic effectiveness."

This problem came to a head in 1999, well over a decade before the general decline in oil prices. Venezuela elected Hugo Chavez, a vocal advocate of Venezuela's poor, as president, and he initiated a radical economic agenda featuring heavy subsidies of the poor like very cheap gasoline and free housing, financed by Venezuelan oil revenues. The results included great damage to oil revenues: between 1999 and 2013 oil production dropped 25 percent, and it has virtually dried to a trickle since. The result has been to stop the flow of wealth into the country (despite a $50 billion loan from China, according to Sabatini). The 2019 crisis has been a direct result of this dynamic.

The nature of Venezuelan oil reserves contributes to the problem. The vast stores of petroleum in the Orinoco Belt are primarily imbedded in oil and tar sands not entirely unlike those in Canada. They are thus more expensive and technologically difficult to extract than other forms. Petroleum must be separated from the sand deposits in which it is deposited, and the captured oil must then be refined, itself difficult because it is so-called heavy oil. The process is expensive and requires considerable skilled management and technology, which Venezuela currently lacks.

Politics is an even greater problem with two aspects. Chavez nurtured a highly egalitarian, socialized approach to the economy, and this caused him to participate in an international coalition with socialist states in the region—notably Cuba and Nicaragua. This arrangement alienated the United States (Trump National Security Advisor John Bolton referred to it as the "troika of tyranny" in 2019). This has worsened never close relations between the United States and Venezuela, and the fear of an American invasion in 2019 was one prominent claim that current president Nicolas Maduro employed to justify retaining power in the 2019 crisis.

Political figures have changed in Venezuela, but as of mid-2019, there has been little substantive change that would help ameliorate the human disaster in the country. Chavez died of cancer in 2013 and was replaced by his chosen successor, Maduro, who has maintained power through the 2019 crisis. Sabatini describes Maduro as "deeply corrupt and fraudulently elected," and moderate president of the National Assembly Juan Guaido declared himself the legitimate ruler in early 2019, a declaration supported by many foreign governments that has not resulted in his rise to power. The United States is among those countries, and American support has been cited by Maduro as a reason he must maintain power as a counterweight to American "imperialism." As of mid-2019, Maduro remains in power, largely because of support from the Venezuelan military.

There seems no easy short-term solution to the problem. As the horrors of the humanitarian crisis were broadcast worldwide in early 2019, there were calls for physical international intercession by states, including advocacies of a possible U.S. military intervention either in the form of limited air strikes against the regime or even a full-scale intervention. Moro denigrates these possibilities, arguing the United States "would almost certainly get sucked into a long, difficult campaign . . . that would cost American lives and money and hurt the United States' standing in Latin America." Such talk strengthens the hand of Maduro by stoking latent fears of the "colossus of the north." As the Guaido challenge has waned, so has support of an active U.S. response.

Conclusion

Petroleum has played a deeply ambivalent role in the human history of the last century. Its discovery and emergence as the principal global energy source of the twentieth and early twenty-first centuries has allowed a process of accelerated development unchallenged in world history, but the realization that it also pollutes the atmosphere and thus threatens that same enhanced environment will also inevitably lead to its wane as a global world force. We used to worry about running out of oil; now we worry about out how to free ourselves from its toxic embrace.

Oil has proven to be politically corrosive in places where its discovery, exploitation, and enormous created wealth occurs in the developing world and transforms countries into petrolist states with all the baggage that conversion entails. Nigeria and Venezuela are two examples of that corroding influence. Exploration in the past decade or so has revealed that there are prospects for oil booms to occur generally around the globe. The only thing that may stand in the way of the petrostate could be a decreased global reliance on oil as the energy source that powers, but also pollutes and corrodes, the human condition.

Study/Discussion Questions

1. What has the international role of oil been in the last century? How has that effect been ambivalent for the world and countries that possess it? Discuss.
2. What is petropolitics? According to the "first law of petropolitics," what is its pernicious effect? How does it make oil "the lubricant that corrodes"?
3. What is the resource curse/Dutch disease? How did the oil price crash of the early 2010s make it an issue?
4. What areas of the world are most vulnerable to the resource curse? What are its consequences for them?
5. Compare and contrast Nigeria and Venezuela as petrostates. How are they similar and different?
6. Summarize the effects of petropolitics on Nigeria.
7. Summarize the effects of petropolitics on Venezuela.
8. Is the possession and use of petroleum a blessing or a curse for its possessors and the world generally? Why?

Bibliography

Azuagi, Penelope Plaza. *Culture as Renewable Oil: How Territory, Bureaucratic Power, and Culture Coalesce in the Venezuelan Petrostate*. New York and London: Routledge, 2018.

Baena, Cesar E. *The Policy Process in a Petro-State: An Analysis of PDVSA's (Venezuela) Internationalization Strategy* (first edition). New York and London: Routledge, 2019.

Campbell, John. "Civil War within Nigerian Islam." *The Cipher Brief* (Council on Foreign Relations online), August 25, 2016.

Carroll, Rory. *Commandante: Hugo Chavez's Venezuela*. New York: Penguin Books, 2014.

Castenada, Jorge C. "Latin America's Left Turn." *Foreign Affairs* 85, no. 3 (May/June 2006), 33–41.

Colgan, Jeff D. "Oil, Domestic Politics, and International Conflict." *Energy Research and Social Science* 1 (March 2014), 198–205.

———. *Petro-Aggression: When Oil Causes War*. Cambridge, UK: Cambridge University Press, 2013.

Corrales, Javier. *Dragon in the Tropics: Venezuela and the Legacy of Hugo Chavez* (second edition). Washington, DC: Brookings Institution Press, 2015.

Dowden, Richard. *Africa: Dancing on the Brink*. New York: PublicAffairs, 2009.

Ellner, Steve, and Daniel Hellinger, eds. *Venezuelan Politics in the Chavez Era: Class, Polarization, and Conflict*. Boulder, CO: Lynne Rienner, 2007.

Falola, Toyin, and Matthew M. Heaton. *A History of Nigeria*. Cambridge, UK: Cambridge University Press, 2008.

Friedman, Thomas L. "The First Law of Petropolitics." *Foreign Policy*, May/June 2006, 36–44.

Kendhammer, Brandon. "Nigeria's New Democratic Dawn?" *Current History* 114, no. 772 (May 2015), 170–76.

Gallagos, Raul. *Crude Nation: How Oil Riches Ruined Venezuela*. Washington, DC: Potomac Books, 2016.

Hausman, Ricardo, and Francisco Rodriguez. *Venezuela Before Change: Anatomy of and Economic Collapse*. State College, PA: Pennsylvania State University Press, 2015.

Klare, Michael T. "The Desperate Plight of the Petro-States." *The Blog* (HuffPost), December 6, 2017.

Lavinder, Kaitlin. "Niger Delta Militants Compound Nigeria's Security Crisis." *The Cipher Brief* (Council on Foreign Affairs online), August 4, 2016.

McCoy, Jennifer L., and David J. Myers, eds. *The Unravelling of Representative Democracy in Venezuela*. Baltimore, MD: Johns Hopkins University Press, 2007.

Meagher, Kate. "The Jobs Crisis Behind Nigeria's Unrest." *Current History* 112, no .754 (May 2013), 169–74.

Mora, Frank O. "What Military Intervention in Venezuela Would Look Like: Getting in Would Be the Easy Part." *Foreign Affairs Snapshot* (online), March 19, 2019.

Page, Matthew. "Instead of Cutting Waste, Nigeria Racks Up Debt to Replace Oil Revenues." *The Cipher Brief* (Council on Foreign Relations online), March 38, 2016.

Sabatini, Christopher. "Trump's Flawed Plan to Oust Maduro." *Foreign Affairs Snapshot* (online), March 21, 2019.

Smith, Mike. *Boko Haram: Inside Nigeria's Unholy War*. London: I.B. Tauris, 2016.

Snow, Donald M. *Cases in International Relations* (fourth edition). New York: Longman, 2010.

———. *Regional Cases in Foreign Policy* (second edition). Lanham, MD: Rowman & Littlefield, 2018.

Stronen, Iselin Asedotter. *Grassroot Politics and Oil Culture in Venezuela: The Revolutionary Petro-State*. London: Palgrave Macmillan, 2017.
U.S. Department of State. "U.S. Relations with Nigeria." Washington, DC: U.S. Department of State Bureau of African Affairs, June 20, 2016.
Wilpert, Gregory. *Changing Venezuela by Taking Power: The History and Politics of the Chavez Government*. New York: Verso, 2008.

PART II

Issues and Problems

10

Nuclear Proliferation

The Contrasting Lessons of North Korea and Iran

Avoiding the spread of nuclear weapons to countries that do not currently possess them has been a global problem since the United States exploded the first nuclear device in 1945. This priority arises from two sources: the enormous destructive power of the weapons and the fear that *someone else* in possession of these weapons might use them against you. Proliferation first occurred when the Soviet Union exploded a nuclear bomb in 1949. Despite efforts by the growing nuclear "club" of weapons possessors, proliferation has continued to the present. The argument for avoiding proliferation is that those states seeking the capability are less stable than current possessors and thus more likely to start a nuclear war.

The current concern focuses on two states that have or may become nuclear possessors: North Korea and Iran. North Korea is the most recent failure of proliferation and the world's ninth acknowledged nuclear power. Iran is a potential nuclear state that has not yet developed or deployed nuclear weapons. Keeping Iran nonnuclear is the current focus of nonproliferation efforts.

Dealing with the spread of nuclear weapons has been a concern since the late 1940s. The post–World War II concern with the spread of nuclear weapons reached a crescendo with the negotiation of the nuclear Non-Proliferation Treaty (NPT) of 1968. The NPT prohibited additional states that did not already have nuclear weapons from acquiring (or trying to acquire) them. It also required current possessors not to aid in the spread of nuclear weapons and made them promise to reduce and eliminate their own arsenals.

Concern about proliferation has ebbed and flowed. When the membership in the nuclear "club" (the countries that possess the weapons) was very small during the 1950s and 1960s, there was great concern that many countries would acquire them, and nuclear proliferation thought was developed to deal with that contingency. During the 1970s and 1980s, concern became more muted, both because the number of nuclear weapons states did not grow perceptibly, and because of concern with other matters, notably the end of the Cold War. Interest in proliferation returned after the turn of the millennium. It has been tied closely to the problem of international terrorism, because of the fear that terrorists might acquire and use nuclear weapons.

The current concern with weapons of mass destruction (WMDs) has two basic sources. The first worry is over the countries that might acquire such weapons, and it focuses currently on the Democratic People's Republic of Korea (DPRK, or North Korea) and Iran. The second source of concern is the various types of WMDs that might be acquired. Ultimately, the WMDs that most matter are nuclear weapons because of their enormous destructive capacity, but other forms such as biological and chemical weapons are of importance as well, as the Syrian crises of 2013 and 2017 have demonstrated.

Principle: Nuclear Proliferation

Proliferation is a delicate problem, largely because its underlying aim is both discriminatory and condescending to those at whom it is aimed. The desire to limit possession of nuclear weapons largely comes from countries that already possess those weapons and is aimed at those who do not. Thus, the strongest current efforts to reverse the DPRK's program come from countries like the United States, Britain, and China. The possessors' implication is clear: we are responsible enough to have these weapons; you are not.

The delicacy of the situation thus arises from rationalizing why it is all right for some states to have nuclear weapons when others should not. The assertions and arguments are inherently discriminatory and condescending, and the question that must be answered is, why some but not others? Invariably, the answer comes back to the assumption regarding responsibility.

The proliferation problem is structurally complex. To understand it, one can look at three questions: What is the nature of the problem? Why is it a problem? And what can be done about it? The answers collectively form the context for analyzing the case applications to North Korea and Iran.

The Nature of the Proliferation Problem

The roots of the contemporary proliferation problem lie in the Cold War fear of nuclear war. The major purposes were to prevent the spread of nuclear weapons to states that did not have them, and to limit the size and destructiveness of the arsenals of possessing states. These two intents were related. In addition, there was concern about the destabilizing impact of burgeoning nuclear possession, which in turn spawned two additional concerns. One was about the kind of capability that countries were attempting to proliferate (what forms of WMD), and the other was the mechanics of how proliferation could occur and thus what steps had to be taken to prevent it from happening.

There are two basic forms of proliferation: vertical and horizontal. *Vertical proliferation* refers to the impact of additional weapons a nuclear state may gain. It is a concern both because additional increments add to the potential deadliness of confrontations and because those increments can spawn arms races in which additions by one side cause the other to build more, resulting in a potentially destabilizing arms spiral. Efforts to control vertical proliferation generally aim at curbing or reducing current levels of arms and are the traditional object of arms control. Most of the nuclear arms treaties negotiated by the United States and the Soviet Union during the Cold War (such as the Strategic Arms Limitations Talks and the Strategic Arms Reduction Talks) were attempts to limit vertical proliferation. Contemporary proliferation efforts center on ***horizontal proliferation***: the spread of nuclear weapons to states that currently do not possess them; generally, when the term ***proliferation*** is used, it is in reference to horizontal proliferation. Both kinds of proliferation efforts can be and are aimed at other weapons capabilities such as so-called nuclear, biological, and chemical weaponry. This chapter focuses on nuclear weapons.

How to produce and avoid the production of these capabilities have been matters of major concern, centering particularly on nuclear weapons and ways to get them to target. The problem of nuclear weapons production is straightforward and has two components. The first is the knowledge of how to fabricate a nuclear device. Nuclear physics has been taught openly for over sixty years now in the world's (and notably American) universities, so that knowledge is widely available both to most governments and undoubtedly to many private groups. The knowledge genie is clearly out of the bottle. The other requirement for building nuclear weapons is possession of adequate supplies of weapons-grade (i.e., highly enriched) isotopes of uranium/plutonium, which generally are byproducts of nuclear reactions in certain types of power generators. Access to such materials is highly guarded and restricted, and aspirants to nuclear weapons must either possess nuclear reactors that produce weapons-grade materials or be able to purchase or steal such material from those who possess it. Nonproliferation efforts have been concentrated on denying access to weapons-grade material to potential proliferators. The other aspect of nuclear proliferation surrounds the ability to deliver those weapons to targets—specifically to targets in the United States and other Western countries. Analyses focus on the ability of nuclear pretenders to build or buy ballistic missiles to deliver these weapons. The question of ballistic delivery systems has been a serious problem in dealing with the DPRK.

The Problem Proliferation Poses

The short answer to why proliferation is a problem is that one has much less to fear from a weapons capability that one's actual or potential adversaries do not possess than from a capability that they do possess. In classic Cold War thinking about nuclear proliferation, the problem was how to keep additional sovereign states from achieving nuclear capability. The more additional countries obtained the weapons, the more "fingers" there would be on the nuclear "button," and thus as a matter of probability, the more likely someone would push the button and start a nuclear war. That problem has been augmented by the fear that some of the potential proliferating states might share their capabilities with terrorist nonstate actors.

In classic terms, the problem of the spread of nuclear weapons to nonpossessors is known as the *N+1* problem. The idea is straightforward. In the formulation, *N* stands for the number of states that currently possess nuclear weapons and refers to the dynamics among them. *+1*, on the other hand, refers to the added problems that would be created for the international system (notably the states that form *N*) by the addition of new (*+1*) states to the nuclear club.

Current members (*N*) and potential proliferators (+*1*) see the problem essentially from opposite ends of the conceptual spectrum. The current members generally believe that the current "club" represents a stable, reliable membership. Viewed this way, the emphasis of the club is on the problems created by new members, and the criterion for concern is the likelihood of destabilization created by new members. Members of *N* tend to look for and find sources of destabilization that should be opposed and want to restrict membership to existing levels.

Members of +*1*, however, see the problem differently. Nonmembers do not see their own acquisition of nuclear weapons as destabilizing and are righteously indignant at the notion that their acquisition would destabilize the system. The accusation by "club" members is a backhanded way of suggesting that new members would be less responsible possessors than those who already have the weapons. Put more bluntly, the imputation that a new state would destabilize amounts to accusing such a state of a greater likelihood of starting a nuclear war than those who already have them and have refrained from doing so.

Indeed, in the current context, nonpossessors are more likely to make the argument that their membership in the nuclear club will stabilize their situations and even global politics generally, because it is a fact that no state that possesses nuclear weapons has ever been the victim of a nuclear aggression against it. Indeed, one of the arguments that both the Iranians and North Koreans (among others) have made in recent years is that gaining nuclear weapons capability is a useful—even necessary—means to avoid being attacked by an aggressive United States. Would, for instance, the United States have attacked Iraq had it possessed, rather than being accused of trying to get, nuclear weapons? Some nonpossessing countries argue the American attack would have been less likely and that Saddam Hussein's major error was in not getting a nuclear capability that might have deterred the United States from invading the country. Some even argue that had he not abandoned his nuclear weapons program, he might still be alive and in power.

There is a further *N*+*1* problem irony—it is generally viewed as a problem only by the current nuclear club. Ironically, a country that aspires to become a member (a +*1* country) may be viewed as a problem before it gets the capability, but once it has done so and has demonstrated its "responsible possession" of the capability, it becomes part of the club and views other aspirants as part of the problem.

The nuclear problem is qualitatively worse when there are more nuclear powers, but one obstacle to sustaining international momentum behind proliferation control has been that it has not occurred at the pace envisioned by those who most feared the prospects. The nuclear club was largely established by 1964, when China obtained nuclear weapons and pushed the number to five—in order of acquisition: United States, the Soviet Union, Great Britain, France, and China. Since the 1960s, five states have gained nuclear capability. One state (Israel) does not formally admit it has the weapons (it also does not deny it), one state obtained and then renounced and destroyed its weapons (South Africa), two countries openly joined the club in 1998 (India and Pakistan), and North Korea exploded a nuclear device in 2006. The total number of currently acknowledged nuclear states thus stands at nine.

Solving or Containing the Problem

Because the roots of thinking about the control of nuclear weapons have their origins in the Cold War, so too does thinking about how to prevent proliferation. The key concept in dealing with nuclear weapons in the Cold War context was deterrence, and that concept dominates historic and contemporary discussions of proliferation as well.

The problem of deterrence changed with the end of the Cold War system. In the past, nuclear deterrence was between states with very large arsenals of nuclear weapons—principally the United States and the Soviet Union. The dynamic of deterrence, captured in the idea of assured destruction, was that any nuclear attack against a nuclear-armed superpower would be suicidal, because the attacked state would retain such devastating capabilities even after absorbing an attack as to be able to retaliate against the attacker and destroy it, making any "victory" decidedly Pyrrhic (costing far more than it was worth). Because potential attackers were presumably rational (or at least not suicidal), the prospects of a counterattack that would certainly immolate them was enough to dissuade (or deter) an attack in the first place.

The Contemporary Problem of Proliferation

The proliferation problem has changed in two important respects. First, nuclear arsenals and policies have changed. All the major weapons states still maintain nuclear arsenals, but they are smaller than they used to be. The primary Cold War antagonists, the United States and the Soviet Union/Russia, had arsenals of weapons capable of reaching the other's territory of 10,000 to 12,000 warheads; the number today is closer to 7,000. China, the rising nuclear power, is moving toward a similar arsenal size. Second, and more important in the current context, the threats in the contemporary environment come from states that will, at best, have a small number of nuclear weapons at their disposal but may not be dissuaded by Cold War threats. Thus, as Joseph Pilat puts it, "There are real questions about whether old, Cold War–vintage concepts . . . really address the needs of today." The question is what replaces those concepts.

In a text published originally in 1996, Eugene Brown and I laid out a framework for categorizing mechanisms that could be used to deter unwanted nuclear behavior. Within this framework, arms proliferation can be dealt with in two ways, acquisition (or front-end) and employment (or back-end) deterrence. Acquisition deterrence consists of efforts to keep states from obtaining nuclear weapons in the first place. The effort consists of related activities. Persuasion, or convincing states that gaining nuclear weapons is not in their best interests (often accompanied by the promise of related rewards for nonproliferation or punitive threats if compliance does not occur), seeks to convince possible proliferating states into not doing so. Successful multilateral efforts through the United Nations and under the NPT to dissuade Iran from making a positive nuclear weapons decision fall into this category. If persuasion does not work, then coercion (threatening or taking punitive—including military—action to prevent proliferation) may occur. Attacks by Israel against an Iraqi nuclear reactor in 1981 and more recently against Syria are extreme examples of coercive options.

The current focus on proliferation has become the spread of nuclear weapons to countries—and especially unstable countries—in the developing world. The stalking horses were Israel and South Africa, both of which conducted highly clandestine weapons development programs that led to their acquisition of nuclear capability. Both countries developed their programs outside the Cold War context: Israel because of its fear its Islamic neighbors might destroy it; South Africa because of the alleged threat posed by neighboring black states (the so-called frontline states). When South Africa dismantled its apartheid system, it also destroyed its nuclear weapons. Israel continues to maintain, and even to expand, its nuclear arsenal, which it argues is necessary to protect its existence in a world of predatory enemies.

The other form of dissuasion is employment deterrence. If efforts to keep states from gaining nuclear weapons fail, then one must turn to efforts to keep them from using the weapons they do acquire. Once again, there are two mechanisms that can be employed. One is the conventional nuclear threat of retaliation. The threat is to retaliate with such devastating—including assured destruction—force that it would not only be suicidal for an attacking state to use its weapons, but the suicide would not necessarily be mutual. Thus, the horror scenario of a possible future North Korean attack against the United States might consist of lobbing a handful of weapons against American targets and inflicting severe but not fatal damage; North Korea would be destroyed in the U.S. retaliation. The other form of employment deterrence threat is denial, the promise that if an attack is launched, it will fail because the potential attacked state has the capability to defend itself from an attack.

The major mechanism by which nonproliferation has been enforced is the NPT. The NPT was negotiated in 1968 and went into effect in 1970. Most countries of the world are or have been members of the regime—Iran and North Korea, for instance—and the question is whether the treaty will remain a viable means to avoid more proliferation in the future.

The Iranian and DPRK cases illustrate both strategies. Iran remains a case of successful acquisition deterrence, whereas the failure to dissuade North Korea into abstaining makes dealing with the DPRK an employment deterrence exercise. The two are related in that the reasons for failing to dissuade the North Koreans may be instructive in how to deal with Iran.

The nonproliferation enterprise remains a work in progress. Since the NPT was launched nearly a half-century ago, there has been little overt nuclear weapons proliferation. Yet proliferation has emerged in the post–September 11 world as a major concern, fueled by the fear some rogue state might acquire such weapons and either use them personally or through some terrorist surrogate. This possibility fuels international concern. North Korea and Iran are the two states about which proliferation fears are arguably the greatest.

Application: North Korea and Iran

The problem of proliferation gains meaning in the specific context of individual states that might or that are suspected of attempting to exercise the nuclear weapons option. North Korea has physically gone several steps through the proliferation process and is a growing nuclear power. It is the only country physically to withdraw from the NPT (in 2003). It is also the only new member of the nuclear club that has conducted nuclear weapons tests since India and Pakistan. Its testing program dates to 2003, and since Kim Jong-un succeeded his father in 2011, the program has accelerated quantitatively and qualitatively. DPRK weapons testing has become progressively aggressive, especially in the mid-2010s, and the North Koreans possess a small arsenal, some of which is wedded to missile launchers. It is also testing missiles capable of delivering a nuclear weapon over an intercontinental range. Estimates vary about when it may achieve that status. Its efforts date back to 1959.

The other state mentioned prominently in proliferation concerns is Iran. Its situation resembles but is distinct from the DPRK's. First, it shares significant foreign policy differences with the United States (although of a different nature and for different reasons than the DPRK). Second, Iran possesses the technology and expertise to produce nuclear weapons and could reasonably easily gain access to the weapons-grade plutonium. Third, Iran denies any interest or desire to build, and especially to use, nuclear weapons. These claims are widely disbelieved in some policy circles, especially in the United States and Israel. Fourth, Iran is a member of the NPT, but it has been deemed to be an untrustworthy, rogue regime whose word cannot be taken at face value in the eyes of prominent political elements in the United States.

Background of the DPRK Problem

North Korea's successful drive to become a consequential nuclear weapons state is the major face of the proliferation problem today, as it has been for a decade or more. The major protagonists have been the United States and North Korea, and in some ways, it is the latest manifestation of a long conflict between the two countries that dates to the Korean War of 1950 to 1953. The DPRK nuclear weapons program is normally dated back to the late 1950s, when a nuclear-armed United States remained the occupying power in South Korea and had nuclear weapons deployed in South Korea to deter another DPRK invasion.

The long-standing animosity between the DPRK and the United States combines with the advanced status of the DPRK program to give it special relevance for the United States, and the strategic location of the DPRK in East Asia adds to the poignancy of the problem, because major East Asian powers and the balance between them are also affected.

The Nature of the North Korean Threat

The North Korean problem has been episodic, at various times in the process of being resolved through negotiation and then flaring up. After several years of off-again, on-again negotiations between the DPRK and the other countries involved in the so-called six-party talks (the United States, Russia, China, Japan, and North and South Korea), a breakthrough occurred in summer 2003 that would have resulted in North Korean disassembly of nuclear facilities capable of producing bomb-grade plutonium, destruction of nuclear bomb materials, and re-accession to the NPT. In return, the DPRK was to be removed from the U.S. State Department's list of terrorist states and the Axis of Evil, and some provisions of the American Trading with the Enemy Act pertinent to the DPRK were lifted.

The rift between Pyongyang and Washington combines proliferation with other concerns. DPRK recalcitrance about its weapons programs is almost certainly motivated partly by American military presence on the peninsula and the fear of absorption by the Republic of Korea in the south as well as a symbiotic relationship with China, which supports the DPRK as a buffer against having a hostile power on its borders. North Korea is one of the most destitute countries on the globe, relies heavily on Chinese assistance to maintain its meager standard of living, and is almost totally ignorable and inconsequential except for its possession of nuclear weapons. As Lankov notes, the nuclear program serves to ameliorate some of the country's woes: "Pyongyang cannot do away with these programs. That would mean losing a powerful military deterrent and a time-tested tool of extortion. It would also relegate North Korea to being a third-rate country, on a par with Mozambique or Uganda."

The history of the North Korean nuclear program—and concerns about it—is long standing and largely framed in terms of U.S.–North Korean relations. The United States and the DPRK have, of course, been antagonists since the 1950s. Aside from the general antagonism this confrontation created, it may have provided the impetus for North Korean nuclear pretensions. As Robert Norris put it in his 2003 *Bulletin of the Atomic Scientists* article, "The fact that North Korea was threatened with nuclear weapons during the Korean War, and that for decades thereafter U.S. weapons were deployed in the South, may have helped motivate former President Kim Il Sung to launch a nuclear weapons program of his own."

The genesis of the ongoing crisis goes back to the Clinton administration. A May 1992 inspection of North Korean nuclear facilities by International Atomic Energy Agency inspectors headed by Hans Blix concluded the North Koreans might be engaged in weapons activity (converting spent nuclear fuel into weapons-grade plutonium). This precipitated a crisis in which the North Koreans threatened the until-then unprecedented step of withdrawing from the NPT in March 1993 (they had joined the treaty in 1984). At this point the Clinton administration intervened, entering into direct talks that produced a negotiated settlement, the Framework Agreement. The North Koreans agreed to freeze and eventually to dismantle their nuclear weapons program under International Atomic Energy Agency supervision. In turn, North Korea would accept light water nuclear reactors to replace those capable of producing weapons-grade materials. The basic policy survived until the George W. Bush administration.

The current, ongoing crisis was precipitated when the Bush administration cut off the flow of heating oil to North Korea and terminated the Framework Agreement in December 2002. The DPRK responded by announcing on January 10, 2003, that it was withdrawing from the NPT, which it did after the mandatory ninety-day waiting period following the announcement of intent. Saber rattling on both sides followed in the ensuing months, and the short-lived six-party negotiations opened on August 28, 2003, at which point North Korea announced it was prepared "to declare itself formally as a nuclear weapons state" (which it did in December 2006).

The breakdown of the six-party talks largely extinguished formal proliferation negotiations with the North Koreans. The acknowledgment that the DPRK has produced and possesses nuclear weapons and that missile development efforts are under way effectively removed the issue from the realm of acquisition deterrence, which had failed. As such, the DPRK is no longer a nonproliferation issue, and it cannot become one again until (or unless) the North Koreans decide to dismantle the forces and to reenter the NPT regime (the "denuclearization" goal of the Trump administration). Despite the summit meetings between Trump and Kim in 2018 and 2019, the prospects of their doing so under the rule of the mercurial Kim Jong-un are not, to put it mildly, encouraging. This means that the problem conceptually has become a matter of keeping them from using those weapons (employment deterrence).

In this light, one is left with what to make of the North Korean nuclear "threat." Given that the North Koreans are nuclear-capable, the question is what would keep them from using their weapons? It is difficult to conjure reasons why North Korea would launch an offensive, preemptive nuclear strike against anyone, given the certain response would be its own utter and certain destruction. Despite this reality, the DPRK leader continues to threaten a nuclear strike against the United States that would have the effect of destroying his country. The threat is less nonsensical if North Korea truly believes they help deter the United States from attacking the DPRK. The idea that the United States needs to be deterred may seem outlandish to most Americans, but not to the North Koreans. As Cumings puts it, "it seems irrational for Pyongyang to give up its handful of nukes when the United States still threatens to attack."

The 800-pound gorilla in all calculations is how to get the North Koreans to change their nuclear weapons policy and belligerency. Because they view their program as a source of prestige and standing in their region and the world as well as a deterrent against predators like the United States, the regime is unlikely to disarm voluntarily. It is generally conceded that China is the key actor in influencing the DPRK. The People's Republic of China joins North Korea as the only remaining communist states in the region, the longest land border the DPRK has with any country is with China, the People's Republic of China is overwhelmingly the largest trading partner and broker of the DPRK, and according to Shirk, "some 85 percent" of North Korean trade "goes to or through" China. In addition, many North Koreans commute to factories on the Chinese side of the frontier to augment their meager existences, and China provides the DPRK with a large amount of foreign assistance without which existence in the Hermit Kingdom would be even grimmer than it is. Despite these sources of leverage, however, the Chinese have not been major contributors to reining in their neighbors. China has the levers to induce North Korea to negotiate its program. As Cha (2017) puts it, "China's diplomatic pique is likely to be part of any successful attempt to get North Korea back to the denuclearization negotiating table."

China does not support the DPRK nuclear program, but it does support what it views as the need for an independent North Korea, for which that program is the major prop. Without nuclear weapons, the peninsular debate would quickly return to reunification, which had support in the early 2000s. From the Chinese vantage point, a unified Korea would be dominated by the Westernized, democratic South Koreans (much as the West Germans have dominated Germany since reunification), and this raises the specter of a potentially hostile country on China's border. That prospect propelled China into the Korean War in 1951, and it is a prospect they feel would violate their basic national interest. For that reason alone, they have been reluctant to pressure Kim Jong-un hard enough to force a sea change in the DPRK nuclear weapons program, which is its chief claim to fame.

The Iranian Contrast

The other state that is prominently mentioned in proliferation discussions is Iran. Like North Korea, Iran is a politically controversial place and has, since 1979, been at major odds with the United States. In 2002, then President George W. Bush included both countries (as well as Iraq) on his "Axis of Evil" list. One of the bases of that list has been that each of those countries at one time or another had nuclear programs with weapons potential. The DPRK obviously fulfilled that ambition; Iran and Iraq have not.

Whether Iran has (or has had) proliferation ambitions is a matter of disagreement. The Iranians have consistently denied that their nuclear program has any pretensions of gaining weapons status, but other countries, led by the United States and Israel, have voiced great skepticism about those claims. The American suspicion is part of the aftermath of the Iranian Revolution of 1979, which overthrew the American-backed Shah, captured the U.S. embassy in Tehran and held its personnel hostage for 444 days, and declared a fundamentalist Islamic Republic of Iran, the chief enemy of which was the "Great Satan" (the United States). The two countries have not had formal relations since. Any Iraqi pretensions were ended by the U.S. invasion and conquest of 2003, part of the rationale for which was destroying Iraq's WMDs, including the nuclear program—which the invaders never demonstrated existed.

The main contrast in the two experiences is that Iran signed an agreement in 2015 with the 5+1 powers (the permanent members of the UN Security Council plus Germany) in which it abjured any right to build nuclear weapons and agreed to international inspection of its nuclear facilities. This agreement has been denounced by Israel and some Americans, led by President Trump, who do not trust the Iranians, do not believe they have honored or will honor their bargain, and rescinded American participation in it in 2018. Nonetheless, it remains in force, and there have been no major demonstrated instances of Iran violating its provisions. Even when the United States dropped out of the agreement, it remained in force due to the continued participation of the other parties. If nothing else, the agreement does demonstrate it is possible successfully to engage in proliferation control efforts: North Korea has been a negative precedent for the future, but it is at least partly countermanded by Iran's restraint.

Iran is still an acquisition deterrence problem, in contrast to the DPRK. The Iranians have not reneged on their nonproliferation agreement despite the withdrawal of the Americans from the Joint Comprehensive Plan of Action and strangling American sanctions against them. The Iranian government has never wavered on its commitment to nonproliferation, American concerns about Tehran's sincerity and honesty notwithstanding. What would make them change their minds?

Proliferation has often occurred when a country feels threatened by a nuclear-armed rival and develops nuclear weapons to deter that rival. This dynamic was evident in the Cold War and in Indian and Pakistani proliferation. The same condition affects Iran, which faces an antagonistic nuclear-armed Israel and is part of the bloody advocacy of a Palestinian state, thereby confronting it with the Israelis. If the United States (and others) truly want to "disincentivize" any change in Iranian commitment not to "go nuclear," this may be a priority the opponents of proliferation should put more publicly on the table.

Conclusion

Is the North Korean case study or its Iranian counterpart the potential harbinger for other proliferation cases? The DPRK has defied the proliferation regime and gotten away with it, but its nuclear program had enough momentum and resolve to allow it to maintain control of its nuclear fate in a regional situation that did not force a negative decision on them. The DPRK case demonstrates that if a state is determined enough to "go nuclear," international restraints like the NPT may not be robust enough to stop them. Israel is another example of this dynamic.

No one, except potential proliferating countries that are part of *+1*, argue that the spread of nuclear and other WMDs to nonpossessing states is in principle a good idea that should be encouraged. On the other hand, the empirical evidence of the impact of individual proliferations (when individual countries joined the nuclear weapons "club") hardly provides incontrovertible proof of the dire perils that have been predicted. What is the evidence, for instance, that the world is a less stable place because Israel, India, or Pakistan possesses the bomb? One can contend it would be better if they did not, but the peril remains theoretical, not demonstrated. Is the DPRK qualitatively different?

How should future potential proliferators like Iran view the scene? Should they conclude that their attempts to attain nuclear weapons status will be viewed as internationally dangerous and destabilizing enough to prompt an international response that will reduce their security if they do not eschew proliferation? Or will they decide a positive nuclear weapons decision will protect them—provide them a deterrent—from attacks by predators, thereby increasing their security?

Nuclear-possessing states have one answer to that question, but recent experience may offer a different interpretation to nonpossessors. Some ask themselves if Saddam Hussein would have been immune from an American invasion had he not stopped pursuing nuclear weapons, and many answer "yes" and believe he made the wrong choice. At a minimum, recent experience does not unambiguously warn potential proliferators not to pursue the nuclear option. Who might be next to follow the DPRK rather than the Iranian precedent? It is an open question.

Study/Discussion Questions

1. What is proliferation? What forms does it take? How do these relate to types of nonproliferation effort? Explain.
2. What is the *N+1* problem? Define it and explain why it illustrates the delicacy of the proliferation problem. Why is it so difficult to resolve?
3. What means are available to deal with proliferation? Distinguish between acquisition and employment deterrence. How does each work?
4. Discuss the evolution of nuclear proliferation. How has it changed over time?
5. Compare and contrast the DPRK and Iran as proliferation problems. How are they similar and different from one another? Elaborate.
6. Why did the DPRK reject nonproliferation? Why is being a nuclear weapons state important to them? What is the likelihood they will "denuclearize"?
7. What is the Iranian position and physical commitment on nuclear weapons possession? Why could Israel provide an incentive for them to change their posture?
8. If you were representing a country contemplating getting nuclear weapons but in an adversarial relationship with the United States, how would that fact affect your decision? Refer to the DPRK and Iran precedents.

Bibliography

Amanat, Abbas. *Iran: A Modern History*. New Haven, CT: Yale University Press, 2017.

Axelworthy, Michael. *A History of Iran: Empire of the Mind*. New York: Basic Books, 2016.

Bluth, Christoph. "North Korea: How Will It End?" *Current History* 109, no. 728 (September 2010), 237–43.

Cha, Victor. "Making China Pay on North Korea: Why Beijing's Coal Ban Isn't Enough." *Foreign Affairs Snapshot* (online), March 21, 2017.

Cha, Victor D., and David C. Kang. *Nuclear North Korea: A Debate on Engagement Strategies*. New York: Columbia University Press, 2008.

Cohen, Michael D. *When Proliferation Causes Peace: The Psychology of Nuclear Crises*. Washington, DC: Georgetown University Press, 2017.

Cumings, Bruce. "The North Korea Problem: Dealing with Irrationality." *Current History* 108, no. 719 (September 2009), 284–90.

Debs, Alexandre, and Numo P. Mantiero. *Nuclear Politics: The Strategic Causes of Proliferation* (Cambridge Studies in International Relations). Cambridge, UK: Cambridge University Press, 2017.

Delury, John. "Trump and North Korea: Reviving the Art of the Deal." *Foreign Affairs* 96, no. 2 (March/April 2017), 46–51.

Haynes, Susan Turner. *Chinese Nuclear Proliferation: How Global Politics Is Transforming China's Weapons Buildup and Modernization.* Washington, DC: Potomac Books, 2016.

Kim, Sung Chull, and Michael D. Cohen. *North Korea and Nuclear Weapons: Entering the New Era of Deterrence.* Washington, DC: Georgetown University Press, 2017.

Lankov, Andrei. "Changing North Korea." *Foreign Affairs* 88, no. 6 (November–December 2009), 95–105.

Mendelsohn, Jack. "The New Threats: Nuclear Amnesia, Nuclear Legitimacy." *Current History* 105, no. 694 (November 2006), 385–90.

The National Security Strategy of the United States of America. Washington, DC: The White House, March 2006.

Norris, Robert S. "North Korea's Nuclear Program, 2003." *Bulletin of the Atomic Scientists* 59, no. 2 (March/April 2003), 74–77.

Oberdorfer, Don, and Robert Carlin. *The Two Koreas: A Contemporary History* (third edition). New York: Basic Books, 2014.

O'Reilly, Kelly P. *Nuclear Weapons and the Psychology of Political Leadership: Beliefs, Motivations, and Perceptions.* New York and London: Routledge, 2016.

Perkowich, George. "The End of the Proliferation Regime." *Current History* 105, no. 694 (November 2006), 355–62.

Pilat, Joseph F., Nathan E. Busch, et al. *Routledge Handbook of Nuclear Proliferation Policy.* New York and London: Routledge, 2015.

Ratcliff, Jonathan E. B. *Nuclear Proliferation: Overview, History, and Reference Guide.* New York: CreateSpace Independent Publishing Platform, 2016.

Sagan, Scott, and Kenneth N. *Waltz. The Spread of Nuclear Weapons: An Enduring Debate.* New York: W. W. Norton, 2012.

Seth, Michael J. *North Korea: A History.* London: Red Globe Press, 2018.

Shirk, Susan. "Trump and China: Getting to Yes with Beijing." *Foreign Affairs* 96, no. 2 (March/April 2017), 20–27.

Snow, Donald M. *Regional Cases in Foreign Policy* (second edition). Lanham, MD: Rowman & Littlefield, 2018.

——— and Eugene Brown. *The Contours of Power: An Introduction to Contemporary International Relations.* New York: St. Martin's Press, 1996.

Solingen, Etel, ed. *Sanctions, Statecraft, and Nuclear Proliferation.* Cambridge, UK: Cambridge University Press, 2012.

Wit, Joel S., Daniel Poneman, and Robert Gallucci. *Going Critical: The First North Korean Nuclear Crisis.* Washington, DC: Brookings Institution Press, 2004.

11

Globalization, Protectionism, and Trade

The Cases of the European Union and NAFTA/USMCA

The exchange of goods and services among people and political units is as old as human interaction generally. It has evolved into a main emphasis of economics and internal and international politics. Economic protectionism and globalization have been the competing philosophies in the debate about economic international relations. After the end of the Cold War, free trade under the banner of globalization became the reigning concept in the debate about policy. More recently, protectionism has reappeared on the horizon. Trade, the most prominent current indicator of international economic relations, has clear economic consequences, but it also has political impacts. Economic issues are often exaggerated and politicized by both champions and opponents, which has arguably been the case in contemporary discussions.

Events such as the global economic recession of 2008 and growing European concerns over aspects of the European Union have dampened international enthusiasm over free trade. The North American Free Trade Agreement (NAFTA), which came into force in 1994, has been a focal point of free trade criticism, especially since the 2016 election of Donald J. Trump as president of the United States, and he has proposed replacement by the United States-Mexico-Canada Agreement (USMCA), an indication of the contemporary policy retreat of globalization.

The modern issue of trade probably congealed over whether to import goods and services that were also produced domestically, especially if foreign goods were cheaper and of comparable or better quality. That question is near the top of the agenda in contemporary discussions of trade and is manifested in most disagreements on the subject, from questions of barriers to trade to environmental impacts of importation versus domestic production. Since the economic downturn of 2008, the contribution of trade to prosperity has been a point of concern, particularly in areas such as employment and fairness of competition in the United States and elsewhere. Both were major themes of the Trump campaign and have carried over into his presidency. The European Union and NAFTA/USMCA, featured in the application section of this chapter, have been lightning rods in this debate.

Whether to allow the unfettered movement of goods and services internationally (free trade) or to place restrictions of one kind or another on that flow is a central element in contemporary international relations. The removal of barriers to trade was the centerpiece of the economic globalization movement of the 1990s, one of the engines designed to draw countries into closer collaboration by entwining them in the global prosperity of that decade. The global economic downturn at the turn of the millennium and the rise of the global war on terror took some of the luster from the free trade issue and relegated it to a less prominent place on the international political agenda.

Principle: Globalization and Terms of Trade

The basic poles in the free trade debate have been between those seeking to expand trade (free traders) and those seeking to restrict trade (protectionists). Nestled between the extremes are those who advocate freer, but not necessarily totally free, trade (who often portray themselves as fair traders). All three emphases are vibrant parts of contemporary arguments.

The debates tend to be emotional and hyperbolic. A major conjunction in the emotional side of the debate is between trade practices and jobs, a clearly critical concern for almost everyone. From both economic and political perspectives, a key question is whether policies promoting one or another trading philosophy create, destroy, or have no effect on employment generally or on individual categories of jobs. The result is to add a clearly emotional element to the debate that will be exploited by partisans on all sides of the issue. There is some concern that some philosophies may affect groups differently—creating greater wealth inequalities, for instance.

Trade Advocacies

The economic aspect of the trade debate has been, and is, asymmetrical, and proponents on one side or the other tend to talk past one another, meaning interchange often devolves into monologues. The arguments promoting free and expanded trade tend to be mainly abstract, impersonal, and macroeconomic. Free trade is advocated because it unleashes basic economic principles like comparative advantage that make overall economies (national or international) stronger and economic conditions within and between countries more vital and prosperous. Advocates maintain that arrangements promoting trade have had a net positive impact on the global economy, and because they expand production, they promote closer, friendlier relations between the participants. Additionally, they intertwine the economies of trade partners in ways that make conflict between them impractical and self-destructive.

Anti–free trade arguments, on the other hand, tend to be specific, personal, and microeconomic. Cries to restrict trade tend to be posed in terms of the adverse impact that expanding trade opportunities has on individuals, groups, industrial sectors, and even geographical regions within countries. Trade is not about economic theories; rather, it is about people's jobs and livelihoods. Thus, opponents emphasize things like jobs lost by individuals in individual industries to make their points.

Fair trade is a third alternative. Fair traders seek a compromise somewhere between the extremes, advocating selective trade reductions in conformance with the principle of free trade but seeking to minimize negative microeconomic impact. Frequently, fair traders emphasize the need for compensatory actions for those individuals adversely affected by what they basically see as the beneficial impacts from free trade. They also oppose actions by trade partners that artificially inflate their competitive advantage at the expense of others.

The debate is intensely political at both the domestic and international levels. Within American national politics, the asymmetry is often reflected between branches of the federal government. Historically, the executive branch of government, more concerned with the overall health of the economy and somewhat more removed from the impact on specific individuals or groups (as opposed to the whole country), tends to be more free trade–oriented and macroeconomic. Members of Congress, whose constituents are the people whose jobs are endangered when foreign goods and services enter the country more freely, tend to be more microeconomically oriented.

At the international level, the debate tends to get intermingled with preferences for the general orientation toward political interactions with the world. As discussed in chapter 5, two positions have dominated the global argument. *Internationalists* generally advocate a maximum involvement in the international system, believing such involvement is systemically beneficial and promotes cooperative interactions among states. Free trade and globalization are the economic manifestation of that reasoning. *Isolationists* advocate a minimal and more nationally controlled level of involvement in the world. The "America First" movement in the 1930s reflects this orientation. Isolationists are also protectionist, because protectionism limits international economic interactions by placing prohibitive barriers on incoming trade.

The terms of this debate are not purely economic. Pro-trade advocates of the 1990s, for instance, argued that the globalization process produces political as well as economic benefits. One of the major reasons for promoting trade with China has been to draw that country more intimately into the global political system. At the same time, anti–free trade arguments have expanded to include strictly noneconomic concerns ranging from environmental degradation to compromises of sovereignty, and more recently immigration as well as politico-economic arguments about the effects on different groups within societies.

Trade can also become a political weapon. In 2019, President Trump adopted the strategy of implementing the imposition of tariffs on countries with which the United States had disagreements. Some were based in economic practices (tariffs on Chinese goods) and some were political (threatened tariffs on Mexico over border security). Tariffs are levies (taxes) against goods entering a country, are controversial policy instruments, and are adamantly opposed by free traders. Their use reached a zenith during the protectionist 1930s, and they were identified as one of the culprits in the slide to World War II. They have been in general disfavor since, until Trump's attempt to employ them as an instrument of power.

This introduction frames the structure of the section, which has three purposes. The first purpose is historical, tracing the process whereby free trade has been institutionalized in the international system since the end of World War II. Second, that process has crystalized the principal reasons for advocating and opposing free trade. Finally, it will attempt to apply this institutional framework and the positions of the two sides to the current, ongoing debate on the issue. These provide a framework for examining the European Union and NAFTA/USMCA.

Institutionalizing Trade

Post–World War II planners agreed a major reason for the war was economic conditions during the Great Depression that nurtured protectionism and produced economic chaos that facilitated the descent into the maelstrom of global war. They were determined not to allow these conditions to return.

There are two geographic thrusts in this effort. One of these was universalist, seeking to create arrangements that had global membership, reach, and economic effect. The United States took the lead in this effort, putting forth and advocating the proposals that became known as the Bretton Woods system named after the New Hampshire town in which they were negotiated beginning in 1944. The major outcomes were two international organizations, the International Bank for Reconstruction and Development (or World Bank) and the International Monetary Fund, both aimed at reducing or eliminating protectionism. Both were limited in their reach and were not explicitly forms of economic integration, and both remain important international institutions. The conferees also proposed an International Trade Organization to promote economic cooperation through free trade. It was deferred until 1995, when it came into being as the World Trade Organization (WTO). It has a worldwide but not universal membership.

The WTO has now existed for over two decades. Its membership has increased from approximately seventy in 1995 to 164 as of July 29, 2016 (according to its website). In addition, twenty-one nonmember countries participate in the organization (observers have five years to apply for full membership), including Iraq, Iran, and Afghanistan. The headquarters, including the secretariat, are in Lausanne, Switzerland. The WTO has established itself as a leading international economic organization in the process.

Its brief tenure has been filled with more controversy and a great deal more publicity than functional international organizations (those that deal with a specific policy area rather than generalist organizations like the United Nations) usually attract or desire. In some ways, the acceptance of or opposition to the WTO reflects the status of globalization, whose central principle of free trade it exemplifies. When the charter came into effect in 1995, globalization was at its apex and the new WTO only activated its most ardent opponents. After 9/11, international attention shifted to the problem of terrorism, taking the spotlight off globalization and the WTO. Free trade has continued to grow, but the acceptance of its values and their institutionalization have become more controversial. For different reasons, NAFTA/USMCA and the European Union are examples of these reactions. As a result, continued momentum is a matter of some contention.

The other, and more successful, approach to economic integration has been regional. Regional organizations, as the name implies, are physically bounded and, in practice, all have been associations of countries with similar interests and pasts, and this has facilitated both the development and progress of these schemes. The most successful by far has been the European Union, and all others are compared to the European Union in terms of progress and success. To understand the comparative evolution, one needs to look at forms such association can take.

Forms of Economic Integration

The movement to promote greater international trade has had two related thrusts, one economic and one political, since it burst upon the global scene as a dominant theme in the 1990s. Both underlay the postwar evolution of trade promotion and share two assumptions: that greater trade will increase productivity and prosperity, and that the resulting economic globalization will also promote economically induced interdependence that will contribute to political stability and peace.

The economic dimension is based on how extensive the commitments are and thus how much increased trade they produce. The motivation to enter into economic arrangements is idiosyncratic, but it combines economic and political motives. The economic appeal, on which much of the process is premised, is to create greater prosperity through economic expansion, including easier trade, and at the macro level, this has generally been achieved. The beneficial effects may be selective, with some groups benefiting more than others—a source of potential backlash. Politically, the motives can be geopolitical, as they were in the case of the European Union, or more localized, as in some provisions of the USMCA that benefit some sectors of the economy more than others.

The process of economic integration has progressed through four steps in increasing levels of extensiveness and effect. All are premised on increasing reductions in barriers to trade and commerce within the physical area in question. The "deeper" the commitment involved, the greater the need for political structures to regulate the process, an inevitable cause of some friction in the effort.

Free trade agreements stand at the base of economic integration schemes. The purpose of these arrangements is to stimulate economic activity among the contracting members. They do so by lowering or eliminating barriers to trade among the contracting members, usually in the form of tariff reductions or eliminations. Free trade agreements do not, however, impose uniform regulations on the terms of goods and services entering the area. These are set by the individual members and raise the problem of so-called indirect importation, whereby an exporter avoids tariffs and the like on its goods with one member of the arrangement by trading with another member that does not have that barrier. Once inside the free trade area, goods can move freely among the members, allowing those goods to be sent to the original destination without penalty. The import of automobile parts for American cars from countries like China through Mexico, allowed under NAFTA, is an example.

The second step is a *customs union*. In this arrangement, the members add a common external tariff (or quotas) to all goods and services entering all member-states, thereby eliminating indirect importation into the area. The effects are greater interaction among the members, the further reduction of goods coming into the area from the outside (which increases economic exchange among members), and greater unity among the members, if they can agree politically on the effects.

When a free trade area and a customs union are created in the same area, the result is to create a *single* or *common market*. This action combines the dynamics of each previous form and aims to create the free circulation of goods, capital, people, and services within the market area. This is accomplished by reducing, preferably to zero, all trade barriers among members (a free trade area) and by creating common external barriers for goods and services coming from the outside (a customs union). This was the original form that the European Economic Community took in the 1960s and was the launching pad from which the European Union was formed.

The fourth, and at least to this point, ultimate form of integration is an *economic union*. At the purely economic level, the creation of an economic union culminates the process of economic integration. It is a two-step process that becomes progressively more complicated as it becomes more political.

The first step in creating the economic union is the formation of a *monetary union*, a financial institution that can issue a common currency and make monetary policy binding on all the members. The process becomes more politically controversial at this point, because the second step requires creating political bodies with the authority to make policy binding on all the members, a direct infringement on the national sovereignty of individual members. It is notable that most of the controversy within the European Union has arisen since the process of creating the monetary union began. When an arrangement combines a single common market and a monetary union, a full economic union has been created.

The major objections to free trade do not come over these abstract principles, but from their application. A key element in opposition arises from the presumption that all countries (or whatever entities are part of a free trading arrangement) will in fact find areas of production at which they have a comparative advantage. This is not always the case, and countries lacking comparative advantage (generally the least developed countries) thus tend to avoid involvement to the extent they can. It also presumes that areas of uncompetitive production can be replaced with compensatory equivalent areas where comparative advantage can be developed to replace uncompetitive enterprises. It is central to microeconomic (protectionist) objections to free trade that this is also not always the case.

This contrast in macro-level versus micro-level benefits helps explain why free trade is more popular among economic elites than the general population and why the issue has become a flash point in economic debates since 2016 in the United States. The economic elites—investors, entrepreneurs, and the like—are all more likely to be insulated from negative micro-level impacts but more affected by broader, macro-level effects like the overall impact on the stock market. If these macro-level indicators are expanding, then those elites are likely to benefit and be supportive. Negative micro-level effects have a direct impact on the jobs of individual voters, and candidates for public office are likely to reflect the suffering that displaced individuals and industries feel. These latter effects have been a pillar of Trump administration policy.

Politics and economics can only be separated in the most general sense. Whether trade is good depends on who benefits. Because economic elites tend to receive benefits from the macroeconomic activities that trading associations produce, it is not surprising that internationalists are likely to be free traders who favor trading agreements. Because the impact of those arrangements favor some forms of economic activity and punish others, it is also unsurprising that people adversely affected would favor isolationist solutions that would shield them from negative personal effects.

Like all economic ideas and their institutionalization, trade arrangements are thus inextricably economic and political, and attempts to argue them exclusively on one ground or the other are fundamentally feckless. Politics at heart involves the authoritative allocation of scarce resources, and economic resources like wealth and economic power are prime subjects for politically determined decisions with both political and economic consequences. To argue the case for or against trade arrangements on "purely" economic criteria distorts reality. Whether macroeconomic or microeconomic consequences should be supreme, for instance, is a political determination, because some of those consequences affect who gains scarce economic benefits. Politics and economics are inextricably intertwined, and this is true of both European Union and NAFTA/USMCA.

Application: The European Union and NAFTA/USMCA

The European Union and NAFTA/USMCA are two of the most prominent trade-based international economic arrangements. They are also contrasting institutions with enormously different experiences, making their comparison a study in contrasts that help explain the international trade issue. The European Union is the only trade-based organization to achieve the status of an economic union. That accomplishment, however, has brought with it political problems, notably Brexit, that it had heretofore avoided. The NAFTA/USMCA was begun in 1994 as a free trade agreement among the three sovereign North American states, and it has never progressed beyond that status. In fact, flaws in its limitation caused it to be renegotiated in 2018 at the insistence of the United States. NAFTA has always been a highly political enterprise, and its cosmetic rebirth as USMCA only accentuates that status.

The European Union

The process that has evolved into the European Union reversed the politics/economics chain of motivation. The original idea that became the union was to create an economic structure that would bring together the principal combatants of World War II under a common banner and, in the process, make future wars between them impossible. The original effort was so successful economically and politically that it created the momentum that led the Europeans through the four steps of the economic association process. The institutionalization of that process will reach its seventieth anniversary in 2020.

By 1945, Europe had exploded into two horrific continent-wide wars that had decimated the continent and left most of its combatants prostrate and at the apparent mercy of the Soviet Union poised at their doorstep. Their only ally was the United States, which was both the bulwark of their defense and the only available source of funds to rebuild the continent. Thus, Europe faced two most difficult problems: how to recover and how to defend themselves. With American participation, the two tasks were effectively combined in what became the European union movement. The first task was how to make war between the principal members unlikely or impossible; the second was how to rebuild them economically and militarily.

The impetus for what became the European Union had its origins in wartime discussions about the post–World War II order. There was consensus that a major reason for the war had been exclusionary economic nationalism in the form of high barriers against the movement of goods and services across borders, which resulted in a postwar determination to open the global economic system in the direction of some form of free trade. The Bretton Woods universalist system was one thrust of that determination. What became the European Union was its first and most powerful regional expression.

The genesis was something called the Schumann Plan, named after French Foreign Minister Robert Schumann. His proposal addressed both the free trade issue and the causes of war by proposing a European Coal and Steel Community in 1951. The organization's members were the six original members of the EU movement: France, Germany, Italy, and the Benelux countries (Belgium, the Netherlands, and Luxembourg). The major provision was to pool the coal and iron ore resources of France and Germany so that neither could independently produce steel that could lead to a new military competition. The European Coal and Steel Community was wildly successful and popular, and it spawned interest in wider forms of cooperation. The result was the negotiation of the Treaties of Rome in 1957 that created the European Economic Community among the six countries. Expansion began in 1973 with the addition of Denmark, Ireland, and the United Kingdom, a process that has led to the gradual expansion of the European Union to its current twenty-seven members. As Moravcsik summarizes the evolution, "The EU has enjoyed an astonishingly successful run." Its population is over 500 million in a territory half the size of the United States, and its economy is the world's third largest (behind the United States and China).

The final step in the integration process, implementing the Lisbon Treaty of 2009, was to create the monetary and thus the full economic union. It has been the most problematic and difficult step, reentering national politics into this remarkably successful economic enterprise. The major problem has been that a full monetary union that includes a common currency must also have political decision bodies coterminous with the union, and this entails increased community-wide decision powers wrested from national governments: the strengthening of the union entails weakening the powers of the members. This transfer of authority to community institutions extends to other areas like the movement of peoples within the union area.

Politics and economics clash, and the clearest example has been Brexit. The term, of course, is shorthand for "British exit" from the European Union, the outcome of a 2016 referendum where the citizens narrowly decided to become the only state ever to exercise the option to leave the union. Their reasoning was mainly political based on the loss of British sovereignty over monetary policy implicit in the Lisbon Treaty: monetary decisions affecting the lives of UK citizens would be made at EU headquarters in Brussels, not in London. In addition, an increase in EU authority over immigrants played a role. Free movement across borders had long been part of the European Union, but as a result of immigration problems caused by Syrians fleeing their civil war, the European Union voted on December 18, 2015, to supplant national control over who entered the EU area with an EU force, the European Border and Coast Guard, to catch illegal immigrants. This act enraged many, but especially the British and, in Muller's estimate, "led to an unprecedented politicization of the EU." Luedtke adds, "European unity cannot be separated, institutionally or politically, from issues of immigration." That refrain is clearly present in the debate over NAFTA/USMCA.

NAFTA/USMCA

NAFTA is a free trading agreement between the governments of the United States, Canada, and Mexico that has been in place since 1994. Its prototype is a similar arrangement entered into by Canada and the United States negotiated between the Reagan administration and the administration of Canadian Prime Minister Brian Mulroney in 1987, the Canada-U.S. Free Trade Agreement. That agreement was formally signed and implemented in 1988. NAFTA has been a free trade agreement with no pretensions of becoming more than that. On November 11, 2018, a replacement agreement, the USMCA, was signed with an implementation date in 2019 or 2020 pending ratification, which had not occurred as of June 2019. It is also a free trade agreement.

The major dynamic change introduced by NAFTA was the addition of Mexico to the North American association. If the Canada-U.S. Free Trade Agreement laid the groundwork by producing a working draft for NAFTA, the addition of Mexico represented something more than a simple expansion. The U.S.-Canadian agreement was between two countries with similar economies, cultures, histories, and levels of economic development. Mexico represents a different kind of entity, and the two countries have long-standing disputes, some of which are ongoing, like immigration and drug trafficking. Mexico thus represented a qualitatively different physical and economic entity. Many of the problems predate NAFTA (drugs like cocaine have come across the border since the end of the U.S. Civil War, for instance), but have either increased in intensity or become intertwined with other problems for which NAFTA has become a lightning rod. Likewise, advocacy or opposition to NAFTA also becomes amplified as part of the terms of trade debate.

It is important to note what NAFTA is in terms of international trade arrangements, a depiction that applies equally to USMCA. Free trade agreements do stand at the bottom of that pyramid. The principal goal of NAFTA has been to promote greater trade by reducing barriers to trade between the members. Operationally, that means a removal or tariffs and quotas on trade across those borders, subject to negotiation in the case of individual categories of items: agricultural goods and automobiles have been prime examples. In terms of basic economic obligations incurred by the members, this is basically all that a free trade arrangement does, which is why it is considered the most elemental and, for some purposes, ineffective form of international trade arrangement.

NAFTA has been the subject of criticism, some of it arguably unfair, since it was instituted. The criticisms are not partisan. NAFTA's predecessor was negotiated by a Republican (Reagan), as was the NAFTA agreement itself (George H. W. Bush). Bush's term expired before he could sign the agreement himself, a task Democrat Clinton performed. In the new century, NAFTA has been supported by GOP President George W. Bush and Democrat President Barack Obama. President Donald Trump has negotiated its demise, replaced by USMCA.

NAFTA has become entangled with the highly emotional, often distorting dialogue of trade positions. As trading arrangements go, NAFTA is basically innocuous. Its structure and provisions contain no major controversial additions to the trading dialogue, and the emotional disagreements that do exist tend to arise from other dynamics like the interaction between the United States and Mexico. It has, however, gained visibility as part of the domestic political debate in the United States over jobs, and especially the effort to repatriate jobs allegedly lost to Mexico because of its existence. These debates are more political and isolationist than economic, as exemplified by provisions within USMCA on what percentages of automobile parts and assembly must occur in each member country to exempt finished cars from import duties. Indeed, a major purpose of USMCA has not been to alter the basic structure or purposes of NAFTA, but rather to create altered terms of trade on some categories of goods and services, generally to U.S. advantage.

In terms of the globalization trading process and the debate over globalization, protectionism, and trade, NAFTA and its proposed USMCA successor are comparatively minor components. Both are simple free trade arrangements between neighboring countries, and neither has shown any inclination or likelihood of progressing further through the integration process. Both, and especially the proposed USMCA, have been highly politicized to the point that their economic impacts are mostly politically based in terms of attempting to appeal to voter segments that might benefit from the trading schedules that are at the heart of the revision. The replacement of NAFTA with USMCA is a minor triumph for the protectionists and a small defeat for the free traders.

USMCA may not come into force. It must be ratified by Congress, and if it becomes a political issue in the 2020 campaign (a distinct possibility), it could become the victim of 2020 election politics. That possibility suggests the difference between a primarily economic process with political repercussions

(European Union) and an overwhelmingly political process with some arguable economic impacts (NAFTA/USMCA).

Conclusion

Advocacy or opposition to free trade and its institutionalization has never been an easy or straightforward proposition. At the abstract, theoretical level of international macroeconomics, the case for free trade is convincing, and it is not surprising that many of the defenses of free trade spring from these theoretical arguments. At the applied level of the impact of free trade on individuals and groups (the microeconomic level), the proposition creates more ambivalence. Individual consumers benefit when comparative advantage produces goods and services at lower cost and higher quality through free trade than they otherwise would. Imagine, for instance, the impact on Christmas gift spending if all goods made in China were eliminated. At the same time, removing protection can terminate employment for those in the less-efficient industries. The theory of comparative advantage says that displaced people should find alternative employment in more competitive fields, but that outcome is almost always easier to accomplish in the abstract than in reality.

Institutionalizing free trade is a related but not synonymous question. One can reasonably take one of three positions on the desirability of free trade per se: one can favor free trade unconditionally, one can oppose it equally unconditionally, or one can favor free trade with some restrictions, the heart of fair trade. For the "pure" positions, the answer to whether some organization should be established to promote and enforce free trade is straightforward and flows directly from one's basic position—virtually regardless of empirical circumstances. From either extreme, debate is pointless and the facts almost beside the point.

The free trade movement is under some level of siege that is partly the result of excessive expectations when it burst upon the scene toward the end of the last century. Its virtues and positive impacts were exaggerated, as were its negative effects. Stimulating economic activity by reducing barriers to trade across state boundaries became the mantra of the 1990s, and it did produce positive outcomes. The hype, however, was greater than the dynamics of trade deserved or could sustain. The Trump protectionist backlash evident in the 2020 election campaign reflects that dynamic.

That overselling is apparent in the institutions created in trade's name. The European Union has progressed steadily through the integration process because the organization's efforts benefit EU members. It only became controversial when it became political. The opposite was true of NAFTA, partly because its economic effects have been less than its more publicized political intertwining with the immigration issue in the United States. As Crowie concludes, "The economic impact of the trade deal is far more ambiguous and significantly less interesting than its political impact. Indeed, it is less of a trade deal than an icon to be smashed or revered."

Study/Discussion Questions

1. What are the reasons for trade? What are the basic positions on trade that have evolved? Describe them, including how politics and economics intertwine in trade discussions.
2. What are the three contemporary positions on trade? Describe each, including its genesis and relationship to basic foreign policy schools of thought.
3. How did World War II affect thinking about trade? What perceptions of why the war occurred led to an emphasis on free trade?
4. Globalization embodying free trade was dominant in the 1990s but has receded in dominance since. Discuss the premises and evolution of the free-trade-protectionist debate of the 2010s.
5. Free trade is more than simple economics. Discuss it as an economic and a political phenomenon, including macroeconomic and microeconomic effects and basic argument for and against it.
6. What is the European Union? Discuss its origins, structure, functions, and controversies associated with it.
7. What is NAFTA? What are its history, purposes, controversies surrounding it, and distortions in discussions about it? What is the USMCA, and how does it affect the dynamics of NAFTA?
8. The relationship between the economic arguments on trade and its political dynamics have had an increasing impact on thinking about and conducting trade in recent years. How? Use the European Union and NAFTA/USMCA to illustrate your points.

Bibliography

Bauman, Zygmunt. *Globalization: The Human Consequences.* New York: Columbia University Press, 1998.

Boskin, Michael J. *NAFTA at 20: The North American Free Trade Agreement's Achievements and Challenges.* Palo Alto, CA: Hoover Institution Press, 2014.

Brickerton, Chris. *The European Union: A Citizen's Guide.* New York: Pelican, 2016.

Clarke, Harold D., Michael Goodwin, and Paul Whiteley. *Brexit: Why Britain Voted to Leave the European Union.* Cambridge, UK: Cambridge University Press, 2017.

Coombs, Kevin. "The Brexit Breakup Gets Messier: The United Kingdom and the EU Will Be Tied to Each Other for Years to Come." *Foreign Affairs Snapshot* (online), March 27, 2019.

Crowie, Jefferson. "What Trump Gets Wrong about NAFTA: The Deal Is Not the Source of America's Problems." *Foreign Affairs Snapshot* (online), May 4, 2017.

Delanty, Gerard. "The EU's Indistinct Identity." *Current History* 115, no. 779 (March 2016), 117–19.

Dinan, Desmond. *Europe Recast: A History of the European Union.* Boulder, CO: Lynne Rienner, 2014.

Dregner, Daniel W. *U.S. Trade Strategy: Free Versus Fair.* New York: Council on Foreign Relations Press, 2006.

Dunt, Jan. *Brexit: What the Hell Happens Now? Everything You Need to Know about Britain's Divorce from Europe.* London: Canbury, 2016.

Friedman, Thomas L. *The Lexus and the Olive Tree: Understanding Globalization.* New York: Farrar, Straus and Giroux, 1999.
Heyman, Bruce, and Vicki Heyman, *The Art of Diplomacy: Strengthening Canada-U.S. Relations in Times of Uncertainty.* New York: Simon and Schuster, 2019.
Irwin, Douglas A. "The False Promise of Protectionism: Trump's Trade Policy Could Backfire." *Foreign Affairs* 96, no. 3 (May/June 2017), 56–65.
———. *Free Trade Under Fire* (fourth edition). Princeton, NJ: Princeton University Press, 2015.
McCormick, John. *European Union Politics.* London: Palgrave Macmillan, 2015.
———. *Understanding the European Union: A Concise Introduction.* London: Palgrave Macmillan, 2002.
Moravcsik, Andrew. "Europe: The Second Superpower." *Current History* 109, no. 725 (March 2010), 91–98.
Muller, Jan-Werner. "The EU's Democratic Deficit and the Public Sphere." *Current History* 115, no. 779 (March 2016), 83–88.
Naim, Moises. "Think Again: Globalization." *Foreign Policy* (March/April 2009), 28–34.
O'Connor, David E. *Demystifying the Global Economy: A Guide for Students.* Westport, CT: Greenwood Press, 2002.
Oliver, Craig. *Unleashing Demons: The Inside Story of Brexit.* London: Holder and Staughton, 2016.
Rodrik, Dani. *The Globalization Paradox: Democracy and the Future of the World Economy.* New York: W. W. Norton, 2010.
Rothgeb, John M. J. *Trade Policy: Balancing Economic Dreams and Political Realities.* Washington, DC: CQ Press, 2001.
Shah, Anup. "Free Trade and Globalization." *Global Issues* (online), July 25, 2009.
Shipman, Tim. *All Out War: The Full Story of How Brexit Sunk Britain's Political Class.* New York: HarperCollins, 2016.
Snow, Donald M. *Cases in International Relations* (sixth edition). New York: Pearson, 2015.
Soros, George. *The Tragedy of the European Union: Disintegration or Revival.* New York: PublicAffairs, 2014.
Villareal, M. Angeles, and Ian F. Fergusson. *NAFTA at 20: Overview and Trade Effects.* Washington, DC: Congressional Research Service, 2014.

12

International Population Movement

Restricting Immigration in the United States and Europe

The movement of people from one place to another precedes recorded human history. People have moved for many reasons, most frequently seeking a better life, but also to avoid distress, suppression, and even extinction. Immigrants, refugees, and asylum seekers are a constant that has been increasing in this century and has reached critical proportions in some places. The problem is exacerbated by a burgeoning world population growth rate, mostly in the developing world.

There are competing, contradictory forces at work in this equation. There are two basic stimuli for migration. One directly involves immigration of people from the developing to the developed world. The motive is both economic and political: seeking prosperity and freedom. For receiving countries, immigrants provide necessary augmentation of shrinking labor forces and thus stimulate productivity. The result can be positive for both sides, but its synergism is partially upset by the prospects that undesirables—especially terrorists and criminals—will infiltrate the immigrants. The other stimulus is largely internal to the developing world in terms of privation and atrocity associated with internal conflicts that produce massive refugee and asylum-seeking populations.

Human migration is a two-way proposition. On one hand are those who seek to relocate for one reason or another, including out of fear for their lives. On the other are those in the sovereign jurisdictions to which the migrants seek to relocate who must decide whether to accept them. It is rarely a seamless, smooth process. It is also a difficult, often traumatic, and even dangerous experience.

Migration is one of the most enduring aspects of the human experience. At some level of remove, essentially everyone is an immigrant or the descendant of immigrants; the only humans who can rightfully claim nonimmigrant status are direct descendants of the earliest humans from the Great Rift Valley in Africa who still live there.

Human migration in its various forms is a large, important, and controversial contemporary phenomenon. In 2005, the UN Department of Economic and Social Affairs reported that there were 191 million international immigrants (people residing in countries other than that of their birth). That figure fluctuates from year to year, as some immigrants are repatriated and others leave voluntarily or flee their native lands. The reasons they move are various and complicated, but the net result is a constant flow of people across borders. The arrival of these new peoples has always been a source of controversy of greater or lesser intensity depending on who was trying to settle where in what numbers and for what reasons.

The immigrant question has always been important for the United States. As the admonition to "bring me your tired, your huddled masses" on the Statue of Liberty heralds, the United States is a quintessential immigrant state, with waves of immigrants from various places arriving at different times in the country's history to constitute one of the world's most nationally and ethnically diverse populations. Sometimes the process of new immigrant waves has been orderly, open, and noncontentious, but it has also been surrounded by considerable disagreement and rancor.

In quantitative terms, the American example is not extreme, but its dynamics may be a harbinger of a future where migration is likely to increase, possibly greatly. Europe joins the United States in this concern. It is host to a considerably larger comparative immigrant population than the United States, especially in a few select countries like Germany. To understand the nature of the concern—and to place the current U.S. debate into a global context—it is necessary to look at the immigration question more broadly.

Principle: Human Population Movement

Population movement is a normal occurrence in much of the world. Some countries are more permissive about letting citizens leave (emigrate) or enter from other countries (immigrate), but some population movement is a regular part of international activity, and one that is arguably increasing in a globalizing world in which international population and interaction of all kinds is increasing. Employing an accepted definition used by Koser that an international immigrant is "a person who stays outside his usual country of residence for at least one year," the global total of immigrants today is over 200 million people. Immigration is, however, only one, if the largest, form of human movement. Understanding the problem in a contemporary context requires beginning by classifying different categories of those who traverse borders.

Forms of Movement

There are various categories of people who leave their homes to go to other locations. Immigration is the historically largest and most generic category, but there are others. Two that stand out are refugees and asylum seekers, both because of their prominence in contemporary international relations and because they are often the result (or even the cause) of great human suffering.

Immigrants are often subdivided into categories. Legal immigrants are those individuals who have migrated to a country through prescribed channels, meaning their immigration is recognized and accepted by the host government. Countries allow immigrants into the country for a variety of reasons and in different numbers depending on the needs or uses they may have for such populations. Parts of Europe—notably Germany—have long admitted workers from places like Turkey to augment shrinking workforces as their population ages, and the United States has historically given priority status to people with particularly needed education and technical skills, such as scientists and engineers from developing countries like India.

There are, however, other, more controversial categories of immigrants. In the contemporary debate, the most controversial are so-called *irregular immigrants*. The UN Department of Economic and Social Affairs defines this class of people as "those who enter a country without proper authorization or who have violated the terms of stay of the authorization they hold, including by overstaying." Other terms for irregular status include illegal, undocumented, and unauthorized immigrants. As Koser points out, "there are around 40 million irregular immigrants worldwide, of whom perhaps one-third are in the United States." The most publicized and largest part of that total are irregular by virtue of illegal entry into the country; some of the most problematical, however, are individuals who have entered the country legally but have overstayed the conditions of their residence, as in not leaving after student or temporary work visas have expired.

A special category of immigrants is refugees. Broadly speaking, refugees are the most prominent example of what the UN Commission on Human Rights (UNCHR) calls "forcibly displaced people," who, according to 2017 UNCHR figures, numbered about 65 million worldwide. The largest numbers of people within this category are refugees (displaced people living outside their native countries) at about 21.3 million, internally displaced persons (refugees within their own countries) at about 43 million, and asylum seekers (people who have sought international protection but whose applications have not been acted upon). Those who seek refugee status often come from developing countries where human misery is both economic and political, meaning that it is sometimes difficult to determine why a refugee or group of refugees seeks to migrate. As Koser points out, "though an important legal distinction can be made between people who move for work purposes and those who flee conflict and persecution, in reality the two can be difficult to distinguish."

The dynamics of immigration as a global issue requires looking at the phenomenon from at least three vantage points. The first is the motivation for immigration: Why do people emigrate from one place to another, and what roles do they fulfill when they become immigrants? The second is where the phenomenon of immigration is the most and least evident on a global scale. The third concern is immigration as a problem, both globally and locally. Are there distinctive problems that are created by current, ongoing patterns, and are these likely to get better or worse in the future?

Immigration Motivations and Functions

Why do people migrate? One way to think about the reasons for immigration is in terms of "push" and "pull" factors. Push factors are motives to leave a political jurisdiction—conditions that make people want to leave or that push them out.

Pull factors, on the other hand, refer to perceived positive attributes to attract immigrants to different destinations—or serve to pull people to different locations. When push and pull factors are both present, the immigration pipeline is particularly strong.

The most obvious push factor is to improve one's living conditions by relocation. People decide to leave for both political and economic reasons: politically to avoid conflict or discrimination in their homeland, and economically in the hope or promise of a materially better life. This basic statement of motivation has numerous variations, as Choucri and Mistree enumerate:

> the most obvious patterns of international migration today include the following: migration for employment; seasonal mobility for employment; permanent settlements; refugees who are forced to migrate; resettlement; state-sponsored movements; tourism and ecotourism; brain drains and "reversals" of brain drains; smuggled and trafficked people; people returning to their country of origin; environmental migration and refugees from natural shortages or crises; nonlegal migration; and religious pilgrimage.

The economic motivation, to move somewhere where economic opportunities are better than those where one lives, is nothing new. As Choucri and Mistree summarize, "during good times people migrate to find better opportunities; during bad times people migrate to escape more difficult circumstances." In either situation, the motivating factor is opportunity, which is manifested in the availability of jobs because, as they add, "To the extent that population growth exceeds a society's employment potential, the probability is very high that people will move to other countries in search of jobs."

Demographics also enter the picture. Population growth rates are highest in developing countries, and that means the rising number of job seekers is greatest in these countries relative to the number of jobs available. In the developed world, on the other hand, population growth rates are often below levels to maintain current population sizes, the overall population is aging, and thus the percentage of citizens in the active workforce is diminishing. Goldstone explains the consequence: "the developed countries' labor forces will substantially age and decline, constraining economic growth in the developed world and raising demands for immigrant workers." Indeed, there are estimates that the developed countries that will be most successful in the future are those that are best able to augment their shrinking workforces with immigrant labor. This dynamic creates pressure for population migration from developing to developed countries globally.

The kinds of talents that immigrants can contribute in different categories make their acceptance welcome or not. The smallest and most welcome category of immigrants is what the United Nations refers to as "highly skilled workers." Far more problematic are the economic immigrants who have comparatively low skill levels. Unskilled immigrants—especially irregular immigrants—pose a distinct moral and practical dilemma for receiving states. These immigrants do jobs that the citizens are either unwilling to do or that they will not do at the lower wages that migrants will accept (especially irregular migrants). Thus, without a pool of such laborers, vital services either would not get done or would only be done at higher costs.

Refugees present a separate problem. They can also be divided into skilled and unskilled groups, with the skilled often constituting professionals from the country from which they flee, and the unskilled composed mainly of subsistence farmers and the like. The skilled parts of the population are more likely to be absorbed into the country to which they flee, whereas the unskilled generally cannot be absorbed and become a burden on the country or on international bodies like the UNCHR. Moreover, most refugees are from developing countries and flee to adjacent countries, which are also poor and thus lacking the resources to tend for their new citizens. Most of the Syrian refugees, for instance, have fled to adjacent countries like Turkey, Lebanon, Jordan, and Iraq.

The World Situation: The Human Tragedy Factor

There are two overlapping continuing trends in worldwide immigration. The first is demographic: most of this population movement is from the developing to the developed world, and especially to Europe and North America. In addition, this immigration is increasing numerically: there are more immigrants worldwide now than there have been. A significant element, however, is demographic, based in aging populations in the developed world and the consequent need to import younger workers both to sustain economic activity and to support an aging and unproductive population.

The other trend is political. Fragile countries in parts of the developing world are disintegrating into violence with a multinational basis along ethnic and religious lines, and the result is the furtive, extremely bloody and gut-wrenching violence against populations segments including innocent and often defenseless civilians of which Syria and South Sudan are currently the most publicized examples. The worst cases are currently in the Middle East (see Snow, *The Middle East, Oil, and the United States National Security Policy* for examples).

These demographic and political trends are likely to increase in the future. As Goldstone points out, "the developed countries' labor forces will substantially age and decline, constraining economic growth in the developed world and raising the demand for immigrant workers." The rate at which populations are aging, and how governments respond to this problem, varies greatly, with different consequences. Japan, for instance, has one of the world's most rapidly aging populations and has, for cultural reasons, been very reluctant to allow non-Japanese immigrants into the country. This is already having two effects. First, it means that a shrinking portion of the population is part of the productive workforce that produces, among other things, the wealth needed to support older, retired Japanese. Second, it means a contraction in productivity and population. The cumulative effect of these dynamics is the projection of a smaller and less economically prominent Japan in the future. The problem is not yet severe in the United States but it could become so if current nativist (e.g., "America First") sentiments dampen the desire of developing world economic immigrants to seek homes in America.

The scale of immigration from the developing to the developed world is not going to go away. If anything, it will increase in the future. As Goldstone suggests, "Current levels of immigration from developing to developed countries are paltry compared to those that the forces of supply and demand might soon create across the world." The degree to which this likely trend is a concern depends on whether one views immigration as a problem.

Application: The Continuing U.S. and European Experiences

Those on the receiving end of population migration have various, sometimes contradictory reasons for accepting or rejecting the influx of new peoples into their countries. The largest current incentive to encourage immigration is the need for additional sources of labor in developed countries. Humanitarian concerns over the plight of beleaguered people sometimes enter the calculus. On the negative side in the present system, there is the danger that in admitting desirable new individuals and groups, one will also allow undesirable, even dangerous people into the country in the process. The result is a dynamic tension about immigration.

This concern is greatest today in the United States and in Europe. Both are concerned about the quantity and quality of outsiders who seek entry and especially the quality of immigrants. The United States has a smaller (but not nonexistent) need for immigrant labor than Europe. It has a secondary concern with terrorists entering the country. Europe, on the other hand, has a large need for immigrant labor, which has made it a much larger recipient of that immigration. Because much of that movement comes from the Middle East and North Africa, it has a much larger concern with terrorists entering the EU area. The political challenge in the United States has been over how to restrict immigrants and is symbolized by the debate over building a wall along the U.S.-Mexican border. In the European Union, the debate is over the loss of sovereign control of borders due to EU actions to take over the boundary regulation function. The most dramatic example the role of that dispute in the Brexit decision.

The U.S.-Mexican Border Problem

As noted in chapter 2, the migration of large numbers of people from Mexico and Central America has been an American political issue since the 1990s, when the population of irregular immigrants increased from around 4 million to 12 million or more coming across the long, porous frontier between the United States and its Southern neighbors. There has always been partisan disagreement about how much of a problem this migration creates and what should be done about it. The threat of possible terrorist penetration has been added in the form of proposed bans on immigrants and refugees from certain Muslim countries.

The U.S.-Mexico border case is intensified by the nature of the border. At 1,933 miles of mostly desolate, rural topography, it is a very long and difficult frontier to "seal," as its proponents advocate. At the same time, the U.S.-

Mexico boundary is the world's only direct land border between the developed and developing worlds.

The U.S.-Mexico case is also distinguished by its sheer volume and the accompanying complexity of the problem. No one, of course, knows exactly how many irregular immigrants are in the United States, and those who voice the greatest concern would argue that official estimates of around 12 million cited earlier are probably too low. This is a larger number than for any other country, although there are several countries such as Germany that have a higher percentage of immigrants in the population than the United States. Moreover, the problem is geographically distinct within the United States: About one-quarter of all estimated irregular immigrants in the United States in 2008 were in California (2.85 million), followed by Texas (1.68 million) and Florida (840,000). The issue is also a complex one. The concern about the U.S.-Mexico border not only involves immigration, but the integrity of the frontier also has strong implications for the trafficking of illicit drugs into the United States and potentially for terrorists seeking to penetrate American soil. For present purposes, the immigration problem is most relevant.

Immigration is, and always has been, an integral part of the human, including American, experience. Although for most times and purposes, it has been one of the proud elements of the American heritage, it has had its dark side in the form of negative reactions to the migration of some people to the United States at different times. Throughout American history, what is now referred to as illegal immigration has always been a part of the pattern, and the history of immigration politics is largely an attempt to regulate both the quantity and quality (measured both in point of origin and skill levels) of immigration to the country. For Americans, the immigration problem along the U.S.-Mexico border is the most dramatic current manifestation of a worldwide pattern of international immigration.

The sheer volume of irregular immigrants in the United States is the heart of the perceived problem in the American political debate. More specifically, it is about irregular immigration by Mexicans and Central Americans into the country in larger numbers than many prefer. Efforts to secure the border are aimed at reducing or eliminating the flow of irregulars into the country; efforts to apprehend and deport irregular immigrants already in the country are aimed at reducing those numbers.

There are essentially two groups that make up that community. By far the most numerous are *economic immigrants*. There is no systematic indication that their participation in or contribution to crime is any greater than that of the population at large; indeed, it is probably lower. The other group is comprised of *criminal immigrants*, individuals who enter the country to engage in criminal behavior, most notably people engaged in narcotics trafficking in one way or another. This group brings with it the violent crime that has ravaged Mexico in particular and is the source of virtually all the concern over the impact of immigration on crime.

Dividing the irregular immigrant community into these two categories helps in understanding the problem and what to do about it. One must begin by asking the question, why do immigrants come illegally to the country? In the case of the economic immigrants, the answer is economic opportunity: jobs. This should not be surprising, given the disparity of wealth between the United States and Mexico and Central America, and it is why economic immigrants migrate worldwide.

Most irregular economic migrants have been displaced Mexicans and Central Americans who have come to the United States in the pursuit of economic advancement, including the accumulation of enough money to send remittances back to their local communities and families at home. Their migration is like economic migration everywhere, moving from where there is no economic opportunity (jobs) to where such opportunities exist.

The immigration problem and its solution take on a different complexion put in these terms. If there are jobs available that irregular immigrants fill, then there must be a labor need that these immigrants fulfill. Generally, this means low-skill, low-paying jobs, often with one or more of the so-called 3D characteristics of being dirty, dangerous, or difficult. If there were Americans willing to do these jobs at wages that employers were willing to pay and that produced services at prices consumers could afford, there would not be jobs, and there would be no incentive for migrants to immigrate. That they have done so and continue to do so indicates not only that such opportunities exist, but that they have not been sated. That is simple supply and demand.

A distinction is also made qualitatively about immigrants. Advocates of permitting only documented workers into the country are often implicitly expressing a preference for highly skilled "legal" immigrants like scientists and engineers, about whom there are few objections on other than social grounds. Skilled immigrants are clearly favored and are less controversial, but they quantitatively do not fulfill all the functions that less skilled, "illegal" economic immigrants provide.

The dynamics suggest that there is a continuing market for irregular immigrant labor. This assertion may seem anomalous, but it is nonetheless true. The simple fact is that illegal workers have advantages to employers over legal immigrants: They will work at lower wages (they have no bargaining ability on wages), they will work longer (they are covered by no labor laws or contracts), and they do not require employers to pay benefits like Social Security taxes or health insurance. Moreover, if the kinds of jobs that irregular immigrants typically perform became part of the regular economy, labor costs would increase (to minimum wage, at the least), which in turn would drive up the costs of the services and the wages of other lower-end jobs. Many Americans would feel the impact in their wallets. This fact places the problem in a different context than those who simply call for expelling irregular immigrants like to frame the question.

The European Problem

The immigration problem in Europe is different. The most current concern is specifically related to the problem of terror that has periodically consumed much of northern North Atlantic Treaty Organization–related Europe. Also, the reasons for migration more often involve refugees and asylum seekers than it does irregular immigrants. Terrorism containment is more pressing and difficult because of the existence of enclaves of people from terrorist-vulnerable societies and the difficulty of monitoring new terrorists. At the same time, the continuing influx and EU attempts to take over functions that ultimately affect control of borders has become a highly divisive issue. Border control, for instance, was part of the Brexit appeal in the United Kingdom. All these factors contrast with the American situation.

As events over the past two years or so clearly demonstrate, Europe is in the throes of an "epidemic" of limited, but often spectacular and gruesome, terrorist attacks that have caused some divisions both within and between European countries. The simple fact is that Europe is more proximate to the Middle East crucible of terrorist activity than is North America, and has welcomed and accepted people from these countries for generations. Given European demographics and geography, it has a difficult time excluding all those who want to enter the EU area from the Middle East or North Africa. Europe is proximate to the problem, vulnerable to it, and in a difficult position trying to stanch terrorist penetration.

The mix between immigrants and refugees is different in the American and European situations. This is also a matter of proximity and circumstance. Due to violent instability in the Muslim world, UNCHR statistics for June 2017 show that the three countries with the most refugees are all in the region close to Europe: Syria with 4.9 million, Afghanistan with 2.7 million, and Somalia with 1.5 million. Of these, the victims of the Syrian civil war represent the largest and most compelling problem. The nearly 5 million refugees are part of a larger internal displaced persons problem that more than doubles that number, and the vicious nature of the civil war makes the return of these refugees impossible in the near term. Surveys of Syrians in refugee camps in the region (principally Turkey) indicate all but about 5 percent hope to return to Syria when the civil war ends, but until they can, they are a tragic burden that spreads to Europe. Because Europeans were active in many of these places during the colonial period, they have some historical ties that are hard to ignore.

This juxtaposition creates a unique construction of the problem for Europeans. Countries like Germany both need and already have sizable migrant populations whom they have recruited because of labor shortages and do not want to alienate. In several European countries, these populations have not been well assimilated, and the isolated ghetto environments in which they reside may be prime recruiting grounds for groups like the Islamic State. Alienating or turning away refugees who might become immigrants is not a good way to build the loyalties that will dampen radicalization of parts of the population.

The recent spate of terrorist attacks in major Northern European urban areas has heightened the urgency and salience of the migrant problem. An additional element that makes the identification of potential terrorists difficult is the fact that, in many cases, the countries from which the terrorists come are former colonies. Radicalized Libyans crossing the Mediterranean Sea for destinations in Italy and other Southern European locales is one example, as are people from old French Union countries.

A final special circumstance surrounds how immigrants and refugees enter Europe and the ability of individual countries to regulate their movement and especially their ability to enter the sovereign territory of countries without obtaining permission from the governments of those countries. This problem bears some resemblance to the border issue in the United States. It is not a coincidence that this issue is of salience in both the United States and the United Kingdom.

The migration dilemma pits population movement versus the enduring question of sovereignty. Economic immigration needs create the incentive for much of Europe to make it relatively easy to let people into the EU area and to facilitate their movement. Part of the economic union's structure is free movement of people across sovereign boundaries without restriction or even routine monitoring of who comes and goes, which facilitates the greater integration of the union. That means, however, that anyone who can get by whatever barriers there are to entry into the EU territory cannot be excluded from any part of the union. That, in turn, means that individual states lose control over the gatekeeping function of those borders, a loss of sovereign control. This potential loss has been a rallying cry of those promoting stronger border measures in the United States. The events of 2015 and 2016 in the European Union, depicted in the discussion of Brexit, enlivened that same concern in Great Britain as well.

Brexit has not spread beyond the British Isles to this point. The election of Emmanuel Macron in France signaled that the anti-immigrant, antirefugee option exercised by the United Kingdom has not spread inexorably to the continent, and the fact that terrorist events have subsequently occurred on both sides of the English Channel further suggest the connection between population movement and terror is not inexorable. One reason the United Kingdom voted to leave the European Union was to plug the pipeline of immigrants from the continent to the British Isles—to reassert British sovereign control over who enters the country.

Conclusion

Human migration is one of humankind's oldest and often most difficult phenomena. Most individuals prefer to live where they have always lived, and being uprooted and having to move is often a very traumatic and unpleasant experience. The inducement and trauma were probably less severe when there were far less people and migration was less encumbered by contact with other peoples who viewed the migrating population with fear, suspicion, even hatred. With a world population of over 8 billion people, livable places to migrate are shrinking. Moreover, the entire land surface of the world—other than Antarctica—is now under the sovereign control of some political authority, and those migrating must gain the permission of the occupying authority to take up residence.

The different forms of movement create varying problems and emotions, depending on circumstances. Normally immigration, the most generic description of movement, has been the least traumatic unless the migration of people from one locale to another is so massive as to activate nativist reactions in the receiving country. This has been the pattern in the United States, where people from an earlier generation of immigration have objected when people from somewhere else seek to settle in their sovereign space. The migration of Mexicans and other Central Americans across the Southern border is just the most recent example.

Controversy and emotion increase when the migration consists solely or in large measure of refugees seeking safety or asylum from disastrous conditions in their countries of origin. The causes of refugee flows are normally disputed by the government of the originating country, which may also consider the refugees radicals or political criminals. The decision to accept or reject refugees is difficult for the receiving country, because it likely strains relations with the government of the country of origin and may entangle it in the dynamics of what caused the refugee problem in the first place. The situation is amplified if there are sizable numbers of political asylum seekers among the fleeing refugees. These factors are counterbalanced by humanitarian suffering and deprivation, especially when those seeking refuge are part of an even larger population of internally displaced people in the country of origin. These concerns all swirl around the ongoing tragedy in Syria.

The contemporary situation adds two contradictory factors to the issue: demographic needs and possible terrorist penetration. The demographic imperative is the need for additional young members of the labor force in developed countries where declining birth rates do not produce adequate numbers of entrants into the job market and where outside augmentation is necessary to keep the economy operating at peak levels. The "pull" involved is especially great for highly skilled, educated immigrants, but it means that people from economically disadvantaged developing world countries are attractive, needed commodities pulled toward the more prosperous but labor deficient developed world.

The other side, pushing against this dynamic, is the fact that some of the workforce that is needed comes from parts of the world that also produces terrorists. It is a national imperative everywhere in the developed world to exclude from their sovereign territory those who would do it harm. The difficulty is in how to be certain that economic immigrants can be adequately vetted to exclude terrorists from sneaking in along with legitimate and welcome people willing to migrate.

The final, and most tragic, push factor occurs when governments make refugees of groups by forcing their departure to places where their presence may be unwanted or where it may intolerably strain the receiving country. The most egregious but underpublicized current example are the estimated 900,000 Muslim Rohingya who have been forced out of their native Myanmar by the Buddhist government and into Muslim Bangladesh, which lacks the resources to accommodate them, leaving the Rohingya in an increasingly desperate, impossible situation.

In the contemporary environment, both aspects of this are especially evident in the EU area and less so in the United States. The most prosperous parts of the European Union—especially the industrialized countries of Northern Europe—both need additions to their workforce and face the reality and prospects of terrorist attacks against them. The American border problem is emotional but less dangerous: some Americans dislike the intrusion on their land by such large numbers of people from south of the border, but other than some drug dealers, it has not been conclusively demonstrated that they pose any other major national security problem.

Study/Discussion Questions

1. What is immigration? Into what categories are immigrants normally placed? Define, discuss, and compare each to the others.
2. Why do people migrate? Use the "push-pull" analogy to help describe reasons for the differences. Apply this analysis to migration across the U.S.-Mexican frontier.
3. What are the current demographic and political factors affecting migration trends worldwide? Describe each factor in detail. What basic trends arise from these observations?
4. Define and contrast the problems of sanctuary seeking and political asylum with the problems of immigration as a general phenomenon.
5. Describe the U.S.-Mexico border problem in terms of the threats and positive effects of irregular immigrants crossing that line.
6. What is the nature of the European immigration problem? Discuss this problem in geographic, demographic, and jurisdictional terms, as well as links to terrorism. How does this problem relate to the Brexit decision?
7. What is the "human factor" in immigration, especially when it involves the "human tragedy" factor as well? Why are these problems likely to increase in the future? How important are these concerns in policy making and enforcement? Include the plight of the Rohingya as part of your explanation.
8. Why is the immigration problem like to increase in the future? Discuss in demographic, economic, and push-pull terms. Who has the greatest immigration problem in the world today? Is it receiving countries and areas like the United States or the European Union, or is it those countries whose citizens wish to or feel they must leave?

Bibliography

Alden, Edward. *The Closing of the American Border*. New York: HarperCollins, 2009.

Betts, Alexander, and Paul Collier. *Rethinking Refugee Policy in a Changed World*. Oxford, UK: Oxford University Press, 2017.

Borjas, George J. *Heaven's Door: Immigration Policy and the American Economy*. Princeton, NJ: Princeton University Press, 2016.

———. *We Wanted Workers: Unravelling the Immigration Narrative*. New York: W. W. Norton, 2016.

Chomsky, Avia. *Undocumented: How Immigrants Become Illegal*. Boston: Beacon Press, 2014.

Choucri, Nazli, and Dinsha Mistree. "Globalization, Migration, and New Challenges to Governance." *Current History* 108, no. 717 (April 2009), 173–79.

Collett, Elizabeth. "Destination: Europe: Managing the Migrant Crisis." *Foreign Affairs* 92, no. 2 (March/April 2017), 150–56.
Daniels, Roger. *Coming to America: A History of Immigration and Ethnicity in American Life*. New York: Harper Perennials, 2019.
Fair, C. Christine. "The Making of the Rohingya Genocide and Myanmar's Impunity." *Current History* 118, no. 807 (April 2019), 149–53.
Fiddean-Qasmiyeh, Elena, Gil Loescher, et al. *The Oxford Handbook of Refugee and Forced Migration Studies*. Oxford, UK: Oxford University Press, 2014.
Gest, Justin. *The New Minority: White Working Class Politics in an Age of Inequality*. Oxford, UK: Oxford University Press, 2016.
Goldstone, Jack A. "The New Population Bomb: The Four Megatrends That Will Change the World." *Foreign Affairs* 89, no. 1 (January/February 2010), 31–43.
Haynes, S. Katrick Ramakrishnan, and Jennifer Mosallas. *Framing Immigrants: News Coverage, Public Opinion, and Policy*. Washington, DC: Russell Sage Foundation, 2016.
Jardina, Ashley. *White Identity Politics* (Cambridge Studies in Public Opinion and Political Psychology). Cambridge, UK: Cambridge University Press, 2019.
Jones, Reece. *Border Walls: Security and the War on Terror in the United States, India, and Israel*. New York: Zed Books, 2012.
Kingsley, Patrick. *The New Odyssey: The Story of the Twenty-First Century Refugee Crisis*. London: Liveright, 2017.
Koser, Khalid. "Why Immigration Matters." *Current History* 108, no. 717 (April 2009), 147–53.
Maril, Robert Lee. *The Fence: National Security, Public Safety, and Illegal Immigration Along the U.S.-Mexican Border*. Lubbock, TX: Texas Tech University Press, 2012.
Martin, Susan F. "Waiting Games: The Politics of US Immigration Reform." *Current History* 108, no. 717 (April 2009), 160–65.
McDonald-Gibson, Charlotte. *Cast Away: True Stories of Survival from Europe's Refugee Crisis*. New York: New Press, 2016.
Payan, Terry. *The Three U.S.–Mexico Border Wars: Drugs, Immigration, and Homeland Security*. Westport, CT: Greenwood, 2006.
Rabben, Linda. *Sanctuary Asylum: A Social and Political History*. Seattle, WA: University of Washington Press, 2016.
Rozenthal, Andres. "The Other Side of Immigration." *Current History* 106, no. 697 (February 2007), 89–90.
Snow, Donald M. *Cases in International Relations* (seventh edition). Lanham, MD: Rowman & Littlefield, 2018.
———. *The Middle East, Oil, and the United States National Security Policy*. Lanham, MD: Rowman & Littlefield, 2016.
Van Hear, Nicholas. "The Rise of Refugee Diasporas." *Current History* 108, no. 717 (April 2009), 180–85.
Van-Wolleg-Georges, Pierre. *The EU's Policy on the Integration of Migrants: A Case of Soft-Europeanization?* London: Palgrave, 2018.
Wong, Tom K. *The Politics of Immigration: Partnership, Demographic Change, and American National Identity*. Oxford, UK: Oxford University Press, 2016.

13

Power Changes

The Middle East Sandy Swamp and the Israeli-Palestinian Conflict

Change is constant both in international politics and the politics within individual states. The process is dynamic and not entirely predictable, despite the concerted efforts of analysts and scholars to understand the dynamics involved in individual cases and in general. As the world's premier superpower with global interests, the United States must be especially attentive to the winds of change, because it has interests virtually everywhere that can be affected by what may seem relatively small changes at any place or point in time. The recognition and reaction to change is thus one of the fundamental tasks of statecraft and thus the success of the United States and other countries in the international realm.

No place in the world has been as vulnerable to change since the millennium as the Middle East. The region's political problems, which I described as "intractable conflicts" with "impossible solutions" in a 2016 book (*The Middle East, Oil, and the U.S. National Security Policy*), have been a major source of policy concern throughout the first fifth of this century. The reason for this concentration of concern has been the religiously based terrorism that has dominated international concern and has been symbolized by Al Qaeda and September 11, and more recently the ominous threat posed by the Islamic State (IS). Both organizations have roots in the Middle East that both help define regional problems and contributes to the dynamics of change. In a sense, terrorism has replaced petroleum as the central reason the rest of the world is fixated with the region.

Principle: The Anomaly of Middle East Change

The Middle East is a global anomaly. Its importance historically has derived from two roots. One is religious. The area is the birthplace of the three great monotheistic religions (Christianity, Islam, and Judaism) and thus has religious significant to literally billions of people worldwide with deep and abiding attachments to its holiest places like Jerusalem and Mecca. The religious distinction is a mixed blessing, because the faithful of the three belief systems have fought and sought to subjugate, extinguish, or convert one another whenever they have interacted with one another. The religious factor also divides co-religionists of different sects, such as the Sunni-Shia conflict within Islam that has become a central aspect of inter-Islamic violence. Religion also creates a political conservatism out of sync with most of the rest of the world.

Since the early twentieth century, Middle Eastern oil has been the other variable in the mix. The Persian Gulf littoral contains some the world's largest deposits of petroleum under its sands and beneath its waters. When the world converted from wood as its primary energy source, the Middle East became an area of interest and importance that it never had occupied before. The oil is selectively located, and this has created a caste system where leadership, power, and especially riches are largely monopolized by the oil-rich sheikdoms of the Persian (or Arabian) Gulf region. As the world slowly attempts to wean itself off dependence on this polluting energy source, one question is how the world's tolerance for the medieval politics of much of the region will continue to be tolerated.

Religion and petroleum have been the mainstays of the Middle Eastern claim to international significance, they both contributed to the regional atmosphere in which it conducts its internal and international practices, and they structure how the rest of the world deals with it. This combination helps define the process of international change that dominates the region.

The Middle East has become the most active microcosm of world political change and its ramifications for the international system. It is not the only part of the world undergoing change or with complex politics. Much of the Afro-Asian world has many of the same characteristics as parts of the Middle East, and an understanding of what is happening in the Middle East may contribute to dealing with parts of the Afro-Asian world as well.

What sets the Middle East apart is that it is one of the few areas of the developing world that was not universally part of the European colonial experience. The region was colonized and subjugated: most of what we think of as the Middle East was part of or influenced by the Ottoman Empire until it was dismembered at the end of World War I, and a good deal of northern Africa was under European tutelage. Much of what passes for Westernized modernization simply did not penetrate the Middle East, and the result is a series of anomalies and anachronisms that still plague understanding the region.

Oil is the major geopolitical reason that the rest of the world has a deep and abiding interest in the Middle East, and the need for and exploitation of the petroleum riches of the region have both made it important and interesting and have driven the direction and content of Western, including American, policy toward the region and its multiple conflicts and anomalies. Imagine, for instance, how intimate the relationship between one of the world's few remaining absolutist, religious monarchies and the United States would be if Saudi Arabia had a natural resource dearth.

Oil is, of course, a commodity the centrality of which is part of the change gripping the region and world relations with it. The global demand for oil has decreased selectively, as countries like the United States have moved to alternative sources like shale oil, but the demand has increased in parts of the developing world attempting to modernize and in need of energy to power its expansion; India is a prime example. Looking ahead, however, it seems likely that the world will enter a period of transition from oil to another energy source (the nature of which is unclear), and the likely major victim regionally of such a development could be the Middle East.

The Sources of Change

The winds of change are clearly blowing across Middle East sands, and the structure of interests and policies with which the rest of the world has treated the Middle East over the past century or more require reexamination as a result. Understanding where those relations are headed, however, requires looking briefly at the factors that elevated the Middle East and its oil to the place it now occupies.

The first agents of change are historical, starting with World War I. A minor theater of the Great War was fought over the Middle East, and especially access to its oil. The major impact surrounded the war's conclusion, and notably the defeat and dismembering of the Ottoman Empire and its replacement by League of Nations mandates in parts of the region. As chronicled by authors like Anderson in *Lawrence in Arabia*, the impact was to subdivide responsibility for the region, to divide it into sovereign jurisdictions (most of which were flawed and resulted in current problems) and to allow the emergence of states like Saudi Arabia (which gained independence in 1933), and the reemergence of powers like Iran under the rule of the Shahs. Most of this was done without real detailed knowledge of the region and its ethno-politics. All of this was done, of course, in the name of access to oil and the wealth it could create.

The impact of World War II was also dramatic. A major part of the war (especially between the Soviet Union and Germany) was fought over access and control of Middle Eastern oil, and the war settled that issue, especially after the United States blocked Soviet attempts to impose themselves in Iran. Two other war-related outcomes may have been more important. Largely at American insistence, the European energy system was replaced with one based on cheap, accessible, and secure Middle Eastern oil as the primary energy source. The result was to cement the importance of the oil-rich regions in Western, and later Cold War, terms. The other impact was the inexorable exodus of Jewish survivors of the Holocaust into Palestine. With world public support and embarrassment as pillars, the creation of an independent state of Israel was inevitable, and with it one of the pillars of conflict that frames change today.

The Cold War had an impact as well. Particularly before Russia began the furtive exploitation of its own reserves, access to Persian Gulf oil was a major Soviet priority, as was any action that would complicate Western access to the reserves. These priorities in turn required a Russian presence in the region. The incompatibility of atheistic communism with highly sectarian Islam made the spread of Soviet influence difficult to achieve, and they used the arming of willing Islamic states like Egypt and Syria as their entrée into the region. Russian "mischief" made minimizing the Soviet presence one of the pillars of American Cold War policy in the region.

Finally, there was the impact of the Arab Spring. This movement, largely spawned by younger, more secular Middle Easterners, was a reaction to the highly authoritarian, sectarian rule in many Middle Eastern states. It began in Tunisia and spread more widely, seeming to promise a liberalization and secularization of the region that might bring it closer to the political mainstream emerging in the world. It spread rapidly in 2010 and 2011, but conservative reactions doused it in most places, and it remains only a distant memory in most of the region. One place where it had a lasting—and tragic—effect was in Syria, whose civil war was sparked by an Arab Spring–inspired demonstration.

The Challenge of Change

During the Cold War, the Middle East was, by current standards, relatively stable. The major source of instability and violence was the ongoing battle regarding the existence and status of Israel that resulted in wars between the Israelis and their Muslim neighbors in 1948, 1956, 1967, and 1973, all of which resulted in victories for Israel. Two of these wars' outcomes still color the geopolitics of the region. The most consequential was in 1967, when the outcome included the occupation of former territories of Islamic states by Israel that remain problems, notably on the West Bank and the Golan Heights. The other was 1973, when Israel came closer than it ever had to defeat and threatened nuclear retaliation in the event of imminent defeat. The effect was to centralize possible nuclearization to the region, a prospect that remains not far from the present surface of regional concerns.

Internationally, the Cold War competition dominated the international politics of the region. American policy was based on three partially contradictory pillars. These were a guarantee of the security of Israel, continued secure access to regional petroleum at reasonable prices, and the minimization of Soviet influence. Because many states in the region rhetorically argued for the destruction of Israel, that goal came in some conflict with access to oil. Until the Iranian revolution of 1979, however, the oil situation remained stable and acceptable (despite occasional Organization of the Petroleum Exporting Countries price manipulation): the Persian Gulf states provided the oil, and America's close ally, the Shah of Iran, ensured its secure transit to market. The ideological incompatibility of Islam and Marxism limited Soviet influence to places dependent on Soviet weaponry.

The fall of Shah Reza Pahlavi, the rise of militant Shiism to power in his place, and the Iranian seizure of the American embassy effectively imploded the thirty-year tranquility for the United States. The American arrangement with Iran had been a pillar of U.S. policy in the region, and it dissolved with the 1979 crises that resulted in both sides treating the other as the "great Satan," a dynamic that persists. America remains the major external guarantor of Israeli security, and the problem of Soviet penetration of the region took care of itself in 1991. The result has been change-driven new dynamics to which the system and its members are still adapting.

The New Manifestations of Change

The Arab Spring fizzled in its implicit promise of intellectually liberalizing and modernizing the politics of the Middle East, but it has had residual effects that help form the parameters in which the sands of change are shifting regional politics. Egypt is a prime example. Along with Iran, it is the largest and most populous among regional states, and the Persian and Egyptian empires have historically been the physical and intellectual bulwarks of the region. Having just experienced its own revolutionary experience in 1979, Iran was largely exempt from the Arab Spring, but it had major disruptive effects on Egypt, which has been quiescent and inactive throughout most of the recent turmoil in the region. For now, at least, Egypt concentrates on moderating the internal chaos that has brought the tourist-based economy to its knees and is not a "player" in the regional politics of the area. The power struggle for supremacy as the regional power is now centered on the Persian Gulf and has Iran and Saudi Arabia as its major contestants.

The Syrian civil war has been the major artifact of the Arab Spring, which in turn spawned the most upsetting regional phenomenon of the 2010s, the rise and then decline of the IS. The descendant of the Al Qaeda in Iraq organization, IS emerged as the most effective opponent of the Syrian government and used that role as a springboard to declare and launch its quest to become a sovereign territorial entity, the Caliphate. IS fighters swept through sparsely populated parts of Eastern Syria and Iraq in 2014 and seemed an inexorable and highly frightening force given their Wahhabist, sharia law–based ideology and their reputation as a terrorist organization.

The reign of IS was, however, as unexpectedly short as its ascent. The large credit for stopping and defeating IS goes to Kurdish territorial militias (the *pesh merga*) motivated to evict the IS invaders from territories the Kurds believed were part of their destiny within their own sovereign state, Kurdistan. The Kurds join the Palestinians as the world's two largest and most vocal stateless nations (nationalities that desire but do not have their own sovereign state), and their causes constitute one of the most difficult problems of the region (see chapter 14).

All these dynamics swirl in the current Middle Eastern mix and suggest the desirability of reassessing the interests that states both within and outside the region have. Increasingly, the changes that are accumulating raise questions about how outside countries should assess Middle East dynamics and the politics of the region. The long-standing conflict between Israel and Palestine illustrates this dilemma, of which the issue of Palestinian statelessness discussed in the next chapter is a prominent part.

Application: Dealing with Israel and Palestine

In 1990, the political scientist John Mearsheimer published an article bemoaning the looming crumbling of the Soviet Union and its impact on the international system. His major concern a year before the Cold War ended was that the result would be the parallel invalidation of the ways in which members of the international system had learned to manage relations below the level of war—and especially nuclear conflict—despite the fierce competition of the Cold War. The United States, among others, had devised durable strategies for dealing with the international relations of the Cold War (the American policy of containment, for instance), and the result was reasonable predictability and stability. The end of the Cold War would invalidate those strategies without leaving anything in their place. It is for that reason that Mearsheimer lamented "why we shall soon miss the Cold War" a year before it happened.

The winds of change that are blowing through the Middle East may be producing a similar phenomenon today. Change has been widespread and fundamental: the decline of Egypt as a regional pillar, the Arab Spring, the rise of religiously based international terrorism, and increasing animosity within and between sects of Islam are examples of this depth of change, and it is not clear how the pillars of policy (the three American principles of Israeli security, protection of access to oil, and exclusion of hostile communism) apply to these new conditions. Have circumstances changed so much that new ways of organizing dealing with the shifting sands of the region are necessary?

It is not an easy question to answer, as the preceding discussions have suggested. There are new emphases and problems, and they are all interconnected and interdependent in ways that make the pursuit of organizing principles more difficult, and what can be attempted, however, is a brief overview of prominent elements and how they interconnected. One has been selected as more exemplary than others both as indicators of regional politics and outside actions and impacts: changes in the status of Israel in the territories it has occupied since the 1967 war and particularly the fate of the Palestinian state.

Israel and Palestine

The disposition, rightful ownership, and control over the territory of which pre-1967 Israel is the focus is the longest continuous point of contention in the post–World War II Middle East, and it remains a major point of cleavage within world politics, especially regarding the territories conquered, occupied, and inhabited by increasing numbers of Israelis since the 1967 war. Almost all countries accept and support UN General Assembly resolutions that condemn the continuing military occupation by Israel of territories seized during the war and especially of Israeli policy that has permitted the settlement of upwards of three-quarters of a million Israeli settlers (mostly immigrants) in these territories, largely the West Bank and East Jerusalem, as well as portions of the Syrian Golan Heights overlooking Israel. The major defenders of Israeli policy prominently include the government of Israeli Prime Minister Benjamin Netanyahu and more recently the American administration under Donald Trump.

The genesis of the crisis was the creation of the state of Israel in 1948. This act triggered a massive exodus of Muslim citizens of Palestine into the surrounding Islamic states, notably the West Bank, Lebanon, Syria, and other parts of Jordan. Prior to the establishment of Israel, the world's Jewish population had been a true stateless nation that had been left unprotected in the face of the hideous predation of the Holocaust. Israel gave them a state and the mechanisms to defend themselves. In the process, the Palestinians were forced to abandon their statehood and became a stateless nation, a status they continue to endure.

The current issue surrounding Israel and Palestine was an outcome of the 1967 Six-Day War, in which Israel routed a coalition of Muslim states dedicated to its defeat and destruction and in the process occupied territories contiguous to and thus posing a potential threat to Israel: the West Bank from Jordan, parts of the Golan Heights from Syria, and the Sinai Peninsula and Gaza Strip from Egypt. Sinai was returned to Egypt as part of the 1982 peace treaty between it and Israel, and Gaza was remanded to the Palestinian Authority in 2006. The West Bank and Golan remain the major points of contention. For one thing, Israeli-continued physical occupation, settlement, and potential annexation are opposed by virtually the entire international community, especially because they virtually eliminate the possibility of a peace settlement between Israel and Palestine by depriving the Palestinians of the sovereign territory on which to construct a state, a goal of most of world opinion, including historically the United States. For another, they motivate others in the region to oppose and attack Israel, thereby contributing to destabilizing conflict in the region. They also ignore or defer a demographic reality that works to the ultimate disadvantage of perpetuating Israel as a Jewish and democratic state. The increasingly aggressive posture of the United States behind positions championed by the Netanyahu government and ratified by the Israeli electorate in reelecting him temporarily in April 2019 have been ripple effects beyond the immediate contest between the Israelis and the Palestinians.

The Israeli Position: Bibi's "Dream"

Prior to the ascension of Netanyahu to prime minister of Israel in 2009, the major focus of international debate was on the process by which the creation of a sovereign Palestinian entity would be accomplished, and successive American administrations through the Obama incumbency championed a process that would have resulted in Israeli withdrawal from most of the occupied territories and the creation of an independent Palestine on the West Bank. This position is directly at odds with the highly nationalistic, security-driven worldview of Netanyahu, who has found an international ally in the current American president, Donald J. Trump.

Israeli foreign policy has always been obsessed with the security of the Israeli state to a more conscious degree than other states experience. The obsession is understandable. The prospect of the success of the Holocaust raised the possibility of successful genocide against the Jewish people, and the Israelis, as the symbolic sovereign expression of world Jewry, are acutely aware of that dynamic and the avowed intent of some others to conclude that process. An Israeli lesson from the Holocaust is that Jews did not unite to resist their gory fate, a mistake that Israeli governments have sought to avoid again. The impressive Israeli Defense Force and nuclear weapons possession are eloquent physical expressions of the imperative "Never again."

The Israeli "obsession" with security also reflects an assessment of the physical condition of the Jewish state. Israel within its pre-1967 borders is a long but narrow piece of territory. At its narrowest point near the West Bank, it is only about ten miles wide, creating the defense problem of how to avoid an invasion across that narrow band that would bifurcate the country and create an intractable defense problem. In the northern part of the country, Eastern Israel sits at the base of the low mountains in Syria known as the Golan Heights, and Israeli settlements in the shadow of the Heights have historically been vulnerable to artillery barrages by the Syrians from the top of the Heights into Israeli valleys below. These facts influence Israeli views of controlling both the West Bank and the Heights, which also provide hospitable sites for Jewish immigration when in control of these territories. Conservative Jews (including Netanyahu) also talk about the occupied regions as part of a Greater Israel that creates a religious base for their claims.

These calculations form much of the context when Netanyahu views the region and acceptable political outcomes to the relationship between Israel, the occupied territories, and sovereign control of the West Bank and Golan. In this formulation, the role of the occupied territories is critical for both security and aspirational reasons. Israel is safer from physical attack in possession of Golan and the West Bank than without them. That safety reinforces the formidable Israeli invulnerability from attack that formed its pre-1967 obsession with being attacked and overrun that nuclear possession helps prevent. The latter source of Israeli security arose in 1973 when the Israelis were temporarily in some danger of losing their first conflict with their neighbors and threatened to activate their nuclear arsenal to avoid defeat. Israel's implicit regional nuclear threat has been part of security considerations in the area ever since.

The West Bank is critical to Netanyahu's aspiration for a Greater Israel in two ways. Partly, the West Bank is part of the historic territory that some Jews claim as a necessary part of a God-given Jewish territorial state. Less metaphysically, part of the dream includes the return of as many world Jews to Israel as possible, and there is simply not enough habitable space in pre-1967 Israel to accommodate that return. The settlements are, despite disclaimers from some Israelis, a place to accommodate the immigration of Jewry to Israel. The annexation of East Jerusalem is also part of this calculus and of the symbolism of Jerusalem as the capital of the country.

How is this dream to be realized? The basic, if publicly unstated, premise is that the longer the occupation continues and settlement increases, the more of a fait accompli will be accomplished and the more permanent it becomes. The eventual annexation of West Bank to Israel is critical here. With the formidable Israeli Defense Force and a hegemonic regional nuclear force, Israeli security and survival are less pressing than they once were, meaning that realization of the territorial dream is now the prime goal of that dream. The strategy for achieving it is attrition: the longer Israel occupies the West Bank, the more likely the world will come to accept the situation as permanent.

Problems with the Dream

There are two major barriers to achieving the goal. The first is that virtually nobody outside Israel accepts Bibi's dream as legitimate. The focus of objections is the plight of the stateless Palestinians, the establishment of a state for them being the solution proposed by most of the world. It is a position that Netanyahu rejects. He states his objection in security concerns, but many observers believe the real motive is Palestinian annexation to Israel to create Greater Israel.

Simply put, Israeli nuclear weapons and conventional arms make Israel as secure as anyone is in the Middle East. Without the West Bank to accommodate immigration, Israel is not as big as it needs to be to create Greater Israel. The question is whether international objections will outlast Netanyahu's obstinance.

The other problem is demographic. When the current Jewish population of Israel and the occupied territories are added together, they very slightly outnumber the Palestinian/Muslim population of the same areas (see, among other places, my *Cases in US National Security* for the actual numbers). The demographics, however, demonstrate that the Muslim population is growing much faster than that of the Jewish population. Even with Jewish immigration into the occupied areas, the Palestinians will very soon equal and exceed the Jewish population, with no prospects of that dynamic being reversed.

In that case, Greater Israel is or will soon have a Muslim majority, and if the political expression of Greater Israel is a single Israeli state composed of pre-1967 and West Bank populations, *Israel will no longer be a Jewish state*. Israel has always prided itself in being both Jewish and democratic, but an expanded Israel cannot be both. The Jewish population can remain in power only by granting a more limited franchise to Muslims—no one man, one vote—but instead some form of apartheid solution (a prospect former President Carter disapprovingly suggested in a 2006 book). To remain Jewish, it must be nondemocratic. If it wants to be democratic, it cannot be fully Jewish. The only way to be both is to adopt the two-state solution of independent Palestinian and Israeli states with a boundary based essentially on the pre-1967 frontier. Benn, editor of *Haaretz*, an Israeli newspaper that has been highly critical of Bibi, suggests that Netanyahu's solution is virtually guaranteed to be condemned internationally. It is the Nation State Bill, which "defines Israel as the nation-state of the Jewish people and lacks provisions for the equality of non-Jews." It is the virtual definition of the apartheid option.

The current situation serves the short-term interest of Israel and its long-term interest only if world opposition erodes over time, but that still leaves the demographic time bomb ticking. It is not clear what that outcome will be. If the situation continues and Israel does not have to settle the Palestinian question to the world's satisfaction, the conflict will continue to poison the already venomous politics of the region. Once its civil war is completed, Syria will almost certainly seek to regain the parts of Golan it has lost, and Iran, which through its sponsorship of Hamas and Hezbollah fighters, has been the primary physical supporter of the Palestinians, will continue that support. An effective Syrian-Iranian alliance has major implications for regional power balances in the region and ensures continuing antagonism between nuclear Israel and potentially nuclear Iran. A militant Iran also becomes a more visible and powerful regional competitor for Saudi Arabia in a region in which Egypt is no longer a major factor. The list goes on.

The Trump administration has thrown its weight behind Bibi's dream. Its first act was to agree in 2018 to move the U.S. Embassy from Tel Aviv to Jerusalem, a symbolic recognition of Jerusalem as the Israeli capital. No other state has done so, and East Jerusalem is also claimed by the Palestinians as their capital. In April 2019, Trump also accepted the annexation of the Golan Heights by Israel in the face of universal opposition.

Israel also views Iran as its primary regional foe, presumably because Iran is the country that most easily could break Israel's nuclear monopoly. The Trump administration has also been helpful there. In 2017, Trump removed the United States from the nonproliferation agreement (Joint Comprehensive Plan of Action discussed in chapter 10) on grounds Iran was violating the accord and, according to Mandelbaum, "challenged American values as well as American interests." In 2019, the administration declared an elite core unit of the Iranian armed forces (the Revolutionary Guards) as a terrorist organization. Both actions reinforced what Mandelbaum described as Israel's status as "a dependable counterweight to Persian power."

Conclusion

Some level of turbulence is endemic to the Middle East because of the enormous diversity of its peoples and their loyalties, religions, and histories. The area may be the cradle of much of the world's religions and the location of its holiest sites, but it has also been the location in which some of its bloodiest and most intractable conflicts have played out through history and continue to exist. The result has been a rapid process of change that is itself a changeable factor. Sorting out the complex internal and external politics is a complicated and ongoing process.

There was a period after World War II when the influence of the Cold War helped structure how the world looked at the region and allowed, in the case of the United States, a reasonably coherent and enduring three-legged stool of priorities: Israel, oil, and Soviet exclusion. When the Cold War system collapsed, so did what passed for a Middle Eastern "order" that allowed the development of coherent strategies to deal with the region wherein an action toward one problem did not necessarily have major impacts on other aspects of the region. That condition has now changed, and any policy toward one part of the region may have consequences in other places that are difficult to anticipate and where what outsiders or other regional actors do are also unpredictable.

The conflict between Israel and Palestine, which is now over seventy years in duration in its present form, was purposely chosen for emphasis in the application section. It is important because it is a destabilizing influence that involves multiple parties with different interests, and because it has occupied a central place in American policy in the region. A pillar of the U.S. regional commitment has always been the sanctity and security of Israel, and especially given the Netanyahu-Trump regional condominium over the region, the fate of Palestine has become a prime determinant of regional policy. That emphasis sends tentacles of concern and change more widely into the region into places like Iran and Syria, with not entirely predictable results. Will, for instance, U.S.-Israeli obstinance over Palestine eventually lead to a nuclear arms race in the region, where Iran feels the need to have the "bomb" to deter Israel, and the Saudis feel the need to "go nuclear" to deter Iran? A nuclear arms race in the Middle East is the worst regional horror scenario given the volatility of Middle Eastern conflict. What could cause it? No one knows, and it is important that policies try to avoid finding out.

Study/Discussion Questions

1. Discuss the process and evolution of Middle Eastern change, with an emphasis on how change has affected U.S. policy.
2. How did the end of the Cold War change the international politics of the Middle East? Cite examples, including the impact of the Arab Spring.
3. What new "manifestations" of change have occurred in the Middle East since the end of the Cold War? Discuss.
4. How are the new regional changes related to one another? How do they affect the environment of change, including Israel and Palestine?
5. What has been the historic relationship between Israel and Palestine? How has it changed in the 2010s?
6. What is "Bibi's dream"? Discuss in detail.
7. What are the major problems with realizing Bibi's dream? How are they related? Discuss.
8. What role has the Trump administration played in the recent Israeli-Palestinian conflict? Have these actions been helpful? To whom? Why?

Bibliography

Anderson, Scott. *Lawrence in Arabia: War, Deceit, Imperial Folly and the Making of the Modern Middle East*. New York: Anchor Books, 2013.

Armstrong, Karen. *Jerusalem: One City, Three Faiths*. London: Ballantine Books, 2011.

Avishi, Bernard. "Confederation: The One Possible Arab-Palestinian Solution." *New York Review of Books*, February 3, 2018.

Bellin, Eva. "Democratization and Its Discontents: Should America Push Political Reform in the Middle East?" *Foreign Affairs* 87, no. 4 (July/August 2008), 112–19.

Benn, Aluf. "Netanyahu's Referendum: What's at Stake for the Israeli Prime Minister in the Early Election." *Foreign Affairs Snapshot* (online), February 6, 2019.

———. "The End of the Old Israel: How Netanyahu Has Transformed the Nation." *Foreign Affairs* 95, no. 4 (July/August 2016), 16–27.

Betts, Richard K. "Pick Your Battle: Ending America's Era of Permanent War." *Foreign Affairs* 93, no. 6 (November/December 2014), 15–24.

Bregman, Ahron. *Cursed Victory: A History of Israel and the Occupied Territories, 1967 to the Present*. Trenton, TX: Pegasus, 2015.

Brown, Nathan J. "The Occupation at Fifty: A Permanent State of Ambiguity." *Current History* 116, no. 704 (December 2017), 331–36.

———. "The Palestinians' Receding Dream of Statehood." *Current History* 110, no. 740 (December 2011), 345–51.

Carter, Jimmy. *Palestine: Peace Not Apartheid*. New York: Simon and Schuster, 2006.

Della Pergola, Sergio. "Israel's Existential Predicament: Population, Territory, and Identity." *Current History* 109, no. 731 (December 2010), 383–89.

——— and Rebhun Uzi (eds.) *Jewish Population Identity: Concept and Reality*. New York: Springer, 2018.

Dowty, Alan. *Israel/Palestine* (fourth edition). London: Polity Press, 2017.

Ehrenreich, Ben. *The Way to the Spring: Life and Death in Palestine*. New York: Penguin Books, 2016.

Eland, Ivan. *No War for Oil: U.S. Dependency and the Middle East.* Oakland, CA: Independent Institute, 2011.
Freedman, Robert, ed. *Israel and the United States: Six Decades of U.S.-Israeli Relations.* New York and London: Routledge, 2018.
Haass, Richard N. "The Unraveling: How to Respond to a Disordered World." *Foreign Affairs* 93, no. 6 (November/December 2014), 70–79.
Hammond, Jeremy R. *Obstacle to Peace: The U.S. Role in the Israeli-Palestinian Conflict.* New York: Worldview, 2016.
Harms, Gregory, and Todd M. Ferry. *The Palestinian-Israeli Conflict: A Basic Introduction* (fourth edition). London: Pluto Press, 2017.
Held, Colbert C., and John Thomas Cummings. *Middle East Patterns: Places. People, and Politics* (sixth edition). Boulder, CO: Westview Press, 2013.
Hummel, Daniel R. *Covenant Brothers: Evangelicals, Jews, and U.S.-Israeli Relations.* Philadelphia, PA: University of Pennsylvania Press, 2018.
Jewish Virtual Library. *Vital Statistics: Latest Population Statistics for Israel.* May 11, 2018.
Mandelbaum, Michael. "The New Containment: Handling Russia, China, and Iran." *Foreign Affairs* 98, no. 2 (March/April 2019), 123–31.
Mearsheimer, John J. "Why We Shall Soon Miss the Cold War." *Atlantic Monthly* 266, no. 2 (August 1990), 35–50.
Muravchik, Joshua. *Making David into Goliath: How the World Turned Against Israel.* New York: Encounter, 2016.
Owen, John M. "From Calvin to the Caliphate: What Europe's Religious Wars Tell Us about the Modern Middle East." *Foreign Affairs* 94, no. 3 (May/June 2015), 77–89.
Petras, James. *The Politics of Empire: The U.S., Israel, and the Middle East.* Atlanta, GA: Clarity Press, 2014.
Ross, Dennis. *Doomed to Succeed: The U.S.-Israeli Relationship from Truman to Obama.* New York: Farrar, Straus, and Giroux, 2015.
Said, Edward W. *The Question of Palestine* (reissue edition). New York: Vintage, 2016.
Scheindlin, Dahlia. "Netanyahu's Foreign Policy Is Bad for Israel." *Foreign Affairs Snapshot* (online), February 8, 2019.
Shavit, Ari. *My Promised Land: The Triumphs and Tragedy of Israel.* New York: Spiegel and Grau, 2015.
Snow, Donald M. *Cases in U.S. National Security: Concepts and Processes.* Lanham, MD: Rowman & Littlefield, 2019.
———. *The Middle East, Oil, and the U.S. National Security Policy: Intractable Conflicts, Impossible Solutions.* Lanham, MD: Rowman & Littlefield, 2016.
Stern, Jessica, and M. Berger. *ISIS: The State of Terror.* New York: ECCO Books, 2015.
U.S. Department of Defense. *Assessing the Impact of U.S.-Israeli Relations on the Arab World.* Washington, DC: U.S. Department of Defense, 2015.
Uzi, Rabi. *Yemen: Civil War and Unification.* London: I. B. Tauris, 2015.
Van Creveld, Martin L. *The Land of Blood and Honey: The Rise of Modern Israel.* New York: Thomas Dunne, 2010.

14

Stateless Nations

The Fate of the Palestinians and the Kurds

There are numerous sources of international differences that make world politics disorderly, conflicting, occasionally violent, and often unjust for some or all parties. A major category of those imperfections involves the question of rightful territorial possession both within and between states. The political map of the world does not always reflect the territorial jurisdictions that all people and groups feel reflect their values. The result is disagreement that can be both very deeply felt and the cause of considerable division and disagreement.

Two major manifestations of this disagreement dominate the contemporary problem. One occurs when state boundaries arbitrarily divide members of a group with national aspirations into more than one state. The other exists when a group with national aspirations is housed within a disputed territory where those who exercise sovereignty preclude that national group from forming a state. The dynamics in the two situations are different, but their effect is to create stateless nations where self-determination is denied.

These situations are uncommon, but they represent a dynamic that often roils what might be more tranquil circumstances otherwise. The geographic area where they are most prevalent, predictably enough given its general instability, is the Middle East, the sandy swamp featured in chapter 13. Each is a classic case in its own way.

One example is the Israeli-Palestinian situation. It is fundamentally a question of who—Israelis or Palestinians—has a superior sovereign claim over the West Bank of the Jordan River. Israel has occupied this space since 1967 and has established and expanded Israeli settlements in many parts of the region, an arguable de facto claim of sovereign authority. The Palestinian Arab population, many of whom were displaced during the establishment of the Israeli state, claims the territory as the basis of the Palestinian state. The other example is the Kurds, a distinct and ancient ethnic, nationalist group who inhabit parts of four Middle Eastern states: Turkey, Iraq, Iran, and Syria. They form a majority in each of the areas of those states where they live, but are in a minority in all four of the countries. Kurdish nationalism is very high, and there is virtually unanimous sentiment to carve a state of Kurdistan from the Kurdish regions of each country. Their fate has become more widely known because of their role in defeating the Islamic State (IS).

Principle: Stateless Nations

In ideal world order, national identities and political jurisdictions would be the same. All the people with a distinct self-identity would be able to live in a sovereign state with like individuals, and no national group would be denied a territorial state of their own or be forced to live in a state where their national identity was politically denied or the subject of discrimination. Unfortunately, that is not universally the case, and the results are territorial disputes—situations where multiple population groups claim rightful sovereign authority over the same territory. In the worst cases, the competing claims are very deeply held, mutually exclusive, zero-sum advocacies that are irreconcilable among the parties themselves and where outside parties either cannot or will not assert enough power to create and enforce outcomes that will be acceptable to some, and preferably all, of the affected parties.

These situations pose a fundamental challenge to the international order. Internal conflicts (developing world internal conflicts [DWICs]) have become the most common form of organized violence (war) in the contemporary international system, eclipsing and virtually eliminating traditional wars between states as sources of violent turmoil. Many DWICs arise either from multinationalist or irredentist roots and have arisen at least in part from the efforts of peoples in decolonized locales to come to grips with questions about the physical boundaries and appropriate holders of sovereign legitimacy in different areas. The victims are members of stateless nations: groups with a national self-identity that lack a territorial home of their own.

Irredentism, Multinationalism, and Developing World Internal Conflicts

The key element in understanding the maladies that plague stateless nations begins with the dichotomy between the anthropological term "nation" and the political and legal term "state." The international system is sometimes said to be composed of "nation-states," suggesting a conjunction of the two concepts that would produce stable sovereign entities and result in minimal instability and violence. The problem is that, in a literal sense, there are very few actual nation-states, and in the places where the connection breaks down, instability, often involving territorial boundaries, is most likely to occur.

The term "nation" refers to the identification people have with others. The nation is the primary point of loyalty people have, and this identification extends to political loyalties to the state or some other entity. No list is comprehensive and not all nationally defined groups possess all the characteristics, but common indicators of national identification include race, ethnicity, language, religion, common territorial habitation, and shared historical experience. The national identity that groups adopt is the basis for their loyalty to and support for or opposition to the state.

The most common form of discontinuity between the concepts of nation and state occur where at least two nationally self-identified national groups live within a state, the basic definition of multinationalism. The terms multiethnic and multicultural nationalism, both of which convey much of the essence of nationality, are sometimes used to distinguish this political connotation of multinationalism in developing countries.

This situation is common to almost all the countries of the developing world and, to a lesser degree, in the developed world as well. Writing in 1993, for instance, Welsh surveyed the world's countries and concluded that 160 of the then 180 recognized sovereign states were multinational in one way or another. It becomes a destabilizing source of territorial dispute when one or more of the groups decide they want to change the physical or political balance by eliminating or suppressing one or more other national groups who reside in the state. Either motive can result in internal violence to overthrow the offending national group or even to secede.

Multinationalist-inspired instability is the most common form of disconnection that underlies territorial disputes, but it is neither the only one nor even, in some cases, the most difficult and intractable form that territorial disputes take. Another form, often associated with particularly difficult, intractable territorial situations, arises from instances of irredentism.

Irredentism is a term with an interesting genesis. It derives from the Italian word that means "unredeemed," and it was first used to describe aspirations about Italian lands during the process of unification of Italy in 1870. It is now used more generically to describe what the *Free Dictionary* calls a movement or sentiment the purpose of which is "the recovery of territory culturally or historically related to one's nation but now subject to a foreign government." If the broad purpose of multinationalist efforts is to alter the state to make it more congenial to some or all the national groups that reside in a given sovereign territory, irredentists challenge the rightful possession and exercise of sovereignty by groups in territories they consider rightfully theirs.

The fundamental purpose and impact of these groups is to attack the problem of stateless nations. Groups making irredentist claims are basically arguing one of two pernicious conditions prevent them from achieving what they regard as their rightful national endowment. One of these is territorial occupation that prevents their assertion of sovereign authority over territory that would allow them to serve as a sovereign state. The other is the situation where territory they view as rightfully theirs is within the unjust sovereign jurisdiction of several states and where their intent and purpose is to unite those areas into a single state. These two situations form the bases for the two applications in the next section.

Statelessness can be the basis for violence and instability when a stateless group asserts its determined desire to alter the boundaries of political jurisdictions so that they can refigure the map and create a state of their own. This determination will almost invariably be rejected and resisted by political authorities in the existing territory in which the new state is proposed, and the clash between contending parties will often result in internal violence in the form of a DWIC. The alternative is frustration on the part of members of the stateless group or the group it proposes to replace. Both outcomes are destabilizing for the international system, because the result can be internal warfare that destabilizes the area involved and can result in an intractable conflict and violence.

Territorial disputes arising from statelessness are not common in contemporary international relations, but where they exist, they are particularly difficult and furtive. The question of what group has the legitimate claim to exercising sovereignty in a given territory has various roots and longer or shorter histories depending on the region and the conflict. All share a commonality: the forced cohabitation of antagonistic groups in the same territorial space and the desire of one group or another to break away and seek its own separate state. The disputes tend to be irresolvable in any acceptable political way, because the contesting groups of people dislike or distrust one another to the point they cannot amicably reach mutually acceptable outcomes. The longest lasting conflicts tend to be in the Middle East, where the roots of conflicts can be traced back over millennia and where the basis of disagreement and hatred can be traced to tribal differences, often influenced by religious factors that have defined and deepened the disagreements across time.

Application: Palestine and Kurdistan

Two conflicts exemplify statelessness especially well because of their unique characteristics, because they are both major irritants to regional and world peace, and because they each represent the territorial issue of being contests in which at least one aspirant is a stateless nation. They differ in the context in which the claim to statehood is based and in the structure of the problem and alternative solutions.

They also differ in important factual ways. The Palestinian quest for statehood has deep historical roots in the more or less constant struggle for possession of the various territories included in the Levant, but their current dilemma has its roots in post–World War II events, notably the establishment of the state of Israel and the Israeli occupation of territory in 1967 on the West Bank of the Jordan River that the Palestinians (and most of the international community) have claimed as the site of Palestine. Structurally, it is primarily a dispute between Israel and the Palestinians. The Kurdish desire for statehood is more long standing, and it is a condition in which the Kurds have consistently been denied the right to self-determination. The current problem has its roots in the settlement of World War I, where Kurdistan was made part of several other states. Structurally, it is a contest between the Kurds and those states, notably Turkey, Iraq, Iran, and Syria. In a sense, Kurdistan already exists, but it does as an area within those four states, none of which is willing to allow the Kurds to unite those areas into the sovereign state of Kurdistan. The international community, with the notable exception of the American Trump administration, accepts the Palestinian claim and advocates an end of the Israeli occupation of the West Bank and Golan. There is also considerable support for Kurdistan, but it is measured because of opposition of a North Atlantic Treaty Organization member, Turkey.

The Case of Palestine

The plight of the Palestinians has been a major issue between Israel and the Palestinian Arabs at least since the end of World War II and even before. It is essentially a territorial dispute between the Jewish people of Israel and the mostly Sunni Muslim Arabs who think of themselves as Palestinians. Israel is an accepted sovereign state, but previously the Jews were a stateless nation with a difficult, often tragic history punctuated by Hitler's attempted extinction of the Jewish people in the 1930s and 1940s. Many surviving European Jews heeded the call for a Zionist exodus and ended up in what was then considered Palestine, part of the British mandated zone from the breakup of the Ottoman Empire. Already living in that area (largely in peace with the Jewish settlers already there) were the Palestinian Arabs, another classic stateless nation that sought a sovereign home in the same region. Historic Palestine was the area both wished to claim as their own.

The Arena and the Contestants

There is not universal agreement on exactly what territory conclusively defines Palestine, a common regional malady in the Middle East due to the many states and empires that have ruled all or parts of the region since antiquity. In a general sense, the area is generally thought of in contemporary times as being composed of Israel (pre-1967), the West Bank (including East Jerusalem), and the Gaza Strip. It is not a physically large area: internationally accepted (pre-1967) Israel is about the size of New Jersey, the West Bank is about the size of Delaware, and Gaza is a narrow peninsula along the eastern Mediterranean coast northward from the Sinai Peninsula of Egypt. Gaza is about twice the size of Washington, DC.

The largest physical part of the territorial dispute is the West Bank. As noted in chapter 13, its continued possession by Israel is central to Netanyahu's dream of Greater Israel and the attraction of more of world Jewry to the Israeli state. Without the West Bank, Israel does not consider itself whole: it is not stateless, but neither is there a complete Israeli state that fully marries nation and state. For Palestinians, the situation is stark. Without the West Bank, there is no sovereign Palestinian entity other than the Gaza Strip. Israelis may not enjoy an entirely fulfilled marriage of statehood and nationality without the West Bank. The Palestinians are a stateless nation without full sovereign control of the territory they think of as Palestine.

As suggested in chapter 13, pre-1967 Israel and the West Bank are distinct in terms of population. The population size of pre-1967 Israel is approximately 6 million, of whom about 5 million are Jewish and the rest are mostly Palestinian Arabs and a small number of Christians. The West Bank, on the other hand, has a Palestinian majority of about 3 million and, including East Jerusalem, a Jewish population of nearly a half million settlers. Gaza has a population of about 1.75 million, virtually all of whom are Palestinian Arabs. The detailed numbers are not precise, but when the three parts of historic Palestine are combined, there are slightly more Palestinian Arabs than Jews in that population. Demographic trends (the Arab population is growing at a faster rate than the Jewish population) are unfavorable to the Israelis, and this fact also affects the attractiveness of various solution to the territorial dispute.

Stripped of its historical and religious trappings, the dispute between the Israelis and Palestinians over the West Bank is thus conceptually relatively straightforward: who has the superior claim to sovereign domain over Palestine? Part of the question has been effectively decided. There is little controversy about Israeli sovereignty over territories ceded to the Jewish state in 1948 and as expanded up until the 1967 war. There are also many individual claims by former Palestinian land and homeowners over the rightful ownership of property in Israel that they abandoned when they fled and which were subsequently claimed by Israelis.

That leaves the West Bank, which is an ongoing problem for two basic reasons. The first is the general question of Israeli settlements on the West Bank. These settlements are enclaves (generally on the best land, which effectively means land with adequate water under it) and are residential areas reserved for Jews, often immigrants. They are not claimed as sovereign territory, but they have become increasingly permanent-looking enclaves that it is increasingly impossible to see Israel abandoning to a Palestinian state. Arab control over the West Bank would likely entail displacement of the settlers. The other problem is the old city of East Jerusalem. Both Israel and the Palestinians claim it as their national capital. It rests along the border between Israel and the West Bank, and it has been the destination of much Jewish settlement outside the pre-1967 boundaries. The religious and political significance of Jerusalem make it possibly the most intractable part of the territorial dispute.

Possible Solutions: One State, Two States, or Conflict Without End?

The question of Palestinian statehood and where to locate a sovereign Palestinian state has been one of the most nettlesome international problems of the last half century. Every American president since 1948 has become involved in its solution, and all have failed. In his first pronouncement on the subject, President Trump intoned that he could live with either a one-state or a two-state solution (the only viable alternatives), whichever the parties could agree to. His pronouncement was immediately dismissed as disingenuous: the heart of the problem is that the sides have been unable to agree on *any* solution.

The basic alternatives are easy to state but have proven impossibly difficult to achieve. The first is a one-state solution, where all three of the constituent parts of greater Palestine (Israel, West Bank, and Gaza) are incorporated into a single state. This solution is opposed by the Palestinians, who are convinced the Israelis would dominate such a state and by some Israelis who fear that demographics ensure they will become a minority in that state. It does, however, solve the problem of Jewish immigration onto the West Bank and of the status of East Jerusalem, which would become the capital of the unified state. The two-state solution has the backing of virtually all the international community outside the U.S.-Israeli axis. It calls for an independent Palestine on the West Bank and Gaza and an independent Israel consisting of the pre-1967 territory, some settlements along the border, and presumably some part of East Jerusalem. Most of the opposition comes from factions (including the Netanyahu regime) who favor a concept of Greater Israel and who fear that a sovereign Palestine would be a launching pad for terrorist activities against the Jewish state.

There are three pivotal considerations that affect disposition of the conflict. The first is Israel's demographic dilemma noted in the last chapter. Israel was established and prides itself as a state that is both democratic and Jewish. The problem is how to remain both under different territorial solutions. If there is a single state solution, demographics work in their disfavor. If Israel remains democratic, the Arabs will soon outnumber the Jews at the polls, and the Jews will be in the minority, leaving the outcome a democratic but non-Jewish state. If the Jews renounce one-man, one-vote democracy, the state can remain Jewish, but not fully democratic. The two-state solution may reduce Israel geographically to something like its pre-1967 size, but it will remain solidly Jewish (a five-to-one ratio of Jews in the population), allowing Israel to remain *both* Jewish and democratic.

The second is Israeli security, and it has two parts. The first, already discussed, is the vulnerability Israel faces of being cut in two by hostile forces attacking west from the West Bank. The second is the fear that a hostile West Bank, sovereign Palestine will serve as a sanctuary for terrorists attacking Israel. This fear also motivated Israel to build a barrier fence along the West Bank frontier to regulate Palestinian movement in and out of Israel. Netanyahu has proposed a semi-sovereign Palestine with occupying Israel Defense Forces contingents on the West Bank for security purposes. Virtually all outsiders dismiss this proposal.

The third, and ultimately most vexing, problem is East Jerusalem. It cannot be the capital of two countries, and neither side is willing to accept their exclusion while it becomes the other's capital. Given the emotional ties both have to religious sites in parts of Jerusalem, neither can abandon it. That leaves two unhappy options. One is to partition the city so part is in Israel and part in Palestine. Conceivably, one zone could become the capital of Israel and the other the capital of Palestine. Virtually no one thinks such a solution could work. The other possibility is either to declare Jerusalem a neutral city-state, possibly under international jurisdiction (which has been tried unsuccessfully) or to declare that it will not be the capital of either country. Neither country finds this outcome satisfactory.

I have called this problem "irresolvable" in previous editions of this text. The enmity and distrust between the two sides on virtually all issues makes an amicable division of a dispute over a parcel of land the size of Delaware a major international issue. Because the Palestinians lack the physical power to wrest control from Israel, they cannot assert their claim militarily. Thus, until the sides decide that resolution and the hopeful peace that will follow are more important than what divides them, the result will continue to be Palestinian statelessness.

The Case of Kurdistan

The Kurdish quest to end its long statelessness is physically more imposing than the Israeli-Palestinian conflict: it spans a longer period of time, it involves territory and people in four Middle Eastern states, and it has been and continues to be a major source of geopolitical struggle between the Kurds and all those countries where the Kurds live and in which they claim statehood for Kurdistan. Global awareness appears and then disappears. It arose in the early 1990s when Iraq's threats of genocidal retribution drove thousands of Iraqi Kurds into uneasy exile in Turkey. It has resurfaced with the prominent role that Kurdish *pesh merga* territory-protecting militias have played in the campaign against the IS.

Table 14.1. Kurdish Population Distribution

Location	Designation	Estimated Population
Turkey	Northern Kurdistan	18 million
Iraq	Southern Kurdistan	5 million
Syria	Western Kurdistan (Rojava)	2 million
Iran	Eastern Kurdistan	8 million
All Other		2–3 million
Total		35–36 million

Source: The Kurdish Project, 2016.

The Kurds are concentrated principally in four countries. They are most numerous in Eastern and Southeastern Turkey (Northern Kurdistan), and their other major concentrations are in Northern Iraq (Southern or Iraqi Kurdistan), Northern Syria (Western Kurdistan or Rojava), and Western Iran (Eastern or Iranian Kurdistan). Census figures are not very precise, but the number of Kurds within territories claimed as part of a Kurdish state is in the range of 35 million, which means that were Kurdistan to come into being, its population would be roughly that of Saudi Arabia and greater than Iraq (after the Kurds currently counted as Iraqi were subtracted from the Iraqi population). Its distribution is summarized in Table 14.1.

The Dream of and Demand for a Kurdistan

The concerted movement toward Kurdish statehood emerged in the early twentieth century, and its progress (or lack thereof) has been highlighted by three major events: the Versailles peace negotiations of 1919, the plight of the Iraqi Kurds after Saddam Hussein threatened their slaughter in 1991, and most recently, the prominent role of the Kurdish *pesh merga* (Kurdish for "those who face death") in defeating the IS Caliphate. These calendar highlights do not define the longer-standing desire of the Kurds for statehood so much as they provide road markers of international awareness of the Kurdish situation.

Each is significant for a different reason. A Kurdish delegation petitioned the peacemakers in Paris in 1919 to create a sovereign state of Kurdistan in the Kurdish area as part of carving up the Ottoman Empire. There were multiple claimants to the areas, including European powers like Britain and France, former regional powers like Persia, and the Turkish successor state. Ultimately the claims of non-Kurds prevailed. The precedent of denying the Kurds what they viewed as their destiny was established, but at least a greater part of the world became aware of their fate.

In 1991, after his stunning eviction from Iraq and rebellions against him (in, among other places, the Kurdish region of Iraq), Saddam Hussein threatened to renew chemical warfare and other attacks against the Kurds in reprisal. Fearing their extinction at the hands of their own president, thousands fled to Turkey. Their plight was widely reported on global television, and the United States, in order to please the Turks, announced a no-fly zone in the Kurdish region from which Iraqi forces were excluded to entice the Kurds to go home. In 1992, the Kurdish area was deemed autonomous and the first Kurdish Regional Government (KRG) was elected.

The final element has been the Kurdish role in the fight against the Caliphate. Iraqi and Syrian Kurdistan were prominent parts of the land initially conquered by the IS as it spread eastward toward Baghdad, and especially in the early going, Iraqi *pesh merga* militia forces were the most effective (for a time virtually the *only* effective) barriers to the IS offensive. This experience called for much further Western reliance on the Kurds to push back the Caliphate. Once the Caliphate is effectively dissembled, the Kurds are bound to expect some territorial compensation for their efforts, and the international system will have difficulty denying it to them. If history is a guide, however, they will find some way to frustrate Kurdish aspirations.

The Geopolitical Resistance

Kurdish irredentism is opposed by all four of the existing states from which Kurdistan would be forged. Resistance to the idea is highest in the two states, Turkey and Iraq, where the Kurds are most prominent and where secession would be most harmful to the existing state. The geopolitics of the region plays into these considerations, and although there is considerable support for the Kurdish cause, it is difficult to find outsiders who can or will offer their wholehearted support for the Kurds.

Turkey. Opposition to Kurdish self-determination is strongest in Turkey for several reasons. Kurds constitute roughly 20 percent of the Turkish population, making them numerically close to two-thirds of the population of a future Kurdistan. Kurdish majority territories are concentrated in the Eastern part of the country, including the Anatolia region that has been developed for its water resources and as a tourist destination. The Kurdish area is about the size of the state of Washington in a country that is slightly larger than Texas. In addition, the Kurds, principally under the leadership of the Kurdish Workers Party (PKK), has waged a civil war/terrorist campaign against the government in Ankara that was formally ended in 2013. The PKK, however, is Marxist and the Turks accuse them of collusion with Russia, also a Turkish rival. Turkey routinely accuses the Kurds of being terrorists. Fighting between the PKK and the government flares up occasionally.

The Turks oppose *any* Kurdistan more than any other regional country. Their motivation arises from the belief that a Kurdish state anywhere would be a platform for encouraging secession by the Turkish Kurds, which is almost certainly true. As a result, the Turks have not been particularly supportive of Iraqi *pesh merga* military efforts against IS, which they feel could be a launching pad to establish a fully independent Iraqi Kurdish state along their border. A similar rationale exists toward Syrian Kurdistan, and the Turks, who fundamentally oppose the Caliphate, find themselves in the anomalous situation of opposing (or not supporting) a primary opponent (Iraqi Kurds) of an enemy they would like to see defeated (the Caliphate).

Iraq. Since Saddam Hussein's atrocities against the Kurds and especially since the American invasion and occupation, the epicenter of attention to Kurdistan has centered on the Kurdish Autonomous Region of Northern Iraq. The region is home to roughly 5 million Kurds, and since 2003, they have been increasingly self-reliant and independent of the central government in Baghdad. Their territory abuts the Kurdish regions of all the other candidate countries and contains significant petroleum reserves in the Zagros Mountain region that makes it valuable to Iraq. The Kurds are linguistically and ethnically distinct from the Sunni and Shiite Arabs of the rest of the country. Moreover, there have been predictions that Iraq, which is a classic artificial country, could break apart into three countries, and there is little doubt that the Kurds would be the first to secede. The KRG has progressively acted like a sovereign government in all but name (its border with the rest of Iraq, for instance, is controlled by the *pesh merga*, who act as border guards). This situation would likely form the basis for a fully independent and unified Kurdistan.

Iran and Syria. Iran has the second-most Kurds (about 8 million) and the second-most territory that is potentially part of any state. It contrasts with the others in that it is not Arab or Sunni. Its people are ethnically like the Kurds (whose language is akin to Persian), but they share different religious traditions. In popular discourse, there have been far fewer publicized separatist pronouncements coming from Eastern Kurdistan than from Turkey or Iraq, although the emergence of an independent Kurdistan in Iraq would certainly arouse demands among Iranian and Syrian Kurds to join the new state. The Kurds are least numerous in Syria (about 2 million), and they live in remote, lightly populated parts of Eastern Syria contiguous with Turkey about which the Syrians have shown little interest. Liberating territory in Syria occupied by the Caliphate benefits Syrian Kurds and will likely stimulate demands for an independent state with the expulsion of IS from the region.

Conclusion

Territorial disputes centering on stateless nations are among the most difficult, vexing problems that confront the international system in a world of imperfectly drawn sovereign state boundaries that divide people who want to live together or aggregate people who do not. The problem of multinational states and their trials have been the cause of many ongoing and potential violent conflicts. The situations where a territory is coveted by more than one party (Palestine) and where sovereign boundaries keep nationalities in separate jurisdictions when they yearn for a common national home (Kurdistan) demonstrate the desperation and furtiveness of these difficulties.

Territorial disputes are truly zero-sum situations where one side "wins" at the expense of the other. Compromise is difficult because one side "wins" (i.e., controls the territory) at the other's expense. Turkish Anatolia cannot simultaneously be part of Turkey and Kurdistan, and the West Bank cannot be sovereign Palestine and part of Israel at the same time.

The situations are geopolitically distinct. The continued control of the Occupied Territories by Israel is opposed by virtually all countries except the United States, and actions by the Trump administration (Jerusalem, Golan, and sanctions against Iran) have undoubtedly emboldened the Netanyahu government. It is problematic how Israeli policy might be affected by a return to a less supportive U.S. government. The Kurds have more international advantages. The KRG has been functioning for over a quarter-century and provides a governmental framework for a viable Kurdish state in the autonomous parts of Iraq and beyond, and Kurdish oil reserves could help underwrite its viability. It also faces a formidable array of states, led by Turkey, who vehemently oppose the Kurdish dream. The performance of the *pesh merga* in the defeat of the IS Caliphate, however, gives them useful international support. For both the Palestinians and the Kurds, however, modifying the terms of the zero-sum game is a difficult task.

Study/Discussion Questions

1. What is the heart of the problem of territorial disputes? Discuss the problem of why they exist and why they are so difficult to resolve.
2. What are multinationalism and irredentism? Discuss these as outcomes of the post–World War I and II worlds.
3. Why are territorial disputes important phenomena in contemporary international relations, especially given changes in the overall pattern of violence in the world?
4. Why are territorial disputes so difficult to resolve to the satisfaction of all claimants? How do the Israeli-Palestinian and Kurdish problems illustrate this difficulty?
5. Discuss the structure of the Israeli-Palestinian dispute. Include a discussion of Palestine on the structure of this conflict.
6. What are the possible outcomes to the Israeli-Palestine dispute? Describe each. Why has it proven so difficult to reach an agreement?
7. Who are the Kurds? Where do they live? Why do they desire the creation of a Kurdistan, and from where would it be carved?
8. Who opposes the creation of a Kurdish state, and what is the basis of their objections? Given the resistance that exists, what are the prospects on an independent Kurdistan?

Bibliography

Allsop, Harriet. *The Kurds of Syria: Political Parties and Identity in the Middle East.* London: I. B. Tauris, 2015.

Ambrosio, Thomas. *Irredentism: Ethnic Conflict and International Politics.* Westport, CT: Praeger, 2001.

Atef, Maged. "Sinai Suffering: The Peninsula Has Become a Breeding Ground for Terror." *Foreign Affairs Snapshot* (online), March 13, 2017.

Aziz, Mahir. *The Kurds of Iraq: Nationalism and Identity in Kurdish Iraq.* London: I. B. Tauris, 2014.

Benn, Auf. "The End of the Old Israel: How Netanyahu Has Transformed the Nation." *Foreign Affairs* 95, no. 4 (July/August 2016), 16–27.

Brown, Nathan J. "The Palestinians' Receding Dream of Statehood." *Current History* 110, no. 740 (December 2011), 345–51.

Carter, Jimmy. *Palestine: Peace Not Apartheid.* New York: Simon and Schuster, 2006.

Chaliland, Gerard, and Michael Pallis. *A People without a Country: The Kurds and Kurdistan*. Northampton, MA: Interlink Publishing Group, 1993.
Chazam, Naomi, ed. *Irredentism and International Politics*. Boulder, CO: Lynne Rienner, 1991.
Della Pergola, Sergio. "Israel's Existential Predicament: Population, Territory, and Identity." *Current History* 109, no. 731 (December 2010), 383–89.
Dowty, Alan. *Israel/Palestine* (Hot Spots in Global Politics) (fourth edition). London: Polity Press, 2017.
Eppel, Michael. *A People without a State: The Kurds from the Rise of Islam to the Dawn of Nationalism*. Austin, TX: University of Texas Press, 2016.
Erakat, Noura. *Justice for Some: Law and the Question of Palestine*. Palo Alto, CA: Stanford University Press, 2019.
Gelvin, James L. *The Israeli-Palestinian Conflict: One Hundred Years of War* (third edition). Cambridge, UK: Cambridge University Press, 2014.
Gunter, M. Michael. *The Kurds: A Modern History*. Princeton, NJ: Markus Weiner Publishers, 2015.
Hammond, Jeremy R. *Obstacle to Peace: The U.S. Role in the Israeli-Palestine Conflict*. New York: Worldview Publications, 2016.
Izady, Mehrdad. *The Kurds: A Concise History and Fact Book*. London: Taylor and Francis, 2015.
King, Diane E. *Kurdistan on the Global Stage: Kinship, Land, and Community in Iraq*. New Brunswick, NJ: Rutgers University Press, 2013.
Livni, Tzipi. "Anger and Hope: A Conversation with Tzipi Livni." *Foreign Affairs* 95, no. 4 (July/August 2016), 10–15.
Masalha, Nur. *Palestine: A Four Thousand Year History*. London: Zed Books, 2018.
Meiselas, Susan. *Kurdistan: In the Shadow of History*. Chicago, IL: University of Chicago Press, 2008.
Muravchik, Joshua. *Making David into Goliath: How the World Turned against Israel*. New York: Encounter Books, 2015.
Peleg, Ilan. *The Democratization of the Hegemonic State*. Cambridge, UK: Cambridge University Press, 2007.
Phillips. David L. *The Kurdish Spring: A New Map of the Middle East*. New York: Routledge, 2017.
Ross, Dennis. *Doomed to Succeed: The U.S.-Israeli Relationship from Truman to Obama*. New York: Farrar, Straus, Giroux, 2015.
Shaked, Ayelet. "Ministering Justice: A Conversation." *Foreign Affairs* 95, no. 4 (July/August 2016), 2–8.
Shavit, Ari. *My Promised Land: The Triumph and Tragedy of Israel*. New York: Spiegel and Grau, 2015.
Smith, Charles D. *Palestine and the Arab-Israeli Conflict. A History with Documents* (ninth edition). New York: St. Martin's Press, 2016.
Snow, Donald M. *The Case Against Military Intervention: Why We Do It and Why It Fails*. New York and London: Routledge, 2016.
———. *The Middle East, Oil, and the U.S. National Security Policy: Intractable Conflicts, Impossible Solutions*. Lanham, MD: Rowman & Littlefield, 2016.
———. *National Security* (seventh edition). New York and London: Routledge, 2020.
Van Creveld, Martin L. *The Land of Blood and Honey: The Rise of Modern Israel*. New York: Thomas Dunne Books, 2010.
Welsh, David. "Domestic Politics and Ethnic Politics," in Michael E. Brown, ed. *Ethnic Conflict and International Security*. Princeton, NJ: Princeton University Press, 1993.

15

Global Climate Change

Paris and Beyond

Global climate change represents one of the clearest, yet most controversial, issues facing the world. It is a problem that cannot be solved by the individual efforts of states, but must be done collectively if it is to be done successfully. It is controversial because there is substantial public, if not scientific, disagreement both about the nature and severity of the problem and over the structure and content of proposed solutions to climate change. President Trump is the most prominent of the skeptics.

This chapter examines the problem from two related vantage points. The first is its nature and extent, what does and does not require controlling, and who the most egregious offenders are. The second is the controversial process surrounding international efforts to deal with global climate change. The original lightning rod for this effort was the Kyoto Protocol of 1997, which expired in 2012. Attempts to implement and move beyond the actions prescribed in that treaty failed until the Paris Climate Agreement of 2015, from which the Trump administration withdrew in June 2017.

The issue of climate change—the extent to which the earth's climate is gradually warming due to human actions or natural processes—is one of the most controversial, divisive, and yet consequential problems facing international relations in the twenty-first century. No one, of course, favors a gradual or precipitous change in global climate because the consequences could be catastrophic. The issue contains a perceptual disconnect. Over 97 percent of all disinterested scientists agree the problem is real. Yet, as Helm points out, "the public gets more indifferent or even skeptical." Most of this skepticism is American.

Regardless of how serious the problem is, global warming is clearly a classic, full-blown transnational issue. As Eileen Claussen and Lisa McNeilly put it, "Climate change is a global problem that demands a global solution because emissions from one country can impact the climate in all other countries." Global warming, in other words, will be curbed internationally or likely it will not be controlled at all.

The underlying dynamic, if not its seriousness, can be easily stated. Global warming, the major manifestation of climate change, is the direct result of the release of so-called greenhouse gases into the atmosphere in volumes that are beyond the capacity of the ecosystem to eliminate them naturally. There are several greenhouse gases. The largest part of the problem comes from the burning of fossil fuels such as petroleum, natural gas, coal, and wood, which releases carbon dioxide, methane, and nitrous oxide into the air in large quantities. According to U.S. Environmental Protection Agency figures in 2017, emissions from fossil fuel burning and "forestry" account for 76 percent, methane for 16 percent, and nitrous oxides for 6 percent of emissions. The natural method of containing the amount of carbon dioxide and its ultimate damaging residue, carbon, in the atmosphere is the absorption and conversion of that gas in so-called carbon sinks, which separate the two elements (carbon and oxygen) and release them harmlessly back into the atmosphere. Both levels of emission and carbon dioxide elimination are parts of the problem.

The cumulative effect is that there is more carbon dioxide in the atmosphere than there used to be, and it acts as a greenhouse gas. What this means is that as heat from the sun radiates off the earth and attempts to return in an adequate amount into space to maintain current climate, carbon dioxide acts as a "trap" that retains the heat in the atmosphere rather than allowing it to escape. This blanketing effect keeps excess heat in the atmosphere.

The expired Kyoto Protocol of 1997 (named after the Japanese city where it was finalized) was the most visible symbol of reaction to global warming and has been the lightning rod of the procedural and substantive debate over it. The heart of the protocol was a series of guidelines for the reduction of emissions almost exclusively by the developed countries. The requirements of the agreement were controversial because of the differential levels of reduction they imposed, especially on the United States. The Kyoto Protocol expired in 2012, creating a sense of concern among supporters of international attempts to control climate change through international regulation and a sense of relief among skeptics. The emphasis eventually moved to Paris, where an agreement was reached in December 2015. Like its predecessors, the Paris Climate Agreement has been controversial, and its future effectiveness has been clouded by the announcement by the U.S. withdrawal. The most recent meeting of the Conference of the Parties was held in Santiago, Chile, in December 2019.

Principle: Global Climate Change

The urgency and importance of the Paris climate accord depends vitally on the urgency and importance of the problem. The debate over climate change is contentious. At least three related factors make a calm, rational debate over the extent and consequences of global warming difficult to conduct. The first is the absence of immediate consequences of whatever change is occurring. Over the past quarter-century or more, global warming has indeed been occurring, but until recently the effects have been so gradual and generally small that either they have gone unnoticed by most people or have not been definitively attributable to the phenomenon. As the frequency of violent climatologically induced events like tornadoes and hurricanes and weather fluctuations have increased, the connection is becoming harder to ignore. Global warming is blamed for numerous contemporary events, from the melting of polar ice caps to recent patterns of violent weather, but there is lingering disagreement about whether manmade global warming is the underlying culprit.

Second, there are abundant scientific disagreements about the parameters of the problem and its solution. Some of the disagreement is honest, some possibly self-interested, but for every dire prediction about future consequences, there is a rebuttal from somewhere. This debate often becomes shrill and accusatory, leading to confusion in the public about what to believe.

Third, almost all the projections have until recently been sufficiently far in the future to allow considerable disagreement and to discourage resolution. The scientific evidence to date may be very strong, but the actual consequences are distant enough that extrapolation is subject to enough uncertainty that some scientists can take the same data and reach diametrically opposed conclusions. These extrapolations are sometimes fifty or even one hundred years in the future, when most of the people at whom they are aimed will not even be alive to be held accountable for them.

Parameters of Debate

That global climate is changing is not contested on any side of the debate over global warming. The Intergovernmental Panel on Climate Change (IPCC) has investigated the extent to which this has happened in the past and has concluded that the average surface temperature of the earth increased by about one degree Fahrenheit during the twentieth century and "that most of the warming observed over the past 50 years is attributable to human activities." (Much of the IPCC material in this section is from the 2001 report of Group I–III of the IPCC, cited in the bibliography.) Extrapolating from trends in the last century, the IPCC predicted additional warming between 2.2 to ten degrees Fahrenheit (1.4 to 5.8 degrees Celsius) in this century. The primary culprits are the greenhouse gases cited in the Kyoto Protocol that result from deforestation (and its destruction of carbon sinks), energy production from the combustion of fossil fuels (natural gas, oil, and coal), transportation (primarily cars and trucks, but also trains and other modes), cattle production (methane gases), rice farming, and cement production.

The extent of these effects, of course, depends on the amount of change caused by global warming. IPCC II data project an average rise of between six and thirty-six inches in sea levels by 2100. Using the higher figure, the impact on some countries would be dramatic. A thirty-six-inch rise would inundate territory in which 10 million people live in Bangladesh alone, forcing their relocation to scarce higher land. The same increase would cover 12 percent of the arable land of the Nile River delta in Egypt, which produces crops on which over 7 million people are dependent. Some estimates suggest the island country of Vanuatu in the South Pacific would simply disappear under the rising waters. Many resort and retirement communities along the American Atlantic shoreline and the Florida peninsula could be catastrophically affected. Some already have been. Worldwide, it is estimated that 45 million people would be displaced.

Warming ocean water could also have dramatic effects, for instance, by affecting ocean currents that now have an influence on climate in various parts of the world. The Atlantic Gulf Stream, for instance, could be affected by warmer water coming from polar areas, changing patterns for the coastal United States and Europe. As an example, Gulf Stream effects that tend to keep major hurricanes off parts of the American coast (e.g., the South Carolina Lowcountry) could and in some instances have been diverted, resulting in new patterns of hurricane, tornado, and storm impacts. Large-scale changes in patterns of ocean circulation are possible worldwide.

The Skeptics

The consensus on climate change is not shared universally. As weather patterns have become more volatile and the effects of climate-based events have become increasingly frequent and calamitous, it has become impossible to deny that climate is not changing for the worse. The thrust of counterarguments has drifted from denial of change to causation and the accuracy of apocalyptical projections if something is not done to arrest and reverse current trends. The newer thrust, most vociferously associated with the current American administration, raises questions about whether fluctuations are natural historical anomalies or are "manmade," a euphemism for change resulting from human activity.

Some scientists—admittedly, a relative few—disagree with the accuracy of these projections and the direness of the consequences that they project. There is little disagreement about the historical record (e.g., the amount of climate change in the last century) because that is based on observed data that can be examined for accuracy. There is, however, some disagreement on the precise causes of change (e.g., scientists affiliated with the power industry tend to downplay the impact of energy production as part of denying manmade culpability).

There tend to be three criticisms of climate change scientists that can be phrased in terms of questions. The first is how much effect will global warming have? A second, corollary question is how much those effects will accumulate under different assumptions about natural and manmade adjustments to these effects. Third, how difficult are the solutions?

There is strenuous disagreement on all these matters. Consider, for instance, the projections on how much average surface temperatures will increase in this century if action is not taken. Estimates range from one to ten degrees Fahrenheit, and that is a considerable difference in terms of the consequences to the world and humankind. If the actual figure is at the upper end of that spectrum, the impact of things like snow pack, glacier, and polar ice cap melting will be considerable, with oceans rising at the upper limits of predictions (around three feet). Parts of Tampa Bay and New Orleans, among other places, will be underwater unless levees are constructed to keep the water out, and Vanuatu may become the next Lost City of Atlantis (an analogy often made by climate change scientists).

Who knows which part of the range is correct? The answer is that with any scientific certitude, no one does. The amount of warming is necessarily an extrapolation into a future that does not exist, after all, not an observation of something that does. Clearly, it is in the interests of those who either do not believe in the more severe projections or who would be most adversely affected by concerted efforts to reduce emissions to believe in the lower projections and to deny the more severe possibilities.

Because the effects are not all immediate and unambiguous, the average person has little way to answer the second question: What does all this mean? Is the world headed for an environmental catastrophe if something is not done to slow, stop, or reduce the phenomenon of global warming? Scientists on both sides of the issue are passionate and self-convinced, but they have not made a case to the world's public that is universally compelling, understandable, and convincing.

This leads to the third question: What should be done about the problem? The immediate answer, of course, is that it depends on what and how bad the problem is. Most of the world's scientific community has accepted the basic science of the global warming problem, but largely economic forces in the United States have been prominent among major powers in denying or downplaying the problem and resisting international solutions. The major source of historic U.S. objection is not the veracity of climate change science, but is instead directed at the differential obligations for solving it that efforts like the Paris agreement prescribe: reductions with economic consequences that would make the American economy less competitive and the exclusion of developing world countries with large pollution potentials from regulation. This is the heart of the Trump objection.

There is, of course, a hedge in answering the third question that reflects a deep American belief that technology will somehow find a way to ameliorate the problem. That is the position often taken by the American energy and transportation industries, and it is an approach that has worked to solve other problems at other times.

Application: Kyoto to Paris and the Continuing Crisis and Controversy

Climate change is a classic *transnational issue*, meaning it transcends national boundaries and cannot be dealt with successfully by individual states. The underlying causes are essentially global, and they can only be solved by the efforts of all countries, acting individually or preferably cooperatively.

The process has been difficult for both scientific and political reasons. The scientific community, as already discussed, is virtually unanimous in assigning causation: the production of excess carbon dioxide and other gases injected into the atmosphere, catastrophic fires like the Amazon rainforest fire of August 2019, and the harvesting of trees that historically have served as "sinks" where photosynthesis breaks down carbon dioxide into harmless carbon and oxygen.

The problem is that fossil fuel burning, the chief source of greenhouse gases, is vital in a political and economic sense. Economically, fossil fuel burning creates energy that powers much economic activity. Energy production and use are the strongest correlates of economic activity, meaning the more energy a country uses, the more its economy thrives. The converse is also true. This means that attempts to curb fossil fuel can differentially affect countries, which creates the possibility of geopolitical advantage and disadvantage. Science and commerce are at odds.

Different effects of compliance with climate-based guidelines are central dynamics in the international politics of climate change control. Since the beginning of the movement, this differential has been prominently framed in developed–developing world terms. In the early days of the movement, almost all the pollution was caused by energy production in the developed world. Emission baseline figures for 1990 used in the Kyoto process showed the United States was responsible for 36 percent of global emissions, followed by the European Union (24.2 percent), the Russian Federation (17.4 percent), and Japan (8.5 percent). The next largest polluter was Australia with 2.1 percent.

Excluded from these baseline figures were the largest developing countries, China and India. The Chinese have taken advantage of disparities in becoming a global economic power. U.S. Environmental Protection Agency figures published in 2017 reflect the change: China now produces 30 percent of greenhouse gas emissions, followed by the United States (15 percent), the European Union (9 percent), India (7 percent), Russia (5 percent), and Japan (4 percent). The politico-economic dynamics help explain why the United States has been such a harsh critic and reluctant participant in the climate control process. The Trump administration withdrew from the Paris agreement, largely on discriminatory grounds based in preferences (lower reduction quotas and economic assistance) for developing countries under the accord.

The Road to Paris

The chronology of global warming as a formal international concern was described by the UN Framework Convention for Climate Change (UNFCCC) secretariat in a 2000 publication, *Caring for Climate*. In 1979, the First World Climate Conference was the first step. That meeting brought together international scientists concerned with the effects of human intervention in the climate process and the possible pernicious effects of trends that they observed. It also provided the first widespread recognition of the greenhouse gases phenomenon.

The process has evolved, with important points corresponding to the most important conferences and agreements it produced. The major signposts were the Kyoto Protocol of 1997 that produced the first major, comprehensive agreement on the subject, the Bali-Copenhagen process beginning in 2007 to produce a follow-on to Kyoto (which, by its own provisions, expired in 2012), and the Paris Climate Agreement of 2015. A follow-on to Paris is part of Conference of the Parties 25 in Chile.

The *Kyoto Protocol* was a complicated document, the details of which go beyond present purposes. Several elements can, however, be laid out that provide a summary of what the protocol attempted to do and, based on those purposes, the objections that have been raised to it.

The overarching goal of the protocol was reduction in the production and emission of greenhouse gases and thus the arrest and reversal of the adverse effects of climate changes. The protocol identifies six gases for control and emission reduction. Three of these gases are "most important" based on emission contribution. Carbon dioxide accounted for fully half of "the overall global warming effect arising from human activities" in the UNFCCC's language, followed by 18 percent for methane and 6 percent for nitrous oxide. The other three specified categories, the "long-lived industrial gases," are hydrofluorocarbons, perfluorocarbons, and sulfur hexafluoride. The goal of the protocol was a global reduction in the production of targeted gases of 5 percent below the baseline year for measuring emissions by the period 2008 to 2012.

The Kyoto accord created a complicated set of categories of states that included differential emissions reduction goals for each category. It placed the burden of reduction on the most developed countries, those members of the Organisation for Economic Co-operation and Development with the largest economies, most productive industrial plants, and thus the greatest consumers of fossil-fuel-derived energy.

Most of the rest of the world was exempted from the reduction quotas or was required to make much smaller contributions. Most critically and controversially, some of the emerging developing states were excluded altogether because they had historically not contributed to the problem and it was assumed that they would learn from the pollution mistakes of the developed world and not follow in the polluting footsteps.

Kyoto grew into a source of contention between the United States and China that helped undermine the accord. Although the United States was an early supporter of the Kyoto process during the Clinton years, it never signed the protocol, and the George W. Bush administration was a leading global opponent. The heart of the Bush objection was that Kyoto discriminated unfairly against the United States, and much of this assertion was based on the advantage that China had as a non-emissions reducer under its provisions.

The American position changed almost immediately after Bush took office. On March 13, 2001, Bush announced that he no longer favored U.S. participation in the protocol. In the process, the administration publicly stated that it would not send the treaty signed by Clinton to the Senate for ratification. As a result, the United States remained the most important country in the world outside the protocol and thus did not consider itself subject to its requirements, a position it continued to maintain.

Bush administration objections to the protocol focused on two basic themes. The first was cost and burden to the United States. Although some other countries had higher percentage reduction quotas than the United States, treaty opponents argued that having to bear 7 percent of 36 percent of the total required reductions was an excessive burden. In addition, U.S. emissions were already 15 percent above the 1990 level by the end of the millennium and, according to Victor, rising at 1.3 percent per year, thereby demanding even further reductions. Thus, the United States was being asked to do too much proportionately. Compliance was viewed as economically ruinous in terms of the additional expenses of doing business and the loss of comparative advantage to industries in other countries that are not regulated by these requirements, notably China. This objection has recurred under Trump.

The second objection was the exclusion of developing countries from the requirements of the protocol. In most cases, this exclusion is innocuous, as most of these countries do not and will not contribute meaningfully to greenhouse gas in the foreseeable future.

The Bush administration's criticism was principally aimed at China and India. China has since become the largest greenhouse gas emitter. India does not pose quite as urgent a threat, but with a population the size of China's and an emerging technological and industrial capacity, it could be. As of 2017, these two countries are responsible for about three-eighths of global emission figures. One of the few signals of progress at Copenhagen was a joint Chinese–American accord to address this problem.

The tenth anniversary of the Kyoto accords was marked by a major UNFCCC conference in Bali, Indonesia, in December 2007. Nearly 10,000 delegates attended the meeting to draft a follow-on agreement that would improve upon the results of the Kyoto Protocol. Gaining American participation and support was a major objective of the conferees. Major issues introduced at the Bali meeting included future targets for carbon dioxide emissions reductions and the participation of countries excluded under the annexes of the Kyoto agreement, notably China and India. The American delegation insisted that developing economies like those of China and India agree to participate in the reduction of emissions. These outcomes were sufficiently positive that the Bush administration endorsed the Bali outcome.

Turning the general agreement into a specific, binding, and effective accord proved to be the hard part—the "devil in the details." Among enthusiasts of global warming control (which included President Obama), there were high hopes for the December 2009 Copenhagen summit. The summit was attended by 115 heads of state and generated much anticipation prior to its beginning on December 8. The Copenhagen summit failed. It neither formally proposed nor enacted any binding, mandatory agreements to supersede Kyoto after its 2012 expiration, nor did it create a framework for a global treaty by the date of Kyoto's expiration. As the meeting wound down inconclusively, a group of major countries, including the United States, China, India, Brazil, and South Africa, convened an "Informal High Level Event" on December 18, the day before the summit was to adjourn. The result was something called the Copenhagen Accord calling for a goal of no more than a two-degree-Fahrenheit increase in global temperatures. This accord was noted but not adopted by the conference.

The Paris Climate Agreement

Climate change advocates hoped Paris would mark an important breakthrough in the process begun in the last century. There were hopeful signs. For one thing, President Obama had been an enthusiastic leader in the process from the beginning. When the United States deposited its accession to the accord on Earth Day in April 2016, the global climate control community believed it had taken a major step toward gaining the big power/big polluter support success required. China was also a signatory. The Paris agreement seemed off to a good beginning.

Then the United States acted like it has so often in the past regarding multinational agreements and announced in June 2017 its intention to remove itself from the arrangement. The action was, in a post–World War II context, not really all that unusual. There is a pattern. When an American administration (usually Democratic) leads the United States into international arrangements that may threaten some aspect of American sovereign control, a subsequent administration (often Republican) reverses the initiative and pulls the United States away. This pattern occurred in the 1992 Earth Summit, where the United States enthusiastically supported the Biodiversity Treaty and then renounced it. The Clinton administration was an enthusiastic supporter of Kyoto, and George Bush renounced it almost immediately upon assuming office. The United States has proposed or supported other initiatives from UN-sponsored human rights proclamations (e.g., the UN Declaration on Human Rights and Convention on Genocide), economic initiatives like the International Trade Organization, and the International Criminal Court, and then denounced them. In a real sense, President Trump was just carrying on an American tradition.

At the core of the Rome process is the attempt to reduce global emissions by engaging the largest polluters as active participants—notably China and the United States but also rising polluters like India. These three countries currently account for over half the global carbon dioxide emissions. Including China and India in global efforts served the dual ends of maximizing participation in the effort *and* of placating American concerns. The Obama administration devoted special attention to orchestrating these conditions.

The agreement itself is notably non-coercive. The basic underlying dynamic is a series of emission reduction targets that the signatories agree to implement. These goals are not specified in the agreement itself; they are voluntarily agreed to, and progress is self-reported. These provisions are intended, among other things, to assuage political elements in the United States that react negatively to any appearance of intrusion on American sovereign control of its affairs.

Two major questions surround the Paris agreement. The first, and in terms of climate change most important, is whether it will succeed in achieving its stated purpose of helping arrest global warming. The prospects are mixed. On the positive side, almost all the world's countries are parties to the agreement, and the goals they have set for themselves could make a significant contribution to amelioration. There are possibly conflicting variables at play, however, including whether countries meet their goals (an assessment made difficult by the lack of strict reporting requirements), the continued participation by states that are major emitters, and the pace both of conservation efforts and the spread of alternative, and especially renewable, energy sources.

The second question is the American role in the process. The United States is only the third original participant to renounce its participation (Venezuela and Iraq are the others). Indeed, the withdrawal announcement of President Trump included the possibility the United States might negotiate reentry on terms it considered more favorable to American interests.

The larger impact of American absence may be self-inflicted damage. The United States has been a global leader in researching, developing, and commercializing nonfossil energy sources like solar and wind power. These areas are compatible with and connected to the process, to the point that, as Deese points out, "rapid reductions in the price of renewable energy and increases in the efficiency of energy consumption have made fighting climate change easier, and often even profitable." The result had been to establish the United States on the inside track as the leader both in climate science and in the commercialization of the Paris-based movement. Withdrawing from Paris may forfeit that advantage and open the door for competitors, notably China and even Saudi Arabia, to take over that leadership. Deese, for instance, reports that China plans to invest $340 billion in this sector, and the Saudis plan to invest $50 billion by 2020 (both more than the U.S. government).

China's president Xi Jinping is, as Krupp points out, a chemical engineer by training, understands the potential and science of this endeavor, and has acted to assert Chinese leadership. Krupp points out that, "In 2015, China installed more than one wind turbine every hour on average and enough solar panels to cover two soccer fields every day." They also cancelled construction of one hundred coal-fired power plants, the visual symbol of Chinese pollution, in 2017. China already leads the world in the production of solar panels, wind turbines, and lithium storage panels. Will their burgeoning efforts and the symbolism of the United States turning its back on Paris undercut the American clean energy efforts, which, according to Deese, currently employ "over three million Americans"?

Conclusion

Hardly anyone disputes that climate change is taking place or that its effects are not pernicious to some degree. No one is a pro–global warmer, but there is considerable reluctance to attack and eradicate the problem, and this has until recently been especially true in the United States, whose participation in the effort is critical to its solution.

The United States and China are both at the heart of the problem and its solution. American alienation from the international efforts rose from what some Americans viewed as two unfair aspects of the Kyoto process that have carried over into subsequent international efforts up to and including the Paris agreement. They are the imposition of crippling emissions reduction requirements that disadvantaged the country in the global economy and the exclusion of China from emissions requirements. The two objections were, of course, interrelated, as Chinese exclusion and American inclusion added to Chinese comparative advantage in production costs, largely at the expense of American competitors. Both arguments have abated since Kyoto, but the Trump administration resuscitated them in withdrawing from the Paris accord.

The tables have turned decisively. China had become the world's greatest polluter, but under the leadership of President Xi Jinping, it has become a leader in emission reduction and in the development and marketing of alternative, nonpolluting energy sources. Both efforts can eclipse American initiatives. Thanks largely to the conversion of power plants to natural gas from shale deposits, the Americans are now reducing emissions unilaterally and are even righteously proclaiming their intent to move on their own to the targets established using 1990 baselines.

Like world energy generally, shale gas (including the exploitation of methane hydrate from the world's sea beds) has the potential to change the dynamics of international global warming efforts, but it is an interim, not a permanent, solution. Shale gas is, after all, still a fossil fuel, and it does emit carbon, if in smaller amounts than other fossil fuels like coal. Ultimately, it allows the prospects of a "breather" of sorts in the process, but it only buys time for progress in the ultimate quest of a global energy system freed of dependence on fossil fuels and their emission of carbon residues.

At the beginning of this chapter, climate change was described as a true transnational issue. That uniqueness has at least four significant emphases. First, global warming is truly a global issue that affects the entire planet and can only be solved by essentially universal actions by the countries of the world. Special burdens fall on countries like the United States and China that contribute most to the problem and are the leaders in exploring solutions. It is arguably impossible to see how these problems can be remediated without the active participation of both countries. Second, responding to this problem will have direct impacts on two of the most important motors of the global economy: energy production and use, and transportation. Third, climate change is the only environmental problem that intensifies or is intensified by other major environmental problems. Rising water levels affect the ability of the earth to produce food, and desertification is increased by warming, to cite two examples. Fourth, climate change is a problem that is intimately related to other vital conditions of life. The climate change problem is largely the result of humankind's need for energy, but the process also creates additional natural resource problems such as desertification and shrinking supplies of usable, potable water. The quality of future human life depends on finding and implementing solutions.

Study/Discussion Questions

1. What is a transnational issue? Why is climate change considered a "classic" transnational issue? How does this dynamic affect how we think about the climate change issue?
2. Describe the nature of global warming. What causes it? How does it work? How and why are fossil fuel burning and deforestation the "villains" causing the problem? Who bears responsibility for creating and solving the problem?
3. What factors make a rational debate on climate change difficult? Discuss the positions both of climate change proponents and skeptics. What makes reconciliation of their positions intractable?
4. List and briefly discuss the major efforts on climate change control from 1979 to the present. What is the basis of the tension between environmental and political and economic factors that has been present throughout the process?
5. What has the historic treatment of developing countries like China and India been in climate change negotiations? Why has that position been a sticking point in international efforts to gain cooperation on agreements? Use

the Chinese case to illustrate the point.

6. Discuss the Kyoto Protocol as the landmark agreement on climate change control. What did it propose? Why was it controversial? Why did attempts at a "follow on" agreement fail before it lapsed in 2012?
7. What is the Paris Climate Agreement? What does it try to do? How is it an improvement over previous agreements? For what stated reasons did American President Trump oppose it as grounds for U.S. withdrawal? What are the likely consequences of the American action?
8. The United States has been an obstructionist since the beginning of the climate change process. How? Why? How does reaction to the Paris agreement simply show the "United States being the United States" in international negotiations? What possibilities for an increased or more marginalized role exist?

Bibliography

Ackerman, John T. *Global Climate Change: Catalyst for International Relations Disequilibria*. PhD Dissertation. Tuscaloosa, AL: University of Alabama, 2004.

Black, Richard. "Copenhagen Climate Summit Undone by 'Arrogance.'" *BBC News* (online), March 16, 2010.

Blau, Judith. *The Paris Agreement: Climate Change, Solidarity, and Human Rights*. London: Palgrave Macmillan, 2017.

Browne, John. "Beyond Kyoto." *Foreign Affairs* 83, no. 4 (July/August 2004), 20–32.

Claussen, Eileen, and Lisa McNeilly. *Equity and Global Climate Change: The Complex Elements of Global Fairness*. Arlington, VA: Pew Center on Global Climate Change, 2000.

Crook, Clive. "The Sins of Emission." *The Atlantic* 301, no. 3 (April 2008), 32–34.

Deese, Brian. "Paris Isn't Burning: Why the Climate Agreement Will Survive Trump." *Foreign Affairs* 96, no. 4 (July/August 2017), 83–92.

Enwerem, Michael C. *The Paris Agreement on Climate Change: A Better Chance of Tackling Global Climate Change*. New York: CreateSpace Independent Publishing, 2016.

Helm, Dieter. *The Carbon Crunch: How We're Getting Climate Change Wrong—and How to Fix It*. New Haven, CT: Yale University Press, 2012.

Henson, Robert. *The Thinking Person's Guide to Climate Change* (second edition). Washington, DC: American Meteorological Society, 2019.

Intergovernmental Panel on Climate Change. A Report of Working Groups I–III. *Summary for Policymakers—Climate Change 2001*. Cambridge, UK: Cambridge University Press, 2001.

Klein, Daniel, and Maria Pia Carazo. *The Paris Climate Agreement: Analysis and Commentary*. Oxford, UK: Oxford University Press, 2017.

Krupp, Fred. "Trump and the Environment: What His Plans Would Do." *Foreign Affairs* 96, no. 4 (July/August 2017), 73–82.

Leggett, Jane. *Paris Agreement: United States, China Move to Become Parties to Climate Change Treaty*. Washington, DC: Congressional Research Service, September 12, 2016.

Luterbacher, Urs, and Detlef F. Sprinz, eds. *International Relations and Global Climate Change*. Cambridge, MA: MIT Press, 2001.

Mann, Charles C. "What If We Never Run Out of Oil?" *The Atlantic* 311, no. 4 (May 2013), 48–63.

McKibben, Bill. *Falter: How the Human Game Began to Play Itself Out*. New York: Henry Holt and Company, 2019.

Pirages, Dennis C., and Theresa Manley DeGeest. *Ecological Security: An Evolutionary Perspective on Globalization*. New York: Rowman & Littlefield, 2004.

Podesta, John, and Peter Ogden. "The Security Implications of Climate Change." *Washington Quarterly* 31, no. 1 (Winter 2007–2008), 115–38.

Romm, Joseph. *Climate Change: What Everyone Needs to Know* (second edition). Oxford, UK: Oxford University Press, 2018.

Schelling, Thomas C. "The Cost of Combating Global Warming: Facing the Tradeoffs." *Foreign Affairs* 75, no. 6 (November/December 1997), 8–14.

Schuetze, Christopher F. "Ignoring Planetary Peril, a Profound 'Disconnect' Between Science and Doha." *International Herald Tribune* (online), December 6, 2012.

———. "Scientists Agree Overwhelmingly on Global Warming. Why Doesn't the Public Know That?" *International Herald Tribune* (online), May 16, 2013.

Sivaram, Varun, and Sagatom Saha. "The Trouble with Ceding Climate Leadership to China: Risky for the World, Costly for the United States." *Foreign Affairs Snapshot* (online), December 10, 2016.

Stavins, Robert N. "Why Trump Pulled the U.S. Out of the Paris Accord: And What the Consequences Will Be." *Foreign Policy Snapshot* (online), June 5, 2017.

Stern, Todd, and William Antholis. "A Changing Climate: The Road Ahead for the United States." *Washington Quarterly* 31, no. 1 (Winter 2007–2008), 175–87.

Suzuki, David, and Ian Harrington. *Just Cool It: the Climate Crisis and What We Can Do.* London: Greystone Books, 2017.

UN Framework on Climate Change. *COP 21 Final Agreement: Paris 2015 United Nations Climate Change Conference*. New York: United Nations, 2015.

U.S. Environmental Protection Agency. *Global Greenhouse Gas Emissions Data*. Washington, DC: U.S. Environmental Protection Agency, April 13, 2017 (online).

Victor, David C. G. *Climate Change: Debating America's Options*. New York: Council on Foreign Relations Press, 2004.

Vidal, John, Allegra Stratton, and Suzanne Goldenberg. "Low Target, Goals Dropped: Copenhagen Ends in Failure." *Guardian.co.uk* (online), December 19, 2009.

Wallace-Wells, David. *The Uninhabitable Earth: Life after Warming*. New York: Tim Duggan Books, 2019.

Wirth, Timothy. "Hot Air over Kyoto: The United States and the Politics of Global Warming." *Harvard International Review* 23, no. 4 (2002), 72–77.

16

Resource Scarcity

The Quest for Secure Access to Water and Energy

The desire, even necessity, to control scarce resources, and conflict over those resources, has acted as a major source of friction in the international order throughout history. Major wars have been fought over access to precious metals, water, food, and exotic spices, to name a few examples. In the contemporary world, some of the most publicized resource conflicts have been over access to water and petroleum reserves. Aspects of both problems are geographically widespread. Water and energy are among the most difficult, interrelated problems facing the future.

The parameters of the problems of water and energy security are changing. The need for adequate, usable water supplies is existential: water is literally the necessary basis for life. Energy is more geopolitical: energy is necessary for survival in the world's coldest climates but is also considered the lubricant of economic activity and geopolitical advantage. The quest for potable water is an ongoing human necessity made more difficult by a growing human population. Energy is a resource in transition to alternate sources, a mandate enlivened by climate change.

Conflict over the ability to control, monopolize, or deny access to valued resources is also as old as human history. Men have fought and died, armies have swept across countless expanses, and empires and states have risen and fallen in the name of precious resources. How will this historical theme be acted out in the early twenty-first century? The resources over which there is the most competition are also the most basic resources for the human condition. At the top of the list is potable water. With 70 percent of the earth's surface covered by water, water per se is hardly a scarce resource, but water that is usable for human purposes like drinking, bathing, and agriculture is in selective shortage across the globe. As world population grows, existing shortages will be intensified unless means can be devised to increase supplies.

The other scarce resource is energy. The heart of the global energy debate has centered on petroleum since World War II, making security of access to oil a prime concern for all states. The balance between oil and other sources of energy is, however, changing, and the needs for different energy sources and forms are changing as well. Where resources are in short supply, the political, including geopolitical, competition between those who have adequate or surplus supplies and those who do not has acrimonious consequences for the relations between the haves and the have-nots.

Scarcity is the key concept. It exists whenever all claimants to a resource cannot simultaneously have all that resource they need or want. When scarcity exists between sovereign states, there are three possible solutions. First, if some method can be found to increase supply so that all claimants can have enough of the resource, scarcity abates and so does the basis for conflict. This solution is often easier to state than to accomplish. Increasing water availability can mean better development or distribution of existing resources or tapping new sources, mostly seawater. Energy production faces tough imperatives like conversion to nonfossil fuel sources.

The second approach is to decrease demand for the resource by using less and thereby lowering demand closer to available supply. Human life requires minimum amounts of water and is, in that sense, inelastic. In the case of traditional energy sources like oil, the fact is that global demand is increasing. Calls for conservation must compete with emerging customers and the mandate to move to different forms of energy propagation.

If the other options fail, then a power struggle may remain an option, pitting the suppliers against the consumers over how much energy will be available at what prices. Up until now, the geopolitical struggle over petroleum has received the most publicity, but it exists over water in selected places as well.

Principle: Resource Scarcity

The ancient Greeks, as well as other civilizations in Eurasia, were the world's oldest recorded "chemists," devising schemes to categorize the most important "elements" affecting their universes. The Greek philosopher Plato publicized one of the most famous of these lists—earth, water, air, and fire—in roughly 540 BC. Modern science has gradually expanded and sophisticated this early "periodic table," but two of its four components, water and fire (energy) remain both basic and contentious in the modern world for existential and geopolitical reasons.

The structure of each problem is changing. There is no alternative to water: attacking its inelasticity is at the heart of the global problem, and adjustments of maldistribution and patterns of use may affect more localized difficulties. Changes in the overall energy equation may lessen the stranglehold of petroleum and thus ameliorate climate change, but in the transition, the dynamics of petroleum remain important as the world's central energy source.

Water Resources

Water is simultaneously the world's most abundant and scarce resource. Over 70 percent of the Earth's surface is covered with water, and scientists have determined that the total amount of water on the planet is 1.4 billion cubic kilometers. Of that total, about one-seventh of the water is considered fresh, or potable, water suitable for human use. The rest is saline, almost exclusively seawater. Water is not scarce, but usable water is.

Water scarcity is not uniformly experienced geographically. Hydrologists categorize scarcity among three conditions: physical scarcity (where inadequate supplies are available), economic scarcity (where resources, expertise, or will are inadequate to maximize availability), and imminent scarcity (where environmental changes could precipitate scarcity). Parts of the American West, Mediterranean (Saharan) Africa, and parts of Central Asia including Northern China are examples of physical scarcity. Much of Central Africa represents economic scarcity, and the Arabian Peninsula is a prime example of imminent scarcity. Most of North and South America, Europe, and the rest of Eurasia do not suffer from water scarcity.

The result is that water scarcity selectively affects many people in the world. There are three degrees of water scarcity that are often cited in describing its extent. The least severe are *water shortages*, which are selective crises often caused by weather patterns, pollution, and overuse of water for non-necessary purposes. *Water stress* refers to conditions where it is difficult to obtain adequate amounts of fresh water due to availability or economic scarcity. The Middle East is the most water-stressed part of the world. The third category is *water crisis*, the situation where there is inadequate supply to meet the needs of the people who live in a region. For purposes of measuring these conditions, the standard for water stress exists when there is less than 1,700 cubic meters per person annually available, shortage can arise when that availability is between 1,700 and 1,000 cubic meters, and water is in crisis when the number drops below 1,000 cubic meters. Availability below 500 cubic meters per person threatens human survival.

The problem of water scarcity is less well recognized in the developed compared to the developing world. Partly, of course, this is true because it exists in fewer places in the developed world, and where it does, it has been dealt with reasonably successfully. As an example, the physical water scarcity in parts of the American West centers on states in the desert southwest and northern Mexico, the chief water source for which is the Colorado River. The western American states through which the river flows negotiated the Colorado River Compact in 1922 by which they allocated water from the river and developed hydroelectric and storage dams to produce electricity and to ensure available water remained in the system for measured and designed utilization.

The inelasticity of water adds to the difficulty and frustration of dealing with it. On the demand side, there are bare minimums of water that people must have, and if they do not, they will perish. As world population increases, the quantitative demand can only increase and put further stress on water supplies. The only demand-side alternative is population control, preferably reduction from a strictly hydrological perspective. Supply can be increased by making some of that six-sevenths of the world's water that is unusable for human purposes potable. There are efforts aimed at doing so, primarily in those parts of the world with the greatest water difficulties. Once again, climate change–related variables like the melting of polar ice caps complicate these efforts. The prospects for change are discussed in the applications section of the chapter.

Energy Resources

The energy crisis is structurally different than water scarcity and has received much more attention. Demands for increased energy have come primarily from the developed world until recently, whereas many of the sources of that energy have been in the developing world. Water scarcity is, in important ways, a humanitarian problem with some geopolitical ramifications. Energy scarcity is largely a geopolitical problem.

Energy is also different because, unlike water, it can come from various sources. Petroleum has been the primary energy source in the developed world for nearly a century, during which vast sources of oil have been discovered and exploited, especially in the Middle East. World dependence has become so great that two basic trends important to this century have emerged. One has been fluctuation in estimates of availability of this non-renewable resource (non-renewable because it does not naturally replenish itself when used). One result has been to look for alternative sources of energy for the future, including petroleum from nontraditional sources and alternate energy sources.

The other trend has been to create a changed element in the world power map. Countries and regions like the Middle East that would not otherwise have great geopolitical significance gained such status because they are significant petroleum repositories. New sources from other places endanger the status of traditional suppliers. The result is that the geopolitical map is likely to move away from traditional oil suppliers to possessors of other energy sources.

There are five sources of energy production for the future. All are currently in use at various levels and with different prospects. Three involve the burning of fossil fuels, with the inevitable byproduct of carbon dioxide emission into the atmosphere. These three sources are petroleum, natural gas, and coal. They differ in quantity available, geographic distribution, and contribution to environmental degradation. The other two source categories are nuclear power generation and renewable energy sources, a cover designation for a variety of specific energy-generating technologies. These sources share the characteristic of being non-carbon burning and thus producing no carbon dioxide emission.

Each source creates specific concerns that go beyond the physics of energy production. One of these concerns is the question of supply adequacy: How much of the resource is available, and is that amount enough for current and projected needs? A related matter is the cost of this supply. Can adequate supplies at acceptable and predictable prices be guaranteed or at least reasonably assured? As well, there is the question of energy security: Can necessary supplies at acceptable supplies be guaranteed, or are they potentially subject to uncontrollable fluctuations in amount of resource availability and cost or interdiction? All these concerns have been prominent parts of the debate over petroleum dependency. The other major concern has been environmental impact: Do some energy sources create such environmental degradation that their use should be restricted or precluded because of the damage they do to the global ecosystem?

Petroleum

Oil has been used primarily as an energy source for economic activity (its conversion to electricity) and transportation, but its uses go well beyond the production of energy. Petroleum is the basic commodity used in the petrochemical industry, and thus most of the plastics industry. There are no ready alternative substitutes for petroleum in making plastics, so it is arguable that using oil to produce energy is a waste of a resource indispensable for other, more important purposes. The late Shah Reza Pahlavi of Iran captured this dilemma: "There is a limited amount of petroleum in the earth. Oil is used for making plastics and other products," he said. "Oil is too valuable to burn."

The joker in supply calculations has been the emergence of shale-formation oil and natural gas as an energy source. Since 2008, the United States and Canada have moved aggressively to extract oil and natural gas from shale formations common throughout much of the world and specifically in North America. The prototype of this activity has been the so-called Bakken formation, named after the North Dakota farmer on whose property near Tioga, North Dakota, the initial formation (part of the Williston Basin covering parts of North Dakota, Montana, and Saskatchewan) was exploited. These formations are amenable to exploitation through a process known as "fracking" that yields natural gas and petroleum.

Traditional petroleum remains the dominant source of energy worldwide, but its geopolitical consequences and pressures from the climate change community are creating pressure for the exploration and marketing of other energy forms. Both ecological concerns and price affect these decisions, and energy use appears to be entering a transition from a petroleum to some other base. Candidates include natural gas, coal, nuclear, and a variety of renewable sources.

Natural Gas

The major contemporary change agent in the energy equation has been the expansion of natural gas usage. It has been part of the energy equation since the transition to petroleum as the world's most favored and used fuel, because natural gas is found essentially everywhere there is oil. Natural gas from traditional sources coterminous with oil reserves has always accounted for nearly as much of total U.S. energy production as its major rivals, fellow carbon-based petroleum and coal. In 2011, gas production passed the production of coal as the single greatest source of American energy production at around 22 percent, and the gap is projected to widen by the year 2040, when natural gas production will account for 35 percent of production, with coal and petroleum occupying second and third places, according to U.S. Energy Information Administration (EIA) figures.

The major reason for this change, of course, has been the emergence of shale oil and gas production, which is becoming a transformational factor in the global energy picture. The United States has been the leader of this development and likely will continue to be at the forefront of this technology, and thus it is worthwhile to examine some of the factors for the rising prominence of shale oil in the United States.

The distribution of shale formations globally gives a long-term advantage to the United States and China, which have the world's largest known availability of these formations. U.S. International Energy Agency figures for 2009, for instance, show that the two countries with the greatest proven shale gas reserves are China (1,275 trillion cubic feet) and the United States (862 trillion cubic feet). The other great attraction for the United States is geopolitical, specifically as a substitute for dependence on foreign petroleum and thus as a contributor to greater energy security, even overall sufficiency. The United States is becoming a net energy exporter, and shale oil and gas are major drivers in this shift. The change also means an increasing movement of the United States away from alternate, including foreign, sources of oil. One spinoff has been the ability of the United States to adopt air pollution projections committing the country to carbon-dioxide-emission reductions in international climate change negotiations and to approximate Paris goals without being a formal party to the regime. American reliance on imported, and especially Middle Eastern, petroleum is also decreasing as shale oil and gas supplant traditional petroleum as a component in the American energy equation. This conversion is also accompanied primarily by a decline in the use of energy derived from petroleum.

Shale oil and gas may provide a useful alternative for both the Chinese energy need and pollution problem. China has the world's largest reserves, and it has begun to test fracking techniques to explore the prospects of mining its vast shale oil formations. On the negative side, most of its reserves are in remote parts of China difficult to access, and China lacks the technology and infrastructure (gas pipelines, for instance) to exploit its reserves in the near- to mid-term.

Coal

Coal is the third major carbon-dioxide-emitting fossil fuel. Coal preceded petroleum in helping to power the Industrial Revolution in eighteenth- and nineteenth-century Europe and North America, and it remains a significant source of energy production and consumption in many countries. What is most notable about coal usage is that it is such an important part of the gradual shift in energy patterns toward the developing world. China has been the world's leading coal consumer. Using EIA-supplied data, China now uses nearly 47 percent the coal consumed in the world. In 2011, for instance, China consumed 3.8 billion tons of coal, whereas the rest of the world combined to use 4.3 billion tons. China's known coal reserves rank third in the world behind the United States and Russia.

Coal is rapidly becoming the energy source of the past. It remains a source in countries like India that lack obvious viable alternatives. Coal use is, however, dirty and increasingly economically uncompetitive, to which the decline in the U.S. coal industry testifies. China has cancelled the construction of more coal-powered plants and is moving away from coal-generated power. The rest of the world is following.

Nuclear Energy

Power generation using nuclear rather than carbon-based fuel is an alternative with both advantages and disadvantages. Its primary advantage is that nuclear power does not contribute to carbon dioxide overload in the atmosphere and is thus an environmentally friendly source of energy. Its primary disadvantages are disposal of spent nuclear fuel, dogged questions of plant safety, facilities security, and the expense of building nuclear power plants.

The United States is the world leader in overall nuclear power generation with over one hundred nuclear power plants in operation. These produce a little less than 10 percent of American power needs, and that proportion is forecast to remain flat or slightly decline. No new nuclear plants have been completed in the United States since the 1970s.

Several problems create public resistance to nuclear power. One of these is the problem of waste disposal. The used (or "spent") fuel from a nuclear reactor is highly toxically radioactive, and the half-life of its toxicity (the point at which it is no longer dangerously environmentally threatening) is measured in hundreds of years. Another, and more spectacular, fear arises from the possibility of nuclear power plant accidents fouling the environment. Although these are relatively infrequent, they are often spectacular and memorable. The most recent major disaster occurred in 2011 at the Fukushima nuclear plant in Japan. The most famous and devastating occurrence was the meltdown of a nuclear reactor at Chernobyl in 1986 in the Ukraine.

Renewables

Problems and controversies surround most traditional energy sources and create interest in alternative sources of energy generation, and particularly sources that are nonpolluting and which are not depleted by use for creating energy. A prominent historical example has been hydroelectrically produced power from dams built on rivers where water flow can be stored and released to produce energy. This form is explicitly environmentally friendly, but its application is restricted to places like the American West and Turkish Anatolia where there are streams that flow through canyons.

There has been greater enthusiasm for so-called renewable sources like wind power, captured by powerful wind turbines and converted to electricity, and solar energy, using solar panels to capture the sun's heat and store it for use as energy. Sizable industries have developed in both the United States and China to develop and commercialize these efforts, and their potential to deal with the energy crisis is raised in the next section.

Application: Securing Access to Water and Energy

Any natural resource for which there is demand can become a scarcity issue, and as the planet expands its population and sophisticates and expands its needs for those resources, conflict over them is likely to increase. Lithium is a current example. Both solar and wind power energy propagation are only feasible as alternatives if one can store the energy they produce; lithium-based batteries are the current answer. Different problems are associated with different natural resources; water security and energy security are prominent among them.

Water Security

In both a conceptual and existential sense, the problem of water security is more important and difficult than is the question of energy. Access to potable water is necessary to propagate and sustain life, and it is the adequate abundance of water resources (and climate) that distinguishes Earth from uninhabitable planets both within the solar system and beyond. To paraphrase the Shah about oil, the alternative to adequate supply is to fight over the last drop. It is also a more difficult problem to solve because there is no alternative to water to sustain life.

Water shortage is, for most inhabitants of the developed world, an abstract problem, because relatively few people in the western hemisphere or Europe suffer from current or imminent water crises like those that afflict swaths of Africa and Asia. The developing world is more naturally vulnerable, both because of geography (being the site of most of the world's greatest deserts, for instance) and having the greatest population explosions placing additional strains on existing supplies. In addition, in places like Central Africa, the technology of water extraction is least developed and least applied. Additionally, attempts to develop economically can also have adverse effects on water supply: exploitation of shale formations involves the utilization and fouling of very large amounts of water, for instance. Climate change is also a factor, as monumental storms disrupt the water cycle. All this is particularly true in China. As Krupp points out, Chinese President Xi "has often spoken publicly about his concerns over the effects of climate change on China, where almost twenty percent of the land is desert, an area expanding at a rate of more than 1,300 square miles per year." The Chinese problem is especially great in Western and Northern China, where a combination of desertification and agricultural use has and continues to lower water tables to the point of leaving increasing areas non-arable.

There are available supply and demand methods to deal with the growing crisis of water. The most prominent (and arguably humane) is to increase supply. Because there is a finite amount of water on the planet, this means concentrating on better means of using available water. There are two approaches: expanding the availability of *usable* water by converting more of the world's six-sevenths of currently non-potable water to usable status, and making more efficient use of existing fresh water supplies.

Desalinization is the obvious way to convert saline into usable water, but it has been a relatively expensive process that the least wealthy states cannot afford. It is little surprise that the states leading efforts at perfecting—including lowering costs—have been in the Middle East. Israel, Saudi Arabia, and other Persian Gulf states have led these efforts. Given that seawater is abundant and available in many places, the emphasis is natural.

Conservation also plays a role. Storage dams stop excess flow from running unused into the oceans, where they become saline and unusable. Better forms of distribution of water through enhanced irrigation plays a role, as does restricting use in drought-prone areas to non-water-intensive forms of agriculture. In parts of Africa, simply drilling wells and means of piping water from the source to users represents an important improvement that can lessen the burden on perpetually water-deficient areas.

There is a demand side to the equation. Although a good deal of the water problem is distributional, it is first and foremost a problem of increased human demand for water. Population growth is, in a very real sense, the root cause of water shortage and security, and as long as population continues to increase, water scarcity alleviation will be a catchup enterprise.

There are geopolitical implications as well. It is not clear what the pace of increasing supplies of potable water by desalination, more efficient use, or conservation will be, and it seems fair to assume that shortages will continue to build, and with them so will demands for greater supplies. When situations reach crisis proportion, resulting conflicts will likely be intense.

Energy Security

The traditional energy problem is changing in two basic ways. The first is changes in demand and includes who will make increasing demands and for different forms of energy. The second, and related, change is in the forms that energy demands will take. Will the world gradually have a decline in use of traditional fossil fuel sources and their gradual replacement with alternate and especially nonpolluting, renewable sources of energy?

The countries with the greatest demands for increased energy are China and India. EIA projections estimate that these two countries alone will account for half of the growth in global energy use between now and 2035. Much of this demand will come for petroleum. India and China will need more Persian Gulf oil, for instance, whereas the United States will require less. The EIA projects that by 2035, nearly five-eighths of world energy demands will come from non–Organisation for Economic Co-operation and Development countries.

This differential trend is also illustrated by changes in the American pattern. The United States will remain a major global energy consumer, but the exploitation of shale oil and gas will change its energy profile considerably. The progressive transformation of American energy (notably electricity) production will also result in reduced energy costs for American industries, helping to support a competitive renaissance for American industries in world markets.

Among the more intriguing prospects is the rising trend toward renewable sources like solar and wind. These technologies have long been derided as marginal and economically non-feasible, but recent breakthroughs have included a lowering of the costs of production to the point that these technologies compete economically with some fossil-based sources. The decline of coal, for instance, is largely because both wind and solar *and* shale gas are cheaper to exploit than coal for providing energy.

There are also geopolitical impacts. Consider the mouth of the Persian Gulf as an example. The Persian Gulf has been the point of egress of major amounts of the world's petroleum energy supplies since the period surrounding World War II: Almost all the oil flowing from the major Organization of the Petroleum Exporting Countries states—Saudi Arabia, Kuwait, Iran, and Iraq, for instance—flows on oil tankers out of the Gulf. Traditionally, most of those ships have made a right turn into the Indian Ocean, heading west for destinations in Europe and North America.

The tankers could start making a left turn out of the Gulf toward emerging energy markets in Asia. China (as well as India) is exemplary. Despite massive amounts of shale oil and gas reserves they cannot yet access economically, China is the largest growing market for energy, and that thirst is likely to increase: Oil use will increase as more and more Chinese become automobile drivers, and China is already reducing the percentage of coal it burns for power consumption for environmental reasons. The same imperative applies to India.

The transition also affects the rocky relationship between the champions of energy security and the supporters of environmental imperatives. Shale gas emits only about half the carbon dioxide into the atmosphere as coal. The conversion of power-producing plants from coal to shale gas has already allowed the United States to reduce its carbon dioxide footprint (a factor that softens the blow of quitting the Paris agreement), and China's decision to stop building new coal-powered energy facilities indicates that President Xi, at least, has similar inclinations.

Conclusion

Resource scarcity of one kind or another has been a recurring feature of human history. Humankind has always wanted or needed resources that all claimants could not possess simultaneously in the amount they desired or needed—the definition of scarcity. Which resource has been coveted in question has changed at different points in time, but the basic problem of scarcity seems perpetual in nature.

Two of the most important resources—the Greeks' water and fire (energy)—are perpetual, enduring concerns. Both are critical to life on the planet. Water sustains life, and it is not a coincidence that the first question astrophysicists searching the universe for the possibility of life ask is whether celestial bodies can or do have water. Without water, there is no life. Energy may be scarce, but there are multiple sources and methods for its exploitation. The basic problem surrounding water is the maximum utilization of a finite, basically inelastic supply. Energy can come from many sources; the problem is finding and exploiting acceptable sources.

The dynamics of understanding and dealing with the two resources is different. Water's vitality derives from its absolute necessity as the source for creating and sustaining life. Moreover, it is a finite resource: there is only so much available, and thus the secret of water security is finding better ways to use what there is and making sure there is access for all legitimate claimants.

Several factors help frame the water security problem. One is the volume of water available. If one includes water unfit for human consumption (basically saltwater), the water supply is more than abundant. Because only one-seventh of total global water is usable, however, water is selectively scarce, a problem that increased demand created by a growing population and additional economic uses like shale exploitation and food production for the larger population necessitate.

For water scarcity to decline, there are two clear mandates. First, the expansion of the potable water supply must occur, which largely means converting more ocean water to a form consumable by humans. This imperative requires perfecting desalination technology that can better match supply and demand at affordable costs. Second, if human demand and supply are to be in balance, water availability and location must be matched. Unfortunately, supplies of water are not uniformly distributed: there is abundant water in some places and not enough in others. The challenge is finding ways to increase supply to areas that are deficient.

Energy scarcity is currently the more publicized global resource problem. The pressures of a growing global population, increasing portions of which demand a greater and more reliable supply of energy, and finite, dwindling reserves of traditional sources of energy combine to create this problem. Energy consumption is tied so closely to economic productivity that demand is both a matter of survival and the symbol of an increasingly prosperous physical condition. Economics and geology collide.

Although the world energy map is clearly in the beginnings of a process of considerable change driven largely by advances in the exploitation of shale oil and gas deposits, the effects of this change remain uncertain and speculative. The ecological consequences of shale extraction (fracking) are not entirely known and are matters of controversy. Perversely, a great deal of the shale available is found in geographic locations that are water deficient. Shale technology uses large amounts of water that are not potable afterwards unless they are treated. Technologies are available to restore that water to usable quality, but they are expensive and undercut the economic advantage of moving to shale in the first place. If shale production cannot be the tip of the spear of movement away from traditional fossil fuel energy to some renewable, nonpolluting future, that path becomes more problematic. Although the shale "revolution" has certainly changed energy production patterns to the distinct advantage of the United States, there are remaining problems. Some are geological in terms of fissures and earthquakes that seem to intensify when shale extraction occurs.

There is a unifying possibility hidden within both these sources of resource scarcity and their alleviation—the world's oceans. Desalinated ocean water is a major component of adequate water supplies for many water-deficient areas, principally those that touch the ocean's shores. This leaves the formidable task of getting water to other places that need it but are too far from saline sources to gain access given current technologies. For energy purposes, many problems of harnessing a controlled fusion process from ocean water it requires have not yet been mastered. In the long run, many scientists have long believed the ultimate solution to energy production is through nuclear fusion utilizing the abundant deuterium and tritium of ocean water as the primary source. Advocacies of fusion that surfaced a decade or more ago were premature, but using the ocean's vastness may be the key to an energy and water scarcity solution.

It is always a perilous task to predict the future, because there are always uncertainties that arise and can bedevil even the best laid-out plans and projections. What can be said with some certainty is that the pattern of water and energy usage and production is changing and that the effects will be important. But they will also be unpredicted and unpredictable to some extent. If one doubts that assertion, go back and look at projections made at the turn of the millennium and see how much of a future contribution they predicted for shale energy.

A world of abundant usable water and safe, nonpolluting energy is an aspiration that everyone does, or should, embrace. Harnessing water and fire would greatly enhance the human condition and make life more commodious globally.

Accomplishing these monumental tasks will not end all scarcity and conflict over natural resources, but it certainly would be a good start.

Study/Discussion Questions

1. What is resource scarcity? Why has it always been a problem? Define the term and its implications for resource allocation. What are the possible solutions to a condition of scarcity?
2. What is water security? What makes it unique among resource scarcities? Discuss the nature and structure of water as a scarce resource.
3. How is energy security different from water security? Why is petroleum so important to the nature and structure of the contemporary problem? Place petroleum use in the context of the evolution of different sources of energy. Is petroleum too valuable to burn?
4. What are the five most common sources of energy in use today? Discuss the nature, advantages, and disadvantages of each. Which involve fossil fuel burning and the consequent emission of carbon dioxide into the atmosphere? Relate this distinction to climate change and the desirability of moving away from fossil fuels for energy production.
5. Why does the text argue that water scarcity is "more important and difficult" than energy scarcity? Discuss the parameters of the problem and possible solutions, pointing out the difficulties associated with each solution.
6. How is the energy problem changing? Elaborate on each of the possible solutions identified. Place special emphasis on the movement from fossil fuel to nonfossil fuel alternatives and the implications of such a transition.
7. Discuss the geopolitics of change in energy sources, emphasizing the effects on the Middle East, climate change, and the unique potential role of China in the evolution.
8. How do the world's oceans offer a potential solution to both the problems of water and energy scarcity? Elaborate and speculate.

Bibliography

Bernell, David, and Christopher A. Simon. *The Energy Security Dilemma: U.S. Policy and Practice*. New York and London: Routledge, 2016.

Central Intelligence Agency. *CIA World Factbook 2017*. Washington, DC: U.S. Central Intelligence Agency, 2012.

Dannreuther, Roland. *Energy Security*. Cambridge, MA: Polity, 2017.

Dinar, Shlomi, and Ariel Dinar. *International Water Scarcity and Variability: Managing Resource Use Across Political Boundaries*. Berkeley, CA: University of California Press, 2016.

Fishman, Charles. *The Big Thirst: The Secret Life and Turbulent Future of Water*. New York: Free Press, 2012.

Fleischman, Stephen E. "Too Valuable to Burn." Common Dreams Newsletter (online), November 29, 2005.

Friedman, Thomas L. "The First Law of Petropolitics." *Foreign Policy* (May/June 2006), 36–44.
Holt, Jim. "It's the Oil." *London Review of Books* (online edition), October 18, 2006.
International Energy Agency. *World Energy Outlook, 2012.* Paris: International Energy Agency, November 2012.
Kalicki, Jan H., and David L. Goldwyn. *Energy and Security: Strategy for a World in Transition.* Baltimore, MD: Johns Hopkins University Press, 2013.
Krupp, Fred. "Trump and the Environment: What His Plans Would Do." *Foreign Affairs* 96, no. 4 (July/August 2017), 73–82.
Lankford, Bruce, Karen Brown, Mark Zeitoun, and Declan Conway, eds. *Water Security: Principles, Perspectives, and Practices.* New York and London: Routledge, 2013.
Richter, Brian. *Chasing Water: A Guide to Moving from Scarcity to Sustainability* (second edition). New York: Island Press, 2014.
Schmidt, Jeremy J. *Water: Abundance, Scarcity, and Security in an Age of Humanity.* New York: NYU Press, 2017.
Sedlack, David. *Water 4.0: The Past, Present, and Future of the World's Most Valuable Resource.* New Haven, CT: Yale University Press, 2015.
Smil, Vaclav. *Energy and Civilization, A History.* Cambridge, MA: MIT Press, 2017.
Snow, Donald M. *Cases in International Relations: Portraits of the Future* (third edition). New York: Pearson-Longman, 2008.
———. *National Security for a New Era* (fifth edition). New York: Pearson, 2014.
Solomon, Steven. *Water: The Epic Struggle for Wealth, Power, and Civilization.* New York: Harper Perennials, 2011.
Tindall, James A., and Andrew A. Campbell. *Water Security: Conflicts, Threats, Policies.* Denver, CO: DTP Publishers, 2011.
U.S. Energy Information Administration (Department of Energy). *Annual Energy Outlook 2013, April 15–May 2, 2013.* http://www.eia.gov/forecasts/aeo/index.cfm.
U.S. Government and National Science and Technology Council. *Coordinated Plan to Advance Desalination for Enhanced Water Security.* Washington, DC: U.S. Government, 2019.
Walsh, Bryan. "The Scariest Environmental Fact in the World." *Time* (online), January 29, 2013.
The World Almanac and Book of Facts. "World Fossil Fuel Reserves." New York: World Almanac Books, 2013.
Yergin, Daniel. "Ensuring Energy Security." *Foreign Affairs* 85, no. 2 (March/April 2006), 69–82.
Zweig, David, and Bi Jianhai. "China's Global Hunt for Energy." *Foreign Affairs* 84, no. 5 (September/October 2005), 18–24.

17

The Evolving Nature and Problem of Terror

The Post–Islamic State Threat

The attacks of September 11, 2001, that brought terrorism into full public view were two decades ago, and they punctuated a growing problem that had been building for at least two decades but had not yet achieved global notoriety. Since then, new groups have spread terror to other places. After 2014, the focus was on the Islamic State (IS), but that group's ascendance has clearly passed. What is next?

The answer requires investigating the nature of the terrorist problem, how it is changing, and what can be done about it. It begins by examining briefly the dynamics of and problems created by terrorism and terrorists. It then moves to how terrorism has evolved structurally as a problem since September 11 and what efforts have been mounted against it. It concludes by examining the evolving nature of the threat and how to attack it.

The tragic terrorist attack by the Islamic terrorist group Al Qaeda (AQ) against the World Trade Center on September 11, 2001, was a seminal international and national event. Internationally, 9/11 signaled a new and frightening escalation of a problem that had troubled other parts of the world for over two millennia. Nationally, the attacks traumatized an American population suddenly aware of its vulnerability and spawned a major national priority for dealing with the problem. The antiterrorist movement worldwide has had successes and failures against elements of the old AQ network, most notably the assassination of AQ founder and leader Osama bin Laden in 2011. AQ has lost its prominence but remains a diffused threat in parts of the Middle East and elsewhere. IS has been the most prominent successor, although it may be fading as a threat to global politics. The evolution from AQ to IS to some other threat is a central dynamic of the future.

Terrorist activity has moved geographically. The United States has not experienced a major coordinated attack by a foreign terrorist organization since 2001, although it has endured "lone wolf" attacks by individuals inspired by ideological groups like IS. Instead, much organized terrorism has been against foreign targets, principally in Europe but also in Asia. If it has changed venues for now, terrorism nonetheless remains a major force that poses threats to greater parts of the world.

Principle: The Nature and Problem of Terrorism

The first step in coming to grips with terrorism is defining the term. This is an important consideration, because so many phenomena in the contemporary international arena are labeled terrorist. Without a definition and a set of criteria, it is hard to tell whether a specific movement, or act, constitutes terrorism.

A comprehensive, universally accepted definition of terrorism does not exist. Rather, there are many different definitions people and organizations in the field employ. Some commonalities recur and will allow the adoption of a definition for present purposes. The U.S. government offers the official definition in its 2003 *National Strategy for Combating Terrorism*: "premeditated, politically motivated violence perpetrated against noncombatant targets by subnational groups or clandestine agents." In *Attacking Terrorism*, coauthor Audrey Kurth Cronin says terrorism is distinguished by its political nature, its nonstate base, the targeting of innocent noncombatants, and the illegality of its acts. Jessica Stern, in *Terrorism in the Name of God*, defines terrorism as "an act or threat of violence against noncombatants with the objective of exacting revenge, intimidating, or otherwise influencing an audience." Alan Dershowitz (in *Why Terrorism Works*) notes that definitions typically include reference to terrorist targets, perpetrators, and terrorist acts.

These definitions share three common points of reference: terrorist acts, terrorist targets, and terrorist purposes. The main difference among them is whether they specify the nature of terrorists and their political base: The State Department, Cronin, and Dershowitz all identify terrorist organizations as nonstate-based actors. Cronin emphasizes that "although states can terrorize, by definition they cannot be terrorists." In the rest of this case study, terrorism will be defined as "the commission of atrocious acts against a target population normally to gain compliance with some demands the terrorists insist upon." It does not specify that terrorism must be committed by nonstate actors. Terrorism is terrorism, regardless of who carries it out.

Terrorist Acts

Terrorist acts are the most visible and recognizable manifestations of terrorism. For most people, these acts are synonymous with the broader phenomenon of terrorism. They share several characteristics. First, terrorist acts are uniformly illegal. Terrorist acts upset the normalcy of life by either injuring or killing people or destroying things. Regardless of the professed motives they espouse, these actions break laws wherever they are committed and are subject to criminal prosecution. Terrorists attempt to raise the legitimacy of their actions by proclaiming them "acts of war" (currently holy war or *jihad*), but the simple fact remains that terrorist acts are against the law. Whether terrorism is crime or war (or both) has consequences for how it is treated and how it is countered.

Second, the general purpose of terrorist acts has been to frighten the target audience: The word *terrorism* is derived from the Latin root *terrere*, which means "to frighten." The method of inducing fright is through the commission of acts of violence that induce fear in those who witness or experience the acts or believe they could be the objects of similar future attacks. Terrorists hope the targets conclude that compliance with terrorist demands is preferable to living with the fear of being victims themselves. Fright is accomplished by disrupting the predictability and safety of life within society, one of whose principal functions is public safety. Thus, a major purpose of terrorist mayhem is also to undermine this vital fiber of society. A third and related purpose of terrorist acts is to cause widespread disorder that demoralizes society and breaks down the social order in a country.

A more tactical use of terrorism is to provoke overreaction by a government in the form of repressive action, reprisals, and overly brutal counterterrorism that may lead to the overthrow of the reactive government. This has been a favorite tactic of Boko Haram, the Nigerian-based terrorist group that has attempted to lure the government in Lagos to attack regions that will alienate the inhabitants and help recruit support for the terrorists.

A fourth purpose of terrorist action is punishment. Terrorists often argue that an action they take is aimed at a specific person or place because that person or institution is somehow guilty of a transgression and is thus being meted out appropriate punishment for what the terrorists consider a crime. Although the Israeli government would be appalled at the prospects of designating their actions after Palestinian bombing attacks by bulldozing the homes of the families of suicide terrorists (or bombing the homes of dissident leaders) as acts of terror, from the vantage point of the Palestinian targets of the attacks, they certainly must have seemed so.

Stern (in *Terrorism in the Name of God*) adds another motivation that is internal to the terrorist organization: morale. Like any other organization, and especially terrorist groups in which the "operatives" are generally young and immature, occasional attacks may be necessary simply to demonstrate to the membership the continuing potency of the group to keep the membership focused and their morale high. As Stern puts it, "Attacks sometimes have more to do with rousing the troops than terrorizing the victims."

Terrorist Targets

Terrorist targets can be divided into two related categories. The first is people, and the objective is to kill, maim, or otherwise cause some members of the target population to suffer as an example for the rest of that population. The second is physical targets, attacks against which are designed to disrupt and destroy societal capabilities and to demonstrate the vulnerability of the target society. The two categories are related in that most physical targets contain people who will be killed or injured in the process. Attacking targets in either category demonstrates that the target government cannot protect its members and valued artifices.

There are subtle differences and problems associated with concentrating on one category or the other. Attacks intended to kill or injure people are the most personal and evoke the greatest emotion in the target population, including anger and the will to resist and seek vengeance. From the terrorist vantage point, the reason to attack people is to undercut their will to resist the demands that terrorists make. Dennis Drew and I have referred to this as *cost-tolerance*, the level of suffering one is willing to endure in the face of some undesirable situation. The terrorist seeks to exceed the target's cost-tolerance by making the target audience conclude that it is physically or mentally less painful to accede to the terrorist's demands than it is to continue to resist those demands.

Overcoming cost-tolerance is not easy, and it usually fails. For one thing, terrorist organizations are generally small and have limited resources, meaning that they usually lack the wherewithal to terrorize enough of the target population to make members become individually fearful enough to tip the scales. Should terrorist groups obtain and use weapons of mass destruction, such a turn of events would be a game changer. Attacking and killing innocent members of a target group may and usually does infuriate its members and increase, rather than decrease, their will to resist.

When the targets are physical things rather than people per se, the problems and calculations change. The range of potential physical targets is virtually boundless. In attacking places, the terrorist seeks to deprive the target population of whatever pleasure or value the object may provide for them. The list of what are called ***countervalue*** targets covers a very broad range of objects, from hydroelectric plants to athletic stadiums, from nuclear power generators to military facilities, from highways to research facilities, and so on. Compiling a list for any large community and trying to figure out how to protect it all is a very sobering experience.

Terrorist Objectives

The ultimate goals of terrorist groups are political. To paraphrase the Clausewitzian dictum that war is politics by other means, so too is terrorism politics by other, extreme means. Likewise, the objectives are pursued by means that color perceptions of the objectives. Sometimes, the objectives are clearly articulated, and at other times they are not. Historically, the more grandiose the goals, the less likely they have been achieved.

Terrorism is the method of the militarily weak and conceptually unacceptable. The extremely unorthodox nature of terrorist actions arises from the fact that terrorists cannot compete successfully using the accepted methods of the target society for succeeding. Terrorists lack the military resources to engage in open warfare, at which they would be easily defeated, or in the forum of public discourse and decision, because their objectives are unacceptable, distasteful, or even bizarre to the target population.

The fact that terrorist objectives are politically objectionable to the target sets up the confrontation between the terrorists and the target. Normally, terrorist goals are stated in terms of changing policies or laws repressing them. Because the terrorists are in a small minority, they cannot bring about the changes they demand by normal electoral or legislative means, and their demands are likely to be viewed as so basically lunatic and unrealistic that they are not taken seriously by the target. The demands make perfect sense to the terrorists, and they are frustrated and angered by the dismissal they receive.

Determining whether terrorists achieve their goals or fail is complicated by the contrast between the short- and long-term levels of objectives. Modern terrorists have rarely been successful at the strategic level of attaining long-range objectives. AQ did not force the United States from the Arabian Peninsula (Osama bin Laden's stated goal), and IS failed to institute a sectarian caliphate. At the same time, the terrorist record at achieving tactical objectives (carrying out terrorist attacks) is not a total failure. If terrorists continue to exist and to achieve some tactical goals, they remain a force against the targets of their activities.

Evolving Terrorism since September 11, 2001

The peril posed by terrorism is changing. The events of September 11 reintroduced the world to a 2,000-year-old phenomenon largely forgotten during a century of world wars and a Cold War that could have turned into a nuclear Armageddon. Understanding the new threat introduced by the 9/11 attacks and lone wolf assaults like the Murrah Building bombing in Oklahoma City in 1995 was different for at least two reasons. First, the new form of terrorism was physically and conceptually different from anything encountered before. It was nonstate-based terrorism arising not from specific political communities or jurisdictions but instead flowing across national boundaries like oil slipping under doors. It is religious, demonstrating degrees of fanaticism and intolerance that, while present in many religious communities, are alien to most people's ability to conceptualize. It is also fanatically anti-American and anti-Western in ways and for reasons most Westerners have difficulty comprehending.

Second, understanding contemporary terrorism is made more difficult by its changeable nature and practitioners. The AQ of 2001 was hard enough to understand, but it has evolved and morphed greatly since. Modern terrorism is truly a hydra-headed monster both in terms of who employs it and for what reasons.

Stern, in *Terrorism in the Name of God*, usefully articulates the requirements for a successful terrorist organization: resiliency (the ability to withstand the loss of parts of its membership or workforce) and capacity (the ability to optimize the scale and impact of terrorist attacks). The larger the scale of operations the terrorist organization can carry out without large losses to its members, the more effective the organization is. Conversely, an organization carrying out small, relatively insignificant acts while having large portions of its membership captured or killed is less effective.

Resiliency and capacity are related. To carry out large operations like 9/11 or the IS campaign, an organization must have a sophisticated, coordinated plan involving multiple people or cells who must communicate with one another both to plan and to execute the attack. The Achilles' heel in terrorist activity is penetration by outsiders, and the key element in doing so is to interrupt communications and destroy its ability to operate (in other words, to reduce its resiliency). The most effective way for the terrorist groups to avoid penetration is to minimize communications that can be intercepted, but engaging in such self-denial comes at the expense of the sophistication and extent of its actions (reduction in capacity).

The result is a dilemma that contemporary terrorist organizations face. Historically, according to Stern and others, most terrorist groups have followed an organizational form known as the *commander-cadre* (or *hierarchical*) model. This form of group is not dissimilar to the way virtually all complex enterprises are structured everywhere: Executives (commanders) organize and plan activities (terrorist attacks) and pass instructions downward through the structure for implementation by employees (cadres).

Commander-cadre arrangements have advantages associated with any large, complex organization: They can coordinate activities maximizing capacity; can organize recruitment efforts and absorb, indoctrinate, and train recruits; and can carry out ancillary activities such as fundraising. The disadvantage of these organizations is that they become more permeable by outside agencies because of their need to communicate among units. Modern electronics become a double-edged sword for the terrorist: they facilitate communications in executing attacks, but those communications can be intercepted and lead to resiliency-threatening penetration.

One result of antiterrorist efforts has been to cause these organizations to become what Stern refers to as the "protean enemy." AQ still exists but is no longer a hierarchically organized entity that plans and carries out terrorist missions as it did before. Instead, it has adopted elements of the alternate form of terrorist organization, the *virtual network* or *leaderless resistance* model, and has dispersed itself into a series of smaller, loosely affiliated terrorist organizations that draw inspiration from the center.

Particularly since the assassination of bin Laden, these mutations, sometimes called "franchises," have increasingly become the public face of terrorism both for AQ and other terrorist entities. AQ activities, for instance, are usually carried out by spin-offs like AQ in the Arabian Peninsula in places like Yemen or by AQ in the Maghreb in places like Mali. Al-Shabab, also an AQ affiliate, is a major actor in Somalia. What distinguishes the actions of such groups is a relatively modest size and geographical reach. Since the collapse of the caliphate, IS has followed a similar strategy. The May 2019 attacks in Colombo, Sri Lanka, are a prominent example.

The effect of changes has been to make the competition between terrorist organizations and their suppressors more sophisticated, difficult, deadly, and expensive. The change has organizationally been in both directions. At the more expansive level, IS emerged in 2014 as a much larger, ambitious entity than previous contemporary organizations, none of which had professed an ambition as large as establishing a territorial state. At the other extreme, much operational terror—especially in the United States—has been transferred to leaderless resistance practitioners acting essentially as lone wolves. Each end of the spectrum represents an evolutionary permutation that creates new horrors and problems for target societies. They are also almost certainly not the last forms terrorism will take in the years ahead.

Application: Dealing with Contemporary Terrorism

What kind of threat does terrorism pose today? What kind of threat will it pose in the future? What will that threat look like? Terrorism has been venerable, and its persistent, if episodic, recurrence suggests that it has enough appeal to desperate groups who feel they have no other way to achieve their goals that they are likely to continue to turn to terrorism as a blueprint.

Understanding efforts to deal with terrorism is a two-step process. It begins by looking at the categories of terrorist suppression, the overarching concept under which the various efforts can be grouped. The other perspective is looking at the terrorism problem in organizational terms, from the discontented individual lone wolf to larger terrorist organizations like IS and beyond. In both cases, the distinctions often blend together in practice. Individual terrorists are often recruited by virtual networks, for instance, and successful virtual networks may broaden their purview.

Suppressing Terrorism: Antiterrorism and Counterterrorism

Conventional terrorism suppression is divided into two methods: antiterrorism and counterterrorism. The two terms are sometimes used interchangeably, but each refers to a distinct form of action with a specific and different contribution to the overall goal. Any program of terrorist suppression will necessarily contain elements of both, but not specifying which is which only confuses the issue.

Antiterrorism refers to defensive efforts to reduce the vulnerability of targets to terrorist attacks and to lessen the effects of terrorist attacks that do occur. Antiterrorism efforts begin from the implicit premise that some terrorist attacks will be attempted and some will succeed tactically, and that two forms of suppression effort are necessary. First, antiterrorists seek to make it more difficult to mount terrorist attacks. Airport security to prevent potential terrorists from boarding airliners or the interception and detention of suspected terrorists by border guards are examples. Second, antiterrorists try to mitigate the effects of terrorist attacks that might or do occur. Blocking off streets in front of public buildings like the White House so that terrorists cannot get close enough to destroy them is one approach, and civil defense measures (e.g., hazmat operations) to mitigate the effects of an attack is another way to deal with the problem.

There are three related difficulties with conducting an effective antiterrorist campaign. One is that it is necessarily reactive; terrorists choose where attacks will occur and against what kinds of targets, and antiterrorists must try to anticipate or respond to the terrorist initiative. A second problem is the sheer variety and number of potential targets. The list is almost infinite, and terrorists seek to randomize what they attack so that potential victims are always off guard and antiterrorists will have trouble anticipating where attacks may occur. The third problem is *target substitution*: If antiterrorist efforts are sufficiently successful that terrorists determine their likelihood of success against a specific target (or class of targets) is significantly diminished, they simply go on to other, less well-defended targets.

The other form of terrorist suppression is *counterterrorism*, offensive and military measures against terrorists or sponsoring agencies to prevent, deter, or respond to terrorist acts. Counterterrorism thus consists of both preventive and retaliatory actions. Preventive acts can include actions such as penetrating terrorist organizations or apprehending and using physical violence against terrorists before they carry out their operations. Retaliation is often military and paramilitary and includes attacks on terrorist camps or other facilities in response to terrorist attacks or disruption or elimination of concentrations of terrorists. The purposes of retaliation include punishment, reducing terrorist capacity for future acts, and hopefully deterrence of future actions by instilling fear of the consequences.

Counterterrorism is inherently and intuitively attractive. Preventive actions are proactive, and in their purest form, preventive counterterrorist actions reverse the tables in the relationship, effectively "terrorizing the terrorists." Pounding a terrorist facility as punishment after enduring a terrorist attack at least provides the satisfaction of knowing the enemy has suffered as well as the victim.

Ideally, antiterrorism and counterterrorist efforts act in tandem. Counterterrorists reduce the number and quality of possible attacks through preventive actions, making the task of antiterrorist efforts to ameliorate the effects of attacks that do succeed less difficult. Further counterterrorist action then can hopefully reduce the terrorists' capacity for future mayhem. The result is a more manageable threat confronting the antiterrorists. In practice, however, these efforts sometimes come into operational conflict.

The Contemporary Threats

The shape of the terrorist threat has undergone a major transformation. AQ still exists, and despite losing physical control of the caliphate, IS continues to inspire and to carry out attacks. The growing phenomenon in North America and Europe is random attacks inspired and sometimes carried out by IS or AQ operatives. A growing problem is acts by random, often deranged, individuals who may (or may not) be inspired by major terrorist groups or who may be acting out of perceived mandates from such groups. Lone wolf attacks in the United States and elsewhere and international attacks for which recognizable groups take credit after the fact are examples. The future remains murky, but it seems likely that this pattern will continue as a prominent part of the international environment.

Lone Wolf Terrorists

The phenomenon of terrorism by individuals apparently unconnected to any organized terrorist group has been a recurring part of the terrorism problem for a long time. Because their actions are idiosyncratic, isolated, and often erratic, they have not individually received the level of attention that more systematic, organized movements do. Cumulatively, however, the rise in their prominence, especially in the United States, parallels a decline in activities by larger, more monolithic organizations. For Americans, lone wolves are the living face of terror in their lives.

Awareness of lone wolves in the United States emerged in the 1990s with the unrelated cases of Unabomber Theodore Kaczynski (the deranged university professor who killed three and wounded over twenty others with letter bombs between 1978 and 1995) and Timothy McVeigh, who killed 159 people in the truck bombing of the Murrah Federal Building in Oklahoma City in 1995. Since these highly publicized cases, there have been increasing if episodic instances of domestic lone wolves in various unrelated locations from San Bernardino, California (where a disgruntled and radicalized employee attacked fellow workers at a social service agency) to Orlando, Florida, site of an attack on a packed nightclub that left forty-nine dead. These atrocious events followed other well-publicized attacks such as the massacre of over thirty fellow soldiers by Major Nidal Hasan at Fort Hood, Texas, in fall 2009 and the 2013 bombing at the Boston Marathon by two brothers. Examples continue to mount, although it is often difficult to distinguish between "honest" terrorist activity and the actions of deranged killers.

What are the characteristics of the lone wolf terrorist? The European Union Instituut voor Veiligheids- en Crisismanagement offered a useful set of interrelated characteristics in a 2007 study. First and foremost, lone wolves act individually rather than as parts of organized and directed groups. Second, lone wolves do not belong to any organized terrorist group or network. Third, they act without the direct influence of a leader or hierarchy. Fourth, the tactics and methods they employ are conceived and conducted by the individual without "any direct outside command or direction." Lone wolf terrorist activities are conceived by individuals who act autonomously in designing and carrying out their acts. The extent of their autonomy compounds the difficulty of identifying and suppressing them in advance. Their lack of affiliation means they likely do not appear on terrorist watch lists, and unless they engage in aberrant behavior that causes citizens to report them to authorities, they present no preattack footprint.

The autonomy of lone wolves makes them extremely difficult to identify in advance, because, by definition, these individuals are usually antisocial loners. Belonging to no formal terrorist groups, they have no communications that can be intercepted and traced back to them, and they may be able to evade detection for a long time after they commit their acts, unless they make some crucial mistake that leads to their apprehension.

Two other factors make the isolation and categorization of lone wolf terrorism problematic. One is whether an individual act meets the criteria for terrorism laid out earlier, or whether it is an instance of pure depravity. This difficulty is particularly relevant when trying to determine the objective of a lone wolf attack. McVeigh, in his twisted way, had the apparent objective of avenging the Branch Davidians who had died at Waco, Texas. What, on the other hand, was the objective of those who attacked young people reveling at a nightclub or teenagers attending an English rock concert?

The other factor is the degree of autonomy and independence of the apparent lone wolf. Groups with diverse messages of hate increasingly publicize their causes and exhort their followers on the internet, and it is often unclear whether apparently independent acts have been influenced by such appeals. There is evidence, for instance, that Major Hasan was "inspired" by extreme antiabortion appeals on the internet, and he was influenced by the violent sermons of American-born, Yemen-based Muslim cleric Anwar al-Awlaki, an AQ supporter who exhorted American Muslims and others to rise and attack infidels.

Large-Scale Terrorist Organizations

The IS has been by far the largest terrorist organization to emerge in this century, and its unexpected rise, apparently spectacular success, and more precipitous decline has presented a parable of sorts for the entire threat of contemporary terrorism. IS arose, frightened—terrorized—much of the world, and has slowly faded from the spotlight. Its rise and descent parallel that of the twenty-first century's other large group, AQ. The bin Laden organization was born in the aftermath of the successful Afghan resistance in the 1980s to the Soviet Union and reached its apex in the 9/11 attack. The success, however, made AQ more visible and more the focus of suppression, which has succeeded in reducing its prominence. AQ still exists; it has contracted. The same fate may befall IS. Neither has disappeared; neither is as prominent as it was.

IS began as a limited terrorist group (AQ in Iraq) to resist the American occupation and Shiite intrusion into Anbar Province in Iraq. The death of its founder Abu Musab al-Zarqawi and the Anbar Awakening drove AQ in Iraq underground until it resurfaced in 2014, rebranded as IS. It moved beyond the traditional terrorist purposes of influencing policy to pretensions of statehood as the caliphate, a very different and uncharacteristic terrorist goal. Its ambition became its undoing.

The establishment of the caliphate was a "bridge too far" for Abu Bakr Baghdadi (the self-proclaimed caliph) and his followers. Its early success was possible because it fielded an "army" of 10,000 to 20,000 fighters against a sparse resistance in thinly populated parts of Syria and Iraq. When it began to expand to occupy and administer that territory while fending off attacks by those who wanted it back, it faltered. Its ambitious agenda of worldwide domain also offended those people from places that would be conquered, and its harsh form of governance alienated many it liberated.

What is the next step in the evolution of contemporary terrorism? IS began as a terrorist organization, tried and has failed to be more, and its retreat turned into a rout. Not surprisingly it has returned to its terrorist roots. That campaign, however, has not overcome European cost-tolerance and has instead apparently increased the determination to destroy IS. The result was probably predictable and instructive for the future. Terrorist organizations are neither large nor powerful enough to become sovereign actors. They *are* capable of horrific attacks that kill many people, but that capacity endangers their resiliency. That parameter defined the IS threat; it will probably be a harbinger of the future.

The IS will not disappear in the near term, but neither will it flourish. It will more likely continue to shrink as has AQ. It no longer has the promise of the caliphate to offer recruits or financial supporters, and this will also decrease its appeal. At the same time, there are still abundant "swamps" to provide a steady stream of recruits to IS or some new terrorist enterprise.

Conclusion

The international terrorism problem continues to evolve. Before the 9/11 attacks, acts of terror were considered a horrible aberration, not an integral part of international existence. The single most deadly terrorist act in history changed that perception. The threat of terrorism is now considered ubiquitous, and efforts to suppress it are now a pervasive part of everyday life. The war on terrorism is now an accepted, institutionalized part of the political environment nationally and internationally.

The terrorism phenomenon is dynamic. It has become more diffuse and atomized as the efforts of terrorism suppressors have forced terrorists to adopt different, more clandestine forms and approaches to attaining their lethal goals. Lone wolves epitomize this diffusion. At the same time, the emergence of IS from the Syrian civil war shows large-scale terrorism continues to exist, if precariously. Moreover, history suggests there will be other, newer permutations.

The organized terrorism represented by AQ and IS now share international attention with the actions of individual lone wolves whose motives are difficult to catalog and difficult to discover in advance. "Organized" terror associated with formal organizations like AQ and IS is more concentrated in the developing world, where governments have fewer resources to engage in effective counterterrorism than do the developed countries. This is counterbalanced by the violence of individual terrorists in the most developed countries.

This combination makes the terrorism future hard to predict. If history is a faithful guide, the current spate of international religious terrorism will indeed fade away eventually, although it is not clear how long that will take. Lone wolf activity is largely idiosyncratic, with unclear motives. History also suggests that a new cycle of terrorists will emerge with different, and as-yet unknown, reasons for being. Terrorists come and go, but terrorism persists. Terrorism has been so enduring because its practitioners have indeed emulated Proteus; today the emphasis is on lone wolves and random individual acts. For as long as the big blue marble that symbolizes Earth is dotted with the kinds of human swamps that breed despair and desperation, terrorism will be part of the human condition as well.

Study/Discussion Questions

1. Define terrorism. What are its three common elements? Can states be terrorists?
2. What do terrorist acts seek to accomplish? In what circumstances do they succeed or fail? Include in your answer a discussion of cost-tolerance. Why is the strategic-tactical distinction important in assessing terrorist activity?
3. What kinds of targets do terrorists attack? Why are some more difficult to protect than others?
4. How has international terrorism changed since 9/11, notably in terms of terrorist organizations?
5. What are the standard distinctions among forms of terrorism suppression described in the text? Describe each as an element in

lessening or eliminating the problem of terrorism.
6. How did the emergence of IS represent a major change in the terrorism threat? How was IS different than the others?
7. The text argues that the IS threat is on the wane, because it has attempted to be much more than a terrorist organization. Discuss this argument. How does the IS failure affect the future evolution of terrorist activity?
8. Terrorism changes and evolves. Based on what you have read, what do you think the terrorism pattern will look like a decade from now? Why?

Bibliography

Art, Robert J., and Kenneth N. Waltz. *The Use of Force: Military Power and International Politics* (seventh edition). London: Rowman & Littlefield, 2008.

Atran, Scott. "The Moral Logic and Growth of Suicide Terrorism." *Washington Quarterly* 29, no. 2 (Spring 2006), 127–47.

Benard, Cheryl. "Toy Soldiers: The Youth Factor in the War on Terror." *Current History* 106, no. 696 (January 2007), 27–30.

Berger, J. M. *Extremism* (MIT Press Essential Knowledge Series) (first edition). Cambridge, MA: MIT Press, 2018.

Clarke, Richard A., ed. "Terrorism: What the Next President Will Face." *Annals of the American Academy of Political and Social Science* 618 (July 2008), 4–6.

Cockburn, Patrick. *The Rise of the Islamic State: IS and the New Sunni Revolution.* London: Verso, 2015.

Cole, Juan. "Think Again: 9/11." *Foreign Policy* (September/October 2006), 26–32.

Cronin, Audrey Kurth. "IS Is Not a Terrorist Group: Why Counterterrorism Won't Stop the Latest Jihadi Group." *Foreign Affairs* 94, no. 2 (March/April 2015), 87–98.

———. "Sources of Contemporary Terrorism," in Audrey Kurth Cronin and James M. Ludes, eds. *Attacking Terrorism: Elements of a Grand Strategy.* Washington, DC: Georgetown University Press, 2004.

Dershowitz, Alan M. *Why Terrorism Works: Understanding the Threat, Responding to the Challenge.* New Haven, CT: Yale University Press, 2002.

Fleishman, Charlotte. *The Business of Terror: Conceptualizing Terrorist Organizations as Cellular Businesses.* Washington, DC: Center for Defense Information.

Gerges, Fawaz A. *ISIS: A History.* Princeton, NJ: Princeton University Press, 2017.

Hoffman, Bruce. "From the War on Terror to Global Insurgency." *Current History* 105, no. 695 (December 2006), 423–29.

———. *Inside Terrorism* (second edition). New York: Columbia University Press, 2006.

Instituut voor Veiligheids- en Crisismanagement. "Lone Wolf Terrorism." June 2007. http://www.transnationalterrorism.eu/tekst/publications/Lone-Wolf.%20Terrorism.pdf.

Jenkins, Brian. "International Terrorism," in Robert J. Art and Kenneth N. Waltz, eds. *The Use of Force: Military Power and International Politics,* 77–84. New York: Rowman & Littlefield Publishers, 2004.

Law, Randal D. *Terrorism: A History* (second edition). Boston, MA: Polity, 2016.

Maher, Shiraz. *Salafi-Jihadism. The History of an Idea* (first edition). Oxford, UK: Oxford University Press, 2016.

Martin, Gus. *Understanding Terrorism: Challenges, Perspectives, and Issues* (fifth edition). Thousand Oaks, CA: Sage, 2015.

McCants, William. *The ISIS Apocalypse: The History, Strategy and Doomsday Vision of the Islamic State*. New York: St. Martin's Press, 2015.

Nacos, Brigette. *Terrorism and Counterterrorism* (fifth edition). New York and London: Routledge, 2016.

Rapaport, David C. "The Four Waves of Terrorism," in Audrey Kurth Cronin and James M. Ludes, eds. *Attacking Terrorism: Elements of a Grand Strategy*, 46–73. Washington, DC: Georgetown University Press, 2004.

Snow, Donald M. *The Middle East, Oil, and the United States National Security Policy*. Lanham, MD: Rowman & Littlefield, 2016.

———. *Regional Cases in Foreign Policy* (second edition). Lanham, MD: Rowman & Littlefield, 2018, especially chapter 1.

——— and Dennis M. Drew. *From Lexington to Baghdad and Beyond: War and Politics in the American Experience* (third edition). Armonk, NY: M. E. Sharpe, 2009.

Stern, Jessica. "Mind over Martyr: How to Deradicalize Islamic Extremists." *Foreign Affairs* 89, no. 1 (January/February 2010), 95–108.

———. *Terrorism in the Name of God: Why Religious Militants Kill*. New York: ECCO, 2003.

———. "The Protean Enemy." *Foreign Affairs* 82, no. 4 (July/August 2003), 27–40.

——— and J. M. Berger. *ISIS: The State of Terror*. New York: ECCO, 2015.

Warraq, Ibn. *The Islam in Islamic Terrorism: The Importance of Beliefs, Ideas, and Ideology*. London: New English Review Press, 2017.

Weiss, Michael, and Hassan Hassan. *ISIS: Inside the Army of Terror* (updated edition). New York: Regan Arts, 2016.

White, Jonathan R. *Terrorism and Homeland Security* (ninth edition). East Windsor, CT: Wadsworth, 2016.

Wood, Graeme. "What ISIS Really Wants." *The Atlantic* 321, no. 2 (March 2015), 78–90.

18

Cyberwar and Cybersecurity

May the Force Be with Whom?

The 1960s movie and television versions of *Star Trek* opened with a panorama of space and intoned, "Space, the final frontier" as the starship *Enterprise* appeared and streaked across the screen. The narrator intoned that the five-year mission of the spaceship was "to boldly go where no man has gone before." The adventure, presumably set in the 2260s, was made into a series of movies and a weekly television program that ran from 1966 to 1969. It is still in syndication, fascinating new generations (as well as the cast of *The Big Bang Theory*) with the prospect of exploring, meeting, and possibly interacting with other life forms.

This fascination has also been an obsession of scientists and people generally who have wondered how space might be utilized and exploited, and that curiosity has inevitably included the prospect of militarizing space or otherwise using it for earthly political advantage. The prospects received major notoriety in the 1980s when President Reagan proposed a nuclear missile defense in space—the Strategic Defense Initiative (SDI)—to protect against a Soviet missile attack (Gary Guertner and I coauthored a book on SDI symbolically titled *The Last Frontier: An Analysis of the Strategic Defense Initiative* in 1986). SDI was quietly shelved when Reagan left office as unworkable. Russian cyberattacks on the 2016 U.S. presidential election process provide a more recent example of the fascination—and mischief—potentially involved.

The problem of cybersecurity is widely recognized as a national security problem. As Zegart and Morrell argue, "Today, an assortment of malign actors perpetrate millions of cyberattacks around the world every day." Cumulatively, Brose concludes, "A revolution is unfolding today." In partial (and arguably largely symbolic) response, the Trump administration proposed to consolidate cyber elements of U.S. government activity in cyberspace into a separate U.S. Space Force in July 2018 to better organize military responses.

In fact and fiction, a concern with information, its uses, its protection, and its exploitation for national security and other purposes is thus nothing new, even if the term "cyber" and some of the techniques associated with it are. Adding the prefix cyber changes how these tasks are done, not what is done. The national security question is how it should be handled in the contemporary scene. What difference does *cyber* make?

An example from World War II illustrates the role of cybersecurity concern without the computer-generated and -stored information component that frames the contemporary debate. During the American island-hopping campaign in the

Pacific, a major problem was how to deprive Japanese defenders of information about American military actions. The Japanese routinely intercepted walkie-talkie communications between American units, allowing them to discern U.S. troop movements. It was a cyber protection problem, and the Americans solved it by "encrypting" their communications. The medium was 420 Navajo Marine "code talkers," who communicated exclusively in Navajo, a language with which the Japanese had no familiarity. The Japanese were never able to discover that the "code" was an American Indian language and break it. Some of the cyber problem of today is finding a new Navajo-like language to protect against the challenges presented by the cyber age.

The problem of protecting information, which is the core of cyber concerns at all levels, was both created and made more difficult by the very processes it created. It is pervasive. Once information enters electronic systems that are the habitat of cyberspace, it becomes part of the vast cyber territory where, unless aggressive actions are taken at protection, it becomes prey vulnerable to exposure or theft unintended by the source of the information. Cybersecurity is the dynamic enterprise that attempts to secure computer-generated or -processed information from those whom the original producer did not authorize that access. The information can be individual data like social security or credit card numbers or corporate proprietary science which, if exposed, would undercut product comparative advantage in the marketplace. In the public realm, the information could be voter preferences in elections or private communications between political figures. In national security, it may involve protecting secrets that can reinforce or compromise the country's safety as well as the activation and use of weaponry dependent on cyber direction.

Especially since the highly publicized and debated intrusion on the 2016 election process in the United States by Russian hackers commissioned and directed by the Russian government, the problem of cybersecurity and even the possibility of cyber*war* has intruded into the American political debate, and the prospect that interference would be attempted in the 2020 election has kept this problem in the public eye. The war analogy, generally vaguely drawn and unfocused on any specific set of events or prospects, has extended the rapidly evolving technology of things "cyber" into the national security debate. The subject does not focus on traditional national security problems and solutions, is difficult to conceptualize in familiar national security constructs, and has a slightly ethereal aura that makes it difficult to grasp.

Principle: The Cyber Challenge

The problem begins conceptually. National security centers on maintaining the physical safety of countries (or groups within states) from harm or extinction. Cyber formulations may involve threats to the state and its people, but those threats arise from different bases, notably electronic networks and virtual reality and the application of those capabilities to military problems. The core concentration is thus on the technologies that compose the computer revolution and actions that hostile others may take to interrupt, steal, or subvert that information and formulations. Given the ubiquity of electronic, computer-based, or -extended activities within society, this encompasses a very wide range of activities and operators. As one considers all the actions that can fall under the label of "cyber," the list is almost infinite, and when it is combined with the subjective nature of what threatens different people, it becomes almost unwieldy, leading the authors of a RAND Corporation study on cybersecurity to conclude the "term is applied too inclusively." Many of the challenges to which cyber technology is applied are traditional forms of hostile statecraft like espionage, sabotage, and propaganda. The goals are not new; the "packaging" is.

The medium in which cyber activity takes place, cyberspace, only adds to the confusion. The heart of cyber concern is information technology, which is a pervasive part of modern social interaction. The breadth of concerns that attach to the information revolution provides fertile ground for speculation and the building of a virtually infinite array of potential threats, some of which frighten some people more than others but also diffuses any systematic, focused delineation of the threat and thus the priority that should attach to solving it. "In cyberspace," Zegart and Morrell explain, "the targets are machines or systems that change constantly."

It was probably inevitable that the complex of activities and ideas that share the cyber moniker would find their way into the national security conversation. The electronic revolution, including the information accumulation and transmission that is at its heart, represents the kind of magnet toward which the national security community is drawn: a new technological, scientific endeavor the prospects of which are not known but that could include applications producing military advantage. That motivation is normally double-edged, meaning scientists must ask themselves both how these technologies could be applied for military advantage and how they could ensure that those applications could not successfully be used against their countries. This endeavor exists in an environment of considerable uncertainty because, by definition, one cannot know what one will discover and how it might be applied until the discovery is made and its implications explored. This is as true for non-defense applications of cyber technology with which the reader may be more familiar as it is for national security applications. In either the national security or civilian sectors, the process is ongoing, dynamic, and changing.

Understanding the cyber phenomenon begins by trying to come to grips with its unique vocabulary and concepts. These involve using familiar national security terms with somewhat different meanings than are attached to those terms in more conventional analyses. This exercise in turn makes it possible to describe the kinds of cyber threats that exist and to place them in the traditional national security framework.

Cyber Terms and Definitions

The root term in the discussion is "cyber." It is the adaptation of an old Greek word referring to space, and it has been adapted to the electronic cyber revolution. Universal agreement about what exactly is encompassed by the term does not exist, although the Oxford Dictionary offers this definition: "relating to electronic communications networks and virtual reality." The heart of cyber phenomena is thus computers and their major "products," information technology and virtual reality. As it has been adapted to the national security debate, cyber refers to attempts to manipulate the processes and products of information technology to either intrude on the cyberspace of individuals or national security systems that use information technology as part of their operating base.

It is a slippery term, because it depicts an evolving phenomenon in the national security environment. Is, for instance, cyberspace intrusion a distinct form of activity, or is it a component of other forms of activity? Klimburg, for one, suggests that it is both. "It is difficult to take the measure of cyberconflict," he argues, "because it is now a part of every other form of conflict; it affects everything while deciding very little on its own, at least so far." It is also not the exclusive province of any group.

National security concerns and actions usually involve the actions of foreign actors, especially national governments or subnational groups. Cyber activity as often as not is conducted by individual "hackers" either acting on their own or with some mysterious, hidden relationship to a sponsor, most problematically a foreign government or movement. The practical effect is to muddy even more the identification and priority one assigns to cyber actions. "A cyberattack could be the work of almost anyone," Parker argues, and this makes the subject even more difficult: "a larger problem with cyberwarfare is uncertainty. How does a government respond to an invisible attacker?" This ephemeral quality of intrusion into hyperspace leads to some colorful evocations. Slaughter, for instance, refers to anonymous hackers as "the invading hordes of the twenty-first century." This description may be hyperbolic, but it creates a dilemma that Parker points out, "A cyberattack could be the work of almost anyone."

Much of the discussion of cyber phenomena is directed at how the United States can protect itself from hostile cyber actions, and this is certainly the valid concern of American national security planners. It implicitly suggests a kind of victimization that probably leaves too much of an impression of American innocence in this area. A great deal of the computer revolution at the heart of cyber actions is, after all, American, and a significant part of the networks and manifestations of information technology were products of American science and technology. This means the United States has significant capabilities both to create and counter cyber developments, and focusing that effort is one of the purposes of the proposed U.S. Space Operations Force initiative.

The basic term to describe what former director of the National Security Agency General Michael Hayden has called the largest unregulated and uncontrolled domain in the history of mankind is the idea of *cyberspace*. The heart of the idea is that cyberspace is the internet environment through which ideas flow and the domain of information technology structures. The U.S. national security information collection, control, and dissemination effort is part of this environment and has designated it a part of the country's "critical infrastructure." This network has developed in a basically unplanned, random, and chaotic manner to a size and complexity that is difficult to understand and even more difficult to regulate.

Cybersecurity and Cyberwar

The most common term used in national security discussions is *cybersecurity*. Like other cyber concepts, it is a compound word with a compound meaning. Its heart is the security of its domain, which in the case of cybersecurity is largely the protection of computer-based information and applications in cyberspace that harm the entity that needs protecting. In traditional national security calculations, the safety sought is normally physical and expressed in terms of safety from physical harm and, at worst, extinction.

Definitions of cybersecurity abound, but they all emphasize actions and methods designed to protect electronic information from being stolen, compromised, or successfully attacked. These distinctions are usually attached to notions of computer security, because that is the medium in which most of the information is stored and transmitted. The security aspects of cybersecurity relate to stealing or distorting information in cyberspace for personal, commercial, or national advantage. The aspects of cybersecurity most interesting to national security are those with direct political or geopolitical applications, from the theft of government military secrets, the compromise of military technologies, the applications of which are computer dependent, the discovery and weaponization of new cyber-based possibilities, to more traditional geopolitical activities like interference in the internal politics of target countries or regions within countries.

Cybersecurity can be both an offensive and a defensive tool. Most discussions of the problem tend to focus on the defensive aspect: what can be done to deny access to information, its manipulation, and uses to which it can be put. Vulnerability exists for any entity with information stored or transmitted on computer networks, which is a very broad net of potential targets. Efforts to engage in the development and application of technologies designed to thwart cybersecurity breaches, of course, tend to vary depending on the degree of threat different entities possess and on resources to engage in counter-technology efforts.

Efforts to reinforce cybersecurity are compromised by a conundrum familiar to all scientific phenomena. Knowledge with applications to controlling or channeling the use of scientific advances is not abstract but is dependent on the existence of problems that can be remediated. Countermeasures presume measures to be countered, and this means that those who want to engage in scientifically based mischief are always a step ahead of those who seek to rein in those efforts. For better or worse, the development of countermeasures has generally received less priority than the burgeoning discovery of new applications in the cyber world, and this makes it more difficult to devise technologies that enhance security of the systems themselves and how they can be used.

The concept of *cyberwar* presents a particularly dramatic and potentially traumatic example of this problem. Like cybersecurity, the term "war" is used in a different way than in the traditional military context. The traditional core of definitions of war is that they involve armed conflict between hostile political units, with their key element being physical fighting to subdue or destroy the other side's will or ability to resist the imposition of politically defined terms, up to and including physical subjugation. War in the cyber context normally lacks the employment of organized forces in combat, unless one stretches the meaning of combat to include electronic means and counter-means to protect or subvert the computers, control systems, and networks of one side (which may or may not be engaged in traditional war at the same time). Rather than being direct instruments of war, cyberwar capabilities are generally conceptualized in supportive roles to aid the pursuit of goals by adversaries.

Libicki offers a useful distinction in types of cyberwar, what he calls strategic and operational cyberwar. In his view, strategic use consists of "a campaign of cyberattacks one entity carries out on another," whereas operational cyberwar "involves the use of cyberattacks on the other side's military in the context of a physical war." Operational cyberwar is closer to traditional notions and conduct of military actions, because it can involve actions like interrupting communications between weapons systems being aimed at enemy targets and those who control the attack. Directing drones to targets is an area where this activity could apply, just as cyberwar capabilities can have responsibility for aiming the weapons in the first place. The 2016 Russian election campaign is an example of the strategic application of cyberwar concepts in a non-lethal sense.

The use of the term war suggests the furtiveness, level of effort, and the seriousness with which cyber activities in the national effort are viewed, but it is not a literal description that can be translated from one domain to the other. Cyberwar is a part of an increasing number of military purposes and capabilities, but it is in a supportive, capabilities-enhancing role, not a physical warfighting role. Computers and their operators may clash on virtual battlefields where the object is to make one electronic device outperform the other, but they do not literally fight and kill one another. But things change in the cyber world, and one cannot discount the prospects of what will be possible in the future. When the classic 1940s movie *1984* was filmed, the technology only allowed depiction of intrusions on personal and private behavior through crude cardboard "eyes" watching the population. Its author, George Orwell, would have been shocked by the extent of the ability to monitor and intrude today that is a routine part of the physical capacity of governments and others.

The Cyber Problem

The ubiquity of the cyber phenomena makes it difficult to grasp and solve. It is all part of the domain of cyberspace, which is conceptually limitless. It is not the exclusive, "sovereign" province of any political jurisdiction in the way that the physical atmosphere above national territory is. No country or body has exclusive or effective power to regulate cyberspace or to enforce violations of norms and regulations which, by and large, do not exist beyond those included in the 1967 Outer Space Treaty. Much cyber activity is private in nature, conducted by individuals who may be violating some domestic laws for which they can be prosecuted if they are caught, but the ephemeral nature of cyberspace makes apprehension more difficult than catching someone who holds up a convenience store. When nefarious activity is conducted by governments trying to conceal their role, it is often difficult as well to determine the locus of behavior that travels through cyberspace. It is not impossible to do so, but the "forensics" of cybercrime are far less developed than those covering domestic criminal behavior.

The task is made even more difficult because cyberspace is used to conduct some of the hidden business that governments have historically conducted against one another. The most famous act of cyber aggression for Americans is Russian interference in the 2016 presidential election discussed in the next section. The manipulation of cyberspace to hack into the election process is the unique characteristic of that intrusion, but the idea of interfering in the electoral processes of other countries is a long practiced but officially illegal violation of sovereign states. The United States, principally in the western hemisphere but also in more remote locations like Iran, has long interfered to promote or defeat candidates it opposed. (Kinzer's study of U.S. intrusion into the 1954 Guatemalan elections is a particularly vivid depiction.) What is unique about the 2016 election (and prospects of the 2020 election) is that the United States was or will be the victim rather than the perpetrator and that the intrusions were committed in cyberspace rather than by Central Intelligence Agency personnel on the ground.

Application: Responding to Cybersecurity

Cyber problems can manifest themselves at an increasing number of levels and in different ways. The first is the political level, where the major security issue is the sanctity of national efforts and entities. The Russian interference case of 2016 is a very public manifestation of that problem. The Russians were engaged in sabotaging the American electoral process through a propaganda campaign involving both cyber penetration and conventional espionage efforts. The use of cyberspace to disseminate misinformation was an obvious intrusion that was very difficult to discover, monitor, and interfere with, and the opacity of the effort has made it difficult to assign and prove cupidity against a Russian leadership that denies the entire effort. It did not possess an overtly military component, but it did compromise the integrity and security of the American political system.

The second level is the more overtly military threats to security that cyber activities may pose, and this can happen in at least two distinct ways. One is that space is the medium in which cyber activities take place, and efforts to protect or interfere with the medium can convey potential military advantage for opponents. Second, that same space may provide a platform from which future capabilities will find an increasingly attractive, and menacing, venue. These kinds of concerns are part of the impetus for consolidating efforts in the United States for some form of Space Force or Command.

The potential ability of cyber warriors to obscure their nefarious behaviors is a prime objective of those who must thwart national security–based attacks. This problem can be handled most effectively using the resources of the U.S. federal government, and more specifically by specialized cyber agencies within the government in an increasingly internationally competitive environment. The Chinese are particularly adept at these kinds of activities. Other countries that frequently come into U.S. discussions of cyber activity include Russia, North Korea, and Iran.

The problems created by the cyber revolution are not so much unique additions to the things that countries do to one another as they are about new ways that states attempt to accomplish traditional political actions against one another. The challenges are consequential because of the extent to which the operation of society has become based in information generation, exchange, and protection. The cyber revolution has not yet produced a game-changing military technology and capability like nuclear weapons did seventy years ago. The cyber phenomenon is, however, a driving part of the scientific revolution that is changing life generally, and so even that limit on the impact of cyber capability may change as well.

The 2016 Russian Election Interference Controversy and Beyond

The Russian electronic interference in the 2016 presidential election in the United States was both a unique and simultaneously thoroughly traditional event in the ways in which states intrude on one another's sovereignty. It was unique in the sense that it was conducted by manipulating cyberspace by so-called cyber-warriors and that it represented a large-scale effort to interfere with an *American* election. It was a thoroughly traditional, if extra-legal, event in that states (including the United States) interfere with the politics of other countries all the time.

The unique aspect is that the election intrusion was conducted by hackers who found ways into files of the Democratic National Committee and the private files of certain Democratic politicians, notably presidential candidate Hillary Clinton. The American intelligence community investigated these claims, and their unanimous conclusion was that the hackers were Russian and were probably employed in some manner by the government of Vladimir Putin. The Russian president, of course, has consistently denied the perpetrators were Russian or that his regime was in any way linked to this theft. Complicating the investigation of the hacking has been President Trump's apparent acceptance of Putin's denial and thus his rejection of the accumulated evidence of the U.S. intelligence community. The special commission headed by Robert Mueller tried to reach a definitive conclusion on whether or how the Russians acted to protect against a repeat performance from Moscow in 2020, but controversy and disagreement has continued to swirl about this complex cyber-based action.

The problem posed by cyber dynamics comes from the difficulty of finding a "hard" evidence trail that could definitively link the Russians to the intrusion. The files that were stolen were obviously not theft proof. The intrusions that occurred required some sophistication, but they were actions that dedicated hackers—from paid Russian operatives to President Trump's 400-pound lone wolf—could have carried out. This process left no literal "paper trail," making it difficult to prove cupidity and easy to deny legal responsibility. The certainty of the American intelligence community about who committed these acts, however, suggests there are classified methods available to allow conclusive detection of these kinds of action if they are utilized, which they were not at the time of the intrusions.

The anonymity of hacking creates a dilemma with national security implications that goes far beyond the substantive case. A cyberattack, Parker points out, "can be the work of almost anyone," and this creates a "larger problem of cyberwarfare. How does a government respond to an invisible attacker? How can a state prevent cyberattacks without attribution?" This difficulty extrapolates into the problem of how can you punish an intruder whose guilt you know about but cannot prove? This has been a problem of American attempts to deal with Russian actions, and the answers are not clear, because foreign hackers and propagandists are not afraid to launch attacks against the United States in and through cyberspace, according to some analysts. The RAND analysts translate this into a Department of Defense mandate to "figure how to deter foreign actors in cyberspace as effectively as in nuclear and conventional war." Ramo suggests a strategy of "hard gatekeeping" to make penetration of hardened networks impossible.

This question of penetrability is the unique national security contribution of this episode. It has gained continuing traction because of its connection in time to the 2016 presidential election, the possibility that the Russians sought to undermine the election prospects of the Democratic candidate by their actions, and that the Trump campaign may have had some involvement in the plot. The fact that the Russians felt they could carry out these attacks against the United States adds to the outrage that surrounds the episode. Worse still, it is not entirely clear that capabilities and protocols are in place to prevent a recurrence in 2020 by the Russians or some other cyberspace opponent like China.

Some of the concerns about Russian violations of American sovereignty are disingenuous, if not openly hypocritical. The United States has been a consistent historical intruder in other politics, including those of Russia (the United States was an open champion of Boris Yeltsin against Putin). In his May 8, 2018, announcement removing the United States from the Joint Comprehensive Plan of Action with Iran, President Trump openly suggested the Iranians replace their government, a recurrent theme with Tehran. The Russians interfered clandestinely; the American president did so on global television. Americans may (and do) dislike others turning the tables on them, but their indignation is tainted by historic U.S. practices. The real challenge of the 2016 incident (beyond possible internal political ramifications) lies in the future: finding ways to detect and thwart cyberattacks and unambiguously identifying perpetrators and punishing them.

The Space Force

The idea of war in space has been a staple theme of science fiction for centuries. Much of this speculation has featured alien attacks and invasions on the Earth and its inhabitants. In the twentieth century, sightings of alien "flying saucers" in the skies over the American West created a whole tourist attraction in Roswell, New Mexico. Almost all this emphasis occurred in a milieu of questionable scientific knowledge.

The situation has changed. Military activity in space is a serious area of speculation, inquiry, and development not by alien intruders but by earthbound humans seeking to gain advantage over their rivals. The use of space is regulated internationally by the Outer Space Treaty of 1967, which remains in force and has 108 states as members. The original signatories were the United States, the United Kingdom, and the then Soviet Union, and the only state mentioned in speculation about space but not a member is Iran, which acceded to the document in 1967 but never ratified it.

Two aspects of the treaty are notable here. First, it accepts the conventional definition of outer space as "the physical universe beyond earth's atmosphere." All activity in space is justified by this parameter. Second, the treaty is permissive regarding the military use of space. Its only military restriction is against "placement of weapons of mass destruction (e.g. nuclear weapons) in space." All other activity, notably most uses related to cyberwar, is permitted.

The militarization of cyberspace has become a major area of global military competition that has been formally recognized by the Trump administration. On June 18, 2018, Trump announced a proposal to create a sixth independent branch of the U.S. military, the U.S. Space Operations Force. This "new combatant command," according to Roulo, would include U.S. Space Command (formerly part of the Air Force) and a Space Development Agency staffed by personnel from existing agencies. To become operational, it requires authorization by Congress, which had not occurred by mid-2019. Secretary of the Air Force Heather Wilson is quoted by Roulo as estimating the additional cost of the new force at $15 billion over its first five years. The proposal is controversial, but the point is that it is an institutional response to cybersecurity.

Conclusion

Cyber activity has a strong link to national security. The exploitation of the potential of computers and computer networks operating in space has been influenced greatly by defensive concerns: how cyberspace can be made more secure and what military and other national security potential capabilities can be created to protect that security. One unique characteristic of the information technology revolution, especially from a security vantage point, has been effectively to "democratize" the exploitation of cyberspace for good and not so good ends: individuals and small groups of people can manipulate access to the information and processes of cyberspace, and this creates a thriving enterprise both among those who wish to breach sources of information and those who try to protect those sources.

The problem in the national security area is particularly critical. Government national security–related organizations like the National Security Agency spend great effort and resources both learning how to deny access to vital information by those who would use it for nefarious purposes and devising methods to penetrate the equivalent kinds of efforts by others. For the government, the emphasis is on the protection of privileged or secret information with potential value for enhancing or undermining the security of the country.

At this point in time, cyberspace use in the national security environment has been derivative, not basic. Clearly, the information process has both the discovery of new information with scientific—and by extension—military applications with protection as mandates. The prototype of the internet, after all, was the product of a Defense Advanced Research Projects Agency grant the purpose of which was to allow university research laboratories to communicate scientific findings among themselves more efficiently, thereby enhancing the speed of scientific discovery. Some of those findings inevitably had military and other dramatic applications, which was part of the rationale for the effort. The same dynamic applies to cyberspace.

In the publicly available contemporary environment, cyberspace and its dynamics are difficult to isolate and to solve. Cybercapabilities provided the context in which Russian 2016 hacking occurred and could recur. The motivation came from nefarious Russian political motivations. Cyber activity itself, like all scientific endeavors, is value neutral about how it is used. Billionaire Warren Buffett, addressing Berkshire Hathaway's annual shareholder's meeting in May 2018 (he owns the insurance company), warned that "cyber is uncharted territory and it's going to get worse, not better," he said, adding it "will get more intense as time goes by." He was talking specifically about the insurance business, but his comments surely apply to national security and international concerns. Is what we see of cyber potential the tip of the iceberg of the international and national security future? What does all this say about the cyber phenomenon and how it should be handled?

Study/Discussion Questions

1. What does it mean to talk about cyber phenomena? What are its core concepts? How does its use alter the ways information is collected, stored, protected, and attacked?
2. Are the various cyber concepts basic national security problems per se, or are they examples of the application of cybercapabilities to traditional national security concerns? What are the national security purposes?
3. What is the cyber "problem"? Is it something new or the latest way in which traditional problems are manifested? Cite examples of how problems like protecting intelligence and interfering with other countries have been accomplished in the past.
4. How does cyberwar affect the way calculations of national security are made both about major rivals like China and Russia and others like North Korea and Iran?
5. What are the basic terms used to describe and discuss cyber ideas? What does "cyber" mean? Apply the basic concepts to national security.
6. Discuss the 2016 case of Russian interference in the American presidential election. Is it primarily an example of the basic problem or an illustration of how cyber phenomena can be applied to more traditional national security concerns?
7. What is the U.S. Space Operations Force? Discuss the roots of the concept, why it has come about, what its status is, and whether you think it is a good idea.
8. Can or should the United States have a discrete cyber strategy, or is cyber a part of other aspects of strategy? How does this distinction affect how we think about cybersecurity in the broader context of national security?

Bibliography

Brodie, Bernard, and Fawn M. Brodie. *From Crossbow to H-Bomb: The Evolution of Weapons and Tactics of Warfare*. Bloomington, IN: Indiana University Press, 1973.

Brose, Christian. "The New Revolution in Military Affairs. *Foreign Affairs* 98, no. 3 (May/June 2019), 122–34.

Buchanan, Ben. *The Cybersecurity Dilemma: Hacking, Trust, and Fear Between Nations*. Oxford, UK: Oxford University Press, 2017.

Buffett, Warren. "Cyber Is Uncharted Territory." *Yahoo Online*, May 5, 2018.

Clarke, Richard A., and Robert Knake. *Cyber War: The Next Threat to National Security and What to Do About It*. New York: ECCO Books, 2011.

Futter, Andrew. *Hacking the Bomb: Cyber Threats and Nuclear Weapons*. Washington, DC: Georgetown University Press, 2018.

Guertner, Gary L., and Donald M. Snow. *The Last Frontier: An Analysis of the Strategic Defense Initiative*. Lexington, MA: Lexington Books, 1986.

Harris, Shane. *@ War: The Rise of the Military-Internet Complex*. New York: Mariner Books, 2014.

Hennessey, Susan. "Deterring Cyberattacks: How to Reduce Vulnerability." *Foreign Affairs* 96, no. 6 (November/December 2017), 39–46.

Isikoff, Michael, and David Korn. *Russian Roulette: The Inside Story of Putin's War on America and the Election of Donald Trump*. New York: Twelve Books, 2018.

Jarmon, Jack A., and Pano Yannakogeorgos. *The Cyber Threat and Globalization: The Impact on U.S. National and International Security*. Lanham, MD: Rowman & Littlefield, 2018.

Kaplan, Fred. *Dark Territory: The Secret History of Cyber War*. New York: Simon and Schuster, 2017.

Kinzer, Stephen. *The Brothers: John Foster Dulles, Allan Dulles, and Their Secret World War*. New York: Times Books, 2013.

Klimburg, Alexander. *The Darkening Web: The War for Cyberspace*. New York: Penguin, 2017.

Kramer, Franklin, Stuart H. Starr, and Larry Wentz, eds. *Cyberpower and National Security*. Washington, DC: Potomac Books, 2009.

Libicki, Martin C. *Cyberspace in Peace and War*. Annapolis, MD: Naval Institute Press, 2016.

Nez, Chester, and Judith Schleiss Avila. *Code Talkers: The First and Only Memoir by One of the Original Navajo Code Talkers of WWII*. New York: Penguin Group, 2011.

Parker, Emily. "Hack Job: How America Invented Cyberwar." *Foreign Affairs* 96, no. 3 (May/June 2017), 133–38.

Perkovich, George, and Ariel E. Levite, eds. *Understanding Cyber Conflict: Fourteen Analogies*. Washington, DC: Georgetown University Press, 2017.

Ramo, Joshua. *The Seventh Sense: Power, Fortune, and Survival in the Age of Networks*. New York: Little Brown, 2016.

Rid, Thomas. *Cyber War Will Not Take Place*. Oxford, UK: Oxford University Press, 2017.

Rosenzweig, Paul. *Cyber Warfare: How Conflicts in Cyberspace Are Challenging America and Changing the World*. Westport, CT: Praeger Security International, 2013.

Roulo, Claudette. "Space Force to Become Sixth Branch of Armed Forces." *Department of Defense News* (online). Washington, DC: Department of Defense, August 9, 2018.

Scharre, Paul. *Army of None: Autonomous Weapons and the Future of War*. New York: W. W. Norton, 2018.

———. "Killer Apps: The Real Danger of an AI Arms Race." *Foreign Affairs* 98, no. 3 (May/June 2019), 135–44.

Segal, Adam. *The Hacked World Order: How Nations Fight, Trade, Maneuver, and Manipulate in the Digital Age*. New York: PublicAffairs, 2016.

Singer, P. W., and Allan Friedman. *Cybersecurity and Cyberwar: What Everyone Needs to Know*. New York: Cambridge University Press, 2014.

Slaughter, Ann-Marie. "How to Succeed in the Networked World: A Grand Strategy for the Digital Age." *Foreign Affairs* 95, no. 6 (November/December 2016), 76–89.

Springer, Paul. *Cyber Warfare: A Reference Handbook* (Contemporary World Issues). New York: ABC-CLIO, 2015.

———. *Encyclopedia of Cyber Warfare*. New York: ABC-CLIO, 2017.

Steinnon, Richard. *There Will Be Cyberwar: How the Move to Network-Centric War Fighting Has Set the Stage for Cyberwar*. London: IT-Harvest Press, 2015.

U.S. Senate, Select Committee on Intelligence. *Russian Interference in the 2016 Election*. New York: CreateSpace Independent Publishing Platform, February 19, 2018.

Zegart, Amy, and Michael Morrell. "Spies, Lies, and Algorithms: Why U.S. Intelligence Agencies Must Adapt or Fail." *Foreign Affairs* 98, no. 3 (May/June 2019), 85–96.

Index

absolutist monarchy, 38, 39, 77, 174
Afghanistan, 12, 167; geography of, 107–8; history of conflict in, 107–8; Pashtuns in, 108–9, 110; U.S. and, 62
Afghanistan war, 112; costs of, 111; NATO and, 10, 109, 111; Al Qaeda and, 40, 101, 104, 109, 111; September 11th attacks and, 101, 109, 110; Soviet Union and, 109; Taliban and, 101, 104, 110; U.S. and, 101, 104, 106, 107, 109–11
Africa, 13, 122, 159; resource scarcity in, 213, 218. *See also specific countries*
Allison, Graham, 89
anarchy, 4–5, 6, 46
Antarctica, 168; sovereignty and, 8
AQ. *See* Al Qaeda
Arab Spring, 175; in Egypt, 176–77; Syrian Civil War and, 46, 51, 177
Asia. *See specific countries*
al-Assad, Bashar, 51, 52, 53, 76; ICC and, 78; war crimes and, 10, 78
asymmetrical warfare, 111–12; adaptability and, 103; appeal of, 104; cost-tolerance and, 103, 104, 106; DWICs and, 101–4, 105–7; Eastern-style warfare and, 101; Iraq, U.S. and, 62, 103, 104, 106; military dimension in, 106; nonstate actors and, 104; outside involvement in, 105–7; political dimension to, 107–8; terrorism and, 104–5; Western-style warfare and, 103. *See also* Afghanistan war
autonomy, 9, 22, 59, 108, 233
Axis of Evil, 138, 140
Axis powers, 60, 63, 71

Baghdadi, Abu Bakr, 39, 234
al-Bashir, Omar, 78
Benn, Aluf, 181
Berkowitz, Bruce, 102
bin Laden, Osama, 40, 107, 110, 225, 229
bin-Sultan, Bandar, 37
bin Sultan, Muhammad (MbS), 40, 41
Bodin, Jean, 5
Boko Haram, 122, 123, 227
Bosnia, 11, 12
Bretton Woods meetings, 61, 64, 148, 152
Brexit, 57, 62, 153, 167, 168, 170
Brown, Eugene, 22, 135
Buffett, Warren, 249
Bush, George W., 12, 13, 203, 204; Iran and, 140; North Korea and, 139
Caliphate, 177, 193, 234
Cambodia, 78
Canada, 153, 215
Canada-U.S. Free Trade Agreement, 153
The Case Against Military Intervention (Snow), 80, 105–6
Castenada, Jorge C., 124
Chavez, Hugo, 121, 124
China: climate change and, 202, 204, 205, 206, 207; coal in, 206, 216; communism in, 90; cybersecurity and, 245; economy in, 90–91, 92; election interference and, 49; military and, 90, 91, 101; North Korea and, 138, 139–40; nuclear weapons in, 135; population in, 92; resources and, 92–93, 206, 215–16, 217, 219–20; as rising power, 86, 88–89, 90–92, 96; SEZs in, 90–91, 92; sovereignty and, 6; trade and, 147; U.S. and, 89, 91, 92–93, 147; Xi in, 91, 206, 218, 220
Choucri, Nazli, 162
classic diplomacy, 21; in Europe, 18, 20; secrecy and, 20
Claussen, Eileen, 197
climate change: causes of, 197–98, 201–2; China and, 202, 204, 205, 206, 207; debate over, 198–200; economics and, 201, 207; greenhouse gas emissions and, 197–205; impacts of, 198; IPCC and, 199; Kyoto Protocol and, 197, 198, 199, 202–4; Paris Climate Agreement and, 197, 198, 204–6, 208; politics and, 202; pollution by country and, 202; skepticism and, 197, 200–201; territory and, 199; as transnational issue, 201, 207; Trump and, 197, 201, 202, 203, 205, 206; UNFCCC and, 202, 204; U.S. and, 197, 201, 202, 203–6, 207, 208, 216; warming ocean water and, 199–200, 207
Clinton, Bill, 12, 203; North Korea and, 138
Clinton, Hillary, 77, 246
coal, 119, 199, 214; in China, 206, 216; energy scarcity and, 216, 219–20; European Coal and Steel Community, 152
Cohen, Eliot, 62
Cold War, 12, 74; election interference and, 7; human rights and, 78–79; ICC and, 11; Middle East and, 175, 176, 182, 183; nuclear proliferation and, 132, 133, 135; politics and, 176; power and, 87, 88; Soviet Union and, 85, 87, 88, 93; U.S. and, 61, 87, 88; vertical proliferation and, 132

Praise for THE YOGA SŪTRAS OF PATAÑJALI

"A superb contribution to the secondary literature on *yoga*. Critically grounded in the scholarship on *yoga* and the rich textual history of the tradition, Bryant nevertheless succeeds in transcending both the excessively technical approaches to *yoga* scholarship as well as much of the popular nonsense about *yoga* in the proliferating 'schools' in the New Age marketplace. Bryant impressively communicates the essentials of *yoga* philosophy and practice to the thoughtful but non-specialist general reader. His translations from the Sanskrit are precise and well-grounded, and his interpretations are provocative and persuasive. His book will surely be welcomed by both serious scholars and responsible practitioners."

—Gerald James Larson, Rabindranath Tagore Professor Emeritus of Indian Cultures and Civilizations, Indiana University, Bloomington, and Professor Emeritus of Religious Studies, University of California, Santa Barbara

"Dr. Bryant's translation of and commentary on Patañjali's *Yoga Sūtras* reveal the rich tapestry of schools and viewpoints that form the background for the *yoga* tradition. Dr. Bryant teaches us to delight in the diversity of ideas and commentaries that come along with the equally diverse practices of *yoga*. He helps us to look deeper into a universal pattern of all practices, taking us out of the fundamentalism and exclusivity of our own schools. Grounded in an unbiased sense of ancient history, he clears away any confusion about the meaning of and the connections between different *yoga* philosophies. His book is a well-rounded and inspiring course on the real connections between ideas, practices, and direct experience. I enthusiastically recommend it."

—Richard Freeman, author of *The Yoga Matrix*

"Edwin Bryant has provided us with a sweeping, kaleidoscopic overview of this essential *yoga* text. His clear and engaging prose brings Patañjali's aphorisms to life, taking his reader on an amazing journey through the history of *yoga* philosophy."

—David Gordon White, Professor of Religious Studies, University of California, Santa Barbara, and author of *Sinister Yogis*

"Edwin Bryant unpacks the layers of history and traditional commentaries that are in the suitcase of the *Yoga Sūtras*. Through his depth of understanding and research rendered in this detailed map, we are able to travel a little closer to our soul. I will be reading and referring to his text for a lifetime." —Rodney Yee, author of *Moving Toward Balance*

"The greatest strength of Edwin Bryant's work on the *Yoga Sūtras* is that he has taken the most abstruse commentaries and made of them a fluidly readable work. He has made an academically serious study into a presentation of most symmetrical beauty. He has brought together the views of different schools of philosophy and made them rhyme as though in poetry. We need more of such works of serious and yet readable philosophy."

—Swami Veda Bharati, D.Litt., Chancellor, HIHT University, Dehradun, India

"Bryant's meticulous study of the *Yoga Sūtras* examines its reception throughout the past fifteen hundred years by a variety of commentators. Understanding that all religious books operate in the context of lived communities, Bryant suggests that the worship of Vishnu as taught by Krishna in the *Bhagavad Gīta* has played an important role in how the practice of *yoga* has been understood and communicated, particularly for the past five hundred years. For practitioners of *yoga*, this book provides a fresh look at a complex philosophy of applied spirituality."

—Christopher Key Chapple, Doshi Professor of Indic and Comparative Theology, Loyola Marymount University, and author of *Yoga and the Luminous*

"What I like about Edwin Bryant's edition is that it serves as a concordance of commentaries, a commentary on the commentaries without which this text (or any other compendium of sutras) is unintelligible. It is a pleasure to watch as Bryant uses the commentaries to show how thinking about the *Yoga Sūtras* shifted and evolved over the years."

—Dr. Robert Svoboda, Ayurvedacharya

Edwin F. Bryant

THE YOGA SŪTRAS OF PATAÑJALI

Edwin F. Bryant received his Ph.D. in Indology from Columbia University. He has taught at Columbia University and Harvard University and since 2001 has been professor of Hindu religion and philosophy at Rutgers University. Bryant has written numerous scholarly articles and published five previous books, including a translation of the four thousand verses of the tenth book of the *Bhāgavata Purāṇa* called *Krishna: The Beautiful Legend of God*. In addition to his work in the academy, Bryant teaches workshops on the *Yoga Sūtras* and other Hindu texts in *yoga* communities around the world. His website is www.edwinbryant.org.

ALSO BY EDWIN F. BRYANT

Krishna: A Source Book (as editor, 2007)

The Aryan Invasion: Evidence, Politics, History (as coeditor with Laurie Patton, 2005)

The Hare Krishna Movement: The Post-Charismatic Fate of a Religious Transplant (as coeditor with Maria Ekstrand, 2004)

Krishna: The Beautiful Legend of God (as translator from Sanskrit with notes and introduction, 2003)

The Quest for the Origins of Vedic Culture: The Indo-Aryan Invasion Debate (2001)

THE YOGA SŪTRAS OF PATAÑJALI

THE YOGA SŪTRAS OF PATAÑJALI

A New Edition, Translation, and Commentary

WITH INSIGHTS FROM THE TRADITIONAL COMMENTATORS

EDWIN F. BRYANT

North Point Press
A division of Farrar, Straus and Giroux
New York

North Point Press
A division of Farrar, Straus and Giroux
18 West 18th Street, New York 10011

Printed in the United States of America
First edition, 2009

Library of Congress Cataloging-in-Publication Data
Bryant, Edwin F. (Edwin Francis), 1957–
The Yoga Sūtras of Patañjali : a new edition, translation, and commentary with insights from the traditional commentators / Edwin F. Bryant.
p. cm.
Includes bibliographical references and index.
ISBN-13: 978-0-86547-736-0 (pbk. : alk. paper)
ISBN-10: 0-86547-736-1 (pbk. : alk. paper)
1. Patañjali. Yogasutra. 2. Yoga. I. Patañjali. Yogasutra. English & Sanskrit. II. Title.

B132.Y6B78 2009
181'.452—dc22

2008050183

www.fsgbooks.com

19 20 18

To my daughter, Mohini

And to all teachers of *yoga*, that Patañjali's *Sūtras* may inform and inspire their teachings

CONTENTS

FOREWORD

by B.K.S. Iyengar

I congratulate you on your lucid commentary on the *Yoga Sūtras* of Patañjali. I have appreciated your commentary quoting the traditional commentators Vyāsa, Vācaspati Miśra, Śaṅkara, Bhoja Rāja, Vijñānabhikṣu, and Hariharānanda, and it reads well. You have presented it in simple and fluent language, which I am sure will be easily understandable to readers. As you are dedicating it to the teachers of *yoga*, I am sure your book will provide the readers with plenty of knowledge so that they may grasp the philosophy behind the subject and move toward the higher aspects of life in their *sādhana* (practice).

Pātañjala Yoga is a practical subject and not a discursive one. As each individual is electrically alive and dynamic, so *yoga* is a living, dynamic force in life. In order to savor its essence, one needs a religiously attentive dynamic practice done with awareness and absorption. The life of man is not only the conjunction of *prakṛti* (the sheaths of the body) and *puruṣa* (the soul), but also a combination of these two. *Yoga* is a means to utilizing the conjunction of *prakṛti* and *puruṣa* for freedom and beatitude (*mokṣa*), as the two are interwoven and interrelated.

Patañjali explains the practice of *kriyā-yoga* in *sūtra* I of the *sādhana pāda*, repeating the same ingredients as are found in the *niyama* disciplines, namely, *tapas, svādhyāya*, and *Īśvara-praṇidhāna* (discipline, self-study, and devotion to God). This three-tiered definition clearly indicates the paths of *karma, jñāna*, and *bhakti*. Though Patañjali advises *bhakti* in the beginning of the text in I.23, I consider the disciplines of *yama* and *niyama* (II.30–45) as corresponding to *karma-marga* (the path of action); *āsana, prāṇāyāma*, and *pratyāhāra* (II.46–55) as corresponding to *jñāna-marga* (the path of knowledge); and *dhāraṇā, dhyāna*, and *śamādhi* (*saṁyama*, III.1–4) as corresponding to *bhakti marga* (the path of devotion).

Prakṛti and *puruṣa* being interwoven and interrelated, the practitioners of *yoga* have to understand this relationship clearly and perform *svādhyāya* in the form of *āsana, prāṇāyāma*, and *pratyāhāra. Svā* means "self" and *adhyāya* means "study." These three aspects of Pātañjala Yoga lead the *sādhaka* (practitioner) to understand himself or herself from the skin to the self. Hence, this guides one on the path of *jñāna. Dhāraṇā, dhyāna*, and *samādhi* being the effect of *jñāna* earned through the practices of *āsana, prāṇāyāma*, and *pratyāhāra* along with *yama* and *niyama*, then lead the *sādhaka* toward the path of *bhakti. Bhakti* is the summum bonum of Pātañjala Yoga. But if the *sādhaka* abuses the *sādhana* with selfish motives, he or she ends up with only the joys of sensual pleasure (*bhoga*).

As *yoga* is a lively subject, interpretations of the *sūtras* may vary according to *dharma, lakṣana*, and *avastha pariṇāma* (character, qualities, and conditions) in *sādhana* (III.13). Therefore, I differ from the traditional commentators on two things. The first pertains to the effects of *āsana*: *tato dvandvānabhighātāḥ* (II.48). The entire text speaks of the intelligence of nature and the intelligence of the self. I understand that the perfection of *āsana* brings unity between the various sheaths of the body and the self (*puruṣa*), which Lord Kṛṣna calls *kṣetra-kṣetrajña yoga* in the *Bhagavad Gītā* (XIII.1ff). Hence, perfection in *āsana* means a divine union of *prakṛti* with *puruṣa*.

The practice of *āsanas* develops *sattva guṇa*, sublimating the *guṇas* of *rajas* and *tamas*. The aim of *āsanas* is to make the *prāṇa* (cosmic universal force) move concurrently with the *prajñā* (insight) of the self on its frontier. This means to make the awareness of the self (*sāsmitā*) move and cover the entire body (II.19) so that the mechanisms of nature are sublimated and the intelligence (*prajñā*) of the self engulfs the body with its *śakti*.

The second point pertains to the *virāma pratyaya* of verse I.18 (*virāma-pratyayābhyāsa-pūrvaḥ saṁskāra-śeṣo 'nyaḥ*—the other *samādhi* is preceded by cultivating the determination to terminate [all thoughts]. [In this state] only latent impressions remain). Patañjali himself does not call this other state *asamprajñāta-samādhi* (I.46). He has said that it is part of *sabīja-samādhi* (I.46). The various commentators infer this state to be *asamprajñāta*, and this may be because Patañjali mentions *samprajñāta-samādhi* in the preceding *sūtra*. For me, this *sūtra* is referring to a consolidating state of *samprajñāta-samādhi*, after attaining which the *yogī* can move toward *asamprajñāta* (*nirbīja*) *samādhi*. Hence, this state acts as the intermediary state for *nirbīja-samādhi*. Just as *pratyāhāra* in *aṣṭāṅga-yoga* (II.54) is a consolidating stage, where one needs to integrate the external sheath (*bahiraṅga*) with the innermost sheath (*antaraṅga*), so is the case with the stage of *virāma pratyaya*, for which Patañjali has not coined any term. It is a consolidating stage of *sabīja-samādhi*, after which the *yogī* naturally moves toward *nirbīja-samādhi*.

For me, the state of *pratyāhāra* in *aṣṭāṅga-yoga* and *virāma-pratyaya* in *samādhi* are the touchstones in understanding the purity, clarity, and maturity of *prajñā*, intelligence. When this illuminative and luminous intelligence takes place, the union of *prakṛti* with *puruṣa* happens (*sattva-puruṣayoḥ śuddhi-samye kaivalyam iti* III.56*). Even in this *pratyāhāra* state of *aṣṭāṅga-yoga* and *virāma-pratyaya* state in *samādhi*, if one neglects *śraddhā, vīrya, smṛti, samādhi-prajñā* (faith, vigor, memory, and the insight of *samādhi*, the four legs of *yoga* in I.20), then, even if one has reached the zenith, one is bound to become a *yoga-bhraṣṭa*, a fallen *yogī*. Therefore, the practice of *pratyāhāra* in *aṣṭāṇga yoga* or *virāma-pratyaya* in *samādhi* is to be performed with these four legs of *yoga* so as to maintain and retain that state of seasoned wisdom (*ṛtambharā prajñā*, I.48) that consecrates *citi-śakti* (the power of *puruṣa*). It is this combination only that leads the *yogī* toward the highest state in *bhakti-marga*—the *śaraṇāgati-mārga*—total dependence on *Īśvara*, God. This is how I understand and practice the *aṣṭāṅga-yoga* of sage Patañjali.

Having expressed my feelings, I am sure your good work and expressions, using the attributes of all the earlier commentators on the *Yoga Sūtras*, will turn out as a study book for hundreds and hundreds of students who have embraced the subject in the West in knowing the light of that hidden illuminative intelligence on the inner self, the

*Editor's note: B.K.S. Iyengar accepts fifty-six verses in the third *pada* where other commentators accept fifty-five.

ātman, and making that light surface and active in their *sādhana*, which will help their fellow beings experience this unalloyed and untainted bliss with its stream of virtuous (*śīlatā*) wisdom.

With all my best wishes, I am sure this volume will benefit *yoga sādhakas* and spiritual seekers throughout the world.

Pune, December 5, 2007

SANSKRIT PRONUNCIATION GUIDE

DIACRITICS USED IN THIS TRANSLATION:

ā ī ū ṛ ḷ ḥ ṁ ṅ ñ ṇ ṭ ḍ ś ṣ

The following pronunciation guide attempts to give *approximate* equivalents in English to the Sanskrit sounds used in this text.

VOWELS

Sanskrit vowels have both short forms and lengthened forms (the latter are transliterated by a line over the vowel—*ā, ī, ū*), as well as a retroflex *ṛ* sound articulated by curling the tongue farther back onto the roof of the mouth than for the English *r*. Other Sanskrit vowels alien to English are noted below. Vowels are listed in Sanskrit in the following traditional order (according to their locus of articulation, beginning from the back of the throat to the front of the mouth):

a	as in "but"
ā	as in "tar"; held twice as long as short *a*
i	as in "bit"
ī	as in "week"; held twice as long as short *i*
u	as in "bush"
ū	as in "fool"; held twice as long as short *u*
ṛ	as in "rim"
ḷ	no English equivalent; approximated by *l* followed by *ṛ*, above
e	as in "they"
ai	as in "aisle"
o	as in "go"

au as in "vow"

ḥ (*visarga*) a final "h" sound that echoes the preceding vowel slightly; as in "aha" for *aḥ*

ṁ (*anusvāra*) a nasal sound pronounced like *mm*, but influenced according to whatever consonant follows, as in "bingo," "punch"

CONSONANTS

Sanskrit consonants have both aspirated forms (*kh*, *gh*, *ch*, *jh*, and so on) and unaspirated forms (*k*, *g*, *c*, *j*, and so on); the former involve articulating the consonant accompanied by a slight expulsion of air. There is also a set of retroflexes (transliterated with a dot beneath them—*ṭ*, *ḍ*, *ṭh*, *ḍh*, *ṇ*, *ṣ*), which have no precise English equivalents, and these involve curling the tongue farther back onto the roof of the mouth than for the English dentals. Sanskrit dentals (*t*, *d*, *th*, *dh*) are articulated with the tongue touching the teeth, slightly farther forward than for their English equivalents. The consonants are listed in Sanskrit in the following traditional order (according to their locus of articulation, beginning from the back of the throat to the front of the mouth):

k as in "pick"
kh as in "E*ck*hart"
g as in "gate"
gh as in "dig-hard"
ṅ as in "sing"
c as in "charm"
ch as in "staunch-heart"
j as in "jog"
jh as in "hedgehog"
ñ as in "canyon"
ṭ as in "tub," but with the tongue curled farther back
ṭh as in "light-heart," but with the tongue curled farther back
ḍ as in "dove," but with the tongue curled farther back
ḍh as in "red-hot," but with the tongue curled farther back
ṇ as in "tint," but with the tongue touching the teeth
t as in "tub," but with the tongue touching the teeth
th as in "light-heart," but with the tongue touching the teeth

d	as in "dove," but with the tongue touching the teeth
dh	as in "red-hot," but with the tongue touching the teeth
n	as in "no," but with the tongue touching the teeth
p	as in "pin"
ph	as in "uphill"
b	as in "bin"
bh	as in "rub-hard"
m	as in "mum"
y	as in "yellow"
r	as in "run"
l	as in "love"
v	as in "vine"
ś	as in "shove"
ṣ	as in "crashed," but with the tongue curled farther back
s	as in "such"
h	as in "hope"

THE HISTORY OF YOGA

Everyone by now has heard of *yoga*, and, indeed, with millions of Americans in some form or fashion practicing *āsana*, the physical aspect of *yoga*, the teaching and practice of *yoga*, at least in the aspect of techniques of body poses and stretches, are now thoroughly mainstream activities on the Western cultural landscape. *Yoga* has popularly been translated as "union with the divine"[1] and may refer to a number of different spiritual systems. The *Bhagavad Gītā*, for example, discusses a number of practices that have been termed *yoga* in popular literature: *karma-yoga* (*buddhi-yoga*), the path of action; *jñāna-yoga* (*sāṅkhya-yoga*), the path of knowledge; *bhakti-yoga*, the path of devotion; and *dhyāna-yoga*, the path of silent meditation (which is the subject of Patañjali's text),[2] and terms such as *tantra-yoga, siddha-yoga, nāḍa-yoga,* and so forth are now common in alternative spiritualities in the West. Typically, however, when the word *yoga* is used by itself without any qualification, it refers to the path of meditation, particularly as outlined in the *Yoga Sūtras*—the Aphorisms on *Yoga*—and the term *yogī*, a practitioner of this type of meditational *yoga*.

Patañjali was the compiler of the *Yoga Sūtras*, one of the ancient treatises on Indic philosophy that eventually came to be regarded as one of the six classical schools of Indian philosophy. He presented a teaching that focuses on realization of the *puruṣa*—the term favored by the Yoga school[3] to refer to the innermost conscious self, loosely equivalent to the soul in Western Greco-Abrahamic traditions. The practice of *yoga* emerged from post-Vedic India as perhaps its most important development and has exerted immense influence over the philosophical discussions and religious practices of what has come to be known as mainstream Hinduism, both in its dominant forms in India and in its most common exported and repackaged forms visible in the West. Accordingly, Patañjali's *Yoga Sūtras* is one of the most important classical texts in Hinduism and thus a classic of Eastern, and therefore world, thought. Along with the *Bhagavad Gītā*, it is the text that has received the most attention and interest outside of India. I might add here that Patañjali's *Yoga Sūtras* is not an overtly sectarian text in the sense of prioritizing a specific deity or promoting a particular type of worship as is the case with many Hindu scriptures, including the *Bhagavad Gītā*. Therefore, as a template, it can be and has been appropriated and reconfigured by followers of different schools and traditions throughout Indian religious history[4] and certainly continues to lend itself to such appropriations, most recently in nonreligious contexts of the West.

In its exported manifestation, *yoga* has tended to focus on the physical aspect of the system of *yoga*, the *āsanas*, or stretching poses and postures, which most Western adherents of *yoga* practice in order to stay trim, supple, and healthy. Patañjali himself, however, pays minimal attention to the *āsanas*, which are the third stage of the eight stages, or limbs, of *yoga*, and focuses primarily on meditation and various stages of concentration of the mind.

There are references to awareness of *yogīs* on the Western landscape as early as Greek classical sources, Alexander being perhaps the most notorious early Westener to be fascinated with Indian ascetics. Its initial introduction to the West in modern times was by Vivekānanda at the end of the nineteenth century. More recently, generic *yoga*—particularly as *āsanas*, postures, but also as a meditative technique leading to *samādhi*, enlightenment—was popularized in the West by a number of influential Hindu teachers of *yoga* in the 1960s, most of whom came from two lineages: Sivananda (1887–1963) and Krishnamāchārya (1888–1989). Sivananda was a renunciant and his ashram tradition was transplanted by his disciples Vishnudevananda (1927–1993), Satchidananda (1914–2002), and Chinmayananda (1916–1993), each of whom founded his own independent mission in the West (the Sivananda Yoga Vedanta Centres, the Integral Yoga Institute, and the Chinmaya Mission, respectively). Krishnamāchārya's three principal disciples took his emphasis on the practice of *āsana* in their own direction: K. Pattabhi Jois (1915–) continued to promote his version of *astāṅga-vinyāsa-yoga*; Krishnamāchārya's son, T.K.V. Desikachar (1938–), developed *viniyoga*; and—perhaps most influential of all—Krishnamāchārya's brother-in-law, B.K.S. Iyengar (1918–) established the Iyengar method. Almost all *yoga* teachers trace their lineage to such masters, and the more serious among such teachers or practitioners of *yoga* will have a valued copy of the *Yoga Sūtras*.

YOGA PRIOR TO PATAÑJALI

The Vedic Period

In terms of Yoga's earliest origins, the Vedic period is the earliest era in South Asia for which we have written records, and it provides the matrix from which (or, more typically, against which) later religious, philosophical, and spiritual expressions such as Yoga evolved in India, at least in the north of the subcontinent. We do not wish to invest any further energy into the ongoing debate over whether the Vedic-speaking peoples (Indo-Aryans[5]) were originally indigenous to the Indian subcontinent or Indo-European intruders from an external point of origin (for which, see Bryant 2001 and 2005), except to note the corollaries of these two positions on the protohistory of Yoga. Those accepting an external point of origin for the Vedic-speaking peoples tend to hold that Yoga, both as practice and philosophy, was originally pre-Vedic (and therefore non-Vedic) and indigenous to the subcontinent. From this perspective, since there is no explicit reference to *yogic* practices and beliefs in the earliest Vedic texts, their emergence in subsequent Vedic literature such as the Upaniṣads[6] points to a later period when the Vedic people had long settled and absorbed themselves into the preexisting populations of the Indian subcontinent. In this process, they established their own Vedic rituals as the mainstream "high" religious activity of the day, and also eventually absorbed many non-Vedic religious elements from the indigenous peoples, such as Yoga philosophy and practice.

Those challenging the thesis of external origins for the original Vedic-speaking peoples tend to prefer to see both Vedic ritualism and *yogic* practices as parallel internal developments evolving within Vedic- (Indo-Aryan-) speaking communities indigenous to the subcontinent. It can certainly be argued that the germs of *yogic* thought can be found in embryonic form in the (middle period) Vedic literatures themselves, the Āraṇyakas and Brāhmaṇa texts. Alternatively, there is little that can discount the possibility that Yoga emerged outside Vedic orthodoxy but nonetheless within Indo-Aryan-speaking communities. (And, of course, one can combine components of these two positions and argue for the Vedic or Indo-Aryan origins of Yoga but still hold that the Indo-Aryans were nonetheless originally immigrants into the subcontinent.) What all these positions have in common, and where our own discussion of the early history of Yoga will commence, is that Yoga evolves on the periphery of Vedic religiosity and beyond the parameters of mainstream Vedic orthopraxy. Yoga is clearly in tension with Vedic ritualism, discussed below, and its goals are in stark and explicit opposition to it (for example, *Yoga Sūtras* I.15–16).

Before considering the early literary history of Yoga, however, we must note that the arguments above are all primarily deduced from the fields of linguistics and philology. Archaeology has revealed the remains of an enormous and sophisticated ancient civilization, the Indus Valley civilization, covering modern-day northwest India and Pakistan, dating from circa 3000 to 1900 B.C.E. Mention must be made, when considering the earliest origins of Yoga, to seals found in Indus Valley sites with representations of figures seated in a clear *yogic* posture. The most famous figure is seated with arms extended and resting on the knees in a classical meditative posture.[7] This evidence suggests that, irrespective of its literary origins, Yoga has been practiced on the Indian subcontinent for well over four thousand years.

Like other Old World cultures, the dominant religious expression in the early Vedic period within which Yoga emerges is that of the sacrificial cult wherein animals and other items are offered to various gods through the medium of fire for the purposes of obtaining worldly boons—offspring, cattle, victory over enemies, etc. A genre of texts, the Brāhmaṇas, describe the ritualistic minutiae of a wide variety of sacrifices, both domestic and public, each one specific to the attainment of particular goals. While the intricacies of the Vedic sacrificial rite may seem alien to our modern worldviews and practices, the mentality that supported it—that of attempting to manipulate the external physical environment for the purpose of enjoying the pleasures of the material world through the medium of the sensual body—has remained constant throughout human history. It is for this reason that the post-Vedic reactions to this type of mentality, in the form of developments such as the various systems of *yoga*, remain perennially relevant to the human condition.

Yoga in the Upaniṣads

There is evidence as early as the oldest Vedic text, the *Ṛg Veda*, that there were *yogī*-like ascetics on the margins of the Vedic landscape.[8] However, it is in the late Vedic age, marked by the fertile speculations expressed in a genre of texts called the Upaniṣads, that practices that can be clearly related to classical *yoga* are first articulated in literary sources.[9] The Upaniṣads reveal a clear shift in focus away from the sacrificial rite, which is relegated to an inferior type of religiosity, replacing it with an interest in philosophical and mystical discourse, particularly the quest for the ultimate, underlying reality underpinning the external world, *Brahman*, localized in living beings as *ātman*.[10] The *Muṇḍaka Upaniṣad* (I.2. 7–11) calls the performers of sacrifice "deluded" and "ignorant," however learned and competent they may posture to be, because the boons and fruits gained from the sacrifice—from the manipulation of one's external environment, to use a more modern frame of reference—are temporary. When they expire, one finds oneself frustrated once more. The *Gītā*, too, calls the Vedic ritualists "less intelligent," since any boons accruing from such materialism do not solve the ultimate problems of life—human suffering inherent in the cycle of birth and death (II.42–45). A move toward understanding higher and more ultimate truths of reality is the prime feature of the Upaniṣads.

Although the Upaniṣads are especially concerned with *jñāna*, or understanding *Brahman*, the Absolute Truth, through the cultivation of knowledge, there are also several unmistakable references to a technique for realizing *Brahman* (in its localized aspect of *ātman*) called *yoga*, which are clearly drawn from the same general body of related practices as those articulated by Patañjali.[11] As with the Upaniṣads in general, we do not find a systematic philosophy here, but mystico-poetic utterances, albeit profound in content. The *Kaṭha Upaniṣad* states:

> When the control of the senses is fixed, that is Yoga, so people say. For then, a person is free from distraction. Yoga is the "becoming," and the "ceasing."[12] Not by words, not by the mind, not by sight, can he [the self] be grasped; how else can he be perceived except by saying: "he is!" . . . For one who perceives him as he really is, his real nature becomes manifest. When all desires lurking in the heart are removed, then a mortal person becomes immortal, and attains *Brahman* in this world. When the knots in the heart that bind one to this world are all cut, then a mortal becomes an immortal, such is the teachings . . . A *puruṣa* [*ātman* or soul] the size of a thumb dwells always in the hearts of men. One should extricate him with determination like a reed from *muñja* grass. One should know him as resplendent and immortal. Thus, when Naciketas had received this knowledge and the complete rules of *yoga* from Death, he attained *Brahman*; he became free of disease and death. So, too, will others who know these teachings about the self. (VI.11–18)

The *Śvetāśvatara Upaniṣad* gets a little more specific about the actual technique of *yoga* practice:

> When he holds the body steady, with the three sections erect, and withdraws the senses into his heart with the mind, a wise person will cross over all the frightening rivers [of embodied existence] by means of the boat of *Brahman*. His breathing restrained here [within the body], and his energy under control, he should breathe through one nostril when his breath is depleted. A wise person should control the mind, just as one would a wagon yoked to unruly horses[13] . . . and engage in the practice of *yoga* . . . When, by means of the true nature of the *ātman*, which is like a lamp, a person perceives the truth of

Brahman in this world, he is freed from all bondage, because he has known the Divine, which is unborn, unchanging, and untainted by all things. (II.8–15)

By the later *Maitrī Upaniṣad*, we have a much more extensive discussion of Yoga, including more specific references to the six *aṅgas*, or limbs, of *yoga*: *prāṇāyāma*, breath control; *pratyāhāra*, sense withdrawal; *dhyāna*, meditation; *dhāraṇā*, concentration; *tarka*, inquiry; and *samādhi*, final absorption in the self (VI.18). Five of these limbs correspond to the last five limbs of Patañjali's system (the *Yoga Sūtras* lists eight limbs in Chapter II[14]). Although, like the two older Upaniṣads quoted above, the *Maitrī* is still embedded in the Upaniṣadic context of unity of *Brahman* as the ultimate goal of *yoga* practice (*Brahman* is not mentioned in the *Yoga Sūtras*), the specifics of *yoga* technique (and Sāṅkhya metaphysics, discussed below) receive far more elaborate and technical attention here than in the older Upaniṣads.[15] In this development, the *Maitrī* represents, as does the *Mahābhārata*, a transition between the old Upaniṣadic worldview and the later emergence of the systematic metaphysical traditions such as the one represented in the *Yoga Sūtras*.

Yoga in the Mahābhārata

The *Mahābhārata*, which culminates in 100,000 verses,[16] is the longest epic in the world and, like the *Maitrī Upaniṣad*, preserves significant material representing the evolution of Yoga. Usually dated somewhere between the ninth and fourth centuries B.C.E., the epic exhibits the transition between the origins of Yoga in the Upaniṣadic period and its expression in the systematized traditions of Yoga as represented in the classical period by Patañjali. Nestled in the middle of the epic, the well-known *Bhagavad Gītā* (circa fourth century B.C.E.) devotes a good portion of its text to the practices of *yoga*, which it already considers to be "ancient" (IV.3); indeed, Kṛṣṇa presents himself as reestablishing *yoga* teachings that had existed since primordial times. While the *Gītā* tends to use the term *yoga* interchangeably with *karma-yoga*, and the text focuses primarily on *karma-yoga, jñāna-yoga*, and especially *bhakti-yoga*, the techniques of Patañjalian-type *yoga* are outlined throughout the entire sixth chapter, albeit subsumed under devotion to Kṛṣṇa. The *Gītā* refers to this type of practice as *dhyāna-yoga*,[17] as did most early Indic texts.

> After establishing a firm seat in a clean place, not too high and not too low . . . there, sitting on that seat and fixing the mind on one object, with mind and senses under control, one should practice *yoga* to purify the *ātman*, self, by holding the body, neck and head straight, steady and keeping oneself motionless, focusing on the tip of the nose, and not looking about in any direction. With a peaceful self, free of fear, firm in the *brahmācarya* vow of celibacy, with mind controlled and thoughts fixed on Me [Kṛṣṇa], one should sit in *yoga*, holding Me as the supreme. (VI.11–15)

As can be seen from this verse, the *Yoga Sūtra's Īśvara-praṇidhāna*, dedication to God, which will be encountered in I.23, becomes the essential teaching of the entire *Gītā* and of all the *yoga* systems prescribed in it, rather than the more discreet ingredient promoted by Patañjali. Nonetheless, the *Yoga Sūtras* is an inherently theistic text.

The *Mahābhārata* contains a number of references to practices that are clearly relatable to the system of *yoga* as taught by Patañjali, most of them in the *Mokṣa-dharma* section of Book 12 of the epic.[18] For example, the sage Vasiṣṭha defines *yoga* as *ekāgratā*, concentration, and *prāṇāyāma*, breath control (XII.294.8), both terms and practices essential to Patañjali's system. The terms *yoga* and *yogī* occur about nine hundred times throughout the epic, expressed as noted above in terms midway between the unformulated expressions of the Upaniṣads and the systematized practice as outlined by Patañjali.[19] This, of course, indicates that practices associated with *yoga* had gained wide currency in the centuries prior to the Common Era, with a clearly identifiable set of basic techniques and generic practices, and it is from these that Patañjali drew for his systemization. One passage from the epic (XII.188.1–22) particularly illustrates this, namely Bhīṣma's deliverance to Yudhiṣṭhira of the "four stages of *dhyāna-yoga*," meditation. *Dhyāna* is the term most often used to refer to meditation in the epic, not just, as with Patañjali, the seventh, penultimate, limb of *yoga* but often as synonymous with Patañjali's eighth limb and ultimate goal, *samādhi*. What is of particular interest in this passage (quoted in the commentary for I.17 below) is that even though the final limb in Patañjali's system also contains four basic stages (two of which go by the same name as two of the states mentioned by Bhīṣma[20]), the terminology and correlations of Bhīṣma's four stages of *dhyāna-yoga* seem to have more in common with the four stages of Buddhist *samādhi*.[21] Scholars have long pointed out a commonality of vocabulary and concepts between the *Yoga Sūtras* and Buddhist texts.[22] All this underscores the basic point that there was a cluster of interconnected and cross-fertilizing variants of meditational *yoga*—Buddhist and Jain as well as Hindu—prior to Patañjali, all drawn from a common but variegated pool of terminologies, practices, and concepts (and many strains continue to the present day).

Indeed, one might profitably begin a discussion of the relationship between Yoga and what was much later to be considered its sister school, Sāṅkhya, and for that matter Buddhism, by noting that in this formative late Vedic period, perhaps for even the best part of a millennium prior to the rise of the clearly defined classical philosophical traditions, there were no schools as such to speak of at all; Sāṅkhya and Yoga (and, for that matter, Buddhism) had yet to become systematic schools, such as what was to become known as the Pātañjala Yoga, or even distinct philosophical systems.[23] Moreover, there were a number of variants going under the name of Yoga (and of Sāṅkhya). One might envision a plethora of centers of learning and practice, many ascetic and spearheaded by charismatic renunciants, where parallel and overlapping philosophical doctrines and meditative practices, many going by the name of *yoga*, were evolving out of a common Upaniṣadic-flavored core. These would become distinct schools only at a much later period of time.

Yoga and Sāṅkhya

The history of Yoga is inextricable from that of the Sāṅkhya tradition. Sāṅkhya provides the metaphysical infrastructure for Yoga and thus is indispensable to an understanding of Yoga. Usually translated as enumeration or counting due to its focus on the evolution and constituents of the twenty-four ingredients of *prakṛti*, material reality, Sāṅkhya might best be understood as dealing with calculation in the sense of reasoning, speculation, philosophy, as it is defined in the *Mahābhārata*[24]—in other words, the path striving to understand the ultimate truths of reality through knowledge, typically known as *jñāna-yoga*. While the specifics of Sāṅkhya metaphysics and Yoga practice will be discussed more elaborately below, we can briefly note here that this metaphysics is dualistic, insofar as ultimate reality is conceived as containing two distinct ultimate principles: *puruṣa*, the innermost conscious self broadly synonymous with the notion of soul, and *prakṛti*, the material world with all its variegatedness within which the *puruṣa* is embedded. While Yoga and Sāṅkhya share the same metaphysics and the common goal of liberating *puruṣa* from its encapsulation, their methods differ. Sāṅkhya occupies itself with the path of reasoning to attain liberation, specifically concerning the analysis of the manifold ingredients of *prakṛti* from which the *puruṣa* is to be extricated, and Yoga more with the path of meditation, focusing on the nature of mind and consciousness, and on the techniques of concentration in order to provide a practical method through which the *puruṣa* can be isolated and extricated. (We must note here that while on occasion we use the language, as do the commentators, more appropriate to Vedānta—of *puruṣa* being extricated or liberated—we do so rhetorically; in fact, as will be discussed, *puruṣa* is and has always been eternally free, liberated, and autonomous, according to Sāṅkhya. It is the mind, not *puruṣa*, that must become enlightened).

Sāṅkhya seems to have been the earliest philosophical system to have taken shape in the late Vedic period,[25] and, indeed, it has permeated almost all subsequent Hindu traditions: Vedānta, Purāṇic, Vaiṣnava,[26] Śaivite,[27] Tāntric,[28] and even the medicinal traditions such as *āyurveda*. Larson goes so far as to say, "Buddhist philosophy and terminology, Yoga philosophy, early Vedānta speculation, and the great regional theologies of Śaivism and Vaiṣṇavism are all, in an important sense, footnotes and/or reactions to a living 'tradition text' of Sāṅkhya" (1999, 732). Indeed, Larson has long seen the classical Yoga of Patañjali as a type of "neo-Sāṅkhya," an updating by those within the old Sāṅkhya tradition in an attempt to bring it into conversation with the more technical philosophical traditions that had emerged by the third to fifth centuries C.E., particularly the challenges represented by Buddhist thought (1999, 2008).[29]

While this may have been true for the systematized Yoga articulated by Patañjali in the second century C.E., it has also been argued that Sāṅkhya itself evolved out of much earlier primordial Yoga origins. We can refer here again to the Indus Valley seal from the third millennium B.C.E. of a horned figure sitting in a distinctly *yoga*-like pose, which points to some kind of *yoga* practice as a primordial element on the Indian subcontinent. Schreiner's statistical analysis of the context and content of the references to Yoga and Sāṅkhya in the *Mahābhārata*—the richest literary source for considering the origins of Yoga—finds Yoga to be more original and Sāṅkhya a later appendage formulated to provide the practices with some philosophical rationale. Schreiner provides an intriguing image of the proto-Sāṅkhya philosopher:

> Those [Sāṅkhya] redactors . . . were . . . probably not practicing Yogins, but rather (perhaps) meticulous scholars, scribes with archival ambitions, thinkers with a liking for numbers and classification (but afraid of the existential commitment to a path of Yoga which would lead to death and through dying, literally and spiritually). They may well have been *yogabraṣṭa* [the "fallen" or "unsuccessful" *yogīs* of the *Gītā* 6.37–45], Yogins who did not make it but were close enough to the practices and experiences of Yoga to be able to speak about it and intellectualize it. The *yogabraṣṭa*, one who did not reach the goal of no return, is probably the best candidate for becoming a Sāṇkhya philosopher. But he would have been a Yogin first. (1999, 776)

This provocative view might be kept in mind if we choose to wonder if Patañjali himself, and certainly his commentators, had experienced the truths of which they spoke in the *sūtras* and their commentaries, or whether some of them were even practitioners. In any event, for our present purposes, the metaphysics of Yoga is that of Sāṅkhya, and hence the history of the two traditions requires a few words.

As noted, the first important point to be stressed is that Sāṅkhya and Yoga should not be considered different schools until a very late date. In fact, the first reference to Yoga itself as a distinct school seems to be in the writings of Śaṅkara in the ninth century C.E. (Bronkhurst 1981). There are (to be precise) 884 references to Yoga in the *Mahābhārata*, "and the common denominator of all the epic definitions of Yoga is disciplined activity, earnest striving—by active (not rationalistic or intellectual) means" rather than the more popular translation and cognate "union" (Edgerton 1924, 38). There are 120 references to Sāṅkhya,[30] defined, as noted, as reasoning, and none of these 1,000-odd combined references to the two approaches indicates any difference between them other than one of method in attaining the same goal: Yoga seeks the vision of *ātman,* the Upaniṣadic term for the *puruṣa*, through practice and mind control, and Sāṅkhya through knowledge and the intellect. Otherwise, "The knowers of Truth see that Sāṅkhya and Yoga are one" (XII.304.4[31]).

This is amply expressed by Bhīṣma when specifically asked by Yudhiṣṭhira to explain the difference between Sāṅkhya and Yoga: "Both the followers of Sāṅkhya and those of Yoga praise their own way as the best . . . The followers of Yoga rely on experiential methods (*pratyākṣa-hetavaḥ*), and those of Sāṅkhya on scriptural interpretation (*śāstra-viniścayāḥ*). I consider both these views true: Followed according to their instructions, both lead to the ultimate goal" (XII.289.7). And, again:

> There is no knowledge equal to Sāṅkhya, there is no power (*balam*) equal to Yoga; both of them are the same path, both, according to oral tradition (*smṛtau*), lead to deathlessness. People of little intelligence consider them to be different. We however, O king, see clearly that they are the same. What the followers of Yoga perceive, the same is experienced by the followers of Sāṅkhya. One who sees Yoga and Sāṅkhya as one, is a knower of Truth. (XII.304.1–4)

While presenting Yoga as a more action-based practice, Kṛṣṇa in the *Bhagavad Gītā* reiterates the same point: "A twofold division was established by Me of old . . . *jñāna-yoga*, the *yoga* of knowledge, followed by Sāṅkhya, and *karma-yoga*, the *yoga* of action followed by the *yogis*" (III.3). Both lead to the same goal (V.2), and anyone who considers them to be different is "childish" (V.4–5—even as Kṛṣṇa clearly favors the action-based approach, III.4ff; V.6ff). Even where the *Gītā* articulates a more Patañjalian type of Yoga, which it calls *dhyāna*, it is still contrasted with Sāṅkhya merely in terms of method leading to the same goal: "Some behold the *ātman*, self, by *dhyāna*, meditation, others by Sāṅkhya" (XIII.25). Nowhere in the *Gītā* or the entire *Mahābhārata* is there any indication that these two approaches constitute different schools or metaphysical systems.[32] Sāṅkhya and Yoga are merely different approaches to salvation until well into the Common Era. This continuity and confluence between Sāṅkhya and Yoga is reflected in early sources for well over a millennium, including Patañjali's time of writing as well as that of Vyāsa, the first and primary commentator on the *Yoga Sūtras* in the fifth century C.E. Vyāsa explicitly concludes the chapters of his *bhāṣya* commentary with the colophon *śrī-pātañjale sāṅkhya-pravacane yoga-śāstre*, "Patañjali's Yoga treatise, an exposition on Sāṅkhya."

Another important point to consider when tracing the origins of Yoga is that in the epic, the ultimate liberation accruing from the practice of *yoga* (as with the practice of Sāṅkhya) is conceived in a number of passages (for example, XII.228.38; 231.17; 246.8) in terms of the monistic goal of unity of the individual soul, *puruṣa/ātman* with the one ultimate Absolute called *Brahman* in the Upaniṣads (expressed variously in different Upaniṣads in both personal or impersonal terms). The later classical Sāṅkhya tradition is distinctly dualistic—ultimate reality consists of two ingredients, *puruṣa* and *prākṛti*, consciousness and matter—rather than monistic—subscribing to the one absolute principle called *Brahman* in the Upaniṣads. The *Mahābhārata* evidences a transitional period between the Upaniṣads and the later tradition as expressed in the *Yoga Sūtras*; the dualistic *puruṣa* and *prākṛti* principles associated with Sāṅkhya/Yoga are retained, but they are subsumed under the higher Upaniṣadic union with *Brahman*. This monistic source in the epic is expressed either in terms commonly used for the impersonal *Brahman*, or as personal *Īśvara*, God, Nārāyaṇa.[33] *Brahman* is not mentioned either in the *Yoga Sūtras* or *Sāṅkhya Kārikās* (the text that became to later Sāṅkhya what the *Yoga Sūtras* became to Yoga, that is, the primary text of the system).[34] Both these texts deal with the liberation of the individual *ātman* rather than the relationship of this *ātman* with the supreme *ātman*, or *Brahman*, which was the concern of the Vedānta tradition (however, *Brahman* is mentioned by the commentators, and thus the Upaniṣadic matrix always remains as a backdrop). And, although Patañjali also accepts a personal *Īśvara*, which he equates with the sonic form of *Brahman* in the Upaniṣads, *oṁ* (I.23ff), he introduces him in the context of meditation rather than cosmology or metaphysics.

In short, Yoga and Sāṅkhya in the Upaniṣads and epic simply refer to the two distinct paths of salvation by meditation and salvation by knowledge, respectively. Followers of both schools upheld belief in the *puruṣa*'s ultimate union with a developed form of the Upaniṣadic Brāhman, expressed in both personal and impersonal terms, which simply points to the fact that all orthodox Hindus of the day tended to accept those beliefs. The chief difference in the trajectory that Patañjali's Yoga took was its exclusive focus on the psychological mechanisms and techniques involved in *puruṣa*'s liberation. Similarly, later Sāṅkhya concerned itself with the specificities of *prakṛti*'s ingredients from which *puruṣa* was to be extricated, "which in the earlier Upaniṣads had been rather ignored, not because its existence was denied, but because it did not interest the earliest thinkers, who were absorbed in the contemplation of the One Ultimate Reality" (Edgerton 1924, 32).

Before concluding this section on the pre-Patañjali background of Yoga, one might add, as an aside, that from the nine hundred–odd references to *yoga* in the *Mahābhārata*, there are only two mentions of *āsana*, posture, the third limb of Patañjali's system.[35] Neither the Upaniṣads nor the *Gītā* mentions posture in the sense of stretching exercises and bodily poses (the term is used in the *Gītā* verse above in its sense as physical seat rather than bodily postures), *āsana* is not mentioned as one of the six limbs of the *Maitrī Upaniṣad*, and Patañjali himself dedicates only three brief *sūtras* from his text to this aspect of the practice. The reconfiguring, presentation, and perception of *yoga* as primarily or even exclusively *āsana* in the sense of bodily poses, then, is essentially a modern Western phenomenon and finds no precedent in the premodern *yoga* tradition, although the fourteenth-century *Haṭhayoga Pradīpikā* does dedicate one of its four chapters to *āsana*.

PATAÑJALI'S YOGA

Patañjali and the Six Schools of Indian Philosophy

In addition to various heterodox schools such as Jainism and Buddhism, what came to be identified (in much later times) as six schools of orthodox thought also evolved out of the Upaniṣadic period (of course, there were various other streams of thought that did not gain this status but nonetheless emerged as significant presences on the religious landscape of Hinduism). As we have seen with Sāṅkhya and Yoga, the streams of thought that later became associated with these six schools were not necessarily conceived of in that way until the end of the first millennium C.E. In fact, it might be more accurate to consider these traditions distinctive religophilosophical expressions that emerged from the Vedic period with different focuses rather than actual schools in the earlier period. They shared much of their overall worldview but dedicated themselves to different areas of human knowledge and praxis, and while differing quite considerably on metaphysical and epistemological issues, they nonetheless did not necessarily reject the authority of the other traditions in other specific areas where these did not conflict with their own positions. Thus, for example, the Nyāya logician school accepts Yoga as the method to be used to realize the *ātman* as understood within that tradition,[36] and Vedānta objects to it only to the extent that it does not refer to *Brahman* as the ultimate source of *puruṣa* and *prakṛti*, not to its authenticity in meditative technique and practice.[37] Even a *dharmaśāstra* text like the *Yājñavalkya Smṛti*, which occupies itself exclusively with *dharma*, codes of ritual, personal, familial, civic, and social duties, states in its opening section that from the abundance of religious scriptures dealing with the plethora of human affairs: "this alone is the highest *dharma*, that one should see the *ātman* by *yoga*" (I.8). Thus, in early Sanskrit texts Yoga referred to a form of rigorous discipline and concentration for attaining the direct perception of the *ātman* and gaining liberation that was appropriated and tailored by different traditions according to their metaphysical understanding of the self, rather than a distinct school.

In any event, eventually an orthodox school of Yoga came to be identified with Patañjali, the compiler of these *sūtras*, and took its place alongside other traditions that also had distinct *sūtra* traditions, as one of the "six schools of Indian philosophy." These are Sāṅkhya, Yoga, Nyāya, Vaiśeṣika, Mīmāṁsā, and Vedānta. These schools were deemed orthodox because they retained at least a nominal allegiance to the sacred Vedic texts—unlike the so-called heterodox schools such as Buddhism and Jainism, which rejected them. Since various ingredients of these schools are referred to in our commentaries, we can briefly refer to some of their salient features.

As mentioned, probably the oldest Indian speculative tradition is Sāṅkhya, later to be referred to as the sister school of Yoga insofar as they shared the same metaphysics. This featured an analysis of reality in which all categories of the created world were perceived as evolving out of a primordial matter, *prakṛti*, from which the *puruṣa*, which is the term used by Sāṅkhya and Yoga schools for the *ātman*, must be extricated. Vaiśeṣika was another metaphysical system, one that perceived the created world as ultimately consisting of various eternal categories such as atoms rather than as evolutes from a singular category of *prakṛti*. This came to be "sistered" with Nyāya, a school that accepted the basics of Vaiśeṣika metaphysics but became distinguished by the aspect of epistemology dealing with the formulation of categories and conditions of valid reasoning and the refinement of rules of logic, such that the debates between the various schools emerging from this period could be conducted according to agreed-upon conventions of what constituted valid or invalid argumentation. Vedānta was a school dedicated to another aspect of epistemology: attempting to systematize the heterogeneous teachings of the Upaniṣads through a consistent hermeneutics. Its concerns were the relationship between the manifest world; *Brahman*, the Absolute Truth and ground of all being; and *ātman*, the localized aspect of this Truth. This was associated with Mīmāṁsā, since both of these schools occupied themselves with hermeneutics, the interpretation of the ancient Vedic texts. The Mīmāṁsā was the main orthodox school that attempted to perpetuate the old Vedic sacrificial rites by composing a philosophical justification for their continued performance.

Indic schools, both orthodox and heterodox, interacted intellectually and sometimes polemically, debating and mutually enriching each other, and their emergence pushed the old Vedic cult further into the background. From this rich and fertile post-Vedic context, then, emerged an individual called Patañjali whose systematization of the heterogeneous practices of *yoga* came to be authoritative for all subsequent practitioners and eventually reified into one of the six schools of classical Indian philosophy. It is important to stress here again that Patañjali is not the founder, or inventor, of *yoga*, the origins of which, as should be clear, had long preceded him in primordial and mythic times. Patañjali systematized the preexisting traditions and authored what came to be the seminal text for *yoga* discipline. There was never one uniform school of ur-Yoga (or of any Indic school of thought, for that matter); there was a plurality of variants and certainly different conceptualizations of meditative practices that were termed *yoga*. For example, whereas Patañjali organizes his system into eight limbs, and the *Mahābhārata*, too, speaks of *yoga* as having eight "qualities" (*aṣṭaguṇita*, XII.304.7[38]), as early as the *Maitrī Upaniṣad* of the second century B.C.E. there is reference to a six-limbed Yoga (VI.18), as there is in the *Viṣṇu Purāṇa* (VI.7.91), and this numerical schema was retained in the later *Gorakṣa-saṁhitā* and the *Dhyānabindu* and *Amṛtabindu Upaniṣads*. Along similar lines, there are various references to the twelve *yogas* and seven *dhāraṇās* (*dhāraṇā* is considered the sixth of Patañjali's limbs) in the *Mahābhārata*.[39] Yoga is thus best understood as a cluster of techniques, some more and some less systematized, that pervaded the landscape of ancient India. These overlapped with and were incorporated into the various traditions of the day such as the *jñāna*, knowledge-based traditions, providing these systems with a practical method and technique for attaining an experienced-based transformation of consciousness. Patañjali's particular systematization of these techniques in time emerged as the most dominant, but by no means exclusive, version.

Indeed, internal to his own text, in his very first *sūtra, atha yogānuśāsanam*, Patañjali indicates that he is continuing the teachings of *yoga* (the prefix *anu-* indicates the continuation of the action denoted by the verb), and the traditional commentators certainly perceive him in this light. In point of fact, the tradition itself ascribes the actual origins of Yoga to the legendary figure Hiraṇyagarbha (see commentary to I.1). Moreover, evidence that Patañjali was addressing an audience already familiar with the tenets of Yoga can be deduced from the *Yoga Sūtras* themselves.[40] For example, on occasion, Patañjali mentions one member of a list of items followed by "etc.," thereby assuming his audience to be familiar with the remainder of the list. Thus, he refers to *aṇimādi*, "the mystic power of *aṇimā*, etc.," indicating that the other seven mystic powers were a standard, well-known group. He likewise speaks of a "sevenfold" wisdom without further explanation (II.27). But, in short, because he produced the first systematized treatise on the subject, Patañjali was to become the prime or seminal figure for the Yoga tradition after his times and accepted as such by other schools. To all intents and purposes, his *Yoga Sūtras* was to become the canon for the mechanics of generic *yoga*, so to speak, that other systems tinkered with and flavored with their own theological trappings.

As with the reputed founders of the other schools of thought, very little is known about Patañjali himself. Tradition, first explicitly evidenced in the commentary of Bhoja Rāja in the eleventh century C.E. (and continuing to this day in a verse often recited at the beginning of *yoga* classes in the Iyengar community), considers him to be the same Patañjali who wrote the primary commentary on the famous grammar by Pāṇini and also ascribes to him authorship of a treatise on medicine.[41] There is an ongoing discussion among scholars as to whether this was likely or not;[42] my own view is that there is not much to be gained by challenging the evidence of traditional accounts in the absence of evidence to the contrary that is uncontroversial or at least adequately compelling.

Patañjali's date can only be inferred from the content of the text itself. Unfortunately, most classical Sanskrit texts from the ancient period tend to be impossible to date with accuracy, and there are always dissenters against whatever dates become standard in academic circles.[43] Most scholars date the text shortly after the turn of the Common Era (circa first to second century), but it has been placed as early as several centuries before that.[44] Other than the fact that the *Yoga Sūtras* were written no later than the fifth century, the date cannot be determined with exactitude.

The Yoga Sūtras *as a Text*

The *sūtra* writing style is that used by the philosophical schools of ancient India (thus we have *Vedānta Sūtras, Nyāya Sūtras*, etc.). The term *sūtra* (from the Sanskrit root *sū*, cognate with sew) literally means a thread and essentially refers to a terse and pithy philosophical statement in which the maximum amount of information is packed into the minimum number of words. Knowledge systems were handed down orally in ancient India, and thus source material was kept minimal partly with a view to facilitating memorization. Being composed for oral transmission and memorization, the *Yoga Sūtras*, and *sūtra* traditions in general, allowed the student to "thread together" in memory the key ingredients of the more extensive body of material with which he or she would become thoroughly acquainted. Thus *sūtras* often begin with connecting words linking them with the previous *sūtras*, typically, pronouns or conjunctions beginning with *t* (such as *tataḥ* and *tatra*). Each *sūtra* served as a mnemonic device to structure the teachings and assist memorization. I sometimes compare them to a series of bullet points that a lecturer might jot down prior to giving a presentation, to structure the talk and provide reminders of the main points intended to be covered; thus, from a dozen shorthand phrases incomprehensible to anyone else, a lecturer might discourse for a couple of hours.[45]

The succinctness of the *Yoga Sūtras*—it contains about 1,200 words in 195 *sūtras*—indicates that they were construed to be a manual requiring unpacking. That the *sūtras*, or aphorisms, are in places cryptic, esoteric, and incomprehensible in their own terms points to the fact that they were intended to be used in conjunction with a teacher: Feuerstein calls them "maps" (1980, 117). Thus, while some of the *sūtras* are somewhat straightforward, the fact is that we cannot construe meaning from many *sūtras* of Patañjali's primary text. Indeed, some are so obtuse that they are undecipherable in their own terms. Therefore, it is, in my view, an unrealistic (if not impossible) task to attempt to bypass commentary in the hope of retrieving some original pure, precommentarial set of ur-interpretations (and those attempting to do so without extensive training in the philosophical universe of India at the beginning of the Common Era frequently have some sectarian or other agenda underpinning their enterprise).

Before considering the commentaries on the *Yoga Sūtras*, some mention must be made of the view of a number of earlier critical scholars that the text is a composite, composed of a number of layers. Starting with the famous Indologist Max Müller (1899), a number of scholars, including Paul Deussen (1920), Richard Garbe (1897), J. W. Hauer (1958), and Erich Frauwallner (1953), have argued that the text is a patchwork. Deussen, for example, maintains that I.1–16 forms one unit devoted to ordinary awareness; I.17–51, another unit, devoted to *samādhi*, meditative awareness; II.1–27, a third, to *kriyā-yoga*, preparatory practice; and II.29–III.55, along with Chapter IV, a fourth unit devoted to the eight-limbed process and other assorted topics.[46] Hauer, Garbe, Frauwallner, Dasgupta, and others added various nuances to the matter.[47] These efforts, while meritorious, have all been subject to critique.[48] The reason for such lack of consensus is clearly that there is insufficient evidence, hence "the task of finding various layers will always be arbitrary" (Larson 2008, 91). The oral traditions of India and their embodiment in the shape of written primary texts have proved to be remarkably resilient, stemming from the Indian reverence and respect for sacred tradition. While this certainly does not grant them immunity from text-critical scholarship, in a work such as the *Yoga Sūtras*, one is best advised to look very carefully for internal structural, semantic, or logical coherency and rationale before assuming that an apparent sudden break in (modern linear notions of) the sequencing of subject matter indicates a later insertion.[49] More recent scholarship has tended to find internal consistency in most of the text.[50]

In any event, the only disjunction in the text that presents itself to my reading occurs in Chapter II and is best explained by postulating two distinct Yoga traditions that were patched together by Patañjali. The chapter begins with the introduction of a practice called *kriyā-yoga*, which is defined as consisting of *tapas*, austerity; *svādhyāya*, study; and *Īśvara-praṇidhāna*, devotion to God. This practice eliminates the *kleśas*, obstacles to *yoga*, which the text proceeds to discuss in a coherent sequential manner, and the section culminates in II.26–27 by stating that *viveka-khyāti*, discrimination, results from the destruction of *avidyā*, ignorance, the cornerstone of these *kleśas*. *Sūtras* II.28–29 then suddenly announce a new practice, the *yoga* of *aṣṭāṅga*, eight limbs, which culminates in this same state of *viveka-khyāti*. There is no indication of the relationship between this practice and the *kriyā-yoga* outlined in the beginning of the chapter. But that they might represent different traditions is a valid consideration given that the second limb of the eight-limbed practice consists of observing five *niyamas*, ethical observances, three of which are identical to the three ingredients of *kriyā-yoga*. Why these three items comprising the entirety of a *yoga* practice called *kriyā* are then placed alongside two other items (*śauca*, cleanliness; and *santoṣa*, contentment) as the five ingredients comprising the second limb (*niyama*) of a differently arranged type of *yoga* practice called *aṣṭāṅga* is puzzling. But Feuerstein's opinion (1979) that they most likely indicate that Patañjali had drawn upon and merged two different traditions with overlapping but differently organized schemas is certainly very plausible.

We therefore find ourselves sympathetic to an alternative and, in our opinion, fruitful way of looking at the issue that respects the historical integrity of the text without denying the likelihood of its containing various disparate strands. R. S. Bhattacharya is willing to concede that "a large part of the *sūtras* are taken by Patañjali from his predecessors either verbatim or with slight changes" (1985, 52). From this perspective, whatever different strands are contained in the *sūtras* (and we are able to feel any confidence only about the one noted above), it is Patañjali who has pieced them together; the text is not a hodgepodge of successive layers interpolated into some ur-text over the years. This point of view respects the traditional understanding of the text's integrity of authorship (needless to say, in the perspective of the commentators, the work is a harmonious and logical whole[51]), while not ignoring some of the more persuasive observations of modern critical scholars, and one that fits well with the previous discussion of Patañjali as a systematizer of preexisting traditions.

The Commentaries on the Yoga Sūtras

Knowledge systems in ancient India were transmitted orally, from master to disciple, with an enormous emphasis on fidelity toward the original set of *sūtras* upon which the system is founded, the master unpacking the dense and truncated aphorisms to the students, and this system continues in traditional contexts today. Periodically, teachers of particular prominence wrote commentaries on the primary texts of many of these knowledge systems. Some of these gained such wide currency that the primary text was always studied in conjunction with a commentary, particularly since, as noted, texts such as the *Yoga Sūtras* (and, even more so, the *Vedānta Sūtras*) were designed to be "unpacked" and hence contain numerous *sūtras* that are incomprehensible without elaboration. One must stress, therefore, that our understanding of Patañjali's text is completely dependent on the interpretations of later commentators; it is incomprehensible, in places, in its own terms.

This, of course, leaves open the possibility that later commentators might have misinterpreted, or, perhaps more likely, reinterpreted aspects of the text by filtering ancient notions through the theological or sectarian perspectives of their times. Part of the academic approach to a text involves identifying and separating diachronic and synchronic developments and philosophical context. This is of course important, as ideas are never static but develop across time and context, constantly cross-fertilizing with other currents of thought. Thus scholars have always been wary of the extent to which the commentaries are imposing later concerns and perspectives on the text that are alien to Patañjali's intentions. Modern methods of text criticism sometimes bypass the commentaries and, by comparing the context, style, terminology, content, and structure of individual *sūtras* or sequences of *sūtras* themselves, attempt to determine what an author's original intentions might have been prior to exegetical overlay. This includes comparing Patañjali's *sūtras* with other earlier texts, particularly Buddhist ones. Critical observations of this nature can often be very insightful, and I include throughout the text some of the analyses and correlations I hold to be more cogent.[52]

In any event, in terms of the overall accuracy of the commentaries, the present commentary represents the view that there is an a priori likelihood that the interpretations of the *sūtras* were faithfully preserved and transmitted orally through the few generations from Patañjali until the first commentary by Vyāsa in the fifth century (and we will see that some commentators, both traditional and modern, even hold Vyāsa's commentary to be that of Patañjali himself). In other words, unless compelling arguments are presented to the contrary, one must be cautious about questioning the overall accuracy of this transmission. Certainly, the commentators from Vyāsa onward are remarkably consistent in their interpretations of the essential metaphysics of the system for over fifteen hundred years, which is in marked contrast with the radical differences in essential metaphysical understanding distinguishing commentators of the Vedānta school (a Rāmānuja or a Madhva from a Śaṅkara, for example). While the fifteenth-century commentator Vijñānabhikṣu, for example, may quibble with the ninth-century commentator Vācaspati Miśra, the differences generally are in detail, not essential metaphysical elements. And while Vijñānabhikṣu may inject a good deal of Vedāntic concepts into the basic dualism of the Yoga system, this is generally an addition (conspicuous and identifiable) to the system rather than a reinterpretation of it. There is thus a remarkably consistent body of knowledge associated with the Yoga school for the best part of a millennium and a half, and consequently one can speak of the traditional understanding of the *sūtras* in the premodern period without overly generalizing or essentializing. One therefore has grounds to expect compelling reasons as to why this uniformity should not have been the case in the couple of centuries that may have separated Patañjali and Vyāsa.

Be all this as it may, the task we have set for ourselves in the present work is not to engage extensively in textual criticism but to attempt to represent something of the premodern history of interpretations associated with the school of Yoga as it has been transmitted for, at the very least, fifteen hundred years, and as it has been accepted by both scholastics and practitioners over this period. This, surely, constitutes a formidable realm of legitimacy and authority in its own right. One thus has grounds to speak of a tradition, and it is this Yoga tradition that the present commentary sets out to represent through some of its primary expressions prior to the modern explosion of interest in *yoga* in the West.

The first extant commentary by Vyāsa, typically dated to around the fourth or fifth century, attained a status almost as canonical as the primary text by Patañjali himself. Consequently, the study of the *Yoga Sūtras* has always been embedded in the commentary that tradition attributes to this greatest of literary figures. So when we speak of the philosophy of Patañjali, what we really mean (or should mean) is the understanding of Patañjali according to Vyāsa: It is Vyāsa who determined what Patañjali's abstruse *sūtras* meant, and all subsequent commentators elaborated on Vyāsa. While, on occasion, modern scholarship has insightfully questioned whether Vyāsa has accurately represented Patañjali in all instances,[53] for the Yoga tradition itself, his commentary becomes as canonical as Patañjali's (in fact, a number of traditional sources identify Vyāsa as none other than Patañjali himself[54]). Indeed, the Vyāsa *bhāṣya* (commentary) becomes inseparable from the *sūtras*, an extension of it (such that on occasion commentators differ as to whether a line belongs to the commentary or the primary text[55]). From one *sūtra* of a few words, Vyāsa might write several lines of comment without which the *sūtra* remains incomprehensible. It cannot be overstated that Yoga philosophy is Patañjali's philosophy as understood and articulated by Vyāsa.

In traditional narrative, Vyāsa, also known as Vedavyāsa or Vyāsadeva, is the legendary "divider"[56] of the four Vedas. The Vedas are the oldest preserved literature in India and, indeed, in the Indo-European language family. Tradition considers that there was originally only one Veda, and at the beginning of the present world age[57] this was subdivided into four by Vyāsa. Vyāsa is also considered to be the recorder of the immense *Mahābhārata*, as well as the compiler of the Purāṇas, the largest body of Sanskrit writing, containing most of the stories and ritual details that underpin what has come to be known as Hinduism. Irrespective of the historical accuracy of such literary prolifigacy, Vyāsa's status in traditional Sanskrit sources is that of the primary literary figure of ancient India. Modern scholars, even accepting the actual existence of a sage Vyāsa, consider our Vyāsa, the primary commentator of Patañjali's text, to be a later figure who penned his commentary under the name of the legendary sage in order to invest it with indisputable authority. Be that as it may, it is essential to recognize that Patañjali's Yoga system has essentially been handed down through the centuries as Patañjali's system as understood by the commentary attributed to Vyāsa. Vyāsa's commentary, the *Bhāṣya*, thus attains the status of canon and is almost never questioned by any subsequent commentator. Later commentators base their commentaries on unpacking Vyāsa's *Bhāṣya*—rarely critiquing it but rather expanding or elaborating on it. This point of reference results in a marked uniformity in the interpretation of the *sūtras* in the premodern period as noted above.

The next commentary considered in the present work is the *Vivaraṇa*. Although its authorship is debated, it is attributed to the great Vedāntin Śaṅkara in the eighth to ninth centuries C.E. Śaṅkara was to become the most influential commentator of the Vedānta school, and all subsequent commentators on the Vedānta, whether in agreement or disagreement with his *advaita*, nondual interpretations,[58] were constrained to define their own theologies in relation to his. It has remained unresolved since it was first questioned in 1927[59] whether the commentary on the *Yoga Sūtras* assigned to Śaṅkara is authentically penned by him. The *advaita*, nondual, aspect of Śaṅkara's thought, which is otherwise in stark opposition to the dualism and realism of Yoga metaphysics, is certainly not prominent in the *Vivaraṇa* to my eye—although one must note Hacker's intriguing theory that Śaṅkara was originally an adherent of Patañjali's *yoga* prior to becoming the famous Vedāntin.[60] There is only one surviving manuscript of this text, and all that can be determined with certainty is that it existed in the fifteenth century.

The next best known commentator after Vyāsa, Vācaspati Miśra, was a Maithila Brāhmaṇa from the Bihar region of India, whose commentary, the *Tattva-vaiśāradī*, can be dated with more confidence to the ninth century.[61] Vācaspati Miśra was a prolific intellectual, penning important commentaries on the Vedānta, Sāṅkhya, Nyāya, and Mīmāṁsā schools in addition to his commentary on the *Yoga Sūtras*. Despite the differences among these schools, Vācaspati Miśra is noteworthy for his ability to present each tradition in its own terms, without displaying any overt personal predilection. Erudite scholastics of the Yoga tradition would have been familiar with other commentaries in addition to that of Vyāsa, and Vācaspati Miśra's *Tattva-vaiśāradī* is the next most authoritative for the overall tradition after the *Bhāṣya* of Vyāsa. As an aside, this eclectic scholasticism contrasts with the experiential focus of *yoga* and makes one wonder whether Vācaspati Miśra was a practicing *yogī*.[62]

A fascinating Arabic translation of Patañjali's *Yoga Sūtras* was undertaken by the famous Arab traveler and historian al-Bīrunī

(973–1050), the manuscript of which was discovered in Istanbul in 1922.[63] Al-Bīrunī translates the *sūtras* in the form of a dialogue and interweaves it with "that over-lengthy commentary." However, the translators hold that this commentary to which he refers and had at his disposal does not appear to have been that of Vyāsa and "had probably been written at a time when the *Bhāṣya* of Veda-vyāsa had not attained any great sanctity or authority . . . [and] may represent a hitherto unknown line of interpretation" (Pines and Gelblum 1966, 304). This is a fascinating consideration, if true, since al-Bīrunī's commentary, which seems to be in complete accordance with Vyāsa's, adds weight to our own opinion that there is little evidence to deny the accuracy of Vyāsa's *Bhāṣya*. (In other words, if al-Bīrunī is following another commentary almost contemporaneous with the *Bhāṣya* and it reads Patañjali with the same interpretation as Vyāsa, the notion of an intact oral lineage from Patañjali informing both commentaries is enhanced.)

Roughly contemporaneous with al-Bīrunī is the eleventh-century king Bhoja Rāja, poet, scholar, and patron of the arts, sciences, and esoteric traditions, whose clan asserted independent rule in the Malwa region of Madhya Pradesh, central India, in the mid-tenth century. While Bhoja Rāja is certainly a welcome exemplar of an important political figure who engaged deeply with the Yoga tradition, his commentary, called the *Rāja-mārtaṇḍa*, essentially reiterates the work of Vyāsa without adding much elaboration, although there are occasionally very valuable insights. In contrast, in the fifteenth century, Vijñānabhikṣu wrote to my mind the most insightful and useful commentary after that of Vyāsa's, the *Yoga-vārttika*. Vijñānabhikṣu was another prolific scholar, to whom eighteen philosophical treatises on Sāṅkhya, Vedānta, and the Upaniṣads are attributed. He is noteworthy for his attempt to harmonize Vedānta and Sāṅkhya concepts, subscribing to a metaphysical view of *bhedābheda*, difference in nondifference, with regard to the relationship between the individual soul and the Absolute Truth. (He thus periodically critiques the nondualism of the Vedāntin Śaṅkara.[64]) As a Vaiṣṇava (a follower of an ancient sect holding Viṣṇu to be the supreme *Īśvara*), his commentary also enhances the devotional element and tenor of the text, as indeed do most of the commentaries. His translator, Rukmani, finds him to be "an uncompromising ascetic, steadfast in the principles of Yoga" (1997, 623).

With regard to the question whether he was a practicing *yogī* himself, despite his scholasticism, he claims in another of his publications on Yoga, the *Yoga-sāra*, that he is expounding the secrets of Sāṅkhya and Yoga as he himself directly experienced them.

In the sixteenth century, another Vedāntin, Rāmānanda Sarasvatī,[65] wrote his commentary, called *Yogamaṇi-prabhā*, which also adds little to the previous commentaries. But there are valuable insights contained in the final commentary considered for the present study, the *Bhāsvatī* by Hariharānanda Āraṇya. While it is not always clear to what extent some of the commentators were practicing *yogīs* and to what extent they were scholastics, we can affirm that Hariharānanda certainly was a fully dedicated *yogī*.[66] From his early life, Hariharānanda lived a renounced, ascetic life as a *sannyasī*, including several years in solitude meditating in the caves of west India and the last twenty-one years of his life in a hermitage where he could be contacted by his disciples only through a window looking into a hall. Although he is technically a "modern" commentator (1869–1947), and this present commentary concerns itself with the premodern, that is, the commentaries of the precolonial period, it is included here because, as a Sāṅkhya *ācārya*, master, Hariharānanda inhabited a traditional universe in terms of his own personal perspectives of reality as well as in his lifestyle. His commentary adds useful insight to the Yoga tradition from a context nearer our own times; his is a standpoint exposed to Western thought but still thoroughly grounded in tradition.

THE SUBJECT MATTER OF THE *YOGA SŪTRAS*

The Dualism of Yoga

Although situated as one of what later came to be known as the six schools of classical Hindu philosophy, Patañjali's text is not so much a philosophical treatise as a psychosomatic technique of meditative practice. As a dualistic system that presupposes an ultimate and absolute distinction between matter and consciousness, it is concerned with presenting a psychology of mind and an understanding of human consciousness rather than a metaphysics of all manifest reality. In actuality, Patañjali's text reads more like a manual for the practitioner interested in plumbing the depths of human consciousness than a philosophical exposition.

While the distinction between the material body and a conscious soul has a well-known history in Western Greco-Abrahamic religion and thought, Yoga differs from most comparable Western schools of dualism by regarding not just the physical body but also the mind, ego, and all cognitive functions as belonging to the realm of inert matter. This metaphysical presupposition of Yogic (and, for that matter, much Indic) thought is essential to an understanding of the basics of Yoga. The dualism fundamental to Platonic or Aristotelian thought, or to Paul or Augustine, is not at all the dualism of Yoga. Perhaps Descartes most famously represents the generic Western notions of the dualism between self and body in his *Meditations*: The self thinks and lacks extension, the body is unthinking and extended. In other words, there are two types of realities in classical Western dualism: physical reality, which is extended in space and empirically perceivable, and mental reality, which does not have spatial extension and is not empirically perceivable but private. For Descartes, following early Greek notions of the soul (tellingly called *psychē*), it is the soul that is *res cogitans*, the thinking being engaging in the cognitive functions of *dubitans, intelligens, affirmans, negans, volens, nolens, imaginans quoque, et sentiens.*

In the Yoga tradition, the dualism is not between the material body and physical reality on one hand, and mental reality characterized by thought on the other, but between pure awareness and all objects of awareness—whether these objects are physical and extended, or internal and nonextended. In other words, in Sāṅkhya and Yoga, thought, feeling, emotion, memory, etc., are as material or physical as the visible ingredients of the empirical world.[1] As an aside, in this regard, Yoga has a curious overlap with modern reductive materialism, which holds that the internal world of thought and feeling is ultimately reducible to neurological brain functioning and other purely material phenomena,[2] as well as with the computational procedures of "artificial intelligence." It thereby offers an unexpected overlap with modern functionalist accounts of mind that merits further exploration (avoiding some of the pitfalls in the Cartesian view in this regard, while, simultaneously, unlike Artificial Intelligence, retaining consciousness itself as independent of cognition[3]). Pure consciousness, called *puruṣa* in this system, animates and pervades the incessant fluctuations of thought—the inner turmoil of fears, emotions, cravings, etc.—but the two are completely distinct entities.

There is thus a radical distinction between the mind, which is considered to be very subtle but nonetheless inanimate matter, and pure consciousness, which is the actual animate life force. Animated by consciousness, it is the mind that imagines itself to be the real self rather than a material entity external to consciousness. The mind is therefore the seat of ignorance and bondage; *puruṣa* is "witness, free, indifferent, a spectator and inactive" (*Sāṅkhya Kārikā* XIX). Therefore, while the goal of the entire *yoga* system, and of Indic[4] soteriological (liberation-seeking) thought in general, is to extricate pure consciousness from its embroilment with the internal workings of the mind as well as the external senses of the body, in fact, according to Sāṅkhya, "no one is actually either bound or liberated, nor does anyone transmigrate; it is only *prakṛti* in her various manifestations who is bound, transmigrates and released" (*Sāṅkhya Kārikā* LXII). *Puruṣa* is eternal and therefore not subject to changes such as bondage and liberation;[5] in the Yoga tradition, the quest for liberation, in other words human agency, is a function of the *prākṛtic* mind, not of *puruṣa*. (We will revisit the implications of this fundamental principle and—since it is perceived by its detractors as the Achilles' heel of an otherwise meritorious system—the reactions to it from other Indic schools of thought in our concluding reflections.) Thus, although the traditional commentators (and the present commentary) sometimes say "*puruṣa* misidentifies itself with *prakṛti*" or "*puruṣa* seeks freedom," these are rhetorical or pedagogical statements. *Puruṣa* has never been bound; all notions of identity whether bound or liberated are taking place in the *prākṛtic* mind. In conclusion, then, Yoga claims to provide a system by which the practitioner can directly realize his or her *puruṣa*, the soul or innermost conscious self, through mental practices.

The Sāṅkhya Metaphysics of the Text

We have discussed how Yoga and Sāṅkhya are not to be considered distinct schools until well after Patañjali's time, but instead as different approaches or methods toward enlightenment. While there are minor differences between the two traditions, Sāṅkhya provides the metaphysical or theoretical basis for the realization of *puruṣa*, and Yoga offers the technique or practice itself.[6] While the Yoga tradition does not agree with the Sāṅkhya view that metaphysical analysis, that is, *jñāna*, knowledge, constitutes a sufficient path toward enlightenment in and of itself,[7] the metaphysical presuppositions of the Yoga system assume those of Sāṅkhya. Therefore, an understanding of the infrastructure of Sāṅkhya metaphysics is a prerequisite to comprehending the dynamics underpinning both the essential constituents of Yoga psychology and practice, as well as the supplementary aspects of the system such as the *siddhi* mystic powers of Chapter III.

As with the cluster of Yoga traditions, there were numerous variants of Sāṅkhya, amply attested in the *Mahābhārata*[8] (the Chinese Buddhist pilgrim Hsüen Tsang's disciple in the seventh century reports eighteen schools,[9] and the *Bhāgavata Purāṇa* also refers to several). Only fragments quoted by other authors have survived from the works of the original teachers of the system—Kapila, the divine sage whom tradition assigns as the original expounder of Sāṅkhya, is mentioned as early as the *Ṛg Veda* (X.27.16), the earliest Indo-European text, as well as in a number of other ancient treatises.[10] Additionally, there are quotes from Pañcaśikha, who is sometimes quoted by our commentators,[11] and Āsuri, the latter's disciple. There are various references to the original Sāṅkhya tradition as *Ṣaṣṭi-tantra*, containing sixty topics (for example, *Sāṅkhya Kārikā* LXXII),[12] but the original text appears to be lost. The later *Sāṅkhya Kārikā* of Īśvarakṛṣṇa, which scholars assign to the fourth or fifth century, has by default become the seminal text of the tradition, just as Patañjali's *Yoga Sūtras* has become for the Yoga tradition, and represents its developed, systematic form. It is quoted throughout the present commentary (as it is in the traditional commentaries).

In the Sāṅkhya (literally, numeration) system, the universe of animate and inanimate entities is perceived as ultimately the product of two ontologically distinct categories; hence this system is quintessentially *dvaita*, or dualistic in presupposition. These two categories are *prakṛti*, or the primordial material matrix of the physical universe, "the undifferentiated plenitude of being,"[13] and *puruṣa*, the innumerable conscious souls or selves embedded within it. As a result of the interaction between these two entities, the material universe evolves in stages. The actual catalysts in this evolutionary process are the three *guṇas*, literally, strands or qualities, that are inherent in *prakṛti*. These are *sattva*, lucidity; *rajas*, action; and *tamas*, inertia. These *guṇas* are sometimes compared to the threads of a rope; just as a rope is a combination of threads, so all manifest reality consists of a combination of the *guṇas*. These *guṇas* are mentioned incessantly throughout the commentaries on the text,[14] as are the various evolutes from *prakṛti*, and thus require some attention.

Given the meditative focus of the text, the *guṇas* are especially significant to *yoga* in terms of their psychological manifestation; in Yoga, the mind and therefore all psychological dispositions are *prakṛti* and thus also composed of the *guṇas*—the only difference between mind and matter being that the former has a larger preponderance of *sattva*, and the latter of *tamas*. Therefore, according to the specific intermixture and proportionality of the *guṇas*, living beings exhibit different types of mind-sets and psychological dispositions. Thus, when *sattva* (from the root *as,* "to be"[15]) is predominant in an individual, the qualities of lucidity, tranquillity, wisdom, discrimination, detachment, happiness, and peacefulness manifest; when *rajas* (from the root *rañj*, to color, to redden) is predominant, hankering, attachment, energetic endeavor, passion, power, restlessness, and creative activity manifest; and when *tamas*, the *guṇa* least favorable for *yoga*, is predominant, stillness, ignorance, delusion, disinterest, lethargy, sleep, and disinclination toward constructive activity manifest.

The *guṇas* are continually interacting and competing with each other, one *guṇa* becoming prominent for a while and overpowering the others, only to be eventually dominated by the increase of one of the other *guṇas* (*Gītā* XIV.10). The Sāṅkhyan text the *Yukti-dīpikā* (13) compares them to the wick, fire, and oil of the lamp which, while opposed to each other in their nature, come together to produce light. Just as there are an unlimited variety of colors stemming from the mixture of the three primary colors, different hues being simply expressions of the specific proportionality of red, yellow, and blue, so the unlimited psychological dispositions of living creatures (and of physical forms) stem from the mixture of the *guṇas*, specific states of mind being the reflections of the particular proportionality of the three *guṇas*.

The *guṇas* underpin not only the philosophy of mind in Yoga but the activation and interaction of these *guṇa* qualities result in the production of the entirety of physical forms that also evolve from the primordial material matrix, *prakṛti*, under the same principle.[16] Thus the physical composition of objects like air, water, stone, fire, etc., differs because of the constitutional makeup of specific *guṇas*: air contains more of the buoyancy of *sattva*; stones, more of the sluggishness of the *tamas* element; and fire, more *rajas* (although its buoyancy betrays its partial nature of *sattva* as well). The *guṇas* allow for the infinite plasticity of *prakṛti* and the objects of the world.

The process by which the universe evolves from *prakṛti* is usefully compared to the churning of milk: When milk receives a citric catalyst, yogurt, curds, or butter emerges. These immediate products can be manipulated to produce a further series of products—toffee, milk desserts, cheese, etc.[17] Similarly, according to classical Sāṅkhya,[18] the first evolute emerging from *prakṛti* when it is churned by the *guṇas*

DIAGRAM OF THE TWENTY-FIVE *TATTVAS* OF CLASSICAL SĀṄKHYA

Illustrating the evolution of *prakṛti* according to the *Sāṅkhya-Kārikā* of Īśvarakṛṣṇa

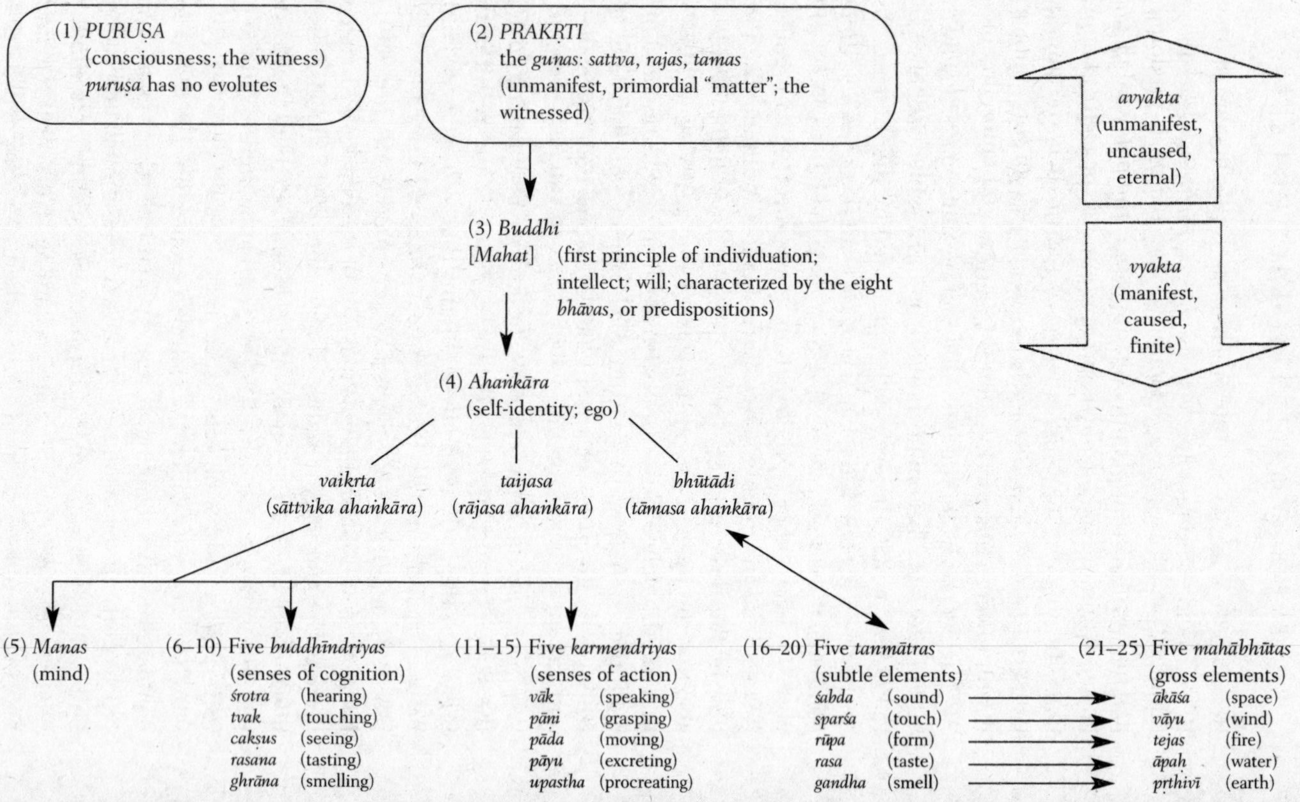

(*sattva* specifically) is *buddhi*, intelligence. Intelligence is characterized by the functions of judgment, discrimination, knowledge, ascertainment, will, virtue, and detachment,[19] and *sattva* is predominant in it. This means that in its purest state, when the potential of *rajas* and *tamas* is minimized, *buddhi* is primarily lucid, peaceful, happy, tranquil, and discriminatory, all qualities of *sattva*. It is the interface between *puruṣa* and all other *prākṛtic* evolutes. From this vantage point, it can direct awareness out into the objects and embroilments of the world, or, in its highest potential, it can become aware of the presence of *puruṣa* and consequently redirect itself toward complete realization of the true source of consciousness that pervades it.

From *buddhi, ahaṅkāra*, or ego, is produced (*aham*, I + *kāra*, doing; referred to as *asmitā* in this text). This is characterized by the function of self-awareness and self-identity. It is the cognitive aspect that processes and appropriates external reality from the perspective of an individualized sense of self or ego—the notion of I and mine in human awareness. The *Sāṅkhya Kārikās* refers to it as conceit, *abhimāna*. It is essential in conceptualizing and distinguishing subject and object, the knower and the known. It creates the notion of an individual self, but additionally, it is from *ahaṅkāra* that both the objective external world, and the instruments through which one can interact with the world (the sense organs, etc.) evolve; in order for there to be a subject, there needs to be a world of objects and instruments through which to access this world. *Ahaṅkāra* also limits the range of awareness to fit within and identify with the contours of the particular psychophysical organism within which it finds itself in any one embodiment, as opposed to another. In other words, the *ahaṅkāra* of a bug acts almost like a concave screen that refracts consciousness to pervade and appropriate the contours of the bug. If the bug dies and becomes, say, a dog and then a human in subsequent lives, the *ahaṅkāra* aspect of the *citta* adjusts to accommodate and absorb consciousness into these new environments. Thus the bug thinks it is a bug, the dog thinks it is a dog, and the human thinks he or she is a human.

Ahaṅkāra is thus not only pivotal in all experience but also is the critical midpoint in the choice between material identification or spiritual pursuit, the external material world or the pure *puruṣa*. Turned inward, *ahaṅkāra* (*asmitā*) can reflect awareness toward its source, *pu-*

ruṣa; turned outward, it can misidentify the self with its *prākṛtic* entrapment.[20] It is the *ahaṅkāra* that determines whether one's notion of self is spiritual or phenomenal.

When ego in turn is churned by the *guṇa* of *sattva* inherent in it, *manas*, the mind, is produced. The mind is the seat of the emotions, of like and dislike, and filters and processes the potentially enormous amount of data accessible to the senses. It primarily receives, sorts, categorizes[21] and then transmits. It serves as the liaison between the activities of the senses transmitting data from the external world, and *buddhi*, intelligence; indeed, the only two times the term occurs in the *sūtras* is in connection with its relationship with the external senses. It therefore partakes both of internal and external functioning: internally, it is characterized by reflective synthesis (*saṅkalpa*) as noted above, while simultaneously being "a sense because it acts similar to the senses" (*Sāṅkhya Kārikā* XXVII).

The *Kaṭha Upaniṣad* (3.9) compares the body to a chariot, the senses to the horses, the mind to the reins that control the horses, the *buddhi* to the driver who controls the reins and charts the course, and the *puruṣa* to the inactive passenger. *Buddhi*, intelligence; *ahaṅkāra*, ego; and *manas*, mind, together comprise the internal body (*antaḥkaraṇa*), the inner noetic world of thoughts, emotions, feelings, determination, will, cognitions, memories, etc. The *puruṣa* soul is cloaked in these psychic layers prior to receiving a gross body and senses. As noted, the Yoga school, while using the terminology of (especially) *buddhi*, but also *ahaṅkāra* and *manas*, differs somewhat from that of Sāṅkhya in conceiving these three as interacting functions of the one *citta*, mind, rather than as three distinct metaphysical layers. *Citta*, then, is the term used by Patañjali and the commentators to refer to all three of these cognitive functions combined (thus it is not a separate evolute from *prakṛti*).

Moving onto more physical levels of reality, from the ego stirred by *tamas* emerge the *tanmātras*, or subtle elements—the energies or powers underpinning sound, sight, smell, taste, and touch. These are the generic energies behind the sensory powers, not specific sounds or varieties of tastes, etc., hence their name, *tanmātra*, only that (namely, the essences of these energies, not their particular individualized expressions).[22] Since knowledge and illumination are qualities of *sattva*, the *tanmātras* are still very *sāttvic* in nature. These, in turn, sequentially produce the five *mahābhūtas*, or gross elements—ether, air, fire, water, and earth—the world of form, the actual physical, tangible stuff of the universe. This evolutionary sequence must be kept in mind in order to understand the metaphysics behind a number of *sūtras* in the *Yoga Sūtras*, particularly those that deal with the mystic powers.

The Sāṅkhya system is classified in Indian thought as *satkārya*, namely, that the effects of the world are present in their cause. This is one of the important points to keep in mind: Gross matter is actually an evolute or derivative of something subtler, the subtle elements, and these of something subtler still, the ego, which is an evolute of *buddhi*, intelligence. This means *buddhi* underpins all reality, even as *buddhi* itself is a manifestation of *prakṛti* and the *guṇas*, or, put differently, any expression of reality, subjective or objective, is nothing other than a manifestation of the *guṇas*. These evolutes are all called *tattvas*, thatnesses; they are the real constituents of "that" world out there perceived by the self.

The Goals of Yoga

According to Patañjali's definition in the second *sūtra, yoga* is the cessation (*nirodha*) of the activities or permutations (*vṛttis*) of the *citta*. The *vṛttis* refer to any sequence of thought, ideas, mental imaging, or cognitive act performed by the mind, intellect, or ego as defined above—in short, any state of mind whatsoever. It cannot be overstressed that the mind is merely a physical substance that selects, organizes, analyzes, and molds itself into the physical forms of the sense data presented to it; in and of itself it is not aware of them. Sense impressions or thoughts are imprints in that mental substance, just as a clay pot is a product made from the substance clay, or waves are permutations of the sea. The essential point for understanding *yoga* is that all forms or activities of the mind are products of *prakṛti*, matter, and completely distinct from the soul or true self, *puruṣa*, pure awareness or consciousness.

The *citta* can profitably be compared to the software, and the body to the hardware. Neither is conscious; they are rather forms of gross matter, even as the former can do very intelligent activities. Both software and hardware are useless without the presence of a conscious observer. Only *puruṣa* is truly alive, that is, aware or conscious. When uncoupled from the mind, the soul, *puruṣa*, in its pure state, that is, in its own constitutional, autonomous condition—untainted by being misidentified with the physical coverings of the body and mind—is free of content and changeless; it does not constantly ramble and flit from one thing to another the way the mind does. To realize pure awareness as an entity distinct and autonomous from the mind (and, of course, body), thought must be stilled and consciousness extracted from its embroilment with the mind and its incessant thinking nature. Only then can the soul be realized as an entity completely distinct from the mind (a distinction such clichés as "self-realization" attempt to express), and the process to achieve this realization is *yoga*.

In conventional existence, *puruṣa*'s awareness of objects is mediated by means of *buddhi*, the intellect. As the discriminatory aspect of the mind, the intelligence is the first interface between the soul and the external world. More specifically, the soul becomes aware of the outside world when images of sense objects are channeled through the senses, sorted by the *manas*, the thinking and organizing aspect of *citta*, and presented to the intellect. Although inanimate, the intellect, in addition to its functions of discrimination noted earlier, molds itself into the form and shape of these objects of experience, thoughts, and ideas, and, due to the reflection of the consciousness of *puruṣa*, appears animated. Since the soul is adjacent to[23] the intellect (and the *citta* in general), the intellect is the immediate covering of *puruṣa*; hence it is through the intellect that *puruṣa* becomes aware of these forms and therefore of the objects of the world. The pure consciousness of the soul pervades the *citta*, animating it, just as a torch, although distinct in its own right, pervades an inanimate object with light and makes it appear luminous.

Pervaded by this consciousness, the *citta* mind appears as if it itself were conscious, as metal placed into intense fire becomes molten and appears as if fire. But the mind animated by consciousness is in reality unconscious—just as an object appears illuminated in its own right but is in actuality dependent on an outside light source for its illumination and visibility. Most important, the soul, the pure and eternal power of consciousness, never changes; as a spectator or witness, it does not itself transform when in contact with the ever-changing states of mind. It simply becomes aware of them. Just as light passively reveals gross and subtle objects in a dark room and yet is not itself affected or changed by them, consciousness passively reveals objects, whether in the form of gross external physical objects or subtle internal thoughts, *vṛttis*, including the higher stage of discrimination, but is not itself actually affected or touched by them. But the awareness of the pure soul does permeate or shine on the *citta*, like a projector light permeating inanimate pictorial forms of a movie reel, thereby animating these pictures as if they had a life of their own. In so doing the animated mind misidentifies consciousness with itself, equating consciousness with the churnings of thought, *vṛttis*, as if consciousness were inherent within itself rather than the effulgence of an entity outside and separate from itself. This misidentification is ignorance, *avidyā*, and the cause of bondage in *saṁsāra*. It is the mysterious glue that binds the self to the world of matter in all Indic soteriological traditions. (Ignorance is mysterious, since the question of how it comes to arise in the first place is bypassed by all Indic metaphysicians by stating that it is beginningless.[24])

According to some commentators, such as Vijñānabhikṣu, the intellect functions like a mirror. Just as light bounces off an illuminated reflective object back to its source, the consciousness of the soul bounces off this animated intellect that presents a reflection to the soul (Vijñānabhikṣu's double-reflection theory is sometimes referred to in this commentary, being in my view more cogent than Vācaspati Miśra's single-reflection theory[25]). Because *sattva* is predominant in the intellect, it is able to reflect pure consciousness back to itself. Just as we become conscious of our appearance in a mirror due to its reflectivity, the soul becomes conscious of its reflection in the animated intellect. But since the intellect is constantly being molded into the images presented to it by the mind and senses, this reflection presented back to the *puruṣa* soul is distorted or transformed by changing forms, *vṛttis*, just as our reflection in a mirror is distorted if the mirror is warped. The soul, that is, the actual source of consciousness, is mistaken to be this distorted reflection by the mind, which considers awareness to be inherent within itself rather than a feature of the *puruṣa*, an entity completely outside of and separate from itself. The soul is thus identified with the world of change through these changing states of mind, the *vṛttis*, just as we may look at our reflection in a dirty mirror and mistakenly think that it is we who are dirty.

Whether the *vṛttis* of the *citta* are reflected back to the *puruṣa* soul, or whether consciousness simply becomes aware of them by proximity and pervasion, the soul nonetheless is identified with the experiences of the body and mind—birth, death, disease, old age, happiness, distress, peacefulness, anxiety, etc., even though these are merely transformations occurring in the inanimate and external body and mind, and therefore unconnected with the *puruṣa*. They are nothing other than the permutations of gross and subtle matter external to the soul that are pervaded by the soul's awareness. But awareness is misidentified with these permutations, as a result of which the self (that is, the mind animated by consciousness) considers itself to be subject to birth and death, happiness and distress, etc., and it is this misidentification, or ignorance, that is the root of bondage to the world. *Yoga* involves preventing the mind from being molded into these permutations, the *vṛttis*, the impressions and thoughts of the objects of the world, such that *puruṣa* can regain its autonomous nature.

To accomplish this, one of the goals of Yoga meditation, as discussed repeatedly by our commentators, is to maximize the proportion of the *guṇa* of *sattva* in the mind and correspondingly decrease that of *rajas* and *tamas*. When all trace of *tamas* and *rajas* is stilled, the mind attains the highest potential of its *prākṛtic* nature—illumination, peacefulness, discernment, etc., all qualities inherent in *sattva*. When the *citta* mind has cultivated a state of almost pure *sattva*,[26] the discriminative aspect of *buddhi*, intelligence, can reveal the distinction between the ultimate conscious principle, the *puruṣa* soul, and even the purest and most subtle (but nonetheless unconscious) states of *prakṛti*. When manifesting its highest potential of *sattva* and suppressing its inherent potential of *rajas* and *tamas*, which divert consciousness from its source, *puruṣa*, and into the external world of objects and internal world of thought, the pure *sattva* nature of the mind can recognize the distinction between *puruṣa* and *prakṛti*, and redirect consciousness back inward toward this inner self (one of the ultimate goals of *yoga*), just as a dusty mirror can reflect things clearly when cleaned. In short, *yoga* can also be viewed as the process of stilling the potential of *rajas* and *tamas*, and allowing the maximum potential *sattva* nature of the mind to manifest, and the commentators often promote it this way.

The means prescribed by Patañjali to still the *vṛtti* states of mind or fluctuations of thought is meditation, defined as keeping the mind fixed on any particular object of choice without distraction. God, *Īśvara*, comes highly recommended in this regard; Yoga is clearly, but nondogmatically, a theistic system. By concentration and meditation (or by the power of God's grace), the distracting influences of *rajas* and *tamas* can be curtailed, and the *sattva* constitution of the mind can exhibit its full potential.

Through grace or the sheer power of concentration, the mind can attain an inactive state where all thoughts remain only in potential but not active form. In other words, through meditation one can cultivate an inactive state of mind where one is not cognizant of anything. This does not mean to say that consciousness becomes extinguished, Patañjali hastens to inform us (as does the entire Upaniṣadic/Vedāntic tradition); consciousness is eternal and absolute. Therefore, once there are no more thoughts or objects on its horizons or sphere of awareness, consciousness has no alternative but to become conscious of itself. In other words, consciousness can either be object-aware or subject-aware (loosely speaking).[27] The point is that it has no option in terms of being aware on some level, since awareness is eternal and inextinguishable. By stilling all thought, meditation removes all objects of awareness. Awareness can therefore now be aware only of itself. It can now bypass or transcend all objects of thought, disassociate from even the pure *sāttvic citta*, and become aware of its own source, the actual soul itself, *puruṣa*. This is self-realization (to use a neo-Vedāntic term), the ultimate state of awareness, the state of consciousness in which nothing can be discerned except the pure self, *asamprajñāta-samādhi*. This is the final goal of *yoga* and thus of human existence.

The Eight Limbs of Yoga

Asamprajñāta-samādhi is the highest stage of the eighth and final limb of *yoga* presented by Patañjali to attain this lofty goal. These eight limbs are *yama*, abstentions, moral restraints; *niyama*, ethical observances; *āsana*, posture; *prāṇāyāma*, breath control; *pratyāhāra*, withdrawal of the senses; *dhāraṇā*, concentration; *dhyāna*, meditation; and *samādhi*, full meditative absorption. The first limb, the *yamas*, are nonviolence, truthfulness, refraining from stealing, celibacy, and refraining from coveting. They deal with how the aspiring *yogī* relates to others. Obviously, if one's goals are to remove consciousness from identification with the body and the mind, one must curb activities that pander to the grosser urges of the body—violence, stealing, deceit, sexual exploitation, and coveting are generally performed with a view to improving one's bodily or material situation and must be resisted by one striving for transcendent goals. The second limb, the *niyamas*, are cleanliness, contentment, austerity, study [of scripture], and devotion to God. These deal with how the *yogī* cultivates his or her own lifestyle. Once the cruder and more destructive potentials of the body are curtailed by following the *yamas* of the first limb, consciousness can be turned more inward toward personal refinement. Each limb furthers and deepens this internal progression. The third limb, *āsana*, focuses on stretches and postures with a view to preparing the *yogī*'s body to sit for prolonged periods in meditation. It is this aspect of *yoga* that has been most visibly exported to the West but too often stripped from its context as one ingredient in a more ambitious and far-reaching sequence.

While successful performance of the third limb begins the focusing of attention and stilling of the mind, the fourth limb, *prāṇāyāma*, furthers this process through fixing the mind on breath control. By regulating and slowing the movement of breath, the mind too becomes regulated and quiescent. The fifth limb, *pratyāhāra*, withdrawal of the senses, deepens the process by removing consciousness from all engagement with the sense objects (sight, sound, taste, smell, touch). This is followed by the three final limbs: *dhāraṇā, dhyāna*, and *samādhi* (which Patañjali divides into seven rather esoteric stages). The last three limbs are essentially different degrees of concentrative intensity and culminate in the realization by awareness of its own nature, *asamprajñāta-samādhi*. The *Yoga Sūtras*, in fact, is primarily a manual for the practitioner rather than an exposition of Yoga philosophy.

THE PRESENT TRANSLATION AND COMMENTARY

There are dozens of modern translations of the *sūtras*, which have been marketed to the *yoga* community or nonspecialized reading public interested in esoteric Eastern practices. There are also a number of outstanding scholarly editions marketed to an academic audience, which typically include elaborate and highly specialized translations of one of the traditional Sanskrit commentaries on the text. Much of the traditional intellectual background is understandably often bypassed or watered down, in an effort to make the material accessible to a modern, primarily Western, nonspecialized audience. On the other hand, much of the scholarly translations are not very accessible to the nonspecialized reader with little or no background in ancient Indian philosophical thought. The present translation attempts to bridge these two worlds of discourse. It attempts to ground the text in its traditional intellectual context but to articulate the subject matter in a way that is accessible to the educated nonspecialist as well as to scholars and students of Indic philosophy. This is a daunting challenge and perhaps by its very nature destined to draw some criticism from all sides, but it is the result of teaching this text over the years to students in the university setting as well as to *yoga* practitioners in numerous workshops in *yoga* communities around the world.

This commentary draws material from all (rather than just one) of the principal historical traditional Sanskrit commentaries, from which I have selected relevant explanatory comments. However, since a good deal of the commentarial tradition deals with abstruse philosophical minutiae of interest only to the specialist, my extracts primarily consist only of material that is essential to understanding the *sūtras* in their own right. I have trimmed superfluous or peripheral philosophical specificity from this commentary, as a thorough representation of these would require extensive background or presentation of Hindu philosophical concepts and issues.

This is not to say that I have watered down this commentary. I have tried to make it user-friendly but still academically rigorous: Readers unfamiliar with Hindu philosophical discourse will unavoidably encounter novel philosophical issues here. The *Yoga Sūtras* is classified as a *darśana*, classical school of philosophical thought, after all, written and handed down over the centuries by scholastics, and so a commentary that claims to represent the Yoga tradition cannot be presented outside this context. Western practitioners of *yoga* have excelled in mastering the rigors of *āsana*, and I would like to think that the more serious and committed among them will be eager to engage intellectually with the traditional interpretations of the *Yoga Sūtras*.

I have included the commentarial sections critiquing Buddhist views of mind and consciousness, since—apart from the fact that they occupy a large portion of Chapter IV (and surface elsewhere)—it seems useful to establish the main points of divergence on these topics between these traditions and classical Yoga, given the popularity of Buddhist traditions in the West. I do, additionally, include frequent snippets of information and other material from the commentaries that are of genuine historical, cultural, and spiritual interest to those for whom this edition is intended: scholars and students of ancient Indian thought, both within academia and without, seeking a synopsis of the text and its commentaries; the educated but nonspecialized lay readership; and aspiring *yogīs* approaching the text as an historical source of authority for meditative practice and willing to marshal some intellectual rigor in this quest. With this latter community in mind, I have attempted to eschew hyperacademic jargon and vocabulary when a topic can be articulated in less technical terms. I might add that the commentaries can be repetitive in parts—after all, the core of the teachings are very simple: to remove consciousness from its absorption in *prakṛti*. Any type of pedagogy involves repetition, and this is especially true of the Indic traditions and their history of oral transmission. This commentary has preserved some of this character.

In many ways, this commentary shares features of traditional exegesis insofar as it primarily seeks to unpack and represent Patañjali as well as the traditional commentaries, although there is plenty of my own elaboration, critical analysis, and, I hope, contributive insight. In classical India, proponents of knowledge systems have a tendency to perceive themselves as members of disciplic successions, *paramparās* (for example, *Gītā* IV.2). Knowledge is perceived as divine revelation and is divided into two categories. Revelation is either *śruti* (that which is heard, namely, the Vedic corpus), transhuman revelation emanating from *Īśvara*, God, for the theist schools,[1] or *smṛti* (that which is remembered, the Purāṇas and epics and other later texts including the *sūtra* traditions), intrahuman revelation emanating from enlightened *ṛṣi* sages. But both genres are descending bodies of knowledge. Consequently, the exegete plays the role of transmitter of information perceived as a priori universally and inherently valid. His or her role, then, is to take the existing traditions and expand upon them according to time and context as existing Truths, rather than formulate new Truths. While I consider the content of the *Yoga Sūtras* text to stem from a core of meditational and enstatic experiences attained in *yogic* practice that has been subsequently systematized and scholastized by Patañjali (who may very likely have been a practicing *yogī*), I have attempted to ground my commentary in the traditional commentaries to provide a chronological variety of premodern traditional perspectives and insights on the *sūtras*. Of course, while attempting to represent these traditional perspectives, I offer plenty of elaboration, interpretation, illustration, cross-referencing, and further clarification, and, as noted above, inform the commentary with the more persuasive observations of modern critical scholars.

With regard to representing tradition, as with all Sanskrit literature, philosophical or other, Hindu cosmology flavors the worldview underpinning the text—there are references to various divinities, celestial realms, mystic powers, and so forth. While such beliefs obviously conflict with the parameters of modern post-Enlightenment rational thought, I have not attempted to sterilize the text from these elements, as some modern translations tend to do, but have retained these teachings within their greater traditional context and presented them with all the trappings accepted by the commentators. Indeed, I probe the metaphysical rationale of the mystic powers (*siddhis*) from the perspective of Sāṅkhya metaphysics and argue that they are an inherent part of the presuppositions of the system. Readers are left to extract whatever aspects of the text are meaningful to them or do not conflict fatally with their own worldviews (and, in any event, such conflict, or cognitive dissonance, affords an opportunity to probe and perhaps reevaluate one's own intellectual and cultural preconceptions and predispositions).

In short, I have adopted something of the phenomenological approach in the study of religion in presenting this material. One of the approaches of phenomenology involves presenting—in its own terms and frame of reference—material that conflicts with or is inexplicable from within the parameters of our modern world knowledge systems. The material is presented without imposing reductionist[2] interpretational models from our very different modern time and context upon it, without value judgment, and in as neutral a fashion as possible. Phenomenology concerns itself with representing the claims and beliefs of a religious tradition as accurately and objectively as possible as phenomena in their own right and within their own context—suspending judgment on issues of "truth" from the perspective of scientific validity. The goal of this commentary is to present the traditional Yogic worldview not as an imagined monolith but through some of the permutations and configurations it has taken in the hands of the commentators over the centuries.

Additionally, the commentaries are replete with references to other texts such as the *Bhagavad Gītā* and Upaniṣads and, with Vijñānabhikṣu, frequently the *Bhāgavata Purāṇa.* I include some of them in the present commentary and add numerous cross-references of my own. Again, since, in traditional Hindu perspectives, these texts are all divine revelation,[3] traditional exegetes draw freely from other (usually) classical sources where these might serve to bolster a particular point. Sometimes the demarcation of ancient Indian thought into Hindu and Buddhist and the former into six schools of philosophy (a much later development in any case) can take on contours that are far more rigid than was likely the case in Patañjali's time. Thinkers drew broadly from a common pool of ideas, and even when they aligned themselves with specific sects, these were demarcated not so much along lines of outright rejection of other sects but to a great extent on the specific areas of interest that a particular sect chose to focus on and develop—from the orthodox side: Mīmāṁsā on epistemology, hermeneutics, and *dharma*; Nyāya on logic; Vaiśeṣika and Sāṅkhya on metaphysics; Vedānta on interpretation of the Upaniṣads from the perspective of knowledge of *Brahman*; Yoga on praxis, etc. All (with the exception of early Mīmāṁsā) are dedicated to a common goal of freeing the *ātman* from the world of suffering. Even where other doctrines are refuted, through the ubiquitous category of the *pūrvapakṣa*,[4] only very specific areas or items of dogma are rejected, not the entirety of a school's metaphysics. Thus, Yoga is partially rejected by the Vedānta tradition only insofar as strains of it subscribe to the (later) Sāṅkhya view of causation from *prakṛti* rather than *Brahman*, which, while all-important to Vedānta, is a peripheral topic of no great concern to Patañjali in the *Yoga Sūtras*. There is no rejection of the central enterprise of the Yoga tradition, namely, presenting a psychology of the mind and a technique of extracting the *ātman* from the mind's machinations. Likewise, the *Nyāya Sūtras*, while differing in their metaphysics, nonetheless accept Yoga as the means to realize the *ātman* (IV.2.46).

In parallel fashion, the Yoga commentators from Vyāsa onward draw freely from sources and concepts associated with the Upaniṣadic/Vedānta tradition, most conspicuously in the case of Vijñānabhikṣu. I am not as uncomfortable with this as some scholars seem to be: To my reading, these types of references do not always impose material on the text that necessarily conflicts with Patañjali's teachings. Patañjali was an orthodox Hindu, which means he accepted the Truths of Divine Revelation, *āgama*—even if he holds that the experience of these Truths is higher than simply belief in them. Moreover, he *requires* the study of scripture, *svādhyāya*, as a mandatory ingredient of his system, both in the practice of *kriyā-yoga* and in that of *aṣṭāṅga*. As an ascetic, Patañjali would certainly have been interested in the Upaniṣadic strata of *āgama* (rather than the earlier ritualistic corpuses, which he indirectly dismisses[5]). He therefore does not present his teachings as separate from this tradition, even as his own *sūtras* are focused on one ingredient within the Upaniṣadic corpus, meditational *yoga*. Thus, even though he makes no mention of the central Upaniṣadic concern, *Brahman* as source of all reality (unlike the commentators, beginning with Vyāsa, who do correlate *puruṣa* with *Brahman*), we cannot say he rejected this notion simply because his particular treatise concerned itself with a related but specific subject matter, the individual *puruṣa*. He does adopt Upaniṣadic language on occasion and incorporate Upaniṣadic concepts into the *sūtras* even if only in passing.

Therefore, we do not know where Patañjali stood in terms of the relationship between the *puruṣa* and *Brahman* or *Īśvara* (*Brahman* can refer to the Absolute Truth as either impersonal or personal, whereas *Īśvara* is exclusively a term for the personal aspect), but we certainly cannot presume that he rejected at least whatever conventional views on these concepts were standard (even as there were a plethora of interpretative differences, some fundamental, among Vedāntins). What we do know is that there are both Sāṅkhya and Yoga traditions preceding Patañjali expressed in the Upaniṣads and in the *Mahābhārata* that accommodated their *puruṣa-prakṛti* metaphysics within a *Brahman* or *Īśvara* framework. We also know that by the time of Bādarāyaṇa, who wrote the *Vedānta Sūtras*, Sāṅkhya is extensively critiqued for jettisoning *Brahman* as the original source of reality (that is, as the source of both *prakṛti* and *puruṣa*), and a passing comment is made that on the same grounds Yoga is rejected (*etena yogaḥ pratyuktaḥ*). But since there were numerous strains of Yoga, many of them represented in the Purāṇas (and most readily visible in the *Gītā*), which undoubtedly *did* preserve the *Brahman/Īśvara*-based theism of the *Mahābhārata* and Upaniṣads, Bādarāyaṇa can be referring only to particular strains of Sāṅkhya and Yoga. In any event, apart from anything else, Bādarāyaṇa wrote his *sūtras* centuries before Patañjali's, so we really have no grounds to deduce that Patañjali departed from the shared presuppositions of the Vedāntic tradition on these matters (although later Vedānta commentators likely are referring to Patañjali's text when they deem Yoga as culpable in this regard). I argue strongly that Patañjali's *Īśvara* cannot be excised or sterilized from the theistic context and *Īśvara*-related options of the second and third centuries. Similarly, it seems probable that he would have seen his teachings as elaborating on one aspect of the greater orthodox corpus stemming from the Upaniṣads, rather than as departing from other essential aspects of it. One must be wary of assuming he rejected standard Vedāntic teachings simply because he does not explicitly direct attention to topics not connected to the specific project he is focusing on in his succinct 195 *sūtras*, namely, the uncoupling of *puruṣa* from *prakṛti*. And the commentators certainly correlate *puruṣa* with *Brahman* as if this were a perfectly standard thing to do.

In any event, I have chosen to represent some of these quotations from the commentators even when, as with Vijñānabhikṣu, sectarian Vedāntic specificities are introduced that may not have been subscribed to by Patañjali. I indicate the source of these quotes, since my goal is to give an overall sense of the methods, exegetical practices, and perspectives of the principal traditional commentators of the Yoga tradition, and to suggest how traditions cross-fertilize. This is especially visible with Vijñānabhikṣu's blending of Yoga with Vedāntic concerns. I also introduce plenty of quotes from the Upaniṣads, *Gītā*, and other texts, as well as the occasional illustration from my ongoing translations of the *Bhāgavata Purāṇa*. There is nothing like a colorful story from the Purāṇas to lighten up and exemplify elements in what is otherwise a dense and demanding text (and these Purāṇa texts have yet to receive the scholarly attention they deserve, as they are a vast repository of not just mythological narrative, but sometimes quite ancient philosophical material transmitted through epic-type narrative which is very relevant to the early history of the Indic intellectual traditions). Nonetheless, while one would be hard put to consider that Patañjali was not well read in texts such as the *Gītā*, Upaniṣads, epics, and the developing Purāṇic corpus of his day, the reader should always keep a healthy awareness of the distinction between the theological concerns underpinning a commentary and what is explicitly stated in the primary text.

For this commentary, I read Vyāsa's commentary in the Sanskrit and used this as the springboard for my own commentary. For the other later commentaries, due to the sheer bulk of the material involved, I availed myself of various English translations in determining which material to extract for this commentary, for which I then consulted the original Sanskrit. I am therefore indebted to the following translators: of Vācaspati Miśra's *Tattva-vaiśāradī*, Rāma Prasāda (1912), and Woods (1914); of Śaṅkara's *Vivaraṇa*, Leggett (1992); of Bhoja Rāja's *Vṛtti*, Ballantyne (1852); of Vijñānabhikṣu's *Yoga-vārttika*, Rukmani (1981); and of his *Yoga-sāra-saṅgraha*, Jhā (1923); of Rāmānanda

Sarasvatī's *Yogamaṇi-prabhā*, Krishnan (1996); of Hariharānanda (1963), Mukerji (1968); and of al-Bīrunī, Pines and Gelblum (1966–89). All translations from the Upaniṣads, *Bhagavad Gītā*, and other texts are my own unless otherwise stated. I do not provide the Sanskrit for translations from these classical sources, since these are easily available to specialists. Also, I provide the Sanskrit in footnotes only for the material I have selected from the Yoga commentaries for direct quotations, not for my own paraphrases.

In addition to the debt I owe these translators or primary sources, and, of course, the insight of the commentators themselves, I would like to acknowledge my indebtedness to the insights I have gained from the work of critical scholars whose secondary sources are mentioned in the bibliography (some of which are represented throughout this commentary in the relevant places). Although the present work concerns itself primarily with presenting how the traditional commentators have understood the text over the centuries, how it has been handed down for over a millennium and a half, I have gained great insight from the work of modern text critical scholars into ways of making sense of certain obscure *sūtras* in particular, and in thinking about the overall text itself. I hesitate to pull out any names for fear of neglecting others, but I would be remiss not to mention at least the various contributions of Koelman, Larson, Feuerstein, Chapple, and Whicher, who have dedicated such rigorous yet sympathetic scholarly analysis to the text for so many years.

In conclusion, while the old Vedic sacrificial cult from which *yoga* emerged no longer defines our modern religious or cultural horizons, a number of the traditions that it spawned, such as Yoga, remain. Modern societies no longer sacrifice animals to the gods, recite Vedic hymns, or pour ghee into the fire in order to attain material goals. But we share many of the same attitudes as the Vedic ritualists—that the goal of life is the pursuit of ever-increasing levels of material abundance and sensual gratification—and we manipulate our environment to attain this goal in other, more damaging ways. From a certain perspective, one might say that the only difference between our modern goals of life and those of the ancient Vedics is the technologies we use in attempting to attain them. They tried to achieve the good life through technologies of *mantra* and ritual, and we use machine-based industrial technologies. Our modern world has universalized, idolized, and mass-produced consumerism—the indulgence of the senses and the mind—as the highest and most desirable goal of life. From the perspective of the Yoga tradition, our *vṛttis*, the restlessness of the mind caused by ignorance and desire, are out of control.

And so, proportionately to our material attachments, according to Yoga, a sense of malaise and dissatisfaction is engendered since, as the *Gītā* informs us, desire is never satisfied and burns like fire (III.39). It is thus our "eternal enemy." According to almost all schools of Indic thought, including Buddhism and Jainism, the more we desire, the more we are frustrated. The more we are frustrated, the more we strive to remove our frustration with more sensory stimuli. And the more we strive, the more we damage ourselves and our environment, and perpetuate our *saṁsāric* existence. It is in the critique of this mind-set of consumption that Patañjali claims to offer an alternative that remains perennially relevant to human existence. But it is a solution that requires an abandonment of the consumer mentality by the practice of the full eight limbs of *yoga*, beginning with the *yamas* and *niyamas*. Without these, attempts to perfect the third limb of *yoga*, *āsanas*, postures, are simply physical gymnastics. To equate the practice and purpose of *yoga* with this limb alone is to miss the whole point of Patañjali's system (particularly and ironically if this is done with a view of improving the sensual prowess of the body and mind in order to maximize physical and mental pleasure). Without recognizing the actual goal of *yoga*, the realization of the true self as other than the body, mind, and sensual apparatus, modernity may not have progressed in attitude and presupposition concerning life's goals from those lusty performers of Vedic sacrifice. It is this attitude that the ancient spiritual teachers of India such as Patañjali were so concerned to redress, and it is in this regard that the teachings of *yoga* will remain perenially relevant to the human condition.

THE YOGA SŪTRAS OF PATAÑJALI

प्रथमः समाधिपादः ।

prathamaḥ samādhi-pādaḥ

CHAPTER I

MEDITATIVE ABSORPTION

The chapter begins by introducing the subject of the work and providing a definition of *yoga*—the cessation of *citta-vṛtti*, the fluctuating states of the mind [1–2]. This is followed by a discussion of the two possible functions of awareness [3–4]; a description of the *vṛttis* [5–11]; and how to control them by practice [13–14] and dispassion [15–16]. Then comes the division of *samādhi* into *samprajñāta* [17] and *asamprajñāta* [18] *samādhis* and how to attain it [20–22], after pointing to other states that might resemble it [19]. *Īśvara* is then introduced as the easy method of attaining *samādhi* [23], along with his nature [24–26], name [27], worship [28], and the fruits accruing therefrom [29]. The chapter describes the distractions of the mind [30] and their accompanying effects such as grief, etc. [31]; outlines the means to combat these by dwelling on one truth [32], practicing benevolence, etc., [33], breath control [34], and other means [35–39] that are conducive to *samādhi*. Additionally, the variety of *samāpatti* meditative states [42] with definitions [42–44] and their fruits [46–48] and object [49] are presented. The chapter concludes with a discussion of *samprajñāta-samādhi* preceding the final stage of *asamprajñāta* [50–51].

Oṁ namo bhagavate Vāsudevāya; I offer obeisances to Lord Vāsudeva (Kṛṣṇa).[1]

Commentators and authors of traditional texts typically begin their commentaries with an invocation, *nāndi-śloka*, to their personal deity, the particular form of *Īśvara*, God, that they revere, soliciting blessings and inspiration for the enterprise they are about to undertake. This, notes Vijñānabhikṣu, is in order to remove any obstacles that might arise either in the completion of the work by the author, or in the students' ability to grasp its meaning. By so doing, one also strives to remove personal ego so that one can become a conduit, accurately transmitting the essence of the text. Most commentators on the *Yoga Sūtras*, in addition to an invocation to God, offer homage to Patañjali himself, the author of the text, usually invoking him in his traditional form as an incarnation of Śeṣa, the bearer of Viṣṇu.[2]

अथ योगानुशासनम् ।। १ ।।

I.1 atha yogānuśāsanam

atha, now; *yoga, yoga*; *anuśāsanam*, teachings

Now, the teachings of *yoga* [are presented].

It is common for authors of philosophical works to commence their treatises by announcing the specific nature of their subject matter, thereby indicating how their undertakings are to be distinguished from other strains of philosophical thought or knowledge systems. Thus, while from the six classical schools of Hindu philosophy[3] the followers of the Vedānta school see their tradition as explaining the nature of the absolute Truth (*Brahman*), and the followers of the Vaiśeṣika and Mīmāṁsā schools as explaining the nature of *dharma*, duty, and these respective points of focus are announced in the first *sūtras* of the primary texts associated with those schools,[4] the Yoga school is interested in the subject of *yoga*.[5] Patañjali accordingly uses the first *sūtra* of his text to announce the topic of his teachings: The primary subject matter of his text differs from that of other systems insofar as his work will be about *yoga*.

It is also standard in the commentarial literature, as will become apparent throughout this work, for the later commentators to analyze each word in every *sūtra* (as discussed in the introduction, *sūtra* means aphorism or extremely succinct verse), and words are analyzed in various ways—etymologically, semantically, contextually, philosophically, etc. Commentaries thus unpack the meaning of words, both individually and collectively, in the *sūtras* of primary texts. Vyāsa, Vācaspati Miśra, Vijñānabhikṣu, Śaṅkara, Bhoja Rāja, Rāmānanda Sarasvatī, and

Hariharānanda Āraṇya are, in chronological order, the main commentators recognized as the most important of the premodern period and their interpretations form the basis of the present commentary.

Accordingly, the first word in this *sūtra*, and thus of the entire *Yoga Sūtras*, is *atha*, now, that is, in the present work Patañjali is about to deliver, demarking these teachings from those in other texts (the word also initiates the opening *sūtras* of other philosophical works[6]). As will be seen below with Vijñānabhikṣu's comments, the word *atha* is also sometimes read as differentiating the text in question from other texts in a hierarchical or sectarian fashion, as indicating that when one has exhausted dabbling with other philosophical or religious systems as represented in other texts, one has now finally come to the summum bonum of Truth, namely, that represented by the text in question.[7] The commentators add, as an aside, that the word *atha* is deemed somewhat sacred[8] and thus also functions as an auspicious opening to the text.

Vyāsa, the primary and most important commentator (whose commentary is almost as canonical as Patañjali's primary text), then proceeds to discuss *yoga*, the second word in this *sūtra*. In accordance with the famous Sanskrit grammarian Pāṇini, he glosses *yoga* with *samādhi*, the ultimate subject matter of the *Yoga Sūtras*. *Samādhi* consists of various contemplative stages of mental concentration that will be described in detail throughout the text. Indeed, the commentator Vācaspati Miśra traces the etymology of *yoga* to one of the meanings of the root *yuj*, to contemplate, which, he points out, is the correct etymology here. The more established etymology from the perspective of modern historical linguistics is, of course, derived from the same Indo-European root as the English word "yoke."[9] *Yoga* can thus mean that which joins, that is, unites one with the Absolute Truth, and while this translation of the term is popularly found (and may be apt in other contexts, such as the *Gītā*, IX.34[10]), it is best avoided in the context of the *Yoga Sūtras*, since, as was pointed out over a hundred years ago by the famous Indologist Max Müller (1899, 309ff) (and long before that, by the sixteenth-century Indian doxographer Mādhava[11]) the goal of *yoga* is not to join, but the opposite: to unjoin, that is, to disconnect *puruṣa* from *prakṛti*.[12] If the term is to mean "yoke," it entails yoking the mind on an object of concentration without deviation.

Elaborating on this, Vyāsa notes that when the mind is directed toward an object, it can manifest five different degrees of focus (*bhūmis*): wondering, confused, distracted, concentrated, and restrained. It is the last two that are of interest to Yoga: when the mind, *citta*, is restrained and concentrated, or fixed on one point, a type of *samādhi* known as *samprajñāta* can be attained.[13] *Samprajñāta-samādhi* entails concentrating the mind in various degrees upon an object of concentration[14] (all of which will be discussed at length below). Vyāsa also introduces the notion of *asamprajñāta-samādhi* in these opening comments. This is the seventh and ultimate level of *samādhi*, when all activities of the mind have been fully restrained—including those involved in *samprajñāta-samādhi* of one-pointed concentration on an object. Since *asamprajñāta-samādhi* will also be discussed at length in the text, we will simply note here that in this state, pure objectless consciousness alone remains, that is, self-contained consciousness conscious only of its own internal nature of pure consciousness rather than of any external object. Vyāsa thus provides a minipreview of the subject matter of the *Yoga Sūtras* in his opening comments.

Vyāsa makes a point of noting that a distracted mind, the third on his list of states, is not to be confounded with *yoga*. Vācaspati Miśra elaborates that while it is obvious that the other two states of mind, wondering and forgetfulness,[15] are not *yoga*, a distracted state of mind may appear to be so because it is periodically fixed. However, since such steadiness soon relapses into wondering and forgetfulness, it cannot be considered real *yoga*. Only the fully concentrated or one-pointed state of mind is *yoga*.

Vācaspati Miśra notes that the third and final term from this *sūtra, anu-śāsanam*, strictly speaking means further teaching.[16] He points out that the *Yājñavalkya Smṛti* states that a sage known as Hiraṇyagarbha was the original teacher of *yoga*. Hence Patañjali is using the prefix *anu-*, which indicates the continuation of the activity denoted by the noun to which it is prefixed, in this case, *śāsanam*, teachings. The *Mahābhārata* also identifies Hiraṇyagarbha as the founder of Yoga (XII.326.65; 337.60). In the Purāṇic tradition (e.g., *Bhāgavata Purāṇa*, X.71.8), Hiraṇyagarbha is considered to be an epithet of Brahmā, the celestial being responsible for engineering the forms in the universe. In Purāṇic lore—for example, *Bhāgavata Purāṇa*, which is quoted frequently herein (III.8)—Hiraṇyagarbha is born on a lotus emanating from the navel of Viṣṇu, the supreme Godhead, who is reclining on the divine serpent Śeṣa on the cosmic waters pervading the entire universe prior to creation. (As an aside, Patañjali himself is considered an incarnation of Śeṣa; see commentary in II.47.) Awakening to consciousness atop the lotus, Hiraṇyagarbha has no means of knowing who he is, or what is the source of the lotus or the all-expansive waters, indeed, no means of discerning or knowing anything at all. Confused and disoriented, he stills his mind (in accordance with the next verse), and enters into the ultimate state of *yoga* (*samādhi*), as a result of which he is granted a divine vision of Lord Viṣṇu. Hiraṇyagarbha is thus the first *yogī* in primordial times, and deemed to have written the original treatise on the subject.

Although mentioned in various texts, the Hiraṇyagarbha treatise is no longer extant, but information about its twelvefold content, all overlapping with the material found in Patañjali's *sūtras*,[17] is preserved in the Vaiṣṇava text the *Ahirbudhnya Saṁhitā*.[18] Indeed, the information provided in this text suggests that Patañjali has, indeed, preserved the ancient formulation of the original philosophy ascribed to Hiraṇyagarbha, rather than patching together some innovative Yogic collage.[19] Elsewhere, Vyāsa also refers to the teachings of one Jaigīṣavya as a forerunner of Yoga (II.55). Mādhava in his sixteenth-century doxography (compendium of philosophical schools) states that Patañjali, out of kindness, seeing how difficult it was to make sense of all the different types of *yoga* scattered throughout the Purāṇas,[20] collected their "essences" (111). Patañjali is not the founder of the practice of *yoga*, which, Vācaspati Miśra stresses, is an ancient practice that preceded even Patañjali. Thus, by using the prefix *anu*, Patañjali himself implies that he has articulated and systematized a method from preexisting sets of teachings. His opening *sūtra, atha yogānuśāsanam*, thus informs the reader about the subject matter of the text.

Although Yoga becomes one of six schools of orthodox Hindu thought, its adherents naturally consider it to supersede the other schools. Vijñānabhikṣu, the most philosophical of the commentators, quotes a number of scriptural passages that point to the supremacy of *yoga*. For example, Kṛṣṇa, in the *Bhagavad Gītā* (which Vijñānabhikṣu quotes frequently) states, "The *yogī* is higher than the ascetic, and also considered higher than the *jñānī*, one who pursues knowledge. The *yogī* is higher still than the *karmī*, one who performs action; therefore, Arjuna, become a *yogī*" (VI.46). Just as all rivers such as the Gaṅgā are present as parts of the ocean, says Vijñānabhikṣu, so all other schools of thought are fully represented as parts of Yoga. While he allows that one can certainly obtain genuine knowledge from these other schools, all knowledge is, by its very nature, a faculty of the intellect, *buddhi*; it is not a faculty of the soul proper. Sectarianism apart, it is perhaps useful to consider the argument so as to establish a preliminary understanding of the mind and intellect from Yoga perspectives. All aspects of mind, intellect, and cognition in Yoga psychology are external to or distinct from the true self, or soul. As will become clearer, the soul, which is pure consciousness, is autonomous and separable from the mind, and lies behind and beyond all forms of thought.

It is essential to fully grasp this fundamental point in order to understand the Yoga system. Just as in most religious systems the body is commonly accepted to be extraneous to and separable from some notion of a soul or life force, and discarded at death, so (in contrast to certain major strains of Western thought), according to the Yoga system (and Hindu thought in general), the mind is also held to be extraneous to and separable from the soul (although it is discarded not at death but only upon attaining liberation). The soul is enveloped in two external and separable bodies in Yoga metaphysics:[21] the gross material body consisting of the senses, and the subtle body consisting of the mind, intellect, ego, and other subtle aspects of the persona.[22] At death, the soul discards the gross body (which returns to the material elements, to "dust") but remains encapsulated in the subtle body, which is retained from life to life, and eventually attains a new gross body, in accordance with natural laws (*karma*, etc.). In order to be liberated from this cycle of repeated birth and death (termed *saṁsāra* in ancient Indian thought), the soul has to be uncoupled from not just the gross body but the subtle body of the *citta* as well. The process of *yoga* is directed toward this end. For our present purposes, then, in contrast to the Cartesian model, knowledge, as a feature of the intellect, or the discriminatory aspect of the mind, is extraneous to the pure self and thus not the ultimate aspect of being.

The point here is that while knowledge is initially essential in leading the *yogī* practitioner through the various levels of *samādhi*, concentrative states, it is only through *yoga*, for Vijñānabhikṣu, that one can transcend the very intellect itself and thus the base of knowledge, to arrive at *puruṣa*, the ultimate state of pure, unconditioned awareness.

From this perspective, Yoga is therefore superior to other schools of thought that occupy themselves with knowledge and thus remain connected to the material intellect. Just as a person with a torch in hand gives up the torch upon finding treasure, says Vijñānabhikṣu, so, eventually, the intellect, and the knowledge that it presents, also become redundant upon attaining the ultimate source of truth, *puruṣa*, the soul and innermost self. The self is pure subjectivity[23] and transcends all knowledge, which is of the nature of objectivity: One knows, that is, one is aware or conscious of, something, hence some other object distinct from the knower or power of consciousness itself, whether this is an external object of the physical world, or an internal object of thought.

Thus, Vijñānabhikṣu says (paraphrasing *Sāṅkhya Kārikā* XXXV), knowledge and the intellect are the door and doorkeeper, and both lead the practitioner of *yoga* from the domain of material cognition to the highest goal of existence, realization of *puruṣa*, consciousness itself, but this ultimately lies beyond even the intellect. This state of pure consciousness, which is not conscious of anything other than consciousness itself, is termed *asamprajñāta-samādhi*. The attainment of this state is the ultimate goal for the school of Yoga, not any type of knowledge however profound or mystical. Hence, from this perspective, Yoga is superior to knowledge-centered paths.

The origins of Yoga are rooted in direct perception of its subject matter, says the commentator Hariharānanda Āraṇya. He too notes that Yoga is based not on the mere logical reasoning of the intellect but on direct experience, and in this regard differs from some of the other schools of orthodox thought, which are highly philosophical. Patañjali's *Yoga Sūtras* is more a psychosomatic technique than a treatise on metaphysics; the truths of Yoga cannot be experienced by inferential reasoning but only by direct perception. As will be seen in I.49, the Yoga school prioritizes experience over other forms of attaining knowledge. These personal realizations, says Hariharānanda, are handed down from teacher to disciple, generation after generation. The teachings of Yoga are an attempt to encapsulate those truths as best as possible through the medium of words and concepts. Since the ultimate truth of the soul, attained in *asamprajñāta-samādhi*, is by definition beyond the intellect, and thus beyond words and concepts, the primary purpose of this text is, as far as possible, to point the reader toward the actual practice of *yoga*. While the *Yoga Sūtras* provides much interesting information on the nature of Hindu psychology and soteriology, it is useful to keep in mind that its intended function is as a manual for the practitioner (hence its cryptic nature from the perspective of the intellect).

योगश्चित्तवृत्तिनिरोधः ॥२॥

I.2 yogaś citta-vṛtti-nirodhaḥ

yogaḥ, *yoga*; *citta*, the mind; *vṛtti*, fluctuation, state;
nirodhaḥ, restraint, control

***Yoga* is the stilling of the changing states of the mind.**

There are various definitions of *yoga* expressed in different traditions which, while all overlapping, reflect the fact that *yoga* referred to a cluster of practices featuring various forms of discipline and mind control practiced by many differing ascetics and communities on the landscape of ancient India with a view to liberation from the sufferings of embodied life; it was not associated with a distinct school until well into the Common Era.[24] In the *Kaṭha Upaniṣad*, for example, "*yoga* is believed to be when the senses are firmly under control" (VI.11), while in the *karma-yoga* (path of action) section of the *Bhagavad Gītā, yoga* is defined as *samatvam*, evenness of mind (II.48) and as *karmasu kauśalam*, skill in action (II.50). Elsewhere, the text defines *yoga* as *duḥkha-saṁyoga-viyogam*, separation from union with pain (VI.23), which is essentially the definition given in the *Vaiśeṣika Sūtras: duḥkhābhāvaḥ*, the absence of pain (V.2.16[25]), a definition that finds its roots in the *Kaṭha Upaniṣad* (II.12).[26] The *Nyāya Sūtras* associate the practice of *yoga* with the attainment of liberation (IV.2.46). While his teachings will incorporate all the above definitions, Patañjali here gives his formal definition of *yoga* for the classical school of Yoga itself: "*Yoga* is the stilling of all thought."

The commentators have packed a considerable amount of rather dense information into their commentaries in this *sūtra*, since Patañjali has basically defined and summarized the entire system of Yoga here, and the commentaries use this *sūtra* to lay out the infrastructure of the psychology and metaphysics of the *yoga* process. Although an attempt will be made here to present the information in stages, the unfamiliar reader might well feel alarmed or overwhelmed by the sudden immersion in *yogic* concepts and Sanskrit terms presented in the commentary to this *sūtra*. The task is complicated somewhat since the commentators presuppose that their readers are aware of the system of Sāṅkhya, one of the other six schools of orthodox Indian thought with which the Yoga school is typically coupled.[27]

Having said this, there are advantages to the "sudden-immersion" technique into Yoga psychology that follows, since once the basics are grasped, the teachings of Yoga become progressively clearer as one advances through the text. The reader unfamiliar with Hindu metaphysics is reassured that if a clear and coherent picture of Yoga psychology is not gained at this early stage, the material presented in the commentary for this *sūtra* will be unpacked, explained, reiterated, and elaborated upon repeatedly and in great detail throughout the remainder of the text such that one soon becomes familiar with the system. Additionally, there are a dozen or more technical Sanskrit words that are retained throughout this translation, which do not translate succinctly into English, and a number of them will be introduced here in rapid succession, but, again, readers will become familiar with them by dint of sheer repetition. That said, the commentary for this *sūtra* remains unavoidably challenging since it presents something of a synopsis of Yoga psychology and practice, and an understanding of these requires a prior discussion of Sāṅkhya and Yoga metaphysics.

The first of the *Yoga Sūtras* introduced the subject matter of the text, a discussion of *yoga*, and this second *sūtra* proceeds to define what this *yoga* is. According to Patañjali's definition in this *sūtra, yoga* is the cessation (*nirodha*) of the permutations or activities (*vṛttis*) of the *citta*. In order to define *citta*, perhaps the most important entity in *yoga* practice, one must become familiar with ultimate reality as elaborated upon in the Sāṅkhya (literally, numeration) system. As we know, in Sāṅkhya, ultimate reality is perceived as the product of two distinct ontological categories: *prakṛti*, or the primordial material matrix of the physical universe, and *puruṣa*, pure awareness, the innermost conscious self or soul (the terms "consciousness" and "awareness," although problematic,[28] will be used interchangeably in this commentary to refer to the nature of the *puruṣa*). As a result of the contact between these two distinct entities, *prakṛti* and *puruṣa*, the material universe evolves in a sequential fashion.

To reiterate, the first and subtlest evolutes from the material matrix, according to Sāṅkhya, are, in order: *buddhi*, intelligence; *ahaṅkāra*, ego; and *manas*, mind. These layers, which are grouped together under the rubric of the "internal body,"[29] constitute the inner life of an individual, and the *puruṣa* soul is cloaked in these psychic layers prior to receiving a gross physical body equipped with senses. The term *citta* (from *cit*, to think, consider, fix the mind on) is used in this *sūtra* and throughout the text by Patañjali and the commentators to refer to all three of these cognitive functions combined (the Yoga school differs somewhat from that of Sāṅkhya in conceiving these three as interacting functions of the one *citta*, mind, rather than as three distinct metaphysical layers[30]), but the main point, as stressed in the last *sūtra*, is that they are distinct from the soul proper.

Buddhi, intelligence, is the aspect of *citta* that produces, among other things, the functions of thought connected to judgment, discrimination, knowledge, ascertainment, and will[31] (from *budh*, to wake up, be aware of). It is the most important aspect of the *citta* as it is from its function of discrimination that liberation is achieved. Additionally, it is *buddhi* that molds itself into the forms of the data funneled to it by *manas*, below, and presents these images to the *puruṣa* soul, to which it is immediately adjacent. *Buddhi* is thus the liaison between *puruṣa* as pure awareness, and the objects, whether physical or psychic, of which *puruṣa* can be aware.

Ahaṅkāra, or ego,[32] produces the function of thought related to self-awareness, self-identity, and self-conceit (the personal pronoun *aham* means I, and *kāra*, the doer). This is the aspect of *citta* that causes notions of I-ness and my-ness: "I know," "I am a man," "I am happy," "This is mine." It also delimits awareness, which is potentially omnipresent,[33] and refracts it to fit into the contours of the particular body and mind within which it finds itself. It is because of ego that the awareness of an ant is limited to the range of the ant's senses and the conceptual structure of its mind, while the awareness of an elephant has a larger range, and that of a human an even larger range. This restructuring of the lens of *ahaṅkāra*, so to speak, is the result of specific sets of *saṁskāras* (imprints from present and past lives, which will be discussed in I.5), relevant to any particular form—bug, dog, or human—activating at the appropriate time.

Manas, the mind, is the aspect of *citta* that engages in the functions of thought especially related to organizing sensory input and directing the senses; it imposes a conceptual structure on the chaotic field of raw sensations, recognizing and identifying sensual impetuses and categorizing them (from *man,* to think, believe).[34] It exhibits attraction to some sensory possibilities and aversion to others—in other words, the functions of feeling, emotion, and desiring. It is the bridge connecting the world of the sense objects as accessed through the sense organs; the ego, which appropriates this under the notion of I; and the intelligence, which judges, evaluates, and strategizes over the input to determine what its duty (*dharma*[35]) is in relation to the data it is receiving from the mind and senses (that is, what to do about it, how to respond or act). In his commentary to the *Sāṅkhya Kārikā* (36), Vācaspati Miśra says:

> As the village chief collects rent from the heads of the families and presents it to the district chief, who delivers it to the chief superintendent, who delivers it to the king, so the sense organs, having perceived an external object, deliver it to the mind, who considers it and delivers it to the ego, who appropriates it and delivers it to the intelligence, the chief superintendent of all. Thus it is said "they present it to intelligence, [thereby] illuminating the purpose of the *puruṣa.*"[36]

I will gloss the Sanskrit word *citta* throughout this discussion with the term mind for ease of reference, since this is how it is usually translated, but it should be noted that the term encapsulates all of the functions of thought outlined above,[37] and not just that of *manas*, which is also usually translated as mind (when I use mind in the latter sense, I will qualify it by the Sanskrit term *manas*). Vijñānabhikṣu states that the *citta* is the one unified internal organ, and this becomes manifest in the various functions of intelligence, ego, and mind because of *vṛttis*.

The *vṛttis* indicated by Patañjali in this *sūtra* will be categorized into five basic types in I.5 and discussed thereafter, and so we will simply note at this point that they ultimately refer to any permutation or activity of the mind, in other words, any sequence of thought, ideas, mental imaging, or cognitive act performed by either the mind, intellect, or ego as defined above, or any state of the mind at all including deep sleep. The verbal root *vṛt* means to revolve, turn, proceed, move, and underscores the always active, sequential, rambling aspect of the mind. The mind is a physical substance in Hindu thought in general and assumes the forms of the sense data presented to it. The ensuing sense impressions, thoughts, or states are products made of that mental substance, just as a gold statue is a form made from the substance gold, or a clay pot is a form from the substance clay. These constantly moving mental images, states, or formations in the *citta* are *vṛttis.* If *citta* is the sea, the *vṛttis* are its waves, the specific forms it takes. (They will be defined in I.5 below.) I will gloss the term *vṛtti* with states or activities of mind or fluctuations of thought, and I will refer to *puruṣa* as pure consciousness or pure awareness. The essential point Patañjali is making here is that since all forms or activities of the mind are products of *prakṛti,* matter, and completely distinct from the soul or true self, *puruṣa,* they must all be restrained in order for the soul to be realized by the *yogī* as an autonomous entity distinct from the mind.

Since, as Vyāsa notes, the soul in its pure state is considered to be free of content and changeless—it does not transform and undergo permutations in the way the mind constantly does—Vijñānabhikṣu raises the issue of how it can be aware of objects at all in the first place. Awareness of objects is brought about by means of *buddhi*, the intellect. The intelligence is the first interface between the soul and the external world. The sense objects provide images that are received through the senses, sorted by the *manas*, the thinking and organizing aspect of *citta*, and presented to the intellect. Although inanimate, the intellect molds itself into the form and shape of these objects of experience, thoughts, and ideas. Vijñānabhikṣu compares this process to liquid copper being poured into a mold and taking the exact shape of the mold, although the forms into which *buddhi* is molded are extremely subtle and psychic in nature. This molding of the *citta* into these thoughts and ideas is the *vṛttis* referred to by Patañjali in this *sūtra*.

This process can be compared to dull, opaque external objects being captured as photographic images on film, which is both translucent and representational, or to geometric patterns on a stained-glass window (Schweitzer 1993, 853), which are again both translucent and representational. That is to say, images on film or in stained glass are translucent enough to allow the light to filter through them, which, on account of the opaqueness of matter, is not the case with the original external gross objects they represent (due to the greater *tāmasic* component).[38] But they are also representational, insofar as these external objects are still indirectly represented as images on the film or forms in the stained-glass windows, becoming visible when pervaded by light. Due to adjacency, the pure consciousness of the soul shines onto the intellect and animates it with consciousness, like a lamp illuminates the film or stained glass with light and makes it appear luminous. Because the pure highly translucent *sattva* element is maximized in *buddhi*, it is able to absorb and reflect the soul's power of consciousness. Enveloped in the soul's consciousness, the workings of the *citta* mind appear to be themselves conscious, but they are in reality unconscious, just as the film or stained glass appears illuminated in their own right but are in actuality dependent on light external to themselves for their illumination and visibility. The awareness of the pure soul permeates the *citta*, animating the churnings of thought, *citta-vṛttis*, but due to ignorance, this animated *citta* considers consciousness to be inherent within itself, rather than an entity outside and separate from itself. It is this ignorance that is the ultimate cause of bondage and *saṁsāra*.

According to some commentators (most notably, Vijñānabhikṣu),[39] just as light bounces off an object back to its source, the consciousness of the soul is reflected off this animated intellect and back to the soul. From this perspective, the intellect also functions like a mirror, the soul becoming conscious of its reflection in the animated intellect, just as one becomes conscious of one's appearance in a mirror. However, since the intellect is constantly being transformed into the images presented to it by the mind and senses, this reflection presented back to the *puruṣa* soul is constantly obscured and distorted by *vṛttis*, just as one's reflection in a mirror is distorted if the mirror is dirty or warped. When this distorted reflection is considered to be inherent within the actual *puruṣa*, rather than the product of the *citta*, an entity outside of and separate from it, the soul becomes misidentified with the world of change, through the changing states of mind, the *vṛttis* noted in this *sūtra*, just as one may look at one's reflection in a dirty mirror and mistakenly think that it is oneself who is dirty. Consider a young child looking at herself in one of those "crazy mirrors" that make one appear grotesquely fat or thin (or, in the premodern analogy used by Śaṅkara, a face reflected in a long sword, making the face appear elongated, III.35). If the child does not realize that her deformed appearance in the mirror is merely a distorted reflection and not her actual self, she may experience fear or panic.

The soul, in short, is neither the physical body in which it is encased nor the mind that exhibits psychic functions. It is pure autonomous consciousness. The *Sāṅkhya Sūtras* refer to a quaint traditional story to illustrate this point:

> A certain king's son, due to being born under an afflicted astrological constellation, is expelled from the city and raised by a member of the forest dwelling Śabara tribe. He thus thinks: "I am a Śabara!" Upon finding him to be still alive, one of the king's ministers informs him: "You are not a Śabara, you are a king's son." Thereupon, the son gives up the idea that he is a Śabara, accepts his true royal identity, and thinks: "I am a king's son." In the same way, the soul, by means of the instruction of a kind soul [the *guru*], is informed: "You are manifest from the first Soul [*Brahman*], who is made of pure consciousness." Thereupon, giving up the idea of being made of *prakṛti*, the soul thinks: "Because I am the son of *Brahman*,[40] I am *Brahman*, not a product of *saṁsāra*." (IV.1)

Thus, the soul appears to undergo the experiences of the body and mind—birth, death, disease, old age, happiness, distress, peacefulness, anxiety, etc., but these are mere transformations of the body and mind. In other words, they are the permutations of gross and subtle matter external to the soul that are pervaded by the soul's awareness. The mind misidentifies the pure self with these permutations and considers the pure self to be subject to birth and death, happiness and distress, etc. This misidentification, or ignorance, is therefore the root of bondage to the world, as will be discussed in the beginning of Chapter II. As stated in this *sūtra* by Patañjali, *yoga* involves preventing the mind from being molded into these permutations, the *vṛttis*, the impressions and thoughts of the objects of the world.

An understanding of the process underpinning the workings of the mind—the *citta-vṛttis* noted here—requires the introduction of a further set of categories: the three *guṇas*, strands or qualities. They are *sattva*, lucidity; *rajas*, action; and *tamas*, inertia.[41] Vyāsa and the commentators waste no time discussing these *guṇas* here and continue to do so continuously in their commentaries throughout the text. Since they are pivotal to an understanding of *yoga* meditation and practice, they require some attention.

The *guṇas* are inherent in *prakṛti*, matter, and are the catalysts in the evolution of the mind and all manifest reality from primordial *prakṛti*. Just as threads are inherent in the production of a rope, says Vijñānabhikṣu, so the *guṇas* underpin and permeate the material matrix of *prakṛti*. *Prakṛti* is constituted by the three *guṇas*. Therefore, since everything evolves from this material matrix, the *guṇas* are present in varying proportions in all manifest reality, just as the three primary colors are present in all other colors produced from them. As one can create an unlimited variety of hues by simply manipulating the relative proportions of red, yellow, and blue, so the unlimited forms of this world, as well as psychological dispositions of all beings, are the product of the interaction and intermixture of the *guṇas*. The *Mahābhārata* states that as one can light thousands of lamps from one lamp, so *prakṛti* can produce hundreds of thousands of transformations of the *guṇas* (XII, 301, 15–16). For our present purposes, the *citta*, as a product of matter, also consists of the three *guṇas: sattva, rajas,* and *tamas*.

Although all of *prakṛti*, including the cosmological and physical aspect of the universe, is also a product of the three *guṇas*, the Yoga tradition is interested in their psychic aspect. The *guṇas* are usually portrayed, and perhaps best understood in the context of Yoga, by their psychological manifestations (indeed Dasgupta translates them as "feelings"[42]). *Sattva*, the purest of the *guṇas* when manifested in the *citta*, is typically characterized, among a number of things, by lucidity, tranquillity, wisdom, discrimination, detachment, happiness, and peacefulness; *rajas*, by hankering, energetic endeavor, power, restlessness, and all forms of movement and creative activity; and *tamas*, the *guṇa* least favorable for *yoga*, by ignorance, delusion, disinterest, lethargy, sleep, and disinclination toward constructive activity. The

Bhagavad Gītā (XIV, XVII, and XVIII) presents a wide range of symptoms connected with each of the *guṇas*.[43] Kṛṣṇa makes the useful observation that the *guṇas* are in continual tension with each other, one *guṇa* becoming prominent in an individual for a while and suppressing the others, only to be dominated in turn by the emergence of one of the other *guṇas* (*Bhagavad Gītā* XIV.10).

One of the goals of *yoga* meditation, as discussed repeatedly in the traditional literature, is to maximize the presence of the *guṇa* of *sattva* in the mind and minimize those of *rajas* and *tamas*. According to Sāṅkhya metaphysics, all three *guṇas* are inherently present in all the material by-products of *prakṛti* including the *citta*, so *rajas* and *tamas* can never be eliminated, merely minimized or, at best, reduced to a latent and unmanifest potential. Clearly, *sattva* is the *guṇa* most conducive—indeed, indispensable—to the *yogic* enterprise, but while *rajas* and *tamas* are universally depicted as obstacles to *yoga*, a certain amount of each *guṇa* is indispensable to embodied existence. Without *tamas*, for example, there would be no sleep; without *rajas*, no digestion or even the energy to blink an eye. Nonetheless, *yoga* is overwhelmingly about cultivating or maximizing *sattva*. Another way of putting this is that *sattva* should control whatever degree of *rajas* and *tamas* are indispensable to healthy survival—sleeping for six or seven hours, for example, rather than ten, eating a modest amount of food, rather than gorging, etc.

The etymological meaning of *sattva* is the nature of being. This indicates material reality in its purest state, and is characterized by the desirable qualities of discrimination, lucidity, and illumination, since it is *sattva* that can reveal matter for what it is before *rajas* and *tamas* cause it to transform. On the other hand, *rajas* and *tamas* are the active influences in the production of the changing states of the mind and fluctuations of thought, the *vṛttis* mentioned in this *sūtra*, by disrupting the *citta*'s placid and lucid aspect of *sattva*. Vyāsa states that when *rajas* and *tamas* become activated, the mind is attracted to thoughts of the sense objects.[44] But both direct the consciousness of the soul, the pure *puruṣa* self, outward, drawing it into the external world and thus into awareness of action and reaction, the cycle of birth and death, in short, *saṁsāra*.[45] When all trace of *tamas* and *rajas* is stilled, however, the mind attains the highest potential of its nature, which is *sattva*, illumination, peacefulness, and discernment.

When the *citta* mind attains the state of *sattva*, the distinction between the ultimate conscious principle, the *puruṣa* soul, and even the purest and most subtle (but nonetheless unconscious) states of *prakṛti*, matter, become revealed. *Buddhi*, intelligence (the subtlest product of *prakṛti*), is the aspect of the mind that produces such discrimination when manifesting its highest potential of *sattva* and suppressing its inherent potential of *rajas* and *tamas*. When freed from the obscuration of these other two debilitating *guṇas*, which divert consciousness from its source, *puruṣa*, and into the external world of objects and internal world of thought, the pure *sattva* nature of the mind redirects consciousness inward toward this inner self. It is like a mirror that, freed from the coverings of dirt, can now reflect things clearly, say the commentators, and can ultimately reflect the true nature of the soul back to itself as it is without distortion. The ensuing state of contemplation is known as *samprajñāta-samādhi*, which, while not the ultimate level of *samādhi*, is the highest level of discriminative thought. In short, the goal of *yoga* is to eliminate, that is, still, the potential of *rajas* and *tamas*, and allow the full potential *sattva* nature of the mind to manifest. This is another way of conceptualizing the *citta-vṛtti-nirodha* of this verse.

The means prescribed by Patañjali to still the states of mind or fluctuations of thought is meditative concentration, defined as keeping the mind fixed on any particular object of choice without distraction. By concentration, the distracting influences of *rajas* and *tamas* are suppressed, and the *sattva* aspect of the mind can manifest to its full potential. Since *sattva* is by nature discriminating, it recognizes the distinction between *puruṣa* and *prakṛti*, the soul and matter, when not distracted by the other two *guṇas*. But, since *sattva* is also by nature luminous and lucid, it is able to reflect the soul in an undistorted way, once the disruptive presences of *rajas* and *tamas* have been stilled, and thus the soul becomes aware of itself in the mirror of the mind, so to speak. Once the dust has been removed, a person can see his or her true face in the mirror. One of the goals of *yoga* is for the mind to develop such discrimination and to reflect the true image of the soul to itself.

The commentators point out, however, that the very faculty of discrimination—even its ability to distinguish between matter and spirit—is nonetheless a feature of the *guṇa* of *sattva*, and *sattva* itself is still an aspect of *prakṛti* matter. The point is that discrimination is not a function of the soul, the innermost conscious self. The soul, notes Vyāsa, the pure and eternal power of consciousness, never changes—a fundamental axiom of Indic thought in general; it does not transform when in contact with states of mind. Rather, consciousness passively pervades and illuminates objects, whether in the form of gross external sense objects or subtle internal thoughts including the higher stage of discrimination, just as light passively reveals gross and subtle objects in a dark room and yet is not affected by them. Hariharānanda points out that the consciousness of the soul, *citi-śakti*, is pure, infinite, immutable, detached, and illuminating. Therefore, as Vijñānabhikṣu outlined in the last *sūtra*, discriminative intelligence, even the ultimate pure *sāttvic* act of discrimination, which is recognition of the distinction between the soul and the subtlest aspect of matter, although indispensable in the *yogī*'s progress, still connects the soul to matter albeit in its subtlest aspect. It, too, must eventually be transcended for full liberation to manifest. As Śaṅkara puts it, the mind sees the limitation in its own nature and deconstructs itself. When lead is burned with gold, says Bhoja Rāja, it not only burns away the impurities in gold, but burns itself away too; discrimination discerns that it itself is not the final aspect of being and pushes the *citta* to dissolve itself and transcend discerning thought altogether so as to reveal the ultimate consciousness beyond. There is thus a still higher goal in *yoga* beyond discrimination.

When the mind restrains even the ability to discriminate, continues Vyāsa, and exists in an inactive state where all thoughts remain only in potential but not active form, in other words, when all thoughts have been stilled (*nirodha*), one has reached a state of mind where nothing is cognized—all cognition, after all, is connected to some external reality (since cognition requires a subject, the cognizer, and an object of cognition distinct from or external to this subject). With no further distractions including discrimination and even the reflection of itself in the mirror of the *sāttvic buddhi* intelligence, consciousness can now abide in its own autonomous nature, the actual soul itself, *puruṣa*. This is the *samādhi* called *asamprajñāta*, the state of awareness in which nothing can be discerned except the pure self. In this stage, the mind, which is ultimately an interface between the *pu-*

ruṣa and the external world, becomes redundant and can be discarded by the *yogī* upon attaining full liberation.[46] This is the ultimate goal of *yoga* and thus of human existence. This stage, however, must be preceded by *samprajñāta-samādhi*, uninterrupted meditation, that is, concentration on an external object (which, by definition is a product of matter) so that the states of mind and fluctuations of thought mentioned in this *sūtra* can first be fully stilled.

Bhoja Rāja raises a possible objection to the existence of *puruṣa*, the soul, which is most likely an implicit reference to Buddhism (although it could in principle apply to the Nyāya and Vaiśeṣika schools). If the soul, or pure consciousness, has no object of consciousness, then would it not cease to exist altogether, like fire ceases to exist when the wood upholding it is destroyed? In other words, if the *vṛttis*, fluctuations of thought, are eliminated, then what would consciousness be conscious of? Buddhists hold that the human persona consists of five sheaths, *skandhas*,[47] one of which is consciousness itself, but none of these are eternal or autonomous as almost all Hindu philosophical thought considers the *puruṣa*, or conscious self, to be. There is thus a fundamental and intractable difference between Buddhism and Hindu and Jain philosophies on this point.

For Buddhists, when the objects of consciousness are removed, so is consciousness. There is thus no ultimate, eternal, essential entity such as a *puruṣa*, soul, that is separable from an object of consciousness; indeed, clinging to such notions of an autonomous self is the very cause of *saṁsāra*. Buddhist theologians used the analogy of the wood and fire mentioned by Bhoja Rāja to argue that consciousness is generated by an object. It is not an entity sui generis with an independent existence—one cannot have consciousness that is not conscious of some object, any more than one can have fire without a substratum such as wood.[48] Even the orthodox Nyāya and Vaiśeṣika schools, which do accept the existence of an autonomous *puruṣa*, hold that when the *puruṣa* becomes liberated and uncoupled from the mind and the objects of the senses, it ceases to be conscious. They, too, hold that consciousness requires contact with the mind as an external object in order to manifest in the *ātman*; it does not manifest independently.[49] To answer such objections, says Bhoja Rāja, Patañjali offers the next *sūtra*.

तदा द्रष्टुः स्वरूपेऽवस्थानम ॥३॥

I.3 tadā draṣṭuḥ svarūpe 'vasthānam

tadā, then, at that point; *draṣṭuḥ*, of the seer, of the soul; *svarūpe*, in its own real essential nature; *avasthānam*, abiding, remaining, being absorbed in

When that is accomplished, the seer abides in its own true nature.

There are various terms in Hindu philosophical thought to refer to the soul according to context or the partiality of different texts and schools, *ātman* being perhaps the most commonly encountered.[50] The Yoga tradition in general favors *puruṣa*, but Patañjali here uses (the genitive case of) *draṣṭṛ*, the seer (from the root *dṛś*, to see), a term he uses on several occasions throughout the text, and, indeed, along with other cognates of the root *dṛś*, is used almost as often as *puruṣa*.[51] By seeing, he does not intend the gross power of sight as manifest through the physical organ of sight but as a metaphor for consciousness itself, which "sees" in the sense of exhibiting awareness.

Having stated in the last *sūtra* that *yoga* means the cessation of all thought, Patañjali now immediately reassures his audience. Some might worry that cessation of thought—the elimination of all objects of consciousness—entails the cessation of the subject of consciousness, *puruṣa*, itself. After all, our only experience of reality is one mediated by the thinking process. Does the elimination of thought entail the elimination of experience and of existence itself? *Is* it existential suicide? What happens to the *puruṣa* self, asks Vyāsa, when the mind is void of content, as prescribed in the last *sūtra*?

Vijñānabhikṣu rhetorically considers three possibilities that might transpire once all the *vṛttis*, states of mind, have been removed: (1) Does the *puruṣa* soul remain as pure consciousness that is conscious only of itself? (2) Does it remain unconscious, like a log of wood (becoming conscious only when confronted by a state of mind, as held by the followers of the Nyāya and Vaiśeṣika schools)?[52] or (3) Does it cease to exist like a lamp on the destruction of the wick (as held by followers of the materialistic Cārvāka school[53])? The Yoga school subscribes to the first view. Once freed from its association with the states of the mind, the soul can abide in its own nature, the highest state of pure consciousness, *asamprajñāta-samādhi*. It is devoid even of knowledge, says Vijñānabhikṣu, since knowledge implies an object of knowledge and thus requires a connection with the states of mind and the external world.

In fact, Vyāsa and the commentators make the point that the soul has always abided in its own nature, even though, when it is absorbed in the outgoing mind and the world of thoughts and sense objects, it appears not to be. The nature of the soul is pure consciousness, just as, says Śaṅkara, the nature of the sun is and has always been to shine. It needs no external instrument to shine, nor does it exert any effort to do so; indeed, it has no alternative but to shine. Similarly, it is the inherent and inescapable nature of *puruṣa* to be conscious.

To illustrate the nature of the soul as pure consciousness alone, devoid of content, the commentators often refer to the example of a pure transparent crystal used frequently (and variously) in philosophical discourse to illustrate the relationship between consciousness and the mind (or between the mind and its object). When a red flower is placed next to a crystal, the flower's color is reflected in the crystal, and so the crystal itself appears to be red. The true nature of the crystal, however, is never actually red, nor is it affected or changed by the flower in any way—even while it reflects the flower—nor does it disappear when the flower is removed.[54] Similarly, consciousness reflects or illuminates external objects and internal thoughts, *vṛttis*, but is not itself affected by them. *Puruṣa*, although an autonomous entity separable from the *citta* with its *vṛttis* placed in its vicinity, is as if colored by them. Since its awareness animates the *citta*, which is "colored," it is consequently (and understandably) misidentified with the *vṛttis* by the *citta*. But in actuality it is not tainted by them, nor does it disappear upon the disappearance of the objects of consciousness. As a crystal is essentially an autonomous entity separable from the red flower placed in its vicinity and retains its pure transparent nature when separated from the flower, so consciousness is an autonomous entity separable from the *citta* with its *vṛttis* placed in its vicinity, and thus retains its pure nature of awareness when detached from the *citta* through the practice of *yoga*. The commentaries frequently utilize another example favored by the Vedānta school to illustrate a related point: Mother-of-pearl does not give up its own essential nature simply because someone mistakes it for the actual pearl itself. Likewise, consciousness does not change its nature simply because it may be confounded with the physical body or the changing states of the mind and intelligence.

The *Śānti-parvan* section of the *Mahābhārata* abounds in similes illustrating the continued existence of *puruṣa* when apart from its *prākṛtic* encapsulation.[55] It is like a silkworm that continues to exist after the destruction of the cell made by its threads, a deer that abandons its horn or a snake its slough after shedding it, a bird that goes elsewhere when the tree on which it is perched falls (XII 212.47–49), or a fish and the water that surrounds it (XII 303.17). Elsewhere, the epic compares the direct vision of the soul within the body indicated by this *sūtra* to the perception of a lamp blazing forth from a pot (XII 187.44), the effulgent sun, a smokeless flame, a streak of lightning in the sky (XII 232.18), or the streak of gold in a stone (XII 198.4).

वृत्तिसारूप्यम् इतरत्र ॥ ४ ॥

I.4 vṛtti-sārūpyam itaratra

vṛtti, fluctuation; *sārūpyam*, identification;
itaratra, otherwise, at other times

Otherwise, at other times, [the seer] is absorbed in the changing states [of the mind].

Patañjali states here that at other times—that is, when not abiding in its own nature as pure consciousness devoid of content—the seer is absorbed, *sārūpyam*, in the *vṛttis*, the mind's changing states. Vyāsa calls the soul the master and the mind its property: He compares the mind to a magnet that attracts iron within its proximity—the consciousness of *puruṣa*. The mind serves its master, the soul, by presenting objects of experience in the form of *vṛttis*. When these ever-changing states of mind are presented to the soul, the soul becomes conscious of them, but is mistakenly identified with them by the *citta*, and thereby appears affected by them. This misidentification, or ignorance, *avidyā*, is the cause of the soul's apparent bondage in the physical world of matter. Vācaspati Miśra repeats the analogy of someone looking in a dirty mirror, identifying with the dirty reflection, and then becoming anxious thinking he or she is dirty. Likewise, when one is not aware of the distinction between consciousness and the mind, one wrongly attributes the states of the mind to the self. The cause of the person's anxiety, frustrations, and experiences is misidentification with something that he or she is not.

The notion of misidentifying the true self with a false reflection goes back to the Upaniṣads. In the *Chāndogya Upaniṣad* (VIII.8–12), there is a charming narrative about Indra, lord of the celestials, and Virocaṇa, lord of the demons. Upon hearing that by attaining the *ātman*, one conquers the universe,[56] the two rivals approached the sage Prajāpati for instruction as to where to find this *ātman*. Perceiving their misguided intent for this enterprise (their interest was in gaining control over the universe, for which the gods and demons are perennially battling), Prajāpati decides to test them. He tells them that they can find the *ātman* by looking into a pan of water. Peering into the waters, the two see their bodies reflected back. They take their leave, thinking that their bodies are this *ātman*, and, while Virocaṇa remains content with this surface realization, Indra sees the inadequacy of this view of the *ātman* and so returns to Prajāpati. "I see no worth in this," he complains, "for this self will die when the body dies." Prajāpati then takes him through progressively more subtle understandings of the self until he teaches him the true nature of *ātman*.

Although the mind is actually inert and unconscious, say the commentators, as a result of being permeated by the consciousness of the soul, its states and fluctuations appear to be states of the true self and are as if experienced by the self. (Recall the analogy of a dark object appearing to be luminous due to contact with an illuminating lamp.) And so, says Vācaspati Miśra, the soul, which has no misconceptions, appears to have misconceptions and, although completely pure and transcendent, appears to be affected by mundane states of mind such as pleasure, pain, or delusion. This is like the phenomenon of a lake appearing to have trees on it due to the reflection of the trees on its bank, says Vijñānabhikṣu. Bhoja Rāja gives the well-known illustration of the moon appearing to be altered and rippled when reflected on rippling water, but it is the water, not the moon, that constantly fluctuates due to the wind. Similarly, the mind is constantly experiencing and processing the forms of sense objects through the senses. It is thus constantly changing, like the flame of a candle, says Vijñānabhikṣu, and, depending on the experiences of the moment, producing temporary states such as happiness, distress, etc. The self, although pure, is then misidentified with these changing states of the mind, due to proximity, and appears also to be affected. It seems to experience the emotions of the mind triggered by the senses and their objects, and thus to be the enjoyer or sufferer of the things of this world. In reality it is not affected, any more than the moon is affected by the ripples on its reflection in water. Vijñānabhikṣu quotes the *Gītā*: "One who sees that all activities are being performed by *prakṛti*, and that the self is not the doer, truly sees" (XIII.29).[57]

Śaṅkara here alludes to the image of a dancing girl in the *Sāṅkhya Kārikās*, the primary text for the Sāṅkhya school: "As a dancer ceases from the dance after having been seen by the audience, so also *prakṛti* ceases after having manifested herself to the *puruṣa*" (LIX). In the same vein, a more modern analogy comes to mind for the process by which *prakṛti* is conjoined with *puruṣa*. Consider a group of people watching a film. The film itself consists of just a sequence of inert flickering images and sounds, which are nothing more than light particles and frequency waves—material energy. The people watching the film, however, can become so absorbed in this spectacle of light and sound that they forget their own existence. If the film is a good one, two or three hours can pass during which the viewers forget about their real lives and personal issues they are undergoing, such as mental anxieties or fears, or bodily needs or aches and pains. Moreover, the viewers can become so wrapped up in the illusory world of the film that they experience, let us suppose, sadness when the hero or heroine is killed, or happiness when hero and heroine live happily ever after. In other words, the viewers forget their own separate existences and experience emotions produced by intense identification with the illusory and separate world of the film. Indeed, a good performance (and this is also the case in classical Hindu dramaturgy) aims to stir precisely such absorption and identification. When the film is over, the viewers are thrust back into their own realities—they are suddenly returned to the world of their own problems, perhaps they become aware of being hungry or thirsty.

In the same way, due to the mind's ignorance and illusion, the soul appears absorbed in the lights and sounds and emotions of the external objective world and forgetful of its own real nature as pure consciousness, even though it is merely the witness of all these, which are actually taking place in the mind's *vṛttis*. *Yoga* is about stilling the *vṛttis,* stopping the film midway so that the mind can realize that the emotions, fears, happiness, pains, births and deaths, etc., it has been experiencing do not exist in the soul but are the inert flickerings and permutations of the material spectacle. Thus *yoga* is ultimately about liberation from the external material world, or, in traditional Hindu terms, from *saṁsāra,* the cycle of birth and death.

Vācaspati Miśra raises the question of the cause of the soul's association with the mind in the first place, in other words, the cause of ignorance. It is eternal, he answers, like the relationship between seed and sprout. Almost all schools of Indic philosophy conceive of ignorance as eternal and do not speculate over any first impetus that caused the individual to be associated with ignorance and *saṁsāra*. As the Buddha is reputed to have said, if a man is shot by an arrow, it is useless to inquire as to the nature of the arrow, its point of origin, etc. One should more profitably first remove the arrow.[58] Likewise, for one drowning in the ocean of birth and death, *saṁsāra,* it is fruitless to speculate as to how one originally fell in; it would be more productive to find first a means to get out. Such a means, of course, is *yoga*.

वृत्तयः पञ्चतय्यः क्लिष्टाक्लिष्टाः ॥ ५ ॥

I.5 vṛttayaḥ pañcatayyaḥ kliṣṭākliṣṭāḥ

vṛttayaḥ, the changing states of mind; *pañcatayyaḥ,* fivefold;
kliṣṭa, detrimental, harmful, damaging, afflicted;
akliṣṭāḥ, nondetrimental, unafflicted

There are five kinds of changing states of the mind, and they are either detrimental or nondetrimental [to the practice of *yoga*].

Patañjali defined *yoga* in I.2 as *citta-vṛtti-nirodha* and now dedicates *sūtras* I.5–12 to discussing the *vṛttis* and I.13–16 to discussing *nirodha.* We here get a sense of the systematic nature of the *sūtra* traditions, in contrast to the more spontaneous but unsystematic nature of the earlier Upaniṣadic corpus from which a number of knowledge systems stemmed. As has been noted, *vṛtti* is used frequently throughout the *Yoga Sūtras* essentially to refer to any sensual impression, thought, idea, cognition, psychic activity, or mental state whatsoever. Since the mind is never static but always active and changing, *vṛttis* are constantly being produced and thus constantly absorb the consciousness of *puruṣa* away from its own pure nature, channeling it out into the realm of subtle or gross *prakṛti.* Vijñānabhikṣu compares *vṛttis* to flames of a fire or waves of the sea. In other words, if the *citta* is the sea, the *vṛttis* are its waves, the never-ending but ever-changing temporary forms and permutations produced by the constant flux of the tides, undercurrents, and eddies of the *citta.* In I.2, Patañjali defined *yoga* as the complete cessation of all *vṛttis.* Here, he addresses the consequent question: What are these *vṛttis* that must be eliminated? There are five categories, *pañcatayyaḥ,* of *vṛttis* (which will be discussed in the following *sūtras*); Patañjali indicates that these can be either *akliṣṭa,* conducive (at least initially) to the ultimate goal of *yoga,* or *kliṣṭa,* detrimental.

Vyāsa states that the detrimental *vṛttis* are caused by the five *kleśas,* the impediments to the practice of *yoga,* ignorance, ego, attachment, aversion, and clinging to life, that will be discussed in II.3. The term for detrimental, *kliṣṭa,* comes from the same root as *kleśa* (*kliś,* to trouble or torment). These types of mental states are detrimental to the goals of *yoga* because they are the fertile soil from which the seeds of *karma* sprout; the *kliṣṭa-vṛttis* culminate in bondage. They are essentially the products of *rajas* and *tamas. Akliṣṭa-vṛttis* are *sāttvic* and have the opposite effect; they are born of insight and culminate in liberation. When under the influence of the detrimental *vṛttis,* the mind becomes attracted or repelled by sense objects drawing its attention. In its attempt to attain that which attracts it, and avoid that which repels it, the mind provokes action, *karma,* which initiates a vicious reactive cycle.

Karma, from the root *kṛ,* to do or make, literally means work, but inherent in the Indic concept of work, or any type of activity, is the notion that every action breeds a reaction.[59] Thus *karma* refers not only to an initial act, whether benevolent or malicious, but also to the reaction it produces (pleasant or unpleasant in accordance with the original act), which ripens for the actor either in this life or a future one. Hence (as will be seen in II.13–14), people are born into different socioeconomic situations, and pleasant or unpleasant things happen to them throughout life in accordance with their own previous actions.

This cycle of action and reaction, or *saṁsāra*, is potentially eternal and unlimited since not only does any one single act breed a reaction, but the actor must then react to this reaction, causing a rereaction, which in term fructifies and provokes rerereactions, and so on ad infinitum. Thus, since the vicious cycle of action and reaction for just one solitary momentary act is potentially unlimited, and since one has to act at every moment of one's life (even blinking or breathing is an act), the storehouse of *karma* is literally unlimited. Since these reactions and rereactions cannot possibly be fitted into one life, they spill over from one lifetime to the next. It is in an attempt to portray the sheer unlimited and eternal productive power of *karma* that Indic thinkers, both Hindu and Buddhist, use such metaphors as the ocean of birth and death. Thus, *karma,* which keeps consciousness bound to the external world and forgetful of its own nature, is generated by the *vṛttis,* and the *vṛttis,* in turn, are produced by the *kleśas.*

The *akliṣṭa* nondetrimental mental *vṛttis,* on the other hand, are produced by the *sāttvic* faculty of discrimination that seeks to control the influence of *rajas* and *tamas* and thereby the detrimental *vṛttis* that they produce. Vyāsa notes that this type of *vṛtti* is beneficial even if situated in a stream of detrimental *vṛttis*.[60] In other words, for the novice struggling to control his or her mind, even if the emergence of *sattva* occurs only periodically, it is always a beneficial occurence, and it can be gradually increased and strengthened by a *yogic* lifestyle. The reverse also holds true, adds Vyāsa: Detrimental *vṛttis* also can surface periodically in a predominantly *sāttvic citta* (hence the *Gītā*'s statement in II.60 that the senses can carry away the mind even of a man of discrimination).

Vācaspati Miśra mentions activities such as the practice of *yoga* and the cultivation of desirelessness born from the study of scripture as nondetrimental, that is, mental activities beneficial to the goal of *yoga*. These actions, like any actions, produce seeds of reactions and create *saṁskāras* (discussed further below), but these seeds are *sāttvic* and beneficial to the path of *yoga* and the ultimate goal of *samādhi*. In time, and with practice, these seeds accumulate such that they eventually transform the nature of the mind. The mind then becomes more and more *sāttvic*, or illuminated and contemplative, such that the beneficial *vṛttis* eventually automatically suppress any stirrings of *rajas* and *tamas*—the detrimental *vṛttis*—until the latter remain only as inactive potencies. When the *citta* manifests its pure *sattva* potential, it becomes "like" the *ātman*, says Vyāsa. He means that, becoming aware of the true nature of reality, it no longer distracts the *puruṣa* with permutations of *prakṛti*, the world of *saṁsāra*, but provides it insight into its true nature and reflects *puruṣa* undistorted, allowing it to contemplate its true nature as per the mirror analogy.

Rāmānanda Sarasvatī notes here that, essentially, the *citta* mind is nothing but *saṁskāras*, mental imprints or impressions (not to be confused with *saṁsāra*, the cycle of birth and death). *Saṁskāras* are a very important feature of Yoga psychology: Every sensual experience or mental thought that has ever been experienced forms a *saṁskāra*, an imprint, in the *citta* mind. Essentially, any *vṛtti* leaves its copy on the *citta* before fading away, like a sound is imprinted on a tape recorder or an image on film. The mind is thus a storehouse of these recorded *saṁskāras*, deposited and accumulated in the *citta* over countless lifetimes. However, it is important to note that these *saṁskāras* are not just passive imprints but vibrant latent impulses that can activate under conducive circumstances and exert influence on a person's thoughts and behaviors. Vyāsa notes that there is thus a cycle of *vṛttis* and *saṁskāras*. *Vṛttis*, that is, sense experiences and thoughts, etc. (and their consequent actions), are recorded in the *citta* as *saṁskāras*, and these *saṁskāras* eventually activate consciously or subliminally, producing further *vṛttis*. These *vṛttis* then provoke action with its corresponding reaction, which in turn are recorded as *saṁskāras*, and the cycle continues.

Memories in Hindu psychology, as we will see in I.11, are considered to be vivid *saṁskāras* from this lifetime, which are retrievable, while the notion of the subconscious in Western psychology corresponds to other less retrievable *saṁskāras* (accumulated, in Hinduism, primarily in previous lives), which remain latent as subliminal impressions. *Saṁskāras* also account for such things as personality traits, habits, compulsive and addictive behaviors, etc. For example, a particular type of experience, say smoking a cigarette, is imprinted in the *citta* as a *saṁskāra*, which then activates as a desirable memory or impulse, provoking a repetition of this activity, which is likewise recorded, and so on until a cluster or grove of *saṁskāras* of an identical or similar sort is produced in the *citta*, gaining strength with each repetition. The stronger or more dominant such a cluster of *saṁskāras* becomes, the more it activates and imposes itself upon the consciousness of the individual, demanding indulgence and perpetuating a vicious cycle that can be very hard to break. The reverse, of course, also holds true with benevolent *akliṣṭa-vṛttis*: One can become addicted, so to speak, to benevolent *yogic* activities and lifestyle by constant repetition. *Kleśas, vṛttis, saṁskāras*, and *karma* are thus all interconnected links in the chain of *saṁsāra*.

Through the practice of *yoga*, the *yogī* attempts to supplant all the *rājasic* and *tāmasic saṁskāras* with *sāttvic* ones until these, too, are restricted in the higher states of meditative concentration. This is because while *sāttvic saṁskāras*, the nondetrimental *vṛttis*, mentioned by Patañjali in this *sūtra*, are conducive to liberation, they nonetheless are still *vṛttis* and thus an external distraction to the pure consciousness of the *ātman*. Of course, as Vijñānabhikṣu points out, all *vṛttis*, including *sāttvic* ones, are ultimately detrimental from the absolute perspective of the *puruṣa*, as they bind consciousness to the world of matter, so the notions of detrimental and nondetrimental are from the relative perspective of *saṁsāra*; the detrimental (*rājasic* and *tāmasic*) *vṛttis* cause pain, and the nondetrimental (*sāttvic*) ones at least lead in the direction of liberation, even though they too must eventually be given up. Vijñānabhikṣu quotes the *Bhāgavata Purāṇa* here to make the point: "Other things [the obstacles to *yoga*] must be eliminated by *sattva*, and [then] *sattva* is eliminated by *sattva*" (XI.25.20). Also, *vṛttis* that are truly and literally *akliṣṭa*, not subject to any ignorance at all, can point only to the state of *jīvanmukta*, liberated while still embodied. This verse thus gives a clear indication that it is possible to act in the world in one's *prākṛtic* body and mind from an enlightened perspective free from ignorance.

प्रमाणविपर्ययविकल्पनिद्रास्मृतयः ॥ ६ ॥

I.6 pramāṇa-viparyaya-vikalpa-nidrā-smṛtayaḥ

pramāṇa, epistemology, source of right knowledge; *viparyaya*, error; *vikalpa*, imagination, fancy; *nidrā*, sleep; *smṛtayaḥ*, memory

[These five *vṛttis* are] right knowledge, error, imagination, sleep, and memory.

The *vṛttis*, which bind *puruṣa* to the world of *saṁsāra*, are enumerated here. Patañjali lists five distinct types of *vṛttis*. The implication, in essence, is that the human mind finds itself in one of these five states at any given moment. According to the Yoga tradition, all possible mental states that can be experienced can be categorized as manifestations of one of these five types of *vṛttis*. Any other states of mind that one might conceive of would be considered by the Yoga tradition as a subset of one of these five essential categories. The commentators reserve their comments for the ensuing *sūtras*, which explain each of these items in turn.

प्रत्यक्षानुमानागमाः प्रमाणानि ॥ ७ ॥

I.7 pratyakṣānumānāgamāḥ pramāṇāni

pratyakṣa, sense perception; *anumāna*, inference, logic; *āgamāḥ*, testimony, verbal communication; *pramāṇāni*, epistemology

Right knowledge consists of sense perception, logic, and verbal testimony.

The first of the five *vṛttis* to be discussed is *pramāṇa*, the central concern of epistemology, that is, what sources constitute valid knowledge of an object, the methods of attaining accurate information about reality.[61] Philosophy and, of course, science—Sāṅkhya, after all, sees itself as dealing with physical verifiable truths—have as their goals the attainment of knowledge about reality, so it is standard in Indic philosophical discourse for scholastics to state which methods of attaining such knowledge of reality they accept as valid. The Yoga school accepts three sources of receiving knowledge, as does the Sāṅkhya tradition (*Sāṅkhya Kārikā* IV), but other philosophical schools accept differing numbers from one to six.[62]

The first method of attaining valid knowledge listed by Patañjali is sense perception: We can know something to be true or valid if we experience it through one or more of our senses—if we see, smell, touch, hear, or taste it. So, for example, you "know" this book is real because you see it and feel it. Śaṅkara notes that sense perception, empiricism, is placed first on the list of *pramāṇas* because the other *pramāṇas* are dependent on it.[63]

Vyāsa defines sense perception as the state or condition of the mind, *vṛtti*, that apprehends both the specific (*viśeṣa*) and generic (*sāmānya*) nature of an external object through the channels of the five senses. The generic and specific nature of objects are categories especially associated with the Vaiśeṣika school of Hindu philosophy and are technical ways of attempting to analyze physical reality. The generic nature of a dog that one might happen to come upon, for example, is that it belongs to the canine species, the specific nature is that which demarcates it from other members of this generic category, that it is, let us say, a ginger Irish terrier. (Technically speaking, *viśeṣa* is what differentiates ultimate irreducible entities such as the smallest subatomic particles of matter from each other, but Vyāsa is using the term in a more general sense, since dogs, as all material objects, are made up of conglomerates of atoms.[64]) When one sees a particular dog, the mind typically apprehends both its generic and specific natures.[65] This is accomplished by the *citta* encountering a sense object through the senses and forming an impression of this object, a *vṛtti*.[66] More specifically, the *tāmasic* natures of sense objects imprint themselves upon the mind and are then illuminated in the mind by the mind's *sāttvic* nature. Due to pervading the mind, the *puruṣa*'s awareness then becomes conscious of this mental impression, as if it were taking place within itself, indistinguishable from itself. In actual fact, the impression is imprinted on the *citta*, mind, which is pervaded by consciousness.

Vācaspati Miśra raises a question here. If the impression is imprinted on the mind, which, according to the metaphysics of Yoga, is a totally separate entity from the *puruṣa* soul, then how is it that the latter is aware of it? Or, as he puts it, if an axe cuts a *khadira* tree, it is not a *plakṣa* tree that is thereby cut. In other words, if an impression is something that is made on the mind, then how does it end up being made on the *puruṣa*? Here, again, Vācaspati Miśra introduces the analogy of the mirror. It is the mind and intelligence, not the soul, that take the form of the object as a result of sense perception. According to the reflection model of awareness, consciousness is reflected in the intelligence due to their proximity and then is misidentified with the reflection by the mind. This reflection, in turn, is altered according to the form assumed by the intelligence—just as a reflection appears dirty if the mirror is dirty. Thus, since the mind and intelligence have taken the form of the object in question, consciousness sees its own reflection as containing that form. This corresponds to the analogy of the moon appearing rippled when reflected in rippling water. According to the nonreflection model, awareness simply pervades the *citta* just as it pervades the body and is misidentified as being nondifferent from the forms of *citta* in the same way as it is misidentified with the form of the body. According to either manner of conceptualization, this misidentification of the awareness of *puruṣa* with the forms of the intellect is the essence of ignorance.

Moving on to the second *pramāṇa*, source of receiving valid knowledge, mentioned by Patañjali in this *sūtra*, Vyāsa defines *anumāna*, inference, as the assumption that an object of a particular category shares the same qualities as other objects in the same category, qualities that are not shared by objects in different categories. He gives the rather clumsy example of the moon and stars, which belong to the category of moving objects because they are seen to move, but mountains belong to a category of immobile objects, because they have never been seen to move. Thus, if one sees an unfamiliar mountain or hill, one can infer that it will not move, because other known objects in this category, all mountains and hills with which one is familiar, do not move.

The more classical example of inference among Hindu logicians is that fire can be inferred from the presence of smoke. Since wherever there is smoke, there is invariably fire causing it, the presence of fire can be inferred upon the perception of smoke even if the actual fire itself is not perceived. So if one sees clouds of smoke billowing forth from a distant mountain, one can say with certainty that there must be fire on it, even if one cannot actually see the blaze itself. It is in this regard that inference, *anumāna*, differs from the first source of knowledge, *pratyakṣa*, sense perception. *Pratyakṣa* requires that one actually see the fire. In *anumāna*, the fire itself is not actually seen, but its presence is inferred from something else that is perceived, smoke.[67] The principle here is that there must always be an absolute and invariable relationship (*vyāpti*, concomitance) between the thing inferred, say, the fire, and the reason on which the inference is made, the presence of smoke—in other words, wherever there is or has ever been smoke there must at all places and at all times always be or have been fire present as its cause with no exceptions. If these conditions are met, the inference is accepted as a valid source of knowledge. If exceptions to the rule can be found, even one instance of smoke ever that does or did not have fire as its cause, then the inference is invalid.

Finally, *āgama*, verbal testimony, the third source of valid knowledge accepted by Patañjali, is the relaying of accurate information through the medium of words by a trustworthy person who has perceived or inferred the existence of an object, to someone who has not. Vyāsa describes a trustworthy person as someone whose statements cannot be contradicted. Vācaspati Miśra adds that such a person should have keen sense organs and be trustworthy and compassionate, and Vijñānabhikṣu, that a reliable or trustworthy person is one who is free from defects such as illusion, laziness, deceit, dull-wittedness, and so forth. The words of such a reliable authority enter the ear and produce an image, *vṛtti*, in the mind of the hearer that corresponds to the *vṛtti* experienced by the trustworthy person. The person receiving the information in this manner has neither personally experienced nor inferred the existence of the object of knowledge, but valid knowledge of the object is nonetheless achieved, which distinguishes this source of knowledge from the two discussed previously.

The most important category of valid knowledge in the form of *āgama*, verbal testimony, is divine scripture, which is also referred to as *śruti*,[68] that which is heard, or *śabda*, the word. Since scriptures are considered to have been uttered by trustworthy persons in the form of enlightened sages and divine beings, their status as trustworthy sources of knowledge is especially valuable. In order to elaborate on this, Vācaspati Miśra raises the issue of how sacred scriptures can be considered valid given that all accurate verbal knowledge must itself originally come either from perception or inference (hence the Cārvāka and Vaiśeṣika schools do not even consider them separate sources of knowledge[69]), but scriptures deal with certain subjects that no human being has either seen or inferred (such as the existence of heavenly realms). Vācaspati Miśra responds that the truths of scripture have been perceived by God, *Īśvara*; thus divine scripture, too, is based on perception—and God, quips Rāmānanda Sarasvatī, is surely a trustworthy person! However, Vācaspati Miśra, in his commentary to the *Sāṅkhya Kārikā* (V), precludes the blind acceptance of scripture by qualifying that revelation may be a useful means of attaining knowledge only if it has a solid foundation, contains no internal contradictions, is supported by reason, and is accepted by people in general.

Vyāsa makes a telling comment in I.32 relevant to the hierarchy of Yoga epistemology. Perception is superior to any other sources of knowledge—indeed, the other sources of knowledge are based on it. If we consider the syllogism there is fire on the mountain because there is smoke, even though the fire is not seen by direct perception and therefore an inference is required to establish its existence, this inference is dependent on perception insofar as the sign (*liṅga*) of the fire, namely, smoke, is perceived. So valid inferences are also dependent on perception. And, as indicated, verbal authority is predicated on the original perception of the object of information by the relayer of the information. Additionally, it can be argued that accepting knowledge from a verbal authority is nothing other than making an inference—one makes an inference that a verbal authority is reliable and does not counter perceivable data. Verbal authority too, then, is indirectly derived from direct perception. Therefore some schools of thought, like that associated with the materialist Cārvāka, accept the need for only one *pramāṇa*, that of sense perception. The Yoga school accepts three sources but is very clear that it considers *pratyakṣa* the highest, not just because the other *pramāṇas* depend on it, but (as will become clearer in I.49) because it is the only way of truly knowing the essential nature of an object.

Different schools of thought prioritized different *pramāṇas*. The

Nyāya school features *anumāna*, dedicating itself for centuries to refining categories of logic, and Sāṅkhya, too, was associated with this epistemology.[70] The Vedānta school occupied itself with *āgama* (*Vedānta Sūtras* I.1.3), dedicating itself to the interpretation and systematization of the Upaniṣads and the *Vedānta Sūtras* derived from them; the Mīmāṁsā school, too, prioritized *āgama* and became especially associated with developing hermeneutics, the methods of scriptural interpretation.[71] While Patañjali accepts *āgama* as a valid source of knowledge, he does not quote or even indirectly refer to a single verse from scripture in his treatise (in contrast with the *Vedānta Sūtras*, which are almost entirely composed of references from the Upaniṣads). The very fact that he categorizes *āgama* as a *vṛtti* and thus comparable in one sense with other *vṛttis* such as *viparyaya*, error, the subject of the next *sūtra*, points to correspondences with aspects of post-Enlightenment thought, namely, that verifiable (in this case *yogic*) experience trumps scripture. This has been termed a "radical mystico-yogic orientation,"[72] since, certainly, as with the Enlightenment, such claims would have challenged the mainstream Vedic authority of the day. As for *anumāna*, while Patañjali uses this source of knowledge on occasion, such as in his arguments against certain Buddhist views, (IV.14–24), clearly almost his entire thrust throughout the *sūtras* is on *pratyakṣa* as the ultimate form of knowledge. *Anumāna* and *āgama* are forms of knowledge, but mediate forms, the truths of which are indirect, where the Yoga tradition bases its claims to authoritativeness on direct, personal experience.

It is because of this orientation that *yoga* is, in my view, destined to remain a perennial source of interest to the empirical dispositions of the modern world. One must also note that there are different types of *pratyakṣa*: the commentary on the *Sāṅkhya Kārikā*, the *Yukti-dīpikā*, speaks of *yogic* perception as well as sensual perception (38.2). Indeed, several schools make a distinction between *apara-pratyakṣa*, conventional perception, and *para-pratyakṣa*, supernormal perception, or, as the *Sāṅkhya Sūtras* put it, external perception, *bāhya-pratyakṣa*, and internal perception *abāhya-pratyakṣa* (I.90).[73] As will become clearer later in the text, the perception of interest to Yoga is the latter, that of a supernormal nature. But even the startling claims of omniscience that occur later in the text are relevant only as signposts of *ex-*

periences that the *yogī* will encounter on the path of Yoga, not as articles of faith.

विपर्ययो मिथ्याज्ञानम् अतद्रूपप्रतिष्ठम् ॥८॥

I.8 viparyayo mithyā-jñānam atad-rūpa-pratiṣṭham

viparyayaḥ, error; *mithyā*, false; *jñānam*, knowledge; *atat*, not that, incorrect; *rūpa*, form; *pratiṣṭham*, established in

Error is false knowledge stemming from the incorrect apprehension [of something].

Patañjali now proceeds to the second of the five different types of *vṛttis*, error. Vyāsa defines error as considering something to be what it is not, *atad-rūpa*, a state that can be subsequently removed by true knowledge of the actual nature of the thing in question. As an example he gives the perception of two moons. After consuming alcohol, a person may see double. This error of perception nonetheless produces a *vṛtti* in the mind of this person, but this *vṛtti* differs from *vṛttis* produced by valid sources of knowledge insofar as the seeing of two moons is an apparent perception that can be contradicted and dismissed by a later accurate perception that there is only one moon in reality, whereas valid knowledge cannot be contradicted. Vijñānabhikṣu notes that error is the result of the superimposition of wrong knowledge, *mithyā-jñānam*, onto an object (in our example, an extra moon is superimposed onto the actual solitary one).

The classical example of error, especially among the followers of Vedānta, is mistaking a rope for a snake: If one happens upon a rope on the path as one is walking home at dusk, and imagines it to be a snake, one is superimposing the form of a snake upon something that is not a snake. This is error according to the Yoga school (different schools of philosophy hold differing views on what constitutes error[74]). The Nyāya school, which especially concerns itself with epistemology, the methods of accurate knowledge, has a similar definition, giving as an example of error considering mother-of-pearl as containing silver. (Specifically, Nyāya defines knowledge, *pramā*, as apprehending an object as it is, correctly identifying the attribute of that object, and error as the opposite, considering an object to have an attribute that in fact it does not have—the mother-of-pearl does not contain silver.[75]) Vyāsa considers error to be essentially the five *kleśas,* the impediments to the practice of *yoga*: ignorance (*avidyā*), ego, attachment, aversion, and clinging to life. However, *avidyā* is the root of the other *kleśas* (II.4), and we will argue in II.5 that it is a fundamentally deeper and more subconscious type of ignorance than the surface-level error represented in this *sūtra* by *viparyaya.*

शब्दज्ञानानुपाती वस्तुशून्यो विकल्पः ॥९॥

I.9 śabda-jñānānupātī vastu-śūnyo vikalpaḥ

śabda, words; *jñāna*, knowledge; *anupātī*, resulting from, followed in sequence; *vastu*, actual object; *śūnyaḥ*, devoid of; *vikalpaḥ*, conceptualization, fancy, imagination; here, figurative language

Imagination consists of the usage of words that are devoid of an actual object.

The commentators take the third type of *vṛtti,* imagination, to be metaphor, words or expressions that do not correspond to any actual physical reality, *vastu-śunya*, but are understood in common parlance, *śabda-jñāna-anupatī.* When we say "consciousness is the essence of *puruṣa*" (*caitanyaṁ puruṣasya svarūpam iti*), says Vyāsa, we are, strictly speaking, making an incorrect statement. Using the genitive case, as in the "essence of *puruṣa*," implies a distinction between the possessor and the thing possessed, as in the phrase "the cow of Citra." But consciousness is not a separate entity owned by another separate entity *puruṣa* as this phrase suggests. Consciousness is *puruṣa*, not something owned by *puruṣa.* Likewise with negative predictions such as "the *puruṣa* has the characteristic of not being born": there is not a factual positive state of "not being born"; something that does not exist has no sensible existence, yet such phrases do bear meaning. Using language in this way is *vikalpa.*

Vyāsa gives other examples of this nature,[76] but if we, along with the commentators, can extend the technical denotative range of *vikalpa* somewhat, perhaps a more straightforward example from English usage might be "the sun rises and sets" or "time flies." The sun doesn't actually either rise or set, nor is there a tangible entity called time flapping about with wings, but common usage has assigned meaning to these imaginary states of affairs, and no one bats an eye when such expressions are uttered. In other words, metaphors and similes might be considered types of *vikalpas*. Indeed, Vācaspati Miśra notes that these expressions, which, if dissected to their literal meanings, do not correspond to actual objective reality, are normal everyday expressions and ubiquitous in human language, since language is largely figurative.

In this way, although other schools, such as Nyāya and Vaiśeṣika, consider *vikalpa* to be a category of error rather than a *vṛtti* in its own right, the Yoga school considers the *vṛtti* of *vikalpa*, imagination, to differ essentially from the previous two *vṛttis*. This is because the first *vṛtti*, right knowledge, corresponds to accurate knowledge of an actual objective reality, recognized as such by others, and error corresponds to a misperception or misunderstanding of something, and therefore it is perceived as an error by other people who can see the actual nature of the misunderstood object. *Vikalpa*, on the other hand, while, like error, referring to an object that lacks actual objective physical reality, yet, unlike the *vṛtti* of error but like the *vṛtti* of right knowledge, is not based on an error of judgment and is intelligible to other people in practice, producing a *vṛtti* impression in the mind of the listener without being perceived as an error or attracting any attention. It thus paradoxically represents a meaningful expression that yet has no actual reality in the real world. It is therefore held to be a different category of *vṛtti* from *pramāṇa* or *viparyaya*.

We thus see what a meticulous thinker Patañjali is. Let us keep our eye on the ball: In order to understand what *puruṣa* is, one has to understand what it is not (I.4). It is not the mind. Therefore, Patañjali is directing very careful attention to what the mind is such that the *yogī* can be clear about what the *puruṣa* should not be identified with. The mind can be recognized by what it does. Patañjali is thus identifying the things that the mind does, that is, its functions. Since *vikalpa*, conceptual thought, does not fit into the other types of *vṛttis* such as *pramāṇa* and *viparyaya* even as it shares features of both of these, he has concluded that it must belong to a category of its own.

Vijñānabhikṣu accepts the more common understanding of this *vṛtti* of *vikalpa*—the usage of nonsensical expressions such as sky-flower, hare's horn, or son of a barren woman, which are the typical motifs in Hindu philosophical discourse that correspond to expressions in English such as pie in the sky. These are all nonexistent objects, but they nonetheless produce some sort of an intelligible *vṛtti* in the mind of the listener. It is curious that the commentators do not direct specific attention to more common aspects of imaginative thought, such as daydreaming, fantasy, make believe, and wishful thinking, which actually occupy major portions of most people's waking attention. Such things might also be considered types of *vikalpas* but, since they depend on the activation of *saṁskāras*, which are imprints of real things, they overlap with other *vṛttis*, particularly the function of memory, the fifth type of *vṛtti* discussed below, and/or error, since they have no reality.

अभावप्रत्ययालम्बना वृत्तिर्निद्रा ॥१०॥

I.10 abhāva-pratyayālambanā vṛttir nidrā

abhāva, absence; *pratyaya*, cause; *ālambanā*, support, basis; *vṛttiḥ*, state of mind; *nidrā*, sleep

Deep sleep is that state of mind which is based on an absence [of any content].

The commentators acknowledge here that there is some difference of opinion regarding whether or not sleep is an actual *vṛtti*. Based on the *Chāndogya Upaniṣad* (VI.8.1), the Vedāntins do not consider any *vṛtti* to be present in the *citta* during deep sleep, but that the *ātman*, or *puruṣa*, undisturbed by any *citta vṛtti* in the state of deep sleep, experiences *Brahman* (*Vedānta Sūtra* I.4.18; II.3.31). Vyāsa and the Yoga commentators, in contrast, view deep sleep as a type of *vṛtti* on the grounds that when one awakes, one remembers that one has either slept well or restlessly or in a stupor. One would not be able to do so, in their view, if these impressions did not relate back to a state of mind that existed during deep sleep. In Yoga psychology, memory is the product of *saṁskāra*, and *saṁskāra* is caused by experience. Therefore, the memory of having slept well must relate to a state of mind experienced during deep sleep, which is recorded in the *citta* as memory (the topic of the next *sūtra*) and remembered upon awakening. This state of mind according to this line of reasoning must therefore pertain to a category of *vṛtti* distinct from others.

It might be useful to note along with Vācaspati Miśra that the fourth *vṛtti* being discussed by Patañjali in this *sūtra* does not refer to the state of mind represented in the dream state—dream sleep corresponds to the *vṛttis* of memory (since it involves the activation of *saṁskāras*). *Nidrā,* sleep, then, refers to deep dreamless sleep. It takes place when the *tāmasic* element of the mind densely covers the *sāttvic* nature of *buddhi*, the intellect; in dream, more *rajas* is active, and this churns up past *saṁskāras*, which produce dream experiences. In deep sleep, *rajas* is inactive, and so the mind is not stimulated to assume the form of the objects of knowledge, as it does during the waking and dream states; thus *puruṣa* is conscious of darkness alone. Another way to put this is that due to the preponderance of *tamas*, there is a suppression of the other *vṛttis*. However, needless to say, while deep sleep can be considered a type of *citta-vṛtti-nirodha*, cessation of thought (at least of the four *vṛttis* other than sleep), since the *sattva* or knowledge aspect of the *citta* is smothered by *tamas*, as is any *rājasic* stirring of *citta*, this is not the *citta-vṛtti-nirodha* defined by Patañjali as the goal of *yoga* in I.2. In the *samādhi* state, *sattva* is at its maximum, and the *yogī*'s *citta-vṛtti-nirodha* occurs in full vibrant wakefulness and in complete lucidity as to the nature of reality; in deep sleep, awareness is simply aware of the dense motionless darkness of *tamas* in which it is enveloped. Additionally (and importantly), this verse informs us that consciousness is eternal; it is never "switched off," not even in deep sleep. In deep sleep, it remains fully aware, since it is eternally and inherently fully aware, but its object of awareness is (almost) pure *tamas*; hence there is nothing to recollect when one awakens (other than whether one has slept well or not).

If the *tāmasic* element that covers the intellect during deep sleep is accompanied by a measure of *sattva*, the commentators inform us, a person feels refreshed and lucid upon awakening; if accompanied by *rajas*, one feels that one has slept restlessly and one is confused and distracted; if *tamas* has almost completely dominated *sattva* and *rajas* during sleep, one feels sluggish and tired upon awakening. Pointing back to I.3 where Patañjali states that *yoga* is the cessation of all *vṛttis*, which therefore includes deep sleep as well, Vācaspati Miśra notes that sleep, too, can be controlled in *samādhi*, meditative absorption. And certainly the hagiographies of saints the world over are replete with claims that many indulged in a very minimal amount of sleep.

There are two important technical terms introduced in this *sūtra: pratyaya* and *ālambanā. Pratyaya* has a number of meanings, two of which are relevant to the *sūtras*. It can mean cause, as it is used in Buddhist sources, which is how Vācaspati Miśra takes it here (as also in I.19).[77] Elsewhere (II.20; III.2, 12, 17, 19, 35)—and it can also be read here in this sense—it refers to the image of an object imprinted on the mind, that is, a cognition, which is how it is understood in the Vedānta tradition. In Yoga cognition, the powers behind the five senses, *jñānendriyas*, flow out through the senses with the mind (as the *antaḥkaraṇa*), to grasp their objects (*pratyaya*, from *prati* + *i*, to go forth), and then imprint images of these objects on the mind (which then presents them to *puruṣa* as outlined previously via its faculty of *buddhi*). These imprints or cognitions are *pratyayas*.[78] Although sometimes used synonymously with *vṛtti* by the commentators, it differs in my understanding insofar as it represents a singular momentary imprint, while a *vṛtti* is more a flow of thoughts or images and may contain a series of *pratyayas*. The second term, *ālambana*, is the support for the mind and refers to any object upon which the *yogī* has chosen to focus or concentrate the mind. A list of possible *ālambanas* for meditation is presented by Patañjali in I.23–39.

अनुभूतविषयासंप्रमोषः स्मृतिः ॥११॥

I.11 anubhūta-viṣayāsampramoṣaḥ smṛtiḥ

anubhūta, experienced; *viṣaya*, sense objects; *asampramoṣaḥ*, not slipping away, retention; *smṛtiḥ*, memory

Memory is the retention of [images of] sense objects that have been experienced.

Vyāsa notes that memories are generated from and thus dependent on the other types of *vṛttis* described in the preceding *sūtras*: right knowledge, error, imagination, and sleep (one has memories of objects of knowledge, error, etc.). Therefore, says Vācaspati Miśra, memory is mentioned last on the list of *vṛttis*. Nonetheless, the Yoga school considers memory a *vṛtti* in its own right. Patañjali here describes memory as the retention or, more literally, the not slipping away, *asampramoṣa*, of an object of experience, *anubhūta viṣaya*. As noted, every object that has ever been experienced forms a *saṁskāra*, an imprint, in the *citta* mind. The mind forms an impression of an object, called a *pratyaya*, through the sense organs. As noted in the previous *sūtra*, a *pratyaya* is the specific content of a *vṛtti*, a unitary image like the individual still of a movie, where a *vṛtti* is more a sequence and thus a series of *pratyayas*, comparable to the reel itself containing the series of stills. Once this *pratyaya* or active image of this object is no longer of interest to the mind, it becomes an inactive, or latent, *saṁskāra*. Thus *vṛttis*, and their *pratyaya* content, are retained as *saṁskāras* when they fade.

A person approaching a red rose, for example, receives an impression through the senses of the sight and smell of a red object of a particular shape with a certain odor. This input is recognized by and imprinted on the mind as a rose, a fragrant member of the flower family. However, even after the mind has moved on to other things, this cognition or impression remains embedded in the *citta* mind in the form of a *saṁskāra*, imprint. Since the mind is exposed to numerous sense objects all the time, and has been for numerous lifetimes, there are unlimited *saṁskāras* continually being embedded in the *citta*, which are all potentially retrievable. Memory, then, the fifth and final type of *vṛtti* listed by Patañjali, consists of the retrieval of these *saṁskāras*; memories are the reactivation of the imprints of sense objects that one has experienced and recognized in the past.[79] (Vijñānabhikṣu makes a distinction here between memory and recognition.[80]) When these *saṁskāras* do not slip away (fall into the unconscious), or, in Sāṅkhyan categories, when they do not become overly covered by *tamas*, they constitute memory. The *citta* can perhaps be compared to a lake, and *saṁskāra* memories to the pebbles at the bottom of the lake. If the lake is peaceful and crystal clear (*sāttvic*), the pebbles are easily visible; if it is choppy (*rājasic*), less so; and if murky (*tāmasic*), the pebbles become very hard or impossible to perceive.

Vyāsa states that memory is of two types—real, namely, recollection of things that actually happened; and imagined, such as in dreams, which involve the spontaneous and more random activation of *saṁskāras* but are still memories of sorts. Bhoja Rāja says that the *saṁskāras* that activate during dreams do so because of the force of the impression that created them. In other words, they were vivid events. On this topic, Rāmānanda Sarasvatī raises the question that if all *saṁskāras* consist of, and only of, events or objects that have been actually experienced, then how can we account for those dreams where one might imagine oneself, for example, as having the body of an elephant? What *saṁskāras* produced these? Surely one has not had such an experience in real life. Such memories, he answers, are the result of error, which affects the dream state just as it does the waking state.

One might add that one cannot dream of, or for that matter even imagine, something that does not exist as a *saṁskāra* or set of *saṁskāras* in one's *citta*, and *saṁskāras*, in turn, correspond to something one has actually experienced. However, *saṁskāras* can be clustered together in a way that corresponds to something that has never been experienced in reality, such as a flying elephant or the horns of a hare. What is taking place in such imaginative instances is the merging together of two sets of actual *saṁskāras*; in other words, one set of memory experiences, recollections of the act of flying or of horns, are superimposed on and blended with other memory imprints, those of an elephant or a hare. (As a point of interest, in addition to the fantasy nature of most dreams, *Vedānta Sūtra* III.2.4 allows that some dreams can also serve as omens of real events.)

The Jains accept memory, *smṛti*, as a *pramāṇa* (I.6) in its own right, but this is rejected by the Hindu schools since memory does not present immediate or new knowledge, which *pramāṇa* for these philosophical schools must do, but re-presents something that has already happened in the past. However, *smṛti* is used by Hindus to refer to a category of *āgama*, sacred text, which is a *pramāṇa*. This category of *smṛti* includes in practice more or less everything other than the *śruti*, or the Vedic corpus[81]—the epics, Purāṇas, and *sūtra* traditions including Patañjali's *Yoga Sūtras*. However, since *smṛti* sacred texts present themselves, at least nominally, as dependent on or derivative from the *śruti* for their authoritativeness,[82] *smṛti* texts are not considered *pramāṇa* on the same level as *śruti*[83] in orthodox discourse, at least not officially (although in practice, it has been the *smṛti* that has determined the beliefs and practices of Hindus throughout the ages). Or, put differently, as in the Vedānta tradition, *smṛti* can be accepted as *āgama-pramāṇa* to the extent it does not conflict with the *śruti*.[84]

This concludes the discussion on what constitutes a *vṛtti*. According to Vyāsa, the five types of *vṛttis* identified by Patañjali are either experienced as pleasurable in nature, resulting in attachment (*sattva*); unpleasurable, resulting in aversion (*rajas*); or deluded, resulting in ignorance (*tamas*). Of course, as Vijñānabhikṣu notes, from the absolute perspective pleasure also results in pain, because pleasure generates attachment to the object of pleasure, and this attachment ultimately results in pain upon the loss of this object; attachment also perpetuates *saṁsāra*, as we will discover in II.2ff.

One might add here that Patañjali indicated in I.5 that these five *vṛttis* are either *kliṣṭa*, detrimental, or *akliṣṭa*, beneficial, conducive to the goal of *yoga*. Thus, for example, the *vṛtti* of sleep might be considered nondetrimental when it is not excessive but simply adequate for the well-being of the body, but detrimental when in excess of this; the *vṛtti* of memory may be nondetrimental when one keeps the goals of *yoga* in mind, but detrimental when one harps back on past sensual indulgences. Perhaps the hardest *vṛtti* to envision in this regard is how error could be *sāttvic* and *akliṣṭa*, conducive to the goal of *yoga*, but irrespective of the state of one's *citta*, if the instruments of the senses are defective error may nonetheless occur. For example, if he has poor eyesight, even the accomplished *yogī* will still perceive things erroneously and thus be subject to error. One can play around creatively with other possible scenarios of error being *akliṣṭa*: One might walk into a *yoga* studio taught by dedicated teachers grounded in Patañjali's teachings, mistaking it for a health spa, but, once there, become inspired to undertake the practices and philosophy of the system, and thus one's initial error becomes conducive to the goals of the *yoga*. There are certainly plenty of examples in the Purāṇas that might illustrate error from a *bhakti*, devotional, perspective. In the Bhāgavata tradition, the residents of Vraj, where Kṛṣṇa spent his childhood, unaware of Kṛṣṇa's divinity, mistook him to be their son, or friend, or lover, etc., but such error is highly favorable to the goal in this Yoga tradition and fundamental to its theology of *līlā*, the pastimes of the incarnation of God in the world (as well as indicative of the extraordinary past-life *yogic* attainments of those residents, which allowed them this opportunity of such intimate association with God in this form).[85] Whatever their nature, says Vyāsa, *vṛttis* must be restrained for any type of concentrative state—either *samprajñāta* or *asamprajñāta*—to take place, as Patañjali announced at the beginning of his *sūtras*.

अभ्यासवैराग्याभ्यां तन्निरोधः ॥१२॥

I.12 abhyāsa-vairāgyābhyāṁ tan-nirodhaḥ

abhyāsa, practice; *vairāgyābhyām*, dispassion, renunciation, nonattachment; *tat*, their [the *vṛtti* states of mind]; *nirodhaḥ*, controlled, restrained

[The v*ṛtti* states of mind] are stilled by practice and dispassion.

At the beginning of the text (I.2), Patañjali defined *yoga* as *citta-vṛtti-nirodha*, the restraint of the *vṛttis*, the changing states of the mind. Having explained what constitutes a *vṛtti*, he now turns his attention to *nirodha*, restraint. How, exactly, are the *vṛttis* to be restrained? In this *sūtra* he identifies two ingredients necessary for such restraint: practice and dispassion (renunciation). Vijñānabhikṣu quotes the *Gītā* here: "The mind is undoubtedly fickle and difficult to control, O Arjuna, but it can be controlled by *abhyāsa-vairāgyābhyām*, practice and dispassion" (VI.35). The same two ingredients are indicated by Patañjali in this *sūtra*. As was seen in I.6, Patañjali's typical method is to introduce a list in one *sūtra* and then explain the items on this list in the subsequent *sūtras*, so his definitions of practice and dispassion follow in the next *sūtras*.

Before proceeding to an analysis on practice and dispassion, Vyāsa notes that the stream of the *citta*, mind, can flow two ways: toward its upliftment or toward its downfall. He analogizes the mind to a river, which normally flows down the channels of the senses toward their objects and into the sea of *saṁsāra*, the cycle of birth and death. However, by dispassion toward the sense objects, the flow of this river of the mind toward the sea of *saṁsāra* is checked, and by discrimination, the current of the river is reversed and the mind flows back, away from *saṁsāra*, and toward realization of the self. By flowing along the course of discrimination, the mind leads to upliftment and ultimate liberation; contrarily, if it flows along the course of nondiscrimination in the form of sensuality, it produces *karma*, which may be good or bad depending on whether the actions the mind provokes are pious or impious, and perpetuates the vicious cycle of repeated birth and death. By practice and dispassion, the flow of the mind toward sensual attractions, which might entice the mind toward vice, becomes drastically diminished. Rather, by practice, which of course refers to the practice of *yoga*, the flow of the mind toward higher knowledge becomes unobstructed, and the mind becomes immersed in discrimination.

Another way of putting this from the perspective of the *guṇas* is that *sattva* becomes enhanced and *rajas* and *tamas* minimized. Discrimination, dispassion, and the impetus to seek a practice in order to realize Truth are inherent in the mind when its *sāttvic* potential is not overwhelmed by *rajas* and *tamas*, which are the influences provoking the flow of the mind toward sensuality. Bhoja Rāja adds that by practice and renunciation, eventually all fluctuating states of the mind, whether *sāttvic, rājasic*, or *tāmasic*, can be controlled. He understands dispassion as the realization by the wise of the negative repercussions of sensuality, which results in avoidance of it—the pursuit of sensual pleasure always bears a hidden price.

तत्र स्थितौ यत्नोऽभ्यासः ॥१३॥

I.13 tatra sthitau yatno 'bhyāsaḥ

tatra, of these [*abhyāsa* and *vairāgya*]; *sthitau*, in the matter of steadfastness; *yatnaḥ*, effort; *abhyāsaḥ*, practice

From these, practice is the effort to be fixed in concentrating the mind.

Patañjali now describes the first ingredient required to restrain the mind, *abhyāsa*, practice, and defines practice as the effort to concentrate the mind. Vyāsa, in turn, defines concentration (one-pointedness) as the peaceful flow of the mind when it has become freed from its fluctuating states or *vṛttis*. The effort to secure this state is practice. It is important to recognize that a controlled mind is not going to manifest by itself: Effort, *yatna*, is required. One is reminded here of the comment of Arjuna (who, as a warrior, had no history of serious *yoga* practice), that the mind is "harder to control than the wind" since it is "fickle, powerful, and obstinate." As noted by Vijñānabhikṣu in the last *sūtra*, Kṛṣṇa assures him that without doubt the fickle mind is hard to control, but it can be subdued with "practice and dispassion" (VI.34–35). In this *sūtra*, Patañjali indicates that this practice requires effort, and Vyāsa associates this effort with enthusiasm and vigor.

Vyāsa also uses the term *sādhana*, which typically refers to one's specific daily spiritual practices. In the context of classical *yoga*, Vācaspati Miśra understands this *sādhana* to be the eight limbs of *yoga* that will be discussed in Chapters II and III. So the *vṛttis* of the mind can be restrained when one is enthusiastic, vigorous, and steadfast in the practice of these eight steps.

The commentators reiterate that one can only hope to be concentrated or one-pointed—the mind can only flow peacefully—when its *rājasic* and *tāmasic* potential have been stilled. Practice is the effort involved in attaining this end. Rāmānanda Sarasvatī introduces the next *sūtra* by wondering how practice can ever achieve steadfastness, since it is constantly disturbed by *rājasic* and *tāmasic saṁskāras*, distracting memories and tendencies inherited from time immemorial, a question with which aspiring *yogīs* can surely relate.

स तु दीर्घकालनैरन्तर्यसत्कारासेवितो दृढभूमिः ॥१४॥

I.14 sa tu dīrgha-kāla-nairantarya-satkārāsevito dṛḍha-bhūmiḥ

saḥ, it [practice]; *tu*, but; *dīrgha*, prolonged; *kāla*, period of time; *nairantarya*, uninterruptedly; *satkāra*, reverence; *āsevitaḥ*, attended to, cultivated, practiced; *dṛḍha*, firm; *bhūmiḥ*, ground

Practice becomes firmly established when it has been cultivated uninterruptedly and with devotion over a prolonged period of time.

Patañjali here gives further specifics pertaining to what the effort underpinning practice consists of. First, in order to become unshakable, practice must be performed *nairantarya*, without interruption. One cannot take breaks from one's practice whenever one feels like it or the mind dictates and expect to attain the goal of *yoga*, which is precisely to quell such whimsical *vṛttis*. Second, one's practice must continue *dīrgha-kāla*, for a long time. One cannot attain success in a few months or even after many years of practice unless one is exceptionally dedicated. Indeed, the *Gītā* speaks of the *yogī* maintaining the *yatna*, effort, of the last *sūtra*, for many births: "Through effort and restraint, cleansed of all impurities, the *yogī* who has cultivated perfection over several lives, eventually attains the supreme destination" (VI.45). Practice is at the very least a lifelong commitment, to be undertaken, Patañjali goes on to say, *satkāra-āsevitaḥ*, with respect and devotion. One is, after all, pursuing the ultimate goal of life—realization of the innermost self—and cannot expect to attain this in a halfhearted or frivolous fashion, or in a random manner.

Vyāsa states that the practice of *yoga* becomes successful, that is, firmly established, when accompanied by austerity, celibacy, knowledge, and faith. Under these conditions, it is not immediately overwhelmed by the ingrained habits of the mind. Vācaspati Miśra calls these habits, which are *saṁskāras* that impel the mind outward into the sensual realm, "highway robbers." He acknowledges that the *sāttvic* nature of the mind—tranquillity and calmness—is often overcome by *rajas* and *tamas*, but if one maintains one's practice, then eventually the mind becomes steadfast and concentrated. If one gives up one's practice, however, one's mind immediately becomes overwhelmed again. Hence this verse indicates that the practice of *yoga* has to be cultivated uninterruptedly and with devotion for a long period of time.

If we correlate *citta* with a garden, *sattva* with a beautiful bed of fragrant and attractive flowers, and *rajas* and *tamas* with weeds and pests, then we have a useful metaphor for the practice of *yoga*. As any gardener knows, maintaining a garden takes devotion and uninterrupted weeding and pest control for a prolonged period of time. In fact, these processes can never be interrupted, since within a remarkably short period of time, even the most devotedly cultivated garden becomes overwhelmed by weeds and pests; if left unattended, all one's hard work is easily undone.

Likewise with *yoga*: The cultivation of *sattva* takes constant attention and cultivation—the minute the *yogī* relaxes his or her practices and vigilance, Vācaspati Miśra's highway robbers of *rājasic* and *tāmasic saṁskāras* overwhelm the *sāttvic* qualities so arduously developed. This is because, like weeds, *saṁskāras* are never actually eliminated or destroyed; they remain in a latent subconscious state and thus can become activated at any moment, unless constantly curtailed (although, as will be discussed below, they can be "burnt" by certain practices, rendering them inoperable); hence Patañjali's notion of devoted uninterruptedness over a prolonged period.

As an aside, many Hindu *gurus* and *yogīs* have been embroiled in scandals that have brought disrepute to the transplantation of *yoga* and other Indic spiritual systems to the West. This *sūtra* provides a mechanism of interpreting such occurrences. If one reads the early hagiographies of many Hindu *gurus* whose integrity was later found compromised, one is struck by the intensity, devotedness, and accomplishments of their initial practices. Nonetheless, however accomplished a *yogī* may become, if he or she abandons the practices of *yoga* under the notion of being enlightened or of having arrived at a point beyond the need of practice, it may be only a matter of time before past *saṁskāras*, including those of past sensual indulgences, now unimpeded by practice, begin to surface. The result is scandal and traumatized disciples. There is no flower bed, however perfected, that can counteract the relentless emergence of weeds if left unattended. As Patañjali will discuss later in the text, as long as one is embodied, *saṁskāras* remain latent, and therefore potential, in the *citta*. Hence one can read this *sūtra* as indicating that since the practices of *yoga* must be uninterrupted, one would be wise to politely avoid *yogīs* or *gurus* who claim to have attained a state of enlightenment such that they have transcended the need for the practice and renunciation prescribed by Patañjali here.

दृष्टानुश्रविकविषयवितृष्णस्य वशीकारसंज्ञा वैराग्यम् ॥१५॥

I.15 dṛṣṭānuśravika-viṣaya-vitṛṣṇasya vaśīkāra-saṁjñā vairāgyam dṛṣṭa, visible, perceptible; *anuśravika*, heard about [from Vedic scriptural revelation]; *viṣaya*, sensual objects; *vitṛṣṇasya*, from one who is freed from craving; *vaśīkāra*, subdue, exert control; *saṁjñā*, consciousness; *vairāgyam*, renunciation, dispassion

Dispassion is the controlled consciousness of one who is without craving for sense objects, whether these are actually perceived, or described [in scripture].

After defining practice, Patañjali turns to the second element in the restraint of the mind, *vairāgyam*, dispassion, renunciation. He defines dispassion as the absence of craving for sense objects, *viṣaya*. As examples of sense objects, Vyāsa mentions members of the opposite sex, food, drink, and power. He notes that such dispassion or detachment precludes the inclination either to accept or reject such objects, even when they are available. That renunciation involves disinterest toward indulging in sense objects is straightforward, but Vyāsa's observation that it also involves disinterest to overly rejecting them merits attention. Too much energy and fanfare dedicated to overly rejecting sense objects can often indicate a hidden attachment to those very objects that is being overcompensated for. Real detachment is indifference to sense objects whether in their absence or presence. As Vācaspati Miśra points out, one might be free from desires for objects because one knows nothing about them, but this does not qualify as dispassion; dispassion is indifference to objects even when these are available. *Vaśīkāra* means to have control over; thus Bhoja Rāja states, with regard to desires, "I am not in their control—they are in my control."

With II.33–34 in mind, Vyāsa states that one who is renounced understands the defects of sensuality from reflection on its consequences, or, as Vijñānabhikṣu puts it, renunciation arises specifically from perceiving the defects of indulging in the objects of the senses, in other words, from discrimination. This is significant: The tradition does not take the position that sensual desires somehow disappear; desires are imprints of past pleasurable experiences that are recorded in the *citta* as *saṁskāras*. *Saṁskāras* never disappear; they always remain latent (except in the exceptional cases when they are burnt by *yogic* practice). When they reactivate, they create desires, the impulse to re-create the pleasurable experience (the desire to avoid unpleasant experiences works along parallel lines). As Vācaspati Miśra notes, the power of renunciation comes not from being free from desires but from being indifferent to them.

The discriminating *yogī* cultivates this indifference by recognizing that any sensual gratification, irrespective of how pleasurable, is temporary. Sooner or later, one is separated from the object of gratification and consequently experiences frustration. Through discrimination, one recognizes this inherent defect of sensual indulgence. One is also astute enough to realize realistically that there is always a *karmic* price to pay for the pursuit of pleasure (all actions, good or bad, when based on seeking gratification, generate correspondingly good or bad reactions and thus perpetuate *saṁsāra*). Simply put, renunciation "consists in the idea of 'enough'" of this sense gratification, says Vijñānabhikṣu.[86] One becomes exhausted with the unending pursuit of seeking fulfillment in this way but attaining only temporary and unfulfilling (from an ultimate perspective) pleasures. Therefore, the wise strive for detachment and the eternal experience of the soul rather than the never-ending pursuit of ephemeral pleasure. This is a recurring theme in the *Gītā*:

> Detached from the external contact [of the senses with their objects] a person finds happiness in the *ātman*. Such a person, engaged in practicing the *yoga* of *Brahman* [the Absolute Truth], experiences eternal happiness. Material pleasures are born from the contact [of the senses with the sense objects]; they have a beginning and an end, and so they are the source of unhappiness. The wise do not delight in them. (V.21–22)

However, Vijñānabhikṣu also cautions that renunciation in and of itself does not guarantee success in *yoga*, and mentions the case of the sage Saubhari. The *Bhāgavata Purāṇa* (IX.6.40ff) tells the story of a sage whose desire for renunciation was so intense that he resolved to meditate under water so as to eliminate all the distractions of the sensual temptations of the world. However, he happened to open his eyes one day and notice two fish mating. This activated latent erotic *saṁskāras* in his own mind (perhaps from experiences recorded from previous births), and he again became overwhelmed with fantasies of sexual enjoyment, abandoned his meditation, and returned to worldly life. As noted, in normal circumstances, *saṁskāras* are not destroyed; they remain latent until suitable conditions arise for reactivation. Therefore, excessive renunciation in and of itself does not necessarily guarantee that one is freed from the potential reemergence of undesirable *saṁskāras*.

Vijñānabhikṣu outlines various stages of detachment: One begins by making an effort to break attachment; next one determines that detachment has been accomplished toward certain objects, while others still need some work; and then, when detachment from all the external objects of the senses has been achieved, one begins to target internal attachments. These include such things as the attachment to honor and respect, and the opposite, the dislike of dishonor and disrespect. One may be externally very renounced and austere but internally be very attached to the prestige renunciation can bring (for example, the reputation of being a great *yogī*, or of having many followers). In this way, one slowly starves the *karmāśaya*, the storehouse of *karma* discussed in II.12, by giving up all desires for the fruits of actions, thereby preventing the further planting of *karmic* seeds.

The commentators elaborate on Patañjali's comment here that there are two types of sense objects: There are the *dṛṣṭa*, those seen in this world, the everyday sensual pleasures of life; and those that are not seen here but are *anuśravika*, heard about (*anu* + *śru* = to hear from authorities). This is a reference to Vedic texts,[87] more commonly referred to as *śruti* (from the same root), texts that are transmitted and recited orally, and thus heard, and therefore is an indirect reference to the pleasures of the celestial realms referred to in these texts. Vyāsa states that detachment requires that one be indifferent also to the heavenly enticements described in the Vedas and such texts (as well as attainments from *yoga* practice such as those outlined in the next verse, and the mystic powers outlined in Chapter III).

The celestial realms mentioned in various Sanskrit literature as early as the Vedic hymns, but more elaborately in the Purāṇas, point to other worlds or dimensions within the material universe where the level of enjoyment, duration of life span, and quality of experience far exceed anything available in this world. These worlds are the destination of the pious—that is, the good *karma* accrued by the performance of *dharma*, socioreligious duty, can translate into sojourns in these celestial realms. By the later Upaniṣadic period, however, these realms were perceived to have a defect in that they, too, involve embodied existence within the confines of *saṁsāra*—they are not the ultimate or permanent destination of the soul. When the good *karma*, or righteous deeds, of the pious that earned them a place in these realms has expired, such souls return again to this world. Good *karma* is accumulated like money in the bank. When one starts to draw on one's credit, however much one has accumulated, sooner or later the account will be depleted. Likewise, upon attaining the celestial realms as a result of the accumulation of merit while on earth, souls are able to remain there until their karmic bank account is inevitably depleted, at which point they again return to this world where suffering is much more pronounced.

In this *sūtra*, Patañjali is implicitly criticizing aspects of Vedic ritualism, which, while on the decline due to the rise of the ascetic traditions including Buddhism and the great theistic devotional traditions of Vaiṣṇavism and Śaivism, would still have been a mainstream religious presence in his day. One of the expressed goals of Vedic ritualism is the obtainment of the good things in life in this world, followed by the pleasures of the celestial realms in the next.[88] The Vedic hymns often express a lusty desire for very earthly boons such as cows, offspring, victory over enemies, etc., which the sacrificer in the earlier Vedic period attempted to obtain by cajoling the gods who controlled such things and, in the middle Vedic period, by mastering the technology of ritual such that the gods were constrained to bestow these boons.[89]

One can read the entire religious and philosophical history of post-Vedic India as a rejection of Vedic ritualism by communities that were eventually to become heterodox to the Vedic matrix—the Buddhists and Jains—and as a demotion or radical reinterpretation of it by those, such as Patañjali and the Yoga school, who remained in the orthodox Vedic fold. Among this latter category, a sometimes quite scathing critique of the ritualistic mind-set can be found in texts as early as the *Muṇḍaka Upaniṣad*, a late Vedic text:

> The fools, who proclaim [the Vedic sacrifices] as the ultimate, return again to old age and death. Wallowing in ignorance, but imagining themselves wise and thinking themselves learned,

> the fools go about harming themselves, like blind men led by a man who is himself blind. Wallowing in ignorance again and again, these foolish people imagine, "We have attained our goals!" Because of their desires, these ritualists do not have foresight, therefore they fall back down, wretched and despondent, when their time in the celestial realms expires. Deeming sacrifices and gifts [to the ritual priests] as the highest, these idiots know nothing better. When they have enjoyed their pious work [i.e., the fruits of their *karma*] in the celestial realms, they return again to this miserable world.
>
> But those [seekers of the self] in the forest, peaceful and wise, who practice austerity and faith, as they wander around as mendicants, pass through the doorway of the sun, spotless, to where that immortal *puruṣa* is, the eternal *ātman*. (I.7–11)

The Upaniṣadic/Yogic view, expressed in this early context, is that pleasures in this world or the next are temporary and simply entwine one in the cycle of birth and death. The *Gītā*, too, is forceful in its rejection of Vedic ritualism in language that parallels that of the Yoga commentarial tradition.

> Those who are ignorant subscribe to the flowery words [of the Veda], Arjuna. Reveling in the Vedic rites, they proclaim "there is nothing else but this." Their hearts filled with desires, intent on the celestial realms, they take to the path of performing numerous variegated rites, which are dedicated to the attainment of opulence and sensual enjoyment, but which bestow rebirth as the fruit of action. To such people, attached to sensual enjoyment and opulence, whose minds have been stolen by these flowery words, a mind fixed in *samādhi* is not granted. (II.42–44)

Patañjali's reference to disinterest in *ānuśravika-viṣaya*, the sense objects available from Vedic ritualism, falls in this same vein: Clearly the goals of *yoga* are in complete contrast to the lusty goals of the normative Vedic sacrificial cult that was still a mainstream presence in his day. Therefore, disinterest in this type of ritualism, whether Vedic or other, is a prerequisite to *yoga*.

Essentially, the critique here is one of materialistic religiosity—religiosity performed with the motive of enjoying the good things of the world. This criticism is thus perennially relevant to the attitudes underpinning religious traditions other than Hindu ones, which likewise promote worldly boons as the goal of religious practice. In other words (connecting this verse to modes of religiosity on our own horizons), engaging in religious activities with material motives for mundane goals conflicts with the transcendent goals of *yoga*. In sum, renunciation means not only disinterest in the visible things of this world but also disinterest in some of the worldly or celestial boons that might be promoted in sacred scripture itself.

One more comment is in order here. A general principle of Sanskrit hermeneutics is that a first item mentioned on a list carries more importance than any subsequent items. Thus, of the five *vṛttis, pramāṇa*, right knowledge, is listed first—it is the most important state of mind. And even within the three subdivisions of *pramāṇa*, the Yoga school prioritizes *pratyakṣa*, direct experience; hence this is situated as the first item of the *pramāṇa* sublist. Of the two ingredients of *nirodha*, then, by this principle, *abhyāsa* is situated before *vairāgya*, since, by practice, the by-products of dispassion, detachment, and renunciation arise spontaneously. It is therefore generally a precondition of the latter.

तत्परं पुरुषख्यातेर्गुणवैतृष्ण्यम् ॥ १६ ॥

I.16 tat-paraṁ puruṣa-khyāter guṇa-vaitṛṣṇyam

tat, that [renunciation]; *paraṁ*, higher; *puruṣa*, the soul, self, innermost consciousness; *khyāteḥ*, knowledge, perception; *guṇa*, qualities of *sattva, rajas*, and *tamas*; *vaitṛṣṇyam*, indifference

Higher than renunciation is indifference to the *guṇas* [themselves]. This stems from perception of the *puruṣa*, soul.

There are two levels of renunciation or detachment: indifference toward the sensual objects of the world or of the celestial realms, as outlined in the last *sūtra*, and a higher level of detachment stemming from indifference to the very *guṇas* themselves, *guṇa vaitṛṣṇyam*. We should bear in mind that the *guṇas* of *prakṛti* are the subtle stuff from which all objects are made, whether physical or mental, since matter, mind, and everything else in existence—except for the *puruṣa*, pure consciousness itself—are evolutes from *prakṛti* when it is stirred by the *guṇas* inherent in her. So indifference toward the *guṇas* automatically includes indifference to all *prākṛtic* objects external to pure consciousness. Vyāsa states that this higher and ultimate level of dispassion or renunciation referred to here stems from *puruṣa-khyāti*, awareness of *puruṣa* itself. Complete loss of interest in *all* things material can realistically take place only when the *yogī* has attained something far superior.

Vācaspati Miśra reiterates the metaphysics underpinning this notion. First, when the influences of *rajas* and *tamas* have been eliminated, the mind's natural quality of *sattva* can manifest without disturbance. *Sattva*, in addition to producing a sustainable experience of happiness (unlike the fleeting pleasures of the senses), is by nature pure, transparent, luminous, and insightful. With no disturbing influences, *sattva* is maximized, and the inherent lucidity of the mind can manifest. *Tamas* and *rajas* taint the mind, which is filtering consciousness, distracting it from its source, the *puruṣa* soul, and out into the realm of sense objects. When these two *guṇas* are stilled, the mind's natural lucidity of *sattva* allows it to peacefully and blissfully contemplate the distinction between the *guṇas* (and their products, which include the mind itself) and the pure *puruṣa* soul. Thus, this natural discriminative knowledge of the difference between *puruṣa* and the *guṇas* (that is, *puruṣa* and *prakṛti*), referred to in this *sūtra* by Patañjali is the highest and ultimate function that the *sāttvic citta* can perform and manifests when other types of knowledge have faded away.

Vācaspati Miśra adds, though, that ultimately the *yogī* must transcend even attachment to this *sāttvic* recognition of the distinction between the *guṇas* and *puruṣa*. Vijñānabhikṣu elaborates that the *yogī* must attain the state where the realization occurs that even discriminative knowledge of the distinction between the *guṇas* and *puruṣa* is a function of the *prākṛtic citta*; it is not a function of *puruṣa*. Besides, even elevated and ultimate knowledge can be transitory and therefore defective; after all, pure *sattva* is nonetheless a *guṇa* and therefore unstable by nature since the three *guṇas* are always in flux. Therefore, upon attaining the highest awareness of *puruṣa*'s own nature, the pure mind checks and restraints itself, and hence *puruṣa*'s awareness becomes disassociated from all types of knowledge whatsoever. This, says Vijñānabhikṣu, is called the highest dispassion by Patañjali because it is dispassion toward the most subtle aspects of matter, the very *guṇas* themselves, whereas the renunciation in the previous *sūtra* primarily refers to the grosser aspects of matter, the *guṇas* as manifest in their most physical and solid products, the gross sense objects (or subtler internal thoughts).

Vijñānabhikṣu mentions Jaḍa Bhārata from the *Bhāgavata Purāṇa* as an exemplar of *vairāgya*.[90] Jaḍa Bhārata had been an advanced *yogī* in a previous life but, due to attachment to a deer, had failed to attain the ultimate goals of *yoga* (see III.7 for the details). Consequently, upon being reborn, although internally his mind was completely immersed in thought of Lord Viṣṇu, he presented himself to the world as being insane, stupid, blind, and deaf so as never again to become attached to anything material. Although his pious and well-meaning father tried to teach him the duties of a *Brāhmaṇa* (the scholarly and priestly caste of Vedic India), Jaḍa Bhārata refused to engage with the world in any way at all, such was his disregard for anything made of the *guṇas*, to use Patañjali's terminology in this *sūtra*. He simply wandered around barefoot and clad in filthy rags "like a precious jewel covered by dirt,"[91] slept on the ground, neglected his personal cleanliness, and subsisted on broken rice, husks, worm-eaten grains, and the discarded rice left sticking on the bottom of pots. Since he was nonetheless stout in limb, some worshippers of Kālī eventually seized him and brought him unresisting to the Goddess to be offered as a human sacrifice. But the Goddess burst forth from the deity and decapitated her own devotees so as to save this enlightened *yogī*. In short, Jaḍa Bhārata is an exemplar in popular narrative of the complete renunciation indicated by Patañjali in this *sūtra*.

Vyāsa states that the *yogī* who has attained the state of *vairāgya* can now think, "Whatever was to be achieved has been achieved; the obstacles to the path that were to be destroyed have been destroyed; and the cycle of repeated existence—one who is born, dies, and one who dies is reborn—has been broken."[92] Vācaspati Miśra reiterates that the links holding this cycle together are the myriad individual acts of virtue and vice, *karma*. As discussed, *karma* means action, the performance of any type of act, and since every action performed generates a reaction, and one acts at every moment, the cycle of action and reaction is potentially eternal. Vācaspati Miśra draws attention to II.12–13, which states that this reservoir of *karma* has its roots in nescience—mistaking the pure eternal self to be a product of the impure noneternal products of the *guṇas*. It fructifies only if this root exists. Thus, through the discrimination and knowledge ensuing from the dispassion, renunciation, and desirelessness discussed in these two *sūtras*, nescience, the root of *karma* and thus of *saṁsāra*, the cycle of birth and death, is destroyed. Vācaspati Miśra states that the *yogī* whose intellect is saturated with this recognition of the distinction between the *guṇas* and *puruṣa* is said to be situated in the *samādhi* state of IV.29 known as *dharmamegha*, the cloud of virtue.

This *sūtra* concludes Patañjali's definition of *yoga* given in I.2, *citta-vṛtti-nirodhaḥ*; *sūtras* I.5–12 discussed the *vṛttis*; and I.13–16, *nirodha*. The only analysis Patañjali has not undertaken is a definition of *citta*. One might suppose that he did not feel the need to do so because the word was so well-known at the time. This is regrettable because the term is actually used somewhat differently in different philosophical contexts. In Vedānta, for example, it is perceived as a fourth aspect of the internal organ, in addition to *buddhi, ahaṅkāra*, and *manas*, and corresponds to memory (see Śaṅkara's commentary to *Vedānta Sūtras* II.4.6, and *Yoga-vāsiṣṭha* III.96.55), as it does in a reference in the *Mahābhārata* (XII.274[93]), and in the *Bhāgavata Purāṇa* (III.26.14). Considering his overall remarkably systematic treatment of his subject matter, it is puzzling that Patañjali did not provide a definition of *citta*, the most important term in the entire system. However, given that other than for its latent function as reservoir of *saṁskāras*, the *karmāśaya* of II.12, the *citta* is essentially known only through its *vṛttis*, that is, anything the *citta* does or can do manifests as one of the *vṛttis*, then one might surmise that by carefully analyzing the *vṛttis*, Patañjali has, in effect, analyzed and described the *citta* itself (some comments to this effect or otherwise would have been welcome, nonetheless!).

वितर्कविचारानन्दास्मितारूपानुगमात् संप्रज्ञातः ॥१७॥

I.17 vitarka-vicārānandāsmitā-rūpānugamāt samprajñātaḥ

vitarka, absorption with physical awareness; *vicāra*, absorption with subtle awareness; *ānanda*, absorption with bliss; *asmitā*, absorption with the sense of I-ness; *rūpa*, form; *anugamāt*, accompanied by; *samprajñātaḥ*, a type of *samādhi* state [which still uses the mind and an object of meditation]

***Samprajñāta* [*samādhi*] consists of [the consecutive] mental stages of absorption with physical awareness, absorption with subtle awareness, absorption with bliss, and absorption with the sense of I-ness.**

Having discussed *yoga* in general as the cessation of all thought, Patañjali here and in the next verse turns his attention to two basic categories of *samādhi*, the state of consciousness ensuing when all thought has, in fact, been stilled, and therefore the final goal of *yoga*: *samprajñāta* and *asamprajñāta samādhis*. This *sūtra* addresses the former category.

In instances such as this, English translations such as "absorption with physical awareness" for *vitarka* and "absorption with subtle awareness" for *vicāra* do not convey the sense or meaning or difference between these two levels of *samādhi*. The technical way that these Sanskrit terms are being used here cannot be captured by a suitable English equivalent, so the reader is advised not to try to understand these terms through the clumsy English words a translator choses to convey them. In fact, even the Sanskrit terms are an artificiality, as Vijñānabhikṣu points out, and not to be correlated with how they are used in other contexts, that is, their conventional Sanskrit dictionary meanings (see, e.g., II.34 for a different usage of the term *vitarka*, and II.3 for *asmitā*). So, since these English terms are little better than heuristic indicators, the Sanskrit terms will be retained in the ensuing discussion. This *sūtra* initiates the esoteric teachings of Yoga. That this *sūtra* is so succinct—yet understood as encapsulating a universe of esoteric significance—points to the nature of the *sūtras*, aptly expressed by Feuerstein, as

> originally and primarily maps for meditative introspection, intended to guide the *yogin* in his exploration of the *terra incognita* of the mind. Thus these models served a very practical

> psychological purpose. This hypothesis helps to explain why so many of these models . . . in early texts, are without apparent logical coherence. These "maps" are records of internal experiences rather than purely theoretical constructions. They are descriptive rather than explanatory. The "map" character of the ontogenetic model of Classical Yoga is beyond question. (1980, 117)

As the symbols of a map denote far greater entities than might be evident from the simple signs themselves (circles, squares, triangles, etc.), and alert the traveler to what to expect on the road ahead, so the technical terms in this *sūtra* represent altered states of consciousness far beyond those of conventional awareness, and thus beyond the ability of conventional words or labels to describe. They are guides for the *yogī*, alerting him or her to some of the meditative experiences that will be encountered on the path.

Vyāsa is curiously not very detailed in his explanation of this complex *sūtra* at this point, but these stages of *samādhi* are discussed in more depth in I.40–45. He notes that these are four stages of *samprajñāta-samādhi*, all of which have an *ālambana*, a support (see discussion in I.10). He means by this that the consciousness of the *puruṣa* is still flowing through the *prākṛtic citta* to connect with or be supported by an object of meditational focus (albeit in progressively more subtle ways). In this state, the mind is fixed on one *pratyaya* (discussed in I.10), or undeviating *vṛtti*, that of the object of concentration, and resists all change into other states. The object of concentration, whatever it might be, is the *ālambana*, the unwavering image the object produces on the concentrated mind (the *pratyaya*).

It is Vācaspati Miśra who unpacks this *sūtra* in detail. He considers the first state on Patañjali's list, *vitarka-samādhi*, to be contemplation on a gross physical object, that is to say, meditating on an object that one experiences as a manifestation or construct of the gross physical or material elements. It is thus the first level of experiencing an object in *samādhi*. Keeping the metaphysics of Sāṅkhya in mind, we know that the five gross elements that constitute gross physical objects evolve from elements that are more subtle, that is, they are actually evolutes from the *tanmātras*, the five subtle elements. Vācaspati Miśra states that *vicāra samādhi*, the second level of *samādhi* concentration mentioned by Patañjali in this *sūtra*, involves absorption on this more subtle aspect of the object of meditation, perceiving the object as actually consisting of these more subtle ingredients. In fact, I.44 informs us that the subtle substructure of external reality can refer to any of the evolutes from *prakṛti*, as even the *tanmātras* evolve from *ahaṅkāra* which, in turn, evolves from *buddhi*. Thus, the latter can also be considered *sūkṣma*, subtle. As a new archer first aims at large objects, Vācaspati Miśra says, and then progressively smaller ones, so the neophyte *yogī* first experiences the gross nature of the object in meditation and then its progressively more subtle nature. Instead of experiencing the object as composed of compact quantum masses, the *bhūtādi* gross elements, as in the first state of *vitarka*, in *vicāra*, the *yogī* experiences the object as composed of vibratory, radiant potential, subtle energy (a sublevel of reality normally imperceptible to the senses[94]).

Vijñānabhikṣu gives us a theistic example of these two states of *samādhi*. If one wishes to fix the mind on God, *Īśvara*, as Patañjali will encourage in I.23–29, how does one do so? *Īśvara* is also a type of *puruṣa* (I.23) and thus beyond *prakṛti*—and we know that the *prākṛtic* mind cannot fix itself on something more subtle than and metaphysically distinct from itself. Vijñānabhikṣu speaks of fixing the mind on a divine form of *Īśvara* such as that of Viṣṇu. Essentially, this can only entail fixing the mind on some *saṁskāra* connected with God, some image, perhaps from one's temple or favorite artistic rendition. When this entails concentrating on *Īśvara* in the form of a *saṁskāra* of some gross *prākṛtic* form (such as a deity), it is *vitarka*, and when in a more subtle *prākṛtic* form, such as God's characteristics, it is *vicāra*. We will see that, for Vijñānabhikṣu, as for most of the *bhakti* traditions, this theistic meditation will eventually culminate in direct, non-*prākṛtic* perception of *Īśvara* as *puruṣa*, that is, a non-*prākṛtic* supreme being of pure consciousness. Patañjali has not discussed this particular type of practice (he will recommend fixing the mind on *Īśvara* in the form of *oṁ* in I.27–28), but Vijñānabhikṣu's approach is certainly acceptable within the framework of this system, and most of the commentators do refer to such conventional *bhakti* modes of *Īśvara*-centered meditation. Whatever the object of meditation, the sine qua non at this point is undeviated concentration on it. In the state of *samādhi*, the mind is fixed so intensely on its *ālambana* that it essentially merges with it, like, says Vijñānabhikṣu, fire in a red-hot iron ball.

There is no consensus among the commentators as to the exact nature of the last two stages of *samādhi, ānanda* and *asmitā,* underscoring the fact that such states do not lend themselves to scholastic categorization and analysis.[95] Vācaspati Miśra's version perhaps surfaces most commonly and seems predicated on the information we will encounter later in the chapter. Specifically, with an eye on I.41, he utilizes the three components of knowledge identified in Hindu philosophical discourse to demarcate the differences among these four stages of *samādhi*. In any act of knowledge, there is the knower or subject of knowledge, the instruments of knowledge (mind and senses, etc.), and the object of knowledge; these are termed *gṛhitṛ, grahaṇa*, and *grāhya*, respectively (literally, the grasper, the instrument of grasping, and that which is grasped). For Vācaspati Miśra, in the first two stages of *samādhi* outlined above, *vitarka* and *vicāra*, the object on which the mind is fixed, whether perceived as its grosser outer form or subtler inner constituents, is nonetheless an external object and therefore considered *grāhya* (that which is grasped). Now, in the third stage, *ānanda-samādhi*, the *yogī* transfers awareness from the objects of the senses, *grāhya*, to the organs of the senses themselves, *grahaṇa* (the instruments of grasping). He specifies that these are the powers (*śakti*) behind the sensual abilities of seeing, touching, smelling, tasting, and hearing, rather than the gross physical organs of eye, ear, nose, etc. The *citta* now becomes aware of the mechanisms of cognition, the instruments of the senses. In other words, it becomes aware of the internal organ through which external objects are grasped, rather than the external objects themselves, whether experienced in their gross or subtle constitutions.

Since, in Sāṅkhya, the *grahaṇa* includes the internal organs, *manas, buddhi*, and *ahaṅkāra*, which comprise the *citta* in Yoga, Bhoja Rāja understands the support of the mind in *ānanda-samādhi* to be the *citta* itself, specifically in its aspect as *ahaṅkāra*, thus differing somewhat with Vācaspati Miśra (who correlates *ahaṅkāra* with the next stage). Thus in this perspective, in this third stage, awareness becomes aware of the *citta* itself in its capacity of acquiring knowledge, as an instrument that grasps the objects of the senses. In other words, the mind focuses on its own cognizing nature. Since the *guṇa* of *sattva* predominates in *ahaṅkāra* and *buddhi* (although, as Bhoja Rāja notes, traces of *rajas* and *tamas* are still present at this stage, which for him demarcates this level of *samādhi* from the fourth), and *sattva* is the source of bliss, Patañjali calls this stage *ānanda-samādhi*, blissful absorption. This is because it involves experiencing a much more rarefied, purer, and more sustainable (and thus supernormal) form of *sāttvic* bliss. *Gītā* XIV.6 warns, however, of becoming attached to this *sāttvic* happiness, and so there is a danger at this stage that the *yogī* may mistake this sense of bliss and unprecedented insight with the ultimate goal of *yoga*. In other words, there is a danger that the *yogī* or mystic will mistake this rapturous state of supernormal perception for the ultimate experience of *puruṣa* (or for Vedāntins, of *ātmānanda*, the bliss of the self).

Vijñānabhikṣu is uncharacteristically vague about this third stage of *ānanda-samādhi*, although he explicitly disagrees with Vācaspati Miśra that it is supported by the sense organs. He states that in *ānanda-samādhi*, the mind transcends the previous stage and experiences bliss due to an increase of *sattva*, but he does not specify the location of this bliss. He merely notes that at this point the object of meditation is no longer perceived as consisting of even the subtle elements, as was the case in the previous stage, but is experienced as pure *sāttvic* bliss (about which all the commentators agree, understandably, given the name Patañjali assigns this third type of *samādhi*). Again, this is not the bliss inherent in *puruṣa* (inherent therein at least according to the Vedānta tradition, but also, as we will suggest in II.5, arguably, to Yoga as well); awareness is still flowing through the mind and focused on an external object, but by contacting the *sāttvic* dimension of the object of meditation, the mind is simply aware of all-pervading happiness and is immersed in an ocean of bliss. Vijñānabhikṣu quotes Kṛṣṇa's description of this state in the *Gītā* (a state which the text actually defines as *yoga*):

> When the *yogī* experiences that endless happiness (*sukha*) which is grasped by the discriminative faculty (*buddhi*), but beyond the grasp of the senses, he remains fixed in this state and never strays from the truth . . . This state, free from any trace of suffering, is called *yoga*. (VI.21–23)

Vijñānabhikṣu notwithstanding, the prevalent view seems to be that in the third state of *samādhi*, the mind becomes absorbed on some aspect of the instruments of cognition themselves, rather than supported by or concentrated on the gross or subtle constituents of an external object of the senses. All commentators at least agree that at this stage of *ānanda-samādhi*, the mind becomes immersed in the *sattva* prevalent in this state of awareness.

Finally, by involuting awareness further and penetrating the internal organ of meditation to its still more essential nature, one transcends even the instruments of knowledge and arrives at *ahaṅkāra*, if one follows Vācaspati Miśra, or *buddhi*, if one follows Bhoja Rāja—either way, to the closest *prākṛtic* coverings to the *puruṣa* itself. Relentless in the pursuit of true and ultimate knowledge, at this point the *yogī* attains the fourth and final stage of *samprajñāta-samādhi* listed by Patañjali in this *sūtra, asmitā-samādhi*. Now, following Bhoja Rāja's schema, having penetrated the constituents of the external object of meditation through its gross and subtle elements consecutively in the first two stages of *samādhi*, and having withdrawn itself from external cognition and into a state of contemplating the powers behind the very organs of cognition in the third, awareness penetrates the *citta* further, absorbing itself in the *citta*'s feature of *buddhi*, the *grahitṛ*, the grasper, the closest *prākṛtic* covering to the *puruṣa* itself. Hariharānanda states that awareness bypasses the feeling of bliss in the previous stage to contact the experiencer of bliss. *Buddhi*, in this highly *sāttvic* state, is so pure and luminous it can reflect the consciousness of *puruṣa* back to itself. At this point, since it has already transcended all objects outside of itself, including the internal organs of cognition, *buddhi* focuses inward, reflecting *puruṣa* itself as its object of meditation.

Another way of putting this is that the *yogī* now finally becomes aware of *puruṣa* itself as pure consciousness by means of its reflection in *buddhi*; in other words, the *citta* of the *yogī* becomes indirectly aware of *puruṣa* (since this awareness is still mediated by *buddhi*). Nonetheless, the *yogī* becomes aware of I-am-ness (the etymological meaning of *asmitā*) rather than any external material *prākṛtic* object, or even internal organ of cognition. *Asmi*, "I am," is the first-person singular of the root *as*, "to be," and *tā* is a suffix added to adjectives to denote "ness," but Śaṅkara notes that this I-am-ness, *asmitā*, is not the same as the *asmitā* listed as an obstacle to *yoga* in II.3. *Asmitā* in the context of the *kleśas* in II.2 and 7 involves a misidentification of *puruṣa* with what it is not and thus corresponds to *ahaṅkāra*.[96] *Asmitā* as *kleśa* involves an *object* of I am—"I am fat," "I am sad," "I am a male." The *asmitā* in the context of *samādhi* occurs when the *citta* contemplates the awareness of *puruṣa* by means of *puruṣa*'s reflection in the pure mirror of the *sāttvic citta*. The mind now experiences an I-am-ness in the sense of the true *subject* of awareness: "the source of my awareness is *puruṣa*." *Asmitā* is consciousness reflecting on the mirror of the mind, as a result of which the *citta* gains a genuine absolute knowledge of the real source and identity of the consciousness pervading it. Whereas in the previous level the mind was aware that "I am blissful," in this fourth level it is now simply experiencing a state of I am. This is pure I-am-ness with no external object or specific content of self-identification, so it is very close to the goal of direct realization of *puruṣa*. This fourth stage is still within the realm of *prakṛti*, however, still at a stage of *samprajñāta-samādhi*. In other words, it is "supported" by some connection with *prakṛti*, because the *citta* is still being used as an instrument to channel awareness (even though the object of awareness is now *puruṣa* itself rather than any external manifestation of *prakṛti*). The *puruṣa* at this point is still not fully autonomous and extricated from its appropriation by the mind.

Before proceeding, we must note that, as with his explanation of *ānanda*, Vijñānabhikṣu also parts company with Bhoja Rāja and Vācaspati Miśra in his understanding of *asmitā*. For him, as a Vaiṣṇava theist, this stage involves a direct vision of God, *Īśvara*,[97] whom we will encounter in I.23, below. Vijñānabhikṣu claims that in the second stage of *savicāra-samādhi* noted in this *sūtra*, the *yogī* fixes the mind on the characteristics (*sopādhi*) of God. Essentially, this can only entail fixing the mind on some *saṁskāra* connected with God. But this fourth stage of *asmitā-samādhi* for him entails transcending this gross (*prākṛtic*) level of meditation of the previous stages and having a direct experience of *Īśvara* as a conscious being. This notion that the *puruṣa* can have a transcendent personal vision of a divine form of God is standard in the Hindu theistic traditions. As the Yoga tradition has always been adamant that the *puruṣa* is an entity that can be directly perceived, so have the *bhakti* devotional traditions always held that

Īśvara as supreme *puruṣa* (*Gītā* XIV.16–18) can likewise be personally perceived (for example, *Gītā* XI.54). Patañjali, however, gives no information pertaining to the experiential relationship between the liberated *yogī* and *Īśvara*, but this does not discount Vijñānabhikṣu's interpretation.

However one takes the various levels of *samprajñāta-samādhi*, one final step remains where this ultimate uncoupling of *puruṣa* from all connection with *prakṛti* and involvement whatsoever with the *citta* occurs. This is *asamprajñāta-samādhi, samādhi* without support (an *a-* prefixed to any noun in Sanskrit negates that noun[98]), which will be outlined in the next *sūtra*. Also, the first two stages of *samādhi* noted in this *sūtra, vitarka* and *vicāra*, will later, in I.42, be further subdivided and refined into *savitarka* and *nirvitarka*, and *savicāra* and *nirvicāra*, respectively (the prefix *sa-* means with, and *nir* means without). This will therefore result in a total of six stages of *samprajñāta-samādhi*, before the final stage of *asamprajñāta-samādhi*.[99] Therefore, including the latter, there will be a total of seven stages of *samādhi* explicitly expressed by Patañjali in his system.

Vyāsa notes that each progressively grosser level of *samādhi* includes the others (just as the grosser aspects of matter include the subtler ones): *Vitarka* includes *vicāra, ānanda*, and *asmitā* (although obviously the latter have yet to be fully experienced by the *yogī* in their own right); *vicāra* includes *ānanda* and *asmitā*; and *ānanda* includes *asmitā*. Also, it is important to reiterate, along with Bhoja Rāja, that any type of *samādhi* involves meditation on the chosen object to the exclusion of all other objects, irrespective of the level of meditation outlined in this *sūtra*. In other words, the mind has attained *citta-vṛtti-nirodha*; it is completely undeviating in focus, which is the prerequisite of all stages of *samādhi*. Additionally, even as there are differences pertaining to the *states* of mind corresponding to these stages, the *object* that the mind uses as its support, that is, on which to fix itself, can, as Bhoja Rāja notes, be either any material object or evolute of *prakṛti*, or *Īśvara*, God, with Patañjali clearly prioritizing the latter. But, as Vijñānabhikṣu in turn notes, the object must remain the same, "whether it be the four-armed form of Viṣṇu, or an ordinary object, such as an earthern pot."[100] Otherwise, if objects are whimsically changed, the *yogī* will be displaying fickleness of mind and thus be disqualified from this stage of *samādhi*.

In conclusion, we have noted that there are minor differences among the commentators' understanding of the metaphysical nature of the two final types of *samprajñāta-samādhi*—*ānanda* and *asmitā*—but all commentators agree that in principle this *sūtra* describes refining one's awareness during consecutive stages of meditation through progressively more subtle states of cognition in quest of the source of awareness itself, *puruṣa*. Also, we can note that in the last two stages of *samādhi*, one cannot technically speaking *know* the *grahaṇa* or *grahitṛ*, because acts of knowing can take place only via these instruments of knowledge and the knowers themselves. Knowing cannot know the very instruments of knowledge any more than cooking can cook itself. Rather, awareness becomes aware of them. This consideration can help us better appreciate this relentless progression toward the source of awareness: from gross objects of knowledge to their subtle substrates, to the instruments of knowledge themselves, and, beyond again, to the ultimate *prākṛtic* knower, until finally one arrives at *puruṣa* itself.

The relationship between the four stages of *samādhi* outlined here and the four *jhānas* (*dhyānas* in Sanskrit) outlined in Buddhist meditation has long been noted.[101] *Dhyāna* occurs as the seventh of the eight limbs of Patañjali's system (III.2), but it is used in Buddhism and also in older Hindu texts such as the *Gītā* and *Mahābhārata* as a synonym for *samādhi*, the final stage. The Buddha speaks of attaining the first *dhyāna*, which consisted of *vitarka, vicāra*, and *viveka*, and then proceeding to attain the other three stages of *dhyāna* (*Majjhima Nikāya* I.246–47). There are several different lists of the four *dhyāna* (*samādhi*) states in the Buddhist *abhidhamma* schools, and the most important of these include *vitarka* and *vicāra*, the first two items mentioned in this *sūtra* under the first *dhyāna*.[102] Moreover, *ānanda*, the third item mentioned by Patañjali (or its correlate, *sukha*), is experienced in the first three of the four stages of *dhyāna*. Only the final item from this *sūtra, asmitā,* I-am-ness, does not have a clear parallel in Buddhism—hardly surprising given the Buddhist rejection of an autonomous *puruṣa*.

It is worth noting again in this regard Bhīṣma's mention of the four *dhyānas* in the Hindu *Mahābhārata* (Bhīṣma too is clearly using the term as a synonym of *samādhi*). Bhīṣma includes in his first stage of *dhyāna* three features (*vitarka, vicāra*, and *viveka*), thereby paralleling the Buddhist system:[103]

O son of Pṛthu, I will now explain to you the fourfold *yoga* of *dhyāna* (meditation), knowing which the great seers [of old] attained eternal perfection. The *yogīs*, great seers, blissful in knowledge, their minds set on *nirvāṇa*, perform *dhyāna* that has been well-practiced. A sage should fix his mind so that it becomes one-pointed . . . [He should withdraw all the senses from the sense objects] . . . Then, being wise, he should merge his five senses into the mind and concentrate[104] his wandering mind and senses . . . When such a sage concentrates his mind on the first *dhyāna* from the beginning, the meditative states of *vicāra, vitarka* and *viveka* manifest . . . Immersed in that bliss, *yogīs* delight in the performance of *dhyāna* and thereby attain *nirvāṇa*, which is free from distress. (XII.188.1–22)

Although the understanding of these terms differs—the Yoga tradition's understanding tends to situate the psychological basis of these states within the more cosmological framework of Sāṅkhyan metaphysics[105]—it is impossible not to recognize a common substratum of practice and terminology. Thus, it is important to be aware of the shared context of meditational practices in ancient India; Hindu, Buddhist, or Jain expressions in their formative periods were not as distinctly demarcated as they later became in scholastic literature. Whatever may have been the direction of influence,[106] the shared or interfertilizing context of meditation in ancient India is undeniable.

विरामप्रत्ययाभ्यासपूर्वः संस्कारशेषेऽन्यः ॥ १८ ॥

I.18 virāma-pratyayābhyāsa-pūrvaḥ saṁskāra-śeṣo 'nyaḥ

virāma, termination, cessation; *pratyaya*, idea, notion, thought; *abhyāsa*, practice; *pūrvaḥ*, previous; *saṁskāra*, mental imprints, memories, subconscious impressions; *śeṣaḥ*, remainder; *anyaḥ*, the other [*samādhi*, *asamprajñāta-samādhi*]

The other *samādhi* [*asamprajñāta-samādhi*] is preceded by cultivating the determination to terminate [all thoughts]. [In this state] only latent impressions remain.

In the last *sūtra*, Patañjali discussed *samprajñāta-samādhi*, which was subdivided into four. Here he uses *anya*, the other, to refer to another state beyond this, which the commentators take to be *asamprajñāta* (a term that actually never occurs in the *sūtras* themselves). As we have seen, the four states of *samprajñāta* all involved the *citta* in various ways. *Asamprajñāta* is beyond the mind. It is therefore beyond thought and word. Perhaps to underscore this, Patañjali has used the simple pronoun *anya* rather than a descriptive term, thereby pointing to *asamprajñāta* as a state that transcends all conceptualization, descriptive categories, and nomenclatures (which are all products of *citta*). In the same vein, the Māṇḍūkya Upaniṣad calls it "the fourth" (beyond the other three states of consciousness: waking, dream, and deep sleep).

The commentators present *asamprajñāta-samādhi, saṁādhi* without support, as being the state where the awareness of *puruṣa* is no longer aware of any external entity at all, including the *citta*, since the latter has dissolved itself. This state corresponds with *nirbīja*, without seed (I.51). In this final and ultimate state, the supreme goal of *yoga*, the mind is not supported by any active thought, including even the object of meditation; latent seeds, or *saṁskāras*, will not sprout into active thoughts. The *vṛttis* of the mind exist simply as potential, and the *saṁskāras*, the subconscious imprints that trigger thoughts, memories, and *karma*, are also latent. Since the mind is now empty of all thoughts, or, as Vyāsa puts it, appears as if nonexistent, the awareness of *puruṣa* now no longer has any object whatsoever to be aware of, and thus, for the first time, can become only self-aware.[107] The final goal of *yoga* has been attained.

Another way of considering this is that awareness is eternal, it cannot ever cease being aware. Following the Upaniṣads, the first spiritual teaching of the *Gītā* in Chapter II articulates this repeatedly—the soul is indestructible, it cannot be slain, it does not die when the body is slain, nor is it ever born, it is birthless, eternal, perpetual, original, it cannot be burnt, pierced by weapons, wetted, blown by the wind, it is unmanifest, beyond thought, unchanging, etc. (II.17ff). Awareness cannot be switched off like a light. That being the case, the soul's only options are what it is aware of: It can be object-aware, or (again, loosely speaking) subject-aware—that is, aware of entities or objects other than itself, or exclusively aware of itself as awareness with no reference to any other entity. After myriad births being aware of the unlimited varieties of *prākṛtic* objects, *puruṣa* has now come to the point of self-realization—realizing itself as distinct from not just objects of thought but the very faculty and process of thought itself, the *citta* and its *vṛttis*. When there are no objects to detain its awareness, *puruṣa* has no alternative but to be self-aware. This is *asamprajñāta-samādhi*.

Now, there must be, in principle, some kind of final thought or mental activity before the mind enters the state of complete inactivity in the *asamprajñāta-samādhi*. Patañjali states in this *sūtra* that the last thought or cognitive act immediately before *asamprajñāta-samādhi* is the thought of terminating thoughts (any thoughts, even the highest kinds, such as thoughts discriminating between *puruṣa* and *prakṛti*). This last thought is termed the *virāma-pratyaya* in this *sūtra*.

Although this very notion of terminating all thoughts is itself a thought, Vyāsa considers it a notion devoid of any objective phenomenon. One might say that it is the last mental state prior to final liberation (the terminator thought, so to speak!). Vyāsa states that this *virāma-pratyaya* is born of the dispassion discussed in I.16. By the constant mental cultivation of the notion of ceasing all thought, says Vyāsa, the mind is deprived of any other object of thought and becomes without support, that is, with nothing to sustain it. It becomes completely empty—all its *saṁskāras* remain latent, *saṁskāra śeṣa*, as Patañjali points out here. Bhoja Rāja states that at this stage the mind constantly dwells on this sole notion of terminating thought and rejects all other *vṛttis*. This type of mental cultivation is the penultimate stage of *yoga* and immediately precedes *asamprajñāta-samādhi*. Śaṅkara compares this *virāma-pratyaya*, terminator thought, to an ebbing flame, which is still nonetheless a flame until all its fuel expires and it is turned to dust—a latent *saṁskāra*. Thus, when even this notion of terminating all thoughts ceases, *asamprajñāta-samādhi* ensues. Al-Bīrunī compares the embodied soul to a grain of rice with its husk. As long as the grain retains the husk (the active *citta* with its *saṁskāras*), it has the potential for sprouting and ripening. When the husk is removed, this potential ceases.[108]

भवप्रत्ययो विदेहप्रकृतिलयानाम् ॥१९॥

I.19 bhava-pratyayo videha-prakṛti-layānām

bhava, becoming, material existence, birth; *pratyayaḥ*, idea, cause;[109] *videha*, unembodied, without a gross body; *prakṛti-layānām*, of those [entities] merged in matter

For [some], those who are unembodied and those who are merged in matter, [the state of *samprajñāta* is characterized] by absorption in [subtle] states of *prakṛti*.

Although Vyāsa and most of the other commentators understand this abstruse *sūtra* as following the topic of *sūtra* I.18 and thus pointing to a type of *asamprajñāta-samādhi* where only latent *saṁskāras* remain in the mind, this seems impossible, given the nature of the states described in this *sūtra*. We thus agree with Bhoja Rāja that this *sūtra* continues from I.17, elaborating on certain *yogīs* whose minds are still absorbed in some state of *prakṛti* paralleling the *prākṛtic* attainments outlined there. The *asamprajñāta-samādhi* of I.18 involves uncouplement from *prakṛti* and thus cannot refer to the *prākṛtic* states attained by the kind of practitioners referred to in this *sūtra*. The type of quasi *samādhi* indicated here is still connected with *bhava*, literally, becoming (which I have translated as states of *prakṛti*), and points to a state that can also be attained by those other than practitioners of "real" *yoga*. The beings in this category remain absorbed in various subtle dimensions of *prakṛti* and thus stranded, as it were, at various heights of supernormal attainments accrued from the *yoga* path; thus Bhoja Rāja considers the states indicated in this *sūtra* to point to "semblances of *yoga*."

Patañjali here refers to two categories of such beings: the *videhas*, those who are unembodied, and the *prakṛti-layas*, those who are merged in matter; their common denominator is that these entities still maintain notions of self-identity that are connected with material (*prākṛtic*) existence. The commentators hold that these categories refer to two types of quasi-perfected *yogīs* who do not have gross physical bodies but exist on some other level within *prakṛti*. *Prakṛti*, as has been discussed, evolves into a number of evolutes: *buddhi*, intelligence; *ahaṅkāra*, ego; *manas*, the mind; and the *tanmātra* subtle elements, *mahābhūta* gross elements, and organs of action. None of these levels represents the real self, *puruṣa*; they are all subtler or grosser evolutes from inanimate matter that cover the *puruṣa* in various layers. But just as normal people misidentify the self with the gross physical body, there are higher beings who, through some type of practice, have managed to transcend the grosser levels of self-misidentification but who nonetheless remain stranded at more subtle levels of misidentification. They remain in these states of pseudoliberation until their latent *saṁskāras* activate once more, at which time they return again to grosser levels of *saṁsāra*.

More specifically, Vyāsa and Vācaspati Miśra identify the fist category of beings mentioned by Patañjali, the *videhas*, as the celestial beings.[110] Śaṅkara specifies that the celestial beings referred to here are only those engaged in the path of *yoga*, and Vijñānabhikṣu says that these are the higher-level celestials that do not have gross physical bodies but bodies made out of *buddhi*, pure intelligence. Some categories of celestials are nourished by subtle forms of *prakṛti* instead of gross food, some even subsisting on the insight of *buddhi*, the subtlest form of *prakṛti*.[111] The Purāṇas indicate that there are different categories of gods, who become progressively superior in terms of life span, powers, sensual facilities, and insight; in the celestial realm called *satyaloka*, for example, the celestials have surpassed all the realizations that are encompassed in *samprajñāta-samādhi* (S. Bhattacharya, 1968).

The commentators hold the second category mentioned by Patañjali in this *sūtra*, those merged in *prakṛti*, matter, to refer to entities who consider themselves to be either unmanifest, primordial *prakṛti* herself, or *buddhi*, the first evolute from *prakṛti*, or the second evolute *ahaṅkāra*, or even the *tanmātras*, five subtle elements. In other words, more or less anyone who does not identify himself or herself as being the gross material body made of the five gross elements, but still identifies the self as being some other, more subtle, aspect of *prakṛti*, could be considered *prakṛti-laya*, merged in matter. In this they follow the *Sāṅkhya Kārikā* (XLV), where the state of *prakṛti-laya* in question is held to come from *vairāgya*, nonattachment (I.15). In his commentary to this verse in the *Sāṅkhya Kārikā*, Gauḍapāda states: "One might have *vairāgya* but without knowing the 24 evolutes of *prakṛti*. This state, which is founded on ignorance, is . . . *prakṛti-layānām*. At death, such a person is not liberated, but is merged into the eight evolutes of *prakṛti—pradhāna,*[112] intelligence, ego and the five subtle elements. From there, he returns again to *saṁsāra*."[113] However, "one merged in this state thinks 'I am liberated.' This is a type of ignorance."[114]

Vācaspati Miśra takes *bhava*[115] in this *sūtra* as a reference to *avidyā*, ignorance; thus these two categories of *yogīs* are still immersed in ignorance, mistaking the self with the nonself. Vijñānabhikṣu, on the other hand, takes *bhava* to mean birth, perhaps in resonance with Patañjali's comment in IV.1 of birth as being a cause of *yogic* attainment, and holds that the two types of *yogīs* mentioned here have attained their respective states due to their births, or practices performed in a past life. The celestials certainly fall into this category. Bhoja Rāja takes *bhava* to refer to *saṁsāra*. He considers the *videhas* of this *sūtra* to be those who have attained the state *ānanda-samādhi*, and *prakṛti-layas* to be those who have attained *asmitā-samādhi* mentioned in I.17. Rāmānanda Sarasvatī considers these individuals to be those who, after the dissolution of their gross bodies, remain in a state of existence devoid of the traditional bodily sheaths.[116]

Whether we take *bhava* to be ignorance, *saṁsāra*, or birth, it should be clear by now that the overall significance remains the same: *Bhava* points to the world of being or becoming, namely, *prakṛti*. Thus, the *videha-layas* and *prakṛti-layas*, whether gods or *yogīs* stranded on one of the levels of *samprajñāta-samādhi* outlined in the previous *sūtra*, are beings who remain absorbed in one of the above evolutes of *prakṛti* until the activation of their *saṁskāras* eventually thrusts them back into lower forms of *saṁsāra* to experience the fruits of their previous activities. Thus, despite difference in detail,[117] the commentators agree that while such *yogīs* may have transcended grosser notions of self-identity, they have not yet realized their true essential nature as *puruṣa* but still identify themselves with some other, finer aspect of matter. Therefore, says Bhoja Rāja, their attainments are to be considered semblances of real *yoga*. They are "as if" liberated, says Vyāsa or, as Vācaspati Miśra puts it, they still have their work cut out for them, namely, realization of the actual true self. The point holds, but since the *puruṣa* is in fact covered by *buddhi* and *ahaṅkāra*, etc., the *prakṛti-laya yogīs* have nonetheless attained legitimate and insightful realizations of the embodied self that can be attained only by discipline and meditation.

Even if they are nonultimate, their realizations certainly surpass the notions of those who identify themselves with the gross physical body.

These two categories of entities, which we can perhaps refer to as imperfect *yogīs*, exist in a state that approximates absolute freedom because they are free from the *citta-vṛttis*, fluctuating states of mind, and their minds consist only of *saṁskāras*, subconscious impressions or latent propensities. They are thus, from normal perspectives, highly evolved beings, but they are still immersed in some aspect of *prakṛti*, and, say Vyāsa and Vācaspati Miśra, they have to return to the cycle of birth and death when their latent *saṁskāras* start to fructify. One might infer from all this that imperfect *yogīs* have at some point, through introspection, attained the realization over time that they are not the gross body but one of the other layers of *prakṛti*. As with any type of devoted and consistent meditation, such prolonged cultivation results in their minds being saturated with *saṁskāras* pertaining to this particular insight. These are highly refined *saṁskāras* and not productive of *citta-vṛttis*. Such *yogīs* remain in their respective states for as long as these accumulated *saṁskāras* dominate the *citta* and other more active *saṁskāras* do not surface.

Perhaps we can conclude that the *videhas* and *prakṛti-layas* have attained some sort of *samprajñāta-samādhi* insofar as they have attained a state of complete cessation of thought, with all their *saṁskāras* inactive, but their awareness, rather than being absorbed in the source of awareness, *puruṣa* itself, is still absorbed in some subtle dimension of *prakṛti*. In time, then, unlike with ideal *yogīs* absorbed in *puruṣa*, or self-awareness, these other two types of *yogīs* are eventually pulled back down into the more mundane states of mind when their latent *saṁskāras* reactivate. They are once more prone to *bhava*, becoming, that is, embodied existence.

Several commentators quote a verse from the *Vāyu Purāṇa* that states that those who identify themselves as beings constituted by the sense organs remain in their particular state for a period corresponding to ten Manus;[118] those identifying themselves with the subtle elements, one hundred periods of the same; those with *ahaṅkāra*, ego, one thousand periods; those with *buddhi*, ten thousand; and those with unmanifest, primordial, preevolutionary *prakṛti*, a full hundred thousand. Whatever the details, the point seems to be that one can remain identified with and absorbed in extremely subtle dimensions of *prakṛti* for prolonged periods of time, but not eternally. Only realization of the *puruṣa* by means of the *asamprajñāta-samādhi* is eternal.

Otherwise, sooner or later, other *saṁskāras*, perhaps connected with grosser objects of thought cultivated in prior lifetimes, begin to activate—like frogs, says Vācaspati Miśra, during the rainy season. Such reactivated memories and impressions awaken and impel these *yogīs* back into the cycle of action and reaction, and hence of birth and death, *saṁsāra*—unless, says Vācaspati Miśra, while in their disembodied state, they develop true discrimination of the difference between any aspect of *prakṛti* whatsoever and the real self, *puruṣa*. Vijñānabhikṣu also points out that these *yogīs* need not necessarily return to *saṁsāra* when their *saṁskāras* reactivate; from their ethereal states they can gradually strive further for ultimate liberation. In this case, as the *Vāyu Purāṇa* quoted above acknowledges, they are eligible to remain eternally immersed in awareness of *puruṣa*.

श्रद्धावीर्यस्मृतिसमाधिप्रज्ञापूर्वक इतरेषाम् ॥२०॥

I.20 śraddhā-vīrya-smṛti-samādhi-prajñā-pūrvakaḥ itareṣām

śraddhā, faith; *vīrya*, vigor; *smṛti*, memory; *samādhi*, absorption; *prajñā*, discernment; *pūrvakah*, preceded by; *itareṣām*, for others

[But] for others, [the state where only subconscious impressions remain] is preceded by faith, vigor, memory, *samādhi* absorption, and discernment.

Vyāsa contrasts this *sūtra* with the previous one by introducing the term *upāya-pratyaya*; the state where only subconscious impressions remain can be attained by the *bhava-pratyaya* of the previous *sūtra*, that is, can have *prakṛti* as its cause, or by *upāya-pratyaya*, can have *upāya*, practice, as its cause. The implication is that the means adopted by real *yogīs* to attain this state are the proper means indicated in this *sūtra*: faith, vigor, memory, *samādhi* absorption, and discernment. If these means are adopted, the practitioner will not return to *prakṛti* like the *bhava-pratyaya* beings of the last *sūtra*.

The commentators take this *sūtra* as promoting a progression of events that must be undertaken by the aspiring *yogī*. Vyāsa takes *śraddhā*, faith, to be clarity of mind, which perhaps indicates that since any type of enterprise requires faith that it will lead to the attainment of a goal, when one sees things clearly, one can understand which kind of endeavor best merits one's trust. Vācaspati Miśra states that faith is belief in the goal of the enterprise, which in this case is *asamprajñāta-samādhi*. Vyāsa states that faith sustains like a benevolent mother; it supports the *yogī* until the very end. Deep faith gives rise to the second item on Patañjali's list, *vīrya*, vigor or energetic endeavor, which the commentators take to be the pursuit of the eight limbs of *yoga* that will be described in some detail in Chapter II. Faith, then, inspires energetic action in pursuing the practices of *yoga*. We can note that according to II.38, the attainment of *vīrya*, vigor, is specifically achieved by the practice of celibacy, an indispensable ingredient in the eight limbs of *yoga*. This *vīrya*, in turn, produces the next item, *smṛti*, memory, which is taken by Vyāsa to mean an undisturbed mind; by Vācaspati Miśra to indicate always keeping the goal in mind; and by Śaṅkara to refer to scriptural knowledge.

This focused state of mind passes into the penultimate stage mentioned in this *sūtra, samprajñāta-samādhi*, or undeviated concentration on an object, which Patañjali addressed in I.17. As a result of the complete absence of distraction in *samādhi*, the final item on the list, *prajñā*, discernment, the ability to see things as they really are, manifests. The ultimate act of discrimination is the ability to distinguish *puruṣa* from any aspect of *prakṛti*. The mind, says Vyāsa, has now accomplished its goal and fulfilled the purpose of its existence and thus need no longer continue to operate. Consequently, preceded by the five stages indicated in this *sūtra, asamprajñāta-samādhi*—the complete uncoupling of the *puruṣa* from the mind—now ensues.

As scholars have long noted, these five stages find a parallel in the Buddha's preenlightenment training under his two *yogī* teachers, Āḷāra Kālāma and Uddaka son of Rāma,[119] which, while understood differently between the traditions, underscores once again the shared context of meditational practices in ancient India.

तीव्रसंवेगानाम आसन्नः ॥ २१ ॥

I.21 tīvra-saṁvegānām āsannaḥ

tīvra, keen; *saṁvegānām*, for those with intensity;
āsannaḥ, near, proximate

[This state of *samprajñāta*] *is near for those who apply themselves intensely.*

Patañjali indicates here that the speed at which the goal of *yoga* is attained depends on one's degree of commitment. Although Patañjali mentions only intensity, the commentators, following Vyāsa, infer that there are three degrees of application implied in this *sūtra*: gentle and moderate as well as intense [*tīvra*]. Categorizations and subcategorizations are ubiquitous in Indic knowledge systems.[120] Indeed, the next *sūtra* indicates that each of the three levels mentioned here is subdivided into three more levels of intensity, resulting in nine different levels of commitment, or degrees of application to the process of *yoga*. These lead to the ultimate goal of *yoga* with different degrees of rapidity.

Otherwise, says Vācaspati Miśra, success would accrue to all without distinction, which is not the case: Success is noticed in some *yogīs* but not in others. Vācaspati Miśra considers these differences to be due to the strength (or weakness) of ingrained habits from previous lives—in other words, disruptive *saṁskāras* from past births—exerting their influence on the various *yogīs* in this life, and these may interfere with their practices. In short, this *sūtra* states that the attainment of *samādhi* and its fruit are near, *āsannaḥ*, for those most intensely committed.

मृदमध्याधिमात्रत्वात ततोऽपि विशेषः ॥ २२ ॥

I.22 mṛdu-madhyādhimātratvāt tato' pi viśeṣaḥ

mṛdu, mild; *madhya*, middling; *adhimātratvāt*, because of intensity;
tataḥ, from this, consequently; *api*, also; *viśeṣaḥ*, distinction

Even among these, there is further differentiation [of this intensity into degrees of] mild, mediocre, and extreme.

As noted above, each of the three levels identified by the commentators is subdivided; thus there is mild, *mṛdu*, intensity of application to the requirements of *yoga*, mediocre, *madhya*, intensity to these requirements, and extreme, *adhimātra*, intensity. Likewise, there are the same three degrees of mediocre application (intense or above-average mediocrity, middling or average mediocrity, and mild or below-average mediocrity) and the same triad of possibility for mild application. In other words, there is a spectrum of application in *yoga* practice, and, expectedly, the speed of success depends on the degree of commitment.

Śaṅkara says the purpose of this *sūtra* is to fortify the enthusiasm of the practitioner. By learning that all *yogīs*, whether slow or swift in their application, eventually attain the goal, practitioners are encouraged and those who have become despondent due to fatigue from excessive effort regain confidence. But that there are gradations in the attainment of the goal of *yoga*, he says, is just as in the world, where, in a race, the prize goes to the person who runs the fastest!

Chapple (1994), who considers Patañjali's text to be a concatenation of summaries of *yoga* texts extant in his day, suggests that Vyāsa tends to comment on *sūtras* individually, in isolation, and sometimes misses or neglects groupings or units. Chapple argues that such is the case here: Vyāsa has overlooked the possibility that Patañjali intended this *sūtra* to qualify the three previous *sūtras*. The word *tataḥ*, consequently, in this *sūtra* suggests its connection with these preceding *sūtras*. Given that there are three qualitative degrees mentioned in this *sūtra*, and the three previous *sūtras* can be read as three progressively advancing states of attainment, he connects the three degrees of application mentioned here with *sūtras* I.19–22. Thus, the mild of this *sūtra* should be taken as describing those merged in *prakṛti* in I.19; the mediocre, as referring to those practicing faith, etc., described in *sūtra* I.20; and the ardent, as those mentioned in the previous *sūtra* who are near to the goal.

ईश्वरप्रणिधानाद् वा ॥ २३ ॥

I.23 Īśvara-praṇidhānād vā

Īśvara, the Lord; *praṇidhānāt*, from devotion, dedication; *vā*, or

Or, [this previously mentioned state is attainable] from devotion to the Lord.

Patañjali here states that the goal of *yoga* can be attained by the grace of God, *Īśvara*. In this *sūtra*, the theistic element of the *sūtras* is encountered for the first time. The theistic, or *Īśvaravāda*, element in Indic thought stretches back at least to the late Vedic period;[121] *īśvara*, from the root *iś*, to have extraordinary power and sovereignty, is already used six times by the *Atharvaveda* in circa 1000 B.C.E. and refers in the oldest texts to a personal but unnamed god. It is the term preferred in philosophical discourse concerning the existence of a personal god. In partial contrast to the term *bhagavān*,[122] *Īśvara* is often concerned more with a philosophical category in these contexts than with specific divine personal supreme beings such as Viṣṇu, Śiva, and Kṛṣṇa, who all lay claim to the title *Īśvara* in Purāṇic and epic texts. Of the six schools of traditional thought that stem from this period, five—Nyāya, Vaiśeṣika,[123] Vedānta, Yoga, and Sāṅkhya—were or became theistic. Sāṅkhya, although often represented as nontheistic, was in fact widely theistic in its early expressions and continued to retain widespread theistic variants outside of the classical philosophical school thereafter, as evidenced in the Purāṇas (for example, *Bhāgavata* third canto).[124] Yoga has always been theistic: As Feuerstein and others have enjoined emphatically, "The popular academic notion that the conception of God was interpolated into classical Yoga is completely unfounded" (1974, 90).

In his commentary, Vyāsa asks rhetorically whether there is any other effective way to attain *samprajñāta-samādhi* without delay. As Patañjali indicates in this *sūtra*, devotion to God is such an option. This notion of attaining a vision of the self by the grace of God goes back to the Upaniṣads (*Katha* II.20; *Śvetāśvatara* III.20). Reflecting Patañjali's undogmatic and nonsectarian sophistication, *Īśvara-praṇidhāna*, devotion to God, may not be the exclusive or mandatory way to attain realization of the self (given the particle *vā*, or, in this *sūtra*), it is clearly favored by him. One of the earliest references to being granted, by a supreme being, the boon (*prasāda*) of perceiving the *puruṣa* (*ātman*) occurs in the *Kaṭha Upaniṣad*: "Greater than the great, smaller than the small, is the *ātman* situated in the heart of beings. One without desires and free of sorrows sees the majesty of the self by the grace of the Creator" (II.20). Etymologically, *praṇidhāna* means to place oneself down, prostrate, submit, etc.,[125] and while not a common term, means devotional submission (for example, *Gītā* XI.44). Devotion to God, according to Vyāsa, involves a particular type of devotion, *bhakti-viśeṣa*; simply by the *yogī*'s longing, God bestows his grace upon the *yogī*. When this happens, the fruits of *samādhi* become quickly available. As Rāmānanda Sarasvatī puts it, God turns toward the *yogī* as a result of such devotion and says, "Let this that he desires be his!" Vācaspati Miśra considers such special devotion to consist of submission to the Lord with body, mind, and word. Bhoja Rāja, with an eye on the *Gītā*'s "desireless action," adds that it entails devoting all one's actions to the Lord, desiring no fruit for oneself. Hariharānanda describes this state as feeling the existence of God in the innermost core of the heart and considering everything to be done by the Lord. As one meditates on the Lord in this way, and loses interest in everything else, one becomes free from ego, and the mind becomes concentrated and calm.

Śaṅkara states that this *sūtra* describes *bhakti*, the *yoga* of devotion, where the Lord reaches out to the *yogī* who is fully devoted to him, indeed, comes face-to-face with him, and bestows his grace upon him in accordance with how the *yogī* has meditated upon him. Thus, in line with the Yoga tradition's prioritization of experience, one can attain a direct vision of God, by his grace. This grace, through which *samādhi* and the goals of *yoga* are attained, is effortless and imparted by the Lord's omnipotence. Along the same lines, Vijñānabhikṣu states that by meditating on the Lord with love, the *yogī* earns the Lord's favor. He quotes a number of scriptures stating that knowledge of God is the cause of liberation and, indeed (and here Vijñānabhikṣu is reflecting the position of the *bhakti* traditions), knowledge of *Īśvara* is more important even than knowledge of the *puruṣa* self. Consequently, the path of devotion for Vijñānabhikṣu (and for the overall Yoga tradition) is the best means of attaining *samprajñāta-samādhi*, since it does not require one to be solely dependent on one's own steam and resources in the intense application noted in the previous *sūtras*.

It seems useful to present a synopsis of the theistic element in the *sūtras* at this point. *Īśvara* occurs in three distinct contexts in the *Yoga Sūtras*. The first, beginning with this *sūtra*, is in the context of how to attain the ultimate goal of *yoga*—the cessation of all thought, *samprajñāta-samādhi*, and realization of *puruṣa*. Patañjali presents dedication to *Īśvara* as one such option, and his discussion of *Īśvara* begins with this *sūtra* and continues to I.28 (or perhaps, indirectly, up to I.33). It is important to note *vā*, or, in this *sūtra*, indicating that Patañjali presents devotion to *Īśvara*, the Lord, as an optional rather than an obligatory means of attaining *samādhi* (although some commentators state that *puruṣa* cannot detach itself from *prakṛti* without the grace of *Īśvara*).

The only information Patañjali gives concerning the nature of God is provided in the next few *sūtras*. In I.24, he states, "The Lord is a special soul." He is untouched by the deposits of *saṁskāras*,[126] fructification of *karma*,[127] *karma*, or the obstacles to the practice of *yoga*, the *kleśas* of II.3: nescience, ego, attachment, aversion, and the will to live. *Sūtra* I.25 informs the reader that "in him, the seed of omniscience is unsurpassed," and, in *sūtra* I.26, that "He was also the teacher of the ancients, because he is not limited by Time." Given the primary context of the *sūtras*, fixing the mind on an object without deviation, *sūtras* I.27–28 specify how *Īśvara* is to be meditated upon: "The name designating him is the mystical syllable *oṁ*," and "its repetition and the contemplation of its meaning [should be performed]." As a result of this devotional type of meditation comes the realization of the inner consciousness and freedom from all obstacles.

The second context in which Patañjali refers to *Īśvara* is in the first *sūtra* in Chapter II: "*Kriyā-yoga*, the path of action, consists of self-discipline, study, and dedication to the Lord." The following two *sūtras* inform us that by performing such *kriyā-yoga*, *samādhi* is attained and the obstacles to this (the *kleśas*) are weakened. Finally, *Īśvara* surfaces again in a third context in II.32, where the *niyamas* are listed. The *niyamas*, which are the second limb of the eight-limbed path of *yoga*, consist of cleanliness, contentment, austerity, study and, as in the other two contexts, *Īśvara-praṇidhāna*, devotion to *Īśvara* (thus, the three ingredients of *kriyā-yoga* are all *niyamas*). The various benefits associated with following the *yamas* and *niyamas*, ethics and morals, are noted in the ensuing *sūtras* of the chapter, and II.45 states that the benefit from the *niyama* of devotion to God is the attainment of *samādhi*. This is the final reference to *Īśvara* in the text.

These, then, are the gleanings that can be extracted from Patañjali's characteristically frugal *sūtras*. From the first context, we learn that the highest *samādhi* can be attained by dedication to *Īśvara*, a claim Patañjali will repeat in the third section. This suggests that *Īśvara* has the absolute power to manipulate the laws of nature; to circumvent the normal procedures required for practitioners to fix their mind, by removing the obstacles to *yoga*; and somehow to pluck the devoted *yogī* from his or her material embeddedness simply by an act of grace. We learn that *Īśvara* is a special *puruṣa* insofar as he has never been touched by *karma* and *saṁskāras* and the *kleśas*, in short, by the normative influences and conditions to which all *puruṣas* in the world of *saṁsāra* are subject. In other words, *Īśvara* has never been subject to *saṁsāra*. He is an eternal being, since he is untouched by time, and thus he taught the ancients. This indicates that *Īśvara* is concerned with the well-being of the souls in this world and actively involved in their upliftment by promoting knowledge. He makes himself available in the form of the repetition of the sound *oṁ*, which should be recited, Patañjali seems to imply, in a devotional mood (since its meaning, which should be contemplated, is *Īśvara* the subject of devotional surrender).

In the second context in which the term is used, Patañjali briefly alludes to the three ingredients of a practice he terms *kriyā-yoga*, which is a more action-based aspect of *yoga* than the intense meditational regimen outlined in Chapter I. Here, devotion to *Īśvara* is mandatory, in contrast to the meditational path, where it is optional, as a means of attaining *samādhi*. Finally, in the third context in II.32, Patañjali again lists *Īśvara-praṇidhāna* as a *niyama*, a mandatory prerequisite for the higher stages of *yoga*. Moreover, he notes that from this practice, *samādhi* is attained. Again this is significant, because all the boons mentioned as accruing from the other *yamas* and *niyamas* (there are ten in all) represent *prākṛtic*, or material, attainments—vitality, knowledge of past lives, detachment, etc. It is only from *Īśvara*-

praṇidhāna, the last item on the list of *yamas* and *niyamas*, that the ultimate goal of *yoga* is achieved, *samādhi*.

Thus we can conclude that Patañjali is definitely promoting a degree of theistic practice in the *Yoga Sūtras*. Although in the first context commencing with the present *sūtra, Īśvara-praṇidhāna*, devotional surrender to God, is optional as a means of attaining *samādhi*, Patañjali does direct six *sūtras* to *Īśvara*, which is not insignificant given the frugality of his *sūtras*. This devotional surrender is not optional in the second context, *kriyā-yoga*. Since it is likewise not optional in the third context as a *niyama*, which is a prerequisite to meditational *yoga*, Patañjali seems to be requiring that all aspiring *yogīs* be devotionally oriented in the preparatory stages to the higher goals of *yoga*, and although in the higher, more meditational stages of practice they may shift their focus of concentration to other objects (I.34–38)—even, ultimately, to any object of their pleasing (I.39)—they would be best advised to retain *Īśvara* as object thereafter, since this special *puruṣa* can bestow perfection of *samādhi*, which other objects cannot (II.45).

Another way of putting this is that any object can serve as the focus of meditation, but only one object can, in addition to this function, accelerate the attainment of *samādhi*. Therefore, one would be hard-pressed to find a rationale to pick some other object that does not have this ability. Who would not opt for two for the price of one? To my reading, then, Patañjali, while not blatantly demanding that *yogīs* maintain their devotion to *Īśvara* in the higher stages of their meditations, does seem to be discreetly, or perhaps not even so discreetly, promoting it. I envision Patañjali as being too sophisticated a thinker and practitioner to be insistent about this dimension of the tradition, and too delicate about the sensitivities of the nontheistic orientations of other *yogī* practitioners on the horizons of his day to be dogmatically exclusivistic. But he is clearly recommending submission to God as the best and most expedient path.

When Kṛṣṇa was asked by Arjuna who is superior, those worshipping him with devotion or those trying to fix their minds on their own self (by their own prowess), Kṛṣṇa replied that the devotee is the best of those engaged in *yoga* (*yuktatama*), even though those whose minds are fixed on the individual self also attain him (XII.1–4):

> The difficulty of those whose minds are attached to the *ātman*[128] is greater [than those who fix their minds on Kṛṣṇa in devotion]. The path of the impersonal *ātman* is attained with difficulty by embodied beings. But those who, meditating on Me [Kṛṣṇa], worship Me, considering Me to be the Supreme, and renouncing all actions in Me, with undeviating Yoga, for those whose thoughts are immersed in Me, it is I who quickly become the deliverer from the ocean of death and transmigration. (XII.5–7)

Patañjali, like the *Gītā*, is not denying that the *ātman* can be attained by self-effort, but he is clearly favoring a theistic approach.

The optionality noted above is expressed in the Sanskrit particle *vā*, or, in this *sūtra*. There has been some discussion among modern scholars as to what the "or" relates to, that is, *Īśvara-praṇidhāna* devotion to God, is being presented here as an alternative to what? Some have argued that the "or" of the *Īśvara-praṇidhāna* of this *sūtra* is being presented as an alternative to the *abhyāsa*, practice, and *vairāgya*, dispassion, of I.12.[129] While this is not the view of the traditional commentators considered here, it does seem to reflect at least one traditional source. The Muslim traveler al-Bīrunī, who relied on an unknown commentary (that may not be much later than Vyāsa's), takes it in the former sense. He structures his representation of the *Yoga Sūtras* in a question-and-answer format, which, although it takes on a mildly Islamic flavoring in the segments dealing with *Īśvara*, is nonetheless remarkably faithful to his sources:

> QUESTION 11: Is there a way to liberation other than the two ways, namely habituation and asceticism [*abhyāsa*, practice, and *vairāgya*, dispassion]?
>
> ANSWER: [Liberation] may be attained by devotion. This is constituted by withdrawal from the body and [directing oneself] towards knowledge, certainty, and sincerity in the heart, and towards praise, exaltation, and laudation with the tongue, and action with the limbs. God alone and nothing else is aimed at in all these, so that succour should come from Him with a view to achieving eternal bliss.[130]

In my view, it is unfeasible that devotion can be construed as an alternative to the practice and dispassion of I.12, as no Indic (Hindu, Buddhist, or Jain) soteriological tradition promotes practice or dispassion as optional, not even the much misrepresented *tantric* traditions. The *vā* of this *sūtra* is best read as an option to the self-reliance of the immediately preceding *sūtras* I.20–22. Thus, one can apply faith, vigor, memory, *samādhi* absorption, and discernment under one's own steam, or apply these in devotion to God, which, can expedite the process.

The succeeding section on *Īśvara* will be followed by additional options for supports that can be used for stilling the mind, all using the particle *vā*.

क्लेशकर्मविपाकाशयैरपरामृष्टः पुरुषविशेष ईश्वरः ॥२४॥

I.24 kleśa-karma-vipākāśayair aparāmṛṣṭaḥ puruṣa-viśeṣa Īśvaraḥ

kleśa, obstacle to the practice of *yoga*; *karma*, action; *vipāka*, fruition, maturing; *āśayair*, by the receptacle, storage, or deposit of *saṁskāras*; *aparāmṛṣṭaḥ*, untouched; *puruṣa*, soul; *viśeṣaḥ*, special; *Īśvaraḥ*, the Lord

The Lord is a special soul. He is untouched by the obstacles [to the practice of *yoga*], *karma*, the fructification [of *karma*], and subconscious predispositions.

Vyāsa, Vācaspati Miśra, and other commentators dedicate their longest commentaries to this *sūtra*. Patañjali notes here that *Īśvara*, too, is a *puruṣa*, but he is *viśeṣa*, special, that is, different and distinct from other *puruṣas*. He briefly lists four conditions of *saṁsāra* from which *Īśvara* is free, and these are elaborated upon by Vyāsa and the commentators. The cause of *saṁsāra* is the *kleśas*, obstacles—ignorance, ego, attachment, aversion, and the will to live—which are discussed in II.3. Under the influence of these, the individual engages in the second item on the list, *karma*, which consists of one's actions, whether good or bad. As discussed, actions produce a corollary, their fructification, listed here as *vipāka*, which is the effect they produce—every action has a corresponding reaction. Chapter II will discuss in detail how these reactions manifest as the situation into which one is born, one's life expectancy, and one's life experience (II.13–14). Vyāsa glosses the final term in the list, *āśaya* (that which lies stored), with *vāsanās*, habits, or clusters of *saṁskāras*. While the terms are often used interchangeably, *vāsanās* tend to refer to latent *saṁskāras* of past lives, which lie dormant, albeit subconsciously molding personality, habit, and choice, and *saṁskāras* to the more active imprints of this life generated at every moment. *Saṁskāras* have to be contained somewhere, and the *āśaya* is their bed or container in the *citta*. Vācaspati Miśra adds that these *vāsanās* and *saṁ-skāras*, subliminal imprints or subconscious impressions that eventually fructify, lie stored as potencies in the field of the mind. *Īśvara* is free from all of these conditions of *saṁsāra*; hence he is a special type of *puruṣa*.

Since *yogīs* who have broken the three bonds[131] and attained liberation are free from these influences, Vyāsa makes a point of noting that *Īśvara* is distinct from liberated *puruṣas*, since he never had nor ever will have any relation to these bonds. Unlike all other *yogīs*, then, he never was bound and never will be. He is eternally the transcendent God, not some sort of a liberated *yogī*. As Śaṅkara points out, *akliṣṭa*, untouched, means *never* touched by the four conditions for *saṁsāra* noted above, whether in time past, present, or future. A liberated *yogī* was once touched by all these in the past but is no longer in the present. *Īśvara* was never touched to begin with. He is therefore in a different category from liberated *yogīs*.

The notion in some modern commentaries that *Īśvara* is some sort of "archetypal" *yogī* (Eliade 1969) is nowhere to be found in the traditional commentarial tradition of the Yoga school, nor, for that matter, in the usage of the term *Īśvara* in the history of Indic philosophical discourse. In later classical Indic philosophical circles there were *Īśvara-vādins*, those believing in *Īśvara*, and *nir-īśvara-vādins*, those who rejected the notion of an *Īśvara*, a supreme God, but whether *Īśvara-vādin* or *nir-īśvara-vādin*, there was no debate at least as to the basic and general referent of the term, *Īśvara*. The arguments were philosophical, revolving around whether the existence of a personal god was philosophically defensible, not semantic, in terms of what *Īśvara* meant.[132] While the term can, on occasion, refer by extension to a being with extraordinary power,[133] texts such as the *Mahābhārata*, the *Gītā*, and later Upaniṣads indicate that *Īśvara* was associated with a personal God, a supreme being, by Patañjali's time, and one would need compelling grounds to renegotiate the meaning of the term as it is used and understood by the entire later Indic philosophical tradition in general in the premodern period. The term cannot be extricated from its traditional context.

On a related note, it is generally held, including in traditional philosophical discourse, that Patañjali's *Īśvara* is not a creator sort of God. Sāṅkhya is criticized in Vedānta for considering creation to evolve from inanimate *prakṛti* (*pradhāna*)[134] rather than the conscious *Brahman* of the Upaniṣads, and the only criticism levied against Yoga by this school is that it is viewed to hold the same position (*etena yogaḥ pratyuktaḥ*[135]), so Patañjali's *Īśvara* seems to have been seen in this light, and this is, of course, significant. Now, there are two types of creatorship: God as material cause (the material stuff of the world emanates from God) and God as efficient cause (God does not create the actual material substance of the world, which is eternal as is He, but it is He who manipulates this stuff to create the world). But Patañjali nowhere indicates how he envisioned the relationship of *Īśvara* with the creation of the world. *Argumentum ex silentio* is not the strongest type of evidence, especially since Patañjali is not talking about creation in the sections of the text where he mentions *Īśvara*. He introduces *Īśvara* in the context of meditation, since that is his project in this text. While he does briefly mention a few attributes of *Īśvara*, they are relevant to the ongoing discussion on meditation and liberation from *saṁsāra*. Creation is an entirely different topic not connected with the subject matter of the *sūtras* and thus one has no explicit grounds from the text itself to determine how Patañjali envisioned the relationship of *Īśvara* with creation. He does correlate *Īśvara* with *oṁ*, in I.27, and would have been well aware that *oṁ* is the designation for *Brahman* in the Upaniṣads, and that *Brahman* is depicted there and consequently in the Vedānta tradition as the source of creation.[136] And certainly all the commentators do accept the creatorship of *Īśvara*, that is, *Īśvara* as efficient cause.[137]

This seems a fairly important point. Patañjali's compact *sūtras* provide succinct information germane to his specific and immediate project, *citta-vṛtti-nirodha* (*samādhi*). He thus provides whatever information related to *Īśvara* is immediately relevant: that *samādhi* can be attained by *Īśvara*; that this is possible because *Īśvara* is omniscient and beyond the *kleśas* and other sources of ignorance dealt with in the text that impede *samādhi*; that this can be attained by reciting *oṁ*, etc.

There was no need to extrapolate further since, apart from this commitment to a very delimited focus, there was anyway no paucity of other theistic texts dealing with all manner of additional theological specificities in circulation at the time. (Certainly Vijñānabhikṣu, although much later and clearly a Vedāntin, explicitly states this: "Now what is *Īśvara*? What is devotion to Him? . . . He has been very thoroughly analyzed in the *Vedānta Sūtras* . . . Consequently, it is only touched upon in passing here.")[138]

To make this point, one could wonder why Patañjali has nothing to say about, for instance, disease, which he mentions in I.30. Again, this solitary reference is in the context of disease being an obstacle to *samādhi*, and in this regard only is it relevant to and therefore introduced in Patañjali's project. There was an extensive body of knowledge in *āyurveda* on other aspects of disease available at the time. That greater body of knowledge is not relevant to Patañjali's project, but this does not mean Patañjali did not consider texts that do focus on *āyurveda* essential to human existence, or did not accept their jurisdiction. Likewise, Patañjali's text focuses on *puruṣa*, not *Īśvara*. But this does not mean he minimizes or rejects the jurisdiction and contours of those texts that focus on other aspects of *Īśvara* such as creation, or, for that matter, the varieties of *praṇidhāna*.

To my knowledge, all unambiguous theistic traditions taking root in Patañjali's day—epic, Purāṇic, Vedānta, Nyāya—accepted *Brahman/Īśvara* at least as efficient creator (if not, with the Vedāntins, material creator)—understandably because the Upaniṣadic and epic usages of the term cast *Īśvara* (or the more common Upaniṣadic term, *Īśa*) in this role.[139] What grounds do we have from this period to insist that Patañjali's notion of *Īśvara* was an exception other than the *Vedānta Sūtras* reference? And even here the evidence simply points to some form of Yoga being associated with some form of Sāṅkhya as denying material creatorship to *Brahman*. But, even prior to the *Vedānta Sūtras*, the *Mahābhārata* states that he whom both Sāṅkhya and Yoga call the Supreme Soul, Nārāyaṇa, is the source of *prakṛti*, so both prior to the *Vedānta Sūtras* and also after their composition, there were mainstream strains of Sāṅkhya and Yoga that did accept the creatorship of *Īśvara*. We have no grounds to consider the author of the *Vedānta Sūtras* to be referring to Patañjali's version of Yoga in the quote noted above, since the *Yoga Sūtras* postdated him.[140] Rather, the very fact that

Patañjali makes no reference to the creatorship aspect of *Īśvara* suggests he accepted the status quo. We must, I suggest, accept that Patañjali considered *Īśvara* at least as efficient cause of creation.

Moreover, the fact that this *sūtra* indicates that *Īśvara* is not touched by the *kleśas* and *karma* does not indicate that *Īśvara* could not be a personal God for Patañjali. If he is the teacher of the ancients (I.26), the bestower of liberation (II.45), and omniscient (I.25), then he must have some sort of personality (even to accept a form of pure *sattva* as held by the commentators), and clearly Patañjali does not consider his involvement with *prakṛti* in this capacity to compromise him or subject him to the laws of *prakṛti*—the *kleśas* and *karma*, etc. Our commentators differ on how to make sense of this important point, but practically any theistic tradition of the world envisions God as a personal being involved in some way with the world and yet simultaneously absolute and temporally untouched, and the notions of *Īśvara* prevalent in Patañjali's time are no exception. One need only consider the *Gītā*, where Kṛṣṇa as *Īśvara* unambiguously claims to be the creator and source of everything (VII.4ff; IX.8; X.8; and throughout), the *Īśvara* who enters into the world of *prakṛti* and supports it (XV.16–18)[141] and yet remains untouched and unchanged by all such things (IV.13–14; IX.8–9). The point here is not to project the theology of the *Gītā* onto Patañjali but to stress that Patañjali's *Īśvara* cannot be extracted from the context of *Īśvara*-related theologies of the time. The entire *Śvetāśvatara Upaniṣad*, too, presents Śiva as *Īśvara*, who actively creates, rules, and engages with the world and yet remains distinct and transcendent to it.[142] Moreover, the largest body of Sanskrit written material, the Purāṇic genre, while yet to attain its final form, was absorbing oral traditions that predated Patañjali's time, and these are pervaded with Viṣṇu/Kṛṣṇa and Śiva theologies of this sort.[143] We have no grounds to insist that Patañjali's *Īśvara* be distinct from such theistic expressions, and thus stress that in our view Patañjali's reference to *Īśvara* cannot be excised from this context of his time.

Fewer than twenty-five words have been utilized in the *sūtras* descriptive of *Īśvara*. Far too much has been made, in our view, by extracting from the greater theistic landscape of Patañjali's day his terse statements toward a description of *Īśvara* and focusing on them as if they exist in some sort of isolated bubble specific to Patañjali and immune from the mainstream *Īśvara* theologies that were enveloping the

Indian landscape. We have noted how earlier scholars opted to consider the entire *Īśvara* element as a later interpolation, in the hope, we suspect, of preserving a rational core to Patañjali, possibly stemming from discomfort with this vivid background of Hindu *Īśvara* theologies. Even with the more careful attention of later scholars who recognize that the *Īśvara* element is inherent to the text, one senses an aversion to pursuing the implications of this. In Patañjali's day and age (and subsequently, for that matter), what options would there have been for any type of *Īśvara* theism other than the Nārāyaṇa/Viṣṇu- and Śiva-derived traditions? Viṣṇu and Śiva had risen to prominence centuries before Patañjali, and their worship was widespread across the subcontinent by the beginning of the Common Era. The *Īśvara* theological options of the time are amply preserved in the epic and much neglected Purāṇic traditions, and thus we have gone so far as to speculate whether, given the theistic options of the second and third centuries, one can legitimately reject the probability that Patañjali would have envisioned *Īśvara* as either Viṣṇu or Śiva, as I have considered (only somewhat gratuitously) elsewhere.[144]

Many centuries prior to Patañjali, there were Sāṅkhya/Yoga traditions preserved in the *Mahābhārata* that were theistic, all with Vaiṣṇava flavorings. Ramakrishna Rao (1966) has extensively sieved through the Sāṅkhya and Yoga (*Mokṣadharma*) sections of the great epic and determined that there were several variant schools subscribing to Sāṅkhyan metaphysics, all of them theistic in some form or fashion.[145] These theistic expressions were Vaiṣṇava in orientation,[146] that is, they used the language of Viṣṇu/Nārāyaṇa when referring to *Īśvara* (even in those variants that conceived of the Supreme Truth in less personal terms).[147] And, of course, the epic's *Bhagavad Gītā* (generally dated between the fourth and second centuries B.C.E.) has Viṣṇu in his form as Kṛṣṇa emphatically stating throughout that he is *Īśvara* and that *prakṛti* and her Sāṅkhyan evolutes are his "lower nature" (VII.4). The only extant description of the supposed original source Sāṅkhyan text, the *Ṣaṣṭi-tantra-śāstra* in the (admittedly later and sectarian) Vaiṣṇava *Ahirbudhnya Saṁhitā*, also accepts a Sāṅkhyan *Īśvara* and considers him to be Viṣṇu, and these Vaiṣṇava Sāṅkhyan traditions were preserved in the Purāṇas, as in the later Vedānta traditions (including that of Śaṅkara who clearly conceived of *Īśvara* as Viṣṇu[148]).

There was thus a widespread variety of Vaiṣṇava-flavored *Īśvara* traditions preserved in a variety of genres long preceding Patañjali.

Indeed, every characteristic Patañjali will make about *Īśvara* being transcendent to *karma*, of unsurpassed omniscience, teacher of the ancients, untouched by Time, represented by *oṁ*, and awarding enlightenment seem extracted from the *Gītā*. In the *Gītā*, Kṛṣṇa claims to be a distinct (but supreme) sort of *puruṣa*, the *uttamaḥ puruṣas anyaḥ*, specifying that this *puruṣa* is distinct from not only nonliberated *puruṣas* but also liberated ones (XV.16–18)[149]; beyond *karma* and the *kleśas* (IV.14; IX.9); of unsurpassed omniscience (VII.26; X.20, 32; XI.43); the teacher of the ancients (IV.1, specified as Vivasvān the sun god, who in turn imparted knowledge to Manu, the progenitor of mankind); transcendent to Time (X.30); the sound *oṁ* (IX.17); the remover of obstacles impeding the progress of his devotees, and the bestower of liberation (VII.14; IX.30–32; X.10–11; XII.7; XVIII.58). There is thus perfect compatibility in quality between Patañjali's unnamed *Īśvara* and Kṛṣṇa as depicted in the *Gītā*. Similarly with the attributes assigned to Nārāyaṇa/Viṣṇu throughout the *Nārāyaṇīya* portion of the *Mokṣa-dharma* section in the twelfth book of the *Mahābhārata* epic, which unambiguously presents Viṣṇu as the supreme deity possessing all these characteristics throughout.[150]

Of course, the *Mahābhārata* with its *Gītā* was not the only well-known philosophical text on the religious landscape at the beginning of the Common Era promoting theism to an identified *Īśvara*. A definite theism had also long emerged in the late Upaniṣads, particularly the *Śvetāśvatara Upaniṣad* (generally dated from the fourth to second century B.C.E.), which vigorously identifies Śiva (named Rudra and Hara in this text) as *Īśvara*. Indeed, the *Śvetāśvatara Upaniṣad* assigns to Śiva several of the same generic characteristics associated with *Īśvara* that Patañjali uses: He is distinct from other souls;[151] he is the awarder of liberation (or, more precisely, by meditating on him all illusion disappears, I.10); he is omniscient and the maker of Time (VI.2, 16); and he supported (taught) the ancient sage Kapila, the founder of the Sāṅkhyan system. This text is very relevant to our line of argument as it promotes *yogic* practice; Chapter II gives the most extensive (and almost sole) description of *yoga* in the earlier Upaniṣads (along with the later Maitrī).[152] Moreover, the *sūtra* is situated in the context of

Sāṅkhyan metaphysics,[153] which is the infrastructure within which Patañjali situates his *yoga* system.[154] The *Gītā* (by most dating estimates[155]) and the *Śvetāśvatara Upaniṣad* had preceded Patañjali by centuries, as had many of the Purāṇic stories, even if they were still being organized into their final literary forms, and there is no evidence that Patañjali's rendition of *Īśvara* is a departure from such specific theistic orientations. Indeed, the question must be raised as to what alternatives to Viṣṇu or Śiva would there be anyway in that period. We thus suggest that the evidence points to the conclusion that the theism in Patañjali's system can stem only from these preexisting Vaiṣṇava or Śaivite strains.

One might add a final note here, that Patañjali not only stipulates the practice of *svādhyāya*, literally self-study, understood in all the commentaries as referring to the study of scripture (which teaches of the self) and recitation of *japa* (II.1, 44), but also states that from such study and recitation one connects with an *iṣṭa-devatā*, one's divinity of preference (a term used in the Upaniṣads and earlier Vedic texts to refer to the Vedic gods). That Patañjali was well versed in the *śāstras*, sacred texts—and thus hardly immune to the theistic currents of the day—is already obvious; this *sūtra* suggests he was himself oriented toward a specific divinity of preference. It is hard to conceive that this divinity would have been one of the (by this time) minor Vedic deities for reasons outlined in the commentary to II.44 (where I again take up the matter of Patañjali's own personal theistic orientations), but which can be summarized by pointing out that the minor deities are approached for worldly boons. Obviously the *yogī* has no interest in worldly boons, as Patañjali has already specified. The *yogī* is interested only in *samādhi*, and the only divine being who can bestow this is *Īśvara*. Thus, *iṣṭa-devatā* might better be read, as it is taken in the theistic traditions, as a reference to a form of *Īśvara* to which the *yogī* is partial.[156] This is underscored by the fact that all the commentators understand *svādhyāya* as also referring to the recitation of *mantra, japa*, which Vyāsa, following Patañjali (I.27–28) takes as reciting *oṁ*. *Oṁ*, we will see, specifically refers to *Īśvara*. So whether *svādhyāya* is taken to be study or *mantra, iṣṭa-devatā* can conceivably refer only to a preferred form of *Īśvara*. The preferred forms of *Īśvara* in the second century had long been associated with Śiva or Viṣṇu or one of his incarnations such as Kṛṣṇa. There were no other candidates.

If one felt inclined to push the matter, the scanty inferential evidence that can be brought to bear on the case for Viṣṇu as Patañjali's *iṣṭa-devatā* might include the facts that, apart from the evidence of the earlier Vaiṣṇava-flavored Yoga streams preserved in the *Mahābhārata* noted above, the later tradition considered Patañjali to be an incarnation of Śeṣa, Viṣṇu's serpent carrier in the Ocean of Milk (rather than, say, Nandi, Śiva's bull carrier) and assigns the primary commentary on Patañjali to the famous Vyāsa, who is embedded in Vaiṣṇava narrative traditions. Indeed, the *Mahābhārata* (XII.337.4–5) considers Vyāsa a manifestation (*aṁśa*) of Viṣṇu/Nārāyaṇa and the son of the latter. This might suggest the preservation of a tradition that was partial to *Īśvara* as Viṣṇu. For this and other reasons,[157] a case can thus be made that Patañjali personally subscribed to the Vaiṣṇava/Viṣṇu-flavored theism of the older epic and Purāṇic Sāṅkhya and Yoga traditions. But one can also make a case for Śiva. Perhaps any such reading of the sparse evidence reflects preexisting dispositions, but one can certainly argue that *Īśvara* in Patañjali's time had long been associated with Viṣṇu and Śiva, and thus Patañjali would in all likelihood have been either a Vaiṣṇavite or a Śaivite.

Having said all this, one cannot ignore the fact that Patañjali chose not to disclose his understanding of *Īśvara* other than in the most general categories of relevance to the specific focus of the *sūtras, citta-vṛtti-nirodha*. I like to imagine that Patañjali is too sophisticated and broad-minded a thinker to risk sectarianizing the otherwise universalistic tenor of the *sūtras* and thereby alienating the sensitivities of aspiring *yogīs* with theistic (or nontheistic) orientations different from his own. That millions of people worldwide continue to find his text personally relevant today speaks to his foresight in this regard.

On a related note, the Yoga tradition in America today primarily stems from the Vaiṣṇava (Viṣṇu-centered) traditions. Krishnamacharya, his son Desikachar, and his son-in-law Iyengar are all devoted members of the Śrī lineage of Vaiṣṇavism, best associated with the twelfth-century Vedāntin Rāmānuja. This is a devotional lineage, prioritizing *bhakti*, which accepts Viṣṇu as the Supreme *Īśvara*.[158] This aspect of their heritage is unknown to most of their followers, since it was not stressed by these *ācāryas* upon coming to Western shores (although it can be perceived more readily in the *viniyoga* writings of Desikachar than in those of Iyengar).[159] The transplantation of Vaiṣṇava *bhakti* to the West in modern times as a *yogic* path unto itself is to be credited to the efforts of A. C. Bhaktivedānta Swami, founder of ISKCON (the Hare Krishna movement), whose devotion to Lord Kṛṣṇa inspired him to spread Kṛṣṇa-centered *bhakti-yoga* (Kṛṣṇa Consciousness) around the world. Noteworthy, too, in the same time period, is the transplantation of the Kashmiri form of Śaivism featuring *bhakti* to Lord Śiva popularized by Swami Muktānanda, founder of Siddha Yoga.[160]

Returning to our commentators, *Īśvara* is unsurpassed by any other power, continues Vyāsa; he has no competitor. Nor does he have an equal. As Vyāsa puts it rhetorically, if, among two equals, one says of a desired object: "Let it be old," and the other says: "Let it be new," the wishes of one of the two will be thwarted since they cannot both have their way. And if, on the other hand, their wishes never contradict, adds Vācaspati Miśra, then what is the point of having more than one *Īśvara* in the first place? Thus, *Īśvara* has no equal but is the one sole being who is unexcelled and unequaled. Therefore, Patañjali states that he is a special *puruṣa*. His existence is substantiated by the scriptures, add the commentators (Vijñānabhikṣu lists a variety of passages in this regard, such as the occurrence of the term *Īśvara* in the *Gītā* [for example, XV.17]). The scriptures are themselves the product of *Īśvara* when he associates with pure *sattva*. Thus there is circularity among *Īśvara*, pure *sattva*, and scripture: *Īśvara* produces scripture from his adoption of pure *sattva*, and scripture directs one to *Īśvara*.[161] Obviously this means that, since *Īśvara* is omniscient, and it goes without saying that he is beyond any cheating propensity due to his nature of pure *sattva*, the scriptures emanating from him are absolute and free from error.

Vācaspati Miśra raises an issue here concerning *Īśvara*'s "personality." If *Īśvara* has knowledge and the power to act, as the previous *sūtras* indicate that he does (since he has the power to bestow liberation on the devoted *yogī* and thus must be aware of his devotion, and I.27 informs us that he taught the ancients), does this not mean he has a *citta* mind? Pure consciousness, Vācaspati Miśra reminds us, is unchanging and without object according to the Yoga school (and an axiom of Hindu thought in general), and therefore removed from all knowledge and the desire to act. Knowledge and desire are thus functions of *citta*, in other words, *citta-vṛttis*. Did not the opening *sūtras* of the text inform us that these very *citta-vṛttis* are responsible for bondage in *saṁsāra*? The *citta* itself is the product of *prakṛti* and thus has its origin in ignorance, *avidyā*. How can *Īśvara*, who is forever free, be bound by *prakṛti* and its products and subject to ignorance in the form of *citta-vṛttis*?

Vācaspati Miśra resolves this dichotomy by supposing that the Lord, even though untouched by nescience, appears to assume the nature of ignorance out of his freedom, just as an actor imitating Rāma freely assumes the character of Rāma. But the actor does not forget his real self. In the same way, *Īśvara* associates with pure *sattva*, free from the influence of *rajas* and *tamas*, out of his own free will, says Vācaspati Miśra.[162] A parallel notion of *Īśvara* is expressed in the *Gītā*:

> Although I am unborn and my nature is imperishable
> And although I am the *Īśvara* of all beings
> Yet I come into being by my own power
> By controlling *prakṛti*, which is mine. (IV.6)

Nonetheless, even if *Īśvara* associates with *prakṛti* out of freedom rather than bondage, his inclination to do so still indicates desire on his part, and desire, for Vācaspati Miśra, is also a symptom of ignorance. To address this philosophical objection, Vācaspati Miśra patches together a rather complicated argument (that will not meet the approval of Vijñānabhikṣu). He argues that *Īśvara* is transcendent to Time. Before the dissolution of the universe,[163] *Īśvara* determines, or wills, that he will again associate with *sattva* when the next universal manifestation occurs. This wish or *saṁskāra* is deposited into *sattva* along with the collective *saṁskāras* of all embodied beings. When dissolution occurs, all *saṁsāric puruṣas* remain in a latent state until the next manifestation. The *saṁskāras* each *puruṣa* had accumulated in past lives also remain latent but are again regrouped around the appropriate *puruṣa* when the next cosmic manifestation takes place. This, for Vācaspati Miśra, applies to *Īśvara*: After dissolution, *Īśvara* disconnects from *sattva* and all acts of volition (i.e., from the *citta*), as do all other *puruṣas*. But when the universe manifests again, *Īśvara*'s determination from the previous cycle is activated, like a cosmic alarm clock, and *Īśvara* again associates with *prakṛti* (just as, says Vācaspati Miśra, Caitra who contemplates "tomorrow I must get up at daybreak" and then, after sleeping, gets up at that very time because of the *saṁskāra* he had deposited into the *citta* the previous day to this effect). This cumbersome explanation is construed to explain how desire, knowledge, and the will to act, which in conventional Yoga understanding are *citta-vṛttis* indicative of unliberated *puruṣas* in *saṁsāra*, can exist in *Īśvara*, whom Patañjali says in this *sūtra* has always been pure and liberated and free from ignorance.

Vācaspati Miśra does not explain how, in the new cycle of creation, the pure and independent *Īśvara* can become influenced by the reactivated *sattva* containing his deposited wish from the previous cosmic cycle. Vijñānabhikṣu draws attention to this problem, pointing out that it is ignorance that causes *puruṣa* to associate (or, after cosmic dissolution, reassociate) with *prakṛti*—but how can ignorance be applicable to *Īśvara*? Rather, for Vijñānabhikṣu, desire, knowledge, and the power to act exist in *Īśvara* eternally. Here, he again reflects the position held by certain Vedānta schools, which also hold that *Īśvara*'s mind and, for that matter, body are not *prākṛtic* productions, even in its pure *sāttvic* potential, but made of pure *Brahman* and thus part of the essential nature of *Īśvara* rather than an external *prākṛtic* covering as is the case with the mind and bodies covering the *puruṣas* in *saṁsāra*.[164]

Vijñānabhikṣu uses this *sūtra* as an opportunity to argue on behalf of the view of the Sāṅkhya and Yoga schools that there is an eternal plurality of *puruṣas*, in opposition to the position of the *advaita*, nondualistic, school of Vedānta, which posits one ultimate, single all-pervading *puruṣa* (*ātman*). The Yoga view holds that, both in the liberated state as well as in the world of *saṁsāra*, there is a plurality of individual souls, while the *advaita* school holds that the apparent plurality of *puruṣas*, including the *puruṣa* known as *Īśvara*, is a product of ignorance occurring only in the world of *saṁsāra*. In *advaita Vedānta*, from a liberated perspective, there is only one undivided *ātman*. Other Vedānta schools, such as Rāmānuja's *viśiṣṭādvaita*, oppose this view, and Vijñānabhikṣu presents various arguments against the *advaita* position that can be found in the writing of Rāmānuja and other post-Śaṅkara Vedāntins. For example, if there were only one ultimate undivided *ātman*, then if any one *jīva* (the *ātman* in *saṁsāric* bondage) becomes liberated, it attains to this undivided state. How, then, can other *jīvas* continue to exist in *saṁsāra*? In other words, if there is only one undivided *ātman* in reality, how can it exist in both liberated as well as *saṁsāric* states? This contradicts the supposed undividedness of *ātman*. For this reason alone, there must therefore be a plurality of *puruṣas*, some liberated and some in *saṁsāra*, as held by the *Sāṅkhya Kārikās* (XVIII).[165] The argument has a history in the polemics of Vedāntins opposed to Śaṅkara's extreme *advaita* form of monism. Thus, *Īśvara* is distinct from the *puruṣas*, and the individual *puruṣas* from each other.

And, importantly, clearly in response to the Vedānta criticism of Sāṅkhya (and, by extension Yoga[166]), Bhoja Rāja notes that it is by the will (*icchā*) of *Īśvara* that the union between *puruṣa* and *prakṛti* takes place. The Vedāntins point out that since *prakṛti* is inert and unconscious, and *puruṣa* in its pure form is free of all desire or any content of consciousness, how could the union between the two ever occur? For Bhoja Rāja, as for the Vedānta and all other theistic traditions, it is the desire of *Īśvara* (in conjunction with the previous activities of each *puruṣa*) that brings about the union between the two in each cycle of creation (the issue of first time primordial beginnings is avoided in Indian philosophy in general by positing that this cycle is beginningless). Thus, with Bhoja Rāja, Vijñānabhikṣu, and, of course, Śaṅkara and other commentators, Vedāntic concerns are blended into the commentaries on the *Yoga Sūtras* (which is an organic and quintessentially orthodox exegetical thing to do).

तत्र निरतिशायं सर्वज्ञबीजम ॥ २५ ॥

I.25 tatra niratiśāyam sarvajña-bījam

tatra, in him; *niratiśāyam*, unsurpassed; *sarvajña*, omniscience; *bījam*, seed

In him, the seed of omniscience is unsurpassed.

Although, by definition, omniscience, *sarvajña*, means to know everything, and thus degrees of omniscience would seem to be something of an oxymoron, Patañjali here indicates that there is a difference between the omniscience of *Īśvara* and any comparable state obtainable by any other entity: *Īśvara*'s omniscience is unsurpassed, *niratiśāyam*.

Vyāsa states that the metaphor of a seed is used because there are in fact degrees in omniscience, as there are in the germination of a seed. He defines the seed of omniscience as the ability to understand anything, large or small, individual or collective, either in the past, present, or future—in other words, the ability to understand all things from all time. An omniscient person is one in whom this seed of understanding keeps growing. As in any form of measurement, there is a maximum attainable dimension of all individual things or subjects; the smallest subatomic particle, for example, says Bhoja Rāja has a certain dimension, as does the vastest entity in manifest reality, space itself. These dimensions of things reach their limit somewhere and so, therefore, does knowledge of them. Omniscience is knowing the totality of the dimensions of all individual things, whether past, present, or future. *Īśvara* must be omniscient in this sort of sense, adds Śaṅkara, to be able to supervise the vast totality of all things in the planned and regulated universe.

Where Bhoja Rāja focuses on the dimension of individual things to define omniscience, Hariharānanda focuses on the knowledge of individual beings. All created beings, whether a worm or a human, have some degree of knowledge, whether greater or lesser. This knowledge of all individual beings, continually grows (new *saṁskāras* are being implanted in the *citta* every second). Since there are unlimited beings whose knowledges are continually growing, the collective knowledge is limitless. The being who has attained the maximum attainable level of this expanding collective of knowledge is omniscient. He is the special *puruṣa* known as *Īśvara*.

Although, by this process of inference, one can reach the conclusion that there must be a highest attainable state of knowledge, omniscience, one does not know the specifics of such an omniscient being by this process, says Vyāsa. The followers of all kinds of sects consider their masters to be omniscient—even in the *Yoga Sūtras* there are several *sūtras* that indicate that the accomplished *yogī* becomes omniscient (for example, I.40; III.49). Are all these on a par with *Īśvara*? The difference is that prior to becoming accomplished, such *yogīs* were not omniscient. Śaṅkara points out here that the Buddhists and Jains themselves state that the Buddha and Mahāvīra[167] attained enlightenment, and this indicates that there was a time when they were not enlightened; in other words, there was a time when they were once subject to ignorance. Their enlightenment and hence omniscience is therefore limited by time—it is not eternal, without beginning.

Vācaspati Miśra makes the same point about Kapila, the founder of the Sāṅkhya system. Vyāsa notes in his commentary that Kapila, the original sage (*ādi-vidvān*), adopted a manufactured *citta* (*nirmāṇa-cittam adhiṣṭhāya*) out of compassion and presented the Sāṅkhya teachings to Āsuri, whom tradition considers to be the first disciple. Kapila was the first teacher of the lineage and attained liberation, says Vācaspati Miśra, but this is not the same as *Īśvara*, the Supreme Teacher, who was always liberated. Even as Kapila is accepted as an incarnation of Viṣṇu in some sources,[168] he still had to attain absolute knowledge, according to Vācaspati Miśra, which, as indicated in the *Śvetāśvatara Upaniṣad* V.2, he received from Śiva Maheśvara. Again, this means there was a time when he—unlike *Īśvara*—was not in possession of absolute knowledge. As an aside, Vyāsa's comment about Kapila points to the Hindu belief that enlightened beings may chose to return to the world out of compassion for those still enmeshed in *saṁsāra*, a notion more fully developed in the Mahāyāna Buddhist notion of the Bodhisattva.

Therefore Patañjali's *Īśvara*, who is not limited by Time, is of a different category from that of all other enlightened beings. We will engage in some additional speculations as to how *Īśvara*'s "extra" omniscience might be read through certain Vedāntic lenses in III.49, which is not irrelevant to the commentarial tradition since, as Vācaspati Miśra states, specific knowledge about *Īśvara*, such as his various names such as Śiva and Viṣṇu, and his activities and other details, can be gained from other scriptures.

Although *Īśvara* has no personal benefit to gain, Vyāsa notes that the purpose of his activities is for the benefit of living beings. *Īśvara* thinks as follows: "During the various creations and dissolutions of the universe, I will uplift beings caught in *saṁsāra* by disseminating knowledge and *dharma*, social duty."[169] Vyāsa is paraphrasing the famous verse from the *Gītā* here, where Kṛṣṇa states: "I appear in every *yuga*, cyclical age,[170] to protect the pious and establish *dharma*"[171] (IV.8). This notion of *Īśvara* periodically bestowing instruction to humanity is relevant to the next *sūtra*.

Śaṅkara makes some useful comments here. *Īśvara*'s body is pure *sattva* and thus free of the limitations of the senses of conventional bodies; therefore, *Īśvara*'s awareness can be in simultaneous contact with everything, that is, omniscient. The awareness of embodied beings is limited by the *tāmasic* element in the senses of their particular bodies. Thus humans can see only a certain distance, hear only a certain range of sounds, etc. Other animals have senses with different ranges, and thus the limitations imposed on consciousness vary—vultures can see farther than humans, for example, and dogs hear and smell more acutely. Śaṅkara analogizes this with a light inside a clay jar with holes in it—the light of the jar is visible and can illumine only through the holes. The body with its senses is like a jar with holes; awareness can penetrate outside reality only through the holes of the senses (often called "gates" in texts like the *Gītā* V.13 and Śvetāśvatara Upaniṣad III.18), and even then its range is limited depending on the type of sense (the sight of a vulture vs. that of a human, which can be compared with different-sized holes in the jar). But when the jar with its holes has been removed, the light that had been contained within can now pervade everything without being dependent on the holes for its path. Similarly, since *Īśvara* is free from *karma*, his awareness is not limited by sensual limitations and thus can perceive everything at the same time. Hence he is omniscient.

Vācaspati Miśra considers the atheistic position that God could not have created the world because it is full of pain. If there were a compassionate God, he would have created a world of undisturbed enjoyment (such arguments surface periodically in the writings of atheistic schools such as the Jain and Mīmāṁsā[172]). His response to this is that God informs mankind of the means of liberation and thus is not cruel. Vijñānabhikṣu considers a further charge that since *Īśvara* is partial to his devotees, showering his blessings on them and not on others, he is a flawed individual, since partiality is not a sign of transcendence. Not so, he says. Just as fire has the nature of heat, so God's nature is such that he is controlled by his devotees, but anyone can avail himself or herself of this nature by cultivating pure *sattva*.

Thus, all have access to his blessings. He quotes *Gītā* IX.29: "I am equal to all beings—there is no one dear to me nor disliked by me. But those who worship me with devotion are in me and I in them." Pleasure and pain, asserts Vijñānabhikṣu, are the result of one's own past actions and have nothing to do with *Īśvara*'s partiality.

पूर्वेषाम् अपि गुरुः कालेनानवच्छेदात् ॥ २६ ॥

I.26 pūrveṣām api guruḥ kālenānavacchedāt

pūrveṣām, of the ancients; *api*, also; *guruḥ*, guru, teacher; *kālena*, by time; *anavacchedāt*, because of not being limited or conditioned by

***Īśvara* was also the teacher of the ancients, because he is not limited by Time.**

Vyāsa states that the ancients, *purvāḥ* (those who went before), were subject to Time, *kāla*; that is, they were mortal beings with finite life spans. The one who is not so subject to Time—*Īśvara*, who transcends Time—is the *guru* of even the ancients. Moreover, just as *Īśvara* existed as the perfect being at the beginning of this creation, so was he the same in previous creations. The commentators hold that this *sūtra* differentiates *Īśvara* from beings like the secondary deity Brahmā[173] (not to be confused with *Brahman*), whose immense life span encompasses the duration of one universal cycle but who ultimately and eventually dies like all created beings and is reborn in the next cycle of creation. *Īśvara* is not such a created being subject to birth, death, cyclical creation, or any other manifestation of Time.

Time for the Yoga school simply means the movement of the *guṇas* of *prakṛti*, that is, the movement of matter. A day is simply the apparent movement of the sun in the heavens; a season, the movements of nature; a year, the earth's movement around the sun; a lifetime, the movement of one's body over the years; a civilization or world epoch, the movement of people and events and the rise of edifices or monuments that eventually crumble and return to their *prākṛtic* source. Everything in Sāṅkhya and Yoga is nothing other than the product of the interaction and movement of the *guṇas* underpinning *prakṛti*. Being subject to Time, embodied beings of the present day are not free to receive teachings directly from, say, Patañjali, Kṛṣṇa, Christ, Buddha, Abraham, or Muhammed, etc., because our situation in Time is different from theirs—they were present in a different configuration of the *guṇas*, which we call a previous age, than the present configuration. But since *Īśvara* is transcendent to Time and to the laws of *saṁsāra* (such as *karma*, which limits ordinary embodied beings' capacity to control their destiny in terms of when and where they are injected into *prakṛti*), *Īśvara* can break into human history at will, so to speak, and impart teachings to sages throughout the ages. In the Muslim traveler/scholar/historian al-Bīrunī's (somewhat Abrahamically flavored) understanding of this *sūtra*:

> It is He who addressed in various ways Brahmā and other primal [sages]. To some of them God sent down a book, to others He opened a gate for intermediation [with respect to Him]. Again, to others He made a prophetic revelation so that they grasped in thought that which He bestowed upon them.[174]

Śaṅkara gives the following purport to this *sūtra*: Just as *gurus*, who are teachers of knowledge and *dharma*, are offered homage by their pupils who have taken shelter of them, so *Īśvara*, who is the teacher of all other teachers, should be meditated upon in the heart by his devotees who know him by such names as Nārāyaṇa (Viṣṇu). And just as human teachers bestow their grace upon their disciples wholly devoted to them, so the Supreme Teacher bestows his grace upon his devotees who purely contemplate him.

Vijñānabhikṣu uses this opportunity to again promote the Vedāntic philosophy of *bhedābheda*, difference and nondifference, which, while not a topic Patañjali chooses to engage with in the *sūtras*, is of general philosophic interest as it touches upon one of the chief concerns of Vedānta thought: the relationship of the *puruṣa* with *Īśvara*. According to *bhedābheda* (and related Vedāntic views[175]), *Īśvara* (the personified *Brahman*) is one with the living entities, but also different. Their relationship is that between the whole and the part, the fire and its sparks. Although there is oneness between the whole and the part on one level, the relationship is not one of absolute unity, as the *advaita*, nondualist, schools of Vedānta hold; it is rather one of nondifference. The point is not one of mere semantics; it is subtle and significant. The spark is nondifferent from the fire in substance, yet not absolutely identical to the fire; it has its own individuality. Thus a measure of duality or difference is maintained even in unity. In this way, the *puruṣa* is one with *Brahman* in quality but also eternally distinct in that it has inherent individuality. Thus, although through categories alien to the *sūtras* themselves, Vijñānabhikṣu is actually defending at least one central tenet of the Yoga tradition—the eternal individuality of the *puruṣa* (whether *Īśvara* or other).

The issue of whether the soul retains its individuality in the liberated state is one of the main metaphysical questions differentiating *advaita Vedānta* from most other Hindu theologies. From the six schools of orthodox philosophy, five—Nyāya, Vaiśeṣika, Sāṅkhya, Yoga, and Mīmāṁsā—and significant branches of the sixth, Vedānta, posit that the *ātman* is eternally individual both in *saṁsāric* and liberated states. The *advaita*, nondual, school of Vedānta (as well as other non-dual, monistic, traditions such as the cluster of *Śakta* schools) holds that individuality is a feature of *saṁsāra* only, but that upon attaining liberation, the soul loses its individuality and realizes its oneness with the Absolute (hence the term *advaita*, literally, nondual, one). The Yoga school rejects this view and subscribes to the position that the soul retains individuality even in the liberated state.[176]

तस्य वाचकः प्रणवः ॥ २७ ॥

I.27 tasya vācakaḥ praṇavaḥ

tasya, his; *vācakaḥ*, designation; *praṇavaḥ*, the mystical syllable *oṁ*

The name designating him is the mystical syllable *oṁ*.

Patañjali states here that *Īśvara* is represented by the mystical syllable *oṁ* referred to here by its synonym, *praṇavaḥ*. *Oṁ* has been understood as a sonal incarnation of *Brahman* (which is the most common term used for the Absolute Truth in the Upaniṣads) since the late Vedic period.[177] The *Taittirīya Upaniṣad*, for example, states: "*Brahman* is *oṁ*, this whole world is *oṁ*" (I.8.1), as does the *Kaṭha Upaniṣad* (II.16), the *Praśna Upaniṣad* (V.2–5), and the *Māṇḍūkya Upaniṣad*, which concerns itself entirely with the relation of manifest reality with this syllable. The *Muṇḍaka Upaniṣad* describes *oṁ* as the bow, the self as the arrow, and *Brahman* as the target that must be struck, paralleling Patañjali's statement in the next *sūtra*. The *Śvetāśvatara Upaniṣad* states that through the practice (*abhyāsa*) of meditating on *oṁ*, one "can see God" (I.14).[178] A scholastic such as Patañjali would most certainly have been well schooled in the Upaniṣads (especially given his own mandate of the prerequisite of study for success in *yoga*, II.1 and 44), which, as an orthodox thinker, he would have accepted as *śruti*, divine revelation. Even though he never refers to *Brahman* in the *sūtras*, here again we must allow for the possibilty that, along with texts such as the *Gītā*,[179] the *Śvetāśvatara Upaniṣad*,[180] the epic, and the theologies of the Purāṇas—indeed, along with *all* the *Īśvara* theologies of his time, to my knowledge—he is consciously equating the Upaniṣadic *Brahman* with this personal *Īśvara*, by means of this common denominator of *oṁ*.

Vyāsa raises the question, which touches upon various Indian theories of language, of whether the relationship between the person *Īśvara* and the designation (*vācaka*) *oṁ* is conventional—a socially agreed upon usage—or inherent and eternal. The relationship of word and meaning (signifier and object signified)[181] has an extensive history in Indian intellectual thought. Briefly, from conventional perspectives, "elephant" refers to a particular type of creature, but "camel" (or any other term, such as "abracadabra") would do just as well provided it becomes a designation for this creature agreed upon by the speakers of the language. Different languages use different terms for the same object. The term "elephant" is thus conventional; it does not have an eternal or absolutely binding relationship with its referent. The same obviously holds true for personal names given to people, as Vijñānabhikṣu notes: The name Devadatta is given adventitiously to a son by his father—he could just as well have called him Viṣṇupriya.[182]

An inherent relationship, on the other hand, is eternal and not dependent on social usage. Vyāsa gives the example of the relationship between a lamp and light; wherever there is a lamp there must always and necessarily be light. Such is the relationship between *Īśvara* and *oṁ*; it is not a culturally agreed upon designation. *Īśvara* was known by the syllable *oṁ* in previous creations, and will be for all eternity; it is an eternal designation not assigned by human convention or socially agreed upon usage (we will further explore the *yoga* understanding of language in general in III.17).

How can this be? wonders Vācaspati Miśra. After all, *oṁ* is just a sound and merges back into *prakṛti* along with all other sounds and all material objects at the dissolution of the universe, and its powers must thereby disappear. At a new creation, how can this particular phoneme regain its power from the previous creation? It remanifests with all its previous power, he continues, just like life-forms that disappear into the earth during the dry season burst back into the same life-forms after the rains. This particular and specific phoneme is eternally invested by *Īśvara* with his power.[183] One can conclude, then, that not being subject to Time, *Īśvara* is not subject to cyclical creation and therefore can invest his potency eternally into the sacred syllable *oṁ*.

This process of *Īśvara* investing his potency in the sound of *oṁ* has been compared to fire permeating an iron ball. When an iron ball is placed into the fire, it becomes permeated by the fire such that the iron exhibits all the qualities of fire. In other words, it becomes fire-ized, so to speak, manifesting the powers of fire, such as heat and light, by dint of being pervaded by fire. In this regard, on one level, it becomes non-different from fire even as on another level, it remains an iron substance and fire remains a distinct physical substance. In the same way, *oṁ* becomes permeated by *Īśvara* such that it manifests the qualities of *Īśvara*. It becomes *Īśvara*-ized, so to speak, manifesting the powers of *Īśvara*, such as the powers of illumination and purification, by dint of being pervaded by *Īśvara*. On one level, then, it becomes non-different from *Īśvara* even as on another level, it remains a *prakṛtic* sound vibration and *Īśvara* remains a distinct transcendent entity. In this way the mind, which, as a *prakṛtic* entity cannot "grasp" that which is finer than itself, namely, *puruṣa* (*Īśvara*, as we know, is a "special" *puruṣa*), can grasp or focus on the *prakṛtic* sound *oṁ*. But since *Īśvara* has invested his presence in this sound (as an act of grace), the mind is, for all intents and purposes, coming into direct contact with *Īśvara*. In this way, the *prakṛtic* mind can absorb itself in an unmediated fashion on the non-*prakṛtic* *Īśvara*.

Hariharānanda believes that this empowered syllable *oṁ* along with its designation, *Īśvara*, is reintroduced to humanity in each new cycle of creation by omniscient beings, or sages with recollection of their past lives. He feels that no other word can bring about comparable calmness of mind. Moreover, it is easy to pronounce since, unlike consonants, vowels can be pronounced in prolonged continuity. The sound, he holds, moves from the throat to the brain, where it aids contemplation. Certainly, the repetition of *oṁ* has been performed by mystics and meditators in India for many centuries and is one of the most common forms of Hindu meditation.

Śaṅkara gives a popular etymology for *praṇava*, the term used here by Patañjali to refer to *oṁ*. Popular etymologies are common in exegetical literature and usually break a word down into its components, assigning extended theological meaning to each segment. While they are not always accepted by modern-day historical linguists as etymologically accurate, such derivations are a good example of how many of the important Vedic terms are reconfigured to conform to specific theological principles of later times. The prefix *pra-*, of *praṇava*, he says, stands for *prakarṣeṇa*, perfectly; and *nava* is a derivative of the root *nu*, in its third-person passive form of *nūyate*, he is praised. Thus, through the recitation (*japa*) of *oṁ*, *Īśvara* is praised perfectly. Alternatively, he continues, substituting the *va* of *praṇava* with *dhā*, one can construe *praṇidhā*, surrender to the Lord; *praṇava* is thus a sound representation of the Lord through which one can meditate on him in a devotional mode, as the next *sūtra* will indicate.

One more general comment seems useful here. *Īśvara* is the generic name for God in the Hindu theistic traditions. That is, when used alone it tends to refer to a philosophical category in these contexts—that of a supreme personal Creator—rather than specific divine manifestations of this Supreme Being in the forms of Viṣṇu, Śiva, and Kṛṣṇa, who all lay claim to the title *Īśvara* in Purāṇic and epic texts. Factually, however, most *yogīs* over the last two millennia have been associated with these devotional sects and hence tend to add the specific name of their *iṣṭa-devatā*, their preferred personal form of divinity (the object of their personal devotion, a notion discussed in II.44) onto the *oṁ mantra*. Thus, for the Viṣṇu/Nārāyaṇa traditions, that is, those that conceive of *Īśvara* as Viṣṇu/Nārāyaṇa, the favored *mantra* is *oṁ namo Nārāyaṇāya*; for the Śiva traditions, *oṁ namaḥ Śivāya*; and for the classical Kṛṣṇa traditions, *oṁ namo bhagavate Vāsudevāya*. Even in the by now far more popular and universalized Kṛṣṇa *mantra*—Hare Kṛṣṇa, Hare Kṛṣṇa, Kṛṣṇa Kṛṣṇa, Hare Hare, Hare Rāma, Hare Rāma,

Rāma Rāma, Hare Hare—introduced to the Western world by the great Vaiṣṇava teacher A. C. Bhaktivedānta Swāmi, the medieval Kṛṣṇa theologians from which his lineage stems proposed that this *mantra* both inherently contains and also supersedes *oṁ*.[184] The point is that even in the more developed *bhakti* traditions, *oṁ* retains its primordial status as encapsulating the Absolute Truth but is incorporated into more sophisticated understandings of *Īśvara* and, consequently, more personalized and elaborate varients of the *oṁ mantra*. These, too, can be (and have long been) used as *mantras* upon which to fix the mind, by those more steeped in *bhakti*.

तज्जपस्तदर्थभावनम् ॥ २८ ॥

I.28 taj-japas tad-artha-bhāvanam

taj, its [of the syllable *oṁ*]; *japaḥ*, repetition; *tat*, its [of the syllable *oṁ*]; *artha*, meaning; *bhāvanam*, dwelling upon

Its repetition and the contemplation of its meaning [should be performed].

Continuing this discussion of *oṁ*, Patañjali here gives a specific indication as to how to fix the mind on *Īśvara*. After all, since *Īśvara*, as a type of *puruṣa*, is beyond *prakṛti*, and therefore beyond conceptualization or any type of *vṛtti*, how is one to fix one's mind upon him since the *prākṛtic* mind cannot perceive that which is more subtle than itself? Patañjali provides the means: through the recitation of the syllable in which *Īśvara* manifests. As early as the *Kaṭha Upaniṣad*, *oṁ*, which is considered there to be, "non-different from *brahman*" is described as "the best *ālambana*," support (I.10, 38) for the mind in meditation: "when one knows this support one delights in *brahman*." The recitation of *oṁ* is called *japa*. *Japa* is an old Vedic term common in the old Brāhmaṇa texts, where it referred to the soft recitation of Vedic *mantras* by the priest.[185]

Vyāsa states that by constantly repeating *oṁ* and contemplating its meaning, *artha*, namely *Īśvara*, the mind of the *yogī* becomes one-pointed—the goal of all *yoga* practice. Vyāsa quotes a verse from the *Viṣṇu Purāṇa*: "From *svādhyāya* [reciting *mantras*], let *yoga* be practiced, and from *yoga* let reciting *mantras* be performed; by perfection in both, the supreme *ātman* shines forth"[186] Elaborating on this, Vācaspati Miśra takes this *sūtra* as specifying how to engage in meditation on *Īśvara*, that is, the devotion to *Īśvara* referred to in *sūtra* I.23. He understands the *bhāvana*, dwelling upon, of this *sūtra* as permeating the mind again and again,[187] and Bhoja Rāja considers it the entrance into the mind of an object again and again to the exclusion of all other objects"[188] (*bhāvana* occurs also in II.2, 33, 34). Repeating *oṁ* and contemplating its meaning, that it is the sound representation of *Īśvara*, the object of the *yogī*'s surrender, when coupled with Patañjali's usage of *praṇidhāna*, devotion, in I.23, points to chanting the *mantra* in a devotional mood. According to the *bhakti* traditions—recall that Vyāsa considers *Īśvara-praṇidhāna* a special sort of *bhakti*—by doing this, thoughts of the Lord become the very substance of the *citta*, a sort of "*Iśvarizing*" parallel to the "*sāttvicizing*" activities of the *yogic* lifestyle.[189] Just as an image and associations of, say, a cow, arise upon hearing the word "cow," so thoughts of the Lord arise in the *citta* upon reciting and hearing his name, *japa*. Śaṅkara notes that such *japa* can be mental or softly audible. By such recitation, *japa*, the *citta* becomes saturated with *saṁskāras* connected to God (of course, in meditation proper, the mind remains fixed on one such *saṁskāra*, specifically, the *mantra* encapsulating *Īśvara*). This results in a feeling of bliss. More important, continues Vācaspati Miśra, the Lord then becomes gracious to such a devotee and awards him or her *samādhi*.

Śaṅkara's analysis of this *sūtra* reflects the widely held view in Hindu traditions touched upon previously that in addition to perception of *puruṣa*, the *yogī* whose practice is imbued with devotion can also directly perceive God as a distinct but supreme *puruṣa*. Since *oṁ* has an inherent relationship with *Īśvara*, says Śaṅkara, by reciting *oṁ* the *yogī* can meet *Īśvara* face-to-face, that is, the recitation of *oṁ* with intense concentration not only brings *Īśvara* to mind but also takes one to a supersensory face-to-face encounter with *Īśvara*: "By perfecting the repetition of *oṁ* and meditation on the supreme *Īśvara*, the supreme *ātman* (*paramātman*) situated in the highest place (*parameṣṭhin*) shines forth for the *yogī*."[190] Vijñānabhikṣu articulates the same view:

> His name is the *praṇava* (*oṁ*). And *praṇidhāna*, devotion, consists in contemplating Him, preceded by chanting *oṁ* and

> culminating in direct perception of Him. This absorption [*saṁyama*] with regard to the supreme *Īśvara* is the primary practice in *asamprajñāta-samādhi* and [the attainment of] liberation . . . Absorption on the personal *ātman*, on the other hand, is secondary.[191]

Here we find the Vaiṣṇava view articulated that the realization and perception of *puruṣa* is a secondary, less important goal of *yoga*. The higher goal is the realization and perception of *Īśvara*, the Supreme form of whom both Śaṅkara and Vijñānabhikṣu consider to be Viṣṇu. Be that as it may, as Coward (1985, 356) recognizes, "According to the Yoga tradition, it was this route to *Īśvara* that was chosen by the majority of *yogīs* as their path to release."

Coward gives a fascinating correlation of Śaṅkara's comments here with the various stages of *samādhi*. He attempts a hermeneutic of the mechanics underpinning this perception of *Īśvara* through chanting *oṁ*. Coward's representation of the stages involved in this process involves the subdivision of the *vitarka* and *vicāra* states of *samādhi* into *sa* and *nir* forms (the prefix *sa-* means with, and *nir* without). This will be explained fully in I.42–44.

In the *savitarka* stage of chanting, *oṁ* is mixed up with the conventional meanings and ideas associated with it. For example, one may have a mental image of *Īśvara* derived from some picture or a description in a Purāṇic scripture, or one's ideas on *Īśvara* will be molded by some sectarian theological notions, or even from pure imagination. In other words, one's mind will be conditioned by convention in some form or fashion. Therefore, at this stage, even though one is fully absorbed in chanting the *mantra* without external distraction, which is the prerequisite of any of the levels of *samādhi*, nonetheless this stage of *samādhi* is obscured by these habitual ways of conceiving *Īśvara*. At the *nirvitarka* stage, these conventional ways of thinking are weakened, and the object of meditation, in this case *Īśvara*, appears in its own pure nature, unobstructed by mental clutter and imposition. Coward states:

> From the reports of *yogīs* like Patañjali and Vyāsa, in this experience, one comes to know *Īśvara* as the original speaker of the Vedas to the *Ṛṣis*, although, of course, to put this into conven-

> tional words, as we have just done, already reduces us back to the level of *savitarka*. To know it in its *nirvitarka*[192] purity, one must experience it for oneself. (1985, 354)

At the third stage of *savicāra*, as the mental concentration on the recitation of the *mantra* deepens, one penetrates into the essence of the sound and begins to perceive *Īśvara*'s body as consisting of pure *sattva*. The *yogī*'s mind is now so completely identified with *Īśvara* that it is no longer aware of its own separate existence; one is so absorbed in this vision that one has lost all self-awareness. One has merged into *Īśvara*, although one must always bear in mind that this is not the merging of *advaita-vedānta* where the soul is held to actually ontologically lose its separate identity. *Puruṣa* never loses its separate identity in Yoga. The merging here is psychological—one forgets one's own self in the rapture of the divine vision of *Īśvara*, but one nonetheless remains a distinct individual. In the final stage, one's absorption in this vision of *Īśvara* is purged of all notions of Time and Space: "*Īśvara*'s relationship with the *praṇava* and all the Vedas (of which it is the seed) is seen to have existed in all previous cycles [world ages] (beginninglessly), to be manifest in the preset cycle, and to be potential in all future cycles" (ibid., 355). Since the late Vedic period, as Coward points out: "*Īśvara-praṇidhāna* and *svādhyāya* (in the form of chanting *AUM*) has been the core practice of most *yogīs*" (357).

It is unfortunate that adequate attention has not yet been directed to the Purāṇic traditions, which were being compiled and organized into the Purāṇic corpus in Patañjali's time, where the "bare bones" directives of the *Yoga Sūtras* are brought to life. It is in the colorful narratives and stories of the great and manifold manifestations of *Īśvara* in the form of Viṣṇu, Śiva, and the Goddess, and in the stories of the great devoted paradigmatic *yogīs* who undertook *tapas*, *Īśvara-praṇidhāna*, and *svādhyāya* in unique and incredible ways, that one finds the inspirational exemplars of Hindu *yoga*. Notwithstanding that these stories have been dismissed by most Western scholars as too mythological to merit serious philosophical attention, it is from these stories and renditions that the living Yoga traditions of Hinduism have found their inspiration and the spiritual practices of hundreds of millions of Hindus over the centuries have taken shape.

The Purāṇic Dhruva story is one such well-known story. Dhruva was a young boy of five who was offended by his father the king (see II.12, 51 for this part of the narrative). Desiring revenge due to his *kṣatriya*, warrior, spirit, the boy took to the forest, where he performed *japa* on the *mantra* given to him by his *guru* Nārada—*oṁ namo bhagavate Vāsudevāya*—with undeviating concentration. (The devotional traditions typically retain the ancient syllable *oṁ*, given its correlation with *Īśvara* and with *Brahman*, but adjoin to it the specific name of *Īśvara* they revere, in this case Kṛṣṇa.) As a result of his constant focus, and incredible austerities (see II.51), Viṣṇu appeared to the boy despite his *tāmasic* motive in undertaking this meditation. Connecting this story with the *vitarka* stage of *samādhi* described in I.17, Vijñānabhikṣu remarks that (in the *Bhāgavata Purāṇa* and Vaiṣṇava tradition in general), there are two ways of gaining a vision of God through meditative practice, that is, two types of Divine epiphany. God can appear either in an external physical form and be perceived externally by the physical eyes of the dedicated devotee, as in the Dhruva story, or internally to the meditating devotee. Put more precisely in this latter case, the *yogi*'s awareness can be transported to another non-*prākṛtic* plane of consciousness (*saguṇa Brahman*[193]), even as the devoted *yogī* still retains his physical body, an experience that Vijñānabhikṣu correlates with *vitarka* meditation:

> The direct perception of *vitarka-samādhi* is different in character from the perception of the form of four-armed Viṣṇu by Dhruva and others attained by the practice of *japa* and penance, etc. The Supreme *Īśvara*, being satisfied with the penance and meditation of such [devotees,] . . . created a body for Himself and manifested before them and interacted with them by talking to them and so forth. *Yogīs*, on the other hand, by the power of their *yoga* practice, directly perceive the four-armed body of the Lord situated in the eternal Divine realm, even though they themselves are somewhere else.[194]

Thus Dhruva here experiences both an internal and an external vision of Viṣṇu. It was (and remains) primarily scholastics or dedicated practitioners who would have seriously studied or engaged intellectually with Patañjali's *Yoga Sūtras* (which remains true for most *yoga* practitioners in the West today). For everyday Hindus, the teachings of the classical knowledge systems are translated into and transmitted through popular stories. We include here a translation of the episode from the *Bhāgavata Purāṇa* (IV.8.43–9.2) referred to here by Vijñānabhikṣu, which describes part of Dhruva's *mantra* meditation and the resulting manifestation of *Īśvara* (Viṣṇu) before him, as an example of how the technical and esoteric stages of classical *yoga* are made accessible and come to life in the popular and colorful narratives that form the core of real-life Hindu religious identity. (In III.3 we provide another description of *yoga* practice from the *Bhāgavata Purāṇa* using the same form of *Īśvara* as the *ālambana*). We take up the narrative where Dhruva's *guru*, the great sage Nārada, instructs the child:

> . . . Seated on a prepared seat (*āsana*).
>
> One should cast off the impurities of the senses, breath and mind by the three practices of *prāṇāyāma*,[195] one should contemplate (*dhyāna*[196]) with a steady mind the [Supreme] Teacher (*guru*, i.e., *Īśvara*). He has pleasing face and eyes and is always inclined to bestow his grace. He has beautiful nose and eyebrows, charming cheeks, and is the most attractive of the divine forms.
>
> Youthful, with charming limbs, and reddish eyes and lips, he is the refuge of his devotees, the shelter of humankind and an ocean of compassion.
>
> He is a *puruṣa*, his color is that of a dark cloud, and he bears on his chest the mark of *śrīvatsa*. He wears a forest garland, and his four arms bear the conch, discus, club, and lotus flower.[197]
>
> He wears a helmet and earrings, and is bedecked with bracelets and armlets. His neck is adorned with the *kaustubha* gem, and his garment is of yellow silk.
>
> He sports a belt with dangling bells, and shining golden anklets. He is the most attractive person in existence, serene, and delightful for the mind and eyes to behold.
>
> He is endowed with two feet shining with a row of gem-like nails. He is to be found within, having taken up his seat in the lotus of the heart of his worshippers.[198]

He is the supreme boon-giver, and one should meditate (*dhyāna*) on his smiling countenance and loving glances with a steady and concentrated mind.

The mind of one meditating on the most auspicious form of God, *Bhagavān*, becomes perfected due to this highest form of mental control, and never refrains from meditating.

Now hear the supreme secret *mantra* which should be chanted (*japa*). A person reciting this *mantra* for seven days and nights attains a vision of the *siddhas*.[199]

It is: *oṁ namo Bhagavate Vāsudevāya*.

With this *mantra*, a wise person should perform the Lord's worship with devotional offerings, understanding the appropriate articles to use in worship according to place and time.

The Lord manifests in the form of the *mantra*. One should perform worship in the same manner as he has been worshipped by the ancients, while reciting this intimate *mantra* . . .

Dhruva withdrew his mind, which is the support of the senses and their objects, from all other objects. Meditating on the form of God in his heart, he ceased to be aware of anything else . . .

Then, he observed that form, which was as brilliant as a flash of lightning, [that he had been perceiving internally] in the lotus of his heart on account of his insight honed by dedicated *yoga* practice, suddenly disappear, and [opening his eyes] he beheld that same form standing externally.

As elsewhere, Vijñānabhikṣu introduces a Vedāntic element to the discussion. As we know, his philosophy is one of *bhedābheda*, oneness in difference, and he quotes a variety of scriptural passages emphasizing the oneness of the *puruṣa* with *Brahman*, or *Īśvara*—that is, between the soul and God—and a selection of passages focusing on the difference between the two (Vijñānabhikṣu is correlating *Brahman* with *Īśvara* here since, in theistic Vedānta, where *Brahman* is conceived of as a personal being, they are essentially one and the same). In Vijñānabhikṣu's view, such apparently conflicting statements can be reconciled by holding that *puruṣa* and *Brahman* are simultaneously both one and different. As he has attempted to illustrate in previous passages, the oneness of the equation holds good insofar as both are pure consciousness and thus belong to the same class, or category, of existence. However, both *Īśvara* and *puruṣa* retain their identities eternally, hence the difference, as Vyāsa will specify in the next verse.[200] While this is a Vedāntic concern, it holds for the Yoga tradition (at least with regard to *puruṣa* and *Īśvara*).

Vijñānabhikṣu adds that the oneness of *puruṣa* with *Brahman* results from the absorption of the consciousness of the former into the latter; in other words, it is a psychological, not an ontological or a metaphysical, oneness. Put differently, the pure *puruṣa* forgets its own separate existence by being absorbed in thoughts of *Īśvara*, but this does not mean such a *puruṣa* actually loses its distinct individuality as certain nondualist schools hold (hence the difference indicated in *bhedābheda* philosophy). Vijñānabhikṣu quotes the well-known verse from the *Mahābhārata* (XII.306.76) stating that those who are wise worship the twenty-sixth category of existence, *Īśvara*, not *puruṣa*, the twenty-fifth. Thus, *Īśvara*, like *puruṣa*, is an eternally separate category of reality, and, although the two are alike in nature insofar as both are conscious beings, they are nonetheless eternally separate and distinct individuals. Through repetition of *oṁ*, and meditation on *Īśvara*, one can realize the latter as *paramātman*, the Supreme Soul.

Additionally, in Vijñānabhikṣu's view, one cannot chant *oṁ* and meditate on *Īśvara* at the same time. Therefore, he suggests that *oṁ* be repeated as a prelude and postlude to devotional meditation. Hariharānanda, on the other hand, holds that the *oṁ mantra* be recited while thoughts of *Īśvara* are simultaneously cultivated, because if *oṁ* is chanted correctly, its designation, *Īśvara*, automatically comes to mind anyway. In his perspective (which is representative of most *bhakti* theologies), eventually both the *mantra* and its referent, *Īśvara*, come naturally to mind, at which time the devotee is established in *Īśvara-praṇidhāna*, submission to God.

ततः प्रत्यक्चेतनाधिगमोऽप्यन्तरायाभावाश्च ।। २९ ।।

I.29 tataḥ pratyak-cetanādhigamo' py antarāyābhāvāś ca

tataḥ, from this; *pratyak*, inner; *cetanā*, consciousness; *adhigamaḥ*, realization; *api*, also; *antarāya*, interruptions; *abhāvāḥ*, absence; *ca*, also, as well

From this comes the realization of the inner consciousness and freedom from all disturbances.

According to Patañjali, as a result of submission to the Lord, the various disturbances, *antarāya* (disease, idleness, etc., listed in the next *sūtra*), do not manifest; rather, the *yogī*'s inner consciousness or real self manifests, *pratyak-cetanādhigamaḥ*. The *yogī* is granted a vision of his own *puruṣa* by *Īśvara*'s grace, a benediction repeated in II.45. Not only this, but the dedicated *yogī* is also bestowed physical health and freedom from all the bodily and psychological disturbances of embodied life. In other words, if we follow Śaṅkara and Vijñānabhikṣu's thrust from the last *sūtra*, by the dedicated absorption in *Īśvara* as manifest in the sound *oṁ*, the *yogī* attains direct experience of his or her own *puruṣa*, physical and psychological well-being in the *prākṛtic* state, and a vision of *Īśvara* in his form of pure *sattva* (that is, a vision of the supreme Lord).

Vyāsa states that just as *Īśvara* is a *puruṣa* who is "pure, peaceful, independent, and free from change," so also is the ordinary *puruṣa*. Elaborating on this, Vācaspati Miśra defines "purity" as free from birth and death; "peaceful" as undisturbed by the obstacles (the *kleśas* of ignorance, ego, attachment, aversion, and clinging to life discussed in II.3); "independent" as beyond virtue and vice; and "freedom from change" as freedom from consequences of *karma*, namely, type of birth and duration and quality of life (II.13–14).

Bhoja Rāja raises the question as to how realization of the self can be attained from devotion to *Īśvara* who is different from the self. The answer, he says, is that *Īśvara* is similar in constitution to the self. Drawing once again on this Vedāntic philosophy of *bhedābheda*, Vijñānabhikṣu elaborates that by understanding the whole, the part is automatically understood; in other words, by absorption in *Īśvara*, God, one realizes one's own self as part of *Īśvara*. Regarding devotion to *Īśvara*, whom he notes the ancients speak of as Vāsudeva and Bhāgavata (Viṣṇu/Kṛṣṇa), he quotes a verse from the *Bṛhan-nāradīya Purāṇa*: "For one who desires liberation, the path that is blissfully performed is devotion to Viṣṇu. Meditate constantly on him with the mind, otherwise one will be cheated. If one is looking for protection, he is your protector in the greatest difficulty."[201] Regarding the removal of obstacles and the revelation of the self by his grace noted by Patañjali,

Vijñānabhikṣu quotes another verse from the same Purāṇa: "For people who have staunch faith in Viṣṇu, the remover of *māyā*, Viṣṇu reveals the self, which is different from *prakṛti*, just like a lamp."[202] The Purāṇa texts are pervaded by statements of this nature.

व्याधिस्त्यानसंशयप्रमादालस्याविरतिभ्रान्तिदर्शनालब्ध
भूमिकत्वानवस्थितत्वानि चित्तविक्षेपास्तेऽन्तरायाः ॥ ३० ॥

I.30 vyādhi-styāna-saṁśaya-pramādālasyāvirati-bhrānti-darśanālabdha-bhūmikatvānavasthitatvāni citta-vikṣepās te'ntarāyāḥ

vyādhi, disease; *styāna*, idleness, apathy; *saṁśaya*, indecision, doubt; *pramāda*, carelessness, negligence; *ālasya*, sloth; *avirati*, lack of detachment; *bhrānti*, confusion, error; *darśana*, perception; *alabdha*, not obtaining; *bhūmikatva*, place, ground, not attaining a base [for concentration]; *anavasthitatvāni*, instability; *citta*, mind; *vikṣepāḥ*, distractions; *te*, these; *antarāyāḥ*, the disturbances

These disturbances are disease, idleness, doubt, carelessness, sloth, lack of detachment, misapprehension, failure to attain a base for concentration, and instability. They are distractions for the mind.

Patañjali lists the disturbances he indicated in the previous *sūtra* are removed by devotion to *Īśvara*. We use "disturbances" here for *antarāya* (literally, that which intervenes) rather than "obstacles," since the latter term is often used for the *kleśas*, which are far more permanent and deep-rooted than the *antarāyaṣ* listed in this *sūtra*. Vyāsa notes that these nine disturbances occur along with the *vṛttis*, the changing states of the mind, and if these disturbances were removed, there would be no *vṛttis*, and thus the goal of *yoga*, the cessation of all *vṛttis*, would be accomplished. He proceeds to define these interruptions. In accordance with the traditional theoretical understanding underpinning *āyurvedic* medicine, he considers disease, *vyādhi*, the first item on the list, to be an imbalance of the bodily fluids, or an imbalance of the *doṣas*, the three humors of Āyurveda (*kapha*, *vāta*, and *pitta*[203]). In other words, disease occurs when one of these is in excess of its requirements. Idleness, *styāna*, is the disinclination of the mind toward work; a sort of mental paralysis, says Śaṅkara. Following the

Nyāya school, doubt, *saṁśaya*, is taken as the consideration of two sides of an issue and thinking, "It might be this way, if not, it might be that way" (or, as Bhoja Rāja quips, "Is the practice of *yoga* doable or not?!").[204]

Carelessness, *pramāda*, is lacking the foundations to practice *samādhi*, presumably a reference to neglecting the eight limbs of *yoga*, which will be discussed in Chapters II and III (a lack of persistence, says Śaṅkara). Sloth, *ālasya*, is lack of effort in mind and body[205] due to heaviness (which is caused by *kapha*, excess phlegm, says Vācaspati Miśra). Lack of detachment, *avirati*, is mental greed due to the mind contemplating the sense objects (due to past addictions, says Śaṅkara), a theme discussed at length in texts such as the *Gītā* (II.44). Misapprehension, *bhrānti-darśana*, is mistaken knowledge, like mistaking mother-of-pearl for silver, says Bhoja Rāja[206] (Śaṅkara considers this to be misconceptions about the *yoga* path itself). Failure to attain a base for concentration, *alabdha-bhūmikatva*, is failure to attain a state of *samādhi*. Finally, instability, *an-avasthitatva*, is the inability to maintain any such state that one might attain; only when *samādhi* is maintained will the mind be stable. Vijñānabhikṣu quotes a verse in this latter regard: "Even an elevated *yogī* can fall down due to worldly attachments; what to speak, then of a neophyte *yogī*?"[207] One is reminded of the *Gītā*'s comment that "the senses are so strong, that they forcefully carry away the mind even of a discriminating person who is striving to control them" (II.60).

These disturbances, concludes Vyāsa, are the impurities of *yoga*, its enemies and obstacles produced by *rajas* and *tamas*. They are called disturbances, *antarāya*, says Śaṅkara, because they move, *aya*, and make a gap, *antara*, in one's practice.

दुःखदौर्मनस्याङ्गमेजयत्वश्वासप्रश्वासा विक्षेपसहभुवः ।। ३१ ।।

I.31 duḥkha-daurmanasyāṅgam-ejayatva-śvāsa-praśvāsā vikṣepa-saha-bhuvaḥ

duḥkha, pain, suffering; *daurmanasya*, dejection; *aṅgam-ejayatva*, trembling of the limbs; *śvāsa*, inhalation; *praśvāsāḥ*, exhalation; *vikṣepa*, distraction; *saha-bhuvaḥ*, occur with, accompany

Suffering, dejection, trembling, inhalation, and exhalation accompany the distractions.

Accompanying the disturbances noted in the previous *sūtra* is a further set of secondary disturbances of the mind which, as always, the commentators explain individually. Vyāsa refers to the three standard sources of suffering or pain, *duḥkha*, the first item on Patañjali's list, recognized in Hindu knowledge systems (e.g., Sāṅkhya Kārikā I.1), which will be discussed in II.15: suffering from one's own body and mind, suffering from other entities, and suffering from the gods, that is, from nature. Vācaspati Miśra gives disease as an example of suffering from one's own body, and desire as suffering of the mind (or, for Rāmānanda Sarasvatī, romantic love!); a tiger's mauling as an example of pain from other living entities, and planetary influences as an example of suffering from nature (which includes natural effects such as excessive heat and cold). Vijñānabhikṣu notes that these three categories are not comprehensive since they do not include pain arising from items such as pots and cloth, by which he seems to be referring to pain caused by inanimate objects. Pain, says Vyāsa, is essentially that which living beings attempt to avoid, as Patañjali will state in II.16. (The ability to perceive the pervasiveness of suffering is discussed in some detail in II.15, since it is an essential prerequisite for undertaking the spiritual path.)

Dejection, *daurmanasya*, the second item on the list, is the disturbance of the mind that arises when one's desires are obstructed. Trembling, *aṅgam-ejayatva*, is self-explanatory, that which causes the limbs to shake, and which, according to Bhoja Rāja, interferes with one's *āsana, yogic* sitting posture. Inhalation, *śvāsa*, is the excessive intake of external air, which Vācaspati Miśra specifies is a defect when it occurs involuntarily and interferes with the *prāṇāyāma* breathing technique known as *recaka*. Vyāsa glosses exhalation, *praśvāsa*, with expelling gas, which, again, Vācaspati Miśra specifies is a defect when it occurs involuntarily and interferes with the *prāṇāyāma* breathing technique known as *pūraka*.

Thus, the nine disturbances mentioned in I.30 are not only disruptions to the practice of *yoga* in their own right, but they produce a further set of disruptions. Vyāsa states that although these symptoms accompany the nine disturbances, they do not manifest for the *yogī* whose mind is fixed. Such obstacles disappear when the mind is not distracted, and consequently a person who has control over the mind does not experience pain and dejection, etc. Ultimately, according to Patañjali in I.29, they all disappear by devotion to *Īśvara*.

तत्प्रतिषेधार्थम् एकतत्त्वाभ्यासः ॥ ३२ ॥

I.32 tat-pratiṣedhārtham eka-tattvābhyāsaḥ

tat, their [these distractions and their accompaniments]; *pratiṣedha*, repel, eliminate, negate; *artham*, for the sake of; *eka*, one, single; *tattva*, object; *abhyāsaḥ*, practice

Practice [of fixing the mind] on one object [should be performed] in order to eliminate these disturbances.

Vyāsa states that the disturbances mentioned in *sūtra* I.30 are to be counteracted by the practice and dispassion mentioned in *sūtra* I.12—in fact, he considers this *sūtra* to conclude Patañjali's discussion on practice. Although in consonance with I.39, the one object, *eka-tattva*, mentioned in this *sūtra* as the support for the mind can be any object, the commentators take it to be *Īśvara*, thereby also concluding this section of the text relating to *Īśvara*.[208] This seems the correct reading, given that this *sūtra* is a continuation of the theme stemming from I.29, which states that from the repetition of *Īśvara*'s sound designation *oṁ* comes freedom from these very obstacles. In other words, by fixing the mind on *oṁ* in a devotional mood, the obstacles to *yoga* are removed and the goal of the entire system is attained.

Vyāsa then launches into a lengthy engagement with Buddhist notions of the mind, which is summarized here for those interested in the history of Indic philosophical dialectic and debate on this subject. (Those primarily interested in *yogic* practice might choose to skim the following section and proceed to the next *sūtra*.) Unlike other schools of thought, such as the Vedānta tradition, which dedicates one of its four chapters to refuting other philosophical views, the Pātañjalian Yoga commentarial tradition, with a few exceptions such as Śaṅkara and Vijñānabhikṣu (themselves Vedāntins), does not concern itself excessively with this type of disputation, since its main claim to truth is based on experiences rather than logical debate (I.6). However, as we find here, the commentators on occasion (and Patañjali himself later in the fourth chapter) do make a point of discussing certain Buddhist notions of mind, since these directly oppose the essential fundamentals of Yogic metaphysics on which the practice of the entire system is based. Indeed, the two systems hold diametrically opposing understandings on certain basic premises pertaining to mind and consciousness. In the early centuries of the Common Era, Buddhism was a significant presence on the Indian subcontinent, so it would be expected, in accordance with normative commentarial conventions, for the metaphysicians of the Sāṅkhya Yoga tradition to establish their perspectives with reference to the primary philosophical alternatives of the day, especially where these encroached on or undermined their own views.

The standard technique for refuting rival views is for a commentator to introduce the view of the opposing school, called the *pūrvapakṣa*, critique it, and then establish the perspective of his own school, the *siddhānta*. Naturally, the representation of the *pūrvapakṣa*, the opponent's view, was sometimes selective or partial, but the ensuing discussion will provide a flavor of the rich debate and keen dialectical interaction between schools that forced theologians to fine-tune their perspectives and kept the Indic intellectual traditions alive and fertile throughout the centuries. While the present work concerns itself with the commentaries of the Yoga tradition on the *sūtras*, and thus will be considering their side of the dialectic and debate with Buddhism here and in several later *sūtras*, it seems fair to point out that Buddhist scholastics participated vigorously in debates with the orthodox schools, particularly the Nyāya school, over the centuries.[209]

The feature of Buddhism targeted here by Vyāsa is fairly generic and normative, not sect-specific, although the later commentators identify the Vaibhāṣika school of Buddhism as the *pūrvapakṣa*. Vyāsa himself does not refer to Buddhism by name but uses one of several terms for Buddhist doctrine common in orthodox Hindu philosophical discourse: *kṣaṇikavāda*,[210] the view that all reality is momentary. What is intended by this, according to all mainstream Buddhist positions, is that nothing in reality has inherent, eternal, independent, and essential existence, that is, nothing has its own durable essence that can be separated from its connection and interdependence with other entities.

Naturally, such a metaphysics is diametrically opposed to the Sāṅkhya Yoga position that both *puruṣa* and *prakṛti* are precisely inherent, eternal, independent, and essential durable entities that, at least in the case of *puruṣa*, do not need to be interconnected or interdependent. Indeed, the extraction and isolation of the eternal and independent *puruṣa* from its codependence on all other reality is precisely the goal of the entire system. Another term for the Buddhists in orthodox commentaries is thus *anātmavāda*, the position that does not accept an eternal, separable, conscious entity called *ātman* (*puruṣa*). As noted above, while the Yoga commentaries do not occupy themselves as much as some of their contemporary schools with disputation on these issues (since, after all, this would counter the experiential focus of Yoga), the Nyāya school debated the Buddhists on the issue of *ātman* for centuries,[211] as did the Mīmāṁsā[212] and Vedānta schools.[213]

The need for raising the Buddhist position at this point arises for Vyāsa because Patañjali's entire system focuses on concentrating the mind on one object, as the present *sūtra* specifically indicates, eliminating all distractions to this end. The implication of the Buddhist view, says Vyāsa, is that the mind can never be distracted in the first place—it can only ever be focused on one object. This is because Buddhists do not accept a constant substratum of mind—a fixed, durable entity with its own distinct essential nature. Cognition, for them, consists of a collection or flow of momentary perceptions or ideas strung together, each one unique and distinct from its predecessor and successor cognitions and ideas. This mental flow rests on a point, or object, for a moment, then exhausts itself, followed in the next moment by another distinct mental idea that fixes fleetingly on the object, and so on. Since these point moments succeed each other sequentially, they give a semblance of stability, a flow of ideas, like a movie that appears to be a flow of events but is in actuality a rapid sequence of completely distinct individual images. With the partial exception of the Idealist school of Vijñānavāda Buddhism,[214] in most schools of Buddhist psychology there is a series of point moments, each of which exists as both the momentary effect of the previous instant and simultaneously the momentary cause of the succeeding instant, in a flow of cognitive instances, but there is no durable underlying entity called mind underpinning this process as the Yoga school holds. Since the Buddhist view threatens to undermine Patañjali's entire system, Vyāsa feels bound to challenge it by offering a number of arguments.

If each point moment of this process is fully fixed on its object for the instant of its existence, says Vyāsa, Patañjali's reference to a distracted mind, or the practice of concentration by fixing the mind on one object, should be meaningless for Buddhists. If there is no enduring underlying substratum of mind in the first place that can concentrate on an object one minute but be distracted the next, there can be no such thing as a distracted mind: Distraction requires a permanent entity that can waver from one thing to another. In Buddhism there is no permanent mind, simply individual cognitions that arise and fade away instantaneously but are fully fixed for their momentary life span on their objects. These cognitions do not take place within a fixed substratum called *citta* as *yogīs* hold (except, as noted, in the partial case of Vijñānavāda). Thought is just a flow of distinct moments in the Buddhist system, and the individual point moments of this flow, the series of thoughts, are each fully and intrinsically concentrated by nature; they do not survive long enough to be distracted. In the absence of a substratum, an individual thought does not last long enough to think of one thing and then get distracted and think of another, so what does it mean to speak of a distracted mind that needs to be concentrated? In short, if each point moment of the mental flow is fully concentrated on its object during the brief instant it occurs, then why do the Buddhists promote concentration? posit the commentators. The very notion of concentration, from the perspective of the Yoga school, presupposes an enduring entity that can either concentrate or be distracted, not a flow of cognitive moments that exhaust themselves as soon as they arise as Buddhism holds.

The Buddhist, Vyāsa supposes, will respond that there is a flow of identical cognitions, each one succeeding the other, and thus the Buddhist concept of concentration should be understood as *keeping* this mental flow of point moments sequencing on the same thought, that is, prolonging the flow of momentary cognitions centered on one object. Distraction therefore entails the interrupting of this flow. Vācaspati Miśra and Vijñānabhikṣu step in here. If the Buddhist notion of concentration entails keeping the flow of mental moments fixed on the same object, then *what* is it that connects this flow of momentary cognitive moments together? Since each thought lasts only an instant, it has no past and future.[215] This means that there can be no overlap between thoughts. What, then, connects each moment of thought to the previous and succeeding moments such that a flow of concentrated thought can occur? Vyāsa's thrust is to establish that there must be something that endures, underpins, and connects the individual cognitions and images—something like the *citta* animated by the consciousness of the *puruṣa* as posited by the Yoga school, that is, a nonmomentary but permanent mind that can think of one thing or focus on one image one minute and then get distracted and think of another thing the next. The momentary slides or stills of a movie require the reel to connect them. Only if the mind is a permanent entity that endures from one moment to the next does the notion of a distracted mind, and hence the viability of a practice of concentration to focus it, become meaningful.

A Buddhist response to this, as Śaṅkara notes, is that before extinguishing itself, a thought leaves a trace or imprint of itself on its succeeding thought, which does the same for the thought succeeding it, and so on, in a sequence of cause and effect, and thus a flow of thought manifests (like a line of red ants, he says). The problem here, says Śaṅkara, is that these thoughts are arising and perishing at different times: When one thought arises in the present as effect, its predecessor, causal thought, has already expired in the past—they are not overlapping. A thought would need to overlap with the previous thought in order to receive such an imprint or influence, and then overlap with the following thought to leave its trace on that, which, in turn, would have to undergo the same process . . . and this overlapping of the individual thoughts might then provide the continuity of thought that we all experience. But such a process would involve at least two moments or instances for each thought: a moment of overlap with the previous thought and a moment of overlap with the subsequent thought (with perhaps an intervening moment in its own right), which conflicts with the Buddhist premise of single momentariness. How does a momentary object as cause connect or come into contact with another momentary object as effect occurring in the next moment? Since it itself endures only one moment, there is no room for overlap. In the absence of a substratum such as mind, as the Yoga school posits, what is it that binds them together into a continuum?

A continuation of this argument, alluded to by Śaṅkara, in his commentary here and elsewhere,[216] is that without a binding receptacle or agent like the *citta*, and if thoughts cannot last long enough to overlap with and leave their imprint on each other, why shouldn't the thought of one moment be completely different from the thought of another? Why shouldn't the thought of an apple, say, arise one instant, followed by the random thought of an orange in the next instant, and then perhaps a cow, followed in turn by the thought of a clay pot for an instant, or anything else in existence, in an eternal whirlpool of incoherent, unconnected momentary images? If all thoughts cannot overlap as cause and effect for the reasons noted above, and last only an atemporal instant, what serves as the cohesive mental factor such that a person can retain sanity and functionality by thinking of the same object for a prolonged period of time, focusing on the same apple from one moment to the next such that one can eat it and a coherent picture of reality can be perpetuated?

The next two objections raised by Vyāsa against the Buddhist position have a well-known history in the orthodox Hindu schools and concern memory and the transferral of *karma*.[217] If each thought comes into being on its own, unconnected with the substratum of a mind, then how would the thought of one instant remember the experience of a previous thought in an earlier instant? In other words, how is memory accounted for? In the Hindu view, an experience is recorded on the mind, *citta*, as a *saṁskāra*, and when this *saṁskāra* is activated, memory occurs. The point is, this all takes place within the receptacle of the mind—the *saṁskāra* needs to be lodged somewhere, in a permanent substratum, such as the *citta* posited by the Yoga school, in order to be retrievable and remembered and, one might add, the *saṁskāra* itself needs to have permanency and not be momentary. But if such an enduring receptacle is done away with, and each thought arises and extinguishes in an instant to be followed by a distinct subsequent thought in the next instant, how can the first thought be retrieved and remembered if it is not deposited somewhere (leaving aside the problem that it does not even exist for long enough to be deposited anywhere in the first place)?

Moreover, in the Buddhist system, one thought would be the experiencer of the *karmic* reactions of a completely different thought. In other words, if there were no eternal *ātman* and no enduring mind, as the Buddhists hold, then how is *karma* preserved and transferred from one life to the next, or even from one moment to the next? And even if one allows that it were transferred, somehow, the entity experiencing it would be a completely different entity from the one who earned it, since everything is momentary and there are no enduring entities. In other words, since, in Buddhism, individuals are just conglomerates of momentary phenomena that exist for only one instant and are then succeeded by a new set of momentary phenomena and so on in every instant of existence, activities performed by an individual in one moment of this flux would bear fruit that would be experienced by a completely different individual at a later moment. Where would be the moral justice in such a view? As Vācaspati Miśra puts it: The thought experienced by the person Maitra is not remembered by some different person such as Chaitra, nor is the *karma* accrued by the former experienced by the latter (an unborn son does not receive the *karma* of the father, says Śaṅkara). However the problem might be explained away, says Vyāsa, it rests on faulty logic, like deciding that since milk comes from a cow, and milk is a palatable substance, cow dung, which also comes from the cow, must also be a palatable substance.

Vyāsa's final argument is that the Buddhist view denies one's very own experience of existence. How can one think "I touch what I saw, and I see what I touched," where the enduring idea of "I" survives without changing, if each idea is distinct from every other? In other words, why is the thought or idea of "I" not momentary, if all ideas are momentary? Why does it endure in everyone's experience such that the "I" that does one act, like seeing something one day, is the same as the "I" that touches the same thing another day? The same and continued notion of "I" endures. How could it do so if all notions were momentary?

Thus, the very notion of a distracted mind and, as a consequence, the concept of concentration, is incompatible with Buddhist teachings for Vyāsa and the Yoga school and, for that matter, all schools of Hindu philosophy, who all oppose the Buddhist notion of momentariness when it comes to consciousness. For the Yoga commentators, the mind as a product of the eternal *guṇas* is not momentary. It is one and constant. The same mind grasps and then relinquishes objects of thought; there may be a continual flow or sequencing of *vṛttis*, but these take place within the stable receptacle of a durable mind (durable in the sense of being composed of the eternal *guṇas*, even as these are always in motion when manifest, as will be discussed later). Therefore, the mind can indeed become concentrated when distractions are eliminated. In Patañjali's teachings there must be one durable mind that either settles on different objects when distracted, or, during concentration, that serves as a substratum that binds together the flow of thought allowing focus on one and the same object. Hence the need to address the Buddhist challenge on this score.

मैत्रीकरुणामुदितोपेक्षणां
सुखदुःखपुण्यापुण्यविषयाणां भावनातश्चित्तप्रसादनम् ॥ ३३ ॥

I.33 maitrī-karuṇā-muditopekṣāṇāṁ sukha-duḥkha-puṇyāpuṇya-viṣayāṇāṁ bhāvanātaś citta-prasādanam

maitrī, friendship; *karuṇā*, compassion; *muditā*, joy; *upekṣāṇām*, equanimity, indifference; *sukha*, happiness; *duḥkha*, suffering; *puṇya*, virtue; *apuṇya*, vice; *viṣayāṇām*, toward objects; *bhāvanātaḥ*, from the mind-set or attitude; *citta*, mind; *prasādanam*, lucidity

By cultivating an attitude of friendship toward those who are happy, compassion toward those in distress, joy toward those who are virtuous, and equanimity toward those who are nonvirtuous, lucidity arises in the mind.

Since the commentators have pointed out some fundamental differences between Buddhism and Yoga when it comes to consciousness, we can note with this *sūtra* a similarity. The four practices noted in this *sūtra*—friendship, *maitrī*; compassion, *karuṇā*; joy, *muditā*; and equanimity, *upekṣā*—correspond exactly to the four *brahma-vihāras* outlined in various Buddhist *suttas* (rendered, in Pali, as *mettā, karuṇā, muditā, upekkā*). Once more, the common context of these practices is underscored—indeed, the Buddhist *Saṁyutta Nikāya* and the *Saṁyukta Āgama* texts contain explicit reference to the fact that these practices were also cultivated by those who did not follow the teachings of the Buddha.[218]

In this *sūtra,* Patañjali outlines a practice essential for enhancing lucidity, the prerequisite for attaining steadiness in the mind. Vyāsa pairs the set of attitudes specified by Patañjali in the first part of this *sūtra* sequentially with the conditions listed in the second part. As a result of cultivating an attitude of friendship with those who find themselves in a situation of happiness, one of compassion toward those in distress, one of joy toward pious souls, and one of equanimity or indifference toward the impious, *sattva* is generated. Consequently, the mind becomes lucid, clarity being the nature of *sattva*. Once the mind is clear, one-pointed concentration or steadiness can be achieved.

Vācaspati Miśra elaborates on this. By being a well-wisher toward those who are happy, as well as those who are virtuous, the contamination of envy is removed. By compassion toward those who are miserable, that is, by wishing to remove someone's miseries as if they were one's own, the contamination of the desire to inflict harm on others is removed. By equanimity toward the impious, the contamination of intolerance is removed. By thus removing these traits of envy, desire to inflict harm, and intolerance, which are characteristics of *rajas* and *tamas*, the *sattva* natural to the mind can manifest. In the ensuing state of lucidity, the inclination toward controlling the *vṛttis,* in other words toward cultivating a focused state of mind by the practice of *yoga*, spontaneously arises, because the inclination for enlightenment is natural to the pure *sāttvic* mind.

Hariharānanda suggests that envy generally arises when we encounter people whom we do not care about experiencing happiness. Even a pious person can invoke our jealousy, and we take cruel delight when we find an enemy in misery. One should rather try to practice projecting the happiness we feel when our friend is happy or virtuous onto an enemy who is happy, he continues, and the compassion we feel for our friends when they are unhappy should be cultivated for our enemies. By these practices of equanimity, the mind can become lucid and fixed in the goal of *yoga*. Vijñānabhikṣu and Śaṅkara quote the *Gītā* in this regard: "A self-controlled person attains peace by engaging with sense objects with the senses freed from attachment and aversion and under his control. With clear mind, his intelligence becomes fixed" (II.64–65). As arithmetic is important, says Bhoja Rāja, not so much in its own right as in order to arrive at the total sum of something, so the attitudes mentioned in this *sūtra* are important in order to prepare the mind for meditation.

This *sūtra* prescribes a kind of mindfulness or mental cultivation off the mat, so to speak, that is, in day-to-day affairs outside of the context of *citta-vṛtti-nirodha*–type meditation. Cultivating the higher qualities of *sattva* is a continuous and constant requirement of the *yogic* path and spills over into all aspects of life's affairs and social interactions. It speaks to the fact that *yoga* need not be perceived as a world-renouncing tradition but is perfectly compatible with engaged and benevolent social action in the world.

प्रच्छर्दनविधारणाभ्यां वा प्राणस्य ॥३४॥

I.34 pracchardana-vidhāraṇābhyām vā prāṇasya

pracchardana, by exhaling; *vidhāraṇābhyām*, by retention; *vā*, or; *prāṇasya*, of the breath

Or [stability of mind is gained] by exhaling and retaining the breath.

Sūtra I.32 indicated that the obstacles to *yoga* can be overcome by fixing or concentrating the mind on an object, and the next few *sūtras* outline various options and methods for accomplishing this. Patañjali has already presented *Īśvara* as an object of concentration in the form of recitation of the sound *oṁ*, and by placing *Īśvara* first on the list of options and dedicating so many *sūtras* to him, Patañjali has clearly prioritized an *Īśvara*-centered form of meditation. The following *sūtras* up to I.39 all also contain the particle *vā*, or. Thus they are all alternative and optional techniques for fixing the mind and, as with the *Īśvara* verses, are to be read as referring back to I.32, that practice on one object eliminates the distractions to *yoga*. One or more of them might be more suitable to a particular person, time, and place, says Śaṅkara, hence the options. Here, Patañjali lists another method of fixing the mind: through the control of breath, *prāṇa*. Although breath control can also bring stability of mind, the "or" introducing this *sūtra* does not indicate that the previous *sūtra* is optional, Vācaspati Miśra hastens to add. The "or" is in relation to the following *sūtras*, not the previous one—friendliness, compassion, etc., from I.33 must be cultivated in all instances.

Exhalation, *pracchardana*, says Vyāsa, is the expulsion of the stomach air through the nostrils by means of special techniques, and retention, *vidhāraṇā*, is the restraint of the breath. These special techniques, elaborates Vācaspati Miśra, involve slowing the exhalation and lengthening the retention of the breath within the body according to the texts delineating such matters (discussed here in II.50). Obviously, point out the commentators, inhalation is not specified in this *sūtra* because it occurs naturally—retention can only follow inhalation; thus, all three aspects of breath control involved in *prāṇāyāma* are intended: *recaka*, exhalation; *pūraka*, inhalation; and *kumbhaka*, retention. Vijñānabhikṣu holds that since *sūtra* II.29 situates *prāṇāyāma*, breath control, as the fourth in a series of the eight limbs of *yoga*, its separate mention in this *sūtra* as a prop for gaining control of the mind, a feature of the higher limbs of *yoga*, is for the advanced practitioner.

As a result of such breathing techniques, the body becomes light and the mind steady, says Hariharānanda. If the breath is subdued, the mind also becomes so because the two are intimately connected. Thus these techniques produce steadiness of the mind and one-pointed concentration. Hariharānanda notes that during the exhalation and retention of breath, the nerves of the body relax. He specifies that the chest and body should be kept still so that the process of breath control is undertaken by the abdominal muscles. At a certain stage, retention and exhalation occur in a unified fashion; no separate effort need be taken for each. After prolonged practice, a happy feeling of lightness spreads over the whole body. But the most important point for Hariharānanda is to practice meditation along with breath control. Otherwise, he warns, the mind can get more disturbed rather than less so. Only when one-pointed concentration of the mind is cultivated along with the *prāṇāyāma* does the mind become free from *vṛttis* and approach *samādhi* states.

विषयवती वा प्रवृत्तिरुत्पन्ना मनसः स्थितिनिबन्धनी ॥ ३५ ॥

I.35 viṣayavatī vā pravṛttir utpannā manasaḥ sthiti-nibandhanī

viṣayavatī, containing a sense object; *vā*, or; *pravṛttiḥ*, activity, inclination; *utpannā*, arises; *manasaḥ*, of the mind; *sthiti-nibandhanī*, causing steadiness

Or else, focus on a sense object arises, and this causes steadiness of the mind.

While *viṣaya* can refer to any sense object (in this section it is also used in I.33 and I.37), Vyāsa and the commentators understand this *sūtra* to refer to supersensuous experiences. Vyāsa states that if one concentrates on the tip of the nose, one can experience a divine or supernormal sense of smell; on the palate, one can experience supernormal color; on the tip of the tongue, supernormal taste; on the middle of the tongue, supernormal touch; and on the root of the tongue, supernormal sound. These experiences fix the mind, eliminate doubt, and are the doorway to *samādhi*. The term *manas* for mind is likely used here and in II.53 & III.48 by Patañjali rather than *citta* because in traditional Sāṅkhya it is the specific aspect of *citta* directly interfacing with the senses.

This *sūtra* clearly states that a sense object can be used as *ālambana*, support, for the mind. It is sometimes stated that the recitation (*japa*) of *oṁ* must be performed mentally, rather than audibly. This finds no support in the *sūtras*. Although silent meditation can certainly be used as an *ālambana* (since, after all, anything can be used provided the mind is fixed on it), this *sūtra* informs us that sound as a sense object—which would include audible *japa*, as Śaṅkara has noted previously—is perfectly legitimate.

Vyāsa makes the important observation that even though the true nature of reality may be revealed by the scripture, or by the process of inference, or by the teachings of the masters (I.7), if one does not experience these higher realities personally through one's own senses, then one's knowledge remains secondhand. Moreover, one will always be afflicted by doubt of the sometimes grandiose or incredible claims of the sacred texts. If even one out-of-the-ordinary scriptural claim can be experienced, then other more esoteric claims, such as the nature of liberation, can be more readily believed. It is for this reason, he says, that if a practitioner can experience one of the claims pertaining to, say, supernormal smell as outlined in this *sūtra*, then faith in the scriptures becomes strengthened. More specifically, one's faith in *Īśvara* becomes strengthened, as does one's ability to concentrate on him, say the commentators. This is like seeing smoke appear upon the rubbing of two sticks, says Śaṅkara, giving one confidence that fire is on the way.

Hariharānanda claims to have experienced these effects and to have also subsequently experienced an accompanying increase of faith in the validity of other Yoga truth claims. He describes a novel aroma pervading the air when the mind is fixed on the tip of the nose. He states that in order to achieve results, such concentration needs to be practiced continuously for a couple of days in a state of fasting or meager diet in a place where there are no disturbances.

विशोका वा ज्योतिष्मती ।। ३६ ।।

I.36 viśokā vā jyotiṣmatī.

viśokā, painless; *vā*, or; *jyotiṣmatī*, effulgent, luminous

Or [steadiness of mind is gained when] the mind is pain free and luminous.

Patañjali here presents another cryptic *sūtra*, part of which the commentators interpret from the perspective of the esoteric anatomy of the subtle body most typically associated with the *siddha/śākta/tantra* cluster of traditions. Vyāsa says that this *sūtra* continues from the last, that is, the phrase "causes steadiness of the mind," *sthiti-nibandhanī*, is to be carried over from the previous *sūtra* to this one. So steadiness of the mind can be attained through the *viṣayavatī*, object-focused, prescription of the last *sūtra*, and/or the painless and luminous one mentioned in this *sūtra*, which Vyāsa understands as having both objective and subjective varients. Actually, in their pure form, all of these experiences are free from pain and luminous, and the commentators point out that these are called painless, *viśokā*, and luminous, *jyotiṣvatī*, by Patañjali because they are free from *rajas* and *tamas*, the sources of pain and obscuration. *Sattva*, we recall, is luminous and blissful by nature.

One means of attaining stability of mind, says Vyāsa, is to concentrate intelligence on the lotus *cakra* in the heart.[219] When one becomes skilled in doing this, one's sense activities attain luminosity like that of the sun, moon, planets, and gems. (Luminosity here is not merely optical light but also the illumination of knowledge inherent in *sattva* that reveals things as they really are.) This is because intelligence, when manifesting its pure *sāttvic* nature, is luminous and all-pervading, like the ether.[220] It is a preponderance of *tamas* that limits this all-pervading potential.[221] (It is essential to note this principle of the *citta*'s all-pervading potential in order to understand the mechanics behind the *siddhis*, mystic powers, of the third *pāda*.) Since intelligence pervades all forms, it can perceive the true nature of all things when its highest *sāttvic* potential is manifest. Hence, when such *sāttvic* intelligence flows through the senses, the senses also become luminous, like the sun, etc. And, of course, another characteristic of *sattva* is happiness, hence the painless reference in this *sūtra*. This is object-focused meditation.

According to Vyāsa, Patañjali in this *sūtra* also implies subject-focused meditation, when the mind is fixed on the sense of I-am-ness (*asmitā*). Free from *rajas* and *tamas*, it becomes calm and unlimited in this state, like a waveless ocean, and is aware only of a sense of I am. Vyāsa states that the *yogī* in this state can ponder the *ātman* within the heart, which is the size of an atom, and realize the self in the form of I am. Vijñānabhikṣu explains that this type of I-am-ness is not the function of the ego refracting out into the objects of the world, as is the case with the *asmitā* of II.6,[222] but is the highest function of the ego reflecting the soul itself. This type of cognition, says Vijñānabhikṣu, is different from cognitions having an external object, such as smell, since the object is the *ātman* itself. In other words, in this highly *sāttvic* state, by reflecting the light and consciousness of *puruṣa*, *asmitā*, the luminous reflective *sāttvic* covering of *puruṣa*, redirects *puruṣa*'s awareness onto *puruṣa* itself. Contemplating the *ātman* in this state, ego loses awareness of any other object and is aware only of pure I-am-ness. This all seems to correspond to the state of *asmitā-samādhi* of I.17.

This state is not the ultimate goal of yoga, which is *nirbīja-samādhi* when *puruṣa* ceases to be aware of anything other than itself, but it is nonetheless indirect awareness of *puruṣa* by the faculty of ego. This perception of the *ātman*, adds Vijñānabhikṣu, taking the opportunity to present his theistic perspectives, is the base for perception of *Īśvara*, the former preceding the latter.

वीतरागविषयं वा चित्तम् ॥ ३७ ॥

I.37 vīta-rāga-viṣayaṁ vā cittam

vīta, without; *rāga*, desire; *viṣayaṁ*, object; *vā*, or; *cittam*, mind

Or [the mind becomes steady when it has] one who is free from desire as its object.

In this *sūtra*, Patañjali indicates that the goal of *yoga* can be attained by meditation on a pure-minded *yogī*. Vyāsa says that when contemplating the minds of those who are free from desire, *vīta-rāga*, one's own mind becomes tinged by the purity of their minds. Vācaspati Miśra says that Vyāsa himself is such a personage. Many of us have at some point in our lives had the experience of being in the presence of someone who, if not "free from desire," at least has a noteworthy level of selflessness and compassion, and have felt our own potential higher qualities emerge by this association.

The commentators do not elaborate much on this *sūtra*, but, naturally, one is affected by the company one keeps. The *guru*-disciple relationship that this *sūtra* hints at is sacrosanct in most Hindu spiritual lineages. The *Gītā* states, "A knower of truth can impart knowledge to you. Know that truth by surrendering to such a person, serving him and asking questions" (IV.34).[223] By intense dedication and service to a *yogī* with a pure *sāttvic* mind, one's own mind can become fixed and free from personal desires. Many Hindu spiritual traditions promote surrender and service to the *guru* as the highest form of meditation,[224] and this type of focus seems reflected in this *sūtra*.

Having noted this, it would be irresponsible not to make some mention here of the recurrence of sometimes very serious scandals and abuses of power associated with numerous charismatic and high-profile *gurus* who have traveled to the West, initiated large numbers of western disciples, and taught their followers absolute dedication and surrender to the *guru*. Since many of these individuals have, explicitly or implicitly, presented themselves as enlightened beings and allowed cultures of absolute allegiance to develop among their followers, the lives of their disciples, many of whom had dedicated their prime years to serving and following such teachers, are thrown into turmoil when confronted with such scandals (very similar patterns of response can be traced across differing *yoga* communities who have had to deal with such problems). The cognitive dissonance resulting from the conflict between the idealized notions of the *guru* and the sordid facts of some of these scandals almost invariably causes trauma, denial, defensiveness, and demonization of the victims and exposers, etc., within the group, and cynicism from observers outside the group. Therefore, it seems prudent to stress that, according to Patañjali, the type of meditation proposed here should be directed only toward a *yogī* who is free from desire. Aspiring *yogīs* seeking a *guru* might benefit by considering Kṛṣṇa's responses in the *Gītā* when asked by Arjuna how, in the real world, one can practically and realistically recognize a *yogī* who has "realized the true self." After all, if one has not realized one's own *puruṣa*, how can one identify someone else who has? Arjuna phrases the question in very basic categories:

> Arjuna asked:
>
> How does one describe one whose insight is steady and who is situated in *samādhi*, O Kṛṣṇa? How does one whose intelligence is fixed speak? How does he sit? How does he move about?
>
> Lord Kṛṣṇa replied:
>
> A person is said to be of steady insight when he is contented in the *ātman* by means of the *ātman*,[225] and when he has renounced all desires, which are produced by the mind. A person is said to be a sage of steady intelligence whose mind is not agitated in misfortune, whose desire for material pleasures is gone, and whose passion, fear and anger have disappeared. A person is of steady insight who is renounced on all sides, who

> does not rejoice or bemoan upon attaining anything, whether pleasant or unpleasant . . . and who completely withdraws the senses from the sense objects, like a tortoise withdraws its limbs [into its shell]. (II.54ff)

Arjuna's question here is in the Vedānta context of the *ātman*. He asks the identical question later in the Sāṅkhya context of the three *guṇas*:

> Arjuna asked:
>
> Oh master, by what signs is a person who has transcended these three *guṇas* [recognized]? What is his conduct? And how does he transcend these three *guṇas*?
>
> Lord Kṛṣṇa replied:
>
> . . . A person is said to have transcended the *guṇas* who is situated in detachment and not disturbed by the *guṇas*; who stands firm and is not affected, thinking: "it is only the *guṇas* that are operating" [i.e., not the soul]; who is situated in the self; equipoised in pain and pleasure; to whom gold, a stone and a lump of earth are one and the same; who is equal to those who are dear, as well as to those who are not dear; who reacts neutrally to criticism and praise of himself; who is equal in honor and dishonor, equal to friends and enemies, and who renounces all [self-centered] enterprises. He who serves me with the *yoga* of undeviating devotion (*bhakti*), he transcends these *guṇas* and is qualified for absorption into *Brahman*; for I am the support of *Brahman*. (XIV.21–27)

Thus, freedom from desire and tranquillity in all circumstances are the minimum qualities of one who has realized his or her *puruṣa* self. By rephrasing this information at some length in two different contexts, as well as sprinkling the entire text repeatedly with parallel descriptions of the true sage[226] the *Gītā* makes a point of stressing the qualities of a genuinely accomplished *yogī* such that charlatans or (initially) sincere but fallen *yogīs* can better be recognized. Being free of desire (and its correlate, anger) is nonnegotiable.

While on this topic, one might also note that Patañjali later stresses that observance of the *yamas*—nonviolence, truthfulness, celibacy, nonstealing, and noncovetousness—are absolute and universal for all *yogīs* (II.31). There are no exceptions. Any *guru* claiming to have transcended the need to follow these basic rules, or of being qualified to compromise them in the name of some sort of higher esoteric spirituality or *yogic* technique, is thus not in line with Patañjali's teachings.

स्वप्ननिद्राज्ञानालम्बनं वा ।। ३८ ।।

I.38 svapna-nidrā-jñānālambanaṁ vā

svapna, dream; *nidrā*, sleep; *jñāna*, knowledge; *ālambanaṁ*, support; *vā*, or

Or [the mind can become steady when it has] the knowledge attained from dreams and sleep as its support.

Vyāsa has little to say about this curious *sūtra* except to state, without clarification, that the *yogī*'s mind can take the form of objects of sleep, *nidrā*, and dream, *svapna*. Vācaspati Miśra and Rāmānanda Sarasvatī are a bit more specific: When the *yogī* reaches the point that he dreams of *Īśvara*, he awakes full of joy. Vācaspati Miśra identifies *Īśvara* here with Śiva as described in the Purāṇas—appearing like the moon in a secluded spot in a lonely forest, enrapturing the mind with his beauty, with limbs as soft as the lotus stem and a form like shining moonstone, draped with sweet-smelling garlands of *mālatī* and *mallikā* flowers. Then, awake, the *yogī* remembers this form and, absorbed in that vision, the mind becomes steady in meditation on *Īśvara*. One might add that, in order to be able to have such dreams of *Īśvara* at night, one has to think consistently of *Īśvara* during the day such that one's *citta* is full of *saṁskāra* imprints of these meditations, which can then activate during the dream state. Dreaming occurs when the external senses are inactive and the *saṁskāric* imprints on the mind are active (in contrast to the deep sleep of I.9, when both the sense objects in the external realm and their *saṁskāric* imprints in the internal realm are quiescent). But the *saṁskāras* that activate in dream tend to be those experiences that were the most vivid when awake.

Śaṅkara has a different take on this *sūtra*, which again reflects a Vedāntic perspective.[227] During deep sleep, he says, the *citta* is free from all thought, which is a type of *citta-vṛtti-nirodha* (cessation of all thoughts) and thus approximates the goal of *yoga*. By meditating on this when awake, one tries to attain this state. (Of course, in normal deep sleep, this objectless state is due to *tamas* and is beyond the sleeper's control; in meditation, one strives to attain this state as a result of cultivating *sattva* while fully awake.) The Vedānta tradition holds that the *ātman* achieves a state of union with *Brahman* during deep sleep, albeit still mediated by ignorance (*Vedānta Sūtras* III.2.7–8).

Vijñānabhikṣu puts a different Vedāntic spin on this *sūtra* and reads it as indicating that the waking state is actually like a dream from the perspective of the self-realized state because the objects of life are as perishable as those in a dream. Accordingly, contemplating dreams from this perspective produces realization of the ephemeral reality of life. Through the detachment from the world that results from such contemplation, the mind attains its desired steadiness and stability, which is the theme of this series of *sūtras*. Thus this somewhat curious *sūtra* allows a number of cogent interpretations, all in line with Yogic metaphysics.

यथाभिमतध्यानाद् वा ॥ ३९ ॥

I.39 yathābhimata-dhyānād vā

yathā, according to; *abhimata*, that which is agreeable; *dhyānāt*, from meditation; *vā*, or

Or [steadiness of the mind is attained] from meditation upon anything of one's inclination.

Patañjali wraps up this series of *sūtras*, which have described various meditational options for producing a steady mind, by acknowledging that ultimately the *yogī* may meditate on any desired object whatsoever, *yathābhimata*, according to his or her inclination. This is about as undogmatic a position as one can take! As Vācaspati Miśra puts it, "What more can one say?"! The commentators note that whether the object of meditation is external or internal, the point is to fix the mind. Janácek articulates this well: "Patañjali [does not] concern himself with a particular method, but the realization of a methodical principle, no matter by what methodical approach this principle may become manifest . . . to reach the Yoga goals" (1951, 555–56).

One should note here the remarkable accomplishments of B.K.S. Iyengar, who—along with fellow Krishnamacharya disciples Pattabhi Jois and T.K.V. Desikachar—has arguably done more over the last half century to popularize the spread of *āsana* practice (bodily postures, the third limb of *yoga*) than anyone in the recorded history of Yoga. (One must also mention here Swami Śivānanda's disciples, Swami Vishnu-Devānanda, Swami Satchidānanda, and Swami Chinmayānanda, who have also contributed much to the spread of *yoga* in the West.) In his *Tree of Yoga*, Iyengar presents *āsana, yogic* posture, as not just the third of the eight limbs of *yoga* but also as a self-contained object of meditation that can itself bring about *samādhi*, the ultimate goal of *yoga*, if approached and undertaken correctly.

While this is something of an innovation in the history of Yoga, at least in terms of how the commentarial tradition has viewed the practice of *āsana*, Patañjali himself specified in I.34 that practices associated with the fourth limb of *yoga, prāṇāyāma*, can bring about steadiness of mind, the prerequisite of *samādhi*, and here in this *sūtra* allows that *any* object of one's inclination can be used as a meditational prop (*ālambana*) to achieve this goal. Approaching *āsana* in this way—as a bona fide support for fixing the mind (and one for which many people in the West might be best suited)—is thus fully defensible within Patañjali's system, *provided it is performed with this intent* rather than some other superficial motive. Indeed, this approach constitutes a unique contribution not just to the history of Yoga as it has been transmitted over the centuries but, more important, also to the participational possibilities of the practice of *yoga* as it is being transmitted in a present-day mainstream context. People who might otherwise be disinterested in some of the other truth claims of Yoga are very attracted to *āsana*, albeit often for physical rather than spiritual reasons. Even if this is the case, if the mind is fully fixed and absorbed *without distraction* on the practice of *āsana*, for whatever motive, it can still attain fixity and stillness. Thus an essential goal of *yoga* is nonetheless attained. Moreover, as Śaṅkara notes, once the mind has attained steadiness in one area, this steadiness can be readily transferred to other areas. Perhaps more important, once the mind becomes stilled, its *sāttvic* nature can manifest, as a result of which the qualities of *sattva*, insight and lucidity, also gradually manifest. These qualities, in turn, start to pervade all aspects of a practitioner's life and can thus transform one's understanding and relationship with one's own practice over time, such that he or she opens to other aspects of the tradition. Ultimately, when *sattva* gains prominence, the inclination to cultivate wisdom and enlightenment manifests automatically.

परमाणुपरममहत्त्वान्तोऽस्य वशीकारः ॥ ४० ॥

I.40 paramāṇu-parama-mahattvānto 'sya vaśīkāraḥ

parama, most distinguished, finest, greatest; *aṇu*, atom; *parama*, greatest, ultimate; *mahattva*, totality of matter; *antaḥ*, up to; *asya*, his (the *yogī*'s); *vaśīkāraḥ*, mastery

The *yogī*'s mastery extends from the smallest particle of matter to the ultimate totality of matter.

Vyāsa explains that the mind can become steady by entering into anything at all in manifest reality, from the minutest object—the *paramāṇu*, the smallest subatomic particle in existence—to the largest—the totality of all *prākṛtic* matter, *mahattva*. As will be discussed later in the text, since the mind is potentially all-pervading and underpins all physical forms, it can pervade any form of any dimension and assume that form's shape and qualities. Later verses elaborate on the states of omniscience that ensue according to the Yoga traditions. By such mastery, says Vyāsa, the *yogī* bypasses the need for the processes outlined in the previous *sūtras*, since nothing can obstruct the *yogī* who has mastery over his or her mind. The other commentators have little to add.

The previous *sūtras* presented suggestions as to how the mind can be fixed, says Śaṅkara. When this has been accomplished by one or more of the methods proposed, what happens next? What kind of *samādhi* ensues? To answer this, Patañjali offers the next *sūtra*.

क्षीणवृत्तेरभिजातस्येव मणेर्ग्रहीतृग्रहणग्राह्येषु
तत्स्थतदञ्जनता समापत्तिः ॥ ४१ ॥

I.41 kṣīṇa-vṛtter abhijātasyeva maṇer grahī tṛ-grahaṇa-grāhyeṣu tat-stha-tad-añjanatā samāpattiḥ

kṣīṇa, weakened; *vṛtteḥ*, the fluctuating states of the mind; *abhijātasya*, of high quality (here, transparent); *iva*, like; *maṇeḥ*, of a jewel; *grahītṛ*, the knower; *grahaṇa*, the instrument of knowledge; *grāhyeṣu*, in the object of knowledge; *tat*, that; *stha*, situated; *tat*, that; *añjanatā*, colored, influenced (here, taking the form of); *samāpattiḥ*, engrossment, complete absorption on an object

Samāpatti, complete absorption of the mind when it is free from its *vṛttis*, occurs when the mind becomes just like a transparent jewel, taking the form of whatever object is placed before it, whether the object be the knower, the instrument of knowledge, or the object of knowledge.

Patañjali has considered various objects that can be used to support the mind in meditation. Now he returns to the analysis (begun in I.17) dealing with stages within the meditative state itself, irrespective of its object. When the mind is freed from all distractions in the form of the *vṛttis*, it becomes like a pure crystal, *maṇi*, says Vyāsa. Just as a crystal exactly reflects the color of whatever object is placed adjacent to it, so the peaceful and fixed mind is colored, *añjanatā*, by any object presented to it, and, in advanced meditation, actually inherently assumes the form of that object. The comparison expressed in this *sūtra* by Patañjali is encountered numerous times throughout the commentaries and has attained wide usage in Hindu philosophical circles: Just as a pure crystal shines with a red color when placed next to a red hibiscus flower, so the calm, pure, and luminous *sāttvic* mind, when freed from the effects of *rajas* and *tamas*, shines with the form of any object presented to it. This occurs when the mind is focused one-pointedly on the object in question. Patañjali states here that the mind can reflect and assume the form of any object: an external object made of gross or subtle elements, *grāhya*; the very instruments of knowledge themselves such as the sense organs, *grahaṇa*; or the intelligence, *grahītṛ*, the knower, even in its purest and most subtle function of indirectly being aware of *puruṣa* itself. This *sūtra*, as we noted, has influenced the commentators interpretation of I.17.

The gross and subtle elements evolve out of *citta* (intelligence and ego) in Sāṅkhya, and thus the mind, being more subtle than its evolutes and, indeed, their very essence, can pervade them. This includes not only the *grāhya*, objects of knowledge, that is, sense objects, but also, as Patañjali indicates here, the *grahaṇa*, instruments of knowledge, that is, the sense organs themselves, and the *grahītṛ*, faculty of *buddhi*, the knower. The mind can not only internally mold its own *guṇas* into the *prākṛtic* form of an object or sense organ, but can actually externally penetrate into the object's very essence. In a sense it becomes the object by merging with it and thereby gains ultimate insight into its deepest nature. This is the *samāpatti* introduced in this *sūtra*. Additionally, when completely pure and steady, the mind can ultimately reflect *puruṣa* to itself, the penultimate stage of *yoga* practice.

Obviously, the mind cannot know *puruṣa* in its own true nature, as Śaṅkara points out, since it is inanimate and *puruṣa* is more subtle than the mind. Things can grasp or perceive only things grosser than themselves: The senses can grasp only the sense objects, but not vice versa; the mind can perceive the senses, but not vice versa; and the *puruṣa* can perceive the mind, but not vice versa. This is a favorite trope of the Upaniṣads: "That which one cannot grasp with one's mind [*ātman/Brahman*], by which, they say, the mind is grasped" (*Kena* I.5). "By what means can one know the knower?" (*Bṛhadāraṇyaka* II.4.13). "You can't see the seer who does the seeing; you can't hear the hearer who does the hearing; you can't think the thinker who does the thinking; you can't perceive the perceiver who does the perceiving" (*Bṛhadāraṇyaka* III.4.2). "Sight does not go there, nor does thinking or speech. We don't know it, we can't perceive it, so how would one express it?" (*Kena* I.3). "Not by speech, not by the mind, not by sight can he be grasped. How else can that be experienced, other than by saying 'He is'?" (*Kaṭha* VI.12). "The self cannot be grasped by multiple teachings or by the intellect" (*Muṇḍaka* III.2.3). Only *puruṣa* can know itself. But mind can, however, redirect awareness back to its own original source and thus indirectly reflect *puruṣa*, just as a mirror can reflect a face. In other words, *puruṣa* can become aware of itself by means of the reflective nature of the pure *sāttvic* mind.

Although *samāpatti*, introduced in this *sūtra* for the first time, and *samādhi* can be correlated in a general way, and the states of mind they represent overlap, they are not technically synonymous: Vijñānabhikṣu points out that the various types of *samāpatti* occur as results of *samprajñāta-samādhi*. *Samādhi* in general might best be understood in terms of the goal of *yoga*: the state when all *vṛttis* of the mind have been stilled. *Samāpatti* is, more specifically, the complete identification of the mind with the object of meditation. Put simply, the former is the more general or overall state of the stilled mind, the latter the more specific content or object upon which the mind has settled itself in order to become still. Complete mental identification with and absorption in an object, by definition, can obviously occur only when all other *vṛttis* have been stilled and the mind is without distraction; hence *samāpatti* occurs only in the context of *samādhi* as indicated in this *sūtra*.

तत्र शब्दार्थज्ञानविकल्पैः संकीर्णा सवितर्का समापत्तिः ।। ४२ ।।

I.42 tatra śabdārtha-jñāna-vikalpaiḥ saṅkīrṇā savitarkā-samāpattiḥ

tatra, there; *śabda*, word; *artha*, meaning; *jñāna*, knowledge, idea; *vikalpaiḥ*, with conceptualization, notions; *saṅkīrṇā*, mixed with; *savitarkā*, with physical awareness, conceptualization; *samāpattiḥ*, absorption

In this stage, *savitarkā-samāpattiḥ*, "*samādhi* absorption with physical awareness," is intermixed with the notions of word, meaning, and idea.

Recall that *vitarka-samādhi* is listed as the first of four stages of *samādhi* in I.17, the other three being *vicāra, ānanda*, and *asmitā*. Here and in the next *sūtra* this first stage is refined by Patañjali and separated into two subdivisions: *sa-*, with *vitarka*, and *nir-*, without *vitarka* (as will be the case with *vicāra* in I.44).

Vyāsa takes a cow as his example of an object of meditation to illustrate the nature of the *samādhi* indicated by *savitarka*. The actual physical object, *artha*, cow; the one-syllable word *śabda*, cow, used in speech to refer to that object; and the idea, *jñāna*, of a cow produced in the mind of a person who hears that word—all are different categories of things, says Vyāsa. They have different characteristics, even though they are conflated in normal cognition: The first is a real-life object made of flesh and blood eating grass in the field, the second is an uttered sound, a linguistic indicator consisting of a spoken phoneme, and the third is a mental image or idea, a *pratyaya* (discussed in I.10) or *saṁskāra*.

When the *yogī* uses an object such as a cow as the meditational support, or object of concentration (*ālambana*, discussed in I.10), but the *yogī*'s awareness of this object is conflated with the word for and the concept of a cow, this absorption is known as *savitarka-samāpatti*, absorption with physical awareness. In other words, the *yogī*'s experience of the object is still subtly tinged with awareness of what the object is called and with the memory or idea corresponding to that object—*śabdārtha-jñāna-vikalpa*. So in conventional experience as well as in the nonconventional experience of the *savitarka-samāpatti* of this *sūtra*, the experience of an object is mixed up, *saṅkīrṇa*, with *vikalpa*, here, mental images, in the form of words and ideas. In this sense, direct experience of the object in its own right and on its own ground of being is tainted by the imposition of conceptual thought on it.

Vācaspati Miśra calls this type of *samādhi apara-pratyakṣa*, lower perception (with an eye to the *para-pratyakṣa*, higher perception, that Vyāsa will call the next type of *samādhi* outlined in I.43). This awareness of the object's word, meaning, and idea is not to be confused with the *vṛttis* discussed in the opening *sūtras* of the text (or with the *vitarkas* of II.33–34[228]). The *yogī* is not deliberating or reasoning about the object in any kind of an analytical or intellectually rambling fashion at the level of discursive thought, nor is he or she consciously activating a *saṁskāra* to recognize the object, since that would involve the activation and presence of *vṛttis*. We are at the level of *samādhi* here, when all *vṛttis* have been stilled. Nonetheless, the *yogī*'s complete absorption on the object still includes some kind of an intuitive level of awareness or spontaneous (nondiscursive) insight as to the object's name and its meaning. In other words, the subconscious *saṁskāras* of recognition are still not fully latent or inactive.

Savitarka might be better understood in comparison with the next stage of *samādhi, nirvitarka*, described in the next *sūtra* as when, in contrast, the object stands out in its own right without being conflated with the conventional terminologies of language that might refer to it, or with any idea or meaning it might generate. Indeed, the commentators begin their discussion of the subject here. *Nirvitarka* means nonconceptual or, perhaps more accurately, superconceptual. This occurs when the *yogī*'s *citta* has been purged of any memory awareness of what the object is and what it is called. In other words, no *saṁskāric* imprints pertaining to cow activate on any subconscious or intuitive level whatsoever. Vācaspati Miśra states that this type of object-awareness is real *yogic* perception, because conceptual or artificial notions and names are not superimposed upon the object. After all, any word could denote the object cow, if socially agreed upon, and of course the object is referred to by many different terms in various languages. And the idea of cow is a mental construction, a *saṁskāric* imprint on the *citta*; neither word, meaning, nor idea is the real cow.

Actually, as the commentators point out, conflating word, meaning, and object can be considered a type of *vikalpa*, imagination (I.8), because three distinct things—a conventionally agreed-upon sound for an object, a *saṁskāric* memory imprint of the object in the *citta*, and the actual physical object itself—are being conflated as if they were one thing. Word and idea are different from the ultimate *prākṛtic* metaphysical ingredients that make up a cow in reality, so in a sense they share features of the *vastu-śūnyam* of I.8. In *nirvitarka-samāpatti*, the object itself stands forth in its own right, free of designation or mental image.

Vyāsa notes that the type of insightful perception into the true nature of an object gained through *samāpatti* supersedes the other two means of gaining right knowledge of reality recognized by the schools of Yoga: inference (logic) and sacred word (I.7). Both inference and scripture depend on words and ideas to impart knowledge. *Nirvitarka-samāpatti* is based on direct perception that transcends words and ideas, and penetrates the essential nature of an object itself at a far more profound level than that of word and meaning or idea. Vyāsa calls it *para-pratyakṣa*, supreme perception, and therefore it is distinct from what he will call *loka-pratyakṣa*, mundane perception. However, says Vyāsa, *nirvitarka-samāpatti* can and does become the seed from which logic and scripture may sprout. In other words, says Vācaspati

Miśra, *yogīs* who have experienced the lofty levels of *samādhi* discussed in these *sūtras* might use words and logic in order to share their experiences with ordinary people—as, indeed, Patañjali is doing—and their words thus become the basis of scripture, as is the case with the present text. In other words, scripture is the product of a *nirvitarka* level of awareness of reality expressed by God or by the sages through words and concepts.

Once these truths become filtered and expressed through words, ideas, and logical thought, however, they become subject to the faults and imperfections inherent in the adoption of words and ideas (one need only consider, for example, how different commentators sometimes understand cryptic *sūtras* differently, especially in the Vedānta tradition[229]). Therefore, in Yoga, direct perception is the highest means of gaining knowledge. One must practice and experience the truths of Yoga, not merely read about, discuss, or try to understand them theoretically.

स्मृतिपरिशुद्धौ स्वरूपशून्येवार्थमात्रनिर्भासा निर्वितर्का ॥ ४३ ॥

I.43 smṛti-pariśuddhau svarūpa-śūnyevārtha-mātra-nirbhāsā nirvitarkā

smṛti, memory; *pariśuddhau*, upon the purification (here, termination); *svarūpa*, own nature; *śūnyā*, empty of; *iva*, as if; *artha*, object; *mātra*, only, alone; *nirbhāsā*, shining; *nirvitarkā*, without physical awareness

***Nirvitarka* [*samāpatti*], "absorption without conceptualization," occurs when memory has been purged and the mind is empty, as it were, of its own [reflective] nature. Now only the object [of meditation] shines forth [in its own right].**

Vyāsa explains that when the mind has been purged of all *saṁskāric* memory in terms of any recognition of what the object of meditation is, or what its name or function are, *smṛti-pariśuddhau*, that is, when it allows itself to be colored exclusively by the object of focus itself without any cognitive analysis of the object's place in the greater scheme of things and without the normal instinctive impulse to identify it and recall its name, then the *yogī* has attained the stage of *nirvitarka-*

samāpatti, or *nirvitarka-samādhi*. In this state, the mind has also given up its own nature of being an organ of knowledge, *svarūpa-śūnya*, in other words, awareness is not even aware of the mind as being an instrument channeling awareness onto an object. In a sense, all knowledge of the object as conventionally understood has been suspended, and the mind has completely transformed itself into the object, free from any cognitive identification or self-awareness.[230] The object can now shine forth in its own right as an object with its own inherent existence, *artha-mātra-nirbhāsa*, free from labels, categorizations, or situatedness in the grand scheme of things. Additionally, we can note that the object has in effect become the *yogī*'s entire universe, since awareness is focused exclusively on it and is thus unaware of anything else, even the cognitive process itself.

A brief discussion of the two stages of conventional perception as understood by a number of Indic philosophical traditions,[231] including (with differences in vocabulary) Sāṅkhya,[232] is useful here. In essence, when for instance, one ambles along the road and encounters an unexpected object, one first becomes aware of it in a vague sort of way, as raw sense data, without assigning a name or identification to it, like the preconceptual awareness of an infant. After this moment, the mind processes the data, and memory *saṁskāras* identify the object in terms of its specific name, the category of thing that it is, and its function in the grand scheme of things, for example, "This is a red clay pot for carrying water."[233] The first stage of indeterminate awareness is called *nirvikalpa*, and the second, *savikalpa*. Thus, in conventional perception, *nirvikalpa-pratyakṣa*, preverbal, preconceptual awareness, is followed by *savikalpa-pratyakṣa*, the recognition of name, category, and function of an object, the latter being considered a more exact form of cognition. In *samādhi* the reverse holds true—*savitarka*, when there is still awareness of an object's name and function, is superseded by *nirvitarka*, where the object stands out freed from the mental clutter of naming, identification, and recognition. Thus, in contrast to mundane perception, in *samādhi*, *nirvitarka* is considered to be a higher level of awareness.

By definition, then, *nirvitarka-samādhi* is a state beyond the ability of words and concepts to describe (so a commentary on *sūtras* such as this is a priori somewhat oxymoronic). Vijñānabhikṣu adds that words and ideas are subject to error, and thus so are inference and scripture, since they are composed of words. Therefore, one must turn to a *guru* who has experienced such states. Even then, says Vijñānabhikṣu, despite the fact that the *guru* may have realized the true nature of things, it is not possible to give experiential insight into such things through words, any more than one can convey the actual taste of sugarcane and milk through words to one who has not experienced them. Therefore, ultimately, one returns to the *yogic* truism that one must experience these states for oneself. Analyses such as this are useful only insofar as they might inspire individuals to take up the actual practice of *yoga*.

When one has attained this stage, says Hariharānanda, one loses any attachment to wealth and family, etc., as one sees all such things as essentially combinations of elements and subtle energies.

एतयैव सविचारा निर्विचारा च सूक्ष्मविषया व्याख्याता ॥ ४४ ॥

I.44 etayaiva savicārā nirvicārā ca sūkṣma-viṣayā vyākhyātā

etayā, by this; *eva*, also; *savicārā*, with subtle awareness; *nirvicārā*, beyond reflection; *ca*, and; *sūkṣma*, subtle; *viṣayā*, objects; *vyākhyātā*, are described

The states of *samādhi* with "subtle awareness" and without "subtle awareness," whose objects of focus are the subtle nature [of things], are explained in the same manner.

I should note again that terms such as "subtle awareness" are somewhat artificial attempts at finding English equivalents to technical Sanskrit terms. In point of fact, the Sanskrit terms themselves may also be something of an artificiality, since they are standard terms in Indic philosophical treatises that carry different meanings in other contexts but are appropriated by Patañjali as labels to point to supernormal states of consciousness (just as, say, we appropriate existing Latin terms to denote new and previously unknown species of flora we might discover). As the purport of terms such as *nirvitarkā* indicates, how can a term denote something that is by its very definition beyond word and meaning? Be that as it may, it is best, in my view, to retain the Sanskrit terms, rather than perpetuate clumsy English translations, which sometimes can be just as abstruse and incomprehensible and thus are of no greater usefulness to the reader than the Sanskrit terms they replace.

Vicāra-samādhi is the second of the four stages of *samādhi* in I.17, and, like *vitarka*, is here also separated into two subdivisions of *sa-*, with, and *nir-*, without. The overall difference between *savitarka-* and *nirvitarka-samāpatti*, and *savicāra-* and *nirvicāra-samāpatti*, as noted in I.17, Vyāsa reminds us, is that the former focus is on the gross physical elements that comprise an object, and the latter is on the subtle elements, *sūkṣma-viṣayatvam*, that underpin these gross elements in objects. Vijñānabhikṣu defines "subtle" as that which is the source or cause of something that evolves from it (recall that the gross elements are evolutes from the subtle elements, which are thereby their causes). Additionally, the subtle aspects of *prakṛti* cannot be perceived by the gross senses; as noted, subtler things can be perceived only by things even subtler than themselves.

The implication of this from the Sāṅkhyan perspective on this *sūtra* is that one can experience an object as consisting of the gross elements—earth, air, water, fire, and ether—as is the case in conventional perception, or one can penetrate this immediate and more physical nature of the object and perceive it as consisting of the essences underpinning these elements—the subtle essences of sound, touch, taste, sight, smell, which are the sources from which the gross elements evolve. This is the perception arising in *savicāra-samādhi*. Vijñānabhikṣu gives an outline here of the Yoga understanding of how *aṇus*, the smallest subatomic particles of gross matter, which form the basis of *vitarka* perception, are produced from their causes, the subtle elements.[234] *Vicāra*, then, is when meditative focus becomes absorbed in the *tanmātras*, the subtle elements underpinning any object of meditation.

This process of penetrating into the subtle or essential nature of an object might be analogous to seeing a piece of ice as a hard chunk of solid substance, or perceiving its deeper nature as essentially the fluid element of water, or, deeper still, as solidified vapor. And one can go further in the analogy and see all of these as a combination of yet finer entities—hydrogen and oxygen molecules—and these can in turn be dissolved into their still finer subatomic physical constituents. As this principle that a gross object is in fact constituted of finer and then still finer energies and elements holds good in modern physics, so it does for Sāṅkhyan physics. One difference is that in modern science, the atomic or subatomic structures of matter can be perceived only by advanced mechanical instrumentation, or inferred as existing, whereas Patañjali and the Yoga tradition claim that the *yogī* can actually and personally perceive or, more accurately, experience with the mind the subtle essences of an object without any such props. They are directly experiential, since the subtle (and gross) elements are evolutes of a substratum of mind stuff, and the Sāṅkhyan principle is that subtler dimensions of *prakṛti* can experience grosser ones. In other words, since one's mind is composed of the same substance as the *buddhi* substratum of any object, gross or subtle, it can blend with this substratum and thus percolate the object intimately from within, so to speak.

When the intensity of focus on the object of meditation deepens such that the *yogī* penetrates its gross externalization and experiences the object as consisting of subtle elements, the *tanmātras*, but subtle elements circumscribed as existing in time and space, then the ensuing concentrative state of awareness is known as *savicāra*. In other words, in *savicāra* meditation, an object is perceived as consisting of subtle elements, but the object is still experienced as existing in the present time, rather than in the past or future, and is still bounded by space, that is, it is taking up some distinct physical space in the presence of the meditator rather than being situated anywhere else. Briefly put, at this stage, the *yogī* still has some level of awareness of space and time. All this will become clearer when contrasted with *nirvicāra* below.

When, on the other hand, the *yogī* can focus on the object unconditioned by such dimensionality, when he or she can focus not just on the subtle nature of an object but can transcend space and time and perceive that these subtle essences pervade and underpin all things at all times, then the *yogī* has attained the state of *nirvicāra*. In this state, the *yogī* is no longer aware of dimensionality and temporality—the here and now. The object is no longer a distinct object taking up extension in a portion of space different from other spatial objects and existing in the present, rather than any other time, because the *yogī* experiences the subtle elements of the object as underpinning all objects at all times. In other words, the form of the object dissolves, as it were, under the power of the *yogī*'s focus, and the *yogī* now is simply experiencing vibrant subtle energies pervading all reality everywhere and eternally.

Hariharānanda uses the sun as a rough but useful example for the four types of *samāpatti*. *Savitarka-samādhi* is analogous to focusing without distraction on the sun, cognizing it as an object of a certain shape composed of fire atoms and situated at a certain distance, with some intuitive awareness of its name and function in the natural scheme of things. *Nirvitarka-samādhi* can be compared to the deepening of one's focus until one sees the sun only as a luminous object in the heavens but without awareness of its name, size, distance, function, shape, composition, etc. *Savicāra* corresponds to perceiving that the fire element of the sun is actually the *tanmātra*, subtle element, of light, but one's awareness is still circumscribed by the specific location of the sun in the universe and by the fact that it is perceived in the present, rather than the past or future. When, however, all awareness of Space and Time dissolves, and one sees the pure light, devoid of color, pervading not just the sun but all things at all times, in other words, one is aware only of omnipresent eternal light, then one's meditative state is known as *nirvicāra*.

We can now return to Śaṅkara's claim that the recitation of *oṁ* along the lines indicated in these *sūtras* culminates in a supersensory face-to-face encounter with *Īśvara*: "By the perfection of repetition [of *oṁ*] and meditation on the supreme *Īśvara*, the supreme *ātman* (*paramātman*) situated in the highest place (*parameṣṭhin*) shines forth for the *yogī*." Given the centrality of the chanting (*japa*) of *oṁ*, it is important to bring the greater insight from the technical information of these *sūtras* to bear on the discussion of the recitation of *oṁ* initiated in I.28, following Coward (1985).

In the *savitarka* stage of chanting, *oṁ* is mixed up with the conventional meanings and ideas that we now know define *vitarka* meditation—perhaps a mental image of *Īśvara* derived from the deity in one's local temple, or from some painting, or the sectarian tradition in which one has been raised or to which one has dedicated oneself.

One's mental notions of *Īśvara* will be molded by one's *saṁsāric* background and *saṁskāric* makeup. Therefore, at the *savitarka* stage of *samādhi*, one's chanting is obscured by these conventional notions of conceiving *Īśvara*. At the *nirvitarka* stage, these are eliminated, and *Īśvara* begins to manifest from the sound *oṁ* in his own pure nature, unobstructed by the concocted images and associations that the *yogī* has fostered. At the third stage of *savicāra*, as the *citta*'s focus on the recitation of the *mantra* deepens, one penetrates into the inner essence of the sound and actually begins to experience, that is, directly perceive, *Īśvara* in his pure *sāttvic* body. The *yogī*'s mind is now so completely absorbed in this vision of *Īśvara* that he or she has lost all self-awareness. One forgets one's own self in the rapture of this divine vision (but, it is imperative to note, contra *advaita Vedānta*, one nonetheless always remains a distinct individual). In the final stage, one's absorption in this vision of *Īśvara* is extracted from any notion of Time and Space, and *Īśvara* (and the sound of *oṁ* of which *Īśvara* is the seed) is experienced as the infinite and eternal Supreme Being.

There is some difference among commentators, both traditional and modern, regarding whether there are six or eight levels of *samprajñāta-samādhi*. Vācaspati Miśra suggests that just as there are *sa-* and *nir-* forms of *vitarka* and *vicāra*, by a parallel logic there should be *sa-* and *nir-* forms of *ānanda* and *asmitā*. In other words, Vācaspati Miśra envisions *sānanda* and *nirānanda* as well as *sāsmitā* and *nirasmitā*, resulting in eight stages of *samprajñāta-samādhi*. Vijñānabhikṣu specifically disagrees with Vācaspati Miśra on this point, rightly in my view. First, he says, there is no authority for such a claim; in other words, neither Patañjali nor Vyāsa mentions any such subdivision of *ānanda* and *asmitā*. But in any event, *ānanda* means bliss and *asmitā* means awareness of consciousness, he says, and there simply are no states corresponding to *nirānanda*, without bliss, or *nirasmitā*, without awareness of consciousness, at this lofty stage of enlightenment.

Recent analyses, both scholarly and from the *yogic* tradition itself, have accommodated themselves around both sides of the issue.[235] My own view is that it is a priori in Vijñānabhikṣu's favor that neither Patañjali nor Vyāsa mentions such a taxonomy. Most obviously and simply, this *sūtra* specifically states that *savicāra* and *nirvicāra* are to be *vyākhyāta*, explained, in the same way; if Patañjali had intended *sānanda* and *nirānanda* and *sāsmitā* and *nirasmitā* to be explained in the same fashion, he would have specified this here. And if one argues that, out of *sūtraic* briefness, he chose not to do so, Vyāsa would have certainly been expected to fill in the gap. The difference of views, however, remains valid, and I acknowledge that I found Koelman's speculative foray into what might possibly be the experiential constituents of hypothetical *sānanda, nirānanda, sāsmitā,* and *nirasmitā* states to be cogent as well as accomodatable within the metaphysical parameters of Yoga psychology.[236]

In the higher stages of *samādhi* (which will be discussed next), Hariharānanda notes that the *tanmātras* are not the only subtle elements underpinning the metaphysics of an object—they themselves are evolutes from still subtler entities such as *ahaṅkāra* and *buddhi*. These subtler elements too can be the object of *samādhi*, as the next *sūtra* indicates.

सूक्ष्मविषयत्वं चालिङ्गपर्यवसानम् ॥ ४५ ॥

I.45 sūkṣma-viṣayatvaṁ cāliṅga-paryavasānam

sūkṣma, subtle; *viṣayatvaṁ*, things having the nature of;
ca, and; *aliṅga, prakṛti*, that which has no sign;
paryavasānam, concluding, terminating

The subtle nature of things extends all the way up to *prakṛti*.

In the context of this *sūtra*, recall that an entity with a subtle nature, *sūkṣma-viṣayatva*, can be defined as something that can generate a product grosser than itself. The five gross elements do not produce any products or evolutes—they are the last link in the chain, so to speak—so they are not considered subtle. The *tanmātras* are considered subtle elements because they can produce grosser by-products. But the *tanmātra* subtle elements are themselves the product of something subtler still, *ahaṅkāra*. As the subtle cause of the *tanmātras, ahaṅkāra* is by extension also the indirect subtle cause of the gross elements, but twice removed, so to speak. And *ahaṅkāra* itself, also has a still subtler cause, *buddhi*. The term *liṅga*, literally, that which is a sign, is used in II.19 for *buddhi*, which is in turn an evolute of *prakṛti*, referred to here as *aliṅga* (that which has no sign).[237] *Prakṛti* is the ultimate subtlest cause of everything because it cannot dissolve into anything subtler.

With all this in mind, Patañjali indicates in this *sūtra* that the *samāpatti* or meditative focus of the *yogī* can penetrate the nature of the object and experience it on progressively even more subtle levels than those indicated in the previous *sūtra*: that of *ahaṅkāra* and *buddhi* (according to the Sāṅkhya schema of things). As one approaches the more subtle levels of *prakṛti*, the *sattva* element becomes more dominant. One of the inherent qualities of *sattva* is joy, *ānanda*. Thus, when the *yogī*'s focused mind becomes absorbed in the *ahaṅkāra* essence of all reality (space, dimensionality, time, etc., having already been surpassed in the previous stage of *nirvicāra*), it comes in contact with the *sāttvic* and blissful quality not only inherent in the object of meditation but also underpinning all reality, hence the *yogī* experiences all-pervading bliss. It is important to note that this is not the bliss of *Brahman* indicated in Upaniṣads such as the *Taittirīya* (II.8ff); the bliss indicated here is *prākṛtic*. The *citta* of the *yogī* is immersed in the *sāttvic* aspect of *prakṛti*, which results in an experience of *sattva* that produces a very refined but nonetheless still *prākṛtic* type of blissfulness. One must be wary of confounding this with the bliss of *Brahman* (see II.18).

Finally, penetrating the essence of reality further still, the *yogī* encounters pure *buddhi*, from which all the other evolutes have evolved. Having nothing further external or outside of itself on which to meditate, at least in the realm of *prakṛti*, since it itself is the source of all *prākṛtic* evolutes, only *puruṣa* now remains as an object of contemplation for the *yogī*'s *buddhi* (*citta*, as discussed, is composed of *buddhi*, *ahaṅkāra*, and *manas* in Yoga). Contemplating *puruṣa*, that is, reflecting consciousness back to its source, the pure *citta* of the *yogī* at this point experiences an awareness simply of I-am-ness, which is the etymological meaning of *asmitā*, rather than of any material *prākṛtic* object however subtle (but this is a particular, *puruṣa*-based type of I-am-ness, not to be confused with the *kleśa* of *asmitā*, as will be discussed below). There now remains one final step, which will be discussed in *sūtra* I.51.

The *puruṣa*, acknowledges Vyāsa, is subtle too—it cannot be perceived by *prakṛti* or its evolutes. But it is not subtle in the sense of being the cause of *prakṛti* or of anything else, and therefore does not come under the definition of subtleness outlined at the beginning of this *sūtra*, namely, that it produces evolutes grosser than itself. *Puruṣa* is changeless, according to the Yoga school, and therefore does not transform to produce evolutes. (*Puruṣa* is, however, the instrumental cause of *prakṛti* insofar as the latter exists for fulfilling the objectives of the former, notes Vācaspati Miśra, with II.18 in mind.)

While on the topic of ultimate causes, Patañjali does not refer to *Īśvara*, who we recall is a special *puruṣa* (I.24), as the material or, for that matter, the efficient cause of the world, that is, the creator of *prakṛti*. However, Vijñānabhikṣu and other commentators connect the *Īśvara* of the *sūtras* with the *Īśvara* of the *Gītā*, where Kṛṣṇa unambiguously states that, as *Īśvara*, he is indeed the efficient cause of *prakṛti*: "*Prakṛti* produces animate and inanimate things with me as overseer. It is from this cause, that the universe revolves" (IX.10). Kṛṣṇa is also the material as well as efficient cause of the universe: "Everything emanates from me" (X.9).

ता एव सबीजः समाधिः ।। ४६ ।।

I.46 tā eva sa-bījaḥ samādhiḥ

tāḥ, they (the four types of *samāpattis* outlined above); *eva*, indeed, very, only; *sa-bījaḥ*, with seed; *samādhiḥ*, meditative absorption

These above-mentioned *samāpatti* states are [known as] *samādhi* meditative absorption "with seed."

Vyāsa explains that the four *samāpatti* states outlined in the previous *sūtras* are known as *samādhi* with seed, *sa-bīja*, because they have something external as their object of focus, whether the gross form of an object, as in the case of the *savitarka* and *nirvitarka* states, or the subtle form of an object, as in the case of *savicāra* and *nirvicāra*. Therefore, *sabīja-samādhi* is fourfold, he says. (We should note that these stages of *samādhi* are referred to here as *sabīja-samādhi* but as *samprajñāta-samādhi* in I.17.) While some modern commentators[238] have argued that there are nuances of differences between these terms (and their counterparts of *nirbīja-samādhi* and *asamprajñāta-samādhi*), they are essentially used synonymously by our commentators. According to Vyāsa, here *bīja* technically refers to a seed in the sense of *saṁskāra*. Any object perceived in the mind leaves a *saṁskāra* imprint, even if the mind is fixed on it in the intense stages of *samprajñāta*, hence the latter's synonym, *sa-bīja*. The object of meditation, *ālambana*, even if the mind is fixed on it exclusively and with the penetrative insight discussed in these verses, still leaves its imprint as a seed, *saṁskāra*, on the mind just as any other object does. Since the object of concentration as well as the concentrating mind itself become redundant in *nirbīja*, no seeds of *saṁskāras* are deposited.

To sum up, in *samprajñāta*, or *sabīja-samādhi*, there are four levels, listed in I.17, two of which, *vitarka* and *vicāra*, are further subdivided into four *samāpattis* in II.42–44. One can thus speak of six levels of *samprajñāta-samādhi*, followed by a final stage of *asamprajñāta-samādhi*. This makes seven types of *samādhis* in toto (or nine types, if one subscribes to Vācaspati Miśra's *sānandā/nirānandā, sāsmitā/nirasmitā* schema).

निर्विचारवैशारद्येऽध्यात्मप्रसादः ॥ ४७ ॥

I.47 nirvicāra-vaiśāradye' dhyātma-prasādaḥ

nirvicāra, superreflective; *vaiśāradye*, in the clarity; *adhyātma*, of the inner self; *prasādaḥ*, lucidity

Upon attaining the clarity of *nirvicāra-samādhi*, there is lucidity of the inner self.

Vyāsa defines *vaiśāradya*, clarity, as the constant pure flow in the *yogī's citta* of the *sattva* inherent in it. *Sattva* is by nature luminous when all impure coverings have been removed (when it is not overpowered by *rajas* and *tamas*). When such clarity arises at the stage of *nirvicāra-samādhi*, the *yogī* gains lucidity of the inner self, *adhyātma-prasāda*. This insight occurs as a flash of illuminating wisdom, which instantly sees things for what they really are. It does not follow the normal processes of experience. It is more or less synonymous with the *prajñā* (wisdom) of the next *sūtra*. Vijñānabhikṣu adds that when *nirvicāra-*

samādhi arises, the truth not only of *prakṛti* and *puruṣa* but of *Īśvara* as well is perceived. Of course, even the purest *sāttvic citta* cannot directly perceive that which is subtler than itself, but it is able to understand that the source of its awareness is behind and beyond it. In this sense it indirectly perceives that there is a *puruṣa* higher than itself, that it is not the ultimate conscious entity.

Vyāsa quotes an adage: "Just as one who is situated on a mountain sees everything that is situated on the plains, so one who has climbed to the heights of the lucidity of wisdom becomes free from suffering, but sees all people suffering."[239] Vijñānabhikṣu adds the insightful comment that normally a person who is suffering perceives others as happy relative to himself or herself. But an enlightened person sees all beings as suffering. We are reminded here of the first Noble Truth of Buddhism: "All is suffering," a topic that will be taken up in the next chapter.

ऋतंभरा तत्र प्रज्ञा ॥ ४८ ॥

I.48 ṛtam-bharā tatra prajñā

ṛtam, truth; *bharā*, bearing; *tatra*, there; *prajñā*, wisdom

In that state, there is truth-bearing wisdom.

Vyāsa states that the word *ṛta*, truth, says all that there is to say. *Ṛta* is an old Vedic term denoting the order underlying and controlling the harmony of the cosmos.[240] In post-Vedic texts it comes, by extension, to denote the underlying truth of reality.[241] In the state of *prajñā*, wisdom, that now manifests, there is absolutely no trace of false knowledge. With an eye on the next *sūtra*, he quotes another adage: "One gains the highest *yoga* by means of cultivating discernment through the threefold practice of scripture, inference, and meditation."[242] Hariharānanda qualifies this by noting that although from the scripture one may learn that life is suffering and that the soul is different from the body, and although one may also arrive at these truths by the process of inference and logic, such theoretical knowledge does not actually prevent one from experiencing this suffering, nor, for that matter, does it give one direct perception of the soul. Therefore, in an immediate sort of way, one is hardly better off than an ignorant person who does not know these things. But when scripture and inference are coupled with meditation and insight, or wisdom, then one can come to the point of actual realized insight rather than theoretical knowledge. It is from such actual lucidity that the cessation of suffering and perception of the self as noted in the last *sūtra* arise. The path of *yoga*, as always, stresses direct experience over other forms of knowledge, as Patañjali clearly expresses in the next *sūtra*. Such direct experience, in this *sūtra*, takes the form of perceiving the ultimate truth of reality.

श्रुतानुमानप्रज्ञाभ्याम् अन्यविषया विशेषार्थत्वात् ॥ ४९ ॥

I.49 śrutānumāna-prajñābhyām anya-viṣayā viśeṣārthatvāt

śruta, that which has been heard, sacred scripture;
anumāna, inference; *prajñābhyām*, from the wisdom, knowledge;
anya, other, different; *viṣayā*, object; *viśeṣa*, the particular, specific;
arthatvāt, as its object

It [seedless *samādhi*] has a different focus from that of inference and sacred scripture, because it has the particularity of things as its object.

The term *viśeṣa*, particularity or specificity, as discussed in I.7, is typically associated with the schools of Nyāya and Vaiśeṣika. In the metaphysical system of these schools, all of manifest reality can be ultimately broken down to seven basic categories, two of which are *viśeṣa*, particularity, and *sāmānya*, generality.[243] *Viśeṣa* is best understood in contrast to *sāmānya*, which refers to the general category of an object. Let us consider a cow, or the standard item used to exemplify a generic object in philosophical commentarial discourse, a pot. The word "cow" refers to a generic category of bovine creature with udders and horns, who gives milk and goes "moo"; and "pot" to a roundish container usually made of clay (in India) that holds liquids or other substances. Although there are millions of cows in the world, and each and every one is distinct, individual, and unique in some way, the term "cow" does not particularize or distinguish one cow from another. It is a general term that refers to an entire category of creatures. Likewise with "pot." The term *sāmānya*, then, refers to the genus, species, or general category of something; terms like "cow" and "pot," indeed all words, refer to objects only in terms of their generic characteristics. *Viśeṣa*, by contrast, is what particularizes ultimate entities from each other—one atom from another (the character an atom has that makes it a unique specific individual, distinct from any other atom). These categories are discussed further in III.44.

Vyāsa says that the three forms of knowledge accepted by Yoga in I.7—*āgama*, scripture, referred to here as *śruta*; *anumāna*, logic (inference); and conventional *pratyakṣa*, sense perception—are all limited because they cannot provide information about particulars or specifics. Scripture and other types of verbal authority are dependent on words, and words, like "cow," can only point to the cow as a member of a general class of things. There is an infinite number of cows in the world, as Śaṅkara points out, and, even though they are all unique and distinct from each other in some way, one cannot come up with a different name for each individual one, hence we use the generic term "cow." So when we say something like, "There is a cow in the field," we are really giving information only about the cow as a member of a species and not about particulars: We are not conveying precise information about the specific individual cow in that field.

Inference, also, deals only with generalities (and is, in fact, dependent on perception in the first place). The standard Indic example of inference is whenever there is smoke there is fire, yet the statement gives us no information about any specific fire. As for empirical sense perception, *pratyakṣa*, it is true, say the commentators, that when we look at a particular cow or pot, we might be able to pick up on some characteristic that distinguishes the cow or pot in front of us from other cows and pots—perhaps this cow has an unusual skin color or the pot an odd shape. But conventional sense perception, says Vyāsa, cannot provide us information about the very specific or subtle nature of an object—its atomic composition, for example—or about distant or hidden objects beyond the range of the senses.

Only through the clear, unobstructed insight of *samādhi* can one fully grasp the *viśeṣa*, particularity, of an object, its subtle substructure of distinct atoms and essences. Patañjali will later claim that the *yogī* can tell the difference between two "identical" items, since although they appear identical to normal perception, the atoms comprising them are different, and it is these that the *yogī* can perceive. We must keep in mind that the Yogic tradition claims one can actually *perceive* these essences, not merely theorize their existence, through the undeviatingly concentrated focus of mind in the higher stages of *samādhi*. This perception, then, is actually a form of *pratyakṣa*, but not that of conventional sense perception. As noted, the *Yukti-dīpikā* commentary on Sāṅkhya points out that *yogic pratyakṣa* transcends normal sense-based perception. It is *para-pratyakṣa*, higher, supreme, supernormal, perception.

Following on the previous verse, Śaṅkara states that scripture provides us with information about the path that is to be followed, and inference or logic helps remove doubts about that path, but ultimately these must be followed by eagerness for meditation on what has been established by these other two sources of knowledge, that is, for direct *experience* of their truths. Patañjali is here clearly asserting that *samādhi* surpasses the ability of scripture and inference in their ability to fully experience an object at its subtlest level rather than understanding it in an indirect, generic, and mediated sort of way. And, ultimately, says Vyāsa, it is only through *samādhi* that one can grasp the distinct particularity of the soul itself.

The ingredients of the mind itself are the same as those underpinning the object in external reality; remember that the gross and subtle elements are nothing other than *tamas*-dominant evolutes from *sattva*-dominant *buddhi* and *ahaṅkāra*. Thus, when fully *sāttvic*, the mind can transcend its own *kleśa* limitations and merge into the common substratum of all things. This corresponds to such states as *savicāra* described above, when the *yogī*'s awareness perceives that the subtle nature of the object of meditation as well as the meditating mind itself actually pervade all objects and thus all reality. As Vācaspati Miśra puts it, once the obstructing qualities of *rajas* and *tamas* have been removed, then the pure luminosity of consciousness is able to pass beyond the limitations of all boundaries and finite objects. What, then, is there in existence that does not fall within its purview? In other words, the commentators claim that in the higher stages of *samādhi*, the *yogī* becomes essentially omniscient since awareness is no longer limited to the body or dimensionality but can radiate out infinitely and permeate the subtle substratum, in the form of *buddhi, ahaṅkāra*, the *tanmātra*, etc. (as well as the specific conglomeration of atoms that emerge from these *tanmātras*), underpinning all objects. It can thus perceive the *viśeṣa*, particularity, that is, the specific atomic composition, of any object, as Patañjali states in this *sūtra*.

तज्जः संस्कारोऽन्यसंस्कारप्रतिबन्धी ॥५०॥

I.50 taj-jaḥ, saṁskāro 'nya-saṁskāra-pratibandhī

tat, that (*prajnā*-bearing); *jaḥ*, born; *saṁskāraḥ*, subconscious imprint; *anya*, other; *saṁskāra*, subconscious imprints; *pratibandhī*, obstructs

The *saṁskāras* born out of that [truth-bearing wisdom] obstruct other *saṁskāras* [from emerging].

Patañjali here states that the truth-bearing wisdom, *ṛtambharā-jñāna* of I.48, produces a certain type of *saṁskāra* of its own. Evidently, these *pratibandhī* or blocking *saṁskāras* are effectively the *virāma-pratyaya*, the thought of terminating all thoughts, of I.18. Such truth-bearing wisdom *saṁskāras*, Vyāsa hastens to add, do not provoke the mind into *vṛtti* activity or activate as thought or in any way agitate the *citta*, which would be counterproductive to the goal of *yoga*. Their function is solely to block the activation and emergence of other conventional *saṁskāras* that lie dormant in the *saṁskāric* deposit of the *citta*. When these conventional *saṁskāras*, which produce mundane thoughts and ideas—the *citta-vṛtti*—are blocked, *samādhi* is enhanced, says Vyāsa. *Samādhi*, in turn, produces beneficial *saṁskāras* of wisdom, or discrimination, which further block the conventional *saṁskāras* and are in turn deposited in the *citta*. These then are activated and further enhance *samādhi*, triggering more *saṁskāras* of wisdom, and the cycle goes on, although the more wisdom *saṁskāras* that are deposited, the more the *citta* is transformed, and the more readily the *yogī* can enter into and maintain *samādhi* states. These beneficial *saṁskāras* (*nirodha-saṁskāras*) have been compared to a thorn used to extract another thorn, which are then both discarded.[244]

This is because wisdom, or discrimination, is still a function of *citta*, says Vyāsa, and therefore produces its *saṁskāras* just as all activities of *citta* are bound to do. So although it, too, must ultimately be bypassed when its function is served, the conventional activities of the mind must first come to a halt by the rise of discrimination. But the wisdom *saṁskāras* born of *samādhi* do not impel the mind to activity; rather they destroy the conventional *saṁskāras* and make them impotent. When this happens, the ability of the mind to produce its *citta-vṛtti* effects is curtailed, and the goal of *yoga* achieved. The wisdom or discriminatory *saṁskāras* reveal the distinction between the *puruṣa* and *prakṛti*, while the conventional *saṁskāras* operate under ignorance, defined in II.5 as the failure to distinguish between the self and the nonself, that is, between the *puruṣa* and its coverings of body and mind. When discrimination arises, this illusion is destroyed; therefore, the wisdom *saṁskāras* are indispensable. Vijñānabhikṣu describes these truth-bearing *saṁskāras*, these *saṁskāras* of discernment, as being of different strengths, perhaps, in resonance with I.22, in accordance with the intensity of *samādhi*, hence the need to reinforce them by the cycle outlined by Vyāsa.

Vācaspati Miśra states that there are only two possibilities for the mind: Either it pursues the objects of the senses, or it cultivates discrimination; put differently, it can be used either for enjoyment or for liberation, as Patañjali notes in II.18. This difference in how the mind is put to use reflects the difference between the *kliṣṭa*, detrimental, and *akliṣṭa*, nondetrimental, *vṛttis* of I.5. The inclination of the mind to aspire after worldly objects of enjoyment occurs only as long as it does not experience lucidity and discriminative awareness of reality, which ultimately means perceiving the distinction between *puruṣa* and *prakṛti*. As will be discussed, when such discrimination arises, ignorance is destroyed and thus the deposit of *karma* and the afflictions of the mind are also destroyed, and the tendency of the mind to seek external enjoyment comes to an end. Rāmānanda Sarasvatī states that upon the rise of discrimination, the mind becomes disgusted with sensual experience and turns toward the self. In this vein, Hariharānanda redirects attention to *sūtra* I.16, where Patañjali indicates that disinterest in the entire productivity of the *guṇas*, which means everything in *prakṛti*, results from realization of the *puruṣa* soul.

Vijñānabhikṣu states the Sāṅkhya and Vedāntic view here: the wisdom-bearing *saṁskāras* destroy only the dormant and unmanifest store of *karma*, and not the *prārabdha-karma*, the *karma* that has already activated. *Karma* exists in various stages, the exact specifications of which differ from school to school, but essentially it lies dormant awaiting later fructification, *sañcita-karma*, or is being accumulated by ongoing activity under ignorance in the present, *sañcīyamāna*; or it has already been activated and is now manifest, *prārabdha*. *Samādhi*, then, destroys all the dormant *karma*. However, the already activated *karma* of the *yogī*'s present experience—life span, type of body, ongoing happenings, etc. (II.13)—is terminated only upon the manifestation of the *nirbīja-samādhi*, the subject of the next *sūtra*.

तस्यापि निरोधे सर्वनिरोधान् निर्बीजः समाधिः ॥ ५१ ॥

I.51 tasyāpi nirodhe sarva-nirodhān nirbījaḥ samādhiḥ

tasya, of that [truth-bearing *saṁskāras*]; *api*, also, even; *nirodhe*, upon cessation of; *sarva*, of everything; *nirodhāt*, from the cessation; *nirbījaḥ*, seedless; *samādhiḥ*, meditative absorption

Upon the cessation of even those [truth-bearing *saṁskāras*], *nirbīja-samādhi*, seedless meditative absorption, ensues.

We now come to the end of the road of the *yogic* process outlined by Patañjali. In *nirbīja*, seedless, *samādhi*, explains Vyāsa, both the illumined insight and discernment born in *sabīja-samādhi* and the truth-bearing wisdom *saṁskāras* that accompany it, are themselves rendered inactive. Vyāsa notes that the *nirodha-saṁskāras* of I.50, the restraining or suppressing *saṁskāras*, block or eliminate even these beneficial truth-bearing *saṁskāras* of discrimination. In the ensuing state of *nirbīja-samādhi*, the *yogī*'s awareness has no contact whatsoever with *prakṛti*, external reality, either in its gross or subtle aspects. In other words, the *citta* is not focused on any aspect of an object, gross or subtle; completely uncoupled from *citta*, all mental and cognitive processes, *puruṣa* is now aware simply of itself. There is a *saṁskāra* that facilitates this by suppressing all *saṁskāras* whatsoever, including those of insight and wisdom. This is the *nirodha-saṁskāra* (as its name suggests, the ultimate *saṁskāra* that produces absolute *citta-vṛtti-nirodha*). All thought is now latent, *sarva-nirodhān*.

Nirbīja-samādhi is different from the *asmitā* stage of *sabīja-samādhi*

discussed in I.17. In the latter, the consciousness of the *puruṣa* is still emanating out and being channeled through *citta*. Because *citta* is so pure in this state, the commentators compare it to a luminous mirror in which *puruṣa* can see its own reflection. But *puruṣa* is not seeing itself directly; it becomes aware of itself indirectly by seeing a reflection of itself through the medium of *citta*. In *nirbīja-samādhi*, the consciousness of *puruṣa* is not radiating out and aware of itself as a reflection in *citta*, because the *citta* has uncoupled itself completely from *puruṣa*, who can now remain purely self-absorbed, that is, no longer aware of *prakṛti* at all.

The term *nirbīja*, seedless, indicates that this state is not related to any object that can plant a *saṁsāric* seed in the *citta*, not even the *nirodha-saṁskāra* of the last *sūtra*. It therefore does not leave any record of itself in the *citta*. The existence of the *nirodha-saṁskāras* can therefore be inferred, says Vyāsa, only by the "lapse of time in the *nirodha* state."[245] What he means is that when one enters into *nirbīja-samādhi*, one is not aware of Time, since one has no external awareness of anything *prākṛtic* at all, and thus, since there is absolutely no frame of reference leaving its imprint on the mind by which one can gauge the passage of Time; one can only infer that one has been in such a state after emerging from it and noticing the amount of Time that has passed since one first sat down to meditate. In other words, if a *yogī* were to fall into such a meditative state in the morning, he or she would be made aware of it only if, upon coming out of such a state, it were now evening.[246] The *yogī*, says Vācaspati Miśra, can have no perception or cognition in this state, since all *vṛttis*, mental functionings, have ceased—the mind is completely inactive. Therefore, there are no cognitive imprints relating to the passage of Time being deposited into the mind as memories of this state as is the case with all other normal or even paranormal activities. This is obviously relevant when considering why there are differences in attempts to describe these states in the various mystic traditions of the world. With no imprints in the mind to recollect, of what categories does the *yogī* avail in attempting to describe them? Hence the repeated assertions in mystical texts such as the Upaniṣads that this experience of *ātman* is beyond words, thoughts, and therefore descriptive categories.

Vijñānabhikṣu sees the eradication of all discriminatory or truth-bearing *saṁskāras* during *nirbīja* or *asamprajñāta-samādhi* to be a gradual process, which explains how a *yogī* can enter into the *nirbīja-samādhi* state and then return to discriminatory consciousness—the total elimination of all such wisdom *saṁskāras* is not instantaneous. When they reactivate, one is thrust back into external *prākṛtic* consciousness. According to Vijñānabhikṣu, only when the very last *saṁskāras* born of *sabīja* (*samprajñāta-samādhi*) are eradicated by the series of *nirodha-saṁskāras* born of *nirbīja* (*asamprajñāta-samādhi*), does one enter fully into the *nirbīja* state permanently. This points to the death of the physical frame. There thus appears to be a progression even within *nirbīja*.

To summarize, Vyāsa is suggesting here that for such a total state of internal absorption to occur, there must be a certain type of *saṁskāra*, the *nirodha-saṁskāra*, that blocks all cognitive functioning of the *citta*, even the hitherto beneficial faculty of pure insight and discrimination. Discrimination, after all, is a function of the mind, which produces a *saṁskāra* that discriminates between *prakṛti* and *puruṣa*. So, by definition, the mind at this point is still engaged and functioning within the contours of *prakṛti* and therefore actively engaging awareness to this extent.

On another note, Bhoja Rāja understands discriminatory *saṁskāras* to take the form of the famous aphorism in the *Bṛhadāraṇyaka Upaniṣad* (IV.5.15): "*neti neti*," not this, not this. In other words, pure *Brahman*, pure consciousness, is not anything *prākṛtic*—not the body, not the mind, not a table, not a chair, not a mountain, not a universe, not anything external whatsoever. But the act of discriminating in this way is nonetheless still a function of *citta*, which is itself *prākṛtic*. The *nirodha-saṁskāras* block all and every type of such mental functioning. They stand guard, so to speak, over *citta* and ensure that no thought, not even an insightful discriminatory one of pure wisdom, arises. I have sometimes half jokingly referred to these as the "terminator" *saṁskāras*.

Hariharānanda understands *nirodha* as a break in mental activity rather than an actual *saṁskāra* in its own right, like the spaces in a dotted line, which can be conceived of either as the break in a line or as no line. This interval between the functions of thought, the spaces in the line, can be prolonged by practice and supreme detachment manifesting as absolute disinterest toward anything knowable. This is the *kaivalya*, absolute liberation of III.50. There is now no possibility of rebirth, which under normal circumstances is triggered by the deposit of latent *saṁskāras* awaiting fruition.

Despite this, Hariharānanda states that some *yogīs*, wishing to do good to humanity, can enter *nirbīja* for a specified time and then later reactivate their mind so as to be able to function in the world for the benefit of others. This is something akin to the Bodhisattva of Mahāyāna Buddhism who postpones irrevocably entering *nirvāṇa* out of compassion for all other embodied beings left suffering in *saṁsāra*. To do this, it would seem that, prior to entering the state of *nirbīja-samādhi*, such a *yogī* would have to intentionally deposit a *saṁskāra* in his or her *citta* to activate later as a thought that will pull the awareness of the *yogī* away from total absorption in the self and back into external consciousness mediated by the *citta*—a type of *saṁskāric* alarm clock arousing the *yogī* from *samādhi*.

Vyāsa continues that when one fully enters into *nirbīja-samādhi*, the mind, along with all the beneficial *saṁskāras* that were produced during *sabīja-samādhi*, dissolves into its primary matrix, the undifferentiated *prakṛti*. The *nirodha-saṁskāras* that allow this, Vācaspati Miśra notes, do not provide the mind with a raison d'être—they do not perpetuate the mind's very reason to exist, as even the *sabīja-saṁskāras* do by providing discriminating wisdom—and so the mind no longer has any purpose to accomplish whatsoever. Vācaspati Miśra points to II.18, which informs us that the mind exists solely to accomplish either of two functions: to provide material experience of *saṁsāra*, or to lead the soul to liberation. Now that the latter has been achieved in *nirbīja-samādhi*, the mind, along with the beneficial truth-bearing wisdom *saṁskāras* that have brought it to this point, ceases all action. The mind therefore, now unemployed, dissolves back into its matrix, *prakṛti*, as a clay pot, once its function has been accomplished, is discarded and dissolves back into the earth. Then, as Rāmānanda Sarasvatī puts it, "Where there is no cause, there is no effect." *Saṁsāra* ceases.

Now, says Vyāsa, the *puruṣa* can exist in its own right—free, pure, and completely detached. Actually, says Vijñānabhikṣu, it has always been free: Notions of freedom and bondage in relation to the *puruṣa* are figurative conventions of scripture. *Saṁsāra* and all it entails exists in the mind, not in the *puruṣa* itself. The *puruṣa* becomes apparently ensnared in *saṁsāra* by dint of the mind erroneously misidentifying with it, and, because of this identification, *puruṣa* apparently becomes ensnared with the universe of experiences that the mind presents to it. But now, in *nirbīja-samādhi*, all vestiges of association with the *citta* have been discontinued, and the final and ultimate goal of *yoga* has been attained—*puruṣa*'s unmediated absorption in its own conscious eternal essential nature. Therefore, says Vyāsa, in this state one refers to the free *puruṣa* as "the pure (*śuddha*), the self-contained (*kevala*), and the liberated (*mukta*)." Actually, it has been that way all along.

इति पतञ्जलिविरचिते योगसूत्रे प्रथमः समाधिपादः ।

iti Patañjali-viracite yogasūtre prathamaḥ samādhi-pādaḥ

Thus ends the first chapter on *samādhi* in the *Yoga Sūtras* composed by Patañjali.

CHAPTER SUMMARY

The chapter begins by introducing and defining *yoga* [1–2]. This is followed by a discussion of the two possible options for awareness [3–4], a description of the *vṛttis* [5–11], and how to control the *vṛttis* by practice and dispassion [12–16]. Then comes the division of *samādhi* into *samprajñāta* and *asamprajñāta* [17–18] and how to attain these [20–22], after the discussion of other states that might resemble it [19]. *Īśvara* is then introduced as the easy method of attaining *samādhi* [23], along with his nature [24–26] and the chanting of his name [27–29]. The chapter describes the distractions of the mind and their accompanying effects [30–31], and prescribes meditation on any object to combat them, with various examples presented [32–40]. *Samāpatti* is introduced with its varieties [41–45] and their fruits [46–48] and object [49]. The chapter concludes with a discussion of *samprajñāta-samādhi* preceding the final stage of *asamprajñāta* [50–51].

द्वितीयः साधनपादः ।

dvitīyaḥ sādhana-pādaḥ

CHAPTER II

PRACTICE

तपःस्वाध्यायेश्वरप्रणिधानानि क्रियायोगः ॥१॥

II.1 tapaḥ-svādhyāyeśvara-praṇidhānāni kriyā-yogaḥ

tapaḥ, austerity, self-discipline; *svādhyāya*, study/recitation; *Īśvara*, the Lord; *praṇidhānāni*, submission to; *kriyā*, action; *yogaḥ*, *yoga*

***Kriyā-yoga*, the path of action, consists of self-discipline, study, and dedication to the Lord.**

Yoga for one with a controlled mind was described in the first chapter. Vyāsa asks, what about for one whose mind is not so fixed? He reads this *sūtra* as indicating how one whose mind is not fixed may practice a more action-oriented type of *yoga* referred to here by Patañjali as *kriyā-yoga* and consisting of discipline, *tapas*; study, *svādhyāya*; and dedication to God, *Īśvara-praṇidhāna*. Vācaspati Miśra points out that *abhyāsa* and *vairāgya*, practice and dispassion, were mentioned in the first chapter (I.15) as the means of *yoga*, whereas here in *kriyā-yoga*, *tapas*, *svādhyāya*, and *Īśvara-praṇidhāna* are being presented as the means. Practice and dispassion, however, require a predominance of *sattva* and so are difficult for the active and outgoing mind that is still under the influence of *rajas* and *tamas*. For such a temperament, the means outlined in this *sūtra* produce the required purity of mind. This is not to say that practice and dispassion are not to be cultivated by the beginner, but that *sattva* is especially easily cultivated through the practice of *kriyā-yoga*. Once the mind is more *sāttvic*, it is more capable of remaining fixed in practice and dispassion. Vijñānabhikṣu (and Mādhava[1]) quote the *Gītā* here: "Action is said to be the means for the sage desirous of *yoga*, but for one who has already attained *yoga*, tranquility is said to be the means" (VI.3). For the commentators, then, Patañjali is now presenting a more accessible and action-oriented method for approaching the goals outlined in the previous chapter.

Patañjali will be delving into a deeper level of psychological analysis, here, at least as pertaining to the conventional functioning of the mind. *Yoga* was defined as *citta-vṛtti-nirodha*, but in the following section he analyzes the mechanisms underpinning the production of the *vṛttis*. One cannot hope to still *vṛttis* until one confronts their underlying cause, hence this chapter is an organic continuation of the previous one (and not reflective of a hodge-podge textual collage as held by earlier scholars of the text as noted in the introduction).

Tapas means the control of the senses—controlling the quantity, quality, and regularity of one's food intake, for example; the quality of what one listens to or reads or talks about—in other words, the "*sāttvicizing*" of one's sensual engagements. There is no question of *yoga* for one who does not practice *tapas*, self-discipline, that is, austerity, the first item on Patañjali's list, says Vyāsa, making no bones about the matter. Impurities, by which he means the influences of *rajas* and *tamas*, which take various forms due to endless *karma*, the *kleśas* (obstacles to *yoga* such as ignorance, ego, and attachment), and the *vāsanās* (clusters of subliminal imprints), have propelled the mind toward the snares of sense objects since beginningless time, *anādi*.[2] These deeply ingrained habits cannot be removed without self-discipline.

Vijñānabhikṣu agrees that the tendency of the mind to pursue sense gratification can be broken only with self-discipline, but he adds that this should be of a gentle kind that will not disrupt the clarity of mind or weaken the body (otherwise, says Śaṅkara, if austerity and self-discipline are practiced in a way that disturbs the mind, they defeat the entire purpose of *yoga*—to still the mind). One does not have to look far to encounter the severity of the practices of certain extreme ascetics in Hindu texts, as even the hagiographical records of the practices of the Buddha indicate.[3] Even the ancient Greeks were struck with the extreme practices they encountered among some Indian ascetics more than two millennia ago—standing on one leg, or with one arm raised aloft (Strabo XV.61), practices still encountered abundantly in India if one attends, for example, a Kumbha Melā festival.

The Yoga commentators take a gentler approach. Rāmānanda Sarasvatī considers self-discipline to consist of celibacy, service to the *guru*, speaking truthfully, gravity, silence, the performance of appropriate duty, tolerance of extremes, and controlled intake of food. Hariharānanda states that it entails renouncing all sensual actions that bring only momentary pleasure. Śaṅkara stresses that *yoga* does not bear fruit for one who does not practice austerity, that is, for one who is too fond of the body, considering it to be one's very self, and overly inclined to avoid discomfort. The mind has been addicted to sense objects since time immemorial, he continues, and is caught up by them like a fish in a net. This primordial propensity cannot be destroyed without *tapas*, austerity. Patañjali will have more to say about *tapas* later.

Vyāsa defines *svādhyāya*, the second item mentioned in this *sūtra*, as *japa*, the repetitive chanting of *mantras* such as *oṁ*, and the study of scripture, which is a *jñāna* practice most especially associated with the Vedānta tradition (it will be further discussed in II.32, 44). From studying scripture, the aspiring *yogī* gains knowledge and inspiration. Vyāsa defines the third ingredient of *kriyā-yoga*, *Īśvara-praṇidhāna*, as the dedication of all action to God, *Īśvara*, and the renunciation of the desire of all fruits that might accrue from one's action. Vijñānabhikṣu notes that the submission to *Īśvara* mentioned in this *sūtra* is different from the interaction with *Īśvara* noted in the last chapter. In I.28, devotion to *Īśvara* was in the context of God as the object of meditation and took the form of concentration on his name and its meaning, whereas here, *kriyā-yoga* being more action oriented, devotion to *Īśvara* takes the form of renunciation of self-centered deeds and the offering of action to God. The implication is that total inward concentration on *Īśvara* is for the more advanced *yogīs*, and the more outward or action-centered practices associated with this chapter are for those whose minds are still outwardly inclined. However, it is important to note that surrender to God is not an option in *kriyā-yoga* as it was when it was presented as an object of meditation; it is a mandatory part of this practice. Patañjali's theistic orientations are thus more forcefully evident in this *sūtra*.

The commentators take this dedication of one's fruits of action to *Īśvara* as an implicit reference to the *bhakti*-centered *karma-yoga* of the *Gītā*, where, of course, Kṛṣṇa identifies himself as *Īśvara*. Indeed, the term *kriyā* overlaps considerably with the term *karma*—action, deed, etc.—both being nominal derivatives of the root *kṛ*, to do. Vācaspati Miśra quotes the quintessential *karma-yoga* verse from the *Gītā* in this regard: "You have a right to perform your duties, but not to their fruits; do not consider yourself to be the doer of your activities, and do not become attached to inaction" (II.47). According to the laws of *karma*, all action, good or bad, when performed out of self-interest, or, more precisely, when performed under the influence of ignorance—mistaking the self to be the body and mind (II.5)—plants a seed of reaction, which in this or a future life must eventually bear fruit, good or bad, in accordance with the original deed (II.12). *Karma-yoga*, as outlined in the *Gītā*, is an action-oriented path through which one can avoid the vicious cycle of *karmic* reaction by acting purely out of *dharma*, duty, rather than self-interest. It is subsequently surpassed and culminates, in the *Gītā*, in action performed not just for duty but in devotion for *Īśvara*. It is in this *bhakti* sense that the *Yoga Sūtras* commentators take this aspect of *kriyā-yoga*.

Thus, Vijñānabhikṣu quotes the verses from the *Gītā* where Kṛṣṇa says: "Whatever you do, whatever you eat, whatever you give away, whatever austerity you perform, do it as an offering to me" (IX.27). "I am the enjoyer of sacrifice and self-discipline, and the great *Īśvara*, Lord, of all the worlds" (V.29). "Those who worship other gods, endowed with faith, are really worshipping me, but they do so in ignorance" (IX.23). In these verses, as elsewhere in the *Gītā*, an alternative but overlapping path to *karma-yoga*, namely, *bhakti-yoga*, is expressed: Even as both paths require the abandonment of self-interest, action is better performed as an offering to Kṛṣṇa, that is, *Īśvara*. Thus, devotion rather than duty for duty's sake (as is the case with *karma-yoga*) becomes the primary motivating principle for activity. In the *Gītā*, Kṛṣṇa most conspicuously establishes the primacy of *bhakti* when he advises Arjuna to abandon all *dharma*, duties, and devote himself exclusively to him, thereby underscoring the primacy of *bhakti* over *dharma* (XVIII.66). (The text ends, however, with Arjuna performing his duty nonetheless, but doing so out of devotion because Kṛṣṇa tells him to, rather than out of the call of duty per se.)

Vijñānabhikṣu notes, therefore, that the *kriyā-yoga* of this *sūtra* denotes more than the *karma-yoga* of the *Gītā*, as it includes *bhakti* in the form of *Īśvara-praṇidhāna*, and *jñāna* in the form of *svādhyāya*, study. Therefore, Patañjali's *kriyā-yoga* actually incorporates three of the *yogic* paths outlined in the *Gītā: karma-yoga, jñāna-yoga*, and *bhakti-yoga*. The term *kriyā-yoga* is found infrequently in older texts.[4] Gelblum (1992, 80), states that the term is to be understood more accurately as ritual or worshipful act rather than the too broad meaning, action. This would tie the term more specifically with the practices of *bhakti-yoga*, which eventually take the form of *pūjā* in theistic Hinduism (for example, the *upāsanā* in *Gītā* IX.14).

Vijñānabhikṣu draws attention to the fact that, as the outer or preparatory aspects of *yoga*, the three ingredients of *kriyā-yoga* specified in this *sūtra* are also three of the five *niyamas*, the second of the eight *aṅgas*, limbs, of *yoga*. He considers the first five limbs, which Patañjali calls outer, also a preparatory aspect of *yoga*, as is *kriyā-yoga*. *Tapaḥ-svādhyāya* and *Īśvara-praṇidhāna* are the most important preparatory ingredients, says Vijñānabhikṣu; hence they have been selected here by Patañjali under the rubric of *kriyā*, in addition to their treatment later as *niyamas*.

Of interest here is the observation that *tapaḥ* and *svādhyāya* are ancient *brāhmaṇa* practices, the former central to Vedic purificatory rites and the latter to the recitation and study of the Vedic texts. Accordingly, one can suggest that Patañjali is providing something of a continuum with mainstream tradition here, incorporating ancient and familiar Vedic activities into the more marginal practices of meditation that he was systematizing.[5]

समाधिभावनार्थः क्लेशतनूकरणार्थश्च ॥ २ ॥

II.2 samādhi-bhāvanārthaḥ kleśa-tanū-karaṇārthaś ca

samādhi, meditative absorption; *bhāvana*, bringing about; *arthaḥ*, for the purpose of; *kleśa*, afflictions; *tanū*, weak; *karaṇa*, making; *arthaḥ*, for the purpose of; *ca*, and

[The *yoga* of action] is for bringing about *samādhi* and for weakening the afflictions [to *yoga*].

Patañjali states here that by the performance of *kriyā-yoga*, the *kleśas*, afflictions—nescience, ego, attachment, aversion, and the clinging to life—which are the subject of the next *sūtra*, are weakened. Etymologically, *kleśa*, from the root *kliś*, means to torment, trouble, cause pain, afflict. The word is often translated as obstacles, since in addition to tormenting the living entities, the *kleśas* obstruct the mind from realizing the nature of the true self. As *yoga* was defined in I.2 in terms of the suppression of *vṛttis*, so here *kriyā-yoga* is defined in terms of the weakening, *tanū-karaṇa*, of what we will discover are the underlying cause of the *vṛttis*, the *kleśas*. We are thus moving into a deeper psychological level of the *citta*.

In fact the *kleśas* become like burnt seeds, scorched by the fire of discrimination, and thus they become unproductive, and one is no longer subject to these afflictions and the *kliṣṭa* (detrimental) *vṛttis* they produce. (We noted earlier that *kliṣṭa* is from the same root as *kleśa*.) In Vācaspati Miśra's understanding, *kriyā-yoga* weakens the afflictions, at which point discrimination, no longer overcome by these powerful enemies, can manifest and burn them further. Otherwise, the *kleśas* are present at all times. Without performing *kriyā-yoga*, says Śaṅkara, one may know theoretically from the scriptures and the teachings of the *gurus* that *prakṛti* and *puruṣa* are different, but this type of knowledge in and of itself will not remove the *kleśas*, and thus there will be no experiential realization of these theoretical ideas.[6] Consequently, one will remain victimized by these *kleśas*—ignorance, ego, desire, etc. Hence Patañjali is prescribing that one must actively perform *kriyā-yoga*.

Recall that under normal circumstances, every seed of *karma* must at some point bear its fruit. Since there are unlimited seeds of *karma*, which cannot all fructify during a single lifetime, one must be reborn in order to experience all one's just *karmic* fruits lying in storage. Upon being reborn and experiencing the fruits of these previously stored seeds of *karma*, however, more actions are performed in response, each one planting more seeds of *karma*, and the vicious cycle of birth and death is perpetuated. As has been discussed, any single action triggers a potentially unending series of reactions, since one solitary action produces a reaction, which, when it eventually bears fruit, prompts a response or rereaction, prompting a rerereaction, provoking a rererereaction and so on unlimitedly. By *kriyā-yoga*, these seeds are burnt and so no longer ripen and bear the fruit of repeated experiences in the world of *saṁsāra*. Simultaneously, as the *kleśas* are weakened, *sattva* is enhanced, and, as this happens, the discrimination of the difference between the *puruṣa* soul and *prakṛti* matter can arise.

Some scholars feel that the jump in subject matter from the previous chapter on *samādhi* to the *kriyā-yoga* orientation of this chapter points to the patchwork nature of the text. After all, the path to *samādhi* was defined earlier as stilling the mind, and here as actively engaging in devotion, austerity, and study. As Feuerstein (1979) has long argued, however, there is an organic transition and fundamental structural coherence between the two. *Sūtra* I.2 defines the primary goal, *citta-vṛtti-nirodha*, the pacification of the mind, and II.1ff concern themselves with those subconscious mechanisms triggering these *vṛttis*, the *kleśas*. The distinction in terminologies and practices in this chapter merely reflects the requirements of a deeper level of psychological analysis and subsequent remedial activity. This chapter is thus an indispensable continuation of the first, providing more specific technical information as to the psychological mechanisms underpinning the *citta-vṛttis* that *sūtra* I.2 requires the *yogī* to still. Without eliminating the *kleśas*, there is no question of bringing about this ultimate state, *samādhi-bhāvana*.

अविद्यास्मितारागद्वेषाभिनिवेशाः क्लेशाः ।। ३ ।।

II.3 avidyāsmitā-rāga-dveṣābhiniveśāḥ kleśāḥ

avidyā, ignorance; *asmitā*, ego; *rāga*, attachment; *dveṣa*, aversion; *abhiniveśāḥ*, clinging to life, will to live; *kleśāḥ*, impediments

The impediments [to *samādhi*] are nescience, ego, desire, aversion, and clinging to life.

The *kleśas* have been referred to throughout the commentaries thus far, and implicitly referred to at the beginning of the text itself in I.5 where the *vṛttis* are stated as being *kliṣṭa* or *akliṣṭa*. Patañjali now formally introduces them here. As we have encountered elsewhere, Patañjali's method when he presents a *sūtra* containing a list is to discuss each item subsequently in separate *sūtras*, so the five *kleśas* will be examined individually in the next *sūtras*. *Kleśa* is often used as a synonym for *duḥkha*, suffering, and, indeed, *saṁsāric* existence, which

Patañjali will describe below as *duḥkha*, is perpetuated as a result of the *kleśas*.

When these *kleśa* impediments to *samādhi* are in full force, says Vyāsa, they strengthen the influence of the *guṇas*, produce *karma*, the law of cause and effect, and, by mutual interaction, bring forth the fruits of *karma*. Patañjali will later define these fruits as the type of birth, life duration, and life experience a person generates in accordance with the quality of actions he or she performs. By "mutual interaction," elaborates Vijñānabhikṣu, anticipating the next *sūtra*, Vyāsa intends that the *kleśa* of ignorance breeds the remainder—attachment, ego, aversion, and clinging to life—and these produce further ignorance in a vicious cycle. Thus, when ignorance is destroyed, so are the other *kleśas*. In short, these five impediments, which are all located in the mind, trigger and perpetuate *saṁsāra*, the world of change, that is, of birth and death.

Recall that Patañjali stated in I.5 that the *vṛttis* can be *kliṣṭa*, that is, produced by these *kleśas*, or *akliṣṭa*. If we take the latter term literally, this seems to indicate that there can be *vṛttis* that are *not* produced by the *kleśas*, that is, not subject to ignorance, attachment, etc. This can point only to the notion of the *jīvanmukta*: someone who is still embodied and thus functioning with a *citta*, but a *citta* that generates *vṛttis* that are not subject to ignorance, ego, attachment, etc. Recent scholarship (Whicher, 1998, Chapple 2008) has consistently and persuasively argued that it is a misconception to consider Yoga to be a radical withdrawal from the world; rather, it entails enlightened engagement with the world, that is, action stemming from *akliṣṭa-vṛttis*. There are certainly solid grounds to support this position.

अविद्या क्षेत्रम् उत्तरेषां प्रसुप्ततनुविच्छिन्नोदाराणाम् ॥ ४ ॥

II.4 avidyā kṣetram uttareṣām prasupta-tanu-vicchinnodārāṇām

avidyā, ignorance; *kṣetram*, field; *uttareṣām*, of the others; *prasupta*, dormant; *tanu*, weak; *vicchinna*, interrupted, intermittent; *udārāṇām*, activated, manifest

Ignorance is the breeding ground of the other *kleśas*, whether they are in a dormant, weak, intermittent, or fully activated state.

Patañjali gives the important information here, in resonance with all Indic soteriological thought, that ignorance, *avidyā*, is the foundation of all the other *kleśas*, the field, *kṣetra*, within which they grow, and hence the ultimate cause of *saṁsāra*. Like a piece of land is the substratum for bushes, creepers, grass, plants, etc., says Śaṅkara, so ignorance supports the other *kleśas*; when ignorance is dispelled, the other *kleśas* disappear.

Adopting what one might nowadays consider a psychoanalytical tone, Patañjali also differentiates among four different states in which the five *kleśas* manifest. Vyāsa defines these as the dormant state, *prasupta*, when the *kleśas* reside in the mind in potential form as seeds. Śaṅkara qualifies this by noting that only the *kleśas* other than ignorance can be found in a dormant state. Ignorance is never dormant, since it is the cause and support of the others and thus is always manifest. Otherwise, according to Vijñānabhikṣu, a *kleśa* may be dormant for a long time, even two or three births, before reactivating. These dormant seeds eventually germinate when a person encounters particular situations or contexts that serve as triggers. They then develop into the fully activated, *udāra, kleśas* mentioned in this *sūtra*—*kleśas* that are actually exerting their influence on the mind at a given time.

When the *kleśas* are continually interrupted—appearing and then fading away—they are described as intermittent, *vicchinna*, the third state listed in this *sūtra*. For example, says Vyāsa, when the *kleśa* of attachment for something is present, aversion for it is absent. Aversion may succeed attachment, but the two do not occur simultaneously.[7] In other words, clarifies Vijñānabhikṣu, aversion is not totally absent from a person when some other emotion like attachment is present; it is just in abeyance or latent (and, of course, vice versa). Therefore, it can be considered intermittent. Or, continues Vyāsa with a rare touch of humor, just because Caitra is attracted to one particular woman at one point in time does not mean he is disinterested in other women. He happens to be interested in one particular woman in the present, but he may become interested in some other woman in the future. These future attachment *kleśas* featuring other women remain either in dormant, weak, or interrupted states while the present *kleśa* is running its course. Intermittent *kleśas* differ from dormant *kleśas*, the first item on the list, insofar as they remain inactive for shorter periods of latency, according to Vijñānabhikṣu.

When, according to Vyāsa, one consciously cultivates a state of mind that is the opposite of the *kleśas*, they become weak, *tanu*, the second state noted by Patañjali. Indeed, Vācaspati Miśra and Vijñānabhikṣu note that one desiring liberation should actively counteract these *kleśas*. One can accomplish this by the practice of *kriyā-yoga*, which Patañjali has indicated weakens the *kleśas, tanū-karaṇa* (I.2). The practice of cultivating their opposites and pondering their consequences, which we will encounter in II.34, also weakens the *kleśas*: Thus, right knowledge dispels its opposite, the *kleśa* of ignorance; discrimination of the difference between *puruṣa*, the real self, and *prakṛti* dispels its opposite, the *kleśa* of ego, the false self; detachment dispels its opposites of both the *kleśas* of attachment and aversion, since they are two sides of the same coin; and the realization of the eternality of the soul dispels the *kleśa* of clinging to life. More than being weakened, Vyāsa continues, ultimately these *kleśas* can be burnt by *yogīs* who have cultivated deep meditation, and they then completely lose their power to activate even when the *yogī* encounters situations that would under normal circumstances trigger their activation. Such *yogīs* are said to have had their last birth.

The *kleśas* therefore can actually be found in five states, according to Vyāsa. Since they continue to exist when they have been burnt, but have lost their power to produce effects, the burnt or impotent state can be added to the list of four mentioned in the *sūtra*, making a total of five. Śaṅkara says this burnt state was not included by Patañjali in this *sūtra* because burnt seeds are not common to all living beings as is the case with the other four states, and this *sūtra* concerns itself with the *kleśas* as generally found present among embodied beings. Only in the *yogī* is a burnt category to be found.

अनित्याशुचिदुःखानात्मसु नित्यशुचिसुखात्मख्यातिरविद्या ॥५॥

II.5 anityāśuci-duḥkhānātmasu nitya-śuci-sukhātma-khyātir avidyā

anitya, noneternal, temporal; *aśuci*, impure; *duḥkha*, painful; *anātmasu*, the nonself, that which is not *ātman; nitya*, eternal; *śuci*, pure; *sukha*, joyful; *ātma*, self; *khyātiḥ*, notion, perception; *avidyā*, ignorance

Ignorance is the notion that takes the self, which is joyful, pure, and eternal, to be the nonself, which is painful, unclean, and temporary.

Patañjali here gives a very important definition of ignorance, the primary cause of all bondage: *Avidyā*, ignorance, entails confounding the nature of the soul with that of the body. The body is here described as painful, *duḥkha*; unclean, *aśuci*; and temporary, *anitya*, unlike the *puruṣa* who is joyful, *sukha*; pure, *śuci*; and eternal, *nitya*. We notice from the prefixes to these two sets of phrases that these two entities are exact opposites.[8] Thus, by adding the negating prefix *a-* or *duḥ-* to the adjectives in the first part of this *sūtra* to the same adjectives in the second part, Patañjali is efficiently underscoring the fact that conventional awareness is the exact opposite of true knowledge. To confuse the two, or misidentify the latter with the former, is *avidyā*.

While anyone can understand that the body is temporary,[9] what does Patañjali intend by saying it is "unclean"? Vyāsa quotes a verse: "The learned consider this body to be unclean, on account of its location, origin, sustenance, excretions, death, and the continual need to keep it clean." As always, the commentators elaborate on why the body might be considered unclean due to these things. The location of the body can be seen as unclean because in its embryonic form it is situated near the mother's excrement and urine; its origin is sperm and blood; its sustenance is fluids produced from food and drink; and its excretions are the discharges from the various outlets of the body—urine, feces, sweat, and mucus.

There are various views of the body in Hindu knowledge systems. *Āyurveda* depicts the body as a complex combination of substances, *dhātus*, that need to be kept in appropriate balance; the *kāma-śāstras*, desire texts, see the body as a means through which one can experience intense sensual enjoyment in skillfully manipulated circumstances; *tantra* considers the body to be a manifestation of *citi-śakti*, divine energy; *bhakti* construes the body as a temple that can be used in the service of God. These views are not mutually exclusive, but the ascetic tradition tends to view the body as a rather unpleasant bag of obnoxious substances.

In reality, as the cliché goes, beauty is skin deep, and a beautiful body is just a bag of bodily fluids and organs, which can be unpleasant and repulsive when taken out of their natural biological context. Thus, part of Patañjali's definition of ignorance in this *sūtra* is that in the unclean or impure there is an illusion of purity or beauty, which, as Vyāsa puts it, means considering this "very distasteful" body to be pure, like the man enamored of a "woman, beautiful like the rising new moon, with limbs made of honey and nectar and eyes as large as the blue lotus, who enthuses the world of men with flirtatious glances."[10] But despite such surface-level attractions, all in all, any body is in reality a sack of potentially rather embarrassing substances. Its real nature is evidenced by the need to constantly clean it (and Patañjali will later refer to the practice of cleanliness, essentially an act of removing the discharges and excretions of the body, as a catalyst that, if performed with the goals of *yoga* in mind, can lead to dispelling any erotic fantasies about the reality of the body). Realization of the nature of the body becomes most vivid during old age and at death: Nobody wants to linger around a decomposing body.

In this same vein, the Buddha advised his followers to actually contemplate the reality of the impurities of the body, that is, the bodily substances which, taken out of context, would be considered obnoxious, specifically that the body is simply a collection of "hair, nails, teeth, skin, flesh, sinews, bones, marrow, kidney, heart, liver, membranes, spleen, lungs, stomach, bowels, intestines, excrement, bile, phlegm, pus, blood, sweat, fat, tears, serum, saliva, mucus, synovial fluid, urine."[11] Indeed, he actually prescribes a series of visual meditations on these realities:

> And moreover bhikkus [monks], a brother, just as if he had seen a body abandoned in the charnel field, dead for one, two, or three days, swollen, turning black and blue, and decomposed, applies that perception to this very body (of his own), reflecting: "this body, too, is even so constituted, is of even such a nature, has not gone beyond that (fate)." . . . And moreover bhikkus [monks], a brother, just as if he had seen a body abandoned in the charnel field [reduced to] a chain of bones hanging together by tendons, with flesh and blood yet about it, or stripped of flesh but yet spotted with blood; or cleaned of

> both flesh and blood; or reduced to bare bones, loosed from tendons, scattered here and there, so that the bones of a hand lie in one direction, in another the bones of a foot, in another, those of a leg, in another a thigh bone, in another the pelvis, in another the pineal vertebrae, in another the skull, applies that perception to this very body (of his own) thinking: "this body, too, is even so constituted, is of such a nature, has not gone beyond that (fate)."[12]

In short, the Yoga tradition does not consider the body a suitable place to seek happiness for those interested in enlightenment. Patañjali will make the same point in II.15 by pointing to the notion of finding pleasure in what is really pain, says Vyāsa. Patañjali and the commentators have a good deal more to say about the nature of the body below.

The nonself, *an-ātman*, referred to by Patañjali here, says Vyāsa, actually consists not only of the body, which is the locus for enjoyment, and the mind, which is an instrument through which the awareness of *puruṣa* can contact the world, but also the accessories or paraphernalia of the body, whether animate (such as spouse, animals, and offspring) or inanimate (such as furniture or food). Although one may think that one's body, one's mind, and even one's possessions are one's real self, they are not, and to confound them as such is ignorance. Vyāsa quotes a verse that the commentators ascribe to Pañcaśikha, an ancient authority in the Sāṅkhya tradition: "One who regards objects, whether animate or inanimate, as part of one's self, rejoicing when these things prosper, and lamenting upon their demise, is deluded."[13] As the *Gītā* puts it: "The wise (*paṇḍitāḥ*) lament neither for the living nor the dead" (II.11).

I must acknowledge a Vedāntic slant in my translation of this *sūtra*, where joy, purity, and eternality are imputed to the soul. Most translators, traditional and modern, translate the *sūtra* perfectly appropriately along the following lines: Ignorance is the apprehension of the joyful, the pure, the eternal, and the self in that which is painful, unclean, temporary, and the nonself. Unlike the Vedānta tradition, the Sāṅkhya Yoga tradition (along with the Nyāya and Vaiśeṣika traditions), at least in their classical expressions, generally do not speak of the experience of the liberated *puruṣa* as blissful but rather as an absence of suffering.[14] Even Vijñānabhikṣu, who otherwise does not hesitate to blend Vedāntic notions into his commentary, states in his *Yoga-sāra-saṅgraha* that "we do not subscribe to the Neo-Vedāntics who imagine that ultimate liberation consists of the attainment of supreme bliss."[15] However, an argument can be made that, in contrast to the qualities of the nonself, Patañjali is alluding to the Upaniṣadic view that the real self—and he uses the Upaniṣadic term *ātman* for the soul here—is *sukha*, blissful. Both scholars and some traditional commentators have disregarded the possibility that Patañjali might be explicitly introducing an Upaniṣadic concept, the blissfulness of the self, underscored by his specific usage of the Upaniṣadic term *ātman*. In Vedānta, the highest self consists of bliss, *ānandamayo 'bhyāsāt* (*Vedānta Sūtras* I.1.13), but there is an assumption in some expressions of the Yoga tradition that the nature of the self is pure consciousness without any content whatsoever, including bliss. Vyāsa himself speaks of the bliss of liberation, compared to which even the highest bliss of worldly pleasure including the states of *sattva* are considered suffering. (Vyāsa in general is quite comfortable correlating *puruṣa* with the *Brahman* of the Upaniṣads [for example, III.34], as has always been standard for any orthodox Hindu thinker.) Whatever direction the later tradition took in this matter, this *sūtra* can be read as indicating that Patañjali, too, subscribed to this view.

Overall, Patañjali has very little to say about the nature of the actual experience of *puruṣa* attained in *nirbīja-* or *asamprajñāta-samādhi*, since, naturally, this state is beyond words and conceptualization, and thus beyond description. But this *sūtra* can be read as suggesting that it is a state of *sukha*, happiness, compared to all experiences other than that of the self, which are ultimately various shades of *duḥkha*, suffering, frustration. (Clearly, the prospect of a positive experience of ultimate bliss in the liberated state is far more enticing for one considering the arduous path of *yoga* than merely the prospect of the cessation of pain!)

The term *sukha* or *ānanda* is used in the Vedānta tradition as an inherent characteristic of the ultimate self[16]—the *Gītā* uses the term a number of times to describe the experience of the self (V.21; VI.21, 27–28; XIV.27), making it clear, however, that this type of *sukha*, unlike the ephemeral and fleeting *sukha* of sensual indulgence, is *akṣayam*, imperishable (V.21); *ātyantikam*, infinite (VI.21, 28); *uttamam*, the highest (VI.27); and *ekāntika*, absolute (XIV.27). The *Taittirīya Upaniṣad* goes a step further and, in a rhetorical or figurative mode, attempts to quantify the unquantifiable experience of bliss inherent in the self according to the Upaniṣadic tradition:

> Let us take a young man—a first class young man who is the most learned, cultured and strong person. And let us suppose that he owns this whole world with all its resources. This situation would constitute one measure of human bliss. A single measure of the bliss of earthly *gandharva* celestials . . . equals one hundred measures of human bliss; a single measure of the bliss of celestial *gandharvas* . . . equals one hundred measures of the bliss of earthly *gandharvas*; a single measure of bliss of the forefathers, who live long in their realm . . . equals one hundred measures of the bliss of celestial *gandharvas*; a single measure of the bliss enjoyed by the gods who attained their status by birth . . . equals one hundred measures of bliss of the forefathers; a single measure of bliss of the gods who attained their status by good deeds . . . equals one hundred measures of the bliss of those gods who attained their status by birth; a single measure of the bliss of Indra, king of the gods . . . equals one hundred measures of the bliss of the [other] gods; a single measure of the bliss of the sage of the gods, Bṛhaspati, . . . equals one hundred measures of the bliss of Indra; a single measure of the bliss of Prajāpati, the progenitor of species, . . . equals one hundred measures of the bliss of Bṛhaspati; a single measure of the bliss of *Brahman* equals one hundred measures of the bliss of Prajāpati. (II.8)

In other words, the bliss of *Brahman* is countless times greater than whatever might constitute the highest level of human bliss. With such figurative language, these texts try to point to the experience of *Brahman/ātman/puruṣa* as not only a state of bliss, but one that is far more blissful than any pleasurable experience connected with *prakṛti*, the world of matter.

A further somewhat technical point is that in Sanskrit, the word for ignorance is *avidyā*. As in English words like "a-theist" or "a-temporal," an *a*-prefixed to a noun in Sanskrit indicates an absence of the thing in question, so *avidyā* literally means a lack of *vidyā*, knowledge. However, ignorance, says Vyāsa, is not just the absence of right knowledge but is an actual type of perception in its own right, a perception of reality that is the opposite of true knowledge. Just as *amitra*, enemy (literally, *a* + *mitra*, not + friend), does not merely mean the absence of a friend but an actual real inimical person in his or her own right, so *avidyā* is a real mental state, not just an absence of knowledge. Thus the *kleśas* are actual in the *citta*. There are differences among the Hindu philosophical schools as to what constitutes ignorance, and Vijñānabhikṣu points out in this regard that Yoga philosophy differs from its sister school of Sāṅkhya, which takes ignorance to be lack of discrimination rather than an actual state of mind in its own right.

Also, although Vyāsa seems to equate *avidyā* with the *vṛtti* of *viparyaya*, error, in I.8, *avidyā* appears to be a more fundamental element in the subconscious. It underpins all the *vṛttis*, including *pramāṇa*, right knowledge, by which the *viparyaya-vṛtti* is dispelled. Error simply means to perceive reality incorrectly on occasion and thus may come and go. Ignorance here, *avidyā*, means much more fundamentally to confuse *puruṣa* with *prakṛti* and remains permanent until enlightenment is attained (even though the other *kleśas*, as noted above, can be intermittent, etc.). In other words, even if surface-level error, *viparyaya*, has been dispelled by surface-level *pramāṇa*, right knowledge, both these *vṛttis* are still underpinned by a deep-structure level of ultimate ignorance. *Viparyaya* is a conscious state but not necessarily a permanent or fundamental one; *avidyā*, in contrast, operates constantly at the very deepest level of the subconscious (until it is dispelled by true knowledge prior to liberation).

The topic of ignorance is discussed extensively by all philosophical schools—since it is, after all, the cause of bondage for almost all soteriological traditions of Indic thought—and the commentators introduce Vedāntic analogies here. Vijñānabhikṣu gives the familiar example of silver and mother-of-pearl to illustrate ignorance: Taking the body and the things of the manifest world to be real and eternal is like mistaking mother-of-pearl to be silver. Hariharānanda gives the other classic Vedāntic example of the snake and the rope: A person walking along at dusk happens upon a rope lying on the path but mistakes it for a snake and is alarmed. Similarly, ignorance is taking one thing for another (in this case, perceiving the nonself as the real self), a false cognition but a cognition nonetheless. Therefore, although ignorance can be dispelled by *vidyā*, its opposite or (to use the more specific Yogic term) *viveka*, discrimination, ignorance in Yoga philosophy is an actual state of mind (rather than just an absence of *vidyā* or discrimination as some other schools hold).

One might note, given the Yoga school's engagement with aspects of Buddhist teachings, that Patañjali defines ignorance in exactly the same terms as used by the Buddha, with one essential and dramatic reversal. Instead of ignorance being defined as the notion that takes the *self*, which is joyful, pure, and eternal, to be the *nonself*, which is painful, impure, and temporary, as Patañjali has done here, Buddhist teachings consider ignorance to be the notion that takes the *an-ātman*, the *absence* of self, which is a joyful, pure, and eternal state, to be an autonomous independent *ātman*, a notion that results in a painful, impure, and temporary state (*Paṭisambhidā Sutta* I.8.2.3). This essential difference will be addressed at various places below, but we can note here that in Buddhism there is no autonomous *ātman* (*puruṣa*) self that can be separated from its interdependence with *prakṛti*. Not only is there no *puruṣa*, but clinging to notions of such an entity is a primary cause of ignorance rather than enlightenment. The two views are thus diametrically opposed—the very goal of *yoga* and of human existence in the Yoga school is the very cause of bondage and ignorance in Buddhism.

दृग्दर्शनशक्त्योरेकात्मतेवास्मिता ॥ ६ ॥

II.6 dṛg-darśana-śaktyor ekātmatevāsmitā

dṛk, the subjective power of seeing, the seer; *darśana*, instrumental power of seeing, sight; *śaktyoḥ*, of the powers; *eka*, one; *ātmatā*, nature; *iva*, as if; *asmitā*, ego

Ego is [to consider] the nature of the seer and the nature of the instrumental power of seeing to be the same thing.

Moving on to *asmitā*, the second of Patañjali's *kleśas*, *dṛk*, the seer, is a reference to the awareness of *puruṣa* (referred to in I.3 as *draṣṭṛ*, another derivation of the same verbal root *dṛś*, to see[17]). The instrumental power of sight, *darśana*, on the other hand, refers to the intelligence aspect of the *citta*, that is, to *buddhi* as the instrument of awareness. *Buddhi* is the first *prākṛtic* layer enveloping *puruṣa* and presents images of the sense objects in the world, and indeed all *vṛttis*, to the *puruṣa*. It is therefore the primary instrument in the power of sight; the senses proper, such as the actual physical sense of sight, although also instruments, can make their impressions known to *puruṣa* only through *buddhi*, when it molds itself into their forms (the metaphor for this process, we recall, is that of liquid copper poured into a mold). In other words, without *buddhi* as primary instrument, *puruṣa* would have no awareness of *prakṛti*. Patañjali thus defines ego, *asmitā,* as the attribute of misidentifying *buddhi*, the instrumental power of sight, with the *puruṣa* soul, the actual seer. I like to give the example of a person wearing spectacles to see clearly, but due to mental disorder refusing to remove them, imagining that the spectacles are his very self rather than an instrument perched on his nose facilitating perception. In a sense, the ego entails doing just this, imagining that the mind and body, which are simply instruments allowing awareness to perceive the world, are the actual self.

Another way of putting this is that the act of experience, says Vyāsa, becomes possible when the experiencer and that which is experienced—two completely distinct categories and metaphysical entities—are considered to be one and the same, *ekātmatā*. It is ego that promotes this confusion. Ego is the specific aspect of ignorance that identifies the nonself, specifically the intelligence, with the true self, *puruṣa* (*ātman*). It is the knot in the heart, says Rāmānanda Sarasvatī, that ties these two entities together. Indeed, says Vijñānabhikṣu, the very act of experience itself *means* the identification of *puruṣa* with *buddhi*: Experience *means* experiencing an object other than the subject of experience. However, when one understands the true natures of these two distinct entities, continues Vyāsa, one no longer attempts to enjoy this world, and complete uncoupling of *puruṣa* from *prakṛti*, liberation, becomes possible.

Vyāsa quotes a verse: "Not perceiving the *puruṣa* self to be distinct from the *buddhi* intelligence in form, nature, and awareness, one makes the mistake of considering the intelligence to be the true *ātman* self as a result of illusion."[18] The difference between the two, notes Vācaspati Miśra, is that the self is unchanging, and the intelligence ever changing. As a result of this misidentification, says Vijñānabhikṣu, one identifies with the states of the intelligence, and so one thinks oneself to be peaceful, or awake, or learned, or whatever state is present in the intelligence. But in reality, it is the intelligence that is experiencing these states.

Vijñānabhikṣu points out that the two *kleśas* of ego and ignorance are to some extent the same thing, but there is a difference in degree. Ignorance initially involves a not yet specific notion of I-ness, a sense of self as being something as yet undefined other than *puruṣa*, a partial identification of the real self with *buddhi*, the intelligence, while ego involves a more developed or complete identity between the *puruṣa* self and *buddhi*. For example, he says, identifying oneself with one's spouse and children is analogous to ignorance, but actually feeling their happiness and distress is analogous to ego. Thus the difference is one of degree; ego evolves out of ignorance and makes the misidentification of nonself with self more concrete and specific.

It should be reiterated here that the *asmitā*, ego, as the effect of *buddhi* under the influence of ignorance, is different from that produced in the higher stages of *samādhi* by the pure *sāttvic buddhi*, as has been discussed. The *asmitā* in the context of *samādhi* in *sūtra* I.17 is true discrimination manifest in the *citta*, that is, correct identification of the *puruṣa* as the real source of I-am-ness. *Asmitā* in the present context of the *kleśas* is false identification, considering the I am to be the *prākṛtic* mind and body, due to the absence of such true discrimination ("I am female," "I am fat," "I am hungry," "I am a dog"). Therefore, *asmitā*, referred to as *ahaṅkāra* in Sāṅkhya, is pivotal in terms of determining the choice the mind will take, in terms of whether it wishes to direct its attention to *puruṣa* or to *prakṛti*:

> That choice will be either the observable world or a quest for liberating wisdom (*jñāna*). *Ahaṅkāra* then is that critical moment during which one of these goals must be chosen; the choice is either spiritual *puruṣa* or *prakṛti*, this is to choose be-

> tween infinity and finitude . . . wisdom or unwisdom, knowledge or ignorance . . . This is the Sāṅkhyan either . . . or, the human plight which points to the need for the healing medicine of Yoga spirituality and discipline . . . Although this definitive choice certainly exists, phenomenal individuality and material identity unfolded by *ahaṅkāra* also threaten to become a prison of bondage; humans may chose to lock themselves into such a phenomenal world and fail to search further for liberating wisdom. (Podgorski 1984, 164)

One might mention here that *asmitā* and the *ahaṅkāra* of the Sāṅkhya system are roughly synonymous but etymologically can be taken to refer, perhaps, to slightly different functions of the ego. *Ahaṅkāra* is not used by Patañjali (but occurs in Vyāsa's *Bhāṣya* in I.45 and III.47, where it is treated synonymously with *asmitā*). The etymological meaning of *ahaṅkāra* is I am the doer and is defined in the *Gītā* as the channeling of consciousness outward through the mind and senses into the world of objects, with the individual imagining himself or herself, due to illusion, to be the doer of actions in the world—actions that are actually being carried out by the mechanical forces of nature, *prakṛti*. In Kṛṣṇa's words, "The soul, bewildered by *ahaṅkāra*, thinks 'I am the doer' of deeds that are actually being done by the *guṇas* of *prakṛti*." (III.27). *Asmitā* is an unusual grammatical construction: *Asmi* means I am, the first-person singular of the present tense of the verb *as*, to be, and hence *asmitā* literally means I-am-ness.[19] Both *ahaṅkāra* and *asmitā* therefore involve consciousness refracting outward away from its source and being falsely identified with its *prākṛtic* embeddedness. But if there is a difference between *ahaṅkāra* as defined in the *Gītā* and *asmitā* as defined in this *sūtra* as a *kleśa*, it is that the emphasis of the former is on the false I as a doer of action, while the emphasis of the latter is on the false I as a *prākṛtic* entity (I am a man, a woman, sad, etc.). In other words, the *Gītā* emphasizes the mistaken notion of I-am-the-doer-ness, whereas Patañjali emphasizes the false sense of I-am-ness, a difference that resonates with the different concerns of the two texts (the former with action in the world and action in devotion, and the latter with realization of the true self).

सुखानुशयी रागः ॥७॥

II.7 sukhānuśayī rāgaḥ

sukha, happiness; *anuśayī*, the consequence; *rāgaḥ*, attachment

Attachment stems from [experiences] of happiness.

Moving on to the third *kleśa*, Vyāsa simply says that the hankering, desire, or craving for pleasure, *sukha*, or the means to attain pleasure by one who remembers past experiences of pleasure is attachment, *rāga*. The key ingredient in this process is memory. One who has experienced pleasure in the past recollects it and hankers to repeat the experience in the present or future, or to attain the means of repeating the experience; it is this dwelling on past experiences that constitutes attachment. Vāçaspati Miśra adds that ego is the root of attachment, just as ignorance is the root of ego; consequently, ego precedes attachment in the list of *kleśas* as ignorance precedes ego.

The commentators outline the psychology of attachment in the following manner: When a new means of pleasure is perceived, it is memory that infers that this new means of pleasure is the same as or similar to something that produced pleasure in the past, and hence it promises to provide the same or similar pleasure in the present or future. Therefore, memory precedes attachment, that is, attachment is predicated on memory. Hariharānanda adds that previous impressions, *saṁskāras*, of pleasure can remain latent in the mind, and thus even when memory is not consciously activated, these latent *saṁskāras* cause the mind and senses to be unconsciously drawn toward objects that have produced pleasure in the past. Hence one might find oneself partial to something for no particular conscious reason, which, from the perspective of Yoga psychology, could correspond to latent imprints from previous lives (the phenomenon of déjà vu is explainable in similar manner). Ignorance and ego cause the deluded mind to associate the self with these latent *saṁskāras* as well, identifying the self with the senses through which these latent impulses toward pleasure can be expressed. These *kleśas* thus cause the mind to identify the self with the nonself, namely, the body and the mind.

Hariharāṇanda also makes the important observation that when desire deepens into greed, the sense of right and wrong, morality, becomes neglected. The stronger the greed, the more a person is liable to pursue immoral means of obtaining the objects of desire. The *Gītā* outlines the sequence of events:

> From contemplating the objects of the senses, an attachment to them is born, from attachment, desire arises, and from desire is produced anger.[20] From anger comes illusion, and from illusion, confusion of memory. From confusion of memory, intelligence is destroyed, and from the loss of intelligence, one is lost. (II.62–63)

Vijñānabhikṣu adds as an aside that the desire of the *jīvanmukta*, or liberated but still embodied soul (most probably a reference to the desire to help other embodied beings), is not an attachment at all and thus not a *kleśa* perpetuating *saṁsāra*. This is because the desire of a liberated soul is not for personal pleasure or gratification, or, ultimately, stemming from ignorance at all.

दुःखानुशयी द्वेषः ॥८॥

II.8 duḥkhānuśayī dveṣaḥ

duḥkha, pain; *anuśayī*, the consequence; *dveṣaḥ*, aversion

Aversion stems from [experiences] of pain.

Vyāsa explains aversion, *dveṣaḥ*, the fourth *kleśa*, in a parallel manner to the previous *kleśa* of attachment: The feeling of resistance, anger, frustration, and resentment toward pain and its causes, by one who remembers past experiences of similar pain, is aversion. The commentators state that this *sūtra* is to be understood along the same lines as the last one: Aversion, *dveṣaḥ*, after all, is the flip side of the same coin as attachment. When we resist or resent something, or are angry or frustrated over something, it is because of a remembrance that this thing caused us pain in the past.

स्वरसवाही विदुषोऽपि तथारूढोऽभिनिवेशः ॥९॥

II.9 svarasa-vāhī viduṣo 'pi tathārūḍho 'bhiniveśaḥ

sva, own; *rasa*, potency, juice; *vāhī*, carrying, bearing; *viduṣaḥ*, the possessor of wisdom, the wise; *api*, even; *tathā*, also; *rūḍhaḥ*, pervaded, grown, established; *abhiniveśaḥ*, clinging to life

[The tendency of] clinging to life affects even the wise; it is an inherent tendency.

The commentators consider this clinging to life *kleśa*, *abhiniveśaḥ*, to be a synonym for the fear of death. All living beings, says Vyāsa, wish that they would never die and could live forever. The inherent nature of such a wish, he says, suggests that the nature of death has been experienced in the past. From this one can conclude that one has undergone previous births. In other words, just as the previous *sūtras* indicated that attachment or aversion to something is caused by positive or negative memories of that thing, aversion to death likewise indicates that one's memory retains unpleasant recollections of past deaths, although these are latent or subconscious in the present life. It is perhaps because fear of death pertains to past-life rather than present-life *saṁskāras*, suggests Balslev (1991), that clinging to life is characterized as an independent *kleśa* rather than relegated under the category of the previous *kleśa* of *dveṣa*, aversion.

Even a newly born worm is afraid of death, Vācaspati Miśra argues to make this case. This fear cannot be explained by the standard means of attaining knowledge established by Patañjali in I.7: direct perception, inference, or verbal testimony. In other words, Vijñānabhikṣu elaborates, one might argue that a person's fear of death need not be based on previous death experiences in past lives but can easily be accounted for by the fact that one directly perceives death around one and can thus infer that one, too, is going to die. Or, one might attain this knowledge of the imminence of death from the testimony of reliable people such as parents or teachers, or from scriptures or books of knowledge. But a newly born worm has not had these perceptions or inferences or testimonies yet nonetheless displays a fear of death.

The same innate fear of death is visible in the human infant, says Vācaspati Miśra. A newborn infant cannot have inferred the reality of death or heard about it any more than the worm. Given the Yoga position indicated in the last verse that *dveṣa*, aversion, like *rāga*, attachment, is the product of memory, how can this innate fear of death be accounted for unless all creatures have latent recollections of previous deaths? Such experiences are embedded in the *citta* in the form of *saṁskāras*, or mental imprints, that subconsciously cause creatures to avoid death. These *saṁskāras* underlie the clinging to life of all creatures noted in this *sūtra*. This seems to be a form of a long-standing argument offered by most Hindu sects in defense of the existence of the soul:[21] that instinctive memories in the newborn and, indeed, any type of memories whatsoever, require a preexisting substratum, or soul, on which to initially inhere, or find their support.

As Patañjali indicates in this *sūtra*, the *kleśa* of clinging to life is found even in the learned, not just the ignorant. The *vidvān* (here in the genitive form *viduṣo*) is one who has *vidyā*, knowledge, that is, one who is learned in the scriptures. Even the wise pursuing liberation, who are aware of the temporality of all things, are subject to this *kleśa*, say the commentators. This is because it is a stronger *saṁskāra* than other *saṁskāras*, says Vijñānabhikṣu (although Vācaspati Miśra adds that this is the case only for those whose wisdom is based on perception, inference, and testimony, not for those who have actually attained *samādhi*).

ते प्रतिप्रसवहेयाः सूक्ष्माः ।।१०।।

II.10 te pratiprasava-heyāḥ sūkṣmāḥ

te, these [five *kleśas*]; *pratiprasava*, return to original state; *heyāḥ*, are eliminated; *sūkṣmāḥ*, subtle

These *kleśas* are subtle; they are destroyed when [the mind] dissolves back into its original matrix.

Vyāsa's only comment here is that when the mind of the *yogī* has fulfilled its purpose, that is, when the *yogī* has attained a permanent state of *nirbīja-samādhi*, it dissolves back into *prakṛti*. As Śaṅkara puts it, no fire is needed for something that has already been burnt, nor grinding mortar for what has already been ground. The mind, having fulfilled its objectives, becomes redundant. The five *kleśas* are lodged in the mind. Consequently, becoming like burnt seeds as discussed above, they too dissolve along with it. Patañjali in *sūtra* II.4 referred to only four possible states for the *kleśas* (dormant, weak, intermittent, or fully activated), but we recall that Vyāsa in his commentary for that *sūtra* mentioned that the burnt state constituted a fifth state. Vācaspati Miśra suggests that in this *sūtra* Patañjali is indirectly confirming that fifth state. This is a good example of how Vyāsa's commentary has become almost as canonical as Patañjali's original text: It is almost never questioned by all subsequent commentators, but reinforced. The task of the traditional exegete is not to probe *if* an authoritative text is true, but *how* it is true.

Like burnt seeds, *kleśas* do not disappear as long as the mind of the *yogī* is still active; they remain embedded there but in their burnt state, like an empty shell, with their potency to sprout or produce effects (unwanted *vṛttis*) terminated. Their total dissolution occurs only when the mind of the liberated *yogī* dissolves back into its original *prākṛtic* source upon the *yogī*'s death, *pratiprasava*. One might mention here that in the Yoga metaphysics of *satkāryavāda*, matter cannot be totally destroyed, it can only transform.[22]

Hariharānanda states that the difference between the burnt seed state of the *kleśas* and their total dissolution along with the mind into *prakṛti* corresponds to the difference between *samprajñāta* and *asamprajñāta-samādhis*. In the former state, the mind is still active. Even the enlightened wisdom *saṁskāra* that "I am not this body" is nonetheless a thought of the mind. In this sense, it is a *vṛtti* and therefore has a form similar to any *vṛtti*, including its opposite, the unenlightened thought, "I am this body." The difference between them is that the former is *akliṣṭa*, beneficial to the goal of *yoga*, and the latter *kliṣṭa*, detrimental (I.5). In the same way, a burnt or parched seed still has a form that is similar to a normal seed; the difference is that one produces fruit and the other does not. However, there is always the possibility of even a burnt or parched seed unexpectedly sprouting, says Vijñānabhikṣu, so it is not until after the death of the *yogī* who has attained *asamprajñāta-samādhi* that the mind completely dissolves along with the *kleśas* and thus completely ceases to function as a mind with no possibility of capturing the awareness of *puruṣa* and of again producing misidentification, rebirth, and *saṁsāric* existence. In *samprajñāta-samādhi*, says Hariharānanda, there is still the sense of I, a faint trace of personal ego, *asmitā*, and thus the mind, along with its *kleśas*, is still not ready to dissolve away completely.

ध्यानहेयास्तद्वृत्तयः ॥११॥

II.11 dhyāna-heyās tad-vṛttayaḥ

dhyāna, meditation; *heyāḥ*, eliminated; *tat*, their [the *kleśas*]; *vṛttayaḥ*, changing states of mind

The states of mind produced by these *kleśas* are eliminated by meditation.

We had suggested at the beginning of the chapter that the relationship of *yoga* defined in I.2 as *citta-vṛtti-nirodha*, with *kriyā-yoga* as defined in II.1, is that by the former the *vṛttis* are weakened, and by the latter the *kleśas* or mechanisms underpinning the production of the *vṛttis* are eliminated. By the phrase *tad-vṛttayaḥ*, Patañjali here confirms that the *kleśas* produce the *vṛttis*. They are thus a deeper element of the psyche and unavoidably need to be confronted if one wishes to *nirodha* the *vṛttis* produced by them, as I.2 requires the *yogī* to do.

Patañjali indicated in II.2 that the *kleśas* are destroyed by *kriyā-yoga*, yet here he states that the *vṛttis* produced by them are destroyed by meditation, *dhyāna*. Vyāsa clarifies that the seed power, or fructifying ability, of the *kleśas* is weakened by the practice of *kriyā-yoga* and then eradicated by the practice of meditation,[23] until they become like burnt seeds. He gives the useful example of washing garments: gross dirt is first removed from soiled clothes, and then efforts are directed at the finer dirt. In the same way, the gross manifestations of the *kleśas* can be easily removed by *kriyā-yoga*, but the more subtle ones require greater efforts.

The commentators understand the process of eradicating the *kleśas* as a threefold sequence: First the cloth is cleaned by shaking it in the air or washing it in water, and this removes the larger chunks of dirt. It is then washed more carefully by adding a cleaning agent or beating it against a stone (as is still the custom in India), and this removes the finer, more ingrained dirt. But to completely and absolutely remove all subtle impressions of the soiled spots, says Rāmānanda Sarasvatī, you ultimately have to destroy the cloth itself. Likewise, the grosser aspects of the *kleśas* are eliminated by *kriyā-yoga*, the more subtle aspects by meditation, but, as indicated by the last *sūtra*, the actual burnt seeds, or residual impressions of the now impotent *saṁskāras*, are not completely dissolved until the mind, along with all its latent *saṁskāras*, merges back into its matrix at the death of the *yogī* who has attained the highest state of *samādhi*.

क्लेशमूलः कर्माशयो दृष्टादृष्टजन्मवेदनीयः ॥१२॥

II.12 kleśa-mūlaḥ karmāśayo dṛṣṭādṛṣṭa-janma-vedanīyaḥ

kleśa, impediments; *mūlaḥ*, root; *karma*, actions; *āśayaḥ*, deposit, stock; *dṛṣṭa*, seen; *adṛṣṭa*, unseen; *janma*, birth; *vedanīyaḥ*, is experienced

The stock of *karma* has the *kleśas* as its root. It is experienced in present or future lives.

Vyāsa states that the deposit, or stock of *karma* mentioned by Patañjali here, the *karma-āsaya*, is produced from *kāma*, *lobha*, *moha*, and *krodha*: desire, greed, delusion, and anger. Vyāsa appears to be using a variant set of terms overlapping the *kleśas*, perhaps taken from the *Gītā* (for example, XVI.21). Desire and its uncontrolled form of greed are ultimately the *kleśas* of attachment, and its flip side, aversion (which stem from the *kleśas* of ego and ignorance); anger is the frustration of this desire or attachment (*Gītā* II.62–63); and delusion is a manifestation of the *kleśa* of ignorance.

Vyāsa then discusses varieties of *karma*, good and bad, and its fructification. The examples Vyāsa gives of good *karma* include performing austerities, chanting *mantras*, cultivating *samādhi*, and worshipping *Īśvara* or the great sages, with enthusiasm and determination. Such activities bear fruit in this lifetime. He illustrates bad *karma* as harmful activities directed against the fearful, infirm, or helpless; those who have placed faith in oneself; the noble minded; or those performing austerities. If these activities are performed intensely, they can bear their fruits during the present life. Vyāsa illustrates the instant fructification of good *karma* by referring to the youth Nandīśvara, whose human form was transformed into a celestial one in that very life due to his intense performance of pious activities. He illustrates the immediate fructification of bad *karma* by the story of Nahuṣa, who was cursed by a sage to immediately abandon his celestial form as Indra and assume the form of a snake in the earthly realms due to his arrogance. Neither of these individuals had to undergo the normal process of old age and death but experienced their just fruits instantly. Similarly, the *Bhāgavata* (X.10) tells the story of two celestials who were cursed to become trees in the courtyard of Kṛṣṇa's family home due to offending sage Nārada with their shameless licentious behavior. Baby Kṛṣṇa pulls down the two trees by dragging a mortar behind him that becomes wedged between them, and the two celestials are immediately released from their curse and regain their celestial forms.

Whether good or bad, all *karma* is stored or imprinted as *saṁskāra* in the *citta* and, in general, may manifest its fruits in either this life or the next. Activities are virtuous or nonvirtuous and produce corresponding fruits. In the next *sūtra*, Patañjali states that the particulars of one's life—the type of birth, quality of life experience, and life span—are all the fruits or results of one's *karma*. But the fruits of *karma* ultimately have the *kleśas* as their root, *mūla*; it is these *kleśas* that influence one to act in good or bad ways. Therefore, there is a vicious cycle: *kleśas* provokes *karma*, and *karma* fuels the *kleśas*.

Vācaspati Miśra gives a few examples of how the desire, greed, delusion, and anger noted by Vyāsa might produce either bad or good *karma*. Desire can obviously produce bad *karma* when one performs impious acts out of avarice, such as stealing another person's property, but desire can also produce good *karma*, as when one performs pious acts motivated by a desire to enjoy the rewards of piety. Bad *karma* caused by anger, says Vācaspati Miśra, hardly needs exemplification—murder of the righteous, etc.—but there are also instances when anger produces good *karma*. Here he refers to the famous Purāṇic story of prince Dhruva, a child devotee of Viṣṇu (*Bhāgavata Purāṇa* IV.9–12ff). Once, Dhruva attempted to climb onto his father's lap but was rebuked by his co-mother, who wanted her own son, Dhruva's half brother, to be the king's favorite and eventual successor to the throne. Offended that his father did not step in when he was humiliated in this way, Dhruva determined in anger to gain a kingdom greater than his father's. Upon asking his own mother to advise him as to who might help him achieve his ends, she told him that he should worship Viṣṇu, since Viṣṇu can bestow any boon. Even though the boy was only five years old, and even though the great sage Nārada tried to dissuade him on account of the perils and hardships of the forest where he was heading, the boy persisted and performed intense austerities with his mind fixed on Viṣṇu. Eventually, as a result of concentrating his mind so exclusively on the supreme Lord in this way, Viṣṇu appeared to him and Dhruva was purified and received immeasurable boons, both material and spiritual. The point is that even though Dhruva worshipped Viṣṇu out of anger at the offense he had suffered, his mind was completely fixed without deviation on *Īśvara* and from this perspective created good *karma* (although a vision of Viṣṇu is, of course, an act of grace and beyond the jurisdiction of any mundane laws of *karma*).

A verse in the *Bhāgavata Purāṇa* states that "those who always dedicate their desire, anger, fear, affection, sense of identity, and friendship to Hari [Kṛṣṇa], enter for certain into his state of being" (X.29.15). According to the *Bhāgavata*, the highest meditation and goal of life is total absorption in God, even if this is generated out of animosity, as was the case with Kaṁsa, who, along with other demoniac adversaries of Kṛṣṇa, attained liberation simply by virtue of their minds being fixed undeviatingly on God, albeit in animosity. The text states: "The king of the Cedis, Śiśupāla, attained perfection despite hating Kṛṣṇa; what then of those dear to him?!" (X.29.13). The bottom line for the *Bhāgavata* is a *samādhi* with the mind fixed exclusively on Kṛṣṇa as *Īśvara*, whether in anger and hatred, or in a mood of intense desire and love, as with the *gopī* cowherd-women—all qualities which, under any other circumstances, would be considered *kleśas*.

Returning to Vyāsa's list, delusion can generate bad *karma*, as in the case of taking the life of another under the belief that doing so is a virtuous act, but delusion, according to Vācaspati Miśra does not beget good *karma*. However, even here, one might think of instances where delusion provokes a positive outcome in Purāṇic narratives. Bali, the king of the demons, for example, was deluded by Viṣṇu who appeared before him in the form of a *brāhmaṇa* boy, Vāmana, and tricked him out of his lordship of the three worlds. Yet the episode ends in Bali's upliftment (see IV.2 for story) since he attained pure devotion to Viṣṇu (*Īśvara*).[24]

Vijñānabhikṣu notes that the laws of *karma* apply only when they are performed out of ego, which, we recall, Patañjali defines as confounding the true *puruṣa* self with the mind and body. He quotes the *Gītā*, where Kṛṣṇa is encouraging the despondent warrior Arjuna to fight a righteous war out of a sense of duty rather than out of concern for the outcome that might result for him personally: "One whose intelligence is not tainted by ego, though he kills people in this world, does not kill, nor is he bound by his actions" (XVIII.17).

Hariharānanda provides the following useful synopsis of the workings of *karma*: Any state of mind leaves an imprint of itself on the *citta*, and, as we know, this imprint is called a *saṁskāra*. Imprints of good and bad *karma* produce an accumulation of *saṁskāras* called the *karmāśaya*, or stock of *karma* (II.12). These *saṁskāras* are either born from the *kleśas*, or are not: Those produced out of ignorance are born from the *kleśas*, but those resulting from true understanding are not (such as the "terminator" *saṁskāra* of I.50). It is the former category of *saṁskāras* born from the *kleśas*, whether pious, impious, or mixed in nature, that produces the store of *karma*, the *karmāśaya*. This store of *karma* then fructifies and brings about the threefold conditions of one's life that are the subject of the next *sūtra*. The time it takes for the seeds of *karma* to fructify—whether in this life or a future one—depends on the intensity of the original *saṁskāra*.

सति मूले तद्विपाको जात्यायुर्भोगाः ॥१३॥

II.13 sati mūle tad-vipāko jāty-āyur-bhogāḥ

sati, when in existence; *mūle*, the root; *tat*, its; *vipākaḥ*, fruition; *jāti*, birth; *āyuḥ*, age, span of life; *bhogāḥ*, experience

As long as the root [of the *kleśas*] exists, it fructifies as type of birth, span of life, and life experience [of an individual].

Vyāsa dedicates a long commentary to this *sūtra*. He begins by reiterating that *karma* can bear fruit only when the *kleśas* exist. Just as grains of rice can germinate only when they are not burnt and when they are connected with the husk, and not when the seeds are burnt or removed from their husks, so *karma* cannot fructify when burnt or removed from its husk or its root, *mula*, of the *kleśas*. As long as the *kleśas* remain active, all the pious and impious actions born of them during one's lifetime, *karma*, whether dominant or subordinate, combine at the time of death and determine one's next life. In other words, at the moment of death, the accumulated *karmāśaya*, or storehouse of *karma*, determines and establishes the "three fruits": type of birth, *jāti* (human, animal, etc.); life span, *āyus*; and life experience, *bhoga* (the aggregate of pleasure and pain that one will experience).

This store of *karma*, Vyāsa adds, containing the impressions of deeds, *saṁskāras*, performed throughout countless previous lives, is like a fishing net covered with knots, and the entire collective determines one's future birth. At death, says Vijñānabhikṣu, the subtle body, or *citta*, which is where the *karmāśaya* and all the *saṁskāras* are stored, transfers into the new body. The subtle body is not destroyed at death as the gross body is, and thus *saṁskāras* are preserved from life to life. Now, whereas some *karma* contained in the *karmāśaya* fructifies in the very next life, not all *karma* is destined to do so. Some *karma* might be mutually exclusive with other *karma* and not be able to coexist in the same life, says Śaṅkara; for example, one might have some *karma* that merits a celestial birth and other *karma* that requires an animal birth for fruition. Clearly those two sets of *saṁskāras* require distinct births in which to fructify. In general, the cluster of *karma* that does not fructify in the next life, says Vyāsa, may undergo three possible outcomes: It can be destroyed, it can merge with more dominant *karma*, or it can remain dormant for a long time, overshadowed by more powerful *karma*.

The destruction of such dormant *karma*, if it is bad, occurs by the performance of good *karma*, such as *yoga*-related activities, and this can be accomplished even in this lifetime, adds Vyāsa. He substantiates this with a verse: "Of the two types of known *karma*, one is bad, but it can be destroyed by deeds that are good. Therefore desire to perform good deeds in this world."[25] On the other hand, although good *karma* can destroy bad *karma*, the reverse does not hold true: Bad *karma* cannot destroy good *karma*. But bad *karma* can merge with good as per the second outcome noted by Vyāsa above and cause some slight diminution or interference in enjoying the fruits of good *karma*—such as indigestion after the pleasure of a good meal, says Vijñānabhikṣu.

As for the third option, lying dormant, not all *karma* is destined to activate in the next life, and so the balance lies dormant until the appropriate conditions manifest for it to fructify (unless, as outlined above, it is destroyed by good *karma*, or merges with more powerful good *karma* in the interim). Hariharānanda gives the example of a man who performed pious deeds as a boy, but due to greed he acted like a beast as he grew older. The beastly acts he performed as an adult developed into the dominant *karma* for that particular lifetime, determining that his next life would be that of a beast. His earlier pious *karma* performed as a boy, which required a human form in which to fructify, would meanwhile lie dormant during his life as a beast until the appropriate conditions manifest for it to activate in a future birth as a human. This means that at the moment of death, the particular cluster of *saṁskāras* destined to fructify in the next life arise like a wave, according to Vācaspati Miśra, and not only propel the *citta* into the next body but also determine the specific mind-set of that body. Thus, the portion of beastly *saṁskāras* of a person during the period when he or she was thinking and acting in a beastly manner, which require an animal birth as *karmic* consequence, reactivate in the mind and solidify into a beastly mind-set for the corresponding period as an animal. Meanwhile, the portion of human *saṁskāras* remains dormant until it is its turn to fructify in a life requiring a human mind-set and birth. Since the time and place of the conditions surrounding the fruition of *karma* are so complex that they cannot be fathomed, the unfolding of *karma*, says Vyāsa, is mysterious. As Kṛṣṇa states: "Difficult to understand are the ways of *karma*" (*Gītā* IV.17).

Vācaspati Miśra notes that, ultimately, the store of *karma* results in pleasure and pain. After all, the type of birth, life experience, and life span mentioned by Patañjali in this *sūtra* basically correspond to experiences of pleasure and pain. And pleasure and pain inevitably produce a mutually dependent relationship with the *kleśas* of attachment and aversion: The latter are dependent on the former. Nor can attachment and aversion exist without producing pleasure and pain. Acting out of attachment, for example, will produce pleasure if the object of attachment is available, or, if it is unobtainable or fails to live up to expectations, pain; likewise with aversion. Therefore, says Vācaspati Miśra, the mind can become a fertile field for the *karmāśaya* only when it is watered by the *kleśas*. Conversely, the *karmāśaya* becomes impotent when the *kleśas* are destroyed. Hence Patañjali calls the *kleśas* the root of worldly existence.

Vijñānabhikṣu quotes various verses pointing to attachment as the cause of *karma* and hence of rebirth: "Being attached, a person, along with his *karma*, attains the result of that to which his mind is attached" (*Bṛhadāraṇyaka Upaniṣad* IV.4.6). "The *puruṣa* soul, situated in *prakṛti* matter, experiences the *guṇas* born of *prakṛti*. It is attachment to these *guṇas* that is the cause of a person's birth in pious or impious wombs" (*Gītā* XIII.21). "Birth is not seen for one who has no attachment" (*Nyāya Sūtras* III.1.24). Of course, attachment itself comes from ego, which in turn comes from ignorance, hence the ordering of the *kleśas* in Patañjali's list in II.3.

When knowledge arises, Vijñānabhikṣu says, two results accrue. We know that ignorance is destroyed and so the *kleśas* are deprived of their base, and thus further *karma* is no longer generated. But additionally, already existing *karma* generated previously that is not due to manifest in this life, the *sañcita-karma*, collection or store of *karma* lying latent, is burnt (since *karma* can exist only where the *kleśas* exist). He quotes the *Gītā* again: "The learned call that person wise whose *karma* is burnt by the fire of knowledge" (IV.19). Vijñānabhikṣu points out that the texts all speak of *karma* being burnt, not destroyed, since nothing can be destroyed—*karma* is fully dissolved only when the mind, where *karma* is lodged, is itself dissolved back into its *prākṛtic* matrix after the death of the enlightened *yogī*.

While the enlightened *yogī* is still alive, says Vijñānabhikṣu, he experiences only the *karma* that has already begun to fructify, called *prārabdha-karma*. When the *citta* is transferred from one body to another, it brings its residual *karma* with it, only some of which is destined to bear its fruit in that birth. Once this next life begins, this portion of *karma* relevant to this birth is called the *prārabdha-karma*. If a person becomes enlightened in that life, all the other residual dormant *karma* that had not been activated for that life, the *sañcita-karma*, is destroyed, and, of course, no ongoing *karma, sañcīyamāna-*

karma, is being generated since the *kleśas* of an already liberated but still embodied *yogī* are destroyed when ignorance, the first *kleśa* and support of the other *kleśas*, is destroyed upon enlightenment. Therefore, an enlightened *yogī* experiences only the *prārabdha-karma* already activated and set in motion for this lifetime, and thus may still be subject to, for example, illness or injury. Such a *yogī* is called a *jīvanmukta*, embodied but liberated, and does not return to *saṁsāra* after death.

The *Sāṅkhya Kārikā* dedicates a specific verse to this phenomenon: "Upon attaining complete enlightenment . . . the embodied self remains [subject to embodiment for the balance of that life] because of the force of past *saṁskāras*, like a potter's wheel" (LXVII). The potter's wheel does not immediately come to a stop when the potter stops turning it; it slows gradually due to the force already invested in it. Or, as per the illustration used in the Vedānta tradition, the archer has no control over the arrow that has already been discharged; it will rest only when its momentum is exhausted (IV.1.15). Or, in more modern terms, if we pull the plug of a fan out of its socket such that no further electric current is entering the appliance, it does not immediately come to a standstill; it needs to use up the energy already transmitted to it. Likewise, even as no further *karma* is being produced by the *yogī* and all latent *karma* is destroyed, the *karma* already activated for this life nonetheless has to run its course.

ते ह्लादपरितापफलाः पुण्यापुण्यहेतुत्वात् ॥१४॥

II.14 te hlāda-paritāpa-phalāḥ puṇyāpuṇya-hetutvāt

te, these [type of birth, span of life, and life experience]; *hlāda*, pleasure; *paritāpa*, pain; *phalāḥ*, fruits; *puṇya*, virtue; *apuṇya*, vice; *hetutvāt*, as a result of

These [the type of birth, span of life, and life experience] bear the fruits of pleasure and pain, as a result of [the performance of] virtue and vice.

This *sūtra* states that vice, *apuṇya*, bad *karma*, produces a short life span and distressful, *paritāpa*, type of birth and life experience; virtue, *puṇya*, good *karma*, produces pleasurable, *hlāda*, experiences. So the *kleśas* provoke *karma*, and *karma*, depending on its nature, produces different qualities of births, life spans, and life experiences, and these in turn produce corresponding pleasure and pain. Vijñānabhikṣu reminds us that pleasure and pain exist in experience, and any experience is ultimately the result of the false identification of oneself with the body and its senses. Therefore, the *kleśas* of ego and ignorance always remain the ultimate root cause of all suffering. And even so-called pleasure can be seen as suffering from an ultimate perspective, since it is temporary and there is always some type of pain or undesirable element mixed in with every pleasurable situation. Vyāsa, anticipating the next *sūtra*, notes that a *yogī* sees suffering even in what others would consider pleasurable situations.

As for the *jīvanmuktas*, says Vijñānabhikṣu, since they are free from ignorance and ego, they experience only the pleasure and pain of the *karma* that has already started to fructify. They have extinguished attachments and desires and so do not produce fresh *karma*. He quotes the *Bṛhadāraṇyaka Upaniṣad*: "If one knows oneself as 'this' [i.e., the pure *ātman* self], then desiring what, and for the sake of whom, will one identify with this body?" (IV.4.12).

परिणामतापसंस्कारदुःखैर्गुणवृत्तिविरोधाच्
च दुःखम् एव सर्वं विवेकिनः ॥ १५ ॥

II.15 pariṇāma-tāpa-saṁskāra-duḥkhair guṇa-vṛtti-virodhāc ca duḥkham eva sarvaṁ vivekinaḥ

pariṇāma, result, consequence, change; *tāpa*, distress; *saṁskāra*, mental impression; *duḥkhaiḥ*, as a result of the pains; *guṇa*, qualities, influences; *vṛtti*, fluctuating states of mind; *virodhāt*, conflict; *ca*, and; *duḥkham*, suffering; *eva*, indeed; *sarvam*, everything; *vivekinaḥ*, one who has discrimination

For one who has discrimination, everything is suffering on account of the suffering produced by the consequences [of action], by pain [itself], and by the *saṁskāras*, as well as on account of the suffering ensuing from the turmoil of the *vṛttis* due to the *guṇas*.

Patañjali here makes a seemingly radical statement that everything is seen as *duḥkha*, suffering, by the wise. In the previous *sūtra*, he noted that pious activities produced *hlāda*, pleasure, but lest anyone take this to indicate that the pursuit of pleasure through piety be a fitting goal of life, he here informs us that even the so-called pleasure of *prakṛti* is only deemed pleasure relative to more obvious forms of *paritāpa*, pain. To the *vivekin*—one who has *viveka*, discrimination—all is suffering, even the so-called *hlāda* of good birth, experiences, and life span mentioned in the last *sūtra*. Indeed, *hlāda* is particularly insidious and especially perpetuates *saṁsāra*, since it is the memories of pleasure that propel people to try to re-create and reexperience that pleasure, and thus get caught in the vicious cycle of *karma* that perpetuates *saṁsāra*.

The term *viveka*, discrimination, comes from the root *vic*, to separate. *Vivekin* is the possessor of *viveka*.[26] Thus, those possessing discrimination, the wise, can separate *puruṣa* from *prakṛti* (to discriminate entails distinguishing between different entities). Hence they can discriminate that even the *hlāda* described in the previous *sūtra* belongs to the world of *prakṛti* and is therefore, from an ultimate perspective, actually *duḥkha*.

A better translation of *duḥkha* than suffering might be, in my view, frustration, since suffering often has physical connotations, and, in addition to referring to physical pain, *duḥkha*, perhaps even primarily, is the frustration that follows from the attempt to find permanent satisfaction in objects of the senses and mind that are by their very nature temporary. This perception of the world as a place of frustration is fairly ubiquitous in the Yogic traditions. The first Noble Truth of Buddhism, *sarvaṁ duḥkham*, all is suffering, consists of the exact same terms adopted by Patañjali. Indeed, the other three Noble Truths are predicated upon the first (that there is a cause of this suffering, that there is a possibility of putting an end to suffering, and that there is a path to accomplish the removal of suffering). Thus the Buddhist path is based on a perception that the world—that is, the world as experienced under the influence of ignorance—is a place of suffering. Patañjali makes the same claim.

In fact, most of the soteriological systems of ancient India shared this perception. As early as the *Bṛhadāraṇyaka Upaniṣad* we find that, other than the *ātman*, "everything else is grief" (III.4.2), and the *Gītā* calls the world *duḥkhālayam aśāśvatam*, a "place of suffering which is temporary" (VIII.15). The *Sāṅkhya Kārikās* state in the very first verse: "Because of the torment of the threefold *duḥkha* [discussed below], the desire to know the means of counteracting them arises" (I.1). In the *Nyāya Sūtras, duḥkha* is one of the nine objects of "right knowledge," and liberation is defined as the removal of suffering (I.1.9, 22). Similarly, the very definition of *yoga* in the *Vaiśeṣika Sūtras* is the elimination of *duḥkha* (V.16).[27]

This *sūtra* is actually the pivot of this chapter, which, in turn, is the heart of the entire text. Verses II.1–14 discuss the causes, the *kleśas*, that produce *duḥkha*, and verses 16 onward focus on the path to remove *duḥkha* as well as the state beyond. The chapter thus echoes the Four Noble Truths.

One might ask, without an experience of the world as frustrating on some level, what would motivate one to seek fulfillment elsewhere and take up the rigors and challenges of the *yoga* path? If one perceives the world of experience as a jolly fine place in which to be, why would one wish to seek a higher truth? From this perspective, a recognition of the world as a place of suffering is actually a preliminary realization for the path of *yoga* or, it might be argued, for any serious spiritual practice, as indicated in the *Sāṅkhya Kārikās* quote above.

Vyāsa sets out to examine the nature of suffering and its apparent opposite, pleasure. Pleasure, says Vyāsa, means attachment to the objects that give pleasure, whether inanimate objects or living beings. It is this attachment to pleasure that motivates action, and, as we know, action produces the *karmāśaya*, the store of action, that is, the cycle of reaction inherent in *karma*. Aversion to suffering is the flip side of this—the attempt to avoid the objects that cause suffering. Therefore, it is attachment and aversion that produce the *karmāśaya*. More specifically, pleasure is the appeasement that occurs when the senses are gratified with the objects of enjoyment, and suffering the lack of such appeasement, in other words, the agitation that results from unfulfilled desire.

However, Vyāsa points out that the senses are never really freed from hankering by repeated indulgence, because such indulgence simply increases the attachment to pleasure as well as the demands of the senses. One remains even more dissatisfied than before. The *Gītā* considers lust "the eternal enemy . . . insatiable as fire" (III.39). The more fuel one pours on a fire, the stronger it burns. Therefore, indulgence is not the means to gain ultimate pleasure, and one who gets addicted to sense pleasure ends up immersed in dissatisfaction and in this sense enmeshed in frustration. This is the frustration born of consequences, *pariṇāma*, the first type of suffering on Patañjali's list. *Pariṇāma* also means change, transformation, as well as consequences, and can be read as pointing to the ever-changing nature of everything. From this perspective, the experience of any happiness, even our "Kodak moments," which appear so satisfying at the moment of experience, are changing or temporary by nature. Hence, when the pleasurable moment inevitably passes, the sense of frustration is enhanced. Therefore the *yogī*, says Vyāsa, sees suffering inherent even in the moment of pleasure.

Vācaspati Miśra continues this theme by pointing out that attachment to pleasure is itself a source of pain because one is never satisfied with what one has but constantly craves additional objects of pleasure. And on the occasions when one gains possession of such perceived sources of pleasure, one finds that they do not provide the anticipated satisfaction, and thus one craves more or different objects. The *Mānava-dharma-śastra*[28] makes the observation that "desire is never extinguished by the enjoyment of what is desired; it just grows stronger, like a fire that flares up with the oblation of butter" (II.94). This constant hankering for more enjoyment is itself suffering. Vācaspati Miśra cites a similar verse in the *Gītā*: "Happiness derived from the contact of the senses appears like nectar in the beginning, but in the end becomes like poison. Such happiness is born from *rajas*." Like honey mixed with poison, he says, there is always suffering inherent as a consequence of pleasure; indeed, there is always suffering mixed in with the actual experience of pleasure itself.

The suffering of pain, *tāpa*, the second type of suffering listed in this *sūtra*, is identified by Vyāsa as the three standard sources of suffering identified in traditional texts. (*Tāpa* here refers to involuntary pain experienced by the mind and senses, in contrast to the spiritual practice of *tāpa* as an ingredient of *kriyā-yoga* or the *niyamas*, where it refers to the voluntary control of the senses.) These three are *ādhyātmika, ādhibhautika,* and *ādhidaivika*: suffering produced by one's own body and mind (such as illness, injury, insecurity, or anxiety); suffering produced by other beings (such as mosquitoes, enemies, obnoxious neighbors, even one's own sometimes troublesome family members and loved ones); and suffering produced by nature and the environment (such as storms or earthquakes). Through body, speech, and mind, a person tries to avoid distressful situations and instead attain the means of pleasure. A small amount of suffering is felt more than an abundance of pleasure, says Vijñānabhikṣu, and so aversion to pain is stronger than desire for pleasure. Therefore, people pray to God that their happiness be perpetuated and suffering be avoided.

A further result of the pursuit of pleasure and avoidance of pain, says Vyāsa, is that it inevitably causes one to harm others in this endeavor, even if some benefit, and thus binds one to accumulate merit and demerit, *karma*. He states that pleasure can be attained only at some direct or indirect cost of harm to others, and thus the seeds of aggression are added to one's store of *karma*. Even in such seemingly innocuous activities as preparing food and cleaning, violence is performed against other living creatures. Tiny creatures are harmed unknowingly in the performance of household chores, as Vācaspati Miśra illustrates with another well-known verse from Manu (III.69) that the householder must atone for the five slaughterhouses of the household: the fireplace, the grindstone, the broom, the mortar, and the pestle.[29]

Saṁskāras, subliminal impressions, the next item mentioned by Patañjali as a source of suffering, are, as we know, the latent imprints deposited in the mind of every past experience of pleasure and suffering. When these ripen as *karma* and fructify, one again experiences pleasure and suffering. The desire for pleasure and aversion to pain trigger these latent *saṁskāras*, which fructify and become memories of past pleasures or pains. These memories generate fresh craving or aversion, the desire to re-create past pleasurable experiences (or avoid known miseries). This is a form of mental torment or suffering: One is constantly lamenting the loss of past pleasures and hankering for the attainment of pleasures one does not at present have. Additionally, of course, inspired by such memories, a person acts, producing further experiences, and these produce a new set of *saṁskāras* that add to the accumulation of *karma*. Thus the river of *karma*, which, as Vyāsa will argue next, is all ultimately suffering, swells continuously. Since one cannot experience the fruition of all this *karma* in one life, one is bound to experience it in future lives, and so the cycle of embodied existence, *saṁsāra*, is perpetuated across lifetimes.

This vicious cycle causes concern only to the *yogī*, however, who can recognize it as being a highly undesirable state of affairs. As the Buddha notes, what others call pleasure, *sukha*, the Noble Ones call *duḥkha*.[30] A wise person cannot enjoy something sweet if he or she knows it will eventually cause sickness, says Śaṅkara. A *yogī* is as sensitive as an eyeball: If a strand of thread falls on the eyeball, says Vyāsa, it causes distress, but if it falls on any other part of the body, it is hardly felt at all. Similarly, the pain of existence even in so-called situations of happiness troubles only the *yogī*; it does not trouble other people. Others, say the commentators, cannot see the long-term repercussions of activities that produce limited so-called happiness in the present. Consequently, they repeatedly experience the suffering accrued due to their *karma*, try to avoid this suffering and pursue happiness but, planting more seeds of *karma*, continue to reexperience it. This is rather like a person running away from a scorpion who gets bitten by a poisonous snake, says Vyāsa.

Everything is painful to the ignorant as well, says Vijñānabhikṣu, but they do not realize it, whereas the *yogī* does. Vijñānabhikṣu illustrates this with a verse from the *Viṣṇu Purāṇa*: "There is more pain created for a person through spouse, friends, children, income, home, property and wealth, etc., than there is pleasure" (VI.5.56). Thus, Patañjali notes that for a wise person, everything is called pain, rather than happiness mixed with pain. Also, fools realize their mistake upon attaining the consequences of the pursuit of pleasure after the event, Vyāsa continues, whereas for the *yogī*, pain is evident at the very time of the experience of pleasure. Moreover, most people relate only to present pain, whereas the *yogī* is aware of past pain, which influences the present, and future pain, which is inherent in and a consequence of the present.

One might give the example of a person who wakes up with a terrible hangover after a night of alcohol excess, swears he or she will never drink again, but, come the next weekend, is back at the bar, destined to awake with another hangover the next morning. The *saṁskāras* of so-called pleasure produced from a night on the town are imprinted in one's *citta* mind. When these reactivate, if one's desire to enjoy in this way is sufficiently strong, it overrides discernment, or the memory of the negative consequences, and one again feels the urge. Thus the cycle of attempting to find happiness but, instead, ultimately being subject to suffering, is perpetuated. The compulsion to experience happiness is so strong that one typically resigns oneself to the inevitable inconveniences that accompany it, under the rationalization, "That's just life." For Cārvāka, an ancient materialist philosopher, all the pleasures of life have some inconveniences, and one must simply tolerate them. In one of his well-known quotes, the enjoyment of fish inevitably requires that one first remove the fish bones.[31] For *yogīs*, of course, such an attitude perpetuates *saṁsāra*, but there are other possibilities, namely, the freedom from all suffering, which is the nature of *puruṣa* itself.

The fourth item on Patañjali's list of the causes of suffering, being constantly subject to the *citta-vṛttis*, the agitations of the mind, refers to the fact that the mind is always changing, never peaceful or satisfied. This is because the *guṇas*, which constitute the *citta*, are always in flux, as Kṛṣṇa states in the *Gītā* (XIV.10). Depending on whether *sattva, rajas*, or *tamas* is dominant at any particular time, the mind temporarily experiences mundane (*prākṛtic*) happiness, distress, or illusion, respectively. But this very turmoil is ultimately a condition of suffering, since the mind craves continuous happiness. Vijñānabhikṣu also quotes the *Gītā*: "For those whose intelligence is not fixed in *yoga* . . . there is no peace, and how can there be real happiness without peace?" (II.66). As he points out, since any one of the *guṇas* is never exclusively present, when *sattva* is temporarily dominant and one experiences the *prākṛtic* happiness that is a characteristic of *sattva*, even then, *rajas* and *tamas* are also present to a subordinate degree. Therefore, this *prākṛtic* happiness is always mixed with some degree of pain (*rajas*) and dejection or illusion (*tamas*)—just like the fruit of the *harītakī* tree contains at the same time all six tastes known to Hindu gastronomy (sweet, sour, salty, pungent, bitter, and astringent). And, besides, since the *guṇas* are always in flux, even one's mixed happy state eventually evaporates and one is plunged into a predominantly *rājasic* or *tāmasic* state that is primarily distressful or dejected. Therefore, every state contains some degree of suffering, hence Patañjali's claim that all is suffering to the wise.

These sources of pain and suffering all stem from ignorance, which is lack of discrimination, that is, being attached to mistaken notions of I and mine—considering the I to be the temporary body, senses, and fluctuating mind rather than pure awareness, and the mine to be one's spouse, children, and possessions, says Vācaspati Miśra. In this way, by attempting to find happiness through one's body, mind, relationships, and possessions, one perpetuates the cycle of birth and death. Vijñānabhikṣu quotes the *Bhāgavata Purāṇa*: "Real happiness is to transcend mundane pleasure and distress" (XI.19.45), and the means to do this is to remove all desire of the senses for the sense objects by ceasing to misidentify the real self with the sensual body.

Seeing himself and all other beings caught up in this tide of suffering, says Vyāsa, the *yogī* takes shelter of true knowledge—that he is not the body or mind. Just as the science of medicine has four parts, he says—disease to be removed, cause of disease, freedom from disease, and the means of removal (medicine)—so the science of *yoga* has four parts: *saṁsāra*, the cause of *saṁsāra*, freedom from *saṁsāra*, and the means of liberation. *Saṁsāra* is the disease that is to be removed, its cause is the contact between *puruṣa* and *prakṛti*, freedom from *saṁsāra* is the cessation of this contact (liberation), and the means of removing this contact is pure knowledge.

Śaṅkara quotes this fourfold division of Vyāsa in the opening words of his *Vivaraṇa* commentary on the first *sūtra* of the *Yoga Sūtras*. The notion of life as suffering is clearly a pivotal tenet of the *Yoga Sūtras* and certainly dominates the present section of the text. This fourfold schema can be correlated with the following *sūtras*: *Sūtra* II.16 states that future suffering is to be avoided; II.17 considers the cause of suffering (with II.18–24 an extended discussion of its characteristics); II.25, freedom from suffering; and II.26, the means of attaining this freedom.

This four-part schema obviously echoes the Four Noble Truths of Buddhism,[32] but Vijñānabhikṣu reads Vyāsa's understanding of these four truths as a rejection of the Buddhist view that considers liberation to be not the cessation of contact between *puruṣa* and *prakṛti* but the giving up of the very notion of *puruṣa/ātman* itself. In Buddhism, consciousness is the fifth and most subtle of five *skandhas*, aggregates or ever-fluctuating interdependent coverings that constitute personhood. In this system, consciousness is not an immutable and eternal entity that can be uncoupled from objects of consciousness, as in the orthodox Hindu view, but an ever-changing noneternal layer that exists only in interdependent relation to objects of consciousness and not separately or autonomously from them.

As has been discussed at length, the Yoga school holds that not only is consciousness, *ātman/puruṣa*, separate from the objects of consciousness, but the goal of the entire system is precisely for consciousness to be aware of itself as a separable, unchanging entity and thereby be extricated from its enmeshment in the world of objects. It is autonomous and independent. In contrast, liberation in Buddhism, *nirvāṇa*, is attained precisely when one *ceases* to identify with consciousness as an eternal, unchanging self and realizes that consciousness *depends* on objects of consciousness and does not exist without them. Consciousness is *not* autonomous or independent; it is dependent or interdependent on its objects—the very opposite of the Yoga position. In other words, whereas in Yoga, one must identify with and strive to realize the *ātman*, in Buddhism, one must cease identifying with or clinging to the notion of and striving for the liberation of an *ātman*; hence, in philosophical discourse, Buddhism is sometimes referred to as *an-ātmavāda* the system that does *not* believe in an *ātman*.

But, argues Vijñānabhikṣu, in order to reject something, there must be two entities: the rejecter and the thing to be rejected. If the notion of *ātman* becomes the thing to be rejected, who is the rejecter of the notion? Or, as Hariharānanda puts it, if one aspires to liberation by thinking, "Let me be free from misery by suspending the activities of the mind," there will remain a pure me free from the pangs of misery. The self behind or beyond the mind is the real experiencer of this process. If one denies the ultimate existence of such an agent, then one is faced with the often-marshaled question: For whose sake is liberation sought? In any event, Vyāsa puts forth the position of Yoga in distinction to the Buddhist view: Consciousness, *puruṣa*, is eternal and immutable, the subject of experience, and liberation involves detaching it from the objects of experience in the form of the evolutes of *prakṛti*.

As an interesting aside, the term for suffering, *duḥkha*, seems to have been coined by analogy to its opposite, *sukha*, happiness. *Kha* refers to the axle of a wagon, and *su-* is a prefix denoting good (and *duḥ-*, bad). Thus in its old Indo-Aryan, Vedic usage, *sukha* denoted a wagon with good axles (that is, a comfortable ride). The Indo-Aryans were tribal cowherders, and one can imagine that comfortable wagons for their travels on the rough, unpaved trails of their day would have been a major factor in their notions of happiness and comfort.

हेयं दुःखम् अनागतम् ।।१६।।

II.16 heyaṁ duḥkham anāgatam

heyam, to be avoided; *duḥkham*, pain, suffering;
anāgatam, yet to come

Suffering that has yet to manifest is to be avoided.

Past suffering has already been experienced, says Vyāsa, and presently experienced suffering has already activated and is bearing its fruits. Therefore, only suffering accruing in the future, *anāgatam*, can be avoided, *heyam*, and it is this suffering that is of concern to the *yogī* who Vyāsa, in the last verse, considered as sensitive as an eyeball. How can one give up suffering that has yet to come, in other words, suffering that does not yet exist? asks Vijñānabhikṣu rhetorically. By removing its cause, the subject of the next *sūtra*. Just as the present is the result of previous causes, and was once that which had yet to come, so future suffering has its seeds in the present and past. There are examples of this everywhere, says Vijñānabhikṣu: The earth has the potential to give rise to many effects that are as yet unmanifest, but their seeds lie stored in the present.

However, the absolute removal of future suffering can be attained only by liberation, say the commentators—removing the identification between *puruṣa* and *prakṛti*. Again, this is the standard view: Gautama, the author of the *Nyāya Sūtras*, states that relief from suffering comes only from liberation (I.1.22). Likewise, Kaṇāda, the author of a series of *sūtras* foundational to the Vaiśeṣika school of philosophy, states that only when the mind is removed from its objects is one free from pain (V.2.16).

दृष्टृदृश्ययोः संयोगो हेयहेतुः ॥१७॥
II.17 draṣṭṛ-dṛśyayoḥ saṁyogo heya-hetuḥ

draṣṭṛ, of the seer; *dṛśyayoḥ*, of the seen; *saṁyogaḥ*, conjunction; *heya*, to be avoided; *hetuḥ*, the cause

The conjunction between the seer and that which is seen is the cause [of suffering] to be avoided.

The seer, *draṣṭṛ*, of this *sūtra*, says Vyāsa, is the *puruṣa* soul who cognizes through *buddhi*, intelligence. The discussion of the mind so far has generally focused on *citta*, which, we recall, consists of *manas*, the sorting and processing aspect of cognition; *ahaṅkāra*, the aspect of cognition underpinning self-identity and ego; and *buddhi*, intelligence, the discriminating aspect of the mind. The ensuing discussion will focus more specifically on *buddhi*. This is the aspect of *citta* immediately adjacent to the *puruṣa* (in the sense of being the first interface between the awareness of the *puruṣa* and the world of *prakṛti* and her effects), the first and most subtle covering, so to speak.

Patañjali's reference to that which is seen, *dṛśya*, consists of all objects that present themselves to the intelligence. These objects act like magnets attracting the awareness of *puruṣa* because of proximity. On account of seeing these objects, the *puruṣa* becomes like their master, says Vyāsa, and, on account of being seen, the objects of experience become, as it were, the property of *puruṣa*, the seer, though they do not exist within *puruṣa*. Though different from and external to *puruṣa*, these objects as if take on the nature of *puruṣa*, becoming animated due to reflecting the consciousness of *puruṣa*. This beginningless association, *saṁyoga*, between these two is the cause of suffering that is to be avoided. Therefore, the absolute remedy for suffering is ceasing the association between *puruṣa* and intelligence.

We see, continues Vyāsa, that there are remedies for suffering in this world. For example, the sole of the foot is capable of being pierced, and the thorn of piercing it. The remedy is to remove the thorn from the foot (or, better still, not to put the foot on the thorn). Likewise, the remedy for the suffering of embodied existence is to remove *puruṣa* from its association with *prakṛti*. One who knows these three features—the locus of pain, the cause of pain, and the remedy for pain—need not undergo suffering.

Vyāsa further notes that on a metaphysical level, suffering is the result of *rajas* disturbing *sattva*. When undisturbed, *sattva* produces a type of happiness; it is *rajas* that causes suffering. Everyone has experience that well-being, peace, and happiness are the result of moderation, says Hariharānanda. When *rajas* activates and one becomes overactive—overindulgent or hyperenergetic—one's peace of mind is destroyed and is replaced by suffering, either mental (in the form, say, of incessant anxiety or craving) or physical (in the form, say, of ulcers, indigestion, or sexual disease). Likewise, if *tamas* activates and inertia sets in, one cannot feel satisfied or self-content at all. Since the natural state of the mind is *sattva*, it is *rajas* and *tamas* that are the disrupters. When *sattva* is disrupted, suffering is the result.

When the *puruṣa*'s awareness pervades this *sattva* disrupted by *rajas* and *tamas*, continues Vyāsa, it becomes aware of this suffering. However, the suffering is not actually located in the *puruṣa*, which is changeless and actionless; it is located in the *buddhi*, intelligence, whose pure *sattva* nature is being disturbed by *rajas*. Vācaspati Miśra elaborates on this: The intelligence is molded by the objects of the senses—sound, etc.—and takes on their characteristics, like liquid copper takes on the form of the mold into which it is poured. The intelligence is thus transformed by input transmitted through the senses. The awareness of *puruṣa* pervades the intelligence and is misidentified with it by the mind, or more precisely, by the *kleśas* in the mind. Thus *puruṣa* becomes aware of intelligence in whatever forms it is molded into by the objects of the senses. Since intelligence is inert and animated only by the consciousness of *puruṣa*, if this connection between *puruṣa* and *buddhi* is not made, the knowable cannot be known—objects cannot be experienced. It is due to the conjunction between the two that the consciousness of *puruṣa* can become aware of this transformed *buddhi*, and through it all the objects of experience.

Due to being pervaded by *puruṣa*, the states of *buddhi* are assigned to *puruṣa* by the mind. If the state of *buddhi* is of undisturbed *sattva*, it appears as if the *puruṣa* is happy, and if of *sattva* disturbed by *rajas* and *tamas*, it appears as if *puruṣa* is suffering. Either way, neither state is ultimately an actual state of *puruṣa*, but of the intelligence and mind with which *puruṣa* is misidentified. Pleasure and pain, in and of themselves, are unconscious characteristics of *buddhi*; it is only when they are pervaded by the conscious self that "I am happy" or "I am sad" becomes a conscious state of awareness. Experience of pain is just experience of *buddhi*, the intelligence, says Vijñānabhikṣu, not of anything actually transpiring in *puruṣa* itself; but due to ignorance, one thinks that *puruṣa* is in pain.

Puruṣa, says Vyāsa, is changeless and actionless; it is the subject, and pain can reside only as an object (pain is an *object* of experience). Vijñānabhikṣu gives the example of water on a leaf: The water does not change the leaf—even though there is contact between them, their properties are different. Likewise, the ever-changing states of the *buddhi* do not change consciousness—even though there is conjunction between them, the properties of *puruṣa* and *prakṛti* are different. But, Vyāsa adds, even the wise must work to rid themselves of this identification with pain caused by conjunction between the two.

Vācaspati Miśra raises the issue of whether the relationship between *puruṣa* and the intelligence is innate or coincidental. It cannot be innate, he says, since then it would never cease to exist and thus there would be no hope of liberation; so it must be coincidental. However, this conjunction between these two entities must have existed eternally. This is because the mind is the product of *karma* and the *kleśas*, etc., but *karma* and the *kleśas* can exist only if the mind is there as their substratum. Like the chicken and the egg, one cannot come into being without the other. Therefore, as with all other Indic soteriological schools, Yoga avoids this dilemma by positing that they must be beginningless. Since the mind, with its inherent *karmas* and *kleśas*, exists only for fulfilling the purpose of *puruṣa*, the conjunction between mind and *puruṣa* must also be beginningless by a similar logic. At the end of each creation cycle,[33] the mind with its *karmas* and *kleśas* dissolves into *prakṛti* to be reactivated at the beginning of the next cycle in the same state in which it was found at the end of the previous cycle, just as the earth becomes parched after the summer season but springs back into life after the rainy season, before eventually becoming parched again.

While one might question Vācaspati Miśra's logic,[34] as a point of information, no Indic school of thought considers speculation into how the soul originally became enmeshed in *saṁsāra* to be fruitful—embodied existence is considered to have been eternal in terms of its origins. But, as Hariharānanda notes, just because this conjunction is beginningless does not mean that it has to be endless. How it began is a question that cannot be answered and thus is fruitless to pose,[35] but inquiring how it can be ended is the goal of human life. It can be terminated by *yoga*. Actually, this conjunction between *puruṣa* and *prakṛti* is brought about by *Īśvara*, says Vijñānabhikṣu, presenting the theistic perspective; it cannot be understood by even the best of *yogīs*, nor by the process of logic. He quotes the *Bhāgavata Purāṇa*: "The bondage and pitiful circumstance of the independent and free soul goes against all logic; such is the *māyā* potency of the Lord" (III.7.9).[36]

प्रकाशक्रियास्थितिशीलं भूतेन्द्रियात्मकं भोगापवर्गार्थं दृश्यम् ।। १८ ।।

II.18 prakāśa-kriyā-sthiti-śīlaṁ bhūtendriyātmakaṁ bhogāpavargārthaṁ dṛśyam

prakāśa, illumination; *kriyā*, activity; *sthiti*, inertia; *śīlam*, having the nature of; *bhūta*, elements; *indriya*, senses; *ātmakam*, having the nature of; *bhoga*, experience; *apavarga*, liberation; *artham*, object, purpose; *dṛśyam*, the knowable

That which is knowable has the nature of illumination, activity, and inertia [*sattva, rajas,* and *tamas*]. It consists of the senses and the elements, and exists for the purpose of [providing] either liberation or experience [to *puruṣa*].

Patañjali here describes the ultimate metaphysical ingredients of the seen, *dṛsyam*, the manifest world, and states its ultimate purpose for existing. The commentators correlate the illumination, *prakāsa*, noted here with *sattva* (the light inherent in *buddhi*); activity, *kriyā*, with *rajas* (all movement and effort); and inertia, *sthiti*, with *tamas*.[37] These three *guṇas* are always in flux, as long as the world is manifest,[38] and their nature is to assert themselves in various proportions and then ebb away, thus giving rise to the ever-changing world of manifest forms. Although one or the other of the three *guṇas* appears dominant and the others secondary at any given moment, the presence of the secondary *guṇas* can always be detected. This never-ending flux is what is called the known, says Vyāsa, and it transforms itself into both the elements and the senses, *bhūtendriyātmakam*. As the former, it manifests subtly as the elements of sound, etc., and grossly as the elements of earth, etc.; as the latter, it manifests subtly as hearing, and also as intelligence and ego, etc.

Hariharānanda correlates *sattva* with the knowledge or awareness aspect of any entity, such as a tree's impulse toward the source of light; *rajas* as the factors that cause any activity or motion, such as a tree's growth toward the source of light; and *tamas* as when any potentiality is retained or stored, such as the winter season for trees, when sap descends to the roots and is stored (or hibernation for animals). As noted, these *guṇas* pervade all manifest reality, whether of the nature of *grahaṇa*, the instruments or organs of cognition such as the ear, or *grāhya*, the objects of cognition such as sound; everything other than the *puruṣa* itself is composed of these three *guṇas*. The *sāttvic* aspect of the ear, for example, says Hariharānanda, manifests when it makes sound known; its *rājasic* aspect is represented by the ear's nervous impulse excited by vibration; and the *tāmasic* aspect, by the energy stored in its nerves and muscles. And sound itself has a knowledge-bestowing aspect, which is *sattva*; a vibrational aspect, which is *rajas*; and a stored energy aspect, which is the *tamas* element.

Patañjali makes the important statement here that the purpose of these *guṇas*, and thus of their *prākṛtic* productions, is to provide either experience, *bhoga*, or liberation, *apavarga*, for the *puruṣa*, as indicated also in the *Sāṅkhya Kārikā* (XVII, XXI, XXXI). Experience, says Vyāsa, consists of occupying oneself with the desirable and undesirable nature of the *guṇas* as discussed in II.14—in other words, with pursuing pleasure and avoiding pain—while liberation entails the realization by *puruṣa* of its own true nature. There is no other reason for the existence of *prakṛti*.

Vyāsa then raises a very important question: How can either the experience or liberation noted in this *sūtra* be imposed on *puruṣa* when they are the constructs and products of *buddhi* and exist only in *buddhi* and not in *puruṣa* itself? Or, as Śaṅkara puts it, how can the deeds of one person be the work of another? The laundryman is not the dyer of clothes. Although experience and liberation are concepts of intelligence, says Vyāsa, they are attributed to the *puruṣa* because the *puruṣa* experiences their fruit, just as the victory and defeat of soldiers are attributed to their chief, even though he may only be witnessing the battle, because he experiences the fruits of victory or defeat.

Perception, memory, deliberation, critical reasoning, knowledge of the truth, determination, and, indeed, any cognitive functioning, all of which in actual fact are existing in *buddhi*, are superimposed on *puruṣa*, continues Vyāsa. As long as the awareness of *puruṣa* remains focused on and is erroneously identified with *buddhi* and its manifestations, *puruṣa* remains as if bound by that connection. But bondage is a state of mind, a product of *buddhi*, not an actual condition of *puruṣa*, and it exists only for as long as the real goal of *puruṣa* is not realized. Liberation is when that goal is attained, namely, the uncoupling of *puruṣa* and *buddhi* by the mind. It, too, is a state of mind, or, put differently, the state of *puruṣa* after the mind has eliminated its own *kleśas* and ceased to superimpose itself onto consciousness. Vācaspati Miśra etymologizes the term for liberation, *apavarga*, as *apa-* + *vṛj* (prefix + verbal root), that which is separated from something else.

Expanding on the notions that bondage and freedom are in *buddhi*, and that the *puruṣa* is merely a witness, Hariharānanda adds that when *buddhi* is impure due to the dust of *rajas* and darkness of *tamas*, it does not discriminate between seer and seen. He notes that *rajas* can mean dust, and as such, it tarnishes the pure lucidity of *sattva; tamas*, in turn, means darkness, and this obscures *sattva* even more densely than does *rajas*. When purified and the natural illumination of *sattva* is able to manifest, the knowledge of the distinction between these two entities becomes clear. This is what *vidyā*, knowledge, is. However, ultimately, even this knowledge is taking place in *buddhi* and, as will be discussed below, is transcended in the higher stages of *samādhi*. *Buddhi* has to deconstruct itself. Therefore the *Sāṅkhya Kārikā* states: "No one is actually bound, nor is anyone liberated from *saṁsāra*. Only *prakṛti* in its myriad forms transmigrates, is bound and then freed" (LXII).

विशेषाविशेषलिङ्गमात्रालिङ्गानि गुणपर्वाणि ।। १९ ।।

II.19 viśeṣāviśeṣa-liṅga-mātrāliṅgāni guṇa-parvāṇi

viśeṣa, particularized; *aviśeṣa*, unparticularized; *liṅga*, distinctive; *mātra*, only, just; *aliṅgāni*, indistinctive; *guṇa*, the modes, influences; *parvāṇi*, stages

The different stages of the *guṇa* qualities consist of the particularized, the unparticularized, the distinctive, and the indistinctive.

This *sūtra* follows on the previous one by outlining the basic categories of evolutes that emerge from the primordial interaction of the *guṇas* in *prakṛti*. The first category noted by Patañjali, the particularized, *viśeṣa*, refers to all final evolutes of *prakṛti*, that is, to end products that do not produce further products or evolutes out of themselves. The second category, the unparticularized, *aviśeṣa*, refers to the evolutes that do produce further products or evolutes out of themselves. Thus, if we glance at the Sāṅkhya chart in the introduction, the gross elements (ether, air, fire, water, earth) are the particularized aspects of the unparticularized subtle elements (sound, touch, sight, taste, smell).[39] Along similar lines, the powers behind the five organs of knowledge (ears, eyes, skin, tongue, and nose), as well as those behind the five organs of action (speech, hands, feet, anus, and genitals), along with the internal organ of mind are the particularized aspects of the unparticularized ego, *ahaṅkāra*.[40] (Since the mind works through these ten organs, it also is considered an organ.[41]) Thus, there are sixteen particularized items including mind, none of which produces further evolutes, and six unparticularized ones including ego, which do produce evolutes. (This schema is found in the *Sāṅkhya Kārikā* III).

Beyond these there is *mahat*, which is another name for the cosmological *buddhi*, referred to in this *sūtra* as *liṅga* by Patañjali and translated here rather loosely as distinctive. The commentators have different views on why *liṅga* is used in this regard. Vijñānabhikṣu, for example, states that *liṅga*, literally mark or sign, is so called because it marks all the other effects of the world, that is, everything emanates from *buddhi*.[42] (Ego, which is the immediate source from which all the particularized and unparticularized elements mentioned above have evolved, is itself a manifestation of *buddhi*.) *Liṅga* in Hindu logic is something that is the sign of something else—smoke is the sign of fire. So whereas *prakṛti* herself is unperceivable, *buddhi* is perceivable—it has signs or characteristics that distinguish it. *Buddhi* is like the root of a tree, says Śaṅkara: It is the closest to the seed that produced it, and it is also the cause of the trunk, branches, leaves, etc., which stem from it.

But *buddhi*, too, is ultimately a transformation of the *guṇas*, specifically that of *sattva*. It is pure beingness, says Vyāsa, neither existence nor nonexistence, neither real nor unreal. The world of manifest reality has yet to emerge from it. It is like the mind just awakened from sleep but prior to the activity that occurs in the ego stage, says Vijñānabhikṣu. He quotes the *Bhāgavata Purāṇa*: "Then, impelled by the Time factor, the entity *mahat* came into existence from the unmanifest. Its nature is knowledge, which dispels ignorance, and it manifests the universe which is situated within itself" (III.5.27).

Finally, the unmanifest mentioned in this *sūtra* is a yet more subtle manifestation of these *guṇas*, the primordial matrix from which even *buddhi* itself, along with all its evolutes, originates. At this level, we have arrived at *prakṛti* herself, and it is this that Patañjali refers to here as *aliṅga*, that without signs, the undistinctive (see also I.45). There are no signs by which one can discern *prakṛti* prior to the movement of the *guṇas* (thus the Sāṅkhya school holds that *prakṛti* cannot be perceived, its existence can only be inferred [*anumānita*], and thus it is called the inferred one[43]). This stage is eternal; the other three stages—*buddhi, ahaṅkāra*, and all subsequent evolutes—are temporary manifestations, or permutations of *prakṛti*.

Therefore, says Vyāsa, the world created by the *guṇas* may appear to have the nature of birth and death, but all that is really occurring is that the evolutes of the *guṇas* are manifesting and unmanifesting the various bodies and things of this world due to the constant flux of the *guṇas* themselves. If Devadatta's cows die, he analogizes, we may think Devadatta has become poor, but his poverty is due to the death of his cows, not his own death. Similarly, there is no birth and death of *puruṣa*, simply the constant mutation and transformation of the *guṇas* of *prakṛti* within which *puruṣa* appears to be embedded, which temporarily produce bodies and forms in certain configurations, and then dissolve them back into their matrix. Vijñānabhikṣu quotes the *Gītā*: "All beings are unmanifest in their beginning, manifest in their interim stage, and unmanifest in their end. What is there to lament in this?"

(II.28). The evolutes, such as bodies and states of mind, are temporary configurations; only the cause is eternal: *prakṛti* herself.

Vācaspati Miśra reiterates that everything one experiences in manifest reality, whether on the grossest level of sensual indulgence or the most subtle level of discrimination between *buddhi* and *puruṣa*, is ultimately taking place in *buddhi* or its evolutes. He notes that *liṅga* and *aliṅga* are called nonexistent by Vyāsa because the *guṇas* are quiescent in this stage, devoid of effects (the senses and sense objects of the world), and therefore cannot fulfill the objectives of *puruṣa*, which, we recall, is for the purpose of providing either experience or liberation to the *puruṣa*. At the same time, Vyāsa also states that they are not totally nonexistent (like the lotus in the sky), because they produce effects. In other words, they exist as cause.

Quoting various passages from the *Vedānta Sūtras*, Vijñānabhikṣu again takes this opportunity to distinguish the philosophy of the Yoga school from that of the *advaita*, nondualist Vedāntic school founded by Śaṅkara. The *advaita* school posits that *prakṛti*, the *guṇas*, and the entirety of the manifest world are all ultimately not real but are mental constructions produced by ignorance, superimpositions on the only real existent, *Brahman*. Outlining the position of the Yoga school, Vijñānabhikṣu stresses that the world in its essence—*prakṛti*—is real and eternal, and therefore the evolutes from this matrix, the world, are also in this sense real, albeit temporary and constantly changing, mutating, and eventually dissolving back into their source. He quotes the well-known verse from the *Chāndogya Upaniṣad* in reference to objects made out of clay, which we call pots or plates, etc., out of convenience, but which remain, essentially, clay: "By means of just one lump of clay, one can perceive everything made out of clay—the transformation is just a verbal handle, a name—while the reality is just this: 'It is clay' " (VI.1.4). The manifestations of *Brahman* are not false, Vijñānabhikṣu argues, contra Śaṅkara, any more than the modifications of clay are false. But they are temporary.

Vācaspati Miśra further states that manifest reality has to follow the sequence of evolution noted by Patañjali in this *sūtra*. It is not that the seed of a *nyagrodha* tree will spontaneously and immediately produce a fully grown, stocky tree with its leaves and branches, he says. The tree comes about gradually, the seed becoming a shoot and slowly evolving in contact with light and water. At the same time, says Vijñānabhikṣu, seed, sprout, and tree are nondifferent from each other, and so, in the same way, are *buddhi* and its effects nondifferent. *Puruṣa*, on the other hand, is a totally different entity. When *puruṣa* and *prakṛti* combine, living beings come into existence, just as when air and water combine, bubbles are formed.

द्रष्टा दृशिमात्रः शुद्धोऽपि प्रत्ययानुपश्यः ॥ २० ॥

II.20 draṣṭā dṛśi-mātraḥ śuddho 'pi pratyayānupaśyaḥ

draṣṭā, the seer; *dṛśi*, the power of seeing; *mātraḥ*, only; *śuddhaḥ*, pure; *api*, although; *pratyaya*, ideas or images of the mind; *anupaśyaḥ*, witnesses

The seer is merely the power of seeing; [however,] although pure, he witnesses the images of the mind.

The seen—the *guṇas* of *prakṛti* and their effects—has been discussed in the above *sūtras*, and now Patañjali turns his attention to the seer, *draṣṭṛ*. The seer is the *puruṣa*, the soul or innermost conscious self. He is the pure undiluted power of consciousness—pure because untouched by any attribute, qualification, object, or predicate. He is neither the same as, nor, at least when embodied, totally different from *buddhi*, intelligence, insofar as his knowledge of *prakṛti* arises from his awareness of *buddhi*.

He is not the same as *buddhi*, because *buddhi* has external things (cows, pots, etc.) as its object of attention and is therefore always changing, while *puruṣa* is unchanging and has only *buddhi* as the object of its attention. Moreover, *buddhi* exists solely for the sake of *puruṣa*, while *puruṣa* exists for its own sake only. Finally, *buddhi* is inert, unconscious, and composed of the three *guṇas*, whereas *puruṣa* is the active spectator, the source of consciousness, and beyond the three *guṇas*. On the other hand, *puruṣa* is not totally distinct from *buddhi* in practice because, even though *puruṣa* is pure and self-contained in essence, by witnessing the transformations of *buddhi* in the form of thoughts and cognitions, *pratyayas*, etc., it appears as if those thoughts pertain to *puruṣa* itself, that they are *puruṣa* rather than the flickerings of an external and inert but subtle substance. *Puruṣa* sees its reflection in the mirror of *buddhi*, say the commentators, and the mind mistakes this reflection in the mirror, which is distorted due to the transformations of the *guṇas*, to be the real self. *Puruṣa* does not change or transform; *buddhi* does.

Therefore, it is said, says Vyāsa, that although *puruṣa* is the experiencer and does not change or pursue the objects of the senses, it appears to do so by its identification with the transformations of *buddhi*, which does change and does pursue the objects of the senses. Indeed, it is only when *buddhi* takes the form of the objects of the senses, the *pratyayas*, noted here (see I.10), that these objects become known to *puruṣa* via the medium of *buddhi*. And it is only *puruṣa* who can inherently know, says Vijñānabhikṣu; *buddhi* does not know, that is to say, is not conscious of the objects of the senses that it is processing and that it exhibits to *puruṣa*. One might analogize that the software of a computer is not conscious of the material that it is processing and that it exhibits on its screen. As the computer needs a witness to know the data, so does *buddhi*.

Thus, as a result of being identified with *buddhi*, *puruṣa* appears to assume the qualities of *buddhi*. The consciousness of *puruṣa*, although not in reality changing, witnesses or follows as a spectator the transformations of *buddhi* and therefore rests on (is aware of) each object that comes into the sphere of the ever-changing *buddhi*. Whatever *buddhi* is transformed into is colored by consciousness, says Vācaspati Miśra, as a result of their contact. Although the moon is not transformed into water, he continues, it appears to be so due to its reflection in water. This Vedāntic analogy works well: Water in a lake or an ocean is transformed or agitated by waves, ripples, foam, etc. When the moon shines upon this disturbed surface, its reflection also becomes rippled and agitated due to the disturbed surface of the water. Ignorance is mistaking the disrupted reflection to be the true moon. Due to ignorance, *puruṣa* is misidentified with the disturbed reflection of *buddhi*, which is taken to be the real self. Like an echo, says Vijñānabhikṣu, a sound that emanates from a source and then bounces off an object to return back to that source in somewhat distorted fashion, the consciousness of *puruṣa* bounces back from *buddhi* in the form of a distorted reflection, and thus *puruṣa* becomes aware of the disturbed *buddhi* along with its *bhāva*, or quality, of ignorance. The *Sāṅkhya Kārikās* speaks of *buddhi* as having eight *bhāvas* (virtue, knowledge, nonattachment, potency, and their opposites, including ignorance) (XXIII). *Buddhi* thus becomes aware of ignorance even though the ignorance is not in *puruṣa*—which, by definition, is pure awareness—but rather in *buddhi*.

Not only does *puruṣa* appear changed due to this symbiosis, but inert *buddhi* appears to be conscious due to being energized by consciousness, continues Vijñānabhikṣu, just as sunlight falling on the sea makes the sea appear to be luminous like the sun. (Verse XX of the *Sāṅkhya Kārikās* states that that which is unconscious appears as if conscious.) Therefore, *puruṣa* is witnessing not only its own reflection but one that appears to be energized, or animate, and this further enhances the tendency of misidentification.

This misidentification of *puruṣa* with *buddhi* transformed or agitated by the three *guṇas*, the objects of this world, is the cause of bondage. Its freedom, says Vijñānabhikṣu, cannot come about through the conventional means of knowledge—the senses, mind, intelligence, etc.—since its nature is essentially different from these. It can come about only through its own nature. Its own nature is pure knowledge, that is, exclusive awareness of its own self, rather than of the objects of *prakṛti*.

Hariharānanda adds to this that the existence of *puruṣa* is evidenced by the fact that the sense of I is constant at all times. One may say, "I know something," where the thing one knows pertains to whatever is being presented at any point in time by *buddhi* and is always changing, but the I who knows remains constant. Likewise even with the notion "I know myself": The myself that is known also pertains to ever-changing *buddhi*—one may think of oneself in many different ways throughout the various stages of one's life—but the I is always constant. As soon as this I begins to know something—anything—then the misidentification of *buddhi* with *puruṣa*, the erroneous notion that *puruṣa* is *buddhi*, has occurred, since all knowable things are the products of *prakṛti*. All knowledge thus requires the presence of the overseer, *puruṣa*, and of something seen, an object in *prakṛti*.

This misidentification of the seer and the seen, continues Hariharānanda, is the product of *ahaṅkāra*, the ego. As a result of this misidentification, the distinction between *puruṣa* and *buddhi* is not perceived in ordinary consciousness. *Buddhi* resembles *puruṣa* to some extent, and vice versa. Inanimate *buddhi* appears to be animate because it is energized by the consciousness of the animate *puruṣa*, and the unchanging *puruṣa* appears to be ever-changing and mutable because its consciousness pervades the ever-changing and mutable *buddhi*; hence Vyāsa's statement that they are neither the same nor different.

तदर्थ एव दृश्यस्यात्मा ॥ २१ ॥

II.21 tad-artha eva dṛśyasyātmā

tat, his [the seer, *puruṣa*'s]; *arthaḥ*, purpose; *eva*, only; *dṛśyasya*, of the knowable, of that which is seen; *ātmā*, essential nature, existence

The essential nature of that which is seen is exclusively for the sake of the seer.

The seen, that is, the knowable—*buddhi* (and ultimately *prakṛti* herself)—exists only for the sake of *puruṣa*, who is the seer, reiterates Vyāsa, and is thus dependent on another, not on itself. As II.18 informed us, the purpose or function of the seen, *prakṛti*, is to provide either experience or liberation to *puruṣa*, and this purpose is fulfilled when experience or liberation has been attained. The nature of experience consists of pleasure and pain, and pleasure and pain are not conscious of themselves; they are experienced by an other. This other is *puruṣa*. Therefore, the purpose of the seen is not for itself but for the seer, just as the purpose of a bed, continues Vijñānabhikṣu, is for the sleeper, not for itself. Or, as Vācaspati Miśra puts it, the relationship of *puruṣa* and *prakṛti* is like that of the king and his possessions.

Since *prakṛti* has nothing more to do once its purposes are fulfilled, asks Rāmānanda Sarasvatī rhetorically with an eye to the next *sūtra*, does this mean that, deprived of its function, *prakṛti* would no longer be perceived? Might it even cease to exist?

कृतार्थं प्रति नष्टम् अप्यनष्टं तदन्यसाधारणत्वात् ॥ २२ ॥

II.22 kṛtārthaṁ prati naṣṭam apy anaṣṭaṁ tad-anya-sādhāraṇatvāt

kṛta, accomplished, fulfilled; *artham*, purpose; *prati*, toward, with regard to; *naṣṭam*, destroyed; *api*, although; *anaṣṭam*, not destroyed; *tat*, that; *anya*, other [*puruṣas*]; *sādhāraṇatvāt*, because of being common

Although the seen ceases to exist for one whose purpose is accomplished [the liberated *puruṣa*], it has not ceased to exist altogether, since it is common to other [not-liberated] *puruṣas*.

This *sūtra* situates the Yoga tradition as realist (the view that the world is objectively and externally real irrespective of whether we perceive it) as opposed to idealist (the world is not objectively or externally real but a product of the mind); indeed, Dasgupta uses the term "reals" for the *guṇas*.[44] Patañjali and the commentarial tradition will take some pains to refute the idealist viewpoint in Chapter IV. The "seen" may have accomplished its purpose, *kṛta-artha*, for the fortunate successful *yogī* who has attained liberation, and thus may cease to exist, *naṣṭam*, for such a soul, but only in the sense that the liberated soul ceases to be aware of it; it has not accomplished its purpose for all other *puruṣas*, says Vyāsa. It needs to provide objects of experience for everyone else. Therefore, it still has a purpose and does not cease to exist, *anaṣṭam*. Color may not be seen by a blind man, says Vācaspati Miśra, but it does not cease to be, since it is seen by those who are not blind. In this sense, the conjunction between the seers (in the sense of the totality of *puruṣas*) and the seen is said to be eternal, because the *puruṣas* are innumerable, so one need not posit the hypothetical possibility that eventually all *puruṣas* will become liberated, causing *prakṛti* to become redundant due to an absence of *puruṣas* needing experience.

This *sūtra* is important to the Yoga school, Vijñānabhikṣu points out, since otherwise its opponents might question its tenets such as that *prakṛti* is eternal, creation is ongoing, and *Īśvara* is eternally sovereign. Moreover, the commentators are motivated by this *sūtra* to argue the position of the Yoga and Sāṅkhya schools, which posit an eternal plurality of *puruṣas*, whether in the liberated or nonliberated state, in distinction to the *advaita*, or nondualist, school of Vedānta, which holds that the plurality and individuality of the *puruṣas* exist only in the nonliberated state of ignorance. This particular school of Vedānta posits that upon attaining enlightenment, the *puruṣa* (more typically referred to as *ātman* by followers of Vedānta) realizes that all plurality and individuality is the product of illusion, and merges into the all-encompassing, nondual, absolute truth, *Brahman*.

To buttress their view of an eternal plurality of *puruṣas* scripturally, several commentators point to the verse in the *Śvetāśvatara Upaniṣad* (IV.5) that speaks metaphorically of a nanny goat (*prakṛti*), whose nature is that of the *guṇas* and who produces evolutes of the same nature, being enjoyed by one passionate billy goat (*puruṣa*) but abandoned by another billy goat who has finished enjoying her. This resonates with Patañjali's *sūtra* here. Just because one billy goat may leave the nanny goat, she nonetheless remains to be enjoyed by another billy goat: One *puruṣa* may become liberated, but all the other unliberated *puruṣas* remain experiencing *prakṛti*. Therefore, whether in the liberated or nonliberated states, there must be a plurality of *puruṣas*, and each one must be individual. This is the view of all six schools of classical Hindu thought except the subbranch of the Vedānta school, *advaita* Vedānta.

But what about the numerous verses in the Upaniṣads that seem to imply the oneness of all *ātmans*? the commentators ask. Vijñānabhikṣu quotes the *Mārkaṇḍeya Purāṇa* (XXXVII.42) to exemplify this notion of oneness as plainly as possible: "Just as the ether, although one, may exist as divided into many in pots, jars, and water-containers, so I, and the mighty armed king of Kāśī and others [are divided] into different bodies with physical distinctions [but are one *ātman*]." One could point to numerous similar verses in the Upaniṣads. Perhaps the most famous are a series of verses from the *Chāndogya Upaniṣad* (VI.9–13) such as:

> These rivers, son, the easterly ones flow to the East, and the westerly ones to the West. Coming from the ocean, they merge back into the ocean. They become that very ocean. When they are in that state, they are not aware that "I am this river," "I am that river." In the same way, son, all creatures, upon attaining "the existent" [*Brahman*], do not think: "We are attaining *Brah-*

> *man.*" Whatever they were in this world—a tiger, a lion, a wolf, a boar, an insect, a moth, a gnat or mosquito—they all become *Brahman*. The finest essence in this world, that is the self of all this. That is Truth. That is the *ātman*. That is who you are . . .

Do not such verses point to one ultimate *ātman* that is perceived as being divided only as a result of ignorance?

The enlightened *yogī* sees that all differences are the product of *ahaṅkāra* and *buddhi*, says Vijñānabhikṣu, and that therefore all *puruṣas* are one, in the sense that they have the same essence, but this does not mean that there is factually only one *puruṣa* metaphysically. The myriad *puruṣas* are identical in the sense that their true nature transcends all distinctions, which are the product of *prakṛti* and her *guṇas*, but this does not mean that they become identical in the sense of loosing their individuality upon attaining liberation, nor that they merge into one ultimate *ātman/Brahman*. (One must keep in mind here, and indeed, Vijñānabhikṣu reminds us, that he is also a Vedāntin who has written a commentary on the *Vedānta Sūtras*, in which he has already critically discussed the one *ātman* theory of the *advaita* non-dual school of Vedānta.)

If there were only one *ātman*, continues Vijñānabhikṣu, how could some *ātmans* be liberated and others still in *saṁsāra*? A number of the commentators draw attention to this argument, which also surfaces in the Vedānta schools opposing the *advaita* viewpoint: If there were ultimately only one *ātman* as the *advaita* school posits, then when any one *puruṣa* attains liberation, so would all other *puruṣas* (since according to the *advaita* school, they are all in reality one *puruṣa/ātman*). In other words, if one *puruṣa* became liberated by realizing that all distinctions among *puruṣas* were illusory and that all *puruṣas* were in actuality one undivided *ātman*, then, with the ignorance of duality removed, there would no longer be any more divided *ātmans* or independent *puruṣas*. If one responds that the realization of the oneness of *ātman* applies only to the liberated *puruṣa*, but not to the other nonliberated *puruṣas*, then one has implicitly accepted a duality in the supposed oneness of *ātman*, a duality between liberated and nonliberated *puruṣas*. Such a conclusion would be awkward for the defenders of this position, say the commentators, contradicting the nondualistic position of the *advaita* school but approaching the position of the Yoga school.

Vijñānabhikṣu continues to argue that not only are individual *puruṣas* different from each other, but the supreme *puruṣa*, God, is different again from all the individual souls. He points to the *Vedānta Sūtras*: "Brahman is greater [than embodied beings] because of the statement of difference [between them]" (II.1.22) and "[The embodied souls] are parts of God because of the statement that they are different" (II.3.43). Patañjali has anyway already established that *Īśvara* is a distinct *puruṣa* and superior to other *puruṣas*.

स्वस्वामिशक्त्योः स्वरूपोपलब्धिहेतुः संयोगः ॥ २३ ॥

II.23 sva-svāmi-śaktyoḥ svarūpopalabdhi-hetuḥ saṁyogaḥ

sva, the possessed; *svāmi*, the possessor; *śáktyoḥ*, of the powers; *svarūpa*, nature, true form; *upalabdhi*, understanding; *hetuḥ*, the cause; *saṁyogaḥ*, conjunction, contact, association

[The notion of] conjunction is the means of understanding the real nature of the powers of the possessed and of the possessor.

Tying the verses in this chapter together, as touched upon in II.15, and echoing the Four Noble Truths of Buddhism, the theme of this second *pāda* (chapter) is suffering, the cause of suffering, the state beyond suffering, and the means to attain this state. Specifically, II.1–14 were dedicated to the immediate causes of suffering on a psychological level (the *kleśas* and their consequences); II.15 to the reality of suffering itself; II.16, to future suffering that can be avoided; II.17, to the cause of suffering on a metaphysical level as the union, *saṁyoga*, between the seer, *draṣṭṛ*, and the seen *dṛśya*; II.18–19, to the seen; II.20, to the seer and the state beyond suffering; and II.21–22, to the seen again. This *sūtra* through II.27 will deal with *saṁyoga*, union, the metaphysical cause of suffering, and *saṁyoga*'s removal, and the remainder of the chapter will be devoted to the means to accomplish this.

This *sūtra* was composed with the intention of explaining the nature of the conjunction, or association, *saṁyoga*, between *prakṛti* and *puruṣa*, says Vyāsa. *Puruṣa* is the possessor, *svāmi*, and he is conjoined with that which he possesses, *sva*, namely *prakṛti* and her objects (the seen of the previous *sūtra*), for the sake of experience. Worldly experience means perceiving the seen, and liberation means perceiving the real nature of the seer. Ignorance is the cause of the conjunction between the seer and the seen, and true knowledge dispels ignorance and is therefore the cause of liberation.

Strictly speaking, continues Vyāsa, true knowledge is not the real cause of liberation because when ignorance does not exist, bondage does not exist, and so technically it is this absence of ignorance that corresponds to liberation. It is because knowledge removes ignorance that it is said to be the cause of liberation, but it is actually the indirect cause of liberation. Vijñānabhikṣu points out that true knowledge, or discrimination, operates right up until the immediate moment prior to liberation. He reminds his readers that discrimination is still a product of the material intelligence, but full liberation involves complete separation between *puruṣa* and *buddhi*. This is the difference between *sabīja* and *nirbīja samādhis*.

With an eye on the next *sūtra*, Vyāsa turns his attention to different views on what constitutes ignorance—the synonym he uses for ignorance here is *adarśana*, the lack of perception (of the real nature of the *puruṣa*). He lists the following possibilities, which are further discussed by the commentators.

(1) Is ignorance the result of the play of the *guṇas*? This, says Hariharānanda, is correct insofar as ignorance continues for as long as the *guṇas* are active, but it doesn't explain the cause of ignorance any more than heat in the body explains the cause of fever.
(2) Is ignorance due to the mind, which fails to modify itself into the true object of knowledge, that is, the knowledge of the distinction between *puruṣa* and *prakṛti*, even though this object is present before it? This possibility is of limited value, says Hariharānanda, like saying, "Illness means to be unwell."
(3) Does ignorance spring from the *guṇas*, which fail to produce the true object of knowledge, namely, discrimination, even though this is latent within them? The same limitations from the previous option apply to this possibility. Another problem with this type of view, says Śaṅkara, is that

since the *guṇas* are eternally in flux, if ignorance were a product of the *guṇas*, it too would be eternal and so there would be no liberation.

(4) Does ignorance remain dissolved as latent *saṁskāras* in the *guṇas* of *prakṛti* at the end of each creative cycle, becoming reactivated in the next creative cycle, at which time it produces an appropriate mind to serve as its substratum or container? This position, say the commentators, is acceptable to the Yoga school and is discussed further in the next *sūtra*, but it does not explain ignorance.

(5) Is ignorance the latent impetus that impels movement in *prakṛti* itself? The same objections apply here.

(6) Is it the very power and capability of *prakṛti* to reveal herself to *puruṣa* that is the ultimate cause of ignorance? This option, says Vijñānabhikṣu, is a variant of item 3. Vijñānabhikṣu quotes a charming verse from the *Sāṅkhya Kārikās* (LXI) personifying *prakṛti* when her game is up and she has been seen by the enlightened *puruṣa* for what she is: "The other one [*prakṛti*] thinks 'I have been seen!' "

(7) Is ignorance the characteristic of both *prakṛti* and *puruṣa*? *Prakṛti* is inert, lifeless matter, but its evolute *buddhi* appears to be ignorant due to being animated by the presence of *puruṣa*; likewise, *puruṣa* appears to be ignorant due to its awareness of *buddhi*, even though, in its pure state, it does not contain either ignorance or knowledge.[45] It is only when the power behind knowledge contacts the objects of knowledge—when the consciousness of *puruṣa* shines on *prakṛti* and her manifestations—and is reflected back to *puruṣa* that ignorance is produced, so is ignorance the product of both? The problem with this, says Hariharānanda, is that it may be correct, but it doesn't explain ignorance: It is like saying sight is dependent on the sun, which doesn't explain sight.

(8) A final opinion is that ignorance is ultimately and paradoxically knowledge itself. To know, after all, is to know something. All things are *prākṛtic*. Therefore, knowledge of things occurs only when *puruṣa* is joined with *prakṛti*.

There are thus many views on ignorance, says Vyāsa. They all contain some element of truth. The common denominator of all them is the conjunction of *puruṣa* with the *guṇas* of *prakṛti*. Ultimately, the origin of ignorance remains mysterious in all Indic philosophical schools; indeed, it is considered beginningless, and thus the question of its origin is bypassed altogether. In the theistic schools, it is a power of *Īśvara*, God.

तस्य हेतुरविद्या ॥२४॥

II.24 tasya hetur avidyā

tasya, of it [conjunction]; *hetuḥ*, the cause; *avidyā*, ignorance

The cause of conjunction is ignorance.

Vācaspati Miśra and Vijñānabhikṣu elaborate somewhat on the fourth possible cause of ignorance outlined in the previous *sūtra*. Creation in Hindu cosmology is cyclical. At the end of each cosmic cycle, all manifest reality, the world and the evolutes of *prakṛti*, dissolve back into their original source matrix along with the souls in *saṁsāra*—the *puruṣas* who have not attained liberation—and remain there latent and inactive until the next cosmic cycle begins anew. This primordial soup, called *pradhāna*, thus contains all the *saṁskāras* from all the *cittas* of all the individual *puruṣas* that had not had a chance to fructify during the last cycle.[46] At the beginning of the new cycle, these *saṁskāras* reactivate and cause *pradhāna* to produce an individual *citta* for each *puruṣa* appropriate to the specific *saṁskāras* possessed by that same *puruṣa* at the end of the last cycle. The *puruṣa* is thus like a fish trapped in a net of its previous *saṁskāras* and *karma*, says Rāmānanda Sarasvatī. As a result of the *puruṣa* being reconnected with a *citta*, its previous *saṁskāras*, most notably the *saṁskāra* of ignorance (i.e., the misidentification between the *puruṣa* and *prakṛti*), reexert their influence. In other words, the *puruṣa* picks up where it left off. The point is, from this perspective, that it is the *saṁskāras* that cause ignorance. This cycle of creation and dissolution is eternal for the Yoga school until liberation occurs (*saṁsāra* has no beginning, but it has an ending). Since the eternality of this cycle is axiomatic, the Yoga school avoids having to account for any primordial *saṁskāra* of ignorance that may have activated the whole cycle in the first place.

When intelligence contains the *saṁskāras* of ignorance, says Vyāsa, it remains active in the realm of *prakṛti* and thus does not produce discrimination about the true nature of *puruṣa*. *Saṁskāras* impel the intelligence to perform the first of its two functions, as expressed in II.18, namely, to provide experience of *prakṛti*, and it is this that is the cause of bondage. Intelligence ceases its activity only when it has attained its alternative and ultimate function, which is to provide discrimination about the distinction between *puruṣa* and *prakṛti*. As was discussed in some detail in I.50, the *saṁskāra* of discrimination overpowers all other *saṁskāras*. When this happens, ignorance, *avidyā*, the cause, *hetu*, of bondage, is removed, and ignorance, we recall, is the support of the other *kleśas*, obstacles (II.3–4), so they, too, dissolve.

In other words, complete liberation occurs only when intelligence first provides discrimination and then ceases to act altogether. Although discrimination, a function of *buddhi*, is initially indispensable in attaining the goal of *yoga*, as long as it remains active, *puruṣa* is still connected with *buddhi*, and thus complete liberation is not realized. But discrimination eventually completely destroys ignorance and thus its own base, like fire destroys its own fuel, says Hariharānanda. This results in *asamprajñāta-samādhi*, the final goal of *yoga*.

One might argue, says Vyāsa, that this claim that full liberation occurs only after discrimination has dissolved itself is rather like an impotent man who, when asked by his wife why she does not have children as her sister has children, replies that he will beget children in her after he is dead. If intelligence cannot provide liberation while it is alive and active, why should one believe that it will do so after it becomes lifeless and inactive? Vyāsa affirms, again, that full and final liberation occurs precisely when the intelligence ceases to act. Intelligence ceases to act when ignorance is removed. And ignorance is removed by knowledge. In other words, bondage is caused by ignorance, ignorance is removed by knowledge, the discriminatory aspect of intelligence, and then intelligence, having performed its grand finale, ceases to operate, and the full freedom of *puruṣa* occurs. Thus, intelligence and knowledge are not the direct cause of liberation, but by removing ignorance, they are the indirect cause.

तदभावात् संयोगाभावो हानं तद्दृशेः कैवल्यम् ॥ २५ ॥
II.25 tad-abhāvāt saṁyogābhāvo hānam tad-dṛśeḥ kaivalyam

tat, of it [ignorance]; *abhāvāt*, from absence, removal; *saṁyoga*, conjunction; *abhāvaḥ*, absence, removal; *hānam*, freedom, escape, liberation; *tat*, that; *dṛśeḥ*, of the seer; *kaivalyam*, absolute freedom, liberation

By the removal of ignorance, conjunction is removed. This is the absolute freedom of the seer.

Keeping our eye on the ball thematically, in II.15 Vyāsa identified four aspects covered by the science of *yoga: saṁsāra*, the cause of *saṁsāra*, liberation from *saṁsāra*, and the means of liberation from *saṁsāra*. This *sūtra* discusses the third aspect of *yoga*: liberation, or freedom from suffering and its cause.

Freedom, *hānam*, is the eternal cessation of bondage, says Vyāsa. This occurs when ignorance is fully removed, as a result of which the conjunction, *saṁyoga*, between *puruṣa* and *buddhi*, the cause of suffering, is removed—in other words, says Vyāsa, *puruṣa* never gets mixed up with the *guṇas* again. When the cause of suffering has been removed, suffering disappears, and *puruṣa* is established in its own true nature. This is liberation, referred to in this *sūtra* and elsewhere as *kaivalyam*.[47] *Kaivalyam* is usually translated as aloneness (in the sense that the *puruṣa* has severed itself from *prakṛti* and her effects and is now situated in its own autonomous nature), but is perhaps better understood as wholeness. The term *kevalin*, one who has attained the state of *kaivalya*, is most commonly used in the Jain tradition to refer to an enlightened being.

विवेकख्यातिरविप्लवा हानोपायः ॥ २६ ॥
II.26 viveka-khyātir aviplavā hānopāyaḥ

viveka, discrimination; *khyātiḥ*, discernment; *aviplavā*, undeviating, undisturbed; *hāna*, freedom, liberation; *upāyaḥ*, the means

The means to liberation is uninterrupted discriminative discernment.

If suffering is eliminated by the removal of its cause, ignorance, and this results in *puruṣa* being established in its own true nature, then what is the means, *upāya*, to accomplish this? asks Vyāsa rhetorically, as he prepares to discuss the fourth aspect of the science of *yoga*, the means of liberation. The means indicated here by Patañjali is *viveka-khyāti*, discriminative discernment. *Viveka*, Vyāsa reiterates, is defined as the cognition of the distinction between *buddhi* and *puruṣa*, but as long as false knowledge has not been removed, discrimination remains shaky (false knowledge, Vijñānabhikṣu reminds us, consists of *saṁskāras* of ignorance, *avidyā,* which keep arising in the mind). Śaṅkara quotes a verse here: "As unrefined gold does not shine forth, so the knowledge of an immature person attached to the world does not shine forth."[48]

When false knowledge becomes like a burnt seed that is incapable of sprouting, says Vyāsa, or, put differently, when the *sattva* of the intelligence has been cleansed of the dirt of *rajas*, then cognition attains a state of utmost clarity. At this point, the pure flow of discriminative discernment can proceed unchecked. Therefore, concludes Vyāsa, the path to liberation, namely, the disassociation of *puruṣa* from *buddhi*, occurs when false knowledge is destroyed like burnt seeds. Vijñānabhikṣu adds to this that it is *viveka-khyāti*, discriminative discernment itself, that burns the seeds of false knowledge, at which time all latent *saṁskāras* of ignorance become like a barren woman incapable of giving birth.

Vyāsa notes that discriminative discernment is initially shaky, as it begins to take up the task of destroying the seeds of ignorance, the distracting *saṁskāras* imprinted in the *citta* that surface continually as a result of *rajas* and *tamas*. Only once this task is fully accomplished by practice, and these *saṁskāras* become impotent and can no longer arise, can discriminative awareness reign supreme, and the *sattva* of the mind and intelligence remain undisturbed, *aviplava*. Then, says Śaṅkara, "As seeds burnt by fire no longer sprout, so is the case with *kleśas* burnt by the fire of knowledge; the *ātman* no longer encounters them."[49] Vyāsa calls this stage *vaśīkāra-saṁjñā,* which literally means knowledge that exerts control. In other words, discriminating discernment controls and eventually burns up the emergence of unwanted *saṁskāras*.

The commentators state that discriminating discernment is initially awakened by listening to the *śāstras*, the sacred texts, and becomes strengthened by contemplation on their content, pursued with reverence, for a long time. It then develops further by the practice of *yoga* that will be outlined in the following *sūtras*. This discrimination exposes and undermines one's attachments in the form of desires for worldly or heavenly enjoyment, continues Hariharānanda. In time, discrimination becomes so powerful that the possibility of falling into illusion again becomes completely eradicated, all wrong notions remaining like parched seeds deprived of their potency. Discrimination has now reached a state where it can flow undisturbed. With discrimination in absolute control, the *citta* is no longer disturbed, and, free from distraction, can now reflect on the *puruṣa*. The *yogī* thus approaches liberation.

तस्य सप्तधा प्रान्तभूमिः प्रज्ञा ॥ २७ ॥

II.27 tasya saptadhā prānta-bhūmiḥ prajñā.

tasya, his [the *yogī*'s]; *saptadhā*, sevenfold; *prānta-bhūmiḥ*, final place; *prajñā*, true insight, wisdom

The *yogī*'s true insight has seven ultimate stages.

This *sūtra* introduces a sevenfold, *saptadhā*, division of *prajñā*, insight. We see here that Patañjali did not specify what these seven stages were, which indicates that he assumed his audience would be familiar with this seven-stepped insight (and that, therefore, as noted in the introduction, Patañjali was not the founder of *yoga*; this type of knowledge was already in circulation). It also reinforces the point that these *sūtras* served as manuals that required unpacking by a teacher.

Upon examination of how this sevenfold division is understood by the commentators, it seems that several of these stages are essentially different ways of looking at the same state rather than actual sequential stages. With regard to *prajñā*, it seems useful here to note Rukmani's (reassuring) observation that "of the six schools of philosophy, Yoga is perhaps the one school which has a profusion of technical words used interchangeably. Thus we have *dharma-megha, prasaṅkhyāna, anyathā-khyāti, sattvapuruṣānyatā-khyāti, viveka, viveka-*

khyāti, prajñā, ṛtambharā, prātibha-jñāna, ekāgra-citta, sa-bījaḥ and more being used more or less in the same sense" (1997, 619). While commentators try to tease out different semantic nuances, at the very least these terms overlap considerably. Rukmani concludes that it might not always be fruitful to attempt to extract logical consistency in the usage of terms and concepts in the system:

> The conviction grows that this [Yoga] is not something that can be logically described. It is a system that has brought in a number of ideas from so many sources and tried to make sense of them. Yoga was a practical school in which the various steps of *prajñā* and *asamprajñāta* were clearly intelligible to the adept in Yoga . . . This is one school which has believed all along in . . . following some well laid down yogic practices. So it is best to accept it as a discipline to be followed rather than to be understood intellectually. (623)

The *yogī* referred to by Patañjali in this *sūtra* refers to the one in whom discrimination has arisen, says Vyāsa. When the impure *rājasic* and *tāmasic* coverings of the *citta* have been removed, and no further *pratyayas*, notions, arise in the mind of the discriminating *yogī*, true insight manifests in seven aspects,[50] which Vyāsa lists as follows:

(1) That which is to be avoided (suffering) is known, and there is nothing further to be known in this regard. The very desire to know ceases, says Hariharānanda, and thus knowledge itself can cease.
(2) The causes of this suffering have been completely eradicated. These causes are the *kleśas*, ignorance, desire, etc., and the ensuing *karma*, as we know.
(3) By *nirodha-samādhi*, the *samādhi* of restraint, which, we recall is how Patañjali defines the entire enterprise of *yoga* (*citta-vṛtti-nirodha*), the removal of the misidentification of *puruṣa* with *buddhi* becomes directly realized. Once this misidentification is removed, *asamprajñāta-samādhi* can manifest.
(4) The means to accomplish this removal of misidentification in the form of discriminative knowledge has been attained.

These first four aspects, says Vyāsa, pertain to liberation from action, or external events. One should note their obvious parallel to the Four Noble Truths of Buddhism. The next three pertain to liberation of the *citta*. Moreover, the first four are the result of the personal effort of the *yogī*, say the commentators, unlike the following three, which arise spontaneously. In other words, one need no longer strive to practice *yoga* at this point. These final three stages represent the complete cessation of the activities of *buddhi*.

(5) Intelligence has fulfilled its purpose: to provide either worldly experience or liberation. It has now become redundant.
(6) The *yogī*'s *guṇas* dissolve back into their causal matrix, *prakṛti*, and emerge no more, since they no longer have a function. Vyāsa compares this to boulders falling from the tops of mountains when deprived of their support. Hariharānanda hastens to point out that the *guṇas* to which Vyāsa is referring are the effects of the *guṇas*, not the primordial *guṇas* themselves, which are constituent ontological categories inherent in *prakṛti* and thus as eternal as is *prakṛti*. Specifically, it is the subtle body of the *citta*, says Vijñānabhikṣu, that dissolves.
(7) *Puruṣa*, removed from the bonds of the *guṇas*, is now eligible to shine forth in its own pure luminous nature. This is called *kevala*, absolute freedom. The *puruṣa* who has surpassed the *guṇas* and attained these seven stages of realization is known as an adept, says Vyāsa. In this state, one doesn't actually realize anything, because now, by definition, one is fully detached and separated from the organ of realization or discrimination, *buddhi*. But just as one realizes upon awakening one has slept well, even if one cannot recall the actual experience of sleep, so does the *yogī* coming out of the state of *asamprajñāta* back into external awareness realize that this has been a state free from all suffering.

There are differing views among Hindu schools as to whether this ability to remain embodied despite having attained *asamprajñāta-*

samādhi (called *jīvanmukti*, liberation, while still in the body) is possible, or whether ultimate and absolute liberation can take place only after death.[51] One can attain this stage even while living, say the Yoga commentators, although this will be such a person's last birth. According to Vijñānabhikṣu, the *jīvanmukta*, the liberated *yogī* who is still embodied, may, if he or she wishes, merely witness the stages of insight, *prajñā*, produced by *buddhi*. There is no sense of *ahaṅkāra*, of wishing to appropriate *prajñā* or misidentify with it, as in normal consciousness.

One must remember that in the Yoga system, *prajñā* is still a function of *buddhi* and thus of *prakṛti*'s connection with *puruṣa*. Therefore, according to Hariharānanda, these seven steps do not yet represent the *puruṣa* being in itself, *asamprajñāta-samādhi*, but the highest or final level of insight prior to this ultimate *samādhi*. As has been discussed, in *asamprajñāta-samādhi*, the mental function, *citta*, ceases completely and the *yogī* consequently ceases to function in the world. In the *jīvanmukta* stage, the *yogī* still retains the *prākṛtic citta*, since, of course, by definition, embodiment entails association with the mind and intelligence, etc. (although the *jīvanmukta* is fully capable of discarding all *prākṛtic* coverings and entering the state of *asamprajñāta*, notes Hariharānanda). The *jīvanmukta*, who has, by definition, no personal desire or reason to do so, might choose to remain embodied so as to help other beings who are still suffering. Obviously, says Hariharānanda, the *jīvanmukta* can rise above any suffering that might come his or her way due to any *saṁskāras* that might still be left, by use of the *buddhi* in the form of discrimination and detachment.

Thus the *yogī* is completely free from the control of the *guṇas*. Vijñānabhikṣu quotes the *Gītā* here: "One who renounces all endeavour is known to have transcended the *guṇas*" (XIV.25). In this section of the *Gītā*, Arjuna asks Kṛṣṇa to describe the symptoms by which one might recognize someone who has transcended the *guṇas*, in other words, what are the characteristics of the *jīvanmukta*? It might be useful for the reader to refer to the translation of this section in I.37, since this material overlaps with what the commentators have to say in their commentaries for this *sūtra*.

योगाङ्गानुष्ठानाद् अशुद्धिक्षये ज्ञानदीप्तिराविवेकख्यातेः ।। २८ ।।

II.28 yogāṅgānuṣṭhānād aśuddhi-kṣaye jñāna-dīptir-āviveka-khyāteḥ

yoga, yoga; *aṅga*, limbs; *anuṣṭhānād*, from the practice of; *aśuddhi*, impurity; *kṣaye*, on the destruction of; *jñāna*, knowledge; *dīptiḥ*, light, lamp; *ā*, up to; *viveka*, discrimination; *khyāteḥ*, knowledge

Upon the destruction of impurities as a result of the practice of *yoga*, the lamp of knowledge arises. This culminates in discriminative discernment.

Patañjali here introduces the long-awaited *aṅgas*, limbs of *yoga*. It has by now been well established, says Vyāsa, that discriminative discernment, *viveka*, when achieved, is the cause of removing the conjunction between *puruṣa* and *prakṛti*, in other words, of removing ignorance such that liberation manifests. But what is the cause of achieving discriminative discernment? A means is required to achieve this. Milk may exist in the udders of the cow, says Vācaspati Miśra, but one needs a means or process to extract it. The means presented in this *sūtra* of attaining discriminative discernment is the practice of the eight limbs of *yoga*, *yogāṅgānuṣṭhāna*, which will occupy the rest of the chapter.

By the practice of *yoga*, Patañjali states, impurity, *aśuddhi*, is destroyed, which, Vyāsa, reminds us, consists of the five *kleśas*, obstacles to *yoga* (ignorance, ego, attachment, aversion, and clinging to life). The notion of *yoga* destroying impurities goes back as far as the *Āpastamba-dharma-sūtra* of the fifth and fourth centuries B.C.E., which lists fifteen *doṣas*, faults, that are eliminated by its practice.[52] When impurity is removed, the light of full knowledge, *jñāna-dīpti*, noted in this *sūtra* can shine forth, like the sun after the cold season, says Śaṅkara. Another way of putting this is that as the impurities of *tamas* and *rajas* dwindle, the luminosity and clarity inherent in *sattva* can manifest unimpeded. An impurity is something that intrudes on or contaminates another entity, in this case, *rajas* and *tamas* covering *sattva* (of course, *sattva* itself is ultimately a covering of *puruṣa*). The more the eightfold path is practiced, the more these impurities dwindle, and the more they dwindle, the more this light can correspondingly increase. This increase culminates in the desired discriminative discernment, a feature of pure *sattva*. Just as the axe slices wood from a tree, so the practice of these eight limbs slices the impurities away from the *citta*, says Vyāsa.

There is the widespread view that the continuity of the text comes to something of an abrupt end after II.27, with this *sūtra* typically deemed as initiating a new self-contained unit on the eight limbs. It is true that Patañjali does not make reference to the eight limbs prior to this point. Nor is there any explanation of the relationship among *tapas, svādhyāya*, and *Īśvara-praṇidhāna* as the three ingredients of *kriyā-yoga*, and their occurrence as three of the five *niyamas*, the second limb, discussed below. And our modern notions of discursive continuity might have put the eight-limbed section in a separate *pāda* of its own, beginning with this *sūtra*.

But, again, one must be wary of submitting the cryptic *sūtra* style to modern notions of structural coherence. Just as the *kriyā-yoga* section introduced a new set of terms and conceptual analyses indispensable to explaining the mechanics (*kleśas*) underpinning the *vṛttis* such that the attainment of the goal of *yoga* might be better understood, so does this ensuing section dedicate itself to a necessarily more specific elaboration of the *abhyāsa*, practice, touched upon in I.12. As with the *kriyā-yoga* section, this increase of detail requires new terms and categories, but now pertaining to practice, articulated accordingly with less philosophical tone and content.

It is likely that Patañjali drew upon an existing tradition of eight-limbed *yoga* when composing his text (or modified the older tradition of six limbs), as well as a distinct tradition featuring *kriyā-yoga*. In other words, as a systematizer of existing traditions, Patañjali might well have merged two distinct but overlapping systems. This possibility is enhanced by the fact that the relationship between the three ingredients of *kriyā-yoga* and the identical three ingredients reappearing in the second limb of *yoga*, the *niyamas*, but now alongside two other ingredients, is not addressed by Patañjali.

यमनियमासनप्राणायामप्रत्याहारधारणाध्यानसमाधयोऽष्टाव्
अङ्गानि ॥ २९ ॥

II.29 yama-niyamāsana-prāṇāyāma-pratyāhāra-dhāraṇā-dhyāna-samādhayo 'ṣṭāv aṅgāni yama, abstentions, moral restraints; *niyama*, observances; *āsana*, posture; *prāṇāyāma*, breath control; *pratyāhāra*, withdrawal of the senses; *dhāraṇā*, concentration; *dhyāna*, meditation; *samādhayaḥ*, absorption; *aṣṭāu*, eight; *aṅgāni*, limbs

The eight limbs are abstentions, observances, posture, breath control, disengagement of the senses, concentration, meditation, and absorption.

In I.12, practice and dispassion were presented as the means to control the *vṛttis* and thus attain *samādhi*; in II.1, self-discipline, study, and submission to the Lord were identified as practices conducive to eliminating the *kleśa* obstacles to *yoga* and attaining *samādhi*. The following *sūtras* offer further prescriptions for attaining the goal of *yoga*. Actually, both sets of injunctions in I.12 and in II.1 can be located within the first two limbs, the *yamas*, abstentions, and *niyamas*, observances; practice and dispassion find correlates in the *yamas*; and the three ingredients of *kriyā-yoga* are repeated verbatim under the *niyamas*. Śaṅkara also adds that there are other requirements of the path, such as practicing *dharma*, righteous conduct, and accepting a *guru*. The commentators save their analyses of the eight items listed in this *sūtra* for the following *sūtras*, which take up each limb individually.

One might add, here, that the notion of *yoga* having *aṅgas*, limbs, is derived in all likelihood from the older Veda-*aṅgas*. The successful performance of Vedic ritual in the later Vedic period was seen as dependent on the mastery of the six limbs of the Vedic ritual: phonetics, meter, grammar, etymology, astronomy, and ritual (mentioned in, e.g., Muṇḍaka Upaniṣad I.1.5). Likewise, the goal of *yoga* expressed in I.2 is dependent on the successful performance of the eight auxiliary limbs of *yoga* indicated in this verse. Just as none of the Vedic limbs individually represented the goal of Vedic sacrifice, but each was an essential contributing part of it, so is the case with the limbs of *yoga*.

अहिंसासत्यास्तेयब्रह्मचर्यापरिग्रहा यमाः ॥ ३० ॥

II.30 ahiṁsā-satyāsteya-brahmacaryāparigrahā yamāḥ

ahiṁsā, nonviolence; *satya*, truthfulness; *asteya*, refraining from stealing; *brahmacarya*, celibacy; *aparigrahāḥ*, refrainment from acquisition or coveting; *yamāḥ*, the abstentions

The *yamas* are nonviolence, truthfulness, refrainment from stealing, celibacy, and renunciation of [unnecessary] possessions.

From the five *yamas* listed here, *ahiṁsā*, nonviolence, the principal motto of Gandhi's noncooperation approach, is the *yama* singled out by the commentators and Patañjali for special attention. In traditional methods of scriptural interpretation, introductory (and concluding) statements carry more weight than other statements.[53] *Ahiṁsā* is the most important *yama*, say the commentators, and therefore leads the list. (It seems important to note that the *yamas* themselves lead the list of the eight limbs, suggesting that one's *yogic* accomplishment remains limited until the *yamas* are internalized and put into practice.)

Vyāsa accordingly takes *ahiṁsā* as the root of the other *yamas*. He defines it as not injuring any living creature anywhere at any time. Just as the footprints of an elephant cover the footprints of all other creatures, says Vijñānabhikṣu, so does *ahiṁsā* cover all the other *yamas*. According to Vyāsa, the goal of the other *yamas* is to achieve *ahiṁsā* and enhance it, and he quotes an unidentified verse stating that one continues to undertake more and more vows and austerities for the sole purpose of purifying *ahiṁsā*.

Although *ahiṁsā* has been defined by Vyāsa as not harming any creature anywhere at any time, one must continue to perform one's *dharma*, duty, cautions Vijñānabhikṣu, even though it is impossible to avoid harming tiny living entities such as bacteria or insects when one engages in activities such as bathing or cleaning. Nonetheless, one must strive as far as possible to avoid harming even an insect. Certainly, one can be very clear about the fact that eating meat, nourishing one's body at the expense of the flesh of other living beings, is completely taboo for aspiring *yogīs*. One should avoid harming even trees, says Hariharānanda. Manu, who composed the primary *dharmaśāstra*, law book, in classical India, states, "To protect living creatures one should inspect the ground constantly as one walks, by night or day, because of the risk of grievous bodily harm" (VI.69).

As an aside, but in this vein, certain communities of observant

Jains, who have taken the principle of nonviolence further than any other tradition recorded in human history, are required to follow strict principles to minimize any possible violence to other creatures. For example, they are admonished not to eat root vegetables, since creatures in the soil may be harmed when uprooting these and not to engage in any farming activities, for the same reason. Needless to say, they must reject any type of military career. Observant members of this community do not cook after sunset, since insects would be attracted to the flame of the fire and perish; strain their water to remove any hapless microscopic creatures that might have fallen in; wear gauze over their mouths so as not to inhale any tiny airborne creatures; and sweep the road before them as they walk, again so as not to step on any creature, etc. Since embodied existence inevitably entails that one will sooner or later inadvertently harm some creature or other, no matter how hard one attempts to avoid this, the ultimate act of nonviolence performed in rare instances by exemplar Jains is to fast to death, sacrificing their own life to save those of other creatures. Sacrificing one's life to save others is the definition of heroism (and, indeed, the perfected Jain *yogī* is called *mahāvīra*, great hero[54]).

This practice may seem extreme (it is of course not mainstream but performed on very rare occasions by exemplar ascetic Jain monks), but it needs to be considered within the parameters of the Jain (and Hindu) belief that all living beings contain an *ātman* (*puruṣa*), and all *ātmans* are spiritually equal. Even as our modern world respects the heroism involved in sacrificing one's life for the protection of fellow humans in recognition of a common humanity or humanness, and certain moral commentators are presently taking a hesitant step beyond the concept of human equality by grappling with the extent of our commonality with the great apes, and the moral issues this might present in our responsibilities to them, so Jains (there are similar instances among Hindu ascetics[55]) extend this principle and, from their perspective, deepen it, by recognizing the common *ātman*-ness among all beings.

The *sūtras* and the commentators do not advocate this degree of commitment to nonviolence, but at the very least, eating meat is to be shunned by anyone with even the minimum pretensions of aspiring to be a practicing *yogī* as understood by Patañjali.

A *sāttvic* person is empathetic and compassionate toward other embodied beings and would never countenance inflicting violence upon them, what to speak of eating their flesh. Moreover, being insightful, such a person understands the *kārmic* consequence of violent actions, as will be indicated in II.34: Any involvement in violent acts of any kind requires that the perpetrator be subjected to the same violence at some future time as *kārmic* consequence. Moreover, inflicting violence is a quality of *tamas*, and thus eating meat increases the *tāmasic* potential of the *citta*, further enhancing ignorance. A vegetarian diet is nonnegotiable for *yogīs*.

Nonviolence, Hariharānanda continues, also encompasses giving up the spirit of malice and hatred, since these produce the tendencies to injure others. This includes avoiding violence in the form of harsh words, or causing fear in others. *Ahiṁsā* must be followed in thought, deed, and word, says Śaṅkara. The degree of violence is determined by intent—acts of violence performed without malice and hatred by a normal person, he notes, such as self-defense or cutting the grass, are not the same as murdering one's parents in cold blood. But *yogīs* avoid even retaliating in self-defense against an attacker, he says, and will shoo off a snake rather than kill it, and thus attempt to inflict as little aggression as possible on their environments.

Vyāsa defines truth, the second *yama*, as one's words and thoughts being in exact correspondence to fact, that is, to whatever is known through the three processes of knowledge accepted by the Yoga school (sense perception, inference, and verbal testimony). Speech, he continues, is for the transferral of one's knowledge to others and should not be deceitful, misleading, or devoid of value. It should be for the benefit of all creatures, and not for their harm, otherwise it is sinful. Posing deceptively as a truthful or virtuous person causes one's downfall, he warns; therefore, one should consider these things carefully and speak only the truth for the welfare of all creatures. Śaṅkara quotes Manu here: "Let him not speak what is true but unkind; let him speak what is kind and not untrue. This is eternal righteousness" (IV.138).

The commentators give a well-known episode from the *Mahābhārata* involving Yudhiṣṭhira as an example of deception. During the *Mahābhārata* war, Droṇa, on the opposing side to Yudhiṣṭhira and his brothers, the five Pāṇḍavas, was unstoppably decimating their army. With a view to breaking his fighting spirit, Droṇa was misinformed that his son Aśvatthāmā had been killed in the battle. In Vācaspati Miśra's rendition of the event, Droṇa asked the righteous son of *dharma* himself, Yudhiṣṭhira, who was renowned for never having told a lie, whether it was true that Aśvatthāmā had been killed. Yudhiṣṭhira answered in the affirmative, but since he was incapable of lying, he forced himself, as he responded, to think of an elephant named Aśvatthāmā who had also been killed in the field that day. Although this resulted in a technically truthful reply to the question, since the thought in Yudhiṣṭhira's mind was of an elephant, the knowledge transferred to Droṇa's mind was in relation to his son. Thus Yudhiṣṭhira's words were purposely deceitful and misleading, as per Vyāsa's definitions above, since their intention was to mislead. This led to Droṇa's downfall, but the deceit also caused Yudhiṣṭhira's chariot wheels, which had up to that point floated above the ground due to the power of his *dharma*, to touch the ground.

On the other hand, continue the commentators, given that the other *yamas* are subservient to *ahiṁsā*, truth must not cause harm to others. Here an example is introduced of a man of truth who is asked by robbers if merchants they are pursuing had passed that way, and, since he had seen them do so, replies truthfully. Although speaking the truth, his compliance with the robbers resulted in harm, *hiṁsā*, being caused to the merchants. Therefore, this also does not qualify as real truth. This underscores Vyāsa's view of the centrality of *ahiṁsā*: Truth must never result in violence. In other words, if there is ever a conflict between the *yamas*—if observing one *yama* results in the compromise of another—then *ahiṁsā* must always be respected first. Hariharānanda applies this principle on a psychological level: *Ahiṁsā* includes not always speaking bluntly and truthfully to people about their shortcomings. Here he follows Manu's injunction that "one should not tell the truth unkindly" (IV.138). Also, avoiding untruth extends to the point of abstaining from reading fiction, for Hariharānanda. The *yogī* is always contemplating spiritual truths and does not occupy his or her mind with fictional or worldly trivia, silly fantasy, daydreaming, or imagination.

Refrainment from stealing, the third *yama*, is described as not taking things belonging to others and not even harboring the desire to do so. This latter aspect is important, explains Vācaspati Miśra, since action is initiated in the mind—the more one desires something, the more inclined one becomes to acquire it. Thoughts of stealing obviously cannot exist in those free of desire, says Śaṅkara. Even if one finds a treasure trove or jewel by chance, it should not be taken since it belongs to someone else, says Hariharānanda.

Vyāsa defines celibacy as the control of the sexual organs, and this is refined by Vācaspati Miśra as not seeing, speaking with, embracing, or otherwise interacting with members of the opposite sex as objects of desire. He quotes the *Dakṣa-saṁhitā*: "The eight kinds of sexual indulgences are thinking, talking, and joking about sex; looking [at the opposite sex with passion], talking secretly about sex, determining to engage in it, attempting to do so, and actually performing the act" (7.31–32).[56] Hariharānanda, ever ready with practical suggestions, says that a frugal diet and moderate sleep are important for celibacy. Plenty of milk and butter may be *sāttvic* for an ordinary person, he says,[57] but not for a *yogī*. In short, ultimate self-realization cannot be attained if one is sexually active because this indicates that one is still seeking fulfillment on the sensual level and thus misidentifying with the nonself.

Vyāsa defines renunciation of possessions as the ability to see the problems caused by the acquisition, preservation, and destruction of things, since these only provoke attachment and injury. There is trouble involved in acquiring things in the first place, says Hariharānanda, trouble again in trying to preserve and upkeep them, and trouble and distress when we inevitably lose them. For such reasons, possession produces *saṁskāras*, and these activate in the future to cause distress in the form of hankering for objects, or lamentation for having lost them. Hoarding wealth without sharing it is sheer selfishness and points to a complete lack of sympathy for the plight of others, says Hariharānanda. Therefore, *yogīs* attempt to give up all objects of enjoyment and take only what is required for their maintenance. No enjoyment can be gained without some level of direct or indirect injury to others, says Vācaspati Miśra, reaffirming Vyāsa's comments about the centrality of *ahiṁsā* among the *yamas*. The more something is enjoyable, the more one becomes attached to it and strives to repeat the experience often without consideration of the consequences for others, and thus, correspondingly, more harm is generated to others.

Rāmānanda Sarasvatī notes that the *yamas* are situated as the first limb of *yoga* because they produce their effects without being aided by any other factors. The *niyamas*, observances, of the next *sūtra* are dependent on the successful cultivation of the *yamas* for their full fruition. In his view, each subsequent limb of *yoga* thus requires the completion of the previous limbs in order to be pursued fruitfully (but Hariharānanda disagrees with this in his comments to *sūtra* II.34, below).

जातिदेशकालसमयानवच्छिन्नाः सार्वभौमा महाव्रतम् ॥ ३१ ॥

II.31 jāti-deśa-kāla-samayānavacchinnāḥ sārva-bhaumā mahā-vratam

jāti, class, caste, occupation; *deśa*, place, country of origin; *kāla*, time; *samaya*, circumstance; *anavacchinnāḥ*, unconditioned, unlimited by; *sārva*, every; *bhaumāḥ*, place on earth; *mahā-vratam*, great vow

[These *yamas*] are considered the great vow. They are not exempted by one's class, place, time, or circumstance. They are universal.

In this very important *sūtra*, Patañjali states that the *yamas* are absolute and universal for aspiring *yogīs*—they cannot be transgressed or exempted under any circumstance such as class, *jāti*; place, *deśa*; time, *kāla*; or circumstance, *samaya*. They are nonnegotiable for *yogīs*. Patañjali is being conspicuously (and uncharacteristically) emphatic here. Not only are the *yamas* a *vrata*, vow, but a *mahāvrata*, great vow. This great vow is further qualified as being *sārva-bhauma*, universal. The term "universal" by definition should make any further qualification redundant, but Patañjali makes a point of additionally naming and eliminating any possible grounds or pleas for exception: These *yamas* are *anavicchinnāḥ*, not exempted because of one's class, *jāti*; place, *deśa*; time, *kāla*; or circumstance, *samaya*. This is as absolute a statement as can be made. As noted, items placed first on a list carry greater importance than subsequent items, underscoring the importance of the *yamas* (and, by the same token, *ahiṁsā* as first of the *yamas*).

At the time of writing this section, there is a discussion in certain quarters of the Yoga community in America about the jurisdiction of the *yamas* in the twenty-first-century West. Whatever direction such discussions may take, and whatever hybrid practices evolve in the West under the rubric of *yoga*, this *sūtra* makes it very clear that as far as Patañjali is concerned, there are no exceptions to these rules at any time in any place for anyone aspiring to be a *yogī* as defined by his system. One might imagine that in Patañjali's own circle, there would have been followers or disciples angling for exceptions to one or other of the *yamas*—perhaps arguing that the sacred Vedic law books, *Dharma-śāstras*, themselves allowed the *brāhmaṇa* caste, for example, to offer animals in Vedic sacrifices, or the *kṣatriya* caste to eat meat, or engage in sexuality. He is therefore being as emphatic here as the straightforward and plain use of human language allows.

One might add that these *yamas* are more or less universal among all the liberation-based spiritual traditions of ancient India, and even in the more worldly *Dharma-śāstra* traditions, the Vedic law books that concern themselves with more conventional sociocivic duties (for example, Manu X.63). This is so not only in orthodox Vedic traditions, but in heterodox ones too. The eightfold noble path of Buddhism, requires the observance of five *sīlas*, four of which—*ahiṁsā, satya, brahmacarya*, and *asteya*—are identical to the first four *yamas*, and one, abstinence from intoxication, replaces *aparigraha*, noncoveting. The Jains, too, have five great vows, for which they use the same term we find in this *sūtra, mahāvrata*, and these are identical to Patañjali's *yamas*.[58] The *Nyāya Sūtras* acknowledge *yoga* as the means to realize the *ātman* but specify that it entails the following of *yama* and *niyama* (IV.2.46). With certain nonmainstream exceptions such as the *tāntric* left-handed practices,[59] these *yamas* are more or less standard across sectarian traditions, even if not listed in the specific format chosen by Patañjali. The *Gītā*, for example, lists some of the *yamas* in its description of the divine attributes (*ahiṁsā* and *satya* in XVI.2); in its description of the qualities of *sattva* (*brahmacarya* and *satya* in XVII.14–15); in its prescriptions for the *yogī* (*aparigraha* in VI.10); and under qualities emanating from Kṛṣṇa himself (*brahmacarya* and *satya* in X.4–5).

The commentators elaborate on this *sūtra* through a discussion of nonviolence, since it is the most important *yama* and, as first member of the list, represents the others; however, the following discussion applies to all the *yamas*. The *yama* of nonviolence conditioned by caste, *jāti*, says Vyāsa, can be seen in the case of, say, a fisherman who, because of his caste occupation inflicts violence only on fish but nowhere else. *Kṣatriyas*, the warrior class, too, are allowed to engage in violence in certain contexts—hunting, for example, and, of course, on the battlefield. While this may hold in other circumstances such as these, nonviolence has no conditions for Patañjali. *Jāti* literally means family of birth; therefore, being born into a family or caste that eats meat does not constitute an exception to the practice of nonviolence. If, say, a *kṣatriya* wishes to become a *yogī* as understood by Patañjali, he must abandon violence even if such violence is legitimate for persons of this caste and, indeed, condoned or even required by *dharmic* prescriptions in the *Dharma-śāstra* texts, and even if such texts are also considered sacred scripture and authoritative. Manu, for example, who wrote one such law book, states, "Kings who try to kill one another in battle and fight to their utmost ability, never averting their faces, go to the celestial realms" (VII.89ff). One can envision that there would have been spiritual seekers in Patañjali's entourage who would have been coming from *kṣatriya* or other *jātis*, castes, who might have pointed to such passages in sacred scripture.

Here we see a distinction between the requirements of *yoga* covered in, for example, the *karma-yoga* section of the *Gītā*, where Kṛṣṇa exhorts Arjuna to do his civic duty as a *kṣatriya* warrior and fight, to specifically engage in violent warfare, and the ascetic tradition represented by Patañjali. What may be acceptable—or even required—in a sociocivic context must be renounced in an ascetic *yogic* one. Indeed, it is with this ascetic alternative in mind that Arjuna initially precisely wishes to renounce violence and take up the ascetic life of mendicancy (II.5). The *Gītā*, of course, while accepting the Pātañjalian-type path as an acceptable means to attain liberation (e.g., chapter VI) has, for the most part, a different objective, one directed to sociocivic concerns, and thus construes a different means to attain perfection from within the parameters of the idealized social system, namely *karma-yoga*, the path of action. While it has long been argued persuasively that the *Yoga Sūtras* are not incompatible with social and civic engagement in the world (e.g., Whicher 1998, 1999, 2005)—that is, once *avidyā*, ignorance, is eliminated, one can act in the world from a position of enlightenment[60]—Patañjali's position on the role of the *yamas* could not be made much clearer.

As an example of nonviolence conditioned by place, *deśa*, Vyāsa points to a person who abstains from injury only when in a sacred place but kills animals elsewhere (or, one might add, vice versa for the Vedic ritualist). For Patañjalī, nonviolence must be upheld everywhere, irrespective of the ritualistic, gastronomic, or culinary practices of a particular country or place. He defines nonviolence conditioned by time, *kāla*, as when one abstains from violence on certain calendar occasions (for example, during religious observances, such as, in a Catholic context, abstaining from meat at Lent), but not at other times. *Yogīs* must be nonviolent at all times. Nonviolence conditioned by circumstance, *samaya*, is exemplified by a person who avoids violence on all occasions except in the context of religious rites. The ancient Vedic *yajña* sacrificial rites, which were still the mainstream religious practices of Patañjali's time, involved offering animals into the sacred fire; thus violence in the sacrificial context is prescribed in the ancient Vedic texts.[61] Vyāsa also gives the example of soldiers who engage in violence on the battlefield but nowhere else. Although legitimate in other contexts, none of these circumstances applies to *yogīs*.

In short, even if one's very *dharma*, righteous duty, allows for exceptions of this sort, if one wishes to be a *yogī*, such exceptions no longer apply. One can also mention allowances made in *āyurveda*, the traditional Hindu system of medicinal knowledge, for temporarily imbibing certain meat substances to cure very specific medical conditions, which would also come under the category of *samaya*. All these exceptions may hold good elsewhere in other contexts but, for the *yogī* wishing to attain the goals of *yoga* outlined in this text, say the commentators, this *sūtra* emphatically specifies that any such mitigating factors or conditions no longer apply. Nonviolence and the other *yamas* must be practiced at all times, in all conditions, everywhere, irrespective of any considerations whatsoever.

One can take this or leave it, but Patañjali's intent cannot be expressed much more clearly. The *yamas* are universal prescriptions—there are no exceptions, says Vyāsa. Aspiring *yogīs* in the modern context are thus informed in this *sūtra* that renegotiations of the *yamas* due to the exigencies of modern times and the Western landscape are emphatically not recognized by the classical Yoga tradition. Hence Patañjali states that the *yamas* are the great vow. So too, say the commentators, are the *niyamas* of the next *sūtra*.[62]

On a separate note, Gokhula (1995) considers the charge that Yoga cannot strictly speaking be considered a moral system, since its goals are not altruistic or focused on the welfare of others, but focused on the liberation of the individual self; it is thus self-centered or egoistic. He concludes, however, that even though Yoga's ultimate goal of self-liberation is individualistic, it cannot be attained except through moral means of interacting with others, as indicated by the five *yamas*, and never obtained through immoral means. It can thus be categorized as a moral system.

शौचसंतोषतपःस्वाध्यायेश्वरप्रणिधानानि नियमाः ॥३२॥

II.32 śauca-santoṣa-tapaḥ-svādhyāyeśvara-praṇidhānāni niyamāḥ

śauca, cleanliness; *santoṣa*, contentment; *tapaḥ*, austerity; *svādhyāya*, study [of the scriptures]; *Īśvara*, God, the Lord; *praṇidhānāni*, devotion to; *niyamāḥ*, observances

The observances are cleanliness, contentment, austerity, study [of scripture], and devotion to God.

In contrast with the *yamas*, which are concerned with how the *yogī* interacts with others, the *niyamas* are centered on one's own personal discipline and practice. Vijñānabhikṣu rationalizes the categorization of these two sets by pointing out that the former deal with *desisting* from certain activities, which, being universal, are not qualified by time and place, and the latter with *engaging* in certain activities, which are qualified by time and place.[63]

Vyāsa divides the first item on Patañjali's list, cleanliness, *śauca*, into external and internal types. External cleanliness pertains to the body and consists (in the premodern world of our commentators and rural India today) of cleaning with water and clay, as well as cow dung and cow urine, which are considered pure substances, and of ingesting pure foodstuff (which, Vācaspati Miśra notes, should be limited in quantity). In terms of ingestion, Hariharānanda reiterates that meat and intoxication cause the mind to be agitated and stimulated—they incite *rajas* and *tamas*—and *yoga* requires a steady and peaceful mind. Therefore, a *yogī* never imbibes such substances. He quotes Caraka, a traditional authority on *āyurveda*: "Whatever is good or most desired in this life or the next is attained by intense concentration of the mind. Alcohol creates a disturbance in the mind. Those blinded by addiction to alcohol lose sight of their best self-interest." Internal cleanliness consists of purifying the mind of all contamination. The commentators speak of jealousy, pride, vanity, hatred, and attachment as examples of mental contamination. Bhoja Rāja states that internal cleanliness is to be accomplished by benevolence—exuding a friendly attitude toward all.

Contentment, *santoṣa*, the second *niyama*, manifests as disinterest in accumulating more than one's immediate needs of life (Vācaspati Miśra points out that the desire to appropriate the possessions of others has in actuality already been given up in the *yama* stage). As the *Gītā* informs us, desire is the real enemy of the embodied soul, since it is never satisfied and burns like fire (III.37–39). True happiness comes from contentment with whatever one has, not with thinking that one will be happy when one gets all that one desires. Even if there is some lack, says Śaṅkara, one thinks, "It is enough." Or, as Hariharānanda puts it, to avoid injury from thorns, one only has to wear one pair of shoes—one doesn't need to cover the entire earth with leather!

The next *niyama*, austerity, *tapas*, is the ability to tolerate hunger and thirst as well as all the dualities of life (hot and cold, etc.), to avoid useless talk, and to perform fasts. Hariharānanda says that *yoga* requires one to tolerate sufferings of the body, endure hardships, and remain undisturbed by the lack of physical comfort. He cautions, however, that inflicting hardship on the body in the form of voluntary austerity and penance should be undertaken only for the expiation of sins and not otherwise.

Study, *svādhyāya*, refers to reading sacred scriptures whose subject matter is liberation,[64] and the commentators also include the repetition of *oṁ* here. Hariharānanda expands this to include devotional *mantras*. He notes that by practicing this *niyama*, one's desire for worldly objects diminishes, and one's taste for spiritual objects increases.

Vyāsa here defines the last item on Patañjali's list, devotion to God, *Īśvara-praṇidhāna*, which has already received a good deal of attention

(I.23ff), as offering all one's activities to *Īśvara*, the original teacher (I.26). In resonance with the *Gītā* II.47, where this is one of the primary teachings, such offerings must be done without desire for the fruit. Rāmānanda Sarasvatī quotes two devotional verses to illustrate this: "Whatever I do, whether with or without desire, whether auspicious or inauspicious, I do it to offer it all to you as directed by you" and "Let all my daily activities, in this life or future lives, whether in deed, thought or word, be dedicated in devotion to Kṛṣṇa." One might draw attention here to numerous verses in the *Gītā* where Kṛṣṇa makes statements such as, "Whatever you do, whatever you eat, whatever you sacrifice, whatever you give away, whatever austerities you perform, O Arjuna, do it as an offering to me" (IX.27). Vijñānabhikṣu, despite his own personal Vaiṣṇavite orientations, which are usually evident in his references when discussing the *Īśvara* element, displays the admirable Hindu penchant for conceptualizing *Īśvara* as manifest in a myriad of forms by quoting in his *Yogasāra* commentary on this *sūtra* a verse to Śiva: "The worship (*pūjā*) of *Īśvara* consists of firm devotion to Śiva by means of praise, remembrance, and worship, through one's words, thoughts, body and actions."[65]

Vyāsa sees fit to quote another verse in his commentary here: "While lying down, sitting, or wandering on the road, one who is focused within and whose net of doubts are weakened, sees the seeds of *saṁsāra* weakening. Such a person, always firm in *yoga*, becomes eternally free and partakes in immortality."[66] He adds that it is from devotion to *Īśvara* that this takes place—obstacles are removed and one is able to realize the innermost consciousness.

Vācaspati Miśra considers devotion to *Īśvara* to be the most important of all the *yamas* and *niyamas*. As we will see below, cultivating the *yamas* and *niyamas* produces beneficial results, but it is only from *Īśvara-praṇidhāna* that the ultimate result of *yoga*, namely, *samādhi*, is gained (II.45). Also, it is important to note again here, that although *Īśvara-praṇidhāna* was optional as a method of meditation in the first chapter, it is not optional here in the context of the *niyamas*. As with the requirements of *kriyā-yoga* at the beginning of this chapter, Patañjali is requiring a theistic practice at least at this point in his system.

वितर्कबाधने प्रतिपक्षभावनम् ॥ ३३ ॥

II.33 vitarka-bādhane pratipakṣa-bhāvanam

vitarka, negative thoughts; *bādhane*, on the harassing of; *pratipakṣa*, the opposite; *bhāvanam*, cultivation

Upon being harassed by negative thoughts, one should cultivate counteracting thoughts.

In the next verse, Patañjali defines "negative thoughts," *vitarkas*, as thoughts countering the *yamas* and *niyamas*. Thus they are thoughts directed toward violence, untruthfulness, stealing, sexual indulgence, accumulation, uncleanliness, discontentment, luxury, disinterest in scripture, and lack of devotion to *Īśvara* (or, contrarily, devotion to ungodly persons). What is reassuring about this *sūtra* is that Patañjali is essentially stating that "when one is harassed by negative thoughts . . ." In other words, negative thoughts *will* arise in the *citta*. How can they not? Negative thoughts are simply the cropping up of *saṁskāras* that are eternally recorded in the *citta* of past indulgences or immoral behaviors that all embodied beings have performed at some point just by being subject to the ever-changing *guṇas*. In even the best-tended gardens, weeds inevitably pop up from time to time. As indicated in the *Gītā*, "One in whom all desires flow by [but who remains undisturbed by them] like the ocean into which the rivers flow but which remains undisturbed, attains peace" (II.70) and "One who neither begrudges or hankers for the presence or absence of lucidity, activity or delusion [*sattva, rajas*, and *tamas*], but who remains as if indifferent, and is not disturbed by the *guṇas* thinking 'the *guṇas* alone are operating' . . . is said to have transcended the *guṇas*" (XIV.22–25). Desires will crop up; *rajas* and *tamas* will manifest in the *citta*. Hence, Patañjali implies in this *sūtra* that the task is not to berate oneself upon finding oneself contemplating a negative thought but to deal insightfully with such occurrences. This, according to Patañjali, means considering their consequences, *pratipakṣa-bhāvana*.

When one is tormented by perverse thoughts, says Vyāsa, such as, "I will kill this evildoer," "I will lie," "I will appropriate this person's wealth," "I will commit adultery with that person's wife," "I will take control over this other person's possessions,"[67] one should cultivate counterthoughts. One should rather think, "Burning in the fire of this world, I have taken shelter of *yoga* by committing myself to the welfare of all creatures; after having renounced such perverse thoughts, by again resorting to them, I am behaving like a dog who licks its vomit."[68] This practice of cultivating counterthoughts should be applied to negative thoughts that arise and obstruct the practice of the other limbs of *yoga* as well, says Vyāsa.

Actually, this *sūtra* is profound in its implications and provides a means of performing a type of mindfulness meditation for *yogīs*, whereby one consciously adjusts the types of *saṁskāras* one allows in one's *citta*. If we consider the *citta* to be essentially a warehouse of *saṁskāras*, negative thoughts are merely the activation of some of these previous *saṁskāras* lying in storage; *saṁskāras* are never destroyed, we recall (although they can be burnt by *yogic* practice). In other words, thoughts of violence, dishonesty, etc., arise because of the past practices of such things imprinted on one's *citta*. If, when the *yogī* becomes aware of a perverse thought arising in the *citta*, he or she makes a conscious effort to counter it by invoking a benevolent thought, then a new more *sāttvic* type of *saṁskāra* is planted in the *citta* warehouse. For example, if an aspiring *yogī* experiences feelings of dislike for a person, which is a type of *hiṁsā*, violence, resulting from ignorance (ignoring the true self of the person), then, upon becoming aware of this feeling, the *yogī* can make the effort to think of the person in a nonviolent fashion, perhaps viewing him or her as simply an embodied being victimized by the *guṇas* and *karma*, etc., and ultimately as a pure *puruṣa* soul. One might additionally consider how the world might be a better place to live if people could go beyond the superficial impressions and view others as fellow spiritual beings and so forth (a practice that has been referred to as a sort of autosuggestion[69]). The *yogī* might also ponder the negative consequences of perverse thinking, as outlined in the next *sūtra*. These newly cultivated *sāttvic* thoughts are then recorded in the *citta*.

The more one practices this type of *sāttvic* thinking in opposition to the *rājasic* and *tāmasic* thoughts that underpin inclinations toward violence, untruthfulness, and the other qualities opposite to the *yamas* and *niyamas*, the more the texture of the *citta* is transformed from *rājasic* and *tāmasic* to *sāttvic*. The more the *citta* becomes "*sāttvicized*" in this way, the less frequently *rājasic* and *tāmasic* thoughts will surface, and the less effort one will have to make to actually cultivate *sattva* (artificially, so to speak)—*sāttvic* thoughts will start to arise more naturally and spontaneously. As in a garden, the more one makes an effort to uproot weeds, the more the bed will eventually become a receptacle for fragrant flowers, which will then grow and reseed of their own accord until there is hardly any room for the weeds to surface. In other words, as *sattva* is cultivated in this way, the personality of the *yogī* becomes altered. Weeding, of course, can never be abandoned completely, and even the most saintly and accomplished *yogī* must be ever vigilant for old *rājasic* and *tāmasic saṁskāras* lying latent in the subconscious depths of the *citta*, like the latent seeds of dormant weeds.

वितर्का हिंसादयः कृतकारितानुमोदिता लोभक्रोधमोहपूर्वका
मृदुमध्याधिमात्रा दुःखाज्ञानानन्तफला इति प्रतिपक्षभावनम् ।। ३४ ।।

II.34 vitarkā hiṁsādayaḥ kṛta-kāritānumoditā lobha-krodha-moha-pūrvakā mṛdu-madhyādhi-mātrā duḥkhājñānānanta-phalā iti pratipakṣa-bhāvanam

vitarkāḥ, negative or perverse thoughts; *hiṁsā*, violence; *ādayaḥ*, etc.; *kṛta*, performed; *kārita*, caused to be done; *anumoditāḥ*, allowed; *lobha*, greed; *krodha*, anger; *moha*, illusion; *pūrvakāḥ*, preceded by; *mṛdu*, slight; *madhya*, medium; *adhi-mātrāḥ*, intense; *duḥkha*, suffering; *ajñāna*, ignorance; *ananta*, never-ending; *phalāḥ*, end results; *iti*, thus; *pratipakṣa*, the opposite; *bhāvanam*, cultivation

Negative thoughts are violence, etc. They may be [personally] performed, performed on one's behalf by another, or authorized by oneself; they may be triggered by greed, anger, or delusion; and they may be slight, moderate, or extreme in intensity. One should cultivate counteracting thoughts, namely, that the end results [of negative thoughts] are ongoing suffering and ignorance.

The *vitarkas* are the thoughts of violence, etc., contrary to the *yamas* and *niyamas* outlined in the previous commentary. Patañjali divides them into three categories: those one performs oneself, *kṛta*; those that one has others perform on one's behalf, *kārita*; and those that one approves of or authorizes in some way, *anumodita*. So, taking, along with the commentators, violence, *hiṁsā*, to exemplify the *yamas* and *niyamas* (but bearing in mind that this verse applies to all the other *yamas* and *niyamas*), killing an animal oneself would come under the first category, purchasing meat that has been killed by someone else is in the second category, and allowing meat consumption to occur in one's sphere of influence, even if one does not consume the meat oneself, would come under the third category. This seems to resonate with Manu, the primary composer of the regulations of *dharma* for Hindus in the ancient period: "The one who gives permission [to eat meat], the one who butchers, the one who slaughters, the one who buys and sells, the one who prepares it, the one who serves it, and the eater—they are all killers" (V.51).[70] The Buddha, too, made a similar statement: "Monks, one possessed of three qualities is put into Hell according to his deserts. What three? One who is himself a taker of life, one who encourages another to do the same, and one who approves thereof."[71]

Patañjali is being fairly specific here, says Bhoja Rāja, otherwise some dull wit (to use his term) may think that since the violence involved in killing is performed by someone else, then the consumer of meat avoids *karmic* responsibilities. Vijñānabhikṣu includes here even violence condoned in the scriptures (that animals can be killed and eaten under certain conditions, such as in the context of Vedic sacrifice), as does Hariharānanda, who rejects the idea that God has allowed certain types of animal consumption. The emergence of a vegetarian ethic such as that expressed here and in most post-Vedic Hinduism from the matriarchal culture of ritual slaughter inherent in the ancient Vedic sacrificial texts is an interesting phenomenon that I have examined elsewhere (Bryant 2006).

Each of these categories, continues Vyāsa, has been subdivided into three degrees of intensity by Patañjali: *mṛdu-madhya-adhimātrāḥ*, slight, moderate, or extreme. Additionally, they may be provoked in three ways: by greed, *lobha*, such as a person inflicting violence on animals out of lust for their meat or with an eye to profit from their skins; anger, *krodha*, such as a person lashing out violently upon being insulted by someone else; or illusion, *moha*, such as a person engaging in violence under the impression that it is his or her duty, or that it is religiously condoned (as in killing animals in a religious context, says Vijñānabhikṣu).

Since greed, anger, and delusion can underpin acts done oneself, on one's behalf, or authorized by oneself, and can be experienced in three degrees of intensity, there are twenty-seven divisions of violence noted by Patañjali in this *sūtra*. Characteristic with the penchant for categorization found in traditional Indic commentaries, Vyāsa trebles this number, by proposing that the intensity of greed, anger, and delusion can be mildly mild, moderately mild, and extremely mild; mildly moderate, moderately moderate, and extremely moderate; and mildly extreme, moderately extreme, and extremely extreme (probably with the set of subdivisions from I.21–22 in mind). This brings the possibilities up to eighty-one! Actually, continues Vyāsa, the possibilities are innumerable since there are other factors qualifying violence such as customary rules (which Vijñānabhikṣu exemplifies as the view that violence can be inflicted on fish but not animals) and other types of options (particular animals can be killed and eaten only on certain days), etc. All these multiple divisions pertain to each of the *yamas* and *niyamas*.

To oppose thoughts of this kind, one should cultivate counterthoughts—thoughts on the consequences of such activities, such as Patañjali's suggestion that violence leads to unlimited suffering and ignorance. The perpetrator of violence, says Vyāsa, first overpowers the strength of the victim (by binding it, says Vācaspati Miśra), then inflicts violence on it by weapons, and then takes its life. As a result of this, the perpetrator's own life forces are weakened in this life, and in the next life, he or she takes birth in hell,[72] or in a lower species of life, where, says Vijñānabhikṣu, the very same violence previously inflicted on other creatures is experienced by the perpetrator. Hence, Patañjali's statement that inflicting violence eventually brings suffering to the agent.

Ultimately, all creatures are parts of *Īśvara*, God, explains Vijñānabhikṣu, like sons to the father and sparks to the fire. Therefore, violence against others is violence against God. He quotes the *Gītā*: "Envious people act hatefully towards me [Kṛṣṇa] in their own and in others' bodies. I continually hurl such cruel hateful people, the lowest of mankind, into *saṁsāric* existence, into only the impure wombs of demons" (XVI.19).

Violent people live every moment as though dead, Vyāsa continues. Indeed, they may even crave death but are forced to live on because, by the law of *karma*, some of the fixed fruits of their activities have to be experienced in this life (for example, says Vijñānabhikṣu, a person may be tormented by a horrible prolonged disease as a *karmic* consequence). Even if a violent person experiences happiness in this life, notes Vyāsa, this is due to good *karmic* reaction accrued from simultaneously performing pious activities along with the impious ones in a past life. These good reactions balance out some of the bad *karmic* reaction from the violence being committed in the present (just as seeds of grain are sown along with seeds of grass, says Vijñānabhikṣu), but the negative *karma* will manifest in some other fashion—a person may experience a short life span, for example, or the seeds of violence being sown in this life may lie dormant until the next life. By the law of action and reaction, violence always eventually breeds suffering for the perpetrator, who has to personally experience the same violence he or she inflicted on other beings. It also breeds ignorance, the second consequence of perverse thoughts mentioned here by Patañjali. Vācaspati Miśra states in this regard that violence is the result of *tamas*, and perpetuating violence increases the *tamas*, ignorance, of the *citta*. Real knowledge is thus further covered over. One becomes less likely to ponder the reactions of one's violence or other harmful activities, and thus is less aware of the *karmic* consequences one is creating for oneself.

Reflecting on the undesirable consequences of negative thoughts in some of these ways, one should not allow the mind to contemplate them. Cultivating the opposite types of thoughts is the means to remove such perverse notions. Although the commentators have focused on violence for this discussion, since it has been presented as the basis of all the *yamas* and *niyamas*, Vyāsa makes it clear that the discussion here can be applied to thoughts that are contrary to all the other *yamas* and *niyamas* in turn. Also it seems important enough to reiterate, and aspiring *yogīs* might be relieved to do so, that Patañjali specified in the previous *sūtra* "when" one is afflicted by negative thoughts, not "if." Negative thoughts are nothing other than old *saṁskāras*, present in great abundance in the *cittas* of all embodied beings. They *will* surface until the *yogī* is very advanced and has burnt up the productive power of all latent seeds by practice. The task, then, is not to become despondent upon their periodic and inevitable emergence but to counter them as outlined here.

When negative thoughts are eliminated, powers accrue to the *yogī*. These are indicative of the *yogī*'s success in this regard and are the subject of the next *sūtras*.

अहिंसाप्रतिष्ठायां तत्सन्निधौ वैरत्यागः ।। ३५ ।।

II.35 ahiṁsā-pratiṣṭhāyām tat-sannidhau vaira-tyāgaḥ

ahiṁsā, nonviolence; *pratiṣṭhāyām*, upon the establishment; *tat*, his; *sannidhau*, in the presence; *vaira*, enmity; *tyāgaḥ*, giving up of

In the presence of one who is established in nonviolence, enmity is abandoned.

In the following section (II.35–45), Patañjali selects some of the boons that accrue to the *yogī* by following, *pratiṣṭhāyām*,[73] each of the ten *yamas* and *niyamas*. Vyāsa states that all living beings give up their enmity in the presence of one who is established in nonviolence. In other words, a saint exudes qualities that rub off on his or her associates. That is to say, the *yogī*'s *sāttvic* mind can pervade out, and *sāttvicize* the minds of other beings in the vicinity, countering their *rajas* and *tamas*, and stimulating their own *sāttvic* potentials. The commentators state that even natural enemies such as cat and mouse or mongoose and snake give up their enmity in the presence of the *yogī* who has fully renounced all thoughts of violence, due to being influenced by the *yogī*'s state of mind. One is reminded here of an episode in the hagiography of the fifteenth-century mystic Chaitanya Mahāprabhu, who caused the deer and tigers in the forest to dance and embrace each other upon hearing him recite the holy names of Kṛṣṇa.[74] Such accounts surface in numerous traditions: one might mention Saint Francis of Assisi, and his taming of the wild wolf; and the Moroccan Sufi woman saint, Rabi'a, who lived on a hill surrounded by wild animals[75]; and the furious elephant Nālāgiri who became quiet in the presence of the Buddha.[76]

According to Hariharānanda, perverse thoughts such as violence can take many subtle forms in the mind that are not always readily visible; these have to be exposed and rooted out through the force of meditation. Specifically, the fifth limb of *yoga*, fixing the mind, *dhāraṇā,* is essential for perfecting the *yamas* and *niyamas* such as non-violence. In this, Hariharānanda adds nuance to the view of some commentators who say that each limb of *yoga* has to be practiced first, before the next one can be undertaken. Of course, all the limbs must eventually be perfected, but *dhāraṇā* deepens the ability to practice the earlier limbs, in his view, and, indeed, it is through *dhāraṇā* and its successive limbs of *dhyāna*, pure concentration, and *samādhi*, meditative absorption, that the *yamas* and *niyamas* become faultless, and the *āsanas*, postures, perfected.

सत्यप्रतिष्ठायां क्रियाफलाश्रयत्वम् ॥ ३६ ॥

II.36 satya-pratiṣṭhāyāṁ kriyā-phalāśrayatvam

satya, truth; *pratiṣṭhāyām*, upon the establishment of; *kriyā*, activity, work; *phala*, fruits; *āśrayatvam*, the nature of being a support or basis

When one is established in truthfulness, one ensures the fruition of actions.

The commentators understand this *sūtra* as indicating that the words of a truthful person invariably bear fruit, *phala*. Their utterances are infallible. If the *yogī* who has perfected this *yama* says to someone, "Be virtuous," says Vyāsa, then the person will be virtuous. Vijñānabhikṣu qualifies this somewhat by stating that the *yogī* will utter the words "Be virtuous" only to one who is fit to be so. He adds that the *yogī* need merely think something pertaining to someone and it will come about. Hariharānanda also qualifies Vyāsa's comment by noting that *yogīs* do not make whimsical or fruitless pronouncements beyond the reach of their power, that is, their will. He understands the ability mentioned in this *sūtra*, like the one discussed in the previous *sūtra*, to be brought about by willpower. Truthfulness, *satya*, is cultivated by willpower—the determination never to tell a lie. This power of simple truth can sway the mind of the listener to act in accordance with the *yogī*'s words. When one meets a saintly person who is situated in truthfulness, one senses that, unlike all other people with whom one comes into contact, this person has no desire or inclination to exploit or manipulate others for personal interest. Such a person is qualified to act as a *guru*, and one can accordingly entrust oneself to his or her guidance.

Vācaspati Miśra has a slightly different take on this *sūtra*. For him, the actions, *kriyā*, referred to by Patañjali here refer to pious and impious activities, and their respective fruition means future births that are correspondingly desirable or undesirable. By ensuring the fruition of actions, *kriyā-phalāśrayatva*, he understands Patañjali as saying that the *yogī* who has perfected the *yama* of truthfulness has control over actions and, consequently, the fruits they bear in future births.

अस्तेयप्रतिष्ठायां सर्वरत्नोपस्थानम् ॥ ३७ ॥

II.37 asteya-pratiṣṭhāyāṁ sarva-ratnopasthānam

asteya, refrainment from stealing; *pratiṣṭhāyām*, upon the establishment of; *sarva*, all; *ratna*, jewels; *upasthānam*, approach, come into the presence of

When one is established in refrainment from stealing, all jewels manifest.

Vyāsa simply says, in regard to one following the *yama* of nonstealing, *asteya*, that jewels, *ratna*, approach the *yogī* from all directions. Vācaspati Miśra's only comment is, "This verse is easy!" and Vijñānabhikṣu and the other commentators offer nothing to explain this *sūtra*. Hariharānanda, however, offers some useful interpretations that save us from having to imagine jewels suddenly flying through the air toward the accomplished *yogī*. Established in nonstealing, a glow of detachment and indifference radiates from the face of the *yogī*. People are inspired by this to feel that this person is trustworthy and has absolute integrity; they thus feel honored to bestow their most valued things on such a *yogī*, confident that they will be put to the best possible selfless use. Hariharānanda takes *ratna*, jewel, to mean the best of every class of things. Thus, the pure-hearted *yogī* attracts the best of human beings and is offered the best of material things by those he or she inspires. R. S. Bhattacharya (1985, 153) takes the jewels to refer to noble-hearted people as well as useful things. Thus, noble-hearted people approach the *yogī* who is firmly fixed in honesty with a view of acquiring divine wisdom; likewise, useful things are offered to the *yogī* in service.

ब्रह्मचर्यप्रतिष्ठायां वीर्यलाभः ॥ ३८ ॥

II.38 brahmacarya-pratiṣṭhāyām vīrya-lābhaḥ

brahmacarya, celibacy; *pratiṣṭhāyām*, on the establishment of; *vīrya*, potency, power; *lābhaḥ*, the gain

Upon the establishment of celibacy, power is attained.

Vyāsa states that when celibacy, *brahmacarya*, is established, a *yogī* perfects his or her qualifications without obstruction. Established in celibacy, the *yogī* becomes capable of imparting knowledge to disciples. Otherwise, the words of wisdom of an incontinent person, says Hariharānanda, do not go deep into the mind of a disciple.

Vijñānabhikṣu understands the power, *vīrya*, Patañjali is referring to as the power of knowledge and action. Bhoja Rāja speaks of it as vigor in one's bodily organs and mind. Other commentators connect the power mentioned in this *sūtra* with the eight mystic powers that will be discussed in the next chapter. Hariharānanda, for example, says that celibacy prevents the loss of vitality, and thus *vīrya*, potency, is retained. This accumulates until it culminates in physical and spiritual power, including the mystic powers described below.

In *āyurvedic* physiology, *ojas* is a subtle vital energy or substance that forms the essence of all the seven bodily tissues (*dhātus*[77]), and, along with *prāṇa*, controls the life functions. It is the essential ingredient in vigor and potency, both physical and spiritual. When semen is dissipated by excessive orgasmic activity, the body and immune system are deprived of this vital resource and the individual becomes susceptible to psychosomatic ailments. *Brahmacarya*, celibacy, then, enhances potency. Hariharānanda adds that celibacy involves abstaining even from thoughts of objects of desire through a firm control of one's mind, as well as through a controlled diet and sleep; it cannot be attained if one indulges in too much sleep or food intake.

There are many stories of *yogīs* attaining tremendous powers by the practice of celibacy, some of which will be touched upon on the next chapter. Indeed, one does not even have to be a *yogī* to accrue the benefits of celibacy: In the *Ādi-parva* section of the *Mahābhārata*, the great Bhīṣma, grandfather to the opposing Pāṇḍava and Kaurava cousins, became the most powerful and invincible warrior of his time partly due to his unbreakable vow of celibacy. Once, his father, the great king Śantanu, fell in love with the beautiful daughter of the chief of the fishermen. Upon approaching the girl's father for her hand in marriage, the chief of the fisher community indicated that he would grant the king his daughter's hand only if the son born of their union would succeed Śantanu on the royal throne. The king declined, since Bhīṣma was his eldest son from a prior union with the goddess of the river Gaṅgā and thus the rightful heir, but he languished with his unfulfilled desire.

Upon learning of the reason for his father's moroseness, the noble Bhīṣma approached the fisher chief to ask him for his daughter's hand for his father, assuring him that he would allow the offspring of this union to supersede him to the throne. Still the chief of the fishing community demurred, stating that while he had no doubts about the inviolability of Bhīṣma's words, he did entertain doubts as to whether Bhīṣma's own progeny might one day agitate for the throne. Bhīṣma then uttered a vow in the presence of all that he would, from that day on, adopt a life of *brahmacarya*. Since his vow was unbreakable once made (even though it resulted in all kinds of intrigues when the two sons born of Śantanu's marriage to this second wife both died without leaving an heir to the throne), Bhīṣma was awarded the boon of dying at will. This boon was perhaps more technically the result of his following the *yama* of *satya*, truthfulness, since his word was inviolable, but his adoption of a life of *brahmacarya* enhanced his already semi-divine powers.

अपरिग्रहस्थैर्ये जन्मकथंतासंबोधः ॥ ३९ ॥

II.39 aparigraha-sthairye janma-kathantā-sambodhaḥ

aparigraha, refrainment from covetousness; *sthairye*, on the steadfastness, constancy; *janma*, birth; *kathantā*, the howness; *sambodhaḥ*, knowledge

When refrainment from covetousness becomes firmly established, knowledge of the whys and wherefores of births manifests.

On perfecting the *yama* of refrainment from covetousness, *aparigraha*, the knowledge of the circumstances of the *yogī*'s present birth as well as of previous and future births, *janma-kathantā*, is automatically revealed if the *yogī* desires it, according to Vyāsa and the commentators. The *yogī* knows exactly who he or she was in a previous birth, specifies Bhoja Rāja, what sort of a person in what sort of circumstance. The connection between cause and effect is hereby revealed, says Rāmānanda Sarasvatī—every type of birth, after all, whether human, animal, or celestial, is the fruit of previous activities, *karma*. The *yogī* is able to perceive precisely how the present birth is the consequence of previous activities, and how present activities will fructify in the form of a specific future birth. Again, the ability to access previous births surfaces frequently in Indic texts: The Buddha, for example, by marshaling "all the techniques of *dhyāna*, meditation" on the night of his ultimate enlightenment, was able to bring to mind all his previous births, according to his hagiography. "He remembered thousands of past lives, as if reliving them again, that 'I had been such and such a person at that time, and then, passing out of that life I had come to this other life' " (*Buddha-carita* XIV.2–3).

Bhoja Rāja elaborates here that refrainment from covetousness involves not coveting the means of enjoyment, and this includes the body, which is the mechanism of enjoyment. In normal life, due to desiring enjoyment, one's consciousness is directed outward and thus the type of knowledge mentioned in this *sūtra* does not reveal itself. In other words, when awareness is not dissipated externally, it can be channeled internally into one's *citta* where all the imprints of past life experiences are recorded. By accessing these *saṁskāras*, the *yogī* can gain awareness of the past lives in which they were recorded. Along the same lines, Hariharānanda states that delusion stemming from attachment to one's body obstructs knowledge of the past and future. When this is given up and one becomes conscious of the body as separate from the self, the body becomes a superfluous burden, and the power of clairvoyance, which means awareness that is not limited to the bodily organs of sight, etc., is developed.

One might imagine the *citta* as a lake, and *saṁskāras* as pebbles within it. When a lake is crystal clear, one can see the pebbles clearly and easily retrieve them. When the lake is choppy or murky, one cannot. Similarly, when the *sattva* potential of the *citta* is maximized, it is clear, and therefore its *saṁskāras*, including those of previous lives, can be more easily extracted. When *rajas* and *tamas* are prevalent, in contrast, it becomes choppy and murky, and even recent memories are difficult to bring to recollection.

R. S. Bhattacharya (1985, 149–51) takes the *janma-kathantā-sambodhaḥ* of this *sūtra* to refer not to knowledge of previous births arising in the mind of the *yogī* free of coveting, but to thoughts arising in the minds of people associated with the *yogī*. The *janma-kathantā* in his reading refers to people's curiosity about the circumstances of the *yogī*'s personal life. Specifically, impressed by the *yogī*'s attitude of *aparigraha*, refrainment, people wonder about the birth of the *yogī*. In other words, they wonder in awe how an embodied being can be free from attachment, etc.

The next few *sūtras* are directed toward the side effects generated by the perfection of the *niyamas*.

शौचात् स्वाङ्गजुगुप्सा परैरसंसर्गः ॥ ४० ॥

II.40 śaucāt svāṅga-jugupsā parair asaṁsargaḥ

śaucāt, from cleanliness; *svāṅga*, one's body; *jugupsā*, distaste; *paraiḥ*, with others; *asaṁsargaḥ*, cessation of union, intercourse, or contact

By cleanliness, one [develops] distaste for one's body and the cessation of contact with others.

Perceiving the defects of the body, says Vyāsa, one develops a distaste for it, *jugupsā*, keeps it clean, and becomes self-controlled. The *yogī* reflects on the nature of his or her own body, *svāṅga*, seeing that it is never clean no matter how much it is washed with water and cleansing agents; indeed, the *yogī* desires to free *puruṣa* from the body. So how, questions Vyāsa, could a *yogī* engage in intimate contact with the bodies of others, which might be all the more unclean?

By the practice of cleanliness, *śauca*, say the commentators, attraction to the opposite sex evaporates, as it does by the contemplation of the realities of the body. Cleansing the body essentially consists of wiping away sweat, urine, feces, mucus, and other discharges and substances which, in and of themselves, are not erotic but obnoxious. By meditating on the realities of the act of cleanliness, the *yogī* ceases to see the body as an erotic object. One is thus freed from the oppressive and ultimately disappointing pressures of erotic illusion and fantasy.

There is the story of a king who, becoming thirsty after hunting in the forest, approaches a secluded hermitage in quest of water. He is greeted by a beautiful but spiritually enlightened young maiden who had been raised as a fully enlightened *yoginī* by the resident sage of the hermitage. Overcome by desire for this beautiful maiden, the king propositions her. Deciding to enlighten the lusty king as to the realities of bodily lust, the maiden requests him to return within a month, at which time she will allow him to taste the nectar of her beauty. During this period, however, the maiden takes laxatives and purges, and collects all the resulting vomit, urine, feces, and other physical discharges in earthen pots. When the king returns after the stipulated period, he is greeted by the maiden, now haggard and wasted and a shadow of her previous self. Upon asking her what had become of her beauty, she presents the king with the earthen pots with their rancid contents and indicates that therein lay the juices of her beauty. She thus acts as the *guru* of the king, enlightening him as to the reality of the body, the foolishness of bodily identification, and the superficiality of bodily attraction.[78]

Along these lines, in this *sūtra*, Patañjali indicates that when one meditates on the act of cleanliness, and the reality of the body and its temporary and skin-deep beauty, one develops a distaste for it, *jugupsā*, and consequently for sensual contact with other bodies, *parair asaṁsargaḥ*. After all, one has to work rather hard to present the body as an erotic and enticing object—cleaning it carefully; decorating it with makeup, cosmetics, and fashionable clothing; pruning its outgrowths of hair; and overpowering its natural odors with artificial scents. Even then, the body can at any moment emit embarrassing odors or noises beyond one's control if one is not attentive, and a romantic moment can be quickly dispelled if one unexpectedly is impelled to vomit or is suddenly overcome by an irrepressible onset of diarrhea or gas. The *yogī* sees through the hype and illusoriness of bodily embellishment and uses the act of cleanliness to meditate on the reality of the physical body, which, from this perspective, can be seen as a bag of obnoxious substances. Seeing bodily reality in this way, the *yogī* ceases to see other bodies as erotic objects and thus ceases fantasizing about sexually enjoying or exploiting others.

This, of course, does not preclude appreciating the body in nonerotic ways—as a vehicle of enlightenment or a temple of God, for example. Hariharānanda notes that animals express their love for other animals by licking their bodies. Indeed, just as animals are aroused by sniffing each other's excrement, which most humans would consider to be unclean or distasteful, humans, in turn, engage in other types of expressions of sensual bodily intimacy, which, in parallel fashion, are seen by the *yogī* as unclean and distasteful. The *yogī* conveys love for other beings through compassion, friendliness, spiritual exchanges, and other expressions that rise above physical sensuality.

As an aside, there are nonmainstream radical ascetics who use bodily discharges as part of their practice. Some extreme Śaivite groups, for example, smear themselves with taboo substances and meditate in cremation grounds as catalysts in transcending bodily identification. While this is by no means a normative or common Hindu practice, it can nonetheless constitute a serious *yogic* practice if performed with the right intent. After all, ash from human corpses and bodily fluids are ultimately simply transformation of *prakṛti*: The *Gītā* (VI.8) informs us that the enlightened sage sees everything—"whether it be a stone, pebble or gold"—as the same. From an ultimate, metaphysical perspective, what is the difference between feces and fragrant or precious substances if they are all ultimately merely transformations of the *guṇas* of *prakṛti*? By means of such extreme practices, the practitioner strives to rise above the dualities of tastefulness and distastefulness on the sensual level. Additionally, upon being subject to the scorn and abuse that such practices might engender from society, the practitioner is called upon to transcend the dualities of honor and dishonor on a psychological level.

In the *Bhāgavata Purāṇa* (V.9.1–11), afraid of getting attached to anyone or anything—his attachment to a deer in a past life having caused him to undergo two further births (see the commentary to III.6 for the story)—the erstwhile king Bharata behaved like a dullard, dressed in a filthy rag, and never washed his body, such that people abused him. Yet, immersed internally in full awareness of his real self as *puruṣa* despite his ragged appearance without, he was "like a jewel covered by dust." His father too, the great king Ṛṣabha, an incarnation of Viṣṇu himself, when the time came to renounce his kingdom, wandered around naked with disheveled hair like a madman, such that ignorant people passed urine on him, spat at him, and threw stones and feces at him (*Bhāgavata* V.5.1ff).

Again, such practices are by no means mainstream in Yoga traditions, but they are certainly theologically defensible and, by virtue of their practitioners' willingness to abandon the most basic civilized notions of personal behavior in their intense quest for truth, deserve respect when undertaken with the true goals of *yoga* in mind. Patañjali is not recommending such practices here—on the contrary, he is promoting cleanliness as an indispensable limb of *yoga*—but a similar type of meditation on the realities of the constituents of the body underpins the intent of this *sūtra*.

सत्त्वशुद्धिसौमनस्यैकाग्र्येन्द्रियजयात्मदर्शनयोग्यत्वानि च ॥ ४१ ॥

II.41 sattva-śuddhi-saumanasyaikāgryendriya-jayātma-darśana-yogyatvāni ca

sattva, the *guṇa* of *sattva*; *śuddhi*, purification;
saumanasya, cheerfulness; *ekāgrya*, one-pointedness; *indriya*, senses;
jaya, control; *ātma*, self; *darśana*, direct seeing;
yogyatvāni, qualification, fitness; *ca*, and

Upon the purification of the mind, [one attains] cheerfulness, one-pointedness, sense control, and fitness to perceive the self.

Sattva, as used in the context of this *sūtra*, is another term for *buddhi*, intelligence, since the constitution of *buddhi* is primarily *sattva*.[79] The previous *sūtra* dealt with the boons accruing from cleanliness of the body; Patañjali here deals with the results ensuing from purification, or cleanliness of the mind. Vyāsa reads a chronological sequence to the qualities listed by Patañjali: From cleanliness, *śuddhi*, the mind is purified, that is, becomes *sattvīc*; from purification of the mind, cheerfulness, *saumanasya*, a by-product of *sattva*, arises; from this, one-pointedness, *ekāgrya*, ensues; and this, in turn, leads to sense control, *indriya-jaya* (when the mind is pure and focused, the senses are automatically under control). Sense control causes *rajas* and *tamas* to be subjugated and enhances the *sattva* of the mind, and a *sāttvic* mind qualifies the *yogī* to become eligible to perceive the *ātman*. All this is attained by cleanliness of the mind, says Vyāsa.

Hariharānanda says that cheerfulness or mental bliss arises when the mind has given up the obstacles of arrogance, pride, and attachment, and becomes aloof toward the body and material possessions. This feeling of happiness, which is inherent in the *sāttvic* potential of the mind, is necessary for mental one-pointedness, he adds, which in turn is a prerequisite for realizing the *ātman*.

संतोषाद् अनुत्तमः सुखलाभः ॥ ४२ ॥
II.42 santoṣād anuttamaḥ sukha-lābhaḥ

santoṣāt, from contentment; *anuttamaḥ*, the highest;
sukha, happiness; *lābhaḥ*, the attainment
From contentment, the highest happiness is attained.

Vyāsa limits his comments here to quoting a verse: "Whatever happiness there may be in enjoyment in this world, and whatever greater happiness there may be in the celestial world, they do not amount to one sixteenth of the happiness attained from the cessation of desire."[80] Vijñānabhikṣu reminds us of a similar verse from the *Taittirīya Upaniṣad* (II.8), quoted fully in II.5 of this commentary, that the bliss of *Brahman* is countless times greater than that experienced by the most fortunate of embodied beings. He explains that when hankering is removed, the *citta* becomes content, *santoṣa*, as indicated in this *sūtra*. *Sattva* thus becomes undisturbed, and the highest happiness, *anuttama-sukha*, which is inherent in the nature of *sattva*, manifests spontaneously. At other times, the innate happiness of *sattva* is covered by *tamas*. This *sāttvic* happiness does not depend on external objects, which are vulnerable and fleeting, but is inherent in the mind when it is tranquil and contented.

कायेन्द्रियसिद्धिरशुद्धिक्षयात् तपसः ॥ ४३ ॥

II.43 kāyendriya-siddhir aśuddhi-kṣayāt tapasaḥ

kāya, the body; *indriya*, senses; *siddhiḥ*, perfection; *aśuddhi*, impurities; *kṣayāt*, from the removal; *tapasaḥ*, from austerity

From austerity, on account of the removal of impurities, the perfection of the senses and body manifests.

As early as the Vedic Brāhmaṇa texts, *tapas* has been recognized as a vital form of preparatory ascetic purification to be undertaken by the sponsor of the Vedic sacrifice, the *yajamāna*,[81] and has remained a fundamental ingredient of Indic soteriological traditions. As austerity is practiced, says Vyāsa, the impure covering of dirt, *aśuddhi* (*tamas* and *rajas*), is destroyed, and as this happens, the *siddhis*, or mystical powers of the body such as clairvoyance and clairaudience, manifest. The commentators thus take Patañjali's perfection of the body, *kāyendriya-siddhi*, as a reference to the various mystical powers, *siddhis*, that are the by-product of *yoga*, which will be discussed in the next chapter. Bhoja Rāja and Rāmānanda Sarasvatī take Patañjali's impurities here to refer to the *kleśas*. Hariharānanda understands them to be subjection to the limitations of the body, such as hunger, thirst, and other cravings. According to him, by the performance of austerities in the form of sleep control, abstention from food, retention of the vital energies of the body (celibacy), etc., and by the practice of *prāṇāyāma* and *āsana*, one can overcome these limitations by sheer willpower (which is how he approaches all the *yamas* and *niyamas*), and this leads to the manifestation of the *siddhis*.

Hariharānanda notes that *jñānīs*, those following the path of *jñāna-yoga*, the *yoga* of knowledge, generally do not develop these *siddhis* because they cultivate renunciation and discrimination rather than austerity. *Siddhis*, then, are specifically the by-product of *tapas*, in this view. Jñānis are unlikely to be interested in such attainments anyway, continues Hariharānanda, and neither are the *yogīs*, who use them, if at all, only to further their spiritual goals.

स्वाध्यायाद् इष्टदेवतासंप्रयोगः ॥ ४४ ॥

II.44 svādhyāyād iṣṭa-devatā-samprayogaḥ

svādhyāyāt, study of scripture; *iṣṭa*, desired, preferred; *devatā*, with the deity; *samprayogaḥ*, connection

From study [of scripture], a connection with one's deity of choice is established.

Svādhyāya literally means self-study, but it more commonly refers to the study of sacred texts (in a sense the two meanings overlap, since sacred texts typically teach about the self). In the earlier Vedic period it involved recitation of the sacred Vedic texts by the student until they were memorized, thus providing the basis for the later tradition to construe the term as referring to both study of sacred texts and the recitation of sacred syllables. From study, according to Vyāsa and the other commentators, the *ṛṣi* sages, celestial beings, and perfected *siddhas* become visible, and they assist in the *yogī*'s work. The commentators take this at face value: Whatever deity the *yogī* wishes to see, says Vijñānabhikṣu, will appear.

Vyāsa has indicated that *svādhyāya* includes the recitation of *oṁ*, in II.32, and the commentators reiterate here that the recitation of *mantras* is one of the ingredients of *svādhyāya*. Hariharānanda makes the interesting observation that ordinarily, during *japa*, the repetition of *mantras*, thought does not remain fixed on the meaning of the *mantra*, and the practitioner typically repeats the *mantra* aimlessly while the mind is roaming here and there. When *svādhyāya* is established, however, the *mantra* and the deity it represents remain uninterruptedly present in the mind. He states that deities invoked with such ardor and faith are sure to appear before their devotees. This does not occur when the mind is sometimes fixed on the *mantra* and sometimes distracted.

Scriptures typically present themselves as encapsulating the life and teachings of divine or saintly beings. Patañjali can be read as saying here that by reading scriptures, one becomes spontaneously attracted to a particular *iṣṭa-devatā*, a manifestation of divinity. *Iṣṭa* means desired or preferred, and *devatā* means deity, so *iṣṭa-devatā* refers to one's deity of choice. By reading the various scriptures of the world, the aspiring *yogī* at some point starts to become partial to or especially attracted to a particular spiritual persona—whether Kṛṣṇa, Viṣṇu, Śiva, Devī, Jesus Christ, Buddha, or any other divine figure, or empowered sage. Such a personage becomes one's *iṣṭa-devatā*, and one worships God in the form of or through this *devatā*. This involves the *japa* recitation of the *mantra* associated with this form of divinity.

In my view, it is most unlikely that Patañjali is using the term *devatā* in its older sense of the minor Vedic deities who are propitiated in Vedic rituals and later derivative Hindu *pūjās* for worldly boons. The notion of *vairāgya* has already been thoroughly established as a prerequisite for *yoga* (I.12–16), and the *yogī* has long been disinterested in the enticements of Vedic ritualism, *ānuśravika*, in I.15. Indeed, we will see in Vyāsa's commentary in III.51 that the minor gods try to distract the *yogī* from the path and lure him or her back to worldly sensory stimulation. In the hymns of the Vedic period, the gods, *devatā*, are solicited most especially for victory over enemies, for cows, and for offspring. In the Purāṇic period they are propitiated for *siddhi* powers and other material boons.[82] Their jurisdiction is exclusively over the workings of *prakṛti* and, consequently, to be avoided by *yogīs* as bad association, so to speak. Given Patañjali's goals, *iṣṭa-devatā* here must therefore refer to the forms of *Īśvara*, as it is used in theistic texts,[83] rather than some minor deity.

This correlation of forms of *Īśvara* with *iṣṭa-devatā* is further supported by Vyāsa and the commentators considering *svādhyāya* to include the recitation of *oṁ*. Patañjali has indicated that *oṁ* is *Īśvara* manifest as sound, and that meditation on *Īśvara* is to be performed by *japa* of *oṁ*. Moreover, one must recite this *tad-artha-bhāvanam*, bearing its meaning in mind. Therefore, if by *svādhyāya* one encounters one's *iṣṭa-devatā* as indicated in this *sūtra*, and *svādhyāya* entails reciting *oṁ* while meditating on *Īśvara*, then the *iṣṭa-devatā* one encounters from this process must be none other than a form of *Īśvara* and not some minor Vedic deity. Therefore, Patañjali must be using *devatā* to refer to the established forms of *Īśvara* evidenced on the mainstream theistic landscape of his time and not the secondary gods (with a lowercase *g*) whose jurisdiction is the bestowing of temporary material boons in which the *yogī* has long lost interest. Therefore, by reciting *oṁ* and studying the *Īśvara* scriptures, one becomes attracted to a particular form of *Īśvara*. One might suppose that this process of study in some cases involves the reactivation of *saṁskāras* from past lives, when one might have already developed a devotional relationship with a particular form of divinity, which becomes spontaneously reactivated in a subsequent life upon encountering this form in some scriptural source.[84]

One might also note here that typically in Hinduism, theistic meditation on *Īśvara* is performed by reciting the name of one's *iṣṭa-devatā* in the form of *japa*, usually appending this name onto the generic and long-revered syllable *oṁ*. As noted, the *mantras* most likely to be encountered in Hindu meditative practices are *oṁ namo Nārāyaṇāya*, the most commonly recited Viṣṇu-based *mantra*; *oṁ namaḥ Śivāya*, the Śaivite equivalent; *oṁ namo bhagavate Vāsudevāya*, the more classical Kṛṣṇa *mantra*; and the by now ubiquitous Kṛṣṇa *mantra* popularized by A. C. Bhaktivedānta Swāmi: *Hare Kṛṣṇa, Hare Kṛṣṇa, Kṛṣṇa Kṛṣṇa, Hare Hare, Hare Rāma, Hare Rāma, Rāma Rāma, Hare Hare*.

An interesting question, broached earlier, can again be raised at this point as to whether anything can be inferred about the identification of Patañjali's own *iṣṭa-devatā*. My own view is that he must necessarily have been either a Vaiṣṇava—follower of Viṣṇu/Kṛṣṇa—or a Śaivite—follower of Śiva. Of the six schools of traditional thought that stem from this period, four—Nyāya, Vaiśeṣika, Yoga, and Vedānta—were theistic and Sāṅkhya had both theistic and nontheistic variants.[85] While the sectarian affiliations of the reputed founders of these theistic schools cannot be determined with certainty, the overall later Nyāya Vaiśeṣika tradition seems to have been Śaivite,[86] and the Vedānta, including Śaṅkara, Vaiṣṇava. Patañjali, like the authors of the root texts of other theistic schools, is not specific about the persona of *Īśvara*, God. Certainly, if we accept the consensus dating Patañjali in the second and third centuries, Vaiṣṇava and Śaiva theisms had long emerged as prominent, if not dominant, religious expressions around the subcontinent. It is thus probable that Patañjali was associated with one of these traditions. The Vaiṣṇavite *Gītā*, according to most dating estimates, and the theistic Upaniṣads such as the Śaivite *Śvetāśvatara* certainly had been around for several centuries, and the massive Purāṇic corpus, which focused primarily on these two streams of devotional religiosity stemming from Viṣṇu and Śiva, was well on its way to its final state of compilation sometime during the Gupta period within which Patañjali penned his treatise.

From a close study of the *sūtras*, it is clear that Patañjali is not just a *yogī* but also an astute intellectual,[87] and thus it seems impossible that he was unfamiliar with such sources. As we see from this *sūtra*, he not only stipulates the practice of *svādhyāya* but also states that from such study one connects with one's *iṣṭa-devatā*, deity of preference. This suggests that Patañjali was not only well versed scripturally, but was himself oriented toward a specific deity of preference. As has been seen throughout the text, Patañjali accepts and promotes the notion of *Īśvara*, God, a category which, given the context of the time, had long been associated with Viṣṇu and Śiva by their respective devotees (and, later, with *Īśvarī*, by the goddess tradition too[88]). A Patañjali with Vaiṣṇava or Śaivite orientations is thus not a frivolous consideration. It is curious that none of the seminal texts of the four theistic philosophical schools identifies *Īśvara*, but it is unlikely that this indicates a time before sectarian quibbling became more pronounced, a time when theological dogma was less important, given the fairly pronounced sectarian tone of the *Gītā* and, indeed, but to a lesser extent, of the *Śvetāśvatara Upaniṣad* (and of course of the Purāṇic corpus that was under compilation by Patañjali's time).

Of course, nothing prevents Patañjali from favoring an inclusivism, which has long been noted as a characteristic of Hindu theism, and identifying *Īśvara* with both Viṣṇu and Śiva in different contexts. Vācaspati Miśra, for example, who identified Viṣṇu as *Īśvara* above, nonetheless speaks of Śiva as *Īśvara* elsewhere in the *sūtras*, with his trademark catholicism.[89] Hindu devotion is typically not exclusivistic; it tends toward inclusivism of a hierarchical nature, an inclusivistic sectarianism: Vaiṣṇava texts, while accepting the multiplicity of other divine manifestations, subordinate them under Viṣṇu, as do the Śaiva texts under Śiva (for example, *Gītā* IX.23). Despite what sometimes appears to be the partisan nature of the texts associated with one or the other of these two Supreme Beings, both accept and indeed extol the transcendent and absolute nature of the other, and of the Goddess, Devī, too, merely affirming that the other deity is to be considered a derivative or secondary manifestation of their respective deity, or, in the case of Devī, the *śakti*, or power of the male divinity. Monotheism, if the term is to be applied to the Purāṇic tradition, needs to be understood in the context of a Supreme Being, whether understood as Viṣṇu, Śiva, or Devī, who can manifest himself or herself into other Supreme Beings (albeit all of them secondary to the original godhead).[90]

Thus, in the *Bhāgavata*, Viṣṇu, in addition to being able to manifest unlimited other identical Viṣṇu forms (e.g., X.13), manifests himself in the form of Śiva for a specific function—to perform the task of destruction at the end of the universe (X.71.8); and into the goddess Devī or Śakti for another function—to manifest the actual stuff of the universe, *prakṛti*, and perform other tasks such as cover the souls with illusion, in her capacity of *māyā*.

In any event, such hierarchical inclusivism aside, we find in this *sūtra* the notion of *iṣṭa-devatā*. Since, as we have seen, *svādhyāya* is mandatory as an ingredient of *kriyā-yoga* and as a *niyama*, we can conclude that all *yogīs* are expected to have an *iṣṭa-devatā* for the practice of *yoga*. By his own prescription, therefore, Patañjali would have been oriented toward one specific deity. Given his focus on *Īśvara* (rather than some lesser *deva*[91]) throughout the *sūtras*, and the fact that the category of *Īśvara* on the religious landscape of his time was associated with Śiva and Viṣṇu, it seems reasonable to conclude that Patañjali would in all likelihood have been either a Śaivite or Vaiṣṇavite.

I have considered this issue in whatever depth is allowed by the available data elsewhere, comparing Patañjali's scanty theology of *Īśvara* with those of the Vaiṣṇava *Gītā* and Śaivite *Śvetāśvatara* (Bryant 2005). I will merely note here that, despite the paucity of explicit data, the strongest evidence for a Vaiṣṇava orientation is the fact that Patañjali himself is considered an incarnation of Viṣṇu's carrier, Śeṣa. Had he been a Śaivite, it is a priori likely that the traditions stemming from him would have preserved a mythology of him being an incarnation of, say, Nandi, Śiva's bull, or some other associate. Moreover, as I have already noted, the Yoga tradition has associated the primary commentator, Vyāsa (circa fourth to fifth century), with the renowned sage Vyāsa of *Mahābhārata* and Purāṇic lore, grandfather of the Pāṇḍavas—who is embedded in Vaiṣṇava contexts and considered a manifestation of Nārāyāṇa/Viṣṇu,[92] which is relevant here for the same reasons (all the more so if those who posit the *Vyāsa-bhāṣya* to have been written by Patañjali himself are correct), and Vyāsa implicitly refers to Kṛṣṇa as *Īśvara* in, for example, his commentary on I.25.

In terms of the *sūtras* themselves, if we accept the commentarial correlation of Patañjali's *kriyā-yoga* with the *Gītā*'s devotionalized *karma-yoga*, a practice most associated with the latter text—which seems reasonable given the common etymology of the two terms from the root *kṛ*, as well as the action-based context of *kriyā-yoga*—then one might have further grounds to suggest a closer connection with the *Gītā*. Other than this, Patañjali's notion of *Īśvara* teaching the ancients raises obvious associations with Kṛṣṇa's assertion in the *Gītā* that he comes every age to reestablish *dharma*, etc., and is read this way by the commentarial tradition. Finally, one might also note that the *Gītā*'s usages of the three types of *puruṣas* (XV.16–18) match those of Patañjali's reference to *Īśvara* as a special *puruṣa* in I.23.[93] In short, while any and all of these assertions can be easily problematized, we can at least say that Patañjali's *iṣṭa-deva* must have been either Viṣṇu or Śiva, with the scanty evidence perhaps favoring the former.

One cannot make too much of this, since, while the Viṣṇu-related evidence might have a few snippets more with which to recommend itself, the question is theoretical and one cannot ignore the fact that Patañjali chose not to proclaim who his *iṣṭa-devatā* is. I prefer to imagine a Patañjali who, while himself a devotee, was too sophisticated a thinker to overly sectarianize the theistic element in the *sūtras* and thereby risk alienating the sensitivities of those dedicated to other conceptualizations of *Īśvara*, or, for that matter, of those devoid of any devotional inclinations. Indeed, while clearly guiding his readers toward a theistic orientation, and while he must have been either a Vaiṣṇava or a Śaivite given the *Īśvara-vāda* options of the second and third centuries, Patañjali is not actually even insistent in his promotion of the theistic element itself in the higher practices of *yoga*. He has thus articulated a more universal, or at least universally adaptable practice pertaining to plumbing the most profound depths of human consciousness that can be appropriated by any number of sacred as well as secular belief systems. That his teachings continue to be so appropriated even in the twenty-first-century West might point to his foresight in this regard.

समाधिसिद्धिरीश्वरप्रणिधानात् ॥ ४५ ॥
II.45 samādhi-siddhir īśvara-praṇidhānāt

samādhi, ultimate meditative state; *siddhiḥ*, perfection; *īśvara*, the Lord, God; *praṇidhānāt*, from submission, surrender
From submission to God comes the perfection of *samādhi*.

Of all the boons noted in the *sūtras* as accruing from the observance of the *yamas* and *niyamas*, it is only from *Īśvara-praṇidhāna* that *samādhi*, the actual and absolute goal of *yoga*, is attained. The other boons are all attainments still bound by the realm of *prakṛti*: mystic powers, knowledge of past births, jewels, etc. These other boons are thus temporary blessings; only the boon accruing from the *niyama* of *Īśvara-praṇidhāna* is ultimate. This fact in and of itself is significant.

In the first *sūtra* of this chapter, Patañjali includes *Īśvara-praṇidhāna* as a mandatory ingredient of *kriyā-yoga*, and we have seen (II.32) that *Īśvara-praṇidhāna* is a mandatory part of *aṣṭāṅga-yoga* as well. Although Patañjali does not mandate that the *yogī* mediate on *Īśvara* in the *samādhi* section of the first chapter, he certainly dedicates far more attention to *Īśvara* than any other meditative alternative. Those six *sūtras* when coupled with this *sūtra* suggest that Patañjali is promoting *Īśvara* as the best object of meditation. Granted, he allows that one can meditate on any object and attain the goal of *yoga* (I.39), but only one object out of the universe of possible objects can, in addition to serving as a meditational prop for the mind, intervene and bypass or at least accelerate the normal process of practice by bestowing *samādhi* on the practitioner as an act of grace. That object is *Īśvara*. One thus gets two for the price of one, so to speak. What advantage, from this perspective, could there be in opting for some other object of meditation that cannot speed up or even bypass the process? It is hard to avoid the fact that Patañjali is promoting a theistic system, albeit in a discreet and nondogmatic fashion, and the commentarial tradition certainly reads it in this way. This notion of receiving a vision of the self as an act of grace is an ancient one. The *Kaṭha Upaniṣad* states: "By the grace of the creator one perceives the glory of the *ātman*" (II.20); as does the *Śvetāśvatara* (III.20).

Patañjali here indicates that *samādhi* is perfected in the *yogī* who has dedicated everything to God. By such dedication, the *yogī* knows all he or she desires to know, says Vyāsa, whether it pertains to other places, other times, or other bodies. Here, Vyāsa refers to the *siddhi* of omniscience (discussed in *sūtra* III.50ff).

This *sūtra* does not mean that the other seven limbs of *yoga* are redundant, say the commentators. Whether one's object of concentration is *Īśvara* or some other object, one still needs to practice the limbs of *yoga*; *samādhi*, as full and undistracted meditation, presupposes all the other limbs. According to Vācaspati Miśra and Rāmānanda Sarasvatī, the other seven limbs of *yoga* help the *yogī* to develop the requisite mental state that allows complete devotion to *Īśvara*. Vijñānabhikṣu puts it differently: One can say either that by mastering the other limbs of *yoga* by the grace of *Īśvara, samādhi* is born, or that the other limbs bring about *samādhi* by the grace of *Īśvara* but do not have this power themselves. Either way, surrender to *Īśvara* is indispensable for the perfection of *yoga*, and the *yogī* cultivates all the limbs of *yoga* but directs them toward God. Bhoja Rāja states that success is attained in this way because *Īśvara*, being pleased, removes the *kleśa* obstacles and awakens *samādhi*, and other commentators also speak of grace in this connection.

Rāmānanda Sarasvatī states that devotion to *Īśvara* has a different object from *yoga*, the goal of which is realization of *puruṣa*, and thus can be considered to be an additional limb of *yoga*. In this he resonates with certain theistic traditions of the Purāṇas, as exemplified in the most important of the Purāṇas, the *Bhāgavata*: Realization of one's personal *puruṣa* is a secondary or even irrelevant by-product of devotion to God, *Īśvara*. The *bhakta*, or devotee, wishes to bathe in the bliss of God's, the supreme *puruṣa*'s, presence rather than in that of his or her own personal *puruṣa*, and is often disinterested in self-realization: The attainment of God realization is the goal. (The *gopīs* of the *Bhāgavata*, for example, had no interest in self-knowledge; they were simply crazed in their love for Kṛṣṇa.[94]) Patañjali's focus in his text, of course, is the individual *puruṣa*, but the *Īśvara* element remains a tantalizing presence throughout, and he does not inform us what he considers to be the relationship between the liberated *puruṣas* and the special *puruṣa* that is *Īśvara* in the liberated state. While one cannot randomly project sectarian Purāṇic theologies onto the *sūtras*, one also cannot extricate and immunize Patañjali's *Īśvara* from the theological landscape of his time. We have stressed that, in our view, this greater theistic landscape cannot be avoided in considering how Patañjali envisioned *Īśvara*.

Rāmānanda Sarasvatī reiterates that, although one has an option, devotion to *Īśvara* hastens the attainment of *samādhi*: If one lacks faith in *Īśvara, samādhi* remains remote, but if one's *yoga* is permeated with the nectar of devotion, it is very near. One is reminded of Arjuna's question to Kṛṣṇa in the *Gītā* (XII.1), as to which *yogīs* are the best—those who are devotees and continually worship Kṛṣṇa as a personal object of devotion, or those who follow the *akṣara-avyakta* path, literally, the imperishable unmanifest path, which most commentators take to be a reference to the quest for the individual soul.[95] Kṛṣṇa states that although the followers of the latter path also attain him, such a path is difficult and troublesome (XII.3–5), but one who is always absorbed in him personally with faith and devotion is considered the best *yogī* (XII.2). As in the *Gītā*, then, in the *sūtras*, Patañjali subtly indicates that devotion to *Īśvara* is the best and safest path for the aspiring *yogī* dedicated to self-realization.

One might note here that although Patañjali is promoting a theistic practice, he does not develop a psychology or methodology of *bhakti*, devotion, other than the recitation of *oṁ* with awareness of its meaning (I.28). This is not his project in this text. The task he has set before him in these *sūtras* is a discussion of *yoga* in the context of the psychology of mind and the attainment of *puruṣa*. Different traditions in the Hindu intellectual tradition focus on specific areas of knowledge but often presuppose awareness of traditions that are dedicated to other systems of knowledge. While there may be disagreement on specific points and different traditions may focus on different aspects of human existence, these systems generally accept the overall validity of other bodies of orthodox knowledge where they do not contradict their own. Thus, in Patañjali's time, a variety of traditions specifically occupying themselves with theologies and methods of *Īśvara-praṇidhāna*, more commonly known as *bhakti*, would have long gained wide currency. Such traditions were already developing sophisticated and extensive theologies, so one might infer that Patañjali, albeit a theist himself, given the growing availability of *Īśvara*-centered theologies saw rather a need to articulate and contribute a more specific and focused psychology and theology of *puruṣa* in its relationship with *citta*. In other words, one might speculate that he did not focus extensively on *Īśvara* because this dimension of metaphysical enquiry had already been amply covered elsewhere and thus Patañjali could direct his disciples to already existing systems in that particular area of spirituality.

The streams of devotion most dominantly associated with *Īśvara* on the widest scale across the Indian subcontinent over the last two and a half millennia have been the Viṣṇu- and Śiva-centered traditions. The Viṣṇu traditions have been the most dominant in literary circles, expressed on a popular level in the two great epics of India, the *Mahābhārata* and the *Rāmāyaṇa*; on a more theological but still popular level, in the Purāṇas, especially the *Bhāgavata* (and *Viṣṇu*) Purāṇas; and on a more philosophical level in the *Bhagavad Gītā* and in the most influential stream of Indian philosophy, the Vedānta commentarial tradition. But *bhakti* to other aspects of divinity, especially the great Lord Śiva, as well as various forms of Goddess worship, pervades all the Purāṇas. The Śiva traditions, although not producing epics of the stature of the *Rāmāyaṇa* and the *Mahābhārata* (in which Śiva is an important presence), or influencing philosophical discourse to the extent that the Vaiṣṇava Vedānta tradition did (although the Nyāya Vaiśeṣika tradition was to become primarily Śaivite), nonetheless developed sophisticated Śiva-centered theologies and primary Purāṇas such as the *Śiva* and *Skandha*. The Goddess, too, has a Purāṇa, the *Devī Bhāgavata* (although this is likely a later compilation), and Goddess-based *śākta* traditions, while less mainstream in terms of the high or classical literary traditions, have also contributed much to the intellectual and theological history of the Indic traditions, especially on a more grassroots level. In any event, to all intents and purposes, popular Hinduism all across India today is essentially an expression of the various forms and traditions of *Īśvara-praṇidhāna* as expressed in these *bhakti* traditions.

And it is from this vast array of *Īśvara-praṇidhāna* practices that *samādhi*, as variously conceived in the myriad and multifaceted sectarian traditions of India, is most commonly attained.

We must note before considering the next limb of *yoga* that Patañjali dedicated sixteen *sūtras* to the *yamas* and *niyamas* (II.30–45), almost a tenth of the entire text, far more than he dedicates to any limb other than *samādhi*. They are a crucial and indispensable prerequisite of *yoga*.

स्थिरसुखम् आसनम् ॥ ४६ ॥

II.46 sthira-sukham āsanam

sthira, steady; *sukham*, comfortable; *āsanam*, posture

Posture should be steady and comfortable.

Patañjali now moves on to the third limb of *yoga*. The term *āsana* is rarely found in the ancient mystical Upaniṣadic texts, except on occasion in the sense of a seat (*Bṛhadāraṇyaka* IV.2.1, VI.2.4; *Taittirīya* I.11.3), although it is used in the *Gītā* (VI.11) in the same sense—*sthira*, steady—in which it is found here. Although the entirety of *yoga* is typically understood and presented as *āsana*, physical posture, in the popular representations of the term in the West, it is actually only the third limb of *yoga*, not an end or goal unto itself (although see the comments on Guruji Iyengar in I.39). Indeed, given that he has just dedicated sixteen *sūtras* to the *yamas* and *niyamas*, Patañjali has relatively little to say about *āsana*, leaving us with only three *sūtras* on the topic consisting of a total of eight words; or, put differently, considerably less than one percent of the text occupies itself with *āsana*.

However, we should not conclude that this limb is irrelevant. That Patañjali does not give more detail about specific *āsanas* does not mean he considers them unimportant practices for *yogīs*. One could also suppose that other extant texts concerned themselves with the specifics of *āsanas*. While *āsana*-specific texts may not have survived from that time, we cannot conclude they did not exist. Vyāsa, below, knew of twelve *āsanas* in the fifth century (more, in fact, since he adds "etc." after his list). The fourteenth-century *Haṭhayoga Pradīpikā*

(I.17ff) speaks of 84 *āsanas* taught by Śiva, from which it outlines 15 (the Gorakṣa-śataka states that there are as many *āsanas* as species—8,400,000—and that Śiva chose 84 of these, from which *siddhāsana* and *padmāsana* are the best[97]), as do the seventeenth-century *Gheraṇḍa Saṁhitā* (II.2) and the *Śiva-saṁhitā* (III.100). Mādhava in the sixteenth century mentions 10 (465ff). Although these texts are much later, we can assume they drew to some extent on much older sources, as the *Mahābhārata* already makes passing reference to more than one kind of *āsana* (XII.142; XIII.304). Thus, one has grounds to suppose that Patañjali saw no need to elaborate on the details of *āsana* since information was available in texts or traditions specifically dedicated to that purpose. Vijñānabhikṣu takes this position: "An elaboration of *āsana* is not undertaken here, because our subject matter is *rāja-yoga*,[98] and a full and detailed treatment of this subject is to be found in works on *haṭha-yoga*."[99]

Essentially, posture is a limb of the actual goal of *yoga* to the extent that it allows the meditator to sit firmly, *sthira*, and comfortably, *sukha*, for meditation. Indeed, as noted, *āsana* literally means seat (*Gītā* VI.11). Obviously one cannot fix one's attention onto something if one is sleeping or running about; one must sit, and sit without fidgeting or discomfort. In other words, *āsana*'s relevance and function for the classical Yoga tradition are to train the body so that it does not disturb or distract the mind of the *yogī* in any way when sitting in meditation. Śaṅkara quotes a verse stating that mastery of postures does not produce the goals of *yoga*; only getting rid of the *kleśa* obstacles to *yoga*, and *samādhi*, undeviated absorption on the object of meditation, can produce the goals of *yoga*.[100] The point is that *yogic* postures are useful only to the extent to which they facilitate fixing the mind completely.

Along similar lines, Vijñānabhikṣu quotes the *Garuḍa Purāṇa*, which states that *āsanas*, or *yogic* postures, are not the goal of *yoga*; meditative practice is: "The prescriptions pertaining to postures and *āsanas* are not the producers of *yoga*; all such rules so elaborately described generate delay: Śiśupāla attained perfection by dint of the force of memory and *abhyāsa*, 'practice.' "[101] The Śiśupāla story is recounted in the *Bhāgavata Purāṇa* (X.74). Śiśupāla, Kṛṣṇa's enemy, attained perfection simply by fixing his mind without deviation on Kṛṣṇa—his enmity against Kṛṣṇa was so strong that he could think of nothing but Kṛṣṇa. The story illustrates the benefits of undeviated meditation on *Īśvara*, even, as in this case, if performed with hatred (that is, with the *kleśa* of *dveṣa*, indeed, all *kleśas*, in full force). This motif adds a new dimension by indicating that although the *kleśas* must under any other circumstances be eliminated for *samādhi* to become possible (II.2, 13, etc.), by the grace and power of intense *Īśvara-praṇidhāna*, however performed (and in this context and this context only), one can attain perfection even despite the *kleśas*. This is not in disharmony with what we can glean from Patañjali's own frugal statements (I.24; II.2, 42).

Posture, says Vācaspati Miśra, is the way one sits. Vyāsa names eleven *āsanas* as examples, and these are elaborated upon somewhat by the commentators. Vijñānabhikṣu quotes Vasiṣṭha as Vyāsa's source for the first four *āsanas*,[102] and the *Yoga-pradīpa* for the remainder. Yoga teachers might be interested in considering which *āsanas* were thought to be the most noteworthy for inclusion by Vyāsa in his commentary more than a millennium and a half ago. The names of the poses along with their descriptions as given by the commentators are as follows (Śaṅkara notes that only the highlights of these poses have been described):

(1) *Padmāsana*, the lotus pose. As Vācaspati Miśra notes, this pose is well-known to all and needs no description (the lotus *āsana* is worshipped by all, according to sage Vasiṣṭha, says Vyāsa). It involves placing the two feet on the two opposite thighs and holding the two toes with the opposite two hands. Śaṅkara adds that the hips, chest, and neck should be straight, the eyes fixed on the tip of the nose (as indicated in *Gītā* VI.13), lips closed like a casket, teeth not grinding against each other, chin a fist's distance away from the chest, the tip of the tongue resting inside the front teeth, and hands joined and resting on the two heels (see *Gītā* VI.11ff for similar prescriptions). These basic principles apply to all the poses listed below, he adds. Once there is no effort involved in holding this posture, he says, it can be called the lotus posture.

(2) *Virāsana*, the hero pose. One foot is placed on the oppo-

site thigh, and the other is placed on the ground below the other thigh.

(3) *Bhadrāsana*, the gracious pose. The ankles are placed below the scrotum, on the sides of the frenum of the prepuce, and the soles are held tight by both hands interlocked.

(4) *Svastikāsana*,[103] the auspicious pose. One sits with the left foot placed between the right thigh and knee, inclined slightly downward, and the right foot placed in the same fashion between the left thigh and knee. The toes should not be seen, says Śaṅkara, and the testicles should rest comfortably between the feet.

(5) *Daṇḍāsana*, the staff pose. This involves sitting down and stretching the thighs and legs along the ground, like a staff, with the soles and toes touching each other closely.

(6) *Sopāśraya*, the support pose. This *āsana* involves sitting down with a *yoga-paṭṭaka*. There is difference of opinion as to what a *yoga-paṭṭaka* is,[104] but, as the name indicates, it was some sort of a prop: Śaṅkara takes it to be a table or chair, but *paṭṭaka* can also refer to a piece of cloth or a board. Whatever is involved, followers of the Iyengar method may care to note that this *sūtra* indicates that props for *āsanas* have been used for centuries and are, in this sense, authentic.

(7) *Paryaṅka*, the bed pose. This *āsana* involves lying down with the arms stretched by one's knees. This is also known as the corpse pose (*śavāsana*), says Hariharānanda.

(8) *Krauñca-niṣadana*, the curlew pose. This *āsana* and the next two are to be performed by watching the seating postures of curlews and the other animals referred to.[105]

(9) *Hasti-niṣadana*, the elephant pose.

(10) *Uṣṭra-niṣadana*, the camel pose.

(11) *Sama-saṁsthāna*, the level pose. Vācaspati Miśra says that the heels and the tips of the feet are pressed together with the knees bent somewhat. Vijñānabhikṣu says that one places the hands over the thighs and remains with body, head, and neck straight up.

Vācaspati Miśra states that the steadiness Patañjali refers to in this *sūtra* means that these postures must be held without motion. "No fidgeting!" says Vijñānabhikṣu. Comfortable means that the poses must not cause trouble to the *yogī*. Also, all of them require that the chest, neck, and head—in other words, the spine—be kept straight, says Hariharānanda. Śaṅkara notes that Vyāsa had written "etc." after listing these poses, indicating that there can be variations prescribed by the *guru*. On this note, Śaṅkara states that *yoga* should be performed in a quiet and pure place, after performing obeisances to the supreme *Īśvara*, the sages, and one's own *guru*.

One might include in this discussion the reference to *āsana* in the *Vedānta Sūtra* tradition (IV.1.7–10), where sitting firmly is a prerequisite for fixing the mind. Moving around requires effort and is distracting, says the great theistic Vedānta commentator Rāmānuja, and lying down provokes sleep; therefore, one should sit on some support without any bodily effort.

प्रयत्नशैथिल्यानन्तसमापत्तिभ्याम् ॥ ४७ ॥

II.47 prayatna-śaithilyānanta-samāpattibhyām

prayatna, effort; *śaithilya*, relaxation; *ananta*, the infinite, the cosmic serpent Śeṣa who holds the worlds upon his heads; *samāpattibhyām*, the power of thought transformation, engrossment, absorption of the mind

[Such posture should be attained] by the relaxation of effort and by absorption in the infinite.

Āsana becomes perfect when all effort or strain, *prayatna*, ceases and the body no longer trembles, says Vyāsa, and when the *citta* is absorbed in the infinite, *ananta*. Hariharānanda elaborates that the practice of *āsana* involves a level of pain at first. After a time, this disappears by complete relaxation, *śaithilya*, into the pose, and by meditating on infinite space so that eventually the body feels nonexistent, like infinite space. The essential idea is that by the practice of *āsana*, the body should be so relaxed that the *yogī* ceases to be conscious of it at all, and the mind can thus be directed toward meditation without any bodily distraction or disturbance.

Since one of the names of Śeṣa, the thousand-headed cosmic serpent upon whom Viṣṇu reclines, and who holds the universe on his hoods, is *Ananta*, some commentators also consider the *ananta* from Patañjali's *sūtra* here to be a possible reference to him, since, as Rāmānanda Sarasvatī notes, he holds the worlds very firmly. In other words, *āsana* should be held as firmly and comfortably as Śeṣa holds the worlds on his hoods. As is well-known, Patañjali himself is considered to be an incarnation of Śeṣa. According to tradition, Śeṣa, desiring to teach *yoga* on earth, fell (*pat*) from the celestial realms into the palm (*añjali*) of a virtuous woman named Goṇikā. The eleventh-century commentary of Bhoja Rāja contains the following invocation to Patañjali in the form of Śeṣa, which is still recited at the beginning of *āsaṇa* classes in the Iyengar tradition:

> I bow with folded hands to Patañjali, best of sages, who removed the impurities of the mind through *yoga*; the impurities of speech, through grammar; and the impurities of the body, through medicine. To he whose upper body has a human form, who holds a conch and *cakra* (disc weapon), who is white and has a thousand heads, to that Patañjali, I offer obeisances.[106]

ततो द्वन्द्वानभिघातः ।।४८।।

II.48 tato dvandvānabhighātaḥ

tataḥ, consequently, from this; *dvandva*, by the opposites; *anabhighātaḥ*, not afflicted

From this, one is not afflicted by the dualities of the opposites.

By mastering posture, says Vyāsa, one is not overcome, *anabhighāta*, by dualities, *dvandva*, such as hot and cold. This language of transcending such dualities is very common in the Vedānta tradition (for example, *Gītā* VI.7; XII.18). Hot and cold (and all shades in between) represent the spectrum of sensations of the body, so this *sūtra* indicates that once *āsana* is mastered, one loses all awareness of the sensations of the body. The mind can now be focused elsewhere in meditation without being distracted by the body. Hariharānanda notes that upon mastering *āsana*, a state of calmness is experienced in the body, which allows for a detachment from the body's sensations such as hunger and thirst. In other words, the purpose and perfection of *āsana* indicated by Patañjali are when one loses all awareness of the body and, consequently, its sensations. It is a preliminary ingredient in a far larger undertaking.

तस्मिन् सति श्वासप्रश्वासयोर्गतिविच्छेदः प्राणायामः ॥ ४९ ॥

II.49 tasmin sati śvāsa-praśvāsayor gati-vicchedaḥ prāṇāyāmaḥ

tasmin, that; *sati*, is attained; *śvāsa*, inhalation; *praśvāsayoḥ*, exhalation; *gati*, movement; *vicchedaḥ*, regulation; *prāṇāyāmaḥ*, breath control

When that [*āsana*] is accomplished, *prāṇāyāmaḥ*, breath control, [follows]. This consists of the regulation of the incoming and outgoing breaths.

Patañjali now moves on to the next limb of *yoga*, *prāṇāyāma*, but we can note that the first phrase of the *sūtra*, *tasmin sati* (known in Sanskrit grammar as a *sati saptamī*, a locative absolute construction), indicates that this is to be undertaken while *āsana* is being perfected. Similar phrases introduce several of the other limbs as well (II.53; III.2). One can thus argue for a consecutive interdependence among the limbs, each one presupposing that the *yogī* is cultivating and mastering the previous ones. Most important for aspiring *yogīs*, one cannot bypass the *yamas* and *niyamas* and expect to be able to fix the mind in the serious and prolonged meditation of the subsequent limbs of *yoga*. Without cultivating the *yamas* and *niyamas*, the mind will not manifest the requisite state of *sattva*, without which there can be no meditation and thus no serious practice of *yoga* as defined by Patañjali. It is *rajas* and *tamas* that provoke the *vitarkas*, the thoughts, tendencies, or urges contrary to the *yamas* and *niyamas* (II.33–34), and it should be very clear by now that the higher goals of *yoga* cannot be attained while *rajas* and *tamas* are prominent in the *citta*.

Prāṇāyāma as breath control is an ancient practice that can be found in the old Brāhmaṇa texts.[107] Vyāsa explains that the *śvāsa* from this *sūtra* is the intake of air from the outside, and *praśvāsa*, the exhalation of air from the stomach. He defines *prāṇāyāma* to be the suspension, or absence, of both—in other words, the suspension of breath. Since Patañjali speaks of a type of suspension of breath as the fourth type of *prāṇāyāma* in II.51, the commentators clarify that here Patañjali is implicitly referring to three other types of breath suspension, *gati-vicchedaḥ: recaka*, where breath is suspended after *praśvāsa*, exhalation; *pūraka*, where breath is suspended after *śvāsa*, inhalation; and *kumbhaka*, the simultaneous suspension of both.

Hariharānanda, however (while accepting the definition given by the other commentators), states importantly that there is more to the *prāṇāyāma* referred to here than just these techniques, some of which receive attention in the fourteenth-century *yoga* manual *Haṭhayoga Pradīpikā*. He stresses that concentration on one's object of meditation has to accompany the practice of *prāṇāyāma*. One must clear the mind of *vṛttis* in conjunction with suspending the breath, not just devote oneself to suspending the breath alone. In his commentary to the next *sūtra*, he notes that *yogic prāṇāyāma* in turn, done properly, reciprocally helps to arrest the *vṛttis* of the mind and make it one-pointed. Thus this practice can lead the mind toward *samādhi*. In any case, without such arresting of the mind, *prāṇāyāma* is not *yoga* but merely a physical feat. He further notes that in *samādhi*, the breath becomes imperceptible, or even wholly suspended.

बाह्याभ्यन्तरस्तम्भवृत्तिः देशकालसंख्याभिः परिदृष्टो दीर्घसूक्ष्मः ॥५०॥

II.50 bāhyābhyantara-stambha-vṛttiḥ deśa-kāla-saṅkhyābhiḥ paridṛṣṭo dīrgha-sūkṣmaḥ

bāhya, external; *ābhyantara*, internal; *stambha*, restrained, suppressed; *vṛttiḥ*, movements; *deśa*, place; *kāla*, time; *saṅkhyābhiḥ*, and number; *paridṛṣṭaḥ*, is manifest; *dīrgha*, long; *sūkṣmaḥ*, subtle

[*Prāṇāyāmaḥ*] manifests as external, internal, and restrained movements [of breath]. These are drawn out and subtle in accordance to place, time, and number.

Vyāsa defines the external, *bāhya*, of this *sūtra* as when there is no flow of breath after exhalation; internal, *ābhyantara*, when there is no flow of breath after inhalation; and restrained, *stambha*, as the simultaneous cessation of both (the commentators specify that these refer to the *recaka, pūraka*, and *kumbhaka* suppressions mentioned in the last *sūtra*[108]). *Vṛtti* means anything that turns or revolves and thus can apply to breathing, as in this verse, or anything else, in addition to the churnings of thought. The movement, *vṛtti*, of breath ceases, he notes, just as water shrinks and contracts from all sides and evaporates when it is sprinkled on a heated stone. The breath remains within the body when it ceases to move in and out, adds Vācaspati Miśra (like motionless water filling a jar, says Rāmānanda Sarasvatī).

Moving on to the second part of the *sūtra*, all these different types of breath restraint are regulated by place, *deśa*, that is, the surface area that is reached by the breath, says Vyāsa. He understands time as the seconds of duration of these cessations of the flow of breath, and number as how many sequences of inhalations and exhalations are restrained, and whether they are mild, middling, or intense in nature. The commentators elaborate on this schema. In terms of place, the surface area covered by breath is either external or internal. The external range of breath here is measured by a piece of cotton or blade of grass placed at a certain distance—a hand span or twelve fingers—from the nose to see at what point it is moved by the breath. The internal range of breath is measured from the soles of the feet to the head and can be sensed like "the touch of an ant." In *kumbhaka*, breath ceases in both these spheres. This external and internal range or surface area of breath constitutes Patañjali's place.

Time, *kāla*, refers to the differing durations of each individual exhalation, inhalation, and retention, and is calculated by *kṣaṇa*, a unit that is taken here to correspond to a quarter of the time it takes to blink the eye (but see III.52 for a more metaphysical definition). *Prāṇāyāma* is regulated by the number of *kṣaṇas* involved in the restraint, etc., of the breath. Number, *saṅkhyā*, is the number of repetitions, or rounds of each cycle of inhalations, exhalations, and retentions at one sitting. Time differs from number, says Vijñānabhikṣu, in terms of the method used in calculation. Number is determined by *mātrā*. Vijñānabhikṣu quotes a verse[109] that states that a *mātrā* corresponds to a single clap of the hands, the opening and closing of the eyes once, or the utterance of a phoneme (for example, the *ga* sound in *yoga*), Vācaspati Miśra takes a *mātrā* to correspond to the time it takes to rub one's kneecap three times and then snap one's fingers. According to Vijñānabhikṣu, twelve *mātrās* are the unit used for *prāṇāyāma*. He prescribes drawing in the breath through the right nostril for the duration of sixteen *mātrās* and, once the lungs are full, holding the breath for sixty-four *mātrās*, after which one exhales for the duration of thirty-two *mātrās*. This is to be accompanied by meditation on the *oṁ mantra*.

Vācaspati Miśra and Vijñānabhikṣu also differ in their understanding of Vyāsa's mild, middling, and intense demarcations. Vācaspati Miśra takes mild to be thirty-six *mātrās*, middling twice that, and intense thrice that amount, whereas Vijñānabhikṣu quotes the *Kūrma Purāṇa* (IX.32) in which mild is understood as twelve *mātrās*, middling as twenty-four, and intense as thirty-six.[110] Hariharānanda recommends the internal chanting of *mantras* as an alternative to the various *mātrā* techniques, using the repetition of a certain number of *mantras* to demarcate the duration of the periods separating inhalation, exhalation, and suppression.

The common denominator of all this is simply that some consistent system of time demarcation is used in *prāṇāyāma*. By practice, says Vyāsa, these restrictions of breath become drawn out, *dīrgha*, and subtle, *sūkṣma*. In other words, say the commentators, one can increase the duration of these intervals of breath restraint so that they become more and more prolonged and imperceptible in terms of the movement of air (such that with practice cotton wool does not move even when placed at the tip of the nose, specifies Hariharānanda).

बाह्याभ्यन्तरविषयाक्षेपी चतुर्थः ।।५१।।

II.51 bāhyābhyantara-viṣayākṣepī caturthaḥ

bāhya, external; *ābhyantara*, internal; *viṣaya*, the sphere, range; *ākṣepī*, surpassing; *caturthaḥ*, the fourth

The fourth [type of *prāṇāyāma*] surpasses the limits of the external and the internal.

The fourth, *caturthaḥ*, type of *prāṇāyāma,* says Vyāsa, refers to the total suppression of breath and so, like the *kumbhaka* mentioned previously, also involves the cessation of inhalation and exhalation. Vijñānabhikṣu calls it *kevala-kumbhaka*, pure *kumbhaka*. In his *Yoga-sāra* commentary, he quotes the *Bṛihan-nāradīya Purāṇa* as referring to it as *śūnyaka*. The commentators are not overly helpful in clarifying the precise difference between the third type of *prāṇāyāma, kumbhaka*, and the fourth type, *caturthaḥ*. As is the case with so much in the *sūtras*, it is clear that these are techniques to be experienced by practice rather than understood intellectually. Vyāsa states that the third type of suppression is brought about by a single effort, whereas the fourth takes place gradually with prolonged effort. Apparently, *kumbhaka* is performed independently of the suppression of breath in *recaka* and *pūraka* that utilizes the system of measurements; it is thus limited in duration. *Caturthaḥ,* in contrast, says Vijñānabhikṣu, involves an extension of the cessation of breath that occurs after exhalation and inhalation in *recaka* and *pūraka* that is not determined by time and number, and the adept of this stage of *prāṇāyāma* can maintain the suppression of breath at will, even for a month or a year. It thus surpasses the other three stages of *prāṇāyāma*. One might also suppose that in this state the body is being maintained by the internal circulation of *prāṇa* rather than any external flow of breath.

Accounts of suspending the functions of conventional breathing are fairly standard throughout the ascetic Yoga traditions of ancient India. In the Pāli Buddhist tradition (*Majjhima Nikāya* I.121ff), the Buddha describes his own experiences with stopping breathing, and similar accounts are found in Jain literature (*Uttarajjhayaṇa* 29).[111] The *Gītā* also speaks of *prāṇāpānau samau*, the equalizing of the incoming and outgoing breath (V.27), and the practice plays a central role in the *Haṭhayoga Pradīpikā* (II.74ff; IV.112). Hariharānanda mentions that he knew of someone who could remain buried alive for ten or twelve days as a result of his ability to restrain the breath, and even the great philosopher of modern times, Dasgupta, claimed to have witnessed a *yogī* remaining in a state of suspended animation for nine days, without intake of food or drink, and devoid even of heartbeat.[112] Accounts were also documented during the colonial period, such as the case of one Haridas, buried alive in 1837 in the Lahore court of Rāja Runjeet

Singh, with extensive precautions taken against fraud, all of which was documented by Sir Claude Martin Wade.[113] The Yoga tradition has long been full of accounts of *yogīs* who have suspended their breath and been buried alive for prolonged periods and then exhumed alive, at which time they reactivated the normal breathing processes. (Indeed, related phenomena have recently attracted some degree of scientific attention.[114])

In its beginning stages, Vijñānabhikṣu continues, this fourth type of *prāṇāyāma* is accompanied by sweating; in higher stages, by shivering; and in advanced stages, by a feeling of "flooding." When mastered, one attains mystic powers such as the ability to fly and go anywhere at will. He cites Dhruva from the *Bhāgavata Purāṇa* (IV.8ff) as an example of someone who had mastered this type of *prāṇāyāma*. The Dhruva story is well-known in the Purāṇic tradition: Offended by his co-mother, who would not allow him to climb on the lap of his father the king, Dhruva is advised by his own mother, the neglected cowife of the king, to practice austerities and worship the supreme Lord Viṣṇu if he wished to sit on the lap of his father. Dhruva is given further directions by the sage Nārada for specifically how to meditate and worship Lord Viṣṇu, and these include the practice of *recaka, pūraka*, and *kumbhaka*, and meditation on the *mantra* "*oṁ namo bhagavate Vāsudevāya*."

Although he was only five years old, the boy betook himself to the forest and practiced severe austerities with a view to attaining an audience with the supreme Lord Viṣṇu. Worshipping the Lord as he had been directed, the lad ate some simple fruits only every third day for the entire first month of his austerities; for the second month, he abstained from all food except for withered grass and leaves consumed every sixth day; for the third, he renounced all food and subsisted only on water drunk every ten days; for the fourth, his only form of sustenance was air inhaled every fourteen days, and then every fifteen days. It is here that Dhruva's story becomes relevant to this *sūtra*: Suppressing the breath for fourteen or fifteen days at a time indicates a mastery of the "fourth" type of *prāṇāyāma* noted by Patañjali in this *sūtra*. For the fifth month Dhruva refrained from all activities whatsoever, including breathing (thereby extending this particular process of *prāṇāyāma* to its maximum extent), stood on one leg in some variant of the *ekapāda-vṛkṣāsana* [tree] pose, and focused exclusively on Lord Viṣṇu.

Because of his complete absorption on the Lord of the universe, Dhruva's personal condition emanated out and pervaded the whole universe, such that all other beings also became deprived of breath. We can note here, given that the topic is the subject of much of the next chapter, that this process by which the *yogī* absorbs the qualities of the object of meditation by absolute unflinching absorption on that object is called *saṁyama*. In this case, since Viṣṇu is the supreme soul pervading the entire universe, Dhruva became as if one with Viṣṇu due to his complete mental absorption on Viṣṇu, and thus his own personal condition of *kevala-kumbhaka* pervaded the entire universe.

Although the boy's worship and meditation were tinged with personal motive, Viṣṇu was nonetheless moved by the incredible determination of the lad, appeared before him, purified his heart of all desires (*kleśas*), and bestowed various boons upon him. A further example from the *Bhāgavata Purāṇa* of a *yogī* who had mastered the techniques of *prāṇāyāma* is described in II.55 below.

ततः क्षीयते प्रकाशावरणम् ॥ ५२ ॥

II.52 tataḥ kṣīyate prakāśāvaraṇam

tataḥ, then; *kṣīyate*, is weakened; *prakāśa*, illumination; *āvaraṇam*, covering

Then, the covering of the illumination [of knowledge] is weakened.

Prakāśa, illumination, as we know from II.18, is a synoynm for *sattva*. The covering of illumination, *prakāśa-āvaraṇa*, says Vyāsa, is ultimately *karma*, and this is destroyed by the practice of *prāṇāyāma*. He quotes a verse that speaks of *karma* as the "net of great illusion" that covers *sattva* and impels one to commit immoral deeds. *Karma*, we recall, consists of actions that are all recorded in the *citta* as *saṁskāras* and that fructify at the appropriate time, conditioning one to act in certain ways. *Karma* is in this sense synonymous with the storehouse of *saṁskāras*, which trigger the behavioral patterns and preconditioned attitudes, perspectives, or responses to the world, such as the immoral deeds mentioned by Vyāsa. It is a net of illusion because, like a net with many knots, when the myriad *saṁskāras* fructify, they channel awareness away from its source and absorb it in conditioned patterns of behavior (the *sattva* of the mind forgets the true nature of the *puruṣa* and becomes enamored by the objects of the senses, says Vijñānabhikṣu). Pursuing these sense objects, additional *karma* is produced, and thus the mind remains further trapped and entangled in this net of action and reaction. In this sense it is *karma* that sustains ignorance, the covering of knowledge, the misconception that the body and senses are the true self.

Although, technically, only knowledge can ultimately destroy ignorance, says Hariharānanda, it is only when the covering of *karma* is weakened that knowledge can shine forth unobstructed. This covering of *karma* is weakened, says Vyāsa, by the practice of *prāṇāyāma*. He quotes a verse that "there is no greater ascetic practice than *prāṇāyāma*, from which defects are purified and the light of knowledge shines forth."[115] Manu, too, states that from the performance of *prāṇāyāma* accompanied by the repetition of the *oṁ mantra*, "the impurities of the sensory powers are burnt away, just as the defiling impurities of metal ore are burnt away in the heat of the furnace" (VI.72).

धारणासु च योग्यता मनसः ।।५३।।

II.53 dhāraṇāsu ca yogyatā manasaḥ

dhāraṇāsu, for concentration; *ca*, and; *yogyatā*, fitness, competency; *manasaḥ*, mind

Additionally, the mind becomes fit for concentration.

Manasaḥ is used here rather than *citta*, as it is the specific aspect of *citta* that interacts with the senses, and awareness must now make a transition from the sensory involvements of *prāṇāyāma* and the next limb, *pratyāhāra*, to the transsensory stage of *dhāraṇā*, concentration.[116] *Dhāraṇā* is the sixth limb of *yoga*, which will be discussed shortly. The commentators assume this *sūtra* to be self-explanatory and have little to add. For the mind to be able to fix on an object of concentration, it must be *sattvic*, that is, *rajas* and *tamas* must be minimized. Bhoja Rāja says that once freed from its defects by these breathing techniques, the mind can remain fixed wherever it is directed; in other words, the correct performance of *prāṇāyāma* prepares the mind for concentration, the preliminary stage of meditation and ultimate *samādhi*. Again, the sequential nature of the limbs is indicated in this *sūtra*. But one more step is required before the mind can successfully undertake the practice of *dhāraṇā*, concentration; this is the fifth limb of the next verse.

स्वविषयासंप्रयोगे चित्तस्य स्वरूपानुकार
इवेन्द्रियाणां प्रत्याहारः ॥५४॥

II.54 svaviṣayāsamprayoge cittasya svarūpānukāra ivendriyāṇāṁ pratyāhāraḥ

sva, their own; *viṣaya*, sense objects; *asamprayoge*, not coming into contact with; *cittasya*, of the mind; *svarūpa*, nature; *anukāraḥ*, imitation, resemblance; *iva*, as if; *indriyāṇām*, of the senses; *pratyāhāraḥ*, withdrawal

***Pratyāhāra*, withdrawal from sense objects, occurs when the senses do not come into contact with their respective sense objects. It corresponds, as it were, to the nature of the mind [when it is withdrawn from the sense objects].**

Patañjali now introduces the fifth limb of *yoga*, *pratyāhāra*, which is when the senses do not come into contact with the sense objects, *svaviṣaya-asamprayoga*, a practice referred to as early as the *Chāndogya Upaniṣad* (VIII.15). This is accomplished through the mind: When the mind is under control, says Vyāsa, the senses are automatically under control; they do not need to be restrained separately. He illustrates this with a metaphor that is drawn from the *Praśna Upaniṣad* (II.4): Just as when the queen bee flies up, all the other bees fly up along with her, and when the queen bee settles down, all the other bees automatically settle down, so the mind and senses are directly interconnected. When the mind is fixed on the object of meditation, says

Vijñānabhikṣu, the senses cease their functioning without any separate endeavor, but when the mind is not controlled, it becomes inclined to follow the senses and is dragged out into the sensual world. He quotes Manu here: "If even one of the senses slips away, a person's knowledge slips away through that sense, like water from a water-bag" (II.99). The *Gītā*, too, states: "The senses are so impetuous, O Arjuna, that they forcibly carry away the mind even of a learned person who is endeavoring to control them" (II.60).

ततः परमा वश्यतेन्द्रियाणाम् ॥५५॥

II.55 tataḥ paramā vaśyatendriyāṇām

tataḥ, from this; *paramā*, highest; *vaśyatā*, control;
indriyāṇām, of the senses

From this comes the highest control of the senses.

In order to illustrate Patañjali's qualification here of highest, *paramā*, in relation to sense control, *vaśyatā indriyāṇām*, Vyāsa contrasts it with various other lesser forms of sense control. Some hold, he says, that sense control means enjoying sense objects as long as they are not prohibited; others, that sense control means contact with sense objects according to one's desire rather than according to the dictates of the senses; and still others, that sense control involves engaging with sense objects but without attachment or aversion, happiness or distress. Real sense control, however, says Vyāsa, reiterating the previous *sūtra*, is when the mind is restrained and focused because then the senses are automatically brought under control.

The problem with the other opinions noted by Vyāsa, says Vācaspati Miśra, is that they all still involve contact with the sense objects, and sense objects are like poison: There is always the danger of being overcome by them. Even the greatest expert in the science of poisons, he says, does not sleep with snakes without fear—there is always the danger of being bitten. Therefore, the highest sense control is that in which there is no engagement whatsoever with sense objects, and this occurs when the mind is withdrawn from the senses.

Vijñānabhikṣu refers to the story of sage Saubhari related in the

Bhāgavata Purāṇa (IX.6.40ff). In an attempt to avoid the lure of the senses and the distractions and temptations of the world, the sage was practicing austerities under the waters of the river Yamunā (which provides, as an aside, an example of the fourth stage of *prāṇāyāma* outlined above, allowing him to suppress his breathing for as long as he willed and thus survive peacefully in environments normally inhospitable to human survival). However, even in this most removed of environments, the sage's mind was not fully under control, and so he became distracted by a pair of fish mating.

Witnessing this act, the sage became overwhelmed with sensual desires, abandoned his asceticism, and turned his attention to conjugal indulgence. From the perspective of Yoga psychology, although the sage had mastered great lofty attainments in terms of *prāṇāyāma*, his *citta* nonetheless contained unlimited *saṁskāras* from previous lives, including *saṁskāras* of previous sexual experiences. By meditating underwater, the sage had tried to remove himself from any possible temptation that might awaken these, but these dormant sexual *saṁskāras* were nonetheless activated by the slightest external sexual stimulus, in this case, mating fish. Vijñānabhikṣu introduces a theistic element here by quoting the *Gītā*: "The senses are so agitating, O Arjuna, that they forcibly carry away the mind even of a person who is struggling to control them. But a person who restrains all of them and remains [with mind] fixed on me [Kṛṣṇa] as the Supreme with senses under control, has steady knowledge" (II.60).

Rāmānanda Sarasvatī gives the example of Sītā from the *Rāmāyaṇa* as one who had mastered the highest sense control. Sītā's mind was so fixed on her husband Rāma, that, even though abducted and in captivity, she was immune to all the lures of the powerful demon Rāvaṇa, who was trying to seduce her. Here we see that, in the more *Īśvara*-focused theologies of the theistic traditions, rather than trying to suppress all one's past *saṁskāras* exclusively by one's own will and meditative prowess, and thus run the risk of past *saṁskāras* reactivating as was the case with the sage Saubhari, the *yogī* instead saturates the mind with devotional *saṁskāras* related to thoughts directed to the divine form and activities of God, *Īśvara*. This is a more theologically elaborate expansion of Patañjali's *Īśvara-praṇidhāna*, based on the idea that rather than exclusively suppressing negative mundane *saṁskāras*, one strives to replace them with transcendent ones, a theistic variant of the *pratipakṣa-bhāvana* from II.33.

इति पतञ्जलिविरचिते योगसूत्रे द्वितीयः साधनपादः ।

iti Patañjali-viracite yogasūtre dvitīyaḥ sādhana-pādaḥ

Thus ends the second chapter on *sādhana* in the *Yoga Sūtras* composed by Patañjali.

CHAPTER SUMMARY

The chapter begins with an introduction of *kriyā-yoga* [1], its effects [2], and a discussion of the *kleśas*, which it removes [3–11]. *Karma* and its consequences are outlined [12–14] and the principle of suffering established [15–16]. This is followed by the characteristics of the seer and the seen [17–22], the conjunction between them [23–24], and the definition of liberation [25–27]. Next, the eight limbs of *yoga* are introduced as the means to attain liberation [28–29], and the remainder of the chapter is dedicated to these: the *yamas* and their universality [30–31], the *niyamas* [32], the means to counter tendencies contrary to the *yamas* and *niyamas* [33–34] and the side benefits accruing from observing them [35–45]. Next, *āsana*, the third limb, is presented [46–48], followed by *prāṇāyāma*, the fourth limb [49–53], and *pratyāhāra*, the fifth [54–55].

तृतीयः विभूतिपादः ।

tṛtīyaḥ vibhūti-pādaḥ

CHAPTER III

MYSTIC POWERS

देशबन्धश्चित्तस्य धारणा ॥१॥

III.1 deśa-bandhaś cittasya dhāraṇā

deśa, place; *bandhaḥ*, bound, fixed; *cittasya*, of the mind; *dhāraṇā*, concentration

Concentration is the fixing of the mind in one place.

Patañjali discussed the first five of the eight limbs of *yoga* in the previous chapter and now concludes his discussion of the remaining three. Since the eight limbs of *yoga* would seem to constitute one discrete, self-contained unit in terms of subject matter, the question can be raised as to why Patañjali chose to divide the limbs over two distinct chapters. The classical commentators do not draw attention to this, but an answer, I suggest, lies in III.4 below. The primary subject matter of this chapter is the *vibhūtis* (*siddhis*), the mystic powers, and these are attained by performing *saṁyama* on various objects. III.4 defines *saṁyama* as a progressive application of the last three limbs of *yoga*. Hence, these three limbs are situated prior to the presentation of *saṁyama*, which in turn is pivotal to an understanding of the mystic powers, and thus is the central theme of the rest of the chapter. Moreover, Patañjali considers the five previous limbs of *yoga* to be the external limbs and the final three limbs of *yoga* discussed here to be internal (III.6), a division that further contributes to a logic of separation into different *pādas*, chapters.

In fact we have seen a gradual progression from the external to the internal throughout the limbs. The *yamas* are the most external, proscribing relations with other beings—one doesn't inflict violence, lie, steal, sexually exploit, or covet the possessions of others. The *niyamas* deal more internally with one's own practices, but practices still related to external elements—hygiene, contentment with one's situation, curbing sensual involvement, study, and devotional activity. *Āsanas* focus exclusively on one's personal body, and *prāṇāyāma*, more internal still, on the breath within the body. *Pratyāhāra* continues this progression of internalization by going still deeper within by withdrawing consciousness itself from the senses. This process of consecutive stages of internalization continues throughout the remaining three limbs.

Dhāraṇā, concentration, Patañjali states, involves fixing the mind on one place, *deśa-bandha*. In the *Mahābhārata*, two passages outline seven or ten different types of *dhāraṇās*, respectively (as does the *Mārkaṇḍeya Purāṇa* XXXVI.44–45), which can be directed toward parts of the anatomy or external objects and result in wonderful powers similar to those that will be described later in this chapter.[1] Vyāsa seems have these passages in mind when he mentions the circle of the navel, the lotus in the heart,[2] the light in the brain,[3] the tip of the nose,[4] the tip of the tongue, or any external object as a place upon which the mind can be fixed. Although Patañjali does not specify the nature of the object upon which *dhāraṇā* is to be performed, Vācaspati Miśra and Rāmānanda Sarasvatī quote a series of verses from the *Viṣṇu Purāṇa* (VI.7.77–85) that recommend theistic meditation on the form of Viṣṇu on the grounds that since concentration requires an object, when one concentrates on the beautiful personal form of the Lord, one has no desire to think of anything else, since nothing else can compete in attractiveness. The mind is thus spontaneously fixed. This type of meditation is often referred to as *sa-guṇa*, wherein the personal form of God is the object of meditation, and is typical of the Indian theistic traditions. The passage chosen by the commentators gives a good illustration of the particulars of this type of meditation:

> One should thus meditate on Hari's [Viṣṇu's] pleasing face, his beautiful lotus eyes, his gorgeous cheeks, his broad and shining forehead, and his ear lobes, which wear charming earrings. His neck is like a conch shell, his broad chest is marked with the tuft of hair called *śrīvatsa*, and his belly has a deep navel and

> three folds. He has four arms, his thighs and legs are symmetrical, and he has beautiful lotus feet. He wears a spotless yellow garment, is adorned with a crown, attractive armlets and bracelets, and holds his *śāraṅga* bow, discus, club, sword, conch and rosary.[5] He is *Brahman*, the absolute truth, and the *yogī* should try to concentrate the mind until it is fixed on him alone.

As we have seen, Vācaspati Miśra provides a parallel illustration of *saguṇa* meditation on Lord Śiva in his commentary on I.38 dealing with the *yogic* dream state.

तत्र प्रत्ययैकतानता ध्यानम् ॥२॥

III.2 tatra pratyayaika-tānatā dhyānam

tatra, there, in that; *pratyaya*, conception, idea, thought; *eka-tānatā*, fixed on one point only; *dhyānam*, meditation

Meditation is the one-pointedness of the mind on one image.

Patañjali now defines the seventh limb of *yoga, dhyāna*, meditation, which Vyāsa describes as the continuous flow of the same thought or image of the object of meditation, without being distracted by any other thought. As has been discussed, *pratyaya* used by Patañjali here refers to the image or impression that an object—in this context, the object of meditation—makes on the mind. When the image of the object of meditation flows uninterruptedly, *eka-tānatā*, in the mind, that is to say when the mind can focus exclusively on that object without any other distraction, *dhyāna*, has been achieved.

The sixth and seventh limbs of *yoga* and, as will be seen below, the eighth as well, are not different practices as is the case with the previous five limbs, but a continuation and deepening of the same practice. As al-Bīrunī puts it, they are like the progression between infancy and maturity.[6] Hariharānanda points out that the difference between these limbs of *yoga* is only one of degree: In concentration, the attention on the object is intermittent or distracted; in meditation, it is unbroken and undistracted. Meditation, he states, is when the mind flows on the object of thought without any interruption, like the smooth and even flow of oil or honey, which pours forth in one thick, uninterrupted stream. Concentration, the previous stage, is more like the uneven trickle of water that flows in a series of distinct droplets, each one similar but interrupted by gaps. Hence, this *sūtra* is distinguished from the previous one by the use of the term *eka-tānatā*, the state of retaining one image in the mind, that is, fixing the mind on one place. Vijñānabhikṣu states that *dhāranā*, concentration, can be disrupted if the senses come in contact with objects that are extremely dear to the practitioner, but this does not occur in *dhyāna* when one is fully absorbed: "just like the arrow-maker, his whole being engrossed in the arrow, who was not aware of the king passing by his side" (*Sāṅkhya Sūtras*).[7]

We can note here that *dhyāna* was used in older Indic texts as a synonym for *samādhi*, the culmination of the meditative process, rather than the penultimate limb, as we find here (in fact, *samādhi* does not occur in the older Upaniṣads prior to the *Maitrāyaṇī*[8]). In the *Mahābhārata* and early Buddhism, *dhyāna* denoted the goal of *yogic* practice, as touched upon in I.17, and the same understanding seems to have been the case with the Upaniṣads (*Śvetāśvatara* I.3) and the *Gītā* (XIII.24). As a point of interest, we include here the section of the *Mahābhārata* that describes the eight-limbed practice of *yoga*—which it calls the *yoga* with eight characteristics (*aṣṭa-guṇa*)—as an example of how an important pre-Patañjali source renders this system:

SAGE YĀJÑAVALKYA TO KING JANAKA

I have spoken to you about the knowledge of *Sāṅkhya*; now hear from me about the knowledge of *yoga* as I have heard and seen it, O best of kings.

There is no knowledge equal to *Sāṅkhya*; there is no power like that of *yoga*. Both of these are the same path; both are said to lead to immortality.

Only people lacking wisdom say that these are different. But we, O king, see them as one without any doubt.

That which the *yogīs* perceive, the followers of *Sāṅkhya* experience. One who sees that *Sāṅkhya* and *yoga* are one, is a seer of Truth.

Know that [the control of] the vital airs to be the highest [practice] in *yoga*, O chastiser of the enemy. In fact, in their very same body, *yogīs* can wander around the ten directions.[9]

When death occurs, my dear king, having abandoned [the physical body], such *yogīs* wander happily around the worlds in the subtle body, endowed with the eight yogic powers (*guṇas*),[10] O sinless one.

In the Vedic scriptures, the wise speak of *yoga* as having eight qualities,[11] and bestowing eight subtle powers.[12] It is this and nothing else, O best of rulers.

They say that the topmost practice of *yoga* is of two kinds, according to what is revealed in the scriptures: *yoga* with "qualities" and *yoga* without "qualities."[13]

There is concentration of the mind [*dhāraṇā*, see III.2[14]], and there is *prāṇāyama* [II.49ff]. *Prāṇāyama* is *saguṅa*, and *dhāraṇā* is *nirguṇa*.

It is seen that exhaling air in the practice of *nirguṅa*, O Lord of Maithila, causes an excess of wind. Because of this, it should not be practiced.

Twelve ways of restraining [the breath] in the first watch of the night are recorded in the scriptures. After sleeping in the middle watch, the twelve ways of restraining [are prescribed again] for the final watch. Living in solitude, tranquil, and controlled, one should without doubt engage one's *ātman* in *yoga* with the intelligence, delighting in the *ātman* and living in solitude.

One should cast off the fivefold faults of the five senses: sound, form, touch, taste, and smell [*pratyāhāra* II.54].

One should restrain the state of *pratibhām-apavargam*,[15] and fix the senses on the mind (*manas*).

The *manas* should then be fixed on the ego, *ahaṅkāra*, O Lord of men; the *ahaṅkāra* on the intelligence, *buddhi*; and the *buddhi*, in turn, on *prakṛti*.

After undertaking this progression, one should meditate on the *puruṣa*, which is autonomous (*kevalam*; II.25), a spotless lotus, eternal, infinite, pure, unblemished, immovable, existent, indivisible, beyond decay and death, everlasting, immutable, the lord and imperishable *Brahman*.

Consider now, O king, the characteristics of the *yogī*. The character of the *yogī* displays a tranquillity like that of the contented person sleeping blissfully.

The wise speak of the *yogī* as like the upward motionless flame of a lamp full of oil burning in a windless place.

The character of the *yogī* is like a rock, which is incapable of being moved even when pummeled by torrents of rain pouring down from clouds.

The demeanor of the *yogī* is not moved by the noise of assorted conches and drums being played together, nor by outbursts of song.

Just as a person of composed nature might ascend a staircase while holding a container full of oil, and yet, despite being alarmed upon being attacked by assailants armed with swords, does not spill a drop out of fear of them, so, in the same way, the mind of one who is absorbed in the supreme, is fully concentrated.

These are the characteristics of the sage *yogī*, which are displayed due to resolve and to controlling the activities of the senses.

Absorbed in the self, the *yogī* beholds the supreme and imperishable *Brahman*, resembling a lamp situated in dense darkness blazing forth.

It is in this way that, after the passage of much time [in practice], the *yogī* enters the state of transcendent liberation (*kevala*) upon leaving the body, O king. This [is revealed in] the eternal scriptures.

This, indeed, is the *yoga* of the *yogīs*. What else is the character of *yoga*? Knowing this, the wise consider that they have accomplished the goal of life.

तद् एवार्थमात्रनिर्भासं स्वरूपशून्यम् इव समाधिः ॥ ३ ॥

III.3 tad evārtha-mātra-nirbhāsam svarūpa-śūnyam iva samādhiḥ

tat, that [the practice of *dhyāna* from the previous *sūtra*]; *eva*, the same, the very one; *artha*, object; *mātra*, alone; *nirbhāsam*, shining forth; *svarūpa*, own form, own self; *śūnyam*, devoid of; *iva*, as if; *samādhiḥ*, meditative absorption

Samādhi is when that same _dhyāna_ shines forth as the object alone and [the mind] is devoid of its own [reflective] nature.

Patañjali here reaches the final limb of *yoga, samādhi*. We can note that only one *sūtra* has been dedicated to this ultimate stage, despite its status as the goal of the entire system, because Patañjali presented the various stages of *samādhi* in the first chapter, and the commentators have already discussed these in some detail there. He therefore here merely needs to connect that discussion with the eight limbs of *yoga* by situating *samādhi* in its place here as the eighth and final limb. We can also note that, out of the seven different types of *samādhi* discussed in that chapter, Patañjali seems to have defined *samādhi* here in terms similar to his description of *nirvitarka-samādhi* in I.43.

Vyāsa states that when the mind is so fully absorbed in the object of meditation that it loses all notions of itself as a self-conscious, reflective mind, *svarūpa-śunyam*, one has reached the state of *samādhi*. In this state, the mind is no longer aware of itself as meditating on something external to itself; all distinctions—between the *yogī* as the subjective meditator, the act of meditation, and the object of meditation—have disappeared. In other words, any subconscious awareness, however subtle, that "I am meditating on this object" ceases. Also, as Bhoja Rāja reminds us, from the threefold aspect of knowledge—the object itself, the name of the object, and the idea of the object in a person's mind—the latter two are eliminated in the *samādhi* referred to here, and only the object itself occupies the *yogī*'s awareness exclusively. There is no mental recognition of what the object is; the object as raw uninterpreted presence now constitutes the *yogī*'s entire universe of experience, shining forth in its own right, *artha-mātra-nirbhāsam*.

The commentators reintroduce the example of a pure crystal which, when placed next to a red flower, appears to completely lose its own character by reflecting the form and color of the flower exclusively. Meditation has reached a height such that the *yogī* is no longer self-aware and is conscious only of the object of meditation rather than of its function or relevance in the scheme of things, and it is in this level of intensity that *samādhi* differs from *dhyāna*. There is thus a progression of concentrative absorption on the object of meditation in the last three limbs of *yoga*: from *dhāraṇā*, through *dhyāna*, to *samādhi*.

In the previous verse, we included the *Mahābhārata*'s (pre-Patañjali) rendition of the practice of Yoga with eight characteristics as a point of contrast with Patañjali's systematized version. We noted in II.28 that the technical and esoteric eightfold stages of classical *yoga* are brought colorfully to life in the popular narratives that form the core of real-life Hindu religious identity in texts such as the *Bhāgavata Purāṇa* (arguably, along with the *Rāmāyāṇa*, the most popular source of religious narrative in the Indian subcontinent).[16] Before moving into the entirely new direction that the *sūtras* are about to take for the remainder of this chapter, we conclude this section on the eight limbs of *yoga* with another version of the eight-limbed practice of *yoga*, this time from the *Bhāgavata Purāṇa* (III.28.1ff), to illustrate how this practice with *Īśvara* as the *ālambana*, meditational support (I.10), for the mind is construed in the *bhakti* traditions. The discussion is relevant to the Yoga tradition as it transpires between Kapila, the reputed founder of the Sāṅkhya tradition (considered an incarnation of Viṣṇu in ancient sources[17]), and his mother:

> The Lord, *bhagavān*,[18] said:
>
> O daughter of the king, I will outline the characteristics of *sabīja-yoga*;[19] by this method, the mind becomes joyful, and undoubtedly attains the path of Truth. One should follow one's *dharma*, duty,[20] to the best of one's ability, and refrain from activities opposed to *dharma*. Content with what one has attained by Providence, one should worship the feet of a spiritual teacher,[21] one who has perceived the *ātman*.
>
> Ceasing mundane religious activities,[22] but rather being attracted to the *dharma* which leads to liberation, one should always eat a limited amount of pure food, and reside in a peaceful, secluded place.
>
> One should practice nonviolence (*ahiṁsā*), truthfulness (*satya*), non-stealing (*asteya*), and adopt only as many possessions as required (*yāvad-artha-parigraha*). One should practice celibacy (*brahmacarya*), austerity (*tapas*), cleanliness (*śaucya*), study (*svādhyāya*) and worship the supreme being (*puruṣārcana*).[23]
>
> Observing silence, one should become fixed [in a sitting posture] by mastering the appropriate *āsanas*, gradually mastering breath control (*prāṇa*), and practicing withdrawal of the senses from sense objects (*pratyāhāra*) with the mind fixed on the heart.

One should fix the breath on one of the *cakras*[24] of the body with one's mind.

One should contemplate the activities of Lord Viṣṇu and become absorbed (*samādhāna*) in that way.

By these and other processes, alert, and with controlled breath, one should gradually fix one's mind, which is prone to corrupt and unspiritual ways, with one's intelligence.

Once one has mastered *āsana* one should establish a seat (*āsana*) in a clean place, and, sitting comfortably, with the body erect, one should perform practice.

One should cleanse the passageway of the air by performing *pūra-kumbhaka-recaka* breath restraints[25] or by the reverse processes, such that the *citta* can become fixed and undistracted.

The mind of the *yogī* whose breath is controlled should soon become purified, just as iron, [melted by] fire and fanned by wind, releases its impurities.

By *prāṇāyāma* one can burn imperfections;[26] by *dhāraṇā*, one's sins; by *pratyāhāra*, contact with sense objects; and by *dhyāna*, ungodly tendencies. When one's mind is perfectly controlled by the practice of *yoga*, with one's gaze fixed on the tip of the nose, one should meditate on the form of God (*Bhagavān*).

He has pleasing lotus-like features, with reddish eyes like the interior of a lotus, and is dark like the petals of a blue lotus. He bears a conch, discus and club. His shiny silken garments are yellow like the filament of a lotus, the *kaustubha* jewel adorns his neck, and the mark of *śrīvatsa* his chest.[27]

His neck is encircled by a forest garland with intoxicated humming bees swarming about it, and he is adorned by a magnificent necklace, bracelets, helmet, armlets and anklets.

His hips are adorned with a brilliantly shining girdle, and he is seated in the lotus of the heart. His countenance is serene and he has the most beautiful appearance, gladdening the eyes and the mind.

He is eternally gorgeous to behold, and is worshipped by the entire universe. He has the youthful vigor of the prime of youth, and is anxious to bestow his blessings upon his devotees.

The glories of this exalted person are worthy of recitation in hymns, and bring renown to pious people [who glorify him]. One should perform meditation (*dhyāna*) upon the entire form of the Lord, until the mind no longer deviates . . .

A person, at this point, with heart flowing with love for the Lord, Hari, *bhagavān*; with hair standing on end from ecstasy; and constantly overwhelmed with streams of tears from intense love, gradually withdraws the hook of the *citta*.[28]

At this stage, the mind suddenly attains liberation (*nirvāṇa*), and enters the state of freedom, detached and without objects, like the flame of a lamp [when it is extinguished]. Freed from the flow of the *guṇas*, one now perceives the *ātman*, fully manifest and autonomous.

The *yogī*, as a result of this supreme dissolution of the mind, becomes situated in the wonders of the *ātman*, and, attaining the nature of the higher self, realizes that the cause of the experiences of pleasure and pain (*duḥkha*) that he had previously attributed to his own self, were actually occurring in the *ahaṅkāra*, which has no ultimate and enduring reality.

त्रयम् एकत्र संयमः ॥४॥

III.4 trayam ekatra saṁyamaḥ

trayam, three; *ekatra*, together; *saṁyamaḥ, saṁyama*

When these three are performed together, it is called *saṁyama*.

Returning to Patañjali's more frugal *sūtras*, this verse informs us that when *dhāraṇā, dhyāna*, and *samādhi* are performed together, *ekatra*, on an object, the act of concentration is called *saṁyama*. Vyāsa uses the term *tāntrika* to describe this, and, certainly, the *tantras* are a body of texts that, among other things, deal with the types of mystic powers that occupy the bulk of this chapter. The commentators simply state that rather than laboriously list all three each time *dhāraṇā, dhyāna*, and *samādhi* are to be performed together, Patañjali has introduced a technical term, *saṁyama*, to refer to the application of the three of them in sequence.

Hariharānanda raises the obvious question: Why are *dhāraṇā* and *dhyāna* relevant at all at this point, since they are already superseded by the time one attains *samādhi*? His reply seems to be that all three types of contemplation are required in order to know an object thoroughly in all its aspects.[29] Another explanation might be that one would assume that the *yogī* (at least most *yogīs*) cannot just snap instantly into a state of *samādhi*. The mind first has to be gradually eased away from external awareness and progressively stilled through the stages of *dhāraṇā* and *dhyāna*. Thus the *yogī* sits down to meditate and, applying *dhāraṇā* in the transition period from conventional awareness to the concentrated state, progressively focuses the mind until *samādhi* is attained.

तज्जयात् प्रज्ञालोकः ॥ ५ ॥

III.5 taj-jayāt prajñālokaḥ

tat, that; *jayāt*, from mastery; *prajñā*, wisdom; *ālokaḥ*, vision, light

From *saṁyama* comes insight.

The commentators have little to say here except that as one becomes fixed in *saṁyama*, so one becomes immersed in the wisdom of *samādhi, prajñāloka*. Various levels of insight involving *prajñā* have been discussed previously (I.20, 48–49; II.27), as have the various stages of *samādhi* in the first chapter.

तस्य भूमिषु विनियोगः ॥ ६ ॥

III.6 tasya bhūmiṣu viniyogaḥ

tasya, its; *bhūmiṣu*, on the stages or planes; *viniyogaḥ*, application

***Saṁyama* is applied on the [different] stages [of *samādhi*].**

One must proceed along each plane of *samādhi* consecutively, says Vyāsa; one cannot skip a step with one's eye on a higher stage and expect to attain the insight mentioned in the previous *sūtra*. No one who sets off for the river Gaṅgā from Śilāhrada, says Vācaspati Miśra, reaches there without passing across the Meghavana. An archer can pierce more subtle targets only when he has mastered larger ones, says Vijñānabhikṣu, and one can climb stairs only step by step. In short, *yogic* insight is attained in stages. The only exception to this progression recognized by the commentators is for one who has attained the higher stages by the grace of God, *Īśvara*. For such a person, the accomplishments of the lower stages are automatically achieved. Otherwise, it is only by the practice of *yoga* itself that one knows what the next stage is, according to Vyāsa. Or, inversely, sometimes, by trying to fix one's mind on a higher stage, one realizes that one is actually qualified only for a lower stage, says Vijñānabhikṣu.

त्रयम् अन्तरङ्गं पूर्वेभ्यः ॥७॥

III.7 trayam antar-aṅgaṁ pūrvebhyaḥ

trayam, three; *antar*, internal; *aṅgam*, limbs;
pūrvebhyaḥ, than the previous ones

These three [*dhāraṇā*, *dhyāna*, and *samādhi*] are internal limbs compared to the previous limbs [of *yoga*].

It is the three limbs involved in the process of *saṁyama*, here called internal, *antar*, that primarily occupy the attention of Patañjali in the *Yoga Sūtras*, not the five external limbs, says Vācaspati Miśra, even though all eight limbs of *yoga* are essential ingredients. Al-Bīrunī states that internal means more removed from the senses;[30] Vijñānabhikṣu says that internal refers to the purification of the mind, and external to the purification of the body. Certainly the higher states cannot be attained without practicing the *yamas* and *niyamas*. Nonetheless, although indispensable, the former limbs are only indirectly relevant to meditation, says Vijñānabhikṣu; the latter are directly relevant. However, as always in the Indic traditions, there is room for rare exceptions, and Vijñānạbhikṣu notes that certain elevated souls like Jaḍabharata directly attain the stage of *saṁyama* simply by virtue of their *yogic* practices in former lives, without the need to practice the other limbs of *yoga* in this life.

In the *Bhāgavata Purāṇa* (V.7–14), Jaḍabharata had been a king named Bharata in a previous life. When the time was appropriate, he gave responsibility for his kingdom to his sons and betook himself to the forest to fix his mind on Lord Viṣṇu without distraction, as per the Purāṇic ideal. One day, as he was sitting in his hermitage, he witnessed a pregnant deer, startled by a nearby lion, leap over the stream where she had been drinking and prematurely deliver her offspring as she leapt, which fell into the river. When the poor deer died from the sheer trauma and exhaustion of the incident, the kindhearted Bharata felt impelled to save the helpless newborn deer drowning in the current. Adopting the orphaned fawn, the saintly king nourished it, protected it, and ended up so completely attached to it that he became diverted from his worship and *yogic* practice, to the point that he was found absorbed in thought of the deer when death came to claim him at his given time.

In resonance with the *Gītā* (VIII.6), where Kṛṣṇa states that "one will attain [after death] whatever state of being one remembers when one leaves one's body," Bharata was reborn as a deer. However, because he had, after all, performed years of *yoga* practice and devotional worship in his previous life, he retained full awareness and past remembrance of the events that had caused his present situation despite being bound in the body of a deer. He thus waited until the *karma* responsible for this condition was exhausted and death came once more to remove him from this deer birth.

Again in resonance with the *Gītā* (VI.42–43), which states that unsuccessful *yogīs* take rebirth in a pious family where they again take up their practices from wherever they had left off in their past life, Bharata was next reborn in the family of a pious *brāhmaṇa*, endowed once more with recollection, this time of his past two births. Determined never again to fall prey to attachment, he postured to the world as an insane mute, so that people would ignore and shun him. Although a fully self-realized *yogī*, Bharata wandered around naked and unkempt, completely disassociated from his bodily functions and social norms. Vijñānabhikṣu thus refers to him to illustrate someone who had attained the highest level of *samādhi* without the need for cultivating the previous limbs of *yoga* in his present life, but, obviously, Bharata had already performed these in his previous life.

The point is that the goal of *yoga* is *samādhi*, and Vijñānabhikṣu goes on to quote the *Garuḍa Purāṇa*,[31] which states that *āsanas* and such external practices, in and of themselves, do not lead to the goal of *yoga*; indeed, these can be impediments to the real goal of *yoga*. Śaṅkara quotes a similar verse in this regard, that *āsanas* alone do not produce the goals of *yoga*; *samādhi* meditation does, and nothing else.

Vijñānabhikṣu draws from another story from the *Bhāgavata Purāṇa* (X.74.46), where the proud and envious Śiśupāla, who had never performed any type of *yoga* practice, attained the supreme goal of meditation simply because his mind was fixed undeviatingly on Kṛṣṇa. Even though his absorption was out of obsessive hatred for Kṛṣṇa, it nonetheless fulfilled the ultimate requirement of *samādhi*, namely, undeviated concentration.[32] Again, the point is that real *yoga* means meditative absorption on one object.

Vijñānabhikṣu quotes the series of verses from the *Bhagavad Gītā* where Kṛṣṇa lays out something of a hierarchy of *yoga* practice:

> Fix your mind on me alone; absorb your intellect in me. You will thus dwell in me without a doubt. If you are not able to fix the mind on me in *samādhi*, then, O Arjuna, desire to reach me by engaging in *abhyāsa-yoga*, the *yoga* of "practice" [see Patañjali I.12ff]. If you are incapable of practicing *abhyāsa-yoga*, then be intent on performing dutiful activity for my sake. (XII.8–10)

The goal here is clearly expressed as absorption, in this case on Kṛṣṇa. *Abhyāsa*, or practice, is relevant only to achieve this state. The *abhyāsa* referred to by Kṛṣṇa here, says Vijñānabhikṣu, is the same *abhyāsa* mentioned earlier in the *Yoga Sūtras* (I.13), "the effort [to be situated] in steadfastness."

तद् अपि बहिरङ्गं निर्बीजस्य ॥८॥

III.8 tad api bahir-aṅgaṁ nirbījasya

tat, these; *api*, even; *bahiḥ*, external; *aṅgam*, limbs; *nirbījasya*, to "seedless" [*samādhi*]

Yet even these are external limbs in relation to "seedless" *samādhi*.

This *sūtra* indicates that *dhāraṇā*, *dhyāna*, and conventional *samādhi*, although internal when compared to the first five limbs of *yoga*, are themselves considered external, *bahir*, in relation to the highest type of *samādhi* known as *nirbīja*. Even the last three limbs involve focusing the mind on an object and, of course, both the mind itself and all its objects are *prākṛtic*, and therefore external, from the perspective of *puruṣa*. *Nirbīja-samādhi* comes about only when all eight limbs of *yoga* have reached their conclusion, says Vyāsa. There are thus three subdivisions in the path of *yoga* outlined by Patañjali in these *sūtras*: The first five limbs are indirect or preparatory causes of *samprajñāta-samādhi*, the three remaining limbs are direct causes of *samprajñāta-samādhi*, and, finally, the ultimate goal is *asamprajñāta-samādhi*.

व्युत्थाननिरोधसंस्कारयोरभिभवप्रादुर्भावौ
निरोधक्षणचित्तान्वयो निरोधपरिणामः ॥९॥

III.9 vyutthāna-nirodha-saṁskārayor abhibhava-prādurbhāvau nirodha-kṣaṇa-cittānvayo nirodha-pariṇāmaḥ

vyutthāna, outgoing, emerging; *nirodha*, suppression, restraint, control; *saṁskārayoḥ*, of the subliminal imprints; *abhibhava*, overpowering, suppression, disappearance; *prādurbhāvau*, manifestation, appearance; *kṣaṇa*, instant, moment; *citta*, mind; *anvayaḥ*, connected, proceeding; *nirodha*, suppression; *pariṇāmaḥ*, development

The state of restraint, *nirodha*, is when there is disappearance of outgoing [i.e., worldly] *saṁskāras* and the appearance of restraining *saṁskāras*. These emerge in the mind at the moment of restraint.

In this *sūtra*, as well as III.11 and 12 below, Patañjali speaks of three types of *pariṇāma*, transformations or developments of the mind. Since change and movement at every moment are the very nature of the *guṇas*, says Vyāsa, the question arises as to what type of change takes place during the moments when the mind is restrained, which by definition should entail no change or movement at all. In other words, the *guṇas* are always in flux, and since the *guṇas* underpin the entirety of *prakṛti* and consequently everything emanating from her, everything in manifest reality is therefore constantly in motion. This includes the mind, which, as we know, is also *prākṛtic*. If the mind, like all *prākṛtic* products, is by its very metaphysical nature constantly in motion and changing because of the ever-shifting *guṇas* that constitute it, how is it possible to still the mind? This would seem to be inherently impossible.

The mind is made of *saṁskāras*, and Vyāsa, following Patañjali in this *sūtra*, divides these into two basic types: *vyutthāna*, outgoing *saṁskāras* that propel the mind into any kind of activity, and *nirodha*, restraining *saṁskāras*, which are activated in meditation and restrain the outgoing *saṁskāras*. Patañjali is now providing more detailed and subtle information as to the mechanics underpinning the state of *citta-vṛtti-nirodha* that he established as the goal of *yoga*. Specifically, *nirodha* is attained by *nirodha-saṁskāras*. According to the psychology of *samādhi*, when the *yogī* sets about meditating, what is actually occurring is that a restraining *nirodha* set of *saṁskāras* is being cultivated to suppress the normal flow of mundane outgoing, *vyutthāna, saṁskāras* active in the turmoil of everyday thought. Thus, when the mind is active and roaming about as in normal consciousness, the restraining *saṁskāras* are latent and therefore absent, and when the restraining *saṁskāras* are active and dominant, the outgoing ones are being suppressed. The idea is that there is always an ongoing dynamic between these two, and therefore, even when the mind is restrained in meditation, there is a tussle between the restraining *saṁskāras* and the others, and consequently ongoing movement, albeit imperceptible to the meditator. In other words, on a metaphysical level, there is always movement in *prakṛti*, however subtle, even when the mind appears to be completely restrained and fixed in the higher stages of *sabīja-samādhi*.

Saṁskāras are not destroyed; they are either active or latent (although, as we know, they can be weakened or burnt and thereby rendered impotent). Even when sense cognition, which produces *saṁskāras*, is checked, the store of *saṁskāras* from previous sense cognition does not just disappear; *saṁskāras* remain latent and can activate at any time—the cloth is not destroyed when the weaver is absent, says Vācaspati Miśra. By practicing meditation, the force or potency of the outgoing *saṁskāras* from the store of *saṁskāras* is gradually lessened, and the emergence and strengthening of *nirodha* ones increased—although, as Vijñānabhikṣu points out, this is a gradual process that increases through practice. This dynamic between these two sets of *saṁskāras* is the movement that takes place during meditation. Therefore, at every moment of meditation, there is suppression of the latent outgoing *saṁskāras* and strengthening of the restraining *saṁskāras* that are performing this task of suppression. Hariharānanda compares it to the struggle of a spring under the stress of weight—the springing potential of the spring does not disappear, it remains latent, but this occurs only when a constant restraining pressure is applied. The relationship between the two sets of *saṁskāras* is thus never static. The reader can refer back to I.18 for further discussion on this aspect of *yoga*.

तस्य प्रशान्तवाहिता संस्कारात् ॥१०॥

III.10 tasya praśānta-vāhitā saṁskārāt

tasya, its [the mind's]; *praśānta*, peaceful; *vāhitā*, flow;
saṁskārāt, from subconscious impressions

The mind's undisturbed flow occurs due to *saṁskāras*.

When one becomes proficient in cultivating the restraining *saṁskāras*, say the commentators, the mind can then flow peacefully in meditation without disturbance, *praśānta-vāhitā*, that is, without being distracted by outgoing *saṁskāras*. Contrarily, when these restraining *saṁskāras* become weakened, they are overpowered by the outgoing *saṁskāras*. Or, as Śaṅkara puts it, meditative absorption lasts for as long as the remaining *saṁskāras* are not overcome by outgoing *saṁskāras*.

It is important to note that the restraining *saṁskāras* are in actuality a continuous series of *saṁskāras*. As will be discussed further below, the restraining (or any type of) *saṁskāras* are actually an ongoing sequence of similar *saṁskāras*, like a movie reel of identical stills. Nothing is static. Even in deep meditation, a continuous sequence of restraining *saṁskāras* is in motion in the controlled mind. Hence Patañjali uses the term flow, *vāhitā*, in this *sūtra*.

One might note here, given the periodic statements in the texts to establishing the Yoga position on mind and consciousness in distinction to the Buddhist one, as well as the dedication of a good portion of Chapter IV by Patañjali and the commentators to this end, that, at least on a surface level, both traditions do accept that external reality consists of a never-ending flow of interdependent, interconnected phenomena. For Yoga, too, the *saṁskāras* that comprise the *citta*, as well as the *aṇus*, the smallest physical subatomic particles of which the more physical aspects of *prakṛti* (the *mahābhūtas*) are composed, are constantly in motion in a successive flow, each individual *saṁskāra* or *aṇu* arising and instantly being followed by a subsequent *saṁskāra* or *aṇu* before disappearing. The difference is that in Sāṅkhya, the *saṁskāras* or *aṇus* do not actually disappear but revolve back into their substratum, which is ultimately *prakṛti*. *Prakṛti*, like *puruṣa*, is an eternal substance with a permanent essence (an autonomous selfhood, to use typical Buddhist phraseology). That is to say, whereas its evolutions and permutations may be in constant flux and temporary, it has an independent essence, an eternal and constant self that is not metaphysically dependent on or interdependent with anything else.[33] As we know, in Buddhism, in contrast, there are no essential, autonomous, independent entities either spiritual or physical. Thus, while both traditions might agree on the basic flux of the surface level of reality—the "flow" of this *sūtra*—their differences lie in whether there is a permanent substratum that underpins it. For Yoga, the two permanent and eternal substrata of reality are *puruṣa* on the one hand and *prakṛti* on the other.

सर्वार्थतैकाग्रतयोः क्षयोदयौ चित्तस्य समाधिपरिणामः ।।११।।

III.11 sarvārthataikāgratayoḥ kṣayodayau cittasya samādhi-pariṇāmaḥ

sarva-arthatā, [focused on] all objects; *eka-agratayoḥ*, focused on one object; *kṣaya*, destruction; *udayau*, rise; *cittasya*, of the mind; *samādhi*, meditative absorption; *pariṇāmaḥ*, transformation

The attainment of the *samādhi* state involves the elimination of all-pointedness [i.e., wandering] of the mind and the rise of one-pointedness [i.e., concentration].

Vyāsa notes that the nature of the mind is to be all-pointed, *sarva-artha*, that is, scattered and roaming about anywhere and everywhere and thinking of all manner of random things. In normal consciousness the propensity of the mind is ever restless and always thinking about sense objects, the past and future, worrying about this and that, etc. However, the mind also has an inherent potential of being one-pointed, *eka-agratā*, or fixed on one object. When the latter propensity is developed to its highest potential, the state of *samādhi* is attained. Vācaspati Miśra reminds us that nothing is ever destroyed—when one of these propensities of the mind arises, that is, when one set of *saṁskāras* discussed in the last verse activates, the other propensity always remains latent. Vijñānabhikṣu adds that changing the nature of the mind is a gradual process; it does not occur instantly, as anyone who has experimented with fixing the mind on one object for a prolonged period will know.

ततः पुनः शान्तोदितौ तुल्यप्रत्ययौ चित्तस्यैकाग्रतापरिणामः ॥१२॥

III.12 tataḥ punaḥ śāntoditau tulya-pratyayau cittasyaikāgratā-pariṇāmaḥ

tataḥ, then; *punaḥ*, again; *śānta*, that which has been subdued, the past; *uditau*, that which has arisen, the present; *tulya*, equal; *pratyayau*, idea, image; *cittasya*, of the mind; *ekāgratā*, one-pointedness; *pariṇāmaḥ*, transformation

In that regard, the attainment of one-pointedness occurs when the image in the mind that has just passed is the same as the image in the mind that is present.

When one says that the mind is one-pointed or fixed, *eka-agratā*, state the commentators, what is actually meant is that the previous cognition or image, *pratyaya*, in the mind that has subsided is identical to the cognition or image that succeeds it. This underscores the fact that the mind is never static but always flowing. Concentration involves replacing a previous mental image with the same image and so on in an ongoing series. This is like the roll of the same identical image on the consecutive slides of a movie reel, thereby producing what appears to be a static picture but is in actuality a flow of identical but separate momentary images—as one momentary image subsides, it is followed by another seemingly identical momentary image.

One might object that this constant change of one image by another, albeit identical, image during meditation nonetheless means that the mind is in reality not actually fixed and unmoving at all, says Rāmānanda Sarasvatī, since these momentary images are constantly succeeding each other and thus coming and going in constant movement. This is technically correct: When we say that the mind is fixed in *samādhi*, we are being rhetorical. What this actually means is that, in meditation, the constant movement of the mind is focused on the same image—it is one-pointed—while during normal consciousness, the constant movement of the mind can randomly flit about and temporarily focus on anything at any given moment. As noted above, everything in *prakṛti* including the mind is constantly in motion because *prakṛti* is constituted by the *guṇas*, and the *guṇas* are in constant flux by their very nature. Technically, it is *rajas* that impels movement; both *sattva* and *tamas* are quiescent by nature. Without *rajas* there would be no motion in anything *prākṛtic*—indeed, there would be no things emerging from *prakṛti* in the first place, since there would be no impetus to stir *prakṛti* into emergence. Since *rajas* is inherent in the very nature of *prakṛti*, everything is in constant motion once creation has been set in motion. Hence meditation is about keeping a flow of *saṁskāras* fixed on an object, rather than a state of actual ontological stillness. Additionally, Vijñānabhikṣu does well to point out that while *yoga* is defined as *citta-vṛtti-nirodha*, technically speaking this entails all *vṛttis* other than the one solitary stable *vṛtti* containing the object of concentration.[34]

एतेन भूतेन्द्रियेषु धर्मलक्षणावस्थापरिणामा व्याख्याताः ॥१३॥

III.13 etena bhūtendriyeṣu dharma-lakṣaṇāvasthā-pariṇāmā vyākhyātāḥ

etena, by this; *bhūta*, an object; *indriyeṣu*, the senses; *dharma*, nature, characteristics; *lakṣaṇa*, qualities, temporal state; *avasthā*, condition, state; *pariṇāmāḥ*, development, change; *vyākhyātāḥ*, is explained

In this way, the change in the characteristics, state, and condition of objects and of the senses is explained.

The above discussion on the changing states of the mind is also applicable to the senses and the sense objects, says Vyāsa, in one of his longest commentaries on the *sūtras*. Patañjali here essentially indicates that the constant change underpinning all manifest reality can be categorized according to *dharma, lakṣaṇa*, and *avasthā*, characteristics, state, and condition. The commentators understand *dharma*, the characteristics of an object mentioned by Patañjali in this *sūtra*, to be that which is specific and distinctive about that object. (It can also refer to the function an object performs.) *Dharma* has a variety of different but overlapping meanings in Hindu and Buddhist knowledge systems[35]—perhaps the best-known usage being that in the *Bhagavad Gītā* where it refers to an individual's social duties or function in society as determined by the person's natural propensities, activities, and psychological inclinations or characteristics (IV.13). This usage overlaps somewhat with the more metaphysical usage of the term here, insofar as it points to the specific inherent characteristics evidenced in an individual.

For example, if clay, at a particular point in time, is made into a pot, it assumes the characteristics of being a pot rather than of being a cup or saucer and its function in the grand scheme of things is that it is a container for substances. The pot is thus a specific *dharma* that is potential in the clay, and the same clay can assume different *dharmas* by being transformed into other things such as saucers and cups. As will be discussed in the next verse, the clay is the *dharmin*, literally, possessor of the *dharmas*, that is, the substratum or underlying substance. Along similar lines, gold bracelets, rings, bangles, or necklaces are *dharmas* of gold (which is the *dharmin*).

In parallel fashion, the *lakṣaṇa*, or state, of an object is understood as its situation in time—a pot can exist in the present, it could have existed in the past or, if yet to be made, exist at some point in the future. The *avasthā*, the third item on Patañjali's list, is taken to refer to the condition of the pot—whether in the past, present, or future, it could be a new pot in good condition, or an old pot, etc. All objects in manifest reality can thus be conceived of as undergoing constant change according to characteristics, state, and condition.

The commentators connect these categories to the mind and the discussion in the previous *sūtras*: The *dharma* of the mind at any given moment is all-pointed—roaming about uncontrolled—or one-pointed. This *dharma*, in turn, is qualified by *lakṣaṇa*, temporal state—the mind could have been one-pointed in the past, or be so in the future, for example, but not in the present. This, too, is qualified by condition—understood in this context to refer to the fact that when the mind is one-pointed, its roaming potential is suppressed, and vice versa.

The point in all this is that the *guṇas*, which underpin all reality whether of the nature of mind or pots, engage in ceaseless activity—things are always changing from future to present to past, from old to new, from pots back into clay and then from clay anew into cups and saucers. But the underlying material substance does not change; only its characteristics, condition, and states change. The clay remains the underlying substance, even when transformed into items with specific characteristics such as pots and then again cups, and irrespective of the time and state in which these items are to be found at any given point. Similarly, the mind remains the same basic substratum whether one-pointed or not. If a gold vessel, says Vyāsa, is melted and made into something else, it does not cease to be gold. Moreover, the gold in any particular object contains the potential of being molded into any other golden object that has been made in the past and might be made in the future. Therefore, in a sense, the past and the future are latent in the present. As the commentators put it, just because a man is interested in one woman at any point in time does not mean he is disinterested in other women; the potential for a change in interest is there, and this may have manifested in the past and may manifest again in the future. And again, along similar lines, a woman might be seen as a mother or daughter or sister or wife depending on context and relationship, just as an object might be perceived differently from different perspectives. But the essential woman herself remains the same, as does the underlying substance constituting all manifest objects.

Patañjali has introduced this somewhat protracted philosophical discussion at this point in the *sūtras* because there is an indispensable metaphysical dimension that needs to be established here. It is essential to grasp the underlying operative principles inherent in material reality according to the Sāṅkhya and Yoga schools in order to understand the mechanics underpinning the *siddhis*, mystic powers, which will occupy most of the rest of the chapter. The Yoga school, along with the Sāṅkhya school, subscribes to a metaphysical view called *satkārya*, that any effect is present in its cause. For these schools, all manifest material reality is simply a transformation of the underlying cause, the *guṇas* of *prakṛti*. All change, then, is simply a change of *prakṛti*'s characteristics, condition, and states. Dasgupta, using the language of loosening of *prakṛti*'s barriers that will be encountered in IV.3, puts this as follows:

> Production of effect only means an internal change of the arrangement of atoms [*aṇus*] in the cause, and this exists in it in a potential form, and just a little loosening of the barrier which was standing in the way of the happening of such a change or arrangement will produce the desired new collocation—the effect. This doctrine is called *satkārya-vāda*, i.e., that the *kārya* or effect is *sat* or existent even before the causal operation to produce the effect was launched. (1922, 257)

The difference between a banyan tree and a bed of roses or anything else is simply its configuration of *aṇus*. When the tree dies, its constituent *aṇus* dissolve back into *prakṛti*, to reappear in new forms and configurations.

One is reminded here of the famous verses in the *Chāndogya Upaniṣad* (VI.1.4ff):

> It is just as from one lump of clay, one can understand everything made of clay, dear boy. The transformation [of a clay object from clay] is just a name, a verbal handle—the reality is actually that "it is just clay."
>
> It is just as from one copper object, one can understand everything made of copper, dear boy. The transformation [of a copper object from copper] is just a name, a verbal handle—the reality is actually that "it is just copper."
>
> It is just as from one nail cutter, one can understand everything made of iron, dear boy. The transformation [of an iron object from iron] is just a name, a verbal handle—the reality is actually that "it is just iron."

In other words, we may call a clay object a pot or plate but essentially it is nothing but a transformation of clay. The names we apply to these transformations of clay are merely verbal handles. As a handle allows us to use the object to which it is attached, names allow us to refer to objects such that useful communication between individuals can take place. The same holds true for any object in *prakṛti*. The Yoga school thus demarcates itself from other schools such as Nyāya and Vaiśeṣika, which, as subscribers to the *asatkārya-vāda* view, hold that the effect is not in one single underlying substratum such as *prakṛti*, as per the *satkārya-vāda* position, but rather in multiple distinct and separate causes,[36] or Buddhism, which holds that there are no ultimate, eternal, autonomous underlying substrata at all. Indeed, Yamashita (1994) considers the specifics of Vyāsa's comments here to be a direct refutation of the view of the fifth-century Buddhist philosopher Vasubandhu in his *Abhidharmakośa-bhāṣya*. It is important to keep the Buddhist challenge in mind given the counterarguments that occupy a fairly significant portion of Patañjali's and our commentators' attention (especially, as we shall see, in Chapter IV).[37]

शान्तोदिताव्यपदेश्यधर्मानुपाती धर्मी ॥१४॥

III.14 śāntoditāvyapadeśya-dharmānupātī dharmī

śānta, ceased, the past; *udita* arisen, the present; *avyapadeśya*, that which has not been named, the future; *dharma*, characteristics; *anupātī*, follows, is a consequence of; *dharmī*, that which possesses characteristics, the substratum

The substratum is that which underpins past, present, and future.

Everything is essentially everything, says Vyāsa, at least potentially, since ultimately *prakṛti* and her *guṇas* are inherent and underpin all reality. Here, the same point is underscored: Beneath all permutations of matter, whether past, *śānta*; present, *udita*; or future, *avyapadeśya*, lies a constant substratum, *dharmin*. In the last *sūtra, dharmas* were discussed—clay can be molded into objects displaying specific characteristics, *dharmas*, such as pots and plates. These *dharmas* are potential in the clay. The *dharmī* (*dharmin*[38]) of this *sūtra* is that which produces (literally, possesses) the *dharmas*; it is the substratum from which specific things with their own character evolve. The *dharmin* underpins and remains common to all past, present, or future manifestations of its *dharmas*. So, in the example given above, the clay itself is the *dharmin*, and the pots and plates produced from it in the past, present, or future, the *dharmas*. However, clay itself is a product of something subtler and more primordial, *prakṛti*, and thus clay and all objects in manifest reality are, in turn, themselves *dharmas* of a more subtle substratum, *prakṛti* herself, the ultimate *dharmin*.

Due to the conditions of time, space, and various other causal factors, this substratum, *prakṛti*, does not manifest everything at one and the same time—saffron grows in Kashmir and not Pañcāla, the monsoon rains come in the summer and not the winter, and a deer gives birth to a deer and not a man, says Vācaspati Miśra—but this is due to different external factors and conditions, the same substratum remains. Therefore, everything is ultimately made of the same stuff and thus is essentially identical to everything else. The past is that which has performed its function and merged back into its substratum, the present is manifest at any given moment, and the future is that which exists in potential (*śakti*). Thus, says Bhoja Rāja, since everything is essentially a temporary manifestation (*dharma*) of *prakṛti*, a cloth is essentially not different from a pot when considered from the perspective of its deepest metaphysical makeup. Or, as Śaṅkara puts it, "The three worlds exist on a finger tip."

This principle is essential in understanding, from the contours of Sāṅkhyan metaphysics, the mechanics of the mystic powers that are to be discussed shortly in this chapter. *Īśvara*, God, as well as advanced *yogīs* who have mastered the techniques that will be encountered in the ensuing *sūtras*, are believed to be able to remove what the commentators call the conditions—what we might call the laws of nature—that cause things to act according to what is considered to be their expected natures. Thus, since everything exists in potential form in *prakṛti*, by manipulating or rearranging the subtle substructure of physical reality and the normal conditions that historically or naturally operate on it in conventional reality, a *yogī* can cause matter to behave in what appears to be supernatural or miraculous ways.

From the perspective of Yoga metaphysics, however, there is nothing magical about such phenomena, once the Sāṅkhyan physics underpinning reality is understood and the techniques for manipulating this reality outlined below are mastered. Specifically, as can be seen from the Sāṅkhya chart in the introduction, all gross physical objects in manifest reality according to this system are manifestations of *prakṛti*'s primary evolutes of mind—*buddhi* and *ahaṅkāra*. These are universalized evolutes—they underpin the universe of all manifest things—but they also exist in individualized form—each individual living being has its own *buddhi* and *ahaṅkāra*. An individual's *buddhi*, according to the Yoga school, is potentially universal (see the commentary on IV.10), which can only mean that it can transcend its limitations and, in principle at least, merge with the cosmic or universal *buddhi* underpinning all objects. Thus, once the delimiting influence of the *kleśas* are removed, by the power of sheer concentration, the *yogī*'s mind can spill out beyond its individualized containment, reconnect with its universal potential, and consequently influence or rearrange the evolutes emerging from its macronature as the universal mind. All this needs to be kept in mind when considering the mystic claims of the succeeding *sūtras*, if we are to consider how *siddhis* might appear rational and logical to a Yoga philosopher.

Before proceeding, Vyāsa takes this opportunity to contrast the metaphysics of the Yoga school with the Buddhist notion of *kṣaṇika-vāda*, momentariness. According to almost all Buddhist sects, there is no underlying substance, *dharmin*, that pervades the temporary forms and states of manifest reality. There is merely the momentary appearance of the characteristics, states, and conditions of III.13 themselves. These are interdependent on each other; they cannot exist in isolation or independence. No autonomous permanent essence or substratum underpins them, either in the form of *prakṛti* and, by extension, its evolute of mind, or *puruṣa*; reality is just a flow of ephemeral, connected moments of existence, all of them interdependent. Thus, while the Buddhists would accept the notion of the "change in the characteristics, state, and condition of objects and of the senses" from the previous *sūtra*, they would consider these to be the ultimate nature of reality and not qualities of a *dharmin*, substratum (*prakṛti*), as indicated in this *sūtra*. There are no *dharmins* in Buddhism, only *dharma-lakṣaṇāvasthā-pariṇāmāḥ*, as per III.13.[39]

Vyāsa presents one of the familiar orthodox Hindu arguments against this view (see, for example, *Vedānta Sūtras* II.2.25): How, from this perspective, does one account for memory? If objects previously seen are subsequently recognized, they must have been previously experienced. If previously experienced, there must be a constant substratum to the mind preserving the memory. Otherwise, if the mind changes at every instant and thereby becomes a different entity from one instant to the next, how would it recognize something recorded by the previous, and entirely different, mind? As Vācaspati Miśra puts it: Yajñadatta does not recall something seen by Devadatta! The argument is taken up again in more detail in the next chapter.

Vyāsa also presents the common Hindu argument of *karma* against the Buddhist *kṣaṇika-vāda* view.[40] If everything is constantly changing, then an actor who acts and thus plants a seed of *karmic* reaction one minute would not be the same person who would receive the fruit later. If personhood, along with everything else, is momentary, a different person emerges every moment. Thus, the person receiving the *karmic* fruit of action at the moment of its fruition would not be the same person as the original actor who merited such fruit. It would be like saying Devadutta receives the fruit of actions performed by Caitra. Where would be the moral justice in this? Further arguments differentiating Yoga perspectives from mainstream Buddhist ones are presented in Chapter IV.

क्रमान्यत्वं परिणामान्यत्वे हेतुः ।।१५।।

III.15 kramānyatvam pariṇāmānyatve hetuḥ

krama, succession, sequence; *anyatvam*, change; *pariṇāma*, transformation; *anyatve*, in change; *hetuḥ*, the cause

The change in the sequence [of characteristics] is the cause of the change in transformations [of objects].

This *sūtra*, immediately preceding the primary topic of this chapter, *siddhis*, mystic powers, reiterates the same basic point: Patañjali and the commentators are ensuring that the metaphysical infrastructure is in place for a correct understanding of the topic that occupies much of this chapter. The transformations, *pariṇāma*, visible in an object are simply the result of the change in the sequence, *krama*, in that object's characteristics, state, and condition: Clay powder, when water is added, becomes clay dough, which becomes a clay pot, which, when broken, becomes clay pot shards, which eventually become clay powder. All change is thus a sequence of characteristics, not a change of substance, in this case, clay (of course, as noted previously, clay itself in this example is in turn a characteristic of an even more subtle substratum, *prakṛti* and her finer evolutes; thus something can simultaneously be a substratum for further transformations and itself a transformation of a substratum even more subtle than itself).

The same applies to temporal changes of state noted in III.13: The clay pot existing in the past has changed into the pot perceivable in the present, which will change into the pot that will exist in the future, but the substratum of clay remains constant. Changes of condition follow the same principle: A new pot gradually starts to become old in successive stages from the moment it comes into existence. Changes of condition, which occur every instant at the atomic level, are not perceivable moment by moment, but they are after the lapse of time—one becomes gradually aware that something is becoming old and no longer new; if grain is left in a grain pit for a great number of years, says Vācaspati Miśra, the structure of its particles becomes reduced to such a state that it will crumble into atoms upon being touched. Although it takes many years to approach such a state that is perceivable in this way, in actuality it is undergoing change in this direction every instant. Vijñānabhikṣu quotes Kṛṣṇa from the *Bhāgavata Purāṇa*: "Actually, the bodies of all creatures are coming into existence and perishing at every moment by the force of Time, but this is not perceived due to the subtle nature of Time" (XI.22.42). In other words, since the *guṇas* underpinning *prakṛti* are in constant motion, change is the inherent nature of all reality, whether physical or psychic.

With regard to the mind, when considered as a substratum it can manifest two *dharmas*, or characteristics, which *sūtra* III.11 termed one-pointed or all-pointed, fixed or distracted. As discussed in III.9, another way of saying this is that the mind consists of either perceived or active cognitions, when the mind is outgoing or roaming about actively, or unperceived or latent impressions when all *saṁskāras* or thoughts are suppressed and the mind is fixed (Vyāsa here refers to seven characteristics of the mind[41]).

With this detailed metaphysical infrastructure in place, the subsequent *sūtras* return to the topic of *saṁyama* introduced in III.4 and its role in the development of mystic powers.

परिणामत्रयसंयमाद् अतीतानागतज्ञानम् ॥१६॥

III.16 pariṇāma-traya-saṁyamād atītānāgata-jñānam

pariṇāma, transformation; *traya*, threefold; *saṁyamāt*, from *saṁyama*; *atīta*, the past; *anāgata*, the future; *jñānam*, knowledge

When *saṁyama* is performed on the three transformations [of characteristics, state, and condition], knowledge of the past and the future ensues.

This *sūtra* introduces the first of the mystic powers that are achievable by advanced concentration and meditation (although mystic powers connected with the *yamas* and *niyamas* have already been touched upon in the previous chapters). Given the grandiose claims that are made in this chapter, it seems useful to begin with a statement of method. There are various methodologies and disciplines used in the academic study of religion that are especially pertinent when attempting to present or represent such things as mystical truth claims that at face value fall outside of the realm of empirical science as currently construed, or beyond the boundaries of human reason as understood in the context of post-Enlightenment, rational thought. For example, the social-scientific approach favored by some scholars might attempt to explain paranormal claims not on their own terms but as the product of psychological or social forces at play on the psyche of the individual. It seems self-evident that individuals are inescapably influenced both by their greater personal, social, cultural, and historical context, and their individual psyches containing the total of formative life experiences, and that individual experience is mediated by or filtered through such constraints. Mystical truth claims that lie outside the boundaries of verifiable observation or reason are therefore explicitly or implicitly dismissed as inaccurate interpretations of experience stemming from such personal filters, and rational "scientific" explanations are sought by the scholar whose more "objective" vantage point is not impinged upon by the same historic-social-psychological influences.

Other scholars find such reductionistic modes of interpretation problematic, not the least because they impose terms and categories on phenomena that are alien to the frame of reference of the system or body of knowledge in question. Moreover, they inevitably assume elitist perspectives, since they suppose that such sociopsychological forces were unknown to the hapless mystic who reported them (who consequently is implicitly construed as a victim of greater forces he or she does not understand or, indeed, is even aware of). More problematic is the assumption that these forces require the specialized and "rational" vantage point of the objective modern scholar to make sense of. And, of course, the limitations of the scholars own "rational" or empirical worldview is also typically left unchallenged.

Accordingly, a method or cluster of methods or approaches in interpretation loosely known as phenomenology developed which, despite meaning rather different things to different scholars, essentially refrains from forcing modern socioscientific hermeneutical methods on religious truth claims. Some phenomenological approaches attempt to present such claims in their own terms and within their own context, without imposing on them interpretational models from a very different time and context, without judgment, and in as neutral a fashion as possible. One should note that phenomenology does not require the acceptance of the truth claims as necessarily true but attempts to suspend or avoid judgment on issues of validity or historicity or scientific accuracy. Some approaches in phenomenology stress empathy, and even participation, bracketing out one's own personal preconceptions as to what is real or true. Obviously, no one can be fully objective, but the attempt is made to situate oneself in the life-world of the other. Phenomenology concerns sympathetic representation and understanding of truth claims as accurately and objectively as possible within their own context—as phenomena in their own right, so to speak—and avoids making sense of them from the perspective of bodies of knowledge such as socioscientific models alien to the system in question. This section, then, will be descriptive and attempt to represent the subject matter through traditional categories (although obviously any attempt at descriptive representation is a priori an interpretation).

The remaining *sūtras* of this chapter contain claims that will seem astonishingly grandiose and fanciful from our modern perspectives. I will adopt some of the basics of the phenomenological method of interpretation here, as I have done throughout, but I will also attempt to make sense of these claims *from within the parameters of the Sāṅkhya school of metaphysics*; in other words, as they might be conceptualized through traditional Yogic perspectives. I thus take a different approach from much recent scholarship, even that penned by scholars otherwise highly appreciative of Yoga's potential contribution to modern theoretical discussions of mind and consciousness but who clearly find the *siddhi* section awkward, typically brushing it off as imagined, or attempting to rationalize it in some way.

Expectedly, earlier, less sympathetic representations of Yoga during the colonial period pointed to the *siddhis* as grounds for a scathing dismissal of the entire system of Yoga:

> The emaciated, bewildered ascetic, reduced to the dimmest spark of life, equally incapable for lack of energy of committing good or evil is . . . but a shrunken caricature of what man ought to be . . . The Yogin . . . is much deceived in the magical powers he ascribes himself. His self-deception, the corresponding self-deception of the user of drugs . . . constitutes one of the most pathetic chapters of human history. To aim so high, and to fall so low, is in truth both deep tragedy and high comedy. Yet the stupefied Yogin is one of the blundering heroes and martyrs who mark the slow progress of humanity. (Leuba 1919, 205)

Even genuinely sympathetic treatments of the *siddhis* from this period attempted to rationalize them from within the contours of the knowledge systems of the day, as Lanman tried to do by separating "these powers which have some basis in scientifically established fact from those which have none" (1918, 134). One finds Lanman struggling sincerely to accommodate as much from these claims as his post-

Enlightenment sensibilities allowed, referring to "reliable" accounts of *yogīs* being buried alive "from the pen of Sir Claude Martin Wade, who was an actual eye-witness" and accepting the *yogic* claims of being able to enter another's body (III.38) as "indubitably a case of hypnosis" (149).

There has been outstanding recent work on the *sūtras*, in contrast, which realizes the legitimate and inalienable place of the *siddhis* in the system (e.g., Whicher 1998, Feuerstein 1980). Feuerstein is right to adamantly point out that

> [In] the consensus of scholarly opinion . . . the supernatural attainments are discordant with Patañjali's rational approach and his philosophical objectives. However, the fact is that one sixth of the aphorisms concerns precisely this recondite aspect of Yoga, and one chapter . . . is actually entitled *vibhūti-pāda*. How can we account for this obvious pre-eminence given to the "magical" side of the *yogic* path? Was Patañjali, after all, not such a staunch rationalist as contemporary interpreters have made him out to be? Has he perhaps unwittingly succumbed to the magical trend in Yoga, betraying its putative shamanistic origins? These questions can all be instantly disposed of by the simple observation that the powers form an integral part of all *yogic* endeavour. (101–102)

However, whether dismissive or accepting, very little effort has been directed toward attempting to provide a coherent explanation of how these *siddhis* are not only a logical corollary of the parameters of Sāṅkhyan metaphysics but actually inevitable and indispensable to them. These powers were not seen as irrational or prephilosophical by scholastics whose intellectual and rational accomplishments continue to impress us today but were inevitable by-products of the presuppositions of these systems; there are no grounds to suppose that any premodern commentators considered them anything other than factual and literal. Narratives of mystical phenomena pervade the entire Indic textual tradition—not only epic and Purāṇic, it might be noted, but philosophical as well (*Vedānta Sūtras* IV.4.17; *Vaiśeṣika Sūtras* IX.1.11ff and commentaries)—and are commonplace also in Jain and Buddhist traditions (e.g., Buddhaghoṣa's *Visuddhimagga* XII and XIII, and the Buddha's hagiography itself[42]).

Pensa is correct that "the question of 'powers' in Yoga and Buddhism in particular has not infrequently been taken into consideration in a biased, oversimple or at any rate excessively summary fashion . . . the prejudice was thus such as to silence the texts, so to speak" (1969, 197). He finds precedent and continuity for this pervasive acceptance of *siddhis* in the *dhīḥ* of the Vedic *ṛṣi* seers in the earliest Vedic texts. Following Gonda (1984, 68), he translates *dhīḥ* as "exceptional and supranormal faculty, proper to 'seers,' of 'seeing' in the mind things, causes, connections, as they really are, the faculty of acquiring a sudden knowledge of the truth, of the functions and influence of diving powers" (196). Like it or not, *siddhis* are integral to the entirety of Hindu beliefs from their earliest Vedic beginnings right up until the ongoing hagiographies of modern Hindu mystics.[43]

Indeed, tracing imagery from the earliest Upaniṣads through the *Mahābhārata*, the *Yoga Sūtras*, and into the tantric traditions, White has argued that the most applicable definition of *yoga* is precisely that of attainment of mystical powers, a definition that "respects both the spirit and the letter of Hindu sources on the uses of the term yoga, in ways that have remained remarkably unchanged from the time of the Upaniṣads down through the Tantras" (2004, 627; see also White, forthcoming).

Now, one might concede this and (again, one suspects, in the hope of salvaging a "rational" Yoga tradition from a more prerational mythological backdrop) suggest that Patañjali has included this section simply out of deference to the popular cultural expectations of the day concerning *yoga*. In support of this position, one can note that the commentators do not really try to explain the mechanics behind the *siddhis*, unlike their extensive technical analysis of the mechanisms underpinning *citta* and the meditative states. Their commentaries on the *siddhis* are some of the shortest in the text. This certainly suggests that they are writing from a position of scholasticism, *āgama*, rather than claiming to represent any sort of experiential authority, *pratyakṣa-pramāṇa*, in the matter of *siddhis*.

This may very well be the case, but I am not fully convinced by this position. First of all, Patañjali is an intellectual and I find it hard to consider that he has dedicated a fifth of this text just to cater to the silly beliefs of uneducated simpletons.[44] Additionally, there is no indication that the commentators take these *siddhis* as anything other than literal—nor, to my knowledge, has any traditional text or commentary in the entire premodern history of the Indic philosophical and literary traditions, whether folk or scholastic, Buddhist, Hindu, or Jain, taken them as anything other than factual. But more fundamental than this, all the preceding *sūtras* in this chapter, particularly III.13–15, precisely do provide the preparatory infrastructure for a metaphysical explanation of the mechanics underpinning the *siddhis*. I will argue, therefore, that *siddhis* are not only fundamental to the Sāṅkhya Yoga tradition but are also an inherent and inevitable corollary of its metaphysical presuppositions. I can certainly appreciate the motives behind attempts to rationalize and minimize the centrality of the *siddhis* since so much else in the *Yoga Sūtras* has much to offer modern discussions on the psychology and philosophy of mind, but, however uncomfortable to our modern sensibilities, we have no grounds to suppose that Patañjali or the commentators considered the *siddhis* to be anything other than literally factual (any more than to suppose that they take the Hindu cosmography of III.26 to be anything other than literal or factual). Even in III.37, where Patañjali speaks disparagingly about the *siddhis*, this is not because they are fanciful or imaginary but, on the contrary, precisely because they are considered actually to arise, they are therefore real dangers to the *yogī*, not imaginary ones. Certainly the commentaries to this *sūtra* take them in this way.

Accordingly, this study will attempt to consider not whether these claims are true or fanciful, but rather *how* they might be construed as fundamental to the knowledge systems in which they are accommodated, in this case, Sāṅkhyan metaphysics. In other words, to adopt the method outlined above, one must suspend notions of true and false in a modern scientific sense. I present the ensuing *sūtras* on *siddhis* as they are best conceptualized (in my reading) from the perspective of the presuppositions of Sāṅkhya metaphysics. Obviously, the reader will ultimately decide how to make sense of these claims from within the presuppositions of our modern knowledge systems and worldviews, but for the duration of this discussion, the reader is invited to step out of his or her own metaphysical/scientific universe and enter into the world of the accomplished *yogī* as I have understood Patañjali and our commentators to conceive of it. We thus embark on a phenomenological engagement with the *siddhis*.

The ingredients from Patañjali's own *sūtras* relevant to a discussion on the metaphysical analysis of the *siddhis* are as follows:

(1) The gross physical elemental makeup and qualities of any object in reality are essentially a transformation of the *tanmātras*, which, in turn, are a transformation of the *guṇas* (III.44). The first evolutes from the *guṇas* are *buddhi* and *ahaṅkāra* in the Sāṅkhya schema (*Sāṅkhya Kārikā* XXIV–XXV), a schema accepted by Yoga in I.17 and throughout. Thus *buddhi* and *ahaṅkara*, that is to say *citta*, are the immediate substratum of the *tanmātras*.

(2) By sheer concentration, the *yogī* can penetrate the subtle substructure of any material object of meditation, experiencing it, in the *savicāra* state, as raw *tanmātra* energy that transcends the limitations of Time and Space, in other words, attain an experience of external reality that is cosmic in scope (I.44). This is an experience of the object, not merely a perception, as all distinctions of subject, object, and process of knowing dissolve, and the object alone stands forth (I.43; III.3).

(3) The *yogī* can penetrate even this *tanmātra* substratum and experience subtler constitutional dimensions of the object, that is, experience its subtler (more *sāttvic*) nature of *ahaṅkāra*, then of *buddhi*, and finally of its ultimate nature as *prakṛti* (I.45).

(4) The *yogī* can experience the subtlest level of not just an object of meditation but also the entirety of *prakṛti* (I.40, 44).

(5) These types of meditative practices culminate in omniscience (III.49). Metaphysically, omniscience means that, since the mind is potentially omnipresent in Yoga, when it regains the ability to manifest this nature in the higher states of *samādhi*, it can pervade the entirety of *prakṛti* and as a consequence be aware of every atomic detail within *prakṛti* (I.40).

(6) The previous *sūtras* have laid the groundwork for this section on *siddhis* by indicating that the change in an object's visible characteristics—the *dharma, lakṣaṇa*, and *avasthā* of III.13ff—are nothing other than surface-level transformations of the substratum of *prakṛti*, the *dharmin*, which, as noted, the *yogī* can permeate entirely with his or her own *citta* (I.40).

From these points I deduce a hermeneutical principle that I hold as fundamental to understanding how these *siddhis* might be accepted as physically possible by minds as rational as Patañjali (as also the Buddha and almost all premodern Indic thinkers). Specifically, external gross perceivable matter in essence consists of subtler matter, and this of subtler matter still, etc., all of which in Sāṅkhya is ultimately nothing other than a combination of three *guṇas*.[45] This preparatory metaphysical information is the rationale behind the previous verses being situated prior to the section on *siddhis*: the "characteristics, state, and condition" of objects in external reality of III.13ff are nothing other than permutations of the *dharmin*, the substratum. Since *buddhi* is the most subtle *dharmin* substructure after the raw *guṇas* of *prakṛti* themselves, it is in a position to manipulate or determine the nature of all effects emanating from it. If, in Sāṅkhya metaphysics, the *yogī*'s *buddhi* is potentially all-pervading in the higher *samādhi* states and can thus permeate all *prakṛti* (I.40), this can only mean that it merges with the *buddhi* substructure underpinning all reality.[46] In other words, the *yogī* is held to be able to transcend the limitations of the *kleśas* and the *ahaṅkāra*, which have restricted or localized or, better, individualized a portion of the universal *buddhi* into the personal *buddhi* of the adept, and thereby merge into the cosmic *buddhi*. This means it is now in a position to manipulate the external effects emanating from *buddhi*. Thus, by manipulating the substructure one can change the nature of the physical products made of that substructure. Koelman has sensed this principle:

> It is more puzzling to understand how concentration leads, not only to the psychological perfection of exhaustive intuition, but even to the acquisition of supernormal powers . . . [but] if then

> a *yogī* has realized a high degree of concentration, could not the psychological aspect of the three *guṇas* metamorphose itself into its physical aspect? . . . Since *prākritic* Nature is, in its entirety, one single substance working for the liberation of the Selves, it does not seem strange that, in proportion that the *yogī* approaches the final goal, *prakriti* Nature looses its hold on him and he gains control over it. (1970, 242–43)

Again, our challenge here is not whether any of this is factually true from the perspective of modern scientific principles, but to acknowledge the centrality of *siddhis* to the Yoga tradition and consequently to consider how these *siddhis* might be construed within the contours of Sāṅkhya metaphysics.

To illustrate this metaphysics in a manner relevant to the discussion on *siddhis*, let us imagine an alien being on some other planet, who, due to the planet's climate, has never seen water but only ice. We take a chunk of ice with which the alien is familiar and rearrange its atomic substructure by applying heat to it (pervading it with this subtle energy of heat) such that it (to the alien) mysteriously completely changes its form and becomes water—a flowing nonsolid entity completely different to perception from the hard, dense physical ice entity known to the alien. We then apply more heat, and the water vanishes into a completely different form, appearing as cloudy, vaporous, nontangible steam. All we have done is to rearrange the imperceptible but consistent substructure of the ice, its hydrogen and oxygen atoms, such that the external forms produced from them appear magically transformed. It is a parallel manipulation of psychic substructure principle that is to be kept in mind when considering the *siddhis* from the framework of Sāṅkhya cosmology.

With this metaphysical preamble in place, we can now turn our attention to these *siddhis*. In the present *sūtra*, Patañjali states that when *saṁyama*, which we recall involves practicing *dhāraṇā, dhyāna*, and *samādhi* simultaneously, is performed on the "characteristics," "conditions," and "states" of manifest reality (III.13), the *yogī* develops the ability to understand the past, *atīta*, and the future, *anāgata*. The previous discussions have made it clear that the past and the future are inherent in the present—the present is the effect of the past as well as the cause of the future. Thus, by perfectly understanding objects in the present, in terms of their characteristics, conditions, and states, the *yogī* is believed automatically to understand the past that produced them and the future that they, in turn, will produce. Such clarity, Bhoja Rāja states, is inherent in the pure nature of the *sāttvic* mind when freed from the obstructive interference of *tamas*.

Hariharānanda points out that everyone has some ability to predict effects from causes and causes from effects. Whatever jokes we make about weather forecasting, in principle at least, the weather of the next few days is forecast daily based on present meteorological causes, and the present weather is understandable from past conditions. Forecasters would likely hold that any mistakes stem from insufficient knowledge of all the variable causes, not from the essential principle of cause and effect itself. Likewise, economists predict cycles based on present economic indicators and explain present conditions by past financial activity. Even on the most basic level, mothers can predict that their children will be hyper if they consume too much sugar before bedtime and can understand their change of mood by past causes. The common denominator in these and numerous other spheres is that the more one studies and concentrates on a phenomenon, the more insight one develops as to its causes and effects. The power of prediction here is essentially an extension of these principles; by *saṁyama* on the characteristics, conditions, and states of the present, the *yogī* can perceive its causes as well as the effects it will produce. This is another way of saying that such a *yogī* is able to determine the past and predict the future.

Vijñānabhikṣu and other commentators make it clear right from the start of the following section on *siddhis* that the practices discussed in the remainder of this chapter, and the supernormal powers that ensue from them, are not to be performed by those desirous of liberation but only by those desiring power (III.37). Those desirous of liberation should perform *saṁyama* only on the distinction between *puruṣa* and *prakṛti*, the real goal of liberation. Indic traditions in general are very clear that powers can distract the *yogī* from the ultimate goal and embroil the practitioner again in *saṁsāra* since, after all, powers are simply extensions of sensual or physical capabilities. Desiring powers, then, is a more ambitious reenactment of the material predicament, namely, desiring to enjoy *prakṛti* and her possibilities (*bhoga* II.18), and desiring to enjoy *prakṛti* on any level, even through supernormal powers, is the cause of the material bondage of *puruṣa*. Consequently, real *yogīs* neither aspire for such powers nor, if they possess them as unsought by-products of their practices, display them for cheap adulation.

शब्दार्थप्रत्ययानाम् इतरेतराध्यासात् संकरस्तत्प्रविभागसंयमात्
सर्वभूतरुतज्ञानम् ॥ १७ ॥

III.17 śabdārtha-pratyayānām itaretarādhyāsāt saṅkaras tat-pravibhāga-saṁyamāt sarva-bhūta-ruta-jñānam

śabda, word; *artha*, meaning, object; *pratyayānām*, of the idea; *itaretara*, one with the other; *adhyāsāt*, superimposition, imposing; *saṅkaraḥ*, mixing together, confusion; *tat*, their; *pravibhāga*, distinctions, separation; *saṁyamāt*, from *saṁyama; sarva*, all; *bhūta*, creatures; *ruta*, cries, sounds; *jñānam*, knowledge

Due to the correlation between word, meaning, and idea, confusion ensues. By performing *saṁyama* on the distinction between them, knowledge of the speech of all creatures arises.

Here, too, the commentators take the opportunity afforded by this *sūtra* to write profuse commentaries outlining the understanding of language according to the Yoga school. There were various competing streams of thought on the topic of language in ancient India, one of which is the *sphoṭa-vāda*, subscribed to by Patañjali here, and outlined by his commentators.[47] As an aside, although Patañjali himself does not use the term, the Yoga school is the only school that accepts the *sphoṭa* theory of the Grammarian school of philosophy, which lends some credibility to the view that Patañjali the author of the *sūtras*, and Patañjali the grammarian could have been one and the same.[48]

First of all, Patañjali notes in this *sūtra* that there is a distinction between a "word," *śabda*; its "meaning" or the object that it denotes, *artha*; and the "idea" or knowledge of the object that it creates in the mind, *pratyaya*. A *pratyaya* is the specific content of the mind at any given moment—an image of the book one is holding, for example—a term that overlaps in meaning with *vṛtti* (although *vṛtti* is more the state of mind within which the *pratyaya* might occur—the state of right knowledge, or error, or whatever, as discussed in I.10). *Śabda*, when manifest as the audible aspect of a word, is, in and of itself, simply an arrangement of sounds or phonemes, which contains meaning of some object, *artha*, that produces an impression on the mind of the listener (and an utterance a string of such words). Therefore, the word is one thing, the meaning or object itself something else, and the idea or knowledge of the object something else again.

The Patañjali who authored the great commentary, the *Mahābhāṣya*, on Pāṇini's grammar raises the question as to what constitutes speech by using the example of the word *gauḥ*, which, when uttered, gives rise to the idea or knowledge of an animal possessing (in India) dewlap, tail, hump, hooves, and horns. His concern was to establish that meaning or knowledge is the primary ingredient in what constitutes a word—that is, a word is more than just the series of letters or sounds (contra the Mīmāṁsā view, critiqued by our commentators here, which holds that a word is simply the series of letters irrespective of whether meaning is construed from them or not). This inherent meaning-bearing aspect of a word is its *sphoṭa*, which will be discussed further below.

Now, while the word for cow, *gauḥ*, consists of the string of sounds *g-au-ḥ*, the actual animal grazing in the pasture is quite another thing—an actual living being with physical shape and form. And the idea or knowledge of a cow that forms in the mind of a listener who hears the word *gauḥ* is still something else again—it is merely a mental impression or image, a *pratyaya* or *vṛtti* made of *citta*, quite different from the real-life, flesh-and-blood creature out there in the pasture made of gross elements, and different again from a string of sounds in words such as *gauḥ*, which may differ depending on pronunciation and other viarables. Thus "word," "meaning," and "idea" are not identical and may cause confusion, says Patañjali in this *sūtra*; that is, in common usage, these three entities are merged or identified together as if they were one.

To explain the next part of the *sūtra* dealing with *saṁyama* and the ability to understand the speech of all creatures, the commentators embark on a discussion of *sphoṭa* theory. By the manipulation of air in the speaker's mouth, the organ of speech articulates the sound or set of sounds, such as those in the word *g-au-ḥ*, which then vibrate in the air and move toward the hearer's organ of ear, the ear drum, which receives the sounds of the word uttered. Sounds have the potential of expressing all objects (as red, yellow, and blue have of manifesting all colors); it is only their particular sequence that determines which specific object the speaker intends to convey. As each sound of a word is uttered, an impression or trace is left on the mind even though the sound fades away. As the last sound is uttered, the memory connects the *saṁskāras* or imprints of the syllables, and the mind construes meaning from the entirety of the impressions of the phonemes.

Up to this point, the enterprise has been sonic—sound vibration, *dhvani*—but once received by the ear, the word manifests its meaning in the mind of the hearer, which is a function of the mind, and not of sound. Thus, the image or idea of a "cow" arises in the *citta* of the listener. The various schools of Indian philosophy theorized over what causes this jump or transformation from word as sound—the vibration of air—to word as meaning or mental image, a *pratyaya* (or *vṛtti*) in the *citta*. How is meaning construed from this jumble of sounds? Is meaning inherent in the sounds themselves, or is it something separate?

According to the *sphoṭa* view, a meaning-bearing word, *śabda*, is an autonomous and permanent entity, which is made manifest through physical sounds, *dhvani*, but independent from them. The *dhvani* sounds are transitory and they succeed each other. For example, the word *g-au-ḥ*, cow, is not a single physical entity whose sounds coexist and form a single unit: at the instant that *au* is pronounced, the *g* has already disappeared and the final *ḥ* is yet to be uttered. Therefore, meaning cannot be considered to be signified by any individual sound, such as *g*, since otherwise uttering the other letters would be redundant (and *g* occurs in numerous different words such as *gaura*). Nor can meaning be associated with the entire group of sounds, since each one has already disappeared before the next one is uttered—they are not pronounced at the same time and thus they cannot coexist in an entirety. Consequently, there must be something else that underpins and unites these letters such that a meaning can be produced from them. This is considered to be the *sphoṭa*, the permanent meaning-bearing aspect of the word. A word or meaning signifier, *śabda*, is called *sphoṭa*, because a meaning, *artha*, bursts forth (*sphuṭati*) from it.

The important point is that the meaning-bearing *sphoṭa* is a whole undivided entity, and thus different from the sounds of words, which consist of parts (*g-au-ḥ* contains three parts). The *sphoṭa* is thus a connected but different entity from the sounds that "reveal" it. It preexists and is autonomous. (The competing school of *varṇavāda* would say that meaning comes out of the total of the phonemes, *varṇas*, and although these *varṇas* are eternal, meaning is not contained in a separate internal entity, as in *sphoṭa*, but the sum of the individual external phonemic parts, the *varṇas*, when pieced together in the mind.)

Let us consider the word "letter-box," for example. The mind cannot construe meaning from the first phoneme only, since "le-" could refer to "leg," "left," "length," and so many other things. The same holds true for the syllable "let." "Letter" could refer to a letter of the alphabet or a piece of mail, and even "letter-bo" is still not clear as it could refer to "letter boy," "letter bomb," etc. It is only when the final "x" is added that the sequence of sounds is united by the mind and meaning instantly emerges in a sudden burst or flash, producing a mental image—a *pratyaya* in the *citta*—of what the word represents. *Sphoṭa* can thus be considered as the internal innate expressiveness of the word as a meaning-bearer. This meaning is manifest externally through the uttered sounds, which are perceived by the organ of hearing, but both of these serve only to manifest the inner *sphoṭa*. The letters (*varṇas*) or sounds (*dhvanis*), are only the outer garment covering the meaning-bearing word, which is distinct from the phonemic clothing in which it is garbed, and the ear is simply the instrument that receives it. By *saṁyama* on the distinction between the word, its meaning and the idea it produces, Patañjali informs us here, one gains knowledge of the speech of all creatures.

We can recall, from I.18, that the Yoga school subscribes to the view that words are eternally connected with their referents (signifiers to their signs). We need not let the transcendent aspect of *sphoṭa* detain us here except in order to understand the *siddhi* outlined in this *sūtra*. One thing that helps us try to uncover the metaphysical suppositions underpinning this *siddhi* is that, as we know, the letters or phonemes of a word serve as the vehicles through which the preexisting meaning or idea of the object in question, inherent within as the *sphoṭa*, can be made manifest. Thus, in principle at least, although in conventional communication an understanding of a speaker's meaning is dependent on the listener's knowledge of the language used, from the Yoga perspective, the advanced *yogī* is able to perform *saṁyama* on any sequence of sounds and gain access to the meaning and idea present as the *sphoṭa* embedded within even if the language is not known. This, according to the commentators, would appear to include the sounds of any creature, which, one might suppose, are simply different types of sound combinations animals use to convey meaning, that is, represent some eternal *sphoṭa* being expressed. Since these sounds are the external phonemic expressions of a particular object or image in the speaker's or creature's mind, and this object or image is actually present as the internal meaning of the sounds in the form of the autonomous *sphoṭa*, the *yogī* can perform *saṁyama* upon sounds and uncover the original *sphoṭa* underpinning them. Put differently, he or she can retrieve the inner meaning of the word from its outer encasement in the audible sounds of a word, and thus one can understand the meaning and idea behind the speech of any person or creature, even if sounds represent an unknown language. Performing *saṁyama* on sound allows the *yogī*'s mind, which is so intensely and exclusively absorbed in the sound, to penetrate the outer physicality of sound and encounter its inner metatphysical reality of *sphoṭa*. Alternatively, Hariharānanda understands the mechanics of this siddhi as the *yogī* being able to trace sounds back to the vocal cords of the speaker, and from there proceed on to the speaker's mind. As an aside, the *yogī* is believed to also be able to pervade the mind of any being directly, not just through the medium of an uttered sound, but this will be discussed in a later *sūtra*.[49]

संस्कारसाक्षात्करणात् पूर्वजातिज्ञानम् ॥१८॥

III.18 saṁskāra-sākṣāt-karaṇāt pūrva-jāti-jñānam

saṁskāra, mental impression; *sākṣāt*, before one's eyes, making evident; *karaṇāt*, by making; *pūrva*, previous; *jāti*, births; *jñānam*, knowledge

By bringing [previous] *saṁskāras* into direct perception comes the knowledge of previous births.

The *yogī*'s ability to perceive previous births, *pūrva-jāti-jñānam*, has already been touched upon in II.39, and this *siddhi* is taken up again in this *sūtra*, which states that accomplished *yogīs* can access the stock of *karma* accumulated from previous lives, that is to say, the stock of *saṁskāras* stored in their *cittas*, by performing *saṁyama* on them. According to the commentators, *saṁskāras* act in various ways: They are the cause of memories, they are the cause of afflictions (ignorance, ego, attachment, aversion, and clinging to life),[50] and they are responsible for the fruits that accrue from any and all activities of vice and virtue (*karma*). In other words, activity, *karma*, is performed and is recorded as *saṁskāra*, just as sound can be recorded on a tape recorder or an image on a film. When the conditions are appropriate, these *saṁskāras* bear fruit and produce the results of *karma*: type of birth, longevity, and life experience (II.13). Since, according to *yoga* psychology, *saṁskāras* are recorded in their original context, that is, embedded with all the clusters of *saṁskāra* imprints of the time and place of origin in which they were performed, the *yogī* can reactivate them as memories and attain knowledge of the details of all previous births. *Yogīs* are held to be able to obtain knowledge of the previous births of others by the same process.

This *siddhi*, like the others in this section, is pan-Indic. According to Aśvaghoṣa's *Buddha-carita* hagiography, on the evening of his enlightenment:

> The Buddha, having attained supreme mastery in all the techniques of *dhyāna*, meditation, during the first watch of the night, remembered the succession of his previous births. He recalled that "Indeed, I had been such and such a person in such and such a place, and falling [at death] from that situation, came into this [other] situation." (XIV.2–3)[51]

Furthermore, in the second watch of the night, "he saw the births and deaths of all creatures, in accordance with their deeds" (9). This is a standard motif in ancient India: Mahāvīra, the contemporary of the Buddha in the Jain tradition, "knew and saw all conditions of the world, of gods, men and demons: whence they come, whither they go, whether they are born as men or animals or become gods or hell-beings" (*Kalpa-sūtra* 120.1).

Vyāsa uses this *siddhi* to make a greater point in the story of the *yogī* Jaigīṣavya, who could directly perceive all his *saṁskāras* from the previous ten cosmic cycles. Once, another sage, Āvaṭya, who generally roamed about in his subtle body, assumed a gross physical form so as to put some questions to him. He asked Jaigīṣavya whether he had experienced more pain or more pleasure in his numerous births among gods and humans. Even though Jaigīṣavya had been able to preserve a pure *sāttvic* mind and avoid the influence of *rajas* and *tamas* during his myriad births, he replied without hesitation that (in resonance with II.15) he considered all his experiences, whether among humans or gods, to be nothing but suffering, even though he had also experienced the suffering of life as an animal as well as of life in hell with which to make comparisons.

Āvaṭya then queried whether Jaigīṣavya's *yogic* control over *prakṛti* and the happiness he experienced from the contentment resulting from his *sāttvic* disposition should also be included under the category of suffering. The happiness of contentment, he replied, is so called only in comparison to what passes as the pleasure of the senses, but when compared to the bliss of ultimate liberation, even the relative happiness of *sattva* is ultimately also nothing but suffering, since it, too, belongs to the realm of *prakṛti* and the three *guṇas*. Vijñānabhikṣu compares this to rice pudding mixed with both honey and poison. The honey of contentment resulting from the avoidance of *rajas* and *tamas* is mixed with the poison ensuing from *puruṣa*'s involvement with *prakṛti*, even if this involvement is with pure *sattva*. As Patañjali informed us in II.15, for the wise, all is suffering.

प्रत्ययस्य परचित्तज्ञानम् ॥१९॥

III.19 pratyayasya para-citta-jñānam

pratyayasya, from the ideas; *para*, of others; *citta*, of the minds; *jñānam*, knowledge

From [their] ideas, one can attain knowledge of others' minds.

This *sūtra* is understood differently by different commentators. Vācaspati Miśra and Bhoja Rāja read it as indicating that by performing *saṁyama* on other people's *pratyayas*—ideas, notions, and mental images—one can attain an understanding of their minds, *citta-jñānam*. Bhoja Rāja states more specifically that by performing *saṁyama* on a person's facial countenance and expression, a *yogī* can understand the person's state of mind. Obviously, anyone can do this to some extent—one can detect fear, or desire, or anger from a person's facial expressions, so this *siddhi* would seem to be an extension of this ability. Vijñānabhikṣu and Hariharānanda, however, read this *sūtra* as indicating that by *saṁyama* on one's own mind, one can then understand other people's minds. One is reminded of the Buddha's reference to the *siddha* described here. In Pāli Buddhist sources, the state of *ceto pariya ñāṇaṁ* allows the adept to "know the minds of other beings by penetrating them with his own mind. He knows the greedy mind as greedy, and so on."[52]

न च तत् सालम्बनंतस्याविषयीभूतत्वात् ॥२०॥

III.20 na ca tat sālambanaṁ tasyāviṣayībhūtatvāt

na, not; *ca*, and; *tat*, that [knowledge]; *sa*, with; *ālambanam*, support, object; *tasya*, of it; *aviṣayībhūtatvāt*, because of not being the object

That knowledge is not accompanied by its object, since this object is not the object [of the *yogī*'s mind].

Continuing the topic of the previous verse, Patañjali here adds that while the *yogī* may be able to perceive the emotional state of mind of others, he or she may not necessarily be aware of the object, *ālambana*, causing that state of mind. The *yogī* may be able to read someone's amorous state of mind, for example, says Vyāsa, but not necessarily know who the beloved is, or perceive fear in someone's mind but not the tiger who caused it. This, says Vyāsa, is because the object of the other person's mind has not been the object of the *yogī*'s *saṁyama*; only the other person's emotion or state of mind has been subject to this. Other commentators, however, are aware that this seems to conflict with the discussion in the previous *sūtra*, where it is stated that *saṁskāras* can be accessed only in their context; this should suggest that the *yogī* should have access to the context of the other person's state of mind—the object of emotion or fear, as well as the emotion itself, since this would be imprinted as an image on the *citta*. One might infer that if the *yogī* wishes to access the actual object causing the other person's state of mind, *saṁyama* would have to be directed to that object specifically.

कायरूपसंयमात् तद्ग्राह्यशक्तिस्तम्भे
चक्षुःप्रकाशासंप्रयोगेऽन्तर्धानम् ॥ २१ ॥

III.21 kāya-rūpa-saṁyamāt tad-grāhya-śakti-stambhe cakṣuḥ-prakāśāsamprayoge 'ntardhānam

kāya, of the body; *rūpa*, form; *saṁyamāt*, by performing *saṁyama*; *tat*, that; *grāhya*, to be grasped or known; *śakti*, power; *stambhe*, on the obstruction; *cakṣuḥ*, eye; *prakāśa*, light; *asamprayoge*, on the absence of contact; *antardhānam*, invisibility

By performing *saṁyama* on the outer form of the body, invisibility [is attained]. This occurs when perceptibility is obstructed by blocking contact between light and the eyes.

The commentators are not very detailed in their explanations of the Sāṅkhyan metaphysics underlying this *sūtra*. Vācaspati Miśra states that a body can be seen because it has color. Rays of light strike this and the body becomes visible to the eyes of others. Apparently, by *saṁyama*, the *yogī* can obstruct this process such that he or she is no longer visible to others, even in broad daylight. (The same process of obstruction can be applied to sound, touch, taste, and smell.) The exact mechanics underpinning this ability to stop light refracting off one's body are left unexplained by our traditional commentators, but Taimni, a *yogī* scholar who wrote an engaging commentary of the *sūtras*, suggests the modus operandi of this *siddhi* is that the body is visible due to the *tanmātra* or subtle element of form, *rūpa*.[53] (As we know, the gross visible elements are transformations of the *tanmātra* subtle elements.) By manipulating the *tanmātra* of form, the *yogī* can prevent light bouncing back off it to the eye of the receiver. The Buddha is reputed to have used this *siddhi* to vanish after giving discourses in various assemblies of nobles.[54]

If we look at the evolution of the *tattvas* on the Sāṅkhya chart in the introduction, we see that form, visibility, and sight emanate from the *tanmātra* of touch, when the *tāmasic* component is increased. One might suppose, then, that the *yogī* is believed to be able to reverse this, that is, minimize the *tāmasic* element that allows sight (or, put differently, maximize the translucent *sāttvic* element), such that light rays do not have a sufficiently dense (*tāmasic*) surface to bounce back to an observing eye (in the same way that air and ether cannot be perceived due to their relatively higher proportion of *sattva*). As always, mind is the substratum of grosser energy that evolves from it, so just as the interaction of hydrogen and oxygen molecules can cause ice to revert to water and then to steam, mind can manipulate the density of the elements that emerge from it, an explanation in accordance with Yoga metaphysics. In support of this explanation, we can note that Vyāsa, in III.45, speaks of invisibility being attained by the *yogī* "covering himself in the element of ether."[55]

सोपक्रमं निरुपक्रमं च कर्म तत्संयमाद्
अपरान्तज्ञानम् अरिष्टेभ्यो वा ।।२२।।

III.22 sopakramaṁ nirupakramaṁ ca karma tat-saṁyamād aparānta-jñānam ariṣṭebhyo vā

sa, with; *upakramam*, approaching, beginning, fruition; *nir*, without; *upakramam*, fruition; *ca*, and; *karma*, action; *tat*, these; *samyamāt*, by performing *saṁyama*; *aparānta*, death; *jñānam*, knowledge; *ariṣṭebhyaḥ*, by omens, portents; *vā*, or

Karma is either quick to fructify or slow. By _saṁyama_ on _karma_, or on portents, knowledge of [one's] death arises.

This *sūtra* divides *karma* according to whether or not it is quick to fructify, *upakramam*. Vyāsa compares *karma* that is quick to fructify to a wet cloth spread out nicely, which dries quickly, and *karma* that is not quick to fructify to a wet cloth twisted and bunched up, which dries slowly; or to fire that when fueled by the wind burns dry hay stacked in one place quickly, as opposed to fire that, when the hay is spread out in different places, burns more slowly. In either event, whenever it is due to fructify, the *yogī* can access this stock of personal *karma* and, through the process of *saṁyama*, understand when its fruition will take place. *Karma*, we recall (II.13), in addition to type of birth and life experience, determines longevity, so through knowledge of one's *karma* and its fructification—the *saṁskāras*, once again—one can determine one's moment and circumstance of death, *aparānta-jñānam*. This is basically the same process mentioned in III.18 involved in the understanding of one's previous births. Here, too, Buddhist sources assign this *siddhi* to the Buddha, who predicted his own death three months in advance,[56] a motif that is not uncommon in hagiographical literature.

An alternative process for understanding one's impending death is noted by Patañjali here—through portents, *ariṣṭebhyaḥ*. The commentaries speak of three types of portents: personal, those associated with other beings, and those associated with divine beings. Examples of personal portents are not hearing any sound when one blocks one's ears—which should otherwise normally produce the sound of fire burning within, says Vijñānabhikṣu (a sound made by one's *prāṇa*, adds Bhoja Rāja)—or not seeing any light when one blocks one's eyes. According to these criteria, one not experiencing these effects is nearing death. Examples of portents heralded by other beings are seeing the messengers of Yama, the lord of death, or unexpectedly seeing one's departed ancestors. Examples of portents involving divine beings are unexpectedly seeing the celestial realms or its denizens, or seeing things contrary to what the *yogī* has been seeing throughout life.

By means of any of these portents one is informed of impending death. Bhoja Rāja states that anyone can be made aware of impending death through such portents, although such information will be vague and not precise with regard to exact specifics such as timing. *Yogīs* adept in the practices indicated in this *sūtra*, in contrast, can see the time and place of their own death precisely, like something visible before their very eyes. The purpose of gaining knowledge of one's death from a *yogic* perspective, says Śaṅkara, is to provoke urgency in fulfilling one's human obligations in not frittering away one's life—in other words, to take up *yoga* seriously and seek liberation.

मैत्र्यादिषु बलानि ॥ २३ ॥

III.23 maitry-ādiṣu balāni

maitrī, friendliness; *ādiṣu*, etc.; *balāni*, strength

By [*saṁyama*] on friendliness and such things, strengths are acquired.

The commentators understand "friendliness and such things" in this *sūtra* to refer to I.33, where *maitrī*, friendship; *karuṇā*, compassion; *muditā*, joy; and *upekṣā*, equanimity were listed by Patañjali. By cultivating friendship toward those who are happy, as prescribed in that *sūtra*, and performing *saṁyama* on this feeling, the *yogī* attains what Vyāsa terms the "power of friendliness." He becomes the well-wisher of all, say the commentators, can make the whole world happy, and his effort to win the friendship of others will not be in vain. He destroys all envy and hatred from his heart, says Hariharānanda, becomes completely free from malice and harshness, and no thoughts of harming others ever darken his heart, such that all people, whether malicious or not, find him to be a source of comfort and friendship. Likewise, by performing *saṁyama* on the feeling of compassion that the *yogī* is prescribed to cultivate toward those in distress (I.33), the power of compassion arises. He can lift the suffering out of their pain, says Vācaspati Miśra. By *saṁyama* on joy toward the pious, one attains the power of joyfulness. The commentators note, however, that *saṁyama* is not directed toward the fourth prescription listed in I.33—equanimity toward the sinful—because equanimity is not a specific feeling but an absence of other feelings; *saṁyama* would thus seem to require a distinct state of mind as an object of focus, otherwise the meditator has nothing on which to focus.

Essentially, the mechanics of this type of *saṁyama* seem to be that through the sheer intensity of total absorption on a feeling such as those listed above, the *citta* of the *yogī* becomes so completely pervaded and charged with that feeling that it emanates out and affects other people. This is just an extension of commonly experienced principles: Laughter, for example, can be contagious, as can sadness, anger, or other emotions. As we have seen, the principle of *saṁyama* simply enhances and expands on these occurrences. All feelings, after all, are potentially inherent in *citta*—the mind is the seat of emotion. So through *saṁyama* the mind simply manifests what is latent within it.

बलेषु हस्तिबलादीनि ॥२४॥
III.24 baleṣu hasti-balādīni

baleṣu, on the power, strength; *hasti*, elephant;
bala, strength; *ādīni*, etc.

[By practicing *saṁyama*] on strengths, [the *yogī*] attains the strength of an elephant, etc.

Here, too, the commentators are curt. By *saṁyama* on the strength of an elephant, *baleṣu hasti*, the *yogī* acquires such strength; by *saṁyama* on Garuḍa, Viṣṇu's eagle carrier, one gets the power of Garuḍa; by *saṁyama* on the power of the wind, one gets such powers, and so on. The principle seems to be that by the *yogī*'s intense concentration on any power, such as the strength of an elephant, his mind can manifest that same power in his body. Once again, everything is potential in the mind, and mind, *citta*, is the substratum of all evolutes, including strength. It can therefore potentially manifest anything at all, since everything inherently exists in latent form within its own nature. Koelman expresses this in his usual profoundly precise way: "Man's individual body and mind are only superficially and relatively individual substances, fundamentally they are only energizations and self-differentiations of and within prakṛtic Nature itself, which is the sole genuine substance. Man, therefore, through his prākṛtic organism, is in communication, is one with prakṛtic Nature in its universality" (1970, 241).

प्रवृत्त्यालोकन्यासात् सूक्ष्मव्यवहितविप्रकृष्टज्ञानम् ॥२५॥
III.25 pravṛttyāloka-nyāsāt sūkṣma-vyavahita-viprakṛṣṭa-jñānam

pravṛttyā, cognition, higher sense activity; *āloka*, light; *nyāsāt*, by directing; *sūkṣma*, subtle; *vyavahita*, concealed; *viprakṛṣṭa*, remote; *jñānam*, knowledge

By directing the light of cognition, one obtains knowledge of subtle, concealed, and remote things.

Vijñānabhikṣu suggests that the *yogī* becomes so powerful that, even without performing *saṁyama*, just by directing his or her mind toward an object, even if it is subtle, *sūkṣma*; concealed, *vyavahita*; or far away, *viprakṛṣṭa*, it becomes revealed—just as one has immediate perception of a nearby pot merely by directing one's eyes to it. This, say the commentators, is because when all traces of *rajas* and *tamas* have been eradicated, the natural luminosity inherent in the *sattva* of the *citta* becomes manifest without hindrance. This light can then be directed toward revealing things beyond normal cognition—the subtle, concealed, and remote things of this *sūtra*. The senses, too, become keener in their operation; as the *Gītā* puts it, "Luminosity manifests in all the gates of the body" (XIV.11). One might add that *citta* in Yoga metaphysics is potentially all-pervading when its *rājasic* and *tāmasic* potentials are suppressed. Thus, when fully *sāttvic* and focused, it can bypass or transcend the senses and contact objects beyond the normal reaches of the senses.

Let us consider this from the perspective of Sāṅkhyan metaphysics. Let us say a *puruṣa*, enveloped in its *citta* as all *saṁsāric puruṣas* are, takes birth as an ant. The awareness of the *puruṣa* or, more precisely, the *vṛttis* of the *puruṣa*'s *citta*, is limited to the contours of the ant's body and sensual range, due to its *kleśas* as per the definitions of *avidyā* and *asmitā* outlined in II.5–6. Now, suppose the ant dies and, due to its particular *karmic* destiny, next takes birth as an elephant. Its *asmitā* now identifies with a new instrument, such that the *vṛttis* produced by it pervade a much larger surface—the body and sensual range of an elephant. This indicates that the range of *citta* can expand and contract. What, then, is to prevent it expanding farther still? Like the light of a small bulb, which could, in principle, continue to emanate out throughout the entire universe were there no obstacles to obstruct it, *citta* is potentially all-pervading (as is the source awareness of *puruṣa, citi-śakti*), were there no *kleśas* to obstruct it. Once the *kleśas* are eliminated, then, one can see how the internal logic of Sāṅkhyan metaphysics requires the *citta* to be all-pervading—and thus, from the perspective of this *sūtra*, able to be aware of anything within *prakṛti* (which is another way of conceptualizing omniscience). This basic theme will be repeated throughout this chapter.

The Jains have an interesting counterpart to these ideas. In Jain metaphysics, the soul's inherent omniscience (which is another way of saying omnipresence) is covered by the obstructing limitations of *karma*.[57] When these *karmic* obstacles are partly destroyed, the *yogī* develops supernormal sensory abilities (*avadhi-jñānam*); when psychological obstacles such as hatred and envy have been overcome, the *yogī* can know the minds of others (*manaḥ-paryāya-jñānam*); and when all *karmic* obstructions have been completely removed, omniscience ensues (*kevala-jñānam*).

भुवनज्ञानं सूर्ये संयमात् ॥ २६ ॥

III.26 bhuvana-jñānaṁ sūrye saṁyamāt

bhuvana, regions, worlds; *jñānam*, knowledge; *sūrye*, on the sun; *saṁyamāt*, by *saṁyama*

By performing *saṁyama* on the sun arises knowledge of the different realms in the universe.

A lengthy description of the Purāṇic concept of the universe is given in the commentaries for this *sūtra*. There are seven *lokas*, worlds or realms, in Hindu cosmography. This world with all its creatures is one, and above it is space with the stars, followed by a series of celestial realms. The first realm is the abode of Indra, king of the gods, and above this the abode of the *prajāpatis*, the progenitors. The threefold realm of Brahmā, the secondary creator[58]—Janaloka, Tapoloka, and Satyaloka—is above these. There are also seven nether regions or lower realms below the earth, as well as seven hells where beings live long and painful lives experiencing the negative *karma* accrued by their impious deeds. Hariharānanda states that entities here have active minds but do not have gross bodies, and thus suffer the torment of not being able to fulfill their desires, like ensnared beasts. Sojourns in hell, however, are never eternal but last only until the specifics of an individual's negative *karma* have been accounted for and borne their due fruits.

The earth realm or region consists of seven islands in the center of which is the golden Sumeru (also known as Meru) mountain. Its peaks are made of silver, emerald, crystal, gold, and jewels. As a result of the reflection from these peaks, the sky in the South is deep blue; in the East, white; in the West, clear; and in the North, golden. The sun revolves around Sumeru, causing day and night, and on the right of this mountain is the Jambū tree, which is why the earth is known as Jambūdvīpa. Jambūdvīpa consists of nine continents. There are three mountains to the north of Meru, surrounding three continents (*varṣa*) consecutively, and three mountains to the south, surrounding three more continents, in addition to which, there is a continent to the east of Meru, one to the west, and one more, the ninth, below Meru. Jambūdvīpa stretches out a distance of fifty *yojanas*[59] in all directions from Meru and is thus one hundred *yojanas* in circumference in its entirety. It is surrounded by a salt ocean twice its size. After this there are six islands (*dvīpas*) in succession, each one surrounded by oceans of different liquids—sugarcane juice, liquor, ghee, curd, milk, and sweet rice. These are encircled by the Lokāloka mountain range. This entire universe is situated within an egglike case. Despite its enormity, it is merely a spark of *prakṛti*, like a firefly in the sky. In these worlds, oceans, and mountains live a variety of gods and celestial beings. The mortals and gods who reside in the islands are pious beings—they gain residency in these realms as a result of good *karma* performed in the past. Various parks are found on Mount Meru, which are the pleasure grounds for the gods. The assembly hall of the gods is also there, along with the city of the gods and their palace. In Indra's realm, the first of the five realms, there are six types of resident gods who have all the mystic powers, such as living for immense life spans (an entire *kalpa*[60]); the ability to fulfill their desires merely by thought; enjoying the pleasures of sex; and they are begotten without parents (in other words, sex is not inconvenienced by pregnancy). The five classes of gods who inhabit the Prajāpati realm have mastery over the material elements (which, says Vācaspati Miśra, means that they can manipulate them at will), subsist on meditation alone (do not require gross *prākṛtic* foodstuffs as their bodies are made of *tanmātra*, the subtle evolutes of *prakṛti*), and live a thousand times longer than the residents of Indra's realm. The four types of gods in Brahmā's realm of

Janaloka live even longer than this (the life span of each of the four types doubling consecutively), have full control over the elements and sense organs, and also subsist on meditation, as do the celibate residents of Tapoloka. In Satyaloka, the highest celestial realm, one of the four classes of resident gods is absorbed in *savitarka* meditation, another in *savicāra*, another in *ānanda* meditation, and the fourth in *asmitā* (see I.17 on these). These various realms and their inhabitants are described in greater detail in the various Purāṇas, particularly in the *Bhāgavata Purāṇa* (V.16–26).

This entire cosmography can be directly perceived by the *yogī* performing *saṁyama* on the "doorway of the sun," says Vyāsa. Some commentators seem to accept this literally, as meditation on the actual sun disk, *sūrye*, but others, such as Vācaspati Miśra and Hariharānanda, take this to be the doorway of the *suṣumnā* channel in the subtle physiology usually associated with *tantric yoga*.[61] Hariharānanda notes that this physiology cannot be directly perceived by the eyes, but by meditation, since it is made of subtle elements, and the eyes can perceive only gross elements. When the entrance to the *suṣumnā* is opened, he states, the various regions noted above are revealed. There is thus a correspondence between the microcosm of the body and the macrocosm of the universe.

The specific mechanics of how the entire universe can be perceived by the sedentary meditator are not explained by the commentators, but one might suppose that since the entire universe is held to evolve from the first evolute of *prakṛti*, *buddhi*, and since one's personal *buddhi* is simply an individualization of this original cosmic *buddhi*, the *yogī* is able to transcend the limitations of the individual *buddhi* and directly perceive the cosmic *buddhi* and all its derivates, such as the various realms of the universe, even when situated motionless in meditation. This perception will thereby appear internal to the *yogī*. As Hariharānanda puts it, from the perspective of the universal *buddhi*, there is no such thing as far or near since *buddhi* underpins all its evolutes; it is thus all-pervading and everything is within it. Therefore, the *buddhi* of each individual creature, as well as the solar systems, which are evolutes from *buddhi*, are indirectly but essentially on the same plane since everything in the universe is a manifestation of the same substratum. The *buddhi* of the *yogī* is supposed to be able simply to pass beyond personal bodily limitations. In any event, this belief is still very much a living tradition. A modern *siddha-yogī*, Swami Muktānanda, who was primarily responsible for establishing the *siddha* tradition in the West in the 1960s, in his remarkable autobiography, *Play of Consciousness*, claimed to have personally experienced internally within himself the various regions of the universe during his own meditations.

The purpose of all this cosmological information, says Hariharānanda, is that by visiting all the realms in creation, the *yogī* is better able to appreciate the greatness of *kaivalya* liberation. There are frequent warnings in the Purāṇas about *yogīs* being sidetracked from their pursuit of liberation by the wonderful realms of the universes; as early as the *Muṇḍaka Upaniṣad* strong language is used to decry the "fools who know nothing better; when they have enjoyed their good *karma* in the higher realms, they return again to this miserable world" (I.2.7ff). The *Gītā* too describes those intent on the celestial realms as "full of desires" and "ignorant" (II.42–43), since the celestial realms "up to the realm of Brahmā are all places of rebirth" (VIII.16).

चन्द्रे ताराव्यूहज्ञानम् ॥ २७ ॥

III.27 candre tārā-vyūha-jñānam

candre, on the moon; *tārā*, stars; *vyūha*, arrangement; *jñānam*, knowledge

[By *saṁyama*] on the moon, knowledge of the solar systems.

The commentators make no comments here, considering this *sūtra* a sequel to the previous one to be understood in parallel fashion. Whereas *saṁyama* on the sun resulted in knowledge of different realms, worlds, mountains, and oceans, *saṁyama* on the moon, *candra*, results in knowledge of the arrangement of the stars, *tārā-vyūha*. Bhoja Rāja notes that this *sūtra* is included separately from the previous one since when the sun is shining, the luster of the stars is not visible (and one can obviously perform *saṁyama* on the moon only when the sun has set). Hariharānanda relates this *sūtra*, too, to *tāntric* physiology.

ध्रुवे तद्गतिज्ञानम् ॥ २८ ॥
III.28 dhruve tad-gati-jñānam

dhruve, on the polestar; *tat*, their [the stars']; *gati*, movement; *jñānam*, knowledge

[By *saṁyama*] on the polestar comes knowledge of the movement of the stars.

Here, too, the commentators take the *sūtra* to be self-explanatory, but all take the polestar, *Dhruva*, to refer to the celestial body and not some aspect of the subtle physiology. By *saṁyama* on the polestar, says Bhoja Rāja, the *yogī* can distinguish stars from planets and determine when a given heavenly body will be situated in any particular sign of the zodiac. Śaṅkara takes this *sūtra* to refer to astrological science: By understanding the movement of the stars, and how their influences neutralize, enhance, and affect each other, one can determine the good and bad fortunes of living beings.

नाभिचक्रे कायव्यूहज्ञानम् ॥ २९ ॥
III.29 nābhi-cakre kāya-vyūha-jñānam

nābhi, navel; *cakre*, on the wheel; *kāya*, body; *vyūha*, arrangement; *jñānam*, knowledge

[By *saṁyama*] on the navel plexus of the body comes knowledge of the arrangement of the body.

Just as one can attain knowledge of different realms by performing *saṁyama* on the sun, and knowledge of the arrangement of the stars by performing *saṁyama* on the moon, Patañjali here states that, on a micro level, one can likewise develop intimate knowledge of the physical body, *kāya-vyūha*, by performing *saṁyama* on the navel, *nābhi-cakra*—that is, one can understand everything about the constituents and inner workings of the body by this means. Vijñānabhikṣu compares the navel wheel to the root of the banana plant from which the entire plant grows. Bhoja Rāja states more specifically that the navel is the root of the *nāḍīs*, subtle veins, that pervade the body.

Vyāsa briefly outlines the understanding of the body according to the traditional medical system of *āyurveda*, by now well-known in the West. There are the three *doṣas*, usually translated as humors—*kapha*, gas; *vāta*, bile; and *pitta*, phlegm—and seven substances—skin, blood, muscle, tendon, bone, fat, and semen—each one layered over the previous one.[62] Disease in *āyurveda* is due to an imbalance in these three *doṣas*. The *yogī* can gain knowledge of any imbalance or malfunctioning in the body by performing the *saṁyama* noted in this *sūtra*. And, from a *yogic* perspective, Vijñānabhikṣu points out that by performing *saṁyama* on the navel the *yogī* can perceive the body to be what it really is, a heap of *doṣas* and substances.

Cakra here is not necessarily a reference to the *cakra* physiology most commonly associated with the cluster of *siddha/tantra/śākta* traditions. Tellingly, Patañjali makes no direct reference to this overall physiology in the *sūtras* other than the mention of *nāḍī* in III.31 below. In fact, classical Yoga does not concern itself with this physiology. Some of the commentators do read some of these *sūtras* from the perspective of the *cakras* (as we have seen in III.26–27), but none of the primary commentators makes any mention of, for example, the primary ingredient of *śākta* physiology, the *kuṇḍalinī*. One might go on to note that the understanding of the goal in classical Yoga clearly differs from the *siddha* notion that the supreme goal of *yoga* is attained, and liberation occurs, when this *kuṇḍalinī* reaches the thousand-petal *sahasrāra-cakra* in the crown of the head. Whatever other references to *cakras* are found throughout the commentaries are peripheral to the classical Yoga tradition (and, indeed, a peripheral topic in mainstream Hinduism).

The cluster of *śākta* traditions is distinct from classical Yoga in a number of ways. First, they are monistic and Yoga is dualistic. The *śākta* traditions see *prakṛti* as ultimately pure consciousness, *citi-śakti* (IV.34); thus they are monist in the sense that they hold that all reality—both the seer and the seen (*puruṣa* and *prakṛti*) of II.17ff—is made up of one substance: consciousness. Accordingly, it is not *prakṛti* that is to be transcended, as is the case with Yoga, but notions of individual separateness from the supreme deity. Once the delimiting ego separating the individual *ātman* from realizing its higher nature as one with the supreme *ātman* has been transcended, ultimate *samādhi* in the *śākta* traditions entails enjoying the spectacle of *prakṛti* as *citi-śakti* in its myriad variegations from the liberated vantage point of oneness with the supreme deity (most usually associated with Śiva or a form of the Goddess). For the dualistic Yoga tradition, on the other hand, *prakṛti* is not *citi-śakti* at all but inert matter obstructing *puruṣa* from realizing its own separate and completely distinct nature as *citi-śakti*; in Yoga, in other words, *citi-śakti* pertains to *puruṣa*, not to *prakṛti*. In line with these monistic presuppositions, in the *śākta* traditions liberation entails the merging of the individual *ātman* into a higher, ultimately transpersonal reality,[63] whereas in Yoga there is a plurality of souls who never lose their individuality whether in the liberated state or not. They do not completely merge into one ultimate Supreme Soul within which personal individuality is ultimately erased, but remain individual *puruṣas*.

Having noted this metaphysical difference, one wonders how different the higher states of the two systems are from an experiential point of view. We have noted how *sattva* is "as if" conscious due to becoming animated by consciousness, *citi-śakti*, reflecting *puruṣa* back to itself when all traces of *rajas* and *tamas* have been made latent. In the higher stages of *samādhi*, the *yogī*'s *citta*, animated by *citi-śakti*, becomes omnipresent and omnipotent due to pervading *prakṛti*—in other words, the animated all-pervading *sāttvic citta* of the *yogī* can become coextensive with *prakṛti*. All this would appear to be a very similar experience to that reported by the *siddha* tradition of enjoying *prakṛti* as *citi-śakti* (put differently, the *siddha* tradition takes *prakṛti* as *citi-śakti*, and Yoga understands it "as if" *citi-śakti*). Moreover, even with regard to the pluralistic versus monistic understanding of liberation in terms of whether there exists a plurality of *ātmans* at the highest level of truth, or only one, one wonders how much difference there might be between experiencing oneself as *the* one supreme absolute soul in a monistic system or to be one of a plurality of liberated *ātmans* who are aware only of their own omnipresent nature and nothing else in a pluralistic system. The Yoga tradition after all gives us no indication that the omnipresent *puruṣa* in *nirbīja/asamprajñāta-samādhi* is aware of other omnipresent *puruṣas*, which, to all intents and purposes, points to a monistic *experience*, even if a plurality of souls are accepted on a metaphysical or scholastic level in principle.

Be this as it may, in terms of method, one can reiterate that *samādhi*, in *tantra*, is attained when *kuṇḍalinī* is first awakened by various techniques and then rises up the central *suṣumnā* channel, piercing the various *cakras* along the way and triggering various supernormal sensual experiences until it finally unites with the *sahasrāra-cakra*. The *siddhi* experiences of *kuṇḍalinī* awakening associated with the *śākta* traditions are indications of *yogic* success and can be enjoyed provided one has realized one's oneness with the supreme deity. As should be obvious by now, liberation is attained entirely differently in classical Yoga, and the *cakra/nāḍī/kuṇḍalinī* physiology is completely peripheral to it—although there is overlap in some (but not all) techniques, such as the use of *mantra* and *prāṇāyāma*. Moreover, and partly as a consequence of this difference in presuppositions, the *siddhis* are considered accomplishments only for one whose "mind is outgoing," that is, who has not attained the *vairāgya*, dispassion, required of *yogic* practice in I.15–16; they are obstacles to the *samādhi* state taught by Patañjali (III.37) and ultimately to be discarded as worthless.

Thus, while *siddhi/śākta/tantra* metaphysics is a wonderful and vibrant spiritual universe in its own right, with deep roots in the ancient Indic past, and with its own internal coherence, logic, and appeal, it is not by any means the same as the system being taught by Patañjali. The integrity and distinctiveness of these traditions have a tendency to be erased into a hodgepodge in their Western exportations—into a kind of *kitchorie* Yoga. In India, a typical meal consists of a *subji*, vegetable dish; *dal*, lentil soup; rice; *chappati*, unleavened bread; and perhaps some other items, each with its own distinct flavorings and spices. After the meal is enjoyed, the leftovers are often combined and served the next day as *kitchorie*, at which point all the flavorings are merged together into a homogenous whole. Similarly, the multiple *yogic* traditions of India such as *tantra* and classical *yoga*, despite their very distinctive features and practices in their traditional settings, tend to be merged into a *kitchorie* sort of *yoga* in many of its Western forms.

Thus one often finds a generic sort of *yoga* typically appropriating bits and pieces of Patañjali-type practices as presented here in the *sūtras* but articulated with neo-*advaita-vedānta/Brahman* terminologies and flavored with elements from *tantric* subtle physiology, all blended together as if representing a single coherent homogenous tradition. This is understandable—and with plenty of antecedents in premodern

Indic traditions themselves one might add[64] (indeed, it can be argued that such blending is the very nature of religious traditions)—and perhaps inevitable in the modern West.

While on this topic, there are a variety of traditions that are clearly influenced by Patañjali, which Larson (2008) calls "satellite traditions," that appropriate important aspects from Patañjali while diverging considerably from him in focus, such as the classical *haṭha yoga* tradition. This, of course, points to the centrality and authoritativeness of Patañjali in *yogic* practice insofar as his system is incorporated into other systems as a source of legitimacy, but then flavored by the sectarian specifics of these other systems.

कण्ठकूपे क्षुत्पिपासानिवृत्तिः ॥ ३० ॥

III.30 kaṇṭha-kūpe kṣut-pipāsā-nivṛttiḥ

kaṇṭha, throat; *kūpe*, pit, hollow; *kṣut*, hunger; *pipāsā*, thirst; *nivṛttiḥ*, cessation, subdual

[By *saṁyama*] on the pit of the throat comes the cessation of hunger and thirst.

Vijñānabhikṣu takes the pit of the throat, *kaṇṭha-kūpa*, to extend from the base of the tongue to the stomach. By *saṁyama* on this spot, *yogīs* can overcome hunger and thirst, *kṣut-pipāsā*, according to Patañjali. No further explanation of how this transpires is provided in our sources, except for Bhoja Rāja's comment that the sensation of hunger is caused by the contact of *prāṇa*, vital air, with this place. One might infer that since the sense of touch or sensation is dependent on the quality of air in Sāṅkhya metaphysics, by manipulating the *prāṇa* life air by means of the power of mind that underpins it along the lines outlined for some of the other *siddhis*, the *yogī* can control its effects, in this case, the sensation of hunger.

कूर्मनाड्यां स्थैर्यम् ॥ ३१ ॥

III.31 kūrma-nāḍyām sthairyam

kūrma, tortoise; *nāḍyām*, subtle channel; *sthairyam*, steadiness

[By *saṁyama*] on the subtle tortoise channel, steadiness is attained.

Below the pit of the throat, or trachea, says Vyāsa, is a particular *nāḍī*, or subtle channel, shaped like a tortoise, *kūrma*. As noted, in *tantra* physiology, just as the gross body is pervaded by innumerable blood vessels, there is a subtle network of thousands of subtle channels called *nāḍīs*. As early as the *Praśna Upaniṣad* the *prāṇa* life airs are held to circulate through the body by means of these *nāḍīs*. The *yogī* can become as steady, *sthairya*, as a snake or an alligator, says Vyāsa, by *saṁyama* on the trachea. Again, although the mechanics behind this *siddhi* are not explained, the same principles can be inferred: Balance is associated with air, so by mentally manipulating the appropriate *prāṇa* associated with balance in the particular *nāḍī* mentioned here by Patañjali, the *yogī* can remain as immobile as snakes and iguanas.[65] From the overall perspective of *yoga*, perhaps more to the point is Hariharānanda's observation that if the body becomes immobile, so does the mind. In his commentary to this *sūtra*, Bhoja Rāja, too, emphasizes firmness of mind as ensuing from this practice.

मूर्धज्योतिषि सिद्धदर्शनम् ॥ ३२ ॥

III.32 mūrdha-jyotiṣi siddha-darśanam

mūrdha, head; *jyotiṣi*, on the light; *siddha*, perfected souls; *darśanam*, vision

[By *saṁyama*] on the light in the skull, a vision of the *siddhas*, perfected beings, is attained.

There is an opening in the skull, says Vyāsa, that contains radiant light. As the radiance of light inside a house is concentrated in the keyhole, says Bhoja Rāja (from the perspective of someone standing outside the house), so the luminosity of *sattva* is concentrated in this opening called the *brahma-randhra*. By performing *saṁyama* on this spot, one has a vision, *darśana*, of the *siddhas*. *Siddhas* are perfected beings who possess mystic powers and inhabit the higher realms of the universe. They often move around in the space between the earth and the sky, and can sometimes be contacted by advanced *yogīs*. Again, this too remains a living tradition: In his autobiography, Muktānanda claimed to have encountered such beings while in states of *samādhi*, as did Yogānanda in his *Autobiography of a Yogi*.

प्रातिभाद् वा सर्वम् ।। ३३ ।।

III.33 prātibhād vā sarvam

prātibhāt, by intuition; *vā*, or; *sarvam*, everything

Or, by intuition, comes [knowledge of] everything.

Intuition, *prātibha*, says Vyāsa, precedes discrimination, the *viveka* of II.26–7, as the light of dawn precedes the light of the sun. The *yogī* is able to attain knowledge of everything, *sarvam*, due to the spontaneous rise of intuition, *prātibha*. Vijñānabhikṣu defines intuition, *prātibha*, as knowledge that is obtained without a teacher. Śaṅkara states that by intuition the *yogī* can automatically attain all of the various powers outlined in the previous *sūtras* that are gained by the practice of *saṁyama* on individual objects. According to the Yoga tradition, intuition is associated with the preliminary phase of omniscience (III.36ff). It is an inherent attribute of pure *sattva*.

हृदये चित्तसंवित् ।। ३४ ।।

III.34 hṛdaye citta-saṁvit

hṛdaye, on the heart; *citta*, the mind; *saṁvit*, knowledge

[By *saṁyama*] on the heart, knowledge of the mind ensues.

Vyāsa calls the heart the "city of *Brahman*, a lotus-like abode," and the place where the intelligence resides. As noted in the introduction, even though Patañjali himself does not refer to *Brahman*, the Absolute Truth of the Upaniṣads, the commentators here and elsewhere do correlate *Brahman* and *puruṣa* as if this is a perfectly natural thing to do, as indeed it is for any classical Hindu thinker. The heart, *hṛdaya*, is taken to be the abode of the *ātman* as early as the *Praśna Upaniṣad* (III.6).

Vācaspati Miśra and Bhoja Rāja describe the lotus as facing down, and in so doing again introduce notions of subtle physiology usually associated with the *haṭha-yoga* and *tantra* traditions in which they play a far more central role than in classical Pātañjalian *yoga*, where they are peripheral. There are seven *cakras* (literally, wheels) or energy centers in the body, and these are usually described as shaped like lotuses. The heart *cakra* is the middle one and considered to be the seat of intelligence. Thus, both the *ātman* and the *citta* are centered in the heart. Consequently, by performing *saṁyama* in this region, one comes to know the *citta* mind and its modifications.

Vijñānabhikṣu notes that the previous powers are minor, insofar as they are peripheral to the real goal of *yoga*, which, as Patañjali wasted no time in informing us at the beginning of the entire text, is to still the *vṛttis* of the *citta*. The knowledge referred to in this *sūtra* facilitates that goal by giving the *yogī* direct perception of the workings of *citta*.

सत्त्वपुरुषयेरत्यन्तासंकीर्णयोः प्रत्ययाविशेषो भोगः
परार्थत्वात् स्वार्थसंयमात् पुरुषज्ञानम् ।। ३५ ।।

III.35 sattva-puruṣayor atyantāsaṅkīrṇayoḥ pratyayāviśeṣo bhogaḥ parārthatvāt svārtha-saṁyamāt puruṣa-jñānam

sattva, of the intellect; *puruṣayoḥ*, and of the *puruṣa*; *atyanta*, complete; *asaṅkīrṇayoḥ*, distinct; *pratyaya*, idea, image, notion; *aviśeṣaḥ*, nondistinction; *bhogaḥ*, experience; *parārthatvāt*, because of having the nature of existing for another; *svārtha*, for itself; *saṁyamāt*, from *saṁyama*; *puruṣa*, the true self; *jñānam*, knowledge

Worldly experience consists of the notion that there is no distinction between the *puruṣa* self and pure intelligence, although these two are completely distinct. Worldly experience exists for another [i.e., for *puruṣa*]. [By *saṁyama*] on that which exists for itself [i.e., on *puruṣa*], comes knowledge of *puruṣa*.

Patañjali here essentially rearticulates the definition of *avidyā* given in II.5: Worldly experience consists of confounding the pure self with the intelligence, which molds itself into the forms and thoughts of this world. As has been discussed repeatedly, *puruṣa*, due to ignorance, considers *buddhi* and all its permutations to be its real self. In addition to the familiar example of the crystal and red flower, Vijñānabhikṣu has us imagine having soot on one's face. As one can be blissfully unaware that one has soot on one's face (a substance that is completely distinct from one's actual face), so, due to *avidyā*, ignorance, the *citta* is unaware that the source of its awareness, *puruṣa*, is completely distinct, *atyantāsaṅkīrṇa*, from the permutations of *buddhi*, which cover it, so to speak.

When the intelligence is completely free from the effects of *rajas* and *tamas*, in other words, when *buddhi* is pure and undisturbed, it becomes luminous and clear. As we know, *rajas* and *tamas* are the influences that pull *buddhi* out into the external world and cause it to mold itself into the external thoughts and forms that have actually nothing to do with pure *puruṣa*. As has been discussed, *buddhi*, when pure, also acts like a spotless mirror, which reflects the face gazing at it without distortion, so to speak. In this luminous state, according to Vijñānabhikṣu, *buddhi* can reflect *puruṣa*'s real image back to *puruṣa*—a pure notion or vision of its true nature, rather than the distorted images of the world of *saṁsāra*. This *sūtra* is taken to indicate that by *saṁyama* on this notion or image of *puruṣa* in the *sāttvic buddhi*, awareness of the existence of the real *puruṣa* emerges.[66] We might infer that the reason Patañjali uses the term *sattva* rather than *citta* or *buddhi* to refer to the mind, is to underscore the fact that, at this point, the mind's *sāttvic* potential is at its maximum, with the other two *guṇas* in a state of as total latency as the constitutional metaphysical makeup of *prakṛti* will allow.

Vyāsa hastens to add that this notion of *puruṣa* in itself is not ultimate self-realization, since it is still a notion or image in *buddhi* which, however pure, is nonetheless a product of *prakṛti* and thus completely distinct from the real *puruṣa*. There is a difference between the reflection in a mirror and the actual face gazing into it. *Puruṣa*, as we know, can know itself only by itself and not through any outside agency, which would involve connection with the world of matter. Vyāsa quotes the *Bṛhadāraṇyaka Upaniṣad* (IV.5.15) here: "By who is the knower to be known?" In other words, *prakṛti* and its products can be known by *puruṣa*, but by what is *puruṣa* to be known? The Upaniṣads are full of verses indicating that the self is higher than the mind or intelligence: "Sight does not reach there, nor thought nor speech; we don't know [it] or perceive [it] so how would one show it?" (*Kena* I.3). Therefore, as the *Gītā* puts it, "*ātmanyeva ātmanā*," "one revels in the self through its own self" (II.55).[67] Hence the coinage of neo-Vedāntic terms such as "self-realization," introduced to the West at the end of the nineteenth century by Vivekānanda and popularized by the Vedānta Society and Paramahansa Yogānanda in the 1930s.[68]

To summarize, then, while *buddhi* cannot reveal the actual *puruṣa*, it can reveal a pure image or reflection of *puruṣa* (Hariharānanda calls this reflection the pure *ahaṅkāra* or ego, since it reveals the "real" *aham*, I, the *puruṣa* self, in contrast to the normal function of *ahaṅkāra asmitā*, which is to cause misidentification with the false self of body and mind). So while this is not the ultimate goal of *yoga*, by *saṁyama* on this pure image or reflection the *yogī* is one step away from *kaivalya*, complete liberation. When this final and ultimate state manifests, *buddhi*, and all its images and ideas, including the pure one described here of the actual *puruṣa* itself, fade away, leaving *puruṣa* with nothing to be aware of except itself.

ततः प्रातिभश्रावणवेदनादर्शास्वादवार्ता जायन्ते ।। ३६ ।।

III.36 tataḥ prātibha-śrāvaṇa-vedanādarśāsvāda-vārtā jāyante

tataḥ, from this; *prātibha*, intuition; *śrāvaṇa*, hearing; *vedanā*, touch; *ādarśa*, vision; *āsvāda*, taste; *vārtāḥ*, smell;[69] *jāyante*, are born

From this, intuition as well as higher hearing, touch, vision, taste, and smell are born.

From the type of *saṁyama* noted in the last *sūtra*, the *yogī* attains the two abilities noted by Patañjali here: intuition, *prātibha*, and higher sense perception. By intuition, says Vyāsa, comes knowledge of "the subtle, the separated, the remote, the past and the future," as expressed in III.25, in other words, of things normally inaccessible to conventional means of knowledge. By higher sense perception one can continually experience divine sounds, sensations, sights, tastes, and smells. Strengthened by the practice of *yoga*, the *yogī*'s senses can experience subtler levels of sense objects. *Sattva*, as we know, becomes much more sensitive, that is, can experience the higher potentials of the senses, when its coverings of *rajas* and *tamas* are removed. Bhoja Rāja takes Vyāsa's reference here to divine sensations to refer to the sense objects of the celestial realms.

According to Vācaspati Miśra, self-realization is impossible until *prakṛti* has revealed herself in her fullness to *puruṣa*, and this entails experiencing the subtler dimensions of *prakṛti*. However, the Indic Yogic tradition in general, as specified by Patañjali in the next *sūtra*, considers all mystic powers, which arise of their own accord even without the *yogī* desiring them, to be impediments to the goal of *yoga*, since they pose the risk of distracting the *yogī* back into sensual (*prākṛtic*) experiences.

ते समाधाव् उपसर्गा व्युत्थाने सिद्धयः ।। ३७ ।।

III.37 te samādhāv upasargā vyutthāne siddhayaḥ

te, they [the powers]; *samādhau*, in *samādhi*; *upasargāḥ*, obstacles; *vyutthāne*, rising up, outgoing; *siddhayaḥ*, accomplishments, perfections, powers

These powers are accomplishments for the mind that is outgoing but obstacles to *samādhi*.

The term *siddhi*, perfection or power, which occurs only four times in the *sūtras*,[70] is used here to mean the supernormal powers. For a *yogī*, the powers noted in the previous *sūtra* hinder the cultivation of *samādhi*, since they entice the mind back out into the realm of *prakṛti* (they cause wonder and pleasure, says Bhoja Rāja) and thus are obstacles, *upasargāḥ*, to the attainment of *samādhi*. But for one whose mind is outgoing, *vyutthāna*, that is, interested in the enticements of the world, they appear to be desirable accomplishments. A beggar, says Vācaspati Miśra, may consider even a meager smattering of wealth to be the fullness of riches, but a *yogī* should not think that these powers, which appear spontaneously, are the goal, and must reject them. For how, he asks, can a genuine *yogī* take pleasure in things that are obstructions to the real goal of *yoga*? That the *siddhis* are potential impediments to the goal of *yoga* is a widespread position in Indic traditions: "The wise speak of the *siddhis* as obstacles; they are the cause of delay to one who is practicing the highest *yoga*" (*Bhāgavata Purāṇa* XI.15.33).

Pensa (1969) suggests that Patañjali's warning here does not apply to all *siddhis* but only to those in the preceding *sūtra*. Meditative states would be disrupted and consciousness would run the risk of again being caught up in sensory experience upon the unexpected eruptions of the quasi-psychedelic, supernormal sensual experiences indicated in the previous *sūtra*. But not all *siddhis* are detriments to *samādhi*; after all, Patañjali (I.35) included supernormal sense experiences as suitable objects for the mind to concentrate on in order to achieve *samādhi*. "Patañjali is thus concerned [in this *sūtra*] with emphasizing something that is an important technical problem and no more" (ibid., 200).[71] Patañjali is informing the practitioner of experiences that might accrue upon the path so that the *yogī* will not be confused, distracted, or sidetracked by them. Additionally, Vyāsa and Vācaspati Miśra noted in I.35 that upon experiencing some of the preliminary truths of *yoga*, the faith of the genuine *yogī* will thereby be reaffirmed and the commitment to proceed strengthened. A *yogī* sidetracked by them has clearly not mastered the *vairāgya*, detachment, required as a preliminary to *yoga* (I.12).

बन्धकारणशैथिल्यात् प्रचारसंवेदनाच् च चित्तस्य
परशरीरावेशः ॥ ३८ ॥

III.38 bandha-kāraṇa-śaithilyāt pracāra-saṁvedanāc ca cittasya para-śarīrāveśaḥ

bandha, of bondage; *kāraṇa*, cause; *śaithilyāt*, from the loosening; *pracāra*, conduct, working, passageway; *saṁvedanāt*, from knowledge; *ca*, and; *cittasya*, of the mind; *para*, others; *śarīra*, body; *āveśaḥ*, settle in, entering

By loosening the cause of bondage, and by knowledge of the passageways of the mind, the mind can enter into the bodies of others.

The mind is restless by nature—like a bouncing ball, says Śaṅkara, or the constant play of flame in glowing coals—but due to the stock of *karma-saṁskāras*, it becomes limited and trapped in one body and cannot experience existence in other bodies until the present body dies. However, by the cultivation of *samādhi*, the strength of this *karma* becomes weakened, *śaithilya*, and knowledge of the workings of the mind arises, *pracāra-saṁvedana*.[72] As a result of these two developments, the *yogī* can remove his mind from its moorings in his own body and settle it into someone else's body, according to this *sūtra*. The powers of the senses follow the mind in this transference, says Vyāsa, just as the swarm of bees follows the queen bee, and so the powers of the senses also settle in the new body when the mind settles into it. Just as the entire subtle body, *sūkṣma-śarīra*, transfers into a new body at death, so the *yogī* can enact this transferal while still alive—but, in this case, after entering into a new body, with the ability to return into the original body. The ability is so widespread in *yogic* narrative that White (forthcoming) calls it "the sine qua non of a yogi's practice."

Bhoja Rāja reminds us that the *citta* is all-pervading. Due to its stock of *karma* (which, we recall, is the result of *dharma* and *adharma*), and of course the *kleśas* underpinning them, it remains confined within the contours of a specific body. To be technically precise, its *vṛttis* are defined in any particular life by the set of *saṁskāras* activated for that specific life (that is, its *karma*) such that it is confined to those contours, and the *kleśas* cement the misidentification with that form. The *yogī* who has transcended these *kleśas* through discernment can perform *saṁyama* on this stock of *karma*, causing it to loose its grip on confining or limiting the *citta*. The *citta* can now transcend its confinement to that particular body and move outside of it, into other bodies if so desired, says Patañjali.

Vācaspati Miśra refers to *nāḍīs* in the body as the passageways through which the mind travels to perform its functions. The relevant *nāḍī* is identified by Bhoja Rāja as the *cittavahā nāḍī*, the *citta*-carrying *nāḍī*, whose function is evident in the name assigned to it. As discussed, the *nāḍīs* carry the *prāṇa* life airs, and thus it appears they carry the mind as well. Vācaspati Miśra also mentions *yogīs* who may have learned how to loosen the bondage of *karma* and thus are no longer bound to the body but who do not necessarily know the passageways that the mind must take to exit from the body to enter the body of others without harming the *yogī*. This is why the loosening of *karma* is mentioned by Patañjali here in combination with knowledge of the passageways of the mind in order to perform the feat mentioned in this *sūtra*. In his *Yoga-śāstra*, the Jain scholar Hemacandra (1088–1172) describes this process:

> After exiting through the aperture at the crown of the head, one should enter [*praviśya*] [another body] through the downward moving breath . . . Then one should spread oneself from the lotus at the navel . . . to the lotus at the heart via the *suṣumnā* or central subtle channel. At that point, one should obstruct the movement of the other's *prāṇa* with one's own breath [*vāyu*]. From that body, he should continue in this fashion until that embodied being falls flat, his movement faded away. When that other body has been completely liberated [of its previous occupant], the *yogin* whose actions and senses have come alive in all the activities [of the other] should commence movement as if in his own body. The intelligent [*yogin*] may play about fully in that other body for half a day or even a day. Again, through that same process one should enter one's own body.[73]

A well-known story featuring this power is found in the traditional hagiographies of our commentator Śaṅkara.[74] One day, Śaṅkara sought out Kumārila Bhaṭṭa, the foremost proponent of the rival Pūrva Mīmāṁsā school in his age, in order to debate with him. However, the great scholar was on his deathbed and directed Śaṅkara to his disciple, Viśvarūpa, more commonly known as (or identified with) the great intellectual, Maṇḍana Miśra. Curiously, the referee at the debate was Maṇḍana's own wife, the learned Bhāratī, regarded as an incarnation of the Goddess Sarasvatī. Bhāratī had much to lose in the affair, since the agreement was that if Śaṅkara won, Maṇḍana would renounce his wife and possessions and become a *sannyāsī*[75] disciple of Śaṅkara. On the other hand, if Maṇḍana won, Śaṅkara would renounce *sannyāsa* and consent to marriage and the life of a householder, a fallen and thus very socially undesirable outcome for a *sannyāsī*.

The debate is said to have lasted for weeks, until Maṇḍana eventually conceded defeat. Bhāratī was a fair judge, but before declaring Śaṅkara the winner, she challenged him with questions pertaining to the Kāma-śāstra, the Sanskrit treatises concerned with eroticism, conjugal love, and desire, about which the ascetic and renunciant Śaṅkara had had no experience. Śaṅkara accordingly requested a delay in proceedings during which time he entered the body of a dying king by the *śarīra-āveśa* technique indicated in this *sūtra* by Patañjali. During this time, he experienced various aspects of conjugal love with the king's queens such that he was able to return equipped with the appropriate answers to Bhāratī's questions (but not before he became so immersed in incessant lovemaking with the king's queen that he forgot all about his mission and was saved in the nick of time by the quick thinking of his disciples from having his original *sannyāsa* body burnt by the king's suspicious ministers!). The honorable Maṇḍana was to become Sureśvara, the most celebrated disciple of Śaṅkara, writing subcommentaries on some of Śaṅkara's Upaniṣad commentaries as well as independent treatises of his own.

A parallel, but slightly different, story occurs in the *Mahābhārata* (XV.33.24ff). Before leaving his mortal frame, the councilor and well-wisher of the Pāṇḍava brothers entered the body of king Yudhiṣṭhira due to his "*yoga* power." He united his life airs and powers of the senses with the king's, such that the latter felt empowered and endowed with more virtues than before. In a similar narrative (XII.31.29ff), the sage Bharadvāja entered the body of Prince Pratardhana from the age of thirteen and empowered him such that he could master at such a young age Vedic as well as military knowledge systems. Elsewhere in the epic (XIII.40–41), the sage Vipula entered into the body of his *guru*'s wife, Ruci, unequaled in beauty, to protect her from the seductive malintentions of the infamous Indra, lord of the celestials, while his *guru* was absent. Unbeknownst to her, "Vipula penetrated her body and joined his eyes with her eyes, and his eyelashes with her eyelashes, like the wind pervades space" (XIII.40.56).

Indra, endowed with *siddhis* such that he could assume any form at will—even that of the wind—adopted a seductive form and entered into the hermitage of the sage who had departed to perform a sacrifice, intending to seduce Ruci. Even though the innocent Ruci was attracted to this beautiful intruder and made to offer him some words of welcome, her senses were restrained due to her being possessed by Vipula, who had decided that this was the only way of protecting her from the powerful celestial. Instead of articulating the words she had in mind, Ruci found herself uttering against her will a blunter accusation, prompted by Vipula within her.

उदानजयाज्जलपङ्ककण्टकादिष्वसङ्ग उत्क्रान्तिश्च ।। ३९ ।।

III.39 udāna-jayāj jala-paṅka-kaṇṭakādiṣv asaṅga utkrāntiś ca

udāna, one of the *prāṇas*, vital airs; *jayāt*, from mastery over; *jala*, water; *paṅka*, mud; *kaṇṭaka*, thorns; *ādiṣu*, etc.; *asaṅgaḥ*, noncontact with; *utkrāntiḥ*, ascension, levitation; *ca*, and

By mastery over the *udāna* vital air, one attains [the power of] levitation and does not come into contact with water, mud, and thorns, etc.

The commentaries briefly discuss the five *prāṇas*, or vital airs, that circulate around the body in connection with this *sūtra*. Vācaspati Miśra quotes a verse stating that the five *prāṇas* are all manifestations of the air element,[76] but Vijñānabhikṣu, following the *Sāṅkhya Kārikās* and the *Vedānta Sūtras*,[77] insists that there is a difference between *prāṇa* and mundane air, which is one of the five gross elements.[78]

The five *prāṇas* are mentioned as early as the *Chāndogya Upaniṣad* (V.19–24). The most important is itself called *prāṇa*, and when it leaves the body, the other vital airs follow. In the *Praśna Upaniṣad* it is stated, "Just as a king appoints administrators stating: 'you oversee these villages, and you these,' so *prāṇa* directs the other life airs to their respective places" (III.4). Vyāsa's understanding of these airs is that *prāṇa* corresponds to the air that moves through the mouth and nose and circulates as far as the heart;[79] *samāna-prāṇa* is present in the navel and distributes (food) equally (around the body); *apāna-prāṇa* is present down to the soles of the feet, and carries away (the waste products of the body); *vyāna-prāṇa* is so called because it is spread all over (the body);[80] and *udāna-prāṇa* manifests up to the head and is so called because it carries up, *ud*. Levitation, *utkrāntiḥ*, is attained by the manipulation of the *udāna-prāṇa*.

More or less the entirety of the Hindu, Buddhist, and Jain Yoga traditions across the centuries have always claimed that the body can be made to levitate by manipulating internal air currents, *prāṇa*. Perhaps the earliest literary reference to such feats is expressed in the oldest Indo-European text, the *Ṛg Veda*, where the long-haired ascetic (*keśin*) flies through the atmosphere (*antarīkṣeṇa patati*) (X.136), and stories of this *siddhi* abound in the hagiographical literatures of Hindu *yogīs* throughout the centuries (and indeed, still surface on the *yogic* landscape of the West, most conspicuously in the "Transcendental Meditation" Organization[81]).

Not only is levitation attained by mastery over the *udāna-prāṇa*, says Vyāsa, but by the manipulation of this *prāṇa*, the *yogī* takes the auspicious upward path out of the body at death. This is a reference to the two pathways that can be taken by the departed soul after death, an upward one toward liberation and a downward one toward rebirth. These are mentioned in the *Bṛhadāraṇyaka Upaniṣad* (VI.15), the *Chāndogya Upaniṣad* (V.10), the *Gītā* (VIII.26), and discussed in the *Vedānta Sūtras* (III.1). And the *yogī* can leave the body at will, adds Rāmānanda Sarasvatī.

समानजयात् ज्वलनम् ॥ ४० ॥

III.40 samāna-jayāt jvalanam

samāna, over the *samāna* vital air; *jayāt*, by mastery;
jvalanam, effulgence

By mastery over the *samāna* vital air, radiance is attained.

By stimulating the fire in the body, one becomes radiant and effulgent, *jvalana*, say the commentators. Hariharānanda notes that the *samāna-prāṇa* is responsible for nourishing all parts of the body, and so, by mastering this *prāṇa*, the *yogī* gets an aura around the body. As with the halo in Christian iconography, auras are commonly associated with saints and *yogīs* in the Indic traditions, explainable in Yogic vocabulary by the prominence of the radiant and effulgent characteristics of *sattva* pervading the *yogī's citta*, and emanating out due to transcending the limitations of the *kleśas*.

Vijñānabhikṣu additionally understands the *jvalanam* of this *sūtra* as referring to the ability to self-combust. He mentions the story of Satī, the wife of Lord Śiva, as an example of someone manipulating the *udāna-prāṇa* in order to cast off her body by self-combustion. Offended by her own father, the proud ritualist Dakṣa, who had disregarded and insulted her husband, Śiva, Satī determined to sever all relations with him to the point of casting off the body that had been begotten by him. Satī, who had mastered *āsana*, first neutralized the up-flowing and down-flowing *prāṇa* and *apāna* airs (as touched on in II.49–50), then raised the *udāna-prāṇa* up from the navel *cakra*, held it in the heart area with concentration, and then drew it up through her throat and to between her eyebrows, from which point her body self-ignited by the power of her *samādhi* concentration (*Bhāgavata Purāṇa* IV.4.25).

King Dhṛtarāṣṭra, the uncle of the five Pāṇḍavas and father of their hundred cousins from the *Mahābhārata*, also self-ignited his body as a result of his *yogic* practice, according to the *Bhāgavata Purāṇa* rendition of his final days (which differs from the account in the epic). After the great Mahābhārata war, in which all his sons and kinsmen had been killed, the old king received persuasive instructions from his half brother and counselor Vidura not to die in a wretched fashion while clinging to his attachments and false sense of security in the royal household—especially since, in addition to being blind from birth, he was now becoming deaf, dull, feeble, and infirm from old age. Enlightened by the words of his well-wisher, Dhṛtarāṣṭra headed for the Himālayas, the destination of those desirous of liberation. We include here the verses spoken by the sage Nārada describing his subsequent practice, since it gives another *Bhāgavata*-flavored version of classical *yoga* featuring meditation on *Īśvara* and culminating in self-combustion, the topic of this *sūtra*:

> With a peaceful mind and free from desire, he [Dhṛtarāṣṭra] subsists on water. He has mastered *āsana* along with

prāṇāyāma, and has withdrawn the six senses (*pratyāhāra*). His impurities of *sattva*, *rajas* and *tamas* have been destroyed, through meditation on Hari [Viṣṇu/Kṛṣṇa] . . . He will cast off his body on the fifth day from today, O king, and it will be reduced to ashes. (I.13.53ff)

श्रोत्राकाशयोः संबन्धसंयमाद् दिव्यं श्रोत्रम् ॥ ४१ ॥

III.41 śrotrākāśayoḥ sambandha-saṁyamād divyaṁ śrotram

śrotra, ear, organ of hearing; *ākāśayoḥ*, ether; *sambandha*, relationship; *saṁyamāt*, by *saṁyama; divyam*, divine; *śrotram*, hearing

By *saṁyama* on the relationship between the organ of hearing and the ether, divine hearing is attained.

Ether, *ākāśa*, in Sāṅkhya thought, is the substratum of sound—sound vibrations require a medium in which to vibrate, and, by a process of elimination, the commentators argue that this substratum must be ether. In fact, ether is itself generated from the *tanmātra*, or subtle element, of sound, so sound is both inherent in ether and conveyed through it. Ether is therefore considered to be present in the ear, such that it can pick up the vibrations of sound. Patañjali here states that by *saṁyama* on the relationship between ether and the ear, the *yogī* is able to surpass the limitations of the physical ear and access divine sounds, *divyam śrotram*. In conventional hearing, says Bhoja Rāja, hearing catches only the sounds that vibrate within the pocket of ether enclosed by the ear; however, since ether is all-pervading, and so potentially is the *sāttvic citta*, the accomplished *yogī*'s *citta* is believed to be able to transcend identification with the body and expand out to access sound beyond the realm of normal hearing vibrating anywhere in the ether (*citta*, being subtler than ether, can pervade it). Parallel abilities can be attained by *saṁyama* on the other four senses and the respective subtle elements with which they are associated: air and the skin, light and the eye, water and the tongue, earth and the nose. In other words, the *yogī* develops supernormal sensual abilities, another long-standing claim of the Yoga tradition.

कायाकाशयोः संबन्धसंयमाल्
लघुतूलसमापत्तेश्चाकाशगमनम् ॥ ४२ ॥

III.42 kāyākāśayoḥ sambandha-saṁyamāl laghu-tūla-samāpatteś cākāśa-gamanam

kāya, the body; *ākāśayoḥ*, ether; *sambandha*, the relationship; *saṁyamāt*, by *saṁyama*; *laghu*, light; *tūla*, cotton; *samāpatteḥ*, a type of intense concentration; *ca*, and; *ākāśa*, sky; *gamanam*, movement, passage

By performing *saṁyama* on the relationship between the body and ether, and by performing *samāpatti* on the lightness of cotton, one acquires the ability to travel through the sky.

Recall that *samāpatti* involves concentrating intensely on an object such that the meditator becomes as if one with the object of meditation. Exactly how this differs from *saṁyama* in this *sūtra* is not discussed by our commentators (although see discussion in I.41), but the two processes appear very similar if not the same. In the commentaries of the Vedānta tradition (IV.2.16), *samāpatti* denotes merging, which in the context of Yoga points to the *citta*'s merger with the *citta* substructure of any object of meditation as a result of its intense focus.

The body moves in ether, or space, and by performing *saṁyama* on this relationship, as well as by total absorption on light entities such as cotton or atoms, one can become so light that one can walk on water, spiderwebs, or rays of light, according to the commentaries. Rāmānanda Sarasvatī takes these abilities as a progression reflecting the density of the medium of travel: First the *yogī* is able to walk on water, then spiderwebs, then light rays, then course through the air at will.

The metaphysical principle operating here seems to be the same one that pervades many of the *siddhis*: By manipulating the substratum, one can transform the nature of its effects. The gross elements are all transformations of ether, which means they are in essence ether. By *saṁyama* on this relationship, it seems that the *yogī* can potentially increase the *sattva* component of the body, thereby minimizing the *tamas* component, and thus manifest the inherent ethereal nature or quality constituting the body such that it takes on the qualities of ether. Ether takes on the form of the body, says Vijñānabhikṣu—the body is pervaded by ether (after all, it *is* essentially ether, from the perspective of the evolution of the material elements). This effect can also be attained by *saṁyama* on light things such as cotton, *tūla*, as well, following a similar principle.

This results in unimpeded freedom of movement, since ether is all-pervading. The *yogī* can thus move freely through the air, and some of the earliest records of Vedic literature preserve references to ascetics who had various powers, such as the ability to fly through the air and appear at will (*Āpastamba-sūtra* II.9.23.6–8; *Sāma-vidhāna* III.9.1). Perhaps the best-known sage in the Purāṇic genre is Nārada Muni, who is always traveling around the universe carrying his *vīṇā*, stringed instrument, visiting his disciples to impart instructions to them and constantly singing the glories of Lord Viṣṇu.

बहिरकल्पिता वृत्तिर्महाविदेहा ततः प्रकाशावरणक्षयः ॥ ४३ ॥

III.43 bahir-akalpitā vṛttir mahā-videhā tataḥ prakāśāvaraṇa-kṣayaḥ

bahiḥ, outside; *akalpitā*, not imagined; *vṛttiḥ*, state of mind; *mahā*, great; *videhā*, out of the body; *tataḥ*, by that; *prakāśa*, light; *āvaraṇa*, covering; *kṣayaḥ*, destruction

The state of mind [projected] outside [of the body], which is not an imagined state, is called the great out-of-body [experience]. By this, the covering of the light [of *buddhi*] is destroyed.

From what can be understood from the commentaries, it seems that this verse is taken to indicate that one can project the mind out of the body in two ways, imagined and nonimagined. The mind, although situated within the body, can focus on something outside the body, which is called *kalpita* or an imagined out-of-body experience. Everyone engages in this all the time: When you focus your mind on the book you are reading, the mind, in a sense, is being projected out of the body. But advanced *yogīs* are believed to be able to actually physically project the mind completely outside of the body at will such that it can function independently from the body. This is called an *akalpita* or nonimagined out-of-body experience. We are all familiar with imaging or thinking about things outside of ourselves, and projecting our minds here and there, but Patañjali here states that the *yogī* is able actually to disconnect the mind completely from the body and roam around at will independent of the body and, if he or she so desires, enter the bodies of others by this method (III.38). As Bhoja Rāja notes, it is because the false ego is removed that the *yogī* develops the ability to exit the body at will (in other words, the *kleśas* have been transcended). False ego, *ahaṅkāra*, means misidentifying with the body, as a consequence of which one is confined to the body until its destruction. So when false ego is destroyed, the bonds that bind the soul to the body are released, and the *yogī* is no longer subject to confinement in the body even while the body is still alive.

Along these lines, Patañjali notes that by this practice, the *yogī* diminishes the coverings, *āvaraṇa*, that envelop the pure light, *prakāśa*, which is to say the *sattva* potential of *buddhi*. These coverings are the *kleśas* and *karma* with its fruits, which are caused by the *guṇas*, says Vyāsa. According to Hariharānanda, this takes place because by such out-of-body experiences it becomes clear that the self is not the body, and so the base of ignorance, namely, any residual thinking that "I am this body," is further eliminated. And as we know, ignorance is the substratum of the other *kleśas* and consequently of the *karma* produced by them.

स्थूलस्वरूपसूक्ष्मान्वयार्थवत्त्वसंयमाद्भूतजयः ॥ ४४ ॥

III.44 sthūla-svarūpa-sūkṣmānvayārthavattva-saṁyamād bhūta-jayaḥ

sthūla, gross; *svarūpa*, essential nature or character; *sūkṣma*, subtle; *anvaya*, constitution; *arthavattva*, purpose, significance; *saṁyamāt*, from the performance of *saṁyama; bhūta*, elements; *jayaḥ*, mastery

By *saṁyama* on the gross nature, essential nature, subtle nature, constitution, and purpose [of objects, one attains] mastery over the elements.

As has been stressed throughout this chapter, to understand the mechanics of the *siddhi* powers from the perspective of Yoga presuppositions, one needs to understand the metaphysics of Sāṅkhya and Yoga. The feats outlined in this chapter have sometimes been called magic,[82] which can carry connotations of harnessing the power of sinister spirits and other notions inappropriate in the context of the *Yoga Sūtras*. The term also has connotations of supernaturalism, of mysteriously transcending the known laws of nature, which is more appropriate to the present context, although, considered from within the parameters of Sāṅkhya philosophy, the principles underpinning the *siddhis* are not actually mysterious but are internally consistent with the metaphysics of the system. This *sūtra* provides further insight into their workings.

As we have seen, the *yogī* performs *saṁyama* on some material object, whatever it might be (sun, moon, sense organ, etc.) and consequently is able to manipulate, rearrange, and tamper with the natural order of things. How does this transpire? In this *sūtra*, Patañjali considers what exactly constitutes physical objects such that they are amenable to such transformations by considering their metaphysical makeup on five progressively more subtle levels of *prakṛti*.

The first two levels, the gross, *sthūla*, and essential, *svarūpa*, natures of an object require a further discussion of two categories in Indic thought initiated in I.49: *viśeṣa* and *sāmānya*. *Viśeṣa*, in the thought of the school of Vaiśeṣika, means particularity, that which makes an entity particular and distinct from other entities. The school of Vaiśeṣika takes its name from *viśeṣa*, which ultimately refers to a metaphysical category or ingredient of reality that distinguishes or individualizes one fundamental entity or subatomic particle from another. Vyāsa uses the term more in the sense of *viśeṣa-guṇa*, or distinguishing quality of an entity. For example, in the present context, each of the five elements has a *viśeṣa-guṇa*: The distinguishing property or particular quality of the water element, for example, is taste. Other substances have taste only to the extent to which they contain some portion of water. Each element's *viśeṣa-guṇa* will be discussed below.

Sāmānya, on the contrary, according to the Vaiśeṣika school, means an essential feature that produces commonality among entities rather than distinguishing between them, as is the case with *viśeṣa*.[83] Here, too, Vyāsa uses the term in a narrower sense to refer to the *dharma*, also a type of property in Hindu philosophical discourse but that

Vyāsa correlates with properties different from those indicated by *guṇa*. This will be clarified below.

In any event, terms such as *viśeṣa* and *sāmānya* and their analyses are especially associated with the Vaiśeṣika school, where they are construed somewhat differently from their utilization here. According to the Yoga tradition, by the first aspect mentioned in this *sūtra*, the *sthūla*, gross nature or aspect of an object, Patañjali is referring to the object's elemental makeup of ether, air, fire, water, and earth—the *mahābhūtas*. As noted, these elements have *viśeṣa-guṇas*, specific qualities, associated with each of them. So the specific quality of ether is sound; the specific quality of air is touch (since air evolves from ether, it also has sound, the quality present in ether); the specific quality of fire is sight (since fire evolves from air, which in turn evolves from ether, it also has the qualities of both, sound and touch); the specific quality of water is taste (since water, in turn, evolves from fire, it also has the qualities of the previous elements, sound, touch, sight); and the specific quality of earth is smell (since earth is the last of the evolutes, it also has the qualities of all four previous evolutes). Thus, as a result of the presence of the wind element, we can feel something; as a result of the presence of the water element, we can taste something; as a result of the earth substance, we can smell something, and so on (therefore pure water has no smell; only muddy water, which contains earth, does).

We notice that each element includes the qualities of the previous elements in addition to its own special quality. Thus earth, which evolves from water which itself evolves from fire which itself evolves from air which evolves from ether, has all the qualities, and each other member of this list progressively has one less. So ether pervades all the elements; air pervades fire, water, and earth; fire pervades water and earth; and so on. Also, it is important to note that at this gross level, sound, touch, sight, taste, and smell are not the generic and nondifferentiated subtle energies corresponding to these sense abilities, the *tanmātras* (which will be encountered at the third level, below), but are sound, touch, etc., as manifest in gross form. This means demarcated by differentiation into the full range of different sounds, smells, tastes, etc., that exist in the perceivable world. For example, sound at this level is manifest in a range of sound in musical notes such as *do*, *ma*, etc., of the Hindu music scale; touch is subdivided into the range of sensations such as hot or cold; sight is determined by the range of colors such as blue or yellow; taste becomes distinctive in the range of flavors such as stringent or astringent; and smell manifests in a variety of odors such as sweet-smelling or otherwise. All this—the elements and their special characteristics—constitutes the gross aspect of an object. The Nyāya and Vaiśeṣika schools in particular have taken it upon themselves to produce lists of all these various qualities, characteristics, and subcharacteristics of gross objects, although there are some significant differences between these schools and those of the Yoga and Sāṅkhya lineages on certain issues.[84]

The second item listed by Patañjali, *svarūpa*, essential nature, is understood as relating to an object's *sāmānya*, its universal or general properties, more abstract or subtle aspects or properties of an object, which Vyāsa discusses in terms of the *dharma* or inherent nature of an object.[85] Universal properties are listed in some detail in the commentaries. For example, in terms of the elements themselves, among the properties of ether noted by Vyāsa and the commentaries is its all-pervadingness and interpenetration (it pervades all objects); of air, its constant motion and the ability to move; of fire, its heat and light; of water, its liquidity and cohesion; and of earth, its shape and weight.[86] These properties are universal insofar as they underpin all objects in their categories. So, for example, everything with the earth element has form (that is, has the universal property of being limited in its extension); everything with water has cohesion in accordance with the proportion of water contained in it.

In sum, Vyāsa notes that form, liquidity, heat, movement, and all-pervadingness are the general properties, *sāmānya*, of earth, water, fire, air, and ether, respectively; and the qualities of smell, taste, visibility, touch, and sound are their corresponding specific or particular qualities, *viśeṣa-guṇas*. A substance, *dravya*, is a combination of these generic and specific qualities, and more specifically, one in which these qualities or properties are inherent, rather than distinct, entities[87] (contra Nyāya and Vaiśeṣika[88]). So when one encounters a physical object, the most immediate aspect of it that one experiences is its gross nature or elemental makeup, and its specific qualities, which are pervaded by the object's essential nature, all of which comprise the first two items listed in this *sūtra*.[89]

Moving on to the third feature, the *sūkṣma*, subtle aspect of an object, consists of the *tanmātras*, subtle elements, from which the gross aspects such as earth, etc., evolve (and it is here that the Sāṅkhya school parts company with the Nyāya and Vaiśeṣika schools). The *tanmātras* are sound, touch, sight, taste, and smell, but these are not specific sounds and touch, etc. (sensations)—the *do* or *mā* of the Hindu music scale, hot or cold, etc.—mentioned above, but generic undifferentiated sound and touch, etc., within which the variations of specific sounds and touch sensations are latent; they have not yet burst forth to manifest their full range of differentiated sounds, tastes, etc., as is the case with level one. Although translated simplistically as sound, touch, taste, etc., the *tanmātras* are a set of vibrational energies that underpin these sense capabilities. The element of ether is produced, according to Sāṅkhya metaphysics, from generic sound; air from generic touch and sound; fire from generic sight, touch, and sound; water from generic taste, sight, touch, and sound; and earth from generic smell, taste, sight, touch, and sound.

Another way of putting this is that the atoms, which correspond to the elements of ether, air, fire, water, and earth, are themselves composed of the *tanmātras*. If one dissects or dissolves any object, penetrates more subtly into its metaphysical makeup, one will realize that the ultimate subatomic particles constituting the physical elements with their qualities are actually individualized densifications, or gross externalizations of a still more subtle energy or set of energies—the *tanmātras*.

The fourth item, constitution, *anvaya*, is taken by the commentators to refer to the three *guṇas*. Penetrating even more deeply into an object's constituents, one comes to its fundamental makeup and realizes that everything in manifest reality, including the *tanmātras*, is ultimately composed of *sattva, rajas*, and *tamas*. Finally, on a less metaphysical and more abstract level, one arrives at the fifth item mentioned in this *sūtra, arthavattva*, purpose, which pertains more to functionality than metaphysics. The purpose of all objects in manifest reality is twofold: to provide to the *puruṣa* either enjoyment (and its consequence, bondage) or liberation, as noted in II.18.

By *saṁyama* on these progressively more subtle ways of perceiving objects in the external world, the *yogī* attains mastery over them. By manipulating the subtle substructure of anything in physical reality with one's will—a function of *citta*—one can rearrange the gross externalization of that object. As Vyāsa puts it, when *saṁyama* is perfected, the elements follow the will of the *yogī*, as calves follow the cow. Since everything is ultimately a product of the three primary *guṇas*, by manipulating the proportion of the *guṇas* in an object one can completely transform its makeup, just as one can completely change the color of something by adjusting the proportions of the primary colors red, yellow, and blue. Or, in Dasgupta's terms, "The difference between one thing and another is simply this, that its collocation of atoms, or the arrangement or grouping of atoms is different from another. The formation of a collocation has an inherent barrier against any change . . . Providing the suitable barriers can be removed, anything could be changed to any other thing" (255–56). Since *buddhi* (and *ahaṅkāra*) ultimately underpin the *tanmātras* which, in turn, underpin the subatomic particles that comprise matter, the Yoga traditions holds that *buddhi* can be manipulated to rearrange the groupings of such atoms, which are nothing but a densification of itself to create new effects. This is not magic from the perspective of Yoga. It is subtle physics.

Vijñānabhikṣu correlates the *vitarka-samādhi* with meditation on the gross nature of an object, which implies other stages of *samādhi* mentioned in the first chapter; specifically, *vicāra* could be correlated with the other, more subtle and rarefied natures of an object, as outlined in this *sūtra* and discussed more specifically in I.42.

ततोऽणिमादिप्रादुर्भावः कायसंपत् तद्धर्मानभिघातश्च ॥ ४५ ॥

III.45 tato 'ṇimādi-prādurbhāvaḥ kāya-sampat-tad-dharmānabhighātaś ca

tataḥ, from that; *aṇimā*, the mystic power of *aṇimā* [lightness]; *ādi*, etc.; *prādurbhāvaḥ*, the appearance of; *kāya*, body; *sampat*, accomplishment, perfection; *tat*, their [the elements']; *dharma*, essential nature; *anabhighātaḥ*, nonresistance, absence of limitations; *ca*, and

As a result of this, there are no limitations on account of the body's natural abilities; mystic powers such as *aṇimā*, etc., manifest; and the body attains perfection.

Here Patañjali lists three consequences of the type of *saṁyama* discussed in the previous *sūtra*. For the removal of "limitations on account of the body's natural abilities," *dharma-anabhighāta*, Vyāsa lists the following:

(1) The earth does not obstruct the *yogī* by its quality of solidness, such that the *yogī* can enter even a stone.
(2) Water, though moist, does not wet the *yogī*.
(3) Fire, though hot, does not burn the *yogī*.
(4) Wind, though moving, does not budge the *yogī*.
(5) Ether, which normally does not cover anything, covers the *yogī* such that he or she remains invisible even to the *siddhas*, or those who have attained these very powers.

The eight mystic powers mentioned in this *sūtra* refer to the standardized list of powers that are ubiquitous in classical Hindu texts. That Patañjali sees fit to note only the first one (*aṇimādi*) followed by etc. indicates that these were already well-known to his audience. The first four powers pertain to *saṁyama* on various gross aspects of *prakṛti*, the remainder on various subtle aspects. These eight powers are:

(1) *Aṇimā*, minuteness: the ability to make one's body atomic in size. This allows one to become small enough to enter into anything (even the dense substructure of a diamond, says Śaṅkara), and by so doing to become invisible to anyone.
(2) *Laghimā*, lightness: the ability to make the body as light as one desires in terms of weight (as light as cotton, say the commentators).
(3) *Mahimā*, largeness: the ability to make the body as heavy in weight as one desires.
(4) *Prāpti*, attainment: the ability to attain anything one desires—one can touch the moon with one's fingertips, says Vyāsa.
(5) *Prākāmya*, freedom of will: the ability to be unobstructed in one's desires—one can dive into the earth just as one plunges into water, says Vyāsa.

(6) *Vaśitva*, mastery: the ability to control the elements and their qualities, and to control other beings.
(7) *Īśitṛtva*, lordship: the ability to control the outward appearance, disappearance, and rearrangement of the elements.
(8) *Yatra-kāmāvasāyitva*: the ability to manipulate the elements at will according to one's fancy.

In short, once one attains perfection in the *siddhis* that accrue from meditation, one becomes practically omniscient and omnipotent. The Hindu and Buddhist traditions are replete with stories pertaining to the magical powers of the accomplished *yogī*.

However, the commentators hasten to add, this does not mean that a *yogī* whimsically disrupts the natural order of things. The *yogī* respects the will of *Īśvara*, the Lord, who is eternally perfect and by whose will the natural order of things was arranged in the first place. Free from personal ego and desire, what reason could the *yogī* have to interfere with *Īśvara*'s plan? To do so, says Śaṅkara, would, quite apart from desire and ego, indicate animosity toward *Īśvara*, and the *yogī*, at this point, has been purified of such base qualities. One might mention here, along with Vijñānabhikṣu, that, according to the *Vedānta Sūtras* (IV.4.17), the *yogī*'s quasi-omnipotent powers do not extend to the ability to create a universe. They are limited in this one regard, and this limitation distinguishes the ordinary *puruṣa* from *Īśvara*, according to the Vedānta school.

The perfection of the body, the third accomplishment mentioned in this *sūtra*, is the topic of the next *sūtra*.

रूपलावण्यबलवज्रसंहननत्वानि कायसंपत् ।। ४६ ।।

III.46 rūpa-lāvaṇya-bala-vajra-saṁhananatvāni kāya-sampat

rūpa, beauty of form; *lāvaṇya*, charm, grace; *bala*, strength; *vajra*, thunderbolt; *saṁhananatvāni*, being of a solid nature; *kāya*, the body; *sampat*, perfection

The perfection of the body consists of [possessing] beauty, charm, strength, and the power of a thunderbolt.

The commentators consider this *sūtra*, which expounds on the perfection of the body, the last item listed in the previous *sūtra*, as self-explanatory and offer no further comments. The *vajra* mentioned here, usually associated in Hinduism with Indra, king of the demigods, is a thunderbolt weapon. Indra is the Indic equivalent to culturally cognate Indo-European figures such as Thor and Zeus, and his *vajra* is fashioned, according to the *Bhāgavata Purāṇa* (VI.10.13), from the bones of the sage Dadhīci and said to be almost unbreakably hard. Rāmānanda Sarasvatī gives Hanumān, the devoted monkey servant of Lord Rāma, as an example of someone who has attained the *siddhi* mentioned in this *sūtra*, and, indeed, one of Hanumān's names is Vajrāṅga—one who has the limbs of a thunderbolt.

ग्रहणस्वरूपास्मितान्वयार्थवत्त्वसंयमाद् इन्द्रियजयः ॥ ४७ ॥

III.47 grahaṇa-svarūpāsmitānvayārthavattva-saṁyamād indriya-jayaḥ

grahaṇa, the process of obtaining knowledge; *svarūpa*, the essence; *asmitā*, the ego; *anvaya*, inherent quality, constitution; *arthavattva*, purposefulness; *saṁyamāt*, by *saṁyama* (concentration) on; *indriya*, the senses; *jayaḥ*, victory, control

By the performance of *saṁyama* on the process of knowing, on the essence [the sense organs], on ego, on the constitution [of the *guṇas*], and on the purpose [of the *guṇas*] comes control over the senses.

This *sūtra* analyzes another set of five progressively more rarefied ways of perceiving reality, in this case the metaphysical makeup of the senses with a view to attaining supreme control over them and thus overlaps with III.44, which in parallel fashion analyzes the objects of the senses in five progressively more rarefied ways. *Grahaṇa*, the process of knowledge, refers to the operation of the senses on the sense objects (the objects of sound, touch, sight, taste, and smell). As we know from I.41, *grahaṇa* literally means grasping and refers here to the process by which the sense objects are grasped or experienced by means of the channels of the senses. It is the act of acquiring knowledge.

Vyāsa and the commentators take the second item on this list, *svarūpa*, the essence, to refer to the *sāttvic* modification of *buddhi* (the intellect), which underpins the illumination, or knowledge-acquiring abilities of the senses. In other words, the *tanmātras*—sound, sight, touch, taste, smell, etc.—which are the powers behind the functions of the senses, are *sāttvic* in essence. As indicated in III.44, these are the general functions of sound, taste, etc., rather than their particulars in specific notes or tastes (which manifest at the level of sense objects).[90] Next, *asmitā*, is specifically correlated with the *ahaṅkāra* by Vyāsa, so these are more or less synonymous terms used in the Yoga and Sāṅkhya schools, respectively, for the ego. Etymologically, *asmitā* means I-am-ness, whereas *ahaṅkāra* means I am the doer, so there is a slight distinction in emphasis, as discussed previously. Regardless, these terms refer to the misidentification of the nonself with the self. It is from *ahaṅkāra* that the senses emerge, as indicated on the *Sāṅkhya* chart in the introduction. So *asmitā* is a still finer cause of sense activity.

As in III.44, *anvaya*, the fourth item, is taken by the commentators to refer to the three *guṇas*, which underpin even ego and, therefore, ultimately also the senses, which are derivatives of ego (see Sāṅkhya chart in the introduction). Since Vyāsa speaks of determination here, and since determination is a feature of *buddhi*, intelligence, Vijñānabhikṣu understands this fourth dimension of the makeup of the senses to refer more specifically to *buddhi* than the *guṇas*. This also works from a metaphysical perspective, as *ahaṅkāra* (*asmitā*), and thus its evolutes such as the senses are themselves derivates from *buddhi*, which is the first evolute from *prakṛti*. Finally, again as in III.44, at the ultimate rarefied level, underpinning the activities of the *guṇas*, is their *arthavattva*, ultimate purpose vis-à-vis *puruṣa*. This purpose is to provide experience or liberation to *puruṣa*.

Thus, paralleling his analysis of the sense objects in III.44, Vyāsa has deconstructed the actual senses themselves into their progressively more subtle constituents: their grossest aspect as their function of acquiring knowledge of the sense objects; their *sāttvic* constitution; their essential nature as evolutes of *ahaṅkāra*; their even more subtle nature as expressions of *buddhi*, which is itself a product of the *guṇas*; and finally their subtlest nature, which is their epistemological purpose for existing in the first place. By performing *saṁyama* on the senses in these progressively more rarefied ways, the *yogī* masters them sequentially, says Vyāsa. Once this is accomplished, the senses can be said to be fully mastered, *indriya-jaya*.

ततो मनोजवित्वं विकरणभावः प्रधानजयश्च ॥ ४८ ॥

III.48 tato mano-javitvam vikaraṇa-bhāvaḥ pradhāna-jayaś ca

tataḥ, from that; *manaḥ*, of the mind; *javitvam*, quickness; *vikaraṇa*, without instruments; *bhāvaḥ*, existence; *pradhāna*, primordial matter; *jayaḥ*, victory; *ca*, and

As a result of this comes speed like the speed of mind, activity independent of the bodily senses, and mastery over primordial matter.

Patañjali here refers to three more sets of powers that accrue to the *yogī* who has conquered the senses in the manner outlined in the previous *sūtra*. Once one has mastered the senses, one's body can move at the speed of mind, *mano-javitvam*; one can act and attain knowledge at any time or place even without one's body and its sense organs of perception, *vikaraṇa-bhāva*; and one attains mastery over the primordial *prākṛtic* matrix[91]—and therefore, specify the commentators, over all its evolutes and thus all manifest reality, *pradhāna-jaya*. Here we again see another articulation of the *yogic* claim to omnipotence and omniscience. Vyāsa groups together the attainment of these three types of abilities under the term *madhu-pratīka*. In his *Yoga-vārttika* commentary, Vijñānabhikṣu connects the latter two powers referred to in this *sūtra* by Patañjali with the attainments of the two types of *yogīs* referred to in I.19: the *videha*, bodiless ones, and the *prakṛti-laya*, those merged in *prakṛti*.

In his *Yoga-sāra* commentary, Vijñānabhikṣu states that it is on account of the first power, *mano-javitvam*, moving at the speed of mind, that great *siddhas* are able to appear in a moment before their disciples merely on the latter's thinking of them.[92] Thus when the traditional Vyāsa—divider of the Vedas, compiler of the Purāṇas, and author of the *Mahābhārata* (whom the Yoga tradition correlates with our commentator Vyāsa), became despondent, his heart unfulfilled despite his immense labors (since he had yet to write the *Bhāgavata Purāṇa* and thus to fully expound the truths of the supreme Lord Viṣṇu), his *guru*, Nārada, appeared before him to council him (I.4.26ff). This belief in the *guru* manifesting before the disciple at a moment of crisis is still evidenced in, for example, Yogānanda's *Autobiography of a Yogi*.

सत्त्वपुरुषान्यताख्यातिमात्रस्य सर्वभावाधिष्ठातृत्वं सर्वज्ञातृत्वं च ॥ ४९ ॥

III.49 sattva-puruṣānyatā-khyāti-mātrasya sarva-bhāvādhiṣṭhātṛtvam sarva-jñātṛtvam ca

sattva, intellect; *puruṣa*, the self, soul; *anyatā*, difference; *khyāti*, discernment; *mātrasya*, of one, only; *sarva*, all; *bhāva*, state of existence; *adhiṣṭhātṛtvam*, state of supremacy over; *sarva*, all; *jñātṛtvam*, state of knowledge; *ca*, and

Only for one who discerns the difference between the *puruṣa* and the intellect do omniscience and omnipotence accrue.

When *buddhi* has been cleansed of its *rājasic* and *tāmasic* ingredients such that only pure *sattva* remains, it attains a state of perfect clarity that Vyāsa calls *vaśīkāra*. In this state, the *yogī* has full realization of the difference between the highest aspect of the cognitive faculty, pure *buddhi*,[93] and the *puruṣa* itself, *sattva-puruṣa-anyatā*. Needless to say, we are still within the realms of *sabīja-samādhi* at this point. The consciousness of *puruṣa* is directed outward insofar as it is still conscious of *buddhi*, albeit *buddhi* in its ultimate purified state, rather than directed inward toward pure self-awareness. But the *yogī* now has complete control, *vaśīkāra*, over manifest reality: The *guṇas*, which are the essence of everything in manifest reality, submit themselves before their owner, the *kṣetrajña*, or master of the field (of *prakṛti*), says Vyāsa, using terms that are likely drawn from the thirteenth chapter of the *Gītā*.[94] They are manipulated by the will of the *yogī*, like iron filings are manipulated by the presence of a magnet, says Vijñānabhikṣu.

Omniscience, *sarva-jñātṛtva*, continues Vyāsa, simply means discriminate awareness of the three *guṇas*. If one perceives the true nature of the *guṇas*, one automatically understands any past, present, or future product emanating from them, just as one can understand the true and ultimate nature of any color, past, present, or future, once one understands how the essential components of the three colors red, yellow, and blue combine to produce the variegated universe of color. Vijñānabhikṣu notes that, in principle at least, all *puruṣas* are masters over the *guṇas*, but, due to the *kleśas* and their ensuing obstacles such as vice, etc.—in other words, due to the prevalence of *rajas* and *tamas*—the *guṇas* do not submit themselves to all *puruṣas* at all times. But the *yogī* who has reached the stage indicated in this *sūtra* has full mastery over them, *sarva-bhāva-adhiṣṭhātṛtva*.

The Jains have an interesting counterpart to this. In the Jain traditions, *karma* is conceived of in a much more physical fashion than in the Hindu/Buddhist schools. It literally sticks onto the *ātman*, depending on the degree of the soul's passions and cravings, which act as a sort of glue, like dirt covering a lamp.[95] When this *karma* is partly destroyed it frees up the *yogī*'s awareness such that it can perceive forms that are normally beyond the purview of the senses, like the light of a lamp can pervade farther when some of the dirt covering it is removed. In other words, the *yogī* develops supernormal powers of the senses (*avadhi-jñāna*). When the soul has overcome hatred and jealousy, etc., the light of the *ātman* can penetrate farther and access subtler dimensions: Its awareness can have direct perception of the thoughts of others, past and present (*manaḥ-paryāya*). Finally, when all *karma* is totally removed, with awareness now unimpeded, like a simple light that can pervade the entire universe if there are no obstructions to impede it, absolute omniscience and omnipotence arise in the soul (*kevala-jñāna*).

Vyāsa uses the term *viśokā*, sorrowlessness, here to describe this state of omniscience. What is sorrow, after all, but the reaction to the loss of something pertaining to *prakṛti*, or the feeling of deprivation when one cannot attain some such thing? Needless to say, the point is theoretical, since to have arrived at this stage the *yogī* has perforce transcended attachment to objects and desire for them. But, if only in principle, if the *yogī* at this point has full control over *prakṛti* and her effects, and thus is obliged neither to lose any object of desire nor submit to powerlessness in attempts to obtain any such object, where is the question of sorrow?

Obviously, grandiose claims of omniscience and omnipotence are hardly likely to appeal to the rational spirit of post-Enlightenment thought. However, recalling our commitment to a phenomenological approach, such claims follow logically from within the parameters of Sāṅkhya or Yoga metaphysics. This metaphysics holds that all material and psychic phenomena are evolutes of *buddhi*. Only the *kleśas* keep one's *buddhi* localized and separate from the universal *buddhi*, the first evolute from *prakṛti*, so once these are transcended, these individualizing limitations are surpassed. Consequently, if one can access and exert mastery over the universality of *buddhi*, one has full knowledge of and control over all its evolutes, namely, the entirety of material and psychic phenomena—the phenomenal world. The claim to omniscience is thus internally consistent with the metaphysics of the Sāṅkhyan system.

Similar claims are fairly standard across Indic traditions: Tantric, Jain, Buddhist, etc., including the Vedānta tradition.[96] In the Jain *Kalpa-sūtra* (120.1), Mahāvīra, the contemporary of the Buddha who is the primary figurehead in the Jain tradition, attains liberation (called *kaivalya*, the same term used in IV.34 below), at which point he becomes omniscient: "Comprehending all objects; he knew and saw all conditions of the world, of gods, men and demons: whence they come, whither they go, whether they are born as men or animals or become gods or hell-beings, the ideas, the thoughts of their minds, the food, doings, desires, the open and secret deeds of all living beings in the whole world."[97] Indeed, the Jains maintain that all souls must necessarily attain omniscience upon liberation. The Buddha, too, makes similar claims about himself: "Whatever . . . in this world with its devas and Māras and Brahmas [celestial beings] is by the fold thereof, gods or men, recluses or Brahmans, seen, heard, felt, discerned, accomplished, striven for, or devised in mind—all is understood by the Tathāgata [Buddha]."[98]

Having said this, we might also revisit the fact that Patañjali in I.25 made a point of noting—and perhaps his comment there can now be considered in a different light—that *tatra niratiśayaṁ sarvajña-bījam*, *Īśvara*'s "omniscience is unsurpassed." Even if the *yogī*'s awareness can pervade all of *prakṛti*, understand its past and future permutations, and access all things knowable as indicated in this *sūtra*, nonetheless *Īśvara*'s omniscience is of a higher order. One might wonder what else there is to know, if the *yogī* already knows everything past and present, but clearly and perhaps expectedly, whatever else there might be must be beyond the range of *citta* and *buddhi*, since the *yogī* already knows all there is to be known within the ranges of these. In other words, if the *yogī* knows everything *prākṛtic*, as indicated in these *sūtras*, yet *Īśvara* knows something that surpasses this (*atiśayam*), then might one have some grounds to infer that *Īśvara*'s additional omniscience, so to speak, might be associated with some level of experience beyond *prakṛti*?

Certainly the theologies of post-Śaṅkara Vedāntins such as Rāmānuja, Madhva, Caitanya, and Vallabha take this view and hold that there are numerous *Brahman* realms and dimensions beyond *prakṛti* made not of *prākṛtic* matter but of pure conscious *Brahman*, and these are inhabited by the unlimited Supreme divine forms of Viṣṇu/Nārāyaṇa/Kṛṣṇa in the company of quasi-omniscient and omnipotent liberated *puruṣas*, also in forms of pure conscious *Brahman*, whose powers are nonetheless inferior to *Īśvara*'s[99] As elsewhere, one cannot project theologies from different times and contexts onto Patañjali's *sūtras*, which—unlike the earlier Sāṅkhya/Yoga traditions as well as the later commentators including Vyāsa—don't even mention *Brahman*. But if one chooses to step beyond Patañjali's characteristically tantalizing references of *Īśvara*'s superomniscience, so to speak, one can find interesting examples of how this notion of graded omniscience and omnipotence gets developed in other later Vedāntic traditions.

In any event, where Patañjali differentiates between the omniscience of liberated *puruṣas* and that of *Īśvara*, the *Vedānta Sūtras* make a parallel statement pertaining to the difference between the omnipotence of liberated *puruṣas* and that of *Īśvara* (IV.4.17). The former has all the divine powers except the creatorship of the universe (*jagad-vyāpāra-varjitam*). Thus, in the Vedānta tradition, *Īśvara*'s omnipotence is unsurpassed, as his omniscience is for Patañjali.

तद्वैराग्यादपि दोषबीजक्षये कैवल्यम् ॥५०॥

III.50 tad-vairāgyād api doṣa-bīja-kṣaye kaivalyam

tat, that [i.e., omniscience and omnipotence]; *vairāgyāt*, from detachment, disinterest; *api*, even; *doṣa*, faults; *bīja*, seeds; *kṣaye*, on the destruction of; *kaivalyam*, supreme independence, ultimate liberation

By detachment even from this attainment [i.e., omniscience and omnipotence], and upon the destruction of the seeds of all faults, *kaivalya*, the supreme liberation ensues.

This *sūtra* announces the ultimate goal of *yoga* or, more specifically, of the practice of *saṁyama*. All other practices of *saṁyamas* are but semblances of this ultimate *saṁyama*, says Vācaspati Miśra. This, as we know, is *nirbīja-samādhi*, which Patañjali here refers to as *kaivalya*. *Kaivalya* carries a range of meanings, including independence, aloneness, not being mixed with anything else. In other words, *puruṣa* has finally reached the state of complete detachment or uncoupling from *prakṛti*. In this state, there is no interest in even the possibility of omnipotence and omniscience, which are obviously states of awareness related to *prakṛti*, albeit *prakṛti* in totality.

When the *kleśas* and subsequent seeds of *karma* have dwindled, says Vyāsa, the *yogī* understands that even the most rarefied stage of discrimination noted in the previous *sūtra* is still a product of *sattva*, and *sattva*, as a *guṇa*, is still a product of *prakṛti* and so also ultimately comes under the category of things to be avoided (as outlined in II.15–16). *Puruṣa*, in contrast, is unchanging and pure and distinct from even *sattva*. Thus, the *yogī* begins to cultivate detachment from pure *sattva*. Since the insight into the need to do this is itself a product of *sattva*, in a sense *sattva* is channeling its own discrimination toward deconstructing itself—toward terminating its own functions.

Consequently, the seeds of the *kleśas* become burnt and incapable of sprouting, *doṣa-bīja-kṣaya*,[100] and, along with the mind that has harbored them, eventually dissolve back into the primordial *prākṛtic* matrix. Once this happens, *puruṣa* does not again experience the threefold miseries,[101] which we know are caused by these *kleśas*. The *guṇas* have now fulfilled their purpose, says Vyāsa, and no longer incite action. Now that they are quiescent, they do not distract the consciousness of *puruṣa*. Now that *puruṣa* is no longer externally conscious of an other, it can be only internally conscious of itself.[102] This is *kaivalya*, absolute independence, in the sense that *puruṣa* is independent of the *guṇas* and their products, and thus of everything in manifest reality. This means it can now be conscious only of itself—there is nothing else for it to be aware of once it ceases to be aware of *prakṛti*. *Puruṣa* is eternally aware; as the *Gītā* stresses throughout the second chapter, the nature of *ātman* can never be destroyed or negated in any way. *Puruṣa* can only and must be aware by its very constitution, so when it ceases to be aware of *prakṛti* it has no other choice by dint of its very nature than to be aware of itself. Awareness can be self-aware or other-aware;[103] there are no other options. Situated exclusively in its own ultimate and autonomous nature, the *puruṣa* is now pure and unadulterated consciousness—*citi-śakti*—that is, consciousness conscious only of itself. This is *kaivalya* or *asamprajñāta-samādhi*.

स्थान्युपनिमन्त्रणे सङ्गस्मयाकरणं पुनर् अनिष्टप्रसङ्गात् ॥५१॥

III.51 sthānyupanimantraṇe saṅga-smayākaraṇam punar-aniṣṭa-prasaṅgāt

sthāni, celestial beings; *upanimantraṇe*, upon the invitation; *saṅga*, attachment; *smaya*, smile, conceit; *akaraṇam*, not performing; *punaḥ*, again; *aniṣṭa*, undesirable; *prasaṅgāt*, inclination toward, attachment

If solicited by celestial beings, [the *yogī*] should not become smug, because the tendency toward undesirable consequences can once again manifest.

As was discussed earlier, according to Hindu cosmology, this material universe contains numerous variegated realms, including celestial realms, attained by the pious performance of good *karma* in the earthly realm (the *puṇya* of II.14). *Karma*, we recall, manifests in type of birth, quality of life experience, and life span, and so the denizens of these celestial realms enjoy the highest births in *saṁsāra*, superb sensual capabilities and quality of experience, and extraordinarily long life spans by human comparison. Such attainments are therefore enticing, and, indeed, were a major goal of the old Vedic ritualism as well as of the Mīmāṁsā school current in Patañjali's time. Patañjali suggests that these celestial beings can attempt to lure the *yogī*, who, having attained omnipotence and omniscience, has powers that have now surpassed even those of the celestials, away from his or her practices.

Vyāsa begins his commentary by noting that there are four classes of *yogī*. First is the *prathama-kalpika*, whom he describes as one who is practicing and in whom the "light" is dawning. Vijñānabhikṣu suggests that such a *yogī* may have attained stages of *samādhi* such as *savitarka*, in which case he or she is an advanced albeit still not fully accomplished practitioner. Next is the *madhu-bhūmika*, one who has attained the *ṛtambharā* insight (referred to in I.48). Vijñānabhikṣu connects this (by the process of elimination) with *nirvitarka-samādhi*. A third type of *yogī* is the *prajñā-jyotiḥ*, who has control over the elements and the sense organs, and who knows all that has been known and all that has to be known. Vijñānabhikṣu says that such a *yogī* has attained the state of *viśokā* noted in III.49, and, indeed, all attainments accruing prior to the state of *asamprajñāta-samādhi*. Finally, there is the *atikrānta-bhāvanīya*, whose sole aim is to dissolve the mind back into *prakṛti*, such that *puruṣa* can now shine forth unfettered. Vyāsa associates the sevenfold insight (referred to in II.27) with this fourth type of *yogī*.

According to Vijñānabhikṣu and Vācaspati Miśra, the specific type of individual referred to by Patañjali in this *sūtra* corresponds to the second category of *yogī* mentioned by Vyāsa, the *madhu-bhūmika*. In other words, when the *yogī* reaches the *madhu-bhūmika* stage, the celestial demigods endeavor to tempt him or her away from proceeding on the path, *sthāni-upanimantraṇa*. This type of *yogī* is the target of the demigods' attention, since the first category of *yogī* is too neophyte to concern the demigods, the third has surpassed temptation, and the fourth has surpassed even the sphere of cognitive thought. The *madhu-bhūmika* then is a prime target for celestial temptations.

In Vyāsa's version of events, the demigods in their various celestial realms, seeing the *yogī* progressing on the path, attempt to divert him:

> Hey there, sit here! Enjoy here! This experience is enjoyable! This maiden is pleasurable! This elixir counteracts disease and old age! This vehicle flies through the air! These are the wish-fulfilling trees![104] Here is the pure Mandākinī river![105] These are the perfected *yogīs* and the sages! Here are the most beautiful and sweetly disposed *apsara* nymphs! Here is clairvoyance and supernormal hearing powers! Here is a body as strong as a

> thunderbolt! You have earned all these by your good qualities! Come and partake of all this! This place, dear to the gods, knows no death, decay, or old age.[106]

The stalwart *yogī*, however, must be guarded against such allurements, and being addressed in this way, should contemplate the dangers of attachment:

> Burnt by the fearsome flames of worldly existence, and tossed around in the darkness of birth and death, I have somehow or other obtained the light of *yoga*, which destroys dense darkness. These winds of sensual enjoyment, which are born of desire, are obstacles [to the goal of *yoga*]. Having obtained that light, how on earth can I be deceived by the illusion of sensual pleasure and again make myself fuel for the burning fire of worldly existence?! Good riddance to you sensual pleasures, which are like a dream, and aspired for only by wretched people![107]

The *yogī* should become firm of resolve, continues Vyāsa, and turn his back on such temptations. But there is a further danger even here: "He should not even give a smile of satisfaction, thinking that he is being entreated even by the demigods! If he becomes smug, thinking himself securely situated, he will fail to realize that he is grasped by the hair by Death."[108] In this way, continues Vyāsa, "forgetfulness [of the true self], which is so hard to overcome, ever on the lookout for a weak spot, will find a point of entry, reactivate the *kleśas*, and undesirable consequences ensue."[109] But the diligent *yogī* becomes neither attached nor, perhaps as important, proud of his nonattachment. Such a *yogī* will eventually attain success.

As early as the *Muṇḍaka Upaniṣad* there is fairly scorching criticism, in this case directed against the Vedic ritualists, of those striving to attain the attractions of the celestial realms by sacrificial rites:

> Because of desire, those who are given to rites, do not understand.
>
> [When] their time in the [celestial] realms has expired, they fall down, tormented.

> Believing sacrifices and gifts to be the highest, fools think there is nothing better than this.
>
> When they have enjoyed [the fruits] of their good deeds in the higher realms, they return back down to this inferior world. (I.2.9–10)

The *Gītā* takes the same view of celestial attainments:

> Ignorant people proclaim the flowery words of the Veda, O Arjuna! Delighting in Vedic doctrine, they say "there is nothing else." Their hearts full of desires and aspiring for the celestial realms, they perform many varied and intricate rituals with the goal of [attaining] enjoyment and power. For those attached to power and opulence, whose minds are stolen by such things, an undeviating *buddhi* fixed in *samādhi* is not attained (II.42–44) . . . After having enjoyed the spacious celestial realm, they then enter the world of mortals when their pious *karma* has expired. (IX.21)

क्षणतत्क्रमयोः संयमादविवेकजं ज्ञानम् ॥५२॥

III.52 kṣaṇa-tat-kramayoḥ saṁyamād viveka-jaṁ jñānaṁ

kṣaṇa, moment, instant; *tat*, its [the moment's]; *kramayoḥ*, sequence, succession; *saṁyamāt*, from performing *saṁyama* on; *viveka*, discrimination; *jam*, born of; *jñānam*, knowledge

By performing *saṁyama* on the moment, and its sequence, one attains knowledge born of discrimination.

The smallest "moment," *kṣaṇa*, in time, referred to here by Patañjali, requires, for its definition, an understanding of the *aṇu*. *Aṇu*, literally minute (in the quantitative sense of tiny), a term typically translated by Indologists of the nineteenth century and subsequently retained as atom, is the smallest individualized particle of matter in existence. An *aṇu* is an irreducible entity in the sense that it cannot be broken down into smaller parts, whereas atoms are reducible into smaller entities (such as electrons and protons, etc.), so atom is not an accurate translation. We will retain the term *aṇu* for this discussion with this in mind (I have, for this reason, sometimes referred to it previously, somewhat unsatisfactorily, as subatomic particle). Of course, as Vijñānabhikṣu rightly points out, *aṇus* themselves are ultimately composed of the *guṇas*; they are simply the smallest entities into which the *guṇas* can exist in the distinct forms of the *mahābhūtas*, gross elements of earth, water, etc., without reverting to subtler energies such as the *tanmātras* or *ahaṅkāra*, etc.[110]

Just as the *aṇu* is the smallest point of matter, the *kṣaṇa*, moment, mentioned in this *sūtra* is the smallest point in time. A *kṣaṇa* is defined as the time it takes for an *aṇu* to move from one point in space to the next point. Vyāsa does not specify how close together these points are, but one can infer that he is referring to the smallest possible distance, which corresponds to a distance equal to the *aṇu*'s own minute size; thus, a moment is the time it takes for the *aṇu* to move to the space immediately adjacent to its previous location. The sequence, *krama*, mentioned by Patañjali refers to a succession of such moments.

Having said this, Vyāsa points out that notions of time such as hour, day, night, year, and so forth have no tangible metaphysical reality—they are simply concoctions of the mind, that is, socially agreed upon constructions that have proved useful in organizing human existence. But in actuality all Time (as a metaphysical category) really consists of in Sāṅkhya is motion—specifically, it is ultimately the motion of the *aṇus* that comprise matter. Human societies assign labels to significant motions of visible matter such as the apparent movement of the sun, which is in essence a large conglomeration of primarily fire atoms. To the apparent motion of this conglomeration through the sky, we assign the term day, to the motion of the earth around the sun, we apply the label year, etc. Such terms, however, have no ultimate metaphysical reality; for the *yogī*, the only metaphysical reality corresponding to the notion of Time is that of the motion of *aṇus*.[111]

With this in mind, continues Vyāsa, there is no reality to the past or to the future. Two moments of the same *aṇu* cannot exist simultaneously—an atom can move only from one moment to the next, which is a sequence. The *aṇu* cannot be perceived in its previous location and its subsequent one simultaneously—this sequence can be viewed only progressively. Therefore, from the perspective of this metaphysics, or perhaps, more accurately, traditional Hindu physics, there is only one moment in all reality—the present. The earlier moment has ceased to be by becoming, or moving into, the present (at which time it no longer exists in its previous location), and the future has yet to be, or be moved into.

Now, since the moments of a succession cannot be perceived simultaneously, from a certain perspective, and as Vācaspati Miśra puts it, they are not real. Hariharānanda elaborates that reality is that which exists, and existence refers to that which is present (that is, has presence). Terms such as past and future actually refer to that which we cannot perceive because they are not present. In this sense, they do not actually exist. Thus, collectivities or successions of moments, such as notions of day or year, have no objective or actual metaphysical reality; they are merely conceptually real. One can, however, notes Vyāsa, say that the past and future are inherent in the present, and that therefore the entirety of reality is compressed or encapsulated in each moment.

With all this in mind, Patañjali is stating here that if one performs *saṁyama* on moments and their succession, which the commentators have presented as being the minute movement of *aṇus*, true knowledge of reality born of discrimination arises. And this reality embodies the past and future, which is nothing other than this very movement of atoms, or, as Patañjali calls it, the "succession of moments." The accomplished *yogī* at this stage can grasp the entirety of reality with its atomic motions, at all times.

Vācaspati Miśra and Vijñānabhikṣu have different views of the relevance of this *sūtra* at this stage of the text. Vācaspati Miśra understands the omniscience previously mentioned throughout the *sūtras* to be rhetorical; for example, when a person states, "We have tasted all vegetables," he or she actually means that a large variety of vegetables has been tasted but not literally that there is not a single vegetable in existence that has not been tasted. In this *sūtra*, however, he understands Patañjali's intent to indicate literal and absolute omniscience. Vijñānabhikṣu, on the other hand, understands the practice of *saṁyama* mentioned here to be an alternate means or technique to obtain the omniscience mentioned previously. The next *sūtra* elaborates on this discussion.

जातिलक्षणदेशैरन्यतानवच्छेदात् तुल्ययोस्ततः प्रतिपत्तिः ॥ ५३ ॥

III.53 jāti-lakṣaṇa-deśair anyatā 'navacchedāt tulyayos tataḥ pratipattiḥ

jāti, species; *lakṣaṇa*, distinguishing characteristic; *deśaiḥ*, location, place; *anyatā*, difference; *anavacchedāt*, not separated; *tulyayoḥ*, of two comparable things; *tataḥ*, from this; *pratipattiḥ*, knowledge, ascertainment

As a result of this, there is discernment of two comparable things that are not distinguishable by species, characteristics, or location.

The previous *sūtra* discussed the role of the moment, that is, the relationship between moment as a construct and the actual movement of *aṇus*, in order to explain how the *yogī* can fully and absolutely understand any material phenomenon. This discussion was prompted by Patañjali attempting to clarify and define the claims of omniscience made in III.49. The present *sūtra* continues that discussion, by presenting yet another schema for analyzing reality.

According to this *sūtra*, any two objects in reality can generally be distinguished according to their species, *jāti*; characteristics, *lakṣaṇa*; and location, *deśa*. Thus, says Vyāsa, if two things have the same characteristics and are in the same place, they can be distinguished if their species or type is different. A cow and a horse are distinguishable because their species are different, even if they have similar characteristics, for example, they are both black with four legs and are herbivores, and even if they are in the same place, they live in the same field. Similarly, two entities can be distinguished if their characteristics are different, even if their species and location are the same. Two cows, despite being of the same species and in the same field, might be distinguishable if one is black and is temperamental and the other is brown and is sweet natured. And, again, two entities can be distinguished even if they are of the same species and have the same characteristics if their location is different. Two identical *āmalaka* fruits can be distinguished if one is situated in front and one at the back of the other despite being of the same species and having identical characteristics.

But what would happen, asks Vyāsa, if someone switched the

placement of the two fruits when the *yogī* wasn't looking (to test his *yogic* discernment, suggests Vācaspati Miśra), such that the fruit that had been in the front was now in the back and vice versa? How could the difference between the two be determined? After all, the claims to higher knowledge and omniscience that have been bandied about throughout the text would require that there be no area of information, however trivial, beyond the purview of the *yogī* adept at *saṁyama*. The two fruits are different, obviously, because, although all other variables such as species, characteristics, and, when switched around, location might be equal, with regard to the latter, they occupy this same location at different times (one fruit was placed in front first and then removed, and the other was placed there a few moments later when the *yogī* wasn't looking).

The qualified *yogī*, says Vyāsa, and of course *Īśvara*, can perceive this difference physically (not just theoretically), even though it is indistinguishable to the common person, because of understanding the moment and its sequences (the atomic movements of *aṇus*), as analyzed in the previous *sūtra*, occupying any particular space. Moving the discussion back to the subatomic level, since *aṇus* are always in motion, and two *aṇus* cannot occupy the exact same space at the exact same time, a *yogī* who has mastery over *saṁyama* can perceive whether the *aṇus* and their sequences occupying a particular space are the same as those that were there previously, even though the cluster of *aṇus* will be identical in all other ways (in species, characteristic, and location). In other words, the *yogī* can perceive that the individual *aṇus* and their sequencing in the second *āmalaka* fruit (the "moments" connected to this fruit) are not the same as those of the *aṇus* occupying the same space in the first fruit and could thus understand that they have been switched around.

Hariharānanda usefully compares this type of knowledge to a scientist who, with a microscope, could (in principle, at least) tell the subtle difference in the atomic makeup of two identical freshly minted coins if their relative positions were switched around, but a normal person could not. In short, whereas a common person can distinguish between things based on differences in their species, characteristics, and location, only a *yogī* can distinguish between things based on their subatomic moments in time.

Vyāsa notes that in the unmanifest stage of *prakṛti*—before the creation of the manifest world, when the *guṇas* are all latent and inactive—there are no distinct material entities, and thus nothing can be discerned. It is from the motion and interaction of the *guṇas* (which we call Time) that matter manifests, as a result of which *aṇus* emerge and things become perceivable. The *yogī*'s perception in *saṁyama* extends to the difference between the specific permutations of the *guṇas* manifesting in the form of one *aṇu* and those manifesting in another. Omniscience thus extends to the minutest levels of physical reality, as Patañjali indicated in I.40.

तारकं सर्वविषयं सर्वथाविषयम् अक्रमं चेति विवेकजं ज्ञानम् ॥५४॥

III.54 tārakaṁ sarva-viṣayaṁ sarvathā-viṣayam akramaṁ ceti viveka-jaṁ jñānaṁ

tārakam, one who liberates; *sarva*, everything; *viṣayam*, object; *sarvathā*, everywhere; *viṣayam*, object; *akramam*, without sequence; *ca*, and; *iti*, thus; *viveka-jam*, born of discrimination; *jñānam*, knowledge

Knowledge born of discrimination is a liberator; it has everything as its object at all times simultaneously.

Tāraka, liberator, says Vyāsa, suggests that the knowledge referred to here comes as a spontaneous flash of insight and not from teachings or books. Books consists of words, and words refer only to generalities, states Vijñānabhikṣu (see discussion in *sūtra* I.49), while the type of perception described in these *sūtras* is so specific it can tell the difference between two identical *aṇus*. It has everything as its object, *sarva-viṣaya*, because nothing is beyond its purview. Past, present, and future are perceived, and perceived without sequence, *akrama*, meaning that the past and the future are seen as inherent in the moment, that is, in the present. This perception is liberating, say the commentators, because it carries one over the ocean of birth and death.

The *yoga-pradīpa*, light of *yoga*, says Vyāsa, begins with the *madhumatī* stage and ends here with knowledge born of discrimination. (Vijñānabhikṣu says that this *madhumatī* is the same stage of *samādhi* as the *madhu-bhūmika* mentioned by Vyāsa in his commentary in

III.51.) *Madhu* means sweet, and Vācaspati Miśra states that this is because this state of *samādhi* causes sweet bliss. *Yoga* starts at the *madhumatī* stage and goes through the seven states mentioned in II.27, say the commentators; it encompasses all stages of *samprajñāta-samādhi*, and all of these stages are parts of and lead to the knowledge born of discrimination, *viveka-jaṁ jñānam*.

सत्त्वपुरुषयोः शुद्धिसाम्ये कैवल्यम् इति ॥ ५५ ॥

III.55 sattva-puruṣayoḥ śuddhi-sāmye kaivalyam iti

sattva, the pure intellect; *puruṣayoḥ*, of the *puruṣa*, pure consciousness; *śuddhi*, purity; *sāmye*, upon becoming equal; *kaivalyam*, absolute independence, *iti*, thus it is said

When the purity of the intellect is equal to that of the *puruṣa*, *kaivalya* liberation ensues.

When the *sattva* element in the *buddhi*, intellect, becomes completely purged of *rajas* and *tamas*, states Vyāsa, and all the *kleśas* have been eliminated, *sattva* becomes almost as pure as *puruṣa*, *śuddhi-sāmya*. Obviously it remains inert *prakṛti*, but, devoid of all obscuring factors, it almost starts to resemble *puruṣa*, as it were, and can now reflect *puruṣa* perfectly—it is in this sense that it becomes "equal to" *puruṣa* insofar as it becomes a perfect reflection of *puruṣa*. When a mirror is completely free of defects or dirt, it can reflect a face back to itself without any distortion and, in this sense, becomes (indirectly) equal to that which it reflects. Now, due to *buddhi*'s transparency, there is no more false state or experience attributed to the self, since the *puruṣa* can now see itself clearly in its original pure state. At this stage, whether or not one has developed the *siddhi* mystic powers, the state of *kaivalya* (described in III.50) is immanent. The ultimate discrimination of the difference between the *buddhi* itself and *puruṣa* is the last cognitive act of *buddhi*. Then *buddhi* ceases to function, says Hariharānanda. After gaining this discrimination, *puruṣa* can rest in its own awareness, as independent of the intellect—as the real face behind the mirror rather than the reflected face peering back, so to speak—hence the term *kaivalya*, aloneness or independence. It is now uncoupled from the intellect and the world of forms that it presents to *puruṣa*.

Vyāsa notes that it is not the mystic powers that bring about *kaivalya* but the discriminative knowledge of the previous *sūtra*. Once discriminative knowledge arises, ignorance is dispelled. Vyāsa uses the term *adarśana* here for ignorance, which literally means nonseeing. Not seeing the real self is what ignorance actually is: The mind is ignoring the self that animates it. Vyāsa reminds us that ignorance is the root of all the *kleśas*; thus, once ignorance is removed, the *kleśas* cease to exist. In the absence of the *kleśas*, there are no more seeds of *karma*, no consequent future births, and therefore no more *saṁsāra*. In this stage, says Vyāsa, the *guṇas* no longer present themselves as objects to be experienced by *puruṣa*. With no more external objects of experience, *puruṣa* is now in the state of *kaivalya* mentioned in this *sūtra*. Since awareness is eternal, and therefore must always be aware of something, now with nothing other than itself of which to be aware—no other—*puruṣa* can be aware only of self. This is *kaivalya*, only aware of selfness. The self now shines freely and purely in its own right. For Vijñānabhikṣu, as a theist, this state additionally entails becoming inseparable (but as distinct individuals) from God, *Īśvara*.

The other commentators ponder Vyāsa's suggestion that the *siddhis*, mystic powers, are unnecessary for ultimate self-awareness. Why would Patañjali spend so much time discussing them? they ask. After all, as Vijñānabhikṣu points out, one has to have some element of desire in order to attain *siddhis*. In any event, all commentators agree that the *siddhis* outlined in this chapter are by-products of the path, not fundamental to it. Indeed, the *siddhis* are still within the realm of suffering, as Hariharānanda notes, since their scope is still *prakṛti*. One might surmise that the *siddhis* are believed to manifest spontaneously and hence Patañjali sees fit to inform the aspiring *yogī* of symptoms that will be encountered on the path so the *yogī* can be alerted not to be distracted and sidetracked by them. In any event, say the commentators, they are certainly not the direct cause of *kaivalya*; only discriminative knowledge is.

इति पतञ्जलिविरचिते योगसूत्रे तृतीयो विभूतिपादः

iti Patañjali-viracite yoga-sūtre tṛtīyo vibhūti-pādaḥ

Thus ends the third chapter on *samādhi* in the *Yoga Sūtras* composed by Patañjali.

CHAPTER SUMMARY

The chapter begins by concluding the definitions of the last three limbs of *yoga* [1–3], which are distinguished from the others by constituting *saṁyama* [4–6] and being internal limbs [7–8]. A discussion of the state of *nirodha* ensues [9–12], followed by the metaphysics of the relationship between substratum and characteristic [13–15]. The remainder of the chapter is then dedicated to an extensive discussion of various mystic powers accrued from the performance of *saṁyama* on a variety of things [16–48], culminating in omniscience followed by ultimate *kaivalya* liberation [49–55].

चतुर्थः कैवल्यपादः

caturthaḥ kaivalya-pādaḥ

CHAPTER IV

ABSOLUTE INDEPENDENCE

जन्मौषधिमन्त्रतपःसमाधिजाः सिद्धयः ॥१॥

IV.1 janmauṣadhi-mantra-tapaḥ-samādhi-jāḥ siddhayaḥ

janma, birth; *oṣadhi*, medicine, herbs; *mantra*, sacred chants; *tapaḥ*, austerity; *samādhi*, meditative absorption; *jāḥ*, born, arise; *siddhayaḥ*, the mystic powers

The mystic powers arise due to birth, herbs, *mantras*, the performance of austerity, and *samādhi*.

Patañjali states that the mystic powers described in the previous section can be produced by a number of means. Powers attained as a by-product of *samādhi*, the last on his list, have already been discussed in detail in the previous chapter, but powers can be attained in four other ways, according to this *sūtra*. Firstly, they can be the result of activities done in a previous birth, *janma*, which have reached their fruition in this birth. For example, celestial beings have mystic powers, and one can be born as a celestial being endowed with various *siddhis* due to the good *karma* one accrued in a previous birth as a human. Fallen *yogīs* too, who may not have attained the ultimate goal of *yoga* (but nonetheless perhaps attained some of the *siddhis*), pick up in a next birth from where they left off in their past life, as indicated in the *Gītā* (VI.37ff) and expressed in the story of Jaḍabhārata outlined in III.7. For that matter, quips Bhoja Rāja, even taking birth as a bird affords one the power of traveling through the air, which is supernormal from human perspectives!

Secondly, Patañjali states that these powers can also be produced from certain herbs, *oṣadhi*, and the commentators mention elixirs used by the *asuras*, supernatural beings, but note that such herbal concoctions are available in this world as well. Śaṅkara refers here to *soma*, a plant described in the early Vedic texts, a favorite beverage of Indra, chief of the celestials, which bestowed supernormal powers when imbibed.[1] Hariharānanda even mentions modern chloroform as sometimes triggering out-of-body experiences.

Thirdly, powers can also be produced by reciting certain *mantras*, say Patañjali and the commentators. The entire ancient Vedic sacrificial cult was predicated on the power of *mantra*—which in the earlier period referred to the Vedic hymns—to manipulate cosmic forces to produce effects, and the power of *mantra* to produce supernormal effects has remained consistent in the Indic traditions ever since.

Finally, one can fulfill one's wishes, whatever they may be, through austerities, *tapas*. There are numerous stories in the *Purāṇas* describing how, by the performance of austerities, even demoniac personalities attained superhuman powers. Desiring immortality, Hiraṇyakaśipu, for example, performed intense austerities. He stood on his toes with arms outstretched in a type of a *vṛkṣāsana* pose for so long that ants covered his body in an anthill and consumed everything except his bones and life airs. As a result of the powers he accrued, the entire universe was disturbed, and so Brahmā appeared before the demon asking him what he sought. Hiraṇyakaśipu asked for immortality, but Brahmā informed him that even he himself, the engineer of the universe, was mortal and thus he could not bestow what he himself did not possess. The demon consequently requested that he not be killed by any created being, inside or outside, during the day or night, on the earth or in the air, or by any weapon. The wily demon thought he had thus circumvented all possible causes of death. However, Viṣṇu incarnated as Narasiṁha, half man half lion (thus neither man nor beast), and killed him on the threshold (neither inside nor outside), at dawn (neither day nor night), on his lap (neither on the ground nor in the air), and with his nails (not with any weapons) (*Bhāgavata Purāṇa* VII.3).

The various legends of practically every culture of the ancient world are replete with stories of magical powers ensuing from birth, incantations, herbal concoctions, etc. In this vein, Patañjali is here stating that these are not exclusively the prerogative of *samādhi* states.

जात्यन्तरपरिणामः प्रकृत्यापूरात् ॥२॥

IV.2 jāty-antara-pariṇāmaḥ prakṛty-āpūrāt

jāti, birth; *antara*, other; *pariṇāmaḥ*, change; *prakṛti*, material nature; *āpūrāt*, because of the filling in

The changes [in bodily forms that take place] in other births is due to the filling in by *prakṛti*.

When one is reborn, one receives a new body. The process by which this new body evolves, its *pariṇāma*, is described in this *sūtra* as due to the filling in of *prakṛti*. We have discussed how, due to the subtle causes of *karma* performed in life, seeds are planted that fructify in future births. These seeds cause an individual to change one body for a completely different body—that of a human, celestial, elephant, ant, or any other being. The process by which the *prākṛtic* configuration of the new body takes place is described here as *prakṛti* filling in, *āpūra*, the new form. The verb *āpṛ* can also mean to pour into so one can perhaps envision the evolutes of *prakṛti* being poured into or filling in the new form as an elephant, human, or whatever being, in accordance with the *kleśas* and *saṁskāras* embedded in the *citta* of the old form (*citta*, of course, is not created anew each birth as the gross body is, but is transferred from birth to birth). So the particular blueprint of the next body embedded in the subtle matter of *citta* in accordance with the *saṁskāras* of that specific *citta* is filled in, or materialized, by the gross elements. There is constant recycling in *prakṛti*. In cosmic terms, too, as any of the evolutes of *prakṛti* propagate further evolutes—as *buddhi* manifests *ahaṅkāra* from itself, or, in turn, *ahaṅkāra* manifests the *tanmātras*—any depletion that is incurred is filled in by *prakṛti* which, being infinite, is never depleted.

To illustrate this principle, Vijñānabhikṣu refers to the story of Vāmana from the *Bhāgavata Purāṇa* (VIII.21ff). Vāmana was an incarnation of Viṣṇu who appeared as a small *brāhmaṇa* boy in the court of Bali, the king of the demons. Bali was harassing the celestial gods, although in fact he was a great devotee of Viṣṇu but had been born to a family of demons due to some quirk of fate in his *karma*. As a result of this birth he was acting inimically toward the celestial demigods, according to the *dharma* of his kind. However, as a devotee Bali also respected the Vedic *dharma* of being dutiful toward *brāhmaṇas*, and so, upon being approached by Vāmana, offered him a boon of his choice. Vāmana simply asked for whatever land could be encompassed by three steps. Bali, as conqueror of the universe, although eager to give much more, was happy to provide this.

With his first step, Vāmana covered the entire earth, and with his second, the universe. With nowhere left to place his third step, Vāmana accused Bali, in a somewhat tongue-in-cheek fashion, of failing to fulfill his promise of granting him his three steps of land. Failing to fulfill a promise is an intolerable notion for a proud and principled monarch of the epic genre. Bali bowed before Vāmana and asked him to place the third step on his head, thereby illustrating his devotion to Viṣṇu. The point of the story in the context of the *Bhāgavata* is that no one is disqualified by birth or status from devotion to God, not even demons, but Vijñānabhikṣu refers to the story to illustrate the principle of *prakṛti* filling in or perhaps rather filling out a body. Vāmana's tiny form was transformed into a form so enormous it could encompass the universe with one step. *Prakṛti* filled in the new, larger form from the old. In short, gross matter emanates out of subtler matter and fills in the various forms of the universe.

निमित्तम् अप्रयोजकं प्रकृतीनां वरणभेदस्तु ततः क्षेत्रिकवत् ।। ३ ।।

IV.3 nimittam aprayojakaṁ prakṛtīnāṁ varaṇa-bhedas tu tataḥ kṣetrikavat

nimittam, instrumental or efficient cause; *aprayojakam*, is not the instigator, motivator; *prakṛtīnām*, of the *prākṛtic* causes, the original causes; *varaṇa*, protective covering; *bhedaḥ*, piercing; *tu*, but; *tataḥ*, from it [*prakṛti*]; *kṣetrika*, farmer; *vat*, like

The instrumental cause of creation is not its creative cause, but it pierces the covering from creation like a farmer [pierces the barriers between his fields].

The *guṇas* of *prakṛti*, as we know, are the creative cause of manifest reality, since all creation emanates from the interaction among them. The issue at stake here is what causes the *guṇas* of *prakṛti* to activate and produce the effects of the world. Is it what Patañjali terms the instrumental causes, *nimitta* [*kāraṇa*], which the commentators take to refer to *dharma* and *adharma*, the meritorious or nonmeritorious activities of human beings? In other words, following up on the previous *sūtra* of *prakṛti* filling in the ever-changing forms of the world, the question is raised indirectly whether it is because of the soul's *dharmic* and *adharmic* activities that *prakṛti* activates the effects of the world, such as the new bodies obtained during reincarnation, as *karmic* reactions to these meritorious or nonmeritorious activities. The Mīmāṁsā school, for example, which denies the existence of *Īśvara*, posits the existence of an unseen power called *adṛṣṭa* (which essentially corresponds to the law of *karma*) as the force responsible for generating the results of *dharma* and *adharma*. Patañjali here rejects *dharma* and *adharma* as ultimate causal agents. *Dharma* and *adharma*, note the commentators, are themselves the effects of *prakṛti*, so they cannot be its causes. But they do remove the obstacles to *prakṛti* taking a certain course. They are thus the instrumental causes that can channel or direct specific effects emerging from within the preexisting substratum creative cause of the *guṇas* of *prakṛti*.

Patañjali analogizes creativity to the acts of a farmer, *kṣetrika-vat*. When a farmer wants to irrigate a field at a lower or equal level to an adjacent field that is already inundated with water, elaborates Vyāsa, he does not personally carry the water from one field to the other with his hands but merely removes the barrier or dam between the two fields, *varaṇa-bheda*, so that the water can spontaneously drain out of the irrigated field and into the adjacent one. Similarly, the farmer does not personally insert water into the roots of the grain; he removes the weeds from the environs that impede the natural tendency of water to flow downward, and the water then penetrates the roots by itself. Likewise, continues Vyāsa, *dharma* and *adharma* counteract each other, and pursuing *dharmic* or *adharmic* activities in life causes the removal of the blockages that obstruct *prakṛti* from creating or filling in a particular *dharmic* or *adharmic* body appropriate to these activities. So *dharma* and *adharma* act as guides or channels through which *prakṛti* can flow, like the barriers and dams in the farmer's field, but they do not instigate the initial motion of *prakṛti* herself in the first place. Hence this *sūtra* says the instrumental cause is not the creative cause, *aprayojaka*, but it does remove barriers within it.

The commentators discuss other instrumental causes that control the movements of *prakṛti*, such as *Īśvara*. Rearticulating the standard theistic argument in (Nyāya) Hindu thought,[2] they note that *Īśvara* is the essential instrumental cause in activating *prakṛti*. In the production of a pot, the other instrumental and material causes—the initial idea or blueprint of the pot, and the clay, water, and potter's wheel—are useless without the instrumental cause of the potter. Like the potter, *Īśvara*, in conjunction with other instrumental causes such as *kāla*, Time, and *dharma* and *adharma*—that is, *karma* and its consequences—is the instrumental cause that awakens the inherent power of *prakṛti* to produce its effects, says Vijñānabhikṣu.[3] And, most important, it is ultimately *Īśvara* who removes the obstacles in *prakṛti* such that *dharma* and *adharma* may generate their respective fruits, says Vācaspati Miśra. *Īśvara* is the ultimate overseer who ensures that deeds are connected to their appropriate fruits. And, of course, on another level, and ironically, one can note that *puruṣa* itself is an indirect cause, since *prakṛti* exists simply for its sake (II.18).

Creation, the initial activation of *prakṛti* from its latent state, as accepted almost universally in classical Hindu thought (with the exception of the early Mīmāṁsā school), is a cyclical process: The universes emanate from their source and then dissolve back into it at the end of each cycle before a new cycle is activated. This is a never-ending process that is considered to be *anādi*, beginningless. Thus, Indic thought in general does not occupy itself with notions of a primordial, precyclical initial impetus—a *prākṛtic* big bang, if you will. This is not seen as a useful topic of speculation (or, rather, any initial impetus is denied by conceiving of cyclical creationality as beginningless). In any event, the point here is that once activated by the instrumental causes, *prakṛti*'s inherent qualities impel it to flow in accordance with the channels of human activity, *dharma* and *adharma*, just as water's own qualities impel it to flow to a lower place once the obstacles damming it have been removed.

निर्माणचित्तान्यस्मितामात्रात् ॥ ४ ॥

IV.4 nirmāṇa-cittāny asmitā-mātrāt

nirmāṇa, created; *cittāni*, minds; *asmitā*, ego; *mātrāt*, only
Created minds are made from ego only.

One of the *siddhis* commonly held to be attainable by accomplished *yogīs* is the ability of an individual *yogī* to create numerous personal bodies (a feat also noted in *Vedānta Sūtras* IV.4.15). The commentators understand this *sūtra* to be addressing the question of whether these multiple bodies each have individual *cittas*, or whether they all have the same *citta*, namely, the *citta* of the *yogī* creating the bodies. The consensus is that each of the bodies created by the *yogī* has its own individual mind, and these minds are all manifested from and are subordinate to the *yogī*'s ego. We recall that *citta*, in the restricted sense of *manas* (as opposed to *buddhi, ahaṅkāra*, and *manas*)[4] is a manifestation of ego, *ahaṅkāra*, in Sāṅkhyan metaphysics. Thus, it would appear that an accomplished *yogī* can manifest multiple minds, rather than just one, from the ego.[5]

If there were just a single mind for multiple bodies, says Śaṅkara, there would be no scope for the different bodies to exhibit different activities, so these bodies would end up as if lifeless. In other words, if all the bodies performed exactly the same thing by virtue of having a single, unitary directing mind, they would effectively have no life of their own, but would all act like synchronized puppets. Or else there would also need to be individual *ātmans* to experience these different bodies and minds, continues Vijñānabhikṣu, not just the one *ātman* of the *yogī* creating the bodies.[6] Even incarnations of *Īśvara* exhibit different minds, he points out: When Rāma, an incarnation of Viṣṇu, exhibited unawareness of his divine nature,[7] he was obviously experiencing a different mental state from that of the omniscient Viṣṇu.

Be this as it may, all commentators accept that a *yogī* can manifest multiple bodies and undertake different experiences—in one body practicing austerities, in another experiencing the objects of the senses, etc., says Vijñānabhikṣu. There is a similar discussion in the *Vedānta Sūtras* (IV.4.15), where the metaphor of a lamp is provided: As one lamp can light numerous individual and separate wicks, which then exhibit their own light, so the *yogī*'s consciousness can animate several bodies. Again, the *Bhāgavata Purāṇa* (III.21–23) provides an illustration of this *siddhi* in the story of the sage Kardama. Kardama, a hermit living on the banks of the Sarasvatī river, accepted the hand of the princess Devahūti on the condition that he depart for the forest once she had conceived a son by him. Despite being accustomed to royal comforts, Devahūti served her husband in his simple hermitage with absolute love and dedication, and consequently became weak and emaciated as a result of her austerities and spiritual practices. Eventually, won over by her devotion, the renounced and reclusive ascetic determined to fulfill her desire for a son. Marshaling some of the mystic powers outlined in the previous chapter, the sage manifested a palace filled with precious gems and all manner of opulence, and arranged for Devahūti to regain her former beauty. In order to fulfill the desires of his beautiful wife, who longed for sexual pleasure, the sage then exhibited the mystic power referred to by Patañjali in this *sūtra* by dividing himself into nine personal forms, so as to better satisfy her completely.

As an aside, the son whom Devahūti eventually bore was named Kapila, the sage who taught the Sāṅkhya doctrine. Tradition thus bears record of perhaps two Kapilas. The Kapila mentioned in the *Śvetāśvatara Upaniṣad*, who received instruction from *Hara* (Śiva) (V.2) is taken by Śaṇkara in his commentary to that verse to be different from the Kapila accepted as an incarnation of Viṣṇu in the *Bhāgavata* (as well as the *Mahābhārata*, the *Gītā*, and the *Ahirbudhnya*, noted earlier[8]), but both appear in theistic contexts. As noted earlier, the theistic Sāṅkhya, also amply evidenced in the *Mokṣa-dharma* section of the *Mahābhārata* and remaining current in the Purāṇic tradition, is in all probability older than the nontheistic variants that surface in Īśvarakṛṣṇa's *Sāṅkhya-kārikā*, despite the fact that the latter text becomes, by default, the seminal text for the Sāṅkhya school (all earlier traditions being lost except in the scattered references noted earlier).

प्रवृत्तिभेदे प्रयोजकं चित्तम् एकम् अनेकेषाम् ॥ ५ ॥

IV.5 pravṛtti-bhede prayojakam cittam ekam anekeṣām

pravṛtti, activity; *bhede*, difference; *prayojakam*, the instigator, director; *cittam*, mind; *ekam*, one; *anekeṣām*, of the many

There is one mind, among the many [created by the *yogī*], which is the director in the different activities [of the different bodies].

What prevents the multiple minds in the various bodies created by the *yogī* from competing with each other in terms of their desires and degenerating into disharmony or conflict? asks Vācaspati Miśra. This *sūtra* is taken to indicate that although the *yogī* is able to create an individual mind for each body he or she chooses to generate, these bodies are all under the guidance or control of a principal mind, *prayojakam cittam*. Just as the one mind can control the multiple limbs of a person's body and its sense functions, say the commentators, so the master mind of the *yogī* controls the subordinate minds inserted into the created bodies. Here the Yoga tradition follows the position of the Vedānta tradition, which, as noted, also raises this topic (IV.4.15).[9] Mind is potentially omnipresent, after all, Hariharānanda reminds us, thus there is no far or near for it, nor any impediment to it manifesting in multiple, distinct bodies. The controlling mind is the perfected mind of the *yogī*, says Vijñānabhikṣu, and the intention or will of this mind governs the activities of the other minds. Thus, through these multiple bodies, the *yogī* can engage in multiple experiences simultaneously. He can then withdraw these bodies into his original form as the sun withdraws its rays, says Vācaspati Miśra.

तत्र ध्यानजम् अनाशयम् ॥ ६ ॥

IV.6 tatra dhyāna-jam anāśayam

tatra, from these [the minds who have attained *siddhis* indicated in IV.1]; *dhyāna-jam*, born from meditation; *anāśayam*, is without the storehouse or stock [of *karma*]

From these [five types of minds that possess *siddhis*], the one born of meditation is without the storehouse of *karma*.

The first *sūtra* of this chapter stated that *siddhis* could be attained by five different means, only one of which is through meditation (the others being through birth, herbs, *mantras*, and the performance of austerity). However, says Vyāsa, only the mind that has attained the *siddhis* through meditation is free from the vice and virtue accruing from the performance of *dharma* or *adharma*, and thus from the *karma* that is accrued thereby, which is stored in the *citta* in what is termed the *āśaya*, a type of receptacle, stock, or store of all the accumulated *karma* (I.24; II.12). As discussed, this *karma* eventually fructifies, perpetuating the cycle of birth and death.

Therefore, although a person may possess and exhibit *siddhis* gained as a result of birth, herbs, *mantras*, or austerities, such a person is not freed from the *kleśas*, which underpin all *saṁsāric* actions and in turn provoke *karma* and its ensuing results (see II.12–13). Such people may have astonishing powers, but they are nonetheless as helplessly bound by the laws of *saṁsāra* as anybody else, as was illustrated in the story of Hiraṇyakaśipu. This is not the case, however, with the *yogī* who has attained the *siddhis* by meditation, *dhyāna-ja*, in other words, as a by-product of *samādhi*. According to Patañjali, only through the practice of *yoga* is one free from the *kleśas* and their consequences.

Therefore, one should not assume that someone with mystical powers is automatically a *yogī* or, indeed, even a benevolent person as is underscored in Hindu folklore. The Purāṇas are full of stories of *asuras*, demons, who attain powers by *tapas*, austerities. Hiraṇyakaśipu utilized the powers that were bestowed on him to harass the entire universe. This included his own saintly son Prahlāda, since the demon could not tolerate his son's devotion to Viṣṇu. Rāvaṇa from the *Ramāyāṇa*, who was also eventually destroyed by Viṣṇu in the form of Rāma, likewise received his awesome supernormal powers by performing austerities, as, indeed, did almost all the great demons in Hindu lore.

In short, the Yoga tradition, along with most other soteriological traditions of ancient India, takes the position that real *yogīs* do not display their powers; therefore, anyone doing so may very well have attained any semblance of *siddhi* power from birth, herbs, *mantras*, or austerity and is likely exhibiting them to manipulate gullible people. Except in very rare circumstances (and then for pedagogical purposes), the cheap display of *siddhis* is not viewed as the sign of an enlightened being in popular *yogic* narrative.

कर्माशुक्लाकृष्णं योगिनस्त्रिविधम् इतरेषाम् ॥ ७ ॥

IV.7 karmāśuklākṛṣṇaṁ yoginas tri-vidham itareṣām

karma, action and its reaction; *aśukla*, not white; *akṛṣṇam*, not black; *yoginaḥ*, of the *yogī*; *tri*, three; *vidham*, types; *itareṣām*, of the others

The *karma* of a *yogī* is neither white nor black; of everyone else, it is of three types.

Vyāsa elaborates on the four types of *karma* alluded to by Patañjali here and divides them into four categories (a widespread schema that surfaces in Buddhist teachings[10]). Black, *kṛṣṇa*, *karma* predictably consists of evil acts performed by the wicked. Black and white *karma* is the performance of both evil and pious acts. It is everyday action in the external world determined by how one acts toward others. The actions of ordinary people are mixed: People certainly often perform good deeds, but the drive toward self-preservation and gratification invariably sooner or later involves causing harm to others on some level. Thus most people perform both black and white *karma*. Hariharānanda points out, by way of example, that in tilling the soil, many creatures are killed, and in saving wealth for oneself, others are denied.

Purely white, *śukla*, *karma* is internal; it is not determined by actions toward others in the external world and thus generative of *karma*, but is the product of the mind alone. Vyāsa specifies that it consists of the performance of austerity, study, and meditation, which are more or less the ingredients of *kriyā yoga*. Finally, that which is neither white nor black pertains to the *yogī* or *sannyāsī*, total renunciant, whose *kleśas* are destroyed and who is finishing up his last birth. Having renounced all the fruits of activity, such a person does not receive either black or white *karma*. Vijñānabhikṣu hastens to add that this does not apply to someone who has simply donned the garb of a mendicant without giving up personal desire. Rather, he quotes the *Muṇḍaka Upaniṣad*: "The wise man, knowing [the truth], does not speak excessively. Sporting in the *ātman* and delighting in the *ātman*, such a person performs work [in the world] and is the best of the knowers of *Brahman*" (3.1.4). He also quotes the *Gītā*: "Having given up attachment [to the fruits of work,] the *yogīs* perform action [in the world] through their body, mind, intelligence and purified senses for the purpose of purifying the *ātman*" (V.11).

All others, including those who have attained *siddhi* powers through the four means other than *samādhi*, accrue *karma* of the other three types, *tri-vidha*: black, white, or mixed. This is because all other actions ensue from the *ahaṅkāra*, ego (the *kleśa* of *asmitā*). As long as the *kleśas* underpin actions, more specifically, as long as there is a false sense of self (considering oneself to be the body and mind) underpinning any action, good or bad, or, put differently, as long as one thinks that it is one's *prākṛtic* self who is acting (etymologically, *ahaṅkāra* means "I am the doer"), then the results of action, whether good or bad, accrue to this self. Vijñānabhikṣu again quotes the *Gītā*: "Always satisfied, without any dependency, having given up attachment to the fruits of activity, [the *yogī*], although engaged in activity, does not actually do anything" (IV.20); and "When action (*karma*) is performed because it is prescribed, Arjuna, having renounced attachment [to its fruits], then that renunciation is considered to be *sāttvic*" (XVIII.9). Also of relevance here is the *Gītā*'s description of the *yogī* as "one who remains fixed and does not waver, being undisturbed by the *guṇas* and seated as a detached witness, thinking 'it is only the *guṇas* that are active' " (XIV.23; the *Gītā* is pervaded by verses of this nature). As the *Gītā* informs us, desire is situated in the senses, mind, and intelligence (III.40). The soul does not desire, since it is complete, and fully self-fulfilled; desires pertain to the stimulation of the body or mind. The point is that, since Patañjali has informed us that desires are the product of misidentification with the body and mind, one who realizes the true nature of *ātman* gives up all desires pertaining to the body and mind and hence accrues no *karma*. As outlined in the second chapter, *karmic* reactions accrue only to those actions performed with desire for their fruits.

ततस्तद्विपाकानुगुणानाम् एवाभिव्यक्तिर्वासनानाम् ॥८॥

IV.8 tatas tad-vipākānuguṇānām evābhivyaktir vāsanānām

tataḥ, from this [the three types of *karma*]; *tat*, those; *vipāka*, fruition; *anuguṇānām*, in accordance with; *eva*, only; *abhivyaktiḥ*, manifestation; *vāsanānām*, of the subliminal impressions

From [these three types of *karma*] the activation of only those subliminal impressions that are ready for fruition [in the next life] occurs.

The purport of this *sūtra* according to the commentaries is that at the time of death, most people will contain in their *karmāśaya*, or storehouse of *karma* located in the *citta*, all kinds of mixed *karma* good and bad that has yet to bear its fruit. This *karma* will not all fructify in only one future life. Therefore, if one's next birth happens to be that of a celestial being, to use the example from the commentaries, then only the *karma* and *saṁskāras* from one's storehouse pertinent to that specific birth will activate, *abhivyakti*, that is, only those *saṁskāras* relevant to the celestial realm will surface in one's *citta*. One may have other *saṁskāras* pertaining to a hellish, a human, or an animal existence, which remain dormant until some other future birth, when they will manifest.

The contrary is true: One may be undergoing a hellish, or human, or animal existence, and thus experiencing the fruits of one's impious or mixed activities of a past life, while nonetheless preserving the *saṁskāras* of one's more pious previous activities dormant in one's *citta* until they eventually manifest in some future birth as, say, a celestial. This, of course, addresses the age-old question of why good things happen to bad people, or bad things to good people. From a *yogic* perspective, if a person appears wicked but is experiencing good fortune, in essence that person is reaping the good effects stemming from a segment of pious activities performed in a previous life. However, that person is simultaneously sowing impious seeds in the present, the effects of which will be reaped in some future birth when suffering will be experienced as a consequence. The reverse is the case with the apparently good person who appears to be suffering bad fortune.

The term used for subliminal impression here is *vāsanā*. Patañjali and the commentators do not always seem to distinguish between *vāsanā* and *saṁskāra*; indeed, *saṁskāra* in the next *sūtra* seems to have a very similar denotative range as the sense of *vāsanā* here. *Vāsanā* might best be taken to refer to those innate *saṁskāras* that remain dormant in this life (that are due to fructify in some future life), although they exert subconscious influence on personality in this life, and *saṁskāra* to impressions and thoughts that are constantly being generated in this lifetime.[11] In other words, *vāsanās* are latent and subconscious personality traits, and *saṁskāras* are imprints being actively generated.

The discussion is pertinent to this chapter since it is only when the fructifying power of the *karma-āśaya* has been destroyed that pure liberation can ensue. As long as any type of *saṁskāras* are activating in the *citta*, they will divert the attention and awareness of *puruṣa* from its pure nature.

जातिदेशकालव्यवहितानाम् अप्यानन्तर्यं
स्मृतिसंस्कारयोर् एकरूपत्वात् ॥ ९ ॥

IV.9 jāti-deśa-kāla-vyavahitānām apy ānantaryaṁ smṛti-saṁskārayor eka-rūpatvāt

jāti, type of birth; *deśa*, place; *kāla*, time; *vyavahitānām*, being separated; *api*, although; *ānantaryaṁ*, noninterval, successive; *smṛti*, memory; *saṁskārayoḥ*, of the subliminal impression; *eka-rūpatvāt*, because of the oneness of form or identity

Because they are identical, there is an uninterrupted connection between memory and *saṁskāra*, even though they might be separated by birth, time, and place.

Vyāsa unpacks this *sūtra* by using the example of a cat. If the circumstances of one's specific *karma* at a given point in time require that one take the birth of a cat, one is injected into the womb of a cat and one's *citta* manifests the mind-set of a cat. This particular mind-set manifests partly as a result of the activation of *saṁskāras* lodged in the *citta* from some previous birth as a cat. (There is, of course, a correlation between one's activities as a human and the segment of latent *saṁskāras* these end up activating in the next life. Thus, cat *saṁskāras* are triggered by catlike or cat-appropriate activities performed in the human form.) Now, posits Vyāsa hypothetically, what if this previous birth were a hundred lifetimes ago, or even a hundred aeons, or in some completely different place, *deśa-kāla-vyavahita*? Patañjali in this *sūtra* states that wherever or whenever those *saṁskāras* were lodged in the *citta*, when the appropriate conditions accrue for them to bear their fruit at a particular time, those *saṁskāras* are triggered, reactivating and manifesting the cat-related memories and consequently producing a cat mentality. *Karma* in effect is the storage and eventual fruition of *saṁskāras*, and *saṁskāras* are memories of lived experiences. When the *karmic* conditions for a particular type of birth ripen as a result of their own spontaneous mechanisms, the *saṁskāras* pertinent to that birth activate automatically while other *saṁskāras* remain latent.

One may argue, says Vācaspati Miśra, that the experiences of yesterday should be more fresh than the experiences of a hundred days ago, and that therefore if one had been a human in the most recent past birth and a cat one hundred births earlier, the experiences in the human birth should be fresher and more vigorous in the *citta* and thus more potent in determining one's next birth. But the laws of *karma* do not work this way. *Saṁskāras* remain equally stored in the *citta* like seeds irrespective of whether they are of one's last birth or of a birth aeons ago. When the conditions appropriate for the activation of a particular set of *saṁskāras*, such as those corresponding to a cat experience, are triggered, the relevant *saṁskāras* are automatically activated, just as at the sight of a meal containing something tasty like tamarind, the tongue automatically waters, says Śaṅkara.

One is reminded here of the cicadas, locustlike creatures, which, in the year of first writing this chapter emerged from the earth in countless billions in various parts of the United States. These cicadas remain in hibernation buried underground for seventeen years but, like clockwork, due to whatever internal driving forces or external conditions awaken them after seventeen years, they emerge from the ground when the time is right even though they go on to live for only a few weeks. They then lay eggs before dying, and these eggs drop into the ground where they lie in hibernation for another seventeen years. Likewise, due to the mysteriously complex factors surrounding the activation of a particular subset of *karma, saṁskāras* previously deposited in the *citta* lay dormant until the factors are ripe for their manifestation. When they manifest, they trigger further action, which produces a new set of *saṁskāras* to be recorded in the *citta* in turn.

Although one's next life as a cat draws from the *saṁskāras* of a previous cat life that one underwent one hundred births before, this does not mean that the two cat lives will be identical. Externally, the environment and landscape inhabited by the second cat life will be different, and thus this cat life will respond to different external stimuli and events producing different *saṁskāras* in the *citta*. Internally also, even as the character of one's actions as a human followed by the corollaries of *karma* cause the original set of cat *saṁskāras* to be activated at some point and to dominate the individual's *citta* for a particular period such that it requires the body of a cat to express itself, the previous cat *citta* and the later one are not identical. The later one will have been molded and influenced by all the *saṁskāras* accrued during the intervening hundred lives. While all these intervening *saṁskāras* may not be activated during the second cat life, they have nonetheless affected and changed the *citta* and they do exert subtle influence. So the second cat life, while experiencing the activation of the *saṁskāras* from the first cat life, will not be reliving identical experiences.

तासाम् अनादित्वं चाशिषो नित्यत्वात् ॥१०॥

IV.10 tāsām anāditvam cāśiso nityatvāt

tāsām, of them [the *saṁskāras*]; *anāditvam*, being without beginning; *ca*, and; *āśisaḥ*, desire; *nityatvāt*, because of being eternal

The *saṁskāras* are beginningless, because the desire [for life] is eternal.

The desire for life is eternal, says Vyāsa. Everyone wishes, "May I not die, may I live!"[12] He cites the example of a very young child who shows an instinctive fear of death. If the child starts to slip from his mother's lap, elaborates Vācaspati Miśra, he will exhibit symptoms of fear and grasp his mother's necklace. From where does such a fear arise? Not from the three means of attaining valid knowledge accepted by the Yoga school in I.7 (sense perception, inference, and verbal authority); the child has not perceived or experienced death in this life, is too young to infer its existence, and has obviously not heard about it from verbal authorities. So the fear must spring from previous *saṁskāras*—previous death experiences recorded on the *citta* that are not graphically remembered by the child but that nonetheless exert a latent influence that is sufficient to give the child a sense of fear in a precarious situation.

One cannot argue that such fear or awareness is inherent in the child, say the commentators, since that which is inherent is not in need of an external cause to manifest. Inherent means it is continually present, like heat that is always inherent and manifest in fire, but fear is experienced only in certain situations where there is an external cause, such as when one is attacked by someone wielding a sword. The argument of the commentators is that if fear of death is not inherent, it must be due to memory of past events activated in particular contexts. And the memory of death can be only from a previous life. In this way, the desire for self-preservation is observed in every creature, and this is because the unwelcome experiences of death in previous lives is recorded on every *citta*, manifesting as fear when triggered by a threatening external cause. The arguments found here are essentially those in II.9 in the discussion of the *kleśa abhiniveśa*, clinging to life (fear of death being essentially the same as clinging to life).

The commentaries then launch into a discussion of whether the mind is atomic in size, or omnipresent. The Nyāya school holds that the mind is atomic in size and can attend to only one sensation, or sensory input, at a time. This notion is rejected by the Yoga school on the grounds that one can be eating a piece of corn and simultaneously experiencing the senses of taste, touch, sight, and smell of the corn. The Nyāya school would hold that the mind would be racing backward and forward among the senses of taste, touch, sight, and smell so quickly that these sensory impressions appear to be simultaneous, whereas in fact they are not. The Sāṅkhya view is that the mind is of intermediate size (between atomic and omnipresent) and adjusts according to the size of the body, expanding or contracting, for example, to fit into the body of an ant or elephant. Vyāsa analogizes this view to the light of a lamp, which can illuminate either a pot or a palace depending on the size of the contained space into which it is placed.

Here then is another example of a minor technical difference between the Sāṅkhya and Yoga schools, which otherwise share most of their metaphysics. The Sāṅkhya (and Jain) schools hold that the *citta* expands and contracts depending on the size of the body, expanding to fill the elephant's form and contracting to fit into an ant's form, while the Yoga authorities claim that it is only the *vṛttis* of the mind that expand or contract, not the mind itself. This takes place in accordance with the specifics of the body due to the limitations of *ahaṅkāra*, ego;

the mind itself is omnipresent. Vyāsa states that the expansion of the mind occurs, in the case of the *yogī*, as a result of the practice of *dharma*, whether performed externally or internally (by expansion, he intends, I suggest, the expansion of the *sāttvic* component of the mind). External *dharma* involves the use of the body, and internal *dharma*, which is superior, of the mind. The examples given by the commentators of external *dharma* are such things as acts of worship and charity; the internal ones are those listed in I.20—faith, vigor, memory, *samādhi*, and discernment.

One further implication of the Yoga view that the mind is essentially omnipresent but that its *vṛttis* contract and expand in accordance with the size of the body is noted by Vācaspati Miśra. He points out that at the moment of death there is no transmigration of a subtle body into a new body, in the sense of something exiting one mortal frame and somehow moving into another (Latin: *trāns*, across, *migrāre*, to move from place to place). If something is omnipresent, it cannot move from place to place—it is already everywhere. Therefore, at death, the all-pervading (and therefore motionless) mind encapsulating the *puruṣa* simply adjusts its *vṛttis* to fit the contours of a new body. Vācaspati Miśra clearly differentiates this view to that of the other Hindu and Jain schools including Sāṅkhya, namely, that the subtle body actually somehow relocates in space and time to a new body.

हेतुफलाश्रयालम्बनैः संगृहीतत्वाद् एषाम् अभावे तदभावः ॥ ११ ॥

IV.11 hetu-phalāśrayālambanaiḥ saṅgṛhītatvād eṣām abhāve tad-abhāvaḥ

hetu, cause; *phala*, fruit, effect, motive; *āśraya*, substratum; *ālambanaiḥ*, support; *saṅgṛhītatvāt*, because of being held together; *eṣām*, of them; *abhāve*, in the absence; *tat*, those [the *saṁskāras*]; *abhāvaḥ*, there is absence of

Since [*saṁskāras*] are held together by immediate cause, motive, the mind, and the object of awareness, the *saṁskāras* cease when the latter cease.

Patañjali here identifies four ingredients that underpin and sustain *saṁskāras*. First, the immediate cause, *hetu*, of the *saṁskāras*, says

Vyāsa, is action, more specifically, *dharma* and *adharma*, pious or impious activity, and their consequences. As we know, from *dharma* comes pleasure, and from *adharma* comes suffering. Subsequently, from pleasure comes attachment—everyone wants to perpetuate pleasure—and from suffering comes aversion—everyone wants to avoid suffering. These, in turn, provoke further actions—the effort to gain or preserve pleasure, and the effort to avoid or remove suffering. Such actions, whether in body, mind, or word, have effects in their turn—one's actions either benefit or harm others and are thus *dharmic* or *adharmic*. These perpetuate the chain of reactions noted above and thus the six-spoked wheel of *saṁsāra* (*dharma, adharma*, pleasure, suffering, attachment, and aversion) is perpetuated. The underlying cause of all this (including the more immediate cause of action)—the driver of the wheel—is nescience, the root of the *kleśas*, as discussed in II.4. Ignorance corresponds to the spokes of the wheel, says Śaṅkara, since upon removing the spokes, the wheel collapses, and the *saṁskāras* lose their effectiveness.

Vyāsa defines the second item listed in this *sūtra*, motive, *phala*, as that which underpins the production of *dharma* and *adharma*, etc., indicated above. One's motives prompt action, whether *dharmic* or *adharmic*, and these produce *saṁskāras* and perpetuate the cycle. The term for motive here is *phala*, literally, fruit: one is motivated by the desire for an outcome or fruit. Additionally, in a sense, one's motives are the result of past experiences and thus are the fruits of past *saṁskāras*. *Saṁskāras* tend to perpetuate similar *saṁskāras*, so it is easy to get caught in patterns of behavior—a certain type of *saṁskāra* activates and prompts a corresponding type of action, which plants *saṁskāras* similar to the original *saṁskāras* that prompted the action, and a vicious cycle is perpetuated.

To illustrate this, consider addictive behavior. Due to habitual past indulgence, a person craves, say, a cigarette, intoxicant, certain type of food, or sexual experience, which the person remembers as being the source of pleasure. When memory of this pleasure is activated in the form of *saṁskāras* awakening in the *citta*, the person is impelled, or at least pressured, by the force of the *saṁskāric* memory to repeat this indulgence, thereby planting a new but similar *saṁskāra* that simply reinforces the original *saṁskāra* such that it awakens with even more force next time, only to be indulged and strengthened yet again. Every time one feels like smoking a cigarette, due to the pressure of past memories of smoking, and then smokes, one is adding another set of *saṁskāras* to the original cigarette *saṁskāras*. Thus, clusters of certain types of *saṁskāras* are continually reinforced and perpetuated, and develop into personality traits that can become very hard to break. By changing motive, one can break this cycle.

Ultimately, one has to change one's base motive from desire to enjoy any kind of pleasure whatsoever to the desire for liberation (the desire to destroy the *kleśa* of ignorance), to break the wheel entirely, but initially one can at least aspire for *dharmic* pleasure if one is caught in a cycle of *adharmic* behavior. *Adharmic* behavior produces unhappiness; the indulgence of craving does not bring genuine lasting pleasure but simply perpetuates frustration, hankering, and discontent.

The substratum, *āśraya*, of *saṁskāras* noted as the third item on the list is, of course, the mind, or, more specifically, the *karmāśaya* of II.12, where *saṁskāras* are lodged. And the commentators understand support, *ālambana*, the last item on the list, to refer to an object one encounters that causes any particular *saṁskāra* to activate, in other words, a catalyst. So, for example, the sight of a provocative picture of the opposite sex will likely incite sexually surcharged *saṁskāras* to overpower the mind; thus this picture is the support for the appearance of those *saṁskāras*. In short, as long as cause, motive, substratum, and support exist, *saṁskāras* exist, and when these conditions are eliminated, *saṁskāras* have no infrastructure within which to exist. *Saṁskāras* are like a stream, says Rāmānanda Sarasvatī, so if their source is cut off, they will be brought to an end. And when *saṁskāras* are eliminated, *saṁsāra* comes to an end.

अतीतानागतं स्वरूपतोऽस्त्यध्वभेदाद् धर्माणाम् ॥ १२ ॥

IV.12 atītānāgataṁ svarūpato 'sty adhva-bhedād dharmāṇām

atīta, past; *anāgatam*, not yet happened, the future; *svarūpataḥ*, in reality; *asti*, there is; *adhva*, path, time; *bhedāt*, because of the difference; *dharmāṇām*, of the characteristics

The past and the future exist in reality, since they differ [from the present only] in terms of the time of [manifestation] of their characteristics.

The following four *sūtras* overlap the discussion initiated in III.9–15. There, an understanding of the transformation of matter was relevant to the context of mystic powers, whereas the discussion of the transformation of matter in these *sūtras* is in the context of the metaphysics of objects in external reality.

That which does not exist cannot come into being, says Vyāsa, and that which does exist can never be destroyed. As the *Gītā* notes: "Of the non-existent there is no being, and of the existent there is no cessation of being; this conclusion is seen by the seers of truth from studying the nature of them both" (II.16). The three phases of time—the past as that which has already manifested, *atīta*; the future as that which has yet to manifest, *anāgata*; and the present as that which is manifesting—all actually exist in a sense, says Patañjali in this *sūtra* (and are therefore objects of knowledge for the *yogī*). In III.52, in apparent contradiction, the commentators stated that the past and future do not exist, but actually the same point is being made by both sets of truth claims. To understand the mechanics of this, it is important to keep in mind the principle of *satkāryavāda*—effects are latent in their causes. The past and the future may be unmanifest, but they are latent in the present, and thus their existence is very real in this sense. The future does not come from nothing, nor does the past fade into nothing. Past and future are thus perceivable by those able to recognize the finer causal levels of present reality. The point being made in the earlier discussion was that past and future do not exist as entities separate from the present. But they do exist in terms of their latent presence in the present, and Patañjali here is stressing this latter perspective.

Śaṅkara refers to the standard *satkāryavāda* illustrations from Sāṅkhya:[13] Yogurt as an effect must be potentially present in milk as its cause; otherwise, if an effect were totally nonexistent in its cause, how could yogurt arise from churning milk? If something could arise that was nonexistent in its cause, then why should not anything arise from churning milk, like gold or elephants? The only product that can arise from milk is one whose characteristics are already inherent within milk. If the oilman could make oil from sand, continues Śaṅkara, why would he go to all the trouble of grinding sesame seeds?

So, with reference to the concluding sentence of the commentary on the previous *sūtra*, how can *saṁskāras*, which exist, ever be destroyed, given that things that exist can never be destroyed? As Śaṅkara points out, they are never actually destroyed in a metaphysical sense, but they can become nonproductive, and this is the meaning intended when the texts speak of destroying *saṁskāras*. *Saṁskāras* cannot be existentially destroyed, but they can be rendered obsolete (frequently referred to as "burnt" by the commentators). In terms of the goals of *yoga*, it is their ability to disturb the *citta* that is destroyed.

ते व्यक्तसूक्ष्मा गुणात्मानः ॥१३॥

IV.13 te vyakta-sūkṣmā guṇātmānaḥ

te, they [past, present, and future]; *vyakta*, are manifest; *sūkṣmāḥ*, subtle, latent; *guṇa*, the three *guṇas*; *ātmānaḥ*, having the nature of

The past, present, and future have the *guṇas* as their essence and are either manifest or latent.

Moving this discussion to its deepest metaphysical essence, Patañjali here states that everything is essentially simply a combination of the three *guṇas*, and when these *guṇas* combine in specific ways and manifest the characteristics of any particular object, we consider that object to be present. When the object deteriorates and its ingredients dissolve into their essences, we consider that process to constitute the past. (Actually, the object still exists but not in a manifest form, that is, the essential energy from which the object was a temporary configuration remains eternally existent.) The future is that which remains potentially stored and locked up within the *guṇas* waiting for the right configuration of circumstances to cause the *guṇas* to produce it. The present is simply the configuration of the *guṇas* that happens to be manifest, and the past and future are those which are latent. They are therefore all real in some sort of quasi-concrete way, as Patañjali indicated in the last *sūtra*. However, in essence, all three are just the permutations of the *guṇas*.

Vyāsa quotes an unidentified verse from the *śāstra*: "One does not become absorbed in a direct perception of the ultimate form of the *guṇas*; that which is perceived directly, is the trifles of *māya*.[14] Vijñānabhikṣu quotes the *Gītā* here: "This divine *māyā* (illusion) of mine [Kṛṣṇa], which is hard to overcome, is made up of the *guṇas*" (VII.14).

No doubt in reference to the *advaita* school of Vedānta thought, which holds the world of illusion to be ultimately essentially unreal, Vijñānabhikṣu hastens to add that in the Yoga position, the effects of the *guṇas* may be temporary, but they are not unreal. The Yoga school holds that *prakṛti* and her effects are essentially and physically real, but due to the constant motion of the *guṇas* that comprise *prakṛti*, her effects are ever-changing. Illusion, then, for Yoga, is to hold these effects to be permanent, not to consider them to be essentially unreal.

परिणामैकत्वाद् वस्तुतत्त्वम् ॥१४॥

IV.14 pariṇāmaikatvād vastu-tattvam

pariṇāma, transformation; *ekatvāt*, singleness, unity; *vastu*, thing; *tattvam*, thatness, reality

The things [of the world] are objectively real, due to the uniformity of [the *guṇas* that underpin] all change.

Patañjali here addresses the relationship between unity and diversity among the objects of the world. If everything in manifest reality is ultimately one, in the sense of having a unified source, *ekatva*, in the form of the *guṇas*, then, posits Vyāsa, how is it that we find all the differences among things in our perception? The commentators take this opportunity to expand on the metaphysics of Sāṅkhya and Yoga. Note again that there were nuances of differences circulating among followers of Sāṅkhya—the *Bhāgavata Purāṇa*, for example, speaks of several different schools in existence (XI.22.2–3). According to Vijñānabhikṣu, from primarily the *tāmasic* element in *ahaṅkāra* (itself an evolute from the highly *sāttvic buddhi*) emanates the *tanmātra*, subtle element, of sound. *Ahaṅkāra* interacting with sound then produces *ākāśa*, the gross element of ether (which has sound as its quality). When ether, in turn, interacts with the *tāmasic* element in *ahaṅkāra*, the subtle element of touch is produced. The *tāmasic* element in *ahaṅkāra* then interacts with the subtle element of touch to produce the gross element air. Air is then affected by the same *ahaṅkāra* and produces the subtle element of sight, and the same process involving interaction with the *tāmasic* element in *ahaṅkāra* progressively transforms sight into the gross element of fire, fire to the fourth subtle element of taste, taste to the gross element of water, water to the subtle element of smell, and smell to the fifth and final gross element of earth. The proportion of the *tāmasic* element in *ahaṅkāra* in the above series is progressively increased vis-à-vis the other two *guṇas* as each element becomes progressively denser; thus, as Bhoja Rāja points out, earth, relative to air, contains more *tamas* and air more *rajas*.

Aṇus, atoms (more precisely, subatomic particles), of physical matter, the *mahābhūtas*, are the smallest particles of elemental matter that can exist without matter dissolving back into its subtler substructure of *tanmātra*. Thus, in Vijñānabhikṣu's schema, the atoms of each of the gross elements are formed from a combination of the *tanmātras*, subtle elements, in the following way: Earth atoms are formed from all five subtle elements of sound, touch, sight, taste, and smell; water atoms are formed from the subtle elements of sound, touch, sight, and taste; fire atoms are formed of sound, touch, and sight; air atoms are formed of sound and touch; ether has no atoms as it does not consist of parts. As a point of contrast, the Vedānta tradition has a slightly different schema whereby the atom of any gross element is made up of half its corresponding subtle element, and the other half by equal portions of the remaining four subtle elements. Thus the earth atom is half the smell *tanmātra* and half of equal portions (one-eighth each) of sound, touch, sight, and taste, and similarly with the other gross elements. We should keep in mind here that *tanmātra* refers to the powers, or subtle vibrational energies, manifesting as sound, touch, taste, etc. They are more *tāmasic* in their constitution than their source, the even subtler vibrational energy *ahaṅkāra*, but more *sāttvic* than their products, the *aṇu* subatomic particles. It is these *aṇus* that are the basic building blocks of the physical universe.

The point of all this metaphysical specificity is that although there may be a unified material energy behind all reality in the form of the three *guṇas* of *prakṛti*, individual items of reality emerge when these *guṇas* and their products interact with each other in various ways, that is, when the *sāttvic, tāmasic*, and *rājasic* proportions of *prakṛti* are realigned. So we can see that earth mixing with water produces clay, a product different from both, says Vijñānabhikṣu, and this product itself transforms again when it interacts with fire and is baked in the form of a pot. Individual objects perceivable in external reality are simply individual mutations of the *guṇas*. Just as the lamp, says Śaṅkara, is a combination of wick, oil, and fire, so material products are specific combinations of the *guṇas*.

Changing track, Vyāsa considers the view of those who deny the reality of the external world, the "idealists." Some, he says, argue that there is no physical object external to or independent of thought, that is, an object demonstrably exists only if it is cognized by thought. Proponents of this position note that there are objects that appear to be independent of thoughts but in reality are demonstrably internal to it, such as the objects imagined in dreams. Since there is nothing that can be known independent of thought, and since some so-called external objects, such as those perceived in dreams, are in fact not external at all, this school concludes that there are no demonstrable objects in reality at all that can be proved to be external to thought; they are all just constructions of the mind. Idealism obviously counters the Yoga view that objects are real (II.22), at least in terms of their essential nature of the *guṇas* as Patañjali has specified, a position loosely categorized as "realism." Vijñānabhikṣu identifies the idealists referred to here by Vyāsa as the Vijñānavāda Buddhists.[15]

But objective physical reality is self-evident, says Vyāsa. There are no means to substantiate the claim that objective reality is a construction of the mind; unlike the imagined reality of objects in a dream that is countered upon waking, nothing counters the reality of objects experienced in the waking state.[16] Hariharānanda points out that, as a matter of fact, even the dream analogy supports the position of realism rather than idealism since the objects constructed by imagination in a dream are actually mental imprints or memories (*saṁskāras*) of real physical objects previously experienced in the waking state that then surface in the mind in a confused fashion when asleep. Śaṅkara makes the additional argument that supposing the objects of perceptions to be not real, but merely consciousness, entails consciousness being divided into subject and object. If the perception of a worm is actually merely a construction of consciousness rather than an external physical thing, then consciousness must be divided into consciousness as thing perceived, the worm, and consciousness as the perceiver, in other words, into subject and object. But this is not defensible, he states, and is akin to arguing that one can divide a light into two lights—light as illuminator and light as illuminated.[17]

Vijñānabhikṣu, meanwhile, takes a swipe at the *advaita* school of Vedānta stemming from Śaṅkara, who is considered by his opponents to be quasi Buddhistic in his philosophy that the world is ultimately unreal.[18]

वस्तुसाम्ये चित्तभेदात् तयोर्विभक्तः पन्थाः ॥१५॥

IV.15 vastu-sāmye citta-bhedāt tayor vibhaktaḥ panthāḥ

vastu, a thing; *sāmye*, while remaining common; *citta*, mind; *bhedāt*, because of difference; *tayoḥ*, of it [the mind and object of perception]; *vibhaktaḥ*, different; *panthāḥ*, paths

Because there is a multiplicity of minds [perceiving an object] but yet the object remains consistent, there is a difference in nature between the object and the mind [of the observer].

Patañjali continues his discussion from the previous *sūtra*, distinguishing the realist Yoga philosophy from the philosophy of idealism. Clearly, various forms of idealism, which all the commentators identify primarily with schools of Buddhism, must have been prevalent on Patañjali's landscape, since he dedicates a number of *sūtras* to the subject (IV.14–22); indeed, this is the only section of the text that engages so explicitly with another philosophical school. Consequently, some scholars see Yoga as an internal updating of the old Sāṅkhya tradition partly with a view of bringing it into conversation with the more technical philosophical traditions that had emerged by the second to fifth centuries, particularly the challenges represented by Buddhist thought.[19]

The reader is alerted that the following section is unavoidably philosophical. One reason for this is that, from the sources of knowledge accepted by the Yoga school (*pratyakṣa, anumāna*, and *āgama*, perception, inference, and verbal authority), verbal authority cannot be used in discussions with Buddhists: The sacred texts and human authorities accepted by the Hindus are not the same as those accepted by the Buddhists. In other words, there is no use quoting the Upaniṣads to resolve a philosophical issue, such as whether or not there is an *ātman*, if the opponent does not accept the Upaniṣads as authoritative sacred text. So, in discussions with those outside the Vedic fold such as Buddhists, verbal authority cannot serve as a common framework. Nor can perception. After all, where Hindu *yogīs* might claim that they or their spiritual masters have perceived the existence of the *ātman* in the state of *samādhi*, Buddhist meditators might equally claim that they have perceived precisely the nonexistence of any such *ātman* in the state ultimate to Buddhists, *nirvāṇa*, each laying claim to direct perception. Where does the conversation go from there? Neither perception nor verbal authority, therefore, can serve usefully as a source of knowledge when debating with nonorthodox schools; only inference can. Therefore, the debates between the Hindus and Buddhists, both textual and actual,[20] adopted logic in critiquing the viewpoints of opponents (called *pūrvapakṣa*). This makes for difficult reading for those not schooled in Indic thought, even as an effort has been made here to reduce the technicalities of the following *sūtras* as far as possible.

An object of the world, despite the fact that it remains a unitary object that remains constant in terms of its metaphysical makeup, *vastu-sāmya*, can be experienced very differently by different minds. If the perceiver's mind is pervaded by *sattva*, says Vyāsa, the object might engender *sāttvic* qualities such as happiness in the mind; if pervaded by *rajas*, it might engender pain; if pervaded by *tamas*, forgetfulness; if perceived with the eye of wisdom, detachment. As Vācaspati Miśra, ever ready with more colorful examples, puts it, the same women may be beloved, hated, ignored, or approached with indifference by the individuals Caitra, Viṣṇumitra, Devadatta, and Maitra, even though the woman remains the same object of perception throughout. If the same object produces different feelings in different minds, then the actual object itself, being common to all, must be different from the mind.

But these differences notwithstanding, how is it that different people all perceive essentially the same basic source object in the first place, if the object is a construction of the mind as idealists hold rather than an object with external reality in its own right? If it is a mental construct, says Bhoja Rāja, then surely there would be a complete difference in the original object constructed by one person's mind as compared to the object constructed by another person's mind—not just a difference in the responses the same object invokes due to the differences of the observers' *guṇas*, but a difference in the very nature of the object itself. Why would Caitra and his friends all perceive the same woman in the first place (irrespective of whether she provokes love, hate, or indifference)? Why should an object construed as external in one person's mind be constructed simultaneously in another's mind? And even if we accept this for argument's sake, continues Vācaspati Miśra, if external objects that appear common to all are actually internal mental constructs that are somehow shared, why are not all individual mental thought constructs shared? If one person randomly thinks of the color blue, why is it that other people do not suddenly think of blue at the same time? Why are only supposedly external objects simultaneously perceived by all?

And even if one goes further and accepts that such a common experience of an external object can spontaneously occur simultaneously, as internal mental constructs of numerous people, what is the original cause of the object's appearance? Can an object that has been constructed or imagined in one person's mind be transmitted to another's such that both individuals share the same supposed external perception of it? If so, whose mind, according to the philosophy of idealism, originally imagined all the varied perceptions in (apparent) external reality common to all? Vijñānabhikṣu points out that one person does not share the dream of another, so how can people all share the perception of the same supposed object in the waking state?[21] If this is not due to transmission from one person's mind to another's, then how is it that the same shared object is being imagined by everyone simultaneously? And even if one allows that this can take place somehow or other, then why doesn't everyone have identical impressions all the time, asks Śaṅkara?

For such reasons, says, Vyāsa, there must be a distinction between the object of perception and the instrument of perception, the mind. The minds may be different in terms of the qualities of their perceptions, but the object remains the same. This is Patañjali's thrust in this *sūtra*. The object must be external to and independent of perception, or consciousness. Objects are not constructions of the mind, but *svapratiṣṭham*, grounded in their own right independent of perception, as Patañjali will clearly state in the next *sūtra*, where the discussion continues.

न चैकचित्ततन्त्रं चेद् वस्तु तद् अप्रमाणकं तदा किं स्यात् ।।१६।।

IV.16 na caika-citta-tantram ced vastu tad-apramāṇakam tadā kiṁ syāt

na, not; *ca*, and; *eka*, one; *citta*, mind; *tantram*, dependent; *cet*, if; *vastu*, thing; *tat*, that [mind]; *apramāṇakam*, not evidenced [by cognition]; *tadā*, then; *kim*, what; *syāt*, happens [to it]

An object is not dependent on a single mind [for its existence]; if it were, then what happens to it when it is not perceived [by that particular mind]?

If an object, say a pot, were indeed merely a construction of the mind, what would happen to it, asks Vyāsa rhetorically, if the mind were in a state of *samādhi*, or even if it were just plain distracted, that is, not focused on that particular object? Since it is supposed to be the construction of a single mind, would the pot then simply cease to exist when that person's mind is no longer aware of it? If so, then why can other people still see it? Moreover, the parts of an object not perceived by the mind would not actually exist, says Vyāsa, according to idealism. If one perceives a person only from the front, does this mean the person's back does not exist because it is not within the sphere of perception? If so, how can a person's stomach exist without a back? he asks in a somewhat tongue-in-cheek manner. And, in a world where objective reality is simply the mental construction of the individual, conventional social interactions would completely break down since there is no reason people's mental constructions of social norms should overlap in any coherent manner, adds Śaṅkara. If everything is a construction of consciousness, then why would the student and teacher both construct the same understanding of their respective social roles such that they might cooperate? How could any sane and standardized social system evolve from independently created mental imaginings?

The objects of the world can therefore be only independent entities, as minds, too, are independent entities. They unite to fulfill their purpose, concludes Vyāsa, which is to provide the *puruṣa* with *bhoga*, experience. The objects of the senses provide distractions for the soul absorbed in *saṁsāra*, and the mind and other faculties process these sense objects and present them to *puruṣa*.

तदुपरागापेक्षित्वाच् चित्तस्य वस्तु ज्ञाताज्ञातम् ॥ १७ ॥

IV.17 tad-uparāgāpekṣitvāc cittasya vastu jñātājñātam

tat, it [the mind]; *uparāga*, colored by, pervaded; *apekṣitvāt*, depending on; *cittasya*, of the mind; *vastu*, a thing; *jñāta*, is known; *ajñātam*, is not known

A thing is either known or not known by the mind depending on whether it is noticed by the mind.

Here Patañjali presents the Yoga position as to why, if objects are objectively real, they are sometimes known, *jñāta*, and sometimes not known, *ajñāta*, to an individual. The process of cognition, according to Yoga, occurs when the *citta* comes in contact with the sense objects. The objects of the senses are like magnets, says Vyāsa, and the mind is like iron—sense objects in the vicinity of the mind exert their pull on the mind. Patañjali uses the term *uparāga*, colored, here: When an object colors the mind due to proximity (is pervaded or noticed by the mind), that object becomes known. Things that are not so pervaded remain unknown. In this way the mind is always changing, noticing one thing and then another.

The *citta* assumes the form of a particular object, or is colored by it, like a cloth is colored when it comes into contact with dye, says Vijñānabhikṣu. More specifically, the intelligence aspect of the *citta* internally replicates the external or physical features of the object, that is, it assumes the shape and contours of the object psychically, and then presents this image to *puruṣa*, which becomes aware of it by its consciousness reflecting on or pervading the *citta*. It is important to keep in mind that *citta* remains inert and unconscious throughout this process. It is still a product of *prākṛtic* matter, however subtle; the ultimate experience of being aware of the object is the prerogative of *puruṣa*'s awareness only. In this way, the *citta* itself becomes the object in terms of *puruṣa*'s awareness.

As a parting comment against the idealists, Śaṅkara notes that if physical objects are simply creations of the mind, the mind would either be omniscient—it should theoretically be able to create and thus gain knowledge of anything at all—or it would not create any objects of awareness, and thus nothing would be known.

सदा ज्ञाताश्चित्तवृत्तयस्तत्प्रभोः पुरुषस्यापरिणामित्वात् ॥ १८ ॥

IV.18 sadā jñātāś citta-vṛttayas tat-prabhoḥ puruṣasyāpariṇāmitvāt

sadā, always; *jñātāḥ*, are known; *citta*, mind; *vṛttayaḥ*, changing state, permutations; *tat*, that [the mind]; *prabhoḥ*, of the master; *puruṣasya*, of the *puruṣa*, soul; *apariṇāmitvāt*, because of it not changing

The permutations of the mind are always known to its master, the *puruṣa* soul, because of the soul's unchanging nature.

Here Patañjali presents an axiomatic truth in Hindu philosophy—the unchanging nature, *apariṇāmitva*, of *puruṣa*. Anything that changes cannot be eternal, since, obviously, if a thing changes into something else, the original thing ceases to be. Therefore, since the soul is eternal, it cannot change. The soul must in any event be unchanging, infers Vyāsa, because if it were constantly changing by nature, as is the case of the mind, then its object of awareness, the mind's *vṛttis*, would be sometimes known to it and sometimes not known. This is not the case: *Puruṣa* is always aware of the mind's *vṛttis*, even in deep sleep (which we recall is a *vṛtti* in its own right). The mind itself, on the other hand, is sometimes aware of its objects of awareness, the sense objects, and sometimes not. Since the mind is always changing and roaming about, its objects—the sense objects of sound, etc.—are sometimes in its sphere of perception and sometimes not, but the *puruṣa*'s awareness, in contrast, is constant and unchanging. The object of the *puruṣa*'s awareness is the mind, irrespective of the *vṛtti* of the mind. Again, if the awareness of the *puruṣa* were also changing and roaming about, it, too, would sometimes be aware of its object, the mind, and sometimes not, but the fact is that the *puruṣa* is always aware of the mind, that is, it is always absorbed in one or other of the *vṛttis*. Therefore, says Vyāsa, its core awareness is unchanging. It is accordingly distinct from the ever-changing mind.

न तत् स्वाभासं दृश्यत्वात् ॥१९॥

IV.19 na tat svābhāsam dṛśyatvāt

na, not; *tat*, it, the mind; *svābhāsam*, self-illuminating; *dṛśyatvāt*, because of its nature as that which is to be perceived

Nor is the mind self-illuminating, because of its nature as the object of perception.

In this *sūtra*, Patañjali rejects the position, identified by the commentators as being that of the Vaināśika Buddhists, that the mind is itself self-aware or self-illuminating, *svābhāsa*, like fire, which does not need any outside agent to illuminate itself. In this view, accordingly, there is no need to posit the existence of an outside source of awareness in the form of *puruṣa*—the mind itself is held to be self-aware, the source of awareness.

But in Yoga epistemology, mind is clearly the object of awareness. When one says, "I am afraid," "I am angry," etc., the mind in the form of anger or fear is the object of awareness, requiring a distinct subject of awareness, an "I." Otherwise it would be like saying the "cooking is cooked" or the "cutting is cut" or the "going is gone," says Vācaspati Miśra. The act and the object of activity cannot be the same thing. Any object of awareness, like a pot, cannot also be the subject of awareness; that which is perceivable requires a perceiver, says Bhoja Rāja. If the pot perceived were identical with the perceiving subject, one should rather say "I am the pot," not "I see the pot." Moreover, points out Hariharānanda, if the mind itself were the subject of awareness or I, in the example "I am afraid" there would have to be one part of the mind that would be the I, or knower, and another part that would be the known or object of knowledge, the "afraid." This is tantamount to accepting that there is a part of the mind that is the knower and a part that is the known, which admits a knower distinct from objects of knowledge and therefore approaches the position of the Yoga school.

And even if, in the fire example, one allows that fire illuminates itself without the need of any other agent, nonetheless fire itself is an object that is known by something outside of itself, namely, the perceiver of the fire seeing through the instrument of the eye. Another outside entity is still required to experience and establish the luminosity of fire in the first place. Therefore, the counterargument of fire is inadequate. In short, the mind, being an object of perception, cannot be subjectively aware or self-illuminating. Whatever illumination it seems to exude is the result of it being permeated by the illumination of the awareness of *puruṣa*, like the cloud appearing illumined due to the sun shining through it, or the iron bar becoming fiery due to being placed in and permeated by the fire. In short, subject and object must be distinct entities. Discussion of this issue continues in the next *sūtra*.

एकसमये चोभयानवधारणम् ॥२०॥

IV.20 eka-samaye cobhayānavadhāraṇam

eka, one; *samaye*, time; *ca*, and; *ubhaya*, both;
anavadhāraṇam, nondiscernment

There cannot be discernment of both [the mind and the object it perceives] at the same time.

Once more, Vyāsa specifically directs his comments toward the *kṣaṇika-vādins*, those who believe in momentariness, another generic name for the Buddhists. Continuing from the previous *sūtra* his refutation of the notion that the mind is self-aware, he reads Patañjali here as presenting another argument that it would not be possible for the mind to be aware of itself as well as an object of awareness in the same instance in *kṣaṇika-vāda* metaphysics. The argument is slightly technical. Buddhists hold that all aspects of reality, whether cognitive or material, do not have any essential nature but exist only for a *kṣaṇa*, moment, during which they produce effects before fading, and thus flavor immediately succeeding moments of existence. Since all phenomena are momentary, that is, all ingredients of reality last for only a moment, any object in reality, such as a pot, although appearing to remain the same for a long period of time, is actually undergoing change at every moment in all its parts. Apparent continuity is merely the production of similar but successive effects each moment, like the different stills of a movie reel, which give the impression of a continuous object but are actually distinct images following each other in rapid succession. This includes the mind; it, too, consists of a series of momentary minds (see discussion in II.32).

Obviously, this *kṣaṇika-vāda* position is in opposition to the Yoga school, which holds that the mind (and all objects of reality) does have an essential nature that endures (in the sense that it is an evolute of the eternal *guṇas* of *prakṛti*), and that the subject of awareness, *puruṣa*, also endures eternally. Thus, the main difference between the Buddhist and the Yoga positions in the matter of the momentary perceivable nature of external reality is that Yoga metaphysics holds that, while reality is indeed a flow of ever-changing moments, all such change is caused by the flux of the underlying substructure, *guṇas*, which are eternal essences, where the Buddhists deny any eternal essences at all in reality. But we can note that both schools agree that surface-level reality is always in flux.

Now, in the cognition "I know the pot," there is an element of self-awareness represented in the I and an element of object awareness represented in the pot. The cognition "I know the pot," while appearing to the conscious mind to be a solitary and uniform thought, actually involves two separate cognitions, one for the I, an act of self-awareness, and another for the pot as object of awareness. However, if, as per the *kṣaṇika-vāda* position, everything arises for only one single instant, this would mean that the mind could be aware of itself for only one instant and then aware of any other object such as a pot for another, separate instant. In other words, if one were to posit that there is no *puruṣa*, soul, as subject of awareness, and if everything in objective reality arises and exists for only one instant, as the Buddhists suppose, then during that instant the mind would not be capable of being self-aware—the I inherent in any act of cognition—as well as simultaneously being object-aware of something else such as a pot. If the mind were momentary and self-illuminating, it would use up its momentary existence being self-aware, because self-awareness is an act, and all acts are momentary in Buddhism. Since one cannot be self-aware and object-aware at the exact same time, then the act of self-awareness uses up the existential life span of the *kṣaṇa*, moment, so to speak. The mind would then find itself in the same situation in the next *kṣaṇa*, which would also be spent being self-aware, and so on with the next, ad infinitum. Where, then, would there ever be a moment free in which to be object-aware? There would never be any room for object-awareness if the mind were momentary and self-illuminating as per the *kṣaṇika-vāda* position. One would never be aware of anything in external reality. The argument is a reductio ad absurdum, called *tarka* in Hindu logic, whereby the opponent's position is shown to lead to impossible consequences.

The Yoga position, of course, is that it is the *puruṣa* that is self-aware or self-illuminating, and the mind, which is object-aware, and these two separate entities coexist and are enduring rather than momentary. Thus the functions of illumination or self-awareness on the one hand, and of object-awareness on the other, are divided between two permanent, separate, and distinct entities, thereby bypassing the problems of a *kṣaṇika-vāda* metaphysics in positing a self-illuminating mind that is simultaneously object-aware. Naturally, the entire Yoga premise is that there is an eternal autonomous *puruṣa* that can be realized, hence the need to engage with Buddhist views denying the existence of such an entity.

चित्तान्तरदृश्ये बुद्धिबुद्धेरतिप्रसङ्गः स्मृतिसंकरश्च ॥ २१ ॥

IV.21 cittāntara-dṛśye buddhi-buddher atiprasaṅgaḥ smṛti-saṅkaraś ca

citta, mind; *antara*, other; *dṛśye*, if it is seen; *buddhi*, intelligence; *buddheḥ*, of the intelligence; *atiprasaṅgaḥ*, excessive contact, unwarranted stretch; *smṛti*, memory; *saṅkaraḥ*, confusion, mixing up of; *ca*, and

If [the mind] were cognized by another mind, then there would be an infinite regress of one intelligence [being known] by another intelligence. Moreover, there would also be confusion of memory.

In the last *sūtra*, the Buddhist notion of mind was considered from the perspective of the subject of awareness. Patañjali and the commentators now engage in technical, psychological analysis from the perspective of the objects of awareness. Let us say the momentary mind, as understood in certain schools of Buddhism, becomes aware of a pot and generates the idea of a pot that exhausts the mind's existential moment of existence. By whom would that idea of a pot be known, if there is no *puruṣa*? Vyāsa argued in the previous *sūtra* that the subject of awareness and object of awareness cannot coexist in the same *citta* at the same moment, so, by a logic parallel to that outlined in the previous *sūtra*, the mind's awareness of the pot can be only the object of awareness, but without a subject. The opponent, at this point, could introduce the idea that there is another subsequent momentary idea, and it is this second idea that is the knower of the first idea. First of all, as Hariharānanda notes, this essentially entails postulating a future (that is, subsequent mind) as knower of a present mind. The problem with this is that the two would not overlap since their nature is momentary in Buddhism. In other words, if everything is momentary, how can a future entity know a present entity when the latter would have become past and thus expired when the future entity became present? Furthermore, even if this were not the case, if this second idea is the knower or subject of the first idea, then the first idea becomes the object of the second idea, but one is still left without a subject for the second idea. And if one introduces a third idea as knower of the second idea, then a fourth, and so on, one ends up with the infinite regress, *atiprasaṅga*, noted by Patañjali in this *sūtra*.

Patañjali's second comment in this *sūtra* pertaining to the confusion of memory, *smṛti-saṅkara*, is also somewhat technical and understood by the commentators as pointing to the fact that all the ideas noted above would produce *saṁskāras* of the same form. The pot becomes the object of awareness for the mind during its moment of existence, and is placed as a pot *saṁskāra* in the *citta*, as all objects of awareness are. But then this mind with its image of a pot itself becomes the object of awareness for a subsequent momentary mind, transferring its pot *saṁskāra* to the second momentary mind, and this, in turn, to a third momentary mind, and so forth. There would be knowledge of the pot, knowledge of the knowledge of the pot, knowledge of the knowledge of the knowledge of the pot . . . Now, each of these minds in this momentary series would manifest, imprinted with its own inherited set of *saṁskāras* of this original pot. Patañjali seems to be saying that such multiple sets of consecutive *saṁskāras* of the pot would throw memory into confusion, since, in the absence of an unchanging, unifying agent and of the same enduring *saṁskāra*, there would be no way of knowing which memory of the pot in this series pertained to the original pot or object of knowledge or idea; there would just be a confused multiplicity of duplicated *saṁskāras*. Moreover, the agent perceiving the original pot, being momentary, would not be the same agent recollecting it at a later moment. Thus memory would not be clear in the sense of identifying and connecting one *saṁskāric* memory to its original corresponding object, since there would be no constant witness to connect them.

Memory has always featured in the arguments of the orthodox Hindu schools against Buddhism. To say, "This is the pot that I saw yesterday," requires that the *saṁskāra* of that pot be retained from one day to the next such that one can remember it. This suggests continuity of *saṁskāra*, which goes against the notion of *kṣaṇa*, momentariness. If one argues that there is a stream of momentary *saṁskāras* within which the *saṁskāra* of a previous moment subtly transmits its impression or stamp on the next, and this second on the third, and so forth, such that there appears to be one constant *saṁskāra* but is in reality a stream of successive moments, then other difficulties arise. Such a process of transmission would require that the *saṁskāra* exist for at least two or three distinct *kṣaṇas*, or moments: There must be a moment when the *saṁskāra* receives the impression, perhaps a moment when it exists in its own right, then at the very least a moment when it overlaps with the subsequent *saṁskāra* such that it can transmit its impression upon it (and then, perhaps, another moment in which it dissolves). According to the followers of other systems of Indian thought, most entities endure for at least three moments: origination, duration, and cessation.[22] Without such overlap, there could not be a stream of continuity. This entails more than one moment, which is not admitted by adherents of the momentariness view, *kṣaṇika-vāda*.[23] Such arguments are expressed in the Vedānta tradition and adopted by most Hindu philosophical schools.[24]

Moreover, if the mind continues to exhaust its momentary existence in object-awareness rather than subject-awareness, there would be no awareness of a subjective self, says Śaṅkara. How could we function in the world without any notion of a subjective self? We would all meet each other in bewilderment, he quips! There is thus the need of a subject, in the Yoga view—the *puruṣa* manifesting its awareness through the *citta*—to be the witness of ideas and provide a basis for continuity.

Vyāsa considers another Buddhist view, which Vijñānabhikṣu again identifies as that of the Vijñānavādins, or Yogācāra Buddhists. In Buddhism in general, the human persona consists of five *skandhas*, layers of personhood: form, sensation, perceptions, *saṁskāras*, and consciousness. None of these is permanent—including consciousness. All five layers consist of constantly changing streams of interdependent point moments, each one codependent on and interconnected with others. Some Buddhists, Vyāsa states, hold that there actually is a mind, called *sattva* (literally, beingness[25]), which appropriates these layers, then discards them constantly for new layers every moment (the more common term for this mental substratum in Yogācāra or Vijñānavāda Buddhism is *ālaya-vijñāna*). Since the postulation of such a *sattva* starts to approach the notion of a *puruṣa*, he continues, they become fearful of the implications of this move and hasten to deny its existence as anything other than momentary.

All in all, from the perspective of the Yoga school, confusion arises by attempting to deny the existence of a *puruṣa* as the witness of the mind. Having said this, one can reiterate that, at least in terms of *prakṛti*, Buddhism and Yoga both agree that surface-level reality is momentary and flows in a stream of ever-changing flux. As will be discussed in IV.33, where they differ is that in Yoga this all takes place in a constant, eternal, and enduring substratum, *prakṛti*. In Buddhism, in addition to there being no *puruṣa* as the witness of *prakṛti*, there is no such entity as *prakṛti* underlying the momentary flux of surface reality.

चितेरप्रतिसंक्रमायास्तदाकारापत्तौ स्वबुद्धिसंवेदनम् ॥ २२ ॥

IV.22 citer apratisaṅkramāyās tad-ākārāpattau svabuddhi-saṁvedanam

citeḥ, of consciousness; *apratisaṅkramāyāḥ*, unmoving; *tat*, that; *ākāra*, form; *āpattau*, pervading, entering into a state; *sva*, its own; *buddhi*, intelligence; *saṁvedanam*, knowing

Although it is unchanging, consciousness becomes aware of its own intelligence by means of pervading the forms assumed by the intelligence.

Having argued that the mind is not self-illuminating but rather an object of knowledge, the question now arises as to how the mind is known at all by *puruṣa*, given the Yoga axiom that *puruṣa* is changeless, *apratisaṅkrama*, and does not act in any way. If *puruṣa* were directly aware of external objects (if there were no *citta*), it would itself be an actor, by virtue of interacting directly with the world, as well as ever-changing, by virtue of being aware of, processing, and thinking about one object after another, as is entailed in everyday consciousness. If *puruṣa* were subject to change in this way, it would not be eternal—eternal means unchanging. Therefore, *puruṣa* is passive and unchanging, according to Yoga metaphysics. Consequently it is the *citta* that changes and modifies itself according to the objects of perception—pots or any other objects of the world—molding itself into a replication of these objects, *āpatti*. One recalls the example of copper being poured into a mold and thereby taking the form of that mold. This transformed *citta*, that is, *citta* molded into the particular form of the external object, the pot, is presented to the changeless and eternal *puruṣa*. The consciousness of *puruṣa*, which eternally radiates forth, thereby becomes aware of the *citta* in this particular mold of a pot. *Puruṣa* has not changed or transformed by being aware of *citta* and its machinations, nor has it acted; its awareness has merely encountered the *citta* in its modified forms of pots and so forth. The light of a movie projector does not change or act when it pervades the ever-changing reel flowing in front of it. Its unchanging nature is simply to shine. Pervaded by *puruṣa*'s awareness, the *citta* in its turn becomes animated as the movie reel becomes illuminated when pervaded by light. Thus the *citta* can act and continually change into the forms of the world, meanwhile allowing the *puruṣa*, as witness, to remain inactive and unchangingly aware.

The *citta* is also conceptualized as acting as a mirror and reflecting the *puruṣa*—Vācaspati Miśra presents again the classic illustration of the moon reflected in rippling water. When *puruṣa* becomes aware of its reflection in the modified *citta*, it becomes aware of an apparently transformed *puruṣa* (that is, of its reflection in whatever is going on in the *citta*, which appears animated due to being pervaded by the *puruṣa*'s awareness). This is compared to the moon's reflection in water agitated by the wind, which makes the moon's reflection—and, by extension, the moon itself—appear to be moving with ripples. Of course, it is only the reflection of the moon that moves with the ripples; the moon itself remains unchanged in the sky, but an ignorant person might mistake the rippled reflection of the moon to be the actual moon. Similarly, the *puruṣa* becomes identified with its distorted reflection by the *citta* and thus becomes aware of and identified with *saṁsāric* life despite the fact that, in reality, it itself is autonomous, aloof, and unchanging. Vyāsa quotes the following verse:

> The sages teach that the hidden place in which the eternal *Brahman* is to be found is not the netherworlds, nor the mountain caves, nor deep darkness, nor the caverns of the oceans; it is the *vṛttis* of the intelligence which appears identical to him [by which it is hidden].[26]

We can note here, as an aside, that although the Upaniṣadic term *Brahman* is not used by Patañjali (*ātman*, of course, is), Vyāsa is here clearly equating it with *puruṣa*.

द्रष्टृदृश्योपरक्तं चित्तं सर्वार्थम् ॥ २३ ॥

IV.23 draṣṭṛ-dṛśyoparaktaṁ cittaṁ sarvārtham

draṣṭṛ, the seer; *dṛśya*, the object seen; *uparaktam*, colored; *cittam*, the mind; *sarvārtham*, knows all objects

The mind, colored by the seer as well as by that which is seen, knows all objects.

The *citta* is the pivot of *saṁsāric* existence. On the one hand, it assumes the forms of the objects of the world. On the other hand, it itself is the object of *puruṣa*'s awareness. Thus, says Vyāsa, it is colored by both object and subject, by the inanimate sense objects and by *puruṣa*, the ultimate source of awareness. By reflecting *puruṣa*'s consciousness, as well as the inert objects of the world, it assumes the forms of both consciousness and unconsciousness, and hence, in

Patañjali's terms, is colored, *uparakta*, by them. Like a crystal, it can reflect disparate things in its various facets. Here again we see the mind compared to the crystal. Depending on the point to be made, sometimes the *puruṣa* is compared to a crystal (e.g., Vācaspati Miśra in I.3) and other times, as we find here, the *citta* is compared to the crystal. In the former instance, the point is to illustrate that just as the crystal remains clear even though it might appear to be colored by an adjacent object, so does the *puruṣa* remain pure, even though its awareness appears to be colored by the adjacent *citta* with its *vṛttis*. But here the same example is used to illustrate that it is the mind that is infused with both consciousness distinct from itself on one side, and with the objects of the senses, also distinct from itself, on the other, as the crystal can be infused with both red and other colors distinct from itself in its various facets.

This is why, says Vyāsa, it is easy to subscribe to the idealist views discussed in the previous *sūtras*. Since objects of consciousness are revealed by the mind, it is understandable that some might think they are products of the mind.[27] Likewise, since the mind reflects the consciousness of *puruṣa*, it is understandable that some might suppose that the mind itself is the source of consciousness. These views deserve sympathy, says Vyāsa. However, if one is truly to realize the source of all consciousness, one must develop a clear understanding of the nature of *puruṣa*, of the *citta*, and of the objects of perception; hence the previous *sūtras* were directed by Patañjali at challenging certain views that might bear resemblances to the Yogic position. The correct view according to the Yoga school is that there are three entities in the process of knowledge: the knower, the instrument of knowledge, and the object of knowledge (*puruṣa, citta*, and the sense objects). And true discriminative knowledge, *viveka*, is the understanding of the difference among them.

तदसंख्येयवासनाचित्रम् अपि परार्थं संहत्यकारित्वात् ॥ २४ ॥

IV.24 tad-asaṅkhyeya-vāsanā-citram api parārtham saṁhatya-kāritvāt

tat, that; *asaṅkhyeya*, uncountable; *vāsanā*, subconscious impressions; *citram*, variegated; *api*, also; *para*, other; *artham*, purpose; *saṁhatya*, combination, union; *kāritvāt*, because of acting

That mind, with its countless variegated subliminal impressions, exists for another entity [other than itself], because it operates in conjunction [with other instruments].

Patañjali concludes the discussion concerning the nature of the mind and consciousness. The mind consists of unlimited *saṁskāras*—of pleasure, pain, knowledge, etc. It is therefore a construction made of many parts. It also works in conjunction, *saṁhatya,* with other entities such as the senses, sense objects, and so forth. Things that are combinations of parts and work in conjunction with other entities, state the commentators, have been conjoined for the purpose of something else, not for themselves. In fact, when the parts of a constructed entity are pulled apart, the entity ceases to exist as a coherent entity. Therefore, it has been put together originally for an entity other than itself. A house is a construction of different parts that exist with other entities. It does not exist for itself but for another entity—a resident.

As we know, the mind exists to provide either experience or liberation. The experience of pleasure that it activates is not for itself, nor is its manifestation of the experience of pain, knowledge, etc., for itself. These are to be experienced by some other entity. That other entity cannot itself be a construct consisting of parts, for the reason outlined above; it must be something of a different nature: That other is the changeless, partless *puruṣa.*

विशेषदर्शिन आत्मभावभावनाविनिवृत्तिः ।। २५ ।।

IV.25 viśeṣa-darśina ātma-bhāva-bhāvanā-vinivṛttiḥ

viśeṣa, distinction; *darśinaḥ*, the seer; *ātma*, the self; *bhāva*, nature; *bhāvanā*, meditation; *vinivṛttiḥ*, cessation

For one who sees the distinction [between the mind and the soul], reflecting on the nature of the self ceases.

Just as the existence of seeds is inferred from blades of grass shooting forth in the rainy season, says Vyāsa, so the existence of *saṁskāras* from the practice of *yoga* in a past life is inferred in the case of one whose hair stands on end and whose tears flow when hearing about the path of liberation.[28] The commentators discuss how, due to the performance of *yoga* in a past life, a person is spontaneously attracted to the practices of *yoga* in the present life. In such a person, they say, curiosity about the nature of the self—"Who am I?" "Who was I in the past?" "What is this life about?" "Where will I go when I die?"—arises spontaneously. Just as the lush verdancy of the rainy season points to the existence of seeds that had remained dormant until the onset of the rains, so the *saṁskāras* accumulated from the practice of *yoga* in a past life lie dormant until conditions in a present life reactivate them, at which time they sprout spontaneously. One is then drawn automatically to the practices of *yoga* and the association of fellow *yogīs*, and loses interest in the more superficial aspects of mundane existence. Kṛṣṇa states in the *Gītā* that the unsuccessful *yogī*, that is, the one who does not quite complete his or her journey in life, is reborn into a pious or prosperous family, or a family of *yogīs*. Then "such a person gains a revival of his insight from the previous birth, and strives again for perfection from that point [where he or she had left off in the past life]" (VI.41–43).

However, continues Vyāsa, Patañjali is indicating in this *sūtra* that when one has actually realized the self, questions such as "Who am I" cease; hence, the prioritization of *pratyakṣa*, experience, by Patañjali (I.49) from the three sources of knowledge accepted by the Yoga school in I.6. The other two, *anumāna* and *āgama*, inference and verbal authority, can help remove doubt, says Hariharānanda, but only actual experience completely dissolves all questions. Existential questions are, after all, the products of *citta*—albeit of the *akliṣṭa* variety noted in *sūtra* I.5 which are advantageous to the ultimate goal of *yoga*. But once one actually experiences the distinction between the real self and everything else, all existential questions evaporate. As the *Muṇḍaka Upaniṣad* states, "All doubts are dispelled, for one who has seen [the truth]" (II.2.9).

तदा विवेकनिम्नं कैवल्यप्राग्भारं चित्तम् ॥ २६ ॥

IV.26 tadā viveka-nimnaṁ kaivalya-prāgbhāram cittam

tadā, then; *viveka*, discrimination; *nimnam*, inclined toward; *kaivalya*, aloneness, ultimate liberation; *prāgbhāram*, inclined toward; *cittam*, the mind

At that point, the mind, inclined toward discrimination, gravitates toward ultimate liberation.

When, says Vyāsa, *citta* recognizes this distinction between itself and the *puruṣa*, the mind of the *yogī*, which had previously been interested in sensual gratification, undergoes a transformation. As Patañjali indicates, it becomes inclined toward the knowledge born of discrimination (of this distinction) and gravitates toward liberation, *kaivalya*. As discussed in II.26, it is *viveka* that destroys ignorance and this brings about *kaivalya* (II.25).

तच्छिद्रेषु प्रत्ययान्तराणि संस्कारेभ्यः ॥ २७ ॥

IV.27 tac-chidreṣu pratyayāntarāṇi saṁskārebhyaḥ

tat, that; *chidreṣu*, break, interval; *pratyaya*, ideas; *antarāṇi*, other; *saṁskārebhyaḥ*, subliminal impressions

During the intervals [in this state of discriminate awareness] other ideas [arise] because of previous *saṁskāras*.

Patañjali states that even in the mind that is inclined toward liberation, there are breaks in the flow of *viveka*, discrimination (of the difference between *puruṣa* and *citta*). Conventional thoughts such as, "I am," "This is mine," "I know," "I don't know," etc., pop into the mind of the meditator, says Vyāsa. From where do they come? These are merely the effects of previous *saṁskāras*, which are gradually dwindling away. The sense of I remains even in *samprajñāta-samādhi*, Vijñānabhikṣu reminds us. And even a very renounced *yogī* who begs for his food as an ascetic, says Vācaspati Miśra, must be conscious of his body and of hunger, etc., to do so. Thus, even as they dwindle, thoughts pertaining to the *prākṛtic* body and mind continue to arise even in the minds of advanced *yogīs*.

हानम् एषां क्लेशवदुक्तम् ॥ २८ ॥

IV.28 hānam eṣāṁ kleśavad uktam

hānam, removal; *eṣām*, of them; *kleśavad*, like the afflictions; *uktam*, is said

The removal [of these previous *saṁskāras*] is said to be like [the removal] of the *kleśa* afflictions.

Just as the *kleśas* become burnt seeds incapable of sprouting, says Vyāsa (II.10–11) the seeds of latent *saṁskāras* noted in the previous *sūtra* that might arise and interrupt the *yogī*'s meditation are likewise singed by the fire of knowledge, *jñāna*. The *kleśas*, we recall, are the cause of *sāṁsāric* existence; once they are burnt up, they do not provoke action and thus no further *saṁskāras* are generated. But one is still left with the latent *saṁskāras* accrued prior to the elimination of the *kleśas*, which may activate and pop into the *yogī*'s mind. This *sūtra* states that any such residual *saṁskāras* are also burnt up in the same way as were the *kleśas*. Thus, they can no longer sprout and give birth to any further thoughts.

As for the knowledge, *jñāna, saṁskāras*, which burn up the other *saṁskāras*, says Vyāsa, these continue to exist until the ultimate goal of the mind is achieved—we recall that *saṁskāras* are never actually destroyed; they can, however, become burnt such that they will not produce seeds. They then dissolve back into the *prākṛtic* matrix when the mind itself is dissolved after final liberation.

प्रसंख्यानेऽप्यकुसीदस्य सर्वथा विवेकख्यातेर्धर्ममेघः समाधिः ॥ २९ ॥

IV.29 prasaṅkhyāne 'py akusīdasya sarvathā viveka-khyāter dharma-meghaḥ samādhiḥ

prasaṅkhyāne, in meditative wisdom; *api*, even; *akusīdasya*, of one who has no interest;[29] *sarvathā*, entirely; *viveka*, discrimination; *khyāteḥ*, insight; *dharma*, virtue; *meghaḥ*, cloud; *samādhiḥ*, state of meditative absorption

For one who has no interest even in [the fruits] of meditative wisdom on account of the highest degree of discriminative insight, the *samādhi* called *dharma-megha*, cloud of virtue, ensues.

The commentators sometimes seem to take technical terms such as *prasaṅkhyana* and *dharma-megha* here, and terms such as *prajñā* (I.20, 48; II.27; III.5), *viveka* or *viveka-khyāti* (II.26, 28; III.52, 54; IV.26, 28), or *khyāti* alone (here and I.16; III.49), as more or less synonyms, or with minor nuances of differences.[30] Vācaspati Miśra here takes *prasaṅkhyana* to refer to the means of restraining all outgoing mental activities, and *dharma-megha* as the state ensuing when even *prasaṅkhyana* in its turn is restrained. Both these terms occur here for the first time. The commentators take *dharma-megha* to essentially mean the highest state of *viveka*, discrimination (Hariharānanda says it is the omniscience ensuing from discrimination), but understand this *sūtra* as saying that when the *yogī* has no interest in the benefits accruing from discernment, his discernment has reached its perfection. Specifically, say the commentators, when the *yogī* has absolutely no interest even in the powers by which he gains control over all things, but, contrarily, actually begins to perceive even these attainments as *duḥkha*, suffering, then his unflinching discrimination is secure and total. We recall that in I.16 Vācaspati Miśra considered the *paraṁ vairāgyam*, higher dispassion toward everything made of the *guṇas*, to be *dharma-megha*. For Vijñānabhikṣu, *dharma-megha* is a state of *jīvan-mukti*, liberated while still embodied.[31]

Why this level of *samādhi* is called *dharma-megha, dharma* cloud, is an interesting question, as is the question of which level of *samādhi* in I.17 and I.42–44 it might correspond to. The commentators don't remark on the latter, but in terms of the former question, Vijñānabhikṣu says that, like a cloud, this state rains *dharma*, which totally uproots the *kleśas* and all *karma*. Śaṅkara states that the supreme *dharma* it rains is *kaivalya*, the final and ultimate state of liberation (II.25; III.50, 55; IV.26). In this state, the *yogī*'s body is like an empty house, he says, all desires to enjoy it have evaporated, no further ideas are created in the *citta*, and the *puruṣa* is left alone in the serenity of pure self-knowledge. Rāmānanda Sarasvatī takes *dharma* in another of its semantic meanings, as knowable things, along the lines of its usage in IV.12, and understands this state of *samādhi* to be one in which the *yogī* knows all knowable things. Taking *dharma* in yet another of its etymological meanings, virtue, Hariharānanda says that as a cloud pours rain, so this state of *samādhi* pours the highest virtue effortlessly. This includes knowledge of the self, which the *yogī*, he says, can see as plainly as a piece of fruit in the palm of his hand.

Given that he finds *dharma-megha* used only once in other Hindu sources, Klostermaier examines the meaning of the term in Buddhist sources and, in conjunction with the next *sūtra*, concludes that it is a state reached after many trials, where there is no longer any danger of the *yogī* sliding backward due to the elimination of the *kleśas* and *karma*: "The metaphor of 'rain' appears to be most appropriate since it extinguishes fire, washes away impurities, and provides a necessary condition for growth" (1986, 262). Feuerstein equates *dharma* with the primal *guṇas*, since *dharma*, like *guṇa*, can also mean quality, and the state of *dharma-megha* as when the *yogī* has conquered all other conditionings and nothing but the primary raw undifferentiated *guṇas* still obscure his all-pervasive vision (1974, 46).

All of these interpretations of *dharma-megha* fit within the contours of Yoga philosophy.

ततः क्लेशकर्मनिवृत्तिः ॥ ३० ॥

IV.30 tataḥ kleśa-karma-nivṛttiḥ

tataḥ, from there; *kleśa*, the obstacles, affliction; *karma*, of *karma*; *nivṛttiḥ*, the cessation

From this comes the cessation of the *kleśas* [impediments to *yoga*] and *karma*.

Once this state of *dharma-megha* has been attained, says Vyāsa, the five *kleśas* and all dormant *karma* are destroyed (more precisely, burnt) to their very roots. With the roots burnt, the seeds can no longer sprout and the *yogī* at this point is liberated even while still alive. How so? poses Vyāsa. Because lack of discrimination, *avidyā*, is the cause of *saṁsāra* (II.4, 24–25), so one situated in unwavering discrimination is no longer in *saṁsāra* (II.26), though still alive. This is the *jīvanmukta*. The term *jīva* is used for the *ātman* or *puruṣa* in the context of *saṁsāra*, that is to say, in the sense of the embodied soul, and *mukta* means liberated. So *jīvanmukta* is a soul still embodied in the world but self-realized and liberated. Such a state is accepted by most

Hindu schools.[32] As was discussed, such persons do not create new *karma*; their dormant *karma* is rendered ineffective and thus they are subject only to the *karma* already activated for the present life—that is, they live out the remainder of their natural life. According to the *Vedānta* tradition (IV.1.5), this notion goes back to the *Chāndogya Upaniṣad*: "There is a delay here only until I am liberated; but then I will attain the goal (VI.14.2).[33] The *Sāṅkhya Kārikā* compares this to a potter's wheel: When the potter stops pumping the pedal, the wheel does not suddenly stop but slows down until all the energy already activated or pumped into it has been expended. Similarly, the *karma* already activated at birth for a *yogī*'s life needs to be exhausted. Such a person absolutely never returns to *saṁsāra* after death, adds Vyāsa, as indicated in numerous Hindu texts (e.g., *Gītā* VIII.21; XV.6).

तदा सर्वावरणमलापेतस्य ज्ञानस्यानन्त्याज्ज्ञेयम् अल्पम् ॥ ३१ ॥

IV.31 tadā sarvāvaraṇa-malāpetasya jñānasyānantyāj jñeyam alpam

tadā, from this; *sarva*, all; *āvaraṇa*, covering; *mala*, impurities; *apetasya*, been removed; *jñānasya*, of knowledge; *ānantyāt*, because of being endless; *jñeyam*, that which is to be known; *alpam*, little

At this point, because of the unlimited nature of knowledge when all impurities have been removed from it, that which remains to be known is little.

The nature of the pure mind is *sattva*, and the nature of *sattva* is knowledge and illumination. When covered by *tamas*, the mind is obscured; when affected by *rajas*, it is stimulated. When all traces of *rajas* and *tamas* have been removed, there is nothing impeding the unlimited knowledge inherent in *sattva* from knowing everything. The *citta*, we recall, is all-pervading in the Yoga school, and thus its inherent ability to know, when not obstructed, is likewise all-pervading. It is *ahaṅkāra*, ego, Hariharānanda reminds us (the *asmitā* of II.6) that causes the potential all-pervading nature of the mind to restrict itself to the limited body and its organs. When ego is removed, the mind regains its all-expansive potential. Limited things, like pots, are known when they are pervaded by the mind channeled through the instruments (limitations) of the senses. By extension, when the mind bypasses its identification with the senses and recovers its all-pervasive nature, it can pervade and thereby know everything unlimitedly. Just as after the rainy season, says Vācaspati Miśra, the sun, no longer obscured by monsoon clouds, shines everywhere with intense light, so does knowledge pervade all things after the influences of *rajas* and *tamas* have been eradicated from the mind. That which remains to be known is as irrelevant as a firefly in the sky, says Śaṅkara.[34]

ततः कृतार्थानां परिणामक्रमपरिसमाप्तिर्गुणानाम् ।। ३२ ।।

IV.32 tataḥ kṛtārthānāṁ pariṇāma-krama-parisamāptir guṇānām

tataḥ, from that; *kṛta*, accomplished; *arthānām*, goal; *pariṇāma*, mutation, transformation; *krama*, sequence; *parisamāptiḥ*, cessation; *guṇānām*, of the *guṇas*

As a result, there is a cessation of the ongoing permutations of the *guṇas*, their purpose now fulfilled.

The *guṇas* have now fulfilled their purpose, says Vyāsa, which, as we know, is to provide either material experience or liberation (II.18). They have become redundant and do not care to stay even for a moment. The ongoing permutations, *pariṇāma-krama*, of the *guṇas* refer to the change inherent in *prākṛtic* existence, which is caused by the constant maneuverings and interactions of the *guṇas* with each other. Change is for the purpose of experience. With the *yogī*'s complete detachment from any sort of experience, even those of the *siddhis*, the *guṇas* no longer have any impetus to provide a never-ending variety of stimulation: "As the dancer ceases from the dance after she has been seen by the audience, so *prakṛti* ceases after having revealed her nature to the *puruṣa; prakṛti* says I have been seen and never again comes before the sight of *puruṣa*" (*Sāṅkhya Kārikā* LIX–LXI).

क्षणप्रतियोगी परिणामापरान्तनिर्ग्राह्यः क्रमः ।। ३३ ।।

IV.33 kṣaṇa-pratiyogī pariṇāmāparānta-nirgrāhyaḥ kramaḥ

kṣaṇa, moment, instant; *pratiyogī*, counterpart, correlative, partnership, dependent existence; *pariṇāma*, change, mutation; *aparānta*, utmost limit; *nirgrāhyaḥ*, is perceivable; *kramaḥ*, sequence, progression

The progression [of any object through Time] corresponds to a [series of] moments. It is perceivable at the final [moment] of change.

The *guṇas* are always in flux, and thus material reality is a flow that can be considered a series of moments, *kṣaṇa*. These moments are related together in a *krama*, progression or sequence, which is what Patañjali intends by a progression corresponding to a series of moments, *kṣaṇa-pratiyogī*. The ongoing existence of an object through Time, then, is actually the continuum of a series of imperceptible moments in the life span of the object, as noted in III.52. Time, in Yoga, is nothing other than a series of moments, which is nothing other than the movement of atoms (and subatomic particles). More precisely, the subatomic (*aṇu*) composition of all objects is constantly in motion at every moment, and a moment, *kṣaṇa*, is the period of time it takes an *aṇu* to move to the space immediately adjacent to it. Hence, saying that an object is moving through Time is to say its subatomic composition is in constant motion.[35] On this point, to be sure, the Yoga school agrees with the *kṣanika-vāda* Buddhists: Nothing is static but changes every *kṣaṇa*, minute.

Therefore, when we say a cloth has become old, in reality we are referring to a certain cutoff point in this sequential flux, which Patañjali here refers to as the final moment of change, *pariṇāma-aparānta*, which occurs at the very end of a series of changes. At the moment the cloth is just about to disintegrate, the ongoing sequence of ever-changing moments becomes unavoidably visible such that it becomes clear to all that the cloth is old. But we can infer that preceding stages of change in the object's progression from new to old existed, says Vācaspati Miśra: the stage of slightest change, very slight change, noticeable change, more noticeable change, and unavoidably noticeable change. The cloth does not suddenly become old all at once at the end, says Vyāsa. It constantly undergoes change from its very inception. Thus material reality is never static but always in motion.

Does this mean there is nothing permanent? asks the rhetorical objector,[36] again alluding to the Buddhist view. Specific transformations of *prakṛti* such as the particular sequence of the *guṇas* underpinning the cloth may be impermanent, but the overall and ongoing movement and sequencing of the *guṇas* in general is permanent.[37] Thus *prakṛti* manifest as a pot is impermanent, but *prakṛti* herself, the ultimate ingredient underpinning the pot, is permanent. It is here that Yoga metaphysics departs from Buddhism, which does not recognize any ultimate substratum to reality. There are actually two types of permanence, says Vyāsa, the permanence of change in general, that is, the permanence underpinning the constantly changing *guṇas*, and the permanence of the unchangeable, *puruṣa*. These are both permanent because their essential nature is never destroyed. This essential permanent nature is obvious in terms of all that has been said throughout the text about *puruṣa*, but the same applies to *prakṛti*. *Prakṛti* is constantly in flux because of the agitation and nonstop interactive dynamic of the *guṇas*, and this causes the effects of *prakṛti*, such as pots, to be temporary, but the essential underlying nature of *prakṛti* herself is eternal and constant. Or in other words, says Vijñānabhikṣu, *prakṛti*'s essential causal nature does not become past as does the nature of all *prākṛtic* effects such as pots. Therefore, Vyāsa noted that there are two types of permanency: one in which mutations in the form of effects such as pots keep changing but the underlying essence remains permanent, which is *prakṛti*, and one in which there are no mutations to begin with, simply pure unchanging essence, which is *puruṣa*. The latter is devoid of the six kinds of changes associated with all living beings: birth, endurance, change, growth, decline, and destruction.

The commentators then consider an opponent who might question whether or not there is an end to these constant permutations of the *guṇas*. If one states that there is not, then this would seem to contradict the previous *sūtra*, which indicates that there is an end to these permutations. If one takes the alternative and states that there is an end, one would seem to be contradicting Vyāsa's commentary to this *sūtra*, which states that there is no end to them. Vyāsa accordingly points out that there are some questions that depend on context and cannot be answered categorically. Some questions, such as whether all that is born will die, have categorical replies irrespective of context. But some questions require contextualization. "Is humankind the superior species?" requires a nuanced response: Humankind may be superior to animals but inferior to the gods and sages. Likewise, "Is the sequence of births and deaths eternal?" has no universal answers but requires nuance: It has an end for those in whom discriminate awareness has dawned but not for others. Along the same lines, the permutations of the *guṇas* have an end for the liberated *yogī* but no end for those bound in *saṁsāra*. This answer, says Vācaspati Miśra, addresses the hypothetical notion (that invariably pops up) that if everyone were to get liberated, wouldn't *prakṛti* and her *guṇas* then cease to mutate and transform, having no further role to play? Living beings are endless, he states, because they are countless. And posing certain questions, adds Vijñānabhikṣu, is to engage in fruitless inferential logic and, ultimately, a waste of time.

पुरुषार्थशून्यानां गुणानां प्रतिप्रसवः कैवल्यं
स्वरूपप्रतिष्ठा वा चितिशक्तिरिति ।। ३४ ।।

IV.34 puruṣārtha-śūnyānāṁ guṇānāṁ pratiprasavaḥ kaivalyaṁ svarūpa-pratiṣṭhā vā citi-śaktir iti

Puruṣa, of the soul; *artha*, goal; *śūnyānām*, devoid of; *guṇānām*, of the *guṇas*; *pratiprasavaḥ*, return to the original state; *kaivalyam*, aloneness, liberation; *svarūpa*, essential nature; *pratiṣṭhā*, situated; *vā*, or; *citi-śaktiḥ*, the power of consciousness; *iti*, thus

Ultimate liberation is when the *guṇas*, devoid of any purpose for the *puruṣa*, return to their original [latent] state; in other words, when the power of consciousness is situated in its own essential nature.

Kaivalya literally means the state of *kevala*, or aloneness, onlyness, one's-own-ness, not-connected-with-anything-else-ness. In other words, *puruṣa*'s awareness is now absorbed exclusively in its own nature as *puruṣa* and completely uncoupled from even the highest and finest states of pure *citta* or *buddhi*. In Vyāsa's terms, the *guṇas* have accomplished their function of providing experience or liberation—at this stage, the latter—and are now devoid of any function. *Puruṣa* now lives in total isolation, its power of consciousness no longer aware of anything else except itself, unconnected with the *citta* and the world of *prakṛti* it had mediated. The red rose has been removed from the environs of the crystal, says Vijñānabhikṣu, which regains its original pure hue, devoid of the red reflection of the rose. Actually, *puruṣa* had never been bound; Vijñānabhikṣu quotes the *Sāṅkhya Kārikā*: "Certainly, therefore, no [*puruṣa*] is bound, or liberated, nor does it migrate; it is *prakṛti* abiding in manifold forms that is bound, migrates, and is liberated" (LXII).[38]

The *yogī*'s physical body and cognitive apparatus can now return to the elements through reverse involution, the *pratiprasava* mentioned in this *sūtra* (and in I.10). The *saṁskāras*, etc., dissolve into the mind, the mind into the ego, the ego into the *mahat* (*buddhi*), and the latter into *prakṛti*. The *yogī*'s sojourn in *saṁsāra* is now officially and totally over. What exactly the eternal experience of final liberation consists of is not a topic that Patañjali has chosen to attempt to discuss. Nor does he address the relationship between the liberated *puruṣa* and *Īśvara*. The task he set for himself was to lay out the path by which the bound *puruṣa* can free itself from bondage. Obviously the actual experience of liberation is by definition a state beyond thought and words as repeated so eloquently in the Upaniṣads.

There are, of course, very elaborate and expansive theologies offering an analytic systematization of the experience in liberation, especially among the *Īśvara*-centered theistic schools of thought evidenced in the Purāṇas such as the Vaiṣṇava or Bhāgavata traditions. Such theologies describe in some detail the possible eternal interactions between *Īśvara* and the liberated *puruṣas* in various *Brahman* realms beyond the domain of *prakṛti*. For such theologies, liberation as outlined by Patañjali is just the first step: Once liberated from *prakṛti* and its effects and having gained awareness of its true identity, the *puruṣa* is eligible to enter into a divine relationship with God, *Īśvara*. The Śaivite and Śakta traditions, too, have produced sophisticated elaborations on the experience of liberation from within the contours of their particular clusters of theologies. Such *bhakti*, devotional, movements see themselves as picking up where Patañjali left off. As we have repeatedly stressed, while one must be careful not to project alien theologies onto the author of the *Yoga Sūtras*, a wide variety of these devotional currents had certainly swept across the Indian subcontinent by Patañjali's time, and it is most probable that he would have been affiliated with a devotional sect.[39]

But Patañjali himself chose to be tantalizingly elusive about *Īśvara* and completely silent about the actual experience of liberation. He focused his enterprise on the area of knowledge concerned with the methods for bringing the *yogī* to the point of liberation, rather than on elaborating on this state, or on the nature of *Īśvara* and the relationship between this being and the liberated *puruṣa*, as some of his predecessors, contemporaries, and successors set out to do. One wonders whether this was because *Īśvara* theologies were already adequately accounted for, or at the very least, developing firm roots on the religious landscape of his day, and he felt the need for a more specific and circumscribed treatise on a less ambitious topic. As such, with *puruṣa* embarking in this *sūtra* on an eternal experience of pure self-awareness in a dimension completely uncoupled from *prakṛti* and her permutations, Patañjali's task is now complete.

इति पतञ्जलिविरचिते योगसूत्रे चतुर्थः कैवल्यपादः ।

iti Patañjali-viracite yoga-sūtre caturthaḥ kaivalya-pādaḥ

Thus ends the fourth chapter on *samādhi* in the *Yoga Sūtras* composed by Patañjali.

CHAPTER SUMMARY

The chapter begins by listing other means of attaining the *siddhis* [1]. This is followed by some comments on *prakṛti*'s relationship with her effects [2–3] and by the phenomenon of the creation of multiple minds by the *yogi* [4–5]. A more advanced discussion of *karma* [6–7], *saṁskāras* [8–11], and Time and the *guṇas* [12–14] then ensues. The next section critiques Buddhist idealist notions of the mind [15–21], followed by a discussion on the *yoga* view of the relationship between mind and consciousness [22–26], and of distractions to meditation [27–28]. The chapter ends with *dharma-megha* and its effects [29–33], and then ultimate liberation [34].

CONCLUDING REFLECTIONS

It has been a wonderful, inspiring, and privileged journey engaging so intensely with the *Yoga Sūtras* of Patañjali. It is clear to me that the text is destined to remain the primary manual for meditative practice for the *ātman*-based traditions, but now not just in India, as it has been for almost two millennia, but the world over. Moreover, in addition to its primary function as a spiritual manual containing clear and precise information about how to actually and factually directly experience the human soul in this life, the *citta/puruṣa* dualism of the text has much to offer modern discussions on the philosophy of mind and consciousness, and the *saṁskāra/kleśa* model has enormous contributions to make to contemporary approaches to therapy and psychoanalysis.

A number of issues nonetheless repeatedly presented themselves in the course of this engagement with the Yoga *Sūtras*. I, as others, found myself lamenting the lack of more extensive access to Patañjali's views on topics of great importance that are only touched upon in a peripheral fashion in the text. That these questions present themselves stem from a number of causes: the extreme brevity of the *sūtras*, which sometimes merely refer to or touch upon aspects that remain undeveloped in their specifics; Patañjali's undeviating focus on one very specific goal—the attainment of *citta-vṛtti-nirodha*—with little attention directed to unpacking anything not directly related to this end; and the likely imposition of certain Sāṅkhya elements on Patañjali by the commentators that are not explicit in the *sūtras* themselves. I here briefly touch upon four such areas: *kartṛtva*, agency or free will; the nature of the Sāṅkhya evolutes as both cosmic and individual components of *prakṛti*; the nature of *kaivalya*, liberation; and the role of *Īśvara*.

PURUṢA AND FREE WILL

Although Patañjali himself does not explicitly deny agency (free will) to the *puruṣa*, the Yoga system tends to be associated with the Sāṅkhya view that agency is a function of *buddhi*, not of *puruṣa*. Thus, the *Sāṅkhyā Kārikās* specifically locates agency, *kartṛtva*, in the *guṇas* and not in *puruṣa* (XX); relegates *adhyavasāya*, judgment, as the prime characteristic of *buddhi*, not *puruṣa*; and ascribes the choice of performing *dharma* or *adharma*, right or wrong, as states (*bhavas*) of *buddhi* (XXIII). Despite centuries of criticism by other schools on this point, the later *Sāṅkhya Sūtras* still promote this position: "It is the ego (*ahaṅkāra*) which is the agent, not the *puruṣa*" (VI.54). It is this Sāṅkhya view that Vācaspati Miśra, for example, approvingly imports into his commentary: "Although the self is certainly self-illuminating, it does not perform any act, and so in the absence of acts, it is not an agent."[1]

However, it must be noted that Patañjali neither explicitly endorses this view nor denies free will to *puruṣa*. The question must then be raised whether the denial of agency to *puruṣa* is a Sāṅkhya feature unwarrantedly foisted upon the *Yoga Sūtras*. We must, I suggest, consider that Patañjali may not have subscribed to the Sāṅkhya view, given the prescriptive and effort-centered nature of the system he has outlined in his *sūtras*. But first, let us consider why ascribing free will to *buddhi* rather than to *puruṣa* is problematic.

If agency does not reside in consciousness, but in the intellect, then, in essence, it is the *buddhi* that is attaining liberation, not the *ātman*, as the *Sāṅkhya Kārikās* are quite happy to pronounce: "Actually, no one is bound, no one liberated, no one transmigrates in *saṁsāra*; it is actually *prakṛti* in her various forms who is bound, transmigrates and is liberated" (LXII). It is ultimately *buddhi* that is subject to ignorance, *buddhi* that gains discrimination and insight, and *buddhi* that exerts the will to attain liberation. The entire *yoga* process is undertaken by *buddhi*—the various degrees of slight, mediocre, and ardent practice of I.22 are the product of *buddhi*'s application and enterprise, not *puruṣa*'s. *Puruṣa* eternally remains the detached witness. One must thus accept a *puruṣa* who has no agency or responsibility for its (apparent) condition. The problem with this perspective, of course, is explaining how there can be any impetus from the part of unconscious matter toward liberation (or toward any type of action, for that matter). Even if this could take place, why should the *puruṣa* be connected with decisions made not by itself but by some completely extraneous entity? And why would the *puruṣa* be implicated in the first place?

From the Sāṅkhya perspective, that one *puruṣa* even apparently attains liberation and another does not is an occurrence taking place because of *saṁskāras* manifesting in the *buddhi*: *sāttvic saṁskāras* of discrimination are activated in a *citta* because of previous conducive *saṁskāras*, which are caused by previous *saṁskāras* in turn, in a beginningless series. Why this particular concatenation of *saṁskāras* should follow this trajectory for one *puruṣa* rather than another is a question that is avoided by the tradition by positing that embodiment—albeit with a potential end—is without beginning. Granted, that the cause of initial embodiment is sidestepped in this way by all Indic soteriological systems; the problem of why one *puruṣa* endeavors (or appears to endeavor) for liberation and another does not is particularly acute when free will and agency are denied to the *puruṣa* in the first place.

This stark feature of the system has attracted the criticism of not just modern scholars of the text but traditional scholars from other schools in ancient India. Overall, other than certain strains of Sāṅkhya, the galaxy of Hindu and Jain traditions have recognized agency as a quality of the *puruṣa*. And strains of Sāṅkhya itself, from the period prior to the emergence of the philosophical traditions, such as those represented in the *Maitrī Upaniṣad* (III.3), as well as the *Mahabhārata* (XII.303.8), explicitly accept the self as the agent (*kartṛ*).[2] But by the time the *Vedānta Sūtras* had been compiled, the need was felt to demarcate the Vedānta position in contradistinction to at least certain other strains of Sāṅkhya that had become mainstream.

The *Vedānta Sūtras*, which are explicit about the agency of *puruṣa*, dedicate nine verses to the topic (II.3.33–39; also IV.4.8).[3] The first of the verses points out that the injunctions of scripture would be pointless if *puruṣa* were not a moral agent capable of either following them or rejecting them, and the latter commentators have much to say here. Scripture is not directed at something insentient, says Madhva, but at a conscious being.[4] And anyway, if *prakṛti* were the moral agent, says the Vedānta commentator Rāmāṇuja, then, there being one *prakṛti* common to all, all *puruṣas* should have the same experience—so how would one account for the diversity of experience? The *Sūtrakṛtāṅga*, an early text of the Jain tradition raises the same objection: "They [the adherents of the Sāṅkhya philosophy] boldly proclaim: 'When a man acts or causes another to act, it is not his soul (*ātman*) which acts or causes to act': how can those who hold such opinions explain (the variety of existence) in the world?" (I.1.1.13–14).[5]

The Nyāya, Vaiśeṣika, and Mīmāṁsā traditions all accept will as a quality of the *ātman*,[6] and later scholastics, especially the Nyāya school, take Sāṅkhya to task here. The eleventh-century logician Udayana, in his *Nyāyakusumāñjali* (part I), argues that if will resided in *buddhi*, then either there would always be *saṁsāra* or there would always be *mokṣa*. He builds up his argument by noting that either *buddhi* is eternal or it is not eternal. If it is eternal, there would never be any liberation; *puruṣa* would be eternally bonded with *buddhi*. If, on the other hand, as an evolute of *prakṛti*, *buddhi* is not-eternal, then, prior to coming into being, what would cause it to attach itself to the ever-free, autonomous *puruṣa*? How can *buddhi* come to be associated with the pure *puruṣa*, if the latter is simply a pure witness? Without some impulse or act of will from its side, *puruṣa* could never be bound by *buddhi* but would remain ever free. Hence, it would be in either a state of perpetual *saṁsāra* or one of perpetual *mokṣa*. It is thus philosophically indefensible from within the contours of Sāṅkhya metaphysics to speak of a soul in *saṁsāra* striving for release.

Almost all modern scholars of the text have grappled with this issue, either alighting on this anomaly to critique the system by, for example, arguing for some unavoidable corollary consequence to which the denial of agency leads its proponents, or suggesting, as I have done, that Patañjali himself cannot be assumed to have denied some form of agency in *puruṣa*. Thus Phillips (1985) argues that if free will is situated not in *puruṣa* but in *buddhi*, then no one who had ever attained *kaivalya* by disconnecting from *buddhi* would find any will in the pure *puruṣa* to return and inform others about it. No one could report back about the experience, there being no will to do so in the state of pure consciousness. Therefore, the *Yoga Sūtras* are the product of scholastics, not enlightened *yogīs*. On the other hand, Koelman (1970), in his superb and highly appreciative analysis of Yoga philosophy, strives to resolve the dilemma by separating will as essential freedom, which he assigns to the pure *puruṣa*, and the actual function of choice, which he relegates to the *prākṛtic* organism: "The willing, however, is not necessarily bound up with choosing. Consequently, the characteristic attribute of will, that is freedom, is not the capacity to choose, but rather self-dependence (*svatantratā*). Liberty of choice arises from the conditioning factor of the Self's *prākṛtic* organism, while perfect freedom is, together with pure Awareness, the very essence of the Self" (257–75). Taking this a step further, one might posit that ultimate free will to seek either pure awareness or *prākṛtic* awareness is a quality of *puruṣa*, but how that will manifests in the specifics of choice is a function of *prakṛti*.

Perhaps the most sophisticated argument that provides positive inferential support to a position open to Patañjali accepting agency in *puruṣa* is to be found in the work of Ranganathan (2007, 2008, forthcoming). The basis of Ranganathan's argument is that terms such as *dharma* must be understood as "key philosophical terms" throughout Indian philosophy. Despite an apparent diversity in its semantic range, he argues that *dharma* does in fact have a shared meaning in all schools and one that touches upon morality in one way or another.[7] In his translation of the *Yoga Sūtras*, Ranganathan argues that scholars have failed to recognize the very different position the *Sāṅkhya Kārikā* and the *Yoga Sūtras* have taken on the role of *dharma*, despite the term's consistent meaning for both schools and despite the different emphasis given to morality in general in both texts.

In Sāṅkhya, *dharma* is a function of *buddhi*, with *puruṣa* a mere passive witness. In Yoga, *dharma* takes on a more active and prescriptive role. The failure to recognize the distinction between the passive orientation of Sāṅkhya and the far more active and prescriptive flavor of Yoga has resulted in some of the traditional commentators foisting the Sāṅkhya position of *puruṣa*'s lack of agency onto the *Yoga Sūtras* without warrant. His overall thesis is that once we recognize that the *Yoga Sūtras* and texts such as the *Sāṅkhya Kārikā* have very different things to say about *dharma*, then we can no longer accept that the

Yoga Sūtras hold that *puruṣas* are not agents. Thus, given the fact that there is no explicit rejection of agency anywhere in the text, we need to interpret Patañjali as advancing the position that *puruṣa* is an active agent in its situation:

> In step with this practical and ethical emphasis is [Patanjali's] correlative affirmation that persons (*puruṣa*-s) are not only transcendent beings of consciousness and knowledge, but volitional beings. Indeed, he characterizes *puruṣa*-s as having the characteristic of *cetana* (*Yoga Sūtra* I.29), which in Sanskrit not only denotes consciousness and knowledge, but also the will. Patañjali emphasizes that persons are in control (they are the "Master of the character of the mind" (*Yoga Sūtra* IV.18), that the will is what accounts for the troubled, bound state of the individual (*Yoga Sūtra* IV.9–10), and that this state provides persons with the opportunity to be the cause of their own liberation (*Yoga Sūtra* II.23). Yet popular and scholarly accounts of the *Yoga Sūtra*, blurred with the value theory of Sāṅkhya and Advaita Vedānta, marginalize both the ethical and empowering aspects of Yoga theory (2008, 22).

We concur with this overall position. For there to be any coherence to the law of *karma*, the condition of the living beings in *saṁsāra*, and the decision to take up the path of *yoga* and follow the *yamas* and *niyamas* of II.30–45; or the friendship, compassion, joy, and equanimity prescribed in I.33; or essentially any of the prescriptions of the *Yoga Sūtras*; one must assign free will to the *puruṣa* as the ultimate agent of its condition.

THE TATTVAS: COSMOLOGICAL OR INDIVIDUAL?

Another problem that remains unclarified in the Sāṅkhya and Yoga traditions, and has long vexed scholars, is whether the *tattvas*, or evolutes from *prakṛti*, are to be considered cosmological or psychological. In other words, there is only one source (*mūla*)—*prakṛti*—but how many *buddhis* and *ahaṅkāras* are there? Does each individual have its own *buddhi* and *ahaṅkāra*, or is there one cosmological *buddhi* and *ahaṅkāra* common to all? It seems clear to me from the various normative sources on Sāṅkhya touched upon in the introduction that *buddhi* and *ahaṅkāra* as well as the *tanmātras* and *mahabhūtas* are clearly both cosmic and individual.[8] We have argued in III.16 that the ability to merge the individual *buddhi* into the cosmic *buddhi* is essential to an understanding of the mechanics of the *siddhis* in Sāṅkhya metaphysics—in other words, to understanding how the *yogī* can effect gross matter by the power of *buddhi*. And the ten *karmendriyas* and *jñānendriyas* of Sāṅkhya would appear to be individual rather than cosmic, even as these do not appear in other Sāṅkhya lists.[9]

But with all the evolutes, the question nonetheless remains: How does the cosmic *buddhi* and *ahaṅkāra*, and so on, become fragmented into the plurality of individual ones? How does *prakṛti* "fill in" the forms of nature with its evolutes (IV.2)? I find myself envisioning this process like that of someone poking his fingers into a blown-up balloon without popping it. The fingers are individually tightly covered with the balloon rubber, yet this rubber remains connected with the greater totality of rubber of the rest of the balloon. Similarly, when the *puruṣas* are injected into *prakṛti*, they are enveloped in individualized layers of *prakṛti* such as *buddhi*, and so on, yet these layers remain somehow potentially connected to the cosmic *buddhi*.

While the specifics of such questions remain puzzling, for the purposes of Yoga, it seems safe to assume that these types of cosmological issues were of no concern to Patañjali, hence they remain undeveloped.[10] Just as his incomplete treatment of *Īśvara* shows interest primarily only in *Īśvara*'s relationship with the goal of *citta-vṛtti-nirodha*, so Patañjali's interest in the *tattvas* is individual and psychological rather than cosmological in any sort of a systematic manner. As Larson notes: "Since the classical Sāṅkhya is concerned only with the isolation of pure consciousness or *puruṣa*, the world is irrelevant apart from its function as a means to salvation. In other words, the classical Sāṅkhya is not concerned with the world in itself except in so far as it is instrumental in the discrimination of the isolated or pure *puruṣa*" (1979, 203).

ENLIGHTENED ACTION AND THE NATURE OF *KAIVALYA*

While texts such as the *Gītā* clearly promote action as better than renunciation and inaction (III.4–8; XII.12), scholarship on the *Yoga Sūtras*—primarily modern rather than traditional—has tended to view full *kaivalya* as incompatible with action in the world and occurring only after the demise of the physical body. Most scholars have read the text as suggesting that the complete eradication of primordial *avidyā* ignorance can only result in the total breakdown of biological and psychological embodied existence. Any type of action, after all, can occur only by means of the utilization of the false self, that is, the non-self of mind and body, and thus *puruṣa*'s complete immersion of awareness in its own true self requires the complete withdrawal of its awareness from the external coverings of the body and mind. The *yogī* in the *kaivalya* state thus becomes dysfunctional. The instant awareness externalizes and becomes aware of "other," it loses awareness of the "self," that is, *puruṣa* (I.3–4). Verses such as II.22, II.25, and IV.34 are fairly explicit that *prakṛti* disappears from the purview of *puruṣa* when it attains *kaivalya*, the very meaning of which is precisely "aloneness." Feuerstein ably represents this perspective:

> As we have seen, Vyāsa promoted the view that deliverance is possible even when still alive. But this standpoint is not sanctioned by the *Yoga-Sūtra* . . . As long as the self has not cut all connections with *prakṛti*, it cannot be said to stand in its true form (*sva-rūpa*). What philosopher yogins like . . . Śaṅkara taught as *jīvan-mukti* can, to the follower of classical Yoga, only mean close proximity to final emancipation. For him, as for Rāmānuja, release follows upon death, when the body has fallen off (*vi-deha*), and whenever a liberated person takes on a body again, either composed of gross or subtle matter, he is no longer residing in freedom, but is again subject to the laws governing the machinery of the universe. Even when residing in the highest and purest realms of nature, he remains subject to a thin veil of illusion (*māyā*), since *prakṛti* is *avidyā* or nescience. (Feuerstein 1974, 47)

In this perspective, as long as the *puruṣa* remains embodied, it can necessarily do so only by associating with illusion. Consequently, Yoga has generally been perceived as a world-renouncing tradition that does not reconcile itself with work in the world, or "enlightened action."

The most vociferous opponent of this understanding of *kaivalya*, has been Whicher:

> Yoga allows for an enlightened, participatory perspective that can embody a rich sense of *dharma* suggesting a responsiveness to life that no longer snares the yogin morally or epistemologically . . . At this high level realization in Yoga, action does not end but becomes purified of afflicted impulses [*kleśas*] . . . Nonafflicted [*akliṣṭa*] action remains for the liberated yogin . . . Yoga extends the meaning of purification and illumination of human identity to incorporate an enlightened mode of activity as well as knowledge . . . We need not conclude that liberative knowledge and virtuous activity are incompatible with one another, nor need we see detachment as an abandonment of the world and the human relational sphere. (Whicher 1999, 794–95)

While Whicher has been criticized for suggesting that Yoga as presented by Patañjali specifically means enlightened engagement in the world,[11] there is merit in his insistence that the two are not incompatible. Although the emphasis on enlightened action in the world is clearly much more prominent in the *Gītā* than in Patañjali, it is not incompatible with the *Yoga Sūtras*. Patañjali's teachings seem clearly geared toward promoting a compassionate (I.33), moral, and ethical (II.29ff), that is, a highly sāttvic social, lifestyle. Indeed, this is reflected right at the beginning of the text by the category of *akliṣṭa-vṛttis*, that is, *vṛttis* not subject to ignorance and the other *kleśas*. This can only point to an enlightened mode of acting in the world.

Now, one cannot deny that in the actual state of *nirbīja-samādhi*, the *yogī* is completely dysfunctional; he or she has, after all, withdrawn consciousness from all sensual activities, *pratyāhara* (II.54–55), and completely stilled all *vṛttis* whatsoever, such that the entire psychophysical organism is absolutely closed down. And the Purāṇas and epics are full of stories of *yogīs* who simply check out, so to speak, discarding their bodies and *cittas* by their *yogic* prowess and entering permanently into the liberated state at will.[12] But it seems to me that both these perspectives can be harmonized into the life of the *jīvanmukta*. If we accept agency in *puruṣa*, as we have done, there is nothing preventing the *yogī* from depositing a *saṁskāra* into the *citta* prior to entering the state of *nirbīja-samādhi* to activate and pull consciousness back into the *prākṛtic* state at a certain point—a sort of *saṁskāric* alarm clock. Of course, the only motive to do this would be out of compassion for those still stranded in the cycle of birth and death who have sought (or might seek) shelter and guidance from the *yogī* as *guru*—a notion akin to that richly developed in the Bodhisattva tradition of Mahāyāna Buddhism. But there is nothing in Patañjali that speaks against the possibility that certain *puruṣas* can will to remain embodied in *prakṛti*, utilizing the *akliṣṭa-vṛttis* of I.5, for the purpose of aiding other living beings. This state of *jīvanmukta* is certainly accepted by the commentators.

Again, the Gītā gives more specific instruction as to precisely what action in the world might look like (e.g., II.47ff and throughout), but I see the *Yoga Sūtras* as an indispensable manual for constructing a profound understanding of mind and of the meditational process that can be incorporated very harmoniously with the *Gītā*'s more developed notion of social duty (as its theism can be incorporated into the *Gītā*'s far more developed theology of the role devotion to *Īśvara* plays in all this as will be discussed below).

This leads to a larger discussion on the nature of *kaivalya*. If we are to use human reason to engage with the *sūtras* (which, needless to say, runs counter to the entire thrust of the text, which is to transcend reason!), numerous questions pertaining to the liberated state present themselves. First of all, if *puruṣa*'s pure awareness is all-pervading, as Yoga holds it to be, and *prakṛti*, too, is all-pervading, then how can *puruṣa* ever be unaware of *prakṛti*? How can *puruṣa* be unaware of another entity if *puruṣa*'s all-pervasive awareness is infinitely and eternally coextensive with this other all-pervading entity? How can a light not illuminate objects in a room if it pervades the room? Can *puruṣa* somehow "ignore" this all-pervading fellow entity, *prakṛti*, with which it shares infinity and eternity, and yet be all-pervasively aware?

Is enlightenment *puruṣa* somehow ignoring infinite and all-pervading *prakṛti* and being simply aware in a content-less fashion—an exact opposite of embodied existence where *puruṣa* is "ignoring" its own infinite and all-pervading nature and focusing awareness on *prakṛti*? (Some have gone so far as to attempt to resolve this dilemma by imposing an *advaita Vedānta* position on the text, which, as discussed previously, involves holding that *prakṛti* herself is an illusion, superimposed by ignorance, and thus, when *avidyā* is dispelled, so is the very existence of the manifest world and all *prakṛti*.)[13]

Clearly, rational thinking on this matter is bound by spatial and temporal categories, hence Patañjali does not attempt to lead us into an understanding of *kaivalya*. Such questions require us to either problematize the claims of Yoga or accept the repeated claim of the Yoga/Vedānta/Upaniṣadic traditions that since liberation is, by definition, a state beyond the intellect, then human reason, *ex hypothesi*, cannot fathom its experience. This position is, of course, so frustrating to the philosopher and critical thinker who limits his or her epistemology to rational thought, but so obvious to the mystic, who seeks to transcend it.

ĪŚVARA

Perhaps the most intriguing question raised by the *sūtras* is the relationship of Patañjali's mysterious *Īśvara*, the transcendent "special" *puruṣa*, with other liberated *puruṣas*. According to Koelman, Patañjali's low-key approach to *Īśvara* was diplomatic, the consequence of maneuvering within the contours of certain later Sāṅkhya traditions that had become dominant in his day:

> We believe that *Pātañjala Yoga* is essentially theistic. But as G.R.F. Oberhammer has proved, the *Pātañjala doctrine of the Supreme Lord had to express itself in terms of a philosophical School, the* Sāṅkhya School, which has no room for God. The *Pātañjala* doctrine of the Supreme Lord is the outcome of two different milieus: that of the existential experience of God of the yogis and that of the atheistic conceptualizations of

> *Sāṅkhya* doctrine. Patañjali made use of the existing *Sāṅkhya* doctrine, and was therefore compelled to make use of tenets foreign to *Sāṅkhyan* thinking in a vocabulary proper to that system (1970, 64).

In I.24, we presented our position that *Īśvara*'s identity and role when interacting with the *puruṣas* within the realm of *prakṛti* cannot be extracted from the greater theistic landscape of Patañjali's day; but what of *Īśvara*'s interaction with the liberated *puruṣas* beyond this realm? Obviously such a consideration can only be purely speculative, invoking theologies external to the text, since Patañjali has chosen to focus only on the characteristics of *Īśvara* exclusively relevant to his circumscribed goal of *citta-vṛtti-nirodha*.

Vijñānabhikṣu, situated in a later more theistically saturated milieu, operates under no such constraints. Quoting the *Matsya* and *Kūrma Purāṇas*, he states:

> A *yogī* is said to be of three kinds: the *bhautika*; the *Sāṅkhya*; and, thirdly, the one who has attained the highest level of *yoga*, the *antyāśramī*. In the first category, there is contemplation [of the elements[14]]; in the *Sāṅkhya* [the second] there is contemplation of the imperishable *puruṣa*; and in the third is said to exist the final contemplation of the Supreme *Īśvara*.[15] . . . When you perceive that I [*Īśvara*] am the one pure, eternal, blissful supreme *ātman*, that is called the great theistic *yoga*. All other forms of *yoga* practiced by *yogīs* that are elaborated on in sacred texts are not equal even to the sixteenth part of this *Brahman yoga*. That *yoga*, in which the liberated *yogīs* directly perceive the universal *Īśvara*, is considered to be the highest *yoga* of all *yogas*."[16]

Here we have the Purāṇic notion that the direct realization and experience of *Īśvara* by fully liberated *yogīs* who have already realized the individual *puruṣa* by the classical techniques of Patañjali-type meditation is higher than merely remaining absorbed in the individual self. According to these Vaiṣṇava theistic traditions (there are Śaivite parallels), there is a progressive nature to types of practice. Thus, for example, in the *Gītā*, after asserting that meditation on him is superior to meditation on the *ātman* (XII.1–2), Kṛṣṇa outlines a very definite hierarchy of spiritual practice: The highest possible form of *yoga* is spontaneous and complete absorption on his personal form at all times (XII.8); second to this is regulated meditative practice (*abhyāsa*) to fix the mind on him undeviatingly (XII.9); next best is performing actions directly for his worship and service (XII.10); after which comes performing other types of actions but giving up their fruits to him in worship (XII.11). These devotional practices are followed in the *Gītā*'s hierarchy by three lower forms of *yoga*, which are devoid of devotion: renunciation of the fruit of action, followed by conventional meditation for realizing the individual *ātman* (by fixing the mind on something other that *Īśvara*), followed by knowledge of the *ātman*. There are thus seven levels of spiritual practice in this hierarchy: meditative absorption on *Īśvara* is ranked highest, and conventional meditative absorption on the individual *ātman* is ranked sixth.

What this means, as can be seen from the quote to which Vijñānabhikṣu draws our attention, is that the theistic traditions hold that there are progressive stages even after enlightenment has been attained: *kaivalya*, absorption in *puruṣa*, is preliminary to devotion to the Supreme *puruṣa, Īśvara*, as the *Gītā* clearly indicates (XVIII.54). In the words of the *Bhāgavata Purāṇa*: "Even sages who are freed of the bondage of *saṁsāra* and delight in the *ātman*, practice pure devotion to Viṣṇu; such are the qualities of Hari" (I.7.10). Thus, meditation on *Īśvara* surpasses realization of the *ātman*. The liberated state, consequently, is multidimensional; it is not a universalized or monolithic experience for all *yogīs*. The *Bhāgavata Purāṇa* (along with other Purāṇas and the *Mahābhārata*) even speaks of realms called Vaikuṇṭha, situated in *Brahman* beyond the range of *prakṛti* for the *yogī* who has attained absolute meditative devotion for Viṣṇu, realms wherein the liberated *ātman* eternally interacts with *Īśvara* in love and devotion:

> Vaikuṇṭha [is] the highest realm, where Viṣṇu resides (XII.24.14). This . . . is the highest region (V.12.26); beyond the world of darkness and *saṁsāra* . . . (IV.24.29; X.88.25); the destination of those who have transcended the three *guṇas* . . . even while they are still alive (XI.25.22); and beyond which

> there is no higher place (II.2.18; II.9.9). The peaceful ascetics who reach that place never return (IV.9.29; X.88.25–6). The residents of Vaikuṇṭha do not have material bodies, but have pure forms (VII.1.34). These forms are like that of Viṣṇu (III.15.14ff), also known as Nārāyaṇa. Viṣṇu/Nārāyaṇa resides in Vaikuṇṭha with Śrī, the goddess of fortune, in palaces with crystal walls. (Bryant 2007, xxxvii–viii)[17]

In other words, realizing the individual *puruṣa* is only the first step on the spiritual journey: The higher goal is to then devote oneself to *Īśvara* and, ultimately, attain to his eternal *Brahman* abode, the kingdom of God.

But, even as such theologies had pervaded the theistic landscape of Patañjali's time, all this is taking us far beyond where Patañjali himself has chosen to leave us in the *Yoga Sūtras*. We can only resort to injecting the much more developed theistic theologies developing in his day, such as those that came to be expressed in the *Bhāgavata Purāṇa* (translated by the author[18]), into the text if we wish to speculate on how Patañjali himself might have envisioned the liberated state, and what any connection therein might be between the individual *puruṣa* and *Īśvara*, or where any such relationship might take place. Patañjali has not attempted to use rational conceptual thought to express states beyond reason and conceptualization. He has chosen not to take us into the other side—he has directed his efforts to guiding us how to get there. The task he set for himself was clearly defined in verse I.2 right at the outset of his project, *citta-vṛtti-nirodha*, and he has kept his eye on that ball with remarkably singular focus. On this score, at the very least, his contribution to understanding the nature of mind and of consciousness, and his presentation of a very clear and experience-based path of liberating the individual *puruṣa* self from the cycle of *saṁsāra*, transcends cultural or religious boundaries, and seems destined to remain a living and perennially relevant classic in the spiritual archives of humanity.

CHAPTER SUMMARIES

CHAPTER I: MEDITATIVE ABSORPTION

The chapter begins by introducing and defining *yoga* [1–2]. This is followed by a discussion of the two possible options for awareness [3–4], a description of the *vṛttis* [5–11], and how to control the *vṛttis* by practice and dispassion [12–16]. Then comes the division of *samādhi* into *samprajñāta* and *asamprajñāta* [17–18] and how to attain these [20–22], after the discussion of other states that might resemble it [19]. *Īśvara* is then introduced as the easy method of attaining *samādhi* [23], along with his nature [24–26] and the chanting of his name [27–29]. The chapter describes the distractions of the mind and their accompanying effects [30–31] and prescribes meditation on any object to combat them, with various examples presented [32–40]. *Samāpatti* is introduced with its varieties [41–45] and their fruits [46–48] and object [49]. The chapter concludes with a discussion of *samprajñāta-samādhi* preceding the final stage of *asamprajñāta* [50–51].

CHAPTER II: PRACTICE

The chapter begins with an introduction of *kriyā-yoga* [1], its effects [2], and a discussion of the *kleśas*, which it removes [3–11]. *Karma* and its consequences are outlined [12–14] and the principle of suffering established [15–16]. This is followed by the characteristics of the seer and the seen [17–22], the conjunction between them [23–24], and the definition of liberation [25–27]. Next, the eight limbs of *yoga* are introduced as the means to attain liberation [28–29], and the remainder of the chapter is dedicated to these: the *yamas* and their universality [30–31], the *niyamas* [32], the means to counter tendencies contrary to the *yamas* amd *niyamas* [33–34] and the side benefits accruing from observing them [35–45]. Next, *āsana*, the third limb, is presented [46–48], followed by *prāṇāyāma*, the fourth limb [49–53], and *pratyāhāra*, the fifth [54–55].

CHAPTER III: MYSTIC POWERS

The chapter begins by concluding the definitions of the last three limbs of *yoga* [1–3], which are distinguished from the others by constituting *saṁyama* [4–6] and being internal limbs [7–8]. A discussion of the state of *nirodha* ensues [9–12], followed by the metaphysics of the relationship between substratum and characteristic [13–15]. The remainder of the chapter is then dedicated to an extensive discussion of various mystic powers accrued from the performance of *saṁyama* on a variety of things [16–48], culminating in omniscience followed by ultimate *kaivalya* liberation [49–55].

CHAPTER IV: ABSOLUTE INDEPENDENCE

The chapter begins by listing other means of attaining the *siddhis* [1]. This is followed by some comments on *prakṛti*'s relationship with her effects [2–3] and by the phenomenon of the creation of multiple minds by the *yogī* [4–5]. A more advanced discussion of *karma* [6–7], *saṁskāras* [8–11], and Time and the *guṇas* [12–14] then ensues. The next section critiques Buddhist idealist notions of the mind [15–21], followed by a discussion on the *yoga* view of the relationship between mind and consciousness [22–26], and of distractions to meditation [27–28]. The chapter ends with *dharma-megha* and its effects [29–33], and then ultimate liberation [34].

APPENDIX

Devanāgarī, Transliteration, and Translation of *Sūtras*

CHAPTER I: MEDITATIVE ABSORPTION

प्रथमः समाधिपादः ।
prathamaḥ samādhi-pādaḥ

अथ योगानुशासनम् ॥१॥
I.1 atha yogānuśāsanam
Now, the teachings of *yoga* [are presented].

योगश्चित्तवृत्तिनिरोधः ॥२॥
I.2 yogaś citta-vṛtti-nirodha
Yoga is the stilling of the changing states of the mind.

तदा द्रष्टुः स्वरूपेऽवस्थानम ॥३॥
I.3 tadā draṣṭuḥ svarūpe 'vasthānam
When that is accomplished, the seer abides in its own true nature.

वृत्तिसारूप्यम इतरत्र ॥४॥
I.4 vṛtti-sārūpyam itaratra
Otherwise, at other times, [the seer] is absorbed in the changing states [of the mind].

वृत्तयः पञ्चतय्यः क्लिष्टाक्लिष्टाः ॥५॥
I.5 vṛttayaḥ pañcatayyaḥ kliṣṭākliṣṭāḥ
There are five kinds of changing states of the mind, and they are either detrimental or nondetrimental [to the practice of *yoga*].

प्रमाणविपर्ययविकल्पनिद्रास्मृतयः ॥ ६ ॥

I.6 pramāṇa-viparyaya-vikalpa-nidrā-smṛtayaḥ

[These five *vṛttis* are] right knowledge, error, imagination, sleep, and memory.

प्रत्यक्षानुमानागमाः प्रमाणानि ॥ ७ ॥

I.7 pratyakṣānumānāgamāḥ pramāṇāni

Right knowledge consists of sense perception, logic, and verbal testimony.

विपर्ययो मिथ्याज्ञानम् अतद्रूपप्रतिष्ठम् ॥ ८ ॥

I.8 viparyayo mithyā-jñānam atad-rūpa-pratiṣṭham

Error is false knowledge stemming from the incorrect apprehension [of something].

शब्दज्ञानानुपाती वस्तुशून्यो विकल्पः ॥ ९ ॥

I.9 śabda-jñānānupātī vastu-śūnyo vikalpaḥ

Metaphor consists of the usage of words that are devoid of an actual object.

अभावप्रत्ययालम्बना वृत्तिर्निद्रा ॥ १० ॥

I.10 abhāva-pratyayālambanā vṛttir nidrā

Deep sleep is that state of mind which is based on an absence [of any content].

अनुभूतविषयासंप्रमोषः स्मृतिः ॥ ११ ॥

I.11 anubhūta-viṣayāsampramoṣaḥ smṛtiḥ

Memory is the retention of [images of] sense objects that have been experienced.

अभ्यासवैराग्याभ्यां तन्निरोधः ॥ १२ ॥

I.12 abhyāsa-vairāgyābhyāṁ tan-nirodhaḥ

[The *vṛtti* states of mind] are stilled by practice and dispassion.

तत्र स्थितौ यत्नोऽभ्यासः ॥ १३ ॥

I.13 tatra sthitau yatno 'bhyāsaḥ

From these, practice is the effort to be fixed in concentrating the mind.

स तु दीर्घकालनैरन्तर्यसत्कारासेवितो दृढभूमिः ॥१४॥
I.14 sa tu dīrgha-kāla-nairantarya-satkārāsevito dṛḍha-bhūmiḥ
Practice becomes firmly established when it has been cultivated uninterruptedly and with devotion over a prolonged period of time.

दृष्टानुश्रविकविषयवितृष्णस्य वशीकारसंज्ञा वैराग्यम ॥१५॥
I.15 dṛṣṭānuśravika-viṣaya-vitṛṣṇasya vaśīkāra-saṁjñā vairāgyam
Dispassion is the controlled consciousness of one who is without craving for sense objects, whether these are actually perceived, or described [in scripture].

तत्परं पुरुषख्यातेर्गुणवैतृष्ण्यम् ॥१६॥
I.16 tat paraṁ puruṣa-khyāter guṇa-vaitṛṣṇyam
Higher than renunciation is indifference to the *guṇas* [themselves]. This stems from perception of the *puruṣa*, soul.

वितर्कविचारानन्दास्मितारूपानुगमात् संप्रज्ञातः ॥१७॥
I.17 vitarka-vicārānandāsmitā-rūpānugamāt samprajñātaḥ
Samprajñāta [*samādhi*] consists of [the consecutive] mental stages of absorption with physical awareness, absorption with subtle awareness, absorption with bliss, and absorption with the sense of I-ness.

विरामप्रत्ययाभ्यासपूर्वः संस्कारशेषेऽन्यः ॥१८॥
I.18 virāma-pratyayābhyāsa-pūrvaḥ saṁskāra-śeṣo 'nyaḥ
The other *samādhi* [*asamprajñāta-samādhi*] is preceded by cultivating the determination to terminate [all thoughts]. [In this state] only latent impressions remain.

भवप्रत्ययो विदेहप्रकृतिलयानाम ॥१९॥
I.19 bhava-pratyayo videha-prakṛti-layānām
For [some], those who are unembodied and those who are merged in matter, [the state of *samprajñāta* is characterized] by absorption in [subtle] states of *prakṛti*.

श्रद्धावीर्यस्मृतिसमाधिप्रज्ञापूर्वक इतरेषाम् ॥२०॥
I.20 śraddhā-vīrya-smṛti-samādhi-prajñā-pūrvaka itareṣām
[But] for others, [the state where only subconscious impressions re-

main] is preceded by faith, vigor, memory, *samādhi* absorption, and discernment.

तीव्रसंवेगानाम् आसन्नः ॥ २१ ॥
I.21 tīvra-saṁvegānām āsannaḥ
[This state of *samprajñāta*] is near for those who apply themselves intensely.

मृदुमध्याधिमात्रत्वात् ततोऽपि विशेषः ॥ २२ ॥
I.22 mṛdu-madhyādhimātratvāt tato 'pi viśeṣaḥ
Even among these, there is further differentiation [of this intensity into degrees of] mild, mediocre, and ardent.

ईश्वरप्रणिधानाद् वा ॥ २३ ॥
I.23 Īśvara-praṇidhānād vā
Or, [this previously mentioned state is attainable] from devotion to the Lord.

क्लेशकर्मविपाकाशयैरपरामृष्टः पुरुषविशेष ईश्वरः ॥ २४ ॥
I.24 kleśa-karma-vipākāśayair aparāmṛṣṭaḥ puruṣa-viśeṣa Īśvaraḥ
The Lord is a special soul. He is untouched by the obstacles [to the practice of *yoga*], *karma*, the fructification [of *karma*], and subconscious predispositions.

तत्र निरतिशायं सर्वज्ञबीजम् ॥ २५ ॥
I.25 tatra niratiśāyaṁ sarvajña-bījam
In him, the seed of omniscience is unsurpassed.

पूर्वेषाम् अपि गुरुः कालेनानवच्छेदात् ॥ २६ ॥
I.26 pūrveṣām api guruḥ kālenānavacchedāt
Īśvara was also the teacher of the ancients, because he is not limited by Time.

तस्य वाचकः प्रणवः ॥ २७ ॥
I.27 tasya vācakaḥ praṇavaḥ
The name designating him is the mystical syllable *oṁ*.

तज्जपस्तदर्थभावनम् ॥ २८ ॥

I.28 taj-japas tad-artha-bhāvanam

Its repetition and the contemplation of its meaning [should be performed].

ततः प्रत्यक्चेतनाधिगमोऽप्यन्तरायाभावश्च ॥ २९ ॥

I.29 tataḥ pratyak-cetanādhigamo 'py antarāyābhāvaś ca

From this comes the realization of the inner consciousness and freedom from all disturbances.

व्याधिस्त्यानसंशयप्रमादालस्याविरतिभ्रान्तिदर्शनालब्ध
भूमिकत्वानवस्थितत्वानि चित्तविक्षेपास्तेऽन्तरायाः ॥ ३० ॥

I.30 vyādhi-styāna-saṁśaya-pramādālasyāvirati-bhrānti-darśanālabdha-bhūmikatvānavasthitatvāni citta-vikṣepās te 'ntarāyāḥ

These disturbances are disease, idleness, doubt, carelessness, sloth, lack of detachment, misapprehension, failure to attain a base for concentration, and instability. They are distractions for the mind.

दुःखदौर्मनस्याङ्गमेजयत्वश्वासप्रश्वासा विक्षेपसहभुवः ॥ ३१ ॥

I.31 duḥkha-daurmanasyāṅgam-ejayatva-śvāsa-praśvāsā vikṣepa-saha-bhuvaḥ

Suffering, dejection, trembling, inhalation, and exhalation accompany the distractions.

तत्प्रतिषेधार्थम् एकतत्त्वाभ्यासः ॥ ३२ ॥

I.32 tat-pratiṣedhārtham eka-tattvābhyāsaḥ

Practice [of fixing the mind] on one object [should be performed] in order to eliminate these disturbances.

मैत्रीकरुणामुदितोपेक्षणां
सुखदुःखपुण्यापुण्यविषयाणां भावनातश्चित्तप्रसादनम् ॥ ३३ ॥

I.33 maitrī-karuṇā-muditopekṣaṇāṁ sukha-duḥkha-puṇyāpuṇya-viṣayāṇāṁ bhāvanātas citta-prasādanam

By cultivating an attitude of friendship toward those who are happy, compassion toward those in distress; joy toward those who are virtuous, and equanimity toward those who are non-virtuous, lucidity arises in the mind.

प्रच्छर्दनविधारणाभ्यां वा प्राणस्य ।। ३४ ।।

I.34 pracchardana-vidhāraṇābhyāṁ vā prāṇasya

Or [stability of mind is gained] by exhaling and retaining the breath.

विषयवती वा प्रवृत्तिरुत्पन्ना मनसः स्थितिनिबन्धनी ।। ३५ ।।

I.35 viṣayavatī vā pravṛttir utpannā manasaḥ sthiti-nibandhanī

Or else, focus on a sense object arises, and this causes steadiness of the mind.

विशोका वा ज्योतिष्मती ।। ३६ ।।

I.36 viśokā vā jyotiṣmatī

Or [steadiness of mind is gained when] the mind is pain free and luminous.

वीतरागविषयं वा चित्तम् ।। ३७ ।।

I.37 vīta-rāga-viṣayaṁ vā cittam

Or [the mind becomes steady when it has] one who is free from desire as its object.

स्वप्ननिद्राज्ञानालम्बनं वा ।। ३८ ।।

I.38 svapna-nidrā-jñānālambanaṁ vā

Or [the mind can become steady when it has] the knowledge attained from sleep and dreams as its support.

यथाभिमतध्यानाद् वा ।। ३९ ।।

I.39 yathābhimata-dhyānād vā

Or [steadiness of the mind is attained] from meditation upon anything of one's inclination.

परमाणुपरममहत्त्वान्तोऽस्य वशीकारः ।। ४० ।।

I.40 paramāṇu-parama-mahattvānto 'sya vaśīkāraḥ

The *yogī*'s mastery extends from the smallest particle of matter to the totality of matter.

क्षीणवृत्तेरभिजातस्येव मणेर्ग्रहीतृग्रहणग्राह्येषु तत्स्थतदञ्जनता समापत्तिः ।। ४१ ।।

I.41 kṣīṇa-vṛtter abhijātasyeva maṇer grahītṛ-grahaṇa-grāhyeṣu tat-stha-tad-añjanatā samāpattiḥ

Samāpatti, complete absorption of the mind when it is free from its *vṛttis*, occurs when the mind becomes just like a transparent jewel, taking the form of whatever object is placed before it, whether the object be the knower, the instrument of knowledge, or the object of knowledge.

तत्र शब्दार्थज्ञानविकल्पैः संकीर्णा सवितर्का समापत्तिः ॥ ४२ ॥

I.42 tatra śabdārtha-jñāna-vikalpaiḥ saṅkīrṇā savitarkā-samāpattiḥ

In this stage, *savitarka-samāpatti*, "*samādhi* absorption with physical awareness" is intermixed with the notions of word, meaning, and idea.

स्मृतिपरिशुद्धौ स्वरूपशून्येवार्थमात्रनिर्भासा निर्वितर्का ॥ ४३ ॥

I.43 smṛti-pariśuddhau svarūpa-śūnyevārtha-mātra-nirbhāsā nirvitarkā

Nirvitarka [*samāpatti*], "absorption without conceptualization," occurs when memory has been purged and the mind is empty, as it were, of its own [reflective] nature. Now only the object [of meditation] shines forth [in its own right].

एतयैव सविचारा निर्विचारा च सूक्ष्मविषया व्याख्याता ॥ ४४ ॥

I.44 etayaiva savicārā nirvicārā ca sūkṣma-viṣayā vyākhyātā

The states of *samādhi* with "subtle awareness" and without "subtle awareness," whose objects of focus are the subtle nature [of things], are explained in the same manner.

सूक्ष्मविषयत्वं चालिङ्गपर्यवसानम् ॥ ४५ ॥

I.45 sūkṣma-viṣayatvaṁ cāliṅga-paryavasānam

The subtle nature of things extends all the way up to *prakṛti*.

ता एव सबीजः समाधिः ॥ ४६ ॥

I.46 tā eva sabījaḥ samādhiḥ

These above mentioned *samāpatti* states are [known as] *samādhi* meditative absorption "with seed."

निर्विचारवैशारद्येऽध्यात्मप्रसादः ॥ ४७ ॥

I.47 nirvicāra-vaiśāradye 'dhyātma-prasādaḥ

Upon attaining the clarity of *nirvicāra-samādhi*, there is lucidity of the inner self.

ऋतंभरा तत्र प्रज्ञा ।। ४८ ।।
I.48 ṛtam-bharā tatra prajñā
In that state, there is truth-bearing wisdom.

श्रुतानुमानप्रज्ञाभ्याम् अन्यविषया विशेषार्थत्वात् ।। ४९ ।।
I.49 śrutānumāna-prajñābhyām anya-viṣayā viśeṣārthatvāt
It [seedless *samādhi*] has a different focus from that of inference and sacred scripture, because it has the particularity of things as its object.

तज्जः संस्कारो न्यसंस्कारप्रतिबन्धी ।। ५० ।।
I.50 taj-jaḥ saṁskāro 'nya-saṁskāra-pratibandhī
The *saṁskāras* born out of that [truth-bearing wisdom] obstruct other *saṁskāras* [from emerging].

तस्यापि निरोधे सर्वनिरोधान् निर्बीजः समाधिः ।। ५१ ।।
I.51 tasyāpi nirodhe sarva-nirodhān nirbījaḥ samādhiḥ
Upon the cessation of even those [truth-bearing *saṁskāras*], *nirbīja-samādhi*, seedless meditative absorption, ensues.

इति पतञ्जलिविरचिते योगसूत्रे प्रथमः समाधिपादः ।
iti Patañjali-viracite yogasūtre prathamaḥ samādhi-pādaḥ
Thus ends of the first chapter on *samādhi* in the *Yoga Sūtras* composed by Patañjali.

CHAPTER II: PRACTICE

द्वितीयः साधनपादः ।
dvitīyaḥ sādhana-pādaḥ

तपःस्वाध्यायेश्वरप्रणिधानानि क्रियायोगः ।। १ ।।
II.1 tapaḥ-svādhyāyeśvara-praṇidhānāni kriyā-yogaḥ
Kriyā-yoga, the path of action, consists of self-discipline, study, and dedication to the Lord.

समाधिभावनार्थः क्लेशतनूकरणार्थश्च ॥ २ ॥

II.2 samādhi-bhāvanārthaḥ kleśa-tanū-karaṇārthaś ca

[The *yoga* of action] is for bringing about *samādhi* and for weakening the impediments [*to yoga*].

अविद्यास्मितारागद्वेषाभिनिवेशाः क्लेशाः ॥ ३ ॥

II.3 avidyāsmitā-rāga-dveṣābhiniveśāḥ kleśāḥ

The impediments [to *samādhi*] are nescience, ego, desire, aversion, and clinging to life.

अविद्या क्षेत्रम् उत्तरेषां प्रसुप्ततनुविच्छिन्नोदाराणाम् ॥ ४ ॥

II.4 avidyā kṣetram uttareṣāṁ prasupta-tanu-vicchinnodārāṇām

Ignorance is the breeding ground of the other *kleśas*, whether they are in a dormant, weak, intermittent, or fully activated state.

अनित्याशुचिदुःखानात्मसु नित्यशुचिसुखात्मख्यातिरविद्या ॥ ५ ॥

II.5 anityāśuci-duḥkhānātmasu nitya-śuci-sukhātma-khyātir avidyā

Ignorance is the notion that takes the self, which is joyful, pure, and eternal, to be the nonself, which is painful, unclean, and temporary.

दृग्दर्शनशक्त्योरेकात्मतेवास्मिता ॥ ६ ॥

II.6 dṛg-darśana-śaktyor ekātmatevāsmitā

Ego is [to consider] the nature of the seer and the nature of the instrumental power of seeing to be the same thing.

सुखानुशयी रागः ॥ ७ ॥

II.7 sukhānuśayī rāgaḥ

Attachment stems from [experiences] of happiness.

दुःखानुशयी द्वेषः ॥ ८ ॥

II.8 duḥkhānuśayī dveṣaḥ

Aversion stems from [experiences] of pain.

स्वरसवाही विदुषोऽपि तथारूढोऽभिनिवेशः ॥ ९ ॥

II.9 svarasa-vāhī viduṣo 'pi tathārūḍho 'bhiniveśaḥ

[The tendency of] clinging to life affects even the wise; it is an inherent tendency.

ते प्रतिप्रसवहेयाः सूक्ष्माः ॥१०॥
II.10 te pratiprasava-heyāḥ sūkṣmāḥ
These *kleśas* are subtle; they are destroyed when [the mind] dissolves back into its original matrix.

ध्यानहेयास्तद्वृत्तयः ॥११॥
II.11 dhyāna-heyās tad-vṛttayaḥ
The states of mind produced by these *kleśas* are eliminated by meditation.

क्लेशमूलः कर्माशयो दृष्टादृष्टजन्मवेदनीयः ॥१२॥
II.12 kleśa-mūlaḥ karmāśayo dṛṣṭādṛṣṭa-janma-vedanīyaḥ
The stock of *karma* has the *kleśas* as its root. It is experienced in present or future lives.

सति मूले तद्विपाको जात्यायुर्भोगाः ॥१३॥
II.13 sati mūle tad-vipāko jātyāyur-bhogāḥ
As long as the root [of *kleśas*] exists, it fructifies as type of birth, span of life, and life experience [of an individual].

ते ह्लादपरितापफलाः पुण्यापुण्यहेतुत्वात् ॥१४॥
II.14 te hlāda-paritāpa-phalāḥ puṇyāpuṇya-hetutvāt
These [the type of birth, span of life, and life experience] bear the fruits of pleasure and pain, as a result of [the performance of] virtue and vice.

परिणामतापसंस्कारदुःखैर्गुणवृत्तिविरोधाच्
च दुःखम् एव सर्वं विवेकिनः ॥१५॥
II.15 pariṇāma-tāpa-saṁskāra-duḥkhair guṇa-vṛtti-virodhāc ca duḥkham eva sarvaṁ vivekinaḥ
For one who has discrimination, everything is suffering on account of the suffering produced by the consequences [of action], by pain [itself], and by the *saṁskāras*, as well as on account of the suffering ensuing from the turmoil of the *vṛttis* due to the *guṇas*.

हेयं दुःखम् अनागतम् ॥१६॥
II.16 heyaṁ duḥkham anāgatam
Suffering that has yet to manifest is to be avoided.

द्रष्टृदृश्ययोः संयोगो हेयहेतुः ॥ १७ ॥
II.17 draṣṭṛ-dṛśyayoḥ saṁyogo heya-hetuḥ
The conjunction between the seer and that which is seen is the cause [of suffering] to be avoided.

प्रकाशक्रियास्थितिशीलं भूतेन्द्रियात्मकं भोगापवर्गार्थं दृश्यम् ॥ १८ ॥
II.18 prakāśa-kriyā-sthiti-śīlaṁ bhūtendriyātmakaṁ bhogāpavargārthaṁ dṛśyam
That which is knowable has the nature of illumination, activity, and inertia [*sattva*, *rajas*, and *tamas*]. It consists of the senses and the elements, and exists for the purpose of [providing] either liberation or experience [to *puruṣa*].

विशेषाविशेषलिङ्गमात्रालिङ्गानि गुणपर्वाणि ॥ १९ ॥
II.19 viśeṣāviśeṣa-liṅga-mātrāliṅgāni guṇa-parvāṇi
The different stages of the *guṇa* qualities consist of the particularized, the unparticularized, the distinctive, and the indistinctive.

द्रष्टा दृशिमात्रः शुद्धोऽपि प्रत्ययानुपश्यः ॥ २० ॥
II.20 draṣṭā dṛśi-mātraḥ śuddho 'pi pratyayānupaśyaḥ
The seer is merely the power of seeing; [however,] although pure, he witnesses the images of mind.

तदर्थ एव दृश्यस्यात्मा ॥ २१ ॥
II.21 tad-artha eva dṛśyasyātmā
The essential nature of that which is seen is exclusively for the sake of the seer.

कृतार्थं प्रति नष्टम् अप्यनष्टं तदन्यसाधारणत्वात् ॥ २२ ॥
II.22 kṛtārthaṁ prati naṣṭam apy anaṣṭaṁ tad-anya-sādhāraṇatvāt
Although the seen ceases to exist for one whose purpose is accomplished [the liberated *puruṣa*], it has not ceased to exist altogether, since it is common to other [not-liberated] *puruṣas*.

स्वस्वामिशक्त्योः स्वरूपोपलब्धिहेतुः संयोगः ॥ २३ ॥
II.23 sva-svāmi-śaktyoḥ svarūpopalabdhi-hetuḥ saṁyogaḥ
[The notion of] conjunction is the means of understanding the real nature of the powers of the possessed and of the possessor.

तस्य हेतुरविद्या ॥ २४ ॥
II.24 tasya hetur avidyā
The cause of conjunction is ignorance.

तदभावात् संयोगाभावो हानं तद्दृशेः कैवल्यम् ॥ २५ ॥
II.25 tad-abhāvāt saṁyogābhāvo hānaṁ tad-dṛśeḥ kaivalyam
By the removal of ignorance, conjunction is removed. This is the absolute freedom of the seer.

विवेकख्यातिरविप्लवा हानोपायः ॥ २६ ॥
II.26 viveka-khyātir aviplavā hānopāyaḥ
The means to liberation is uninterrupted discriminative discernment.

तस्य सप्तधा प्रान्तभूमिः प्रज्ञा ॥ २७ ॥
II.27 tasya saptadhā prānta-bhūmiḥ prajñā
The *yogī*'s true insight has seven ultimate stages.

योगाङ्गानुष्ठानाद् अशुद्धिक्षये ज्ञानदीप्तिराविवेकख्यातेः ॥ २८ ॥
II.28 yogāṅgānuṣṭhānād aśuddhi-kṣaye jñāna-dīptir-āviveka-khyāteḥ
Upon the destruction of impurities as a result of the practice of *yoga*, the lamp of knowledge arises. This culminates in discriminative discernment.

यमनियमासनप्राणायामप्रत्याहारधारणाध्यानसमाधयोऽष्टाव्
अङ्गानि ॥ २९ ॥
II.29 yama-niyamāsana-prāṇāyāma-pratyāhāra-dhāraṇā-dhyāna-samādhayo 'ṣṭāv aṅgāni
The eight limbs are abstentions, observances, posture, breath control, disengagement of the senses, concentration, meditation, and absorption.

अहिंसासत्यास्तेयब्रह्मचर्यापरिग्रहा यमाः ॥ ३० ॥
II.30 ahiṁsā-satyāsteya-brahmacaryāparigrahā yamāḥ
The *yamas* are nonviolence, truthfulness, refrainment from stealing, celibacy, and renunciation of [unnecessary] possessions.

जातिदेशकालसमयानवच्छिन्नाः सार्वभौमा महाव्रतम् ।। ३१ ।।
II.31 jāti-deśa-kāla-samayānavacchinnāḥ sārva-bhaumā mahā-vratam
[These *yamas*] are considered the great vow. They are not exempted by one's class, place, time, or circumstance. They are universal.

शौचसंतोषतपःस्वाध्यायेश्वरप्रणिधानानि नियमाः ।। ३२ ।।
II.32 śauca-santoṣa-tapaḥ-svādhyāyeśvara-praṇidhānāni niyamāḥ
The observances are cleanliness, contentment, austerity, study [of scripture], and devotion to God.

वितर्कबाधने प्रतिपक्षभावनम् ।। ३३ ।।
II.33 vitarka-bādhane pratipakṣa-bhāvanam
Upon being harassed by negative thoughts, one should cultivate counteracting thoughts.

वितर्का हिंसादयः कृतकारितानुमोदिता लोभक्रोधमोहपूर्वका मृदुमध्याधिमात्रा दुःखाज्ञानानन्तफला इति प्रतिपक्षभावनम् ।। ३४ ।।
II.34 vitarkā hiṁsādayaḥ kṛta-kāritānumoditā lobha-krodha-moha-pūrvakā mṛdu-madhyādhimātrā duḥkhājñānānanta-phalā iti pratipakṣa-bhāvanam
Negative thoughts are violence, etc. They may be [personally] performed, performed on one's behalf by another, or authorized by oneself; they may be triggered by greed, anger, or delusion; and they may be slight, moderate, or extreme in intensity. One should cultivate counteracting thoughts, namely, that the end results [of negative thoughts] are ongoing suffering and ignorance.

अहिंसाप्रतिष्ठायां तत्सन्निधौ वैरत्यागः ।। ३५ ।।
II.35 ahiṁsā-pratiṣṭhāyāṁ tat-sannidhau vaira-tyāgaḥ
In the presence of one who is established in nonviolence, enmity is abandoned.

सत्यप्रतिष्ठायां क्रियाफलाश्रयत्वम् ।। ३६ ।।
II.36 satya-pratiṣṭhāyāṁ kriyā-phalāśrayatvam
When one is established in truthfulness, one ensures the fruition of actions.

अस्तेयप्रतिष्ठायां सर्वरत्नोपस्थानम् ॥ ३७ ॥

II.37 asteya-pratiṣṭhāyāṁ sarva-ratnopasthānam

When one is established in refrainment from stealing, all jewels manifest.

ब्रह्मचर्यप्रतिष्ठायां वीर्यलाभः ॥ ३८ ॥

II.38 brahmacarya-pratiṣṭhāyāṁ vīrya-lābhaḥ

Upon the establishment of celibacy, power it attained.

अपरिग्रहस्थैर्ये जन्मकथंतासंबोधः ॥ ३९ ॥

II.39 aparigraha-sthairye janma-kathantā-sambodhaḥ

When refrainment from covetousness becomes firmly established, knowledge of the whys and wherefores of births manifests.

शौचात् स्वाङ्गजुगुप्सा परैरसंसर्गः ॥ ४० ॥

II.40 śaucāt svāṅga-jugupsā parair asaṁsargaḥ

By cleanliness, one [develops] distaste for one's body and the cessation of contact with others.

सत्त्वशुद्धिसौमनस्यैकाग्र्येन्द्रियजयात्मदर्शनयोग्यत्वानि च ॥ ४१ ॥

II.41 sattva-śuddhi-saumanasyaikāgryendriya-jayātma-darśana-yogyatvāni ca

Upon the purification of the mind, [one attains] cheerfulness, one-pointedness, sense control, and fitness to perceive the self.

संतोषाद् अनुत्तमः सुखलाभः ॥ ४२ ॥

II.42 santoṣād anuttamaḥ sukha-lābhaḥ

From contentment, the highest happiness is attained.

कायेन्द्रियसिद्धिरशुद्धिक्षयात् तपसः ॥ ४३ ॥

II.43 kāyendriya-siddhir aśuddhi-kṣayāt tapasaḥ

From austerity, on account of the removal of impurities, the perfection of the senses and body manifests.

स्वाध्यायाद् इष्टदेवतासंप्रयोगः ॥ ४४ ॥

II.44 svādhyāyād iṣṭa-devatā-samprayogaḥ

From study [of scripture], a connection with one's deity of choice is established.

समाधिसिद्धिरीश्वरप्रणिधानात् ॥ ४५ ॥
II.45 samādhi-siddhir īśvara-praṇidhānāt
From submission to God comes the perfection of *samādhi*.

स्थिरसुखम् आसनम् ॥ ४६ ॥
II.46 sthira-sukham āsanam
Posture should be steady and comfortable.

प्रयत्नशैथिल्यानन्तसमापत्तिभ्याम् ॥ ४७ ॥
II.47 prayatna-śaithilyānanta-samāpattibhyām
[Such posture should be attained] by the relaxation of effort and by absorption in the infinite.

ततो द्वन्द्वानभिघातः ॥ ४८ ॥
II.48 tato dvandvānabhighātaḥ
From this, one is not afflicted by the dualities of the opposites.

तस्मिन् सति श्वासप्रश्वासयोर्गतिविच्छेदः प्राणायामः ॥ ४९ ॥
II.49 tasmin sati śvāsa-praśvāsayor gati-vicchedaḥ prāṇāyāmaḥ
When that [*āsana*] is accomplished, *prāṇāyāma*, breath control, [follows]. This consists of the regulation of the incoming and outgoing breaths.

बाह्याभ्यन्तरस्तम्भवृत्तिः देशकालसंख्याभिः परिदृष्टो दीर्घसूक्ष्मः ॥ ५० ॥
II.50 bāhyābhyantara-stambha-vṛttiḥ deśa-kāla-saṅkhyābhiḥ paridṛṣṭo dīrgha-sūkṣmaḥ
[*Prāṇāyāma*] manifests as external, internal, and restrained movements [of breath]. These are drawn out and subtle in accordance to place, time, and number.

बाह्याभ्यन्तरविषयाक्षेपी चतुर्थः ॥ ५१ ॥
II.51 bāhyābhyantara-viṣayākṣepī caturthaḥ
The fourth [type of *prāṇāyāma*] surpasses the limits of the external and the internal.

ततः क्षीयते प्रकाशावरणम् ॥ ५२ ॥
II.52 tataḥ kṣīyate prakāśāvaraṇam
Then, the covering of the illumination [of knowledge] is weakened.

धारणासु च योग्यता मनसः ॥५३॥
II.53 dhāraṇāsu ca yogyatā manasaḥ
Additionally, the mind becomes fit for concentration.

स्वविषयासंप्रयोगे चित्तस्य स्वरूपानुकार
इवेन्द्रियाणां प्रत्याहारः ॥५४॥
II.54 svaviṣayāsamprayoge cittasya svarūpānukāra ivendriyāṇāṁ pratyāhāraḥ
Pratyāhāra, withdrawal from sense objects, occurs when the senses do not come into contact with their respective sense objects. It corresponds, as it were, to the nature of the mind [when it is withdrawn from the sense objects].

ततः परमा वश्यतेन्द्रियाणाम् ॥५५॥
II.55 tataḥ paramā vaśyatendriyāṇām
From this comes the highest control of the senses.

इति पतञ्जलिविरचिते योगसूत्रे द्वितीयः साधनपादः ।
iti Patañjali-viracite yogasūtre dvitīyaḥ sādhana-pādaḥ
Thus ends the second chapter on *sādhana* in the *Yoga Sūtras* composed by Patañjali.

CHAPTER III: MYSTIC POWERS

तृतीयः विभूतिपादः ।
tritīyaḥ vibhūti-pādaḥ

देशबन्धश्चित्तस्य धारणा ॥१॥
III.1 deśa-bandhaś cittasya dhāraṇā
Concentration is the fixing of the mind in one place.

तत्र प्रत्ययैकतानता ध्यानम् ॥२॥
III.2 tatra pratyayaika-tānatā dhyānam
Meditation is the one-pointedness of the mind on one image.

तद् एवार्थमात्रनिर्भासं स्वरूपशून्यम् इव समाधिः ।।३।।
III.3 tad evārtha-mātra-nirbhāsaṁ svarūpa-śūnyam iva samādhiḥ
Samādhi is when that same *dhyāna* shines forth as the object alone and [the mind] is devoid of its own [reflective] nature.

त्रयम् एकत्र संयमः ।।४।।
III.4 trayam ekatra saṁyamaḥ
When these three are performed together, it is called *saṁyama*.

तज्जयात् प्रज्ञालोकः ।।५।।
III.5 taj-jayāt prajñālokaḥ
From *saṁyama* comes insight.

तस्य भूमिषु विनियोगः ।।६।।
III.6 tasya bhūmiṣu viniyogaḥ
Saṁyama is applied on the [different] stages [of *samādhi*].

त्रयम् अन्तरङ्गं पूर्वेभ्यः ।।७।।
III.7 trayam antaraṅgaṁ pūrvebhyaḥ
These three [*dhāraṇā*, *dhyāna*, and *samādhi*] are internal limbs compared to the previous limbs [of *yoga*].

तद् अपि बहिरङ्गं निर्बीजस्य ।।८।।
III.8 tad api bahir-aṅgaṁ nirbījasya
Yet even these are external limbs in relation to "seedless" *samādhi*.

व्युत्थाननिरोधसंस्कारयोरभिभवप्रादुर्भावौ
निरोधक्षणचित्तान्वयो निरोधपरिणामः ।।९।।
III.9 vyutthāna-nirodha-saṁskārayor abhibhava-prādurbhāvau nirodha-kṣaṇa-cittānvayo nirodha-pariṇāmaḥ
The state of restraint, *nirodha*, is when there is disappearance of outgoing [i.e., worldly] *saṁskāras* and the appearance of restraining *saṁskāras*. These emerge in the mind at the moment of restraint.

तस्य प्रशान्तवाहिता संस्कारात् ।।१०।।
III.10 tasya praśānta-vāhitā saṁskārāt
The mind's undisturbed flow occurs due to *saṁskāras*.

सर्वार्थतैकाग्रतयोः क्षयोदयौ चित्तस्य समाधिपरिणामः ॥११॥
III.11 sarvārthataikāgratayoḥ kṣayodayau cittasya samādhi-pariṇāmaḥ
The attainment of the *samādhi* state involves the elimination of all-pointedness [i.e., wandering] of the mind and the rise of one-pointedness [i.e., concentration].

ततः पुनः शान्तोदितौ तुल्यप्रत्ययौ चित्तस्यैकाग्रतापरिणामः ॥१२॥
III.12 tataḥ punaḥ śāntoditau tulya-pratyayau cittasyaikāgratā-pariṇāmaḥ
In that regard, the attainment of one-pointedness occurs when the image in the mind that has just passed is the same as the image in the mind that is present.

एतेन भूतेन्द्रियेषु धर्मलक्षणावस्थापरिणामा व्याख्याताः ॥१३॥
III.13 etena bhūtendriyeṣu dharma-lakṣaṇāvasthā-pariṇāmā vyākhyātāḥ
In this way, the change in the characteristics, state, and condition of objects and of the senses is explained.

शान्तोदिताव्यपदेश्यधर्मानुपाती धर्मी ॥१४॥
III.14 śāntoditāvyapadeśya-dharmānupātī dharmī
The substratum is that which underpins past, present, and future.

क्रमान्यत्वं परिणामान्यत्वे हेतुः ॥१५॥
III.15 kramānyatvaṁ pariṇāmānyatve hetuḥ
The change in the sequence [of characteristics] is the cause of the change in transformations [of objects].

परिणामत्रयसंयमाद् अतीतानागतज्ञानम् ॥१६॥
III.16 pariṇāma-traya-saṁyamād atītānāgata-jñānam
When *saṁyama* is performed on the three transformations [of characteristics, state, and condition], knowledge of the past and the future ensues.

शब्दार्थप्रत्ययानाम् इतरेतराध्यासात् संकरस्तत्प्रविभागसंयमात् सर्वभूतरुतज्ञानम् ॥१७॥
III.17 śabdārtha-pratyayānām itaretarādhyāsāt saṅkaras tat-pravibhāga-saṁyamāt sarva-bhūta-ruta-jñānam
Due to the correlation among word, meaning, and idea, confusion en-

sues. By performing *saṁyama* on them separately, knowledge of the speech of all creatures arises.

संस्कारसाक्षात्करणात् पूर्वजातिज्ञानम् ॥१८॥

III.18 saṁskāra-sākṣātkaraṇāt pūrva-jāti-jñānam

By bringing [previous] *saṁskāras* into direct perception comes the knowledge of previous births.

प्रत्ययस्य परचित्तज्ञानम् ॥१९॥

III.19 pratyayasya para-citta-jñānam

From [their] ideas, one can attain knowledge of others' minds.

न च तत् सालम्बनं तस्याविषयीभूतत्वात् ॥२०॥

III.20 na ca tat-sālambanaṁ tasyāviṣayībhūtatvāt

That knowledge is not accompanied by its object, since this object is not the object [of the *yogī*'s mind].

कायरूपसंयमात् तद्ग्राह्यशक्तिस्तम्भे
चक्षुःप्रकाशासंप्रयोगेऽन्तर्धानम् ॥२१॥

III.21 kāya-rūpa-saṁyamāt tad-grāhya-śakti-stambhe cakṣuḥ-prakāśāsamprayoge 'ntardhānam

By performing *saṁyama* on the outer form of the body, invisibility [is attained]. This occurs when perceptibility is obstructed by blocking contact between light and the eyes.

सोपक्रमं निरुपक्रमं च कर्म तत्संयमाद्
अपरान्तज्ञानम् अरिष्टेभ्यो वा ॥२२॥

III.22 sopakramaṁ nirupakramaṁ ca karma tat-saṁyamād aparānta-jñānam ariṣṭebhyo vā

Karma is either quick to fructify or slow. By *saṁyama* on *karma*, or on portents, knowledge of [one's] death arises.

मैत्र्यादिषु बलानि ॥२३॥

III.23 maitryādiṣu balāni

By [*saṁyama*] on friendliness and such things, strengths are acquired.

बलेषु हस्तिबलादीनि ।। २४ ।।
III.24 baleṣu hasti-balādīni
[By practicing *saṁyama*] on strengths, [the *yogī*] attains the strength of an elephant, etc.

प्रवृत्त्यालोकन्यासात् सूक्ष्मव्यवहितविप्रकृष्टज्ञानम् ।। २५ ।।
III.25 pravṛttyāloka-nyāsāt sūkṣma-vyavahita-viprakṛṣṭa-jñānam
By directing the light of cognition, one obtains knowledge of subtle, concealed, and remote things.

भुवनज्ञानं सूर्ये संयमात् ।। २६ ।।
III.26 bhuvana-jñānaṁ sūrye saṁyamāt
By performing *saṁyama* on the sun arises knowledge of the different realms in the universe.

चन्द्रे ताराव्यूहज्ञानम् ।। २७ ।।
III.27 candre tārā-vyūha-jñānam
[By *saṁyama*] on the moon, knowledge of the solar systems.

ध्रुवे तद्गतिज्ञानम् ।। २८ ।।
III.28 dhruve tad-gati-jñānam
[By *saṁyama*] on the polestar comes knowledge of the movement of the stars.

नाभिचक्रे कायव्यूहज्ञानम् ।। २९ ।।
III.29 nābhi-cakre kāya-vyūha-jñānam
[By *saṁyama*] on the navel plexus of the body comes knowledge of the arrangement of the body.

कण्ठकूपे क्षुत्पिपासानिवृत्तिः ।। ३० ।।
III.30 kaṇṭha-kūpe kṣut-pipāsā-nivṛttiḥ
[By *saṁyama*] on the pit of the throat comes the cessation of hunger and thirst.

कूर्मनाड्यां स्थैर्यम् ।। ३१ ।।
III.31 kūrma-nāḍyāṁ sthairyam
[By *saṁyama*] on the subtle tortoise channel, steadiness is attained.

मूर्धज्योतिषि सिद्धदर्शनम् ॥ ३२ ॥
III.32 mūrdha-jyotiṣi siddha-darśanam
[By *saṁyama*] on the light in the skull, a vision of the *siddhas*, perfected beings, is attained.

प्रातिभाद् वा सर्वम् ॥ ३३ ॥
III.33 prātibhād vā sarvam
Or, by intuition, comes [knowledge of] everything.

हृदये चित्तसंवित् ॥ ३४ ॥
III.34 hṛdaye citta-saṁvit
[By *saṁyama*] on the heart, knowledge of the mind ensues.

सत्त्वपुरुषयेरत्यन्तासंकीर्णयोः प्रत्ययाविशेषो भोगः
परार्थत्वात् स्वार्थसंयमात् पुरुषज्ञानम् ॥ ३५ ॥
III.35 sattva-puruṣayor atyantāsaṅkīrṇayoḥ pratyayāviśeṣo bhogaḥ parārthatvāt svārtha-saṁyamāt puruṣa-jñānam
Worldly experience consists of the notion that there is no distinction between the *puruṣa* self and pure intelligence, although these two are completely distinct. Worldly experience exists for another [i.e., for *puruṣa*]. [By *saṁyama*] on that which exists for itself [i.e., on *puruṣa*], comes knowledge of *puruṣa*.

ततः प्रातिभश्रावणवेदनादर्शास्वादवार्ता जायन्ते ॥ ३६ ॥
III.36 tataḥ prātibha-śrāvaṇa-vedanādarśāsvāda-vārtā jāyante
From this, intuition as well as higher hearing, touch, vision, taste, and smell are born.

ते समाधाव् उपसर्गा व्युत्थाने सिद्धयः ॥ ३७ ॥
III.37 te samādhāv upasargāḥ vyutthāne siddhayaḥ
These powers are accomplishments for the mind that is outgoing but obstacles to *samādhi*.

बन्धकारणशैथिल्यात् प्रचारसंवेदनाच् च चित्तस्य
परशरीरावेशः ॥ ३८ ॥
III.38 bandha-kāraṇa-śaithilyāt pracāra-saṁvedanāc ca cittasya para-śarīrāveśaḥ

By loosening the cause of bondage, and by knowledge of the passageways of the mind, the mind can enter into the bodies of others.

उदानजयाज्जलपङ्ककण्टकादिष्वसङ्ग उत्क्रान्तिश्च ।। ३९ ।।
III.39 udāna-jayāj jala-paṅka-kaṇṭakādiṣv asaṅga utkrāntiś ca
By mastery over the *udāna* vital air, one attains [the power of] levitation and does not come into contact with water, mud, and thorns, etc.

समानजयात् ज्वलनम् ।। ४० ।।
III.40 samāna-jayāt jvalanam
By mastery over the *samāna* vital air, radiance is attained.

श्रोत्राकाशयोः संबन्धसंयमाद् दिव्यं श्रोत्रम् ।। ४१ ।।
III.41 śrotrākāśayoḥ sambandha-saṁyamād divyaṁ śrotram
By *saṁyama* on the relationship between the organ of hearing and the ether, divine hearing is attained.

कायाकाशयोः संबन्धसंयमाल्
लघुतूलसमापत्तेश्चाकाशगमनम् ।। ४२ ।।
III.42 kāyākāśayoḥ sambandha-saṁyamāl laghu-tūla-samāpatteś cākāśa-gamanam
By performing *saṁyama* on the relationship between the body and ether, and by performing *samāpatti* on the lightness of cotton, one acquires the ability to travel through the sky.

बहिरकल्पिता वृत्तिर्महाविदेहा ततः प्रकाशावरणक्षयः ।। ४३ ।।
III.43 bahir-akalpitā vṛttir mahā-videhā tataḥ prakāśāvaraṇa-kṣayaḥ
The state of mind [projected] outside [of the body], which is not an imagined state, is called the great out-of-body [experience]. By this, the covering of the light [of *buddhi*] is destroyed.

स्थूलस्वरूपसूक्ष्मान्वयार्थवत्त्वसंयमाद्भूतजयः ।। ४४ ।।
III.44 sthūla-svarūpa-sūkṣmānvayārthavattva-saṁyamād bhūta-jayaḥ
By *saṁyama* on the gross nature, essential nature, subtle nature, constitution, and purpose [of objects, one attains] mastery over the elements.

ततोऽणिमादिप्रादुर्भावः कायसंपत् तद्धर्मानभिघातश्च ।। ४५ ।।
III.45 tato 'ṇimādi-prādurbhāvaḥ kāya-sampat-tad-dharmānabhighātaś ca
As a result of this, there are no limitations on account of the body's natural abilities; mystic powers such as *aṇimā*, etc., manifest; and the body attains perfection.

रूपलावण्यबलवज्रसंहननत्वानि कायसंपत् ।। ४६ ।।
III.46 rūpa-lāvaṇya-bala-vajra-saṁhananatvāni kāya-sampat
The perfection of the body consists of [possessing] beauty, charm, strength, and the power of a thunderbolt.

ग्रहणस्वरूपास्मितान्वयार्थवत्त्वसंयमाद् इन्द्रियजयः ।। ४७ ।।
III.47 grahaṇa-svarūpāsmitānvayārthavattva-saṁyamād indriya-jayaḥ
By the performance of *saṁyama* on the process of knowing, on the essence [of the sense organs], on ego, on inherence [the *guṇas*], and on the purpose [of the *guṇas*] comes control over the senses.

ततो मनोजवित्वं विकरणभावः प्रधानजयश्च ।। ४८ ।।
III.48 tato mano-javitvaṁ vikaraṇa-bhāvaḥ pradhāna-jayaś ca
As a result of this comes speed like the speed of mind, activity independent of the bodily senses, and mastery over primordial matter.

सत्त्वपुरुषान्यताख्यातिमात्रस्य सर्वभावाधिष्ठातृत्वं सर्वज्ञातृत्वं च ।। ४९ ।।
III.49 sattva-puruṣānyatā-khyāti-mātrasya sarva-bhāvādhiṣṭhātṛtvam sarva-jñātṛtvam ca
Only for one who discerns the difference between the *puruṣa* and the intellect do omniscience and omnipotence accrue.

तद्वैराग्यादपि दोषबीजक्षये कैवल्यम् ।। ५० ।।
III.50 tad-vairāgyād api doṣa-bīja-kṣaye kaivalyam
By detachment even from this attainment [i.e., omniscience and omnipotence], and upon the destruction of the seeds of all faults, *kaivalya*, the supreme liberation ensues.

स्थान्युपनिमन्त्रणे सङ्गस्मयाकरणं पुनर् अनिष्टप्रसङ्गात् ।। ५१ ।।
III.51 sthānyupanimantraṇe saṅgasmayākaraṇaṁ punar-aniṣṭa-prasaṅgāt

If solicited by celestial beings, [the *yogī*] should not become smug, because the tendency toward undesirable consequences can once again manifest.

क्षणतत्क्रमयोः संयमादविवेकजं ज्ञानम् ॥५२॥
III.52 kṣaṇa-tat-kramayoḥ saṁyamād-viveka-jaṁ jñānaṁ
By performing *saṁyama* on the moment, and its sequence, one attains knowledge born of discrimination.

जातिलक्षणदेशैरन्यतानवच्छेदात् तुल्ययोस्ततः प्रतिपत्तिः ॥५३॥
III.53 jāti-lakṣaṇa-deśair anyatā 'navacchedāt tulyayos tataḥ pratipattiḥ
As a result of this, there is discernment of two comparable things that are not distinguishable by species, characteristics, or location.

तारकं सर्वविषयं सर्वथाविषयम् अक्रमं चेति विवेकजं ज्ञानम् ॥५४॥
III.54 tārakaṁ sarva-viṣayaṁ sarvathā-viṣayam akramaṁ ceti vivekajaṁ jñānam
Knowledge born of discrimination is a liberator; it has everything as its object at all times simultaneously.

सत्त्वपुरुषयोः शुद्धिसाम्ये कैवल्यम् इति ॥५५॥
III.55 sattva-puruṣayoḥ śuddhi-sāmye kaivalyam iti
When the purity of the intellect is equal to that of the *puruṣa, kaivalya* liberation ensues.

इति पतञ्जलिविरचिते योगसूत्रे तृतीयो विभूतिपादः
iti Patañjali-viracite yoga-sūtre tṛtīyo vibhūti-pādaḥ
Thus ends the third chapter on *vibhūti* in the *Yoga Sūtras* composed by Patañjali.

CHAPTER IV: ABSOLUTE INDEPENDENCE

चतुर्थः कैवल्यपादः
caturthaḥ kaivalya-pādaḥ

जन्मौषधिमन्त्रतपःसमाधिजाः सिद्धयः ।।१।।
IV.1 janmauṣadhi-mantra-tapaḥ-samādhi-jāḥ siddhayaḥ
The mystic powers arise due to birth, herbs, *mantras*, the performance of austerity, and *samādhi*.

जात्यन्तरपरिणामः प्रकृत्यापूरात् ।।२।।
IV.2 jāty-antara-pariṇāmaḥ prakṛtyāpūrāt
The changes [in bodily forms that take place] in other births is due to the filling in by *prakṛti*.

निमित्तम् अप्रयोजकं प्रकृतीनां वरणभेदस्तु ततः क्षेत्रिकवत् ।।३।।
IV.3 nimittam aprayojakaṁ prakṛtīnāṁ varaṇa-bhedas tu tataḥ kṣetri-kavat
The instrumental cause of creation is not its creative cause, but it pierces the covering from creation like a farmer [pierces the barriers between his fields].

निर्माणचित्तान्यस्मितामात्रात् ।।४।।
IV.4 nirmāṇa-cittāny asmitā-mātrāt
Created minds are made from ego only.

प्रवृत्तिभेदे प्रयोजकं चित्तम् एकम् अनेकेषाम् ।।५।।
IV.5 pravṛtti-bhede prayojakaṁ cittam ekam anekeṣām
There is one mind, among the many [created by the *yogī*], which is the director in the different activities [of the different bodies].

तत्र ध्यानजम् अनाशयम् ।।६।।
IV.6 tatra dhyāna-jam anāśayam
From these [five types of minds that possess *siddhis*], the one born of meditation is without the storehouse of *karma*.

कर्माशुक्लाकृष्णं योगिनस्त्रिविधम् इतरेषाम् ।।७।।
IV.7 karmāśuklākṛṣṇaṁ yoginas tri-vidham itareṣām
The *karma* of a *yogī* is neither white nor black; of everyone else, it is of three types.

ततस्तद्विपाकानुगुणानाम् एवाभिव्यक्तिर्वासनानाम् ॥ ८ ॥
IV.8 tatas tad-vipākānuguṇānām evābhivyaktir vāsanānām
From [these three types of *karma*] the activation of only those subliminal impressions that are ready for fruition [in the next life] occurs.

जातिदेशकालव्यवहितानाम् अप्यानन्तर्यं
स्मृतिसंस्कारयोर् एकरूपत्वात् ॥ ९ ॥
IV.9 jāti-deśa-kāla-vyavahitānām apy ānantaryaṁ smṛti-saṁskārayor eka-rūpatvāt
Because they are identical, there is an uninterrupted connection between memory and *saṁskāra*, even though they might be separated by birth, time, and place.

तासाम् अनादित्वं चाशिषो नित्यत्वात् ॥ १० ॥
IV.10 tāsām anāditvaṁ cāśiso nityatvāt
The *saṁskāras* are eternal, because the desire [for life] is eternal.

हेतुफलाश्रयालम्बनैः संगृहीतत्वाद् एषाम् अभावे तदभावः ॥ ११ ॥
IV.11 hetu-phalāśrayālambanaiḥ saṅgṛhītatvād eṣām abhāve tad-abhāvaḥ
Since [*saṁskāras*] are held together by immediate cause, motive, the mind, and the object of awareness, the *saṁskāras* cease when the latter cease.

अतीतानागतं स्वरूपतोऽस्त्यध्वभेदाद् धर्माणाम् ॥ १२ ॥
IV.12 atītānāgataṁ svarūpato 'sty adhva-bhedād dharmāṇām
The past and the future exist in reality, since they differ [from the present only] in terms of the time of [manifestation] of their characteristics.

ते व्यक्तसूक्ष्मा गुणात्मानः ॥ १३ ॥
IV.13 te vyakta-sūkṣmā guṇātmānaḥ
The past, present, and future have the *guṇas* as their essence and are either manifest or latent.

परिणामैकत्वाद् वस्तुतत्त्वम् ॥ १४ ॥
IV.14 pariṇāmaikatvād vastu-tattvam
The things [of the world] are objectively real, due to the uniformity [of the *guṇas* that underpin] all change.

वस्तुसाम्ये चित्तभेदात् तयोर्विभक्तः पन्थाः ।। १५ ।।
IV.15 vastu-sāmye citta-bhedāt tayor vibhaktaḥ panthāḥ
Because there is a multiplicity of minds [perceiving an object] but yet the object remains consistent, there is a difference in nature between the object and the mind [of the observer].

न चैकचित्ततन्त्रं चेद् वस्तु तद् अप्रमाणकं तदा किं स्यात् ।। १६ ।।
IV.16 na caika-citta-tantraṁ vastu tad apramāṇakaṁ tadā kiṁ syāt
An object is not dependent on a single mind [for its existence]; if it were, then what happens to it when it is not perceived [by that particular mind]?

तदुपरागापेक्षित्वाच् चित्तस्य वस्तु ज्ञाताज्ञातम् ।। १७ ।।
IV.17 tad-uparāgāpekṣitvāc cittasya vastu jñātājñātam
A thing is either known or not known by the mind depending on whether it is noticed by the mind.

सदा ज्ञाताश्चित्तवृत्तयस्तत्प्रभोः पुरुषस्यापरिणामित्वात् ।। १८ ।।
IV.18 sadā jñātāś citta-vṛttayas tat-prabhoḥ puruṣasyāpariṇāmitvāt
The permutations of the mind are always known to its Lord, the *puruṣa* soul, because of the soul's unchanging nature.

न तत् स्वाभासं दृश्यत्वात् ।। १९ ।।
IV.19 na tat-svābhāsaṁ dṛśyatvāt
Nor is the mind self-illuminating, because of its nature as the object of perception.

एकसमये चोभयानवधारणम् ।। २० ।।
IV.20 eka-samaye cobhayānavadhāraṇam
There cannot be discernment of both [the mind and the object it perceives] at the same time.

चित्तान्तरदृश्ये बुद्धिबुद्धेरतिप्रसङ्गः स्मृतिसंकरश्च ।। २१ ।।
IV.21 cittāntara-dṛśye buddhi-buddher atiprasaṅgaḥ smṛti-saṅkaraś ca
If [the mind] were cognized by another mind, then there would be an infinite regress of one intelligence [being known] by another intelligence. Moreover, there would also be confusion of memory.

चितेरप्रतिसंक्रमायास्तदाकारापत्तौ स्वबुद्धिसंवेदनम् ॥ २२ ॥
IV.22 citer apratisaṅkramāyās tad-ākārāpattau svabuddhi-saṁvedanam
Although it is unchanging, consciousness becomes aware of its own intelligence by means of pervading the forms assumed by the intelligence.

द्रष्टृदृश्योपरक्तं चित्तं सर्वार्थम् ॥ २३ ॥
IV.23 draṣṭṛ-dṛśyoparaktaṁ cittaṁ sarvārtham
The mind, colored by the seer as well as by that which is seen, knows all objects.

तदसंख्येयवासनाचित्रम् अपि परार्थं संहत्यकारित्वात् ॥ २४ ॥
IV.24 tad-asaṅkhyeya-vāsanā-citram api parārthaṁ saṁhatya-kāritvāt
That mind, with its countless variegated subliminal impressions, exists for another entity [other than itself], because it operates in conjunction [with other instruments].

विशेषदर्शिन आत्मभावभावनाविनिवृत्तिः ॥ २५ ॥
IV.25 viśeṣa-darśina ātma-bhāva-bhāvanā-vinivṛttiḥ
For one who sees the distinction [between the mind and the soul], reflecting on the nature of the self ceases.

तदा विवेकनिम्नं कैवल्यप्राग्भारं चित्तम् ॥ २६ ॥
IV.26 tadā viveka-nimnaṁ kaivalya-prāgbhāraṁ cittām
At that point, the mind, inclined toward discrimination, gravitates toward ultimate liberation.

तच्छिद्रेषु प्रत्ययान्तराणि संस्कारेभ्यः ॥ २७ ॥
IV.27 tac-chidreṣu pratyayāntarāṇi saṁskārebhyaḥ
During the intervals [in this state of discriminate awareness] other ideas [arise] because of previous *saṁskāras*.

हानम् एषां क्लेशवदुक्तम् ॥ २८ ॥
IV.28 hānam eṣāṁ kleśavad uktam
The removal [of these previous *saṁskāras*] is said to be like [the removal] of the *kleśa* afflictions.

प्रसंख्यानेऽप्यकुसीदस्य सर्वथा विवेकख्यातेर्धर्ममेघः समाधिः ।। २९ ।।
IV.29 prasaṅkhyāne 'py akusīdasya sarvathā viveka-khyāter dharma-meghaḥ samādhiḥ
For one who has no interest even in [the fruits] of meditative wisdom on account of the highest degree of discriminative insight, the *samādhi* called *dharma-megha*, cloud of virtue, ensues.

ततः क्लेशकर्मनिवृत्तिः ।। ३० ।।
IV.30 tataḥ kleśa-karma-nivṛttiḥ
From this comes the cessation of the *kleśas* [impediments to *yoga*] and *karma*.

तदा सर्वावरणमलापेतस्य ज्ञानस्यानन्त्याज्ज्ञेयम् अल्पम् ।। ३१ ।।
IV.31 tadā sarvāvaraṇa-malāpetasya jñānasyānantyāj jñeyam alpam
At this point, because of the unlimited nature of knowledge when all impurities have been removed from it, that which remains to be known is little.

ततः कृतार्थानां परिणामक्रमपरिसमाप्तिर्गुणानाम् ।। ३२ ।।
IV.32 tataḥ kṛtārthānāṁ pariṇāma-krama-parisamāptir guṇānām
As a result, there is a cessation of the ongoing permutations of the *guṇas*, their purpose now fulfilled.

क्षणप्रतियोगी परिणामापरान्तनिर्ग्राह्यः क्रमः ।। ३३ ।।
IV.33 kṣaṇa-pratiyogī pariṇāmāparānta-nirgrāhyaḥ kramaḥ
The progression [of any object through Time] corresponds to a [series of] moments. It is perceivable at the final [moment] of change.

पुरुषार्थशून्यानां गुणानां प्रतिप्रसवः कैवल्यं
स्वरूपप्रतिष्ठा वा चितिशक्तिरिति ।। ३४ ।।
IV.34 puruṣārtha-śūnyānāṁ guṇānāṁ pratiprasavaḥ kaivalyaṁ svarūpa-pratiṣṭhā vā citi-śaktir iti
Ultimate liberation is when the *guṇas*, devoid of any purpose for the *puruṣa*, return to their original [latent] state; in other words, when the power of consciousness is situated in its own essential nature.

इति पतञ्जलिविरचिते योगसूत्रे चतुर्थः कैवल्यपादः ।

iti Patañjali-viracite yoga-sūtre caturthaḥ kaivalya-pādaḥ

Thus ends the fourth chapter on *samādhi* in the *Yoga Sūtras* composed by Patañjali.

NOTES

THE HISTORY OF YOGA

1. But see discussion in I.1 for the accuracy of the translation "union" in the context of the *Yoga Sūtras*.
2. The identification of these four *yoga* systems in the *Bhagavad Gītā* was first popularized in *Rāja Yoga* by Vivekānanda, who made his initial impact in the West after his address to the Chicago Parliament of Religions in 1893. See De Michelis (2004) for a genealogy of neo-Vedānta.
3. Throughout the present work, Yoga refers to the philosophical school, or Yoga tradition, while *yoga* indicates various practices or systems of *yoga*.
4. For a good example, see the Jain scholar Haribhadra's *Yoga-dṛṣṭi-samuccaya* (Chapple 2003).
5. Vedic is an older form of Sanskrit; both are members of the Indo-European language family. The earliest Sanskrit-speaking peoples, which are the easternmost branch of this family, are referred to as Indo-Aryans.
6. The earliest Vedic texts are the four Vedas, followed by the Brāhmaṇas, the Āraṇyakas, and the Upaniṣads.
7. Due to the figure's horned headpiece, and the presence of animal motifs on this seal, it received the most attention and was unfortunately hastily identified as the "proto-Śiva" seal. There is no consensus among archaeologists as to the cultural identity of the Indus Valley, but obviously one's position on the origins of the Indo-Aryan people is relevant to this discussion. Those holding the Indo-Aryans to be immigrants perceive the Indus Valley civilization as a non-Vedic culture whose decline more or less coincided with the arrival of the Indo-Aryans. Those considering the Indo-Aryans to be indigenous argue for a Vedic presence in the Indus Valley. See Bryant (2001) for full discussion.
8. For a discussion of scholarship on the *keśin*, long-haired mystic of *Ṛg Veda* X.136, see Werner (1989).
9. Interestingly, all the Upaniṣads wherein Yoga is expressed belong to the same Vedic branch, that of the black Yajur Veda.
10. While the term *Brahman* is used primarily for the absolute truth in its all-encompassing aspect, and *ātman* for the more localized aspect of that same truth in the individual, the two terms are interchangeable in the Upaniṣads.

11. The earliest reference to *yoga* is actually in the *Taittirīya Upaniṣad* (II.5.4), after a discussion of the five *kośas*, or layers, that make up an individual, but whether this refers to a meditative technique is unclear. Werner (1986) argues that this reference points to the merger of an older Vedic spiritual tradition with meditative techniques from non-Vedic traditions.
12. The sense here is that the *yogī* discovers the real self and thus becomes, and by removing awareness from the illusory self, thereby also ceases.
13. The text adds: "One should practice *yoga* in a place that is flat, clean, free of grit, fire and sand, near quiet running water, etc., favorable to the mind, not an eyesore, and protected from the wind in a cave or sheltered place . . . Lightness, health, absence of desire, effulgent complexion, pleasant voice, nice fragrance, and little faeces and urine, these are the first expressions of *yogic* practice."
14. This Upaniṣad adds *tarka*, inquiry, to the last five limbs found in Patañjali and reverses the order of *dhāraṇā* and *dhyāna* from that found in Patañjali's system.
15. This demarcation of Sāṅkhya/Yoga metaphysics in the *Maitrī Upaniṣad* extends to ridiculing the later Vedāntic *advaita*, nondualistic, school of Upaniṣadic interpretation as "not worthy of discussion" (*kiṁ tad avācyam*, VI.7). Advaita Vedānta holds a radically monistic view of the world by rejecting the reality of *prakṛti*, matter, as illusory and considers only *Brahman/ātman* as real. The Sāṅkhya/Yoga traditions are dualist and accept the reality of both the world of *prakṛti* as well as *ātman* (which it calls *puruṣa*).
16. While both traditional narrative and critical scholarship consider the epic to have developed over the centuries, it had reached its present size of 100,000 verses prior the fifth century C.E. (when a land grant refers to it as consisting of this number of verses).
17. E.g., XIII.24; XVIII.52.
18. For further discussion, see Brockington (2005 and 2003).
19. See Hopkins (1901, 336) for discussion.
20. *Vicāra* and *vitarka*; see I.17 for discussion.
21. For extended analysis on this issue, see Bronkhorst (1993).
22. See Dasgupta (1963, I:229–30) for list.
23. See Edgerton (1924, 32) and Larson (1989, 132).
24. Edgerton (1924, 36).
25. Sāṅkhya is first mentioned in the *Śvetāśvatara Upaniṣad* (VI.13.1), where even the name of its reputed founder, Kapila, is found (V.2).
26. See, for example, Bryant (2004).
27. See, for example, Hara (1999).
28. See, for example, Torella (1999).
29. Specifically, this view sees Yoga as a merger of three complexes: "1) one or more Sāṅkhya traditions; 2) one or more Buddhist traditions; and 3) an emerging philosophical Yoga tradition that is compiling various older ascetic and religious strands of speculation" (58ff). More specifically, Larson finds two systematic philosophizing strains in ancient India, that of the *Ṣaṣṭi-tantra* tradition of Sāṅkhya, and the Abhidharma tradition of Sarvāstivāda and Sautrāntika Buddhism, with systematic Yoga emerging as a hybrid of that interaction (1989, 134).

30. Schreiner (1999).
31. See also XII.293.30, and 296.42.
32. This has been amply stressed by Edgerton. Indeed, "any formula of metaphysical truth provided that *knowledge* thereof was conceived to tend towards salvation, might be called 'Sāṅkhya'" (1924, 15). However, see Ramakrishna Rao (1966, 270ff) for an opposing perspective that does find grounds to identify distinctions between Sāṅkhya and Yoga in the *Mahābhārata*.
33. The ultimate Absolute, *Brahman*, is understood as either a supreme personal being or a supreme impersonal consciousness, depending on the sects of Vedānta stemming from the Upaniṣads.
34. Although Patañjali arguably makes implicit reference to *Brahman* in I.26–27, where he correlates *Īśvara* with *oṁ*.
35. *Vīrāsana* is mentioned in XII.292.8 and XIII.130.8–10 (Brockington 2003, 20).
36. *Nyāya Sūtras* IV.2.42.
37. *Vedānta Sūtras* I.2.1.3 and commentaries.
38. See Kane (1977, 1419) for discussion.
39. For further discussion and references, see Brockington (2003).
40. See R. S. Bhattacharyya (1985, 3–15) for discussion.
41. Bhattacharyya (ibid., 101–102) considers the first instance of this identification of the three Patañjalis to be in the commentary by Puṇyarāja on the fifth-century grammatical text the *Vākyapadīya*.
42. See Kane (1977, 1396) and Larson (2008) for discussion and references. Larson does not close the door to the possibility that the Patañjalis could be one and the same, in contrast, for example, to Woods (1914) and R. S. Bhattacharyya (1985). Others, such as Dasgupta (1922), are open to accepting the identity of Patañjali the grammarian and Patañjali of the *Yoga Sūtras*, but not that of the commentator on *āyurveda*. Larson, following Bhattacharyya but drawing different conclusions, raises the relevant observation that connections among the three systems of knowledge were already being made by the philosopher and grammarian Bhartṛhari in his *Vākyapadīya*.
43. A number of scholars have dated the *Yoga Sūtras* as late as the fourth or fifth century C.E., but these arguments have all been challenged. The main rationales for this date were laid by scholars such as Jacobi (1911). These include the claims that the Patañjali of the *Yoga Sūtras* is different from the Patañjali who is the commentator of the grammarian Pāṇini; the *Yoga Sūtras* address, implicitly, the Vijñānavāda Buddhism of the fifth century (IV.15ff) and so must postdate this school; and certain doctrines in the *sūtras* are not evidenced in early Sāṅkhya and Yoga texts, and so must belong to a later period. All such arguments are problematic. Prasad (1930) was one of the first to point out that although the (later) commentaries beginning with Vyāsa identify Patañjali's anti-idealism arguments as directed against Vijñānavāda Buddhism, there are serious reasons to question whether this was the specific school of idealism prevalent at Patañjali's time. Second, whether or not the two Patañjalis noted above are the same is, to all intents and purposes, irrelevant to the date of the *sūtras*. Finally, the doctrines specified as absent in early Sāṅkhya and Yoga texts may nonetheless have been ancient

doctrines and thus do not necessarily point to a late date. See also Dasgupta (1974, 226–38) for further discussion.

44. R. S. Bhattacharyya (1985, 109ff).
45. Not irrelevant here is the maxim of the Grammarian tradition that if even as much as half a phoneme can be saved in the formulation of a rule, the Grammarian rejoices as he would the birth of a son!
46. See Larson (2008, 86ff) for recent discussion and references.
47. Hauer (1958) considered the five strata of the texts to consist of: the *nirodha* section, I.1–22; the *Īśvara-praṇidhāna* section, I.23–51; the *kriyā-yoga* section, II.1–27; the *aṣṭāṅga* section, II.28–III.55; and the fourth chapter on the *nirmāṇa-citta*, constructed mind. Frauwallner (1953) divided the text into three sections: the *nirodha* section, *pāda* I; *kriyā-yoga* leading into *aṣṭāṅga-yoga, pādas* II–III; and *pāda* IV, a later appendage. Dasgupta (1922) argued that the fourth chapter, with its change in style and subject matter, was added later, especially since the particle *iti* concluding the third chapter, indicated that the original text had ended at that point.
48. E.g., Bhattacharyya (1985).
49. As Feuerstein notes, "Our need for 'order' in the sense of logical neatness, linear consecutiveness, is not necessarily shared by non-western cultures" (1979, 41).
50. E.g., Feuerstein (1979); Larson (2008), Whicher (1998), Chapple (1994).
51. From their perspectives, Chapter I deals with the mind and the different levels of consciousness relevant to the goals of *yoga*; Chapter II, with the mechanisms underpinning the relationship between the mind and consciousness, and the practical techniques required to attain higher levels of consciousness; Chapter III, with the results that accrue from such practices; and Chapter IV, with establishing the Yoga position on mind and consciousness in the context of rival views, and with the goal of realization of the true self.
52. Caution is required in attempting to bypass the commentaries and excavate an original set of "pure" Pātañjalian teachings distinct from those of the later Yoga school, since such enterprises, of course, require the projection of very much later philological assumptions and methods onto Patañjali with no means of verification. Even when rigorous attention is directed onto the chronology of philosophical terms and concepts in contemporaneous philosophical literature in an attempt to identify borrowings or influences from other traditions, terms were often drawn from a common pool but sometimes used to denote different things, both diachronically and synchronically in different philosophical contexts and knowledge systems. When seeking extraneous influence on a text, it is rarely certain who has influenced whom or whether commonalities between traditions indicate linear influence or two traditions dipping into this common pool. A fallacy is all too often made, in my view, of assuming that the first instance a concept or term surfaces in a text indicates that this text or tradition has consequently influenced all subsequent traditions wherein this concept or term is used. All that can be said, in fact, is that this concept can first be identified in an (extant) literary source at this time; one must be careful of hastily assuming that the concept itself did not exist prior to it being recorded in this way.

53. See, for example, Chapple (1994).
54. For discussion and references, see Bronkhurst (1985).
55. For examples, see R. S. Bhattacharyya (1985, 43–47).
56. The etymology of Vyāsa is derived from the root *vi* + *as* = divide.
57. There are four world ages in Hindu cosmography, of which the fourth, the *kali yuga*, is considered to have begun in 3108 B.C.E.
58. For Śaṅkara, the entire world of change is an illusory superimposition on an unchanging, formless, qualitiless, and impersonal *Brahman*, Absolute Truth. Thus, everything in the realm of matter, *prakṛti*, is illusory, *māyā*. The changing world of forms simply does not exist from the perspective of absolute reality, or, perhaps more accurately, everything that appears to exist in the external world is, in reality, the changeless *Brahman*. Similarly, the apparent individuality of the multiple and multifarious living beings in the world, the *ātmans*, is also illusory. There is not an infinite number of living entities; there is only the undivided, all-pervading *Brahman*, hence the name of his school of philosophy, *advaita*, nonduality. For Śaṅkara there is only one underlying truth, and all apparent dualities perceived in existence—the world of forms and individuals—are the product of illusion, *avidyā*.
59. *Quarterly Journal of the Andhra Research Society* 2 (1927): 134ff.
60. Hacker (1968) and other Śaṅkara specialists, as well as scholars who have worked more closely with this commentary, are inclined to accept its authenticity. Rukmani, however, in her translation of the *Yogasūtra-bhāṣya-vivaraṇa of Śaṅkara* (2001, xiff), rejects the authorship of the Vedāntin Śaṅkara. She offers as the most convincing evidence the fact that the *Vivaraṇa* contains some explicit references to statements made by Vācaspati Miśra, who lived after Śaṅkara. In contrast to this, Wezler (1983) sees these influences as going the other way—Vācaspati Miśra's work shows clear vestiges of the influence of the *Vivaraṇa*. For this and other reasons, the matter remains unresolved.
61. For discussion of the dates of Vācaspati Miśra (as well as Patañjali and Vyāsa), see Woods (1914, xxiff).
62. In Feuerstein's view, Vācaspati Miśra "approached his subject matter with great candour and sympathy but not from within the yogic tradition. This is corroborated by his whole style, and his preoccupation with philological and epistemological matters as well as his anxious dependence on Vyāsa" (1979, 30).
63. It had, however, been known since the publication of al-Bīrunī's more famous work, *India*, published in 1887, that he had translated the *sūtras*, since it was quoted copiously in that work.
64. There were a number of Vaiṣṇava commentators on the Vedānta who vigorously critiqued Śaṅkara's views, including Rāmānuja in the twelfth century. Rāmānuja presented a position of *viśiṣṭādvaita*, differentiated nonduality, that modified the basic metaphysical infrastructure of *advaita* nonduality by proposing that there were differentiations within ultimate reality. Rāmānuja posited a basic and eternal tripartite subdivision within *Brahman*: *Brahman* as supreme personal Being, or *Īśvara*, whom he correlated with Viṣṇu/Nārāyāṇa; *prakṛti*, matter; and the *puruṣa* souls. For Rāmānuja, these are eternal and real ontological categories, not illusory superimpositions on an undifferentiated *Brahman*, as Śaṅkara had posited, but

they do not compromise the essential nonduality of the absolute since everything emanates from, and remains dependent on, Viṣṇu. In one of Rāmānuja's analogies, the relationship of the personal *Brahman* (Viṣṇu) with *prakṛti* and *puruṣa* is like that of the body and possessor of the body: Although in one sense they are one, the latter is dependent on, and supported by, the former. Madhva, in the thirteenth century, further emphasized the divisions between these categories. Other Vaiṣṇava commentators on the Vedānta added their particular sectarian nuances to the issue, of which Vallabha and the Caitanya school in the fifteenth century are noteworthy, and all of them drew upon the Upaniṣads, the Vedānta, and the *Bhagavad Gītā* as sources of authority. In any event, Vijñānabhikṣu's philosophy of *bhedābheda*, difference in nondifference, overlaps with the main metaphysical tenets of these predecessor Vedāntins, both in asserting the reality of the world and the eternal individuality of the souls, and in his critique of Śaṅkara's *advaita*. For Vijñānabhikṣu, *Brahman* is different from the world and the souls, insofar as the latter are the inherent manifestations of *Brahman*, which is the material and efficient cause of the universe. But *Brahman* is also nondifferent from the souls insofar as they have the same characteristics as *Brahman*.

65. Rāmānanda Sarasvatī wrote a commentary called *Ratna-prabhā* on Śaṅkara's commentary on the Vedānta Sūtra, the *Brahmasūtra-bhāṣya*.
66. See comments by his disciple, P. N. Mukerji in Hariharānanda (1963, preface).

THE SUBJECT MATTER OF THE *YOGA SŪTRAS*

1. As Dasgupta notes, if the mind itself were conscious, then why would its states be sometimes conscious and sometimes unconscious? In other words, if the very nature of the mind were conscious, then all its states should always be conscious—there should be no unconscious or subconscious states in that which is, by definition, conscious. The fact that this is not the case suggests that consciousness lies in another entity behind the mind, which is conscious of some states external to it but not others.
2. See Larson (1983) for discussion.
3. Schweizer states as follows: "If mind and environment are held to belong to the same metaphysical realm, then mental content can both cause and be caused by other physical events. This at least opens the door to explaining mental representation and the evolution of cognitive structure through appeal to the interaction between an organism and its environment, while it is not at all clear that this door is open on a Cartesian account (1993, 853). Along similar lines, he elaborates that AI adopts a computational paradigm, which assumes that all phenomena, whether artificial or natural, are founded on computational procedures evidenced in physical systems. Since the *citta* in Yoga is an unconscious mechanism which manipulates the representational structures involved in perception, it can be characterized as computational (ibid., 854). He further notes that, as in Yoga, "subjective experience is an element which is theoretically extraneous to the research programs of cognitive science and AI."

4. I use Indic throughout to refer to Hindu, Buddhist, and Jain commonalities.
5. It is an axiom in Indic thought that anything eternal cannot be subject to change. If the soul is eternal, it therefore cannot undergo changes.
6. The difference between the two schools is primarily one of focus. Both accept the liberation of *puruṣa* from *prakṛti* as their goal, but Sāṅkhya mostly concerns itself with metaphysics, analyzing what *puruṣa* must extricate itself from, namely, the manifestations of *prakṛti*. In other words, liberation is attained by inference and intellectual reasoning, that is, with the path of knowledge, *jñāna*. Yoga concerns itself more with the nature of the mind and the results accrued from its control, in other words, with active meditative strategies for attaining liberation. But there are also differences of nuance, perhaps the most important of which for our purposes, is that Sāṅkhya conceives of the mind as consisting of three aspects, *buddhi*, intelligence; *ahaṅkāra*, ego; and *manas*, mind, whereas the Yoga school conceives of these as interacting functions of the one *citta*, internal organ, rather than as three distinct metaphysical layers. Sāṅkhya posits fifty components of psychic experience, which are simplified in Yoga to five *vṛttis*, and while some later Sāṅkhya traditions are nontheistic insofar as there is no mention of God (although there were important theistic variants), Yoga is theistic. In addition, since *citta* is all-pervasive, in Yoga there is an immediate transferal to a new body, in contrast to the Sāṅkhyan notion of a subtle body that transmigrates (*Sāṅkhya Kārikā* XL–XLI).
7. Tellingly, Sāṅkhya does not have very much to say as far as the *means* to liberation is concerned. *Sāṅkhya Kārikā* LXIV is the only verse giving any indication as to how to attain release, but even this says little about an actual methodology.
8. The *Mahābhārata* contains various strands. For example, compare Yudhiṣṭhira's dialogue with Bhīṣma and Śuka's dialogue with Vyāsa in XII.187, 239–41, respectively.
9. Houben (1999, 500).
10. Kapila was clearly a renowned sage in ancient lore and is mentioned widely, e.g., *Śvetāśvatara Upaniṣad* V.2; *Mahābhārata* XII.290.3 and 337.59; *Gītā* X.26; *Sāṅkhya Kārikā* LXIX; and as the fifth *avatāra* of Viṣṇu in the *Bhāgavata Purāṇa* (I.3.10).
11. See Motegi (1999) for a compilation of quotes attributed to Pañcaśikha by later authors. This sage is also mentioned several times in the *Mahābhārata* (e.g., *Śānti-parvan* XII.307.211–12).
12. A number of commentators ascribe this original work to Kapila, the primordial disseminator of Sāṅkhya. The sixty topics are specified in the Vaiṣṇava text *Ahirbudhnya Saṁhitā.*
13. Larson (1979, 167).
14. Patañjali himself, however, explicitly mentions only *sattva* (II.41; III.35, 49, 55), and then in its sense of *buddhi*, intelligence. He does, however, refer to synonyms of all the *guṇas* in II.18.
15. *Sattva* literally means "beingness."
16. When the *guṇas* maintain what we might call an equitension, *prakṛti* remains in

a precreative state of dynamic potential called *avyakta*. Once the equilibrium is disrupted, however, creation takes place. See Ramakrishna Rao (1963) for a discussion.

17. The analogy of milk holds only in terms of the evolution of by-products. Where *prakṛti* differs from milk is that it and its evolutes maintain their own separate identity while simultaneously producing further evolutes, unlike milk, which is itself fully transformed when producing yogurt.
18. There were a number of schematic variations of the Sāṅkhya system in circulation, which enumerate the categories differently.
19. Specifically, *Sāṅkhya Kārikā* XXIII uses the term *adhyavasāya*, ascertainment. It notes that the *sāttvic* form of *buddhi* contains detachment; virtue, knowledge, and power, and its *tāmasic* form the opposite of these.
20. See Podgorski (1984) for an excellent discussion of *ahaṅkāra*'s pivotal role.
21. Technically *manas* is the function that ascribes the categories of *sāmānya*, genus, and *viśeṣa*, particularly (mostly associated with Nyāya) to cognition. It is *savikalpa-pratyakṣa* where brute sensory input is *nirvikalpa-pratyakṣa* (see I.43 for discussion of these terms).
22. In technical Sanskritic philosophical terminology, the *tanmātras* can be considered the universals, *sāmānya*, of sound, taste, etc., rather than individuators, *viśeṣa*, of particular notes of the scale, range of tastes, etc.
23. Since *puruṣa* is omnipresent, its adjacency with *buddhi* is not spatial; conceptualizing their relationship is one of the main philosophical problems of Hindu thought.
24. The genesis of ignorance is not a topic deemed resolvable by the human intellect in any Indic knowledge system and therefore not considered a fruitful topic of speculation.
25. Vyāsa uses the term "reflected image," *pratibimba*, only once in his commentary (IV.23), to indicate that it is the objects that are reflected in the mind—not the *puruṣa* in the mind and/or vice versa as per Vācaspati Miśra and Vijñānabhikṣu. Vācaspati Miśra sees the consciousness of *puruṣa* reflected in *buddhi*, which then becomes as if conscious. In actuality, in his view, there is no contact between *puruṣa* and *buddhi*. *Buddhi* is animated by the reflection of the *puruṣa* pervading it and becomes a quasi person, as it were. While this position seems determined to ensure that no change is ascribed to *puruṣa* itself, the problem with it, from the perspective of the detractors of the Yoga school, is that since *buddhi* is essentially inert *prakṛti*, it does not account for experience itself, which is the nature of *puruṣa*. Vijñānabhikṣu, therefore, holds that while *buddhi* may indeed become animated by the reflection of the *puruṣa* reflected in it, *buddhi* and its permutations are then reflected back to *puruṣa*, which then actually experiences its states of mind. In this double-reflection model, there is thus some form of real contact between *puruṣa* and *buddhi*, even as the former remains unchanged and autonomous, insofar as it is the witness of *buddhi*. It is due to ignorance that the states of *buddhi* are imagined to be in *puruṣa*. The problem with this position is that it suggests *puruṣa* is subject to change, which counters an axiom of much

Hindu, and certainly Yoga, philosophy. Such differences underscore the recondite nature of any dualistic system of thought (Eastern or Western) in accounting for the mechanics underpinning the interaction between consciousness and matter, two ontologically distinct entities.

26. *Rajas* and *tamas* can never be completely eliminated due to the inherent constitution of *prakṛti*.
27. I use the notion of the soul as pure subjectivity or as subject-aware loosely throughout this commentary. The notion of subject is meaningful only in contrast to some interaction with an object. In ultimate *asamprajñāta-samādhi*, by definition, there are no interactions with objects; therefore, the notion of subjectivity becomes inapplicable. However, I find it useful to retain the usage with this caveat so as to underscore the difference in the focus of awareness in *yoga* from other to pure self.

THE PRESENT TRANSLATION AND COMMENTARY

1. Or, for the nontheistic Mīmāṁsā, consisting of authorless eternal words.
2. Reductionism seeks to interpret a religious body of knowledge by reducing it to modern categories of explanation external to the knowledge in question, such as seeking known scientific, sociological, or psychological explanations for religious phenomena.
3. The Vedānta tradition accepts *Smṛti* texts where they are not perceived as contradicting the *Śruti* (II.1.1 and commentaries).
4. Literally, the opposing point of view. Commentaries frequently discuss opposing philosophical positions in order to identify their defects.
5. See reference in I.1 to the *Brāhmaṇa* texts, which concern Vedic ritual.

CHAPTER I: MEDITATIVE ABSORPTION

1. This invocation is found preceding the commentary of Vyāsa in some recensions (although it is likely a later insertion). The term used for God here is Bhagavān (the same term used in the *Bhagavad Gītā*, spoken by Kṛṣṇa to Arjuna, and in the *Bhāgavata Purāṇa*, the story of Kṛṣṇa's incarnation). The term used for Kṛṣṇa is Vāsudeva, a patronymic for Kṛṣṇa as son of Vasudeva.
2. Viṣṇu is considered God in the Vaiṣṇava traditions, and either the source of the incarnation of Kṛṣṇa noted above, or derivative from him, depending on the sect. Śeṣa is a multiheaded serpent upon which he reclines. See II.47 for the traditional verse offered to Patañjali in the form of Śeṣa.
3. Traditional sources enumerate six schools of thought that emerged from the Upaniṣadic period of the late Vedic age (although, as noted in the introduction, the first textual reference to such six schools can be attested only very late). Among these, the Mīmāṁsā school, noteworthy for its treatment of epistemology, formulated a rationale for perpetuating the old Vedic sacrificial rites. The Nyāya school was best known for developing rules of logic so that the debates between the var-

ious schools could be conducted according to conventions about what constituted valid argument. The Vaiśeṣika school provided a metaphysics that perceived the created world as ultimately consisting of the combination of various eternal categories such as subatomic particles. The Sāṅkhya school posited a contrasting metaphysical system in which the created world evolved out of primordial matter, *prakṛti*, from which the *puruṣa*, soul, must extricate itself. The Vedānta school was concerned less with the physical constituents of the material world and more with the relationship among *Brahman*, the Supreme Truth of the *Upaniṣads; ātman*, the individualized feature of *Brahman*; and the perceived world as an emanation of *Brahman*. Finally, the Yoga school as represented by Patañjali is less a philosophical school than a practical psychosomatic technique through which the *puruṣa*—the *ātman* of the Upaniṣads—can be realized as distinct from *prakṛti*. As noted in the introduction, Yoga referred to a cluster of meditative techniques, some form of which was common to numerous different schools and sects, rather than a distinct philosophical school.

4. The first *sūtra* of the primary text for the Vedānta school, the *Vedānta Sūtras*, is *athāto brahma-jijñāsā*, now there is inquiry about *Brahman*; that of the primary *sūtra* of the Mīmāṁsā school is *athāto dharma-jijñāsā*, now there is inquiry into duty; and similarly that of the Vaiśeṣika school, *athāto dharmaṁ vyākhyāsyāmaḥ*, now we will explain duty.
5. As noted, throughout the text, Yoga refers to the philosophy, psychology, and metaphysics of the tradition as a school, while *yoga* denotes the techniques, systems, and paths of the tradition as a body of practices.
6. For the *Vedānta, Mīmāṁsā*, and *Vaiśeṣika Sūtras*, see note 3 above. *Athāto* is a compound of *atha* + *ataḥ*.
7. For example, the Vedānta school, as its name denotes, presented itself as the *anta* or conclusion of the Veda. Rāmānuja, the famous twelfth-century theistic commentator of the text, explains that *atha*, now, in the first *sūtra* of the *Vedānta Sūtras* (*athāto brahma-jijñāsā*) refers to one who has exhausted the study of Vedic ritualism and understood that the fruits that are gained from performing the sacrifices and works prescribed in the Vedas are temporary and limited. Such a person, who begins to conceive of the desire for release from the *saṁsāric* cycle of action and reaction, is "now" ready to begin a study of *Brahman*, as expressed in the Vedānta.
8. Vijñānabhikṣu states that Brahmā, the secondary creator god of Hinduism, is said to have uttered *atha* along with *oṁ* in the beginning of creation (quoted by Mādhava from the *Amara Kośa*, traditional dictionary, 87). Mādhava, in his doxography, notes that, among its many meanings, *atha* is also an auspicious particle (*Sarva-darśana-saṅgraha* 43ff).
9. Sanskrit and English are members of the Indo-European language family and thus share many cognate terms.
10. *Mām evaiṣyasi yuktvaivam*, engaged in *yoga*, you will come to me. This sense of union is common in the Upaniṣads (e.g., *Kena* 1.1).
11. *Sarva-darśana-saṅgraha* 150ff.

12. First of all, the notion of uniting or joining requires the existence of two entities that come into contact. While this might work somewhat in certain Vedānta traditions where the *ātman* might be conceived as uniting with *Brahman*, in the Yoga tradition, *ātman* (*puruṣa*) does not come into contact with anything other than itself, and hence union is problematic, unless used very loosely. Second, *yoga* is more accurately a process of disunion, that is, of *puruṣa* breaking its union with *prakṛti* rather than uniting with anything.
13. In one sense, Vyāsa notes, one can argue that *samādhi* underpins all of these five states, since it is inherent in the pure nature of the actual mind itself, and some degree of concentration is evident in any mental state, but it is the last two that are relevant in this preliminary definition of *yoga*.
14. Vyāsa states that all obstacles to *yoga* become loosened by such one-pointed concentration.
15. Vācaspati Miśra defines wondering, *kṣipta*, as a state of mind constantly afflicted by *rajas* toward various external objects; and confused, *mūḍha*, when the mind is possessed by deep sleep on account of lethargy, *tamas*. One-pointed, *ekāgra*, is obtained only when *sattva* is maximized.
16. *Śāsanam*, from the root *śās*, means teaching (*śāstra*, another common derivative, means the implement for teaching, namely, sacred texts), and the prefix *anu* means the continuation of an action.
17. While some of the twelve topics are obscure in connotation, R. S. Bhattacharyya (1985) translates them as follows: (i) the eight limbs of *yoga*; (ii) the impurities of the mind; (iii) the obstacles to *yoga*; (iv) the body; (v) the bodily regions upon which concentration is directed; (vi) the last three meditative limbs of *yoga*; (vii) incomplete *samādhi*; (viii) the highest form of *samādhi*; (ix–xi) mystic powers (or the three means for attaining *samādhi*); and (xii) liberation.
18. This is a work of the Pāñcarātra (Vaiṣṇava or Bhāgavata) school.
19. See Ramakrishna Rao (1966, 292ff) for discussion.
20. The Purāṇas are a huge compendium of texts that essentially contain most of the ingredients of modern Hinduism—the stories of the great divinities and their devotees, royal dynasties, social duties, yogic practices, etc. The most important of these is the Bhāgavata.
21. Or, more correctly, in Sāṅkhya, the metaphysical matrix accepted by Yoga. The introduction describes the difference between these two schools on the matter of the internal body.
22. These two bodies are also referred to as *sthūla-śarīra* and *sūkṣma-śarīra*, respectively.
23. Recall the caveat in the introduction on applying "pure subjectivity" or "subject-aware" to the soul in the context of Yoga metaphysics.
24. The first reference to Yoga itself as a distinct school seems to be the writings of Śaṅkara in the ninth century (Bronkhorst 1981).
25. *Yoga* is also mentioned in IX.1.11 and 13; 2.13 of this text.
26. *Adhyātma-yogādhigamena . . . harṣa-śokau jahāti.*
27. The difference between the two schools is primarily one of focus. Both accept as

their goal the liberation of *puruṣa*, the inner self, from *prakṛti*, matter, but Sāṅkhya mostly concerns itself with a knowledge-based method—analyzing what *puruṣa* must be extricated from, namely, the manifestations of *prakṛti*—and Yoga, with an action-based method—the means by which *puruṣa* can attain such liberation, namely, the psychosomatic process of *yoga*.

28. Although "awareness" and "consciousness" tend to imply an object, when speaking about *puruṣa* I am using them to refer to objectless awareness, for want of a better user-friendly term.
29. These are known in Sāṅkhya as the *antaḥkaraṇa*, or, as noted in the previous *sūtra, sūkṣma-śarīra*.
30. The Yoga tradition also differs from the Vedānta tradition in this regard.
31. The term *adhyavasāya* is used in the *Sāṅkhya Kārikā* (XXIII) for the function of *buddhi*, which denotes determination, resolution, decision, opinion, mental effort.
32. *Ahaṅkāra* is referred to as *asmitā* in this text.
33. See *Sāṅkhya Sūtras* I.50.
34. There are two stages involved in sense perception, discussed more fully in other Indic traditions such as Jainism and Nyāya. The first is preconceptual, when a sense object is not recognized or identified but is perceived as raw impression, like a baby's impression of the world, called *nirvikalpa-pratyakṣa*. This is followed by the mind's recognition of the object that it categorizes as a certain type of thing (technically considered to be the recognition of it as a member, *viśeṣa*, of a class, *sāmānya*, in several Indic knowledge systems). This is called *savikalpa-pratyakṣa*. See I.43 for the two types of *pratyakṣa*, and III.44 for further discussion on *viśeṣa* and *sāmānya*.
35. The *Sāṅkhya Kārikās* define *buddhi* as containing eight *bhāvas*, dispositions: knowledge, detachment, *dharma* (duty, righteousness), and power when its *sāttvic* nature is manifest, and their opposites when its *tāmasic* nature is manifest.
36. *Yathā hi grāmādhyakṣaḥ kauṭṭumbhikebhyaḥ karamādāya viṣayādhyakṣāya prayacchati viṣayādhyakṣaś ca sarvādhyakṣāya sa ca bhūpataye tathā bāhyendriyāṇyālocya manase samarpayanti manaś ca saṅkalpyāhaṅkārāya ahaṅkāraś cābhimatya buddhau sarvādhyakṣa-bhūtāyāṁ tad idam uktaṁ puruṣasyārthaṁ prakāśya buddhau prayacchanti iti.*
37. As Vācaspati Miśra notes in his commentary to I.1.
38. The question might arise that if mind is made of the same *prakṛti* as matter, then why cannot the *puruṣa* become directly aware of gross objects? Why does it require the medium of the mind? The Jains, for example, hold that the awareness of the soul can pervade external objects when all its covering of matter has been removed. According to Yoga, the preponderance of *sattva* in *buddhi*, which resembles the consciousness of *puruṣa*, is able by its translucence to absorb the light of the latter and reflect it back to *puruṣa*. The objects of the world are predominantly made of *tamas* and thus too dull and opaque to directly absorb the light of consciousness.
39. For a discussion of the merits of the double-reflection theory of Vijñānabhikṣu vs. the single-reflection theory of Vācaspati Miśra, see introduction and Kumar (1981).

40. *Brahman* is the term for the Absolute Truth in the Vedānta tradition.
41. See *Sāṅkhya Kārikā* XIII, and the *Gītā* XIV, XVII, and XVIII.
42. Dasgupta (1922, I:242ff).
43. These cover such things as prescribed duty and its mode of performance, worship, diet, charity, sacrifice, austerity, knowledge, activity, understanding, determination, attainment of happiness, and future birth. See also Manu XII.24–52; and *Mahābhārata* XII.301–302.
44. When the mind is overcome primarily by *tamas*, it becomes inclined to vice, ignorance, attachment, and impotence, and when it is overcome primarily by *rajas*, it becomes inclined to the opposite types of qualities.
45. *Saṁsāra* in Indic thought is a cycle of birth and death because every action breeds a reaction, which then eventually bears fruit, provoking rereactions, which cause rerereactions, and so on ad infinitum. Living beings have to return life after life to experience the accumulated store of *karmic* reactions, but in doing so simply breed more reactions and thus perpetuate a vicious cycle of birth and death. This is discussed in detail in Chapter II.
46. There is a difference of opinion among Hindu thinkers as to whether full *asamprajñāta-samādhi* can be experienced while alive, or whether it entails the complete abandonment of the physical and cognitive apparatus of the body and mind. For the views of the various schools, see Fort and Mumme (1996).
47. The five *skandhas*, sheaths or aggregates (*khandha* in Pali), are (1) aggregate of matter, *rūpa-skandha*, the elements—fluidity, solidity, motion, and heat—as well as the sense organs and their objects—sound, smell, etc.—in short, the physical body; (2) aggregate of sensations, *vedanā-skandha*, all pleasant and unpleasant sensations experienced sensually or mentally; (3) aggregate of perceptions, *saṁjñā-skandha*, perceptions or recognition of objects through the six faculties; (4) aggregate of mental formations, *saṁskāra-skandha*, all volitional activities good or bad; (5) aggregate of consciousness, *vijñāna-skandha*. This *skandha* of consciousness is of interest here since, for Buddhists, it requires one of the four faculties (eye, etc., including mind) as its basis and an object (i.e., form, etc., including thought) as its support. So consciousness is named according to the means by which it arises—visual consciousness, mental consciousness, etc. The essential point is that consciousness depends on other faculties and objects; it cannot exist separately and therefore is not considered eternal and extractable from its faculties and objects for Buddhists, as it is for the followers of Yoga and almost all Hindu sects. This is perhaps the most essential metaphysical difference between Hindu (and Jain) traditions and Buddhist ones.
48. See, for example, Nāgārjuna's *Mūla-madhyamaka-kārikā*, Chapter X.
49. Liberation, for such schools, entails a state of nonconsciousness, a prospect that was ridiculed by their opponents.
50. The oldest philosophical texts of India, the Upaniṣads, typically favor the term *ātman* for the localized aspect of the self and *Brahman* for the universal aspect of the supreme self (although these terms are sometimes used interchangeably). The *Gītā* uses both these terms, as well as *puruṣa* favored by the Yoga school, and other terms usually used in the context of the soul in *saṁsāra*, such as *jīva; dehī*,

the embodied one; and *kṣetrajña,* the knower of the field [of *prakṛti*]. There are significant differences among schools in the understanding of the nature of the soul, such as those noted previously.

51. *Draṣṭṛ* occurs in various cases in this *sūtra* and in II.17, II.20, and IV.23. Two other derivatives of the same verb with very similar meaning also occur: *dṛś,* to see, in II.6; and *dṛśi,* seeing, in II.20, 25. *Puruṣa* occurs eight times (I.16, 24; III.35 [twice], 49, 55; and IV.18, 34). *Ātman* in the sense of self occurs three times (II.5, 41; IV.25).
52. The Nyāya and Vaiśeṣika schools hold that consciousness itself is adventitious to the soul and is generated only when the soul comes in contact with the mind. When separated from the mind, the soul remains in a state devoid of consciousness, a view of liberation that was derided as rather unenticing by other schools of Hindu thought (as can be sensed from the way Vijñānabhikṣu frames this perspective). While the Yoga school shares the view that the mind and all mental activities are distinct from the soul, it holds that consciousness itself is at all times inherent and manifest in the soul, and not a property that manifests only when in contact with the mind; it thus differs from Nyāya and Vaiśeṣika in this regard.
53. The followers of Cārvāka and other related philosophers were materialists and held consciousness to be a by-product of matter (the body), which is manifest under certain circumstances, and not something distinct from the body in any way, just as alcohol is a by-product generated under certain circumstances from fermented fruit or grain and not something separable from fruit or grain.
54. Depending on the point to be made, sometimes the *puruṣa* is compared to the red flower and the *citta* to the crystal (e.g., IV.23), and sometimes the *puruṣa* to a crystal and the *citta* to a red flower (e.g., Vācaspati Miśra in I.4, 41). In the former, the comparison illustrates that the mind is infused both with sense objects distinct from itself as well as with consciousness distinct from itself, just as the crystal is infused in its various facets with different colors distinct from itself. In the latter, the comparison illustrates that the crystal remains clear even though it might appear to be colored by an adjacent object, as does the *puruṣa,* even though its awareness appears to be colored by the adjacent *citta* with its *vṛttis* (see Murakami 1999 for further references). This metaphor is widely used, for example in Saṅkara's commentary to *Vedānta Sūtra* III.2.11, where *Brahman* is correlated with the crystal, which is not transformed due to the reflections of sense objects within it.
55. See Jacobsen (2005) for a discussion of similes in Sāṅkhya.
56. The idea of this metaphor, of course, is the Upaniṣadic notion that the self is in some way one with *Brahman* (understood variously by different Vedāntic exegetes). Since *Brahman* is the source of all reality, by realizing the self one realizes one's unity with all reality, and in this sense gains the universe.
57. Hariharānanda Āraṇya outlines his version of the process by which the *yogī* can remove the misidentification of the *citta* with *puruṣa* in his commentary. Any act of cognition involves the subject of knowledge, the instrument or means of knowledge, and the object of knowledge. The *manas* aspect of the *citta* is an instrument of knowledge when it has the senses and external things as its objects

of knowledge. But the *manas* can itself become an object of knowledge—one can scrutinize one's mind by introspection. Thus, although an instrument of knowledge, the mind is simultaneously an object of knowledge in its own right. More subtle than the mind is *ahaṅkāra*, ego. This is the aspect of *citta* that produces a sense of personal identity with the *vṛttis* of the mind. It lays claim to the mind. According to Hariharānanda, through the practice of meditation the mind can be stilled, and one can gain a sense or intuition of this *ahaṅkāra*. One can then realize that the mind itself is actually an object of knowledge, and the *ahaṅkāra* the instrument of knowledge that processes the information of the mind through the "I sense." In other words, through meditation, one can determine that the ego, or sense of I, is a different faculty from the knowledge that is presented to it by the *manas* mind. From this perspective, the *ahaṅkāra* ego, as instrument of knowledge, appropriates the knowledge of the *manas* as object of knowledge.

But one can go deeper into the workings of one's *citta* to the *buddhi*. By further meditation on the *ahaṅkāra*, the *buddhi* aspect of the *citta* can determine that this sense of I is different from the real self and therefore to be discarded. Now *buddhi* becomes the instrument of knowledge and *ahaṅkāra* the object of knowledge. By further concentration still, one realizes that even *buddhi*, the source of all discrimination, is also not the ultimate source of awareness, and one becomes aware of a *puruṣa* by which even the discriminatory functions of *buddhi* are illuminated. Such ability to discern this existence of *puruṣa* is the final act of *buddhi* (this is the *viveka-khyāti* that will be discussed in *sūtra* II.26). In other words, *buddhi* realizes that it itself is not the ultimate self—it deconstructs itself, so to speak. When even this final act of discrimination ceases due to supreme detachment, there is no further object of knowledge and therefore no further function for *buddhi* to perform. *Puruṣa* then becomes completely uncoupled from *buddhi* and, hence, *prakṛti*, and exists in isolation (the *kaivalya* of III.55). Thus separated, *buddhi* itself can become an object of knowledge, says Hariharānanda (in principle, at least, although once *puruṣa* is disassociated from *buddhi*, there is no further subject of knowledge to focus on the *buddhi* as an object of knowledge).

58. *Majjhima Nikāya, Sutta* 63.
59. However, the various Lokāyata materialist schools do not accept the notion of *karmic* reactions to action.
60. Just as a *brāhmaṇa* living in the village of Śala, which is full of Kirāṭas (a tribe living in the east of India), says Vācaspati Miśra, does not become a Kirāṭa, so *sāttvic vṛttis* retain their nature even if surrounded by *rājasic* and *tāmasic* ones.
61. *Pramāṇa* comes from the root *pra* + *mā*, to measure or estimate, in this case, the sources of knowledge or instruments through which it is gained. Relevant and related roots include *pramātṛ*, the knower; *prameya*, that which is known; *pramā*, that actual state of correct knowledge, cognition; *pramāṇya*, the validity of knowledge.
62. The extra *pramāṇas* posited by other schools are considered by the Yoga school to be variants of the *pramāṇas* mentioned here.
63. Indeed, some philosophical schools such as that associated with the materialist

Cārvāka accept sense perception as the only *pramāṇa*, arguing that the other means of knowledge are derived from it.

64. In Vaiśeṣika, all manifest reality can be broken down into seven basic categories, one of which is *dravya*, substance. There are nine different types of substances, the minutest particles of earth, water, fire, air, and ether (matter, liquids, energy, gas, space), the mind, the soul, time, and space. The specific aspect of a substance, *viśeṣa* (from which the school gets its name), is that which distinguishes it from another substance, which keeps particles, for example, separate and individual so that one can differentiate between one molecule of earth and another, or between one soul and another. Since one dog, or any object in reality, is different from another by dint of its distinct conglomeration of atoms, *viśeṣa* can be applied in a more general manner to refer to the distinctiveness of any object from another.
65. There are two stages of perception as understood by a number of Indic philosophical traditions (see I.43 for discussion). Briefly, when a person encounters an unfamiliar object, one first becomes aware of it in a vague sort of way, as raw sense data, without assigning a name or identification to it, like an infant's preconceptual awareness. After this moment, the mind processes the data in terms of its specific name, and the category of thing that it belongs to, and its function, that is, recognizing the object's *sāmānya* and its *viśeṣa*. The first stage of indeterminate awareness is called *nirvikalpa*, and the second, *savikalpa*.
66. Technically, the impression of an object is called *pratyaya*. These are single momentary impressions, while *vṛttis* are more a prolonged sequence of different impressions; thus, a number of *pratyayas* may make up a *vṛtti*.
67. Some schools of thought, such as that associated with Cārvāka, hold that *anumāna* is not a separate source of knowledge because it is predicated on sense perception—the smoke is seen, even if the fire is not—and thus it is a variant of *pratyakṣa* rather than an independent source of knowledge.
68. The variant *śruta* is used in I.49.
69. These schools hold that scripture is simply an extension or subcategory of *pratyakṣa*, sense perception.
70. The *Vedānta Sūtras* refer to the *prakṛti* of Sāṅkhya as established by inference (I.3.3, 4.1; II.2.1), which they consider inferior to Truth that can be verified by recourse to *āgama*, scripture. The *Vedānta Sūtras* dedicate a section to refuting Sāṅkhya on the grounds of scripture, and another using *anumāna*. As an aside, that these *sūtras* devote so much attention to refuting Sāṅkhya points to the importance and prevalence of the Sāṅkhya metaphysics.
71. The focus of the Mīmāṁsā, however, was on the scriptures pertaining to ritual, the Brāhmaṇa texts, as opposed to the mysticophilosophical Upaniṣad texts, which were of interest to the Vedānta tradition.
72. Grinshpon (1997, 136).
73. The *Yukti-dīpikā* actually speaks of three types of sense perceptions in this verse: sensual, mental, and yogic.
74. Vijñānabhikṣu, for example, points out that error is considered an action that entails a positive act of misidentification in the Yoga school, a position technically

known as *viparītākhyāti* or *anyathākhyāti*, rather than a negative lack of discrimination, a position subscribed to by the Sāṅkhya and Mīmāṁsā schools, called *ākhyāti*.

75. E.g., *Tarka-saṅgraha* 37–38.
76. Vyāsa gives some slightly complicated examples, including "the arrow stands still, stood still, will stand still." What this actually means in the mind of the listener is that the arrow has ceased (or will cease) to move. Vācaspati Miśra elaborates that in order to understand the meaning of the root "to stand still," the listener has to imagine a state of not moving. In actual fact, standing still, absence of motion, is really an imagined state of affairs dependent on the idea of motion, but it is then projected as an actual characteristic of the arrow. *Vikalpa* is thus verbalization, or the connotative use of words, rather than the denotative.
77. *Pratyaya* is often translated as presented idea.
78. But see Janácek (1957), who takes *pratyaya* in all instances to mean "impulses" that emanate out from objects, which are then grasped by the mind, rather than the images of these objects in the mind.
79. Since a *saṁskāra* consists of both an imprint of a sense object and recognition or conceptualization of that object, Vyāsa notes that if the former aspect of the *saṁskāra* is dominant when it activates, then it is memory; if the latter, then it is an act of intelligence.
80. Recognition of, say, a rose, depends on the senses contacting a red rose and then seeing a rose again at a later time, at which point the *saṁskāra* of the first experience is activated and one recognizes that the rose of the second occasion *is* similar to the first; in other words, recognition is dependent on the contact of the senses with a sense object. This is not the case with pure memory per se, which is when a rose can be recalled to mind even when one is not physically seeing a rose.
81. The Vedic corpus consists of the four Vedas, the Brāhmaṇas, the Āraṇyakas, and the Upaniṣads.
82. Or, at least, are perceived this way by the Vedānta tradition (*Vedānta Sūtras* II.1.1).
83. See Larson (1983) for a discussion on the tripartite interconnectedness of *smṛti* as memory, sacred text and myth, or legendary history.
84. See *Vedānta Sūtras* X.1.1 and commentaries.
85. See, for discussion, Bryant (2003, xxiiff).
86. *Vairāgyaṁ ca alam-buddhi. (Yoga-sāra).*
87. The term occurs also in the *Sāṅkhya Kārikās* (II), where the commentaries (e.g., Vācaspati Miśra's *Tattva-kaumudī*) also take it to refer to the Vedic texts.
88. See, e.g., *Śloka-vārttika* XXIV–XXVI.247ff.
89. In still later Vedic ritualism, as expressed by the Mīmāṁsā school, the gods became essentially irrelevant (demoted to grammatical categories rather than personified), and the ritual itself construed as paramount in the obtainment of wealth and well-being, rather than being attained due to the pleasure or displeasure of the gods.

90. *Yoga-sāra* commentary.
91. Bhāgavata V.9.10.
92. *Prāptaṁ prāpaṇīyaṁ kṣīṇāḥ kṣetavyāḥ kleśāḥ chinnaḥ śliṣṭapurvā bhavasaṅkramaḥ yasya avicchedāj-janitvā mriyate mṛtvā ca jāyate.* Vyāsa is being rhetorical here, since, obviously, the *yogī* at this point has ceased conventional "thinking" altogether.
93. In the discourse of Asita Devala, *citta* is presented as higher than the sense organs, *manas* as higher than *citta*, higher than which is *buddhi*. See, for discussion, Chakravarti (1975, 45). Also see Bedekar (1959) for the variety of ways terms such as *citta, manas,* and *buddhi* are used in the *Mahābhārata*. In the *Abhidharma-samuccaya* of Asaṅga (founder of the Yogācāra school of Mahāyāna Buddhism), *citta* forms part of the *vijñāna-skandha* along with *manas*.
94. Dasgupta expresses this usefully: "The difference of *tanmātras* or infra-atomic units and atoms (*paramāṇu*) is this, that the *tanmātras* have only the potential power of affecting our senses, [they] must be grouped and regrouped in a particular form to constitute a new existence as atoms before they can have the power of affecting our senses" (1922, 252).
95. See, for discussion, Whicher (1998, 238ff), Koelman (1970), Larson (2008).
96. *Asmitā* as *kleśa* and *ahaṅkāra* of the Sāṅkhya system are roughly synonymous and correlated by the commentators (e.g., Vyāsa in II.19) but refer to slightly different functions of the ego as will be discussed in II.7.
97. *Īśvara-cetanatva-sākṣātkāras.*
98. The same phenomenon is preserved in English: *theist/atheist, sexual/asexual*, etc.
99. Some scholars, traditional and modern, infer the existence of eight stages of *samprajñāta samādhi* as will be discussed in II.42.
100. *Catur-bhujādikaṁ vā śarīraṁ ghaṭādikaṁ vā.* (*Yoga-sāra*)
101. For recent examples, see Bronkhorst (1993) and Sarbacker (2005).
102. *Vitarka/vitakka* in Buddhism has the sense of placing the mind on an object and comprehending its name and form as well as its diverse relations, and *vicāra* of keeping it there in absorption, although the term has a history of usage in Buddhist scholastic texts; see Cousins (1992) for discussion. The former is compared to the bee following a scent to a lotus and then dropping down upon it, the latter like the bee wandering over the lotus once it has reached there. Or the former like the hand that firmly grips a dirty vessel, and the latter like the other hand that rubs it with a cloth, or again, the former is like the potter's hand that firmly holds down the clay, and the latter like the hand that moves it here and there to shape it.
103. Curiously, while mentioning the four *dhyānas* several times, the discussion in this section of the epic ends at the first *dhyāna*.
104. The term *samādadhyān* is used here (and another form of this verb is used in the next line), from the same stem *samādhī*, from which the noun *samādhi*, the final limb of Patañjali's system, is derived.
105. For a comparative discussion of *vitarka* and *vicāra* in Buddhism and Yoga, see Cousins (1992).

106. While early Buddhism borrowed much from mainstream Indic meditative practices, the reverse can also be argued: Bhīṣma's reference to these states in the *Śānti-parvan* section of the epic—as well as the structure of Patañjali's fourfold schema outlined in this *sūtra*—might point to borrowings from Buddhist meditative practices into mainstream Sāṅkhya, as Bronkhorst (1993, chap. IV) has argued. However, in my view it is best to speak of a common substratum of meditative practices rather than hazard estimates at the dates of texts containing similar features and then assume the older text to be the source of any shared notion present in an (even slightly) later text. Apart from anything else, dating the various strata of the epic is a highly speculative and tentative undertaking and can never be conclusive; for a survey of dating attempts, see Brockington (1998, 130–58).
107. I use "self-aware" loosely and heuristically, since "self" implies "other," and the ultimate stage of *asamprajñāta-samādhi, kaivalya* (literally, "aloneness," IV.34), by definition, involves the absence of any "other."
108. Pines and Gelblum (1977, 524).
109. *Pratyayaḥ* here means cause rather than image or idea as it means elsewhere. See I.10 for discussion.
110. See also Vijñānabhikṣu on III.48 in this regard.
111. See, for related comparison, the reference in the *Mahābhārata* to the residents of the White Island where a form of Nārāyaṇa resides, whose bodies do not have gross senses (*pañcendriya-varjitāḥ* XII.331.41). Even certain accomplished *yogīs* are held to have transcended mundane foodstuffs, as is the belief in one of the two primary strains of the Jain tradition in regard to Mahāvīra.
112. *Pradhāna* is *prakṛti* prior to creation, full of potential but as yet unmanifest.
113. *Yathā kasyacid vairāgyam asti na tattva-jñānaṁ Tasmāt ajñāna-pūrvād vairāgyāt prakṛti-layaḥ mṛto 'ṣṭāsu prakṛtiṣu līyate pradhāna-buddhy-ahaṅkāra-tanmātresu līyate*.
114. *Tatra līnaṁ ātmanāṁ manyate mukto 'ham-iti tamo-bheda eṣaḥ.* (Gauḍapāda to *Sāṅkhya Kārikā* XLVIII.)
115. *Bhava* is not found in the Upaniṣads. It is first used as a philosophical term in Pali texts. See Dasgupta (1922), I:87).
116. The sheaths are identified in the *Taittirīya Upaniṣad* as food, breath, mind, discrimination, and bliss (II.2ff).
117. See Rukmani (1978) for further discussion.
118. There are fourteen Manus in the life of Brahmā, the secondary creator of the universe. According to the *Gītā* (VIII.17), Brahmā's one day consists of a thousand cycles of the four *yugas* (which, added together, correspond to 4.32 billion human years), as does his night. Brahmā lives a hundred years, so one can thus calculate the life span of Manu.
119. *Majjhima Nikāya* I.164–66; repeated in I.240 and II.212.
120. Even in the *Kāma Sūtras*, the treatises on eroticism, there are various categories of permissible aphrodisiacs, flirtatious gestures, arousal techniques, and sexual postures.

121. For a history of early theism, see Gonda (1975).

122. *Bhagavān* is a term most popularly associated with Kṛṣṇa (as in the two texts best associated with him, the *Bhagavad Gītā* and *Bhāgavata Purāṇa*), although it can be used for other deities and even noteworthy humans as well.

123. God is not mentioned in the *Vaiśeṣika Sūtras*; the first mention of God in this tradition is in the *Padārtha-dharma-saṅgraha* by the commentator Praśastapāda. See Bronkhorst (1996).

124. While later doxographies tend to contrast nontheistic Sāṅkhya with theistic Yoga (e.g., the eighth-century Jain text *Ṣaḍdarśana-samuccaya* by Haribhadra; Rāmānuja's twelfth-century Vedānta commentary I.4.23 and elsewhere; and Mādhava's fourteenth-century *Sarva-darśana-saṅgraha*), this perception seems based on Īśvarakṛṣṇa's *Sāṅkhya Kārikās* (fourth–sixth century). To be sure, there is no mention of any *Īśvara* here (though that is not quite the same thing as an explicit denial of *Īśvara*). But one must bear in mind that the *Sāṅkhya Kārikās* were to become regarded by later philosophers as the seminal or primary source of Sāṅkhya purely by default: The earlier (arguably theistic) original sources had become lost. It is not until the *Sāṅkhya Sūtras* of the fourteenth century that there is an explicit statement that the existence of God "cannot be proven" (I.92; V.10; VI.64—*Īśvarāsiddheḥ, pramāṇābhāvān na tat-siddhiḥ; Kārya-siddhir neśvara-kartṛ-adhīnā pramāṇābhāvāt*).

In any event, the facts seem to indicate that the early Sāṅkhya tradition, or at least strains of it, did accept the existence of an *Īśvara*, God. Although some scholars find evidence in the *Mahābhārata* (*Śānti-parvan* XII.289.3) for a nontheistic Sāṅkhya—the most conspicuous of which is the term *anīśvara*, which can be rendered as "without *īśvara*," used in reference to Sāṅkhya in contradistinction to Yoga, Edgerton (1924, 11) reads the term as a reference to the individual soul. Indeed, in his reading, there is not a single nontheistic passage associated with Sāṅkhya in the entire epic, a position supported by Ramakrishna Rao (1966). There are undoubtedly many passages in the epic that explicitly associate Sāṅkhya with the impersonal monistic absolute Brahman, or with a personal god, adding a twenty-sixth ingredient of reality to the more standard twenty-five ingredients typical of Sāṅkhya (for example, XII.295–96 and of course the entire Nārāyaṇiya section; see Ramakrishna Rao for a full discussion). In the *Mahābhārata*'s *Bhagavad Gītā*, Kṛṣṇa emphatically states that he is *Īśvara* and that *prakṛti* and her Sāṅkhyan evolutes are his "lower nature" (VII.5). Thus, at the very least, there were theistic strains of Sāṅkhya intermingling with nontheistic ones in the epic.

Additionally, one of the oldest Sāṅkhya texts recognized by the later tradition is the *Ṣaṣṭi-tantra-śāstra*. This is described in the Vaiṣṇava *Ahirbudhnya Saṁhitā*, and in this, Kapila, the undisputed founder of Sāṅkhya in all traditional sources, is stated to be theistic and an incarnation of Viṣṇu. The *Mahābhārata*, too, considers Kapila an incarnation of Viṣṇu, and he is certainly accepted as such and associated with theism in the Purāṇas (e.g., *Bhāgavata* III.24), where his narrative as an incarnation of Viṣṇu is described and his theistic form of Sāṅkhya outlined.

This tradition of a theistic Sāṅkhya is thus ancient and widespread, since it pervades a number of Purāṇas as well as the Pāñcarātra tradition. See Dasgupta (1922, IV:24ff) for discussion. For the history of God in Sāṅkhya texts, see Bronkhorst (1983).

125. The prefix *pra-* gives the sense of forward, *ni* the sense of down, and the root *dha*, to place or put. Thus to put oneself forward and down before *Īśvara*, or prostrate.
126. *Saṁskāras* are the imprints on the mind of every deed, thought, and sense impression one has experienced; they essentially correspond to memories and behavioral patterns.
127. *Karma* means action, which in the Indic context involves not just an action per se but also the inherent reaction every action generates.
128. The term *avyakta* in the *Gītā* is used to describe the *ātman* (e.g., II.25).
129. E.g., R. S. Bhattacharyya (1985). See also Larson (2008) for discussion.
130. Pines and Gelblum (1966, 319). The translation is from the Arabic.
131. Vijñānabhikṣu states that these three bonds are attachment to the sense of I, ego; attachment to the objects of the senses; and attachment of householders to sacrifice, sacrificial fee, gifts, and Vedic study, etc. (in other words, ritualism for the sake of its fruits).
132. Of course, different theistic schools had different notions as to the specific role played by *Īśvara*. For example, was *Īśvara* the material and efficient cause of the universe or simply the efficient cause? (e.g., commentaries to *Vedānta Sūtras* II.2.37, contra Nyāya; II.2.3 contra Yoga).
133. See the description of the mystical powers of the *yogīs* that cause them to be referred to as *Īśvara* in *Mahābhārata* XII.289.24ff (my thanks to David White for this reference), or as deluded demoniacal character types who consider themselves *Īśvara* in the *Gītā* XVI.14. In the *Bṛhadāraṇyaka Upaniṣad*, the term is used to refer to *ātman/Brahman* as Lord (IV.4.22). But such usages are figurative and derivative, and their connotative force implies the normative referent of the term to a supreme being.
134. *Vedānta Sūtras* I.1.1ff; II.2.1ff.
135. Ibid., I.1.3; see also Śaṅkara's commentary to II.2.37.
136. *Vedānta Sūtras* I.1.2 and throughout.
137. See, e.g., Vyāsa I.25 for implicit acceptance of *Īśvara*'s creator role, which seems to be taken for granted in this context. See also Vācaspati Miśra IV.3, however, in his characteristically eclectic and nonpartisan manner, when writing his commentary on the *Sāṅkhya Kārikās* (LVI–II) Vācaspati Miśra is quite comfortable representing the Sāṅkhya view that *prakṛti* is the source of creation and presenting all the standard atheistic arguments against accepting *Īśvara* as cause of creation without refuting them. Interestingly, the commentator Gauḍapāda considers *prakṛti* and *Brahman* to be synonyms (*Bhāṣya* to XXII), another interesting twist in blending Vedāntic and Sāṅkhyan categories.
138. *Atha ka Īśvaraḥ kiṁ vā tat-praṇidhānam ucyate . . . sa ca . . . vedānta-sūtrair aśeṣa-viśeṣato mīmāṁsitaḥ. Ato 'tra diṅ-mātreṇocyate.* (*Yoga-sāra*)
139. See, for example, *Śvetāśvatara* VI.6ff; *Gītā* IX.4 and throughout; *Mahābhārata*

XII.290.110, 333.16, 335.11 (*Īśvaro hi jagat-sraṣṭā*), 336.55, and elsewhere. See also, *Nyāya Sūtras* IV.1.19. The *Nyāya Sūtras* were composed by Gautama, the reputed founder of the Nyāya school, which specialized in analyzing categories of logic.

140. Śaṅkara recognizes Yoga as accepting *Īśvara* as efficient cause in II.2.37 (although in II.1.3, Śaṅkara seems to state that *prakṛti* is the sole cause of creation in Yoga). See Rukmani (1993) for discussion.

141. The term *Īśvara* is first used in the *Gītā* IV.6, which is also the first instance where the text unambiguously announces Kṛṣṇa's supreme and divine nature. The opportunity is ostensibly framed by Arjuna's question after Kṛṣṇa had informed him that he had come to reestablish the eternal science of *yoga*, which he had originally imparted to the sun god Vivasvān in primordial time. Given that Kṛṣṇa, his cousin and contemporary, is standing in front of him, how, wonders Arjuna, could he possibly have instructed Vivasvān many aeons ago? Kṛṣṇa replies that he is the *Īśvara* of all living entities, birthless, imperishable, and the controller of *prakṛti*, and that his appearances in the world are through his own power (*ātmamāyā*). This is followed by the well-known verses in which Kṛṣṇa states that he comes whenever there is a decline in *dharma* and an increase in *adharma* in order to protect the pious and destroy the impious.

In V.29, Kṛṣṇa claims that he is *maheśvara* (the great Lord) of all the worlds, enjoyer of sacrifices and austerities, and friend of all creatures, and that one knowing him attains peace. Similar language is used in X.3, where Kṛṣṇa repeats that he is the *maheśvara*, great *Īśvara*, of the world, birthless and beginningless, and that the undeluded among men who know him as such are freed from all evils. A few verses further, Arjuna calls Kṛṣṇa the supreme *Brahman*; supreme abode, *dhāma*; supreme purifier; birthless, all-pervading primal God; and, of relevance here, the eternal divine *puruṣa* (*Īśvara*, for Patañjali, is a special *puruṣa*). In XVIII.61, Kṛṣṇa as *Īśvara* is said to reside in the hearts of all beings, causing them to revolve by the power of illusion, as if fixed on a machine. Although *Īśvara* is used elsewhere in the text with different nuances, the *Gītā* unquestioningly (and, indeed, quite assertively) identifies this supreme being with Kṛṣṇa.

142. Of the three occurrences of *Īśvara* in the Upaniṣads—other derivatives of the root *iś* such as *īśa* and *īśana* are used more frequently—two (supplemented by the adjective *mahā*, great, that is, *maheśvara*, great *Īśvara*) occur in the SU (IV.10; VI.7), in reference to Śiva (that is, under the names of Hara and Rudra).

143. For a discussion of the *Īśvara* theology of the *Bhāgavata Purāṇa*, see Bryant (2003, xixff).

144. Bryant (2005).

145. Specifically, Ramakrishna Rao determines that there were four traditions accepting the basic Sāṅkhya categories: proto-Sāṅkhya, Vedānta, Yoga, and Pāñcarātra. These differed primarily in their understanding of whether there were twenty-five or twenty-six categories, and whether the twenty-fifth or twenty-sixth category was *Īśvara* or a more impersonal notion of an Absolute. Yoga and *Pāñcarātra* accepted the twenty-sixth category of *Īśvara*, which they referred to as Viṣṇu/

Nārāyaṇa. Even proto-Sāṅkhya, interestingly, which accepted twenty-five categories, albeit associating this with a universal rather than an individual self, nonetheless referred to this category as Viṣṇu (1966, Chapter V). Thus the theism of the proto-Sāṅkhya Yoga section of the epic is Vaiṣṇava in orientation. (Incidentally, Ramakrishna Rao finds evidence of Sāṅkhya and Yoga being independent but overlapping strains in this early period, rather than the one system argued by the other scholars.)

146. Vaiṣṇava refers to a devotee of Viṣṇu; Śaivite, to a follower of Śiva.
147. See, e.g., XII.289.62, 290.109–110, 291.37, 306.76 and, of course, the entire Nārāyaṇīya section where, for example, 334.17 specifically states that the followers of Sāṅkhya and Yoga meditate on Nārāyaṇa (*tat-sāṅkhya-yogibhir-udāra-dhṛtaṁ buddhyā yatātmabhir viditaṁ satatam*).
148. For Śaṅkara's understanding of *Īśvara*, see Nelson (2007).
149. In XV.16–8, Kṛṣṇa states that there are two types of *puruṣas, kṣara-puruṣas*, perishable beings, and *akṣara-puruṣas*, imperishable ones. The *kṣara-puruṣas* are all living entities, *sarvāṇi bhūtāni*, and the *akṣara-puruṣas* are *kuṭastha*, literally, situated on the top. This latter term is used twice elsewhere in the *Gītā* (VI.8 and XII.3), the former in reference to the enlightened sage and the latter as a quality of the highest truth realized by the enlightened sage. On both scores, we can take the *kṣara-puruṣa* to refer to the unenlightened being (or, with Minor 1982, the being phenomenally considered), and the *akṣara-puruṣa* as the enlightened being (or, with Minor, the true realized self). XV.17 goes on to describe another, highest *puruṣa*, the *paramātmā*, the supreme self who pervades the three worlds and supports them, and the term *Īśvara* is used for this highest *puruṣa*. XV.18 emphasizes again that this supreme self is higher than both *kṣara* and *akṣara puruṣas*, and XV.19 that one who knows this supreme self to be Kṛṣṇa knows all that there is to know. X.20 goes further and asserts that knowledge of this is the most confidential scriptural teaching. Thus, while more assertive and elaborative than Patañjali, the *Gītā* also articulates a theology of *Īśvara* as a special *puruṣa* of a different order from other *puruṣas*, except that the *Gītā* puts a name to the position—Kṛṣṇa.
150. E.g., Book XII, chapters 199, 200, 202, 271, 321, 323, 326, 336.
151. Moreover, VI.8 specifies that the *ātman* is not *īśa* and remains bound (because of having an enjoying disposition) until he comes to know God. In short, we have the soul in bondage, the liberated soul, and Śiva, an almost exact Śaivite equivalent of the *Gītā* XIV.16–18, with parallels to Patañjali's theistic rhetoric.
152. III.8–11 speak of the *yogī* sitting in a cave or sheltered place in an appropriate setting, where he should keep the body straight and erect, draw the senses and mind into the heart, and compress the breath and exhale through one nostril. The benefits of this practice are described in III.11–15.
153. Proto-Sāṅkhyan metaphysics are clearly referred to in I.9 and IV.5.
154. The text also refers to Rudra as *puruṣa* (III.9–17). However, the reference is more archaic, making a clear association between Rudra and the famous thousand-limbed *puruṣa* of the Ṛg Vedic *puruṣa* hymn.

155. Even if, for argument's sake, one accepts Minor's (2005) very late dating of 150 C.E. for the composition of the *Gītā* (in contrast to his earlier 1982 assignment of 150 B.C.E.), which is more or less coterminus with the common date assigned to Patañjali, it nonetheless at the very least reflects a major theistic expression current at the time that had long been developing its roots, all the more so given that it was deemed worthy of insertion into the great epic. See Minor (1982, introduction) for the range of dates assigned to this text.
156. See, e.g., *Śvetāśvatara Upaniṣad* IV.11 and 17 for the use of *deva* for Rudra (Śiva), which the text presents as the supreme *Īśvara* and, likewise, the *Gītā* XI.38 for Kṛṣṇa. The term is used extensively in the *Mahābhārata* as a reference to Nārāyaṇa/Viṣṇu (e.g., three times in XII.331.47–51) and throughout the Purāṇic corpus (e.g., *Bhāgavata* III.28.18).
157. See Bryant (2005).
158. Older photos of Krishnamacharya as well as Iyengar show them with the *tilak*, sacred clay, of the Śrī lineage—two broad white vertical lines on the forehead, with a red vertical streak in between.
159. See Stern (2005) and Nevrin (2005).
160. See Bryant (2004) for a range of the postcharismatic problems and challenges faced by the Hare Krishna movement. These are authentic classical Indian spiritual traditions and rich in centuries of philosophical and literary developments.
161. Vācaspati Miśra and Vijñānabhikṣu offer the argument that the scriptures must be absolute, because the *mantras* and knowledge of herbs, etc., contained in them are seen to work, and no one person, even in a thousand lives, could have figured out such things independently.
162. Hariharānanda discusses a "fixed" and "unfixed" mind in relation to *Īśvara*. He states that any *yogī* can potentially arrest the fluctuations of the mind and extinguish the latent *saṁskāras*, or subconscious impressions. Consequently, such a *yogī* can close down the working mind for a specified period and enter into a state of meditative absorption, after which he or she can reactivate the mind if desired. This mind will not be the uncontrolled one of ordinary beings but endowed with knowledge appropriate for the benefit of such a *yogī*. Thus, voluntarily adopting such a mind, liberated *yogīs* can work in the world for the benefit of other beings. Hariharānanda understands *Īśvara*'s adoption of a mind at the time of creation and dissolution to be along the same lines: to address a need such as the upliftment of creatures from the world of *saṁsāra*.
163. Creation in all Hindu systems except the Mīmāṁsā school is cyclical. For the Sāṅkhya school tradition, the universe periodically dissolves into its Sāṅkhya *tattva* constituents and ultimately into primordial *prakṛti*, and remains in a state of dissolution until the next cosmic manifestation, when it evolves forth again.
164. This is the view of the theistic Vedāntins (e.g., Rāmānuja's commentary to *Vedānta Sūtras* I.1.21; Baladeva's commentary to *Vedānta Sūtras* III.2.14ff).
165. Vijñānabhikṣu quotes the *Sāṅkhya Sūtras* (I.154) as stating that the supposed *advaita* passages of the Upaniṣads (upon which the *advaita* school is predicated) do not in actuality contradict the existence of a plurality of eternal *puruṣas*, because,

properly understood, they do not point to one ultimate monistic *ātman*, but refer to the oneness of the *category* of *ātman*. In other words, all *ātman* are the same insofar as they belong to the same category of existence, *ātman-ness*; they are not ontologically one.

166. *Vedānta Sūtras* II.1.3.
167. Mahāvīra, while not the founder of Jainism according to its own sources, is the primary teacher (*tīrthaṅkara*) for this age.
168. E.g., *Bhāgavata Purāṇa* III.24.
169. *Jñāna-dharmopadeśena kalpa-pralaya-mahā-pralayeṣu saṁsāriṇaḥ puruṣān uddhariṣyāmīti.*
170. Hindu time is cyclical. There are four *yugas*, or world ages: the *satya* (aka *kṛta*)-*yuga*, or golden age; *tretā-yuga*; *dvāpara-yuga*; and the present world age of *kali-yuga*, the most degenerate age. Once the cycle is completed, it starts anew.
171. *Dharma* in the context of the *Gītā* most commonly refers to the various duties incumbent on every human being—social, religious, political, professional, familial, etc. The term has a wide variety of usages in philosophical discourses (see, for example, its usage in III.13–14).
172. E.g., *Śloka-vārttika* 16.43ff.
173. Brahmā is the secondary creator of the universe insofar as he creates the forms in the world but does not create the primordial stuff from which these forms are created. He is thus more of an engineer than a creator. The point being made here is that he himself is also a mortal being within *saṁsāra* with a finite, albeit immense, life span (see *Gītā* VIII.17).
174. Pines and Gelblum (1966, 321).
175. There are numerous variants or permutations of this basic view of oneness in diversity in post-Śaṅkara Vedāntic tradition: *dvaitādvaita, viśiṣṭādvaita, śuddhādvaita*, etc. See note 63.
176. For Vijñānabhikṣu, the famous statements of the Upaniṣads, such as the *tat tvam asi*, you are that (*ātman = Brahman*), verses of the *Chāndogya*, are to be understood in this light. A series of verses in the *Chāndogya* VI.8ff, perhaps the most quoted verses from the Upaniṣads, point to the oneness of the soul, *ātman*, with *Brahman*, a oneness that Vijñānabhikṣu and other Vedāntins hold is not absolute but some type of oneness-in-difference as exemplified by Vijñānabhikṣu above.
177. See Bedekar (1964) for a discussion of *oṁ* in the *Mahābhārata*.
178. *Devaṁ paśyet.*
179. E.g., XV.17–18; XIII.13; XIV.27.
180. E.g., III.7; V.6; VI.18.
181. This relationship between designator and designatum, *vācaka* and *vācya*, is called *abhidhā*.
182. Devadatta is used ubiquitously in the Hindu commentarial tradition to refer to an everyday individual, a John Doe.
183. The denotative power of all words is eternal, according to Yoga (and certain other schools, such as Mīmāṁsā).
184. For the Chaitanya Gauḍīya tradition, since Kṛṣṇa is the fullest possible manifes-

tation of Godhead who contains and supersedes all other divine manifestations (*Bhāgavata Purāṇa* I.3.28), the name of Kṛṣṇa, as his sonic manifestation, includes and supersedes all other *mantras*.

185. See, in the Upaniṣads, *Bṛhad* I.3.28; VI.3.6; *Chāndogya* V.2.6; *Kauṣītaki* II.2.8, 11.
186. *Svādhyāyād yogam āsīta yogāt svādhyāyam āsate; svādhyāya-yoga-sampattyā paramātmā prakāśate.*
187. *Bhāvanaṁ punaś citte niveśanam* (I.28).
188. *Bhāvanā tavad bhāvyasya viṣayāntara-parihāreṇa cetasi punaḥ-punar-niveśanam* (I.17).
189. This is to say that, in addition to manifesting the *sāttvic* potential of the *citta*, the *bhakti* traditions aspire to fill the *citta* with *saṁskāras* centered exclusively on *Īśvara* (e.g., Gītā IX.27, 34; XII.8).
190. *Tathā ca praṇava-japa-parameśvara-dhyāna-sampattyā para ātmā parameṣṭhī prakāśate yogina iti.*
191. *Tasya praṇavo nāma praṇava-pūrvakaṁ ca tad-anucintaṁ sākṣātkāraparyavasāyi praṇidhānam iti. Ataḥ parameśvare saṁyamo 'samprajñāta-paryanta-yoge mokṣe ca mukhya-kalpaḥ . . . jīvātma-saṁyamas tu tatrānukalpa iti.*
192. The prefix *sa-* means with, the prefix *nir-* means without. (This is explained fully in I.42–44.)
193. *Saguṇa-brahman* in the Vedānta traditions points to realms within *Brahman* that are made of pure consciousness, *Brahman*, but that nonetheless contain forms, individuals, and personalities. These are non-*prākṛtic* forms and personalities, not to be confused with the evolutes of *prakṛti*.
194. *Tapo-japādi-sādhanair Dhruvādīnāṁ catur-bhūjādi-sākṣātkārād ayaṁ sākṣātkāro vilakṣaṇaḥ. Teṣāṁ hi tapo-dhyānādinā tuṣṭaḥ parameśvaraḥ svayaṁ śarīraṁ nirmāya puraḥ prakaṭībhūya vāgādi-vyavahāraṁ cakre. Yoginas tu yoga-balena vaikuṇṭha-śvetadvīpādi-stham eva catur-bhūjādi-śarīram anyatra sthitāḥ.* (*Yoga-sāra*)
195. See commentaries to II.50 for *recaka*, where breath is suspended after *praśvāsa*, exhalation; *pūraka*, where breath is suspended after *śvāsa*, inhalation; and *kumbhaka*, the simultaneous suspension of both.
196. *Dhyāna* is the seventh limb of *yoga* in Patañjali's system (the verbal form *abhidhyāyet* is used here).
197. *Śrivatsa* is a curl of hair on Viṣṇu's chest. All the details here are standardized descriptions of Viṣṇu's form.
198. The *Bhāgavata* school holds that a manifestation of *Īśvara*, the *antaryāmī* or *paramātman*, resides in the heart along with the individual *ātman*.
199. *Siddhas* are perfected beings who have developed mystic powers, such as flying through the air (which is the term used here, *khecara*).
200. This paradoxical relationship of individuality in oneness, *bhedābheda*, is called by such terms as *viśiṣṭādvaita*, differentiated nonduality; *dvaitādvaita*, duality in nonduality; *śuddhādvaita*, pure nonduality; and *acintyabhedābheda*, inconceivable difference and nondifference by different post-Śaṅkara schools of Vedānta, all with nuances of difference as to how this relationship is conceived of metaphysically.

201. *Tasmān mumukṣoḥ susukho mārgaḥ śrī-viṣṇu-saṁśrayaḥ. Cittena cintayanneva vañcyate dhruvam anyathā. Dhatte padaṁ tvam avitā yadi vighna-mūrdhni.*
202. *Māyā pravartake viṣṇau dṛḍhā bhaktiḥ kṛtā nṛṇām sukhena prakṛter bhinnaṁ svaṁ darśayati dīpavat.*
203. *Kapha* roughly corresponds to the biological fluid system of the body and provides the material for its physical structure and lubrication; *vāta*, to the bodily air principle and is primarily associated with movement; and *pitta*, to the body's energy and is especially associated with metabolism.
204. In Nyāya, doubt arises when no distinguishing characteristics are available to differentiate between things. For example, if one sees an object in the distance that is the same size as both a post and a man, one might not be able to make out which of the two it is in the absence of a distinguishing characteristic (such as movement, which would indicate the object is a man). *Nyāya Sūtras* I.1.23–25.
205. R. S. Bhattacharyya (1985, 157) takes it to be weakness of discrimination.
206. This is the classic Vedāntic metaphor for ignorance: mistaking the apparent world, which is illusory and temporary, to be what it is not, real and ultimate. The nature of error is discussed extensively by all Hindu schools since, as with the *Yoga Sūtras* (II.4), it is the fundamental cause of embodied existence.
207. *Viṣṇu Purāṇa* IV.2.124.
208. See Rukmani (1981, I:181–82n8), for discussion.
209. Prominent are the Buddhist scholastics Vasubandhu, Dignāga, Dharmakīrti, Śantarakṣita, and Kamalaśila.
210. The word *vāda* is added to a philosophical or ideological concept or category to indicate the school or point of view associated with that concept (and *vādin* the follower of such a school). Thus *kṣaṇika-vāda* denotes the school that believes all reality is momentary, *kṣaṇika* (and *kṣaṇika-vādin*, an adherent to this view, a Buddhist).
211. For example, Udayanācārya's *Ātma-tattva-viveka*.
212. For example, Kumārila Bhaṭṭa's *Śloka-vārttika* XVIII.
213. For example, Bādarāyaṇa's *Vedānta Sūtras* Chapter II.2.18ff and commentaries.
214. While Vijñānavāda (Yogācāra) Buddhism did posit a substratum to thought, the *ālaya-vijñāna*, it nonetheless held, in accordance with normative Buddhist doctrine, that this *ālaya-vijñāna* itself was not an inherently durable entity, but it too consisted of a flow or series of moments. Hence that school is only a partial exception to the generic Buddhist position outlined by Vyāsa, since the same objections that can be raised against the standard Buddhist notions of mind can be raised against the *ālaya-vijñāna*.
215. Vijñānabhikṣu also argues here that without a past and future, how can one thought be similar to another? Similarity means that something in the present resembles something in the past, but there is no past thing surviving into the present in a theory of momentariness.
216. Śaṅkara on *Vedānta Sūtras* II.2.26.
217. *Vedānta Sūtras* II.2.25; *Nyāya Sūtras* III.1.18 and commentaries; *Śloka-vārttika* XVIII.115ff.

218. See Bronkhorst (1993, 93).
219. Vācaspati Miśra and Vijñānabhikṣu describe how this lotus *cakra* is situated between the chest and the abdomen. It has eight petals and faces downward. It must be reversed by controlling one's exhalation, and one must use it as a support upon which to focus the mind. Different sections of this lotus are connected with different luminous objects, with different aspects of the syllable *oṁ* (*a-u-m*), and with different stages of consciousness in accordance with the *Māṇḍūkya Upaniṣad* (I.9–12). Thus, the middle of the lotus is the sphere of the sun and of waking consciousness, and is connected to the *a* of *auṁ*. Above this is the sphere of the moon and of dreaming consciousness, which is connected with the *u*. Higher still is the sphere of fire and of dreamless sleep, connected with the *m*. Beyond these three spheres lies the highest state of consciousness, connected with the sound of *Brahman* itself. Within the stalk of the lotus is a channel called the *brahma-nāḍī* with its mouth facing upward, and above that the *suṣumnā* channel (these two channels are the same thing according to Vijñānabhikṣu, and they are one branch of a *mano-vaha-nāḍī*, mind-bearing channel, that has a thousand branches). This channel runs through the various spheres of the sun, etc., noted above. Vācaspati Miśra says this *suṣumnā* channel is the seat of the mind, so if one concentrates here, one attains direct awareness of the mind. Since the mind is also all-pervading like *buddhi*, the intelligence, and *ahaṅkāra*, the ego, from which it is derived, one attains full awareness of all objects.
220. The all-pervading quality of the *buddhi, ahaṅkāra*, and *manas* (i.e., the *citta*), in the school of Yoga is in contradistinction to the Nyāya, Vaiśeṣika, and Mīmāṁsā schools, which hold the mind to be minute.
221. It is due to the dense or weighty nature of *tamas* that the creation of any type of distinct form or delimitation in *prakṛti* is possible, even on the level of gross objects. Without *tamas, prakṛti* would be buoyant and ethereal (*sattva*) and/or constantly moving (*rajas*); no physical forms would take shape. It is *tamas* that weighs down *prakṛti* such that it can take material shapes and manifest as gross objects. The same holds true of the mind.
222. *Asmitā* is usually correlated with the *ahaṅkāra* of Sāṅkhya.
223. See also *Chāndogya Upaniṣad* IV.9.3; VI.14; *Śvetāśvatara* VI.23 for verses stressing the importance of a teacher.
224. An extraordinary example of intense absorption on the *guru* as the object of meditation in the Siddha tradition is the case of Muktānanda, as described in his autobiography *Play of Consciousness* (South Fallsburg, NY: SYDA Foundation, 2000). See also, from other traditions, Sridhar Deva Goswami, *Sri Guru and His Grace* (San Jose: Guardian of Devotion Press, 1983).
225. The *puruṣa* can be aware only of itself, since it is beyond the intelligence and mind and other instruments of cognition, hence the common aphorism of the self knowing itself by itself.
226. See, for example, V.18–29 for another extended list of qualifications.
227. In the introduction I stated that Śaṅkara's *advaita* philosophy is not prominent in his Yoga commentary, to my eye. However, this view of sleep is an example of classical *advaita*.

228. While it has been argued that this state of *samādhi* is still afflicted by the *vitarkas* as defined in II.33–34 (e.g., Kenghe 1970), this seems unlikely, as the *yogī* should have suppressed all outgoing *saṁskāras* at this point. If a connection is to be made, it would seem to be that the *yogī* is still afflicted by awareness of the names and concepts of things (unlike in the *nirvitarka* of the next verse) but not by the *vitarkas* of II.33, where the term is used in a different sense. There it refers to thoughts of violence, etc. Technical terms can be multivalent.

229. See, for example, the completely different interpretation given to the *Vedānta Sūtras* I.1.5–9 by Madhva compared to Śaṅkara and Rāmānuja.

230. As an aside, Vyāsa goes on to make the point that although objects of *nirvitarka*, like cows and pots, are ultimately assemblages of atoms that are themselves composed of subtle elements, nonetheless objects are coherent wholes. He rejects the notion that such conglomerations are unreal because everything consists of parts, which are ultimately imperceptible, and thus there is only the illusion of a whole coherent object. The commentators take Vyāsa to be referring to certain Buddhist positions, which believe in neither whole entities nor partless atoms. For the Buddhists, there are no whole irreducible entities of any sort, because everything consists of parts, and these parts themselves consist of parts, and so on ad infinitum.

Of what, asks Vyāsa, would perfect knowledge of reality consist of if there were no real objects of perception? If the whole does not exist because it is made up of parts, and yet the parts are imperceptible and therefore unprovable because they themselves are made up of parts and therefore not wholes in their own right, and so on, then there would be no basis to establish true knowledge, and so all knowledge would be false. Rather, the whole is both different from and the same as its parts. The Sāṅkhya Yoga philosophy is that of *satkārya*: All objects, even though they may consist of parts, are essentially transformations of an ultimate all-encompassing reality, *prakṛti*. The objects of reality are thus parts of a whole.

231. E.g., Vācaspati Miśra in his *Nyāya-vārttika-tātparya-ṭīkā*. See Clear (1990, 307ff) for more detailed discussion.

232. See Vācaspati Miśra's commentary on *Sāṅkhya Kārikā* XXVII. The language used in the *Kārikās* and the *Yukti-dīpikā* for the two types of perception differs from the more standard usage in Nyāya and elsewhere.

233. Technically this process of recognition involves identifying the object's *sāmānya*, generality, and *viśeṣa* (see I.7).

234. The earth atom is produced from all five *tanmātras*, subtle elements, with a preponderance of smell; liquid, from the *tanmātras* excluding smell, with a preponderance of taste; fire, from the *tanmātras* excluding smell and taste, with a preponderance of sight; air, from the *tanmātras* excluding smell, taste, and sight, with a preponderance of touch; and ether, from the *tanmātra* of sound alone. *Aṇus* are the smallest particles in which matter can exist without reverting back to their essential nature of *tanmātra*. There were variant schemas pertaining to the constituents of the various atoms circulating in different Sāṅkhya or Sāṅkhya-related traditions. The Vedānta tradition, for example, held that each atom was constituted of half its own element and an eighth of the other four; thus the fire

atom, for example, was made up of half the fire element and an eighth portion of ether, air, water and earth.

235. E.g., Larson (2000), Koelman (1970), and Taimni (1961) in support of Vācaspati Miśra's schema, and Feuerstein (1980), Whicher (1998), and myself against.
236. Recall from I.17 that *ānanda* refers to being aware of the *grahaṇa*, the instruments of cognition (the senses themselves and/or the mind), and *asmitā* to the *grahitṛ*, the grasper of cognition (the *buddhi* aspect of the *citta*). Very briefly, in Koelman's analytical schema (1970, 197–224), *sānanda* occurs when one's awareness of these instruments of cognition includes the registering of a feeling of bliss, a quality of *sattva* that is the primary *guṇa* manifest in the instruments of cognition. When one goes beyond this emotional veil, one has attained *nirānanda*. Subsequently, *sāsmitā* is awareness of *buddhi* when still stained by *ahaṅkāra* and *nirasmitā* when one transcends the I-am-ness of ego and is aware simply of *buddhi*'s reflecting nature of is-ness.
237. *Liṅga*, common in Nyāya, literally means a sign and indicates that *buddhi*'s existence is inferred by its signs, that is to say, its characteristics. In Hindu logic, an inference (I.7) is made on the basis of a sign or characteristic, e.g., the presence of an unperceived fire is inferred based on the perception of smoke, which is the sign, *liṅga*, of fire. Primordial, precreation *prakṛti* is *aliṅga*, since, being a state in which the *guṇas* are completely latent, it has no signs or characteristics (any characteristics in the form of its evolutes come later, once the *guṇas* have been activated).
238. See Taimni (1961).
239. *Prajñā-prāsādam āruhyā'śocyaś śocato janān / Bhūmiṣṭhān iva śaila-sthas sarvān prājño'anupaśyati.*
240. See *Ṛg Veda* X.190.1.
241. See *Taittirīya Upaniṣad* I.1.1; I.9.1; II.4.1; III.10.6; *Kaṭha* III.1.
242. *Āgamenānumānena dhyānābhyāsa-rasena ca / Tridhā prakalpayan prajñā labhate yogam uttamam.*
243. The other five are *dravya*, substance; *guṇa*, quality; *karma*, motion; *samavāya*, inherence; and *abhāva*, absence.
244. Whicher (2005, 626).
245. *Nirodha-sthiti-kāla-kramānubhavena.*
246. The length of time one remains in *samādhi*, says Vācaspati Miśra, depends on the *yogī*'s complete desirelessness and practice.

CHAPTER II: PRACTICE

1. *Sarva-darśana-saṅgraha* 353ff.
2. Indic philosophical traditions in general consider the soul's sojourn in *saṁsāra* to be *anādi*, without beginning. There is no point at which it fell into *saṁsāra*—it has always been there, and early Indian philosophers considered it a fruitless intellectual endeavor to speculate as to how this state of affairs came about. Better, rather, to reflect on how to bring it to an end.
3. See, for example, the austerities of Hiraṇyakaśipu from the *Bhāgavata Purāṇa*

(VII.3) in IV.1. See also the account of the ascetic in the Buddhist *Kassapa Sīhanāda Sutta*.

4. The term occurs in the *Mahābhārata* III.2.23 and XIII.14.22.
5. Carpenter (2003), Pandit (1985).
6. This is not Śaṅkara's overall position in the *Vedānta Sūtras* (e.g., III.4.12ff), where knowledge is clearly prioritized over any type of activity. See also his *Gītā-bhāṣya* II.10; III.0; V.16; XII.12; XVIII.11, 60.
7. According to the *Bhagavad Gītā* II.62, from contemplating the objects of the senses, one becomes attached to them, and from attachment, anger [aversion] arises, which in turn produces further undesirable consequences. Vyāsa is indicating a similar sequence of events: When attachment is present, aversion has not yet manifested.
8. As discussed previously, the prefix *a-* negates the noun to which it is added. Along very similar lines, the prefix *duḥ-* denotes an unpleasant state of a noun in opposition to *su-*, which denotes the pleasant state.
9. Considering the temporary mentioned in this verse to be eternal, says Vyāsa, is to think that entities like the earth or the sky, along with the moon and stars, are permanent.
10. *Naveva śaśāṅka-lekhā kamanīyeyaṁ kanyā madhv-amṛtāvayava-nirmiteva candraṁ bhitvā niḥsṛteva jñāyate nīlotpala-patrāyatākṣī hāva-garbhābhyāṁ locanābhyāṁ jīva-lokam āśvāsayantīveti.*
11. *Mahā Satipaṭṭhāna Suttanta*, verse 5. (T. W. Rhys Davis and C.A.F. Rhys Davis, *Dialogues of the Buddha* (1910; Delhi: Motilal Banarsidass, 2000).
12. Ibid., verses 7 and 9.
13. *Vyaktam avyaktaṁ vā sattvam ātmatvenābhipratītya tasya sampadam anunandati ātma-sampadaṁ manvānas tasya vyāpadam anuśocati ātma-vyāpadaṁ manyamānaḥ sa sarvo'pratibuddhaḥ.*
14. E.g., see *Sāṅkhya Sūtras* V.74.
15. *Yat tu navīnā vedānti-bruvā nityānandāvāptiṁ parama-mokṣaṁ kalpayanti, tad eva ca vayaṁ na mṛṣyāmahe.*
16. See Fort (1988) for discussion of and references to Śaṅkara's equating of *sukha* and *ānanda* in his commentary to various Upaniṣads.
17. The genitive case *draṣṭuḥ* is used in I.3.
18. *Buddhitaḥ paraṁ puruṣam ākāra-śīla-vidyādibhir vibhaktam apaśyan kuryāt tatrātma-buddhiṁ moheneti.* This verse is attributed to Pañcaśikhācārya by the commentators.
19. Generally the *-tā* (-ness) suffix is used only with nouns. It is very unusual in Sanskrit for it to be affixed to a conjugated verb form.
20. Desire produces anger because either the object of desire is not obtained and one is frustrated, or it is obtained but fails to satisfy for very long and one is again frustrated.
21. *Nyāya Sūtras* III.1.18, 21.
22. In *satkāryavāda*, all physical reality is a transformation of one reality, in Sāṅkhya, *prakṛti*. Thus manifestations or evolutes of *prakṛti* are never destroyed but simply dissolve back into their more subtle matrix.

23. This particular meditation is called *prasaṅkhyāna* by the commentators. This is considered to be the highest type of meditation and will be discussed in IV.29.
24. *Bhāgavata Purāṇa* VIII.21ff.
25. *Dve dve ha vai karmaṇī veditavye pāpakasyaiko rāśiḥ puṇya-kṛto'pahanti. Tad icchasva karmāṇi sukṛtāni kartum ihaiva te karma kavayo vadanti*. Unattributed quote.
26. The *-in* suffix appended onto a noun indicates the possessor of the noun in question. Thus *vivekin* is the possessor of *viveka*.
27. Pre-Socratic Greek sources contain resonances on this perspective of life: "Count no mortal happy until he has reached the very end of his life free from misfortune and pain" (Sophocles, *Oedipus Tyrannus*).
28. These are the ancient law books for the followers of the Vedic civilization, outlining various specificities pertaining to *dharma*, sociocivic and religious codes of conduct.
29. In other words, insects are killed involuntarily even when engaging in innocuous household chores such as cooking, sweeping, or grinding spices.
30. *Sutta-nipāta* III.12.361.
31. Cārvāka, who was evidently not a vegetarian, argued vigorously that the goal of life is the pursuit of sensual pleasure and minimization of discomfort.
32. See Wezler (1984) for an excellent discussion.
33. Time, in Hindu cosmography, is cyclical. At the end of every great cycle, the manifest universe devolves into its subtlest ingredients and ultimately back into its matrix, undifferentiated *prakṛti*, from which it again evolves when the new cycle begins. See *Gītā* VIII.17–19 for an expression of this.
34. Although it seems acceptable to suppose that the mind can exist only if the *puruṣa* exists, the reverse need not hold true. After all, *puruṣa* can exist without the mind upon attaining liberation.
35. Hariharānanda argues at length that the union between *puruṣa* and *prakṛti* cannot be a temporal or spatial relationship; it is beyond Time and Space.
36. *Māyā*, in Hindu thought, is the power of illusion that is the cause of ignorance, the root of the *kleśas*. In the more developed theistic traditions, it is a power of God, *Īśvara*.
37. Although Patañjali uses the term *sattva* (III.35, 49, 55) as a synonym for *buddhi* (and specifically when he refers to the immediate relationship between *buddhi* and *puruṣa*), he never uses the terms *tamas* and *rajas*.
38. When the *guṇas* are in equilibrium, a state called *pradhāna*, there is no creation. This occurs at the end of one new cycle and prior to the evolution of a new one.
39. According to the Sāṅkhya view of the unparticularized subtle elements, upheld by Vyāsa here, sound has one property, touch two, sight three, taste four, and smell five. This is because each progressively grosser evolute of these subtle elements contains the properties of all the previous evolutes. Thus taste contains sound, sight, touch; and smell contains all five properties. As noted in the *Yuktidīpikā*, however, there are two schools or views on the matter, that of Vārṣagaṇya, articulated by Vyāsa, and the other holding that each *tanmātra* has only one property—the principal one associated with it.

40. The *ahaṅkāra* ego, which produces these eleven items, was defined in II.6 (where it was termed *asmitā*) as the misidentification of *puruṣa* with *buddhi*.
41. Vijñānabhikṣu points out that only through the mind can one absorb sounds, etc., and thus if one is distracted, one doesn't hear or see things.
42. In his commentary to the *Sāṅkhya Kārikās* (XX), Vācaspati Miśra takes *liṅga* to refer to any evolutes from *prakṛti*, not merely *buddhi*.
43. E.g., *Vedānta Sūtras* I.4.1; II.2.1.
44. 1922, 246.
45. Knowledge of anything requires change, Vācaspati Miśra reminds us—knowledge is directed from one object to another, from one thought to another, etc., and is thus constantly changing—and *puruṣa*, in the Yoga school, is considered to be constant and changeless. Therefore, *puruṣa* does not actually know anything in its pure state except its own unchanging, eternal self.
46. Each *saṁskāra* in this primordial *pradhāna* would appear to still be connected in some way with its specific owner, the individual *puruṣa*, since *saṁskāras* are reconnected with their previous owners at the time of the next creation. Therefore, they do not dissolve entirely into the primordial soup of *pradhāna*.
47. III.50, 55; IV.26, 34. See also *Sāṅkhya Sūtra* V.20, which states that liberation is the removal of obstacles.
48. *Yathā hemā-vipakvaṁ na virājate tathā 'pakva-kaṣāyasya vijñānaṁ na prakāśate.*
49. *Bījānyagny-upadagdhāni na rohanti yathā punaḥ jñāna-dagdhais tathā kleśair nātmā sampadyate punaḥ.*
50. The *Mahābhārata* refers to seven *dhāraṇās*, but these are explained differently from the descriptions given by Vyāsa here (see Hopkins 1901, 351ff). Also, it is worth noting that Chapple (1994), compares verses II.15–27 here, the content of which deals with Sāṅkhya metaphysics, with the *Sāṅkhya Kārikā*, and finds reason to suggest that the seven *prānta-bhūmis* mentioned here are the seven *bhāvas* inherent in *buddhi* according to Sāṅkhya. In this latter tradition, *buddhi* has eight total modes, four *sāttvic* and four *tāmasic*. The *sāttvic* modes are *jñāna, vairāgya, dharma*, and *aiśvarya*, knowledge, dispassion, duty, and power, and their opposites are *tāmasic*. Only the first, *jñāna*, is conducive to liberation; the remaining seven have to be transcended by the *yogī*. These seven stages manifesting prior to liberation might be what Patañjali is referring to here, according to Chapple.
51. For differing views, see Fort and Mumme (1996).
52. See Kane (1977, 1390) for discussion.
53. See, for example, Śaṅkara's commentary on the *Vedānta Sūtras* I.1.4.
54. Such heroism may not be exclusively altruistic, but it is connected with the Jain notion of *karma*, conceived as an actual physical substance that covers the soul. Violence breeds *karma*, which keeps the soul covered, in Jainism, and thus embodied, and so extensive measures to avoid such *karma* have self-centered implications.
55. See Bryant (2006) for examples.
56. Vācaspati Miśra takes the term for control, *saṁyama*, further and considers it to apply to control over all the senses, not only the procreative one.
57. See, in this regard, *Gītā* XVII.8, which describes *sāttvic* food as *snigdha*, fatty.

58. See, e.g., *Uttarādhyayana* XXIII.12.
59. Certain left-handed *tāntric* rites prescribe (highly) ritually circumscribed imbibing of meat or other prohibited substances, including intoxicating substances, along with indulgence in sexual practices with a view to transcending dualistic notions of purity and pollution, and facilitating an experience of the divine interplay underpinning material reality as conceived of in the *śākta* traditions. But even here, these practices are not performed in a licentious manner but within the context of ritual and meditational conditions. Right-handed *tantra*, however, tends to observe and promote *yama*-type principles.
60. More technically, one can act through the *akliṣṭa-vṛttis* of I.5, namely, *vṛttis* not produced from *kleśas* such as *avidyā*.
61. See Bryant (2006) for discussion.
62. However Manu, in his *Dharma-śāstra* (IV.34) states that the *yamas* are obligatory but the *niyamas* are not.
63. *Anayor yama-niyamayor madhye yamānāṁ nivṛtti-mātratayā deśa-kālādy-aparicchinnatva-sambhavena . . . niyamānāṁ tu pravṛtti-rūpatayā deśa-kālādi-yantritatvena*. (*Yoga-sāra*)
64. *Svādhyāya*, study, appears alongside another of the *niyamas, tapas*, in the list of divine qualities in the *Gītā* XVI.1. Two of the *yamas*—*āhiṁsā* and *satya*—are listed subsequently (XVI.2).
65. *Stuti-smaraṇa-pūjābhir vāṅ-mānaḥ-kāya-marmabhiḥ suniścalā Śive bhaktir etad īśvara-pūjanam*. (*Yoga-sāra*).
66. *Śayyāsana-stho 'tha pathi vrajan vā svasthāḥ parikṣīṇa vitarka-jālaḥ saṁsāra-bīja-kṣayam īkṣamāṇaḥ syān nitya-yukto 'mṛta-bhoga bhāgī*. (*Yoga-sāra*)
67. *Hāniṣyāmy aham apakāriṇam, anṛtam api vakṣyāmi, dravyam apy asya svīkariṣyāmi, dāreṣu cāsya vyavāyī bhaviṣyāmi, parigraheṣu cāsya svāmī bhaviṣyāmīti.*
68. *Ghoreṣu saṁsārāṅgāreṣu pacyamānena mayā śaraṇam upāgataḥ sarva-bhūtābhaya-pradānena yoga-dharmaḥ, sa khalv ahaṁ tyaktvā vitarkān punas tān ādadānas tulyaḥ śva-vṛtteneti.*
69. Kenghe (1970).
70. Doniger and Smith (1991, 104).
71. *Aṅguttara Nikāya* III.17.1.
72. Hell, in Indic thought, is not a situation of eternal damnation but a location to which one goes to suffer the fruits of negative *karma*, until such *karma* expires, at which time one may be reborn as a human. One must remain in such locations until one has finished experiencing all the suffering one inflicted upon others when in the human form. (Madhva and Vallabha, commenting on the *Gītā*, interpret the verse from the *Gītā* quoted by Vijñānabhikṣu later in this commentary as pointing to a class of entity that is eternally condemned; this, however, is an exceptional view in Hinduism.)
73. The term *pratiṣṭhā* (here in the feminine locative case), or, from the same verbal root (*sthā*), *sthairya* (II.39, also in the locative) is repeated throughout the five *yamas* and means to be situated in, to follow fully.
74. *Caitanya Caritāmṛta*, Madhya Līlā, 17.37.

75. Rosen, Steven, *Diet for Transcendence: Vegetarianism and the World Religions*, p. 63.
76. *Vinaya Piṭaka Cullavagga* VII.8.13.
77. These are plasma, blood tissue, muscle tissue, adipose tissue, bone tissue, bone marrow (nerve tissue), and semen. See the works of Vasant Lad for excellent summaries of *āyurvedic* principles accessible to the layperson.
78. I have encountered this story in secondary sources on *yoga* but never with a reference to a primary text. The narrative has the flavor of a Purāṇic tale.
79. The closer to the *prākṛtic* matrix an evolute is, the more *sattva* it contains. Thus, *buddhi*, as first evolute, is highly *sāttvic*, whereas earth, the last, is highly *tāmasic*.
80. *Yac ca kāma-sukhaṁ loke yac ca divyaṁ mahat-sukhaṁ tṛṣṇā-kṣaya-sukhasyaite nārhataḥ ṣoḍaśīṁ kalām iti.* Sadāśivendra Sarasvatī, in his commentary, identifies this as a verse from the *Mahābhārata* but does not provide an exact citation.
81. See Carpenter (2003) for discussion and further references.
82. E.g., Hiraṇyakaśipu, in the *Bhāgavata*, and Rāvaṇa in the *Rāmāyaṇa*.
83. See Chapter I, note 157 for the frequent usage of the term *deva* to refer to *Īśvara* in early epic and Upaniṣadic sources.
84. This possibility is in accordance with Kṛṣṇa's statement in the *Gītā* that *yogīs* who do not attain liberation in one life pick up in the next from where they left off in the last life (VI.41).
85. See discussion in I.23.
86. See, for discussion, *The Tradition of Nyāya-Vaiśeṣika up to Gaṅgeśa*, Vol. II of *Encyclopedia of Indian Philosophies*, ed. Karl Potter (Delhi: Motilal Banarsidass, 1977), 21–23.
87. See, for example, his arguments against Buddhist idealism in IV.19ff.
88. See, for example, the *Devī Gītā*.
89. In I.38, Vācaspati Miśra speaks fondly of the *sāttvic yogī*'s ability to dream of Śiva.
90. Viṣṇu also manifests the *jīvas* or *ātmans*, souls who populate the world, and he can empower certain *jīvas* to perform extraordinary tasks; such *jīvas* are considered empowered incarnations.
91. The lesser *devas* in the late Vedic theistic Hindu pantheon are considered cosmological agents of *Īśvara* (e.g., *Gītā* X.2; IX.23) that oversee the day-to-day maintenance of the universe.
92. *Mahābhārata* XII.337.4–5.
93. The *Gītā* uses *puruṣa* to refer to the individual soul and then states that Kṛṣṇa is another, higher type of *puruṣa*. The *Śvetāśvatara* does not do this; while it uses the term to refer to Hara (but not to the individual soul), its agenda is quite different as it does so with a view to appropriating the cachet of the famous Ṛg Vedic *puruṣa*, where the term is used quite differently.
94. See, for discussion, Bryant (2003, xxxv, xlvii).
95. In VIII.3, *akṣara* is correlated with *Brahman*, and in XIV.26–27, *Brahman* is subordinated to Kṛṣṇa.
96. The *Bhāgavata Purāṇa* also speaks of *sthiraṁ sukham āsanam*, II.2.15.
97. Kaṇe (1977, 1426).

98. *Dhyāna-yoga*, the term used in the *Gītā* for Pātañjalian *yoga*, is often referred to as *rāja-yoga*.
99. *Āsanasya prapañcas tv atra rājayoga-prakaraṇatvān na kriyāte . . . haṭhayogādi-grantheṣvaśeṣa-viśeṣato draṣṭavyāḥ* (*Yoga-sāra-saṅgraha*)
100. Quoted in Leggett (1992, 287).
101. *Āsana-sthāna-vidhayo na yogasya prasādhakāḥ vilamba-jananāḥ sarve vistarāḥ parikīrtitāḥ. Śiśupālaḥ siddhan-āpa smaraṇābhyāsa-gauravāt.* (*Yoga-sāra*, and referred to in Vijñānabhikṣu's *Yoga Sūtras* commentary to this verse.) Rukmani identifies this verse as *Garuḍa Purāṇa* 227.44–45 but notes that Vijñānabhikṣu's rendition is quite different (1981, III:12).
102. Rukmani (1981) suggests this is probably the *Yogavāsiṣṭha*.
103. A *svastika* in India is a symbol of auspiciousness and good luck. Unlike the Nazi symbol that appropriated it, it faces counterclockwise.
104. Woods (1914) quotes the commentator Balarāma, who takes it to be some sort of table used for supporting the arms of the meditator. Hariharānanda and Rāmānanda Sarasvatī take it as a cloth used to tie the back and two legs while sitting. Rāma Prasāda, however, translates it as a tiger or deer skin, or a piece of cloth, upon which one sits.
105. Vijñānabhikṣu also refers to a peacock pose.
106. *Yogena cittasya padena vācāṁ malaṁ śarīrasya ca vaidyakena, yo 'pākarot taṁ pravaraṁ munīnāṁ patañjaliṁ prāñjalir ānato 'smi. Ābāhu-puruṣākāraṁ śaṅkha cakrāsi-dhāriṇaṁ, sahasra-śirasaṁ śvetaṁ, praṇamāmi patañjalim.*
107. See Pandit (1985) for references.
108. Hariharānanda, however, considers there to be a difference between the *vṛttis*, used here as movements of the breath, and *recaka, pūraka*, and *kumbhaka*. He notes, for example, that Vyāsa has defined external as when there is no flow of breath after exhalation, which is not quite the same as *recaka*, which he takes as meaning the active expulsion of air.
109. Identified by Rukmani as the *Mārkaṇḍeya Purāṇa* IIII.X.15 (see Ram Mishra, 1967, for references to *yoga* in this particular Purāṇa).
110. For other systems of demarcation in the Purāṇas, see Kane (1977, 1436).
111. Bronkhorst (1993) argues that the Buddhist inclusion of these practices in their canon represents a tacit disapproval of such forms of extreme asceticism.
112. Dasgupta (1927, 75).
113. Lanman (1917, 148–49). The account was published in *Observations on Trance or Human Hybernation* (Edinburgh, 1850). For an early nineteenth-century account of a *yogī* being buried alive, see the *Calcutta Medical Journal*, 1835.
114. See, for example, www.noetic.org/research/medbiblio/ch1.htm.
115. *Tapo na paraṁ prāṇāyāmāt tato viśuddhir malānām dīptiś ca jñānasya.*
116. I thank Jonathon Freilich for this observation.

CHAPTER III: MYSTIC POWERS

1. XII.228.13ff, 289.30ff. See Bedekar (1962) for discussion.
2. There are a number of *cakras*, also known as lotuses, situated in various parts of the body in tantric (esoteric) Hindu physiology, one of which is in the heart.
3. Śaṅkara says this is the door of a *nāḍī*, a subtle radiant energy channel in Hindu esoteric physiology.
4. See *Gītā* VI.13 for focusing on the tip of the nose, *nāsikāgraṁ*, which Śaṅkara in his commentary to the *Gītā* here takes as fixing the sight within.
5. Most Hindu rosaries (*mala*) consist of 108 beads. The beads are used to count *mantras* performed during *japa* (I.28).
6. Pines and Gelblum (1983, 259).
7. *Yatheṣukāro nṛpatiṁ vrajantam iṣau gatātmā na dadarśa pārśve* (*Yoga-sāra*). Original quote in *Sāṅkhya Sūtras* IV.14.
8. The term *samādhi* occurs in the *Gītā* (II.53–54) but rarely elsewhere in the *Mahābhārata*. See Kane (1977, 1459) for references.
9. Hindus hold there to be ten directions. In other words, accomplished *yogīs* can wander around the universe at will.
10. See III.45 for the eight *siddhis*.
11. The term used here is *aṣṭa-guṇita* rather than Patañjali's *aṣṭa-aṅga* (II.2).
12. The term used here is *guṇa* rather than *siddhi*.
13. *Guṇa* is used again here; there is a play on *guṇa* given that it has been used in three different ways in these two verses.
14. For the occurrence of these terms in Patañjali, I provide the appropriate verse numbers.
15. It is not clear what exactly the state of *pratibhām-apavargam* denotes (but see II.18 for *apavarga*).
16. Both these texts are especially popular in the northern, western, eastern, and central parts of the subcontinent, essentially the areas where the Indo-Aryan languages are spoken. While Rāma and Kṛṣṇa are, of course, popular in the south as well, the worship of Viṣṇu/Nārāyaṇa has been more dominant there. (Śiva, as a point of information, is worshipped all over the subcontinent, but his worship is not embedded in a text comparable to the wide-ranging appeal of either the *Rāmāyāṇa* or *Bhāgavata Purāṇa*.)
17. See Chapter I, notes 96 and 97.
18. Students familiar with the *Bhagavad Gītā* will be familiar with the term Bhagavān (see introduction footnote 1).
19. See I.46 for discussion of *sabīja-samādhi*, also known as *samprajñāta-samādhi*.
20. *Dharma* here refers to the cluster of a person's civic, social, familial, gender, etc., duties.
21. Respect is shown to deities and saints in Indic traditions by worshipping their feet (since the feet are the lowest part of a person's anatomy).
22. Activities that are pursued with the aim of attaining material benefits in this world.
23. Notice that the *Bhāgavata* essentially presents the identical *yamas* and *niyamas* as

Patañjali in II.30ff, with *yāvad-artha-parigraha* as a rewording of *aparigraha*; and *puruṣārcana*, of *Īśvara-praṇidhāna*.

24. See III.29 for discussion on the *cakras*.
25. See II.49.
26. The term *doṣa* here is used as a synonym for *kleśa* (although it could refer to imperfections in the balance of the bodily constitution as understood in *Āyurveda*).
27. *Śrīvatsa* is a curl of hair. These adornments, garments, and other bodily details are all standardized descriptions of the form of Viṣṇu.
28. The idea here is that the mind is used as a hook to catch (contemplate) this vision of *Īśvara*.
29. It is still not clear why *dhāraṇā* and *dhyāna* are relevant at this point, from this perspective, since the knowledge of *samādhi* would seem to make that of the previous stages redundant.
30. Pines and Gelblum (1983, 258).
31. Rukmani (1981) identifies this verse as 227.44–45 but notes that Vijñānabhikṣu's rendition is quite different.
32. One must also note here that Kṛṣṇa's presence is considered so purifying in the *Bhāgavata* that all the demons who were killed by him were purified and liberated from their bondage simply as a result of his divine presence.
33. However, *prakṛti*'s function, or raison d'être, is dependent on something else, that is, *puruṣa*, in the soteriological sense expressed in II.18 and III.35.
34. *Dhyeyātirikta-vṛtti-nirodha-viśeṣaḥ*.
35. In Buddhism, *dharma* most popularly refers to the Buddha's teachings but can refer to a number of more technical things (such as quality, similar to its usage here; cause; and the momentary essenceless nature of a physical object). In Jainism it refers to the metaphysical category that allows motion to take place.
36. The Nyāya and Vaiśeṣika schools (paralleling with various differences other ancient Indic schools subscribing to the *asatkārya-vāda* view such as the Mīmāṁsakas and Jains) hold that all objects in manifest reality are formed by the combination of seven (or other finite number depending on the school) interdependent but distinct underlying causal entities such as atoms and qualities; they are not formed by one ultimate underlying causal substratum substance such as the Yoga school envisions *prakṛti* to be.
37. Since Vasubandhu had presented criticisms of a rival sect of Buddhism, the *Sarvāstivāda*, that can be applied to the Sāṅkhyan view, Vyāsa, in his commentary to the next *sūtra* and elsewhere, according to Yamashita, uses the Sarvāstivāda view as a springboard to elaborate on the Sāṅkhyan view of *dharma* and its transformations as expressed in this *sūtra*. More specifically, Vasubandhu is directing arguments against the view of four teachers of this rival Buddhist Sarvāstivāda school, but he regards this as the same as the Sāṅkhyan view.
38. In Sanskrit, an *-in* suffix appended to a noun indicates possession of that noun. For example, *hasta* means hand, and *hastin* means possessor of a hand, which is one of the terms for elephant in Sanskrit (that which possesses a hand, that is, trunk). Or, better, *yogin* as possessor of *yoga*. In the nominative masculine, the *-in* becomes *-ī* (e.g., *dharmī, yogī*, etc.).

39. See Stcherbatsky (1934) for discussion.
40. See, e.g., Kumārila's *Śloka-vārtika, ātmavāda* 23–25.
41. These seven characteristics are those conducive to *nirodha*, the stilling of all *vṛttis* (II.2); *dharma*, the performance of meritorious or nonmeritorious activities; *saṁskāra*, memory; *pariṇāma*, constant transformation; *jīvana*, the mind's perpetuation of the life air (*prāṇa*), *ceṣṭā*, will and volition; and *śakti*, the mind's power to accomplish all of the above.
42. The *siddhis* are referred to as *abhijñas* in Buddhism; Pensa (1969, 219) notes that they take first place in all the lists of qualities, states, and means favorable to attaining the enlightened state of either a Bodhisattva or a Buddha in Mahāyāna literature.
43. E.g., *The Gospel of Ramakrishna*, 9th ed. (New York: Ramakrishna-Vivekananda Center, 2000); Paramahansa Yogānanda, *Autobiography of a Yogi* (Los Angeles: Self-Realization Fellowship, 1997); Swami Muktānanda, *Play of Consciousness* (South Fallsburg, NY: SYDA, 2000); *Living with the Himalayan Masters: Spiritual Experiences of Swami Rama* (Honesdale, PA: Himalayan International Institute, 1980).
44. As a point of comparison, he has nothing to say about the Vedic "magic" (apart from the dismissive comment in I.15), that is, the sacrificial culture outlined in the introduction where items are offered in the fire to celestial beings in return for worldly boons, and this was the mainstream state-sponsored tradition of the day. If he has nothing to say about the magic of the high culture, why, then, if his intention was to cater to popular belief, would he dedicate so much time to *yogic siddhis* that would have been marginal to this normative type of Vedic ritual magic?
45. In Saṅkhya, subtle energy pervades or underpins gross energy (but not vice versa). Thus *prākṛtic* evolutes pervade evolutes grosser than themselves. Therefore, senses can pervade or perceive the sense objects (but not vice versa), and the mind can pervade the senses, etc.
46. I will say more about the scholarly debate pertaining to the relationship between the Sāṅkhyan *tattvas* as cosmological vs. psychological entities in the Concluding Reflections section (my own view being presaged here).
47. The *varṇa-vāda* position of the Mīmāṁsā school, which held that meaning is contained in the phonemes, *varṇas*, and their accumulation into words and sentences, rather than in a separate metaphysical entity like the *sphoṭa*, was the main opponent of the *sphoṭa* theory. See Coward, Harold (1980), and Beck (1993).
48. See Rukmani (1981, III, 79n), Dasgupta (238n). Sāṅkhya rejected the *sphoṭa* view of Yoga (e.g., *Sāṅkhya Sūtras* V.57).
49. Another possible way of interpreting the mechanics underpinning this *siddhi*, mystic power, is to keep in mind that intelligence and ego, that is, functions of *citta*, are subtle aspects of *prakṛti* from which grosser evolutes such as sound, etc., emanate. Sound from this perspective is nothing but *citta* externalized or manifest in a somewhat more tangible and concrete audible form, just as yogurt is essentially a more solid and acidic form of milk, from which it emanates as an evolute. A person utters sounds in the form of words, or a creature utters sounds

in the form of barks, moos, quacks, or whatever, to convey an image or impression. That impression is essentially a *saṁskāra* imprinted in and emanating from the mind of the person or creature attempting to communicate through sound. The *yogic* premise is that sound itself is nothing other than an evolute of mind, *citta*. Therefore, in principle, it is not internally inconsistent with this metaphysic to propose that a *yogī* can penetrate the external dimension of sound and access its inner substratum of mind stuff, that is, to retrieve from this *citta* the meaning, or idea, embedded within it (as *saṁskāra*) that caused the sound to be uttered in the first place.

50. Vyāsa here refers to this category as *vāsanās*.
51. See also Aṅguttara IV.19.9 for reference to this *siddhi*.
52. *Dīgha Sīlakkhandhavaggo* II.5.93, translated in Tandon (1995, 22).
53. Taimni (1961, 319).
54. *Dīgha Mahāvaggo* III.12.42.
55. *anāvaraṇātmake 'py ākāśe bhavaty āvṛta-kāyaḥ.*
56. *Dīgha Mahāvaggo* III.17.56.
57. The Jains conceive of *karma* as a more physical and solid substance, compared to the Hindu and Buddhist schools.
58. Brahmā is the creator of the forms of this world in the sense of being an engineer, but not of the *prākṛtic* matrix itself, which emanates from Viṣṇu in most Purāṇic narratives (or Śiva, in others).
59. A *yojana* is a unit of measure corresponding, according to some calculations, to four to five miles or, according to others, nine miles.
60. According to the *Gītā* (VIII.17), a thousand *mahāyugas*, which correspond to one day of Brahmā, or 4,320,000,000 human years, equal one *kalpa*.
61. In *tāntric* physiology, just as the gross body is pervaded by innumerable blood vessels, there is a network of thousands of subtle channels that transport and distribute *prāṇa*, life air, around the body. Three of these, which are situated within the spine, are primary, from which one, the central channel, is the most important. This central channel is the *suṣumnā*, and it is within this that the *kuṇḍalinī* energy, which is of primary interest to practitioners of *tantra* (but not of Pātañjalian *yoga*), is situated.
62. Hariharānanda states here that according to the ancient medical authority Suśruta, gas is especially associated with *sattva* and knowledge-acquiring functions, bile with *rajas* and mutation, and phlegm with *tamas* and retention.
63. Although personal forms of *Īśvara*, particularly Śiva and the Goddess (there are also Vaiṣṇava strains of *tantra*), are prominent features of these traditions.
64. For example, the fourteenth-century *Haṭhayoga Pradīpikā* is one example of a mélange of different streams.
65. As I edit this section, I have before me, perched on the side of a pond, a frog that has remained completely immobile for two hours now, such that I walked over to it to see if it were not perhaps a garden statue.
66. On this notion, see Rukmani (1988).
67. See *Gītā* IV.5, 20 for similar phraseology.

68. For an excellent genealogy of the term "self-realization" from its neo-Vedāntic origins in colonial Bengal, see De Michelis (2005).
69. R. S. Bhattacharyya (1985) takes *vārtā* to be a typo for *vartā*, smell.
70. II.43, 45, and IV.1 in addition to this verse.
71. See also Sahay (1988).
72. Knowledge of the mind, for Śaṅkara, entails knowing what excites it, deludes it, or disturbs it.
73. Quoted in Smith (2006, 289). Smith's work is an encyclopedic compilation of possession accounts throughout the history of Indic traditions.
74. The *Śaṅkara-digvijāya* of Mādhava Vidyāraṇya and the *Śriśaṅkara-vijāya* by Anantānandagiri.
75. *Sannyāsa*, the renounced ascetic order of life, is the fourth and final stage of the Hindu social system, *āśrama*. One who enters this order is a *sannyasī*.
76. See also Vācaspati Miśra's commentary on the *Sāṅkhya Kārikās* XXIX.
77. See *Vedānta Sūtras* II.4.9ff and *Sāṅkhya Kārikās* XXIX. The five *prāṇas* are first mentioned in the *Chāndogya Upaniṣad* III.13.1–6.
78. *Prāṇa* is understood variously in different Indic systems. (In the Upaniṣads, *prāṇa* is associated with *Brahman*, e.g., *Kauṣītakī* II.1, or with *prajñā* wisdom, e.g., III.3.) In his commentary to the *Sāṅkhya Sūtras* II.31, where he again disagrees with this commonly accepted notion, Vijñānabhikṣu states that the *prāṇa* is a transformation of the internal organ (*antaḥkaraṇa-pariṇāma*), that is, the subtle body noted previously. According to him the reason it is sometimes called air is that it moves like air and is presided over by the deity Vāyu (I thank Andrew J. Nicholson for this reference). This is a good example of Vijñanabhiksu's overall concern with interweaving Sāṅkhya Yoga and Vedānta, which we have seen in a number of instances. See Bakker (1982) for a discussion of *prāṇa* in the Upaniṣads.
79. *Āyurveda* tells us *prāṇa* is active in breathing and swallowing of food.
80. *Vyāna-prāṇa* is situated in the heart and helps in the circulation of blood.
81. The members of Transcendental Meditation, a *yoga* group that was especially prominent in popularizing meditation in the sixties, promote levitation as a skill that can be learned through the practice of their techniques (see, for example, www.alltm.org/VFlying.html).
82. See, for example, Mircea Eliade, *Yoga: Immortality and Freedom* (Princeton: Princeton University Press, 1958).
83. When we think of cows or pots or any category of reality, we think of a group of entities or objects that have some universal or essential properties in common, cowness or potness, such that they can be lumped together. But what exactly is this commonality that allows them to be grouped together in such coherent ways? Several schools of thought hold that they possess a universal, *sāmānya*, such as cowness. It is because of these universal or essential properties that categories of objects are grouped together and distinguished from other categories of objects in the gross realm, such that we can recognize that something is a pot and that a pot is a pot and not a cloth or anything else.
84. The Vaiśeṣika school is especially criticized in the commentaries for its view that

these categories combine to produce effects that are new and distinct entities not present in their causes, *asatkāryavāda*, rather than, as per the Sāṅkhya and Yoga *satkāryavāda* view, inherent and nonseparable permutations of *prakṛti*, and thus potential and present in *prakṛti*.

85. *Guṇas* and *dharmas* can both be considered universals, or *sāmānyas*, insofar as qualities are shared by numerous entities common to a class (although strictly speaking, for Vaiśeṣika, *guṇas* are not universals; they are tropes: The red of a red shirt is unique to the shirt, and likewise for the red of a hat. But the redness of each *guṇa* of red is universal and repeatable; my thanks to Matthew Dasti for this specification).
86. Some properties, such as weight, are held by more than one element, in this case earth and water; others, such as cohesion, by water alone.
87. Vyāsa elaborates here that an entity that consists of a combination or collection of qualities or parts can be further subdivided in various ways. First, any collection of parts can be divided into whether its parts are distinct or not—in a forest, the trees (the parts) are not distinct from the forest itself, but in a collection such as men and gods, the two parts are distinct. Second, a collection can be categorized as to whether these parts can be separated, as in a forest, or cannot be separated, as in a body or an atom. A forest continues to be a forest if some of its trees are removed, but a body is no longer a body if its limbs are removed, nor an atom an atom if its (subtle) parts are separated. A substance is something in which the qualities or parts are nondistinct and inseparable.
88. For Vaiśeṣika, *guṇas* are not separable because they can exist only as inhering in a substance, *dravya*. There are no uninstantiated *guṇas*. Universals may be instantiated in *karma* actions, *guṇas* or *dravyas*, but ultimately there must be a *dravya* to support them. *Karma* and *guṇas* are thus not separable in the sense of existing separate from *dravyas*.
89. See Malinar (1999) for an insightful discussion of how all the various evolutionary stages of *prakṛti* (that is, all stages other than *prakṛti* herself at one end, and the *mahābhūtas* as final products on the other) can be construed as simultaneously the *viśeṣa* of the prior stage and *sāmānya* of the subsequent one. For example, the *tanmātras* are the *viśeṣas* of *ahaṅkāra* from which they evolve, and the *sāmānya* of the *mahābhūtas* that evolve from them. This is another way of articulating the principles underpinning II.19.
90. Specifically, Vyāsa defines *svarūpa*, the essence, to be the senses as substances consisting of a collection of parts involving the generic and particular aspects, discussed in III.44, which cannot be separated from each other, emanating from the *sattvic*, illuminating nature of *buddhi*.
91. *Prakṛti* is referred to here as *pradhāna*.
92. *Mano-jayitvaṁ yenopāsakādibhiḥ smṛti-mātrāḥ kṣaṇād eva siddhāḥ puro dṛśyante*. (*Yoga-sāra*)
93. *Buddhi* is referred to here, as elsewhere, as *sattva* (as in III.35, 49, 55).
94. The thirteenth chapter of the *Gītā* occupies itself with a discussion of *kṣetra*, the field, and *kṣetrajña*, the knower of the field.
95. Desire, will, pleasure, and pain are *paryāyas*, temporary characters, of the *ātman*

that come and go, but in Jainism they inhere in the *ātman* itself, rather than in the *citta* as per the Sāṅkhyan view.

96. See *Praśna Upaniṣad* IV.10–11; *Vedānta Sūtras* IV.4.17; *Vaiśeṣika Sūtras* IX.1.11ff.
97. Quoted in Jaini (1974, 73).
98. *Pāsādika Suttanta* 29. (*Dīgha Nikāya* iii.136; Rhys Davids 1927, part III, 126.)
99. See Rāmāṇuja on *Vedānta Sūtra* I.1.21 and elsewhere; Baladeva on III.2.14ff and elsewhere; and Bryant (2004, xxxviff) for general discussion in the Bhāgavata tradition.
100. The term Patañjali uses for *kleśa* here is *doṣa*, a term used in the *Mahābhārata* for the *kleśas* (XII.232.4, 289.11, 290.53–54).
101. The *ādhibhautika, ādhidaivika*, and *ādhyātmika* miseries, discussed in II.15.
102. As noted earlier, "internal" and "external" are used loosely and rhetorically.
103. "Self-aware" and "other-aware" also are used rhetorically.
104. The *kalpadruma* trees that can fulfill any desire.
105. The Mandākinī is situated by Citrakūṭa, a well-known mountain in Purāṇic lore. By bathing in this river one is awarded the wealth and majesty of a king.
106. *Bhor ihāsyatām iha ramyatāṁ kamanīyo 'yam bhogaḥ kamanīyeyaṁ kanyā rasāyanam idaṁ jarā-mṛtyuṁ bādhate vaihāyasam idaṁ yānam amī kalpa-drumāḥ puṇyā mandākinī siddhā maharṣaya uttamā anukūlā apsaraso divye śrotra-cakṣuṣī vajropamāḥ kāyaḥ sva-guṇais sarvam idam upārjitam āyuṣmatā pratipadyatām idam akṣayam ajaram amara-sthānaṁ devānāṁ priyam iti.*
107. *Ghoreṣu saṁsārāṅgāreṣu pacyamānena mayā janana-maraṇāndhakāre viparivarttamānena kathañcid-āsāditaḥ kleśātimira-vināśī yoga-pradīpas tasya caite tṛṣṇā-yonayo viṣaya-vāyavaḥ pratipakṣāḥ sa khalv ahaṁ labdhālokaḥ katham anayā viṣaya-mṛga-tṛṣṇayā vañcitas tasyaiva punaḥ pradīptasya saṁsārāgner ātmānam indhanī-kuryām iti svasti vaḥ svapnopamebhyaḥ kṛpaṇa-jana-prārthanīyebhyo viṣayebhya iti.*
108. *Smayam api na kuryād evam aham devānām api prārthanīya iti smayād ayaṁ susthitaṁ manyatayā mṛtyunā keśeṣu gṛhītam iva ātmānam na bhāvayiṣyati.*
109. *Tathā cāsya chidrāntara-prekṣī nityaṁ yatnopacaryaḥ pramādo labdha-vivaraḥ kleśānuttam-bhayiṣyati tataḥ punar aniṣṭa-prasaṅgaḥ.*
110. In this regard, the Sāṅkhya and Yoga schools differ from the Nyāya and Vaiśeṣika ones, since the latter hold that *aṇus* are irreducible and not composed of subtler ingredients such as the *tanmātras* and ultimately the *guṇas*.
111. See Sen (1968) for a discussion of Time in the Hindu philosophical systems.

CHAPTER IV: ABSOLUTE INDEPENDENCE

1. The identity of this plant remains unknown despite various, sometimes ingenious, attempts to identify it.
2. See *Nyāya Sūtras* IV.1.19 and commentaries.
3. The Vedānta tradition (*Vedānta Sūtras* II.2.37) argues that God is not just the instrumental cause of the universe but the material cause as well. In the *Bhāgavata Purāṇa*, it is *Īśvara* as Kṛṣṇa that stirs *prakṛti* through his power of Time (III.6.1ff; see also II.5.17; III.5.26, 32–33).

4. *Citta* is occasionally used in the *sūtras* in the restricted sense of *manas*, as is the case here, but most often in the more widespread sense of *manas, buddhi*, and *ahaṅkāra*.
5. However, since Patañjali uses *citta* here, a term that includes *ahaṅkāra, buddhi*, and *manas*, one might have to assume that the central *asmitā* or *ahaṅkāra* of the *yogī* is manufacturing dependent *ahaṅkāras* in the secondary bodies.
6. Vijñānabhikṣu introduces the concept of *aṁśa* in this regard, a term used in the *Gītā, Bhāgavata*, and other Purāṇas. In the *Bhāgavata*, it is primarily used in connection with Viṣṇu and Kṛṣṇa and means a portion or partial incarnation. The sense is that the supreme deity can maintain his own presence while simultaneously manifesting some aspect of himself elsewhere in a separate and distinct presence (or any number of presences). That secondary or derivative manifestation, which exhibits a part but not the full characteristics or potency of the source being, is known as an *aṁśa*. Vijñānabhikṣu holds that the *yogī* has similar abilities to manifest *aṁśas*.
7. At various places in the *Rāmāyāṇa*, Rāma, despite being an incarnation of God, appears to be unaware of his divinity.
8. See Dasgupta (1922, IV, 37ff) for discussion and references.
9. See Smith (2006) for comprehensive discussion on the commentaries to this verse.
10. *Aṅguttara* IV.24.2.1.
11. See Dasgupta (1922, Vol. 263) for discussion.
12. *Na bhūvam bhūyāsam*.
13. See *Sāṅkhya Kārikā* IX and commentaries.
14. *Guṇanāṁ paramaṁ rūpaṁ na dṛsti-patham ṛcchati yat tu dṛṣṭi-pathaṁ prāptaṁ tan māyeva sutucchakam iti*. *Māyā* is a common Vedāntin term for illusion, sometimes used interchangeably with *avidyā*, that causes one to misidentify with the unreal or temporary.
15. Yamashita (1994), scanning Vijñānavāda literature, finds specific Vijñānavāda terms represented by the Yoga commentators, such as *kalpita* and *parikalpita* (imagined), thus concurring with Vijñānabhikṣu's identification here.
16. The liberated state, for the Sāṅkhya and Yoga schools, entails seeing reality for what it is, a temporary configuration of the *guṇas*, which are real and external, and thus does not contradict the reality of external objects.
17. Vācaspati Miśra makes the argument here that the qualities of grossness and externality, which characterize physical objects of perception, cannot be created by thought alone.
18. In the *advaita* view, all objective reality is ultimately illusory, a superimposition on the only reality, *Brahman*, the Absolute Truth, like a mirage superimposed upon the desert sand. If the products of the physical world are all illusory, then so are the Vedānta texts themselves, says Vijñānabhikṣu. If these texts, which are accepted by the *advaita* school itself as *āgama*, the main source of knowledge and authority for the validity of its philosophy, are illusory, then on what other authority can the illusoriness of the world be established? This argument in more devel-

oped form can be found in Rāmānuja's commentary on *Vedānta Sūtras* I.1.1, where Rāmānuja argues at length that none of the sources of knowledge (*pramāṇas*, listed in Patañjali I.7) can establish the illusoriness of the world (since perception is obviously invalid if all objects of perception are illusory, and inference and verbal authority are extensions of, or predicated on, perception). Hence such a position cannot be defended by any valid source of knowledge and therefore cannot be supported on any grounds.

19. Larson (2008, 58ff).
20. There were public debates sponsored in ancient India, the loser and his disciples often being expected to submit and become disciples of the winner.
21. Here, Vijñānabhikṣu is referring to the analogy common in Indic idealistic thought that objects perceived in the waking state are just mental constructions created by consciousness in the same way that imagined objects are created by consciousness during the dream state.
22. The same argument holds good, obviously, for the continuity of any ingredient of reality, such as atoms, etc.
23. See Shaw (2002) for an excellent discussion on causality in Indic thought.
24. See, for example, from the Vedānta school, *Vedānta Sūtra* II.2.24; from the Mīmāṁsā school, Kumārila's *Śloka-vārttika* V.187ff; from the Nyāya school, Udayana's *Ātma-tattva-viveka* IV (probably the most extensive critique of Buddhist views in orthodox Hindu polemics); from Sāṅkhya, *Sāṅkhya Sūtra* I.35.
25. *Sattva* is a term used for intelligence in Sāṅkhya and Yoga (e.g., III.35, 49, 55), because in Yoga metaphysics the *guṇa* of *sattva* is maximized in the *citta*.
26. *Na pātālaṁ na ca vivaraṁ girīṇāṁ naivāndhakāraṁ kukṣayo nodadhīnām, Guhā yasyāṁ nihitaṁ brahma śāśvataṁ buddhi-vṛttim-aviśiṣṭāṁ kavayo vedayanta iti.*
27. Vyāsa further argues that if one takes this idealist position, then one will have to argue that the insight into the nature of an object gained during *samādhi* is also all a mental construction. In *samādhi*, one gains insight into the nature of an object (i.e., that gross objects are in reality transformations of subtler energies). One then gets another insight, according to the idealist school of thought, that all external objects, whether gross or subtle, are in reality mental constructions. This is tantamount to saying that insight reveals the true nature of insight (i.e., that a second insight gains insight into the first insight). How can insight gain insight into insight? asks Vyāsa. This would be like saying burning can burn itself or cutting cut itself. Insight can be directed only against an object different from itself.
28. The hair standing on end and the outpouring of tears are symptoms of spiritual ecstasy usually associated with the devotional paths of *bhakti*, especially those of the Kṛṣṇa sects.
29. R. S. Bhattacharyya (1985) takes *akusīdasya* in a figurative sense to indicate one who sees the harmfulness, from a *yogic* point of view, of the mystic powers.
30. See Rukmani (2007) for discussion.
31. *Evaṁ jīvan-muktāvasthā.* (*Yoga-sāra*)
32. See Fort and Mumme (1996) for the concept of *jivanmukta* in different Hindu traditions.

33. See commentaries on *Vedānta Sūtras* IV.1.15.
34. It is not clear whether Patañjali is being rhetorical in saying that that which is left to be known is "little." The commentators don't specify what that little bit might be, if anything. Given the seemingly grandiose claims of omniscience presented throughout the text, one would expect that there should be nothing outside of the *yogī*'s sphere of comprehension.
35. See Sen (1968).
36. This, of course, is the *pūrva-pakṣa*, opposing point of view outlined in the previous *sūtras*.
37. Of course, during *pralaya*, universal dissolution, the *guṇas* remain in a latent and hence unmoving state.
38. See also *Sāṅkhya Sūtra* I.58 for bondage being a state of mind rather than a state of the soul.
39. For some speculations on Patañjali's sectarian affiliation, see II.44.

CONCLUDING REFLECTIONS

1. *Na khalv ātmanaḥ svayam-prakāśasyā 'py asti kācit kriyā na ca tām antareṇa kartā* (VM IV.22).
2. Although the Gītā seems to espouse the Sāṅkhya line, XIII.20 and 29 at a surface reading, the commentators to these verses such as Rāmānuja and Madhva do assign *kartṛtva* to *puruṣa* in their commentaries, as does Śaṅkara (however, see next note). Also, as an aside, as Bronkhorst notes, surely this issue would have drawn the attention of rival schools in earlier times, as they had by Rāmānuja's day, so perhaps such objections were discussed in the numerous ancient Sāṅkhya texts that have not survived (1999). The issue remained an ongoing acute bone of contention; in the sixteenth to seventeenth century, the *Yatīndramata-dīpikā* by Rāmānuja's Śrī Vaiṣṇava follower Śrīnivāsacarya, characterizes the notion that agency is a function of *buddhi* as erroneous knowledge held by sophists (VIII).
3. For Śaṅkara, of course, agency is a feature of the soul, but in conventional reality, it is an *upādhi*, or illusory superimposition. In its ultimate pure state, the *ātman* is not an agent. One must bear in mind that, in Śaṅkara's radical *advaita* monism, there is only *Brahman*—everything else is superimposition, like the mirage in a desert; thus there is nothing upon which an agent might act. Nonetheless, within the discourse of conventional reality, he sides with the Vedāntins against the Sāṅkhya view on this point: Agency lies in the *ātman* (as conventionally understood) rather than the *buddhi* (as conventionally understood).
4. The theistic commentators accept that it is by the grace of *Īśvara* that the *puruṣa* can exert its will. Madhva quotes scriptural verses that speak of the activities of the *ātman* in the liberated state, which points to free will in the *ātman* rather than in the *buddhi*.
5. Translation from Hermann, Jacobi, 1895. *Jaina Sūtras: Sacred Books of the East*, Vol. XLV, 237.
6. Since qualities (*guṇas*) including consciousness itself arise in the *ātman* only

when it is in contact with the mind (which, as in Yoga, is external to the *ātman*), these traditions find themselves having to defend a position in which there is no consciousness in the state of liberation (which, as in Patañjali, involves separating the *ātman* from the mind). Their position is ridiculed in turn by their opponents: who would aspire for such a liberated state that does not even consist of a state of consciousness? (See, for example, the ninth-to-tenth-century Naiyāyika Jayanta Bhaṭṭa's *Nyāya-mañjari* for an articulation of this position.)

7. Ranganthan consistently translates the term *dharma* as "moral character" or "ethical life," even where the commentators take it in the more metaphysical sense of, for example, III.12–13; 45; IV.12. His argument that the ultimate justification for reading "dharma" as meaning ethical or moral is based on a text-type theoretic approach to semantics (2008, pp. 11–23). Texts exist in "types" or genres—poetic, philosophical, epic, and so on—and terms such as *dharma* in a "text-type" or genre have a consistent meaning throughout that genre, even as different schools assign these terms different roles or nuances in accordance with their distinctive philosophies.
8. Vācaspati Miśra in II.22 seems to subscribe to the view of individual *buddhis*. Apart from anything else, if *buddhi* were not individualized but cosmic, then upon one *puruṣa* becoming liberated due to discrimination manifesting in his *buddhi*, all others would share the same effect, *buddhi* being common to all. Verse II.22 suggests that the individual *citta* remains individual until liberation when it merges back into its source. Thus the evolutes are both individual and cosmic.
9. These do not appear, for example, in the Gītā's listing of evolutes in VII.4 (but then neither do the *tanmātras*, which I do hold as being cosmic as well as individual).
10. Regarding this dilemma, Hulin suggests that "oppositions, like the one between general and particular . . . were not final to them. They were looking at them, at least implicitly, as belonging to that impure, only half-real sphere of experience that owes its existence to the transcendental confusion between *puruṣa* and *prakṛti* . . . Once it vanishes, in the wake of discrimination, there is no ground anymore to contrast the personal with the universal perspective" (1999, 722).
11. Larson (1999).
12. See Dhṛtarāṣṭra in the *Bhāgavata* (I.14).
13. Thus, rejecting the various standard interpretations that "skirt the issue," such problems cause Burley (2005) to conclude that "the realist-cosmogonic interpretation of Sāṅkhya and Yoga stands no chance of presenting a coherent account of *kaivalya* . . . The central problem for the realist interpretation of *kaivalya* is how to account for the fact that, according to Sāṅkhya and Yoga, the cessation of mental activities coincides (or precipitates) a dissolution of manifest entities when those entities are supposed by the realist to exist independently of any experience of them" (231). Burley finds reason and argument can accommodate only one explanation: *prakṛti* and the world she manifests is not externally or independently real. It is experientially real only relative to the *puruṣa* under the influence of ig-

norance, and therefore ceases to exist when true knowledge dawns. Thus, logical thinking leads Burley to conclude that "the whole metaphysical schema is concerned with factors that are *internal* to experience . . . The empirical world is, precisely, not assumed to exist independently of experience" (234). In other words, *prakṛti* is the product of the *puruṣa*'s ignorance, not real in itself. Thus, it can persist for other *puruṣas*, not because it is real in itself but because others have not yet dispelled their own illusion. This is fairly classical *advaita vedānta*, and in many ways follows Śaṅkara's own utilization of logic, *anumāna*, specifically *tarka*, reducing the opponents view to absurdum, to deconstruct a realist ontology. As with Śaṅkara, of course, Burley finds himself postulating a position that is nowhere explicitly stated in the texts that he strives to exegete or in the entirety of the primary commentarial tradition, as he himself acknowledges (233).

14. We follow Vijñānabhikṣu's exegesis here and throughout these passages.
15. *Yogī ca trividho jñeyo bhautikaḥ sāṅkhya eva ca. Tṛtīyo antyāśramī prokto yogam uttamam āsthitaḥ. Prathamā bhāvanā pūrve Sāṅkhye tv akṣara-bhāvanā. Tṛtīye cāntimā proktā bhāvanā pārameśvarī.*
16. *Yatra paśyasi cātmānaṁ nityānandaṁ nirañjanam / Mām ekaṁ sa mahāyogo bhāṣitaḥ pārameśvaraḥ / Ye cānye yogināṁ yogāḥ śruyante grantha-vistare / Sarve te brahmayogasya kalāṁ nārhanti ṣoḍaśīm / Yatra sākṣat-prapaśyanti vimuktā viśvam īśvaraṁ / sarveṣām eva yogānāṁ sa yogaḥ paramo mataḥ.*
17. The text continues: "The parks there shine like final liberation itself, and contain wish-fulfilling trees, which blossom all the year round. There are fragrant winds, and creepers dripping with honey near bodies of water. Cries of exotic birds mingle with the humming of bees, and magnificent flowers bloom everywhere. Devotees of Viṣṇu along with their beautiful wives travel in aerial vehicles made of jewels, emeralds and gold, but the beautiful smiling residents of this realm cannot distract the minds of the opposite sex, since everyone is absorbed in Kṛṣṇa (III.15.14–25).
18. See Bryant (2003) for Book X of the *Bhāgavata Purāṇa* (the most important) and anticipated future volumes of the remainder. See also the edition of the entire text (twelve books) translated by the great Vaishnava teacher Bhaktivedanta Swami, published in the West by the Bhaktivedanta Book Trust.

BIBLIOGRAPHY

Alquié, Ferdinand. *Descartes, Oeuvres Philosophiques*. II. Garnier: Paris, 1967.

Bakker, Hans. "On the Origin of the Sāṅkhya Pyschology." *Wiener Zeitschrift fur die Kunde Sudasiens und Archiv fur Indische Philosophie* 26 (1982): 117–48.

Ballantyne, James Robert. *The Aphorisms of the Yoga Philosophy of Patañjali with Illustrative Extracts from the Commentary by Bhoja Raja*. Allahabad: Presbyterian Mission Press, 1852.

Balslev, Anindita. "The Notion of *Kleśa* and Its Bearing on the Yoga Analysis of Mind." *Philosophy East and West* 41.1 (1991): 77–88.

Banerjee, Anil Kumar. "Meaning of Chitta in Patanjali's Yoga." *Prabuddha Bharata* 55 (1950): 284–89.

Beck, Guy. *Sonic Theology*. Columbia: University of South Carolina, 1993.

Bedekar, V. M. "The Mokṣadharma Studies: The Place and Functions of the Psychical Organism." *Annals of the Bhandarkar Oriental Research Institute* 40 (1959): 262–88.

———. "The Dhyānayoga in the Mahābhārata (XII.188)." *Bhāratīya Vidya Bhavan* 20–21 (1960–61): 116–25.

———. " 'Dhāraṇā and Codanā' in the Mokṣadharmaparvan of the Mahābhārata in Their Relation with the Yogasūtras." *Bhāratīya Vidyā* XXII (1962): 25–32.

———. "The Place of Japa in the Mokṣadharmaparvan (MB.XII 169–193) and the Yoga-Sūtras: A Comparative Study." *Annals of the Bhandarkar Oriental Research Institute* 44 (1964): 63–74.

Bhattacharya, Krishnachandra. *Studies in Philosophy*, vol. I. Calcutta: Progressive, n.d.

Bhattacharya, Ram Shankar. *An Introduction to the Yoga Sūtra*. Delhi: Bharatiya Vidya Prakasansa, 1985.

Bhattacharya, S. "The Concept of Videha and Prakṛti-Laya in the Sāṅkhya Yoga System." *Annals of the Bhandarkar Oriental Research Institute* 48–49 (1968): 305–12.

Brockington, John. "Mysticism in the Epics." In *Perspectives on Indian Religion* (Delhi: Satguru, 1986), 9–20.

———. *The Sanskrit Epics*. Leiden: Brill, 1998.

———. "Yoga in the Mahābhārata." In *Yoga: The Indian Tradition* (London: Routledge, 2003), 13–24.

———. "Epic Yoga." *Journal of Vaishnava Studies* 14.1 Fall (2005): 123–38.

Bronkhorst, Johannes. "Yoga and Seśvara Sāṅkhya." *Journal of Indian Philosophy* 9 (1981): 309–20.

———. "God in Sāṅkhya." *Archiv Fūr Indische Philosophie* 27 (1983): 149–64.

———. "Patanjali and the Yoga Sūtras" *Studien zur Indologie und Iranistik* 10 (1985): 191–212.

———. *The Two Traditions of Meditation in Ancient India*. Delhi: Motilal Banarsidass, 1993.

———. "God's Arrival in the Vaiśeṣika System." *Journal of Indian Philosophy* 24 (1996): 281–94.

———. "The Contradiction of Sāṅkhya on the Number and the Size of the Different Tattvas." *Asiatische Studien Études Asiatiques* LII.3 (1999): 679–91.

Bryant, Edwin. *The Quest for the Origins of Vedic Culture: The Indo-Aryan Invasion Debate*. New York: Oxford University Press, 2001.

———. *Krishna: The Beautiful Legend of God: The Srimad Bagavata Purana Book X*. Translation from Sanskrit with notes and introduction. London: Penguin Classics, 2003.

———. *The Post-Charismatic Fate of the Hare Krishna Movement*. New York: Columbia University Press, 2004.

———. *The Aryan Invasion: Evidence, Politics, History*. Coedited with Laurie Patton. Richmond, UK: Routledge Curzon Press, 2005.

———. "Was the Author of the Yoga Sūtras a Vaishnava?" *Journal of Vaishnava Studies* 14.1 (2005): 7–28.

———. "Strategies of Vedic Subversion: The Emergence of Vegetarianism in Post Vedic India." In *A Communion of Subjects* (New York: Columbia University Press, 2006), 194–203.

———. *Krishna: A Source Book*. Editor. New York: Oxford University Press, 2007.

Burley, Mikel. " 'Aloneness' and the Problem of Realism in Classical Sāṅkhya and Yoga." *Asian Philosophy* 14.3 (2005): 223–38.

Carpenter, David. "Practice Makes Perfect." *Yoga: The Indian Tradition* (London: Routledge, 2003), 25–50.

Chakravarti, Pulin. *The Origin and Development of Sāṅkhya* (Calcutta: Metropolitan Printing and Publishing House, 1951).

Chapple, Christopher. "The Unseen Seer and the Field: Consciousness in Sāṅkhya and Yoga." *The Problem of Pure Consciousness* (New York: Oxford University Press, 1990), 53–70.

———. "Reading Patañjali Without Vyāṣa." *Journal of the American Academy of Religion* LXII.1 (1994): 85–103.

———. *Reconciling Yogas*. Albany: State University of New York Press, 2003.

———. *Yoga and the Luminous*. Albany: SUNY Press, 2008.

Chattopadhyay, Narayan Kumar. "The Concept of Nidrā in the Pātañjala-Yoga System." *The Calcutta Review* X 1&2 (2001): 92–95.

Clear, Edeltraud Harzel. "Iśvara Kṛṣṇa's Two Level Perception: Propositional and Non-Propositional." *Journal of Indian Philosophy* 18 (1990): 305–40.

Connolly, Peter. "Some Critical Comments on Vyāsa's Interpretation of Selected Yoga Sūtras." *Perspectives on Indian Religion* (Delhi: Satguru, 1986), 35–43.

Cousins, L. S. "Vitakka/Vitarka and Vicāra." *Indo-Iranian Journal* 35:2–3 (1992): 137–57.

Coward, Harold. *The Sphoṭa Theory of Language*. Delhi: Motilal Banarsidass, 1980.

———."Āgama in the Yoga Sūtras of Patañjali." *Indian Philosophical Quarterly* XII.4 (1985): 341–59.

Dasgupta, Surendranath. *A History of Indian Philosophy*. Delhi: Motilal Banarsidass, 1922.

———. *Hindu Mysticism*. Delhi: Motilal Banarsidass, 1927.

———. *Yoga Philosophy in Relation to Other Systems of Indian Thought*. Delhi: Motilal Banarsidass, 1974.

———. *Yoga as Philosophy and Religion*. Mineola, N.Y.: Dover Publications, 2002.

Davids, Rhys C.A.F. *Dialogues of the Buddha*. Reprint, 3 vols. Delhi: Motilal Banarsidass, 2000.

De Michelis, Elizabeth. *A History of Modern Yoga*. London: Continuum, 2005.

Deussen, Paul. *Allgemeine Geschichte der Philosophie*. I.3. Leipzig: F. A. Brockhaus, 1922.

Doniger, Wendy, and Brian K. Smith, trans. *The Laws of Manu*. London: Penguin, 1991.

Edgerton, Franklin. "The Meaning of Sankhya and Yoga." *The American Journal of Philosophy* 45.1 (1924): 1–46.

Eliade, Mircea. *Patanjali and Yoga*. New York: Funk and Wagnalls, 1907.

———. *The Essence of Yoga*. London: Rider and Company, 1974.

Feuerstein, Georg. "Some Notes on the Final Stages of Yoga According to Patañjali." *Bharatiya Vidya* 28 (1968): 1–12.

———. *The Yogasūtras of Patañjali: An Exercise in the Methodology of Textual Analysis*. Delhi: Arnold Heinemann, 1979.

———. *The Philosophy of Classical Yoga*. New York: St. Martin's Press, 1980.

Feuerstein, Georg, and Miller, Jeannie. *A Reappraisal of Yoga*. London: Rider and Company, 1974.

Fort, Andrew. "Beyond Pleasure: Saṅkara on Bliss." *Journal of Indian Philosophy* 16 (1988): 177–89.

———. *Living Liberation in Hindu Thought*. Albany: SUNY Press, 1996.

Frauwallner, Eric. *Geschichte der Indischen Philosophie*, vol. 1. Salzburg: Otto Muller, 1953.

Garbe, Richard. *The Philosophy of Ancient India*. Chicago: The Open Court Publishing Co., 1897.

Gelblum, Tuvia. "Notes on an English Translation of the *Yogasūtrabhāṣyavivaraṇa*." *Bulletin of the School of African and Oriental Studies* 55:1 (1992): 76–89.

Gokhule, P. "Is There a Moral Perspective in Patañjali's Yogasūtras?" *Indian Philosophical Quarterly* XXII.1 (1955): 41–53.

Gonda, J. *The Vision of the Vedic Poets*. The Hague: Mouton, 1963.

———. "The Concept of a Personal God in Ancient Indian Religious Thought." In *J. Gonda Selected Studies, History of Ancient Indian Religion*, vol. IV. Brill: Leiden, 1975.

Grinshpon, Yohanan. "Yogic Revolution and Tokens of Conservatism in Vyāsa-Yoga." *Journal of Indian Philosophy* 25 (1997): 129–38.

Hacker, Paul. "Śaṅkara the Yogin and Śaṅkara the Advaitin, Some Observations." *Beitraüge zur Geistesgeschichte Indiens. Festschrift für Erich Frauwallner*. Wien (1978): 119–48.

Hara, Minoru. "Pāśupata and Yoga." *Asiatische Studien Études Asiatiques* LII.3 (1999): 593–608.

Hariharānanda, Mukerji. *Yoga Philosophy of Patañjali*. Calcutta: Calcutta University, 1963 (reprint, Albany: SUNY, 1977).

Hattori, Maasaki. "On Seśvara Sāṅkhya." *Asiatische Studien Études Asiatiques* LII.3 (1999): 609–18.

Hauer, J. W. *Der Yoga*. Stuttgart: W. Kohlhammer, 1958.

Hopkins, E. W. "Yoga Technique in the Great Epic." *Journal of the American Oriental Society* vol. 22 (1901): 333–79.

Houben, Jan E. "Why Did Rationality Survive, But Hardly Survive in Kapila's 'System.' " *Asiatische Studien Études Asiatiques* LII.3 (1999): 491–512.

Hulin, Michel. "Reinterpreting *Ahaṅkāra* as a Possible Way of Solving the Riddle of Sāṅkhya Metaphysics." *Asiatische Studien Études Asiatiques* LII.3 (1999): 713–22.

Ingalalli, R. I. "Pramāṇas in Yoga Philosophy and Mental Health." *Pathway to God* 34.4 (2000): 28–36.

Jacobi, Hermann. "The Dates of the Philosophical Sūtras of the Brahmans" *Journal of the American Oriental Society* 31 (1911): 1–29.

Jacobsen, Knut A., ed. *Theory and Practice of Yoga: Essays in Honour of Gerald Larson*. Brill: Leiden, 2005.

Jaini, Padmanabh S. "On the Sarvajñātva (omniscience) of Mahavīra and the Buddha." In *Buddhist Studies in Honour of I. B. Horner* (Dordrecht: Reidel, 1974), 71–90.

Janácek, Adolf. "The Methodological Principle in Yoga According to Patañjali's Yoga Sūtras." *Archiv Orientalia* 19 (1951): 514–67.

———. "The 'Voluntaristic' Type of Yoga in Patañjali's Yoga Sūtras." *Archiv Orientalia* 22 (1954): 69–87.

———. "The Meaning of Pratyaya in Patañjali's Yoga Sūtras." *Archiv Orientalia* 25 (1957): 201–61.

———. "Two Texts of Patañjali and a Statistical Comparison of Their Vocabularies." *Archiv Orientalia* 26 (1958): 88–100.

Jha, Ganganath. *The Yogasara Sangraha of Vijnana Bhiksu*. Bombay: Tattva Viveka, 1923.

Joshi, K. S. "On the Meaning of Yoga." *Philosophy East and West* 15.1 (1965): 53–64.

———. "The Concept of Siyama [*sic!*] in Patanjali's Yogasutra." *Yoga Mīmāṁsā* VIII.2 (1965): 1–18.

Jwala, Prasad. "The Date of the Yoga Sūtras." *Journal of the Royal Asiatic Society* 84 (1930): 365–75.

Kane, P. V. *History of Dharmaśāstra*, vol. V.II. Poona: Bhandarkar Oriental Research Institute, 1977.

Karambelkar, P. V. "Yama Niyama." *Yoga Mimamsa* XVIII 3&4: 102–109.

Kenghe, C. T. "The Concept of Vitarka in the Patanjala Yogasastra." *Cosmic Society* 8.4 (1970): 28–30.

———. "The Concepts of 'Viparyaya' and 'Avidya' in the Yogasastra and Depth Psychology." *Darshana* 41 (1971): 93–96.

Klostermaier, Klaus. "Dharmamegha Samādhi: Comments on Yogasūtra IV.29." *Philosophy East and West* 36.3 (1986): 253–62.

Koelman, G. M. *Pātañjala Yoga*. Poona: Papal Athenaeum, 1970.

Krishnan, Balal. *The Yogamaṇiprabhā of Rāmānandasarasvati with the Gloss Svasaṅketa*. Delhi: Nag, 1996.

Kumar, Shiv. "Knowledge and Its Genesis in Sāṅkhya Yoga." *Annals of the Bhandarkar Oriental Research Institute* 62 (1981): 17–32.

Kumar, S., and D. N. Bhargava. *Yuktidīpikā*. Delhi: Eastern Book Linkers, 1992.

Lanman, Charles Rockwell. "Hindu Ascetics and Their Powers." Transactions and Proceedings of the American Philological Association, XIVIII (1971): 133–51.

———. "The Hindu Yoga System." *Harvard Theological Review* XI.4 (1918): 355–75.

Larson, Gerald James. *Classical Sāṅkhya*. Delhi: Motilal Banarsidass, 1979.

———. "An Eccentric Ghost in the Machine: Formal and Quantitative Aspects of the Sāṅkhya-Yoga Dualism." *Philosophy East and West* 33.3 (1983): 219–33.

———. "An Old Problem Revisited: The Relation Between Sāṅkhya Yoga and Buddhism." *Studien zur Indologie und Iranistik* 15 (1989): 129–46.

———. "Krishna Chandra Bhattacharyya and the Plurality of Puruṣas (*puruṣabahutva*) in Sāṅkhya." *Journal of the Indian Council of Philosophical Research* 10.1 (1992): 93–104.

———. "The Trimūrti of *Smṛti* in Classical Indian Thought." *Philosophy East and West* 43 (1993): 373–88.

———. "Classical Yoga as Neo-Sāṅkhya: A Chapter in the History of Indian Philosophy." *Asiatische Studien Études Asiatiques* LII.3 (1999): 723–32.

———. "Introduction to Yoga Philosophy" in *Yoga Philosophy*, eds. Larson, G., and R. S. Bhattacharya. Delhi: Motilal Banarsidass, forthcoming.

Larson, Gerald James, and Ram Shankar Bhattacharya, eds. *Saṁkhya: A Dualist Tradition in Indian Philosophy Encyclopedia of Indian Philosophies*, vol. IV. Trenton: Princeton University Press and Motilal Banarsidass, 1987.

———. *Yoga: India's Philosophy of Meditation Encyclopedia of Indian Philosophies*, vol. XII. Delhi: Motilal Banarsidass, 2008.

Leggett, Trevor. *Śaṅkara on the Yoga Sūtras*. Delhi: Motilal Banarsidass, 1992.

Leuba, James H. "The Yoga System of Mental Concentration and Religious Mysticism." *Journal of Philosophy and Scientific Methods* XVI.8 (1919): 197–206.

Mallinar, Angelika. "Prakṛti as Sāmānya." *Asiatische Studien Études Asiatiques* LII.3 (1999): 619–43.

Masson-Oursel, P. "Sur La Signification du Mot 'Yoga.'" *Revue de l'Histoire des Religions* 68 (1913): 18–31.

Minor, Robert N. *Bhagavad Gita: An Exegetical Commentary*. New Delhi: Heritage, 1982.

———. "Krishna in the Bhagavad Gita." In *Krishna*, ed. Bryant, Edwin. (New York: Oxford University Press, 2007): 77–94.

Mishra, N. "The Conception of Saṅskāra in the Yoga-Sūtra." *Journal of the Bihar Research Society* XXXVII (1951): 48–65.

———. "Saṅskāras in Yoga Philosophy and Western Psychology." *Philosophy East and West* 2 (1953): 308–16.

Mishra, Ram Ugrah. "Yoga in Mārkaṇḍeya Purāṇa." *Journal of the Yoga Institute* 13 (1967): 85–87.

Motegi, Shujun. "The Teachings of Pañcaśikha in the Mokṣadharma" *Asiatische Studien Études Asiatiques* LII.3 (1999): 513–35.

Müller, Max. *The Six Systems of Indian Philosophy*. New York: Longmans, 1899.

Murakami, Sendai. "What Is Chaitanya—Eternal or Non-Eternal." *Asiatische Studien Études Asiatiques* LII.3 (1999): 645–65.

Nelson, Lars. "Krishna in Advaita Vedanta: The Supreme in Human Form." In *Krishna*, ed. Bryant, Edwin (New York: Oxford University Press, 2007): 309–28.

Nevrin, Klas. "Modern Yoga and Śri Vaishnavism." *Journal of Vaishnava Studies* 14.1 (2005): 65–93.

Olivelle, Patrick. *The Early Upaniṣads*. New York: Oxford University Press, 1998.

Pandeya, Ram Chandra. *Yuktidīpikā*. Delhi: Motilal Banarsidass, 1967.

Pandit, Motilal. "Pre-Patañjali Sources of Yoga." *Pathway to God* 19.3 (1985): 42–38.

Parrott, Rodney. "The Problem of the Sāṅkhya Tattvas as Both Cosmic and Psychological Phenomena." *Journal of Indian Philosophy* 14 (1986): 55–77.

Pensa, Corrado. "On the Purification Concept in Indian Traditions with Special Regard to Yoga." *East and West* 19(1–2) (1969): 194–228.

Phillips, Stephen H. "The Conflict of Voluntarism and Dualism in the Yogasūtra." *Journal of Indian Philosophy* 13 (1985): 399–414.

Pines, Shlomo, and Tuvia Gelblum. "Al-Bīrūnī's Arabic Version of Patañjali's *Yogasūtra*: A Translation of the Second Chapter and a Comparison with Related Texts." *Bulletin of the School of Oriental and African Studies* 29:2 (1966): 302–25.

———. "Al-Bīrūnī's Arabic Version of Patañjali's *Yogasūtra*: A Translation of the Second Chapter and a Comparison with Related Texts." *Bulletin of the School of Oriental and African Studies* 40:3 (1977): 522–49.

———. "Al-Bīrūnī's Arabic Version of Patañjali's *Yogasūtra*: A Translation of the Third Chapter and a Comparison with Related Texts." *Bulletin of the School of Oriental and African Studies* 46:2 (1983): 258–304.

———. "Al-Bīrūnī's Arabic Version of Patañjali's *Yogasūtra*: A Translation of the Fourth Chapter and a Comparison with Related Texts." *Bulletin of the School of Oriental and African Studies* 52:2 (1989): 265–305.

Podgorski, Frank R. *Ego Revealer—Concealer*. New York: Lanman, n.d.

Prasad, Rama. *Patanjali's Yoga Sūtras: The Sacred Books of the Hindus*, vol. 4. Allahabad: AMS Press, 1974.

Prasāda, Rāma. *Patañjali's Yoga Sūtras*. Delhi: Munshiram Manoharlal, 2000.

Rao, K. B. Ramakrishna. "The Guṇas of Prakṛti According to the Sāṅkhya Philosophy." *Philosophy East and West* 13 (1963): 61–71.

———. *Theism of Pre-Classical Sāṅkhya*. Mysore: Prasaranga, 1966.

Rukmani, T. S. "Vijñānabhikṣu on Bhava Pratyaya and Upāya Pratyaya in Yoga Sūtras." *Journal of Indian Philosophy* 5 (1978): 311–17.

———. *Yogavārttika of Vijñānabhikṣu*. 4 vols. Delhi: Munshiram Manoharlal, 1981.

———. "Two Interpretations of Samprajñāta Samādhi." In *Rationality and Philosophy* (Delhi: Northern Book Center, 1984).

———. "Vijñānabhikṣu's Double Reflection Theory of Knowledge in the Yoga System." *Journal of Indian Philosophy* 16 (1988): 367–75.

———. "The Problem of the Authorship of the *Yogasūtrabhāṣyavivaraṇam*." *Journal of Indian Philosophy* 20 (1992): 419–23.

———. "Saṅkara's View on Yoga in the *Brahmasūtrabhāṣya* in Light of the Authorship of the *Yogasūtrabhāṣya Vivaraṇa*." *Journal of Indian Philosophy* 21 (1993): 395–404.

———. "Tension Between Vyutthāna and Nirodha in the Yoga Sūtras." *Journal of Indian Philosophy* 25 (1997): 613–28.

———. *Yogasūtrabhāṣyavivaraṇa of Saṅkara*. Delhi: Munshiram Manoharlal, 2001.

———. "Dharmamegha *Samādhi* in the Yogasūtras of Patañjali: A Critique." *Philosophy East and West* 57:2 (2007): 131–39.

Sahay, G. S. "Vibhutis and Its Spiritual Importance." *Yoga Mimamsa* XXVI.3&4 (1988): 103–10.

Sarbacker, Stuart Ray. *Samādhi*. Albany: SUNY Press, 2005.

Schrader, Otto. "Sāṅkhya, Original and Classical." *Adyar Library Bulletin* XIX (1955): 1–2.

Schreiner, Peter. "What Comes First (in the Mahābhārata): Sāṅkhya or Yoga?" *Asiatische Studien Études Asiatiques* LII.3 (1999): 755–77.

Schweitzer, Paul. "Mind/Consciousness Dualism in Sāṅkhya-Yoga Philosophy." *Philosophy and Phenomenological Research* LIII.4 (1993): 845–59.

Sen, Sanat Kumar. "Time in Sāṅkhya Yoga." *International Philosophical Quarterly* 8 (1968): 406–26.

Sharma, R. K. "The Role of Mind (citta) in the Yogasūtras." In *Amṛtadhārā Professor R. N. Dandekar Felicitation Volume* (Delhi: Ajanta, 1984).

Shaw, J. L. "Causality: Sāṅkhya Bauddha and Nyāya." *Journal of Indian Philosophy* 30 (2002): 213–70.

Smith, Frederick M. *The Self Possessed.* New York: Columbia University Press, 2006.

Stcherbatsky, T. "The 'Dharmas' of the Buddhists and the 'Guṇas' of the Sāṅkhyas." *The Indian Historical Quarterly* X (1934): 737–60.

Stern, Eddie. "The Yoga of Krishnamacharya." *Journal of Vaishnava Studies* 14.1 (2005): 95–106.

Taimini, I. K. *The Science of Yoga.* London: The Theosophical House, 1961.

Takagi Shingen. "On the 'Kriyā Yoga' in the Yoga Sūtra." *Journal of Indian and Buddhist Studies* XV (1966): 24–33.

Tandon, S. N. *A Reappraisal of Patanjali's Yoga Sutras in the Light of the Buddha's Teachings*. Dhammagiri: Vipassana Research Institute, 1995.

Torella, Raffaele. "Sāṅkhya as Sāmānyaśastra." *Asiatische Studien Études Asiatiques* LII.3 (1999): 553–61.

Watts, Alan. "Asian Psychology and Modern Psychiatry." *American Journal of Psychoanalysis* 13.1 (1953): 25–30.

Welden, Ellwood. "The Sāṅkhya Teachings in the Māitrī Upaniṣad." *The American Journal of Philology* 35.1 (1914): 32–51.

———. "Religious Practice and Yoga in the Time of the Vedas, Upaniṣads and Early Buddhism." *Annals of the Bhandarkar Oriental Research Institute* LVI (1975): 179–94.

———. *Yoga and Indian Philosophy*. Delhi: Motilal Banarsidass, 1977.

Werner, Karl. "Yoga and the Old Upanisads." In *Perspectives on Indian Religion* (Delhi: Satguru, 1986), 1–7.

———. "The Longhaired Sage of RV 10,136: A Shaman, a Mystic or a Yogi?" In *The Yogi and the Mystic* (London: Curzon, 1989).

Wezler, A. "Philological Observations on the So-Called Pātañjalayogasūtrabhāṣyavivaraṇa." *Indo-Iranian Journal* 25 (1983): 17–40.

———. "On the Quadruple Division of the Yogaśāstra, the Caturvyūhatva of the Cikitsāśāstram and the 'Four Noble Truths' of the Buddha." *Indologica Taurinensia* (1984): 289–337.

Whicher, Ian. *Integrity of the Yoga Darśana*. Albany: SUNY Press, 1998.

———. "Classical Sāṅkhya, Yoga and the Issue of Final Purification" *Asiatische Studien Études Asiatiques* LII.3 (1999): 779–97.

———. "The Liberating Role of *Saṅskāra* in Classical Yoga." *Journal of Indian Philosophy* 33 (2005): 601–33.

White, David. *Sinister Yogis*. Chicago: Chicago University Press, forthcoming.

Woods, James Haughton. *The Yoga System of Patañjali*. Delhi: Motilal Banarsidass, 1998 (reprint).

Yamashita Koichi. *Pātañjala Yoga Philosophy with Reference to Buddhism*. Calcutta: Firma KLM, 1994.

GLOSSARY OF SANSKRIT TERMS AND NAMES*

Abhāva Absence, removal.

Abhyāsa Practice; here defined as the effort to concentrate the mind.

A. C. *Bhaktivedānta* Swami who founded ISKCON (the *Hare Krishna* movement) to spread *Kṛṣṇa bhakti* (*Kṛṣṇa* Consciousness) around the world.

Ādhibhautika Suffering produced by other beings (mosquitoes, enemies, neighbors, family members, etc.).

Ādhidaivika Suffering produced by nature and the environment (storms, earthquakes, etc.).

Ādhyātmika Suffering produced by one's own body and mind (illness, injury, insecurity, anxiety, etc.).

Advaita Monism or nonduality; a philosophical tenet opposed to the dualism and realism of *Yoga* metaphysics. The *Advaita Vedānta* school posits that the entire manifest world is ultimately not real, but a mental construction produced by ignorance and superimposed on the only real existent, *Brahman*. Thus, on attaining liberation the *ātman* (*puruṣa*) realizes that all plurality and individuality is the product of illusion, and merges into the all-encompassing, nondual, absolute truth, *Brahman*.

Āgama Testimony, verbal communication; this includes divine scripture (*śruti* or *śabda*).

Ahaṅkāra "I am the doer"; *sāṅkhya* term for *ego*. The *Gītā* describes the false "I" as thinking of oneself as the doer of action.

Ahiṁsā Nonviolence in thought, word and deed.

Akliṣṭa Nondetrimental (to the ultimate goal of *yoga*).

Ālambana Support, object, basis; refers to the object upon which the *yogī* has chosen to concentrate the mind.

Al-Bīrunī Arab traveler and historian (973–1050 C.E.); translated *Patañjali's Sūtras* into Arabic.

*A Sanskrit word can have multiple meanings depending on the context in which the word is used.

Aliṅga That which has no sign; primordial, pre-creation *prakṛti* is a state in which the *guṇas* are completely latent, therefore *prakṛti* has no "signs" or characteristics.

Anādi Without beginning, beginningless time.

Ānanda-samādhi Absorption with bliss; the third level of *samprajñāta-samādhi*. The *guṇa* of *sattva* predominates in *ahaṅkāra* and *buddhi* and *sattva* is the source of bliss.

Ananta Never-ending, infinite; one of the names of the cosmic serpent Śeṣa, who holds the universes on his hood.

Anātma-vāda Belief that there is no eternal, separable conscious entity called *ātman* (*puruṣa*). Another term for Buddhist doctrine in Hindu commentaries.

Antaḥkaraṇa Internal body composed of *buddhi* (intelligence), *ahaṅkāra* (ego), and *manas* (mind).

Aṇu An irreducible entity in the sense that it cannot be further broken down into smaller parts. Variously translated as minute, tiny, atom, smallest physical subatomic particles. The gross elements (*mahābhūtas*) are comprised of *aṇus*.

Anya Other; refers to a state beyond *samprajñāta-samādhi*, which the commentators take to be *asamprajñāta-samādhi*.

Apāna One of the five *prāṇas*; responsible for eliminating waste products from the body.

Apara-pratyakṣa Conventional perception.

Aparigraha Refraining from acquiring or coveting objects; taking only what is required for maintaining the body.

Apavarga Liberation; realization by *puruṣa* of its own true nature.

Api Also, even, although.

Āraṇyakas Texts which are part of the *Vedic* corpus and are concerned with cosmological and metaphysical topics.

Artha Goal, purpose, for the sake of, object, meaning.

Asamprajñāta-samādhi The highest stage of the eighth and final limb of *Yoga*; ultimate state of awareness in which nothing can be discerned except the pure self.

Āsana Seat, posture, or stretching pose for the purpose of preparing the *yogī*'s body to sit firmly (*sthira*) and comfortably (*sukha*) for prolonged periods in meditation.

Asatkārya-vāda Metaphysical view that the effect is not in one single underlying substratum such as *prakṛti*, but that all objects in manifest reality are formed by the combination of interdependent but distinct underlying causal entities. The *Nyāya*, *Vaiśeṣika*, *Mīmāṁsā* and *Jaina* schools subscribe to *asatkārya-vāda*.

Āśaya Type of receptacle, stock or store of all the accumulated *karma*. This *karma* eventually fructifies, perpetuating the cycle of birth and death (*saṁsāra*).

Asmitā "I-am-ness" or Ego; misidentifying *buddhi* (intelligence or the instrumental power of sight) with *puruṣa* (soul, the actual seer).

Asmitā-samādhi Absorption with the sense of I-ness; the fourth and final stage of *samprajñāta-samādhi*. The *yogī* becomes indirectly aware of *puruṣa* or "I-amness," rather than any external material *prakṛtic* object or internal organ of cognition. *Asmitā* in the context of *samādhi* is not the same as *asmitā* in the context of the *kleśas*.

Aṣṭāṅga Yoga Eightfold path of *Patañjali Yoga* consisting of: *yamas* (moral restraints), *niyamas* (ethical observances), *āsana* (posture), *prāṇāyāma* (breath control), *pratyāhāra* (sense withdrawal), *dhāraṇā* (concentration), *dhyāna* (meditation), and *samādhi* (meditative absorption).

Asteya Refraining from stealing.

Atad Not that, incorrect.

Ātmā/Ātman The innermost self or soul.

Avidyā Ignorance. Considered by the *Yoga* school as a mental state or perception of reality which confuses or misidentifies the nature of the soul (*Puruṣa*) with that of the body.

Āyurveda Knowledge tradition dealing with health.

Bādarāyaṇa Wrote the *Vedānta Sūtras* (also known as the *Brahma Sūtras*), the most significant systemization of the various doctrines expressed in the *Upaniṣads*.

Bhagavad Gītā "Song of God"; a dialogue between the warrior *Arjuna* and *Kṛṣṇa* (his teacher).

Bhāgavata Purāṇa Most important *puraṇa*, and primary scripture for the *Kṛṣṇa* traditions.

Bhakti Devotion to a personal form of divinity.

Bhaktivedānta Swami Important Vaisnava teacher who spread *Kṛṣṇa* devotion around the world.

Bhakti Yoga The path of devotion.

Bhāva Dispositions of *buddhi*.

Bhāvanā Mind-set or attitude, meditation.

Bhāvana Dwelling upon, cultivation.

Bhedābheda Difference-and-nondifference. This Vedānta doctrine posits that *Brahman* is one with the living entities, but also different. The relationship is similar to the fire and its sparks. This paradoxical relationship of difference in oneness is known by various terms by different post-Śaṅkara schools of Vedānta.

Bhoga Experience; refers to experience of the *guṇas*—pursuing pleasure and avoiding pain.

Bhoja Rāja King, poet, scholar, and patron of the arts, sciences, and esoteric traditions; ruled Malwa region of Madhya Pradesh in the mid–tenth century and wrote a commentary titled *Rāja-mārtaṇḍa* on the *Yoga Sūtras*.

Bhūmi Stages (e.g., of *samādhi*).

Bhūta Element; object; creature.

B.K.S. Iyengar Established the *Iyengar* School, the most influential school of modern postural *Yoga*.

Brahmacarya Celibacy.

Brahman Refers to the ultimate absolute reality or principle expressed in the Upaniṣads. *Brahman* is either understood as a supreme personal being (*Īśvara*, God), or as a supreme impersonal consciousness, depending on the sects of *Vedānta* stemming from the Upaniṣads.

Brāhmaṇa Texts that are part of the Vedic corpus describing the ritualistic minutiae of sacrifices for the attainment of specific goals. Also name of one of the four castes, that of the teacher and ritualist specialist.

Buddha Founder of Buddhism.

Buddhi Intelligence, discriminatory aspect of the mind (*citta*). *Buddhi* has the functions of judgment, discrimination, knowledge, ascertainment, will, virtue, and detachment.

Ca Also, and, as well.

Cakra Wheel, centers of subtle energy located at various points along the spine. The *cakra/nāḍī/kuṇḍalinī* physiologies are associated with the *siddha/tantra/śākta* traditions.

Cārvāka Indian philosopher associated with the Materialistic school of philosophy, which believes that the goal of life is the pursuit of sensual pleasure and minimization of discomfort.

Caturtha Fourth; refers here to the fourth type of *prāṇāyāma* where the *yogī* can suppress his breath at will for indefinite time periods.

Chaitanya Mahāprabhu Post–*Śaṅkara Vedāntin* theologian and mystic (15th C.E.); founder of the *Gauḍīya* (Bengal) school of *Vaiṣṇavism*.

Charaka Authority on *Āyurveda*.

Chinmayananda, Swami A disciple of *Swami Sivananda* who established the Chinmaya Mission (1916–1993).

Citi-śakti Divine energy, power of Consciousness.

Citta In the *Yoga* school *citta* refers to the combined functioning of the three cognitive aspects of the internal organ—*buddhi* (intelligence), *ahaṅkāra* (ego), and *manas* (mind).

Devī Goddess.

Dhāraṇā Concentration; fixing the mind on an object of meditation.

Dharma *Dharma* has various meanings. In the *Yoga Sūtras*, *dharma* (nature, characteristics) is understood to be that which is specific and distinctive about an object.

Dharma-megha Cloud of virtue; a state of *samādhi* corresponding to the highest state of discrimination (*viveka*) when the *yogī* has no interest even in the benefits accruing from discernment.

Dharma-śāstra Vedic law books concerning worldly socio-civic duties.

Dhātu Refers to the seven bodily tissues in *Āyurvedic* physiology (plasma, blood, muscle, adipose, bone, bone marrow, semen).

Dhyāna Meditation; the continuous flow of the mind on the object of meditation, without being distracted by any other thought.

Dhyāna Yoga The path of fully concentrated meditation (subject of *Patañjali's Yoga Sūtras*).

Draṣṭṛ/Draṣṭā Seer, *puruṣa*, the soul, or innermost conscious self.

Dṛk Derived from *dṛś* "to see"; subjective power of seeing; the Seer. Refers to the awareness of *puruṣa* (*drastṛ* in I.3).

Dṛśya The seen; all objects which present themselves to the intelligence (*buddhi*).

Dualism A philosophical belief that ultimate reality consists of two metaphysical categories; in *Yoga* philosophy these categories are labeled *puruṣa* and *prakṛti*.

Duḥkha Pain, frustration, aversion, suffering.

Dveṣa Aversion; resentment toward pain by one who remembers past experiences of pain.

Ekāgratā One-pointedness; when the previous thought (*pratyaya*) in the mind is identical to the thought that succeeds it in meditation.

Epistemology The study of knowledge, specifically the methods of attaining accurate information about reality.

Eva Also, indeed, very, only, the same, the very one.

Grahaṇa The instrument of grasping or the instruments of knowledge (mind, senses, etc.); process of obtaining knowledge.

Grahitṛ/Grahitā The grasper; the knower, or subject of knowledge.

Grāhya That which is grasped or the object of knowledge.

Guṇas Strands or qualities; the three *guṇas* inherent in *prakṛti—sattva* (lucidity), *rajas* (action), and *tamas* (inertia). These *guṇas* are like the threads which make up a rope, and all manifest reality consists of a combination of the *guṇas*.

Hāna Freedom, escape, removal, liberation from *saṁsāra*.

Hariharānanda Āraṇya A *yogī* (1869–1947) who wrote a commentary on the *Yoga Sutras* titled *Bhāsvatī*.

Haṭha Yoga The path of Yoga using physical disciplines to direct the vital energies in the body to awaken *kuṇḍalinī-śakti* (serpent power), which is dormant and coiled at the base of the spine.

Haṭhayoga Pradīpikā Manual on *Haṭha Yoga* written by *Swami Swatmaramam* (15th C.E.). The *Haṭhayoga Pradīpikā* includes information about *āsanas*, *prāṇāyāma*, *cakras*, *kuṇḍalinī*, *bandhas*, *kriyās*, *śakti*, *nāḍīs*, and *mudrās*.

Hermeneutics Methods of textual interpretation, here the interpretation of ancient *Vedic* texts.

Heterodox Schools Philosophical schools which rejected the *Vedic* corpus, such as *Buddhism* and *Jainism*.

Hiraṇyagarbha A divine sage; identified by the *Yājñavalkya Smṛti* and *Mahābhārata* as the founder of Yoga.

Idealism The philosophical view that the world is not objectively or externally real, but a product of the mind.

Iṣṭa-devatā One's divinity of preference, a form of *Īśvara* to which a *yogī* is partial.

Īśvara The supreme being; generic name for God.

Īśvara-praṇidhāna Dedication to God (*Īśvara*).

Īśvara-vādin One believing in *Īśvara*; theist.

Iva Like; as if.

Jaḍa Bhārata An advanced *yogī* who, in a prior life as King Bhārata, failed to attain the ultimate goals of *yoga* due to attachment. In a subsequent birth he became an example of the complete renunciation indicated by Patañjali.

Jainism A spiritual tradition handed down by a line of twenty-four teachers (*tīrthaṅkaras*), the last of whom was *Mahavira*, a contemporary of Buddha.

Japa Repetitive chanting of *mantras*; for *Patañjali*, *mantra* means the recitation of *oṁ*.

Jāti Birth, class, species, caste, occupation.

Jaya Mastery, victory, control.

Jīva The embodied self, the soul in *saṁsāra*.

Jīvan-mukta Soul still embodied in the world, but self-realized and liberated.

Jñāna Knowledge, speech.

Jñāna Yoga The path of knowledge, understanding the ultimate truths of reality through discrimination (*viveka*) between the Self (*puruṣa/ātman*) and the not-self (*prakṛti*).

Jñānendriyas Powers behind the five senses of hearing, sight, smell, taste, and touch.

Jñāni One following the path of *jñāna yoga*.

Kaivalya Absolute freedom, supreme independence, liberation, state of wholeness; *puruṣa* shines forth in its own pure luminous nature.

Kāli A manifestation or form of *Devī*, the Goddess.

Kali Yuga Last and most degenerate of the four world ages in Hindu cosmography; the present world age.

Kāma Desire.

Kāma Śāstras "Desire texts"; outlining the aesthetics of sensual enjoyment.

Kapila Sage whom tradition assigns as the original expounder of *Sāṅkhya Yoga*.

Karma From the root *kṛ* to "do" or "make," literally means "work"; refers not only to an initial act but also to the reaction it produces (pleasant or unpleasant in accordance with the original act) either in this life or a future one.

Karmāśaya Stock of *karma*, accumulation of *saṁskāras*. At the moment of death, the *karmāśaya* determines the three aspects of rebirth that one will experience: *jāti* (type of birth—human, animal, etc.), *āyuḥ* (lifespan), *bhoga* (quality of life).

Karma Yoga The path of action; the performance of one's duty without desire for the outcome.

Kevalin One who has attained the state of *kaivalya*.

Khyāti Insight, knowledge, perception.

Kleśas Afflictions, impediments, obstacles. *Patañjali* lists five primary *kleśas* to the practice of yoga—ignorance, ego, attachment, aversion, and clinging-to-life.

Kliṣṭa Detrimental, harmful, damaging, afflicted (to the ultimate goal of *yoga*).

Kośas Layers or sheaths that make up an individual. There are five *kośas*.

Krishnamāchārya Triumalai Krishnamāchārya (1888–1989) A visionary and innovative *Yoga* teacher. His three principal disciples established their own methods of Yoga in the West: *K. Pattabhi Jois* (*Ashtanga vinyasa yoga*), *T.K.V. Desikachar* (*Viniyoga*), and *B.K.S. Iyengar* (*Iyengar yoga*).

Kriyā-yoga Defined by *Patañjali* as a practice consisting of *tapas* (austerity), *svādhyāya* (study), and *Īśvara-praṇidhāna* (devotion to God).

Kṛṣṇa The supreme God descended on earth who instructed *Arjuna* in the *Bhagavad Gītā*; *Kṛṣṇa* is presented in the *Bhagavad Gītā* as the supreme *Īśvara*.

Kṣaṇa Instant, moment, smallest point in time. A *kṣaṇa* is defined as the time it takes an *aṇu* to move from one point in space to the space immediately adjacent to it.

Kṣanika-vāda The view that all reality is momentary—nothing in reality has inherent, eternal, independent, and essential existence; one of several terms for Buddhist doctrine.

Kṣatriya Member of the warrior caste.

Kṣetra-jña The knower of the field (*prakṛti*); another term for the *ātman*.

Kuṇḍalinī Coiled feminine power central to the *siddha* and *tantra* traditions.

Kuṇḍalinī-sakti Serpent power or the creative power (*śakti*) which is dormant and coiled at the base of the spine.

Laghu Light (in terms of density).

Lakṣaṇa Distinguishing characteristic, qualities, temporal state.

Liṅga Sign, that which has a sign, distinctive; used here for *buddhi*.

Lokas Worlds or realms.

Madhva Famous *Vaiṣṇava* theologian (13th C.E.) who interpreted the teachings of the *Upaniṣads* on the basis of *Dvaita Vedānta* (dualism).

Mahābhārata One of India's two great epics (9th–4th B.C.E.); describes the saga of the *Pāṇḍavas* and the *Kauravas* and is the largest epic in the world consisting of 100,000 verses. The *Bhagavad Gītā* is included in the sixth book of the *Mahābhārata*.

Mahā-bhūtas Five gross or material elements—ether, air, fire, water, and earth; the actual physical tangible stuff of the universe.

Mahāvīra A perfected *Jain yogī*; great hero or warrior. *Mahāvīra* is not the founder of Jainism but is considered to be the primary teacher (*tīrthaṅkara*) for this age.

Maheśvara Great Lord; usually used for *Śiva*.

Manas Mind, the thinking and organizing aspect of *citta*.

Mantra Sacred chant; *mantras* encapsulate divine presence in the form of sound.

Manu Dharma Śāstra Ancient law books outlining *dharma*, socio-civic and religious codes of conduct.

Māyā The power of illusion that is the cause of ignorance; *Vedāntin* term for illusion that causes one to misidentify with the unreal. (Sometimes used interchangeably with *avidyā*.)

Mīmāṁsā One of the six schools of orthodox philosophy; noteworthy for its treatment of epistemology, hermeneutics, and *dharma*. Formulated a rationale to perpetuate the old Vedic sacrificial rites.

Moha Delusion, illusion.

Monism A philosophical belief that ultimate reality consists of one absolute principle called *Brahman*.

Mukta Liberated.

Muktānanda Teacher of *Siddha Yoga*, a Kashmiri form of *Śaivism* featuring *bhakti* to Lord *Śiva*; came to the West in the sixties.

Nāḍīs Network of thousands of subtle energy channels (*nāḍīs*) which transport and distribute life force (*prāṇa*) around the body in *tantric* physiology.

Narasiṁha *Viṣṇu* incarnation as half man, half lion.

Nārāyaṇa Another name for *Viṣṇu*; used often in the Mahābhārata.

Nirbīja-samādhi Synonymous with *asamprajñāta-samādhi*; a state where the *yogī*'s awareness has no contact whatsoever with *prakṛti*. *Puruṣa* is now simply aware of itself.

Nirīśvara-vādins Those who reject the notion of an *Īśvara*; atheists.

Nirodha Restraint, control, cessation. When all thoughts have been stilled.

Nirodha-saṁskāras *Saṁskāras* activated in meditation that restrain the outgoing or *vyutthāna-saṁskāras*.

Nirvicāra-samādhi *Samādhi*; beyond reflection; the second of four stages of *samprajñāta-samādhi*. *Vicāra-samādhi* is subdivided by Patañjali into *sa* (with) *vicāra* and *nir* (without) *vicāra*; a state where the *yogī* can focus on the subtle substructure of the object of meditation and transcend space and time.

Nirvikalpa-pratyakṣa Pre-conceptual perception; when a sense object is not recognized or identified but perceived as raw impression. In contrast to *Savikalpa-pratyakṣa* where the mind recognizes the object which it categorizes as a certain type of thing.

Nirvitarka-samādhi *Samādhi*; without physical awareness, without conceptualization; the first of four stages of *samprajñāta-samādhi*. *Vitarka-samādhi* is subdivided by Patañjali into *sa* (with) *vitarka* and *nir* (without) *vitarka*. A state when the mind has been purged of all *saṁskāric* memory in terms of any recognition of what the object of meditation is.

Niyamas Ethical observances—the *yogī*'s own personal discipline and practice. There are five *niyamas*: *śauca* (cleanliness), *santoṣa* (contentment), *tapa* (austerity), *svādhyāya* (study of the scriptures), *Īśvara-praṇidhāna* (devotion to God).

Nyāya One of the six schools of orthodox philosophy, focused on developing rules of logic so that debates between various schools could be conducted according to conventions about what constituted valid argument.

Ojas Subtle vital energy which forms the essence of all the seven bodily tissues (*dhātus*) in *Āyurvedic* physiology.

Oṁ Sonal incarnation of *Īśvara*. The relation between *Īśvara* and *oṁ* is an eternal designation not assigned by human convention.

Orthodox Schools The six schools of Indian Philosophy—*Sāṅkhya*, *Yoga*, *Nyāya*, *Vaiśeṣika*, *Mīmāṁsā*, and *Vedānta* are considered "orthodox" because they retain at least a nominal allegiance to the sacred *Vedic* texts.

Pāda Chapter, quarter, part. There are for *pādas* in the Yoga Sūtras.

Paramātman The supreme *ātman*.

Paramparā Succession, lineage, tradition of teacher/disciple relationship.

Para-pratyakṣa Supernormal perception.

Pariṇāma Result, consequence, change, transformation, development, mutation.

Patañjali Compiler of the *Yoga Sūtras*, one of the ancient treatises on Indic philosophy. Tradition considers him to be the same Patañjali who wrote the primary commentary on the famous grammar by Pāṇini, and who wrote a treatise on medicine.

Pattabhi Jois (1915–) Developed *Ashtanga Vinyasa Yoga*, which emphasizes continuity and fluidity between one movement and the next. Disciple of *T. Krishnamāchārya* (1888–1989).

Phala Fruits, end results, effect, motive.

Phenomenology Representing the beliefs of a religious tradition as accurately and objectively as possible as phenomena in their own right and within their own context.

Pracchardana Exhalation.

Pradhāna Primordial matter with its creative potential latent; a state when the *guṇas* are in equilibrium and there is no creation; used almost synonymously with *prakṛti*.

Prajñā True insight, wisdom, discernment, to see things as they really are. The ultimate discrimination is the ability to distinguish *puruṣa* from any aspect of *prakṛti*.

Prakṛti Also known as *pradhāna*; the material world with all its varieties within which the *puruṣa* is embedded; the raw stuff from which the world is formed.

Prakṛti-laya Merged in matter; refers to quasi-perfected *yogīs* who do not have gross physical bodies but exist on some other level within *prakṛti*.

Pramāṇa Epistemology; the methods of attaining accurate information about reality. For the *Yoga* school, these methods consist of sense perception, inference, logic, and testimony.

Prāṇa Principle life air responsible for directing the other *prāṇas* and for respiration in the body.

Prāṇas Vital airs. There are five *prāṇas* in the body: *prāṇa* (directing the other *prāṇas* and respiration in the body), *samāna* (digesting nutrients and nourishing all parts of the body), *apāna* (eliminating waste products from the body), *vyāna* (circulating all over the body), and *udāna* (upward movements in the body).

Prāṇāyāma Breath control, by regulating and slowing the movement of breath, so that the mind also becomes regulated and quiescent.

Praṇidhāna To place oneself down, prostrate, submit, devotional submission.

Prārabdha-karma *Karma* that has already been activated and is manifest in the present life.

Prasaṅkhyāna Highest type of meditation; means of restraining all outgoing mental activities.

Prātibhā Intuition; knowledge of things normally inaccessible to conventional means of knowledge.

Pratipakṣa Opposite; consequence; practice of generating thoughts that are opposite to any negative thoughts that arise, so that a new more *sāttvic* type of *saṁskāra* is planted in the *citta*.

Pratiprasava Return to the original state; when the *yogī's* mind has fulfilled its purpose (*nirbīja-samādhi*), it dissolves back into *prakṛti*.

Pratyāhāra Withdrawl of the senses from objects.

Pratyakṣa Sense perception; the state of mind (*vṛtti*) which apprehends both the specific (*viśeṣa*) and generic (*sāmānya*) nature of an external object through the five senses.

Pratyaya Conception, idea, thought, cause, presented idea, the imprint or impression of an object in the *citta*.

Purāṇas "That which took place previously"; a compendium of texts which contain the ingredients of modern Hinduism and the stories of the great Divinities and their devotees, royal dynasties, social duties, yogic practices, etc. There are eighteen *Purāṇas*, one of which is the *Bhāgavata Purāṇa* (the story of *Kṛṣṇa*'s incarnation).

Puruṣa Term favored by the *Yoga* school to refer to the innermost conscious self, loosely equivalent to the soul in Western Graeco-Abrahamic traditions.

Pūrva-pakṣa The opposing point of view; commentaries frequently discuss opposing philosophical positions with a view to identifying their defects.

Rāga Attachment. Desire or craving for pleasure by one who remembers past experiences of pleasure.

Rajas One of the three *guṇas*; when *rajas* is predominant in an individual, hankering, attachment, energetic endeavor, passion, power, restlessness, and creative activity manifest.

Rāja-yoga Equivalent to *Dhyāna-yoga*, the term used in the *Bhagavad Gītā* for *Patañjali-Yoga*.

Rāmānanda Sarasvatī Vedāntin who wrote a commentary on the *Yoga Sūtras*, titled *Yogamaṇi-rabhā* (16th C.E.).

Rāmānuja Post-*Śaṅkara Vedānta* philosopher (12th C.E.) who is identified with the doctrine of *viśiṣṭādvaita* (differentiated non-duality)—that *Īśvara* (the personified *Brahman*) is one with the living entites, but also different. *Rāmānuja* prioritized *bhakti* and acknowledged *Viṣṇu* as the Supreme *Īśvara*.

Rāmāyaṇa Epic narrating the story of *Rāma*, the incarnation of *Viṣṇu*; one of two great Epics of India along with the *Mahābhārata*.

Realism The view that the world is objectively and externally real irrespective of whether we perceive it. The Yoga tradition is "realist."

Ṛg Veda The oldest *Vedic* text; consists of hymns to the Gods that are chanted during the performance of sacrifice.

Ṛṣi Vedic Sage; seer of Vedic truths.

Sabīja-samādhi *Samādhi* with seed; synonymous with *samprajñāta-samādhi*. The four levels of *samprajñāta-samādhi* are known as *sabīja-samādhi*, because these mental states have something external as their object of focus.

Sādhana One's specific daily spiritual practices.

Śākta Follower of *Devī*, the Goddess.

Śakti Power; associated with the Goddess or the feminine power of a male divinity.

Samādhi Full meditative absorption or final absorption in the self, *Patañjali* subdivides *samādhi* into seven levels: the six levels of *Samprajñāta-samādhi* (*savitarka*, *nirvitarka*, *savicāra*, *nirvicāra*, *ānanda*, *asmitā*) and the seventh level of *asamprajñāta-samādhi*.

Samāna One of the five *prāṇas* responsible for digesting nutrients and nourishing all parts of the body.

Sāmānya Universals; refers to the genus, species, or general category of an object. (For example, the term "cow" does not particularize or distinguish one cow from another, but refers to the species.)

Samāpatti Intense concentration such that the *yogī* becomes one with the object of meditation.

Sāṅkhya Kārikā Oldest surviving and thus (by default) primary text of the Sāṅkhya School.

Samprajñāta-samādhi Concentration on an object so that the mind can be fully stilled. There are four stages of *samprajñāta-samādhi*: *vitarka*, *vicāra*, *ānanda*, *asmitā*.

Saṁsāra Cycle of repeated birth and death. *Saṁsāra* has no beginning, but will end when liberation occurs.

Saṁskāras Mental imprints, memories, subconscious impressions. Every experience or thought forms an imprint—a *saṁskāra*, in the *citta*. Memory is the product of *saṁskāras*.

Saṁyama The application of *dhāraṇā*, *dhyāna*, and *samādhi* in sequence on an object of meditation.

Saṁyoga Conjunction, contact, association; refers to conjunction between *puruṣa* and *buddhi*.

Sañcita-karma Karma that is dormant awaiting later fructification.

Sañcīyamāna Karma that is being accumulated by ongoing activity under ignorance in the present life.

Śaṅkara The most influential commentator of *Advaita Vedānta* in the 8th–9th C.E.

Sāṅkhya "Enumeration" or "counting"; a philosophical school focusing on the twenty-four ingredients of material reality (*prakṛti*). *Sāṅkhya* is the earliest philosophical system of the six classical Schools and provides the metaphysical framework for the *Yoga* School.

Sāṅkhya-kārikās Primary text of the *Sāṅkhya* school of philosophy by *Iśvarakṛṣṇa* (4th–5th C.E.).

Santoṣa Contentment; happiness that does not depend on external objects, but is inherent in the mind when the mind is tranquil.

Śāstras Sacred Sanskrit texts.

Satchidananda Disciple of *Swami Sivananda* who established the Integral Yoga Institute in the United States (1914–2002).

Satkārya Metaphysical view that any effect is present in its cause. All manifest reality is simply a transformation of the underlying cause *prakṛti*. The *Sāṅkhya* and *Yoga* schools subscribe to this view.

Sattva One of the three *guṇas*; literally means "being-ness." When *sattva* is predominant in an individual, the qualities of lucidity, tranquillity, wisdom, discrimination, detachment, happiness, and peacefulness manifest. Also used as a synonym of *buddhi*.

Satya Truthfulness; one of the *yamas*.

Satya-loka Celestial realm (still within saṁsāra).

Śauca Cleanliness—refers to both external and internal cleanliness.

Savicāra-samādhi The second of four stages of *samprajñāta-samādhi*. *Vicārā-samādhi* is subdivided by Patañjali into *sa* (with) *vicāra* and *nir* (without) *vicāra*. When the *yogī* experiences the object of meditation as consisting of subtle elements (*tanmātras*), circumscribed as existing in time and space.

Savikalpa-pratyakṣa Sense perception involving the mind's recognition of the object, which it categorizes as a certain type of thing. (In contrast to *Nirvikalpa-pratyakṣa*, preconceptual perception.)

Savitarka-samādhi Samādhi with physical awareness, conceptualization; the first of four stages of *samprajñāta-samādhi*. *Vitarka-samādhi* is subdivided by Patañjali into *sa* (with) *vitarka* and *nir* (without) *vitarka*. When the *yogī's* awareness of the object of concentration is conflated with the word for and the concept of the object.

Śeṣa Thousand-headed cosmic serpent upon which *Viṣṇu* reclines and who holds the universes on his hood. Also known as *Ananta*.

Siddhānta A defining tenet of a philosophical school.

Siddha Yoga Spiritual path founded by Swami Muktananda (1908–1982).

Śiva Supreme Being considered by *Śaivites* (followers of *Śiva*) to be the supreme *Īśvara* or God; also known as *Rudra* and *Hara*.

Sivananda Renunciant (1887–1963) whose teachings were brought to the West by his disciples *Swami Vishnu-devananda, Swami Satchidananda, Swami Satyananda*, and *Swami Chinmayananda*.

Skandhas Sheaths or aggregates. Buddhists' belief that the human persona consists of five sheaths: matter, sensations, perceptions, mental formations, and consciousness.

Smṛti That which is remembered, memory. Intra-human revelation emanating from enlightened *ṛṣi* sages (as recorded in the *Purāṇas*, Epics and other texts including the *Sūtra* traditions). Also refers to memory as the retrieval of *saṁskāras*.

Soma Plant described in the *Vedic* texts that bestowed supernormal powers when imbibed.

Soteriology The branch of theology dealing with notions of liberation or salvation.

Sphoṭa That which illuminates; preexisting eternal meaning inherent in a sound that bursts forth in a flash.

Sphoṭa-vāda Metaphysical view that meaning (*sphoṭa*) is an autonomous and eternal entity embedded in words. Phonemes serve as the vehicles through which the preexisting meaning (*sphoṭa*) of the object bursts forth. The *Yoga* school subscribes to the *sphoṭa* theory.

Śruti Revelation of "that which is heard"; refers to the texts of the *Vedic* corpus. Transhuman revelation emanating from God (*Īśvara*) for the theist schools.

Sthūla-śarīra Gross body.

Sūkṣma-śarīra Subtle body. Consists of *buddhi* (intelligence), *ahaṅkāra* (ego), and *manas* (mind), collectively known as the *antaḥkaraṇa*.

Suṣumnā Subtle energy channel situated within the center of the spine.

Sūtra Terse and pithy philosophical statement in which the maximum amount of information is packed into the minimum amount of words.

Svādhyāya Study—refers to the study of sacred scriptures. Also, the repetition of *oṁ* or other devotional *mantras* (*japa*).

Tadā Then, at that point, from this.

Tamas One of the three *guṇas*. When *tamas* is predominant in an individual, ignorance, delusion, disinterest, lethargy, sleep, and disinclination toward constructive activity manifest.

Tanmātras "Only that"; refers to the generic energies underlying sound, sight, smell, taste, and touch. *Tanmātras* sequentially produce the five mahābhūtas (gross elements).

Tāntric Yoga Esoteric practices usually associated with the *Śiva* or *Devī* sects.

Tapaḥ Means either distress, involtunary pain experienced by the senses, or the spiritual practice of *tapaḥ*, which concerns the voluntary control of the senses (part of *kriyā-yoga* and the *niyāmas*). In the context of spiritual practice, *tapaḥ* requires austerity and self-discipline.

Tasya His, of that, of it, its.

Tat That, his, it.

Tataḥ From that, then, consequently.

Tatra There, in that, from these.

Tattva Thatnesses (a general term referring to the evolutes of *prakṛti*); an object in reality.

Te These, they.

T.K.V. Desikachar Developed *Viniyoga* and introduced it to the West, continuing the approach that was originally developed by his guru and father, *T. Krishnamāchārya* (1888–1989).

Udāna One of the five *prāṇas* responsible for upward movements in the body.

Upaniṣads Philosophical texts of the late Vedic period concerned with understanding the ultimate truths of reality.

Vācaspati Miśra Wrote a commentary on the *Yoga Sūtras* titled *Tattva-vaiśāradī*; also wrote commentaries on the *Vedānta*, *Sāṅkhya*, *Nyāya*, and *Mīmāṁsā* schools in the 9th C.E.

Vāda Suffix added to a philosophical category to indicate the school or point of view associated with that concept.

Vairāgya Dispassion, renunciation, non-attachment; absence of craving for sense objects.

Vaiśeṣika One of the six schools of orthodox philosophy, focused on metaphysics; perceived the created world as ultimately consisting of the combination of various eternal categories such as subatomic particles.

Vaiṣṇava Followers of *Viṣṇu/Kṛṣṇa*. Believer that *Viṣṇu* is the supreme *Īśvara*.

Vaitṛṣṇya Indifference; highest dispassion.

Vajra Thunderbolt.

Vallabha Post–*Śaṅkara Vedāntin* (16th C.E.) and *Vaiṣṇava* theologian.

Varṇas Phonemes.

Vāsanās Subliminal imprints (*saṁskāras*) that remain dormant in this life; latent and subconscious personality traits that will manifest in future lives.

Vedānta One of the six schools of orthodox philosophy that is focused on the interpretation and systematization of the Upaniṣads, specifically with determining the relationship between *Brahman* (the supreme Truth of the Upaniṣads), *ātman* (the individualized feature of *Brahman*) and the perceived world.

Vedānta Sūtras The primary text for the *Vedānta* school; also known as the *Brahma Sūtras*.

Vedas Oldest preserved literature in India. Tradition believes there was originally only one *Veda*, subdivided into four *Vedas* by *Vyāsa: Ṛgveda, Sāmaveda, Yajurveda,* and *Atharvaveda*.

Vedic Corpus Consists of: the 4 *Vedas* (*Ṛgveda, Sāmaveda, Yajurveda, Atharvaveda*), the Brāhmaṇas, the Āraṇyakas, and the Upaniṣads.

Vibhūtis Mystic powers.

Vicāra-samādhi Absorption with subtle awareness. Contemplation on the more subtle aspect of the object of meditation, the subtle energies (*tanmātras*) that underpin the gross elements. *Vicāra* is the second level of experiencing an object in *Samprajñāta-samādhi*, and is subdivided into *savicāra* and *nirvicāra* stages.

Videha Unembodied, without a gross body. Refers to quasi-perfected *yogīs* who do not have gross physical bodies but exist on some other level within *prakṛti*.

Vidyā Knowledge of the scriptures.

Vijñānabhikṣu Prolific scholar to whom eighteen philosophical treatises on *Sāṅkhya*, *Vedānta*, and the *Upaniṣads* are attributed; also wrote a commentary titled *Yoga-vārttika* on the *Yoga Sūtras* in 15th C.E.

Virāma-pratyaya The thought of terminating all thoughts.

Vīrya Vigour, potency, power.

Viṣaya Sense objects; sphere, range of senses.

Viśeṣa Particularized, difference; the specific aspect of an object that distinguishes it from another.

Vishnu-Devananda Disciple of *Swami Sivananda* who established *Sivananda Yoga Vedanta* Centres throughout the world (1927–1993).

Viṣṇu Considered by *Vaiṣṇavas* to be the supreme *Īśvara*, or God; incarnates age after age.

Vitarka Negative or perverse thoughts and actions in contradiction to the *yamas* and *niyamas*.

Vitarka-samādhi Absorption with physical awareness; the first level of experiencing an object in *Samprajñāta-samādhi*, consisting of contemplation on a gross physical object. *Vitarka* is subdivided into *savitarka* and *nirvitarka* stages.

Vivaraṇa Commentary on the *Yoga Sutras* by the *Vedāntin Śaṅkara* in the 8th–9th C.E.

Viveka Discrimination; knowing the distinction between *prakṛti* and *puruṣa*.

Vivekānanda *Vedanta* philosopher who became popular in the West after his address to the Chicago Parliament of Religions in 1893.

Vṛttis Any sequence of thought, ideas, mental imaging, or cognitive act performed by either the mind, intellect, or ego (collectively *citta*).

Vyāna One of the five *prāṇas* responsible for circulating all over the body.

Vyāsa Also known as *Vedavyāsa* or *Vyāsadeva*; primary literary figure of ancient India held to be compiler of the *Vedas*, *Purāṇas*, and the *Mahābhārata* Epic. *Vyāsa*, the first and primary commentator of *Patañjali's Yoga Sūtras*, is considered to be a later figure, who penned his commentary *Bhāṣya* in 5th C.E. under the name of the legendary sage.

Vyutthāna Outgoing, emerging; refers here to *saṁskāras* that propel the mind into activity).

Yājñavalkya Smṛti Text discussing *dharma*, codes of ritual, personal, familial, civic, and social duties.

Yamas Abstentions or moral restraints. There are five *yamas*: *ahiṁsā* (non-violence), *satya* (truthfulness), *asteya* (refraining from stealing), *brahmacarya* (celibacy), *aparigraha* (refraining from acquisition or coveting).

yoga The techniques, systems, and paths of various practices aimed at realization of the *ātman*.

Yoga One of the six classical Schools of Indian philosophies; the Yoga school as represented by *Patañjali* presents techniques through which *puruṣa* (soul) can be realized as distinct from *prakṛti* (matter). Patañjali defines *yoga* as the cessation (*nirodha*) of the activities (*vṛttis*) of the *citta*. Historically *Yoga* just referred to a cluster of meditative techniques, some form of which was common to numerous different schools and sects, rather than a distinct philosophical school.

Yoga Sūtras The primary text for Yoga, one of the six classical Schools of Indian philosophy; most scholars place the text circa 1st–2nd C.E.

Yogī A practitioner of Yoga.

Yugas Cyclical world ages; in every cycle there are four world ages known as *satya-yuga* (golden age), *tretā-yuga*, *dvāpara-yuga*, and the present world age of *kali-yuga* (most degenerate age).

Yuj Contemplate, yoke, union; verbal root of the noun *yoga*.

WORD INDEX

This index lists in Roman alphabetical order most of the key words in the *Yoga Sūtras*, together with a guide to the *sūtra(s)* in which each appears. The text of the cited *sūtras* is excerpted to indicate the context of the entry word; however, note that the Sanskrit case endings and rules of *sandhi* dictate that the entry word is often spelled differently, elided, or embedded in a compound word. Brackets around text within the citations provide implied context or indicate a pronoun or adjective reference. Brackets around *sūtra* numbers indicate that the *sūtra* implies only the entry word or refers to it using only an impersonal pronoun.

For the benefit of readers who are not specialized in Sanskrit, participles, pronominal forms, and negatives are listed separately, not under their verbal roots.

The index is not exhaustive, but focuses on key concepts and themes so the reader may easily trace where these are addressed in each *pāda*. Only words from the *Yoga Sūtras* are included; vocabulary of the commentators is not. To highlight prominent topics in the *Sūtras*, words that recur five times or more appear in bold in this index.

The English words in parentheses are those used in the context of the present translation; they are not necessarily literal translations. They are provided not as complete definitions (see the Glossary or the word translations following each *sūtra*), but as a memory aid for those newer to the Sanskrit terms.

ābhāsa (luminosity) *svābhāsam* [*citta*] IV.19

abhāva (absence; removal) *vṛttir nidrā* I.10; *antarāyābhāvaś* I.29; [*avidyā*] *abhāvāt-saṁyogābhāva* II.25 [used twice]; *eṣām-abhāve tad-abhāvaḥ* [*saṁskāras*] IV.11 [used twice]

abhibhava (subjugation) *abhibhava-prādurbhāvau* III.9

abhijāta (transparent) *abhijātasyeva maṇer* I.41

abhiniveśa (will to live) [*kleśa*] II.3; *tathārūḍho 'bhiniveśaḥ* II.9

abhivyakti (manifestation) *evābhivyaktir vāsanānām* IV.8

abhyantara (internal, i.e., *prāṇāyāma*) *bāhyābhyantara-stambha-vṛttiḥ* II.50; *bāhyābhyantara-viṣayākṣepī* II.51

abhyāsa (practice) *abhyāsa-vairāgyābhyām* I.12; *sthitau yatno 'bhyāsaḥ* I.13; [I.14] *virāma-pratyayābhyāsa* I.18; *eka-tattvābhyāsaḥ* I.32

aṇima (mystic power—lightness) [*vibhūti*] III.45
aniṣṭa (undesired) *aniṣṭa-prasaṅgā* III.51
anitya (ephemeral) *anityāśuci-duḥkhānātmasu* II.5
añjanatā (colored, influenced) *añjanatā samāpattiḥ* I.41
antara (other) *jātyantara-pariṇāmaḥ* IV.2; *cittāntara-dṛśye* IV.21; *pratyayāntarāṇi* IV.27
antar-aṅga (internal limbs) *trayam antarāṅgam* [*dhāraṇā, dhyāna, and samādhi*] III.7
antarāya (disturbance) *antarāyābhāvaś* I.29; *citta-vikṣepās te 'ntarāyāḥ* I. 30
antardhāna (invisibility) [*vibhūti*] III.21
aṇu (atom) *paramāṇ-parama-mahattvāntaḥ* I.40
anubhūta (experienced) *anubhūta viṣayāsampramoṣaḥ* I.11
anumāna (inference) [*pramāṇa*] I.7; *śrutānumāna-prajñābhyām* I.49
anupaśya (perceive internally) *pratyayānupaśyaḥ* II.20
anupātin (follows as a consequence) *śabda-jñānānupātī* I.9; *dharmānupātī dharmī* III.14
anuśayin (stem from) *sukhānuśayī* II.7; *duḥkhānuśayī dveṣaḥ* II.8
ānuśravika (revealed in scripture) *dṛṣtānuśravika-viṣaya* I.15
anuṣṭhāna (practice) *yogāṅgānuṣṭhānād aśuddhi-kṣaye* II.28
anuttama (unexcelled) *santoṣād anuttamaḥ sukha-lābhaḥ* II.42
anvaya (connection, constitution) *nirodha-kṣaṇa-cittānvayaḥ* III.9; *anvaya . . . saṁyamād* III.44; [*guṇas*] *anvaya . . . saṁyamād* III.47
anya (other, distinct) *saṁskāra-śeṣo 'nyaḥ* I.18; *anya-viṣayā* I.49; *anya-saṁskāra-pratibandhī* I.50; *tad-anyasādhāraṇatvāt* II.22
anyatā (distinction) *sattva-purusānyatā-khyāti* III.49; *anyatānavacchedāt tulyayoḥ* III.53
anyatva (change) *kramānyatvaṁ pariṇāmānyatve hetuḥ* III.15 [used twice]
aparāmṛṣṭa (untouched) *aparāmṛṣṭaḥ . . . Īśvaraḥ* I.24
aparānta (death; final moment) *aparānta-jñānam ariṣṭebhyaḥ* III.22; *pariṇāmāparānta-nirgrāhyaḥ* IV.33
aparigraha (noncovetousness) [*yama*] II.30; *aparigraha-sthairye* II.39
apariṇāmitva (immutability) *puruṣasyāpariṇāmitvāt* IV.18
āpatti (pervade) [*citta*] . . . *āpattau svabuddhi-saṁvedanam* IV.22
apavarga (liberation) *bhogāpavargārthaṁ dṛśyam* II.18
apramāṇaka (unverifiable) [*citer*] *apramāṇakam* IV.16
apratisaṅkrama (unchanging) *citer apratisaṅkramāyās* IV.22
aprayojaka (noncausing) *nimittam aprayojakam* IV.3
apuṇya (nonmerit) *puṇyāpuṇya-viṣayāṇām* I.33; *phalāḥ puṇyāpuṇya* II.14
āpūra (filling in) *prakṛtyāpūrāt* IV.2
artha (meaning; object; purpose) [*om*] *artha-bhāvanam* I.28; [*antarāya*] *pratiṣedhārtham* I.32; *śabdārtha-jñāna-vikalpaiḥ* I.42; *artha-mātra-nirbhāsā* I.43; *samādhi-bhāvanārthaḥ kleśa-tanū-karaṇārthaś ca* II.2 [used twice]; *bhogāpavargārtham* II.18; [*puruṣa*] *tad-artha* II.21; *kṛtārthaṁ* II.22; [*dhyāna*] *tad-evārtha-mātra* III.3; *śabdārtha-pratyayānām* III.17; *parārthatvāt svārtha . . . puruṣa* III.35; *cit-taṁ sarvārtham* IV.23; *citram api parārthaṁ* IV.24; *kṛtārthānāṁ . . . guṇānām* IV.32; *puruṣārtha* IV.34
arthatva (functionality; purpose) *viśeṣārthatvāt* I.49; *bhogaḥ parārthatvāt* III.35

arthavattva (significance, purpose) [*viṣaya*] III.44; [*guṇas*] III.47
asamprayoga (noncontact) *svaiṣayāsamprayoge* II.54
asaṁsarga (nonassociation) *parair asaṁsargaḥ* II.40
āsana (posture) [*aṣṭāv aṅgāni*] II.29; *sthira-sukham āsanam* II.46; [II.47]; [II.49]
asaṅkīrṇa (distinct) *sattva-puruṣayor atyantāsaṅkīrṇayoḥ* III.35
āśaya (deposit) *vipākāśayair* I.24; *karmāśayo* II.12
āsevita (cultivated) [*abhyāsa*] *satkārāsevito* I.14
āśis (will, desire) *cāśiso nityatvāt* IV.10
asmitā (ego) *asmitā . . . samprajñātaḥ* I.17; *asmitā . . . kleśāḥ* II.3; *ekātmatevāsmitā* II.6; *nirmāṇa-cittāny-asmitā* IV.4
āśraya (substratum) *hetu-phalāśrayālambanaiḥ* [*saṁskāras*] IV.11
āśrayatva (support, basis) *satya . . . āśrayatvam* II.36
aṣṭa (eight) [*aṣṭāv aṅgāni*] II.29
asteya (nonstealing) [*yama*] II.30; *asteya-pratiṣṭhāyām* II.37
aśuci (impure) *anityāśuci-duḥkhānātmasu* II.5
aśuddhi (impurity) *aśuddhi-kṣayāt tapasaḥ* II.43
āsvāda (taste) [*vibhūti*] III.36
atiprasaṅga (infinite regress) *buddher atiprasaṅgaḥ* IV.21
atīta (the past) *atītānāgata-jñānam* III.16; *atītānāgataṁ svarūpato* IV.12; [IV.13]
ātman (self; essence) *nitya-śuci-sukhātma* II.5; *guṇātmānaḥ* IV.13; *dṛśyasyātmā* II.21; *ātma-darśana-yogyatvāni* II.41; *ātma-bhāva-bhāvanā* IV.25
ātmatā (self-ness; nature) *ekātmatevāsmitā* II.6
āvaraṇa (covering) *prakāśāvaraṇam* II.52; *prakāśāvaraṇa-kṣayaḥ* III.43; *sarvāvaraṇa-malāpetasya* IV.31
avasthā (condition) *dharma-lakṣaṇāvastha-pariṇāmā* III.13; [III.16]
avasthāna (abiding) *svarūpe 'vasthānam* I.3
avidyā (ignorance) [*kleśa*] II.3; *avidyā-kṣetram uttareṣāṁ* II.4; *nitya-śuci-sukhātma-khyātir avidyā* II.5; [*saṁyoga*] *hetur avidyā* II.24; [II.25]
aviplava (undeviating) *viveka-khyātir aviplavā* II.26
avirati (lack of detachment) [*antarāya*] I.30
aviśeṣa (unparticularized; nondistinction) *viśeṣāviśeṣa . . . guṇa-parvāṇi* II.19; *pratyayāviśeṣo bhogaḥ* III.35
avyapadeśya (future) *śāntoditāvyapadeśya-dharma* III.14
āyus (lifespan) *jātyāyur-bhogāḥ* II.13; [II.14]

bahir-aṅga (external limbs) *bahir-aṅgaṁ nirbījasya* III.8
bāhya (external) *bāhyābhyantara-stambha-vṛttiḥ* II.50; *bāhyābhyantara-viṣayākṣepī caturthaḥ* II.51
bala (strength) *maitry ādiṣu balāni* III.23; *baleṣu hasti-balādini* III.24; *bala . . . kāya-sampat* III.46
bandha (bound) *deśa-bandhaś cittasya dhāraṇā* III.1; *bandha-kāraṇa-śaithilyāt* III.38
bhauma (places) *sarva-bhaumā mahā-vratam* II.31
bhava (becoming) *bhava-pratyayo* I.19
bhāva (state of existence) *vikaraṇa-bhāvaḥ* III.48; *sarva-bhāvādhiṣṭhātṛtvam* III.49; *ātma-bhāva-bhāvanā* IV.25

bhāvana (contemplation, cultivation) *tad-artha-bhāvanam* I.28; *bhāvanārthaḥ* II.2; *pratipakṣa-bhāvanam* II.33, II.34
bhāvanā (meditation) *ātma-bhāva-bhāvanā* IV.25
bhāvanātas (from the attitude) *bhāvanātaś citta-prasādanam* I.33
bheda (piercing, difference) *prakṛtīnāṁ varaṇa-bhedas tu* IV.3; *pravṛtti-bhede* IV.5; *adhva-bhedād* IV.12; *citta-bhedāt* IV.15
bhoga (experience) *jātyāyur-bhogāḥ* II.13; [II.14]; *bhogāpavargārtham* II.18; *pratyayāviśeṣo bhogaḥ* III.35
bhrānti (misapprehension) *bhrānti-darśana . . . antarāyāḥ* I.30
bhūmi (stage, ground) *dṛḍha-bhūmiḥ* I.14; *prānta-bhūmiḥ* II.27; *tasya bhūmiṣu viniyogaḥ* III.6
bhūmikatva (ground, base) *ālabdha-bhūmikatva* [*antarāya*] I.30
bhūta (element, being) *bhūtendriyātmakam* I.18; *bhūtendriyeṣu* III.13; [III.15]; *sarva-bhūta-ruta* III.17; *bhūta-jayaḥ* III.44
bhūtatva (object, being) *tasyāviṣayībhūtatvāt* III.20
bīja (seed) *sarvajña-bījam* I.25; *doṣa-bīja-kṣaye* III.50
brahmacarya (celibacy) [*yama*] II.30; *brahmacarya-pratiṣṭhāyāṁ vīrya-lābhaḥ* II.38
buddhi (intelligence) *buddhi-buddher atiprasaṅgaḥ* IV.21; *svabuddhi-saṁvedanam* IV.22

cakra (wheel) *nābhi-cakre* III.29
caturtha (fourth) *viṣayākṣepī caturthaḥ* II.51
cetanā (consciousness) *tataḥ pratyak-cetanādhigamo 'py antarāyābhāvaś ca* I.29
chidra (interval) *tac-chidreṣu pratyayāntarāṇi* IV.27
citi (awareness) *citer apratisaṅkramāyās* IV.22; *svarūpa-pratiṣṭhā vā citi-śaktir* IV.34
citta (mind) *citta-vṛtti* I.2; *citta vikṣepāḥ* I.30; *citta-prasādanam* I.33; *cittam* I.37; *citta-sya* II.54; *deśa-bandhaś cittasya* III.1; *nirodha-kṣaṇa-cittānvayaḥ* III.9; [III.10]; *cittasya* III.11; *cittasyaikāgratā-pariṇāmaḥ* III.12; *para-citta-jñānam* III.19; *citta-saṁvit* III.34; *cittasya* III.38; *nirmāṇa-cittāny asmitā-mātrāt* IV.4; *cittam ekam-anekeṣām* IV.5; *citta-bhedāt tayor vibhaktaḥ* IV.15; *caika-citta-tantram* IV.16; *cittasya vastu jñātājñātam* IV.17; *jñātāś citta-vṛttayas* IV.18; [IV.19]; [IV.20]; *cittāntara-dṛśye* IV.21; *cittam* IV.23; [IV.24]; *cittām* IV.26

darśana (perception, vision) *bhrānti-darśanālabdha* I.30; *dṛg-darśana* II.6; *jayātma-darśana-yogyatvāni* II.41; *siddhi-darśanam* III.32
darśin (the seer) *viśeṣa-darśinaḥ* IV.25; [II.21]
daurmanasya (dejection) *daurmanasya . . . vikṣepa-saha-bhuvaḥ* I.31
deśa (place) *jāti-deśa-kāla-samayānavacchinnāḥ* II.31; *vṛttiḥ-deśa-kāla-saṅkhyābhiḥ* II.50; *deśa-bandhaś cittasya dhāraṇā* III.1; *jāti-lakṣaṇa-deśair anyatān-avacchedāt* III.53; *jāti-deśa-kāla-vyavahitānām* IV.9
devatā (deity) *svādhyāyād iṣṭa-devatā-samprayogaḥ* II.44
dhāraṇā (concentration) [*aṣṭāv aṅgāni*] II.29; *dhāraṇāsu ca yogyatā manasaḥ* II.53; *deśa-bandhaś cittasya dhāraṇā* III.1; [III.4]; [III.7]; [III.8]
dharma (nature, characteristics) *dharma-lakṣaṇāvastha-pariṇāmā* III.13; *dharmānupātī dharmī* III.14; [III.15]; [III.16]; *tad-dharmānabhighātaś ca* III.45; *asty adhva-bhedād dharmāṇām* IV.12; *dharma-meghaḥ samādhiḥ* IV.29

hetu (cause) *saṁyogo heya-hetuḥ* II.17; *svarūpopalabdhi-hetuḥ saṁyogaḥ* II.23; *tasya hetur avidyā* II.24; *kramānyatvaṁ pariṇāmānyatve hetuḥ* III.15; *hetu-phalāśrayālambanaiḥ* IV.11

hetutva (result) *puṇyāpuṇya-hetutvāt* II.14

heya (to be avoided, eliminated) *pratiprasava-heyāḥ* II.10; *dhyāna-heyās tad-vṛttayaḥ* II.11; *heyaṁ duḥkham* II.16; *saṁyogo heya-hetuḥ* II.17

hiṁsā (violence) *vitarkā hiṁsādayaḥ* II.34

hlāda (pleasure) *hlāda-paritāpa-phalāḥ* II.14

hṛdaya (heart) *hṛdaye citta-saṁvit* III.34

indriya (sense-organ) *bhūtendriyātmakam* II.18; *saumanasyaikāgryendriya-jayātma* II.41; *kāyendriya-siddhir* II.43; *ivendriyāṇāṁ pratyāhāraḥ* II.54; *paramā-vaśyatendriyāṇām* II.55; *bhūtendriyeṣu* III.13; *indriya-jayaḥ* III.47

Īśvara (the Lord) *Īśvara-praṇidhānād* I.23; *puruṣa-viśeṣa Īśvaraḥ* I.24; [I.25]; [I.26]; [I.27]; *svādhyāyeśvara . . . kriyā-yogaḥ* II.1; *Īśvara-praṇidhānāni niyamāḥ* II.32; *īśvara-praṇidhānāt* II.45

ja (born) *taj-jaḥ saṁskāro* I.50; *saṁyamād viveka-jaṁ jñānam* III.52; *vivekajaṁ jñānam* III.54; *samādhi-jāḥ siddhayaḥ* IV.1; *dhyāna-jam anāśayam* IV.6

janman (birth) *dṛṣṭādṛṣṭa-janma-vedanīyaḥ* II.12; *janma-kathantā-sambodhaḥ* II.39; *janmauṣadhi-mantra-tapaḥ* IV.1

japa (repetition) *taj-japas tad-artha-bhāvanam* I.28

jāti (birth, category) *jātyāyur-bhogāḥ* II.13; [II.14]; *jāti . . . anavacchinnāḥ* II.31; *pūrva-jāti-jñānam* III.18; *jāti-lakṣaṇa-deśair anyatānavacchedāt* III.53; *jāty-antara-pariṇāmaḥ* IV.2; *jāti-deśa-kāla-vyavahitānām* IV.9

javitva (quickness) *mano-javitvam* III.48

jaya (mastery) *jayātma* II.41; *jayāt prajñālokaḥ* III.5; *udāna-jayāj-jvalanam* III.39; *samāna-jayāt* III.40; *bhūta-jayaḥ* III.44; *indriya-jayaḥ* III.47; *pradhāna-jayaś ca* III.48

jāyante (are born) *prātibha-śrāvaṇa . . . jāyante* III.36

jña (knowing) *niratiśāyaṁ sarvajña bījam* I.25 [see *sarvajña*]

jñāna (knowledge, insight) *viparyayo mithyā-jñānam* I.8; *śabda-jñānānupātī* I.9; *śabdārtha-jñāna* I.42; *svapna-nidrā-jñānālambanam* I.38; *atītānāgata-jñānam* III.16; *sarva-bhūta-ruta-jñānam* III.17; *pūrva-jāti-jñānam* III.18; *para-citta-jñānam* III.19; [III.20]; *aparānta-jñānam* III.22; *sūkṣma-vyavahita-viprakṛṣṭa-jñānam* III.25; *bhuvana-jñānam* III.26; *tārā-vyūha-jñānam* III.27; *jñāna-dīptir āviveka-khyāteḥ* II.28; *tad-gati-jñānam* III.28; *puruṣa-jñānam* III.35; [III.36]; *viveka-jaṁ jñānam* III.52, III.54; *malāpetasya jñānasyānantyāj jñeyam-alpam* IV.31

jñāta (known) *vastu jñātājñātam* IV.17; *sadā jñātāś citta-vṛttayas* IV.18

jñātṛtva (knowingness) III.49 [see *sarva-jñātṛtvam*]; [III.50]

jñeya (to be known) *jñeyam alpam* IV.31

jugupsā (distaste) *svāṅga-jugupsā* II.40

jvalana (radiance) *samāna-jayāj jvalanam* III.40

jyotis (light) *mūrdha-jyotiṣi* III.32
jyotiṣmant (illuminating) *viśokā vā jyotiṣmatī* I.36

kaivalya (absolute independence) *tad-dṛśeḥ kaivalyam* II.25; *doṣa-bīja-kṣaye kaivalyam* III.50; *sattva-puruṣayoḥ śuddhi-sāmye kaivalyam* III.55; *kaivalya-prāgbhāraṁ cittām* IV.26; *guṇānāṁ pratiprasavaḥ kaivalyam* IV.34
kāla (time) *kāla-nairantarya* I.14; *kālenānavacchedāt* I.26; *jāti-deśa-kāla-samayānavacchinnāḥ* II.31; *deśa-kāla-sankhyābhiḥ* II.50; *jāti-deśa-kāla-vyavahitānām* IV.9
karaṇa (doing, making) *saṁskāra-sākṣāt-karaṇāt* III.18
kāraṇa (cause) *bandha-kāraṇa-śaithilyāt* III.38
karman (action) *kleśa-karma-vipākāśayair* I.24; *kleśa-mūlaḥ karmāśayaḥ* II.12; *sopakramaṁ nirupakramaṁ ca karma* III.22; *karmāśuklākṛṣṇam* IV.7; [IV.8]; *kleśa-karma-nivṛttiḥ* IV.30
karuṇā (compassion) *maitrī-karuṇā-muditopekṣāṇām* I.33
kāya (body) *kāyendriya-siddhir* II.43; *kāya-rūpa-saṁyamāt* III.21; *kāya-vyūha-jñānam* III.29; *kāyākāśayoḥ sambandha* III.42; *kāya-sampat* III.45, 46
khyāti (discernment, insight) *puruṣa-khyāter guṇa vaitṛṣṇyam* I.16; *viveka-khyātir aviplavā* II.26; *sattva-puruṣānyatā-khyāti* III.49; *viveka-khyāter dharma-meghaḥ* IV.29
kleśa (obstacle, affliction) *kleśa-karma-vipākāśayair* I.24; *kleśa-tanū-karaṇārthaś ca* II.2; *avidyāsmitā-rāga-dveṣābhiniveśāḥ kleśāḥ* II.3; [II.10]; [II.11]; *kleśa-mūlaḥ karmāśayaḥ* II.12; [II.13]; *kleśavad* [*saṁskāras*] IV.28; *kleśa-karma-nivṛttiḥ* IV.30
kliṣṭa (detrimental) *vṛttayaḥ pañcatayyaḥ kliṣṭākliṣṭāḥ* I.5
krama (sequence, succession) *kramānyatvam* III.15; *kṣaṇa-tat-kramayoḥ* III.52; *pariṇāma-krama-samāptir guṇānām* IV.32; *kṣaṇa-pratiyogī pariṇāmāparānta-nirgrāhyaḥ kramaḥ* IV.33
kriyā (action, activity) *kriyā-yogaḥ* II.1; *prakāśa-kriyā-sthiti-śīlam* II.18; *kriyā-phalāśrayatvam* II.36
krodha (anger) *vitarka . . . krodha . . . pūrvakā* II.34
kṛta (done, fulfilled) *kṛtārtham* II.22; *kṛtārthānāṁ pariṇāma-krama-samāptir guṇānām* IV.32
kṣaṇa (moment) *nirodha-kṣaṇa-cittānvayaḥ* III.9; *kṣaṇa-tat-kramayoḥ saṁyamād viveka-jam* III.52; *kṣaṇa-pratiyogī* IV.33
kṣaya (removal, destruction) *yogāṅgānuṣṭhānād aśuddhi-kṣaye* II.28; *aśuddhi-kṣayāt tapasaḥ* II.43; *kṣayodayau cittasya* III.11; *prakāśāvaraṇa-kṣayaḥ* III.43; *doṣa-bīja-kṣaye* III.50
kṣetra (field) *avidyā-kṣetram* II.4
kṣetrika (farmer) *varaṇa-bhedas tu tataḥ kṣetrikavat* IV.3
kṣīṇa (weakens) *kṣīṇa-vṛtter* I.41
kṣīyate (weakened) *kṣīyate prakāśāvaraṇam* II.52
kṣudh (hunger) *kṣut-pipāsā-nivṛttiḥ* III.30

lābha (attained) *vīrya-lābhaḥ* II.38; *sukha-lābhaḥ* II.42
lakṣaṇa (distinctive characteristic) *dharma-lakṣaṇāvasthā* III.13; [III.16]; *jāti-lakṣaṇa-deśair* III.53
lāvaṇya (gracefulness) *lāvaṇya . . . kāya-sampat* III.46
laya (merged) *prakṛti-layānām* I.19
liṅga-mātra (particularized) *viśeṣāviśeṣa-liṅga-mātrāliṅgāni guṇa-parvāṇi* II.19
lobha (greed) *vitarka . . . lobha . . . pūrvakā* II.34

madhya (medium, middling) *mṛdu-madhyādhimātratvāt* [*saṁvegānām*] I.22; *vitarka . . . mṛdu-madhyādhimātrā* II.34
mahant (great) *mahā-vratam* II.31; *vṛttir mahā-videhā* III.43
maitrī (friendliness) *maitrī-karuṇā-muditopekṣāṇām* I.33; *maitryadiṣu balāni* III.23
mala (impurity) *sarvāvaraṇa-malāpetasya* IV.31
manas (mind) *manasaḥ sthiti-nibandhanī* I.35; *yogyatā manasaḥ* II.53; *mano-javitvam* III.48
maṇi (jewel) *abhijātasyeva maṇer* I.41
mantra (sacred chant) *janmauṣadhi-mantra-tapaḥ* IV.1
mātra (only, alone) *śūnyevārtha-mātra-nirbhāsā* I.43; *liṅga-mātrāliṅgāni guṇa-parvāṇi* II.19; *draṣṭā dṛśi-mātraḥ* II.20; *tad evārtha-mātra-nirbhāsam* III.3; *sattva-puruṣānyatā-khyāti-mātrasya* III.49; *asmitā-mātrāt* IV.4
megha (cloud) *dharma-meghaḥ samādhiḥ* IV.2
mithyā (false) *mithyā-jñānam* I.8
moha (delusion) *vitarka . . . moha-pūrvakā* II.34
mṛdu (mild) *mṛdu-madhyādhimātratvāt* [*saṁvegānām*] I.22; *vitarka . . . mṛdu-madhyādhimātrā* II.34
muditā (joy) *maitrī-karuṇā-muditopekṣāṇām* I.33
mūla (root) *kleśa-mūlaḥ karmāśayaḥ* II.12; *sati mūle tad-vipākaḥ* II.13

nāḍī (subtle channel) *kūrma-nāḍyām* III.31
nairantarya (uninterruptedly) *dīrgha-kāla-nairantarya* I.14
naṣṭa (ceased) *naṣṭam apy anaṣṭam* II.22
nibandhanin (steadiness) *sthiti-nibandhanī* I.35
nidrā (sleep) *nidrā-smṛtayaḥ* I.6; *abhāva-pratyayālambanā vṛttir nidrā* I.10; *svapna-nidrā-jñāna* I.38
nimitta (instrumental cause) *nimittam aprayojakam* IV.3
nimna (inclined toward) *viveka-nimnam* IV.26
niratiśaya (unsurpassed) *niratiśāyaṁ sarvajña-bījam* I.25
nirbhāsa (shining forth) *svarūpa-śūnyevārtha-mātra-nirbhāsā* I.43; *evārtha-mātra-nirbhāsam* III.3
nirbīja (seedless) [I.49]; *sarva-nirodhān nirbījaḥ samādhiḥ* I.51; *tad api bahir-aṅgaṁ nirbījasya* III.8
nirgrāhya (perceivable) *pariṇāmāparānta-nirgrāhyaḥ kramaḥ* IV.33
nirmāṇa (created) *nirmāṇa-cittāni* IV.4

nirodha (restraint, cessation) *citta-vṛtti-nirodhaḥ* I.2; *abhyāsa-vairāgyābhyāṁ tan-nirodhaḥ* I.12; *tasyāpi nirodhe sarva-nirodhān* I.51 [used twice]; *vyutthāna-nirodha-saṁskārayor . . . nirodha-kṣaṇa-cittānvayo nirodha-pariṇāmaḥ* III.9 [used thrice]

nirupakrama (without fruition) *sopakramaṁ nirupakramaṁ ca karma* III.22

nirvicāra (*samādhi* state without subtle awareness) *savicārā nirvicārā ca sūkṣma* I.44; *nirvicāra-vaiśāradye* I.47; [I.48]

nirvitarka (*samādhi* state without physical awareness) *smṛti-pariśuddhau . . . nirvitarkā* I.43

nitya (eternal) *nitya-śuci-sukhātma-khyātir* II.5

nityatva (eternality) *cāśiso nityatvāt* IV.10

nivṛtti (cessation) *pipāsā-nivṛttiḥ III.30; ātma-bhāva-bhāvanā-vinivṛttiḥ* IV.25; *kleśa-karma-nivṛttiḥ* IV.30

niyama (observances) [*aṣṭāv aṅgāni*] II.29; *śauca-santoṣa- . . . niyamāḥ* II.32

nyāsa (focusing) *pravṛttyā lokanyāsāt* III.25

pañcatayya (fivefold) *vṛttayaḥ pañcatayyaḥ kliṣṭākliṣṭāḥ* I.5

para (superior, other) *tat param* [*vairāgyam*] I.16; *parair asaṁsargaḥ* II.40; *para-citta-jñānam* III.19; *bhogaḥ parārthatvāt* III.35; *citram api parārtham* IV.24; *para-śārīrāveśaḥ* III.38

parama (greatest) *paramāṇu-parama-mahattva* I.40 [used twice]; *paramā-vaśyatendriyāṇām* II.55

paramāṇu (most minute) *paramāṇu-parama-mahattvānto 'sya vaśīkāraḥ* I.40

pariṇāma (consequence, transformation) *pariṇāma-tāpa-saṁskāra* II.15; *nirodha-pariṇāmaḥ* III.9; *samādhi-pariṇāmaḥ* III.11; *cittasyaikāgratā-pariṇāmaḥ* III.12; *dharma-lakṣaṇāvasthā-pariṇāmā* III.13; *kramānyatvaṁ pariṇāmānyatve hetuḥ* III.15; *pariṇāma-traya* III.16; *jāty-antara-pariṇāmaḥ* IV.2; *pariṇāmaikatvād vastu-tattvam* IV.14; *pariṇāma-krama-samāptir guṇānām* IV.32; *pariṇāmāparānta* IV.33

pariśuddhi (purification) *smṛti-pariśuddhau* I.43

paritāpa (pain) *hlāda-paritāpa-phalāḥ* II.14

parvan (stage) *guṇa-parvāṇi* II.19

paryavasāna (termination) *cāliṅga-paryavasānam* I.45

phala (fruit, result) *hlāda-paritāpa-phalāḥ* II.14; *duḥkhājñānānanta-phalā* II.34; *kriya-phalāśrayatvam* II.36; *hetu-phalāśrayālambanaiḥ* IV.11

prabhu (the lord, *puruṣa*) *jñātāś citta-vṛttayas tat-prabhoḥ* IV.18

pracchardana (exhalation) *pracchardana . . . prāṇasya* I.34

pradhāna (primordial matter) *pradhāna-jayaś ca* III.48

prādurbhāva (manifestation) *saṁskārayor abhibhava-prādurbhāvau* III.9; *tato 'ṇimādi-prādurbhāvaḥ* III.45

prāgbhāra (inclined toward) *kaivalya-prāgbhāraṁ cittām* IV.26

prajñā (wisdom, discernment) *samādhi-prajñā* I.20; *ṛtam-bharā tatra prajñā* I.48; *śrutānumāna-prajñābhyām* I.49; [I.50]; *prānta-bhūmiḥ prajñā* II.27; *pra-jñālokaḥ* III.5

sampad (accomplishment, perfection) *kāya-sampat* III.45, III.46
samprajñāta (*samādhi* state still using mind and object) *vitarka-vicārānandāsmitā-rūpānugamāt samprajñātaḥ* I.17; [I.18]; [I.19]; [I.20]; [I.21]
samprayoga (connection) *iṣṭa-devatā-samprayogaḥ* II.44
saṁśaya (doubt) [*antarāya*] I.30
saṁskāra (subliminal imprint) *pūrvaḥ saṁskāra-śeṣo 'nyaḥ* I.18; *anya-saṁskāra-pratibandhī* I.50; *pariṇāma-tāpa-saṁskāra-duḥkhair* II.15; *nirodha-saṁskārayor abhibhava-prādurbhāvau* III.9; *praśānta-vāhitā saṁskārāt* III.10; [IV.10]; [IV.11]; [IV.28]
saṁvedana (knowing) *-pracāra-saṁvedanāc ca* III.38; *svabuddhi-saṁvedanam* IV.22
saṁvega (intense) *tīvra-saṁvegānām* I.21; [I.22]
saṁvid (knowledge) *citta-saṁvit* III.34
sāmya (equality, commonness) *sattva-puruṣayoḥ śuddhi-sāmye kaivalyam* III.55; *vastu-sāmye citta-bhedāt tayor vibhaktaḥ panthāḥ* IV.15
saṁyama (performing *dhāraṇā*, *dhyāna* and *samādhi* simultaneously on the same object) *trayam ekatra saṁyamaḥ* III.4; [III.5]; [III.6]; *pariṇāma-traya-saṁyamād* III.16; *tat-pravibhāga-saṁyamāt* · III.17; *kāya-rūpa-saṁyamāt* III.21; *karma tat-saṁyamād* III.22; *sūrye saṁyamāt* III.26; *svārtha-saṁyamāt* III.35; *śrotrākāśayoḥ sambandha-saṁyamād* III.41; *kāyākāśayoḥ sambandha-saṁyamāl-laghu-tūla-samāpatteḥ* III.42; *sthūla-svarūpa-sūkṣmānvayārthavattva-saṁyamād* III.44; *grahaṇa-svarūpāsmitānvayārthavattva-saṁyamād* III.47; *kṣaṇa-tat-kramayoḥ saṁyamād* III.52; [III.23, 24, 27–32, 34, 35, 48, 53 also list *siddhis* attained through *saṁyama*; the word is merely implied]
saṁyoga (conjunction) *draṣṭṛ-dṛśyayoḥ saṁyogo heya-hetuḥ* II.17; *svarūpopalabdhi-hetuḥ saṁyogaḥ* II.23; *tad-abhāvāt saṁyogābhāvaḥ* II.25; [II.24]
saṅga (attachment, contact) *saṅgasmayākaraṇam* III.51; *jala-paṅka-kaṇṭakādiṣv asaṅga* III.39
saṅgṛhītatva (held together) *hetu-phalāśrayālambanaiḥ saṅgṛhītatvād* IV.11
saṅkara (confusion) *itaretarādhyāsāt saṅkaras* III.17; *smṛti-saṅkaraś ca* IV.21
saṅkhyā (number) *deśa-kāla-saṅkhyābhiḥ* II.50
saṅkīrṇa (mixed with) *vikalpaiḥ saṅkīrṇā* I.42; *sattva-puruṣayor atyantāsaṅkīrṇayoḥ* III.35
śānta (past, quiescent) *śāntoditau* III.12; *śāntoditāvyapadeśya* III.14
santoṣa (contentment) [*niyama*] II.32; *santoṣād anuttamaḥ sukha-lābhaḥ* II.42
saptadha (sevenfold) *tasya saptadhā prānta-bhūmiḥ prajñā* II.27
śarīra (body) *cittasya para-śarīrāveśaḥ* III.38
sārūpya (identification) *vṛtti-sārūpyam* I.4
sarva (all, everything) *sarvajña-bījam* I.25; *sarva-nirodhān nirbījaḥ samādhiḥ* I.51; *duḥkham eva sarvam vivekinaḥ* II.15; *sarva-bhaumā* II.31; *sarva-ratnopasthānam* II.37; *sarvārthataikāgratayoḥ* III.11; *sarva-bhūta-ruta-jñānam* III.17; *prātibhād vā sarvam* III.33; *sarva-bhāvādhiṣṭhātṛtvaṁ sarva-jñātṛtvam ca* III.49 [used twice]; *tārakaṁ sarva-viṣayaṁ sarvathā-viṣayam akramam* III.54 [used twice]; *cittaṁ sarvārtham* IV.23
sarvathā (everywhere, always) *tārakaṁ sarva-viṣayaṁ sarvathā-viṣayam akramam* III.54; *sarvathā viveka-khyāter* IV.29
satkāra (devotion) *nairantarya-satkārāsevitaḥ* I.14

sattva (*sattva-guṇa*, the intellect) *sattva-śuddhi* II.41; *sattva-puruṣayor atyantāsaṅkīrṇayoḥ* III.35; *sattva-puruṣānyatā-khyāti-mātrasya* III.49; *sattva-puruṣayoḥ śuddhi-sāmye kaivalyam* III.55

satya (truthfulness) [*yama*] II.30; *satya-pratiṣṭhāyām* II.36

śauca (cleanliness) [*niyama*] II.32; *śaucāt svāṅga* II.40

saumanasya (cheerfulness) *saumanasyaikāgryendriya* II.41

savicāra (*samādhi* state with subtle awareness) *etayaiva savicārā nirvicārā ca sūkṣma-viṣayā* I.44

savitarka (*samādhi* state with physical awareness) *savitarkā samāpattiḥ* I.42

śeṣa (remainder) *saṁskāra-śeṣo 'nyaḥ* I.18

siddha (perfected being) *siddhi-darśanam* III.32

siddhi (perfection, mystic power) *kāyendriya-siddhir* II.43; *samādhi-siddhir* II.45; *vyutthāne siddhayaḥ* III.37; *samādhi-jāḥ siddhayaḥ* IV.1; [III.37]

śīla (having the nature of) *prakāśa-kriyā-sthiti-śīlam* II.18

smṛti (memory) *vikalpa-nidrā-smṛtayaḥ* I.6; *viṣayāsampramoṣaḥ smṛtiḥ* I.11; [*asamprajñāta-samādhi*] *smṛti . . . pūrvaka* I.20; *smṛti-pariśuddhau* I.43; *smṛti-saṁskārayor eka-rūpatvāt* IV.9; *smṛti-saṅkaraś ca* IV.21

śraddhā (faith) *śraddhā-vīrya-smṛti-samādhi-prajṇā* I.20

śrāvaṇa (hearing) *prātibha-śrāvaṇa-vedanādarśāsvāda-vārtā* III.36

śrotra (ear) *śrotrākāśayoḥ sambandha-saṁyamād divyaṁ śrotram* III.41 [used twice]

śruta (heard, tradition) [I.15]; *śrutānumāna* I.49

stambha (restrain, obstruct) *bāhyābhyantara-stambha-vṛttiḥ* II.50; *stambhe cakṣuḥ-prakāśāsamprayoge* III.21

sthairya (steadiness) *aparigraha-sthairye* II.39; *kūrma-nāḍyāṁ sthairyam* III.31

sthānin (celestial) *sthānyupanimantraṇe* III.51

sthira (steady) *sthira-sukham āsanam* II.46

sthiti (steadiness, inertia) *tatra sthitau yatno 'bhyāsaḥ* I.13; *manasaḥ sthiti-nibandhanī* I.35; *prakāśa-kriyā-sthiti* II.18; other causes of steadiness: [I.34]; [I.36]; [I.37]; [I.38]; [I.39]

sthūla (gross) *sthūla-svarūpa-sūkṣmānvayārthavattva* III.44

styāna (idleness) [*antarāya*] I.30

śuci (pure) *nitya-śuci-sukhātma-khyātir* II.5

śuddha (pure) *draṣṭā dṛśi-mātraḥ śuddho 'pi* II.20

śuddhi (purity) *sattva-śuddhi* II.41; *sattva-puruṣayoḥ śuddhi-sāmye kaivalyam iti* III.55

sukha (happiness, joy, comfort) *sukha-duḥkha-puṇyāpuṇya-viṣayāṇām* I.33; *nitya-śuci-sukhātma-khyātir* II.5; *sukhānuśayī rāgaḥ* II.7; *santoṣād anuttamaḥ sukha* II.42; *sthira-sukham āsanam* II.46

sūkṣma (subtle) *sūkṣma-viṣayā* I.44; *sūkṣma-viṣayatvam* I.45; *pratiprasava-heyāḥ sūkṣmāḥ* II.10; *dīrgha-sūkṣmaḥ* II.50; *sūkṣma-vyavahita-viprakṛṣṭa* III.25; *sūkṣmānvayārthavattva* III.44; *vyakta-sūkṣmā guṇātmānaḥ* IV.13

śūnya (empty, devoid) *vastu-śūnyo* I.9; *svarūpa-śūnyevārtha* I.43; *svarūpa-śūnyam iva* III.3; *puruṣārtha-śūnyānāṁ guṇānām* IV.34

sūrya (sun) *bhuvana-jñānaṁ sūrye saṁyamāt* III.26

svādhyāya (study of scripture) *tapaḥ-svādhyāyeśvara-praṇidhānāni kriyā-yogaḥ* II.1; [*niyama*] II.32; *svādhyāyād iṣṭa-devatā-samprayogaḥ* II.44

vitṛṣṇa (without craving) *viṣaya-vitṛṣṇasya* I.15
viveka (discrimination) *viveka-khyātir aviplavā* II.26; *dīptir āviveka-khyāteḥ* II.28; *viveka-jaṁ jñānam* III.52; *vivekajaṁ jñānam* III.54; *viveka-nimnaṁ . . . cittām* IV.26; *viveka-khyāter dharma-meghaḥ* IV.29
vivekin (one with discrimination) *duḥkham eva sarvaṁ vivekinaḥ* II.15
vrata (vow) *mahā-vratam* II.31
vṛtti (fluctuation, movement) *citta-vṛtti* I.2; *vṛtti-sārūpyam* I.4; *vṛttayaḥ pañcatayyaḥ kliṣṭākliṣṭāh* I.5; [I.6]; *vṛttir nidrā* I.10; *kṣīṇa-vṛtter* I.41; *dhyāna . . . vṛttayaḥ* II.11; [I.12]; *guṇa-vṛtti-virodhāc ca* II.15; *bāhyābhyantara-stambha-vṛttiḥ* II.50; *bahir-akalpitā vṛttir* III.43; *sadā jñātāś citta-vṛttayas* IV.18
vyādhi (disease) [*antarāya*] I.30
vyakta (manifest) *te vyakta-sūkṣmā guṇātmānaḥ* IV.13
vyavahita (concealed, separated) *sūkṣma-vyavahita* III.25; *jāti-deśa-kāla-vyavahitānām* IV.9
vyūha (arrangement) *tārā-vyūha-jñānam* III.27; *kāya-vyūha-jñānam* III.29
vyutthāna (going forth, wakened) *vyutthāna-nirodha* III.9; *samādhāv upasargāḥ vyutthāne siddhayaḥ* III.37

yama (abstention) *yama . . . 'ṣṭāv aṅgāni* II.29; *ahiṁsā-satyāsteya . . . yamāḥ* II.30; [II.31]
yatna (effort) *tatra sthitau yatno 'bhyāsaḥ* I.13
yoga [left untranslated] *atha yogānuśāsanam* I.1; *yogaś citta-vṛtti-nirodhaḥ* I.2; *kriyā-yogaḥ* II.1; *yogāṅgānuṣṭhānād* II.28
yogin/yogī [left untranslated] [II.27]; *karmāśuklā-kṛṣṇaṁ yoginas* IV.7
yogyatā (fitness) *yogyatā manasaḥ* II.53
yogyatva (capability) *jayātma-darśana-yogyatvāni* II.41

ACKNOWLEDGMENTS

To Patricia Walden: When I was the lecturer in Hinduism at Harvard, I received a request from her Somerville studio to lecture on Yoga philosophy. Patricia subsequently invited me to lecture at various teacher training workshops, and soon I was receiving invitations from Yoga teachers all over the country and internationally. Consequently, I realized that thousands of *yoga* practitioners worldwide were perceiving Patañjali's *Yoga Sūtras* as a paramount source of spiritual authority. This led to the conviction that there was a need for a user-friendly edition of the *Sūtras* that was firmly and authentically grounded in and representative of the intellectual history of the classical Yoga tradition in pre-modern India. Thus the commitment to undertake this translation and commentary took root. This edition is especially dedicated to Patricia and the entire Iyengar community, particularly to Guruji Iyengar himself for his enormous contribution to the well-being of humanity, and for his foreword to this volume.

To Paul Sherbow, for his meticulous editing of the Sanskrit in several drafts of the manuscript. To Bob Gilbo, for editing this manuscript, and creating the word index and the Sāṅkhya chart, and to Snehy Gupta for undertaking the glossary; both went beyond the call of duty. To Valerio Virgini for pasting in the Sanskrit Nagari font and the transliteration. To Chris Chapple for reviewing the manuscript, and to Swami Veda Bharati, Anthony Nickolson, Gerald Larson, Guy Beck, George Cordona, and Matthew Dasti for their comments and insight. To Matthew Ekstrand-Abueg for maintaining the website and to Nina Golder for the computer. And to Rutgers University for a research grant.

To Bo Forbes for her editing, photography, and patience; and, from among many wonderful *yoga* teachers and students whose acquaintance I have been fortunate to make, to her and Eileen Muir in particular for making me a part of their communities and for their loyal friendship. To the Rutgers *Yoga Sūtras* class of fall 2008, and to all the students of Yoga philosophy with whom I have been privileged to study the *Sūtras*, both in the university classroom and in many workshops worldwide, for their interest and enthusiasm in the teachings of the Yoga tradition, and their encouragement in undertaking this translation and commentary. Each new teaching opportunity with the *Sūtras* has furthered my own insight into and consequent appreciation of the text. To Jeff Seroy, Wah-Ming Chang, and the folks at Farrar, Straus and Giroux for being a great team to work with! And, most important, to my daughter, Mohiṇī, for blessing and enriching my life with her presence, and for teaching me so many wonderful things. Finally, to my dad and Pia, for always being there.